Annotated Guide to the Companies Act

Annotated Guide to the Companies Act

Brenda Hannigan, MA, LLM, Solicitor (Ireland)

Professor of Corporate Law, University of Southampton

Butterworths

A Member of the LexisNexis Group

Members of the LexisNexis Group worldwide

United Kingdom	Butterworths Tolley, a Division of Reed Elsevier (UK) Ltd, Halsbury House, 35 Chancery Lane, LONDON, WC2A 1EL, and 4 Hill Street, EDINBURGH EH2 3JZ
Argentina	Abeledo Perrot, Jurisprudencia Argentina and Depalma, BUENOS AIRES
Australia	Butterworths, a Division of Reed International Books Australia Pty Ltd, CHATSWOOD, New South Wales
Austria	ARD Betriebsdienst and Verlag Orac, VIENNA
Canada	Butterworths Canada Ltd, MARKHAM, Ontario
Chile	Publitecsa and Conosur Ltda, SANTIAGO DE CHILE
Czech Republic	Orac sro, PRAGUE
France	Editions du Juris-Classeur SA, PARIS
Hong Kong	Butterworths Asia (Hong Kong), HONG KONG
Hungary	Hvg Orac, BUDAPEST
India	Butterworths India, NEW DELHI
Ireland	Butterworths (Ireland) Ltd, DUBLIN
Italy	Giuffré, MILAN
Malaysia	Malayan Law Journal Sdn Bhd, KUALA LUMPUR
New Zealand	Butterworths of New Zealand, WELLINGTON
Poland	Wydawnictwa Prawnicze PWN, WARSAW
Singapore	Butterworths Asia, SINGAPORE
South Africa	Butterworths Publishers (Pty) Ltd, DURBAN
Switzerland	Stämpfli Verlag AG, BERNE
USA	LexisNexis, DAYTON, Ohio

ISBN 0 406 98864 1

Typeset by Doyle & Co, Colchester
Printed by and bound in Great Britain by The Bath Press, Bath

Visit Butterworths LexisNexis *direct* at www.butterworths.com

Preface

The Companies Act 1985 contains almost six hundred sections ranging from the crucial (unfairly prejudicial conduct: s 459), the complex (financial assistance: s 151), and the convoluted (oversea companies: s 680A et seq), to the mundane (company names: s 25 et seq), the obscure (unregistered companies: s 718), and the obsolete (limited companies may have directors with unlimited liability: s 306). All of corporate life is here, from incorporation to dissolution and striking off.

The statute is only part of the picture, however, and busy corporate practitioners also need at their fingertips the case law which explains, illustrates and defines the scope of the statutory provisions. Company law is a moving target, of course, and on occasion it seemed that the Court of Appeal was intent on overruling decisions and re-interpreting provisions just as soon as the commentary on them was completed. The first few months of 2001 alone saw appellate decisions on schemes of arrangement: *Re Hawk Insurance Co* 23 February 2001, (unreported), CA; the restoration of dissolved companies: *Smith v White Knight Laundry* 11 May 2001, (unreported), CA; take-over offers to overseas shareholders: *Winpar Holdings Ltd v Joseph Holt Group plc* 11 May 2001, (unreported), CA; unlawful distributions: *Bairstow v Queens Moat Houses plc* 17 May 2001, (unreported), CA; and charges on book debts: *Re Brumark Investments Ltd* 5 June 2001, (unreported), PC; all of which are noted in the text.

This book attempts to ease the burden of the busy corporate practitioner in dealing with this great wealth of material by providing a detailed commentary on each section of the Companies Act taking into account all of the statutory amendments since 1985 as well as the latest judicial pronouncements.

I am very grateful to the editorial staff at Butterworths for their assistance at every stage of this project.

The law is stated as of 1 June 2001 and the text of the statute is as amended to the same date, although it has been possible to note some subsequent developments. All references in the commentary to sections are to sections of the Companies Act 1985 unless otherwise stated.

Brenda Hannigan

September 2001

Contents

Table of cases

A

C

PAGE

D

I

PAGE

S

X

Y

COMPANIES ACT 1985

(1985 c 6)

Arrangement of sections

PART I
FORMATION AND REGISTRATION OF COMPANIES; JURIDICAL STATUS AND MEMBERSHIP

CHAPTER I
COMPANY FORMATION

Memorandum of association

A company's membership

CHAPTER II
COMPANY NAMES

CHAPTER III
A COMPANY'S CAPACITY; FORMALITIES OF CARRYING ON BUSINESS

PART II
RE-REGISTRATION AS A MEANS OF ALTERING A COMPANY'S STATUS

Private company becoming public

Limited company becoming unlimited

Unlimited company becoming limited

Public company becoming private

PART III
CAPITAL ISSUES

CHAPTER I
ISSUES BY COMPANIES REGISTERED, OR TO BE REGISTERED, IN GREAT BRITAIN

The prospectus

PART IV
ALLOTMENT OF SHARES AND DEBENTURES

General provisions as to allotment

Pre-emption rights

Commissions and discounts

Amount to be paid for shares; the means of payment

PART V
SHARE CAPITAL, ITS INCREASE, MAINTENANCE AND REDUCTION

CHAPTER I
GENERAL PROVISIONS ABOUT SHARE CAPITAL

CHAPTER II
CLASS RIGHTS

CHAPTER III
SHARE PREMIUMS

CHAPTER IV
REDUCTION OF SHARE CAPITAL

CHAPTER V
MAINTENANCE OF CAPITAL

CHAPTER VIII
MISCELLANEOUS PROVISIONS ABOUT SHARES AND DEBENTURES

Share and debenture certificates, transfers and warrants

Debentures

PART VI
DISCLOSURE OF INTERESTS IN SHARES

PART VII
ACCOUNTS AND AUDIT

CHAPTER I
PROVISIONS APPLYING TO COMPANIES GENERALLY

CHAPTER II
EXEMPTIONS, EXCEPTIONS AND SPECIAL PROVISIONS

Small and medium-sized companies and groups

Exemptions from audit for certain categories of small company

PART VIII
DISTRIBUTION OF PROFITS AND ASSETS

PART IX
A COMPANY'S MANAGEMENT; DIRECTORS AND SECRETARIES; THEIR QUALIFICATIONS, DUTIES AND RESPONSIBILITIES

PART X
ENFORCEMENT OF FAIR DEALING BY DIRECTORS

PART XA
CONTROL OF POLITICAL DONATIONS

PART XI
COMPANY ADMINISTRATION AND PROCEDURE

CHAPTER I
COMPANY IDENTIFICATION

CHAPTER II
REGISTER OF MEMBERS

CHAPTER V
AUDITORS

Appointment of auditors

PART XII
REGISTRATION OF CHARGES

CHAPTER I
REGISTRATION OF CHARGES (ENGLAND AND WALES)

CHAPTER II
REGISTRATION OF CHARGES (SCOTLAND)

PART XIII
ARRANGEMENTS AND RECONSTRUCTIONS

PART XIIIA
TAKEOVER OFFERS

PART XIV
INVESTIGATION OF COMPANIES AND THEIR AFFAIRS;
REQUISITION OF DOCUMENTS

Appointment and functions of inspectors

PART XV
ORDERS IMPOSING RESTRICTIONS ON SHARES
(SECTIONS 210, 216, 445)

PART XVI
FRAUDULENT TRADING BY A COMPANY

PART XVII
PROTECTION OF COMPANY'S MEMBERS AGAINST UNFAIR PREJUDICE

PART XVIII
FLOATING CHARGES AND RECEIVERS (SCOTLAND)

CHAPTER I
FLOATING CHARGES

CHAPTER III
GENERAL

PART XX
WINDING UP OF COMPANIES REGISTERED UNDER THIS ACT OR THE FORMER COMPANIES ACTS

CHAPTER VI
MATTERS ARISING SUBSEQUENT TO WINDING UP

PART XXII
BODIES CORPORATE SUBJECT, OR BECOMING SUBJECT, TO THIS ACT (OTHERWISE THAN BY ORIGINAL FORMATION UNDER PART I)

CHAPTER I
COMPANIES FORMED OR REGISTERED UNDER FORMER COMPANIES ACTS

CHAPTER II
COMPANIES NOT FORMED UNDER COMPANIES LEGISLATION, BUT AUTHORISED TO REGISTER

PART XXIII
OVERSEA COMPANIES

CHAPTER I
REGISTRATION, ETC

CHAPTER II
DELIVERY OF ACCOUNTS AND REPORTS

CHAPTER III
REGISTRATION OF CHARGES

ss 703A–703N – not in force

CHAPTER IV
WINDING UP ETC

PART XXIV
THE REGISTRAR OF COMPANIES, HIS FUNCTIONS AND OFFICES

PART XXV
MISCELLANEOUS AND SUPPLEMENTARY PROVISIONS

PART XXVI
INTERPRETATION

PART XXVII
FINAL PROVISIONS

SCHEDULES

An Act to consolidate the greater part of the Companies Acts

[11 March 1985]

NOTES

Commencement. Unless otherwise indicated, this Act came into force on 1 July 1985; see s 746.

Civil Procedure Rules. The Civil Procedure Rules 1998, SI 1998/3132, Rule 49, states that, as from 26 April 1999, those Rules apply to proceedings under this Act subject to the provisions of the relevant practice direction which applies to those proceedings.

Insider dealing. Note that all references in this Act to the "Insider Dealing Act" are substituted by the words "insider dealing legislation" by the Criminal Justice Act 1993, s 79(13), Sch 5, Pt I, para 4(2), as from 1 March 1994.

European Economic Interest Groupings. As to the application of certain provisions of this Act, with modifications, to European Economic Interest Groupings, see the European Economic Interest Grouping Regulations 1989, SI 1989/638, reg 18, Sch 4.

PART I

FORMATION AND REGISTRATION OF COMPANIES; JURIDICAL STATUS AND MEMBERSHIP

CHAPTER I

COMPANY FORMATION

MEMORANDUM OF ASSOCIATION

1. Mode of forming incorporated company

(1)   Any two or more persons associated for a lawful purpose may, by subscribing their names to a memorandum of association and otherwise complying with the requirements of this Act in respect of registration, form an incorporated company, with or without limited liability.

(2)   A company so formed may be either—

  (a) a company having the liability of its members limited by the memorandum to the amount, if any, unpaid on the shares respectively held by them ('a company limited by shares');

  (b) a company having the liability of its members limited by the memorandum to such amount as the members may respectively thereby undertake to contribute to the assets of the company in the event of its being wound up ('a company limited by guarantee'); or

  (c) a company not having any limit on the liability of its members ('an unlimited company').

(3)   A 'public company' is a company limited by shares or limited by guarantee and having a share capital, being a company—

  (a) the memorandum of which states that it is to be a public company, and

  (b) in relation to which the provisions of this Act or the former Companies Acts as to the registration or re-registration of a company as a public company have been complied with on or after 22nd December 1980;

and a 'private company' is a company that is not a public company.

(3A) Notwithstanding subsection (1), one person may, for a lawful purpose, by subscribing his name to a memorandum of association and otherwise complying with the requirements of this Act in respect of registration, form an incorporated company being a private company limited by shares or by guarantee.

(4)   With effect from 22nd December 1980, a company cannot be formed as, or become, a company limited by guarantee with a share capital.

S 1(1)

Number of persons   The minimum number of persons required is two, save in the case of a private company limited by shares or by guarantee where only one person is required, see sub-s (3A). The requirement is for 'persons' and not individuals and a body corporate (including a limited company) will suffice, subject to the constraints in s 23; see also s 375.

Lawful purpose   The purpose for which the persons are associated must not be illegal or contrary to public policy: see *R v Registrar of Joint Stock Companies*, *ex p More* [1931] 2 KB 197 (registration refused: company formed to promote a lottery which was illegal at the time); *R v Registrar of Companies, ex p A-G* [1991] BCLC 476 (registration quashed – objects were the carrying on of the business of prostitution); *Bowman v Secular Society* [1917] AC 406 (object denying Christianity was not an unlawful purpose).

Subscribers to the memorandum   The signatories to the memorandum are the first members of the company, the subscribers, and their signatures must be witnessed, see s 2(6); the subscribers are members of the company automatically by virtue of s 22(1), see note to that provision. As to the subscribers' obligation to sign the articles, see s 7(1), (3)(c). The statement of first directors and secretary must also be signed by or on behalf of the subscribers: s 10(3). As to the shares taken by the subscribers, see s 2(5); and as to their obligation for payment in cash for their shares, if the company is a public company, see s 106. In the case of a company formed by formation agents, the subscribers (employees of the formation agents) will be replaced as members of the company on a sale of the company.

Requirements for registration   As far as the requirements with respect of registration are concerned, what is required is a memorandum of association (see s 2); articles of association (see ss 7, 8, especially s 8(2)); and a company name (see ss 25–34). The documents which must be sent to the registrar of companies are identified in s 10 and a statutory declaration or statement is required, see s 12. A registration fee (currently £20) is payable (Companies (Fees) Regulations 1991, SI 1991/1206 as amended) and incorporation will usually take four to five working days; for same-day incorporation, the fee is £80 (at time of writing). As to the registrar of companies, see note to s 10. As to the company as a body corporate, see s 13(3).

S 1(2)(a)

A company limited by shares   A member's liability is limited to the amount due and unpaid on the nominal value of his shares: *Ooregum Gold Mining Co of India Ltd v Roper* [1892] AC 125; and the nominal value is identified in the memorandum of association (see s 2(5)(a)). Where a member has contracted to purchase shares at a premium to the nominal or par value (ie the fixed amount specified by the memorandum) then, as a matter of contract, his liability will be to pay the nominal or par value and any share premium due under the contract.

As to the model form of memorandum of association for a company limited by shares, see s 3 and the Companies (Tables A to F) Regulations 1985, SI 1985/805 as amended, Table B and Table F; as to the form of articles, see ss 7, 8 and the Companies (Tables A to F) Regulations 1985, SI 1985/805 as amended, Table A.

S 1(2)(b), (4)

A company limited by guarantee   It is no longer possible to form (or re-register as) a company limited by guarantee with a share capital, although those in existence prior to 22 December 1980 remain on the register (s 1(4)). In the absence of share capital, it follows that such a company must be a private company (see s 1(3)) and it may be a single member company (see s 1(3A)).

Members' guarantee   A company limited by guarantee without a share capital has members necessarily and not shareholders. The members' contribution to the company is limited to a guarantee, stated in the memorandum of association, to pay a certain amount on the winding up of the company with the amount guaranteed being very small, commonly £1: see s 2(4); and IA 1986, s 74(3). No contribution is required until winding up. The amount guaranteed is not capital and it cannot be mortgaged or charged prior to winding up: *Re Irish Club* [1906)] WN 127. Given the absence of share capital, a company limited by guarantee is not subject to the capital maintenance requirements applicable to a company limited by shares.

The absence of share capital means that a company limited by guarantee, if it is to trade (and there is no prohibition on such companies trading), must fund its activities in other ways. In fact, the distinction in this respect between such companies and companies limited by shares is minimal, as the register at 31 March 2000 showed that there are 1,053,400 companies with a share capital of £100 or less, so they too must fund their activities in other ways (DTI *Companies in 1999–2000* Table A7).

Common uses   While there is no prohibition on trading by companies limited by guarantee, such companies are predominantly found in the not-for-profit sector and are widely used for community and sporting groups, local associations, flat management companies, and for educational and charitable purposes. The advantages of incorporation for such organisations are legal personality and limited liability so facilitating the ownership of property and the contracting of obligations despite a fluctuating membership.

Constitutional documents   A company limited by guarantee has a memorandum and articles of association in the same manner as a company limited by shares. The memorandum of association is identical in most respects with the addition of the members' guarantee (s 2(4)) and the deletion of the share capital provision (s 2(5)); see also s 15. The model form of memorandum of association can be found in the Companies (Tables A to F) Regulations 1985, SI 1985/805 as amended, Table C: s 3(1). A company limited by guarantee must register articles of association: s 7(1); and the model form is contained in Table C which includes elements of Table A with appropriate additions and exclusions (for example, the provisions on share capital).

Membership   Membership of a company limited by guarantee is governed by the articles and Table C, reg 3 (if adopted) provides that new members may not be admitted unless approved by the directors. Membership is not transferable and ceases on death and a member can withdraw on giving seven days' notice (reg 4). The duration of membership and the events or matters which will terminate it will also be set out in the articles. For example, if the company is a flat management company, it is common to provide that membership ceases when ownership of one of the flats ceases. As there is no share capital, share transfers are not required nor share certificates. Every member present at a general meeting has one vote on a show of hands and also one vote on a poll (reg 8) but there is no reason why the company cannot adopt different categories of members with differing voting rights (see, for example, *Re NFU Development Trust Ltd* [1973] 1 All ER 135).

Directors   Directors of a company limited by guarantee are subject to the same obligations as directors of a company limited by shares.

Names   A company limited by guarantee must comply with s 25(2) (name to end in 'limited' or 'ltd' or Welsh equivalents) unless it applies under s 30 to be exempt from the use of the word 'limited' in its name (and meets the conditions laid down by that provision). However, there is no requirement for such companies to apply for exemption and many do not (as at October 1998, there were 39,953 companies limited by guarantee on the register of which 10,860 had claimed exemption and 29,093 had not: *Company Law Review: Modern Company Law for a Competitive Economy, Developing the Framework* (March 2000) para 9.12).

Distributions   A common misconception is that companies limited by guarantee are prevented from distributing their profits. The prohibition on distribution of profits is a condition for exemption under s 30 and has nothing to do with a company's status as a company limited by guarantee. Of course, the nature of the activities commonly undertaken by companies limited by guarantee does mean that they are rarely in a position to distribute profits but there is no prohibition on such distribution unless the company has sought exemption under s 30.

Disclosure requirements   Companies limited by guarantee must still file accounts (see s 226) and an annual return with the registrar of companies although they do not give details of their members, see s 364A(1); they are required to maintain a register of members, however, under s 352. They may qualify for exemption from the requirement to have their accounts audited (s 249A) and be able to file abbreviated accounts (s 246).

Re-registration   A company limited by guarantee may re-register as an unlimited company (see s 49) but it cannot re-register as a company limited by shares. There is no mechanism for transfer between the two forms and where that is required, it will be necessary to wind up the company limited by guarantee and form a new company limited by shares.

S 1(2)(c)

An unlimited company   It is possible to form an unlimited company and while it might appear an unattractive option, given the open-ended commitment by the members to meet the company's liabilities on winding up, there were 3,900 on the register at 31 March 2000. An unlimited company requires two persons and it is not possible to have a single member unlimited company: s 1(1), (3A).

An unlimited company is necessarily a private company (see s 1(3)); and it may be formed with or without a share capital. It is not required to make returns of allotments under s 88; nor is it subject to the restrictions on purchase of own shares: s 143; and it may reduce capital without requiring court confirmation: s 135. An unlimited company with a share capital is subject to the restrictions on financial assistance for the acquisition of its own shares in s 151 et seq; and unlimited companies are subject to the distribution rules in s 263 et seq. An unlimited company can be re-registered as a limited company (ss 51, 52) and, provided it has a share capital, as a public company (ss 43–48).

The advantage which an unlimited company has over other forms of registered company is that generally there is no obligation to file accounts with the registrar of companies, see s 254. Where privacy is a major consideration, therefore, and the risk of insolvency is remote (for example, because the company is not trading but holding investments), then unlimited liability may be attractive. However, given that the disclosure requirements have been significantly reduced in recent years for small companies (see s 246), this advantage may not be as attractive as it once was. There may be taxation reasons, however, why an unlimited company may be advantageous.

S 1(3), (4)

A public company   A public company must have a share capital; the only company limited by guarantee which can be a public company, therefore, is any such company with a share capital which was in existence on 22 December 1980 (sub-s (4)). The requirement in sub-s (3)(a) that the memorandum of association must so state is to ensure that there is public notice of the status of the company; sub-s (3)(b) is a reference to the re-classification and definition effected by the CA 1980. Prior to that Act, a private company had to meet certain criteria and any other company was a public company. The position is reversed by this provision which defines a public company while any other company is a private company.

     The general approach to regulating public companies is that the statutory requirements are more onerous than those imposed on private companies so, for example, the share capital requirements are stricter and there are more extensive disclosure requirements. The main differences between a public and private company include the following:

Name   The name of a public company must end in 'public limited company' or its abbreviation or Welsh equivalent while the name of a private company must end in 'limited' or its abbreviation or Welsh equivalent (ss 25, 27); and, in certain circumstances, a private company (but not a public company) may be exempt from ending its name with the word 'limited' (s 30).

Capital   The nominal value of a public company's allotted share capital must be not less than 'the authorised minimum': s 117; which is currently £50,000: s 118. There is no minimum share capital for a private company. The rules regarding payment for share capital are stricter (ss 99–116) including a requirement for public companies that any non-cash consideration be valued (ss 103–108). Stricter rules apply to any purchase by a public company of its own shares (see ss 159–162, 171) or the giving of financial assistance for the purchase of its own shares (see ss 151, 155) or the making of any distribution (see ss 263, 264). Furthermore, a public company formed as such cannot commence trading without a certificate under s 117, whereas a private company can trade immediately on incorporation. The directors of a public company must call an extraordinary general meeting on a serious loss of capital: s 142. A public company may offer its shares to the public (although it is not obliged to do so) while a private company commits an offence if it offers its shares to the public (s 81).

Officers and members   A public company must have at least two directors while a private company requires only one: s 282(1), (3). A public company requires a minimum of two persons to incorporate while there may be a single member in a private company: s 1(1), (3A). Certain qualifications are required of a secretary of a public company: s 286. The restrictions in ss 330–344 on loans etc to directors and connected persons are more stringent with respect to public companies.

Accounts   The disclosure requirements imposed on public companies are more onerous and extensive than those on private companies and a public company cannot qualify, for example, for the exemptions available to small or medium-sized companies: s 247A. Public companies have a shorter period within which to deliver their accounts to the registrar of companies: s 244(1)(b); and must maintain their accounting records for a longer period: s 222(5).

Meetings and written resolutions   Private companies may use the statutory written resolution procedure (s 381A) and can elect to dispense with certain statutory requirements (holding annual general meetings, reappointing auditors annually, etc) under the elective regime provided by s 379A.

S 1(3A)

Single member private limited companies   This provision was added by the Companies (Single Member Private Limited Companies) Regulations 1992, SI 1992/1699, as from 15 July 1992 and it implements the 11th EC Company Law Directive (Council Directive (EEC) 89/667 (OJ L395 12.12.89)).

2. Requirements with respect to memorandum

(1)   The memorandum of every company must state—

    (a) the name of the company;

    (b) whether the registered office of the company is to be situated in England and Wales, or in Scotland;

    (c) the objects of the company.

(2)   Alternatively to subsection (1)(b), the memorandum may contain a statement that the company's registered office is to be situated in Wales; and a company whose registered office is situated in Wales may by special resolution alter its memorandum so as to provide that its registered office is to be so situated.

(3)   The memorandum of a company limited by shares or by guarantee must also state that the liability of its members is limited.

(4)   The memorandum of a company limited by guarantee must also state that each member undertakes to contribute to the assets of the company if it should be wound up while he is a member, or within one year after he ceases to be a member, for payment of the debts and liabilities of the company contracted before he ceases to be a member, and of the costs, charges and expenses of winding up, and for adjustment of the rights of the contributories among themselves, such amount as may be required, not exceeding a specified amount.

(5)   In the case of a company having a share capital—

    (a) the memorandum must also (unless it is an unlimited company) state the amount of the share capital with which the company proposes to be registered and the division of the share capital into shares of a fixed amount;

    (b) no subscriber of the memorandum may take less than one share; and

    (c) there must be shown in the memorandum against the name of each subscriber the number of shares he takes.

(6)   Subject to subsection (6A), the memorandum must be signed by each subscriber in the presence of at least one witness, who must attest the signature.

(6A) Where the memorandum is delivered to the registrar otherwise than in legible form and is authenticated by each subscriber in such manner as is directed by the registrar, the requirements in subsection (6) for signature in the presence of at least one witness and for attestation of the signature do not apply.

(7)   A company may not alter the conditions contained in its memorandum except in the cases, in the mode and to the extent, for which express provision is made by this Act.

General note

Legal status   The legal status of the memorandum of association is determined by s 14. The memorandum is one of the company's two constitutional documents, the other being the articles of association (see ss 7–9). In the event of a conflict, the memorandum, as the document containing the fundamental conditions upon which alone the company is allowed to be incorporated, prevails over the articles which contain the internal regulations of the company: *Guinness v Land Corpn of Ireland Ltd* (1882) 22 Ch D 349. The model forms of memorandum are provided by the Companies (Tables A to F) Regulations 1985, SI 1985/805, as amended: see s 3.

   At common law, persons dealing with a company are deemed under the doctrine of constructive notice to have notice of the company's memorandum and articles of association and various (ill-defined) public documents (including special resolutions and any charges registered with the registrar of companies) and any limitations contained therein: *Ernest v Nicholls* (1857) 6 HL Cas 401; *Mahony v East Holyford Mining Co* (1875) LR 7 HL 869; *Irvine v Union Bank of Australia* (1877) 2 App Cas 366, PC; *Wilson v Kelland* [1910] 2 Ch 306. The application of this doctrine is mitigated, in turn, by the rule in *Turquand's Case* regarding matters of internal management: *Royal British Bank v Turquand* (1856) 6 E&B 327, see note to s 35A(1),(2). However, the doctrine of constructive notice is effectively abolished as regards limits contained in the memorandum on the company's capacity or the powers of the board by ss 35–35B, see the notes to those provisions.

   This section identifies the clauses which must be contained in the memorandum of association. It is possible (though rarely advisable) to include additional clauses and s 17 provides for the alteration of those additional provisions and for their entrenchment.

S 2(1)(a)

Name   The requirements as to the company's name are set out in ss 25–34.

S 2(1)(b), (2)

Jurisdiction   The purpose of this statement is to determine the jurisdiction governing the company. It fixes the company's domicile and, unlike an individual, a company cannot change its domicile other than by dissolving itself and re-incorporating elsewhere: *Gasque v ICR* [1940] 2 KB 80; *Carl Zeiss Stiftung v Rayner & Keeler Ltd (No 3)* [1969] 3 All ER 897 at 914. In so far as nationality can by analogy be applied to a juristic person, the nationality of a company is determined also by the law of the place of incorporation: *Kuenigl v Donnersmarck* [1955] 1 QB 515. An English company can assume an enemy character for the purposes of the prohibitions on trading with the enemy in time of war: *Daimler Co Ltd v Continental Tyre and Rubber Co (Great Britain) Ltd* [1916] 2 AC 307.

The place of residence of a company is mainly relevant for the purposes of revenue law which essentially considers: (i) the place of incorporation: a company incorporated in the UK is regarded as resident here (Finance Act 1988, s 66(1)); and (ii) the place where central management and control is located: a company incorporated outside of the UK can be resident here if its central management and control is in the UK; a consideration of these issues is beyond the scope of this work: see 23 *Halsbury's Laws* (4th edn Reissue).

Choice of jurisdiction   The jurisdiction selected must be either England and Wales, Wales, or Scotland. Where Wales alone is chosen, this entitles the company to submit various forms and accounts in Welsh (although an English translation will either have to be provided by the company or supplied by the registrar of companies, depending on the document: see s 710B). A company can choose Wales initially or, unusually, may change jurisdiction subsequently to Wales by special resolution (as to a special resolution, see s 378).

The memorandum does not contain the actual address of the registered office which is set out in the statement sent to the registrar under s 10.

S 2(1)(c)

Objects of the company   The memorandum of association must state the objects of the company which may be altered by special resolution (see ss 4–6); another possibility when a change of activity is contemplated is to set up a subsidiary with appropriate objects. Where a company limited by guarantee wishes to take advantage of an exemption under s 30 to dispense with the word 'limited' in its name, then requirements regarding its objects clause must be adhered to, see ss 30(3), 31(1).

Capacity of the company and the ultra vires doctrine   The capacity of a registered company to act is limited by the company's objects as stated in the memorandum: *Ashbury Railway Carriage and Iron Co Ltd v Riche* (1875) LR 7 HL 653. In addition to its express objects, the court will imply that the company may do all such other things as are incidental or conducive to the attainment of its objects: *A-G v Great Eastern Rly Co* (1880) 5 App Cas 473, HL; although in practice this provision is usually included expressly in the objects clause. The restriction of a company's capacity was intended to protect creditors and shareholders by requiring the company to operate within defined limits. Acts outside of the objects are ultra vires and void: *Ashbury Railway Carriage and Iron Co Ltd v Riche* (1875) LR 7 HL 653; although ratification is now provided for by statute (s 35(3)) and the position of persons dealing with the company is safeguarded by s 35(1).

Statutory reform   As far as persons dealing with the company are concerned, the significance of the ultra vires doctrine and therefore the objects clause is much diminished by the statutory reforms introduced by the CA 1989 and now contained in ss 35–35B. These provisions prevent the validity of any act done by a company from being questioned on the ground of lack of capacity. The ultra vires doctrine is retained as an internal matter and the shareholders can seek injunctive relief with respect to anticipated acts which are ultra vires (s 35(2)) and directors, and others, may be personally liable for losses arising from ultra vires transactions (see s 35(3) and the note to that provision). The doctrine retains some internal potency, therefore, which in turn is reflected in the drafting of objects clauses which attempt to ensure that the company has the widest possible capacity.

Short form objects   Essentially, a company may adopt short or long form objects. Short form objects involve the adoption of the statutory object, that the company is a 'general commercial company', as provided by s 3A: see the note to that provision.

Long form objects   Long form objects involve the setting out of every conceivable activity which the company might wish to undertake such that the objects clause may run for 30 or 40 or more provisions which obscure rather than clarify the company's objectives and which give no clue as to which activity the company might actually be pursuing.

In addition to what is in effect a dictionary list of objects, there will be a *Cotman v Brougham* clause. Attempts by the courts to limit the company's objects by applying a main objects rule of construction, ie identifying an initial number of main objects and construing the remaining provisions as subsidiary to those main objects, were met by the inclusion of an independent objects clause, ie a clause stating that each clause in the objects clause is to be construed independently and is not to be regarded as subsidiary to any other clause. The validity of such clauses was confirmed in *Cotman v Brougham* [1918] AC 514, HL; see also *Anglo-Overseas Agencies Ltd v Green* [1961] 1 QB 1.

A further addition will be a *Bell Houses* clause, ie a provision allowing the directors: '... to carry on any other trade or business whatsoever which can, in their opinion, be advantageously carried on by the company in connection with or as ancillary to the general business of the company': *Bell Houses Ltd v City Wall Properties Ltd* [1966] 2 QB 656, CA. A clause of this nature ensures that the bona fide opinion of the directors is sufficient to decide whether an activity of the company is intra vires even though it has no objective connection with or relationship to the company's main business: '... it matters not how mistaken the directors may be. Providing they form their view honestly, the business is within the [plaintiff] company's objects and powers' (at 690, per Salmon LJ).

Objects and powers   As noted above, the objects clause usually contains a power enabling the company to do all such other things as are incidental or conducive to the attainment of its objects although the courts would imply a provision to this effect in any event: *A-G v Great Eastern Rly Co* (1880) 5 App Cas 473, HL; see also *Evans v Brunner, Mond & Co Ltd* [1921] 1 Ch 359.

In addition, it is common practice for the objects clause to contain a lengthy list of express powers, for example, the power to borrow, to rent property, to employ persons, to operate bank facilities, to promote the company's products through advertising, to buy insurance, to give guarantees, etc. This is done to ensure that the company is not dependent on the court implying a particular power.

Powers do not and cannot stand alone; and an independent objects clause (see *Cotman v Brougham* [1918] AC 514, above) cannot convert a mere power into a substantive stand-alone object of the company: *Re Introductions Ltd* [1970] Ch 199, CA (court refused to accept that the borrowing of money could be an independent object, despite the presence of an independent objects clause: the power to borrow was by its nature incapable of constituting a substantive object and could only be exercised for the legitimate purposes of the company's business); *Rolled Steel Products (Holdings) Ltd v British Steel Corpn* [1985] 3 All ER 52, CA (power to lend and advance money was a mere power, despite the presence of an independent objects clause).

Powers exist for, and must be exercised for, the purposes of the company but no such limitation exists with respect to an act construed to be within the terms of a substantive object because, by definition, this is something which the company is formed to do: *Re Horsley & Weight Ltd* [1982] 3 All ER 1045, CA. In that case, the court construed a power to grant pensions as a substantive object of the company (cf *Re Introductions Ltd* [1970] Ch 199) and so it was irrelevant whether the grant of a pension pursuant to that object would benefit or promote the commercial prospects of the company. It is for this reason that, despite the protection of ss 35 and 35A, lenders like to ensure that a company which gives a guarantee of the liabilities of another company or companies in a group have the power to give guarantees in their objects clause drafted as an independent substantive object so as to prevent any issue arising as to the benefit to the guaranteeing company of issuing the guarantee. Where the power is drafted as a substantive object, no issue of ultra vires arises but there remains the issue of whether the directors were acting bona fide in the interests of the company when they entered into the transaction.

In fact, whether a provision is a power or a substantive object is of little significance now in terms of the ultra vires doctrine, as a result initially of the decision in *Rolled Steel Products (Holdings) Ltd v British Steel Corpn* [1985] 3 All ER 52, discussed below, and subsequently because of the provisions of s 35. But the distinction still has relevance to the question of whether the directors have exceeded or abused their authority, for powers are more limited in their scope than substantive objects.

See s 719 which implies a power to make provision for employees on the cessation or transfer of business, even if it is not in the best interests of the company.

Ultra vires acts   The position as to what constitutes an ultra vires act was clarified by the Court of Appeal in *Rolled Steel Products (Holdings) Ltd v British Steel Corpn* [1985] 3 All ER 52. The court distinguished between acts which are beyond the capacity of the company and acts which are carried out by the directors in excess or abuse of their powers. Only the former are ultra vires transactions and void.

Whether a transaction is beyond the capacity of the company and ultra vires is a matter of construction of the memorandum. The objects clause must be construed to see whether there is explicit provision for the activity or transaction in question, whether expressed as an object or a power, or whether the transaction is capable of being performed as reasonably ancillary or incidental to the objects. If the transaction falls within either of these categories (ie either expressly provided for, whether as an object or as a power, or within an implied power) then it is intra vires; otherwise it is ultra vires. This approach coupled with the practice of using long form objects means that it would be rare now for a transaction to be ultra vires.

The consequences of a transaction being ultra vires are dealt with by s 35 which ensures that a person dealing with the company is unaffected although the matter has internal repercussions as the directors have failed to observe limitations on their powers flowing from the company's memorandum hence the importance of continuing to draft long form objects in as expansive a manner as possible, see note to s 35 and, in particular, to s 35(3). Where the transaction is intra vires but the directors have exceeded or abused their authority, the position of the other party is safeguarded by s 35A but the directors, and others, remain potentially liable for breach of duty, see note to s 35A and, in particular, to s 35A(5).

Gratuitous transactions   A particular problem which had concerned the courts prior to the decision in *Rolled Steel* and prior to the statutory reforms, was transactions which could be classed as gratuitous transactions: see *International Sales and Agencies Ltd v Marcus* [1982] 3 All ER 551 (payments to clear deceased director's debts); *Re Horsley & Weight Ltd* [1982] 3 All ER 1045 (ex-gratia payments to retired employees); *Re Halt Garage Ltd* [1982] 3 All ER 1016 (payments to inactive director); *Simmonds v Heffer* [1983] BCLC 298 (political donations).

A long form objects clause will invariably contain provisions relating to pensions, remuneration, guarantees, donations etc as well as an independent objects clause. An express provision appropriate to the gratuitous transaction, whether expressed as an object or as a power, will usually exist therefore so, applying *Rolled Steel,* the transaction would be intra vires. No question of ultra vires will arise (and even if it did, the other party is protected by s 35) although there may be an issue as to whether the directors have acted in the best interests of the company in entering into the transaction and the identity of the recipient will be relevant to that issue.

The position of the other party where the directors have exceeded or abused their powers is safeguarded by s 35A (if the other party is in good faith and see s 35A(2)) but directors remain potentially liable for breach of duty. In determining whether the directors have acted in breach of their duties, the distinction between powers and objects will retain some significance since, as noted above, powers must be exercised for the purposes of the company whereas no such limitation applies to substantive objects.

S 2(3)

See note to s 1(2)(a), (b), above.

S 2(4)

See note to s 1(2)(b). The specified amount cannot be increased thereafter as no provision has been made for its alteration, see s 2(7). A company limited by guarantee may create multiple classes of members, however, a point confirmed by s 352(4).

S 2(5)(a)

An unlimited company with a share capital must set out its share capital in the articles, see Companies (Tables A to F) Regulations 1985, SI 1985/805, as amended, Table E, reg 3.

The amount of share capital   For a private company limited by shares, a typical clause will specify that the company's authorised capital is £100 divided into 100 £1 shares. There is no requirement to issue up to this amount and it is common to find such companies with only two (or one) issued shares. There is no minimum share capital with respect to a private company. In the case of a public company formed as such, the amount of the share capital stated in the memorandum must not be less than the authorised minimum: s 11; which is currently £50,000: s 118; see also note to s 117.

The fixed amount of the share (£1, in the example above) is the nominal or par value of each share and it can be any figure including fractions of a penny. There are no restrictions on the number of shares or on their nominal value and many companies have shares of 25p or 10p or 1p. It is for the company to determine the appropriate figure. The significance of the amount of the nominal or par value is that companies cannot issue shares at less than this amount (see s 100), so setting the figure too high may prove a problem if the shares cannot be sold at that price. Hence the preference for very low nominal values.

There is no requirement to denominate share capital in sterling other than, it seems, in relation to the minimum authorised capital for a public company: see ss 117, 118, and *Re Scandinavian Bank Group plc* [1987] BCLC 220. A company may have its share capital divided into several different classes of shares, each with a different nominal amount, and each, if so desired, denominated in a different currency: *Re Scandinavian Bank Group plc* [1987] BCLC 220. This will permit the denomination of shares in euros in the memorandum of association. The redenomination of existing capital is more problematic, see note to s 121(2) below.

Increasing the amount of the share capital   The capital figure as stated in the memorandum is a ceiling on the amount of capital which can be issued. An allotment in excess of the authorised capital is void: *Bank of Hindustan, China and Japan Ltd v Alison* (1867) LR 6 CP 222; *Re a Company (No 00789 of 1987), ex p Shooter* [1990] BCLC 384 at 389; although in view of the fact that the ceiling may be raised by an ordinary resolution, it may be (assuming the articles authorise an increase in the authorised capital) that the allotment should be voidable and not void. To avoid any problems, the correct procedure is to raise the ceiling by an ordinary resolution under s 121 which permits, subject to authorisation in the articles, a range of alterations to the capital figure as specified in the memorandum. See also ss 135, 138(5).

S 2(5)(b),(c), (6)

These provisions establish the requirements with respect to the subscribers to the memorandum who are identified by s 1(1). See also s 106.

S 2(6A)

This provision was inserted by the Companies Act 1985 (Electronic Communications) Order 2000, SI 2000/3373, art 2(1),(3), as from 22 December 2000 to facilitate electronic incorporation; as to the delivery of documents to the registrar using electronic communications, see s 707B.

S 2(7)

Alteration of the memorandum of association   In keeping with its status as one of the constitutional documents of the company, the memorandum of association is not freely alterable but only to the extent where express provision is made for its alteration. However, provision has been made for the alteration of many of the provisions although no alteration can be made, without a member's consent, to increase his obligation to contribute to the company: s 16.

Name The name of the company may be changed under s 28.

Status The status of the company as a public company (which must be stated in the memorandum, see s 1(3)(a)) must be deleted from the memorandum when the company is re-registered as a private company, see s 53; and a private company re-registering as a public company may add this clause: s 43(2)(a).

Jurisdiction This clause cannot be altered with the exception that a company may change jurisdiction subsequently to Wales by special resolution (see note to sub-s (2), above).

Objects The objects may be altered under ss 4–6.

Limited liability Where the company is a company limited by shares, it may re-register as an unlimited company under s 49 and the memorandum may be altered to reflect its new status: see s 49(5); likewise, if an unlimited company re-registers as a limited company: see s 51(3)(a). The statute does permit a limited company to provide in its memorandum for directors with unlimited liability and to alter the memorandum so as to subject the directors to unlimited liability (ss 306, 307) but these provisions, unsurprisingly, are obsolete now.

Capital The authorised share capital may be altered by resolution, see s 121; or as part of a reduction of capital, see s 135(2).

The court has power to order alterations to the memorandum of association as required under various provisions: see ss 5, 54, 177, 461. As to the alteration (or entrenchment) of provisions in the memorandum which could have been contained in the articles, see s 17.

Where an alteration is made to the memorandum, a printed copy of the memorandum as altered must be delivered to the registrar of companies: s 18(2); and all copies of the memorandum issued after any alteration must embody the alteration: s 20.

3. Forms of memorandum

(1) Subject to the provisions of sections 1 and 2, the form of the memorandum of association of—

    (a) a public company, being a company limited by shares,

    (b) a public company, being a company limited by guarantee and having a share capital,

    (c) a private company limited by shares,

    (d) a private company limited by guarantee and not having a share capital,

    (e) a private company limited by guarantee and having a share capital, and

    (f) an unlimited company having a share capital,

shall be as specified respectively for such companies by regulations made by the Secretary of State, or as near to that form as circumstances admit.

(2)   Regulations under this section shall be made by statutory instrument subject to annulment in pursuance of a resolution of either House of Parliament.

General note

A similar provision with respect to the form of the articles of association can be found in s 8(4). The Tables provided by the regulations are intended to provide a model but not a straitjacket and they do not determine the contents of the constitutional documents. The general form of the relevant Table, setting out matters in numbered paragraphs, should be followed and the statutory requirements but otherwise the draftsman is free to add, subtract or vary, as the needs of the case suggest: *Gaiman v National Association for Mental Health* [1971] Ch 317.

In practice, there is little flexibility with the memorandum of association because of: (i) the prescribed clauses in s 1(3)(a) and s 2, and (ii) the dangers of including additional provisions in the memorandum in the light of s 2(7) which restricts the alteration of the memorandum. There is greater flexibility with the articles.

S 3(1)

The forms of memorandum of association are contained in the Companies (Tables A to F) Regulations 1985, SI 1985/805, as amended. The respective tables are for (a): Table F; (b) Table D, Pt I; (c) Table B; (d) Table C; (e) Table D, Pt II; (f) Table E.

3A. Statement of company's objects: general commercial company

Where the company's memorandum states that the object of the company is to carry on business as a general commercial company—

    (a)   the object of the company is to carry on any trade or business whatsoever, and

    (b)   the company has power to do all such things as are incidental or conducive to the carrying on of any trade or business by it.

General note

See note to s 2(1)(c) as to the requirement for a company to state its objects in the memorandum and as to the ultra vires doctrine.

This provision was inserted by the CA 1989, s 110(1) as part of the package of ultra vires reforms reflected in ss 35–35B. It was thought that companies which did not wish to retain the ultra vires doctrine as an internal matter (see s 35(3)) could effectively opt out of it by adopting this object. In fact, doubts about the scope of this provision have made it an unattractive option for companies.

Uncertain scope of the provision   As to (a), it is not clear whether the entitlement to carry on any trade or business would allow a company, say, to sell its entire undertaking or pursue charitable objectives. As to (b), companies prefer to include this type of provision expressly in their objects clause and to make the issue a matter for the subjective opinion of their directors rather than an objective matter as here; see discussion in note to s 2(1)(c). Moreover, the scope of what is meant by 'incidental or conducive to the carrying on of any trade or business' has preoccupied the courts for many years, particularly with respect to gratuitous transactions such as gifts, donations, and guarantees.

It is also unclear as to whether a company must adopt only this object ('... memorandum states that *the* object of the company ...'). In practice, it is not uncommon to see companies adopt a long form of objects (see note to s 2(1)(c)) as well as this provision. It is unclear what approach the court would take when confronted with such a combination.

Given these uncertainties, and given that the decision in *Rolled Steel Products (Holdings) Ltd v British Steel Corpn* [1985] 3 All ER 52, CA (see note to s 2(1)(c), above) shows clearly the merits of having extensive express provisions in the objects clause so reducing the risk of a transaction being ultra vires and the directors being liable for breach of duty under s 35(3), it is not surprising that companies are reluctant to adopt this provision as a stand-alone object.

4. Resolution to alter objects

(1)   A company may by special resolution alter its memorandum with respect to the statement of the company's objects.

(2)   If an application is made under the following section, an alteration does not have effect except in so far as it is confirmed by the court.

General note

This provision, giving an unrestricted power to alter the objects, was introduced by CA 1989, s 110(2). Prior to 1989, only specified types of alterations to the objects clause were permitted although it was rare for any challenge to be made to an alteration. When a significant change of activity is contemplated, it may be more appropriate to set up a subsidiary with the required objects and name than to change the objects of an existing company.

Statutory constraints on alteration   A company limited by guarantee which is exempt from the requirement that its name end with 'limited' under s 30 is prevented from making certain alterations to its objects: see s 31(1), (5); and the power to alter the objects is subject to any pre-existing court order restricting alterations to the memorandum, without the leave of the court, which order might arise under a variety of provisions: see ss 5(6), 54(8), 177(4).

Objections to alterations   The power to alter is subject to any objections lodged under s 5 and to the requirements of s 6. An alteration which reflects a significant change of activities by a company may also require a change of name (see s 28) to avoid a direction from the Secretary of State for Trade and Industry under s 32 (power to require company to abandon misleading name): see *Re Governments Stock Investment Co (No 2)* [1892] 1 Ch 597.

S 4(1)

Special resolution   As to a special resolution, see s 378; a private company may use a written resolution: s 381A(1), (6). In either case, the resolution must be forwarded to the registrar of companies within 15 days after it is passed or made: s 380(1), (4)(a); and, as a document making or evidencing an alteration in the company's memorandum or articles, the resolution must be gazetted under s 711(1)(b) and is subject to s 42 which limits the company's ability to rely on the alteration until officially notified in the Gazette. The resolution takes effect when passed, subject to s 42. However, as objectors have 21 days in which to go to court (s 5(3)), it is inadvisable to act on the resolution until 21 days have passed. A printed copy of the memorandum as altered must be delivered to the registrar, see s 6; and any copy of the memorandum issued thereafter must embody the alteration: s 20.

   Informal unanimous consent is also effective to alter the objects: *Re Home Treat Ltd* [1991] BCLC 705; *Re Duomatic Ltd* [1969] 1 All ER 161; see also *Wright v Atlas Wright (Europe) Ltd* [1999] 2 BCLC 301, CA.

---

5. Procedure for objecting to alteration

(1)   Where a company's memorandum has been altered by special resolution under section 4, application may be made to the court for the alteration to be cancelled.

(2)   Such an application may be made—

   (a) by the holders of not less in the aggregate than 15 per cent in nominal value of the company's issued share capital or any class of it or, if the company is not limited by shares, not less than 15 per cent of the company's members; or

   (b) by the holders of not less than 15 per cent of the company's debentures entitling the holders to object to an alteration of its objects;

but an application shall not be made by any person who has consented to or voted in favour of the alteration.

(3)   The application must be made within 21 days after the date on which the resolution altering the company's objects was passed, and may be made on behalf of the persons entitled to make the application by such one or more of their number as they may appoint in writing for the purpose.

(4)   The court may on such an application make an order confirming the alteration either wholly or in part and on such terms and conditions as it thinks fit, and may—

   (a) if it thinks fit, adjourn the proceedings in order that an arrangement may be made to its satisfaction for the purchase of the interests of dissentient members, and

   (b) give such directions and make such orders as it thinks expedient for facilitating or carrying into effect any such arrangement.

(5)   The court's order may (if the court thinks fit) provide for the purchase by the company of the shares of any members of the company, and for the reduction accordingly of its capital, and may make such alterations in the company's memorandum and articles as may be required in consequence of that provision.

(6)   If the court's order requires the company not to make any, or any specified, alteration in its memorandum or articles, the company does not then have power without the leave of the court to make any such alteration in breach of that requirement.

(7)   An alteration in the memorandum or articles of a company made by virtue of an order under this section, other than one made by resolution of the company, is of the same effect as if duly made by resolution; and this Act applies accordingly to the memorandum or articles as so altered.

(8)   The debentures entitling the holders to object to an alteration of a company's objects are any debentures secured by a floating charge which were issued or first issued before 1st December 1947 or form part of the same series as any debentures so issued; and a special resolution altering a company's objects requires the same notice to the holders of any such debentures as to members of the company.

In the absence of provisions regulating the giving of notice to any such debenture holders, the provisions of the company's articles regulating the giving of notice to members apply.

S 5(2)

Application to the court   This provision identifies the thresholds for those objecting, whether in a company limited by shares or by guarantee, although in practice objections are rare. The applicants must either hold 15% in nominal value of the shares or of the class or have been appointed in writing by the holders of 15% at the date of the application and not merely when it comes on for hearing: see *Re Sound City (Films) Ltd* [1947] Ch 169; *Re Suburban and Provincial Stores Ltd* [1943] Ch 156 (on identical wording in s 127). Shareholders who do not meet the thresholds have no locus standi in their own right to apply and can only be heard in support of the contentions of a qualified applicant: *Re Hampstead Garden Suburb Trust Ltd* [1962] Ch 806. The right of debenture holders to object is obsolete now, see s 5(8).

The Jenkins Committee in 1962 criticised the proviso which excludes those who voted for the alteration. The effect is to exclude a nominee or trustee who casts his votes in favour of a proposed alteration on behalf of some beneficiaries but against the alteration on behalf of others: he cannot apply to the court on behalf of the latter (Report of the Company Law Committee, Cmnd 1749, para 49(iii)).

The grounds for the application are not specified but possibilities would include that the new object would not be lawful or that there was a procedural irregularity in the holding of the meeting or the passing of the resolution.

S 5(3)

As to the date of the passing of a written resolution, see s 381A(3); see s 6(4) on the consequences of the expiry of the 21-day period.

S 5(4)–(5)

Powers of the court   The purchase of shares envisaged by sub-s (4)(a) need not be by the company but may be by other members of the company; where, under sub-s (5), the court orders the company to purchase the shares of any members, any such purchase is exempt from the prohibition on a company purchasing its own shares: s 143(3)(c). The court must order the purchase of the entire holding; but the order is not necessarily limited to dissenting members although in practice this will be the case.

Nothing in s 125(2)–(5) requiring consent to a variation or abrogation of class rights affects the court's powers under this provision: s 126.

S 5(6)–(7)

The effect of sub-s (7) is that a court ordered alteration is open to subsequent alteration by the company in the normal manner, subject to sub-s (6).

S 5(8)

Given the passage of time, this limitation on the class of debenture holders who may object ensures that there are probably no debenture holders now who would qualify under this provision.

6. Provisions supplementing ss 4, 5

(1) Where a company passes a resolution altering its objects, then—

    (a) if with respect to the resolution no application is made under section 5, the company shall within 15 days from the end of the period for making such an application deliver to the registrar of companies a printed copy of its memorandum as altered; and

    (b) if such an application is made, the company shall—

        (i) forthwith give notice (in the prescribed form) of that fact to the registrar, and

        (ii) within 15 days from the date of any order cancelling or confirming the alteration, deliver to the registrar an office copy of the order and, in the case of an order confirming the alteration, a printed copy of the memorandum as altered.

(2) The court may by order at any time extend the time for the delivery of documents to the registrar under subsection (1)(b) for such period as the court may think proper.

(3) If a company makes default in giving notice or delivering any document to the registrar of companies as required by subsection (1), the company and every officer of it who is in default is liable to a fine and, for continued contravention, to a daily default fine.

(4) The validity of an alteration of a company's memorandum with respect to the objects of the company shall not be questioned on the ground that it was not authorised by section 4, except in proceedings taken for the purpose (whether under section 5 or otherwise) before the expiration of 21 days after the date of the resolution in that behalf.

(5) Where such proceedings are taken otherwise than under section 5, subsections (1) to (3) above apply in relation to the proceedings as if they had been taken under that section, and as if an order declaring the alteration invalid were an order cancelling it, and as if an order dismissing the proceedings were an order confirming the alteration.

S 6(1), (2)

Notification to the registrar   To allow for objections, the company must wait 21 days from the passing of the resolution (s 5(3)). It then has a further 15 days within which to deliver to the registrar of companies a printed copy of the memorandum as altered. The registrar will already have received (within 15 days after the passing of the resolution) notice of the resolution altering the objects (see note to s 4(1)) and the resolution too must be gazetted under s 711(1)(b) and is subject to s 42; so while quite a long period may elapse before the amended memorandum appears on the public record, notice of the resolution will have appeared at a much earlier stage. If objectors apply to the court, the company must notify the registrar of companies of that fact and then await the outcome of the court hearing. The receipt of the memorandum as altered must be gazetted by the registrar of companies: s 711(1)(b); and s 42 applies.

S 6(3)

As to penalties, see s 730, Sch 24; 'officer in default' is defined in s 730(5).

S 6(4), (5)

The provision in sub-s (4) was included when the power to alter objects was restricted to a number of set alterations. The intention was to limit disputes as to whether or not an alteration was within one of the specified cases. The Jenkins Committee recommended that if the limitations on alterations were removed, as they have been, this provision should be repealed (Report of the Company Law Committee, Cmnd 1749, para 48). However, it remains in the legislation.

The time limit applies to proceedings either under s 5 or 'otherwise'. As proceedings under s 5 are limited to objections by shareholders or members (and a limited and obsolete category of debenture holder), this presumably envisages objections by others, such as creditors, although it is unlikely that today any creditor would wish to challenge an alteration to the objects. Where they do so object, they too are limited by the 21-day period (a suggestion to the contrary in *Re Home Treat Ltd* [1991] BCLC 705 at 710 seems to ignore the words 'or otherwise' in sub-s (4)).

Where a creditor or any other person wishes to object, sub-ss (1)–(3) apply so as to ensure that the registrar of companies is kept informed.

ARTICLES OF ASSOCIATION

7. Articles prescribing regulations for companies

(1)   There may in the case of a company limited by shares, and there shall in the case of a company limited by guarantee or unlimited, be registered with the memorandum articles of association signed by the subscribers to the memorandum and prescribing regulations for the company.

(2)   In the case of an unlimited company having a share capital, the articles must state the amount of share capital with which the company proposes to be registered.

(3)   Articles must—

  (a) be printed,

  (b) be divided into paragraphs numbered consecutively, and

  (c) subject to subsection (3A), be signed by each subscriber of the memorandum in the presence of at least one witness who must attest the signature.

(3A) Where the articles are delivered to the registrar otherwise than in legible form and are authenticated by each subscriber to the memorandum in such manner as is directed by the registrar, the requirements in subsection (3)(c) for signature in the presence of at least one witness and for attestation of the signature do not apply.

General note

Legal status   The legal status of the articles of association is determined by s 14. A company has two constitutional documents, one being the articles, the other being the memorandum of association (see s 2). In the event of a conflict, the memorandum, as the document containing the fundamental conditions upon which alone the company is allowed to be incorporated, prevails over the articles which contain the internal regulations of the company: *Guinness v Land Corpn of Ireland* (1882) 22 Ch D 349.

  The articles are a commercial document and, in the event of any ambiguity, the courts will construe them so as to give them business efficacy, if possible: *Holmes v Keyes* [1959] Ch 199; and see note to s 14 as to the extent to which the courts might imply terms in the articles. The court has no jurisdiction to rectify the articles even if the articles do not accord with what was the intention of the subscribers to them: *Scott v Frank F Scott (London) Ltd* [1940] Ch 794; instead the members must alter the articles using the mechanism in s 9.

S 7(1)

Model forms of articles are provided by the Companies (Tables A–F) Regulations 1985, SI 1985/805 as amended: s 8. As to a company limited by shares, see s 1(2)(a);

this provision is permissive since, for such companies, the model form of articles (Table A) applies by default: s 8(2). As to a company limited by guarantee, see s 1(2)(b). As to an unlimited company, see s 1(2)(c). As to the subscribers to the memorandum of association, see s 1(1).

S 7(2)

See Companies (Tables A–F) Regulations 1985, SI 1985/805, as amended, Table E, reg 3.

S 7(3)

These requirements as to form must be followed but otherwise the draftsman is free to add, subtract or vary the articles, as the needs of the case suggest: *Gaiman v National Association for Mental Health* [1971] Ch 317. The requirement that the articles be signed can be overlooked which will result in them being rejected by the registrar of companies.

S 7(3A)

This provision was inserted by the Companies Act 1985 (Electronic Communications) Order 2000, SI 2000/3373, art 3(1),(3), as from 22 December 2000 to facilitate electronic incorporation; as to the delivery of documents to the registrar using electronic communications, see s 707B.

8. Tables A, C, D and E

(1)   Table A is as prescribed by regulations made by the Secretary of State; and a company may for its articles adopt the whole or any part of that Table.

(2)   In the case of a company limited by shares, if articles are not registered or, if articles are registered, in so far as they do not exclude or modify Table A, that Table (so far as applicable, and as in force at the date of the company's registration) constitutes the company's articles, in the same manner and to the same extent as if articles in the form of that Table had been duly registered.

(3)   If in consequence of regulations under this section Table A is altered, the alteration does not affect a company registered before the alteration takes effect, or repeal as respects that company any portion of the Table.

(4)   The form of the articles of association of—

    (a)   a company limited by guarantee and not having a share capital,

    (b)   a company limited by guarantee and having a share capital, and

    (c)   an unlimited company having a share capital,

shall be respectively in accordance with Table C, D or E prescribed by regulations made by the Secretary of State, or as near to that form as circumstances admit.

(5)　Regulations under this section shall be made by statutory instrument subject to annulment in pursuance of a resolution of either House of Parliament.

S 8(1)

Table A is the model form of articles for companies limited by shares provided by the Companies (Tables A to F) Regulations 1985, SI 1985/805 as amended, and any company may adopt all or part of it; see also s 8(2).

S 8(2), (3)

Options　This provision offers public or private companies limited by shares a number of possibilities:

(1)　A company limited by shares need not register articles at all and Table A will apply automatically. It is unusual for any company, public or private, not to register any articles at all.

(2)　A company may draw up a number of articles concerning matters of particular interest to the shareholders and adopt the remainder of Table A by stating that Table A applies except to the extent that it is excluded. This common practice can give rise to difficulties as it is not always clear whether the specific provisions have excluded or modified Table A. Moreover, it requires the shareholders and anyone using the articles to refer to the specific provisions and to Table A and there may be inconsistencies as between the two documents. Given that private companies typically have a very small number of shareholders and the costs of printing an entire set of articles are minimal, this method of adoption of articles should be avoided.

(3)　A company may expressly exclude all of Table A and register an entire set of articles. This allows the company to adopt a combination of specific provisions drafted to meet its circumstances and those provisions of Table A which seem appropriate. Registering such articles as a stand alone document is the most desirable method of proceeding, not least because by including all of the provisions within one document, it can be reviewed for internal consistency before adoption so avoiding subsequent disputes.

The articles may be in Welsh if the company's registered office as stated in the memorandum of association is in Wales: s 710B.

It is Table A as in force at the time of the company's registration which applies, which explains why many companies on the register are still governed by the 1948 Table A; and see, exceptionally, ss 369(4F), 379A(2F).

S 8(4), (5)

The Tables provided by the regulations (Companies (Tables A to F) Regulations 1985, SI 1985/805, as amended) are intended to provide a model but not a straitjacket and they do not determine the contents of the constitutional documents. The general form of the relevant Table, for example, setting out matters in numbered paragraphs, should be followed and the statutory requirements met but otherwise the draftsman is free to add, subtract or vary, as the needs of the case suggest: *Gaiman v National Association for Mental Health* [1971] Ch 317. These tables, unlike Table A, are not default provisions, see s 8(2) above. See also s 15.

8A   Table G

(1)   The Secretary of State may by regulations prescribe a Table G containing articles of association appropriate for a partnership company, that is, a company limited by shares whose shares are intended to be held to a substantial extent by or on behalf of its employees.

(2)   A company limited by shares may for its articles adopt the whole or any part of that Table.

(3)   If in consequence of regulations under this section Table G is altered, the alteration does not affect a company registered before the alteration takes effect, or repeal as respects that company any portion of the Table.

(4)   Regulations under this section shall be made by statutory instrument which shall be subject to annulment in pursuance of a resolution of either House of Parliament.

General note

This provision was inserted by the CA 1989, s 128 but was not brought into force. It was intended to provide a model form of articles for a company limited by shares where there was substantial employee participation. It is not expected that it will be brought into force.

9. Alteration of articles by special resolution

(1)   Subject to the provisions of this Act and to the conditions contained in its memorandum, a company may by special resolution alter its articles.

(2)   Alterations so made in the articles are (subject to this Act) as valid as if originally contained in them, and are subject in like manner to alteration by special resolution.

General note

Statutory power to alter the articles   Any agreement or article purporting to deprive a company of the power to alter its articles is invalid on the ground that it is contrary to the statute: *Walker v London Tramways Co* (1879) 12 Ch D 705; *Malleson v National Insurance and Guarantee Corpn* [1894] 1 Ch 200; *Allen v Gold Reefs of*

West Africa Ltd [1900] 1 Ch 656 at 671; *Punt v Symons & Co Ltd* [1903] 2 Ch 506; *Southern Foundries (1926) Ltd v Shirlaw* [1940] AC 701 at 740–741, per Lord Porter; *Cumbrian Newspapers Group Ltd v Cumberland & Westmorland Herald Newspaper & Printing Co Ltd* [1986] 2 All ER 816 at 831; *Russell v Northern Bank Development Corpn Ltd* [1992] BCLC 1016.

Entrenching a provision   Notwithstanding that a company cannot be deprived of the power to alter the articles, there are a number of mechanisms which make it possible to entrench a provision and render it unalterable:

(1) Weighted voting rights may be granted to a shareholder or group of shareholders to ensure that a resolution to alter the articles cannot be passed: see *Bushell v Faith* [1969] 1 All ER 1002.

(2) The statutory power to alter the articles is subject to the provisions of the Act which include s 125 which governs the variation or abrogation of any class rights (as to which, see note to s 125) and which generally requires the consent of the class. Class rights can be used therefore to prevent particular provisions from being altered without the consent of the class: see *Cumbrian Newspapers Group Ltd v Cumberland & Westmorland Herald Newspaper & Printing Co Ltd* [1986] 2 All ER 816. See also *Harman v BML Group Ltd* [1994] 2 BCLC 674 where quorum provisions constituted as class rights operated to prevent a shareholders' meeting being called so preventing any resolutions being passed.

(3) Shareholders may reach an agreement outside of the articles as to how they would exercise their voting rights on any resolution to alter the articles: *Russell v Northern Bank Development Corpn Ltd* [1992] 3 All ER 161, HL. The company must not be a party to the shareholders' agreement: *Russell v Northern Bank Development Corpn Ltd* [1992] 3 All ER 161.

(4) The provisions of the memorandum of association, unlike the articles, are not generally alterable, see s 2(7). It is possible therefore to entrench provisions by including them in the memorandum of association, subject to s 17; and see the note to that provision as to making such provisions unalterable.

S 9(1)

Subject to the provisions of the Act   Various provisions in CA 1985 either prevent certain types of alterations or permit alterations by methods other than by a special resolution under this section:

(1) an alteration cannot require a member to take more shares or in any way increase his liability to the company without his consent (s 16);

(2) a company limited by guarantee which is exempt under s 30 from the use of the word 'limited' in its name may not alter its memorandum or articles so as to defeat the conditions in s 30(3) without losing the exemption (s 31(1));

(3) an alteration cannot vary or abrogate class rights without compliance with s 125, which governs such matters;

(4) certain provisions are required or excluded in some situations so alterations to delete required provisions or include excluded provisions are impermissible: see s 7(2) (articles of an unlimited company with a share capital must state the amount of that share capital); s 15 (articles of a

company limited by guarantee must not make provision for the division of the company's undertaking into share capital);

(5)   various provisions enable the court to order an alteration of the articles or to prohibit an alteration: see ss 5(4)–(6), 54(5)–(8), 177(2)–(4), 461(2)–(4), although these powers are rarely used;

(6)   where a company re-registers (for example, changes from a public company to a private company), such alterations to the articles as are requisite may be effected as part of the re-registration process: see ss 43(2), 49(6), 51(3), 53(2);

(7)   a resolution to give, vary, revoke or renew the authority of the directors to allot shares under s 80 may be an ordinary resolution notwithstanding that it alters the company's articles: ss 80(8), 80A(3);

(8)   a directors' resolution that title to a class of shares may be in uncertificated form and transferred by means of the CREST system is effective (unless overturned by the shareholders) notwithstanding that this is inconsistent with the company's articles so, in effect, the directors alter the articles in this way: Uncertificated Securities Regulations 1995, SI 1995/3272, reg 16(3).

Subject to conditions in the memorandum   The power to alter the articles is also subject to any conditions in the memorandum. Simply including provisions in the memorandum of association which could have been in the articles is not sufficient to entrench them for such provisions are alterable as if they were in the articles: s 17(1); although they may be entrenched by provisions in the memorandum prohibiting their alteration or requiring a higher majority than that necessary for a special resolution. Such entrenchment, while possible, may not be advisable, see note to s 17.

Acceptance of alterations   Within the limits set by the statute, and by the memorandum, the rights of members, so far as they depend on the regulations of the company, are subject to alteration and a member joins a company on the understanding that the articles may be changed: *Allen v Gold Reefs of West Africa Co Ltd* [1900] 1 Ch 656 at 672, 673; *Greenhalgh v Arderne Cinemas Ltd* [1951] 2 All ER 1120 at 1127; *Malleson v National Insurance and Guarantee Corpn* [1894] 1 Ch 200 at 205, 206.

Special resolution   As to a special resolution, see s 378; a private company may use a written resolution: s 381A(1), (6). In either case, the resolution must be forwarded to the registrar of companies within 15 days after it is passed or made: s 380(1), (4)(a); and, as a document making or evidencing an alteration in the company's articles, the resolution must be gazetted under s 711(1)(b) and is subject to s 42 which limits the company's ability to rely on the alteration until officially notified in the Gazette. A copy of the articles as altered must be sent to the registrar of companies with the resolution: s 18(2); and a copy of the resolution must be embodied in every copy of the articles issued after the alteration: s 380(2). Informal unanimous consent is also effective to alter the articles: *Cane v Jones* [1981] 1 All ER 533; *Re Duomatic Ltd* [1969] 1 All ER 161; *Wright v Atlas Wright (Europe) Ltd* [1999] 2 BCLC 301, CA.

Bona fide for the benefit of the company as a whole   The statutory provision provides the mechanism by which an alteration of the articles can be affected. However, any exercise of the power to alter the articles must be exercised 'not only in the manner required by law but also bona fide for the benefit of the company as a whole and it must not be exceeded': *Allen v Gold Reefs of West Africa Ltd* [1900] 1 Ch 656 at 671, per Lindley MR; *Shuttleworth v Cox Bros & Co (Maidenhead) Ltd* [1927] 2 KB 9; *Greenhalgh v Arderne Cinemas Ltd* [1950] 2 All ER 1120. In this context, 'the company as a whole' does not mean the company as a commercial entity but rather the corporators as a general body: *Greenhalgh v Arderne Cinemas Ltd* [1950] 2 All ER 1120 at 1126.

The test of whether an alteration is bona fide for the benefit of the company as a whole is not one of (i) bona fides and (ii) benefit of the company as a whole, but is a single test requiring the shareholders to act honestly, having regard to and endeavouring to act for the benefit of the company: *Sidebottom v Kershaw, Leese & Co Ltd* [1920] 1 Ch 154 at 172; *Shuttleworth v Cox Bros & Co (Maidenhead) Ltd* [1927] KB 9 at 23; *Greenhalgh v Arderne Cinemas Ltd* [1950] 2 All ER 1120.

It is for the shareholders, and not for the court, to say whether an alteration is for the benefit of the company, provided that it is not such that no reasonable man could consider it for the benefit of the company: *Shuttleworth v Cox Bros & Co (Maidenhead) Ltd* [1927] KB 9 (rejecting support for an objective test in *Dafen Tinplate v Llanelly Steel Co* [1920] 2 Ch 124). If, applying this test, an alteration is bona fide for the benefit of the company as a whole, the fact that it will prejudice an individual shareholder is irrelevant: *Sidebottom v Kershaw, Leese & Co Ltd* [1920] 1 Ch 154; *Greenhalgh v Arderne Cinemas Ltd* [1950] 2 All ER 1120; *Shuttleworth v Cox Bros & Co (Maidenhead) Ltd* [1927] KB 9 at 23; *Allen v Gold Reefs of West Africa Ltd* [1900] 1 Ch 656; the position is different if the alteration is targeted at an individual for malicious or dishonest reasons.

The onus of proof is on those who assert that the alteration is not bona fide: *Peter's American Delicacy Co Ltd v Heath* (1939) 61 CLR 457.

Some examples The courts have permitted alterations to enable a company:
- to issue preference shares (*Andrews v Gas Meter Co* [1897] 1 Ch 361);
- to extend a lien from partly paid shares to fully paid shares (*Allen v Gold Reefs of West Africa Ltd* [1900] 1 Ch 656);
- to relax restrictions on the transfer of shares (*Greenhalgh v Arderne Cinemas Ltd* [1950] 2 All ER 1120);
- to facilitate the vacating of office by a director (*Shuttleworth v Cox Bros & Co (Maidenhead) Ltd* [1927] KB 9); and
- to permit the removal of a competing shareholder (*Sidebottom v Kershaw, Leese & Co Ltd* [1920] 1 Ch 154).

Compulsory acquisition It is rare for a challenge to an alteration to succeed, the court being reluctant to disagree with the subjective opinion of 75% of the shareholders who voted on the alteration. The courts have rejected alterations, however, where majority shareholders have sought an unrestricted power, in their own interests, to expropriate the shares of the minority: see *Brown v British Abrasive Wheel Co* [1919] 1 Ch 290; *Dafen Tinplate v Llanelly Steel Co* [1920] 2 Ch 124. Such alterations confuse the interests of the majority with the benefit of the company as a whole. However, benefit to the company was found in *Sidebottom v Kershaw, Leese & Co Ltd* [1920] 1 Ch 154, where an alteration was permitted which provided for the compulsory purchase (at full value) of the shares of a shareholder who was actively interested in a rival business. A provision allowing for compulsory purchase, applicable to all members equally, can be included in the original articles: *Phillips v Manufacturers' Securities Ltd* (1917) 116 LT 290; *Borland's Trustee v Steel Bros & Co Ltd* [1901] 1 Ch 279.

Reformulating the test   The 'bona fide for the benefit of the company as a whole' test has been criticised as being inappropriate when what is at issue is a conflict between groups of shareholders: see *Peter's American Delicacy Co Ltd v Heath* (1939) 61 CLR 457; and the Australian High Court, in a controversial decision, has rejected it with respect to alterations giving rise to a conflict of interests and alterations involving the expropriation of shares or of valuable proprietary rights attaching to shares: see *Gambotto v WCP Ltd* (1995) 182 CLR 432, noted Prentice [1996] 112 LQR 194. The Australian court considered that the test to be applied where an alteration involved a conflict of interests was whether the alteration was ultra vires, beyond any purpose contemplated by the articles or oppressive. An alteration providing for the expropriation of shareholdings or other valuable proprietary rights attaching to shares would be permissible only if the power to expropriate was exercisable for a proper purpose and was not oppressive and the onus was on those proposing the alteration to establish its validity. This approach is not necessarily any more certain in its application than the 'bona fide for the benefit of the company as a whole' test of which the Australian court was so critical.

Here, in *Greenhalgh v Arderne Cinemas Ltd* [1950] 2 All ER 1120 at 1126, Evershed MR did attempt a reformulation of the test. In his view, a special resolution altering the articles would be liable to be impeached if the effect of it was to discriminate between the majority and the minority shareholders so as to give the former an advantage of which the latter were deprived. However, there are difficulties with this formulation too, not least that it sits somewhat uneasily with the line of authorities since *Allen v Gold Reefs of West Africa Ltd* [1900] 1 Ch 656 which might have been resolved differently had the test being applied actually been a test of discrimination as between shareholders. Moreover, this type of approach to the issue is probably unnecessary now in view of s 459 (the unfairly prejudicial remedy).

Notwithstanding the criticisms aired in *Gambotto*, the English courts may be reluctant to disregard a line of authority established for over a century and may prefer to continue to rely on the orthodox formulation of 'benefit to the company as a whole', particularly, perhaps, when an aggrieved shareholder may be able to obtain redress by way of a petition under s 459: see note to that provision, below.

Indeed, it might be argued that the existing settled state of the law coupled with statutory redress in cases of unfairly prejudicial conduct (under s 459) has struck the correct balance between freedom for the majority to make constitutional changes and the need to protect the minority against oppressive and discriminatory conduct.

Alterations and implied or express contracts   An alteration of the articles potentially has an impact on a contract entered into by the company in a number of situations:

(1)   A member has a contractual relationship with the company by virtue of s 14 and the articles form part of that contract. As noted above, a member joins a company on the basis that that contract is alterable and so cannot claim that an alteration amounts to a breach of the statutory contract.

(2)   The articles cannot confer rights on an outsider or on a member other than qua member: see note to s 14. However, a person (who may or may not be a member) may wish to rely on the articles as evidence of an implied contract extrinsic to the articles but, in that case, any implied contract is subject to alteration in the same manner as the articles on which it is founded: *Shuttleworth v Cox Bros & Co (Maidenhead) Ltd* [1927] 2 KB 9; *Swabey v Port Darwin Gold Mining Co* (1889) 1 Meg 385.

(3)   A person may have a contract entirely extrinsic to the articles but an

alteration to the articles renders performance of the contract impossible. The position in that case is that a company cannot be precluded from altering its articles thereby giving itself power to act upon the provisions of the altered articles, but so to act may nevertheless be a breach of contract if it is contrary to a stipulation in a contract validly made before the alteration: *Southern Foundries (1926) Ltd v Shirlaw* [1940] AC 701 at 740–741; *Cumbrian Newspapers Group Ltd v Cumberland & Westmorland Herald Newspaper & Printing Co Ltd* [1986] 2 All ER 816 at 831; *Punt v Symons & Co Ltd* [1903] 2 Ch 506.

In *Southern Foundries (1926) Ltd v Shirlaw* [1940] AC 701, a director was appointed as managing director for a ten-year period. The articles provided that any person who ceased to be a director automatically ceased to be managing director. The company altered the articles to facilitate the removal of any director. It then removed Shirlaw under the new provision with the effect that his contract as managing director was terminated. The House of Lords held that it was an implied term of his contract as managing director that the company would not terminate his appointment as director so making it impossible for him to continue as managing director. The company could not be constrained from altering its articles but it was liable for damages for breach of contract. See also *Shindler v Northern Raincoat Co Ltd* [1960] 2 All ER 239.

There has been some discussion in the cases as to whether injunctive relief might be available in this situation. In *Cumbrian Newspapers Group Ltd v Cumberland & Westmorland Herald Newspaper & Printing Co Ltd* [1986] 2 All ER 816 at 831, Scott J thought there was no reason why an injunction could not be obtained to prevent a company calling a meeting to alter its articles when it had contracted not to alter the articles. However, he also thought that a company could not be prevented from calling the meeting for the same purpose on a requisition of the shareholders, since it had a statutory obligation to do so; nor could an injunction be obtained to prevent the company from acting on the altered provisions.

REGISTRATION AND ITS CONSEQUENCES

10. Documents to be sent to registrar

(1) The company's memorandum and articles (if any) shall be delivered—

    (a) to the registrar of companies for England and Wales, if the memorandum states that the registered office of the company is to be situated in England and Wales, or that it is to be situated in Wales; and

    (b) to the registrar of companies for Scotland, if the memorandum states that the registered office of the company is to be situated in Scotland.

(2) With the memorandum there shall be delivered a statement in the prescribed form containing the names and requisite particulars of—

(a) the person who is, or the persons who are, to be the first director or directors of the company; and

(b) the person who is, or the persons who are, to be the first secretary or joint secretaries of the company;

and the requisite particulars in each case are those set out in Schedule 1.

(3)   The statement shall be signed by or on behalf of the subscribers of the memorandum and shall contain a consent signed by each of the persons named in it as a director, as secretary or as one of joint secretaries, to act in the relevant capacity.

(4)   Where a memorandum is delivered by a person as agent for the subscribers, the statement shall specify that fact and the person's name and address.

(5)   An appointment by any articles delivered with the memorandum of a person as director or secretary of the company is void unless he is named as a director or secretary in the statement.

(6)   There shall in the statement be specified the intended situation of the company's registered office on incorporation.

S 10(1)

The reference to articles, 'if any', reflects the fact that a company limited by shares need not register articles, in which case Table A will apply: see s 8(2).

The registrar of companies   The main office of the registrar of companies for companies registered in England and Wales is Companies House, Crown Way, Cardiff, CF14 3UZ and there are also offices in London, Birmingham, Manchester and Leeds. Documents may be delivered to the registrar at any of these offices which also provide search facilities for those wishing to search the register of companies. Increasingly, provision is made by Companies House for electronic filing of documents and for on-line searching. For further information, see the Companies House web site: www.companies-house.gov.uk.

  The main office of the registrar of companies for companies registered in Scotland is Companies House, 37 Castle Terrace, Edinburgh, EH1 2EB and there is also an office in Glasgow.

S 10(2)–(3), (5)

Appointments   The appointment of the first directors or secretary by naming them in the articles is insufficient and it is the persons named in the statement required by sub-s (2) who are deemed to have been appointed to the respective positions on incorporation: see s 13(5). The signatures 'by or on behalf of the subscribers' must not be overlooked; and those appointed must sign to indicate their consent; there is no requirement that such signatures be witnessed (cf s 2(6)).

Particulars   The particulars of the directors and the company secretary which must be provided to the registrar of companies are the same as those which must be included on the company's own register of directors and secretaries which is required by s 288: see notes to ss 288–290, below. Any changes among the directors or in its secretary or any change in the particulars contained in the register must be notified to the registrar of companies within 14 days, see s 288(2).

S 10(6)

The memorandum simply states whether the registered office is in England and Wales, Wales or Scotland: s 2(1); hence the need for the actual location to be specified in this statement. As to changes to that location, see s 287.

11. Minimum authorised capital (public companies)

When a memorandum delivered to the registrar of companies under section 10 states that the association to be registered is to be a public company, the amount of the share capital stated in the memorandum to be that with which the company proposes to be registered must not be less than the authorised minimum (defined in section 118).

General note

This requirement arises from the 2nd EC Company Law Directive, art 6 (Council Directive (EEC) 77/91 (OJL 26 31.1.77, p 1), which requires public limited companies to have a minimum authorised share capital which is set at £50,000 by s 118. As to the capital statement in the memorandum, see s 2(5)(a).

See also s 117, which requires a company registered as a public company on its original incorporation to obtain a certificate from the registrar of companies to the effect that the nominal value of the company's allotted share capital is not less than the authorised amount before it can do business or exercise any borrowing powers.

12. Duty of registrar

(1) The registrar of companies shall not register a company's memorandum delivered under section 10 unless he is satisfied that all the requirements of this Act in respect of registration and of matters precedent and incidental to it have been complied with.

(2) Subject to this, the registrar shall retain and register the memorandum and articles (if any) delivered to him under that section.

(3) Subject to subsection (3A), a statutory declaration in the prescribed form by—

    (a) a solicitor engaged in the formation of a company, or

    (b) a person named as a director or secretary of the company in the statement delivered under section 10(2), that those requirements have been complied with shall be delivered to the registrar of companies, and the registrar may accept such a declaration as sufficient evidence of compliance.

(3A) In place of the statutory declaration referred to in subsection (3), there may be delivered to the registrar of companies using electronic communications a statement made by a person mentioned in paragraph (a) or (b) of subsection (3) that the requirements mentioned in subsection (1) have been complied with; and the registrar may accept such a statement as sufficient evidence of compliance.

(3B) Any person who makes a false statement under subsection (3A) which he knows to be false or does not believe to be true is liable to imprisonment or a fine, or both.

S 12(1)–(2)

If the requirements are met, the registrar of companies must register the company: *R v Registrar of Companies, ex p Bowen* [1914] 3 KB 1161.

S 12(3)

By 'sufficient evidence' of compliance, it is meant that the registrar of companies can proceed on this basis unless the contrary is shown.

If the company is to be registered with a name for which consent must be obtained from any body under s 29, the statutory declaration must be accompanied with the statement required by s 29(3). If a private company limited by guarantee is to be registered with a name which does not include the word 'limited', a statutory declaration under s 30(4) is also required.

S 12(3A), (3B)

These provisions were inserted by the Companies Act 1985 (Electronic Communications) Order 2000, SI 2000/3373, art 4(1),(3), as from 22 December 2000 to facilitate electronic incorporation; as to the delivery of documents to the registrar using electronic communications, see s 707B; as to 'sufficient evidence', see note to sub-s (3), above.

As to penalties, see s 730, Sch 24; the intention is to provide the same penalties for false statements as is provided by the Perjury Act 1911 for false statutory declarations.

13. Effect of registration

(1) On the registration of a company's memorandum, the registrar of companies shall give a certificate that the company is incorporated and, in the case of a limited company, that it is limited.

(2)　The certificate may be signed by the registrar, or authenticated by his official seal.

(3)　From the date of incorporation mentioned in the certificate, the subscribers of the memorandum, together with such other persons as may from time to time become members of the company, shall be a body corporate by the name contained in the memorandum.

(4)　That body corporate is then capable forthwith of exercising all the functions of an incorporated company, but with such liability on the part of its members to contribute to its assets in the event of its being wound up as is provided by this Act and the Insolvency Act.

This is subject, in the case of a public company, to section 117 (additional certificate as to amount of allotted share capital).

(5)　The persons named in the statement under section 10 as directors, secretary or joint secretaries are, on the company's incorporation, deemed to have been respectively appointed as its first directors, secretary or joint secretaries.

(6)　Where the registrar registers an association's memorandum which states that the association is to be a public company, the certificate of incorporation shall contain a statement that the company is a public company.

(7)　A certificate of incorporation given in respect of an association is conclusive evidence—

　　(a)　that the requirements of this Act in respect of registration and of matters precedent and incidental to it have been complied with, and that the association is a company authorised to be registered, and is duly registered, under this Act, and

　　(b)　if the certificate contains a statement that the company is a public company, that the company is such a company.

S 13(1), (6)

The issue of the certificate must be gazetted by the registrar: s 711(1)(a); as to a public company, see s 1(3).

S 13(3),(4)

The date of incorporation　'From the date of incorporation' means precisely that and it includes any portion of the day on which the company is incorporated, it does not mean from the commencement of the next day: *Jubilee Cotton Mills Ltd v Lewis* [1924] AC 958, HL (certificate dated 6 June, the company was from the commencement of 6 June a body corporate); and the date on the certificate will be the date on which the certificate is processed in Companies House. See s 117 as to the requirements for public companies formed as such which require a trading certificate under s 117 before they are capable of exercising all the functions of a body corporate.

It is only from this date that the company is a body corporate, hence the use of same day incorporation or the purchase of a company from a formation agent when the need for a body corporate is urgent. As to potential personal liability when contracting by or on behalf of a company not yet formed, see s 36C.

A separate legal entity   Once incorporated, 'the company is at law a different person altogether from the subscribers to the memorandum; and, though it may be that after incorporation the business is precisely the same as it was before, and the same persons are managers, and the same hands receive the profits, the company is not in law the agent of the subscribers or trustee for them. Nor are the subscribers as members liable, in any shape or form, except to the extent and in the manner provided by the Act': *Salomon v A Salomon & Co Ltd* [1897] AC 22 at 51, per Lord Macnaghten, HL; *Maclaine Watson & Co Ltd v Department of Trade and Industry* [1989] 3 All ER 523.

The mere fact that a person owns all the shares in a company does not make the business carried on by that company his business. The company is not his agent and he is not its principal, without more: *Gramophone and Typewriter Ltd v Stanley* [1908] 2 KB 89. However, exceptionally, it may be that there is an agency relationship between a company and its individual shareholders: *Rainham Chemical Works Ltd v Belvedere Fish Guano Co Ltd* [1921] 2 AC 465; or between a parent company and a subsidiary: see *Firestone Tyre and Rubber Co Ltd v Llewellin* [1957] 1 All ER 561; *Smith, Stone & Knight Ltd v Birmingham Corpn* [1939] 4 All ER 116; but this will depend on an investigation of all aspects of the relationship between the parties and there is no presumption of such agency: *Adams v Cape Industries plc* [1991] 1 All ER 929 at 1020.

Within a group of companies, the fundamental principle is that each company in a group is a separate legal entity possessed of separate legal rights and liabilities: *Woolfson v Strathclyde Regional Council* 1978 SLT 159, HL; *Adams v Cape Industries plc* [1991] 1 All ER 929; *Ord v Belhaven Pubs Ltd* [1998] 2 BCLC 447; *Re Polly Peck International plc* [1996] 1 BCLC 428 (although statute will require the preparation of group accounts, see s 227 et seq).

As a separate legal entity, a company enjoys perpetual succession (until steps are taken to have it wound up and dissolved or it is stuck off the register as defunct under s 652 et seq), the ability to contract on its own behalf, to own property in its own name, to sue and be sued. It follows that sole shareholders and directors may be charged with theft of the company's property: *A-G's Reference (No 2 of 1982)* [1984] 2 All ER 216; *R v Philipfou* (1989) 89 Cr App Rep 290.

Liability in tort   A company may be vicariously liable for tortious acts committed by its employees acting within the scope of their employment: *Lloyd v Grace, Smith & Co* [1912] AC 716, HL; *Citizens Life Assurance Co v Brown* [1904] AC 423.

Criminal liability   There are some offences which a company cannot commit, such as bigamy, and others for which a company could not be prosecuted, such as murder, since imprisonment is the only penalty. For all other offences, a company may be liable provided that the required actus reus and mens rea can be established. There are two methods of holding a company criminally liable: (i) under the identification principle; and (ii) on the basis of vicarious liability although recent decisions have blurred the distinction between the two categories.

Identification   The identification principle requires the identification of those controlling officers and managers who are the embodiment of the company such that their acts and intentions are the acts and intentions of the company and their guilt is the guilt of the company: *Tesco Supermarkets Ltd v Nattrass* [1971] 2 All ER 127 at 134, HL; *Seaboard Offshore Ltd v Secretary of State for Transport* [1994] 2 All ER

99, HL; *A-G's Reference (No 2 of 1999)* [2000] 3 All ER 182 at 186, CA. See also *HL Bolton (Engineering) Co Ltd v T J Graham & Sons Ltd* [1957] 1 QB 159; *DPP v Kent and Sussex Contractors Ltd* [1944] KB 146; *R v ICR Haulage Ltd* [1944] KB 51; *Moore v I Bresler Ltd* [1944] 2 All ER 515.

The directors of a company are, prima facie, likely to be regarded as its directing mind and will but different persons may for different purposes satisfy the requirements of being the company's directing mind and will: see *El Ajou v Dollar Land Holdings plc* [1994] 2 All ER 685 (non-executive chairman was the directing mind and will with respect to the transaction in question).

Where the application of the identification principle in a particular case with respect to a statutory offence not giving rise to vicarious liability would defeat the intended application of the statutory provision to a company (for no controlling person who was the embodiment of the company would ever carry out the act in question) then the principle has to be modified in that instance: *Meridian Global Funds Management Asia Ltd v Securities Commission* [1995] 3 All ER 918 at 923–924. It is necessary instead to ask 'whose act, knowledge or state of mind was for this [statutory] purpose intended to count as the act etc of the company' taking into account the language of the rule and its content and policy (at 924). The Court of Appeal subsequently considered that the approach in *Meridian* was not departing from the identification principle but was confirming its existence: *A-G's Reference (No 2 of 1999)* [2000] 3 All ER 182 at 192, CA.

The identification principle has been criticised as setting too high a threshold for liability and it has proved particularly difficult to secure a conviction of a company for corporate manslaughter on this basis. This is due to the difficulty of establishing that someone identified as the embodiment of the company itself has done an act which fulfils the prerequisites of the crime of manslaughter: see *R v HM Coroner, ex p Spooner* (1987) 88 Cr App Rep 10 at 16; *R v P & O European Ferries (Dover) Ltd* (1990) 93 Cr App Rep 72 at 84; *A-G's Reference (No 2 of 1999)* [2000] 3 All ER 182 at 191. For a case where a conviction for manslaughter was secured in respect of a one-man company, see *R v Kite and Oll Ltd* (9 December 1994, unreported).

Vicarious liability   The alternative basis for criminal liability is where a statutory offence gives rise to vicarious liability on the part of a company, as with any employer, for the acts of its employees in the ordinary course of their employment: see *R v British Steel plc* [1995] 1 WLR 1356; *National Rivers Authority v Alfred McAlpine Homes (East) Ltd* [1994] 4 All ER 286. The courts have been content to find such liability even though the legislation in question limited the offence in some way (such as by a requirement to ensure, so far as is reasonably practicable, a safe system of working): *R v British Steel plc* [1995] 1 WLR 1356; and even where the company management had forbidden its employees to behave in a particular way: *Re Supply of Ready Mixed Concrete (No 2), Director General of Fair Trading v Pioneer Concrete (UK) Ltd* [1995] 1 All ER 135.

Piercing the corporate veil   The court will 'pierce the corporate veil' where special circumstances exist indicating that it is a mere facade concealing the true facts: *Woolfson v Strathclyde Regional Council* 1978 SLT 159, HL; *National Dock Labour Board v Pinn and Wheeler Ltd* [1989] BCLC 647; *Adams v Cape Industries plc* [1991] 1 All ER 929; *Ord v Belhaven Pubs Ltd* [1998] 2 BCLC 447. In identifying what is a mere façade, the motive of those behind the company will be relevant: *Jones v Lipman* [1962] 1 All ER 442; *Adams v Cape Industries plc* [1991] 1 All ER 929 at 1022.

While not offering a comprehensive definition of the principles guiding the courts in determining whether or not arrangements amount to a façade, the Court of Appeal was prepared to assume in *Adams v Cape Industries plc* [1991] 1 All ER 929 at 1025–1026 that the courts will pierce the veil:

(1)   where the corporate structure has been used to evade limitations imposed on conduct by law: see *Jones v Lipman* [1962] 1 All ER 442 (to avoid an order of specific performance imposed on an individual); *Gilford Motor Co Ltd v Horne* [1933] Ch 935 (to carry out activities which it was unlawful for the defendant to conduct); *Re Bugle Press Ltd* [1961] Ch 270 (to take advantage of statutory provisions allowing the compulsory purchase of minority shareholders).

(2)   where the corporate structure has been used to evade rights of relief which third parties already possess against a defendant: *Re a Company* [1985] BCLC 333 (chain of companies used to dispose of assets otherwise susceptible to a Mareva injunction treated in same way as owner would have been); *Bank of Credit and Commerce International SA v BRS Kumar Bros Ltd* [1994] 1 BCLC 211 (company shifted assets to another company to avoid reach of charges granted to creditors of first company: receiver appointed over assets of second company).

However, there is no general jurisdiction to pierce the veil in the interests of justice nor is the court entitled to lift the veil merely because the corporate structure has been used so as to minimise or avoid liabilities which might arise in the future: the use of a corporate structure (for example, through the use of subsidiary companies) for this purpose is inherent in our company law: *Adams v Cape Industries plc* [1991] 1 All ER 929 at 1020, 1026. A company is in law entitled to organise the group's affairs in the manner that it does, and to expect that the court should apply the principles of *Salomon v A Salomon & Co Ltd* [1897] AC 22 in the ordinary way: *Ord v Belhaven Pubs Ltd* [1998] 2 BCLC 447 at 458.

For the purpose of taxation, there are numerous statutory provisions which in effect require the corporate veil to be pierced.

S 13(5)

The first appointments of the directors and secretary take effect from the date of incorporation. As to the register of directors and secretaries, see s 288.

The power to appoint directors, thereafter, is commonly vested by the articles in the company in general meeting although the board will have power to fill casual vacancies, defined as 'any vacancy not occurring by effluxion of time, that is any vacancy occurring by death, resignation or bankruptcy': *York Tramways Co v Willows* (1882) 8 QBD 685 at 694, per Lord Coleridge CJ. See Table A, regs 73–80; also s 288 on the register of directors and secretaries.

S 13(7)

Conclusive evidence   This 'conclusive evidence' provision is common to a number of sections in the Act, namely ss 47(5), 48(3), 50(3), 52(3), 55(3), 139(5), 147(4), 688(3) (company re-registration); s 117(6) (public company certificate to commence trading); s 138(4) (reduction of capital); and s 401(2) (registration of company charges); and see the note to s 401(2), below.

The purpose of the 'conclusive evidence' provision is to provide certainty in commercial matters and to avoid any need for third parties to investigate whether all the formalities for incorporation (or registration of charges etc) have been complied with: see *R v Registrar of Companies, ex p Central Bank of India* [1985] BCLC 465 at 482–483; *Re Yolland, Husson & Birkett Ltd* [1908] 1 Ch 152. The conclusive nature of the certificate avoids in this jurisdiction the problems which arise elsewhere when incorporation can be declared a nullity. In view of the certificate, the court cannot reject the objects clauses before it but must construe them as they stand: *Cotman v Brougham* [1918] AC 514. The date of incorporation as stated on the certificate is conclusive as to the date even if it is shown to have been wrongly stated: *Jubilee Cotton Mills Ltd v Lewis* [1924] AC 958.

Evidence cannot be adduced to challenge the correctness of the registrar's decision to register the company as a body corporate in any judicial proceedings including an application for judicial review, save on the application of the Attorney General: *Bowman v Secular Society Ltd* [1917] AC 406; *R v Registrar of Companies, ex p Central Bank of India* [1985] BCLC 465 (on registration of charges). As the Companies Act does not bind the Crown, the Attorney General may take action to quash a registration which the registrar of companies has improperly or erroneously allowed: *Bowman v Secular Society Ltd* [1917] AC 406; see *R v Registrar of Companies, ex p A-G* [1991] BCLC 476 (incorporation of business of prostitution was contrary to public policy and would be quashed).

The section does not render all of the company's objects legal, if otherwise illegal, but does preclude anyone from going behind the certificate or from alleging that the company is not a corporate body with the status and capacity conferred by the Acts: *Bowman v Secular Society Ltd* [1917] AC 406.

14. Effect of memorandum and articles

(1) Subject to the provisions of this Act, the memorandum and articles, when registered, bind the company and its members to the same extent as if they respectively had been signed and sealed by each member, and contained covenants on the part of each member to observe all the provisions of the memorandum and of the articles.

(2) Money payable by a member to the company under the memorandum or articles is a debt due from him to the company, and in England and Wales is of the nature of a specialty debt.

S 14(1)

The statutory contract created by this provision is subject to the provisions of the Act, which includes provisions allowing for its alteration (see, for example, ss 4, 9) and a wide variety of provisions which apply notwithstanding any provision in the company's articles (see, for example, ss 16(2), 164(5), 174(3), 183(1), 187, 303(1), 368(1), 379A(5)).

While the contract comprises the memorandum and the articles of association, the issues here relate almost exclusively to the articles, given the predominantly external focus of the memorandum of association, and that emphasis is reflected in this note.

A contract with distinctive features   The articles form a statutory contract with its own distinctive features deriving its binding force not from a bargain struck between parties but from the terms of the statute: *Bratton Seymour Service Co Ltd v Oxborough* [1992] BCLC 693 at 698, CA. The articles can be altered by a special resolution without the consent of all the contracting parties under s 9 but the articles cannot be rectified by the court even if the articles do not accord with what is proved to have been the intention of the parties: *Scott v Frank F Scott* [1940] Ch 794; nor can terms be implied from extrinsic circumstances to give business efficacy to the contract: *Bratton Seymour Service Co Ltd v Oxborough* [1992] BCLC 693, CA; *Mutual Life Insurance Co of New York v Rank Organisation Ltd* [1985] BCLC 11. On a more limited basis, and as a matter of necessity to make the articles workable, the court will imply terms to give effect to the obvious intention of the parties: *Tett v Phoenix Property and Investment Co Ltd* [1986] BCLC 149; and see *Re Benfield Greig Group plc* [2000] 2 BCLC 488 at 510–512.

The contract formed by the articles is also, unlike an ordinary contract, not defeasible on the grounds of misrepresentation, common law mistake, mistake in equity, undue influence or duress: *Bratton Seymour Service Co Ltd v Oxborough* [1992] BCLC 693.

Enforcing the contract   A key issue is the extent to which the statutory contract confers contractual rights which can be enforced:

    (1)   by the company;

    (2)   by the members against the company;

    (3)   by the members against other members; and

    (4)   by outsiders (ie non-members or members claiming in a capacity other than as a member).

Enforcement of the statutory contract by the company against the members   The articles generally as such create rights and obligations between the members and the company respectively which the company can enforce: *Hickman v Kent or Romney Marsh Sheep-Breeders' Association* [1915] 1 Ch 881.

Enforcement of the statutory contract by the members against the company   A member may bring an action to restrain a threatened breach of the articles: *Irvine v Union Bank of Australia* (1877) 2 App Cas 366. A more difficult issue is whether a member can bring an action where the breach has already occurred. Despite argument to the contrary (most notably by Professor Wedderburn [1957] CLJ 194, [1958] CLJ 93), the courts have not accepted that members are entitled to bring a personal action with respect to every breach of any provision in the articles. Instead, it is only those articles regulating the rights and obligations of the members generally as such which create rights and obligations between them and the company respectively and which a member might enforce: *Hickman v Kent or Romney Marsh Sheep-Breeders' Association* [1915] 1 Ch 881.

This question of enforcement is linked to the rule in *Foss v Harbottle* (1843) 2 Hare 461 which establishes that the proper plaintiff in the event of a wrong done to the company is the company itself and:

> 'where the alleged wrong is a transaction which might be made binding on the company or association and on all its members by a simple majority of the members, no individual member of the company is allowed to maintain an

action in respect of that matter for the simple reason that, if a mere majority of the members of the company or association is in favour of what has been done, then *cadit quaestio.*'

(*Edwards v Halliwell* [1950] 2 All ER 1064 at 1066.)

The courts have reconciled the requirements of this rule and the fact that the statute creates a contract between the company and the members, by drawing a distinction between: (1) provisions in the articles which create enforceable personal rights conferred on a member qua member (as a matter of contract); and (2) provisions which relate to matters of internal management of the company, breaches of which are mere internal irregularities open to ratification by the majority and not actionable by individual shareholders (in keeping with the rule in *Foss v Harbottle*).

Those provisions in the articles which the courts have accepted are enforceable as a personal right fall into a variety of categories including:

(1)   Rights with regard to meetings. Members will frequently be able to seek relief where the complaint is as to non-compliance with provisions governing the conduct of a meeting: see, for example, *Kaye v Croydon Tramways Co* [1898] 1 Ch 358; *Tiessen v Henderson* [1899] 1 Ch 861 (inadequate notice); *Pender v Lushington* (1877) 6 Ch D 70 (members' right to have their vote recorded). Cf *MacDougall v Gardiner* (1875) 1 Ch D 13 (a member was denied relief when a chairman refused to call a poll in circumstances prescribed by the articles, the court regarding the matter as one of internal management: this case has been much criticised and is best confined to its facts).

(2)   Rights with respect to dividends. Members may enforce provisions governing the payment of dividend: see, for example, *Wood v Odessa Waterworks Co* (1889) 42 Ch D 636.

(3)   Rights with respect to requirements of special majorities. A member may bring an action if the matter in respect of which he is suing is one which could validly be done, not by a simple majority of members, but only by a special majority, for otherwise the majority are in effect altering the articles by a simple resolution: *Edwards v Halliwell* [1950] 2 All ER 1064, CA.

However, this category may be quite limited in application: cf *Grant v United Kingdom Switchback Rly Co* (1888) 40 Ch D 135; *Irvine v Union Bank* (1877) 2 App Cas 366. In these cases, the directors acted in breach of restrictions imposed by the articles but the matter was found to be a mere internal irregularity which was ratifiable and could not be the subject of a personal action by a shareholder. Ratification of an unauthorised act is not the same as an alteration of the articles as to the future which would require a special majority. See also *Mozley v Alston* (1847) 1 Ph 790 (directors continued in office despite requirement in the articles of retirement by rotation: mere internal irregularity).

The debate as to the scope of s 14 may be of diminishing importance. The Law Commission in reviewing the section considered that the difficulty in identifying the precise personal rights of the members posed few practical problems. Moreover, shareholders with a grievance are unlikely to look to enforce the statutory contract but will prefer to seek relief using the broader remedy provided by s 459 (unfairly prejudicial conduct): see Law Commission *Shareholder Remedies* (Law Com no 246 (1997), para 7.10.

Enforcement of the statutory contract by the members against the members   While the expectation is that the contract will be enforced through the company (see *Welton v Saffery* [1897] AC 299 at 315), it was accepted in *Rayfield v Hands* [1960] Ch 1 that a member could enforce the articles directly against the other members.

Enforcement of the statutory contract by outsiders or members claiming in a capacity other than as a member   The articles of association can neither constitute a contract between a company and an outsider (ie a non-member) nor give any individual member special contractual rights beyond those of the members generally: *Pritchard's Case* (1873) 8 Ch App 956; *Melhado v Porto Alegre Rly Co* (1874) LR 9 CP 503; *Eley v Positive Government Security Life Assurance Co* (1876) 1 Ex D 88; *Browne v La Trinidad* (1887) 37 Ch D 1; *Hickman v Kent or Romney Marsh Sheep-Breeders' Association* [1915] 1 Ch 881; *Beattie v E & F Beattie Ltd* [1938] Ch 708. Any right claimed by an outsider must be conferred by a separate agreement outside the articles. This point is confirmed by the Contracts (Rights of Third Parties) Act 1999, s 6(2), which provides that the Act does not confer any rights on a third party in the case of any contract binding on a company and its members under CA 1985, s 14.

That extrinsic contract may be made by the company with an outsider on the basis of the articles and such a contract may even be inferred from the conduct of the parties: *Swabey v Port Darwin Gold Mining Co* (1889) 1 Meg 385; *Re New British Iron Co, ex p Beckwith* [1898] 1 Ch 324. Such a contract will be on the basis that the articles can be unilaterally changed by the company by special resolution under s 9 so altering the implied contract but such alteration must not be retrospective: *Swabey v Port Darwin Gold Mining Co* (1889) 1 Meg 385.

S 14(2)

The effect of this provision is to ensure that where a debt is due by a member to the company, it is a specialty debt and subject to a 12-year limitation period. On the other hand, debts owed by the company to the members (for example, in respect of declared dividends) are not specialty debts (the contract is not deemed sealed by the company, see s 14(1)) and to those debts a six-year limitation period will apply: *Re Compania de Electricidad de la Provincia de Buenos Aires Ltd* [1978] 3 All ER 668 at 697.

15. Memorandum and articles of company limited by guarantee

(1)   In the case of a company limited by guarantee and not having a share capital, every provision in the memorandum or articles, or in any resolution of the company purporting to give any person a right to participate in the divisible profits of the company otherwise than as a member, is void.

(2)   For purposes of provisions of this Act relating to the memorandum of a company limited by guarantee, and for those of section 1(4) and this section, every provision in the memorandum or articles, or in any resolution, of a company so limited purporting to divide the company's undertaking into shares or interests is to be treated as a provision for a share capital, notwithstanding that the nominal amount or number of the shares or interests is not specified by the provision.

General note

This provision is designed to prevent a company limited by guarantee which can no longer be incorporated with a share capital (see s 1(4)) attempting through provisions in the memorandum or articles or by resolution to create share capital by the back door, either by provisions distributing profits in a particular way or by dividing the interest or undertaking into shares.

S 15(1)

The restriction is on participation in profits otherwise than as a member. There is no restriction on members of a company limited by guarantee participating in profits unless the company has sought exemption from the use of the word 'limited' in its name under s 30.

16. Effect of alteration on company's members

(1)   A member of a company is not bound by an alteration made in the memorandum or articles after the date on which he became a member, if and so far as the alteration—

    (a) requires him to take or subscribe for more shares than the number held by him at the date on which the alteration is made; or

    (b) in any way increases his liability as at that date to contribute to the company's share capital or otherwise to pay money to the company.

(2)   Subsection (1) operates notwithstanding anything in the memorandum or articles; but it does not apply in a case where the member agrees in writing, either before or after the alteration is made, to be bound by the alteration.

General note

A company cannot, even if so provided in the memorandum or articles, increase a member's liability as a member without his consent in writing.

S 16(1)

The restriction extends to any requirement to pay money to the company as a member.

17. Conditions in memorandum which could have been in articles

(1)   A condition contained in a company's memorandum which could lawfully have been contained in articles of association instead of in the memorandum

may be altered by the company by special resolution; but if an application is made to the court for the alteration to be cancelled, the alteration does not have effect except in so far as it is confirmed by the court.

(2)   This section—

(a)   is subject to section 16, and also to Part XVII (court order protecting minority), and

(b)   does not apply where the memorandum itself provides for or prohibits the alteration of all or any of the conditions above referred to, and does not authorise any variation or abrogation of the special rights of any class of members.

(3)   Section 5 (except subsections (2)(b) and (8)) and section 6(1) to (3) apply in relation to any alteration and to any application made under this section as they apply in relation to alterations and applications under sections 4 to 6.

S 17(1), (3)

Provisions which must be included in the memorandum are specified in s 2 and the memorandum is unalterable save to the extent permitted by s 2(7). This provision provides for some ease of alteration where the company has included within the memorandum provisions which might have been included in the articles and which would therefore have been alterable under s 9. This possibility of alteration is subject, however, to important limitations in s 17(2).

If the condition included in fact is an object of the company, then alteration is governed by ss 4–6 and not by this provision: *Re Hampstead Garden Suburb Trust Ltd* [1962] Ch 806.

Where an objection is made to the court, the procedure is governed by ss 5–6: sub-s (3); and see notes to those provisions, above.

S 17(2)(a)

The ability to alter provisions under s 17(1) does not permit any alteration which would increase a member's liability to the company without his consent in writing (s 16); or an alteration contrary to any court order made under s 461 (relief against unfairly prejudicial conduct).

S 17(2)(b)

Memorandum provides for or prohibits alteration   The ability to alter provisions under s 17(1) does not apply if the memorandum already provides a method of altering the condition in question. The method provided must require at least a majority sufficient to pass a special resolution (see s 378); otherwise, companies could sidestep the requirements of s 9 by including in the memorandum provisions which rightly belong in the articles.

The provision does not apply if a condition is included in the memorandum and its alteration prohibited. That condition is then entrenched to what might turn out to be an unacceptable degree. The only method of altering the condition would be to use a scheme of arrangement sanctioned by the court under s 425 which is a time-consuming and expensive procedure (see, for example, *Re RAC Motoring Services Ltd* [2000] 1 BCLC 307). Where a degree of shareholder protection is required, it is better to consider alternatives such as class rights, voting structures and shareholder agreements rather than entrenchment in the memorandum in this way (see general note to s 9, above).

Special rights of any class   This ability to alter provisions contained in the memorandum as if they were contained in the articles does not extend to any variation or abrogation of 'the special rights of any class of members', a phrase which encompasses companies with or without share capital and which must be interpreted in the same manner as 'rights attached to any class of shares' in s 125, so far as companies with a share capital are concerned: *Cumbrian Newspapers Group Ltd v Cumberland & Westmorland Herald Newspaper & Printing Co Ltd* [1986] 2 All ER 816 at 829, per Scott J. The variation or abrogation of such rights is a matter for s 125 not s 17; and see note to s 125. Class rights are the type of clause most commonly added to the memorandum of association but the effect of this provision is that s 17 is inapplicable in that case.

18. Amendments of memorandum or articles to be registered

(1)   Where an alteration is made in a company's memorandum or articles by any statutory provision, whether contained in an Act of Parliament or in an instrument made under an Act, a printed copy of the Act or instrument shall, not later than 15 days after that provision comes into force, be forwarded to the registrar of companies and recorded by him.

(2)   Where a company is required (by this section or otherwise) to send to the registrar any document making or evidencing an alteration in the company's memorandum or articles (other than a special resolution under section 4), the company shall send with it a printed copy of the memorandum or articles as altered.

(3)   If a company fails to comply with this section, the company and any officer of it who is in default is liable to a fine and, for continued contravention, to a daily default fine.

S 18(2)

Alterations of objects under s 4 are exempt from the requirements of this provision as s 6(1) provides for the delivery to the registrar of a copy of the memorandum as altered in that case. Alterations which are subject to this requirement are alterations to the articles under s 9, to the name of the company under s 28, and to the capital clause under s 121.

As a matter of good practice, where there has been a change of name, the memorandum of association should reflect the new name but a footnote to the text should set out the previous names by which the company was registered.

S 18(3)

As to penalties, see s 730, Sch 24; 'officer in default' is defined in s 730(5).

---

19. Copies of memorandum and articles to be given to members

(1) A company shall, on being so required by any member, send to him a copy of the memorandum and of the articles (if any), and a copy of any Act of Parliament which alters the memorandum, subject to payment—

- (a) in the case of a copy of the memorandum and of the articles, of 5 pence or such less sum as the company may prescribe, and
- (b) in the case of a copy of an Act, of such sum not exceeding its published price as the company may require.

(2) If a company makes default in complying with this section, the company and every officer of it who is in default is liable for each offence to a fine.

S 19(1)

In practice, it is rare for any charge to be made for a copy of these documents; as to sub-s (1)(b), this provision is effectively obsolete.

S 19(2)

As to penalties, see s 730, Sch 24; 'officer in default' is defined in s 730(5).

---

20. Issued copy of memorandum to embody alterations

(1) Where an alteration is made in a company's memorandum, every copy of the memorandum issued after the date of the alteration shall be in accordance with the alteration.

(2) If, where any such alteration has been made, the company at any time after the date of the alteration issues any copies of the memorandum which are not in accordance with the alteration, it is liable to a fine, and so too is every officer of the company who is in default.

S 20(2)

As to penalties, see s 730, Sch 24; 'officer in default' is defined in s 730(5).

---

21. *(Repealed by the Welsh Language Act 1993, ss 30(1), (2), 35(1), Sch 2, as from 21 December 1993.)*

A COMPANY'S MEMBERSHIP

22. Definition of 'member'

(1)   The subscribers of a company's memorandum are deemed to have agreed to become members of the company, and on its registration shall be entered as such in its register of members.

(2)   Every other person who agrees to become a member of a company, and whose name is entered in its register of members, is a member of the company.

General note

Entry on the register   Entry on the register of members is required in all cases save that of the subscribers: see *Re Florence Land and Public Works Co, Nicol's Case, Tufnell and Ponsonby's Case* (1885) 29 Ch D 421, CA. The register of members is governed by ss 352–362; it is not conclusive but prima facie evidence of membership: s 361; and it is subject to rectification by the court under s 359.

S 22(1)

Subscribers   The subscribers are the first members who sign the memorandum of association on incorporation and who must take at least one share in the company: see ss 1(1), 2(5). They are automatically members of the company and must be entered in the register of members.

S 22(2)

Agreement   For all other persons, there are two elements to becoming a member: (1) agreement; and (2) entry on the register. For the purpose of 'agreeing' to become a member, it is sufficient that a person assents to registration as a member and there is no requirement of a binding contract between that person and the company (otherwise the section would be inoperable in the case of a share transfer as opposed to an allotment): *Re Nuneaton Borough Association Football Club Ltd* [1989] BCLC 454, CA.

If a person whose name is entered on the register of members did not agree to become a member, he can seek rectification of the register under s 359. Where he takes no action on discovering that his name has been entered on the register, his agreement to the registration may be implied. As to entry on the register, see notes to ss 352 and 359, below.

The requirement for entry on the register ensures that membership of the company is concerned only with the legal owner of the shares and not with the beneficial owner so, for example, overseas investors holding American Depository Receipts (ADRs) will not be members of the company as the shares are held by a depository as the legal owner; likewise, if shares are held by a custodian on behalf of a pension fund.

Members and shareholders   A member is not necessarily a shareholder; for example, where the company is a company limited by guarantee without a share capital; equally, a shareholder who holds bearer warrants is not a member, unless the articles so provide, see s 355(5).

Corporate members   A company may be a member of another company and may appoint a corporate representative to attend meetings on its behalf: s 375. A company cannot be a member of itself: *Trevor v Whitworth* (1887) 12 App Cas 409, HL; s 143(1); and although it may acquire its own shares in certain circumstances, those shares are then cancelled, see ss 160(4), 162(2). A company cannot be a member of its holding company, subject to various exceptions: s 23.

Minors   There is no prohibition on minors (persons under the age of 18 in England and Wales: Family Law Reform Act 1969, s 1) as members but a contract to purchase shares is voidable by a minor before or within a reasonable time of attaining his majority. If the minor repudiates the contract, he will not be liable for future calls but he cannot recover the purchase price unless there has been a total failure of consideration: *Steinberg v Scala (Leeds) Ltd* [1923] 2 Ch 452, CA, which is unlikely to be the case. Until the minor repudiates, he has full rights of membership.

23. Membership of holding company

(1)   Except as mentioned in this section, a body corporate cannot be a member of a company which is its holding company and any allotment or transfer of shares in a company to its subsidiary is void.

(2)   The prohibition does not apply where the subsidiary is concerned only as personal representative or trustee unless, in the latter case, the holding company or a subsidiary of it is beneficially interested under the trust.

For the purpose of ascertaining whether the holding company or a subsidiary is so interested, there shall be disregarded—

(a)   any interest held only by way of security for the purposes of a transaction entered into by the holding company or subsidiary in the ordinary course of a business which includes the lending of money;

(b)   any such interest as is mentioned in Part I of Schedule 2.

(3)   The prohibition does not apply where shares in the holding company are held by the subsidiary in the ordinary course of its business as an intermediary.

For this purpose a person is an intermediary if that person—

(a)   carries on a bona fide business of dealing in securities;

(b)   is a member of an EEA exchange (and satisfies any requirements for recognition as a dealer in securities laid down by that exchange) or is otherwise approved or supervised as a dealer in securities under the laws of an EEA State; and

   (c) does not carry on an excluded business.

(3A) The excluded businesses are the following—

   (a) any business which consists wholly or mainly in the making or managing of investments;

   (b) any business which consists wholly or mainly in, or is carried on wholly or mainly for the purpose of, providing services to persons who are connected with the person carrying on the business;

   (c) any business which consists in insurance business;

   (d) any business which consists in managing or acting as trustee in relation to a pension scheme or which is carried on by the manager or trustee of such a scheme in connection with or for the purposes of the scheme;

   (e) any business which consists in operating or acting as trustee in relation to a collective investment scheme or is carried on by the operator or trustee of such a scheme in connection with or for the purposes of the scheme.

(3B) For the purposes of subsections (3) and (3A)—

   (a) the question whether a person is connected with another shall be determined in accordance with the provisions of section 839 of the Income and Corporation Taxes Act 1988;

   (b) 'collective investment scheme' has the meaning given in section 75 of the Financial Services Act 1986;

   (c) 'EEA exchange' means a market which appears on the list drawn up by an EEA State pursuant to Article 16 of Council Directive 93/22/EEC on investment services in the securities field;

   (d) 'insurance business' means long term business or general business as defined in section 1 of the Insurance Companies Act 1982;

   (e) 'securities' include investments falling within paragraphs 7, 8 and 9 of Schedule 1 to the Financial Services Act 1986 and, so far as relevant to any of those paragraphs, paragraph 11 of that Schedule;

   (f) 'trustee' and 'the operator' shall, in relation to a collective investment scheme, be construed in accordance with section 75(8) of the Financial Services Act 1986.

(3C) Where—

   (a) a subsidiary which is a dealer in securities has purportedly acquired shares in its holding company in contravention of the prohibition in subsection (1); and

   (b) a person acting in good faith has agreed, for value and without notice of that contravention, to acquire shares in the holding company from the subsidiary or from someone who has purportedly acquired the shares after their disposal by the subsidiary,

any transfer to that person of the shares mentioned in paragraph (a) shall have the same effect as it would have had if their original acquisition by the subsidiary had not been in contravention of the prohibition.

(4)   Where a body corporate became a holder of shares in a company—

(a) before 1st July 1948, or

(b) on or after that date and before 20th October 1997, in circumstances in which this section as it then had effect did not apply,

but at any time on or after 20th October 1997 falls within the prohibition in subsection (1) above in respect of those shares, it may continue to be a member of that company; but for so long as that prohibition would apply, apart from this subsection, it has no right to vote in respect of those shares at meetings of the company or of any class of its members.

(5)   Where a body corporate becomes a holder of shares in a company on or after 20th October 1997 in circumstances in which the prohibition in subsection (1) does not apply, but subsequently falls within that prohibition in respect of those shares, it may continue to be a member of that company; but for so long as that prohibition would apply, apart from this subsection, it has no right to vote in respect of those shares at meetings of the company or of any class of its members.

(6)   Where a body corporate is permitted to continue as a member of a company by virtue of subsection (4) or (5), an allotment to it of fully paid shares in the company may be validly made by way of capitalisation of reserves of the company; but for so long as the prohibition in subsection (1) would apply, apart from subsection (4) or (5), it has no right to vote in respect of those shares at meetings of the company or of any class of its members.

(7)   The provisions of this section apply to a nominee acting on behalf of a subsidiary as to the subsidiary itself.

(8)   In relation to a company other than a company limited by shares, the references in this section to shares shall be construed as references to the interest of its members as such, whatever the form of that interest.

General note

This prohibition is intended to reinforce the rule in *Trevor v Whitworth* (1887) 12 App Cas 409 that a company cannot be a member of itself.

S 23(1), (7)–(8)

Scope of the prohibitions   A body corporate (defined s 740) cannot be a member of its own holding company (defined s 736) and any transfer or allotment (see s 738) of its shares to a subsidiary (defined s 736) is void. The prohibition only applies where the companies fall within these defined categories and it is possible therefore to devise interlinked holdings which fall outside of the prohibition. The prohibition also applies to a company without a share capital with appropriate modifications, see sub-s (8); and it cannot be evaded by a transfer or allotment to a nominee acting on behalf of the subsidiary: sub-s (7). There are a number of exceptions in sub-ss (2)–(6).

S 23(2)

Personal representatives and trustees   A subsidiary may be a member of its holding company as a personal representative or as a trustee provided that neither the holding company nor a subsidiary of it is beneficially interested under the trust, but excluding any interest arising as a security interest under sub-s (2)(a) or any of the limited interests identified in Sch 2, Pt I, being any residual interest arising under pension and employee share schemes, or any rights to enforce any charge, lien or set-off, or to recover any refund under any pension and employee share scheme.

S 23(3), (3A)–(3C)

Dealers in securities   These provisions were substituted by the Companies (Membership of Holding Company) (Dealers in Securities) Regulations 1997, SI 1997/2306, and they exempt a subsidiary company from the prohibition if it carries on business as a certain class of dealer in securities. The intention was to ensure that intermediaries who deal in securities (as defined) are not inhibited from dealing in the ordinary course of business by the fact that the intermediary is a subsidiary of a company in whose shares they would deal in the ordinary course of business.

Subsection (3C) provides for the protection of a bona fide purchaser for value without notice purchasing from a subsidiary which is a dealer in securities which is not so exempt and therefore is within the prohibition in s 23(1). Without this protection, the subsidiary would have no title to the securities to pass to the purchaser.

S 23(4), (6)

This provision ensures that a company which acquired shares in circumstances in which these provisions (prohibiting membership) as they then had effect did not apply, but which has now fallen within the prohibition in respect of those shares (because of the changed definitions of holding and subsidiary companies), may continue to be a member of the holding company. It may also receive bonus issues in respect of its holding but it has no right to vote any of its shares in general or class meetings.

S 23(5), (6)

This provision ensures that where a company becomes a holder of shares in another company in circumstances where it is not within the prohibition in s 23(1) but subsequently becomes a subsidiary of that other company and so would be within the prohibition, it may continue to hold those shares and to receive bonus issues in respect of its holding. However, it has no right to vote any of its shares in general or class meetings.

24. Minimum membership for carrying on business

If a company, other than a private company limited by shares or by guarantee, carries on business without having at least two members and does so for more than 6 months, a person who, for the whole or any part of the period that it so carries on business after those 6 months—

    (a) is a member of the company, and

    (b) knows that it is carrying on business with only one member,

is liable (jointly and severally with the company) for the payment of the company's debts contracted during the period or, as the case may be, that part of it.

General note

This section removes the protection of limited liability where the number of members falls below the two required for incorporation by s 1(1) for a period of more than six months.

Applies only to public companies   The provision applies only to public companies, since private companies limited by shares or by guarantee with only one member have been permitted since 1992: s 1(3A); Companies (Single Member Private Limited Companies) Regulations 1992, SI 1992/1699. A company which has a public company as a subsidiary must take care to ensure that it is not (and does not become) the sole member and so potentially liable for the subsidiary's debts under this provision.

    The company must have carried on business for more than six months with less than two members so there is a six-month period of grace to allow the company to secure a further shareholder to bring the number back up to two. In practice, all that is required is the transfer of one share to a nominee so it is not difficult to avoid the reach of the section and it will only catch those unaware of the need for this simple transaction: see, for example, *Nisbet v Shepherd* [1994] 1 BCLC 300.

Liability   Where liability arises, it falls on the remaining member and not the directors. It only arises, however, if the remaining member knew that the company was carrying on business with only one member which will not necessarily be the case. The liability is for debts contracted after the six-month period of grace has lapsed. In *Nisbet v Shepherd* [1994] 1 BCLC 300 the business had continued with only one shareholder for seven years.

    Enforcement may be by an individual creditor but it is more likely to be by a liquidator on the company having gone into winding up: see *Nisbet v Shepherd* [1994] 1 BCLC 300.

CHAPTER II

COMPANY NAMES

General note to this Chapter

The regulation of company names is a matter for the Secretary of State for Trade and Industry, whose functions in this regard are carried out by the registrar of companies.

Overview   The scheme governing company names is as follows:
- (1)   certain designations or their alternatives are required: ss 25, 27; unless exempt under ss 30, 31; with criminal penalties for misuse; ss 33, 34;
- (2)   certain names are prohibited: s 26(1);
- (3)   the use of certain other names requires the consent of the Secretary of State for Trade and Industry (ie the registrar of companies) or some other designated body: s 26(2);
- (4)   a company may change its name by special resolution: s 28(1);
- (5)   a company may be directed to change its name in certain circumstances: ss 28(2), 31, 32;
- (6)   there are special rules governing names for Open-Ended Investment Companies: see the Open-Ended Investment Companies Regulations 2001, SI 2001/1228, regs 18–20;
- (7)   there are restrictions on the use of certain names by a person who was a director or shadow director of a company which has gone into insolvent liquidation: see IA 1986, s 216; IR 1986, rr 4.228–4.230.

Publicity   The company's name must be set out in the memorandum of association (s 2(1)(a)); and on correspondence (s 349); and engraved on the company's seal, if it has one (s 350); and displayed on the company's premises (s 348). In addition to its name, a company on registration is allotted a registered number (s 705) which is crucial in distinguishing between companies.

Business names   A company may trade under a business name and must then comply with the Business Names Act 1985 as well as the Companies Act 1985; see also the Company and Business Names Regulations 1981, SI 1981/1685, as amended. The Business Names Act 1985 will require the disclosure of the corporate name on all business letters, written orders, invoices and receipts and on the premises where the business is carried on and to which customers and suppliers have access.

Passing off   In addition to complying with the statutory rules governing company names, a company needs to consider any risk of being sued for passing off by other businesses (see note to s 28(2), below) and any possibility of an infringement of an existing trade mark.

Guidance notes   Detailed guidance as to the practice of the registrar of companies regarding company names can be found in the Companies House Guidance Booklet, *Company Names*, which is available on the Companies House web site: www.companies-house.gov.uk.

25. Name as stated in memorandum

(1)   The name of a public company must end with the words 'public limited company' or, if the memorandum states that the company's registered office is

to be situated in Wales, those words or their equivalent in Welsh ('cwmni cyfyngedig cyhoeddus'); and those words or that equivalent may not be preceded by the word 'limited' or its equivalent in Welsh ('cyfyngedig').

(2) In the case of a company limited by shares or by guarantee (not being a public company), the name must have 'limited' as its last word, except that—

    (a) this is subject to section 30 (exempting, in certain circumstances, a company from the requirement to have 'limited' as part of the name), and

    (b) if the company is to be registered with a memorandum stating that its registered office is to be situated in Wales, the name may have 'cyfyngedig' as its last word.

General note

The penalties for non-compliance with the requirements of this section will arise as a consequence of breaches of ss 348–351 (company identification).

S 25(1)

In the specified case, the Welsh equivalent may be used, although there is no requirement to do so; the common alternatives for the statutory designations are provided for by s 27. Misuse of the designation or omission of the designation is an offence under s 33. As to a public company, see s 1(3).

S 25(2)

In the specified case, the Welsh equivalent may be used although there is no requirement to do so; the common alternatives for the statutory designations are provided for by s 27. Misuse of the designation is an offence under s 34. As to a company limited by shares, see s 1(2)(a); as to a company limited by guarantee, see s 1(2)(b). There is no requirement for an unlimited company to end its name with 'unlimited' but see s 26(1).

26. Prohibition on registration of certain names

(1) A company shall not be registered under this Act by a name—

    (a) which includes, otherwise than at the end of the name, any of the following words or expressions, that is to say, 'limited', 'unlimited' or 'public limited company' or their Welsh equivalents ('cyfyngedig', 'anghyfyngedig' and 'cwmni cyfyngedig cyhoeddus' respectively);

    (b) which includes, otherwise than at the end of the name, an abbreviation of any of those words or expressions;

(bb) which includes, at any place in the name, the expression 'investment company with variable capital' or 'open-ended investment company' or their Welsh equivalents ('cwmni buddsoddi â chyfalaf newidiol' and 'cwmni buddsoddiant penagored' respectively);

(bbb) which includes, at any place in the name, the expression 'limited liability partnership' or its Welsh equivalent ('partneriaeth atebolrwydd cyfyngedig');

(c) which is the same as a name appearing in the registrar's index of company names;

(d) the use of which by the company would in the opinion of the Secretary of State constitute a criminal offence; or

(e) which in the opinion of the Secretary of State is offensive.

(2) Except with the approval of the Secretary of State, a company shall not be registered under this Act by a name which—

(a) in the opinion of the Secretary of State would be likely to give the impression that the company is connected in any way with Her Majesty's Government or with any local authority; or

(b) includes any word or expression for the time being specified in regulations under section 29.

'Local authority' means any local authority within the meaning of the Local Government Act 1972 or the Local Government (Scotland) Act 1973, the Common Council of the City of London or the Council of the Isles of Scilly.

(3) In determining for purposes of subsection (1)(c) whether one name is the same as another, there are to be disregarded—

(a) the definite article, where it is the first word of the name;

(b) the following words and expressions where they appear at the end of the name, that is to say—

'company' or its Welsh equivalent ('cwmni'),

'and company' or its Welsh equivalent ('a'r cwmni'),

'company limited' or its Welsh equivalent ('cwmni cyfyngedig'),

'and company limited' or its Welsh equivalent ('a'r cwmni cyfyngedig'),

'limited' or its Welsh equivalent ('cyfyngedig'),

'unlimited' or its Welsh equivalent ('anghyfyngedig'),...

'public limited company' or its Welsh equivalent ('cwmni cyfyngedig cyhoeddus');

'investment company with variable capital' or its Welsh equivalent ('cwmni buddsoddi â chyfalaf newidiol'); and

'open-ended investment company' or its Welsh equivalent ('cwmni buddsoddiant penagored');

(c) abbreviations of any of those words or expressions where they appear at the end of the name; and

(d) type and case of letters, accents, spaces between letters and punctuation marks;

and 'and' and '&' are to be taken as the same.

General note

As to the application of this provision to oversea companies, see s 694.

S 26(1)

Prohibitions　This provision specifies the prohibited names. Categories (a)–(bb) are self-explanatory other than to note that where 'unlimited' is included in a company's name (and there is no requirement to do so, see s 25(1)), then it must appear at the end of the name.

'Same' name　Guidance is provided in s 26(3) to assist with the determination of what is the 'same' name for these purposes. If a name is registered despite being the same as an existing name, the company may be directed at a later date to change its name: see s 28(2). The composition of the index of names is much broader than companies registered under CA 1985 (see s 714) so the prohibition is much wider than initially appears.

Criminal offence　The use of certain names such as 'Bank' or 'Building Society' without authorisation may be a criminal offence, as may be the use of the titles of various professions such as 'Dentist', 'Optician', 'Pharmacist', see Companies House Guidance Booklet, *Company Names*, Appendix C, for the full list; see also *R v Registrar of Companies, ex p Bowen* [1914] 3 KB 1161.

Offensive names　For an example of names considered offensive, see *R v Registrar of Companies, ex p A-G* [1991] BCLC 476 (company formed to incorporate business of prostitute).

S 26(2)

Names which fall into these categories require the consent of the Secretary of State which means the consent of the registrar of companies or any other designated body. A number of words have been specified in this way under regulations made under s 29 including, for example, 'Association', 'British', 'English', 'National', 'Holding', 'Group', 'Council', and 'Society'. See also the Company and Business Names (Chamber of Commerce, Etc) Act 1999 which came into force on 10 May 2001: (SI 2001/258): the consent of the Secretary of State for Trade and Industry (in practice the registrar) is required in order to make use of any of the specified names, for example, Chamber of Trade, Chamber of Commerce, Chamber of Enterprise, Chamber of Business. Companies House has published guidance as to the manner in which this discretion will be exercised which is available on its web site, see www.companies-house.gov.uk.

S 26(3)

This provision assists in determining whether names are the 'same' and therefore prohibited under s 26(1)(c).

Plurals　An omission from this provision is whether a name and its plural (where 's' has been added to one or more of the elements of the name) should also be specified in this provision as rendering two names the 'same'. At present, a name which is distinguished from an existing name only by being the plural would not be prohibited as being the 'same' but a company registered with such a name runs the risk of a direction under s 28(2) on the grounds that the name is 'too like' an existing name.

Symbols   The section make no allowance for the current practice of incorporating symbols into names such as @ or * or .com with the result that a company name which is distinguishable from an existing name simply by a symbol is not treated as the same as the existing name and will be allowed on to the register, but again a company registered with such a name runs the risk of a direction under s 28(2) on the grounds that the name is 'too like' an existing name.

27. Alternatives of statutory designations

(1)   A company which by any provision of this Act is either required or entitled to include in its name, as its last part, any of the words specified in subsection (4) below may, instead of those words, include as the last part of the name the abbreviations there specified as alternatives in relation to those words.

(2)   A reference in this Act to the name of a company or to the inclusion of any of those words in a company's name includes a reference to the name including (in place of any of the words so specified) the appropriate alternative, or to the inclusion of the appropriate alternative, as the case may be.

(3)   A provision of this Act requiring a company not to include any of those words in its name also requires it not to include the abbreviated alternative specified in subsection (4).

(4)   For the purposes of this section—
    (a)   the alternative of 'limited' is 'ltd.';
    (b)   the alternative of 'public limited company' is 'p.l.c.';
    (c)   the alternative of 'cyfyngedig' is 'cyf.'; and
    (d)   the alternative of 'cwmni cyfyngedig cyhoeddus' is 'c.c.c.'.

S 27(1)

The requirement to include these words as the last part of the name is contained in s 25; the entitlement to include the words refers to companies with their registered office in Wales who are entitled to adopt the Welsh equivalent of these terms: s 25.

S 27(2)

This provision ensures that where the Act requires, for example, the display of the company's name on its premises or on correspondence (see ss 348, 349), the requirement is satisfied either by the full name or by the use of the approved alternatives.

S 27(3)

There are prohibitions on the use by a company of 'public limited company' when it is not entitled to do so and of 'limited' when not entitled (see ss 33–34) and this provision extends the criminal penalties arising from misuse of those terms to misuse of the alternatives.

S 27(4)

Strictly speaking, the only permitted abbreviations are those set out in this provision. In practice, 'ltd.' is commonly presented as 'Ltd' and 'p.l.c.' as 'plc' or 'Plc', none of which are in conformity with the requirements of this section. The common use of these abbreviations is now so established that a court might be willing to overlook this misuse of the name but, equally, companies and their directors should be aware of the dangers of misuse of the name, in particular in the light of the requirements in s 349(4); see the note to that provision, below.

28. Change of name

(1)   A company may by special resolution change its name (but subject to section 31 in the case of a company which has received a direction under subsection (2) of that section from the Secretary of State).

(2)   Where a company has been registered by a name which—

   (a)   is the same as or, in the opinion of the Secretary of State, too like a name appearing at the time of the registration in the registrar's index of company names, or

   (b)   is the same as or, in the opinion of the Secretary of State, too like a name which should have appeared in that index at that time,

the Secretary of State may within 12 months of that time, in writing, direct the company to change its name within such period as he may specify.

Section 26(3) applies in determining under this subsection whether a name is the same as or too like another.

(3)   If it appears to the Secretary of State that misleading information has been given for the purpose of a company's registration with a particular name, or that undertakings or assurances have been given for that purpose and have not been fulfilled, he may within 5 years of the date of its registration with that name in writing direct the company to change its name within such period as he may specify.

(4)   Where a direction has been given under subsection (2) or (3), the Secretary of State may by a further direction in writing extend the period within which the company is to change its name, at any time before the end of that period.

(5)   A company which fails to comply with a direction under this section, and any officer of it who is in default, is liable to a fine and, for continued contravention, to a daily default fine.

(6)   Where a company changes its name under this section, the registrar of companies shall (subject to section 26) enter the new name on the register in place of the former name, and shall issue a certificate of incorporation altered to meet the circumstances of the case; and the change of name has effect from the date on which the altered certificate is issued.

(7)   A change of name by a company under this section does not affect any rights or obligations of the company or render defective any legal proceedings by or against it; and any legal proceedings that might have been continued or commenced against it by its former name may be continued or commenced against it by its new name.

S 28(1)

Procedural matters   As to a special resolution, see s 378; it must be registered with the registrar of companies within 15 days: s 380(1), (4)(a); if the company is a private company, a written resolution may be used: s 381A; a resolution of the directors suffices if the company is ordered to change its name under s 31. As to when the resolution takes effect, see s 28(6). If the change of name is part of an application for exempt status under s 30, compliance with the additional requirements of that provision is also necessary.

As a change of name alters a term of the company's memorandum of association (see s 2(1)(a)), a printed copy of the memorandum as altered must also be filed with the special resolution: s 18(2); and see s 20. On a change of name, the limitations imposed by s 26 apply as to the choice of name, in the same way as they apply on incorporation. The fee payable to the registrar of companies on a change of name is £10 (at the time of writing) or £80 if a same-day change of name is required.

S 28(2)

Same as an existing name   The registrar of companies may refuse registration of a name which is the same as an existing name (see note to s 26); but if such a name is registered, the registrar can direct the company, within 12 months of the registration, to change its name with all the cost and inconvenience which that entails. The composition of the index of names is much broader than companies registered under CA 1985 (see s 714) so the application of this provision is wider than initially appears.

'Too like' an existing name   More importantly, the registrar can take the same steps with regard to any company which is registered with a name which is 'too like' an existing name; see also note to s 26(3). A company which has been registered with a name which is 'too like' another cannot be sure, therefore, that it will be allowed to retain the name in view of these powers vested in the registrar. In determining whether a name is 'too like' an existing name, the registrar cannot have regard to the ownership of the companies, and must apply the rules equally to companies under separate ownership and companies in the same group.

The issue primarily is one of a visual comparison of the full corporate names of the companies and whether there is a danger of confusion demonstrably to do with the companies' names and only the companies' names: see Companies House, *Policy on Company Names*, The Register, Issue 44. This is a change of practice by Companies House which previously had considered factors such as the nature and location of the companies' trading activities but those considerations will not be treated as relevant now: see Companies House Guidance Booklet, *Company Names*. A direction to a company to change its name is a direction to the company to exercise the powers in s 28(1) and so a special resolution will be required (cf s 31(2)). As to a similar power with respect to oversea companies, see s 694(2).

Many companies register subsidiaries with similar names simply to safeguard the name and larger companies monitor new incorporations to check for 'too like' names. This is to ensure that they register their objections with the registrar in time for him to exercise his powers under this provision. They may also initiate proceedings for passing off against the subsequently registered company.

Business names   As noted in the general note to this Part, companies may use business names and will be regulated in that use by the Business Names Act 1985 and regulations made thereunder. However, there is no register of business names and no provisions on 'same' or 'too like' names in the manner provided here. The only remedy in that situation for an aggrieved business lies in a passing off action at common law.

Opportunistic incorporations   An issue which has given rise to concern is that of opportunistic incorporations where, in anticipation of business developments affecting a particular company or companies, a person incorporates a company or companies with names which are likely to be of interest to those businesses with a view, for example, to requiring payment from those businesses in return for agreeing to change the company's name.

This situation arose in *Glaxo plc v GlaxoWellcome Ltd* [1996] FSR 388 where, in anticipation of the merger of Glaxo and Wellcome, the defendants incorporated a company with the name Glaxowellcome, the two pharmaceutical companies having indicated that the name of the merged company would be Glaxo-Wellcome. The defendants were willing to sell the company to the plaintiffs for £100,000. Lightman J held that the defendants had acted dishonestly. It was, in his view, a dishonest scheme to appropriate the goodwill of the plaintiff and to extort a substantial sum as the price for not damaging the plaintiffs' goodwill. He stated (at 391):

> 'The court will not countenance any such pre-emptive strike of registering companies with names where others have the goodwill in those names, and the registering party then demanding a price for changing the names. It is an abuse of the system of registration of companies' names. The right to choose the name with which a company is registered is not given for that purpose.'

A mandatory injunction was granted requiring the defendants to change the name of the company. Lightman J agreed that a party prejudiced by this type of conduct is not obliged to wait for the registrar of companies to issue a direction for a change of name under the statutory scheme but can proceed with an action for passing off.

S 28(3)

This provision relates to situations where information has been provided or assurances given to secure the consent of the registrar or of some other body to the use of a name, as required by s 26(2), for example, assurances as to the ownership or activities of a company, which turn out to be misleading.

S 28(5)

As to penalties, see s 730, Sch 24; 'officer in default' is defined in s 730(5).

S 28(6), (7)

No change of status   The company receives a new certificate of incorporation with the new name but there is no change in the company's status and its incorporation continues unaffected by the change of name which does not effect any re-formation or re-incorporation of the company: *Oshkosh B'gosh Inc v Dan Marbel Inc Ltd* [1989] BCLC 507. Any litigation in progress is unaffected.

Effective date   The new name comes into effect once the certificate is issued. It is important that the old name is not used after that date and that the new name is not used before that date. The company's officers may be personally liable in some circumstances where the company's name is not described accurately: see s 349(4). The issue of the certificate must be gazetted by the registrar: s 711(1)(a); and s 42 applies.

29. Regulations about names

(1)   The Secretary of State may by regulations—

     (a)   specify words or expressions for the registration of which as or as part of a company's corporate name his approval is required under section 26(2)(b), and

     (b)   in relation to any such word or expression, specify a Government department or other body as the relevant body for purposes of the following subsection.

(2)   Where a company proposes to have as, or as part of, its corporate name any such word or expression and a Government department or other body is specified under subsection (1)(b) in relation to that word or expression, a request shall be made (in writing) to the relevant body to indicate whether (and if so why) it has any objections to the proposal; and the person to make the request is—

     (a)   in the case of a company seeking to be registered under this Part, the person making the statutory declaration under section 12(3) or statement under section 12(3A)(as the case may be),

     (b)   in the case of a company seeking to be registered under section 680, the persons making the statutory declaration under section 686(2) or statement under section 686(2A)(as the case may be), and

     (c)   in any other case, a director or secretary of the company concerned.

(3)   The person who has made that request to the relevant body shall submit to the registrar of companies a statement that it has been made and a copy of any response received from that body, together with—

     (a)   the requisite statutory declaration or statement, or

     (b)   a copy of the special resolution changing the company's name, according as the case is one or other of those mentioned in subsection (2).

(4)   Sections 709 and 710 (public rights of inspection of documents kept by registrar of companies) do not apply to documents sent under subsection (3) of this section.

(5)   Regulations under this section may contain such transitional provisions and savings as the Secretary of State thinks appropriate and may make different provision for different cases or classes of case.

(6)   The regulations shall be made by statutory instrument, to be laid before Parliament after it is made; and the regulations shall cease to have effect at the end of 28 days beginning with the day on which the regulations were made (but without prejudice to anything previously done by virtue of them or to the making of new regulations), unless during that period they are approved by resolution of each House. In reckoning that period, no account is to be taken of any time during which Parliament is dissolved or prorogued or during which both Houses are adjourned for more than 4 days.

General note

Regulations must specify the words for which approval is required under s 26(2) before they can be used in a company name. The regulations to date are the Company and Business Names Regulations 1981, SI 1981/1685, as amended by SI 1982/1653, SI 1992/1196, SI 1995/3022 and SI 2001/259.

S 29(2)

This provision identifies the person responsible for seeking the permission of the relevant body and that person varies depending on the company's circumstances. The relevant body must give reasons where it objects to the proposed name.

S 29(3),(4)

Details of the request for permission and the response of the relevant body must be forwarded to the registrar of companies but they are not put on the public record.

30. Exemption from requirement of 'limited' as part of the name

(1)   Certain companies are exempt from requirements of this Act relating to the use of 'limited' as part of the company name.

(2)   A private company limited by guarantee is exempt from those requirements, and so too is a company which on 25th February 1982 was a private company limited by shares with a name which, by virtue of a licence under section 19 of the Companies Act 1948, did not include 'limited'; but in either case the

company must, to have the exemption, comply with the requirements of the following subsection.

(3) Those requirements are that—

    (a) the objects of the company are (or, in the case of a company about to be registered, are to be) the promotion of commerce, art, science, education, religion, charity or any profession, and anything incidental or conducive to any of those objects; and

    (b) the company's memorandum or articles—

        (i) require its profits (if any) or other income to be applied in promoting its objects,

        (ii) prohibit the payment of dividends to its members, and

        (iii) require all the assets which would otherwise be available to its members generally to be transferred on its winding up either to another body with objects similar to its own or to another body the objects of which are the promotion of charity and anything incidental or conducive thereto (whether or not the body is a member of the company).

(4) Subject to subsection (5A), a statutory declaration that a company complies with the requirements of subsection (3) may be delivered to the registrar of companies, who may accept the declaration as sufficient evidence of the matters stated in it; and the registrar may refuse to register a company by a name which does not include the word 'limited' unless such a declaration has been delivered to him.

(5) The statutory declaration must be in the prescribed form and be made—

    (a) in the case of a company to be formed, by a solicitor engaged in its formation or by a person named as director or secretary in the statement delivered under section 10(2);

    (b) in the case of a company to be registered in pursuance of section 680, by two or more directors or other principal officers of the company; and

    (c) in the case of a company proposing to change its name so that it ceases to have the word 'limited' as part of its name, by a director or secretary of the company.

(5A) In place of the statutory declaration referred to in subsection (4), there may be delivered to the registrar of companies using electronic communications a statement made by a person falling within the applicable paragraph of subsection (5) stating that the company complies with the requirements of subsection (3); and the registrar may accept such a statement as sufficient evidence of the matters stated in it.

(5B) The registrar may refuse to register a company by a name which does not include the word 'limited' unless a statutory declaration under subsection (4) or statement under subsection (5A) has been delivered to him.

(5C) Any person who makes a false statement under subsection (5A) which he knows to be false or does not believe to be true is liable to imprisonment or a fine, or both.

(6) References in this section to the word 'limited' include (in an appropriate case) its Welsh equivalent ('cyfyngedig'), and the appropriate alternative ('ltd.' or 'cyf.', as the case may be).

(7) A company which is exempt from requirements relating to the use of 'limited' and does not include that word as part of its name, is also exempt from the requirements of this Act relating to the publication of its name and the sending of lists of members to the registrar of companies.

S 30(1), (7)

The requirement to include the word 'limited' as the last word of the name is imposed by s 25(2). In addition to the exemption regarding the name, the company is also exempt from the requirements regarding publication of the name (see ss 348–350 with respect to the publication of the company's name on its premises, correspondence and on the company seal, if it has one). The company is also exempt from the requirement to send a list of members to the registrar of companies with the annual return as required by s 364A; but it is still obliged to state on business letters and order forms that it is a limited company: s 351(1)(d); and to maintain a register of members which is open for inspection: ss 352, 356.

S 30(2)

This exemption is only available to companies limited by guarantee, defined s 1(2)(b), and there is a limited transitional category of companies limited by shares which were so entitled under licence.

S 30(3)

The required objects are quite broad and are not restricted to charities as such, as is sometimes thought. The requirement is 'to promote' these objects which would mean to advance or encourage or support them. For members, there is a prohibition on dividends and on a return of capital on a winding up. Any alteration of these provisions is prohibited without a change of name to include 'limited' as required by s 25(2); the registrar of companies can direct a change of name where there has been a failure to adhere to these requirements: s 31(2).

S 30(4)

The registrar of companies can accept the statutory declaration as 'sufficient evidence', ie unless the contrary is shown.

S 30(5)

Exempt status may be sought either from incorporation or subsequently hence the person responsible for the statutory declaration will vary according to the circumstances.

S 30(5A)–(5C)

These provisions were inserted by the Companies Act 1985 (Electronic Communications) Order 2000, SI 2000/3373, art 5(1),(3), as from 22 December 2000; and facilitate the acceptance by the registrar of companies of electronic statements as to certain matters in the same manner as he accepts statutory declarations as to those matters; see s 30(4); as to the delivery of documents to the registrar using electronic communications, see s 707B.

As to penalties, see s 730, Sch 24; the intention is to provide the same penalties for false statements as is provided by the Perjury Act 1911 for false statutory declarations.

31. Provisions applying to company exempt under s 30

(1)   A company which is exempt under section 30 and whose name does not include 'limited' shall not alter its memorandum or articles of association so that it ceases to comply with the requirements of subsection (3) of that section.

(2)   If it appears to the Secretary of State that such a company—

   (a)   has carried on any business other than the promotion of any of the objects mentioned in that subsection, or

   (b)   has applied any of its profits or other income otherwise than in promoting such objects, or

   (c)   has paid a dividend to any of its members,

he may, in writing, direct the company to change its name by resolution of the directors within such period as may be specified in the direction, so that its name ends with 'limited'.

A resolution passed by the directors in compliance with a direction under this subsection is subject to section 380 of this Act (copy to be forwarded to the registrar of companies within 15 days).

(3)   A company which has received a direction under subsection (2) shall not thereafter be registered by a name which does not include 'limited', without the approval of the Secretary of State.

(4)   References in this section to the word 'limited' include (in an appropriate case) its Welsh equivalent ('cyfyngedig'), and the appropriate alternative ('ltd.' or 'cyf.', as the case may be).

(5)   A company which contravenes subsection (1), and any officer of it who is in default, is liable to a fine and, for continued contravention, to a daily default fine.

(6)   A company which fails to comply with a direction by the Secretary of State under subsection (2), and any officer of the company who is in default, is liable to a fine and, for continued contravention, to a daily default fine.

S 31(1), (5)

A company which is exempt under s 30 is prohibited from altering its objects away from those required for the exemption without changing its name; and criminal penalties arise for breach: sub-s (5). As to penalties, see s 730, Sch 24; 'officer in default' is defined in s 730(5).

S 31(2),(6)

Exempt status is lost in the specified circumstances. The direction allows the directors to change the name without the necessity of a special resolution as is required by s 28(1) although this resolution too must be filed with the registrar of companies. As to penalties, see s 730, Sch 24; 'officer in default' is defined in s 730(5).

S 31(3)

This requirement prevents a company which has lost exempt status from simply applying for it again at a later date.

32. Power to require company to abandon misleading name

(1)   If in the Secretary of State's opinion the name by which a company is registered gives so misleading an indication of the nature of its activities as to be likely to cause harm to the public, he may direct it to change its name.

(2)   The direction must, if not duly made the subject of an application to the court under the following subsection, be complied with within a period of 6 weeks from the date of the direction or such longer period as the Secretary of State may think fit to allow.

(3)   The company may, within a period of 3 weeks from the date of the direction, apply to the court to set it aside; and the court may set the direction aside or confirm it and, if it confirms the direction, shall specify a period within which it must be complied with.

(4)   If a company makes default in complying with a direction under this section, it is liable to a fine and, for continued contravention, to a daily default fine.

(5)   Where a company changes its name under this section, the registrar shall (subject to section 26) enter the new name on the register in place of the former name, and shall issue a certificate of incorporation altered to meet the circumstances of the case; and the change of name has effect from the date on which the altered certificate is issued.

(6)   A change of name by a company under this section does not affect any of the rights or obligations of the company, or render defective any legal proceedings by or against it; and any legal proceedings that might have been continued or commenced against it by its former name may be continued or commenced against it by its new name.

S 32(1)

The section is concerned only with misleading names and not with any other means by which the public is misled. It is not sufficient to show that a name is misleading – a likelihood of harm must be shown; in many cases, the latter will follow from the former but this is not necessarily so: *Association of Certified Public Accountants of Britain v Secretary of State for Trade and Industry* [1997] 2 BCLC 307. It is not necessary to show instances of anyone actually having been misled, nor that any particular section of the public might be misled. It simply requires that the name is misleading to at least a substantial number of people: *Association of Certified Public Accountants of Britain v Secretary of State for Trade and Industry* [1997] 2 BCLC 307.

S 32(3)

The direction to change the company's name is automatically suspended once an application is made to the court; and the application is not by way of appeal but requires the court to consider the matter de novo on the evidence brought before it; that evidence may be raised by either side and may relate to matters before or after the direction was given; the court will then form its own view on whether the name offends the provision: *Association of Certified Public Accountants of Britain v Secretary of State for Trade and Industry* [1997] 2 BCLC 307.

S 32(4)

As to penalties, see s 730, Sch 24.

S 32(5), (6)

See note to s 28(6), (7), above.

---

33. Prohibition on trading under misleading name

(1)   A person who is not a public company is guilty of an offence if he carries on any trade, profession or business under a name which includes, as its last part, the words 'public limited company' or their equivalent in Welsh ('cwmni cyfyngedig cyhoeddus').

(2)   A public company is guilty of an offence if, in circumstances in which the fact that it is a public company is likely to be material to any person, it uses a name which may reasonably be expected to give the impression that it is a private company.

(3)   A person guilty of an offence under subsection (1) or (2) and, if that person is a company, any officer of the company who is in default, is liable to a fine and, for continued contravention, to a daily default fine.

S 33(1)

It is an offence for any person, whether trading as a company or not, to use the statutory designation imposed on public companies by s 25(1) (or its alternative, see s 27(2)), when not entitled.

S 33(2)

The essence of this offence is clear – a public company must not pass itself off as a private company. However, the wording is unclear, for example, as to the meaning of '… circumstances in which the fact that it is a public company is material'. It is not clear either what type of name might reasonably be expected to give the impression that the company is a private company other than a failure to include the words 'public limited company' or 'plc' as required by ss 25, 27.

    In practice, it is more likely that a private company will attempt to pass itself off as a public company, an offence under s 33(1).

S 33(3)

As to penalties, see s 730, Sch 24; 'officer in default' is defined in s 730(5).

34. Penalty for improper use of 'limited' or 'cyfyngedig'

If any person trades or carries on business under a name or title of which 'limited' or 'cyfyngedig', or any contraction or imitation of either of those words, is the last word, that person, unless duly incorporated with limited liability, is liable to a fine and, for continued contravention, to a daily default fine.

General note

The requirement to use the designation 'limited' when limited is set out in s 25(1). The prohibitions on its use extend to the use of the approved alternatives: s 27(2). The consequence of breach of this provision is merely the statutory fine; a person in breach of it is not prevented from enforcing contracts or recovering moneys for work done: *Cotronic (UK) Ltd v Dezonie* [1991] BCLC 721. As to penalties, see s 730, Sch 24.

CHAPTER III

A COMPANY'S CAPACITY; FORMALITIES OF CARRYING ON BUSINESS

35. A company's capacity not limited by its memorandum

(1)   The validity of an act done by a company shall not be called into question on the ground of lack of capacity by reason of anything in the company's memorandum.

(2)   A member of a company may bring proceedings to restrain the doing of an act which but for subsection (1) would be beyond the company's capacity; but no such proceedings shall lie in respect of an act to be done in fulfilment of a legal obligation arising from a previous act of the company.

(3)   It remains the duty of the directors to observe any limitations on their powers flowing from the company's memorandum; and action by the directors which but for subsection (1) would be beyond the company's capacity may only be ratified by the company by special resolution.

   A resolution ratifying such action shall not affect any liability incurred by the directors or any other person; relief from any such liability must be agreed to separately by special resolution.

(4)   The operation of this section is restricted by section 65(1) of the Charities Act 1993 and section 112(3) of the Companies Act 1989 in relation to companies which are charities; and section 322A below (invalidity of certain transactions to which directors or their associates are parties) has effect notwithstanding this section.

General note

See s 719 as to the power of the company to provide for employees on the cessation or transfer of business.

S 35(1)

The ultra vires doctrine   The capacity of a registered company to act is limited by the company's objects as stated in the memorandum and acts outside of the objects are ultra vires and void: *Ashbury Railway Carriage and Iron Co Ltd v Riche* (1875) LR 7 HL 653. See the extensive note to s 2(1)(c), above.

Abolition   The ultra vires doctrine is abolished by this provision, as far as persons dealing with the company are concerned, and neither the company nor the other party can challenge the validity of any act (which would include a gratuitous transaction) done by the company on the grounds of lack of capacity by reason of anything in the company's memorandum. There is also no requirement to enquire as to whether a transaction is permitted by the company's memorandum: s 35B, see the note to that provision, below.

Internal significance   The doctrine retains some internal significance: see s 35(2)–(3); an ultra vires act will be a breach by directors of their duties (s 35(3)) and an unauthorised act by the board: that lack of authority is addressed by s 35A.

Common law   A lack of capacity at common law, for example, to make distributions out of capital, remains ultra vires and void; the statutory exemption here applies only to limitations arising under the memorandum of association. See the general note to Part VIII (ss 263–281 distribution of profits and assets) on ultra vires distributions, below.

S 35(2)

Anticipatory relief   Injunctive relief is available to any member (defined in s 22) in advance of an act which is beyond the company's capacity although a member is unlikely to be sufficiently well informed to take advantage of this provision. This personal right to seek relief reflects the position at common law, see *Simpson v Westminster Palace Hotel Co* (1860) 8 HL Cas 712; *Parke v Daily News Ltd* [1962] 2 All ER 929. In practice, modern drafting techniques coupled with the decision of the Court of Appeal in *Rolled Steel Products (Holdings) Ltd v British Steel Corpn* [1985] 3 All ER 52, CA, mean that it is rare now for any act to be ultra vires, see note to s 2(1)(c), above.

Relief is not available once the act is part of a binding legal obligation, as where relief is sought between the company signing a contract and completion or between the execution of a guarantee and payment under that guarantee. In each case, the company is committed to a legal obligation arising from a previous act.

S 35(3)

Directors' duties   This provision retains the ultra vires doctrine internally and directors remain liable for breach of their duties when the company enters into an ultra vires transaction although, as noted above, it is rare now for a transaction by a registered company to be ultra vires.

Ratification   The provision allows for the ratification of an ultra vires act by a special resolution: see s 378; a private company may use a written resolution: s 381A. This reverses the common law position where not even the unanimous agreement of the shareholders would suffice to ratify an ultra vires act: *Ashbury Railway Carriage and Iron Co Ltd v Riche* (1875) LR 7 HL 653. What is unclear is why ratification would be required as ratification to validate the transaction is unnecessary in view of s 35(1).

It would seem that the possibility of ratification is there to offer the other party greater reassurance; s 35(1) validates transactions against challenge on the ground of lack of capacity but the transaction might still be challenged on the ground of breach of duty by the directors and s 35A is not wide enough to protect the other party in such a case: that provision validates a lack of authority but not a breach of duty: see s 35A(5). Ratification may be necessary or desirable, therefore, to satisfy the other party that the act cannot be challenged either on the grounds of ultra vires or on any other basis.

Two resolutions   Ratification would normally have the effect of validating the transaction and 'whitewashing' the directors' conduct so precluding any corporate action against the directors (or any derivative action by a minority shareholder) but, in this case, two separate resolutions are required to achieve that effect. The requirement of two resolutions allows the shareholders to separate two distinct decisions: (1) ratifying the act so as to give the other party the reassurance which he seeks; and (2) absolving the directors and 'any other person' from any liability arising.

In implementing these reforms in 1989, Parliament was concerned to give persons dealing with the company the maximum protection possible while not diluting the ability of shareholders to hold directors to their duties. The requirement of two resolutions, though cumbersome, reflects those concerns.

Third party liability   The second resolution may relieve the directors and 'any other person' from any liability arising from an act which is beyond the capacity of the company and in breach of the directors' duties. A third party may be liable as a constructive trustee on the standard basis of either 'knowing assistance' in a breach of trust (see *Royal Brunei Airlines Sdn Bhd v Tan* [1995] 3 All ER 97) or 'knowing receipt' of trust funds applied in breach of duty (see *Bank of Credit and Commerce International (Overseas) Ltd v Akindele* [2000] 4 All ER 221); see the extensive note on constructive trust liability included in the note to s 151(3), below.

It might be thought that third party liability as a constructive trustee cannot arise in view of s 35A, but that section only deems the powers of directors to be free of any limitation under the company's constitution and preserves the directors' obligation to adhere to their duties to the company: see *Coöperatieve Rabobank 'Vecht en Plassengebied' BA v Minderhoud*: Case C–104/96 [1998] 2 BCLC 507, ECJ; and s 35A(5) specifically preserves the potential liability of directors and 'other persons' for any liability arising from the directors exceeding their powers; see note to that provision; see also *International Sales and Agencies Ltd v Marcus* [1982] 3 All ER 551 at 560.

Derivative actions   An action to recover money or property on behalf of the company in respect of a past ultra vires transaction is an action in respect of a wrong done to the company and the company is the proper plaintiff. An action by a shareholder can only be a derivative action, therefore, on behalf of the company: *Smith v Croft (No 2)* [1987] 3 All ER 909. Where the transaction is ratified and a second special resolution is passed relieving the directors or any other person from any liability arising then no action, corporate or derivative, will lie. This is subject to the possibility that the act of ratification to relieve the directors or any other person of liability, where secured by the wrongdoers, could be seen itself as a fraud on the minority 'depriving the company of some money, property or advantage': see *Burland v Earle* [1902] AC 83; *Menier v Hooper's Telegraph Works* (1874) 9 Ch App 350; *Estmanco (Kilner House) Ltd v Greater London Council* [1982] 1 All ER 437.

S 35(4)

In view of the public interest in the proper conduct of charities, a modified regime contained in the Charities Act 1993 applies to companies which are charities and essentially limits the operation of s 35(1) to parties who deal in good faith and for value or who are unaware that the company is a charity. Where a company is a charity, the ratification of an act under s 35(3) is ineffective without the prior written consent of the Charity Commissioners. CA 1989, s 112(3) made similar provision for Scotland.

Section 322A deals with the situation where one of the parties to a transaction which is beyond the company's capacity and/or the authority of the board is an 'insider' of the company (as defined in s 322A). In that situation, it is thought inappropriate that the insider should avail of the protection afforded by ss 35 and 35A, see note to s 322A.

35A. Power of directors to bind the company

(1) In favour of a person dealing with a company in good faith, the power of the board of directors to bind the company, or authorise others to do so, shall be deemed to be free of any limitation under the company's constitution.

(2) For this purpose—

 (a) a person 'deals with' a company if he is a party to any transaction or other act to which the company is a party;

 (b) a person shall not be regarded as acting in bad faith by reason only of his knowing that an act is beyond the powers of the directors under the company's constitution; and

 (c) a person shall be presumed to have acted in good faith unless the contrary is proved.

(3) The references above to limitations on the directors' power under the company's constitution include limitations deriving—

 (a) from a resolution of the company in general meeting or a meeting of any class of shareholders, or

 (b) from any agreement between the members of the company or of any class of shareholders.

(4) Subsection (1) does not affect any right of a member of the company to bring proceedings to restrain the doing of an act which is beyond the powers of the directors; but no such proceedings shall lie in respect of an act to be done in fulfilment of a legal obligation arising from a previous act of the company.

(5) Nor does that subsection affect any liability incurred by the directors, or any other person, by reason of the directors' exceeding their powers.

(6) The operation of this section is restricted by section 65(1) of the Charities Act 1993 and section 112(3) of the Companies Act 1989 in relation to companies which are charities; and section 322A below (invalidity of certain transactions to which directors or their associates are parties) has effect notwithstanding this section.

General note

Constructive notice Persons dealing with a company are deemed under the doctrine of constructive notice to have notice of the company's memorandum and articles of association and various (ill-defined) public documents (including special resolutions and any charges registered with the registrar of companies) and any limitations contained therein: *Ernest v Nicholls* (1857) 6 HL Cas 401; *Mahony v East Holyford Mining Co* (1875) LR 7 HL 869; *Irvine v Union Bank of Australia* (1877) 2 App Cas 366, PC: *Wilson v Kelland* [1910] 2 Ch 306. The application of the doctrine is mitigated by the rule in *Turquand's* case regarding matters of internal management: *Royal British Bank v Turquand* (1856) 6 E & B 327, discussed below.

 Constructive notice is irrelevant under s 35A since even actual knowledge of itself does not establish bad faith: see note to sub-ss(1), (2); and a party to a transaction with the company is not bound to enquire as to the capacity of the company or the authority of the directors: s 35B. The doctrine of constructive notice for all other purposes was to have been abolished by s 711A to be inserted by CA 1989 s 142 but drafting problems meant that s 711A was never brought into force and it is to be repealed at the earliest opportunity.

S 35A(1), (2)

In favour of a person dealing with a company   This provision, introduced by CA 1989, s 108, operates in favour of the other party only and if the company wants to hold that party to the transaction or other act then it must ratify the transaction or act. An act in excess of the board's authority can be ratified by ordinary resolution (special, if the unauthorised act is also ultra vires: s 35(3)) even though an alteration to the board's powers to authorise the directors so to act in future would require a special resolution: see *Irvine v Union Bank of Australia* (1877) 2 App Cas 366, PC; *Grant v United Kingdom Switchback Rlys Co* (1888) 40 Ch D 135, CA.

'Dealing' is defined by sub-s (2) in a way which ensures that the provision applies to gratuitous acts such as donations or guarantees as well as commercial transactions.

In good faith   The other party must deal in good faith. There is a presumption of good faith, however, and a person is not to be regarded as acting in bad faith by reason *only* of his knowing that an act is beyond the powers of the directors (sub-ss (2)(b), (c)). Constructive notice is irrelevant here since actual knowledge alone of any limitation does not establish bad faith. Furthermore, there is no obligation to enquire as to any limitation on the capacity of the company or the authority of the directors: s 35B; see *TCB Ltd v Gray* [1986] 1 All ER 587 at 596; *Barclays Bank Ltd v TOSG Trust Fund Ltd* [1984] BCLC 1 at 18 (on the previous provision, European Communities Act 1972, s 9(1), which had similar wording).

To establish that the other party has not acted in good faith, it is necessary to show something in addition to knowledge, such as dishonesty or collusion in the breach by the directors of their duties although the precise factors which the courts will take to be indicative of bad faith remain to be identified: *Barclays Bank Ltd v TOSG Trust Fund Ltd* [1984] BCLC 1 at 18.

Powers of the board   The focus of the provision is on the powers of the board: (1) to bind the company; and (2) to authorise others to bind the company and limitations on those powers may be disregarded. The section has no application to individual directors (or the company secretary) acting in breach of their authority: that issue is governed by the ordinary rules of agency dealing with actual and ostensible authority.

Limitations under the company's constitution   The limitations which may be disregarded are those arising under the memorandum and articles of association as the company's constitution (and including the limitations identified in sub-s (3)), such as provisions prohibiting the directors from dealing with a particular matter or requiring directors to execute a transaction in a particular manner.

It is argued that other requirements, such as those relating to quorum requirements or the location of board meetings, are also constitutional limitations on the power of the board of directors to act. The government's position, while the CA 1989 was being debated in Parliament, was that rules as to quorum, for example, are not limitations on the powers of the board of directors but deal with the logically prior question of what constitutes a board of directors and are not within the provision.

The point may be debatable as far as the interpretation of s 35A is concerned but, in any event, the answer to whether the company can be held to transactions which are in breach of such requirements may lie in the existing law, namely the rule in *Royal British Bank v Turquand* (1856) 6 E&B 327.

The rule in *Turquand's Case* The rule in *Royal British Bank v Turquand* (1856) 6 E&B 327 provides that persons dealing with a company are not obliged to inquire into the internal proceedings of a company but can assume that all acts of internal management have been properly carried out, save where an outsider knows or ought to know of the failure to adhere to procedure: *Royal British Bank v Turquand* (1856) 6 E&B 327; *B Liggett (Liverpool) Ltd v Barclays Bank Ltd* [1928] 1 KB 48; *Morris v Kanssen* [1946] AC 459, HL; *Rolled Steel Products (Holdings) Ltd v British Steel Corpn* [1985] 3 All ER 52, CA; or the document on which the outsider relies is a forgery: *Ruben v Great Fingall Consolidated* [1906] AC 439, HL. Requirements as to quorum, for example, are matters of internal management which an outsider, in the absence of knowledge, is entitled to assume have been properly performed.

Obviously, the statutory provision by enabling a person dealing with the company to ignore limitations on authority arising from the memorandum, articles, resolutions in general meeting or shareholders' agreements is much broader in its application than the rule in *Turquand's Case* and this will reduce the need to fall back on the rule. However, cases do remain, such as those involving inquorate boards or invalidly appointed directors, which will be outside s 35A (not being limitations on the board's power to act) and there will still be a need to have recourse to the rule. It remains narrower than s 35A in that notice of the defect will prevent the other party relying on *Turquand*, whereas knowledge of limitations on the powers of the board does not preclude reliance on s 35A.

S 35A(3)

The limitations which may be disregarded include any arising from a unanimous shareholders' agreement or an agreement of a class of shareholders.

Constraints on the board The typical division of authority between the board and the general meeting is provided by Table A, reg 70, which states that, subject to the provisions of the Act, the memorandum and articles and to any directions given by special resolution, the directors may exercise all the powers of the company. It is envisaged, therefore, that the directors' powers may be constrained by provisions of this nature. For example, the consent of the company in general meeting might be needed to authorise the sale of a particular asset, or the articles may limit the power of the board to delegate, or the general meeting might give directions on a particular matter. As constraints on the powers of the board, these limitations are of little value, for persons dealing in good faith may ignore them. Internally, these limitations are useful in establishing that the directors have exceeded their powers for the purposes of liability under sub-s (5), subject always to the possibility of ratification, see note to sub-ss (1), (2) above.

S 35A(4)

Anticipatory relief A member may seek injunctive relief although he is unlikely to be sufficiently well informed to take advantage of this provision; see also note to s 35(2), above, which makes similar but not identical provision in the case of ultra vires transactions.

S 35A(5)

Breach of duty   The intention of the reforms introduced by CA 1989 was that, while persons dealing with a company in good faith should be able to hold the company to a transaction or other act despite any lack of authority on the part of the board, internally, the directors should remain liable for any breach of duty, subject to the ability of the company to ratify acts in excess of their powers. A third party as 'any other person' is also potentially liable as a constructive trustee: see *Rolled Steel Products (Holdings) Ltd v British Steel Corpn* [1985] 3 All ER 52, CA; *International Sales and Agencies Ltd v Marcus* [1982] 3 All ER 551; see the note to s 35(3), above; and the detailed note to s 151(3) on constructive trust liability. This position is confirmed in *Coöperatieve Rabobank Vecht en Plassengebied BA v Minderhoud*: Case C–104/96 [1998] 2 BCLC 507, ECJ.

S 35A(6)

See note to s 35(4), above, and to s 322A, below.

35B. No duty to enquire as to capacity of company or authority of directors

A party to a transaction with a company is not bound to enquire as to whether it is permitted by the company's memorandum or as to any limitation on the powers of the board of directors to bind the company or authorise others to do so.

General note

This provision is not restricted to dealings with the board but it is restricted to transactions. Sections 35 and 35A extend to 'acts' and 'transactions' is a narrower term which is thought not to cover gratuitous dispositions. It is unclear whether the use of 'transaction' here is an oversight or a deliberate narrowing of the provision.

 As noted, prior to these provisions (ss 35–35B), persons dealing with a company were affected by constructive notice of the memorandum and articles and were put on inquiry as to matters arising from their deemed knowledge, mitigated only by the rule in *Royal British Bank v Turquand* (1856) 6 E&B 327 as to matters of internal management. This provision, coupled with s 35A(2)(b), (c), confirms that not only is knowledge alone of a limitation irrelevant but there is no duty to inquire as to the two matters specified: ie as to limitations on capacity in the memorandum or limitations on the powers of the board to bind the company or authorise others to do so. The combined effect is to abolish the doctrine of constructive notice for these purposes.

36. Company contracts: England and Wales

Under the law of England and Wales a contract may be made—

  (a) by a company, by writing under its common seal, or

  (b) on behalf of a company, by any person acting under its authority, express or implied;

and any formalities required by law in the case of a contract made by an individual also apply, unless a contrary intention appears, to a contract made by or on behalf of a company.

General note

The statute distinguishes between an act of the company itself, and actions taken by agents to bind it and so provides that a contract may be made: (i) *by* a company or (ii) *on behalf of* a company.

Contracts by a company   A contract can be made by a company by writing under its common seal (see note to s 36A(2), below). However, a company is no longer required to have a common seal (s 36A(3)) and a document signed by a director and the secretary or by two directors and expressed to be executed by the company has the same effect as if executed under the common seal of the company: s 36A(4). Execution by either of these methods, therefore, is execution by the company under seal.

Contracts on behalf of a company   Alternatively, and more commonly, a contract may be made on behalf of the company and signed by an authorised person on its behalf. This may be in writing or, for more routine matters, will be a parol contract made on behalf of the company by an authorised person without being reduced to writing. A company may ratify contracts entered into without authority. If it chooses not to ratify, the contracting party may still be able to hold the company to its obligations by relying on s 35A (where the issue concerns a lack of authority on the part of the board) or on the actual or ostensible authority of the individual agent who contracted: see *Hely-Hutchinson v Brayhead Ltd* [1968] 1 QB 549; *Freeman and Lockyer v Buckhurst Park Properties (Mangal) Ltd* [1964] 2 QB 480.

    The normal form of contract is for the company to be the named party to the contract which is then signed on its behalf.

    As to bills of exchange and promissory notes, see s 37.

Contracts by foreign companies   In similar fashion, for companies incorporated outside Great Britain, a contract may be made either:

  (1) by a company itself, by writing under its common seal or in any other manner permitted by the territory of incorporation for the execution of documents by such a company; or

  (2) on behalf of a company, by any person who (in accordance with the laws of the territory of incorporation) is acting under the authority, express or implied, of that company: Foreign Companies (Execution of Documents) Regulations 1994, SI 1994/950, as amended.

36A. Execution of documents: England and Wales

(1)   Under the law of England and Wales the following provisions have effect with respect to the execution of documents by a company.

(2)   A document is executed by a company by the affixing of its common seal.

(3)   A company need not have a common seal, however, and the following subsections apply whether it does or not.

(4)   A document signed by a director and the secretary of a company, or by two directors of a company, and expressed (in whatever form of words) to be executed by the company has the same effect as if executed under the common seal of the company.

(5)   A document executed by a company which makes it clear on its face that it is intended by the person or persons making it to be a deed has effect, upon delivery, as a deed; and it shall be presumed, unless a contrary intention is proved, to be delivered upon its being so executed.

(6)   In favour of a purchaser a document shall be deemed to have been duly executed by a company if it purports to be signed by a director and the secretary of the company, or by two directors of the company, and, where it makes it clear on its face that it is intended by the person or persons making it to be a deed, to have been delivered upon its being executed.
   A 'purchaser' means a purchaser in good faith for valuable consideration and includes a lessee, mortgagee or other person who for valuable consideration acquires an interest in property.

General note

This provision deals with two distinct matters:
  (1)   the manner in which any document may be executed by a company (sub-ss (2), (4)); and
  (2)   the manner in which documents which are to be deeds may be executed (sub-s (5)).

An exhaustive analysis of this complex provision can be found in a consultation paper and report from the Law Commission: see *The Execution of Deeds and Documents by or on behalf of Bodies Corporate* (1996) Consultation Paper, No 143; Report (Law Com no 253 (1998)).
   This section, as modified, applies to companies incorporated outside Great Britain: see the Foreign Companies (Execution of Documents) Regulations 1994, SI 1994/ 950, as amended.

S 36A(2)

Execution of a document under seal   As to requirements regarding the company seal, see s 350; a company is no longer required to have a company seal (s 36A(3)). For companies which have retained a seal, there may be good reasons for continuing with the existing practice of executing documents in this way. The Law Commission identified the following advantages to so doing:

(1)   execution under seal, because it carries the company's name and usually also its registered number, probably offers a greater guarantee of authenticity than execution by the signature of officers alone;

(2)   execution under seal involves greater formality and may help focus the attention of the company's officers on the transaction in hand; while provisions dealing with the safekeeping of the seal and the maintenance of a seal register enhance internal controls;

(3)   execution under seal may be important if the documents are executed for use abroad in a jurisdiction which requires execution under seal;

(4)   execution under seal may offer greater flexibility – the articles may extend, for example, the range of authorised persons, beyond directors and the company secretary, who can attest the sealing (*The Execution of Deeds and Documents by or on behalf of Bodies Corporate* (1996) Consultation Paper no 143, para 14.2).

A company which has a common seal may also have a facsimile of it for use abroad and for 'securities' purposes: see ss 39, 40.

Formalities under the articles   If a company chooses to execute a document by affixing its seal, it must comply with any formalities prescribed by the company's constitution for the affixing of the seal: see, for example, Table A, reg 101 (the affixing of the seal must be accompanied by the signature of a director and the secretary or by a second director).

   In any event, applying the rule in *Royal British Bank v Turquand* (1856) 6 E&B 327 (which entitles persons dealing with a company to assume, absent notice, that all matters of internal management have been complied with, see note to s 35A(1)), a party is entitled to assume that the seal has been duly affixed, the directors duly appointed and their signatures duly made: *Gloucester County Bank v Rudry Merthyr Steam and House Coal Colliery Co* [1895] 1 Ch 629; except where the document is a forgery, where the rule in *Turquand's* case has no application: *Ruben v Great Fingall Consolidated* [1906] AC 439, HL. It is debatable whether the protection afforded by s 36A(6) to a 'purchaser' applies to a document executed under seal, see note to that provision.

   In an appropriate case, the other party may also be able to avail of the protection of s 35A with respect to any defect in the authority of the board.

   A company which has a common seal must also comply with s 350.

Seals and deeds   Execution under seal does not automatically make a document a deed. Execution as a deed is a matter for sub-s (5) and will require, in addition to execution by the company, that it is intended to be executed as a deed and that it is delivered.

S 36A(4)

Execution of a document by signature without a seal   A company may use this alternative method of execution, which has the same effect as if executed under seal, even though the company's constitution does not make provision for such alternative method. There is no requirement that these signatures be attested.

The advantages of execution without sealing identified by the Law Commission are:

(a)   execution under seal is an administrative burden and an archaic practice;

(b)   allowing execution without sealing brings company practice into line with requirements for execution by individuals;

(c)   execution without sealing facilitates business with jurisdictions which do not recognise the concept of execution under seal (*The Execution of Deeds and Documents by or on behalf of Bodies Corporate* (1996) Consultation Paper no 143, para 14.3).

Where the officer required to sign is itself a company, the signature required is that of someone authorised on its behalf; and where there are common officers for a number of companies signing on behalf of those companies, they should take care to sign separately on behalf of each individual company which is party to the transaction.

A purchaser, as defined in s 36A(6), has the protection of the irrebuttable presumption of due execution in that provision. In any event, applying the rule in *Royal British Bank v Turquand* (1856) 6 E&B 327 (which entitles persons dealing with a company to assume, absent notice, that all matters of internal management have been complied with, see note to s 35A(1), above), a party is entitled to assume that the officers were duly appointed and their signatures duly made: *Gloucester County Bank v Rudry Merthyr Steam and House Coal Colliery Co* [1895] 1 Ch 629; *Mahony v East Holyford Mining Co* (1875) LR 7 HL 869; except where the document is a forgery where the rule in *Turquand's* case has no application: *Ruben v Great Fingall Consolidated* [1906] AC 439, HL.

In an appropriate case, the other party may also be able to avail of the protection of s 35A with respect to any defect in the authority of the board.

S 36A(5)

Execution of a document as a deed   There are a number of distinct steps involved for a document to be executed as a deed.

(1)   The document must be executed by the company, ie under seal (s 36A(2)) or by signature (s 36A(4)).

(2)   On the face of the document, it must be clear that it is intended by those making it to be a deed. It is best to do this by express words, such as 'this deed', or by stating that it is 'executed as a deed' so as to avoid any uncertainty as to what is intended.

(3)   There must be delivery (ie an intention to be bound) and delivery is presumed where (1) and (2) are present, unless the contrary is proved. 'Delivery' for these purposes will include delivery with immediate effect and delivery in escrow where the intention is to be bound provided certain conditions are met: see *Beesly v Hallwood Estates Ltd* [1960] 1 WLR 549 at 562; *Johnsey Estates (1990) Ltd v Newport Marketworld Ltd* [1996] NPC 81 (*The Execution of Deeds and Documents by or on behalf of Bodies Corporate* (1996) Consultation Paper no 143, para 6.25; Law Com no 253 (1998), para 6.15).

Delayed delivery   Where the company wishes to retain the option of withdrawing from the transaction, it must take care to rebut the presumption of delivery (including delivery in escrow) and provide for delayed delivery. This is commonly done by authorising the company's solicitors to delay delivery until completion.

The Law Commission noted in its Report that delivery in escrow and delayed delivery are legally quite distinct and have very different consequences, the former being irrevocable, where the conditions are met, while the latter can be withdrawn at any time (*The Execution of Deeds and Documents by or on behalf of Bodies Corporate* (1998), Law Com No 253, para 6.5). It also noted that it may not be obvious in practice which of the two methods is being used and the significance is not always appreciated by practitioners and clients.

The Law Commission suggested that practitioners should make it clear in correspondence which method is being used, for example, by using covering letters which ask the client to execute and return the deed to the solicitor 'for delivery on your behalf on completion', so making clear that delivery is something apart from execution (*The Execution of Deeds and Documents by or on behalf of Bodies Corporate* (1996) Consultation Paper, No 143, para 11.60).

S 36A(6)

This provision creates two presumptions: (1) as to the execution of a document; and (2) as to the delivery of a deed, in both cases in favour of a 'purchaser' as defined. The presumptions will not apply where the document is a forgery: *Ruben v Great Fingall Consolidated* [1906] AC 439, HL.

Irrebuttable presumption as to due execution The intention here was to extend the protection available to a purchaser under the Law of Property Act 1925, s 74 (which creates a similar presumption where a deed is executed by affixing a common seal) to the situation where the company has taken advantage of s 36A(4) to execute a document without using a seal (*The Execution of Deeds and Documents by or on behalf of Bodies Corporate* (1996) Consultation Paper No 143, para 5.26).

Irrebuttable presumption as to delivery This provision poses such difficulties that the Law Commission has recommended that it be repealed (*The Execution of Deeds and Documents by or on behalf of Bodies Corporate* (Law Com No 253 (1998) para 6.43). The difficulties identified were as follows:

    (a)   The provision is unnecessary in the light of sub-s (5) (which provides for a rebuttable presumption of delivery) and inconsistent with LPA 1925, s 74 (which it was intended to replicate) as s 74 is concerned only with due execution and contains no presumption of delivery in favour of a purchaser (*The Execution of Deeds and Documents by or on behalf of Bodies Corporate* (Law Com no 253 (1998)) para 6.14).

    (b)   The difficulty with this presumption is that 'by implication this [deemed delivery] is irrebuttable, since it is worded as a deeming provision, and there is no reference to contrary intention being proved, in clear contrast to the presumption in s 36A(5)' (*The Execution of Deeds and Documents by or on behalf of Bodies Corporate* (1996) Consultation Paper, No 143, para 6.23). If the presumption is irrebuttable, then it would seem to rule out delayed delivery in cases within sub-s (6), ie where a purchaser is involved. It seems that, in such cases, the parties must not execute the deed if they are to defeat the irrebuttable presumption of delivery in this section.

    (c)   It is also unclear whether this irrebuttable presumption will apply where the document is executed under seal. It appears not on the wording, leaving the matter to LPA 1925, s 74 where the document is executed under seal. There is unreported authority that it does apply to documents executed under seal, see *Johnsey Estates (1990) Ltd v Newport Marketworld Ltd* [1996] NPC 81, although the Law Commission does not entirely accept this construction and regards the matter as uncertain (*The Execution of Deeds and Documents by or on behalf of Bodies Corporate* (Law Com No 253 (1998)), para 6.12).

36B. Execution of documents by companies

(1)　Notwithstanding the provisions of any enactment, a company need not have a company seal.

(2)　For the purposes of any enactment—
    (a)　providing for a document to be executed by a company by affixing its common seal; or
    (b)　referring (in whatever terms) to a document so executed,

a document signed or subscribed by or on behalf of the company in accordance with the provisions of the Requirements of Writing (Scotland) Act 1995 shall have effect as if so executed.

(3)　In this section 'enactment' includes an enactment contained in a statutory instrument.

General note

This provision clarifies that no seal is required regardless of the provisions of any statute or statutory instrument.

36C. Pre-incorporation contracts, deeds and obligations

(1)　A contract which purports to be made by or on behalf of a company at a time when the company has not been formed has effect, subject to any agreement to the contrary, as one made with the person purporting to act for the company or as agent for it, and he is personally liable on the contract accordingly.

(2)　Subsection (1) applies—
    (a)　to the making of a deed under the law of England and Wales, and
    (b)　to the undertaking of an obligation under the law of Scotland,

as it applies to the making of a contract.

General note

This section is modified in relation to companies incorporated outside Great Britain by the Foreign Companies (Execution of Documents) Regulations 1994, SI 1994/ 950 as amended.

Novation required   A company cannot by adoption or ratification obtain the benefit of a contract purportedly made on its behalf before it came into existence: *Natal Land and Colonization Co Ltd v Pauline Colliery and Development Syndicate* [1904] AC 120, PC. The company will be bound only where the obligations are novated, ie a new contract must come into existence after incorporation on the same terms as the old one: *Natal Land*.

Novation may be express or implied, and express novation is the preferable method of proceeding. Reliance on implied novation runs the risk that the conduct of the company may not be unequivocally referable to the alleged new agreement. It may be seen simply as a continuation of the old agreement in the erroneous belief that it is binding: *Re Northumberland Avenue Hotel Co Ltd* (1886) 33 Ch D 16.

S 36C(1)

Personal liability   The person who purports to contract on behalf of the company is personally liable, however he chooses to express his signature, unless there is the clearest exclusion of personal liability. Although the section does not specify that any such exclusion be express, the decision in *Phonogram Ltd v Lane* [1981] 3 All ER 182 effectively requires it. In that case, the contract in question was signed by the defendant 'for and on behalf of the company'. The Court of Appeal held that that method of signature was insufficient to negate the liability arising under this provision and that to hold otherwise would defeat the purpose of the provision; see also *Braymist Ltd v Wise Finance Co Ltd* [2001] All ER (D) 20, Ch D.

Mutual obligations   A person who purports to contract on behalf of the company can enforce the agreement: *Braymist Ltd v Wise Finance Co Ltd* [2001] All ER (D) 20, Ch D.

Company has not been formed   The operation of the provision is confined to situations where the contract purports to be made by or on behalf of a company which has not been formed. Where a company does exist but is improperly described, it cannot be said that the contract purports to be on behalf of a company not yet formed so as to leave the individual signatory liable: *Badgerhill Properties Ltd v Cottrell* [1991] BCLC 805.

In *Oshkosh B'gosh Inc v Dan Marbel Inc Ltd* [1989] BCLC 507 the plaintiff contracted with a company which had changed its name. At the time of contracting, the company had not secured a certificate of incorporation under that new name. It was argued that the person who contracted for the company should be personally liable since, at the time of contracting, the company had 'not been formed'. The Court of Appeal rejected this argument as it is clear that a change of name does not affect a company's continued existence: see s 28(7). The contract was with a company which was in existence although under a different name.

A contract can purport to be made on behalf of an unformed company, even if both parties know that the company has not been formed and is only about to be formed; liability does not depend upon a representation that the company is already in existence, since the claim is not for damages for breach of warranty of authority: *Phonogram Ltd v Lane* [1981] 3 All ER 182. However, if the formation of the company is not in anyone's contemplation at the time the contract is made, then it cannot be said that the contract purports to be made by or on behalf of that company: *Cotronic (UK) Ltd v Dezonie* [1991] BCLC 721.

37. Bills of exchange and promissory notes

A bill of exchange or promissory note is deemed to have been made, accepted or endorsed on behalf of a company if made, accepted or endorsed in the name of, or by or on behalf or on account of, the company by a person acting under its authority.

General note

A bill of exchange is defined as an unconditional order in writing, addressed by one person to another, signed by the person giving it, requiring the person to whom it is addressed to pay on demand or at a fixed or determinable future time a sum certain in money to or to the order of a specified person, or to bearer: Bills of Exchange Act 1882, s 3(1); a cheque is a bill of exchange drawn on a banker payable on demand: Bills of Exchange Act 1882, s 73.

A promissory note is an unconditional promise in writing made by one person to another, signed by the maker, engaging to pay, on demand or at a fixed or determinable future time, a sum certain in money to, or to the order of, a specified person or to bearer: Bills of Exchange Act 1882, s 83(1). See 4(1) *Halsbury's Laws*, (4th edn reissue) para 306.

See s 349(4) as to the potential personal liability of the signatory to a bill of exchange, promissory note, etc.

38. Execution of deeds abroad

(1)   A company may [...], by writing under its common seal, empower any person, either generally or in respect of any specified matters, as its attorney, to execute deeds on its behalf in any place elsewhere than in the United Kingdom.

(2)   A deed executed by such an attorney on behalf of the company has the same effect as if it were executed under the company's common seal.

(3)   This section does not extend to Scotland.

General note

Table A, reg 71 provides an express power to grant a power of attorney which would include a power to execute deeds within the UK. The purpose of this provision is merely to clarify that a company has the power to grant a power of attorney to execute deeds outside the UK; see Law Commission, *The Execution of Deeds and Documents by or on behalf of Bodies Corporate* (Law Com no 253 (1998)) para 7.8.

S 38(1)

Instead of utilising the company seal, a company may use the alternative method of execution provided by s 36A(4) to grant the power of attorney.

---

39. Power of company to have official seal for use abroad

(1)   A company which has a common seal whose objects require or comprise the transaction of business in foreign countries may, if authorised by its articles, have for use in any territory, district, or place elsewhere than in the United Kingdom, an official seal, which shall be a facsimile of its common seal, with the addition on its face of the name of every territory, district or place where it is to be used.

(2)   The official seal when duly affixed to a document has the same effect as the company's common seal.

(2A) Subsection (2) does not extend to Scotland.

(3)   A company having an official seal for use in any such territory, district or place may, by writing under its common seal or as respects Scotland by writing subscribed in accordance with the Requirements of Writing (Scotland) Act 1995[...] authorise any person appointed for the purpose in that territory, district or place to affix the official seal to any deed or other document to which the company is party in that territory, district or place.

(4)   As between the company and a person dealing with such an agent, the agent's authority continues during the period (if any) mentioned in the instrument conferring the authority, or if no period is there mentioned, then until notice of the revocation or determination of the agent's authority has been given to the person dealing with him.

(5)   The person affixing the official seal shall certify in writing on the deed or other instrument to which the seal is affixed the date on which and the place at which it is affixed.

General note

This provision offers companies with a common seal the option of also having a facsimile of it for use abroad.

S 39(1)

This provision is restricted to companies whose objects meet the specified requirements.

40. Official seal for share certificates, etc

(1)   A company which has a common seal may have, for use for sealing securities issued by the company and for sealing documents creating or evidencing securities so issued, an official seal which is a facsimile of its common seal with the addition on its face of the word 'Securities'.

   The official seal when duly affixed to a document has the same effect as the company's common seal.

(2)   Nothing in this section shall affect the right of a company registered in Scotland to subscribe such securities and documents in accordance with the Requirements of Writing (Scotland) Act 1995.

General note

This provision offers companies with a common seal the option of also having a facsimile of it for securities use.

41. Authentication of documents

A document or proceeding requiring authentication by a company is sufficiently authenticated for the purposes of the law of England and Wales by the signature of a director, secretary or other authorised officer of the company.

General note

As to the definition of 'officer', see s 744.

42. Events affecting a company's status

(1)   A company is not entitled to rely against other persons on the happening of any of the following events—

   (a)   the making of a winding-up order in respect of the company, or the appointment of a liquidator in a voluntary winding up of the company, or

   (b)   any alteration of the company's memorandum or articles, or

   (c)   any change among the company's directors, or

   (d)   (as regards service of any document on the company) any change in the situation of the company's registered office,

if the event had not been officially notified at the material time and is not shown by the company to have been known at that time to the person concerned, or if the material time fell on or before the 15th day after the date of official notification (or, where the 15th day was a non-business day, on or before the next day that was not) and it is shown that the person concerned was unavoidably prevented from knowing of the event at that time.

(2) In subsection (1)—

    (a) 'official notification' and 'officially notified' have the meanings given by section 711(2)(registrar of companies to give public notice of the issue or receipt by him of certain documents), and

    (b) 'non-business day' means a Saturday or Sunday, Christmas Day, Good Friday and any other day which is a bank holiday in the part of Great Britain where the company is registered.

General note

A company cannot rely on any matter within this provision until publication in the London or Edinburgh Gazette and can only conditionally rely on it for 15 days thereafter. The validity of the matter is not affected.

S 42(1)

Not officially notified   If one of the specified events has not been officially notified, ie published by the registrar of companies in the relevant Gazette, the company cannot rely on it against the other party unless they have actual knowledge of it.

Within 15 days of official notification   If the event has been gazetted but the company is seeking to rely on it within 15 days of the gazetting, then it cannot do so if the other person can show that they were unavoidably prevented from knowing of the matter at that time, despite it being gazetted.

Negative effect   The provision is essentially negative in its impact: *Official Custodian for Charities v Parway Estates Developments Ltd* [1984] 3 All ER 679. In this case, a company which had gone into compulsory winding up, the order for which had been gazetted, tried to insist that the gazetting had the effect of imputing knowledge of the winding up to the company's landlord. The Court of Appeal held that the effect of the section was purely negative in that it provided that a company could not rely on an event of which it was required to give notice if that event was not gazetted; the converse did not follow, namely that a company could rely on the gazetting of an event as being notice to all the world. Accordingly, the notice in the London Gazette of the winding-up order did not impute to the landlord either notice or knowledge of the winding up.

PART II

RE-REGISTRATION AS A MEANS OF ALTERING A COMPANY'S STATUS

General note to this Part

This Part provides for the re-registration of companies. The options available are:

(1)   **a private company** with a share capital (ie either limited by shares or an old company limited by guarantee with a share capital (see s 1(4)) or an unlimited company with a share capital, provided it was originally incorporated as unlimited and not re-registered as unlimited) may become **a public company** (ss 43–48);

(2)   **a private limited company** may become an **unlimited company** provided it was a limited company from incorporation and has not been re-registered as limited or as unlimited (ss 49–50);

(3)   **an unlimited company** may become **a limited company** but only as a private company limited either by shares or by guarantee and it must have been unlimited from original incorporation and has not been re-registered as unlimited (ss 51–52);

(4)   **a public company** may become a **private company** limited either by shares or by guarantee (ss 53–55).

The result is that there is freedom to move between public and private company status but there is a restriction on moving between limited and unlimited status. There is no provision for the re-registration of a company limited by shares as a company limited by guarantee or vice versa.

PRIVATE COMPANY BECOMING PUBLIC

43. Re-registration of private company as public

(1)   Subject to this and the following five sections, a private company (other than a company not having a share capital) may be re-registered as a public company if—

(a)   a special resolution that it should be so re-registered is passed; and

(b)   an application for re-registration is delivered to the registrar of companies, together with the necessary documents.

A company cannot be re-registered under this section if it has previously been re-registered as unlimited.

(2)   The special resolution must—

(a)   alter the company's memorandum so that it states that the company is to be a public company; and

(b)   make such other alterations in the memorandum as are necessary to bring it (in substance and in form) into conformity with the requirements of this Act with respect to the memorandum of a public company (the alterations to include compliance with section 25(1) as regards the company's name); and

(c) make such alterations in the company's articles as are requisite in the circumstances.

(3) The application must be in the prescribed form and be signed by a director or secretary of the company; and the documents to be delivered with it are the following—

(a) a printed copy of the memorandum and articles as altered in pursuance of the resolution;

(b) a copy of a written statement by the company's auditors that in their opinion the relevant balance sheet shows that at the balance sheet date the amount of the company's net assets (within the meaning given to that expression by section 264(2)) was not less than the aggregate of its called-up share capital and undistributable reserves;

(c) a copy of the relevant balance sheet, together with a copy of an unqualified report (defined in section 46) by the company's auditors in relation to that balance sheet;

(d) if section 44 applies, a copy of the valuation report under subsection (2)(b) of that section; and

(e) subject to subsection (3A), a statutory declaration in the prescribed form by a director or secretary of the company—

(i)   that the special resolution required by this section has been passed and that the conditions of the following two sections (so far as applicable) have been satisfied, and

(ii) that, between the balance sheet date and the application for re-registration, there has been no change in the company's financial position that has resulted in the amount of its net assets becoming less than the aggregate of its called-up share capital and undistributable reserves.

(3A) In place of the statutory declaration referred to in paragraph (e) of subsection (3), there may be delivered to the registrar of companies using electronic communications a statement made by a director or secretary of the company as to the matters set out in sub-paragraphs (i) and (ii) of that paragraph.

(3B) Any person who makes a false statement under subsection (3A) which he knows to be false or does not believe to be true is liable to imprisonment or a fine, or both.

(4) 'Relevant balance sheet' means a balance sheet prepared as at a date not more than 7 months before the company's application under this section.

(5) A resolution that a company be re-registered as a public company may change the company name by deleting the word 'company' or the words 'and company', or its or their equivalent in Welsh ('cwmni','a'r cwmni'), including any abbreviation of them.

General note

In view of the inconvenient requirements for a trading certificate under s 117, most public companies are formed by way of re-registration under this provision rather than by direct incorporation as a public company, see note to s 117(1).

See s 104 which applies to certain transfers of assets to a company which has re-registered as a public company where those transfers take place within two years of that re-registration.

S 43(1)

A private company is defined in s 1(3); a private company limited by guarantee without a share capital cannot re-register under this provision but a private company limited by guarantee with a share capital (which must have been in existence prior to 22 December 1980, see s 1(4)) could re-register.

A 'public company' is defined in s 1(3); as to a special resolution, see s 378(2) and it must be delivered to the registrar of companies within 15 days after it is passed: s 380; the requirements as to the share capital position at the time when the special resolution is passed are set out in s 45 (these are designed to prevent the evasion of the share capital requirements of s 117 which apply to a company formed as a public company).

An unlimited company can re-register as a public company provided it was formed as such and has not been re-registered as unlimited and, in that case, this provision applies as modified by s 48. Where winding up commences within three years of the re-registration of the unlimited company, past members remain potentially liable in respect of its debts and liabilities contracted prior to re-registration: see IA 1986, s 77.

See also note to s 116, below, which applies various provisions governing payment for share capital to a private company which has passed, and not revoked, a resolution for re-registration as those provisions apply to a public company.

S 43(2), (5)

The requirements of the Act with respect to the substance of the memorandum of association of a public company are set out in ss 1(3)(a) and 2; as to form, see s 3 and the Companies (Tables A to F) Regulations 1985, SI 1985/805 as amended, Table F. The share capital clause must reflect the authorised minimum: see ss 117, 118. The change which may be made to the company's name under this provision is restricted to changing the end of the name to 'public limited company' as required by s 25(1) (or the abbreviation p.l.c. as permitted by s 27 or the Welsh equivalents) and making the deletions permitted by s 43(5) and does not extent to a more substantive change of name which will require a separate resolution under s 28(1). A typical change to the articles of association would be the removal of any restriction on share transfers. These alterations take effect as determined by s 47(4). All of these matters can be dealt with within one composite resolution.

As to the application of these provisions to an unlimited company re-registering as a public company, see s 48(2).

S 43(3)(a)–(d)

Memorandum and articles   The alterations to the memorandum and articles of association must be gazetted by the registrar of companies: s 711(1)(b); and s 42 applies.

Statement by auditors   'Relevant balance sheet' is defined in s 43(4). The balance sheet date must be no more than seven months before the application for re-registration and this statement by the auditors relates only to the position as at that date; see sub-s (3)(e)(ii) as to the subsequent position. 'Called-up share capital' is defined in s 737; 'undistributable reserves' is defined in s 264(3).

Balance sheet and report   An unqualified report, essentially, is a report without material qualification that the balance sheet has been properly prepared in accordance with the Act: see s 46.

Valuation report   A valuation report is required where shares are allotted for a non-cash consideration.

Statutory declaration or statement   As to the effect of the statutory declaration, see s 47(2); as to the time period to which it relates, this follows on from the auditors' statement required by sub-s (3)(b). As to the statement in place of the statutory declaration, see sub-s (3A).

The re-registration fee (at time of writing) is £20 or £80 for same day re-registration; the change of name fee is £10 and the fee for same day simultaneous re-registration and change of name is £160.

S 43(3A), (3B)

These provisions were inserted by the Companies Act 1985 (Electronic Communications) Order 2000, SI 2000/3373, art 6(1),(3), as from 22 December 2000, and facilitate the acceptance by the registrar of companies of electronic statements as to certain matters in the same manner as he accepts statutory declarations as to those matters; as to the delivery of documents to the registrar using electronic communications, see s 707B.

As to penalties, see s 730, Sch 24; the intention is to provide the same penalties for false statements as is provided by the Perjury Act 1911 for false statutory declarations.

---

44. Consideration for shares recently allotted to be valued

(1)   The following applies if shares have been allotted by the company between the date as at which the relevant balance sheet was prepared and the passing of the special resolution under section 43, and those shares were allotted as fully or partly paid up as to their nominal value or any premium on them otherwise than in cash.

(2)   Subject to the following provisions, the registrar of companies shall not entertain an application by the company under section 43 unless beforehand—

   (a)   the consideration for the allotment has been valued in accordance with section 108, and

   (b)   a report with respect to the value of the consideration has been made to the company (in accordance with that section) during the 6 months immediately preceding the allotment of the shares.

(3)   Where an amount standing to the credit of any of the company's reserve accounts, or of its profit and loss account, has been applied in paying up (to

any extent) any of the shares allotted or any premium on those shares, the amount applied does not count as consideration for the allotment, and accordingly subsection (2) does not apply to it.

(4)   Subsection (2) does not apply if the allotment is in connection with an arrangement providing for it to be on terms that the whole or part of the consideration for the shares allotted is to be provided by the transfer to the company or the cancellation of all or some of the shares, or of all or some of the shares of a particular class, in another company (with or without the issue to the company applying under section 43 of shares, or of shares of any particular class, in that other company).

(5)   But subsection (4) does not exclude the application of subsection (2), unless under the arrangement it is open to all the holders of the shares of the other company in question (or, where the arrangement applies only to shares of a particular class, all the holders of the other company's shares of that class) to take part in the arrangement.
    In determining whether that is the case, shares held by or by a nominee of the company allotting shares in connection with the arrangement, or by or by a nominee of a company which is that company's holding company or subsidiary or a company which is a subsidiary of its holding company, are to be disregarded.

(6)   Subsection (2) does not apply to preclude an application under section 43, if the allotment of the company's shares is in connection with its proposed merger with another company; that is, where one of the companies concerned proposes to acquire all the assets and liabilities of the other in exchange for the issue of shares or other securities of that one to shareholders of the other, with or without any cash payment to shareholders.

(7)   In this section—

  (a)   'arrangement' means any agreement, scheme or arrangement, including an arrangement sanctioned in accordance with section 425 (company compromise with creditors and members) or section 110 of the Insolvency Act (liquidator in winding up accepting shares as consideration for sale of company's property), and

  (b)   'another company' includes any body corporate and any body to which letters patent have been issued under the Chartered Companies Act 1837.

General note

This is an anti-avoidance provision designed to ensure that a company cannot evade the requirements of ss 99–116 (payment for shares) by entering into allotments for a non-cash consideration ahead of re-registering as a public company. The provision also applies to a joint stock company, defined in s 680, seeking registration as a public company, see s 685(1), (2). See also note to s 116.

S 44(1)

Shares are taken to be allotted as defined in s 738(1); the date of the relevant balance sheet is determined by s 43(4); shares are deemed to be paid up in cash or allotted for cash in accordance with s 738(2)–(4).

Allotment for a non-cash consideration   This provision applies to any private company seeking re-registration as a public company and lays down valuation requirements where such a company purports to allot any shares for a non-cash consideration between the specified dates. Where the company purports to allot shares for a non-cash consideration after the passing of the resolution but before the company is re-registered as a public company, the valuation rules in s 103 are applied to the company by s 116. In this way, valuation requirements are imposed at each stage when allotments might be made.

S 44(2)

Valuation report   The valuation procedure is that required by s 103 where a public company seeks to allot shares for a non-cash consideration save that a copy of the valuation report need not be given to the allottee (cf s 103(1)(c)). Subsections (3)–(6) make provision for a number of exceptions where there is no valuation requirement.

A failure to adhere to the valuation procedure, when required, means that the registrar of companies cannot entertain an application for re-registration. The allotment remains valid, however, and there is no imposition of statutory liability on the allottee (as under s 103(6)), as the company remains a private company.

S 44(3)–(6)

These provisions are similar to s 103(2)–(5): see notes to that section, below.

S 44(7)

This provision is similar to s 103(7), see note to that section, below.

---

45. Additional requirements relating to share capital

(1)   For a private company to be re-registered under section 43 as a public company, the following conditions with respect to its share capital must be satisfied at the time the special resolution under that section is passed.

(2)   Subject to subsections (5) to (7) below—

   (a)   the nominal value of the company's allotted share capital must be not less than the authorised minimum, and

   (b)   each of the company's allotted shares must be paid up at least as to one-quarter of the nominal value of that share and the whole of any premium on it.

(3)   Subject to subsection (5), if any shares in the company or any premium on them have been fully or partly paid up by an undertaking given by any person that he or another should do work or perform services (whether for the company or any other person), the undertaking must have been performed or otherwise discharged.

(4)   Subject to subsection (5), if shares have been allotted as fully or partly paid up as to their nominal value or any premium on them otherwise than in cash, and the consideration for the allotment consists of or includes an undertaking to the company (other than one to which subsection (3) applies), then either—

    (a)   the undertaking must have been performed or otherwise discharged, or

    (b)   there must be a contract between the company and some person pursuant to which the undertaking is to be performed within 5 years from the time the resolution under section 43 is passed.

(5)   For the purpose of determining whether subsections (2)(b),(3) and (4) are complied with, certain shares in the company may be disregarded; and these are—

    (a)   subject to the next subsection, any share which was allotted before 22nd June 1982, and

    (b)   any share which was allotted in pursuance of an employees' share scheme and by reason of which the company would, but for this subsection, be precluded under subsection (2)(b)(but not otherwise) from being re-registered as a public company.

(6)   A share is not to be disregarded under subsection (5)(a) if the aggregate in nominal value of that share and other shares proposed to be so disregarded is more than one-tenth of the nominal value of the company's allotted share capital; but for this purpose the allotted share capital is treated as not including any shares disregarded under subsection (5)(b).

(7)   Any shares disregarded under subsection (5) are treated as not forming part of the allotted share capital for the purposes of subsection (2)(a).

General note

These provisions are designed to ensure that a private company re-registering as a public company adheres to the share capital payment rules which would apply if the company had been formed as a public company from the outset. This provision also applies to a joint stock company, defined in s 680, seeking registration as a public company: see s 685(1), (2).

S 45(1)

The requirement is that these conditions be met at the time of passing the resolution, not the time of making the application for re-registration.

S 45(2), (7)

Authorised minimum   This provision reflects s 117; the authorised minimum is £50,000 (s 118). In deciding whether a company has the authorised minimum, shares disregarded under s 45(5) (shares allotted pre-June 1982, subject to s 45(6), and shares allotted under an employees' share scheme which are partly paid) are not counted: s 45(7) (see s 117(4)).

Paid up as to one-quarter of the nominal value   This provision reflects s 101. In deciding whether there is compliance with this requirement, shares allotted pre-June 1982 (subject to s 45(6)) and shares allotted under an employees' share scheme which are partly paid are disregarded: s 45(5) and see s 101(2)). Shares are taken to be allotted as defined in s 738(1).

S 45(3)

Undertakings to do work or perform services   Such undertakings may not be accepted by a public company as consideration for an allotment of shares (see s 99(2)) hence the requirement that they be performed or discharged before the company passes a resolution for re-registration. Shares allotted as prescribed by s 45(5), subject to s 45(6), may be disregarded for these purposes.

S 45(4)

Long-term undertakings   Any undertaking within this provision must either be performed or discharged before the company passes a resolution for re-registration, or it must be the subject of a contractual requirement of performance within five years, in keeping with the prohibition on long-term undertakings in s 102. Shares are taken to be allotted as defined in s 738(1); as to when a share is paid up in cash or allotted for cash, see s 738(2). Shares allotted as prescribed by s 45(5), subject to s 45(6), may be disregarded for these purposes.

S 45(5)

Category (a) is subject to s 45(6). 'Employees' share scheme' is defined in s 743; the category of shares disregarded are shares within such a scheme which are not paid up as to one-quarter of the nominal value and the whole of any premium.

---

46. Meaning of 'unqualified report' in s 43(3)

(1)   The following subsections explain the reference in section 43(3)(c) to an unqualified report of the company's auditors on the relevant balance sheet.

(2)   If the balance sheet was prepared for a financial year of the company, the reference is to an auditors' report stating without material qualification the auditors' opinion that the balance sheet has been properly prepared in accordance with this Act.

(3)   If the balance sheet was not prepared for a financial year of the company, the reference is to an auditors' report stating without material qualification the auditors' opinion that the balance sheet has been properly prepared in accordance with the provisions of this Act which would have applied if it had been so prepared.

For the purposes of an auditors' report under this subsection the provisions of this Act shall be deemed to apply with such modifications as are necessary by reason of the fact that the balance sheet is not prepared for a financial year of the company.

(4)   A qualification shall be regarded as material unless the auditors state in their report that the matter giving rise to the qualification is not material for the purpose of determining (by reference to the company's balance sheet) whether at the balance sheet date the amount of the company's net assets was not less than the aggregate of its called up share capital and undistributable reserves.

In this subsection 'net assets' and 'undistributable reserves' have the meaning given by section 264(2) and (3).

S 46(2)

A company's 'financial year' is defined by s 223; the requirements as to a balance sheet 'properly prepared' in accordance with the Act are set out in s 226.

47. Certificate of re-registration under s 43

(1)   If the registrar of companies is satisfied, on an application under section 43, that a company may be re-registered under that section as a public company, he shall—

    (a) retain the application and other documents delivered to him under the section; and

    (b) issue the company with a certificate of incorporation stating that the company is a public company.

(2)   The registrar may accept a declaration under section 43(3)(e) or a statement under section 43(3A) as sufficient evidence that the special resolution required by that section has been passed and the other conditions of re-registration satisfied.

(3)   The registrar shall not issue the certificate if it appears to him that the court has made an order confirming a reduction of the company's capital which has the effect of bringing the nominal value of the company's allotted share capital below the authorised minimum.

(4)   Upon the issue to a company of a certificate of incorporation under this section—

    (a) the company by virtue of the issue of that certificate becomes a public company; and

    (b) any alterations in the memorandum and articles set out in the resolution take effect accordingly.

(5)   The certificate is conclusive evidence—

    (a) that the requirements of this Act in respect of re-registration and of

103

matters precedent and incidental thereto have been complied with; and

(b) that the company is a public company.

S 47(1)

The application of this provision is modified in the case of an unlimited company seeking re-registration as a public company, see s 48(3). The issue of the certificate must be gazetted by the registrar of companies: s 711(1)(a).

S 47(2)

By 'sufficient evidence' is meant that the registrar of companies can proceed on this basis unless the contrary is shown.

S 47(3)

As to a reduction of capital, see ss 135–137; as to the 'authorised minimum', see s 118.

S 47(4)

As to the alterations to the memorandum and articles, see s 43(2).

S 47(5)

As to the conclusiveness of the certificate, see note to s 13(7), above.

48. Modification for unlimited company re-registering

(1)   In their application to unlimited companies, sections 43 to 47 are modified as follows.

(2)   The special resolution required by section 43(1) must, in addition to the matters mentioned in subsection (2) of that section—

(a) state that the liability of the members is to be limited by shares, and what the company's share capital is to be; and

(b) make such alterations in the company's memorandum as are necessary to bring it in substance and in form into conformity with the requirements of this Act with respect to the memorandum of a company limited by shares.

(3)   The certificate of incorporation issued under section 47(1) shall, in addition to containing the statement required by paragraph (b) of that subsection, state that the company has been incorporated as a company limited by shares; and—

(a)   the company by virtue of the issue of the certificate becomes a public company so limited; and

(b)   the certificate is conclusive evidence of the fact that it is such a company.

S 48(1)

Those sections apply only to an unlimited company formed as such and a company which has been re-registered as unlimited on a previous occasion cannot utilise this procedure: see s 43(1); 'unlimited company' is defined in s 1(2)(c).

S 48(2)

These matters are additional to those specified in s 43(2). The requirements as to the substance and form of a memorandum of association of a public company limited by shares are set out in ss 1(3)(a), 2, 3; and see note to s 43(2), above.

S 48(3)

This provision reflects the fact that an unlimited company re-registering as a public company effectively takes two steps: (i) to become a limited company and (ii) to become a public limited company and the certificate needs to reflect both stages. As to the conclusiveness of the certificate, see note to s 13(7). The issue of the certificate must be gazetted by the registrar of companies: s 711(1)(a).

LIMITED COMPANY BECOMING UNLIMITED

49. Re-registration of limited company as unlimited

(1)   Subject as follows, a company which is registered as limited may be re-registered as unlimited in pursuance of an application in that behalf complying with the requirements of this section.

(2)   A company is excluded from re-registering under this section if it is limited by virtue of re-registration under section 44 of the Companies Act 1967 or section 51 of this Act.

(3)   A public company cannot be re-registered under this section; nor can a company which has previously been re-registered as unlimited.

(4)   An application under this section must be in the prescribed form and be signed by a director or the secretary of the company, and be lodged with the registrar of companies, together with the documents specified in subsection (8) below.

(5)   The application must set out such alterations in the company's memorandum as—

    (a) if it is to have a share capital, are requisite to bring it (in substance and in form) into conformity with the requirements of this Act with respect to the memorandum of a company to be formed as an unlimited company having a share capital; or

    (b) if it is not to have a share capital, are requisite in the circumstances.

(6)   If articles have been registered, the application must set out such alterations in them as—

    (a) if the company is to have a share capital, are requisite to bring the articles (in substance and in form) into conformity with the requirements of this Act with respect to the articles of a company to be formed as an unlimited company having a share capital; or

    (b) if the company is not to have a share capital, are requisite in the circumstances.

(7)   If articles have not been registered, the application must have annexed to it, and request the registration of, printed articles; and these must, if the company is to have a share capital, comply with the requirements mentioned in subsection (6)(a) and, if not, be articles appropriate to the circumstances.

(8)   The documents to be lodged with the registrar are—

    (a) the prescribed form of assent to the company's being registered as unlimited, subscribed by or on behalf of all the members of the company;

    (b) subject to subsection (8A), a statutory declaration made by the directors of the company—

        (i)   that the persons by whom or on whose behalf the form of assent is subscribed constitute the whole membership of the company, and

        (ii) if any of the members have not subscribed that form themselves, that the directors have taken all reasonable steps to satisfy themselves that each person who subscribed it on behalf of a member was lawfully empowered to do so;

    (c) a printed copy of the memorandum incorporating the alterations in it set out in the application; and

    (d) if articles have been registered, a printed copy of them incorporating the alterations set out in the application.

(8A) In place of the lodging of a statutory declaration under paragraph (b) of subsection (8), there may be delivered to the registrar of companies using electronic communications a statement made by the directors of the company as to the matters set out in sub-paragraphs (i) and (ii) of that paragraph.

(8B) Any person who makes a false statement under subsection (8A) which he knows to be false or does not believe to be true is liable to imprisonment or a fine, or both.

(9) For purposes of this section—

    (a) subscription to a form of assent by the legal personal representative of a deceased member of a company is deemed subscription by him; and

    (b) a trustee in bankruptcy of a member of a company is, to the exclusion of the latter, deemed a member of the company.

S 49(1)

An 'unlimited company' is a company not having any limit on the liability of its members (s 1(2)(c)) which makes this status generally unattractive for trading companies. The main attraction of such companies is the exemption generally from the requirement to file accounts with the registrar of companies (s 254) although, given the minimal financial disclosure now required of small companies (see ss 246, 249A), this advantage may not be as significant as it once was.

As to limits on a past member's contribution in the event of the re-registered company subsequently going into liquidation, see IA 1986, s 78(2).

S 49(1)–(3)

The wording of these provisions is confusing but essentially there are three restrictions:

    (1) a private limited company cannot re-register as an unlimited company if it was originally unlimited and re-registered as a limited company under either of the specified provisions;

    (2) a public company cannot re-register as an unlimited company in one step under this provision – it must first go from public to private status under ss 43–48 and then go from private to unlimited status under this provision;

    (3) a company which was previously re-registered as unlimited cannot seek that status again.

See s 50(3), a certificate of incorporation on re-registration is conclusive evidence that the company was authorised to be re-registered under this section.

S 49(5)

An unlimited company may or may not have a share capital, hence the permutations in sub-s (5)(a) and (b). As to the form of a memorandum of association of an unlimited company with a share capital, see s 3(1)(f) and the Companies (Tables A to F) Regulations 1985, SI 1985/805, as amended, Table E. The substance is dictated by s 2. The alterations required include that the company's name must no longer end in 'limited': s 34. The name need not include 'unlimited' but if it does, it must be as the last word in the name: s 26(1)(a). Any substantive change to the name will require a resolution under s 28(1). The statement that the members' liability is limited is omitted from the memorandum (see s 2(3)) and the share capital provision is included in the articles rather than in the memorandum: ss 2(5)(a), 7(2), and see Table E.

Where the company is to be an unlimited company without a share capital, no form of memorandum of association is set out in the regulations and the company is free to adopt an appropriate form.

S 49(6), (7)

Whether or not articles have been registered depends on the type of limited company: see s 7(1). As an unlimited company, it must register articles: see ss 7(1), 8(4) and the Companies (Tables A to F) Regulations 1985, SI 1985/805, as amended, Table E. As noted above, the share capital provision is included in the articles rather than in the memorandum: ss 2(5)(a), 7(2), and Table E.

S 49(8), (9)

The consent of all members (defined s 22) is required because of the significance of the change to their position and sub-s (9) assists by further defining who are the members for this purpose. The alterations to the memorandum and articles of association must be gazetted by the registrar of companies: s 711(1)(b); and s 42 applies.

The re-registration fee is currently £20 or £80 for same-day re-registration; the change of name fee is £10 and the fee for same-day simultaneous re-registration and change of name is £160.

S 49(8A), (8B)

These provisions were inserted by the Companies Act 1985 (Electronic Communications) Order 2000, SI 2000/3373, art 8(1), (3), as from 22 December 2000, and facilitate the acceptance by the registrar of companies of electronic statements as to certain matters in the same manner as he accepts statutory declarations as to those matters; as to the delivery of documents to the registrar using electronic communications, see s 707B.

As to penalties, see s 730, Sch 24; the intention is to provide the same penalties for false statements as is provided by the Perjury Act 1911 for false statutory declarations.

---

50. Certificate of re-registration under s 49

(1) The registrar of companies shall retain the application and other documents lodged with him under section 49 and shall—

    (a) if articles are annexed to the application, register them; and

    (b) issue to the company a certificate of incorporation appropriate to the status to be assumed by it by virtue of that section.

(2) On the issue of the certificate—

(a) the status of the company, by virtue of the issue, is changed from limited to unlimited; and

(b) the alterations in the memorandum set out in the application and (if articles have been previously registered) any alterations to the articles so set out take effect as if duly made by resolution of the company; and

(c) the provisions of this Act apply accordingly to the memorandum and articles as altered.

(3)   The certificate is conclusive evidence that the requirements of section 49 in respect of re-registration and of matters precedent and incidental to it have been complied with, and that the company was authorised to be re-registered under this Act in pursuance of that section and was duly so re-registered.

S 50(1)

The issue of the certificate must be gazetted by the registrar of companies: s 711(1)(a).

S 50(3)

As to the conclusiveness of the certificate, see note to s 13(7); the certificate is conclusive not just as to the requirements of re-registration but as to the company's entitlement to be re-registered under s 49.

UNLIMITED COMPANY BECOMING LIMITED

51. Re-registration of unlimited company as limited

(1)   Subject as follows, a company which is registered as unlimited may be re-registered as limited if a special resolution that it should be so re-registered is passed, and the requirements of this section are complied with in respect of the resolution and otherwise.

(2)   A company cannot under this section be re-registered as a public company; and a company is excluded from re-registering under it if it is unlimited by virtue of re-registration under section 43 of the Companies Act 1967 or section 49 of this Act.

(3)   The special resolution must state whether the company is to be limited by shares or by guarantee and—

(a) if it is to be limited by shares, must state what the share capital is to be and provide for the making of such alterations in the memorandum as are necessary to bring it (in substance and in form) into conformity with the requirements of this Act with respect to the memorandum of a company so limited, and such alterations in the articles as are requisite in the circumstances;

(b) if it is to be limited by guarantee, must provide for the making of such alterations in its memorandum and articles as are necessary to bring them (in substance and in form) into conformity with the requirements of this Act with respect to the memorandum and articles of a company so limited.

(4) The special resolution is subject to section 380 of this Act (copy to be forwarded to registrar within 15 days); and an application for the company to be re-registered as limited, framed in the prescribed form and signed by a director or by the secretary of the company, must be lodged with the registrar of companies, together with the necessary documents, not earlier than the day on which the copy of the resolution forwarded under section 380 is received by him.

(5) The documents to be lodged with the registrar are—

(a) a printed copy of the memorandum as altered in pursuance of the resolution; and

(b) a printed copy of the articles as so altered.

(6) This section does not apply in relation to the re-registration of an unlimited company as a public company under section 43.

General note

Where winding up commences within three years of the re-registration, past members remain potentially liable in respect of the company's debts and liabilities contracted prior to re-registration: see IA 1986, s 77.

S 51(2), (6)

An unlimited company (defined s 1(2)(c)) cannot become a public company (defined s 1(3)) under this provision but must do so via ss 43–48 to ensure that the company complies with the capital requirements in ss 44, 45; and a company which is unlimited through re-registration under the specified provisions cannot retrace its steps.

See s 52(3), a certificate of incorporation on re-registration is conclusive evidence that the company was authorised to be re-registered under this section.

S 51(3)

As to a company limited by shares, see s 1(2)(a); as to a company limited by guarantee, see s 1(2)(b).

Limited by shares As to the form of memorandum of association of a company limited by shares, see s 3 and the Companies (Tables A to F) Regulations 1985, SI 1985/805, as amended, Table B. The substance is dictated by s 2. The alterations required would include that the company's name must end in 'limited' (s 25(2), unless exempt under s 30) and a statement that the members' liability is limited (s 2(3)) and as to the share capital position (s 2(5)(a)) must be included. Any substantive changes to the name will require a resolution under s 28(1). The default form of articles for a private company limited by shares is Table A: see s 8.

Limited by guarantee   As to the form of memorandum of association of a company limited by guarantee, see s 3 and the Companies (Tables A to F) Regulations 1985, SI 1985/805, as amended, Table C. The substance is dictated by s 2. The alterations required would include that the company's name must end in 'limited' (s 25(2), unless exempt under s 30) and a statement that the members' liability is limited (s 2(3)) and of the amount of the members' guarantees (s 2(4)) must be included. Any substantive changes to the name will require a resolution under s 28(1). As to the form of articles for a company limited by guarantee without a share capital, see s 8(4)(b) and the Companies (Tables A to F) Regulations 1985, SI 1985/805, as amended, Table C.

S 51(5)

The alterations of the memorandum and articles of association must be gazetted by the registrar of companies: s 711(1)(b); and s 42 applies.

The re-registration fee is currently £20 or £80 for same-day re-registration; the change of name fee is £10 and the fee for same day simultaneous re-registration and change of name is £160.

---

52. Certificate of re-registration under s 51

(1)   The registrar shall retain the application and other documents lodged with him under section 51, and shall issue to the company a certificate of incorporation appropriate to the status to be assumed by the company by virtue of that section.

(2)   On the issue of the certificate—

    (a) the status of the company is, by virtue of the issue, changed from unlimited to limited; and

    (b) the alterations in the memorandum specified in the resolution and the alterations in, and additions to, the articles so specified take effect.

(3)   The certificate is conclusive evidence that the requirements of section 51 in respect of re-registration and of matters precedent and incidental to it have been complied with, and that the company was authorised to be re-registered in pursuance of that section and was duly so re-registered.

S 52(1)

The issue of the certificate must be gazetted by the registrar of companies: s 711(1)(a).

S 52(3)

As to the conclusiveness of the certificate, see note to s 13(7); the certificate is conclusive not just as to the requirements of re-registration but as to the company's entitlement to be re-registered under s 51.

PUBLIC COMPANY BECOMING PRIVATE

53. Re-registration of public company as private

(1) A public company may be re-registered as a private company if—

(a) a special resolution complying with subsection (2) below that it should be so re-registered is passed and has not been cancelled by the court under the following section;

(b) an application for the purpose in the prescribed form and signed by a director or the secretary of the company is delivered to the registrar of companies, together with a printed copy of the memorandum and articles of the company as altered by the resolution; and

(c) the period during which an application for the cancellation of the resolution under the following section may be made has expired without any such application having been made; or

(d) where such an application has been made, the application has been withdrawn or an order has been made under section 54(5) confirming the resolution and a copy of that order has been delivered to the registrar.

(2) The special resolution must alter the company's memorandum so that it no longer states that the company is to be a public company and must make such other alterations in the company's memorandum and articles as are requisite in the circumstances.

(3) A company cannot under this section be re-registered otherwise than as a company limited by shares or by guarantee.

General note

A public company may also be re-registered as a private company under s 147 where, following a cancellation of shares acquired by it under s 146, it falls below the authorised minimum capital for a public company (see s 118) and must re-register as a private company: see ss 146(2), 147.

S 53(1)

A public company is defined in s 1(3); as is a private company; as to the type of private company which may be used, see s 53(3); as to a special resolution, see s 378. The special resolution can be challenged under s 54.

S 53(2)

As to the form of a memorandum of association of a private company limited by shares, see s 3 and the Companies (Tables A to F) Regulations 1985, SI 1985/805 as amended, Table B. The substance is dictated by s 2. The company's name must end in 'limited' (s 25(2), unless exempt under s 30) or the permitted abbreviation (s 27) or the Welsh equivalents. The default form of articles for a private company limited by shares is Table A: see s 8.

As to the form of a memorandum of association of a company limited by guarantee, see s 3 and the Companies (Tables A to F) Regulations 1985, SI 1985/805, as amended, Table C. The substance is dictated by s 2. The alterations required would include that the company's name must end in 'limited' (s 25(2), unless exempt under s 30) or the permitted abbreviation (s 27) or the Welsh equivalents and a statement of the amount of the members' guarantees (s 2(4)) must be included. Any substantive change to the name will require a resolution under s 28(1). As to the form of articles for a company limited by guarantee without a share capital, see s 8(4)(b) and the Companies (Tables A to F) Regulations 1985, SI 1985/805, as amended, Table C.

The alterations to the memorandum and articles of association must be gazetted by the registrar of companies: s 711(1)(b); and s 42 applies.

The re-registration fee is currently £20 or £80 for same-day re-registration; the change of name fee is £10 and the fee for same day simultaneous re-registration and change of name is £160.

S 53(3)

A public company cannot be re-registered as an unlimited company under this provision. It must become a private company limited by shares (defined s 1(2)(a)) or limited by guarantee without a share capital (defined s 1(2)(b), and see s 1(4)) and then re-register under s 49 as unlimited.

54. Litigated objection to resolution under s 53

(1)   Where a special resolution by a public company to be re-registered under section 53 as a private company has been passed, an application may be made to the court for the cancellation of that resolution.

(2)   The application may be made—

   (a) by the holders of not less in the aggregate than 5 per cent in nominal value of the company's issued share capital or any class thereof;

   (b) if the company is not limited by shares, by not less than 5 per cent of its members; or

   (c) by not less than 50 of the company's members;

but not by a person who has consented to or voted in favour of the resolution.

(3)   The application must be made within 28 days after the passing of the resolution and may be made on behalf of the persons entitled to make the application by such one or more of their number as they may appoint in writing for the purpose.

(4)   If such an application is made, the company shall forthwith give notice in the prescribed form of that fact to the registrar of companies.

(5)   On the hearing of the application, the court shall make an order either cancelling or confirming the resolution and—

    (a)   may make that order on such terms and conditions as it thinks fit, and may (if it thinks fit) adjourn the proceedings in order that an arrangement may be made to the satisfaction of the court for the purchase of the interests of dissentient members; and

    (b)   may give such directions and make such orders as it thinks expedient for facilitating or carrying into effect any such arrangement.

(6)   The court's order may, if the court thinks fit, provide for the purchase by the company of the shares of any of its members and for the reduction accordingly of the company's capital, and may make such alterations in the company's memorandum and articles as may be required in consequence of that provision.

(7)   The company shall, within 15 days from the making of the court's order, or within such longer period as the court may at any time by order direct, deliver to the registrar of companies an office copy of the order.

(8)   If the court's order requires the company not to make any, or any specified, alteration in its memorandum or articles, the company has not then power without the leave of the court to make any such alteration in breach of the requirement.

(9)   An alteration in the memorandum or articles made by virtue of an order under this section, if not made by resolution of the company, is of the same effect as if duly made by resolution; and this Act applies accordingly to the memorandum or articles as so altered.

(10) A company which fails to comply with subsection (4) or subsection (7), and any officer of it who is in default, is liable to a fine and, for continued contravention, to a daily default fine.

S 54(1), (2)

In view of the significance of the change of status in this case, which will bring with it the lack of transferability and reduced marketability which is characteristic of shares in a private company, objecting shareholders are allowed to apply to the court. As to the company's issued share capital, see note to s 738, below; as to the members of a company, see s 22. Subsection (2)(b) was a transitional provision since all public companies now must have a share capital: s 1(3). No grounds for the application are specified. Any nominee who acts for a number of members and who has voted on their behalf both for and against the resolution cannot make an application under this provision on behalf of those opposed to the resolution.

S 54(5)

Nothing in s 125(2)–(5) regarding the consent of a class of members to a variation or abrogation of their rights affects the court's powers under this provision: s 126.

S 54(6)

The provision requires that the entire shareholding be purchased; it need not necessarily be the holding of a dissentient member but in practice that will be the case. Where the company is so required to purchase the shares of any member, it is exempt from the prohibition on purchase of its own shares contained in s 143(1): s 143(3). In practice, dissentients are likely to be identified and bought out long before the company seeks to pass the special resolution.

S 54(8), (9)

See notes to s 5(6), (7), above.

S 54(10)

As to penalties, see s 730, Sch 24; 'officer in default' is defined in s 730(5).

55. Certificate of re-registration under s 53

(1)   If the registrar of companies is satisfied that a company may be re-registered under section 53, he shall—
  (a) retain the application and other documents delivered to him under that section; and
  (b) issue the company with a certificate of incorporation appropriate to a private company.

(2)   On the issue of the certificate—
  (a) the company by virtue of the issue becomes a private company; and
  (b) the alterations in the memorandum and articles set out in the resolution under section 53 take effect accordingly.

(3)   The certificate is conclusive evidence—
  (a) that the requirements of section 53 in respect of re-registration and of matters precedent and incidental to it have been complied with; and
  (b) that the company is a private company.

S 55(1)

The issue of the certificate must be gazetted by the registrar of companies: s 711(1)(a).

S 55(3)

As to the conclusiveness of the certificate, see note to s 13(7).

PART III

CAPITAL ISSUES

ISSUES BY COMPANIES REGISTERED, OR TO BE REGISTERED, IN GREAT BRITAIN

THE PROSPECTUS

56. *(Repealed for all purposes)*

57. *(Repealed for all purposes)*

58. Document offering shares etc for sale deemed a prospectus

(1)　If a company allots or agrees to allot its shares or debentures with a view to all or any of them being offered for sale to the public, any document by which the offer for sale to the public is made is deemed for all purposes a prospectus issued by the company.

(2)　All enactments and rules of law as to the contents of prospectuses, and to liability in respect of statements in and omissions from prospectuses, or otherwise relating to prospectuses, apply and have effect accordingly, as if the shares or debentures had been offered to the public for subscription and as if persons accepting the offer in respect of any shares or debentures were subscribers for those shares or debentures.

This is without prejudice to the liability (if any) of the persons by whom the offer is made, in respect of mis-statements in the document or otherwise in respect of it.

(3)　For purposes of this Act it is evidence (unless the contrary is proved) that an allotment of, or an agreement to allot, shares or debentures was made with a view to their being offered for sale to the public if it is shown—

(a)　that an offer of the shares or debentures (or of any of them) for sale to the public was made within 6 months after the allotment or agreement to allot, or

(b)　that at the date when the offer was made the whole consideration to be received by the company in respect of the shares or debentures had not been so received.

(4)　Section 56 as applied by this section has effect as if it required a prospectus to state, in addition to the matters required by that section—

(a)　the net amount of the consideration received or to be received by the company in respect of the shares or debentures to which the offer relates, and

(b)　the place and time at which the contract under which those shares or debentures have been or are to be allotted may be inspected.

General note

This provision has been repealed for all purposes except in so far as it is necessary for interpretation purposes for ss 81, 83, and 744: Financial Services Act 1986 (Commencement) (No 13) Order 1995, SI 1995/1538. The definitions in this section are retained to interpret s 81, which prohibits a private company from offering its shares or debentures to the public either directly or through an intermediary.

S 58(1), (2)

These provisions ensure that any document by which an offer to the public is made which is issued other than by the company is deemed to be a prospectus (defined s 744) issued by the company and so brings the company within the prohibition in s 81(1) and attracts the obligations in s 58.

S 58(3)

Establishing that an allotment or agreement to allot was 'with a view to' the shares being offered to the public is important to the prohibition in s 81(1)(b); and this provision provides rebuttable presumptions in this regard where the purchaser offers the shares or debentures for sale to the public within a short period of time and where the company is still waiting on the whole consideration.

59. Rule governing what is an 'offer to the public'

(1)   Subject to the next section, any reference in this Act to offering shares or debentures to the public is to be read (subject to any provision to the contrary) as including a reference to offering them to any section of the public, whether selected as members or debenture holders of the company concerned, or as clients of the person issuing the prospectus, or in any other manner.

(2)   The same applies to any reference in this Act, or in a company's articles, to an invitation to the public to subscribe for shares or debentures.

General note

This provision has been repealed for all purposes except in so far as it is necessary for interpretation purposes for ss 81, 83, and 744: Financial Services Act 1986 (Commencement) (No 13) Order 1995, SI 1995/1538.

S 59(1), (2)

These provisions, which apply to offers for subscription as well as offers for sale, clarify that an offer can be made to the public although only to a restricted category of the public. The breadth of this provision is balanced by the exceptions provided by s 60; 'prospectus' is defined in s 744.

60. Exceptions from rule in s 59

(1)   Section 59 does not require an offer or invitation to be treated as made to the public if it can properly be regarded, in all the circumstances, as not being calculated to result, directly or indirectly, in the shares or debentures becoming available for subscription or purchase by persons other than those receiving the offer or invitation, or otherwise as being a domestic concern of the persons receiving and making it.

(2)   In particular, a provision in a company's articles prohibiting invitations to the public to subscribe for shares or debentures is not to be taken as prohibiting the making to members or debenture holders of an invitation which can properly be regarded as falling within the preceding subsection.

(3)   For purposes of that subsection, an offer of shares in or debentures of a private company, or an invitation to subscribe for such shares or debentures, is to be regarded (unless the contrary is proved) as being a domestic concern of the persons making and receiving the offer or invitation if it falls within any of the following descriptions.

(4)   It is to be so regarded if it is made to—

  (a) an existing member of the company making the offer or invitation,

  (b) an existing employee of that company,

  (c) a member of the family of such a member or employee, or

  (d) an existing debenture holder.

(5)   For purposes of subsection (4)(c), the members of a person's family are—

  (a) the person's husband or wife, widow or widower and children (including stepchildren) and their descendants, and

  (b) any trustee (acting in his capacity as such) of a trust the principal beneficiary of which is the person him or herself, or any of those relatives.

(6)   The offer or invitation is also to be so regarded if it is to subscribe for shares or debentures to be held under an employees' share scheme.

(7)   The offer or invitation is also to be so regarded if it falls within subsection (4) or (6) and it is made on terms which permit the person to whom it is made to renounce his right to the allotment of shares or issue of debentures, but only in favour—

  (a) of such a person as is mentioned in any of the paragraphs of subsection (4), or

  (b) where there is an employees' share scheme, of a person entitled to hold shares or debentures under the scheme.

(8)   Where application has been made to the competent authority for the purposes of Part IV of the Financial Services Act 1986 for admission of any securities to the Official List of the Stock Exchange, then an offer of those securities for subscription or sale to a person whose ordinary business it is to buy or sell shares or debentures (whether as principal or agent) is not deemed an offer to the public for purposes of this Part.

General note

This provision has been repealed for all purposes except in so far as it is necessary for interpretation purposes for ss 81, 83, and 744: Financial Services Act 1986 (Commencement) (No 13) Order 1995, SI 1995/1538.

S 60(1)

Two exemptions There are two distinct exemptions:
  (1) an offer or invitation not calculated to result (ie not likely to have the consequence), directly or indirectly, in the shares or debentures (defined s 744) becoming available for subscription or purchase (ie either directly from the company or through a purchaser: see *Re VGM Holdings Ltd* [1942] Ch 235) by anyone other than those receiving the offer or invitation; and there are no limits imposed under this element as to the number of persons who might receive the offer or invitation;
  (2) an offer or invitation which is of a domestic concern of the persons receiving and making it; matters which are of 'domestic concern' are identified by s 60(3)–(7).

The question is not who receives the offer or invitation but who can accept the offer put forward: *Governments Stock and Other Securities Investment Co Ltd v Christopher* [1956] 1 All ER 490.

S 60(3)–(7)

Domestic concerns There is a presumption that the offers specified are of domestic concern, unless the contrary is proved; 'employees' share scheme' is defined in s 743. The offer or invitation may be renounceable but only to the restricted categories identified in sub-s (7). If the offer or invitation is generally renounceable, it will be an offer to the public.

S 60(8)

This provision applies where an application for listing has been made and only public companies can be admitted to listing. An offer of shares to a professional intermediary at this stage is deemed not to be an offer to the public for the purposes of this Part (ie for the purposes of ss 58–62 as the only remaining provisions of this Part in effect). The reference to the Official List as maintained by The London Stock Exchange Limited is to be read as a reference to the Official List as maintained by the Financial Services Authority, by virtue of the Official Listing of Securities (Change of Competent Authority) Regulations 2000, SI 2000/968, reg 4.

---

61. *(Repealed.)*

62. Meaning of 'expert'

The expression 'expert', in both Chapters of this Part, includes engineer, valuer, accountant and any other person whose profession gives authority to a statement made by him.

General note

This section is repealed for all purposes except in so far as it is necessary for purposes of s 744 (expressions used generally in this Act): Financial Services Act 1986 (Commencement) (No 13) Order 1995, SI 1995/1538.

63.–79. *(Repealed.)*

PART IV

ALLOTMENT OF SHARES AND DEBENTURES

GENERAL PROVISIONS AS TO ALLOTMENT

80. Authority of company required for certain allotments

(1)   The directors of a company shall not exercise any power of the company to allot relevant securities, unless they are, in accordance with this section or section 80A, authorised to do so by—

    (a)   the company in general meeting; or

    (b)   the company's articles.

(2)   In this section 'relevant securities' means—

    (a)   shares in the company other than shares shown in the memorandum to have been taken by the subscribers to it or shares allotted in pursuance of an employees' share scheme, and

    (b)   any right to subscribe for, or to convert any security into, shares in the company (other than shares so allotted);

and a reference to the allotment of relevant securities includes the grant of such a right but (subject to subsection (6) below), not the allotment of shares pursuant to such a right.

(3)   Authority under this section may be given for a particular exercise of the power or for its exercise generally, and may be unconditional or subject to conditions.

(4)   The authority must state the maximum amount of relevant securities that may be allotted under it and the date on which it will expire, which must be not more than 5 years from whichever is relevant of the following dates—

    (a)   in the case of an authority contained in the company's articles at the time of its original incorporation, the date of that incorporation; and

    (b)   in any other case, the date on which the resolution is passed by virtue of which the authority is given;

but such an authority (including an authority contained in the articles) may be previously revoked or varied by the company in general meeting.

(5)   The authority may be renewed or further renewed by the company in general meeting for a further period not exceeding 5 years; but the resolution must state (or restate) the amount of relevant securities which may be allotted under the authority or, as the case may be, the amount remaining to be allotted under it, and must specify the date on which the renewed authority will expire.

(6)   In relation to authority under this section for the grant of such rights as are mentioned in subsection (2)(b), the reference in subsection (4)(as also the corresponding reference in subsection (5)) to the maximum amount of relevant securities that may be allotted under the authority is to the maximum amount of shares which may be allotted pursuant to the rights.

(7)   The directors may allot relevant securities, notwithstanding that authority under this section has expired, if they are allotted in pursuance of an offer or agreement made by the company before the authority expired and the authority

allowed it to make an offer or agreement which would or might require relevant securities to be allotted after the authority expired.

(8) A resolution of a company to give, vary, revoke or renew such an authority may, notwithstanding that it alters the company's articles, be an ordinary resolution; but it is in any case subject to section 380 of this Act (copy to be forwarded to registrar within 15 days).

(9) A director who knowingly and wilfully contravenes, or permits or authorises a contravention of, this section is liable to a fine.

(10) Nothing in this section affects the validity of any allotment.

(11) This section does not apply to any allotment of relevant securities by a company, other than a public company registered as such on its original incorporation, if it is made in pursuance of an offer or agreement made before the earlier of the following two dates—

    (a) the date of the holding of the first general meeting of the company after its registration or re-registration as a public company, and

    (b) 22nd June 1982;

but any resolution to give, vary or revoke an authority for the purposes of section 14 of the Companies Act 1980 or this section has effect for those purposes if passed at any time after the end of April 1980.

General note

In addition to ensuring that they have the authority to allot shares as required by this provision, directors must exercise the power to allot (as all their powers): (1) bona fide for the benefit of the company as a whole and not for a collateral purpose: *Howard Smith Ltd v Ampol Petroleum Ltd* [1974] 1 All ER 1126 (the power to allot cannot be used solely to destroy an existing majority or create a new one); and (2) fairly as between different shareholders, which does not require that they be treated identically: *Mutual Life Insurance Co of New York v Rank Organisation Ltd* [1985] BCLC 11.

Many attempts by directors to use this power to consolidate their control or prevent a rival body from taking over the company have been held to be invalid, notwithstanding the asserted belief of the directors that they were acting in the best interests of the company: see *Fraser v Whalley* (1864) 2 Hem & M 10; *Punt v Symons & Co Ltd* [1903] 2 Ch 506; *Piercy v S Mills & Co Ltd* [1920] 1 Ch 77; *Hogg v Cramphorn Ltd* [1966] 3 All ER 420; *Bamford v Bamford* [1969] 1 All ER 969; *Howard Smith Ltd v Ampol Petroleum Ltd* [1974] 1 All ER 1126.

S 80(1)–(2)

Any company This provision applies to all companies, public and private, although private companies may take advantage of the relaxation in s 80A; 'company' is defined in s 735. Authorisation is required either from the company in general meeting or by the articles and the consequences of an unauthorised allotment are set out in s 80(9), (10).

Allotments within this provision   The requirement for authorisation applies to the allotment of *any* shares excluding shares taken by the subscribers to the memorandum (see s 2(5)) and shares allotted as part of an employees' share scheme (defined in s 743). It also extends to the grant of any rights to subscribe for shares or to convert any security into shares. It suffices to have authority for the grant of such rights and it is not necessary subsequently to seek authorisation on the allotment of shares pursuant to the exercise of such options.

S 80(3)

Whether the authority granted is to be general or particular will have a bearing on the procedure to disapply pre-emption rights under s 95, see note to that provision, below.

S 80(4)–(6)

While a five-year period is provided for, it is customary for public companies to renew the authority at each annual general meeting rather than to seek authority for the entire period. For a private company, s 80A allows for an indefinite period or a fixed period of the company's choice unconstrained by these provisions. As to the maximum amount of relevant securities: see sub-s (6).

S 80(8)

Only an ordinary resolution is required, even if it has the effect of altering the articles, and it must be delivered to the registrar of companies and the receipt of any such resolution from a public company must be gazetted by him: s 711(1)(d). Where a private company uses a written resolution, the date of the resolution is determined by s 381A(3), (5).

S 80(9), (10)

The requirement that the director act 'knowingly and wilfully' would require evidence of a deliberate intention to make an allotment knowing it was unauthorised as opposed to an allotment made in the mistaken belief that there was authority to do so. As to penalties, see s 730, Sch 24. An unauthorised allotment remains valid, thus avoiding the difficulties which would arise if it was necessary to rescind the transaction.

80A. Election by private company as to duration of authority

(1)   A private company may elect (by elective resolution in accordance with section 379A) that the provisions of this section shall apply, instead of the provisions of section 80(4) and (5), in relation to the giving or renewal, after the election, of an authority under that section.

(2)   The authority must state the maximum amount of relevant securities that may be allotted under it and may be given—

    (a) for an indefinite period, or

    (b) for a fixed period, in which case it must state the date on which it will expire.

(3)   In either case an authority (including an authority contained in the articles) may be revoked or varied by the company in general meeting.

(4)   An authority given for a fixed period may be renewed or further renewed by the company in general meeting.

(5)   A resolution renewing an authority—

    (a) must state, or re-state, the amount of relevant securities which may be allotted under the authority or, as the case may be, the amount remaining to be allotted under it, and

    (b) must state whether the authority is renewed for an indefinite period or for a fixed period, in which case it must state the date on which the renewed authority will expire.

(6)   The references in this section to the maximum amount of relevant securities that may be allotted shall be construed in accordance with section 80(6).

(7)   If an election under this section ceases to have effect, an authority then in force which was given for an indefinite period or for a fixed period of more than five years—

    (a) if given five years or more before the election ceases to have effect, shall expire forthwith, and

    (b) otherwise, shall have effect as if it had been given for a fixed period of five years.

General note

The elective regime set out in s 379A allows members of a private company unanimously to elect to avail of certain exemptions or relaxations of various statutory requirements. In this case, the provision offers private companies flexibility as to the duration of any authority granted under s 80 to allot shares.

S 80A(1), (2), (6)

As to elective resolutions, see note to s 379A; as to the maximum amount of relevant securities, see s 80(6).

S 80A(3)

An authority can be revoked or varied, even if conferred by the articles, by an ordinary resolution which must be forwarded to the registrar of companies: s 80(8).

S 80(7)

An elective resolution ceases to have effect in two circumstances: (1) where the company revokes the elective resolution (s 379A(3)); (2) where a private company is re-registered as a public company and so is no longer entitled to avail of the elective regime: s 379A(4).

81. Restriction on public offers by private company

(1)   A private limited company (other than a company limited by guarantee and not having a share capital) commits an offence if it—

   (a)   offers to the public (whether for cash or otherwise) any shares in or debentures of the company; or

   (b)   allots or agrees to allot (whether for cash or otherwise) any shares in or debentures of the company with a view to all or any of those shares or debentures being offered for sale to the public (within the meaning given to that expression by sections 58 to 60).

(2)   A company guilty of an offence under this section, and any officer of it who is in default, is liable to a fine.

(3)   Nothing in this section affects the validity of any allotment or sale of shares or debentures, or of any agreement to allot or sell shares or debentures.

General note

This section was to be repealed by FSA 1986, s 212(3), Sch 17, Pt 1 but that provision was commenced to only a limited extent (see SI 1986/2246, SI 1988/740) which does not affect the continuing application of this provision to private companies offering unlisted securities to the public.

Public Offers of Securities Regulations   A source of confusion in this area is the relationship between this provision and the Public Offers of Securities Regulations 1995, SI 1995/1537 (the POS regulations) which require the publication of a prospectus where an offer of unlisted securities is made to the public in the UK for the first time. The two distinct but overlapping issues to consider are: (1) whether there is an offer to the public (defined ss 58–60) in breach of s 81; (2) whether there is an offer to the public (as defined differently) within the Public Offers of Securities Regulations 1995 so requiring a prospectus under those provisions.

S 81(1)

The offence   A private company commits an offence if it offers its shares to the public in any way and 'offer to the public' is defined for these purposes by ss 58–60. The prohibition is comprehensive and extends to offers of debentures (defined s 744) although it is unlikely that offers of debentures would be made by a private company.

It applies whether the shares are offered for cash or otherwise; and the prohibition extends, for example, to any offer for sale or placing as well as any offer for subscription; and see s 58(3) as to the rebuttable evidence that the company has allotted or agreed to allot shares 'with a view to' all or any of them being offered for sale to the public. See also s 58(1), (2) which deems any document issued by an intermediary by which the offer for sale is made to be a prospectus issued by the company.

Breach of the Act and the POS regulations If a private company makes an offer to the public in breach of s 81 then the penalties in sub-s (2) apply but, in addition, if the offer to the public which has occurred is also an offer to the public as defined (differently) in the Public Offers of Securities Regulations 1995, SI 1995/1537 (which it is likely to be), then a prospectus will be required under those regulations. As it is unlikely, in such circumstances, that a private company will appreciate that it has made an offer to the public, the most likely outcome will be a breach of s 81 *and* of the POS regulations.

No breach of the Act but within the POS regulations Equally, the company, relying on s 60(1), may make an offer which restricts the availability of the shares or debentures to persons receiving the offer or invitation. In such a case, there being no offer to the public as defined by ss 59, 60, no offence is committed under s 81. However, the unrestricted nature of the class to whom the shares were offered may mean that the offer is an offer to the public within the Public Offers of Securities Regulations 1995, SI 1995/1537, so requiring a prospectus. This is subject to the offer falling within one of the exempted categories set out in the regulations where no prospectus is required.

S 81(2)

As to penalties, see s 730, Sch 24; 'officer in default' is defined in s 730(5).

S 81(3)

The validity of the allotment is unaffected thus avoiding the difficulty of rescinding an allotment when a breach of this provision is discovered.

82. Application for, and allotment of, shares and debentures

(1)   No allotment shall be made of a company's shares or debentures in pursuance of a prospectus issued generally, and no proceedings shall be taken on applications made in pursuance of a prospectus so issued, until the beginning of the third day after that on which the prospectus is first so issued or such later time (if any) as may be specified in the prospectus.

(2)   The beginning of that third day, or that later time, is 'the time of the opening of the subscription lists'.

(3)   In subsection (1), the reference to the day on which the prospectus is first issued generally is to the day when it is first so issued as a newspaper advertisement; and if it is not so issued as a newspaper advertisement before

the third day after that on which it is first so issued in any other manner, the reference is to the day on which it is first so issued in any manner.

(4) In reckoning for this purpose the third day after another day—

(a) any intervening day which is a Saturday or Sunday, or is a bank holiday in any part of Great Britain, is to be disregarded; and

(b) if the third day (as so reckoned) is itself a Saturday or Sunday, or a bank holiday, there is to be substituted the first day after that which is none of them.

(5) The validity of an allotment is not affected by any contravention of subsections (1) to (4); but in the event of contravention, the company and every officer of it who is in default is liable to a fine.

(6) As applying to a prospectus offering shares or debentures for sale, the above provisions are modified as follows—

(a) for references to allotment, substitute references to sale; and

(b) for the reference to the company and every officer of it who is in default, substitute a reference to any person by or through whom the offer is made and who knowingly and wilfully authorises or permits the contravention.

(7) An application for shares in or debentures of a company which is made in pursuance of a prospectus issued generally is not revocable until after the expiration of the third day after the time of the opening of the subscription lists, or the giving before the expiration of that day of the appropriate public notice; and that notice is one given by some person responsible under sections 67 to 69 for the prospectus and having the effect under those sections of excluding or limiting the responsibility of the giver.

General note

This section is repealed for all purposes except for the purposes of prospectuses to which Public Offers of Securities Regulations 1995, SI 1995/1537, reg 8 applies (ie prospectuses issued on an offer of unlisted securities to the public): The Financial Services Act 1986 (Commencement) (No 14) Order 1999, SI 1999/727, art 2.

S 82(1), (6)

This provision applies to offers to the public for subscription and to offers for sale. 'Allotment' is defined in s 738(1); 'debentures' is defined in s 744, as is 'prospectus issued generally'. The intention behind the provision is to allow a period after the prospectus is published both for media comment and for would-be subscribers or purchasers to seek advice and information.

S 82(5)

The validity of the allotment is unaffected by breach of these timing requirements. As to penalties, see s 730, Sch 24; 'officer in default' is defined in s 730(5); note the modification in sub-s (6).

S 82(7)

This obscurely worded provision renders an application irrevocable until a period of six days has elapsed (ie until the expiration of three days from the opening of the subscription lists, defined in sub-s (2), as the beginning of the third day after that on which the prospectus is first issued); or where the person responsible for the prospectus has given public notice repudiating liability under it. By the time the period specified has expired, the offer will have been accepted (ie on the opening of the subscription lists) with the result that it will no longer be possible to revoke the offer.

The intention behind this provision apparently was to prevent stagging of an issue, where potential purchasers having applied for shares would revoke their offers at the earliest opportunity if it seemed unlikely that the shares would attract a suitable premium on trading commencing. That practice is effectively curtailed now by clearing cheques accompanying applications immediately and, if necessary, refunding the money later, so requiring the applicants to be in funds at the time of the application and depriving them of interest on the funds while awaiting a refund.

83. No allotment unless minimum subscription received

(1) No allotment shall be made of any share capital of a company offered to the public for subscription unless—

 (a) there has been subscribed the amount stated in the prospectus as the minimum amount which, in the opinion of the directors, must be raised by the issue of share capital in order to provide for the matters specified in paragraph 2 of Schedule 3 (preliminary expenses, purchase of property, working capital, etc); and

 (b) the sum payable on application for the amount so stated has been paid to and received by the company.

(2) For purposes of subsection (1)(b), a sum is deemed paid to the company, and received by it, if a cheque for that sum has been received in good faith by the company and the directors have no reason for suspecting that the cheque will not be paid.

(3) The amount so stated in the prospectus is to be reckoned exclusively of any amount payable otherwise than in cash and is known as 'the minimum subscription'.

(4) If the above conditions have not been complied with on the expiration of 40 days after the first issue of the prospectus, all money received from applicants for shares shall be forthwith repaid to them without interest.

(5) If any of the money is not repaid within 48 days after the issue of the prospectus, the directors of the company are jointly and severally liable to repay it with interest at the rate of 5 per cent per annum from the expiration of the 48th day; except that a director is not so liable if he proves that the default in the repayment of the money was not due to any misconduct or negligence on his part.

(6) Any condition requiring or binding an applicant for shares to waive compliance with any requirement of this section is void.

(7) This section does not apply to an allotment of shares subsequent to the first allotment of shares offered to the public for subscription.

General note

This section is repealed for all purposes except for the purposes of prospectuses to which Public Offers of Securities Regulations 1995, SI 1995/1537, reg 8 applies (ie prospectuses issued on an offer of unlisted securities to the public): The Financial Services Act 1986 (Commencement) (No 14) Order 1999, SI 1999/727, art 2.

S 83(1), (7)

This provision is of limited significance and applies only on the first allotment of shares offered to the public (defined ss 58–60) for subscription, ie offered by the company for cash: *Governments Stock and Other Securities Investment Co Ltd v Christopher* [1956] 1 All ER 490. It requires (1) that the minimum subscription in cash be stated in the prospectus; and (2) that that sum be received by the company before any allotment takes place. If the allotment is underwritten, no problem will arise since the company will necessarily obtain the minimum subscription. As to the meaning of 'allotment', see s 738(1).

The intention behind this requirement was that companies should not be able to allot shares to those who applied if the amount to be raised would be insufficient to give the company a basis on which to proceed with its undertaking.

As to the consequences where the company proceeds with an allotment in contravention of this provision, see s 85.

S 83(2)

The company does not have to wait for the cheque to be cleared in order to deem the money paid and received for the purposes of s 83(1)(b).

84. Allotment where issue not fully subscribed

(1) No allotment shall be made of any share capital of a public company offered for subscription unless—

    (a) that capital is subscribed for in full; or

    (b) the offer states that, even if the capital is not subscribed for in full, the amount of that capital subscribed for may be allotted in any event or in the event of the conditions specified in the offer being satisfied;

and, where conditions are so specified, no allotment of the capital shall be made by virtue of paragraph (b) unless those conditions are satisfied.

This is without prejudice to section 83.

(2) If shares are prohibited from being allotted by subsection (1) and 40 days have elapsed after the first issue of the prospectus, all money received from applicants for shares shall be forthwith repaid to them without interest.

(3) If any of the money is not repaid within 48 days after the issue of the prospectus, the directors of the company are jointly and severally liable to repay

it with interest at the rate of 5 per cent per annum from the expiration of the 48th day; except that a director is not so liable if he proves that the default in repayment was not due to any misconduct or negligence on his part.

(4) This section applies in the case of shares offered as wholly or partly payable otherwise than in cash as it applies in the case of shares offered for subscription (the word 'subscribed' in subsection (1) being construed accordingly).

(5) In subsections (2) and (3) as they apply to the case of shares offered as wholly or partly payable otherwise than in cash, references to the repayment of money received from applicants for shares include—

    (a) the return of any other consideration so received (including, if the case so requires, the release of the applicant from any undertaking), or

    (b) if it is not reasonably practicable to return the consideration, the payment of money equal to its value at the time it was so received,

and references to interest apply accordingly.

(6) Any condition requiring or binding an applicant for shares to waive compliance with any requirement of this section is void.

General note

This section was to be amended by FSA 1986, s 212(3), Sch 17, Pt 1 but that provision was commenced to only a limited extent (see SI 1986/2246, SI 1988/740) which does not affect the continuing application of this provision to public companies offering unlisted securities to the public.

S 84(1), (4)

This provision prohibits an allotment of a proportion of the capital offered for subscription unless the prospectus had specified the proportion which might be allotted in any event.

    This requirement is quite separate from the requirements of s 83, although there is an element of overlap between the two provisions. This section differs from s 83 in that (1) it applies to all offers for subscription and not just to the first allotment offered to the public for subscription; and (2) offers for subscription, in this case, include shares offered wholly or partly for a non-cash consideration (cf *Governments Stock and Other Securities Investment Co Ltd v Christopher* [1956] 1 All ER 490).

    As to the consequences where the company proceeds with an allotment in contravention of this provision, see s 85.

85. Effect of irregular allotment

(1) An allotment made by a company to an applicant in contravention of section 83 or 84 is voidable at the instance of the applicant within one month after the date of the allotment, and not later, and is so voidable notwithstanding that the company is in the course of being wound up.

(2)   If a director of a company knowingly contravenes, or permits or authorises the contravention of, any provision of either of those sections with respect to allotment, he is liable to compensate the company and the allottee respectively for any loss, damages or costs which the company or the allottee may have sustained or incurred by the contravention.

(3)   But proceedings to recover any such loss, damages or costs shall not be commenced after the expiration of 2 years from the date of the allotment.

General note

This section was to be amended by FSA 1986, s 212(3), Sch 17, Pt 1 but that provision was commenced to only a limited extent (see SI 1986/2246, SI 1988/740) which does not affect the continuing application of this provision where needed to give effect to ss 83 or 84, which remain in effect to the extent indicated in the general notes to those sections.

S 85(1)

The preceding two provisions determine the position regarding repayment of moneys to applicants where no allotment of shares can take place because of a failure to reach the thresholds set by those provisions. This provision determines the consequences where a company proceeds, despite failing to reach the thresholds, to make an allotment in contravention of those provisions.

The allotment is only voidable at the option of the shareholder (and only within the time specified) and the company cannot pay back the application money of its own initiative; the only liability of the directors after allotment is the liability to make good the loss: *Burton v Bevan* [1908] 2 Ch 240.

S 85(2)

'Knowingly contravene' means contravene with knowledge of the facts. A director cannot escape liability by ignorance of the law: *Burton v Bevan* [1908] 2 Ch 240.

86. Allotment of shares, etc to be dealt in on stock exchange

Repealed for all purposes: The Financial Services Act 1986 (Commencement) (No 14) Order 1999, SI 1999/727, art 2.

87. Operation of s 86 where prospectus offers shares for sale

Repealed for all purposes: The Financial Services Act 1986 (Commencement) (No 14) Order 1999, SI 1999/727, art 2.

88. Return as to allotments, etc

(1)   This section applies to a company limited by shares and to a company limited by guarantee and having a share capital.

(2)   When such a company makes an allotment of its shares, the company shall within one month thereafter deliver to the registrar of companies for registration—

(a)   a return of the allotments (in the prescribed form) stating the number and nominal amount of the shares comprised in the allotment, the names and addresses of the allottees, and the amount (if any) paid or due and payable on each share, whether on account of the nominal value of the share or by way of premium; and

(b)   in the case of shares allotted as fully or partly paid up otherwise than in cash—

(i)   a contract in writing constituting the title of the allottee to the allotment together with any contract of sale, or for services or other consideration in respect of which that allotment was made (such contracts being duly stamped), and

(ii)   a return stating the number and nominal amount of shares so allotted, the extent to which they are to be treated as paid up, and the consideration for which they have been allotted.

(3)   Where such a contract as above mentioned is not reduced to writing, the company shall within one month after the allotment deliver to the registrar of companies for registration the prescribed particulars of the contract stamped with the same stamp duty as would have been payable if the contract had been reduced to writing.

(4)   Those particulars are deemed an instrument within the meaning of the Stamp Act 1891; and the registrar may, as a condition of filing the particulars, require that the duty payable on them be adjudicated under section 12 of that Act.

(5)   If default is made in complying with this section, every officer of the company who is in default is liable to a fine and, for continued contravention, to a daily default fine, but subject as follows.

(6)   In the case of default in delivering to the registrar within one month after the allotment any document required by this section to be delivered, the company, or any officer liable for the default, may apply to the court for relief; and the court, if satisfied that the omission to deliver the document was accidental or due to inadvertence, or that it is just and equitable to grant relief, may make an order extending the time for the delivery of the document for such period as the court thinks proper.

General note

The information on returns under this section supplements the information as to share capital and shareholders found on the annual return, see s 364A. Details of any allotments during the financial year must also be included in the notes to the accounts: Sch 4, para 39.

Any return of allotments of a public company must be gazetted by the registrar of companies: see s 711(1)(m).

S 88(1)

As to a company limited by guarantee with a share capital, see s 1(4); unlimited companies with a share capital are excluded from the provision and returns of allotments by such companies are not required although such companies do submit an annual return which requires particulars of share capital and shareholders, see s 364A.

S 88(2), (3)

The return must be delivered within one month of the allotment. On this point, the guidance from the registrar of companies states:

'If shares are allotted over a period of time, particularly in a rights issue, it is not acceptable to delay delivery until all the shares have been allotted if this means the form will be late. Instead, [the company] should complete consecutive forms so that each of them can be delivered within one month of the first allotment stated on each form.'

(Companies House Guidance Booklet *Share Capital and Prospectuses.*) As to 'allotment', see s 738(1); as to when shares are paid up in cash or allotted for cash, see s 738(2)–(4).

Bonus issues   A return of allotment is required on a bonus issue (see Table A, reg 110(d) as to how this is organised) and a bonus issue is to be treated as an allotment for a non-cash consideration so attracting the more onerous obligations under this provision: see s 738(2); also see *Whittome v Whittome* 1994 SLT 114 at 124.

Non-cash consideration   Problems can arise where a non-cash consideration is involved. The statute requires that the contract be delivered and this means that information which is commercially sensitive may have to be disclosed if it is included in the contract.

The registrar of companies will accept a certified copy of the contract but it must be duly stamped: Companies House Guidance Booklet *Share Capital and Prospectuses*. The requirement that the Inland Revenue must already have stamped the written contract, or the statement of the prescribed particulars under sub-s (3), confirming that stamp duty has been paid or that none is payable, before it is sent to the registrar of companies can cause practical problems in filing the return of allotment within the required time period.

Where the allotment for a non-cash consideration is by a public company, the return of allotments must be accompanied by the valuation report made under s 108: s 111(1).

S 88(5), (6)

As to penalties, see s 730, Sch 24; 'officer in default' is defined in s 730(5). As to the court's discretion to grant relief, see s 404 where similar wording is used. In practice, prosecutions for non-compliance are rare and it is unlikely that any director will need to seek relief from the court. A failure to file a return has no effect on the validity of the allotment.

PRE-EMPTION RIGHTS

89. Offers to shareholders to be on pre-emptive basis

(1) Subject to the provisions of this section and the seven sections next following, a company proposing to allot equity securities (defined in section 94)—

(a) shall not allot any of them on any terms to a person unless it has made an offer to each person who holds relevant shares or relevant employee shares to allot to him on the same or more favourable terms a proportion of those securities which is as nearly as practicable equal to the proportion in nominal value held by him of the aggregate of relevant shares and relevant employee shares, and

(b) shall not allot any of those securities to a person unless the period during which any such offer may be accepted has expired or the company has received notice of the acceptance or refusal of every offer so made.

(2) Subsection (3) below applies to any provision of a company's memorandum or articles which requires the company, when proposing to allot equity securities consisting of relevant shares of any particular class, not to allot those securities on any terms unless it has complied with the condition that it makes such an offer as is described in subsection (1) to each person who holds relevant shares or relevant employee shares of that class.

(3) If in accordance with a provision to which this subsection applies—

(a) a company makes an offer to allot securities to such a holder, and

(b) he or anyone in whose favour he has renounced his right to their allotment accepts the offer,

subsection (1) does not apply to the allotment of those securities, and the company may allot them accordingly; but this is without prejudice to the application of subsection (1) in any other case.

(4) Subsection (1) does not apply to a particular allotment of equity securities if these are, or are to be, wholly or partly paid up otherwise than in cash; and securities which a company has offered to allot to a holder of relevant shares or relevant employee shares may be allotted to him, or anyone in whose favour he has renounced his right to their allotment, without contravening subsection (1)(b).

(5) Subsection (1) does not apply to the allotment of securities which would, apart from a renunciation or assignment of the right to their allotment, be held under an employees' share scheme.

General note

This group of provisions, ss 89–95, deals with rights issues and implements art 29 of the Second EC Company Law Directive requiring pre-emption rights whenever equity securities are to be offered for a *cash* consideration: Council Directive (EEC) 77/91 (OJ L26 31.1.77 p 1). As to the scope of art 29, see *Siemens AG v Nold*: Case C-42/95 [1997] 1 BCLC 291.

The general obligation to make a rights issue imposed by s 89(1) is modified by:

(1)   the exemptions in sub-ss (2)–(5);

(2)   the ability of private companies to exclude the operation of this provision under s 91; and

(3)   the ability of any company to disapply this provision under s 95 (and the provision is routinely disapplied to some extent by public companies).

S 89(1)

These requirements apply to all companies, public and private, subject to ss 91 and 95.

Proposing to allot equity securities   To be within the provision, the company must propose to allot equity securities. The effect of the convoluted definitions in s 94 is that equity securities are shares (including rights to subscribe for or to convert into shares) which are not bonus shares, nor shares taken by subscribers to the memorandum, nor shares with restricted rights as to dividends and return of capital, nor shares held or to be allotted in pursuance of an employees' share scheme (defined s 743). An allotment is defined in s 94(3) as including the grant of a right to subscribe for, or to covert securities into, relevant shares in the company or of that class.

It follows that bonus shares, subscriber shares, shares with restricted rights as to dividends and return of capital, and shares allotted in pursuance of an employees' share scheme may all be allotted on a non-rights basis, subject to any requirements in the company's memorandum or articles of association.

The requirement that the amount of securities allotted be 'as near as practicable' allows the directors some discretion as to how to deal with any fractional entitlements which might arise.

Offer to certain shareholders   If the company so proposes to allot, it is required to offer the equity securities to certain shareholders, namely the holders of relevant shares (ie shares with unrestricted rights to dividends and a return of capital: s 94(5)) or holders of relevant employee shares (ie relevant shares held by persons who acquired them in pursuance of an employees' share scheme: s 94(4)). See s 94(7) as to the identification of the holders to whom an offer must be made.

The terms on which the offer must be made must be the same or more favourable than those on which the company would allot the shares to any other person (sub-s (1)(a)). This means that if the rights issue is not taken up by the existing holders, perhaps because they are thought to be too highly priced, the company cannot then offer those securities to any other person at a lower price.

The manner in which the offer must be made is set out in s 90; the duration of the offer is prescribed by s 90(6).

Allotments to any other persons   Where there is a requirement to make an offer to certain holders, the company cannot allot any of those securities to any other person, until the period specified in sub-s (1)(b) has expired (which allows the holders time to accept) or the company has notice of the acceptance or refusal of *every* offer so made. Once the time has expired, the company may allot any share not taken up to any other person but not at a more favourable price.

S 89(2), (3)

Offers on a pre-emptive basis to a class   The effect of these provisions is to exempt from the general pre-emption requirement in s 89(1) any allotment of equity securities which is on a pre-emption basis to a class of shareholders in pursuance of a requirement in the memorandum or articles of association to that effect. A reference to a class of shares is to shares to which the same rights are attached as to voting and as to participation, both as respects dividend and as respects capital, in a distribution: s 94(1), (6).

The proposed allotment must be of equity securities consisting of relevant shares of the particular class which (applying s 94(2), (3)) means the proposed allotment of any share of the class (other than shares taken by subscribers to the memorandum or bonus shares) or the grant of a right to subscribe for or to covert securities into relevant shares of that class.

The manner in which the offer to the class must be made is set out in s 90; the duration of the offer is prescribed by s 90(6); and see s 90(7) which nullifies provisions in the memorandum or articles as to the manner of any pre-emption offer to a class which contravenes the statutory scheme in s 90(1)–(6).

If the shares so offered are not accepted by the holder of those shares, or anyone in whose favour he has renounced his right to their allotment, then it appears from the final proviso to sub-s (3) that any subsequent offer of those shares has to be in accordance with sub-s (1), ie on a pre-emption basis to the rest of the shareholders rather than to the general public. In these cases, therefore, the order of allotment is to the holder of the class of shares or anyone in whose favour he has renounced, then to the existing shareholders on a pre-emption basis, and only then to the general public.

S 89(4)

The first element of this provision offers an easy method of avoiding pre-emption rights, for so long as any part of the consideration is paid up otherwise than in cash (as to which, see s 738(2)–(4), and noting the limitation in s 738(3)), the general rule does not apply. There is no de minimis element here and the provision permits avoidance of s 89(1) where there is any partly paid element. However, if the partly paid element is derisory, the court may doubt the bona fides of the directors in pursuing this course of action and their conduct may be open to challenge as being for a collateral purpose.

The second element of this provision permits a company to make an allotment to the holders (or anyone to whom they have renounced their rights) without regard to the time limits in s 89(1)(b), ie without waiting for the time limit in s 90(6) to expire or for the acceptance or refusal of every offer.

S 89(5)

There is no requirement for a rights issue where the allotment is of securities to be held under an employees' share scheme (defined s 743), even if the scheme permits the renunciation or assignment of the rights to the allotment of the securities.

90. Communication of pre-emption offers to shareholders

(1) This section has effect as to the manner in which offers required by section 89(1), or by a provision to which section 89(3) applies, are to be made to holders of a company's shares.

(2) Subject to the following subsections, an offer shall be in writing and shall be made to a holder of shares either personally or by sending it by post (that is to say, prepaying and posting a letter containing the offer) to him or to his registered address or, if he has no registered address in the United Kingdom, to the address in the United Kingdom supplied by him to the company for the giving of notice to him.

     If sent by post, the offer is deemed to be made at the time at which the letter would be delivered in the ordinary course of post.

(3) Where shares are held by two or more persons jointly, the offer may be made to the joint holder first named in the register of members in respect of the shares.

(4) In the case of a holder's death or bankruptcy, the offer may be made—

     (a) by sending it by post in a prepaid letter addressed to the persons claiming to be entitled to the shares in consequence of the death or bankruptcy by name, or by the title of representatives of the deceased, or trustee of the bankrupt, or by any like description, at the address in the United Kingdom supplied for the purpose by those so claiming, or

     (b) (until such an address has been so supplied) by giving the notice in any manner in which it might have been given if the death or bankruptcy had not occurred.

(5) If the holder—

     (a) has no registered address in the United Kingdom and has not given to the company an address in the United Kingdom for the service of notices on him, or

     (b) is the holder of a share warrant,

the offer may be made by causing it, or a notice specifying where a copy of it can be obtained or inspected, to be published in the Gazette.

(6) The offer must state a period of not less than 21 days during which it may be accepted; and the offer shall not be withdrawn before the end of that period.

(7) This section does not invalidate a provision to which section 89(3) applies by reason that that provision requires or authorises an offer under it to be made in contravention of any of subsections (1) to (6) above; but, to the extent that the provision requires or authorises such an offer to be so made, it is of no effect.

General note

Subsections(1)–(5) (manner of offer) or sub-s (6) (period of offer) may be excluded by a private company in the circumstances prescribed by s 91.

S 90(1), (6)

These provisions, determining the manner in which an offer must be made and the time period of the offer, apply both to general offers under s 89(1) and offers to a class of shareholders as required by any provision in the company's memorandum or articles of association under s 89(3). Subsection (7) negates any provision in the memorandum or articles requiring a pre-emption offer to a class under s 89(3) to be communicated in a manner different to that here prescribed or permitting its revocation at a time contrary to the requirements of sub-s (6).

However, private companies, expressly or by the use of inconsistent provisions, may exclude these provisions as to communication and timing with respect to general offers under s 91; but a private company cannot exclude the operation of sub-s (7) imposing these requirement with respect to an offer to a class of shareholders.

S 90(2)–(5)

As to the 'holder' of shares, see s 94(7). There is a presumption that the offer is made at the time when the letter would be delivered in the ordinary course of post; this is an irrebuttable presumption designed to put the matter beyond doubt: see *St Aubyn v A-G* [1951] 2 All ER 473 at 498; the position would be different if the wording 'unless the contrary is proved' had been included: see Interpretation Act 1978, s 7. As to a share warrant, see s 188.

An overseas shareholder   If an overseas shareholder has no registered address in the UK, and no address has been supplied for notice, sub-s (5) applies. This provision is more generous to such an overseas shareholder than Table A, reg 111 and puts the company to the burden of including him in the offer notwithstanding the lack of a registered address. It may be undesirable to include such a shareholder as it may subject the offer to onerous obligations imposed by the investor's home jurisdiction. The company will usually find it preferable to disapply these provisions under s 95 and proceed with an offer which excludes overseas shareholders.

S 90(6)

This provision does not provide that the offer period starts with the sending of the documentation but rather that the document must indicate 'a period of not less than 21 days' which, for the company, lengthens the period which the rights offer will take. This mandatory period may be excluded by a private company (see s 91); and any company disapplying these provisions in accordance with s 95 may adopt a different timetable.

---

91. Exclusion of ss 89, 90 by private company

(1)   Section 89(1), section 90(1) to (5) or section 90(6) may, as applying to allotments by a private company of equity securities or to such allotments of a particular description, be excluded by a provision contained in the memorandum or articles of that company.

(2)   A requirement or authority contained in the memorandum or articles of a private company, if it is inconsistent with any of those subsections, has effect as a provision excluding that subsection; but a provision to which section 89(3) applies is not to be treated as inconsistent with section 89(1).

S 91(1), (2)

The provisions which may be excluded are:
    (1)   the requirement to have a rights issue under s 89(1);
    (2)   the requirement to make the offer in the manner dictated by s 90(1)–(5); and
    (3)   the requirement to keep the offer open for the period dictated by s 90(6).

The exclusion, which need not be express, may relate to all allotments of equity securities (defined in s 94(2), (5)) or to particular allotments but the option of exclusion is available only to private companies (defined in s 1(3)).

It may not be desirable to exclude pre-emption rights by means of a provision in the memorandum, in particular, because of the difficulty of subsequently altering such a provision (see ss 2(7), 17). It may be preferable to proceed on an ad hoc basis, disapplying s 89(1) as and when appropriate by means of a special resolution under s 95.

A class right of pre-emption contained in the memorandum or articles of association is not an inconsistent provision which operates to exclude the general requirement of a rights offer under s 89(1).

92. Consequences of contravening ss 89, 90

(1)   If there is a contravention of section 89(1), or of section 90(1) to (5) or section 90(6), or of a provision to which section 89(3) applies, the company, and every officer of it who knowingly authorised or permitted the contravention, are jointly and severally liable to compensate any person to whom an offer should have been made under the subsection or provision contravened for any loss, damage, costs or expenses which the person has sustained or incurred by reason of the contravention.

(2)   However, no proceedings to recover any such loss, damage, costs or expenses shall be commenced after the expiration of 2 years from the delivery to the registrar of companies of the return of allotments in question or, where equity securities other than shares are granted, from the date of the grant.

S 92(1)

Penalties   The provisions specified, breach of which attracts the penalties imposed by this provision, are:
    (1)   the requirement to have a rights issue under s 89(1);
    (2)   the requirement to make the offer in the manner dictated by s 90(1)–(5);
    (3)   the requirement to keep the offer open for the period dictated by s 90(6);

(4)   the requirement to make a rights issue to a class under a provision contained in the company's memorandum or articles of association: s 89(3).

There is no criminal sanction but civil liability is imposed on the company and every officer knowingly involved to compensate persons to whom the offer should have been made (which is governed by s 89(1)(a) and, if a class right is involved, s 89(2),(3)) for loss etc arising *by reason of* the contravention.

Settling aside the allotment   No provision is made for improper allotments to be set aside (no doubt because of the difficulty of unravelling matters once an allotment has been made), but see *Re Thundercrest Ltd* [1995] 1 BCLC 117 where the court did set aside an allotment by directors in their own favour which was made in breach of the statutory requirements. The company was a private company with only three members so, as a practical matter, it was possible to rescind the allotment in this case.

Unfairly prejudicial conduct   A failure to comply with the pre-emption provisions may be grounds for a petition alleging unfairly prejudicial conduct under s 459: see *Re a company (No 005134 of 1986), ex p Harries* [1989] BCLC 383 at 396; and an allotment, even on a pre-emption basis, may be challenged if it is being proposed for a collateral purpose: see *Re a company (No 002612 of 1984)* [1985] BCLC 80; *Re Regional Airports Ltd* [1999] 2 BCLC 30.

S 92(2)

As to the return of allotments, see s 88.

93. Saving for other restrictions as to offers

(1)   Sections 89 to 92 are without prejudice to any enactment by virtue of which a company is prohibited (whether generally or in specified circumstances) from offering or allotting equity securities to any person.

(2)   Where a company cannot by virtue of such an enactment offer or allot equity securities to a holder of relevant shares or relevant employee shares, those sections have effect as if the shares held by that holder were not relevant shares or relevant employee shares.

General note

This provision is designed to exempt companies from the obligation to make a rights issue imposed by s 89(1), or s 89(3), where some other prohibition prevents the making of an offer or allotting of equity securities to any person as, for example, where the existing shares are subject to restrictions imposed by Part XV: see s 454(1)(c). It would also apply in cases where prohibitions on trading with the enemy came into play (see Trading with the Enemy Act 1939, s 7) and, previously, in cases where exchange control would have been relevant.

S 93(2)

The provision operates by deeming the holder of the affected shares not to be a holder of relevant shares or relevant employee shares and therefore he is not entitled to receive the offer under s 89(1) or s 89(3).

94. Definitions for ss 89–96

(1)   The following subsections apply for the interpretation of sections 89 to 96.

(2)   'Equity security', in relation to a company, means a relevant share in the company (other than a share shown in the memorandum to have been taken by a subscriber to the memorandum or a bonus share), or a right to subscribe for, or to convert securities into, relevant shares in the company.

(3)   A reference to the allotment of equity securities or of equity securities consisting of relevant shares of a particular class includes the grant of a right to subscribe for, or to convert any securities into, relevant shares in the company or (as the case may be) relevant shares of a particular class; but such a reference does not include the allotment of any relevant shares pursuant to such a right.

(4)   'Relevant employee shares', in relation to a company, means shares of the company which would be relevant in it but for the fact that they are held by a person who acquired them in pursuance of an employees' share scheme.

(5)   'Relevant shares', in relation to a company, means shares in the company other than—

  (a)   shares which as respects dividends and capital carry a right to participate only up to a specified amount in a distribution, and

  (b)   shares which are held by a person who acquired them in pursuance of an employees' share scheme or, in the case of shares which have not been allotted, are to be allotted in pursuance of such a scheme.

(6)   A reference to a class of shares is to shares to which the same rights are attached as to voting and as to participation, both as respects dividends and as respects capital, in a distribution.

(7)   In relation to an offer to allot securities required by section 89(1) or by any provision to which section 89(3) applies, a reference in sections 89 to 94 (however expressed) to the holder of shares of any description is to whoever was at the close of business on a date, to be specified in the offer and to fall in the period of 28 days immediately before the date of the offer, the holder of shares of that description.

S 94(4), (5)

As to the meaning of 'employees' share scheme', see s 743.

S 94(7)

This provision identifies those holders to whom the company must make the offer required by s 89(1) or (3).

---

95. Disapplication of pre-emption rights

(1)   Where the directors of a company are generally authorised for purposes of section 80, they may be given power by the articles, or by a special resolution of the company, to allot equity securities pursuant to that authority as if—

    (a) section 89(1) did not apply to the allotment, or

    (b) that subsection applied to the allotment with such modifications as the directors may determine;

and where the directors make an allotment under this subsection, sections 89 to 94 have effect accordingly.

(2)   Where the directors of a company are authorised for purposes of section 80 (whether generally or otherwise), the company may by special resolution resolve either—

    (a) that section 89(1) shall not apply to a specified allotment of equity securities to be made pursuant to that authority, or

    (b) that that subsection shall apply to the allotment with such modifications as may be specified in the resolution;

and where such a resolution is passed, sections 89 to 94 have effect accordingly.

(3)   The power conferred by subsection (1) or a special resolution under subsection (2) ceases to have effect when the authority to which it relates is revoked or would (if not renewed) expire; but if the authority is renewed, the power or (as the case may be) the resolution may also be renewed, for a period not longer than that for which the authority is renewed, by a special resolution of the company.

(4)   Notwithstanding that any such power or resolution has expired, the directors may allot equity securities in pursuance of an offer or agreement previously made by the company, if the power or resolution enabled the company to make an offer or agreement which would or might require equity securities to be allotted after it expired.

(5)   A special resolution under subsection (2), or a special resolution to renew such a resolution, shall not be proposed unless it is recommended by the directors and there has been circulated, with the notice of the meeting at which the resolution is proposed, to the members entitled to have that notice a written statement by the directors setting out—

    (a) their reasons for making the recommendation,

    (b) the amount to be paid to the company in respect of the equity securities to be allotted, and

    (c) the directors' justification of that amount.

(6)   A person who knowingly or recklessly authorises or permits the inclusion in a statement circulated under subsection (5) of any matter which is misleading, false or deceptive in a material particular is liable to imprisonment or a fine, or both.

General note

This provision allows any company to disapply the operation of the statutory pre-emption requirements in s 89(1) and to allot equity securities for cash on a non-rights basis. The method of disapplication depends on the nature of the authority to allot shares granted to the directors under s 80. The company cannot use this provision to disapply pre-emption rights contained in the company's memorandum or articles of association (see s 89(2), (3)) which must be altered in the usual way, if necessary: see ss 2(7), 9, 17.

S 95(1)

General disapplication   This provision allows for a general disapplication of the pre-emption requirement in s 89(1) where the directors have a general authority to allot under s 80. Pre-emption rights may be disapplied entirely or may be applied with such modifications as the directors determine (for example, a shorter offer period than the 21 days specified by s 90(6)). The power to disapply may be granted by a provision in the articles or by a special resolution (see s 378) of the company. 'Equity securities' is defined in s 94(2). The duration of the disapplication is determined by s 95(3).

S 95(2), (5)

Limited disapplication   This provision allows for a more limited disapplication of the pre-emption requirement with regard to a specified allotment regardless of the nature of the authority granted under s 80. Pre-emption rights may be disapplied entirely with respect to the specified allotment or may be applied to that allotment with such modifications as may be specified by the resolution (not by the directors). 'Equity securities' is defined in s 94(2). The duration of the disapplication is determined by sub-s (3). See sub-s (5) as to the written statement which must be circulated to the shareholders in this case.

   Where a private company wishes to proceed by written resolution, this requirement as to the circulation of a written statement does not apply but such a statement must be supplied to each relevant member at or before the time at which the resolution is supplied to him for signature: s 381A(7); Sch 15A, para 3.

S 95(1)–(3)

The receipt by the registrar of companies of any special resolution passed by a public company under these provisions must be gazetted by him: s 711(1)(e).

S 95(6)

As to penalties, see s 730, Sch 24.

---

96. Saving for company's pre-emption procedure operative before 1982

(1)   Where a company which is re-registered or registered as a public company is or, but for the provisions of the Companies Act 1980 and the enactments replacing it, would be subject at the time of re-registration or (as the case may be) registration to a pre-1982 pre-emption requirement, sections 89 to 95 do not apply to an allotment of the equity securities which are subject to that requirement.

(2)   A 'pre-1982 pre-emption requirement' is a requirement imposed (whether by the company's memorandum or articles, or otherwise) before the relevant date in 1982 by virtue of which the company must, when making an allotment of equity securities, make an offer to allot those securities or some of them in a manner which (otherwise than because involving a contravention of section 90(1) to (5) or 90(6)) is inconsistent with sections 89 to 94; and 'the relevant date in 1982' is—

- (a)   except in a case falling within the following paragraph, 22nd June in that year, and
- (b)   in the case of a company which was re-registered or registered as a public company on an application made before that date, the date on which the application was made.

(3)   A requirement which—

- (a)   is imposed on a private company (having been so imposed before the relevant date in 1982) otherwise than by the company's memorandum or articles, and
- (b)   if contained in the company's memorandum or articles, would have effect under section 91 to the exclusion of any provisions of sections 89 to 94,

has effect, so long as the company remains a private company, as if it were contained in the memorandum or articles.

(4)   If on the relevant date in 1982 a company, other than a public company registered as such on its original incorporation, was subject to such a requirement as is mentioned in section 89(2) imposed otherwise than by the memorandum or articles, the requirement is to be treated for purposes of sections 89 to 94 as if it were contained in the memorandum or articles.

General note

This provision deals with the situation where a company had existing pre-emption procedures prior to the passing of the Companies Act 1980 which introduced the statutory requirements now contained in ss 89–95.

S 96(1), (2)

The statutory scheme does not apply to any public company which had a pre-emption requirement, prior to the relevant date, which is inconsistent with the statutory scheme in some way other than as to the manner of an offer under s 90(1)–(5) or the period of an offer under s 90(6). In practice, most public companies would have altered their schemes to have brought them into line with the statutory scheme by now.

S 96(3)

A pre-1982 pre-emption scheme of a private company which would have been effective under s 91 to exclude the operation of the statutory scheme had it been contained in the memorandum or articles of association is deemed contained in the memorandum or articles for these purposes.

S 96(4)

A pre-1982 pre-emption scheme with respect to a class of shares of a private company which would have been effective under s 89(2), (3) to exclude the operation of the statutory scheme had it been contained in the memorandum or articles of association is deemed contained in the memorandum or articles for these purposes.

COMMISSIONS AND DISCOUNTS

97. Power of company to pay commissions

(1)   It is lawful for a company to pay a commission to any person in consideration of his subscribing or agreeing to subscribe (whether absolutely or conditionally) for any shares in the company, or procuring or agreeing to procure subscriptions (whether absolute or conditional) for any shares in the company, if the following conditions are satisfied.

(2)   The payment of the commission must be authorised by the company's articles; and—

  (a)   the commission paid or agreed to be paid must not exceed 10 per cent of the price at which the shares are issued or the amount or rate authorised by the articles, whichever is the less; and

  (b)   the amount or rate per cent of commission paid or agreed to be paid, and the number of shares which persons have agreed for a commission to subscribe absolutely, must be disclosed in the manner required by the following subsection.

(3) Those matters must, in the case of shares offered to the public for subscription, be disclosed in the prospectus; and in the case of shares not so offered—

(a) they must be disclosed in a statement in the prescribed form signed by every director of the company or by his agent authorised in writing, and delivered (before payment of the commission) to the registrar of companies for registration; and

(b) where a circular or notice (not being a prospectus) inviting subscription for the shares is issued, they must also be disclosed in that circular or notice.

(4) If default is made in complying with subsection (3)(a) as regards delivery to the registrar of the statement in prescribed form, the company and every officer of it who is in default is liable to a fine.

General note

This provision and s 98 must be read together: s 98(1) prohibits commissions of a certain nature unless permitted by s 97(1) or s 98(3). The statutory intention is to prevent the issue of shares at a discount through the payment of large commissions to those subscribing or agreeing to subscribe for any shares in the company.

S 97(1), (2)(a)

These provisions were to have been amended by FSA 1986 but the amendments have been repealed without being brought into force. These provisions apply to all companies which, when duly authorised, may pay commissions which would otherwise be prohibited by s 98(1).

Authority is required for the direct payment of commissions to those who subscribe and to intermediaries who procure or agree to procure subscriptions; 'subscription' means taking or agreeing to take shares for cash: *Government Stock and Other Securities Investment Co Ltd v Christopher* [1956] 1 All ER 490.

S 97(2)(b), (3), (4)

These provisions, which deal with the disclosure requirements with respect to commissions, are repealed to the extent that they relate to any investment which is listed or subject to an application for listing (SI 1986/2246), or to a proposal offering for subscription, or any form of application for, any units in a body corporate which is a recognised scheme (SI 1988/740).

With those exceptions, these provisions remain in force and, in particular, remain applicable to any offer to the public of unlisted securities and to any invitation (not being a prospectus) to subscribe which is issued by a private company (sub-s (3)(b)). 'Prospectus' is defined for these purposes in s 744 and see ss 59, 60 as to the meaning of offer to the public.

A similar disclosure obligation applies under the Public Offers of Securities Regulations 1995, SI 1995/1537, Sch 1, para 23, but this provision has a broader reach applying to offers which are not public offers under those regulations.

A failure to comply with the requirement to disclose the amount of any commission in a circular means that the contract for the payment of the commission is illegal and cannot be enforced: *Andreae v Zinc Mines of Great Britain Ltd* [1918] 2 KB 454 at 498; if the company has already paid the commission and the recipient had no knowledge of the illegality then the commission cannot be recovered: *Andreae v Zinc Mines of Great Britain Ltd* [1918] 2 KB 454.

S 97(4)

As to penalties, see s 730, Sch 24; 'officer in default' is defined in s 730(5).

98. Apart from s 97, commissions and discounts barred

(1)   Except as permitted by section 97, no company shall apply any of its shares or capital money, either directly or indirectly in payment of any commission, discount or allowance to any person in consideration of his subscribing or agreeing to subscribe (whether absolutely or conditionally) for any shares in the company, or procuring or agreeing to procure subscriptions (whether absolute or conditional) for any shares in the company.

(2)   This applies whether the shares or money be so applied by being added to the purchase money of any property acquired by the company or to the contract price of any work to be executed for the company, or the money be paid out of the nominal purchase money or contract price, or otherwise.

(3)   Nothing in section 97 or this section affects the power of a company to pay such brokerage as has previously been lawful.

(4)   A vendor to, or promoter of, or other person who receives payment in money or shares from, a company has, and is deemed always to have had, power to apply any part of the money or shares so received in payment of any commission, the payment of which, if made directly by the company, would have been lawful under section 97 and this section.

S 98(1)–(2), (4)

The prohibition on the application of 'any shares or capital money' as commission etc applies to payments by the company in the form of shares or payments in cash made out of money derived from the issue of its shares: *Hilder v Dexter* [1902] AC 474 at 480 (an option granted to a member to acquire shares at par which he exercised at a time when the shares stood at a premium did not amount to a commission paid directly or indirectly by the company, for the company did not part with any portion of its capital or indeed with any moneys belonging to it).

The prohibition is subject to the exceptions in s 97(1) and sub-s (3); and there is nothing to stop a company using other funds to pay commissions and by s 130(2) the share premium account may be used to pay such commissions as are lawful. Subsections (2), (4) are anti-avoidance provisions.

S 98(3)

By brokerage is meant 'commission to stockbrokers, bankers and the like, who exhibit prospectuses and send them to their customers, and by whose mediation the customers are induced to subscribe' and similar transactions: *Andreae v Zinc Mines of Great Britain Ltd* [1918] 2 KB 454 at 498; see also *Metropolitan Coal Consumers' Association v Scrimgeour* [1895] 2 QB 604. This provision is thought to have little modern significance and adds little to s 97(1), other than that it is not constrained by s 97(2).

AMOUNT TO BE PAID FOR SHARES; THE MEANS OF PAYMENT

99. General rules as to payment for shares on allotment

(1) Subject to the following provisions of this Part, shares allotted by a company, and any premium on them, may be paid up in money or money's worth (including goodwill and know-how).

(2) A public company shall not accept at any time, in payment up of its shares or any premium on them, an undertaking given by any person that he or another should do work or perform services for the company or any other person.

(3) If a public company accepts such an undertaking in payment up of its shares or any premium on them, the holder of the shares when they or the premium are treated as paid up (in whole or in part) by the undertaking is liable—

  (a) to pay the company in respect of those shares an amount equal to their nominal value, together with the whole of any premium or, if the case so requires, such proportion of that amount as is treated as paid up by the undertaking; and

  (b) to pay interest at the appropriate rate on the amount payable under paragraph (a) above.

(4) This section does not prevent a company from allotting bonus shares to its members or from paying up, with sums available for the purpose, any amounts for the time being unpaid on any of its shares (whether on account of the nominal value of the shares or by way of premium).

(5) The reference in subsection (3) to the holder of shares includes any person who has an unconditional right to be included in the company's register of members in respect of those shares or to have an instrument of transfer of them executed in his favour.

General note

The application of this provision to a public company is extended to any private company or joint stock company which has passed and not revoked a resolution to re-register or register, as the case may be, as a public company, see note to s 116, below.

S 99(1)

Money or money's worth　　A company cannot make a gratuitous allotment of its shares: *Re Wragg Ltd* [1897] 1 Ch 796; *Ooregum Gold Mining Co of India Ltd v Roper* [1892] AC 125; *Re Eddystone Marine Insurance Co* [1893] 3 Ch 9. The allottee must pay at least the nominal value of the shares (s 100) and will possibly pay a premium (ie an amount in excess of the nominal or par value) as well.

This provision, which reflects the common law position (see *Re Wragg Ltd* [1897] 1 Ch 796), permits the allottee to pay in money or money's worth. In exercising their powers to allot shares for 'money's worth', the directors must act bona fide in the interests of the company as a whole. Details of any non-cash consideration accepted by the company must be included in the return of allotments to the registrar of companies under s 88(2).

Non-cash consideration　　Where a non-cash consideration is involved, it may disguise what is in effect an issue of shares at a discount contrary to s 100.

'The Court would doubtless refuse effect to a colourable transaction, entered into for the purpose or with the obvious result of enabling the company to issue its shares at a discount but it has been held that, so long as the company honestly regards the consideration given as fairly representing the nominal value of the shares in cash, its estimate ought not to be critically examined ...'

(*Ooregum Gold Mining Co of India v Roper* [1892] AC 125 at 137, per Lord Watson; see also *Re Wragg Ltd* [1897] 1 Ch 796; *Park Business Interiors Ltd v Park* [1992] BCLC 1034 at 1040.)

It is only where the consideration is colourable or illusory or it is manifest on the face of the instrument that the shares are issued at a discount that the court will be prepared to consider the adequacy of the consideration: *Re White Star Line Ltd* [1938] Ch 458; *Mosely v Koffyfontein Mines Ltd* [1904] 2 Ch 108; *Re Wragg Ltd* [1897] 1 Ch 796. The question whether the consideration is colourable is one of fact in each case: *Re Innes & Co Ltd* [1903] 2 Ch 254 at 262.

The inconsistency between prohibiting a discount but allowing payment in money's worth was noted by Lindley LJ in *Re Wragg Ltd* [1897] AC 796 at 831 who accepted that the difference between issuing shares at a discount and issuing them at a price put upon property or services by the vendor and agreed to by the company may not always be very apparent in practice. In his opinion, however, the two transactions were essentially different and, whilst the one was ultra vires, the other was intra vires.

Public companies　　In view of the potential for shares to be issued at a discount as a result of a company accepting a non-cash consideration, stricter rules are imposed for public companies: see ss 99(2), 101–104, 106; although the broad definition of an allotment for a cash consideration in s 738(2)–(4) offers scope for avoidance of these stricter rules.

Shares are taken to be allotted as defined in s 738(1); and a share in a company is deemed paid up in cash or allotted for cash in accordance with s 738(2)–(4). Share premium is governed by ss 130–134.

S 99(2)

Work or services This prohibition on accepting such undertakings as consideration for an allotment of shares can be explained on the basis that the value of such services is difficult to quantify and it would otherwise leave too much scope for abuse. 'Public company' is defined in s 1(3). The prohibition extends to undertakings whether by the allottee or another; and to work or services whether for the company or for another person, such as a subsidiary company.

Despite any contravention of these provisions, any undertaking given, if otherwise enforceable, remains enforceable by the company: s 115(1).

S 99(3)

Liability of the holder The allotment still stands and the holder (defined in sub-s (5)) is potentially subject to a penal liability in that, even if he has performed services in return for the shares, he is required by this provision to pay the full amount of the nominal value and any premium represented by the undertaking together with interest.

The effect is to create an immediate liability as if the allottee had agreed to take up the shares for cash: *Re Bradford Investments plc* [1991] BCLC 224 at 233 (re liability under s 103 but equally applicable here). The appropriate rate of interest is governed by s 107.

The liability of subsequent holders is governed by s 112(1) subject to the exemptions in s 112(3); it is possible for the holder and any subsequent holder to apply for relief from liability under s 113(1); the company and any officer in default are liable to a fine under s 114.

S 99(4)

Bonus shares The requirement in sub-s (1) to pay for shares does not prevent a company from making an allotment of bonus shares; this is not a gratuitous allotment in any event but a capitalisation of reserves, see Table A, reg 110.

S 99(5)

The holder will include the beneficial owner if different from the registered owner; and a person to whom renounceable letters of allotment have been renounced is a holder for these purposes: *Systems Control plc v Munro Corporate plc* [1990] BCLC 659.

100. Prohibition on allotment of shares at a discount

(1)   A company's shares shall not be allotted at a discount.

(2)   If shares are allotted in contravention of this section, the allottee is liable to pay the company an amount equal to the amount of the discount, with interest at the appropriate rate.

S 100(1)

No discount   This provision reflects the long established common law rule that a company cannot allot shares at a discount, ie for less than the nominal value stated in the memorandum of association (see s 2(5)(a)): *Ooregum Gold Mining Co of India v Roper* [1892] AC 125, HL. As Lord Macnaghten explained in *Ooregum* (at 145):

> '…the liability of a member continues so long as anything remains unpaid upon his shares. Nothing but payment, and payment in full, can put an end to the liability … To sum the matter up, I cannot, I think, do better than adopt the language Mr. Buckley has used in speaking of the Limited Liability Acts. "The dominant and cardinal principle of these Acts," he says, "is that the investor shall purchase immunity from liability beyond a certain limit, on the terms that there shall be and remain a liability up to that limit".'

See also *Re Eddystone Marine Insurance Co* [1893] 3 Ch 9; *Welton v Saffery* [1897] AC 299.
    The rule cannot be evaded by issuing convertible debentures at a discount which are capable of being immediately converted to ordinary shares: *Mosely v Koffyfontein Mines Ltd* [1904] 2 Ch 108. An exception to the no discount rule is that which permits companies to pay underwriting commissions (see ss 97, 98).
    While a company may not allot shares at less than the nominal value, shares may be paid up in money or money's worth (s 99(1)) which may disguise the issue of shares at a discount. See the note to that provision, above.
    Shares are taken to be allotted as defined in s 738(1).

S 100(2)

Liability of the allottee   The allotment still stands but the effect of this provision is to create an immediate liability to pay up to the nominal amount: *Re Bradford Investments plc* [1991] BCLC 224 at 233 (re liability under s 103 but equally applicable here). The appropriate rate of interest is governed by s 107.
    The liability of subsequent holders is governed by s 112(1) subject to the exemptions in s 112(3); it is not possible in this case (given that the company has not received the nominal amount) for any allottee or subsequent holder to apply for relief from liability under s 113; the company and any officer in default are liable to a fine under s 114.

Directors' duties   Directors who allot shares at a discount are guilty of a breach of duty to the company and are liable to pay the amount of the discount and interest to the company if that amount cannot be recovered from the allottee or holder of the shares, as where the shares have passed into the hands of a bona fide purchaser for value from the original allottee: *Hirsche v Sims* [1894] AC 654, PC.

Premium   This section provides a statutory entitlement to secure the nominal value of the shares. If a purchaser fails to pay an agreed premium, the company will have a remedy in contract. As to payment up for the shares in the case of a public company, see s 101.

101. Shares to be allotted as at least one-quarter paid-up

(1)   A public company shall not allot a share except as paid up at least as to one-quarter of its nominal value and the whole of any premium on it.

(2)   Subsection (1) does not apply to shares allotted in pursuance of an employees' share scheme.

(3)   If a company allots a share in contravention of subsection (1), the share is to be treated as if one-quarter of its nominal value, together with the whole of any premium on it, had been received.

(4)   But the allottee is liable to pay the company the minimum amount which should have been received in respect of the share under subsection (1) (less the value of any consideration actually applied in payment up, to any extent, of the share and any premium on it), with interest at the appropriate rate.

(5)   Subsections (3) and (4) do not apply to the allotment of bonus shares, unless the allottee knew or ought to have known the shares were allotted in contravention of subsection (1).

General note

The application of this provision to a public company is extended to any private company or joint stock company which has passed and not revoked a resolution to re-register or register, as the case may be, as a public company, see note to s 116.

S 101(1)

One-quarter paid up   A private company may allot shares as nil paid with no part of the capital paid up but this provision requires shares in a public company to be paid up to the extent specified. However, the sum 'paid up' may be paid up in money or money's worth (s 99), which can include an undertaking which need not be performed for up to five years (s 102) so 'paid up' may be something of a misnomer. A very limited exception is where shares are allotted to the subscribers to the memorandum who must pay cash (s 106); even then 'cash' includes an undertaking to pay cash in the future, so it need not be cash in hand: see s 738(2). Shares are taken to be allotted as defined in s 738(1).

Before it can obtain a trading certificate (see s 117), the minimum nominal value of the allotted share capital of a public company must be £50,000 (ss 117, 118) so the application of this provision means that at least £12,500 must be paid up (as defined above) in the case of a public company.

For many public companies, the nominal value of a share will be insignificant (often being fixed at 5p or 10p or 25p) when compared with the premium payable. The effect of this requirement that all of the premium be paid up means that, in practice, a public company will allot its shares as fully paid. For example, if the issue price is £3.50 with a nominal value of 10p, the share must be paid up as to £3.43 so the company is likely to seek the entire amount and allot the shares as fully paid.

S 101(2)

An 'employees' share scheme' is defined in s 743; such shares need not be paid up to the extent required by sub-s (1).

S 101(3)

Effect of breach on allotment   The allotment is still valid and, by treating the allottee as if he has paid the correct amount, this ensures that the shareholder has a right to be registered and to receive dividends although he has not actually paid up for the shares. Given that an allotment of shares in a public company may be to a large number of shareholders and that the problem regarding payment as required by sub-s (1) might not come to light for some time, it would cause considerable confusion if the allotment was void. For example, resolutions might be improperly passed and dividends improperly received. The better solution is to provide, as here, that the allotment is valid as if from the day of allotment and the allottee is liable under sub-s (4) for the outstanding amount.

S 101(4)

Liability of the allottee   The effect is to create an immediate liability: *Re Bradford Investments plc* [1991] BCLC 224 at 233 (re liability under s 103 but equally applicable here). The appropriate rate of interest is governed by s 107.

The liability of subsequent holders is governed by s 112(1) subject to the exemptions in s 112(3); it is not possible in this case for any allottee or subsequent holder to apply for relief from liability under s 113 (the subsection itself provides relief by requiring account to be taken of any consideration actually paid) ; and the company and any officer in default are liable to a fine under s 114.

S 101(5)

Bonus shares   As to bonus shares, see Table A, reg 110. In practice, it would be rare for a bonus issue to be partly paid, although that situation might arise where the company had made an error as to the availability of profits to capitalise in this way, rendering the issue void for mistake: see *Re Cleveland Trust plc* [1991] BCLC 424.

Recipient without knowledge   The wording of this provision is obscure. It provides that sub-ss (3) and (4) (which validate an allotment contrary to sub-s (1) and render the allottee immediately liable to pay the amount due on the shares) do not apply to an allotment of bonus shares in contravention of sub-s (1). The consequence of such an allotment, therefore, must be that the allotment does not stand and the allottee is not liable to pay up the requisite amount on the shares. As a bonus issue is an unsolicited distribution by a company, it would be wrong for the recipient of such shares to be required to contribute a further payment to the company for shares for which he did not apply.

Recipient with knowledge   Where the recipient knows or ought to know of the contravention, for example, where there is some collusion with the company's officers, or the recipients are the company's officers, then sub-ss (3) and (4) do apply with the result that the bonus issue does stand and the recipient is liable to the extent specified in sub-s (4). It follows that it will be possible for a bonus issue to be partially valid and partially void under this provision, depending on the position of the recipient.

102. Restriction on payment by long-term undertaking

(1) A public company shall not allot shares as fully or partly paid up (as to their nominal value or any premium on them) otherwise than in cash if the consideration for the allotment is or includes an undertaking which is to be, or may be, performed more than 5 years after the date of the allotment.

(2) If a company allots shares in contravention of subsection (1), the allottee is liable to pay the company an amount equal to the aggregate of their nominal value and the whole of any premium (or, if the case so requires, so much of that aggregate as is treated as paid up by the undertaking), with interest at the appropriate rate.

(3) Where a contract for the allotment of shares does not contravene subsection (1), any variation of the contract which has the effect that the contract would have contravened the subsection, if the terms of the contract as varied had been its original terms, is void.

(4) Subsection (3) applies also to the variation by a public company of the terms of a contract entered into before the company was re-registered as a public company.

(5) The following subsection applies where a public company allots shares for a consideration which consists of or includes (in accordance with subsection (1)) an undertaking which is to be performed within 5 years of the allotment, but the undertaking is not performed within the period allowed by the contract for the allotment of the shares.

(6) The allottee is then liable to pay the company, at the end of the period so allowed, an amount equal to the aggregate of the nominal value of the shares and the whole of any premium (or, if the case so requires, so much of that aggregate as is treated as paid up by the undertaking), with interest at the appropriate rate.

(7) A reference in this section to a contract for the allotment of shares includes an ancillary contract relating to payment in respect of them.

General note

The application of this provision to a public company is extended to any private company or joint stock company which has passed and not revoked a resolution to re-register or register, as the case may be, as a public company: see note to s 116, below.

S 102(1)

Long-term non-cash consideration This undertaking must be with respect to an allotment otherwise than in cash. A share in a company is deemed paid up in cash or allotted for cash in accordance with s 738(2)–(4); 'public company' is defined in s 1(3).

S 102(2)

Liability of the allottee The allotment stands but the effect of this provision is to create an immediate liability as if the allottee had agreed to take up the shares for cash: *Re Bradford Investments plc* [1991] BCLC 224 at 233 (re liability under s 103 but equally applicable here). The appropriate rate of interest is governed by s 107.

The liability of subsequent holders is governed by s 112(1), (5), subject to the exemptions in s 112(3); and it is possible for the allottee and any subsequent holder to apply for relief from liability under s 113; the company and any officer in default are liable to a fine under s 114. The undertaking remains enforceable by the company: s 115(1).

S 102(3)–(4)

Variation of contracts These provisions are designed to prevent the easy avoidance of sub-s (1) by subsequently varying a contract, including where a public company seeks to vary a contract entered into when it was a private company. See the extended definition of contract in sub-s (7).

S 102(5)–(6)

Undertaking not performed in period allowed The allotment stands but the effect of this provision is to create an immediate liability (at the time when the period for performance of the undertaking elapses) as if the allottee had agreed to take up the shares for cash: *Re Bradford Investments plc* [1991] BCLC 224 at 233 (re liability under s 103 but equally applicable here). The appropriate rate of interest is governed by s 107.

The liability of subsequent holders is governed by s 112(1), (5), subject to the exemptions in s 112(3); and it is possible for the allottee and any subsequent holder to apply for relief from liability under s 113; the company and any officer in default are liable to a fine under s 114.

103. Non-cash consideration to be valued before allotment

(1)   A public company shall not allot shares as fully or partly paid up (as to their nominal value or any premium on them) otherwise than in cash unless—

   (a)   the consideration for the allotment has been independently valued under section 108; and

   (b)   a report with respect to its value has been made to the company by a person appointed by the company (in accordance with that section) during the 6 months immediately preceding the allotment of the shares; and

   (c)   a copy of the report has been sent to the proposed allottee.

(2)   Where an amount standing to the credit of any of a company's reserve accounts, or of its profit and loss account, is applied in paying up (to any extent) any shares allotted to members of the company or any premiums on shares so allotted, the amount applied does not count as consideration for the allotment, and accordingly subsection (1) does not apply in that case.

(3)   Subsection (1) does not apply to the allotment of shares by a company in connection with an arrangement providing for the allotment of shares in that company on terms that the whole or part of the consideration for the shares allotted is to be provided by the transfer to that company (or the cancellation) of all or some of the shares, or of all or some of the shares of a particular class, in another company (with or without the issue to that company of shares, or of shares of any particular class, in that other company).

(4)   But subsection (3) does not exclude the application of subsection (1) unless under the arrangement it is open to all the holders of the shares in the other company in question (or, where the arrangement applies only to shares of a particular class, to all the holders of shares in that other company, being holders of shares of that class) to take part in the arrangement.

In determining whether that is the case, shares held by or by a nominee of the company proposing to allot the shares in connection with the arrangement, or by or by a nominee of a company which is that company's holding company or subsidiary or a company which is a subsidiary of its holding company, shall be disregarded.

(5)   Subsection (1) also does not apply to the allotment of shares by a company in connection with its proposed merger with another company; that is, where one of the companies proposes to acquire all the assets and liabilities of the other in exchange for the issue of shares or other securities of that one to shareholders of the other, with or without any cash payment to shareholders.

(6)   If a company allots shares in contravention of subsection (1) and either—

   (a)   the allottee has not received the valuer's report required by that subsection to be sent to him; or

   (b)   there has been some other contravention of this section or section 108 which the allottee knew or ought to have known amounted to a contravention,

the allottee is liable to pay the company an amount equal to the aggregate of the nominal value of the shares and the whole of any premium (or, if the case so requires, so much of that aggregate as is treated as paid up by the consideration), with interest at the appropriate rate.

(7) In this section—

(a) 'arrangement' means any agreement, scheme or arrangement (including an arrangement sanctioned in accordance with section 425 (company compromise with creditors and members) or section 110 of the Insolvency Act (liquidator in winding up accepting shares as consideration for sale of company property), and

(b) any reference to a company, except where it is or is to be construed as a reference to a public company, includes any body corporate and any body to which letters patent have been issued under the Chartered Companies Act 1837.

General note

See s 104, which may apply to a particular transaction in addition to this provision.

The application of this provision to a public company is extended to any private company or joint stock company which has passed and not revoked a resolution to re-register or register, as the case may be, as a public company: see note to s 116, below.

S 103(1)

Valuation of non-cash consideration   A share in a company is deemed paid up in cash or allotted for cash in accordance with s 738(2)–(4) and the breadth of the definition in that section offers scope for the avoidance of the valuation requirement imposed by this provision. 'Public company' is defined in s 1(3). The timing requirement in sub-s (1)(b) must be observed. A copy of the report must be filed with the registrar of companies at the same time as the company delivers the return of allotments (s 88) for those shares: s 111(1). The receipt of that report by the registrar of companies must be gazetted: s 711(1)(f).

S 103(2)

Bonus issue exempt   This provision exempts bonus issues (shares allotted to members of the company on a capitalisation of reserves or of its profit and loss account) from any valuation requirement: but the exemption is limited to bonus issues to existing members which may not always be the case, for example, under a scheme of arrangement: see note to s 425, below.

S 103(3)–(4), (7)

Takeovers and schemes of arrangement   This provision exempts from the valuation requirement any share exchange between companies 'in connection with' any arrangement which is broadly defined in sub-s (7)(a) to include any take-over offer as well as including any scheme of arrangement under s 425 or within IA 1986, s 110, provided the conditions in sub-s (4) are met. The allotment of shares need be only part of the consideration.

S 103(5)

Mergers   This provision exempts from the valuation requirement shares allotted in accordance with a proposed merger but only a merger as defined in this provision.

S 103(6)

Liability on breach   Liability under sub-s (6)(b) requires that the allottee knew or ought to have known of the facts which constitute the contravention: *Systems Control plc v Munro Corporate plc* [1990] BCLC 659. It is not a requirement that the allottee knew the requirements of the law as to valuation which, given the complexity of the provisions, would be difficult to establish but rather that he knew or ought to have known of the facts which gave rise to the contravention, ie that shares were issued for a non-cash consideration without any valuation having taken place. While the consequence of this approach may be severe, Hoffmann J thought the answer to that concern lay in s 113, which allows the court to grant relief from liability provided that the company has received full value for its shares: *Systems Control plc v Munro Corporate plc* [1990] BCLC 659 at 663.

The allotment stands and the effect is to create an immediate liability as if the allottee had agreed to take up the shares for cash: *Re Bradford Investments plc* [1991] BCLC 224 at 233. The appropriate rate of interest is governed by s 107. The liability of subsequent holders is governed by s 112(1), subject to the exemptions in s 112(3); the company and any officer in default are liable to a fine under s 114. Any undertaking given to the company is still enforceable: s 115(1).

These penalties can be onerous: see *Re Ossory Estates plc* [1988] BCLC 213; *Re Bradford Investments plc (No 2)* [1991] BCLC 688; but it is possible for the allottee and any subsequent holder to apply for relief under s 113.

S 103(7)

The definition of 'another company' or the 'other' company in sub-ss (3) and (5), ie the party to the arrangement or merger as a result of which the public company is allotting shares, is widened to include any body corporate (defined s 740).

---

104. Transfer to public company of non-cash asset in initial period

(1)   A public company formed as such shall not, unless the conditions of this section have been complied with, enter into an agreement with a person for the transfer by him during the initial period of one or more non-cash assets to the company or another, if—

    (a) that person is a subscriber to the company's memorandum, and

(b) the consideration for the transfer to be given by the company is equal in value at the time of the agreement to one-tenth or more of the company's nominal share capital issued at that time.

(2) The 'initial period' for this purpose is 2 years beginning with the date of the company being issued with a certificate under section 117 (or the previous corresponding provision) that it was entitled to do business.

(3) This section applies also to a company re-registered as a public company (except one re-registered under section 8 of the Companies Act 1980 or section 2 of the Consequential Provisions Act), or registered under section 685 (joint stock company) or the previous corresponding provision; but in that case—

(a) there is substituted a reference in subsection (1)(a) to a person who is a member of the company on the date of registration or re-registration, and

(b) the initial period is then 2 years beginning with that date.

In this subsection the reference to a company re-registered as a public company includes a private company so re-registered which was a public company before it was a private company.

(4) The conditions of this section are as follows—

(a) the consideration to be received by the company, and any consideration other than cash to be given by the company, must have been independently valued under section 109;

(b) a report with respect to the consideration to be so received and given must have been made to the company in accordance with that section during the 6 months immediately preceding the date of the agreement;

(c) the terms of the agreement must have been approved by an ordinary resolution of the company; and

(d) not later than the giving of the notice of the meeting at which the resolution is proposed, copies of the resolution and report must have been circulated to the members of the company entitled to receive the notice and, if the person with whom the agreement in question is proposed to be made is not then a member of the company so entitled, to that person.

(5) In subsection (4)(a)—

(a) the reference to the consideration to be received by the company is to the asset to be transferred to it or the advantage to the company of the asset's transfer to another person; and

(b) the specified condition is without prejudice to any requirement to value any consideration for purposes of section 103.

(6) In the case of the following agreements, this section does not apply—

(a) where it is part of the company's ordinary business to acquire, or arrange for other persons to acquire, assets of a particular description, an agreement entered into by the company in the ordinary course of its business for the transfer of an asset of that description to it or to such a person, as the case may be;

(b) an agreement entered into by the company under the supervision of the court, or of an officer authorised by the court for the purpose, for the transfer of an asset to the company or to another.

General note

Overlap with s 103   There is a degree of overlap between the requirement in s 103 for a non-cash consideration for an allotment of shares by a public company to be valued and this provision governing the transfer to a public company of non-cash assets in the initial two-year period, as defined in sub-s (2).

Section 103 applies whenever a public company accepts a non-cash consideration from anyone as consideration for an allotment of shares and requires that the non-cash consideration be valued.

Section 104 applies: (i) to any transfer to the company or another of a non-cash asset by a subscriber to a company's memorandum in certain circumstances within the initial two-year period, whether the consideration for the transfer is an allotment of shares or something else; and (ii) to any such transfer by a member of a company essentially where a private company has re-registered as a public company, in this case, within the first two years after re-registration. In such cases, valuation is required and the agreement must be approved by the company in general meeting. There are also different exceptions to each provision.

The provisions are not mutually exclusive and it is possible for both provisions to be applicable in the same instance, as where an allotment of shares for a non-cash consideration is made to a subscriber within the two-year period. Where the transaction is within both provisions, the procedures required by both provisions must be adhered to although there is an element of duplication.

The type of transaction which is within s 104 but not within s 103 is where the transaction does not involve an allotment of shares but is simply a transfer of non-cash assets by a subscriber to the company, or by a member to the company, within the initial two-year period.

S 104(1)

A public company formed as such   The requirements of this sub-section apply to a public company 'formed as such'; a 'public company' is defined in s 1(3); 'non-cash asset' and the 'transfer of a non-cash asset' are defined in s 739; as to the 'subscribers to the memorandum of association', see ss 1(1), 2(5)–(6), 7(1), (3). The asset need not be transferred to the company but may be transferred to 'another'.

Consideration given by the company   The threshold for value in sub-s (1)(b) relates to the consideration given by the company (and as to the meaning of this, see s 109(3)) and it is determined by reference to the company's issued share capital which is not defined in the legislation but see note to s 738(1), below.

The requirement of valuation imposed by sub-s (4) is subject to the exceptions in sub-s (6). Default is governed by s 105.

S 104(3)

Application to companies re-registered as public companies   This provision extends considerably the scope of the section as sub-s (1) is very limited in the class of transactions to which it applies. Few public companies are formed as such as opposed to being re-registered from private companies to public companies under s 43 et seq. This provision applies the requirements of the section to any transfer of the nature specified in sub-s (1) by a member of a public company which has not been formed as such but which has become a public company through re-registration and the transfer takes place within two years of that re-registration. However, this category is limited to persons who were members of the company on the date of re-registration which provides scope for avoidance.

This provision also applies to a public company which, although formed as such (and so apparently within sub-s (1)), was re-registered as a private company and then re-registered again as a public company. As to re-registration, see ss 43–55.

S 104(4),(5)

Consideration to be valued   Valuation in this case is of the asset or advantage (see sub-s (5)(a)) received by the company (or another) and given by the company (and as to the meaning of consideration given by the company, see s 109(3)). Any valuation required is in addition to any valuation required by s 103 (sub-s (5)(b)). The transfer or acquisition of a non-cash asset is defined in s 739(2).

Report made   The time period is determined by the date of the agreement.

Agreement approved   Approval is required of the terms of the agreement and not of the valuation. A copy of the valuation report and the resolution must be delivered to the registrar of companies within 15 days of passing the resolution: s 111(2). The receipt of that report by the registrar of companies must be gazetted: s 711(1)(f).

Information circulated   The time period imposed here must be observed.

S 104(6)

The exception in sub-s (6)(a) requires that the agreement be entered into in the ordinary course of *that* company's business to acquire, or arrange for others to acquire, the asset in question.

---

105. Agreements contravening s 104

(1)   The following subsection applies if a public company enters into an agreement contravening section 104, the agreement being made with the person referred to in subsection (1)(a) or (as the case may be) subsection (3) of that section, and either—

(a) that person has not received the valuer's report required for compliance with the conditions of the section, or

(b) there has been some other contravention of the section or of section 108(1),(2) or (5) or section 109, which he knew or ought to have known amounted to a contravention.

(2)   The company is then entitled to recover from that person any consideration given by it under the agreement, or an amount equal to the value of the consideration at the time of the agreement; and the agreement, so far as not carried out, is void.

(3)   However, if the agreement is or includes an agreement for the allotment of shares in the company, then—

    (a)   whether or not the agreement also contravenes section 103, subsection (2) above does not apply to it in so far as it is for the allotment of shares; and

    (b)   the allottee is liable to pay the company an amount equal to the aggregate of the nominal value of the shares and the whole of any premium (or, if the case so requires, so much of that aggregate as is treated as paid up by the consideration), with interest at the appropriate rate.

S 105(1)

Liability under sub-s (1)(b) requires that the person specified knew or ought to have known of the facts which constitute the contravention: *Systems Control plc v Munro Corporate plc* [1990] BCLC 659. It is not a requirement that that person knew the requirements of the law as to valuation which, given the complexity of the provisions, would be difficult to establish but rather that he knew or ought to have known of the facts which gave rise to the contravention, ie of the transfer of a non-cash asset without any valuation having taken place.

S 105(2)

Effect of breach on agreement   Recovery by the company is provided for by this provision; the position of the other party is governed by s 113(8) and he may be exempted from liability to the extent of any benefit accruing to the company by virtue of his performance of the agreement. The company and any officer in default are liable to a fine under s 114.

S 105(3)

Transactions within ss 103 and 104   As stated in the general note to s 104, above, it is possible for a transaction to be within s 103 and within s 104 as where shares are allotted for a non-cash asset by the company to a subscriber to the memorandum (or a member of the company where it has been re-registered as a public company) within the initial two-year period. In such cases a valuation under ss 103 and 104 is required.

This provision provides that where there has been a failure to comply with the requirements of s 104 such that a person is within sub-s (1) and the agreement is void under sub-s (2), nevertheless the allotment remains valid and the allottee is subject to an immediate liability under this provision to pay for the shares in cash: see *Re Bradford Investments plc* [1991] BCLC 224 at 233. The appropriate rate of interest is governed by s 107. Any undertaking given in respect of the allotment of shares is enforceable by the company despite the contravention of s 104: s 115(2).

The liability of subsequent holders of the shares is governed by s 112(2) subject to the exemptions in s 112(3); and it is possible for the allottee and any subsequent holder to apply for relief from liability under s 113(1) in relation to payment in respect of the shares.

106. Shares issued to subscribers of memorandum

Shares taken by a subscriber to the memorandum of a public company in pursuance of an undertaking of his in the memorandum, and any premium on the shares, shall be paid up in cash.

General note

This provision is of limited importance since most public companies are formed as private companies and re-registered as a public company under s 43 and so the subscribers are subscribers to the memorandum of a private company and are not subject to this provision.

Section 101 requires that shares allotted by a public company (which would include shares allotted to a subscriber) must be paid up as to one quarter of the nominal value and the whole of any premium. This provision adds the requirement that if the shares in question are those taken by the subscribers, then this amount must be paid up in cash. However, as a subscriber need not take more than one share (s 2(5)(b)), this obligation is not unduly onerous. A subscriber to the memorandum of a private company need not pay anything on subscription.

As to the 'subscribers' to the memorandum, see ss 1(1), 2(6), 7(1), (3); a 'public company' is defined in s 1(3); as to those undertaking to take up shares, see s 2(5)(b); as to when shares are allotted or paid up in cash, see s 738(2)–(4).

In the event of a breach of this provision, the company and any officer in default are liable to a fine under s 114.

The application of this provision to a public company is extended to any private company or joint stock company which has passed and not revoked a resolution to re-register or register, as the case may be, as a public company, see note to s 116.

107. Meaning of 'the appropriate rate'

In sections 99 to 105 'the appropriate rate', in relation to interest, means 5 per cent per annum or such other rate as may be specified by order made by the Secretary of State by statutory instrument subject to annulment in pursuance of a resolution of either House of Parliament.

General note

No statutory instruments have been made under this provision.

VALUATION PROVISIONS

108. Valuation and report (s 103)

(1)   The valuation and report required by section 103 (or, where applicable, section 44) shall be made by an independent person, that is to say a person qualified at the time of the report to be appointed, or continue to be, an auditor of the company.

(2)   However, where it appears to the independent person (from here on referred to as 'the valuer') to be reasonable for the valuation of the consideration, or part of it, to be made (or for him to accept such a valuation) by another person who—

(a)   appears to him to have the requisite knowledge and experience to value the consideration or that part of it; and

(b)   is not an officer or servant of the company or any other body corporate which is that company's subsidiary or holding company or a subsidiary of that company's holding company or a partner or employee of such an officer or servant,

he may arrange for or accept such a valuation, together with a report which will enable him to make his own report under this section and provide the note required by subsection (6) below.

(3)   The reference in subsection (2)(b) to an officer or servant does not include an auditor.

(4)   The valuer's report shall state—

(a)   the nominal value of the shares to be wholly or partly paid for by the consideration in question;

(b)   the amount of any premium payable on the shares;

(c)   the description of the consideration and, as respects so much of the consideration as he himself has valued, a description of that part of the consideration, the method used to value it and the date of the valuation;

(d)   the extent to which the nominal value of the shares and any premium are to be treated as paid up—

(i)   by the consideration;

(ii)   in cash.

(5)   Where the consideration or part of it is valued by a person other than the valuer himself, the latter's report shall state that fact and shall also—

(a)   state the former's name and what knowledge and experience he has to carry out the valuation, and

(b)   describe so much of the consideration as was valued by the other person, and the method used to value it, and specify the date of the valuation.

(6)   The valuer's report shall contain or be accompanied by a note by him—

(a)   in the case of a valuation made by a person other than himself, that it appeared to himself reasonable to arrange for it to be so made or to accept a valuation so made;

(b) whoever made the valuation, that the method of valuation was reasonable in all the circumstances;

(c) that it appears to the valuer that there has been no material change in the value of the consideration in question since the valuation; and

(d) that on the basis of the valuation the value of the consideration, together with any cash by which the nominal value of the shares or any premium payable on them is to be paid up, is not less than so much of the aggregate of the nominal value and the whole of any such premium as is treated as paid up by the consideration and any such cash.

(7) Where the consideration to be valued is accepted partly in payment up of the nominal value of the shares and any premium and partly for some other consideration given by the company, section 103 (and, where applicable, section 44) and the foregoing provisions of this section apply as if references to the consideration accepted by the company included the proportion of that consideration which is properly attributable to the payment up of that value and any premium; and—

(a) the valuer shall carry out, or arrange for, such other valuations as will enable him to determine that proportion; and

(b) his report shall state what valuations have been made under this subsection and also the reason for, and method and date of, any such valuation and any other matters which may be relevant to that determination.

General note

The application of this provision to a public company is extended to any private company or joint stock company which has passed and not revoked a resolution to re-register or register, as the case may be, as a public company, see note to s 116, below.

S 108(1)

Non-cash consideration on allotment   This provision applies to a valuation of a non-cash consideration where a public company makes an allotment of shares otherwise than for cash (s 103) or where a private company is to be re-registered as a public company and shares have recently been allotted for a consideration otherwise than in cash (s 44).

The valuer must be qualified to be the company's auditor (as to the qualifications of an auditor, see CA 1989, Part II) and may be, but need not be, the company's current auditor.

The company's officers are obliged to provide the valuer with any information required for these purposes: see s 110.

S 108(2)

The valuer   The valuer appointed under sub-s (1) may appoint an expert who must be independent of the company to the extent specified under sub-s (2)(b); and note sub-s (3), which allows the company's auditor (or an auditor of a group company) to be appointed as the expert. 'Officer' is defined in s 744; 'body corporate' in s 740; 'subsidiary' and 'holding company' are defined in s 736.

The effect of subs-s (1) and (2) is that the company may appoint anyone qualified to be the company's auditor or the company's auditor to act as the valuer and he in turn may appoint an expert to assist him; equally, where a valuer who is not the company's auditor is appointed, the auditor may be appointed as an expert to assist that valuer.

S 108(4)–(6)

Content of the valuer's report   These provisions specify the content of the valuer's report and that of an expert, if used. The key element is sub-s (6)(d), which provides that the report must show that the consideration received (plus any cash by which the shares are paid up) equals what the company said it was worth in terms of the amount of the nominal value and premium which is treated by the company as paid up. Shares are allotted or paid up in cash as defined in s 738(2)–(4).

The valuer will owe a duty of care to the company with respect to his report and will consequently be liable in the event that he negligently reports in the terms required by sub-s (6)(d), with the result that the company issues shares at a discount or, more likely, at a reduced premium: see *Caparo Industries plc v Dickman* [1990] BCLC 273, HL.

S 108(7)

Consideration referable to the allotment   This provision covers the situation where the non-cash consideration received by the company is partly for an allotment of shares but also partly for some other consideration given by the company. In that case, the valuation must determine the proportion of the consideration received which is referable to the allotment of the shares. This is not necessarily the proportion stipulated by the company for the requirement is for the valuer to determine the proportion which is *properly* attributable to the allotment.

For example, a company allots shares (cost £100,000) to B in return for an asset valued at £500,000, the asset being transferred (i) to pay for the shares but also (ii) to pay for warehouse facilities provided by the company for B. The company would assert that one-fifth of the value of the non-cash asset is referable to the allotment of the shares. A valuer might discover, however, that the value of the warehouse facilities was £500,000. In that case, shares valued at £100,000 and facilities valued at £500,000 have been provided for £500,000 in total so the proportion of the consideration properly attributable to the shares is one-sixth, ie shares costing £100,000 have been transferred in return for a non-cash asset valued at £83,333.

Hence the important in sub-s (7)(a) of requiring the valuer to carry out any other valuations (in this case, of the value of the warehouse facilities) in order to determine the proportion properly attributable to the shares rather than accepting the company's determination of this issue.

109. Valuation and report (s 104)

(1) Subsections (1) to (3) and (5) of section 108 apply also as respects the valuation and report for the purposes of section 104.

(2) The valuer's report for those purposes shall—

(a) state the consideration to be received by the company, describing the asset in question (specifying the amount to be received in cash) and the consideration to be given by the company (specifying the amount to be given in cash);

(b) state the method and date of valuation;

(c) contain or be accompanied by a note as to the matters mentioned in section 108(6)(a) to (c); and

(d) contain or be accompanied by a note that on the basis of the valuation the value of the consideration to be received by the company is not less than the value of the consideration to be given by it.

(3) A reference in section 104 or this section to consideration given for the transfer of an asset includes consideration given partly for its transfer; but—

(a) the value of any consideration partly so given is to be taken as the proportion of the consideration properly attributable to its transfer;

(b) the valuer shall carry out or arrange for such valuations of anything else as will enable him to determine that proportion; and

(c) his report for purposes of section 104 shall state what valuation has been made under this subsection and also the reason for and method and date of any such valuation and any other matters which may be relevant to that determination.

S 109(1)

Transfers of non-cash assets in the initial period   This subsection applies the provisions specified to the valuation of transfers of non-cash assets to a public company within the initial two-year period as required by s 104. The company's officers are obliged to provide the valuer with any information required for these purposes: see s 110.

S 109(2)

Valuation is required of the consideration received by the company and of the consideration given by the company, as defined in sub-s (3). The key requirement is in sub-s (2)(d) that the consideration received must equal, at least, that given. As to the potential liability of the valuer for a negligent report, see note to s 108(6), above.

S 109(3)

Consideration given partly for the transfer   This makes provision for the situation where only part of the consideration given by the company is *properly* attributable to the transfer of the non-cash asset by the specified person in s 104.

For example, Company A gives £200,000 to B, of which £100,000 is attributed to a non-cash asset transferred to the company by B and £100,000 is attributed to a payment by Company A for services provided for the company by B. In that case, sub-s (2)(d) requires the valuation to determine whether the value of the non-cash asset transferred is not less than £100,000. However, the company may be improperly attributing too high a value to the services provided by B, which may be more properly valued at £50,000. If that is the case, then the company has in fact given £150,000 for the non-cash asset which must be worth that amount if the valuer is to be able to report in the terms required by sub-s (2)(d). Hence the requirement that it is for the valuer to determine the amount properly attributable to the transfer of the non-cash asset and the requirement that the valuer be able to seek the valuation 'of anything else' necessary to determine this issue. In this example, he would wish to value the services provided by B.

110. Entitlement of valuer to full disclosure

(1)   A person carrying out a valuation or making a report under section 103 or 104, with respect to any consideration proposed to be accepted or given by a company, is entitled to require from the officers of the company such information and explanation as he thinks necessary to enable him to carry out the valuation or make the report and provide a note under section 108(6) or (as the case may be) section 109(2)(c).

(2)   A person who knowingly or recklessly makes a statement which—

(a) is misleading, false or deceptive in a material particular, and

(b) is a statement to which this subsection applies,

is guilty of an offence and liable to imprisonment or a fine, or both.

(3)   Subsection (2) applies to any statement made (whether orally or in writing) to a person carrying out a valuation or making a report under section 108 or 109, being a statement which conveys or purports to convey any information or explanation which that person requires, or is entitled to require, under subsection (1) of this section.

General note

The application of this provision to a public company is extended to any private company or joint stock company which has passed and not revoked a resolution to re-register or register, as the case may be, as a public company, see note to s 116, below.

S 110(1)

This provision gives the valuer a statutory right to the necessary information. 'Officer' is defined in s 744.

S 110(2)

As to penalties, see s 730, Sch 24.

---

111. Matters to be communicated to registrar

(1)   A company to which a report is made under section 108 as to the value of any consideration for which, or partly for which, it proposes to allot shares shall deliver a copy of the report to the registrar of companies for registration at the same time that it files the return of the allotments of those shares under section 88.

(2)   A company which has passed a resolution under section 104 with respect to the transfer of an asset shall, within 15 days of so doing, deliver to the registrar of companies a copy of the resolution together with the valuer's report required by that section.

(3)   If default is made in complying with subsection (1), every officer of the company who is in default is liable to a fine and, for continued contravention, to a daily default fine; but this is subject to the same exception as is made by section 88(6)(relief on application to the court) in the case of default in complying with that section.

(4)   If a company fails to comply with subsection (2), it and every officer of it who is in default is liable to a fine and, for continued contravention, to a daily default fine.

General note

The application of this provision to a public company is extended to any private company or joint stock company which has passed and not revoked a resolution to re-register or register, as the case may be, as a public company: see note to s 116, below.

S 111(1), (3)

The filing of a return of allotment is required by s 88(2) within one month of the allotment. The receipt of this report by the registrar of companies must be gazetted: s 711(1)(f). As to penalties, see s 730, Sch 24; 'officer in default' is defined in s 730(5).

S 111(2), (4)

The receipt of this report by the registrar of companies must be gazetted: s 711(1)(f). In this instance, the offence is also committed by the company. As to penalties, see s 730, Sch 24; 'officer in default' is defined in s 730(5).

OTHER MATTERS ARISING OUT OF ALLOTMENT, &C

111A. Right to damages, &c not affected

A person is not debarred from obtaining damages or other compensation from a company by reason only of his holding or having held shares in the company or any right to apply or subscribe for shares or to be included in the company's register in respect of shares.

General note

The decision in *Houldsworth v City of Glasgow Bank* (1880) 5 App Cas 317, HL, is reversed by this provision which was inserted by CA 1989, s 131(1), as from 1 April 1990.

   Until the Companies Act 1989, it was the position that a shareholder could not both retain his shares and bring an action against the company for damages for deceit having been induced by fraud to buy shares from the company: *Houldsworth v City of Glasgow Bank* (1880) 5 App Cas 317, HL. In principle, it was thought that such a claim was inconsistent with the contract into which the plaintiff had entered on joining the company and the plaintiff had therefore to sever his connection with the company by agreement or judgment for rescission before he could sue the company for misrepresentation: see *Houldsworth v City of Glasgow Bank* at 324, 325, per Lord Cairns LC.

112. Liability of subsequent holders of shares allotted

(1)   If a person becomes a holder of shares in respect of which—
   (a)   there has been a contravention of section 99, 100, 101 or 103; and
   (b)   by virtue of that contravention, another is liable to pay any amount under the section contravened,

that person is also liable to pay that amount (jointly and severally with any other person so liable), unless he is exempted from liability by subsection (3) below.

(2)   If a company enters into an agreement in contravention of section 104 and—
   (a)   the agreement is or includes an agreement for the allotment of shares in the company; and
   (b)   a person becomes a holder of shares allotted under the agreement; and
   (c)   by virtue of the agreement and allotment under it, another person is liable to pay any amount under section 105,

the person who becomes the holder of the shares is also liable to pay that amount (jointly and severally with any other person so liable), unless he is exempted from liability by the following subsection; and this applies whether or not the agreement also contravenes section 103.

(3)　A person otherwise liable under subsection (1) or (2) is exempted from that liability if either—

　　(a)　he is a purchaser for value and, at the time of the purchase, he did not have actual notice of the contravention concerned; or

　　(b)　he derived title to the shares (directly or indirectly) from a person who became a holder of them after the contravention and was not liable under subsection (1) or (as the case may be) subsection (2).

(4)　References in this section to a holder, in relation to shares in a company, include any person who has an unconditional right to be included in the company's register of members in respect of those shares or to have an instrument of transfer of the shares executed in his favour.

(5)　As subsections (1) and (3) apply in relation to the contraventions there mentioned, they also apply—

　　(a)　to a contravention of section 102; and

　　(b)　to a failure to carry out a term of a contract as mentioned in subsections (5) and (6) of that section.

General note

The application of this provision to a public company is extended to any private company or joint stock company which has passed and not revoked a resolution to re-register or register, as the case may be, as a public company: see note to s 116, below.

　　See s 113, which enables those liable to make payment to the company to apply to the court for relief.

S 112(1)

Liability of subsequent holders　As a general rule, where there has been a breach of the specified payment provisions, the allottee remains liable to pay an amount equal to the nominal amount and any premium together with interest. This provision renders any subsequent holder jointly and severally liable with the allottee unless they are within sub-s (3) and it is designed to prevent collusive agreements between the allottee and subsequent holders.

S 112(2)

Liability of subsequent holders where transfer of non-cash assets　Where a breach of s 104 has occurred (transfer of non-cash assets to a public company within the initial period) and an allotment of shares has been part of that transaction, the liability of the allottee is determined by s 105(3).

　　This provision renders liable any subsequent holder (subject to the exemptions in sub-s (3)) and this liability applies whether or not there has been a breach of s 103, this being a situation where compliance with s 103 and s 104 is required.

　　Where a breach of s 104 has occurred but an allotment of shares is not involved, the position of the parties is governed by s 105(2).

S 112(3)

Exemption – purchaser without actual notice   The exemption from liability for a subsequent holder of shares applies to any purchaser for value without actual notice of the contravention. The nature of the notice required by this provision was considered in *System Control plc v Munro Corporate plc* [1990] BCLC 659, where a non-cash consideration for an allotment of shares had not been valued as required by s 103. The holders of the shares argued that the valuation requirements of s 103 had never crossed their minds so that they could not be said to have actual notice of the contravention of the section. The court rejected this argument; what is required is:

> '… notice of the facts which constitute the contravention. It does not require the offending directors to have been learned in the law. Indeed … the effect of the section would be largely destroyed if that requirement were introduced.' (at 663, per Hoffmann J.)

It suffices to fix the holders with notice that they were aware that shares had been allotted for a non-cash consideration without any valuation having taken place. While the consequence of this approach may be severe, Hoffmann J thought the answer to that concern lay in s 113, which allows the court to grant relief from liability provided that the company has received full value for the shares.

Also exempt are subsequent holders (whether purchasers for value or not) within sub-s (3)(b), ie whose title is derived directly or indirectly from an exempt purchaser for value.

S 112(4)

This broad definition of 'holder' includes any person in whose favour renounceable letters of allotment have been renounced: *Systems Control plc v Munro Corporate plc* [1990] BCLC 659 at 662.

S 112(5)

This provision imposes liability on the subsequent holder (subject to the exemptions in sub-s (3)) where there has been a breach of the requirements concerning long-term undertakings as consideration for the allotment of shares in a public company.

---

113. Relief in respect of certain liabilities under ss 99 ff

(1)   Where a person is liable to a company under—

    (a)   section 99, 102, 103 or 105;

    (b)   section 112(1) by reference to a contravention of section 99 or 103; or

    (c)   section 112(2) or (5),

in relation to payment in respect of any shares in the company, or is liable by virtue of an undertaking given to it in, or in connection with, payment for any such shares, the person so liable may make an application to the court to be exempted in whole or in part from the liability.

(2)   If the liability mentioned in subsection (1) arises in relation to payment in respect of any shares, the court may, on an application under that subsection, exempt the applicant from the liability only—

(a)   if and to the extent that it appears to the court just and equitable to do so having regard to the matters mentioned in the following subsection,

(b)   if and to the extent that it appears to the court just and equitable to do so in respect of any interest which he is liable to pay the company under any of the relevant sections.

(3)   The matters to be taken into account by the court under subsection (2)(a) are—

(a)   whether the applicant has paid, or is liable to pay, any amount in respect of any other liability arising in relation to those shares under any of the relevant sections, or of any liability arising by virtue of any undertaking given in or in connection with payment for those shares;

(b)   whether any person other than the applicant has paid or is likely to pay (whether in pursuance of an order of the court or otherwise) any such amount; and

(c)   whether the applicant or any other person has performed in whole or in part, or is likely so to perform, any such undertaking, or has done or is likely to do any other thing in payment or part payment for the shares.

(4)   Where the liability arises by virtue of an undertaking given to the company in, or in connection with, payment for shares in it, the court may, on an application under subsection (1), exempt the applicant from the liability only if and to the extent that it appears to the court just and equitable to do so having regard to—

(a)   whether the applicant has paid or is liable to pay any amount in respect of liability arising in relation to the shares under any of the provisions mentioned in that subsection; and

(b)   whether any person other than the applicant has paid or is likely to pay (whether in pursuance of an order of the court or otherwise) any such amount.

(5)   In determining whether it should exempt the applicant in whole or in part from any liability, the court shall have regard to the following overriding principles, namely—

(a)   that a company which has allotted shares should receive money or money's worth at least equal in value to the aggregate of the nominal value of those shares and the whole of any premium or, if the case so requires, so much of that aggregate as is treated as paid up; and

(b)   subject to this, that where such a company would, if the court did not grant the exemption, have more than one remedy against a particular person, it should be for the company to decide which remedy it should remain entitled to pursue.

(6)   If a person brings proceedings against another ('the contributor') for a contribution in respect of liability to a company arising under any of sections 99 to 105 or 112, and it appears to the court that the contributor is liable to make such a contribution, the court may exercise the powers of the following subsection.

(7)   The court may, if and to the extent that it appears to it, having regard to the respective culpability (in respect of the liability to the company) of the contributor and the person bringing the proceedings, that it is just and equitable to do so—

(a)   exempt the contributor in whole or in part from his liability to make such a contribution; or

(b)   order the contributor to make a larger contribution than, but for this subsection, he would be liable to make.

(8)   Where a person is liable to a company under section 105(2), the court may, on application, exempt him in whole or in part from that liability if and to the extent that it appears to the court just and equitable to do so having regard to any benefit accruing to the company by virtue of anything done by him towards the carrying out of the agreement mentioned in that subsection.

General note

The application of this provision to a public company is extended to any private company or joint stock company which has passed and not revoked a resolution to re-register or register, as the case may be, as a public company: see note to s 116, below.

S 113(1)

Scope of the provision   This provision identifies those allottees and subsequent holders of shares who, being liable to make payment to the company under the specified provisions, may apply to the court for relief under this provision.

S 113(2)

These provisions apply to those liable in relation to any payment for any shares (liability under s 105, for example, may not relate to any payment for any shares, in which case, see sub-s (8)); the court must consider separately any liability as to payment and as to interest.

S 113(3)

In view of sub-s (5), these matters are not intended to be an exhaustive statement of the matters to which the court should or may have regard: *Re Bradford Investments plc (No 2)* [1991] BCLC 688 at 693.

S 113(4)

This provision applies to those liable by virtue of any undertaking in, or in connection with, payment for any shares. It is subject to sub-s (5).

S 113(5)

Overriding principles   This provision was considered in *Re Bradford Investments plc (No 2)* [1991] BCLC 688, where Hoffmann J concluded that the designation 'overriding principles' does not oblige the court to refuse relief unless the company has received at least the nominal value of the allotted shares and any premium: had that been the intention the requirement would have been framed as a rule:

> 'Instead, it is described as a "principle" and the court is required to 'have regard' to it. That means, in my judgment, that very good reasons would be needed before the court could accept that it was just and equitable to exempt an applicant from liability notwithstanding that the company had not received sufficient value.'

Re Bradford Investments plc (No 2) [1991] BCLC 688 at 694, per Hoffmann J.

In *Re Ossory Estates plc* [1988] BCLC 213, the allottee was relieved from liability as the company had sold some of the property transferred to it in consideration for the allotment of shares at a substantial profit. It had undoubtedly received at least money or money's worth equal in value, and probably exceeding in value, the aggregate of the nominal value of the shares and any premium.

This can be contrasted with *Systems Control plc v Munro Corporate plc* [1990] BCLC 659, where the court said there was no prospect of relief being granted when there was absolutely no evidence that the company had received the minimum amount; and *Re Bradford Investments plc (No 2)* [1991] BCLC 688, where the applicants failed to discharge the burden of showing that the company had received value for the shares.

S 113(6), (7)

These provisions allow the court to make appropriate adjustments between the liabilities of the allottee and a subsequent holder.

S 113(8)

Transfer of non-cash assets in initial period   The preceding provisions have been concerned to exempt parties from liabilities with respect to payment for shares. This provision applies where a person is liable as a result of the transfer to a public company of a non-cash asset in the initial period (restrictions on such transfers are contained in s 104) which need not involve any allotment of shares; where it does not, the liability in consequence arises under s 105(2) and this provision allows the court to grant relief in such cases.

114. Penalty for contravention

If a company contravenes any of the provisions of sections 99 to 104 and 106 the company and any officer of it who is in default is liable to a fine.

The application of this provision to a public company is extended to any private company or joint stock company which has passed and not revoked a resolution to re-register or register, as the case may be, as a public company, see note to s 116.

As to penalties, see s 730, Sch 24; 'officer in default' is defined in s 730(5).

115. Undertakings to do work, etc

(1)   Subject to section 113, an undertaking given by any person, in or in connection with payment for shares in a company, to do work or perform services or to do any other thing, if it is enforceable by the company apart from this Act, is so enforceable notwithstanding that there has been a contravention in relation to it of section 99, 102 or 103.

(2)   Where such an undertaking is given in contravention of section 104 in respect of the allotment of shares, it is so enforceable notwithstanding the contravention.

General note

The application of this provision to a public company is extended to any private company or joint stock company which has passed and not revoked a resolution to re-register or register, as the case may be, as a public company: see note to s 116.

S 115(1)

This provision is not restricted to undertakings to do work or perform services but includes any undertaking 'to do any other thing'. It is subject to s 113, which allows the court to grant relief from liability in certain circumstances.

S 115(2)

Section 105(2), (3) generally render agreements contravening s 104 (transfers of non-cash assets to a public company in the initial period) void, so far as not carried out, save where the agreement involves an allotment of shares. This provision permits the enforcement of any undertaking in respect of such an allotment, despite the breach of s 104.

116. Application of ss 99 ff to special cases

Except as provided by section 9 of the Consequential Provisions Act (transitional cases dealt with by section 31 of the Companies Act 1980), sections 99, 101 to 103, 106, 108, 110, 111 and 112 to 115 apply—

(a) to a company which has passed and not revoked a resolution to be re-registered under section 43 as a public company, and

(b) to a joint stock company which has passed, and not revoked, a resolution that the company be a public company,

as those sections apply to a public company.

General note

This provision is linked to the requirements for re-registration (or registration in the case of a joint stock company) as a public company.

Background   Where a private company decides to re-register as a public company, the process is governed by ss 43–48, which contain rules designed to ensure that the share capital requirements imposed on public companies are met by companies seeking to re-register in this way. As part of the application for re-registration, the auditors, for example, must state that at the balance sheet date, a date not more than seven months before the company's application, the company's net assets are not less than the aggregate of its called-up share capital and undistributable reserves: s 43(3)(b). Section 44 imposes certain share payment rules where the company purports to allot any shares for a non-cash consideration between that balance sheet date and the date of the passing of the special resolution seeking re-registration as a public company. These requirements ensure that the company cannot devalue the auditors' statement by allotting shares for dubious consideration during that period.

Scope of this provision   This provision in turn deals with the period subsequent to the passing of the resolution for re-registration and applies the rules applicable to public companies to the company seeking re-registration, again to ensure that allotments for dubious consideration cannot take place in the period between the resolution for re-registration being passed and the company being re-registered as a public company.

The provision likewise applies these rules to a joint stock company (defined in s 683) seeking registration as a public company which too is subject to s 44 (see s 685(2)). The transitional provision is now spent.

PART V

SHARE CAPITAL, ITS INCREASE, MAINTENANCE AND REDUCTION

CHAPTER I

GENERAL PROVISIONS ABOUT SHARE CAPITAL

117. Public company share capital requirements

(1) A company registered as a public company on its original incorporation shall not do business or exercise any borrowing powers unless the registrar of companies has issued it with a certificate under this section or the company is re-registered as a private company.

(2) The registrar shall issue a company with such a certificate if, on an application made to him by the company in the prescribed form, he is satisfied that the nominal value of the company's allotted share capital is not less than the authorised minimum, and there is delivered to him a statutory declaration complying with the following subsection. This subsection is subject to subsection (3A).

(3) The statutory declaration must be in the prescribed form and be signed by a director or secretary of the company; and it must—

(a) state that the nominal value of the company's allotted share capital is not less than the authorised minimum;

(b) specify the amount paid up, at the time of the application, on the allotted share capital of the company;

(c) specify the amount, or estimated amount, of the company's preliminary expenses and the persons by whom any of those expenses have been paid or are payable; and

(d) specify any amount or benefit paid or given, or intended to be paid or given, to any promoter of the company, and the consideration for the payment or benefit.

(3A) In place of the statutory declaration referred to in subsection (2), there may be delivered to the registrar of companies using electronic communications a statement made by a director or secretary of the company complying with the requirements of subsection (3)(a) to (d).

(4) For the purposes of subsection (2), a share allotted in pursuance of an employees' share scheme may not be taken into account in determining the nominal value of the company's allotted share capital unless it is paid up at least as to one-quarter of the nominal value of the share and the whole of any premium on the share.

(5) The registrar may accept a statutory declaration or statement delivered to him under this section as sufficient evidence of the matters stated in it.

(6) A certificate under this section in respect of a company is conclusive evidence that the company is entitled to do business and exercise any borrowing powers.

(7) If a company does business or exercises borrowing powers in contravention of this section, the company and any officer of it who is in default is liable to a fine.

(7A) Any person who makes a false statement under subsection (3A) which he knows to be false or does not believe to be true is liable to imprisonment or a fine, or both.

(8) Nothing in this section affects the validity of any transaction entered into by a company; but, if a company enters into a transaction in contravention of

this section and fails to comply with its obligations in that connection within 21 days from being called upon to do so, the directors of the company are jointly and severally liable to indemnify the other party to the transaction in respect of any loss or damage suffered by him by reason of the company's failure to comply with those obligations.

General note

If a public company subsequently reduces its share capital such that it falls beneath the authorised minimum required by this provision, it will be required to re-register as a private company (under ss 53–55): s 139; likewise, on the occurrence of any of the matters specified in s 146. An omission from any such requirement for re-registration is where a company redeems or purchases its shares (see ss 160(4), 162(2)) to such an extent that it falls below the minimum amount; as the company is able to issue shares up to the amount of the shares redeemed or purchased (s 160(5)), the expectation would be that a public company would so act to bring its allotted capital back up to the minimum amount. Even if it does not, it retains its status as a public company and cannot avail of any of the exemptions available for private companies (for example, re accounting requirements).

See s 104 as to certain transfers of assets to a public company in the two years following the issue of the trading certificate required by this provision.

A false representation as to the capital position for the purpose of securing this certificate is grounds for disqualification under the Company Directors Disqualification Act 1986: see *Re Kaytech International plc, Secretary of State for Trade and Industry v Kaczer* [1999] 2 BCLC 351 at 363.

S 117(1)

Public companies formed as such This provision applies to a public company formed as such and is of limited significance since most public companies are formed as private companies and re-register (under s 43) as public companies to avoid the inconvenience of requiring a trading certificate under this provision. Where a private company re-registers as a public company, these conditions as to share capital must be satisfied at the time that the company resolves on the re-registration (ss 43, 45(1), (2)) so avoiding any time gap between re-registering and commencing trading.

If a public company formed as such does not secure the required certificate within one year of incorporation, it may be wound up by the court: IA 1986, s 122(1)(b). Re-registration of a public company as a private company is governed by s 53.

S 117(2)

The authorised minimum is £50,000: s 118. As to when share capital is allotted, see s 738(1).

S 117(3)

Contents of the statutory declaration or statement   Shares allotted by a public company must be paid up as to one quarter of their nominal value and the whole of any premium (s 101(1)); subject to an exception for shares allotted in accordance with an employees' share scheme which need not be so paid up (s 101(2)); but note sub-s (4) below. A return of allotments must be delivered to the registrar of companies within one month of the allotment: s 88(2).

There is no definition of 'promoter' in the legislation but the courts have considered the issue on many occasions in the older cases. The term 'promoter' is 'a short and convenient way of designating those who set in motion the machinery by which the [Companies] Act enables them to create an incorporated company': *Erlanger v New Sombrero Phosphate Co* (1878) 3 App Cas 1218 at 1268, per Lord Blackburn, HL. It is someone who 'undertakes to form a company with reference to a given project and to set it going, and who takes the necessary steps to accomplish that purpose': *Twycross v Grant* (1877) 2 CPD 469 at 541, per Cockburn CJ, CA.

The receipt of the statutory declaration under this provision must be gazetted by the registrar of companies: s 711(1)(g).

S 117(3A)

This provision was inserted by the Companies Act 1985 (Electronic Communications) Order 2000, SI 2000/3373, art 9(1),(3), as from 22 December 2000; and it facilitates the acceptance by the registrar of companies of electronic statements as to certain matters in the same manner as he accepts statutory declarations as to those matters. As to the delivery of documents to the registrar using electronic communications, see s 707B.

S 117(4)

As to the meaning of 'employees' share scheme', see s 743. The effect of this provision is that shares allotted under such a scheme which need not be paid up to the required amount (s 101(1),(2)) cannot be counted towards the authorised minimum unless they are paid up to the extent required.

S 117(5)

See note to s 12(3), above.

S 117(6)

See note to s 13(7), above.

S 117(7)

As to penalties, see s 730, Sch 24; 'officer in default' is defined in s 730(5).

S 117(7A)

This provision was inserted by the Companies Act 1985 (Electronic Communications) Order 2000, SI 2000/3373, art 9(1),(5), as from 22 December 2000; as to penalties, see s 730, Sch 24; the intention is to provide the same penalties for false statements as is provided by the Perjury Act 1911 for false statutory declarations.

S 117(8)

Validity of the transaction   Any transaction entered into by a public company when it does not have a trading certificate is not affected by the contravention and remains valid.

Directors' liabilities   The directors may incur personal liability although the wording of the provision is obscure on this point. It renders the directors jointly and severally liable if the company enters into a transaction without a trading certificate (or being re-registered) and fails to comply with its obligations 'in that connection' within 21 days of being called upon to do so.

It is not clear whether this is a reference to its obligations in connection with s 117 (ie to obtain a certificate or re-register) or its obligations under the transaction. If the former, it means that a third party can call on the company to obtain a certificate or re-register and the directors are liable for any loss arising from the company's failure to do so, which loss would be difficult to quantify. If the latter, it means that a third party, having discovered that the company does not have a trading certificate, can call on the company to perform its contractual obligations within 21 days (which makes sense given that the third party will now have doubts about the financial basis of the company) and renders the directors personally liable for any loss arising, should the company fail to honour its obligations under the transaction.

Essentially, the choice is between a narrow and a broad interpretation. The latter broad interpretation, although not without its difficulties (for example, as to whether the third party can call for performance although the time specified for performance in the contract has not arrived: it would seem so), is favourable to third parties and more likely to be effective in deterring directors from trading without the required certificate.

---

118. The authorised minimum

(1) In this Act, 'the authorised minimum' means £50,000, or such other sum as the Secretary of State may by order made by statutory instrument specify instead.

(2) An order under this section which increases the authorised minimum may—

    (a) require any public company having an allotted share capital of which the nominal value is less than the amount specified in the order as the authorised minimum to increase that value to not less than that amount or make application to be re-registered as a private company;

    (b) make, in connection with any such requirement, provision for any of the matters from which provision is made by this Act relating to a company's registration, re-registration or change of name, to payment for any share comprised in a company's capital and to offers of shares in or debentures of a company to the public, including provision as to the consequences (whether in criminal law or otherwise) of a failure to comply with any requirement of the order; and

(c) contain such supplemental and transitional provisions as the Secretary of State thinks appropriate, make different provision for different cases and, in particular, provide for any provision of the order to come into operation on different days for different purposes.

(3) An order shall not be made under this section unless a draft of it has been laid before Parliament and approved by resolution of each House.

General note

Despite the power to alter this figure, the minimum figure remains at the level set in 1980.

S 118(1)

Sterling required   While a company has general freedom to denominate its share capital in any currency or currencies, it would seem, in view of the statutory statement, that a public company must have the authorised minimum amount denominated in sterling: see *Re Scandinavian Bank Group plc* [1987] BCLC 220; although the point is not without difficulty.

119. Provision for different amounts to be paid on shares

A company, if so authorised by its articles, may do any one or more of the following things—

(a) make arrangements on the issue of shares for a difference between the shareholders in the amounts and times of payment of calls on their shares;

(b) accept from any member the whole or a part of the amount remaining unpaid on any shares held by him, although no part of that amount has been called up;

(c) pay dividend in proportion to the amount paid up on each share where a larger amount is paid up on some shares than on others.

General note

This provision is of limited significance now given that most shares are issued fully paid up.

Para (a)   See Table A, reg 17; as to calls generally, see regs 12–22.

Para (b)   There is no current provision for the acceptance of such advances on calls in Table A (reflecting the obsolescence of this provision) although the 1948 Table A, reg 21, did so provide. Such payments in advance are made by way of loan to the company by the member and the articles, as in 1948 Table A, reg 21, may make provision for the payment of interest on such amounts.

Para (c)   See Table A, reg 104.

120. Reserve liability of limited company

A limited company may by special resolution determine that any portion of its share capital which has not been already called up shall not be capable of being called up except in the event and for the purposes of the company being wound up; and that portion of its share capital is then not capable of being called up except in that event and for those purposes.

General note

Setting aside reserve capital in this way is rare today. Where a company does have such capital, the company has no power to create any charge on it: *Re Mayfair Property Co* [1898] 2 Ch 28. As to a special resolution, see s 378; 'called-up share capital' and 'uncalled capital' are defined in s 737. As to the reserve liability of unlimited companies, see s 124.

121. Alteration of share capital (limited companies)

(1)   A company limited by shares or a company limited by guarantee and having a share capital, if so authorised by its articles, may alter the conditions of its memorandum in any of the following ways.

(2)   The company may—

    (a)   increase its share capital by new shares of such amount as it thinks expedient;

    (b)   consolidate and divide all or any of its share capital into shares of larger amount than its existing shares;

    (c)   convert all or any of its paid-up shares into stock, and re-convert that stock into paid-up shares of any denomination;

    (d)   sub-divide its shares, or any of them, into shares of smaller amount than is fixed by the memorandum (but subject to the following subsection);

    (e)   cancel shares which, at the date of the passing of the resolution to cancel them, have not been taken or agreed to be taken by any person, and diminish the amount of the company's share capital by the amount of the shares so cancelled.

(3)   In any sub-division under subsection (2)(d) the proportion between the amount paid and the amount, if any, unpaid on each reduced share must be the same as it was in the case of the share from which the reduced share is derived.

(4)   The powers conferred by this section must be exercised by the company in general meeting.

(5)   A cancellation of shares under this section does not for purposes of this Act constitute a reduction of share capital.

General note

The amount of a company's share capital (its authorised or nominal share capital) and its division into shares of a fixed amount are set out on incorporation in the company's memorandum of association (s 2(5)(a)); and are unalterable save to the extent for which express provision is made by the Companies Act 1985: s 2(7).

Any provision in the articles purporting to fetter the power of the company to exercise these statutory powers is void, although shareholders may reach an agreement, apart from the articles, as to how they would exercise their voting rights on any resolution to alter capital in any of the permitted ways: *Russell v Northern Bank Development Corpn Ltd* [1992] 3 All ER 161, HL. The company must not be a party to the shareholders' agreement: *Russell*.

S 121(1)

Authorisation in the articles is required, see Table A, reg 32. Companies limited by guarantee with a share capital can no longer be formed: s 1(4). For unlimited companies with a share capital, see Companies (Tables A–F) Regulations 1985, SI 1985/805, as amended, Table E.

S 121(2),(3), (5)

Multiple alterations   It is common and permissible for a company to provide for two or more of these alterations to take place although subsequent elements of the re-organisation of capital are necessarily conditional on other steps occurring, as where capital is increased first and then consolidated or subdivided. The resolution relating to consolidation in that case is conditional on the increase occurring but is nonetheless valid: see *Re Tip-Europe Ltd* [1988] BCLC 231; *Re Castiglione, Erskine & Co Ltd* [1958] 2 All ER 455.

Redenomination of capital   While this provision provides for a variety of possible alterations of share capital, it does not provide for the redenomination of any shares from one currency to another, for example, from sterling to euros. One method of effecting such a redenomination is to reduce the capital denominated in sterling (under s 135) and then to issue fresh shares denominated in euros but this is a costly and time consuming process. As an alternative, a company could issue a new class of shares denominated in euros alongside the existing class denominated in sterling. The Department of Trade and Industry is considering the introduction of a more straightforward procedure which would facilitate redenomination.

Increasing the capital   Increasing the company's authorised share capital, so lifting the ceiling imposed by the terms of the memorandum, is a common alteration. The passing of a resolution to increase the authorised share capital does not operate as a grant of authority to the directors to proceed to allot those shares. Authority to allot is a separate matter: see s 80.

Consolidation   It is possible to consolidate shares, ie to combine a number of shares into a new share of commensurate nominal value, thus ten £1 shares may be consolidated into one £10 share. This process is less common now, as investors prefer shares of lower rather than higher nominal value, but it is sometimes used as an element of a capital re-arrangement scheme where that scheme has left the company with shares of an unwieldy nominal value, so 12.5p shares may be consolidated into 50p or £1 shares. See Table A, reg 33, which deals with the situation where fractions of shares remain after consolidation. Before proceeding with a consolidation, the impact which any re-organisation of the capital might have on any outstanding share options should be considered: see *Forsayth Oil and Gas NL v Livia Pty Ltd* [1985] BCLC 378.

Conversion into stock   Stock cannot be issued directly by the company but arises from a conversion of fully paid shares into stock: see *Re Home and Foreign Investment and Agency Co Ltd* [1912] 1 Ch 72. This provision is of limited significance for it is rare now for companies to convert shares into stock; indeed, no provision for conversion is included in Table A, see reg 32. For the purposes of the Act, 'shares' includes 'stock': s 744.

Sub-division of shares   Sub-division is quite a common process and involves dividing a share into a number of new shares. It is usually done to increase the marketability of shares where companies feel their nominal value is too high, so a £1 share may be subdivided in four 25p shares or ten 10p shares. See also sub-s (3).

Cancellation of unissued shares   The only effect of cancellation of authorised but unissued share capital is to reduce the scope for issuing further shares, but power to do so can be restored at any time by increasing the share capital again under sub-s (2)(a) above.

The requirement that the shares have not been 'taken or agreed to be taken' will exclude shares which have been issued ('taken') or shares which have been allotted under a binding contract ('agreed to be taken': see s 738(1)). Shares are not 'agreed to be taken' where a prospective purchaser has offered to the company to take the shares but the company has not accepted the offer: *Re Swindon Town Football Club* [1990] BCLC 467.

A cancellation of unissued capital in this way must be distinguished from a reduction of capital, see sub-s (5). A reduction of issued capital may have implications for a company's creditors, whereas a cancellation of capital not yet taken up or agreed to be taken up has no effect on creditors. Given its limited significance, this power is rarely used other than as part of an overall scheme of reconstruction.

Where cancellation, or any other re-organisation as is permitted by this provision, is carried out as part of a reduction of capital, it should be treated as done as part of the scheme of reduction (see s 135 et seq) and not as a separate matter under s 121: *Re Castiglione, Erskine & Co Ltd* [1958] 2 All ER 455.

Notification   Notification to the registrar of companies of any alteration under sub-s (2)(a) is governed by s 123; notification of any alteration under sub-s (2)(b)–(e) is governed by s 122; and a copy of the memorandum of association as altered must also be delivered to the registrar of companies: s 18(2).

S 121(4)

Ordinary resolution   Although only an ordinary resolution is required, it must be notified to the registrar under s 123.

Written resolution   In the case of a private company, a written resolution may be used: see s 381A. It would seem that a public company, even if it was feasible, cannot use a written resolution in view of the doubts expressed in *Re Barry Artists Ltd* [1985] BCLC 283 as to whether a written resolution, in the absence of a statutory authorisation as in s 381A, could override a statutory procedure based on the need for a meeting and a resolution. See notes to s 381A(6) and s 381C, below.

Informal unanimous consent   Informal unanimous consent would suffice, with the shareholders being entitled to waive the protection afforded to them by this provision: *Wright v Atlas Wright (Europe) Ltd* [1999] 2 BCLC 301, CA.

Direct effect   This provision is derived from Art 25(1) of the Second EC Company Law Directive (EEC) 77/91 (OJ L 26/97 p 1), which article is unconditional and sufficiently precise to be relied on and invoked by an individual against the state: *Karella v Minister of Industry, Energy and Technology*: Cases C-19, 20/90 [1994] 1 BCLC 774 (Greek administrative authorities purported to exercise the power to increase the share capital of a company which the authorities had taken over). It would defeat the protective purpose of the provision if the member states were entitled administratively, even in exceptional cases, to effect an increase in the company's capital which would have the effect either of obliging the original shareholders to increase their contributions to the capital or of imposing on them the addition of new shareholders, thus reducing their involvement in the decision-taking power of the company.

122. Notice to registrar of alteration

(1)   If a company having a share capital has—

    (a)   consolidated and divided its share capital into shares of larger amount than its existing shares; or

    (b)   converted any shares into stock; or

    (c)   re-converted stock into shares; or

    (d)   sub-divided its shares or any of them; or

    (e)   redeemed any redeemable shares; or

    (f)   cancelled any shares (otherwise than in connection with a reduction of share capital under section 135),

it shall within one month after so doing give notice in the prescribed form to the registrar of companies, specifying (as the case may be) the shares consolidated, divided, converted, sub-divided, redeemed or cancelled, or the stock re-converted.

(2)   If default is made in complying with this section, the company and every officer of it who is in default is liable to a fine and, for continued contravention, to a daily default fine.

S 122(1)

Any matter notified which makes or evidences an alteration in the company's memorandum or articles of association must be gazetted by the registrar of companies: s 711(1)(b); matters notified under sub-s (1)(e) must be gazetted under s 711(1)(h); the redemption of redeemable shares is governed by ss 159–160; sub-s (1)(f) is broader than cancellations under s 121(2)(e) and would include cancellations of capital arising under s 146 or on a purchase of a company's own shares: see ss 160 and 162. It would also apply to reductions of capital (and consequent cancellations) under ss 5(5), 54(6) and 461(2).

S 122(2)

As to penalties, see s 730, Sch 24; 'officer in default' is defined in s 730(5).

123. Notice to registrar of increased share capital

(1)   If a company having a share capital (whether or not its shares have been converted into stock) increases its share capital beyond the registered capital, it shall within 15 days after the passing of the resolution authorising the increase, give to the registrar of companies notice of the increase, and the registrar shall record the increase.

(2)   The notice must include such particulars as may be prescribed with respect to the classes of shares affected and the conditions subject to which the new shares have been or are to be issued.

(3)   There shall be forwarded to the registrar together with the notice a printed copy of the resolution authorising the increase, or a copy of the resolution in some other form approved by the registrar.

(4)   If default is made in complying with this section, the company and every officer of it who is in default is liable to a fine and, for continued contravention, to a daily default fine.

S 123(1), (3)

The notification required by this provision is of an increase in the authorised (or registered, as it is called here) capital under s 121(2)(a); an increase in issued capital will be notified via the return of allotments under s 88. As the increase in the authorised capital is an alteration of the memorandum, a copy of the memorandum as altered must also be delivered to the registrar: s 18(2).

The registration of an ordinary resolution is not usually called for (see s 380) but is required here because this resolution involves an alteration to the company's constitution.

S 123(2)

There is an element of overlap between this provision and s 128.

S 123(4)

As to penalties, see s 730, Sch 24; 'officer in default' is defined in s 730(5).

124. Reserve capital of unlimited company

An unlimited company having a share capital may by its resolution for re-registration as a public company under section 43, or as a limited company under section 51—

  (a) increase the nominal amount of its share capital by increasing the nominal amount of each of its shares (but subject to the condition that no part of the increased capital is to be capable of being called up except in the event and for the purpose of the company being wound up), and

  (b) alternatively or in addition, provide that a specified portion of its uncalled share capital is not to be capable of being called up except in that event and for that purpose.

General note

This provision mirrors s 120, which permits limited companies to create a reserve capital of this nature. This provision allows for such reserve capital to be created either by creating partly paid shares where the balance will only be paid in the specified circumstances or by designating existing uncalled capital. For all companies, such capital is rare today. 'Called-up share capital' and 'uncalled capital' are defined in s 737.

CHAPTER II

CLASS RIGHTS

125. Variation of class rights

(1)   This section is concerned with the variation of the rights attached to any class of shares in a company whose share capital is divided into shares of different classes.

(2)   Where the rights are attached to a class of shares otherwise than by the company's memorandum, and the company's articles do not contain provision with respect to the variation of the rights, those rights may be varied if, but only if—

  (a)   the holders of three-quarters in nominal value of the issued shares of that class consent in writing to the variation; or

  (b)   an extraordinary resolution passed at a separate general meeting of the holders of that class sanctions the variation;

and any requirement (howsoever imposed) in relation to the variation of those rights is complied with to the extent that it is not comprised in paragraphs (a) and (b) above.

(3)   Where—

  (a)   the rights are attached to a class of shares by the memorandum or otherwise;

  (b)   the memorandum or articles contain provision for the variation of those rights; and

  (c)   the variation of those rights is connected with the giving, variation, revocation or renewal of an authority for allotment under section 80 or with a reduction of the company's share capital under section 135;

those rights shall not be varied unless—

  (i)   the condition mentioned in subsection (2)(a) or (b) above is satisfied; and

  (ii)   any requirement of the memorandum or articles in relation to the variation of rights of that class is complied with to the extent that it is not comprised in that condition.

(4)   If the rights are attached to a class of shares in the company by the memorandum or otherwise and—

  (a)   where they are so attached by the memorandum, the articles contain provision with respect to their variation which had been included in the articles at the time of the company's original incorporation; or

  (b)   where they are so attached otherwise, the articles contain such provision (whenever first so included),

and in either case the variation is not connected as mentioned in subsection (3)(c), those rights may only be varied in accordance with that provision of the articles.

(5)   If the rights are attached to a class of shares by the memorandum, and the memorandum and articles do not contain provision with respect to the variation of those rights, those rights may be varied if all the members of the company agree to the variation.

(6)   The provisions of section 369 (length of notice for calling company meetings), section 370 (general provisions as to meetings and votes), and

sections 376 and 377 (circulation of members' resolutions) and the provisions of the articles relating to general meetings shall, so far as applicable, apply in relation to any meeting of shareholders required by this section or otherwise to take place in connection with the variation of the rights attached to a class of shares, and shall so apply with the necessary modifications and subject to the following provisions, namely—

    (a) the necessary quorum at any such meeting other than an adjourned meeting shall be two persons holding or representing by proxy at least one-third in nominal value of the issued shares of the class in question and at an adjourned meeting one person holding shares of the class in question or his proxy;

    (b) any holder of shares of the class in question present in person or by proxy may demand a poll.

(7) Any alteration of a provision contained in a company's articles for the variation of the rights attached to a class of shares, or the insertion of any such provision into the articles, is itself to be treated as a variation of those rights.

(8) In this section and (except where the context otherwise requires) in any provision for the variation of the rights attached to a class of shares contained in a company's memorandum or articles, references to the variation of those rights are to be read as including references to their abrogation.

General note

The statutory scheme in this section is intended to provide a comprehensive code setting out the manner in which rights attached to any class of shares can be varied: *Cumbrian Newspapers Group Ltd v Cumberland & Westmorland Herald Newspaper & Printing Co Ltd* [1986] 2 All ER 816 at 824, per Scott J.

    These complicated provisions set out a number of permutations which depend on:

    (1) the origin of the class rights (ie whether they are contained in the memorandum or articles or elsewhere); and

    (2) whether any specific provision has been made for their alteration.

Typically, the articles will provide that the variation of class rights requires the consent of the holders of three-quarters in nominal value of the issued shares of that class in writing or an extraordinary resolution (see s 378) of the class approving the variation at a separate class meeting (and see s 125(4)).

Protective device   The value of a class right is that the section operates to protect those rights against variation or abrogation by a mere alteration of the articles under s 9. A class right can therefore be a valuable element in the protection of minority shareholders or any other special interests.

Class rights   Rights are typically described as class rights when they relate to matters such as voting rights, rights to dividends and rights to a return of capital on a winding up and are 'attached to any class of shares' such that the rights enjoyed by the holders of those shares are not enjoyed by the holders of other shares. Where all the shares in a company fall within the one class, there are no class rights, only shareholder rights.

The concept of rights 'attached to any class of shares' also includes rights conferred on a member of the company in his capacity as a member which rights are not attached to any particular class of shares: *Cumbrian Newspaper Group Ltd v Cumberland & Westmorland Herald Newspaper & Printing Co Ltd* [1986] 2 All ER 816 (the plaintiff shareholder had been given by name certain rights of pre-emption and the right to appoint a director and to transfer shares). In that case, Scott J concluded (at 830):

'For the purposes of s 125, the share capital of a company is, in my judgment, divided into shares of different classes, if shareholders, qua shareholders, enjoy different rights . . . a company which, by its articles, confers special rights on one or more of its members in the capacity of member or shareholder thereby constitutes the shares for the time being held by that member or members a class of shares for the purposes of s 125. The rights are class rights.'

Cf *Re Blue Arrow plc* [1987] BCLC 585 at 590 (a right conferred on an individual not as a member of the company and unrelated to any shareholding in any way cannot be described as a class right).

The fact that the rights are attached to shares issued to a named individual and which might terminate on the transfer of the shares by that person would not of itself prevent the rights, pre-alienation, from being described as class rights: *Cumbrian Newspapers Group Ltd v Cumberland & Westmorland Herald Newspaper & Printing Co Ltd* [1986] 2 All ER 816 at 825.

Setting out class rights   Class rights may be set out in the memorandum or articles or in the resolution creating them (which might be a resolution of the board or of the general meeting). In practice, they are usually set out in the articles. The express attachment of any rights to a share is, prima facie, a defection of the whole of the rights in that respect: *Re National Telephone Co* [1914] 1 Ch 755. In any case of conflict between provisions in the memorandum and rights sets out in the articles or in the resolution authorising the issue, the memorandum prevails: *Guinness v Land Corpn of Ireland Ltd* (1882) 22 Ch D 349, CA. A shareholders' agreement signed by all the shareholders attaching rights to shares must be taken to have the same effect as if the rights had been set out as class rights in the articles: *Harman v BML Group Ltd* [1994] 2 BCLC 674, CA. As to whether such an agreement might need to be registered with the registrar of companies, see the note to s 128(1) and also note to s 380(4).

Where a company has more than one class of issued shares or more than one class of members (in the case of a company which does not have share capital), information as to the class of shares or membership must be included in the register of members: s 352(3)(a)(i), (4). The annual return of a company with share capital must also contain information as to the nature of each class of shares and the membership of the class: see s 364A(3), (5). See also s 128.

S 125(1)

Companies limited by guarantee without a share capital   This provision applies only to companies with share capital so companies limited by guarantee which, since 22 December 1980, cannot be formed with a share capital (s 1(4)) but which may have different classes of members (for example, with different voting rights) are not within the provision. For such companies, the question of the variation of the members' rights will depend to a large extent on whether provision has been made, either in the memorandum or articles, for their variation.

If class rights have been set out in the memorandum and it is contemplated by the provision in the memorandum that those class rights might be varied by a provision for variation contained in the articles filed contemporaneously with the memorandum, then the provision in the articles will apply: *Re Welsbach Incandescent Gas Light Co Ltd* [1904] 1 Ch 87. If class rights have been set out in the memorandum and there is no provision for variation of the class rights in the memorandum or in the articles filed contemporaneously with the memorandum, then a scheme of arrangement would be required under s 425 to alter those rights or, by analogy with sub-s (5), the consent of all of the members of the company would be required.

If the class rights are set out in the articles and the articles make provision for variation, the class rights can be altered only by adhering to the provision in the articles, applying s 14. If the class rights are set out in the articles and the articles make no provision for variation, it would seem that the class rights can be altered in the same manner as the articles, ie by special resolution of the general meeting under s 9.

Rights are varied or abrogated   The protection of the statutory provision only applies where the rights are varied or abrogated (see sub-s (8)); and the insertion or variation of a variation provision in the articles is itself a variation (see sub-s (7)). In *Re House of Fraser plc* [1987] BCLC 293 at 301 the Court of Session thought that 'variation' presupposes the continuance of rights in a varied state, while 'abrogation' presupposes termination of rights without satisfaction or fulfilment.

Judicial interpretation   The courts have restricted the application of the section by interpreting 'variation' and 'abrogation' quite narrowly. The courts have drawn a key distinction between matters affecting the rights attaching to each share (which *do* amount to a variation or abrogation of class rights) and matters affecting the shareholders as a matter of business in the enjoyment of those rights (which *do not* amount to a variation or abrogation). Where only the enjoyment of the rights is affected, the shares may be commercially less valuable but the rights remain what they always were: *White v Bristol Aeroplane Co Ltd* [1953] Ch 65, CA; *Re John Smith's Tadcaster Brewery Co Ltd* [1953] 1 All ER 518, CA; *Greenhalgh v Arderne Cinemas Ltd* [1946] 1 All ER 512, CA.

Dilution   An issue of further preference shares which will dilute the control of the existing preference shareholders does not amount to a variation of class rights, for the rights of the existing shareholders remain exactly as they were before although the enjoyment of those rights might be affected: *White v Bristol Aeroplane Co Ltd* [1953] Ch 65, CA. A subdivision of shares to rank pari passu with and form one class with an existing class likewise does not amount to a variation or abrogation of those class rights, for the rights of the existing shareholders remain exactly what they always were although affected as a matter of business: *Greenhalgh v Arderne Cinemas Ltd* [1946] 1 All ER 512, CA.

Reduction of capital   A scheme for the reduction of capital (see s 135) which involves paying off the preference shareholders is a fulfilment and not a variation of the rights of a preference shareholder, where the reduction is consistent with the preference shareholders' rights as to a prior return of capital on a winding up: see *Re Floating Dock Co of St Thomas Ltd* [1895] 1 Ch 691; *Re Chatterley-Whitfield Collieries Ltd* [1948] 2 All ER 593, affd sub nom *Prudential Assurance Co Ltd v Chatterley Whitfield Collieries Ltd* [1949] AC 512, HL; *Wilsons and Clyde Coal Co Ltd v Scottish Insurance Corpn* 1948 SC 360, Ct of Sess; affd sub nom *Scottish Insurance Corpn Ltd v Wilsons and Clyde Coal Co Ltd* [1949] AC 462, HL; *Re Saltdean Estate Co Ltd* [1968] 3 All ER 829; *House of Fraser v ACGE Investments Ltd* [1987] BCLC 478, affg [1987] BCLC 293. This is so even if the preference shareholders are participating as to surplus while the company is a going concern: *Re Saltdean Estate Co Ltd* [1968] 3 All ER 829;

and, possibly, even if they are participating as to surplus on a winding up, at least if winding up is not imminent: *Re William Jones & Son Ltd* [1969] 1 WLR 146; cf *Re Old Silkstone Collieries Ltd* [1954] Ch 169.

Where preference shareholders have no priority on a return of capital on a winding up, a rateable reduction of capital on all shares, preference and ordinary, though diminishing the actual preference dividend, is not a variation of the rights of the preference shareholders so as to require their consent and is not unfair or inequitable so that the court might refuse confirmation: *Re Mackenzie & Co Ltd* [1916] 2 Ch 450; *Bannatyne v Direct Spanish Telegraph Company* (1886) 34 Ch D 287.

Provisions in the articles   An equally strict approach is taken to equivalent variation provisions in the articles, even if the provision in drafted in broad terms. For example, a typical provision is that the rights of a class may not be 'affected, modified, varied, dealt with or abrogated in any manner' without the consent of a three-quarters majority of the class: see *White v Bristol Aeroplane Co Ltd* [1953] Ch 65, CA; *Re House of Fraser plc* [1987] BCLC 293. The courts have taken the view that the wording of such provisions must be interpreted in the context in which the wording appears (ie the variation of class rights) and, therefore, these terms, 'modification', 'dealt with', etc, must be taken to refer only to modifications to or dealings with class rights which amount to a variation (including abrogation, see sub-s (8)): see *Re House of Fraser plc* [1987] BCLC 293 at 302, aff'd sub nom *House of Fraser v ACGE Investments Ltd* [1987] BCLC 478 at 484, HL; *Re John Smith's Tadcaster Brewery Co Ltd* [1953] 1 All ER 518.

Express protection required   In view of the narrow construction of 'variation' taken by the courts, it will be appreciated that neither s 125, nor equivalent provisions in the articles, however broadly worded, will protect members of a class against changes having a significant impact on their position. The protection afforded to a class can be enhanced, however, if the articles or terms of issue expressly deem certain matters (for example, a reduction of capital or a further issue of shares of that class, etc) to amount to a variation or abrogation of class rights requiring the consent of the class so limiting the scope for a restrictive interpretation by the court: see *Re Northern Engineering Industries plc* [1994] 2 BCLC 704, CA. The courts will construe such provisions in a manner designed to give effect to their protective purpose: see *Re Northern Engineering Industries plc* [1994] 2 BCLC 704, CA. Matters which are typically so expressed include: any alteration to issued or authorised capital; any redemption or purchase of the company's shares; any reduction of capital; any sale of the whole or any substantial part of the undertaking, property or assets of the company; and the passing of any resolution for winding up.

S 125(2)

Rights not in the memorandum but elsewhere – no provision for variation in the articles   This provision covers the standard situation where the class rights are attached not by the memorandum but by the articles or otherwise (for example, by resolution) and no provision has been made in the articles with respect to their variation. Variation in this instance must be in accordance with this statutory procedure. As Table A does not contain a provision for the variation of class rights, this procedure will frequently apply.

Any additional requirements in relation to the variation of those rights, however imposed (eg by the terms of issue), but not comprised within the statutory scheme must also be adhered to. The scope for additional requirements is very limited, however, given that this provision only applies where the articles do not contain a provision with respect to variation, but it might include, for example, requirements concerning additional notice of any proposed resolution.

While the provision envisages either class consent in writing or at a meeting, informal unanimous consent of the class will be equally effective, applying the *Duomatic* principle: *Re Torvale Group Ltd* [1999] 2 BCLC 605; *Wright v Atlas Wright (Europe) Ltd* [1999] 2 BCLC 301, CA; *Re Duomatic Ltd* [1969] 1 All ER 161.

As to when shares are issued, see note to s 738(1); as to extraordinary resolutions, see s 378(1); and the resolution must be forwarded to the registrar of companies: s 380(1), (4)(b). A private company may use a written resolution: s 381A. As to class meetings, see sub-s (6).

S 125(3)

Specified variations   The only acceptable procedure with respect to variations 'connected with' the matters specified in sub-s (3)(c), where the memorandum or articles have made provision for variation, is the statutory procedure in sub-s (2)(a) or (b). This is the minimum protection for the class which is acceptable with regard to variations of this nature which relate to matters which would be of particular concern to a class of shareholders. It is not always easy to determine whether a variation is 'connected with' an authority given under s 80 so as to require adherence to this provision rather than to what may be a more lax regime under sub-s (4). The fact that a variation is in 'connection with' a reduction of capital is usually clear from the facts.

Any additional requirements, however imposed (eg by the terms of issue) but not comprised within the statutory scheme must also be adhered to, which would entitle the company to increase the required percentages, for example, to 90% or even unanimity, although such requirements would be unusual.

S 125(4)

Rights attached by memorandum or otherwise – variation in the articles   Where the class rights are attached by the memorandum or otherwise and there is a provision for variation in the articles as specified and the variation is not 'connected with' the matters specified in sub-s (3)(c), variation is permitted only in accordance with that variation provision in the articles.

In practice, a variation provision in the articles will often replicate the requirements of sub-s (2) so this provision may make little difference but it does enable companies to adopt a less onerous regime, for example, requiring only the consent of a simple majority of a class or, indeed, dispensing with the consent of the class and requiring only the consent of the shareholders in general meeting; or a company may adopt a more onerous scheme, for example, requiring a higher percentage.

There is a qualification where the rights are attached by the memorandum of association. In that case, the variation procedure must have been contained in the original articles of the company drawn up on incorporation. If there is a variation provision in the articles but it was added to the articles subsequent to incorporation, the provision in the articles cannot apply.

In that situation, it is necessary to resort to sub-s (5) which applies where the rights are attached by the memorandum and the memorandum and articles do not contain provision with respect to the variation of *those* rights. In this case, the articles do not contain provision with respect to the variation of *those* rights, for only the original articles drawn up on incorporation can contain provisions with respect to the variation of *those* rights. Sub-s (5) requires the consent of all the members of the company to the variation. Alternatively, the rights might be varied by a scheme of arrangement under s 425.

S 125(5)

Rights in the memorandum – no provision for variation   Where the rights are contained in the memorandum which, in practice, is rare, and no provision is made in the memorandum or articles for the variation of those rights (and see sub-s (4), a provision inserted later in the articles is ineffective), the agreement of all of the members of the company (not of the class) is required which may be impossible to secure so entrenching these rights to what may prove to be an unacceptable degree. Variation could also be achieved by a scheme of arrangement under s 425. As to who is a member, see s 22.

Rights in the memorandum – prohibition on variation   If the rights are set out in the memorandum and there is an express prohibition on variation in the memorandum (it is not therefore a case where there is no provision 'with respect to the variation of those rights' in the memorandum and so is not within this subsection), the rights cannot be altered except by a scheme of arrangement under s 425. But, as can be seen above, even without an express prohibition, it is possible for the rights to be entrenched simply by including them in the memorandum of association and making no provision for their variation in the original articles of the company.

Relationship with s 17   Section 17 allows, subject to certain restrictions, the alteration of provisions which have been included in the memorandum and which could have been included in the articles but this does not permit the 'variation or abrogation of the special rights of any class of member': s 17(2)(b). The wording of that section differs from that of s 125 ('rights attached to any class of shares') but both phrases must be interpreted in the same manner so that the variation of 'any special rights of any class' should be dealt with under s 125 and not by s 17: *Cumbrian Newspapers Group Ltd v Cumberland & Westmorland Herald Newspaper & Printing Co Ltd* [1986] 2 All ER 816 at 829, per Scott J.

S 125(6)

Class meetings   This provision applies the rules in the specified sections (which apply to general meetings of the shareholders) to class meetings in 'connection with' any variation of class rights; and does so whether the class meeting is required by the section or otherwise, for example, by the articles or terms of issue. 'Variation' is defined by the courts, as noted above under sub-s (1), and as expanded by sub-ss (7), (8). This provision also applies any provisions of the articles relating to general meetings, so far as applicable, to such class meetings. Other provisions governing general meetings are applied expressly to any meeting of any members of a class: see ss 372, 374, 375, 381, 381A.

Quorum and right to demand a poll   The application of the statutory provisions and the articles are subject to two modifications regarding quorum and the right to demand a poll. With regard to quorum, a financial threshold is imposed of one-third in nominal value of the issued shares of the class which might be hard to muster (as to issued capital, see note to s 738(1)) although no such threshold applies to an adjourned meeting. If, in fact, the class consists of only one member, the court may order a class meeting of one under s 371: *East v Bennett Bros Ltd* [1911] 1 Ch 163.

It is sometimes suggested that the requirements of sub-s (6)(a) and (b) only apply when the articles make no provision for class meetings and that they may be overridden by explicit provision on these matters in the articles. The origin of this element of the provision is the 1948 Table A, reg 4. Had it been intended to leave these matters to be determined by companies in their articles, it is unlikely that these provisions would have been removed from Table A to the statute. It seems clear that the intention was to lay down a statutory minimum on these matters which cannot be overridden by express provisions in the articles.

Composition of class meeting   Prima facie, a separate meeting of a class should be attended only by members of the class (although they may consent to the attendance of others and, in the absence of objections, the court will consider that they did so consent): *Carruth v ICI Ltd* [1937] AC 707 (separate meetings of deferred and ordinary shareholders were not held; instead there were separate votes of the classes at the general meeting attended by all shareholders, deferred and ordinary: held valid).

At a class meeting so held, the shareholders must have regard to what is in the best interests of the class: *British America Nickel Corpn v MJ O'Brien Ltd* [1927] AC 369; *Re Holders Investment Trust Ltd* [1971] 2 All ER 289.

S 125(7)

Inserting or deleting a variation provision in the articles   This provision gives a deemed meaning to the term 'variation'. It applies only to provisions in the articles. It causes no problems where the company inserts or deletes such a provision when it has no classes of shares but if the company attempts to insert or delete a variation provision when it has a class of shares, the effect of the provision is to require the consent of the class to the insertion or deletion. If a company deletes a variation of rights clause in the articles while still retaining classes of shares, variation would then be governed by sub-ss (2), (5) above.

S 125(8)

An unusual example of the statute determining the interpretation of words in the company's memorandum and articles of association. It applies 'except where the context otherwise requires'.

---

126. Saving for court's powers under other provisions

Nothing in subsections (2) to (5) of section 125 derogates from the powers of the court under the following sections of this Act, namely—

       sections 4 to 6 (company resolution to alter objects),

       section 54 (litigated objection to public company becoming private by re-registration), section 425 (court control of company compromising with members and creditors),

section 427 (company reconstruction or amalgamation),

sections 459 to 461 (protection of minorities).

General note

The specified provisions give certain powers to the court and this provision ensures that the court's power to act is unaffected by any requirement arising under s 125(2)–(5) to secure class consent.

127. Shareholders' right to object to variation

(1)   This section applies if, in the case of a company whose share capital is divided into different classes of shares—

  (a)   provision is made by the memorandum or articles for authorising the variation of the rights attached to any class of shares in the company, subject to—

    (i)   the consent of any specified proportion of the holders of the issued shares of that class, or

    (ii)   the sanction of a resolution passed at a separate meeting of the holders of those shares,

  and in pursuance of that provision the rights attached to any such class of shares are at any time varied; or

  (b)   the rights attached to any class of shares in the company are varied under section 125(2).

(2)   The holders of not less in the aggregate than 15 per cent of the issued shares of the class in question (being persons who did not consent to or vote in favour of the resolution for the variation), may apply to the court to have the variation cancelled; and if such an application is made, the variation has no effect unless and until it is confirmed by the court.

(3)   Application to the court must be made within 21 days after the date on which the consent was given or the resolution was passed (as the case may be), and may be made on behalf of the shareholders entitled to make the application by such one or more of their number as they may appoint in writing for the purpose.

(4)   The court, after hearing the applicant and any other persons who apply to the court to be heard and appear to the court to be interested in the application, may, if satisfied having regard to all the circumstances of the case, that the variation would unfairly prejudice the shareholders of the class represented by the applicant, disallow the variation and shall, if not satisfied, confirm it.

The decision of the court on any such application is final.

(5)   The company shall within 15 days after the making of an order by the court on such an application forward a copy of the order to the registrar of companies;

and, if default is made in complying with this provision, the company and every officer of it who is in default is liable to a fine and, for continued contravention, to a daily default fine.

(6) 'Variation', in this section, includes abrogation; and 'varied' is to be construed accordingly.

General note

In practice, this provision is rarely used, not least because it is unlikely that a court will overturn a variation which has already been agreed to by a majority of the class. A member of a class who feels aggrieved may prefer to bring a more broadly-based case under the unfairly prejudicial remedy (s 459) which would enable him to seek a personal remedy without the constraints of this provision.

S 127(1)

The provision only applies to variations arising under the specified methods; and only if what has occurred is a 'variation' as defined by the courts and expanded by sub-s (6). See note to s 125(1), above.

S 127(2), (3)

The threshold of 15% is high, given that classes of shares are often to be found in larger companies where the number of issued shares of the class may be considerable. Once an application for cancellation is made, the variation has no effect until confirmed. As to when shares are issued, see note to s 738(1), below.

The applicants must either hold 15% of the shares of the class affected or have been appointed in writing by the holders of 15% at the date of the presentation of the petition and not merely when it comes on for hearing: *Re Sound City (Films) Ltd* [1947] Ch 169; *Re Suburban and Provincial Stores Ltd* [1943] Ch 156.

S 127(4)

The court may hear any person appearing to be interested but its powers are limited to confirming or disallowing the variation. There is no power to modify the variation in any way or to add any terms or conditions to its operation. 'Unfair prejudice' will presumably be defined in the same manner as in s 459; and what must be established is unfair prejudice to the class, not to the applicant alone. The provision ruling out any appeal is unusual.

S 127(5)

As to penalties, see s 730, Sch 24; 'officer in default' is defined in s 730(5).

S 127(6)

In *Re House of Fraser plc* [1987] BCLC 293 at 301, the Court of Session noted that 'variation' presupposes the continuance of rights in a varied state while 'abrogation' presupposes termination of rights without satisfaction or fulfilment.

128. Registration of particulars of special rights

(1)   If a company allots shares with rights which are not stated in its memorandum or articles, or in any resolution or agreement which is required by section 380 to be sent to the registrar of companies, the company shall deliver to the registrar of companies, within one month from allotting the shares, a statement in the prescribed form containing particulars of those rights.

(2)   This does not apply if the shares are in all respects uniform with shares previously allotted; and shares are not for this purpose to be treated as different from shares previously allotted by reason only that the former do not carry the same rights to dividends as the latter during the 12 months immediately following the former's allotment.

(3)   Where the rights attached to any shares of a company are varied otherwise than by an amendment of the company's memorandum or articles or by a resolution or agreement subject to section 380, the company shall within one month from the date on which the variation is made deliver to the registrar of companies a statement in the prescribed form containing particulars of the variation.

(4)   Where a company (otherwise than by any such amendment, resolution or agreement as is mentioned above) assigns a name or other designation, or a new name or other designation, to any class of its shares, it shall within one month from doing so deliver to the registrar of companies a notice in the prescribed form giving particulars of the name or designation so assigned.

(5)   If a company fails to comply with this section, the company and every officer of it who is in default is liable to a fine and, for continued contravention, to a daily default fine.

General note

Where a company without a share capital creates class rights, the position is governed by s 129.

S 128(1)

This provision applies if the company allots shares with rights which would not otherwise be notified to the registrar of companies by virtue of an alteration of the memorandum or the articles or by a resolution or agreement requiring registration under s 380. 'Allotment' is defined in s 738(1). A return of allotment must in any case be made within one month of the allotment under s 88 although that return does not require particulars of the share rights. The existence of classes of shares must also be indicated on the register of members: s 352; and on the annual return, see s 364A(3), (5). The receipt of notification under this provision must be gazetted by the registrar of companies: s 711(1)(j). See also s 123, which requires notification of any increase in *authorised* capital including particulars with respect to the classes of shares affected.

This provision presupposes that class rights are created on allotment by the company but, as *Harman v BML Group Ltd* [1994] 2 BCLC 674, CA, illustrates, class rights can be created by all the shareholders acting together in a shareholders' agreement. In that case, there appears to be no mechanism for the particulars of the rights to be notified to the registrar of companies. The creation of such rights would not fall within this provision, nor is there generally an alteration of the memorandum or articles of association so as to require notification or a resolution or agreement within s 380 requiring registration. To argue for the disclosure of such particulars to the registrar of companies, it would be necessary to treat the shareholders' agreement as an informal alteration of the articles which alteration would require registration: see *Harman v BML Group Ltd* [1994] 2 BCLC 674 at 678; *Cane v Jones* [1981] 1 All ER 533.

S 128(3)

This provision applies to the variation of 'rights attached to any shares' which must be given the same meaning as in s 125 (see general note to that provision). As to when rights are 'varied', see note to s 125(1).

S 128(4)

This requirement is sometimes overlooked.

S 128(5)

As to penalties, see s 730, Sch 24; 'officer in default' is defined in s 730(5).

129. Registration of newly created class rights

(1)   If a company not having a share capital creates a class of members with rights which are not stated in its memorandum or articles or in a resolution or agreement to which section 380 applies, the company shall deliver to the registrar of companies within one month from the date on which the new class is created a statement in the prescribed form containing particulars of the rights attached to that class.

(2)   If the rights of any class of members of the company are varied otherwise than by an amendment of the memorandum or articles or by a resolution or agreement subject to section 380, the company shall within one month from the date on which the variation is made deliver to the registrar a statement in the prescribed form containing particulars of the variation.

(3)   If a company (otherwise than by such an amendment, resolution or agreement as is mentioned above) assigns a name or other designation, or a new name or other designation, to any class of its members, it shall within one month from doing so deliver to the registrar a notice in the prescribed form giving particulars of the name or designation so assigned.

(4)   If a company fails to comply with this section, the company and every officer of it who is in default is liable to a fine and, for continued contravention, to a daily default fine.

General note

These disclosure provisions mirror s 128 but apply to a company limited by guarantee without a share capital or an unlimited company without share capital which nevertheless may have different classes of members, for example, with different voting rights.

S 129(4)

As to penalties, see s 730, Sch 24; 'officer in default' is defined in s 730(5).

CHAPTER III

SHARE PREMIUMS

130. Application of share premiums

(1)   If a company issues shares at a premium, whether for cash or otherwise, a sum equal to the aggregate amount or value of the premiums on those shares shall be transferred to an account called 'the share premium account'.

(2)   The share premium account may be applied by the company in paying up unissued shares to be allotted to members as fully paid bonus shares, or in writing off—

 (a) the company's preliminary expenses; or

 (b) the expenses of, or the commission paid or discount allowed on, any issue of shares or debentures of the company,

or in providing for the premium payable on redemption of debentures of the company.

(3)   Subject to this, the provisions of this Act relating to the reduction of a company's share capital apply as if the share premium account were part of its paid up share capital.

(4)   Sections 131 and 132 below give relief from the requirements of this section, and in those sections references to the issuing company are to the company issuing shares as above mentioned.

S 130(1)

Obtaining a premium   There is no requirement that shares be issued at a premium (ie at more than their nominal value as specified in the memorandum, see s 2(5)(a)) but the directors prima facie must obtain the full value for the shares unless there is good reason not to do so and the expectation would be that shares will be issued at a premium, if that is possible: *Hilder v Dexter* [1902] AC 474 at 480; *Lowry v Consolidated African Selection Trust Ltd* [1940] AC 648 at 679.

Premium on acquisitions   A premium may arise whether the shares are issued for cash or for a non-cash consideration; and a non-cash premium may arise where there is a merger or acquisition of another company funded by a share exchange. The decision in *Henry Head & Co Ltd v Ropner Holdings Ltd* [1951] 2 All ER 994, subsequently followed in *Shearer (Inspector of Taxes) v Bercain Ltd* [1980] 3 All ER 295, confirmed that where the assets acquired exceed the nominal value of the shares issued or transferred, a transfer of the relevant premium to the (undistributable) share premium account was required. The effect of these decisions was to render the pre-acquisition profits of the target company undistributable. That result was thought undesirable and the effect of these decisions has been mitigated by ss 131–134.

S 130(2), (3)

Use of the share premium account   Until CA 1947, the position had been that the company could distribute share premium as a dividend, since it was not share capital:

Drown v Gaumont-British Picture Corpn Ltd [1937] Ch 402. The position now is that share premium is treated in most respects as share capital. It is one of the company's undistributable reserves (s 264(3)) and can be applied only to the extent permitted by this provision, ie for bonus issues (only if fully paid) and for expenses, commissions etc (to the extent permitted by ss 97, 98). In addition, the share premium account may be reduced to the extent specified in ss 160(2), 171(5) (redemption of redeemable shares and purchase by a private company of its own shares out of capital). Apart from these specified matters, any other use of the share premium account must be structured as a reduction of capital: see s 135 et seq.

S 130(4)

This relief is in response to the decisions in *Henry Head & Co Ltd v Ropner Holdings Ltd* [1952] Ch 124 and *Shearer (Inspector of Taxes) v Bercain Ltd* [1980] 3 All ER 295, noted above. The net effect is to allow certain mergers and reconstructions to take place either without a transfer to a share premium account (s 131) or requiring only a limited transfer (s 132), so releasing funds which may be distributed as a dividend.

131. Merger relief

(1) With the exception made by section 132(8) (group reconstruction) this section applies where the issuing company has secured at least a 90 per cent equity holding in another company in pursuance of an arrangement providing for the allotment of equity shares in the issuing company on terms that the consideration for the shares allotted is to be provided—

(a) by the issue or transfer to the issuing company of equity shares in the other company, or

(b) by the cancellation of any such shares not held by the issuing company.

(2) If the equity shares in the issuing company allotted in pursuance of the arrangement in consideration for the acquisition or cancellation of equity shares in the other company are issued at a premium, section 130 does not apply to the premiums on those shares.

(3) Where the arrangement also provides for the allotment of any shares in the issuing company on terms that the consideration for those shares is to be provided by the issue or transfer to the issuing company of non-equity shares in the other company or by the cancellation of any shares in that company not held by the issuing company, relief under subsection (2) extends to any shares in the issuing company allotted on those terms in pursuance of the arrangement.

(4) Subject to the next subsection, the issuing company is to be regarded for purposes of this section as having secured at least a 90 per cent equity holding in another company in pursuance of such an arrangement as is mentioned in subsection (1) if in consequence of an acquisition or cancellation of equity shares in that company (in pursuance of that arrangement) it holds equity shares in that company (whether all or any of those shares were acquired in pursuance

of that arrangement, or not) of an aggregate nominal value equal to 90 per cent or more of the nominal value of that company's equity share capital.

(5)   Where the equity share capital of the other company is divided into different classes of shares, this section does not apply unless the requirements of subsection (1) are satisfied in relation to each of those classes of shares taken separately.

(6)   Shares held by a company which is the issuing company's holding company or subsidiary, or a subsidiary of the issuing company's holding company, or by its or their nominees, are to be regarded for purposes of this section as held by the issuing company.

(7)   In relation to a company and its shares and capital, the following definitions apply for purposes of this section—

(a) 'equity shares' means shares comprised in the company's equity share capital; and

(b) 'non-equity shares' means shares (of any class) not so comprised;

and 'arrangement' means any agreement, scheme or arrangement (including an arrangement sanctioned under section 425 (company compromise with members and creditors) or section 110 of the Insolvency Act (liquidator accepting shares etc as consideration for sale of company property)).

(8)   The relief allowed by this section does not apply if the issue of shares took place before 4th February 1981.

General note

The effect of this provision is to exempt a company from any obligation to make a transfer to the share premium account where the issuing company secures at least a 90% equity holding in another company in pursuance of any arrangement.

A company which can avail of this provision for merger relief may not necessarily meet the conditions for the use of merger accounting which are laid down in Sch 4A, para 10.

S 131(1), (2)

The relief will only arise if the 90% equity holding is acquired 'in pursuance of an arrangement' and the manner of determining whether 90% has been secured is dealt with by sub-ss (4)–(6). Relief is available only when the consideration provided by the target company is as specified although the issuing company may provide consideration in addition to the allotment of equity shares; 'equity shares' and 'non-equity shares' are defined in sub-s (7). Any premium arising from the allotment is not share premium for the purposes of s 130. The definition of 'company', other than 'issuing company', is extended by s 133(4). This provision does not apply to a case falling within s 132: s 132(8).

See also s 133(1), which allows the issuing company to show the shares acquired etc at nominal value in the company's balance sheet so allowing for the pre-acquisition profits of the target to be available for distribution.

The allotment of equity shares need not be to the target company but to a nominee; and the shares acquired need not be acquired by the issuing company but by a nominee: s 133(2).

S 131(3)

Any premium arising on the acquisition on non-equity shares is also exempt if the allotment was in pursuance of the arrangement; 'non-equity shares' is defined in sub-s (7).

S 131(4)–(6)

Calculating the 90% equity holding   In deciding whether the 90% threshold has been achieved:

(1)   it is permissible to count shares already held by the issuing company and not acquired in pursuance of the arrangement, provided that with those acquired in pursuance of the arrangement, the overall total has reached at least 90%;

(2)   where there are different classes of equity share capital, 90% of each class is required (there is no need to secure 90% of non-equity shares);

(3)   shares held by those companies and nominees identified in sub-s (6) count towards the 90% threshold.

S 131(7)

'Equity share capital' is defined in s 744; 'arrangement' can involve a number of separate transactions which together amount to an arrangement.

132. Relief in respect of group reconstructions

(1)   This section applies where the issuing company—

(a)   is a wholly-owned subsidiary of another company ('the holding company'), and

(b)   allots shares to the holding company or to another wholly-owned subsidiary of the holding company in consideration for the transfer to the issuing company of assets other than cash, being assets of any company ('the transferor company') which is a member of the group of companies which comprises the holding company and all its wholly-owned subsidiaries.

(2)   Where the shares in the issuing company allotted in consideration for the transfer are issued at a premium, the issuing company is not required by section 130 to transfer any amount in excess of the minimum premium value to the share premium account.

(3)   In subsection (2), 'the minimum premium value' means the amount (if any) by which the base value of the consideration for the shares allotted exceeds the aggregate nominal value of those shares.

(4)   For the purposes of subsection (3), the base value of the consideration for the shares allotted is the amount by which the base value of the assets transferred exceeds the base value of any liabilities of the transferor company assumed by the issuing company as part of the consideration for the assets transferred.

(5)   For the purposes of subsection (4)—

  (a) the base value of assets transferred is to be taken as—

      (i)   the cost of those assets to the transferor company, or

      (ii) the amount at which those assets are stated in the transferor company's accounting records immediately before the transfer,

      whichever is the less; and

  (b) the base value of the liabilities assumed is to be taken as the amount at which they are stated in the transferor company's accounting records immediately before the transfer.

(6)   The relief allowed by this section does not apply (subject to the next subsection) if the issue of shares took place before the date of the coming into force of the Companies (Share Premium Account) Regulations 1984 (which were made on 21st December 1984).

(7)   To the extent that the relief allowed by this section would have been allowed by section 38 of the Companies Act 1981 as originally enacted (the text of which section is set out in Schedule 25 to this Act), the relief applies where the issue of shares took place before the date of the coming into force of those Regulations, but not if the issue took place before 4th February 1981.

(8)   Section 131 does not apply in a case falling within this section.

General note

This provision facilitates group reconstructions by requiring that only a defined amount, the minimum premium value, need be transferred to the share premium account.

S 132(1),(2)

The conditions which govern this relief are that:

  (1)   the issuing company must be a wholly-owned subsidiary (defined in s 736);

  (2)   the shares must be allotted to the holding company (defined in s 736) or a wholly-owned subsidiary of the holding company, subject to s 133(2) (allotment to a nominee);

  (3)   the asset received, which may be but need not be shares, must be transferred by the holding company or a wholly-owned subsidiary of the holding company (if shares, this is subject to s 133(2)).

See also s 133(1), which applies to the amount of premium disregarded under this provision; it is also disregarded for the purpose of determining the amount at which the asset received is to be included in the issuing company's balance sheet.

S 132(3)–(5)

Calculating the minimum premium value   These provisions determine the amount which must be transferred. The first figure to determine is the amount by which the base value (either the cost or book value of the asset, whichever is lower) exceeds any liabilities transferred to the issuing company. The amount by which that figure exceeds the nominal value of the shares allotted is the minimum premium value.

133. Provisions supplementing ss 131, 132

(1)   An amount corresponding to one representing the premiums or part of the premiums on shares issued by a company which by virtue of sections 131 or 132 of this Act, or section 12 of the Consequential Provisions Act, is not included in the company's share premium account may also be disregarded in determining the amount at which any shares or other consideration provided for the shares issued is to be included in the company's balance sheet.

(2)   References in this Chapter (however expressed) to—

  (a) the acquisition by a company of shares in another company; and

  (b) the issue or allotment of shares to, or the transfer of shares to or by, a company,

include (respectively) the acquisition of any of those shares by, and the issue or allotment or (as the case may be) the transfer of any of those shares to or by, nominees of that company; and the reference in section 132 to the company transferring the shares is to be construed accordingly.

(3)   References in this Chapter to the transfer of shares in a company include the transfer of a right to be included in the company's register of members in respect of those shares.

(4)   In sections 131 to 133 'company', except in references to the issuing company, includes any body corporate.

S 133(1)

This section is an essential accounting element of the relief provided by ss 131(2) and 132(2). The reference to the Companies Consolidation (Consequential Provisions) Act 1985, s 12 relates to such merger relief as was available where the shares were issued prior to 4 February 1981.

S 133(2)

This provision provides considerable flexibility in terms of those to, or by, whom the allotment or the transfer etc must be made.

S 133(4)

'Body corporate' is defined in s 740.

134. Provision for extending or restricting relief from s 130

(1)   The Secretary of State may by regulations in a statutory instrument make such provision as appears to him to be appropriate—

    (a)   for relieving companies from the requirements of section 130 in relation to premiums other than cash premiums, or

    (b)   for restricting or otherwise modifying any relief from those requirements provided by this Chapter.

(2)   Regulations under this section may make different provision for different cases or classes of case and may contain such incidental and supplementary provisions as the Secretary of State thinks fit.

(3)   No such regulations shall be made unless a draft of the instrument containing them has been laid before Parliament and approved by a resolution of each House.

General note

No regulations have been laid under this provision.

CHAPTER IV

REDUCTION OF SHARE CAPITAL

135. Special resolution for reduction of share capital

(1)   Subject to confirmation by the court, a company limited by shares or a company limited by guarantee and having a share capital may, if so authorised by its articles, by special resolution reduce its share capital in any way.

(2)   In particular, and without prejudice to subsection (1), the company may—

(a)   extinguish or reduce the liability on any of its shares in respect of share capital not paid up; or

(b)   either with or without extinguishing or reducing liability on any of its shares, cancel any paid-up share capital which is lost or unrepresented by available assets; or

(c)   either with or without extinguishing or reducing liability on any of its shares, pay off any paid-up share capital which is in excess of the company's wants;

and the company may, if and so far as is necessary, alter its memorandum by reducing the amount of its share capital and of its shares accordingly.

(3)   A special resolution under this section is in this Act referred to as 'a resolution for reducing share capital'.

General note

It is a basic principle of company law that share capital cannot be reduced other than in the manner permitted by the statute which reduction must be confirmed by the court: *Trevor v Whitworth* (1887) 12 App Cas 409, HL. A transaction which upon examination can be seen to involve a return of capital (other than one properly sanctioned by the court), in whatever form, under whatever label, and whether directly or indirectly, to a member, is void: *Barclays Bank plc v British and Commonwealth Holdings plc* [1996] 1 BCLC 1; *Aveling Barford Ltd v Perion Ltd* [1989] BCLC 626.

Reduction under other provisions   Apart from the direct statutory procedure laid down in s 135, a reduction of capital may occur as a consequence of the operation of other statutory provisions, for example, on a redemption or a purchase back of shares by a private company out of capital: s 171 et seq. Reduction does not occur in the case of redemption or purchase otherwise than out of capital for, in those instances, an amount equivalent to the amount redeemed or purchased must be transferred to the capital redemption reserve which, for most purposes, is treated as if it were share capital: s 170(4).

   A reduction may also be effected under ss 146, 147, following the acquisition by a public company of its own shares in certain circumstances, without complying with ss 135, 136: see s 147(1).

Reduction by order of the court   A reduction of capital can also arise as a consequence of a court order for the purchase by the company of a member's shares under a variety of provisions, for example, under s 54(6) (objection to public company being re-registered as a private company); s 157(3) (objection to private company giving financial assistance for the purchase of its own shares); s 177(3) (objection to purchase or redemption of shares by private company out of capital); and s 461(2)(d) (relief for unfairly prejudicial conduct).

Forfeiture and surrender   The forfeiture of shares for non-payment of calls, or the acceptance of shares surrendered in lieu, in accordance with the articles (see Table A, regs 18–22) is not a reduction requiring the confirmation of the court; whether surrender amounts to a reduction of capital requiring court confirmation in any other case depends on the facts: *Trevor v Whitworth* (1887) 12 App Cas 409; *Bellerby v Rowland and Marwood's Steamship Co Ltd* [1902] 2 Ch 14; *Rowell v John Rowell & Sons Ltd* [1912] 2 Ch 609; *Re St James' Court Estate Ltd* [1944] Ch 6.

Schemes of arrangement   Reductions are commonly devised as a component of a scheme of arrangement, see notes to s 425 et seq, below.

S 135(1)

Confirmation   As to confirmation by the court, see note to s 137(1).

Type of company   Companies limited by guarantee with a share capital can no longer be formed (s 1(4)), so this provision will apply only to the small number of such companies remaining on the register of companies. The provision does not apply to unlimited companies which may reduce their share capital without requiring court confirmation: *Re Borough Commercial and Building Society* [1893] 2 Ch 242.

Authorisation   A company must be authorised by its articles to reduce capital, see Table A, reg 34. The authorisation in the articles is frequently qualified in the case of public companies by a provision that the reduction must not have the effect of reducing the share capital below the authorised minimum for a public company (£50,000: s 118). Such a provision does not rule out a reduction by a company which momentarily reduces the company's capital to nil before following it with an increase in capital to above that minimum: *Re M B Group plc* [1989] BCLC 672. As to the position when a reduction does result in the capital of a public company falling below the authorised minimum, see s 139.

A company cannot bind itself not to exercise the statutory power to reduce its capital, although the shareholders may agree, apart from the articles, as to how they will exercise their voting rights on any resolution to reduce capital: *Russell v Northern Bank Development Corpn Ltd* [1992] 3 All ER 161, HL.

Special resolution   A special resolution is required, subject to the right of a private company to use a written resolution (s 381A, which removes the doubts expressed in *Re Barry Artist Ltd* [1985] BCLC 283 as to whether written resolutions are acceptable for reduction of capital schemes). As to when the resolution takes effect, see s 138(2). As to the requirements regarding a special resolution, see ss 378, 380; also *Re Moorgate Mercantile Holdings Ltd* [1980] 1 All ER 40 (if the resolution is incorrectly notified and passed, the court has no jurisdiction to confirm the reduction). The special resolution must be forwarded to the registrar of companies within 15 days after it is passed: s 380(4)(a); and, if necessary, a printed copy of the memorandum or articles, as altered: s 18(2).

A resolution to reduce capital can be conditional on other alterations to the share capital taking place and so may refer to the share capital as it will be when the court's confirmation is sought and not as it stands at the date of the resolution: *Re Tip-Europe Ltd* [1988] BCLC 231 (a resolution for the reduction of the share premium account was made conditional on a prior allotment of shares at a premium; the court can confirm such a reduction provided the condition is fulfilled by the time confirmation is sought; *Re Transfesa Terminals Ltd* (1987) 3 BCC 647 distinguished).

Method of reduction   The courts have emphasised on many occasions that there is no question of limiting or controlling the power available to the company to reduce its capital in any way: see *British and American Trustee and Finance Corpn v Couper* [1894] AC 399 at 410, HL; *Poole v National Bank of China Ltd* [1907] AC 229, HL; *Ex p Westburn Sugar Refineries Ltd* [1951] AC 625, HL; *Carruth v ICI Ltd* [1937] AC 707.

A company can reduce its capital to nil momentarily followed by an increase to a positive amount: see *Re Northern Engineering Industries plc* [1994] 2 BCLC 704; *Re Anglo American Insurance Co Ltd* [1991] BCLC 564; *Re M B Group plc* [1989] BCLC 672. A conversion of ordinary shares already issued into deferred shares redeemable on a specified date two years later was a scheme for the reduction of capital in a particular but unusual way: *Forth Wines Ltd, Petitioners* [1991] BCC 638. A cancellation of unissued shares under s 121 does not constitute a reduction of capital: s 121(5).

The share premium account and capital redemption reserve are treated as share capital and are subject to the same possibilities of (and constraints on) reduction: see ss 130(3), 170(4).

See the note to s 137(1) as to a reduction of capital and class rights.

S 135(2)

Possible schemes of reduction   This provision is without prejudice to the company's ability to reduce capital in any way, see note to sub-s (1), above. Apart from the three situations specified, a reduction may be helpful where some error has occurred in a transaction, perhaps involving a purchase by a company of its own shares or a breach of the financial assistance provisions in s 151 et seq, which is best resolved by a reduction of capital and a cancellation of the shares in question (see Law Society Company Law Committee Memorandum *Company Law Reform, Capital Maintenance* (January 2000) p 20).

Capital not paid up   In practice, this category is rarely used, for it is unusual now for shares to be issued as partly paid.

Capital lost or unrepresented by available assets   Reduction in this instance will usually be an exercise to restore reality to the company's accounts and will be essential (in view of the distribution rules in Part VIII) where the company needs to eliminate a deficit on the profit and loss account so as to enable it to pay dividends from current profits. The capital may be lost or it may be unrepresented by available assets, these are alternative grounds: *Re Hoare & Co Ltd* [1904] 2 Ch 208.

If confirmation of a reduction is sought on the basis that the capital is lost, that loss must be proved: *Re Jupiter House Investments (Cambridge) Ltd* [1985] BCLC 222; *Re Grosvenor Press plc* [1985] BCLC 286; *Re Barrow Haematite Steel Co* [1900] 2 Ch 846; and the loss must be permanent (so far as is presently foreseeable) and not just a temporary fall in the value of some capital asset: *Re Jupiter House Investments (Cambridge) Ltd* [1985] BCLC 222.

However, as a company can reduce capital for any purpose and in any way, if the loss cannot be proved to be permanent, the court may still exercise its discretion to confirm the reduction, subject to the standard requirement that the position of existing creditors be safeguarded, usually by an undertaking to create a reserve which is undistributable as long as any creditor at the date of the reduction remains unpaid or does not consent: *Re Grosvenor Press plc* [1985] BCLC 286. Exceptionally, the court may require additional undertakings from the company for the protection of future creditors before it will confirm the reduction: see *Re Jupiter House Investments*

(Cambridge) Ltd [1985] BCLC 222 (reserve was to be made a capital reserve and undistributable). See note to s 136(6) below.

Capital in excess of the company's wants   It is for the company to determine, subject to the statutory provisions for the protection of creditors, whether its capital is or is not excessive of its present wants: *British and American Trustee and Finance Corpn v Couper* [1894] AC 399 at 413, HL; *Ex p Westburn Sugar Refineries Ltd* [1951] AC 625. However, the court will want some proof that it is excessive, as this will be relevant to its consideration as to whether the creditors' position has been safeguarded: see *Re Jupiter House Investments (Cambridge) Ltd* [1985] BCLC 222. It is only in this instance that capital is actually returned to the shareholders. In sub-s (2)(a) above, the capital has never been received and in sub-s (2)(b) above, the capital is lost.

It is not necessary that the shareholders should actually receive cash; non-cash assets may be used instead: *Ex p Westburn Sugar Refineries Ltd* [1951] AC 625 (shares in another company); *Re Thomas de la Rue & Co Ltd* [1911] 2 Ch 361 (debenture stock). In that case, there need not be an exact correlation between the capital reduced and the value of the assets transferred as, in many cases, it is impossible to make any exact valuation of the non-cash assets although the court will be alert to any abuse of this option: *Ex p Westburn Sugar Refineries Ltd* [1951] AC 625 at 631, 636–638. It is possible therefore that a shareholder may receive more or less than the value of his capital and it is for the shareholders to decide as to the adequacy or inadequacy of the consideration but, if what is offered to the shareholder is illusory, the court will refuse to confirm the reduction: *Re Thomas de la Rue & Co Ltd* [1911] 2 Ch 361.

A distribution, whether of cash or assets, in a reduction of capital is not a distribution for the purposes of Part VIII (distribution of profits and assets): s 263(2)(c).

---

136. Application to court for order of confirmation

(1)   Where a company has passed a resolution for reducing share capital, it may apply to the court for an order confirming the reduction.

(2)   If the proposed reduction of share capital involves either—

    (a)   diminution of liability in respect of unpaid share capital; or

    (b)   the payment to a shareholder of any paid-up share capital,

and in any other case if the court so directs, the next three subsections have effect, but subject throughout to subsection (6).

(3)   Every creditor of the company who at the date fixed by the court is entitled to any debt or claim which, if that date were the commencement of the winding up of the company, would be admissible in proof against the company is entitled to object to the reduction of capital.

(4)   The court shall settle a list of creditors entitled to object, and for that purpose—

    (a)   shall ascertain, as far as possible without requiring an application from any creditor, the names of those creditors and the nature and amount of their debts or claims; and

    (b)   may publish notices fixing a day or days within which creditors not entered on the list are to claim to be so entered or are to be excluded from the right of objecting to the reduction of capital.

(5) If a creditor entered on the list whose debt or claim is not discharged or has not determined does not consent to the reduction, the court may, if it thinks fit, dispense with the consent of that creditor, on the company securing payment of his debt or claim by appropriating (as the court may direct) the following amount—

(a) if the company admits the full amount of the debt or claim or, though not admitting it, is willing to provide for it, then the full amount of the debt or claim;

(b) if the company does not admit, and is not willing to provide for, the full amount of the debt or claim, or if the amount is contingent or not ascertained, then an amount fixed by the court after the like enquiry and adjudication as if the company were being wound up by the court.

(6) If a proposed reduction of share capital involves either the diminution of any liability in respect of unpaid share capital or the payment to any shareholder of any paid-up share capital, the court may, if having regard to any special circumstances of the case it thinks proper to do so, direct that subsections (3) to (5) of this section shall not apply as regards any class or any classes of creditors.

S 136(1)

Application procedure   Application must be made to the court having jurisdiction to wind up the company: s 744. The procedure is governed by CPR, Part 49 and by Practice Direction – Applications under the Companies Act 1985 and the Insurance Companies Act 1982, which requires that the application for confirmation be by petition: para 4(1)(d). Petitions are heard by the Companies Court Registrar unless otherwise ordered: para 6(3); and are typically pled with the court as soon as the general meeting has passed the requested special resolution under s 135(1).

S 136(2)

Settling the list of creditors   The settling of a list of creditors entitled to object (defined in sub-s (3)) is required only in the cases specified and is subject to the court's discretion under sub-s (6) to dispense with the settling of the list; and it is standard practice to dispense with the settling of the list.

A settling of the list of creditors is not called for where the capital is lost or unrepresented by available assets, as the reduction in that case is simply an acknowledgment of what has already occurred and there is no role for objecting creditors. They are protected by the court's insistence that there be proof that the capital is lost or unrepresented by available assets (see note to s 135(2), above) before it will confirm the reduction and, if there is any doubt as to the position, the court may require additional undertakings from the company to protect the creditors: see note to sub-s (6), below.

The court does have power 'in any other case' to direct the settling of a list of creditors but the court will so direct only where a strong case is made out: *Re Meux's Brewery Co Ltd* [1919] 1 Ch 28.

S 136(3), (4)

Creditors entitled to object   The creditors entitled to object are those entitled to prove in winding up: see Insolvency Rules 1986, SI 1986/1925, r 4.73 et seq; and their claims may be present or future, certain or contingent, ascertained or sounding only in damages: Insolvency Rules 1986, r 12.3(1). Penalties are imposed by s 141 on the officers of the company in the event of the wilful concealment or misrepresentation of the existence of any creditor or the nature or amount of any debt. See also s 140(2)–(5).

S 136(5)

Dispensing with consent   The consent of a creditor may be proved in such manner as the court thinks sufficient: CPR, Part 49 and Practice Direction – Applications under the Companies Act 1985 and the Insurance Companies Act 1982, para 6(1). Subsection (5)(b) would apply, for example, to a claim by a landlord for future rent or future breaches of covenant: see *Re Lucania Temperance Billiard Halls (London) Ltd* [1965] 3 All ER 879.

S 136(6)

As noted above, it is standard practice to dispense with the settling of the list of creditors.

Dispensing with settling the list of creditors   The special circumstances to justify dispensing with the settling of the list of creditors entitled to object (as defined in sub-s (3)) must be such that the court is satisfied that the creditors will not be prejudiced by the proposed reduction: *Re Lucania Temperance Billiard Halls (London) Ltd* [1965] 3 All ER 879; and the potential for prejudice to creditors exists in all cases save where the reduction is on the basis of a permanent loss of capital, see note to s 135(2).

Margin of safety   In considering whether to dispense with the list of creditors, where capital is being returned, the court will consider whether a company holds sufficient cash and gilt-edged securities to cover all provable liabilities with a reasonable margin of safety (typically 10%), as well as the amount which it is proposed to be returned to the shareholders. However, the court's consideration is not limited to cash and gilt-edged securities and it may also take into account sums due to a company by its sundry debtors provided that the said sums have been written down so as to exclude bad debts: *Re House of Fraser plc* [1987] BCLC 293; *Re Lucania Temperance Billiard Halls (London) Ltd* [1965] 3 All ER 879.

Undertakings by the company   Strictly speaking, the wording of sub-s (2) and s 137(1) is limited to particular types of reduction but court practice has diverged from the procedure envisaged by the statute and the courts look to protect creditors by way of undertakings by the company in all reductions (save where capital is permanently lost) as part of their discretionary jurisdiction to confirm reductions.

Typically, the company will offer certain undertakings to secure the consent of creditors (frequently in the form of bank guarantees to cover the amount owing to non-consenting creditors) or will pay them off. The undertakings need only be adequate to protect the position of creditors at the time of the reduction and not future creditors who must take the company as they find it: *Re Grosvenor Press plc* [1985]

BCLC 286; *Quayle Munro Ltd, Petitioners* [1994] 1 BCLC 410, CS; although, in exceptional cases, long-term undertakings might be sought: see *Re Jupiter House Investments (Cambridge) Ltd* [1985] BCLC 222.

Where capital is reduced by the cancellation of the share premium account, so as to eliminate a deficit on the profit and loss account (which loss may not be permanent), and the capital written off exceeds the deficit, the creditors can be protected by an undertaking to transfer the amount of the share premium account to a special reserve which is undistributable as long as any creditor at the date of the reduction remains unpaid or does not consent: see *Re Grosvenor Press plc* [1985] BCLC 286; *Quayle Munro Ltd, Petitioners* [1994] 1 BCLC 410, CS. This undertaking might be made subject to the company's right to reduce the special reserve where the company subsequently increases its capital by a fresh issue or by a bonus issue.

The undertakings offered by the company perform the dual role of creating the special circumstances which justify the court dispensing with the settling of the list of creditors under this section and also of satisfying the court that the position of creditors has been safeguarded which is central to the question of whether the court can confirm the reduction under s 137.

---

137. Court order confirming reduction

(1)   The court, if satisfied with respect to every creditor of the company who under section 136 is entitled to object to the reduction of capital that either—

(a)   his consent to the reduction has been obtained; or

(b)   his debt or claim has been discharged or has determined, or has been secured,

may make an order confirming the reduction on such terms and conditions as it thinks fit.

(2)   Where the court so orders, it may also—

(a)   if for any special reason it thinks proper to do so, make an order directing that the company shall, during such period (commencing on or at any time after the date of the order) as is specified in the order, add to its name as its last words the words 'and reduced'; and

(b)   make an order requiring the company to publish (as the court directs) the reasons for reduction of capital or such other information in regard to it as the court thinks expedient with a view to giving proper information to the public and (if the court thinks fit) the causes which led to the reduction.

(3)   Where a company is ordered to add to its name the words 'and reduced', those words are, until the expiration of the period specified in the order, deemed to be part of the company's name.

S 137(1)

In practice, assuming that the procedures have been followed properly and the necessary special resolution passed, confirmation is routine. The creditors' consent will usually have been secured by the company and shareholders will have little interest in objecting other than in the context of a variation of class rights (discussed below). Any shareholders who have objections must persuade the court not to confirm the reduction.

A discretionary matter for the court   Subject to the obligation to be satisfied as to the position of the creditors entitled to object under s 136, the court's power to confirm a reduction of capital is entirely discretionary: *British and American Trustee and Finance Corpn v Couper* [1894] AC 399, HL; *Re Thomas De la Rue & Co Ltd* [1911] 2 Ch 361; and this is so even if the application is unopposed: *Re Ransomes plc* [1999] 2 BCLC 591 at 602.

Traditionally, the courts have explained the nature of the jurisdiction in terms of considering whether the scheme would be 'fair and equitable', or 'just and equitable', or 'fair and reasonable'. Generally, however, the courts are reluctant to reject a petition for confirmation as the dissenting shareholders must necessarily be a small number and a reduction of capital is a re-organisation of the company's domestic affairs in which the courts are loath to interfere.

The modern position is set forth by Harman J in *Re Ratners Group plc* [1988] BCLC 685 at 687, where he identified the three principles on which the court will require to be satisfied:

'... first, that all shareholders are treated equitably in any reduction. That usually means that they are treated equally, but may mean that they are treated equally save as to some who have consented to their being treated unequally, so that counsel's word "equitably" is the correct word which I adopt and accept. The second principle to be applied is that the shareholders at the general meeting had the proposals properly explained to them so that they could exercise an informed judgment on them. And the third principle is that creditors of the company are safeguarded so that money cannot be applied in any way which would be detrimental to creditors.'

Harman J added that the reduction should be for some discernible purpose (at 688).

Fair and equitable   The question for the court is whether, looking at the scheme as a whole, the proposed reduction is fair and equitable as between the different classes of shareholders: *British and American Trustee and Finance Corpn v Couper* [1894] AC 399; *Re Thomas de la Rue Ltd* [1911] 2 Ch 361; *Poole v National Bank of China Ltd* [1907] AC 229; *Wilson and Clyde Coal Co Ltd v Scottish Insurance Corpn* 1948 SC 360, Ct of Sess; affd sub nom *Scottish Insurance Corpn Ltd v Wilsons and Clyde Coal Co Ltd* [1949] AC 462, HL.

The position as to where the burden of proof lies is somewhat unclear (see *Carruth v ICI Ltd* [1937] AC 707) but that issue is not decisive in any event, since a petition for confirmation is not ordinary adversarial litigation and the question is simply whether, on the evidence as a whole, the court is satisfied that it is right to give its approval: *Re Ransomes plc* [1999] 2 BCLC 591 at 602, CA; *Carruth v ICI Ltd* [1937] AC 707.

The requirement that the reduction be fair and equitable does not require that all shareholders be treated alike: *British and American Trustee and Finance Corpn v Couper* [1894] AC 399, HL. However, a reduction which does not provide for uniform treatment of shareholders whose rights are similar is narrowly scrutinised to ensure that it is fair and equitable and should be confirmed: *British and American Trustee and Finance Corpn v Couper* [1894] AC 399. In *Re Robert Stephen Holdings Ltd* [1968] 1 WLR 522 it was stated that the better practice in cases where one part of a class are to be treated differently from another part of the same class (unless all the shareholders consent) is to proceed by way of a scheme of arrangement under what is now s 425, as this affords better protection to a non-assenting minority. In this case, the court did confirm the reduction despite it affecting shareholders of the same class in different ways but no shareholder appeared to oppose the confirmation.

Reduction of capital and class rights   A reduction of capital should be dealt with in accordance with the priorities created by the company's constitution which would apply on a winding up although the classes of shareholders affected may agree to some other scheme: *Re Floating Dock Co of St Thomas Ltd* [1895] 1 Ch 691; *Re Chatterley-Whitfield Collieries Ltd* [1948] 2 All ER 593 at 596, per Lord Greene MR. Where a scheme is in accordance with such priorities, it is prima facie fair and equitable: *Re Chatterley-Whitfield Collieries Ltd* [1948] 2 All ER 593 at 596, per Lord Greene MR.

A reduction of capital which involves paying off the preference shareholders is a fulfilment and not a variation of the rights of a preference shareholder, where the reduction is consistent with the preference shareholders' rights as to a prior return of capital on a winding up: see *Re Floating Dock Co of St Thomas Ltd* [1895] 1 Ch 691; *Re Chatterley-Whitfield Collieries Ltd* [1948] 2 All ER 593; affd sub nom *Prudential Assurance Co Ltd v Chatterley Whitfield Collieries Ltd* [1949] AC 512, HL; *Wilson and Clyde Coal Co Ltd v Scottish Insurance Corpn* 1948 SC 360, Ct of Sess; affd sub nom *Scottish Insurance Corpn Ltd v Wilsons and Clyde Coal Co Ltd* [1949] AC 462, HL; *Re Saltdean Estate Co Ltd* [1968] 3 All ER 829; *House of Fraser v ACGE Investments Ltd* [1987] BCLC 478; affg [1987] BCLC 293. This is so even if the preference shareholders are participating as to surplus while the company is a going concern: *Re Saltdean Estate Co Ltd* [1968] 3 All ER 829; and, possibly, even if they are participating as to surplus on a winding up, at least if winding up is not imminent: *Re William Jones & Son Ltd* [1969] 1 WLR 146; cf *Re Old Silkstone Collieries Ltd* [1954] Ch 169. The consent of the preference shareholders is not required, therefore, and, provided that the scheme is otherwise fair, the reduction will be confirmed by the court.

Where preference shareholders have no priority on a return of capital on a winding up, a rateable reduction of capital on all shares, preference and ordinary, though diminishing the actual preference dividend, is not a variation of the rights of the preference shareholders so as to require their consent and is not unfair or inequitable so that the court might refuse confirmation: *Re Mackenzie & Co Ltd* [1916] 2 Ch 450; *Bannatyne v Direct Spanish Telegraph Co* (1886) 34 Ch D 287.

To avoid these restrictive interpretations of when a reduction of capital amounts to a variation of class rights, it is common to specify in the terms of issue that matters such as a reduction of capital are deemed to be a variation of the class rights so ensuring that the consent of the class is required; see note to s 125, above.

If a scheme of reduction does vary or abrogate class rights (and see note to s 125, above as to the meaning of these terms) or is so deemed then, despite the generality of the court's power to confirm (and some suggestions to the contrary in older cases: see *Re William Jones & Sons Ltd* [1969] 1 All ER 913), the court will not confirm a reduction without the consent of the class as required by s 125: *Re Northern Engineering Industries plc* [1994] 2 BCLC 704 at 713, CA. Where the consent of the class is required and obtained, the court still has a discretion as to whether or not to confirm the reduction but it is unlikely that the court would reject a scheme which has been approved by a majority of those affected.

Informed shareholders   The court can confirm a resolution even if there is a factual error in it, provided that it is so insignificant that no one could be thought to be prejudiced by its correction and the way in which it is to be corrected is clear: *Re*

Willaire Systems plc [1987] BCLC 67 (miniscule errors). See also *Re European Home Products plc* [1988] BCLC 690 where a more significant error occurred in the circulars sent out to the shareholders setting out the proposed reduction: the court reluctantly confirmed the reduction as creditors were not affected and no shareholder regarded the mistake as being of such importance as to oppose the reduction. In *Re Ransomes plc* [1999] 1 BCLC 775, affd [1999] 2 BCLC 591, CA, the court confirmed a reduction even though the company had been 'parsimonious' with information to the shareholders for, despite the procedural deficiencies, the scheme was substantially fair.

Protected creditors Creditors are protected either by the settling of a list of creditors entitled to object and the making of provision for those who do not consent under s 136(2)–(5) but this is rarely done. Instead, the practice is to dispense with the requirement for settling the list on the company giving undertakings sufficient to protect the position of creditors: see note to s 136(6), above.

Discernible purpose In *Re Ratners Group plc* [1988] BCLC 685, Harman J required that the reduction should be for some discernible purpose (at 688) which he defined in *Re Thorn EMI plc* [1989] BCLC 612 as meaning '... something which is demonstrated by evidence to the court and is something sufficiently solid and near in expectation to be a real prospect' (at 616). See also *Re Ransomes plc* [1999] 2 BCLC 591 at 603: 'the court needs to know at least the general purpose of what is proposed.'

Public interest Some of the earlier cases suggested that the court should have regard to the interests of creditors and shareholders and to the interests of those members of the public who may be induced to take shares in the company: see *Poole v National Bank of China Ltd* [1907] AC 229 at 239, HL; *Ex p Westburn Sugar Refineries Ltd* [1951] AC 625 at 630. The court appears to give little weight to such considerations now for, in the absence of exceptional circumstances, future creditors and shareholders are adequately protected by the statutory safeguards: *Re Grosvenor Press plc* [1985] BCLC 286.

The court is not concerned with any ulterior purpose for the reduction provided it is lawful. Thus, in the past, reduction schemes to avoid some of the consequences of nationalisation have been approved: *Ex p Westburn Sugar Refineries Ltd* [1951] AC 625.

S 137(2), (3)

In practice, these provisions are obsolete.

---

138. Registration of order and minute of reduction

(1) The registrar of companies, on production to him of an order of the court confirming the reduction of a company's share capital, and the delivery to him of a copy of the order and of a minute (approved by the court) showing, with respect to the company's share capital as altered by the order—

    (a) the amount of the share capital;

   (b) the number of shares into which it is to be divided, and the amount of each share; and

   (c) the amount (if any) at the date of the registration deemed to be paid up on each share,

shall register the order and minute (but subject to section 139).

(2)   On the registration of the order and minute, and not before, the resolution for reducing share capital as confirmed by the order so registered takes effect.

(3)   Notice of the registration shall be published in such manner as the court may direct.

(4)   The registrar shall certify the registration of the order and minute; and the certificate—

   (a) may be either signed by the registrar, or authenticated by his official seal;

   (b) is conclusive evidence that all the requirements of this Act with respect to the reduction of share capital have been complied with, and that the company's share capital is as stated in the minute.

(5)   The minute when registered is deemed to be substituted for the corresponding part of the company's memorandum, and is valid and alterable as if it had been originally contained therein.

(6)   The substitution of such a minute for part of the company's memorandum is deemed an alteration of the memorandum for purposes of section 20.

S 138(1)

This provision is subject to the provisions governing the reduction of a public company's capital below the authorised minimum, see s 139.

Contents of the minute   The court must approve a minute which will state the amounts from and to which capital is reduced. Although the minute is usually limited to the reduction itself, as the matter requiring court confirmation, further information may be included. In *Re Anglo American Insurance Co Ltd* [1991] BCLC 564 the court thought that a minute showing a reduction of capital to nil without referring to an immediate increase to $US50m would be positively misleading and not in accordance with the purpose of the statutory provision; the subsequent increase should also be noted.

   Any cancellation or reduction of the share premium account which forms part of the reduction should not be referred to in the minute: *Re Paringa Mining and Exploration Co Ltd* [1957] 3 All ER 424; and see note to sub-s (5), below.

S 138(2)

Effective date   The resolution for reducing capital takes effect on the registration of the order and the minute by the registrar of companies and not on its delivery to the registrar.

Registration must precede any repayment of capital, since the resolution is not effective until registration and the company is not entitled to make any repayment of capital to shareholders except under and in pursuance of an effective resolution: *Re Lees Brook Spinning Co* [1906] 2 Ch 394. If the capital is not returned, the right of the shareholders to claim it will be barred after 12 years from the date of the notice of the order confirming the reduction: Limitation Act 1980 s 8(1); *Re Artisans' Land and Mortgage Corpn* [1904] 1 Ch 796 at 802.

S 138(3)

The court usually directs that the registration be advertised in the same newspapers as those in which the hearing of the petition was advertised.

s 138(4)

Conclusive certificate   The certificate of the registrar is conclusive and, where there was an irregularity with regard to the passing of the resolution to reduce the capital of the company, the court had no power to inquire into it: *Ladies' Dress Association Ltd v Pulbrook* [1900] 2 QB 376, CA (ineffective alteration of the articles to authorise reduction); see also *Re Walker and Smith Ltd* (1903) 72 LJ 572 (company had no power in its articles to reduce capital, defect cured by the certificate). See generally the notes to ss 13(7) and 401.

See also *Re Ransomes plc* [1999] 2 BCLC 591; affg [1999] 1 BCLC 775, where the party who unsuccessfully opposed the confirmation by the court of the cancellation of a share premium account appealed (also unsuccessfully) to the Court of Appeal seeking the imposition of further conditions with respect to the scheme of reduction which would have had the effect of cancelling the court's confirmation (see, in particular, at 600–601). While dismissing the appeal on other grounds, the court did not explore how such an appeal could be compatible with the conclusive certificate under this provision, which certificate had been issued in the case; see also *Exeter Trust Ltd v Screenways Ltd* [1991] BCLC 888, CA. Finality in these matters is crucial and, in practice, the court order sanctioning the reduction (and minute) will be registered promptly by the registrar of companies and the company will proceed forthwith to carry out the scheme of reduction so any appeal, even if compatible with this provision (and that must be doubtful), is likely to be pointless.

S 138(5)

Minute as part of the memorandum of association   It is because the minute forms part of the memorandum, taking the place of the existing statement of capital in the memorandum, that the minute does not refer to any writing down or off of the share premium account: *Re Paringa Mining and Exploration Co Ltd* [1957] 3 All ER 424; likewise regarding the capital redemption reserve. Such information, if included in the memorandum, would give rise to a conflict between s 2(7) (memorandum cannot be altered except as expressly provided for by the Act) and s 130(2), which enables the share premium account to be used in various ways, and s 170(4), which enables the capital redemption reserve to be used for the issue of fully paid bonus shares.

S 138(6)

Alteration of the memorandum   The effect of this provision is that every copy of the memorandum issued after the date of the registration of the order confirming the reduction must embody the alterations made in accordance with the order so as to comply with s 20.

As the minute effects an alteration to the memorandum of association, it cannot be relied on as against third parties until officially notified: s 42(1)(b); by which is meant that it must be gazetted by the registrar of companies as required by s 711(1)(b), (2); but this only applies if the reduction is a reduction of capital and not a reduction of the share premium account or the capital redemption reserve (which are not reflected in the minute and do not effect an alteration to the memorandum, as noted above, see sub-s (5)).

139. Public company reducing capital below authorised minimum

(1)   This section applies where the court makes an order confirming a reduction of a public company's capital which has the effect of bringing the nominal value of its allotted share capital below the authorised minimum.

(2)   The registrar of companies shall not register the order under section 138 unless the court otherwise directs, or the company is first re-registered as a private company.

(3)   The court may authorise the company to be so re-registered without its having passed the special resolution required by section 53; and where that authority is given, the court shall specify in the order the alterations in the company's memorandum and articles to be made in connection with that re-registration.

(4)   The company may then be re-registered as a private company, if an application in the prescribed form and signed by a director or secretary of the company is delivered to the registrar, together with a printed copy of the memorandum and articles as altered by the court's order.

(5)   On receipt of such an application, the registrar shall retain it and the other documents delivered with it and issue the company with a certificate of incorporation appropriate to a company that is not a public company; and—

  (a) the company by virtue of the issue of the certificate becomes a private company, and the alterations in the memorandum and articles set out in the court's order take effect; and

  (b) the certificate is conclusive evidence that the requirements of this section in respect of re-registration and of matters precedent and incidental thereto have been complied with, and that the company is a private company.

S 139(1)

As to the authorised minimum, see s 118.

S 139(2)

As to the re-registration of a public company as a private company, see ss 53–55; and also sub-ss (3)–(5), below.

S 139(3), (4)

These provisions allow the company to be re-registered as a private company without passing the special resolution required by s 53 since, in this case, re-registration is mandatory in view of the failure to comply with the minimum capital requirements.

S 139(5)

As to the conclusive nature of the certificate, see note to s 13(7).

140. Liability of members on reduced shares

(1) Where a company's share capital is reduced, a member of the company (past or present) is not liable in respect of any share to any call or contribution exceeding in amount the difference (if any) between the amount of the share as fixed by the minute and the amount paid on the share or the reduced amount (if any), which is deemed to have been paid on it, as the case may be.

(2) But the following two subsections apply if—

    (a) a creditor, entitled in respect of a debt or claim to object to the reduction of share capital, by reason of his ignorance of the proceedings for reduction of share capital, or of their nature and effect with respect to his claim, is not entered on the list of creditors; and

    (b) after the reduction of capital, the company is unable (within the meaning of section 123 of the Insolvency Act) to pay the amount of his debt or claim.

(3) Every person who was a member of the company at the date of the registration of the order for reduction and minute is then liable to contribute for the payment of the debt or claim in question an amount not exceeding that which he would have been liable to contribute if the company had commenced to be wound up on the day before that date.

(4) If the company is wound up, the court, on the application of the creditor in question and proof of ignorance referred to in subsection (2)(a), may (if it thinks fit) settle accordingly a list of persons so liable to contribute, and make and enforce calls and orders on the contributories settled on the list, as if they were ordinary contributories in a winding up.

(5) Nothing in this section affects the rights of the contributories among themselves.

General note

As partly paid shares are rare now, this provision is of limited practical significance.

S 140(1)

This provision exempts the shareholder from any liability to pay up to the amount originally due on the share; his liability is to pay up only to the amount as reduced.

S 140(2)–(5)

These provisions make an exception to the rule in sub-s (1), where a creditor's claim was overlooked when the court settled the list of creditors under s 136 and the company has become insolvent before that claim has been met. The position as to ordinary contributories on a winding up is governed by IA 1986, s 76.

---

141. Penalty for concealing name of creditor, etc

If an officer of the company—

    (a) wilfully conceals the name of a creditor entitled to object to the reduction of capital; or

    (b) wilfully misrepresents the nature or amount of the debt or claim of any creditor; or

    (c) aids, abets or is privy to any such concealment or misrepresentation as is mentioned above,

he is guilty of an offence and liable to a fine.

General note

This provision relates to the court's obligation to settle a list of creditors under s 136 and imposes penalties on any officer of the company (defined in s 744) who wilfully obstructs the court in the drawing up of that list. As noted above, the settling of a list in this fashion under s 136 is usually dispensed with in any event by the court under s 136(6).

As to penalties, see s 730, Sch 24.

CHAPTER V

MAINTENANCE OF CAPITAL

142. Duty of directors on serious loss of capital

(1)   Where the net assets of a public company are half or less of its called-up share capital, the directors shall, not later than 28 days from the earliest day on which that fact is known to a director of the company, duly convene an extraordinary general meeting of the company for a date not later than 56 days from that day for the purpose of considering whether any, and if so what, steps should be taken to deal with the situation.

(2)   If there is a failure to convene an extraordinary general meeting as required by subsection (1), each of the directors of the company who—

  (a) knowingly and wilfully authorises or permits the failure, or

  (b) after the expiry of the period during which that meeting should have been convened, knowingly and wilfully authorises or permits the failure to continue,

is liable to a fine.

(3)   Nothing in this section authorises the consideration, at a meeting convened in pursuance of subsection (1), of any matter which could not have been considered at that meeting apart from this section.

General note

This provision applies only to public companies and is thought to be of limited utility.

S 142(1), (3)

Definition of net assets   The phrase 'net assets' is not defined although the phrase is defined elsewhere in the legislation (see ss 152(2), 264(2)); and it was defined for the purposes of this provision when it was originally introduced by CA 1980, s 34 (in that case, as the aggregate of the company's assets less the aggregate of its liabilities: CA 1980, s 87(4)(c)).

  'Called-up share capital' is defined in s 737, although it is unclear whether amounts credited to the share premium account must be included. It is thought not; elsewhere in the legislation, called-up share capital does not include amounts credited to the share premium account. For example, see s 43(3)(b), which requires, for the purposes of that provision, that net assets equal the amount of called-up share capital and undistributable reserves which undistributable reserves are defined by s 264(3) as including the share premium account. But if the provision only applies when the net assets are half or less of the called-up share capital excluding premium, the obligation to call a meeting will rarely arise.

Calling the meeting   If a company has assets which fluctuate in value significantly, the effect may be that there is a recurring obligation to call a meeting. It has been suggested that the obligation to call a meeting should only arise if the loss of capital is permanent (see Law Society Company Law Committee, Memorandum no 389, January 2000). The time scale within which the meeting must be called is triggered by the knowledge of any one director.

Purpose of the meeting The purpose of the meeting is solely to consider whether any, and if so what, steps should be taken to deal with the situation. However, no concrete steps may be taken by the meeting, such as a resolution to wind up the company, unless the proper notice of that matter has been given. Equally, if any other business is to be transacted at the meeting, the appropriate notice must have been given in the usual fashion: sub-s (3). This is subject to the agreement of the shareholders to short notice: see s 378(3).

S 142(2)

As to penalties, see s 730, Sch 24.

143. General rule against company acquiring own shares

(1) Subject to the following provisions, a company limited by shares or limited by guarantee and having a share capital shall not acquire its own shares, whether by purchase, subscription or otherwise.

(2) If a company purports to act in contravention of this section, the company is liable to a fine, and every officer of the company who is in default is liable to imprisonment or a fine, or both; and the purported acquisition is void.

(3) A company limited by shares may acquire any of its own fully paid shares otherwise than for valuable consideration; and subsection (1) does not apply in relation to—

  (a) the redemption or purchase of shares in accordance with Chapter VII of this Part,

  (b) the acquisition of shares in a reduction of capital duly made,

  (c) the purchase of shares in pursuance of an order of the court under section 5 (alteration of objects), section 54 (litigated objection to resolution for company to be re-registered as private) or Part XVII (relief to members unfairly prejudiced), or

  (d) the forfeiture of shares, or the acceptance of shares surrendered in lieu, in pursuance of the articles, for failure to pay any sum payable in respect of the shares.

S 143(1)

Capital maintenance A company cannot be a member of itself, a point originally established in *Trevor v Whitworth* (1887) 12 App Cas 409, HL, which held that a purchase by a company of its own shares, though expressly authorised by the company's articles, was ultra vires and an unauthorised reduction of capital contrary to the interests of the creditors. It is a basic principle of company law that share capital cannot be reduced other than in the manner permitted by the statute which reduction must be confirmed by the court: s 135; *Trevor v Whitworth* (1887) 12 App Cas 409, HL. A transaction which upon examination can be seen to involve a return of capital (other than one properly sanctioned by the court), in whatever form, under whatever label, and whether directly or indirectly, to a member, is void: *Barclays Bank plc v*

British and Commonwealth Holdings plc [1996] 1 BCLC 1; *Aveling Barford Ltd v Perion Ltd* [1989] BCLC 626.

This common law position is now reflected in the statute which expresses the prohibition on a company acquiring its own shares broadly in terms of purchase, subscription or otherwise, though subject to the exceptions in sub-s (3).

This provision does not prohibit a company (A) from acquiring the shares of another company (B) in circumstances where the sole asset of the acquired company (B) is shares in the acquiring company (A): *Acatos & Hutcheson plc v Watson* [1995] 1 BCLC 218. It was argued in this case that if A could not, without authorisation, purchase its own shares then, equally, it could not purchase a company whose sole asset was a holding of approximately 30% of the voting shares of A.

The court accepted that in law what A was purchasing was B and not the assets of that company which were A's shares; therefore, the acquisition did not contravene the prohibition on a company acquiring its own shares. To hold otherwise would be to provide target companies with an effective defence against takeovers, by acquiring shares in a potential bidder. The point is reinforced by s 23, which expressly entitles the target company to retain its shareholding in the bidder although not to vote those shares. In view of the potential for abuse, however, the court would look carefully at any such transaction to ensure that the directors of the acquiring company have acted with an eye solely to the interests of the acquiring company and have safeguarded the interests of shareholders and creditors alike.

S 143(2)

Penalties for contravention   Where none of the exceptions is available, any purported acquisition is void and any contractual obligation to purchase is unenforceable (see *Vision Express (UK) Ltd v Wilson* [1995] 2 BCLC 419); as to potential civil liabilities arising from the acquisition, see note to s 151(3), below. As to penalties, see s 730, Sch 24; 'officer in default' is defined in s 730(5).

S 143(3)

Exceptional cases   A company may acquire its own fully paid shares otherwise than for valuable consideration (for example, as recipient of a legacy) for then there is no erosion of the company's capital but, as the company cannot be a member of itself, the shares must be vested in a nominee to be held on the company's behalf and may be voted as the company directs: *Re Castiglione's Will Trusts, Hunter v Mackenzie* [1958] Ch 549; *Kirby v Wilkins* [1929] 2 Ch 444. Shares so acquired by a public company must be cancelled within three years and no votes may be exercised with respect to them in the meantime: s 146.

Subsection (3)(a)–(c) are the subject of statutory procedures (see ss 159–181 (redemption or purchase); ss 135–141 (reduction of capital)) or require a court order with safeguards for shareholders and creditors in each case and are therefore permissible as exceptional cases; in each case, the shares acquired are cancelled and so the company does not become a member of itself. A failure to adhere correctly to the prescribed procedures will mean that the prohibition in sub-s (1) applies and the acquisition is void: see *Re R W Peak (Kings Lynn) Ltd* [1998] 1 BCLC 193.

Subsection (3)(d) reflects a long-standing exception at common law which was accepted in *Trevor v Whitworth* (1887) 12 App Cas 409, HL. Shares so acquired by a public company must be cancelled within three years and no votes may be exercised with respect to them in the meantime: s 146.

The acquisition by a company (or in certain cases by the company's nominee) of its shares in any of the permitted ways must be disclosed in the directors' report: see Sch 7, paras 7, 8.

144. Acquisition of shares by company's nominee

(1)   Subject to section 145, where shares are issued to a nominee of a company mentioned in section 143(1), or are acquired by a nominee of such a company from a third person as partly paid up, then, for all purposes—

    (a) the shares are to be treated as held by the nominee on his own account; and

    (b) the company is to be regarded as having no beneficial interest in them.

(2)   Subject to that section, if a person is called on to pay any amount for the purpose of paying up, or paying any premium on, any shares in such a company which were issued to him, or which he otherwise acquired, as the company's nominee and he fails to pay that amount within 21 days from being called on to do so, then—

    (a) if the shares were issued to him as subscriber to the memorandum by virtue of an undertaking of his in the memorandum, the other subscribers to the memorandum, or

    (b) if the shares were otherwise issued to or acquired by him, the directors of the company at the time of the issue or acquisition,

are jointly and severally liable with him to pay that amount.

(3)   If in proceedings for the recovery of any such amount from any such subscriber or director under this section it appears to the court—

    (a) that he is or may be liable to pay that amount, but

    (b) that he has acted honestly and reasonably and, having regard to all the circumstances of the case, he ought fairly to be excused from liability,

the court may relieve him, either wholly or partly, from his liability on such terms as the court thinks fit.

(4)   Where any such subscriber or director has reason to apprehend that a claim will or might be made for the recovery of any such amount from him, he may apply to the court for relief; and the court has the same power to relieve him as it would have had in proceedings for the recovery of that amount.

S 144(1)–(2)

This provision is essentially an anti-avoidance provision. If shares are issued to a nominee or he acquires partly paid shares from a third person, the nominee is treated as holding on his own account and liable accordingly in keeping with the doctrine of capital maintenance, subject to the exceptions in s 145. As the nominee may be a person of no substance, the company's position is protected by requiring the other subscribers to the memorandum or the directors, as the case may be, also to meet the liability jointly and severally with the nominee.

S 144(3)

As to whether any person liable might be excused, see the note to s 727, below, which is similarly worded.

145. Exceptions from s 144

(1)   Section 144(1) does not apply to shares acquired otherwise than by subscription by a nominee of a public company, where a person acquires shares in the company with financial assistance given to him directly or indirectly by the company for the purpose of or in connection with the acquisition, and the company has a beneficial interest in the shares.

(2)   Section 144(1) and (2) do not apply—
   (a) to shares acquired by a nominee of a company when the company has no beneficial interest in those shares, or
   (b) to shares issued in consequence of an application made before 22nd December 1980, or transferred in pursuance of an agreement to acquire them made before that date.

(3)   Schedule 2 to this Act has effect for the interpretation of references in this section to a company having, or not having, a beneficial interest in shares.

General note

The obscurely worded exceptions here deal with two situations where a nominee of a company acquiring shares is not treated as holding on his own account, as is the general position dictated by s 144(1). The background to the provision is that it is designed to facilitate the operation of employees' share and pension schemes but its operation is problematic.

S 145(1)

In this instance, where the company has a beneficial interest (see sub-s (3)), the nominee can hold on behalf of the company but he and the subscribers and the directors (to the extent indicated) remain potentially liable under s 144(2). Where the company is a public company, the shares so held must be cancelled within one year and no votes may be exercised with respect to them in the meantime: s 146(1)(d), (2)–(4).

'Financial assistance' is not defined for these purposes: it is assumed that it means financial assistance as defined by s 152, although the definitions there are expressed to apply only to those provisions. The exemption appears to apply whether or not the financial assistance is lawful; however, any purported acquisition financed by unlawful financial assistance will be void under s 151.

S 145(2)

In the situation within sub-s (2)(a), the nominee holds neither on his own account nor on the company's account but as nominee for whosoever is beneficially interested. The nominee, and the subscribers and the directors, are exempt from potential personal liability under s 144(2).

S 145(3)

Schedule 2 provides that residual rights of the company, not vested in possession, arising from a pension scheme (defined in Sch 2, para 5) or an employees' share scheme (defined in s 743) are disregarded in determining whether a company is beneficially interested in any shares for these purposes; as are rights arising with respect to employers' charges and other rights of recovery under any such scheme; and rights of the company in its capacity as a trustee and a personal representative: see Sch 2, paras 1, 3–5.

---

146. Treatment of shares held by or for public company

(1)   Except as provided by section 148, the following applies to a public company—

   (a)   where shares in the company are forfeited, or surrendered to the company in lieu, in pursuance of the articles, for failure to pay any sum payable in respect of the shares;

   (aa) where shares in the company are surrendered to the company in pursuance of section 102C(1)(b) of the Building Societies Act 1986;

   (b)   where shares in the company are acquired by it (otherwise than by any of the methods mentioned in section 143(3)(a) to (d)) and the company has a beneficial interest in the shares;

   (c)   where the nominee of the company acquires shares in the company from a third person without financial assistance being given directly or indirectly by the company and the company has a beneficial interest in the shares; or

   (d)   where a person acquires shares in the company with financial assistance given to him directly or indirectly by the company for the purpose of or in connection with the acquisition, and the company has a beneficial interest in the shares.

Schedule 2 to this Act has effect for the interpretation of references in this subsection to the company having a beneficial interest in shares.

(2)   Unless the shares or any interest of the company in them are previously disposed of, the company must, not later than the end of the relevant period from their forfeiture or surrender or, in a case within subsection (1)(b),(c) or (d), their acquisition—

254

(a) cancel them and diminish the amount of the share capital by the nominal value of the shares cancelled, and

(b) where the effect of cancelling the shares will be that the nominal value of the company's allotted share capital is brought below the authorised minimum, apply for re-registration as a private company, stating the effect of the cancellation.

(3) For this purpose 'the relevant period' is—

(a) 3 years in the case of shares forfeited or surrendered to the company in lieu of forfeiture, or acquired as mentioned in subsection (1)(b) or (c);

(b) one year in the case of shares acquired as mentioned in subsection (1)(d).

(4) The company and, in a case within subsection (1)(c) or (d), the company's nominee or (as the case may be) the other shareholder must not exercise any voting rights in respect of the shares; and any purported exercise of those rights is void.

S 146(1)

This provision is subject to s 148, which applies it to a private company which, after it has acquired its own shares in the specified circumstances, re-registers as a public company.

The intention is to require a public company which acquires shares in any of the specified ways to cancel those shares within the specified time period

Acquisitions of shares   As to sub-s (1)(b), the acquisition must be lawful, ie within one of the exceptions to s 143, and taking into account the exclusion of the exceptions in s 143(3)(a)–(d), the only remaining exception is where the acquisition is of fully paid shares other than for valuable consideration. As to sub-s (1)(c), the acquisition must be of fully paid shares, for the acquisition by a nominee of partly paid shares is within s 144, which would treat the company as having no beneficial interest. As to sub-s (1)(d), note the shorter time limit imposed by sub-s (3)(b) in this instance. This provision does not specify whether it is limited to illegal financial assistance in breach of s 151 or whether it will apply equally if the financial assistance is permissible, for example, under s 153. In the absence of any specific limitation, the provision must apply to financial assistance whether lawful or unlawful.

Schedule 2 provides that residual rights of the company, not vested in possession, arising from a pension scheme (defined in Sch 2, para 5) or employees' share scheme (defined in s 743) are disregarded in determining whether a company is beneficially interested in any shares for these purposes; as are rights arising with respect to employers' charges and other rights of recovery under any such scheme; and rights of the company in its capacity as a trustee and a personal representative: see Sch 2, paras 1, 3–5.

S 146(2)

Cancellation of the shares acquired   In effect, this provision provides a modified reduction of capital scheme not requiring court approval under s 135: see s 147(1).

Any cancellation of the shares must be notified to the registrar of companies, see s 122.

Re-registration   The authorised minimum is £50,000: s 118. As to the re-registration as a private company, see s 147; as to the consequences of non-compliance by a public company (or a private company brought within this provision on re-registration as a public company, see s 148) with the requirement to cancel any shares, see s 149(2).

S 146(3)

Where the company's interest has arisen as a result of certain residual rights vesting in possession, the shares are deemed to have been acquired on the date on which that interest vests in possession: Sch 2, para 2; and this time period for disposal will run from that date.

S 146(4)

Prior to cancellation, the key point is that the voting rights attached to these shares may not be exercised.

147. Matters arising out of compliance with s 146(2)

(1) The directors may take such steps as are requisite to enable the company to carry out its obligations under section 146(2) without complying with sections 135 and 136 (resolution to reduce share capital; application to court for approval).

(2) The steps taken may include the passing of a resolution to alter the company's memorandum so that it no longer states that the company is to be a public company; and the resolution may make such other alterations in the memorandum as are requisite in the circumstances.

Such a resolution is subject to section 380 (copy to be forwarded to registrar within 15 days).

(3) The application for re-registration required by section 146(2)(b) must be in the prescribed form and be signed by a director or secretary of the company, and must be delivered to the registrar of companies together with a printed copy of the memorandum and articles of the company as altered by the resolution.

(4) If the registrar is satisfied that the company may be re-registered under section 146, he shall retain the application and other documents delivered with it and issue the company with a certificate of incorporation appropriate to a company that is not a public company; and—

    (a) the company by virtue of the issue of the certificate becomes a private company, and the alterations in the memorandum and articles set out in the resolution take effect accordingly, and

    (b) the certificate is conclusive evidence that the requirements of sections

146 to 148 in respect of re-registration and of matters precedent and incidental to it have been complied with, and that the company is a private company.

General note

This provision allows for: (1) a modified reduction of capital scheme (cf ss 135–139); and (2) modified provisions for re-registration as a private company (cf ss 53–55).

S 147(1)

This provision authorises the directors to act executively in effecting the cancellation of capital required under s 146(2) without the need for a special resolution and court approval as required by s 135 et seq.

S 147(2)

As the requirement to re-register is mandatory, the procedure for re-registration can be modified by deleting requirements for shareholder approval and for the rights of objecting members under ss 53–55. The resolution to alter the memorandum is by resolution of the directors; and see note to s 53(2) as to the other alterations to the memorandum which are requisite in the circumstances. See s 149 as to the consequences of non-compliance with this requirement.

S 147(3), (4)

See note to s 55; as to the conclusive certificate, see note to s 13(7).

148. Further provisions supplementing ss 146, 147

(1) Where, after shares in a private company—
   (a) are forfeited in pursuance of the company's articles or are surrendered to the company in lieu of forfeiture, or
   (b) are acquired by the company (otherwise than by such surrender or forfeiture, and otherwise than by any of the methods mentioned in section 143(3)), the company having a beneficial interest in the shares, or
   (c) are acquired by the nominee of a company in the circumstances mentioned in section 146(1)(c), or
   (d) are acquired by any person in the circumstances mentioned in section 146(1)(d),

the company is re-registered as a public company, sections 146 and 147, and also section 149, apply to the company as if it had been a public company at the time of the forfeiture, surrender or acquisition, but with the modification required by the following subsection.

(2)　That modification is to treat any reference to the relevant period from the forfeiture, surrender or acquisition as referring to the relevant period from the re-registration of the company as a public company.

(3)　Schedule 2 to this Act has effect for the interpretation of the reference in subsection (1)(b) to the company having a beneficial interest in shares.

(4)　Where a public company or a nominee of a public company acquires shares in the company or an interest in such shares, and those shares are (or that interest is) shown in a balance sheet of the company as an asset, an amount equal to the value of the shares or (as the case may be) the value to the company of its interest in them shall be transferred out of profits available for dividend to a reserve fund and are not then available for distribution.

S 148(1)–(3)

The effect of this provision is that where a private company re-registers as a public company, after having acquired shares in its own company in any of the specified ways, then the obligation to cancel the shares imposed by s 146 will apply, as it applies to a public company, with the time period for cancellation running not from the acquisition etc but from the time of re-registration as a public company.

S 148(4)

In keeping with the doctrine of capital maintenance, the value of the shares or the company's interest in the shares is treated as an undistributable reserve; see also s 264(3)(d).

149. Sanctions for non-compliance

(1)　If a public company required by section 146(2) to apply to be re-registered as a private company fails to do so before the end of the relevant period referred to in that subsection, section 81 (restriction on public offers) applies to it as if it were a private company such as is mentioned in that section; but, subject to this, the company continues to be treated for the purpose of this Act as a public company until it is so re-registered.

(2)　If a company when required to do so by section 146(2) (including that subsection as applied by section 148(1)) fails to cancel any shares in accordance with paragraph (a) of that subsection or to make an application for re-registration in accordance with paragraph (b) of it, the company and every officer of it who is in default is liable to a fine and, for continued contravention, to a daily default fine.

S 149(1)

A public company required by s 146(2) to re-register as a private company which fails to do so is treated as a private company for the purposes of the prohibition in s 81 on private companies making offers of their shares or debentures to the public. For all other purposes, the company is treated as a public company so it cannot take advantage of any of the statutory relaxations (for example, accounting exemptions or use of the elective regime, etc) available to private companies.

S 149(2)

This provision applies to a public company within s 146(2) and any private company which has been brought within the scope of that provision on re-registration as a public company by s 148. As to penalties, see s 730, Sch 24; 'officer in default' is defined in s 730(5).

150. Charges of public companies on own shares

(1) A lien or other charge of a public company on its own shares (whether taken expressly or otherwise), except a charge permitted by any of the following subsections, is void.

This is subject to section 6 of the Consequential Provisions Act (saving for charges of old public companies on their own shares).

(2) In the case of any description of company, a charge on its own shares is permitted if the shares are not fully paid and the charge is for any amount payable in respect of the shares.

(3) In the case of a company whose ordinary business—

    (a) includes the lending of money, or

    (b) consists of the provision of credit or the bailment (in Scotland, hiring) of goods under a hire purchase agreement, or both,

a charge of the company on its own shares is permitted (whether the shares are fully paid or not) if it arises in connection with a transaction entered into by the company in the ordinary course of its business.

(4) In the case of a company which is re-registered or is registered under section 680 as a public company, a charge on its own shares is permitted if the charge was in existence immediately before the company's application for re-registration or (as the case may be) registration.

This subsection does not apply in the case of such a company as is referred to in section 6(3) of the Consequential Provisions Act (old public company remaining such after 22nd March 1982, not having applied to be re-registered as public company).

S 150(2)–(4)

Public companies   For public companies, the acceptance of charges on their own shares is prohibited by this provision subject to three narrow exceptions: (1) where the shares are partly paid and with respect only to the amount due on the shares (sub-s (2)); (2) where the company carries on one of the specified businesses and the transaction is in the ordinary course of its business (sub-s (3)); or (3) where the company altered its structure to become a public company and the charge was in existence prior to that re-registration or registration (sub-s (4)).

Disclosure   Where the company takes a lien or charge over its shares to the extent permitted by sub-ss (2) or (4), details of that lien etc must be disclosed in the directors' report: Sch 7, paras 7, 8.

Private companies   For private companies, there are no restrictions on taking security over their own shares. Table A, reg 8 provides for a charge on partly paid shares with respect to sums due on those shares. Equally, private companies may adopt a wider provision, applicable to fully and partly paid shares and with respect to all moneys due by the shareholder to the company.

CHAPTER VI

FINANCIAL ASSISTANCE BY A COMPANY FOR ACQUISITION OF ITS OWN SHARES

PROVISIONS APPLYING TO BOTH PUBLIC AND PRIVATE COMPANIES

151. Financial assistance generally prohibited

(1) Subject to the following provisions of this Chapter, where a person is acquiring or is proposing to acquire shares in a company, it is not lawful for the company or any of its subsidiaries to give financial assistance directly or indirectly for the purpose of that acquisition before or at the same time as the acquisition takes place.

(2) Subject to those provisions, where a person has acquired shares in a company and any liability has been incurred (by that or any other person), for the purpose of that acquisition, it is not lawful for the company or any of its subsidiaries to give financial assistance directly or indirectly for the purpose of reducing or discharging the liability so incurred.

(3) If a company acts in contravention of this section, it is liable to a fine, and every officer of it who is in default is liable to imprisonment or a fine, or both.

General note

The essence of ss 151–158 is that a company or any of its subsidiaries is prohibited from giving financial assistance (broadly defined), directly or indirectly, for the purpose of the acquisition of any of the company's shares. There is also a prohibition on the discharge, post-acquisition, of any liabilities incurred in so doing. There are a number of specific exemptions from the prohibitions and private companies, if they meet various conditions, are able to avail of a relaxation of the prohibitions. In the event of breach, criminal penalties arise, any financial assistance given is void and directors and third parties involved may face civil liabilities.

Given these consequences, it is of considerable practical importance not to infringe these complex provisions.

Background The prohibition on financial assistance arose out of recommendations of the Greene Committee in 1926 (Cmd 2657) which was particularly concerned with the situation where a company is taken over and the company's assets are used to finance the bidder's acquisition costs. In effect, the company provides financial assistance for the acquisition of shares in the company, a practice which the Greene Committee thought was open to the gravest abuses; see also *Re VGM Holdings Ltd* [1942] 1 All ER 224 at 239. Statutory prohibition followed in successive legislation and is now contained in ss 151–158.

The prohibition on financial assistance has traditionally been seen as an aspect of the doctrine of capital maintenance although financial assistance does not always result in a reduction of capital. The provisions are essentially protective, designed to protect creditors and shareholders against the misuse and depletion of the company's assets, and concerns about the misuse of the target's assets for the benefit of the acquirer remain. A further dimension is where financial assistance is used to ramp share prices, so manipulating the market in the shares of listed companies involved in take-overs: see DTI *Guinness plc, Report of investigation under ss 432(2) and 442 of the CA 1985* (1997). Those practices might more appropriately be regulated by provisions such as the Financial Services and Markets Act 2000, s 118 (market abuse) rather than by company law.

Leaving that aspect aside, most of the transactions which give rise to concerns about financial assistance do remain closely linked to company acquisitions and take-overs where the target company's assets are being used to assist the bidder. Many of the transactions are complex multi-party transactions and it is not always clear whether financial assistance has taken place. In this context, when attempting to identify whether financial assistance has occurred, it can be helpful to bear in mind the comment of Lord Denning in *Wallersteiner v Moir* [1974] 3 All ER 217 at 238:

'The transactions are extremely complicated, but the end result is clear. You look to the company's money and see what has become of it. You look to the company's shares and see into whose hands they have got. You will then soon see if the company's money has been used to finance the purchase.'

Reform   In view of the practical difficulties which arise from applying these provisions, there has been much consultation over the past decade with a view to reform. In 1992 a working party was set up by the DTI to examine the statutory provisions which resulted in a consultation document: DTI *Company Law Review: Proposals for Reform of Sections 151–158 of the Companies Act 1985* (October 1993). Further consultation then ensued with interested parties which prompted a complete re-think by the Department with a view to much simpler reforms than originally envisaged (see revised proposals: DTI *Company Law Reform: Financial assistance by a company for the acquisition of its own shares* (November 1996 and April 1997). The Company Law Review Steering Group has also considered the position and it too proposes further reforms: see *Modern Company Law for a Competitive Economy, The Strategic Framework* (February 1999) pp 86–88; *Modern Company Law for a Competitive Economy, Company Formation and Capital Maintenance* (October 1999) pp 39–45; *Modern Company Law for a Competitive Economy, Completing the Structure* (November 2000) pp 151–152.

Second Company Law Directive   Attempts at reform are hampered with regard to public companies by the requirements of the Second EC Company Law Directive (EEC) 77/91 (OJ L26/1 31.1.1977, pp 1–13), which provides that a public company may not advance funds, nor make loans, nor provide security, with a view to the acquisition of its shares by a third party (art 23).

Directors' duties   It must be borne in mind that, even if a transaction can be structured in a way which puts it beyond the reach of the prohibitions on financial assistance, the directors in entering into any transaction must have regard to their overriding obligation to act bona fide in the interests of the company: see *Plaut v Steiner* (1989) 5 BCC 352.

Key issues   In considering a transaction, the key issues are:
(1)   is there financial assistance as defined in s 152?
(2)   is the financial assistance in breach of the prohibitions in s 151 ? (ie for what purpose was the assistance given?)
(3)   is the financial assistance within any of the specified exemptions in s 153?
(4)   is the company giving the financial assistance a private company which might take advantage of the 'whitewash' procedure in ss 155–158?

(5)   are the directors, in proceeding with the transaction, acting in the best interests of the company as a whole?

S 151(1), (2)

Financial assistance is defined in s 152.

Companies affected   The prohibitions apply to the target company which is prohibited from assisting with the acquisition of its shares; 'company' is defined in s 735 as a company formed and registered under CA 1985 or its predecessors, so excluding foreign companies; this definition includes unlimited companies which are subject to these prohibitions.

The prohibition applies both to the company and 'any of its subsidiaries', which significantly extends the reach of the provisions. 'Subsidiary' is defined in s 736 in a manner which includes foreign companies ('any body corporate': s 736(3)). In *Arab Bank plc v Merchantile Holdings Ltd* [1994] 1 BCLC 330 Millett J held, however, that the wording 'any of its subsidiaries' could not be interpreted in a way which would give the provision extra-territorial effect. The prohibition on financial assistance applies, therefore, only to assistance given by a company formed and registered under CA 1985 or its predecessors and any of its subsidiaries so formed or registered.

A foreign registered subsidiary of an English holding company can give financial assistance for the acquisition of the latter's shares: *Arab Bank plc v Merchantile Holdings Ltd* [1994] 1 BCLC 330; however, the English holding company may still commit the offence of the indirect provision of financial assistance, for example, if it procured the giving of the financial assistance, or otherwise indirectly provided the assistance, as where it hived down assets to the subsidiary to enable it to provide the financial assistance: see *Arab Bank plc v Merchantile Holdings Ltd* [1994] 1 BCLC 330 at 335. It would then be a case of considering which type of financial assistance within s 152(1) has occurred.

Equally, an English subsidiary could give financial assistance to acquire shares in a foreign holding company without infringing the prohibitions but the directors would have to consider whether they were acting in the best interests of the subsidiary in so doing.

If the corporate structure is such that the company providing the financial assistance is not a subsidiary of the company whose shares are being acquired, there are no restrictions on the giving of assistance under ss 151–158 although the directors of that company would have to consider whether the transaction was in the best interests of that company: see *Parlett v Guppys (Bridport) Ltd* [1996] 2 BCLC 34.

Acquisitions of shares   The assistance may be direct or indirect and does not have to be given to the person acquiring the shares. Likewise, the post-acquisition assistance need not be given to the acquirer but to any other person who has incurred a liability for the purpose of the acquisition, such as a guarantor. As to what is meant by 'incurring a liability' and the giving of post-acquisition financial assistance, see s 152(3). The acquisition must be of shares and not, for example, debentures or loan stock and 'acquisition' includes acquisition by purchase and subscription and share exchanges. As the prohibitions only apply to the acquisition of shares, in a particular context, the acquisition of the assets of the target company rather than its shares may be appropriate.

The prohibition applies to financial assistance to whomsoever given, provided that it is *for the purpose of* the acquisition of those shares; or the reduction etc of liability incurred *for the purpose of* that acquisition.

Some examples   The most common example of financial assistance is where a loan is obtained from a bank to finance the acquisition of shares in the target company and the loan is then guaranteed by the target company, or secured on the target company's assets, or the assets of a subsidiary of the target company are charged to secure that loan, or a loan from the target company is used to service the borrowings from the bank. For examples of these type of arrangements, see *Arab Bank plc v Merchantile Holdings Ltd* [1994] 1 BCLC 330 (would have been financial assistance, had the subsidiary not been a foreign registered company); *Coulthard v Neville Russell* [1998] 1 BCLC 143; *Re Continental Assurance Co of London plc, Secretary of State for Trade and Industry v Burrows* [1997] 1 BCLC 48.

Other types of transactions which may amount to financial assistance include the purchase by a target company of an asset at an overvalue so putting the vendor of the assets in funds with which to acquire the company's shares: see *Belmont Finance Corpn v Williams Furniture Ltd (No 2)* [1980] 1 All ER 393, CA; the payment off of a parent company's debt by a subsidiary in order to facilitate an acquisition of the parent company's shares: *Armour Hick Northern Ltd v Armour Trust Ltd* [1980] 3 All ER 833 (vendor of the shares would not sell until the debt due to him was paid); an exchange of assets between companies to facilitate an exchange of shares between shareholders: see *Brady v Brady* [1989] AC 755, HL; *Plaut v Steiner* (1989) 5 BCC 352. Financial assistance can arise where a company agrees to pay over the odds for the services of a director as part of an agreement by which he transfers his shares in the company to his sons: see *Parlett v Guppys (Bridport) Ltd* [1996] 2 BCLC 34.

The financing and structuring of common transactions such as reconstructions, joint ventures and management buyouts can raise issues of potential illegal financial assistance, in particular over attempts to use the target company's assets as security for the financing of the scheme. All sorts of provisions may arise, such as break fees, or group guarantees, or warranties or indemnities with respect to share issues, which can give rise to concerns as to whether they amount to illegal financial assistance. Indeed, the Company Law Review reported that it is estimated that £20m per annum is spent on advice on these provisions: *Modern Company Law for a Competitive Economy, The Strategic Framework* (February 1999) p 87.

Group guarantees   With respect to group guarantees, care must be taken where a bidder for a company has borrowed to finance the bid and, after the successful take-over, the target company is required to join in cross-guarantees which secure the lending of the group including the bidder's borrowings. This could be regarded as post-acquisition financial assistance reducing or discharging a liability incurred by the bidder in acquiring the shares.

Break fees   With regard to break fees (ie sums paid in the event of one party walking away from a transaction in specified circumstances), it might be argued that since no acquisition has occurred (which is why the break fee is payable), there is no breach of sub-s (1). The wording of sub-s (1) (in particular, the final phrase, 'before or at the same time as the acquisition takes place') casts some doubt as to whether the provision prohibits financial assistance given for the purpose of the acquisition of the shares when, for some reason, no acquisition then takes place. Such a prohibition is arguably envisaged by the Second Directive (see general note, above). However, if the financial assistance takes the form of the assumption of a liability to pay certain sums in future, as with a break fee, then the date on which the assistance is given is the date on which the liability is assumed and not when the payment accrues due: see *Parlett v Guppys (Bridport) Ltd* [1996] 2 BCLC 34 at 41–42. Such financial assistance is within sub-s (1), being assistance given to 'someone proposing to acquire shares' before the acquisition takes place.

Financial assistance as defined   Of course, much depends on the purpose of the transaction and whether the assistance provided is financial assistance within s 152. To be within the prohibition, the financial assistance in question must be financial assistance as defined by s 152. For example, a break fee can only be financial assistance if it reduces the net assets to a material extent (see s 152(1)(a)(iv), assuming that it is not drafted as an indemnity) and, if care is taken to set the fee at a figure which does not reduce the net assets to a material extent, the prohibition in sub-s (1) does not arise.

As for the purpose of the financial assistance, it might have been thought that the answer to the concerns about the transactions noted above might lie in s 153(1) and (2), which were designed to exempt transactions where the financial assistance was only incidental or subsidiary to some wider commercial purpose. However, the interpretation of those statutory exemptions adopted in *Brady v Brady* [1989] AC 755, HL (discussed below: see s 153(1), (2)) has ruled out that defence.

In cases of uncertainty, the proposed transaction needs to be reviewed against the key issues identified in the general note to this section.

Perform legally   Where an agreement is capable of being performed in alternative ways, one lawful and one in breach of the provisions on financial assistance, it is to be presumed that the parties intend to carry out the agreement in a lawful and not an unlawful manner: *Brady v Brady* [1989] AC 755, HL; *Plaut v Steiner* (1989) 5 BCC 352; *Neilson v Stewart* [1991] BCC 713; *Parlett v Guppys (Bridport) Ltd* [1996] 2 BCLC 34; *Grant v Lapid Developments Ltd* [1996] BCC 410.

S 151(3)

Penalties   As to penalties, see s 730, Sch 24; 'officer in default' is defined in s 730(5).

The company   The company commits an offence, a provision which has been much criticised; despite this, the company may seek civil remedies (for breach of trust, as opposed to enforcing the agreement for financial assistance) against whose involved in the financial assistance: *Belmont Finance Corporation Ltd v Williams Furniture Ltd* [1979] 1 All ER 118, CA. The statutory provisions do not deal with the civil consequences which remain a matter for the common law.

Directors   A director who authorises the giving of financial assistance in breach of the statutory provisions will be in breach of his duties to the company and liable to make good any loss suffered by the company resulting from the breach: *Selangor United Rubber Estates Ltd v Cradock (No 3)* [1968] 2 All ER 1073; *Steen v Law* [1964] AC 287; *Wallersteiner v Moir* [1974] 3 All ER 217; *Belmont Finance Corporation Ltd v Williams Furniture Ltd* [1980] 1 All ER 393 at 405.

Participation by directors in a scheme which contravenes s 151 may be relied on in disqualification proceedings as evidence of unfitness under the Company Directors Disqualification Act 1986: see *Re Dawes & Henderson (Agencies) Ltd (No 2)* [1999] 2 BCLC 317; also *Re Continental Assurance Co of London plc, Secretary of State for Trade and Industry v Burrows* [1997] 1 BCLC 48. Directors penalised for breaches of the provisions may in turn consider legal action against their advisers for inadequate advice: see *Coulthard v Neville Russell* [1998] 1 BCLC 143; also *Hill v Mullis & Peake* [1999] BCC 325.

Shareholders   A shareholder may seek an injunction to restrain the giving of illegal financial assistance. Once the transaction is completed, he may only bring a derivative action on behalf of the company to recover the sums expended: see *Smith v Croft (No 2)* [1987] 3 All ER 909.

Third parties – knowing assistance   The involvement of third parties such as bankers is often crucial to the carrying out of an illegal financial assistance scheme and the liabilities arising from such 'knowing assistance' were addressed definitively by the Privy Council in *Royal Brunei Airlines Sdn Bhd v Tan* [1995] 2 AC 378.

The key to this liability is dishonesty. A liability in equity to make good any resulting losses to the company will attach to any such third party who dishonestly procures or assists the directors in a breach of their fiduciary duties to the company: *Royal Brunei Airlines Sdn Bhd v Tan* [1995] 2 AC 378, PC; see also *Barnes v Addy* (1874) 9 Ch App 244; *Agip (Africa) Ltd v Jackson* [1992] 4 All ER 385 at 405; *Eagle Trust plc v SBC Securities Ltd* [1992] 4 All ER 488 at 499; *Polly Peck International plc v Nadir (No 2)* [1992] 4 All ER 769 at 777. In this context, acting dishonestly means simply not acting as an honest person would in the circumstances; and, for the most part, dishonesty is to be equated with conscious impropriety: *Royal Brunei Airlines Sdn Bhd v Tan* [1995] 2 AC 378 at 389, PC.

The court when called upon to decide whether a person was acting honestly will look at all the circumstances known to the third party at the time: *Royal Brunei Airlines Sdn Bhd v Tan* [1995] 2 AC 378 at 381, PC. In this area of the law, the nature of the transaction, and whether it would appear to an honest observer as an ordinary commercial transaction, is always a most important factor. There is not any clear dividing-line between commercial and non-commercial transactions, but a need to look at all the circumstances of the particular case: *Grupo Torras SA v Al-Sabah (No 5)* [2001] CLC 221 at 251.

The Court of Appeal in the *Grupo Torras* case emphasised the need for the trial judge to make the basis for his finding crystal clear. If he is finding objective dishonesty, properly so called, he should say so making it clear that, although/even if he accepted that the defendant believed that he was doing nothing wrong, he was nevertheless dishonest by objective standards. If he finds blind eye dishonesty, he should make this clear by saying that the defendant is dishonest by lending assistance after deliberately closing his eyes and ears and/or deliberately not asking questions for fear of learning something he would rather not know: *Grupo Torras SA v Al-Sabah (No 5)* [2001] CLC 221 at 254.

Third parties – knowing receipt   The Privy Council was concerned in *Royal Brunei* solely with accessory liability and did not address the 'knowing receipt' cases.

The key to this liability is knowledge. The older authorities had established that a third party who received company funds may be liable to the company as a constructive trustee if he received the funds with *knowledge* of the directors' breach of duty, whether it be actual knowledge, or knowledge in the sense that he wilfully shut his eyes to the obvious, or wilfully and recklessly failed to make the type of inquiries which an honest and reasonable man would have made, in other words actual knowledge (or its equivalent) was required: *Selangor United Rubber Estates Ltd v Cradock (No 3)* [1968] 2 All ER 1073; *Eagle Trust plc v SBC Securities Ltd* [1992] 4 All ER 488; *Re Montagu's Settlement Trusts* [1992] 4 All ER 308; *Polly Peck*

International plc v Nadir (No 2) [1992] 4 All ER 769; *Cowan de Groot Properties Ltd v Eagle Trust plc* [1992] 4 All ER 700; *Eagle Trust plc v SBC Securities Ltd (No 2)* [1996] 1 BCLC 121.

The issue of 'knowing receipt' liability has been comprehensively reviewed by the Court of Appeal in *Bank of Credit and Commerce International (Overseas) Ltd v Akindele* [2000] 4 All ER 221. The Court of Appeal held that dishonesty is not an essential ingredient of a claim for knowing receipt, and the test for knowledge in such a claim is simply whether the defendant's knowledge made it unconscionable for him to retain the benefit of the receipt. Although such a test could not avoid difficulties of application, the court thought it should avoid those of definition and allocation to which previous categorisations had led. Moreover, it should better enable the courts to give commonsense decisions in the commercial context in which claims in knowing receipt are now frequently made, paying equal regard, on the one hand, to the need to avoid the mischief of paralysing trade and, on the other hand, to the realisation that there are cases in which a commercial man should not be allowed to shelter behind the exigencies of commercial life (at 235–236). See also *Belmont Finance Corporation Ltd v Williams Furniture Ltd (No 2)* [1980] 1 All ER 393.

The agreement   An agreement to provide unlawful financial assistance is unenforceable by either party to it: *Brady v Brady* [1988] 2 All ER 617, HL; *Plaut v Steiner* (1989) 5 BCC 352. Any financial assistance given is void and unenforceable. Hence financial assistance in the form of a loan for the purpose of the acquisition of the shares would be illegal and unenforceable by the company against the borrower (subject to the company's rights against the directors and third parties noted above). Such illegality would also have knock-on effects for the company's accounts, if the loan is shown as an asset: see *Coulthard v Neville Russell* [1998] 1 BCLC 143 at 149.

Where the financial assistance consists of security given by the company for money lent to enable a person to purchase shares in the company, that security is unenforceable: *Heald v O'Connor* [1971] 2 All ER 1105 (*Victor Battery Co Ltd v Curry's Ltd* [1946] Ch 242 to the contrary effect is generally accepted to be wrongly decided: see *Selangor United Rubber Estates Ltd v Cradock (No 3)* [1968] 2 All ER 1073).

The broader transaction, of which the illegal financial assistance is only an element, will stand if the illegal element can be severed: *Herbert Spink (Bournemouth) Ltd v Spink* [1936] Ch 544; *South Western Mineral Water Co Ltd v Ashmore* [1967] 2 All ER 953; *Carney v Herbert* [1985] 1 All ER 438, PC; *Neilson v Stewart* [1991] BCC 713, HL.

Severance can take place provided that the financial assistance is ancillary to the overall transaction and its elimination would leave unchanged the subject matter of the transaction: *Carney v Herbert* [1985] 1 All ER 438 at 446. In this case, the transaction was a contract for the purchase of shares and the illegal financial assistance consisted of mortgages given to secure the payment of the purchase price. The court found that the mortgages could be severed from the agreement for the sale of shares without altering the subject matter and primary obligations of the parties.

---

152. Definitions for this Chapter

(1)   In this Chapter—

    (a)   'financial assistance' means—

      (i)   financial assistance given by way of gift,

      (ii) financial assistance given by way of guarantee, security or indemnity, other than an indemnity in respect of the indemnifier's own neglect or default, or by way of release or waiver,

      (iii) financial assistance given by way of a loan or any other agreement under which any of the obligations of the person giving the assistance are to be fulfilled at a time when in accordance with the agreement any obligation of another party to the agreement remains unfulfilled, or by way of the novation of, or the assignment of rights arising under, a loan or such other agreement, or

      (iv) any other financial assistance given by a company the net assets of which are thereby reduced to a material extent or which has no net assets;

  (b) 'distributable profits', in relation to the giving of any financial assistance—

      (i)   means those profits out of which the company could lawfully make a distribution equal in value to that assistance, and

      (ii) includes, in a case where the financial assistance is or includes a non-cash asset, any profit which, if the company were to make a distribution of that asset, would under section 276 (distributions in kind) be available for that purpose, and

  (c) 'distribution' has the meaning given by section 263(2).

(2)   In subsection (1)(a)(iv),'net assets' means the aggregate of the company's assets, less the aggregate of its liabilities ('liabilities' to include any provision for liabilities or charges within paragraph 89 of Schedule 4).

(3)   In this Chapter—

  (a) a reference to a person incurring a liability includes his changing his financial position by making an agreement or arrangement (whether enforceable or unenforceable, and whether made on his own account or with any other person) or by any other means, and

  (b) a reference to a company giving financial assistance for the purpose of reducing or discharging a liability incurred by a person for the purpose of the acquisition of shares includes its giving such assistance for the purpose of wholly or partly restoring his financial position to what it was before the acquisition took place.

S 152(1)

The structure of this provision is that: (1) certain transactions are identified as financial assistance regardless of whether they have any impact on the company's assets (and there is no de minimis provision to any of these categories); and (2) there is a general provision covering any other financial assistance but only if it reduces net assets to a material extent: see sub-s (1)(a)(iv). It may be, therefore, that the transaction falls within sub-s (1)(a)(iv) but does not have this effect on the net assets, in which case it is not financial assistance for the purpose of s 151.

Financial assistance   By using the words 'financial assistance' in each form of definition, it is a requirement that the actual transaction must be of the type mentioned, and must also amount to financial assistance: *Barclays Bank plc v British and Commonwealth Holdings plc* [1996] 1 BCLC 1 at 38, per Aldous LJ.

Gifts   The payment of a purely compensatory sum by a company to persons acquiring shares in the company is a gift; as is the purchase by a company of assets at an overvalue for the purpose of the acquisition by the vendor (of the assets) of shares in the company: *Plaut v Steiner* (1989) 5 BCC 352 at 364; equally, such a transaction may result in a material reduction of the net assets under sub-s (1)(a)(iv); see also *Parlett v Guppys (Bridport) Ltd* [1996] 2 BCLC 34 at 42–43.

Guarantee, securities etc   Each of the terms used here (guarantee, security, indemnity, release, waiver) has a recognised legal meaning: *Barclays Bank plc v British and Commonwealth Holdings plc* [1996] 1 BCLC 1 at 39, CA. For example, 'an indemnity is a contract by one party to keep the other harmless against loss, but a contract of guarantee is a contract to answer for the debt, default or miscarriage of another who is to be primarily liable to the promise': *Yeoman Credit Ltd v Latter* [1961] 2 All ER 294 at 296, per Holroyd Pearce LJ. The fact that there may be a contract under which a party may recover the same amount by way of damages as he would have recovered under an indemnity is not sufficient to convert that contract into an indemnity: *Barclays Bank plc v British and Commonwealth Holdings plc* [1996] 1 BCLC 1, CA.

Loan or any other agreement   The extension of this category to 'any other agreement' has caused uncertainty although any agreement potentially within this category might in any event fall foul of sub-s (1)(a)(iv).

Any other financial assistance   'Net assets' is defined in sub-s (2). The date at which the reduction falls to be assessed is the date on which the assistance is given: see *Parlett v Guppys (Bridport) Ltd* [1996] 2 BCLC 34. No reduction of net assets arises where a company discharges a debt due to the person who acquires the shares: *Armour Hick Northern Ltd v Armour Trust Ltd* [1980] 3 All ER 833. A reduction occurs where a target company purchases an asset at an overvalue so putting the vendor of the asset in funds with which to acquire the company's shares: see *Belmont Finance Corpn Ltd v Williams Furniture Ltd* [1979] 1 All ER 118, CA. The reduction must be material relative to the company's assets overall and there is no guidance as to what would be a material reduction for these purposes. In *Parlett v Guppys (Bridport) Ltd* [1996] 2 BCLC 34 at 45, Nourse LJ noted that what is 'material' is a question of degree to be answered on the facts of the particular case. In practice, any financial assistance which is greater than 1% of the assets is likely to be regarded as material.

Distributable profits   To be a 'lawfully made' distribution, regard must be had to the requirements of Part VIII (ss 263–281) and the company's own articles.

S 152(2)

In view of the difference in wording between this provision and s 154(2), the requirement is to look to the market value of the assets in contrast to book values: see *Parlett v Guppys (Bridport) Ltd* [1996] 2 BCLC 34 at 42. 'Liabilities' must include reasonable provision for liabilities or losses likely to be incurred or certain to occur but uncertain as to amount or as to the date on which the loss or liability will arise: Sch 4, para 89.

S 152(3)

When determining whether someone has incurred a liability, it is necessary to have regard to a person *changing* his financial position and when determining whether a company gave financial assistance for the purpose of reducing or discharging a liability incurred, it is necessary to see if the company has taken steps wholly or partly to restore that financial position.

153. Transactions not prohibited by s 151

(1)   Section 151(1) does not prohibit a company from giving financial assistance for the purpose of an acquisition of shares in it or its holding company if—

   (a)   the company's principal purpose in giving that assistance is not to give it for the purpose of any such acquisition, or the giving of the assistance for that purpose is but an incidental part of some larger purpose of the company, and

   (b)   the assistance is given in good faith in the interests of the company.

(2)   Section 151(2) does not prohibit a company from giving financial assistance if—

   (a)   the company's principal purpose in giving the assistance is not to reduce or discharge any liability incurred by a person for the purpose of the acquisition of shares in the company or its holding company, or the reduction or discharge of any such liability is but an incidental part of some larger purpose of the company, and

   (b)   the assistance is given in good faith in the interests of the company.

(3)   Section 151 does not prohibit—

   (a)   a distribution of a company's assets by way of dividend lawfully made or a distribution made in the course of the company's winding up,

   (b)   the allotment of bonus shares,

   (c)   a reduction of capital confirmed by order of the court under section 137,

   (d)   a redemption or purchase of shares made in accordance with Chapter VII of this Part,

   (e)   anything done in pursuance of an order of the court under section 425 (compromises and arrangements with creditors and members),

   (f)   anything done under an arrangement made in pursuance of section 110 of the Insolvency Act (acceptance of shares by liquidator in winding up as consideration for sale of property), or

   (g)   anything done under an arrangement made between a company and its creditors which is binding on the creditors by virtue of Part I of the Insolvency Act.

(4)   Section 151 does not prohibit—

(a) where the lending of money is part of the ordinary business of the company, the lending of money by the company in the ordinary course of its business,

(b) the provision by a company, in good faith in the interests of the company, of financial assistance for the purposes of an employees' share scheme,

(bb) without prejudice to paragraph (b), the provision of financial assistance by a company or any of its subsidiaries for the purposes of or in connection with anything done by the company (or a company in the same group) for the purpose of enabling or facilitating transactions in shares in the first-mentioned company between, and involving the acquisition of beneficial ownership of those shares by, any of the following persons—

(i)   the bona fide employees or former employees of that company or of another company in the same group; or

(ii) the wives, husbands, widows, widowers, children or stepchildren under the age of eighteen of any such employees or former employees,

(c) the making by a company of loans to persons (other than directors) employed in good faith by the company with a view to enabling those persons to acquire fully paid shares in the company or its holding company to be held by them by way of beneficial ownership.

(5)   For the purposes of subsection (4)(bb) a company is in the same group as another company if it is a holding company or subsidiary of that company, or a subsidiary of a holding company of that company.

S 153(1), (2)

These provisions provide identical exceptions and apply depending on whether the financial assistance is provided before or at the same time as the acquisition (sub-s (1)) or after the acquisition (sub-s (2)).

The 'purpose' exceptions   The provision allows for two possible defences to an allegation of improper financial assistance. First, it may be argued that the principal purpose in giving the financial assistance was not to give it for the purpose of the acquisition etc although that is usually difficult to argue on the facts. Secondly, it may be accepted that there is financial assistance but, it is argued, the giving of that assistance was incidental to some larger purpose of the company.

The scope of the exceptions   The 'purpose' exception was considered at length in *Brady v Brady* [1988] 2 All ER 617, HL (which involved sub-s (2)). In this case, financial assistance was given by a company to reduce or discharge a liability incurred for the acquisition of shares in the company in prima facie breach of the statutory prohibition. The transaction arose as part of an elaborate scheme for the division of a family business between two brothers. It was argued that this division of the business was the larger purpose, as required by the exception, and the financial assistance was only incidental to it.

The House of Lords adopted a restrictive interpretation of the provision, however, which is thought to have rendered the exemption largely ineffective. In construing 'purpose', Lord Oliver noted that there has always to be borne in mind the mischief against which s 151 is aimed and it is necessary to distinguish between a *purpose* and the *reason* why a purpose is formed.

The fact that a company in giving financial assistance has some more important reason for the transaction than the giving of financial assistance is not the same thing as the company having a 'larger purpose' as envisaged by this provision. The *purpose* of the transaction in *Brady* was to assist in the financing of the acquisition of the shares although the *reason* for the transaction was to facilitate a break up of the business. But the court will not have regard to the financial and commercial advantages in the wider context which are mere by-products of the scheme. The financial assistance in *Brady* was not incidental to a larger purpose, it was not within the exemption therefore, and it was provided in breach of s 151(2). See also *Plaut v Steiner* (1989) 5 BCC 352.

The approach adopted by the House of Lords in *Brady* is driven by a concern that companies will always have a variety of motivations and reasons for transactions and if financial assistance can be justified as being part of wider corporate schemes, the section would be effectively nullified.

Good faith   The assistance must be given in good faith in the interests of the company which requires that those responsible for procuring the company to provide the assistance act in the genuine belief that it is being done in the company's interests; and the time at which this is to be considered is the time at which the assistance is given: *Brady v Brady* [1988] 2 All ER 617 at 632, HL.

S 153(3)

All of the schemes mentioned in this provision are subject to other requirements designed to ensure the protection of creditors and prevent the misuse of assets and, in a number of cases, the schemes require the confirmation of the court. There is no need, therefore, to subject such transactions to the prohibition on financial assistance.

Dividends   The exemption for dividends lawfully declared does offer considerable scope for a successful bidder to use the target company's funds to finance the take-over. The protection for creditors lies in the fact that it can only be a dividend lawfully declared, ie in accordance with the rules of Part VIII and the company's articles. The exemption applies only to distributions by way of dividends or on a winding up.

Unlimited companies   The exemption in sub-s (3)(c) would not be available to an unlimited company as reductions of capital by such companies are not subject to confirmation by the court.

S 153(4)

Public companies wishing to avail of these exemptions may do so only to the extent permitted by s 154.

Lending in the ordinary course of business   The lending of money, to be part of the ordinary business of a company, must be a lending of money in general, in the sense that money lending is part of the ordinary business of a registered moneylender or a bank. Loans deliberately made by a company for the direct purpose of financing a purchase of its shares could never be described as made in the ordinary course of its business: *Steen v Law* [1964] AC 287, PC.

Employees' share schemes   As to the definition of 'employees' share schemes', see s 743. Subsection (4)(bb) ensures that share schemes which enable employee shareholders to buy and sell between themselves are permitted but it would not cover a scheme which allowed sales to outsiders.

154. Special restriction for public companies

(1)   In the case of a public company, section 153(4) authorises the giving of financial assistance only if the company has net assets which are not thereby reduced or, to the extent that those assets are thereby reduced, if the assistance is provided out of distributable profits.

(2)   For this purpose the following definitions apply—

(a) 'net assets' means the amount by which the aggregate of the company's assets exceeds the aggregate of its liabilities (taking the amount of both assets and liabilities to be as stated in the company's accounting records immediately before the financial assistance is given);

(b) 'liabilities' includes any amount retained as reasonably necessary for the purpose of providing for any liability or loss which is either likely to be incurred, or certain to be incurred but uncertain as to amount or as to the date on which it will arise.

General note

This provision limits the availability of the exemptions in s 153(4) (essentially, money lending in the ordinary course of business as money lenders and employees' share schemes) for public companies.

S 154(1)

The requirement is not that there be no material reduction but rather that there be no reduction, unless the assistance is provided out of distributable profits, as defined in s 152(1)(b).

S 154(2)

The definition of 'net assets' here requires that both assets and liabilities be determined by reference to book values (cf s 152(2)); this is not by reference to the last annual accounts but as stated in the company's accounting records immediately before the financial assistance is given. Where appropriate, a company could update its accounting records as to the value of the assets and liabilities prior to, and with a view to facilitating, the giving of the assistance. As to the company's accounting records, see s 221.

PRIVATE COMPANIES

155. Relaxation of s 151 for private companies

(1)   Section 151 does not prohibit a private company from giving financial assistance in a case where the acquisition of shares in question is or was an acquisition of shares in the company or, if it is a subsidiary of another private company, in that other company if the following provisions of this section, and sections 156 to 158, are complied with as respects the giving of that assistance.

(2)   The financial assistance may only be given if the company has net assets which are not thereby reduced or, to the extent that they are reduced, if the assistance is provided out of distributable profits.
   Section 154(2) applies for the interpretation of this subsection.

(3)   This section does not permit financial assistance to be given by a subsidiary, in a case where the acquisition of shares in question is or was an acquisition of shares in its holding company, if it is also a subsidiary of a public company which is itself a subsidiary of that holding company.

(4)   Unless the company proposing to give the financial assistance is a wholly-owned subsidiary, the giving of assistance under this section must be approved by special resolution of the company in general meeting.

(5)   Where the financial assistance is to be given by the company in a case where the acquisition of shares in question is or was an acquisition of shares in its holding company, that holding company and any other company which is both the company's holding company and a subsidiary of that other holding company (except, in any case, a company which is a wholly-owned subsidiary) shall also approve by special resolution in general meeting the giving of the financial assistance.

(6)   Subject to subsection (6A), the directors of the company proposing to give the financial assistance and, where the shares acquired or to be acquired are shares in its holding company, the directors of that company and of any other company which is both the company's holding company and a subsidiary of that other holding company shall before the financial assistance is given make a statutory declaration in the prescribed form complying with the section next following.

(6A) In place of the statutory declaration referred to in subsection (6), there may be delivered to the registrar of companies under section 156(5) a statement made by the persons mentioned in subsection (6) above complying with the section next following.

General note

This 'whitewash' procedure for private companies, though procedurally quite cumbersome and costly to execute, is important in practice given the width of the prohibitions in s 151 and the limited availability of the exemptions in s 153. In some instances, it may be appropriate for a public company to re-register as a private company (see ss 53–55) to take advantage of this procedure.

S 155(1)

Private companies   A private company which complies with these conditions may give financial assistance for the acquisition of its shares or the shares of its holding company: 'company' is defined in s 735; 'subsidiary' and 'holding company' in s 736; and see note to s 151(1) as to the exclusion of foreign companies.

Constitutional matters   A private company which wishes to take advantage of these relaxations will need to ensure that the objects clause in its memorandum of association is suitably all-encompassing. The company's articles must also be checked for any prohibition on the giving of financial assistance. Older companies with the 1948 Table A will need to remove the prohibition on the giving of financial assistance contained in reg 10 of that Table.

Non-compliance   As these provisions are designed primarily for the protection of creditors, non-compliance with these statutory requirements will not be treated as a mere procedural irregularity capable of being waived or dispensed with or validated by unanimous agreement of all the members entitled to vote at meetings of the company: *Re S H & Co (Realisations) 1990 Ltd* [1993] BCLC 1309 at 1316; see *Wright v Atlas Wright (Europe) Ltd* [1999] 2 BCLC 301, CA. Non-compliance will mean a breach of the statutory prohibition on the giving of financial assistance with all the consequences of unenforceability and liability to penal sanctions under s 151(3) which that entails: *Re S H & Co (Realisations) 1990 Ltd* [1993] BCLC 1309 at 1317. The very severity of the consequences of non-compliance may encourage some leniency on the part of the court towards errors in compliance: see *Re S H & Co (Realisations) 1990 Ltd* [1993] BCLC 1309 at 1319.

S 155(2)

'Net assets' are defined in s 154(2). The requirement is not that there be no material reduction but rather that there be no reduction of net assets unless the assistance is provided out of distributable profits, as defined in s 152(1)(b). Financial assistance in the form of a loan, for example, will not reduce the net assets as the money leaving the company is balanced by the borrower's obligation to repay. The position would be different if there are immediate concerns as to the repayment of the loan which required that provision should be made for non-payment or only partial repayment although this would raise issues as to the bona fides of the directors. Whether the net assets are reduced is essentially a question for the accountants: see *Hill v Mullis & Peake* [1999] BCC 326.

S 155(3)

A subsidiary company cannot give financial assistance for the acquisition of shares in its holding company if there is a public company interposed between the subsidiary and that holding company. As to the definition of 'subsidiary' and 'holding company', see s 736.

S 155(4)

Special resolution   As to special resolutions, see s 378. As to the timing requirements regarding the special resolution, see s 157(1); as to objections to the passing of the resolution, see s 157(2), (3). The resolution is ineffective in the circumstances set out in s 157(4). A special resolution must be forwarded to the registrar of companies: s 380(1), (4)(a). 'Wholly-owned subsidiary' is defined in s 736. A written resolution may be used (see s 381A) subject to the modifications to the procedure set out in Sch 15A, para 4.

S 155(5)

Multiple resolutions   This provision requires that where the financial assistance is being provided by a subsidiary for the acquisition of shares in the holding company, the holding company and any intermediate holding company (unless a wholly-owned subsidiary, defined s 736) also must approve by special resolution of the financial assistance (or by written resolution, as noted in sub-s (4)). The number of resolutions required can delay matters.

   As to the definition of 'subsidiary' and 'holding company', see s 736.

S 155(6)

Statutory declaration or statement   As to the contents of the declaration or statement, see s 156. All the directors must make the statutory declaration on the same day but there is no obligation for all the directors to sign the same declaration.

Group directors   Where the financial assistance is being given by a subsidiary for the purpose of the acquisition of shares in its holding company, the statutory declaration (or statement, see sub-s (6A)) must be made by a broader group of directors than simply the directors of the company giving the financial assistance. In this case, the directors of the holding company and any intermediate holding company (whether wholly-owned or not) must also make the declaration.

S 155(6A)

This provision was inserted by the Companies Act 1985 (Electronic Communications) Order 2000, SI 2000/3373, art 10(1), (3), as from 22 December 2000, presumably to facilitate the use of electronic statements although there is a drafting error here in that the provision has omitted the term 'using electronic communications'. The provision should provide for the 'delivery to the registrar using electronic communications' of a statement etc which is the wording used in equivalent provisions inserted by that order: see, for example, ss 2(6A), 7(3A), 12(3A) and 117(3A).

---

156. Statutory declaration under s 155

(1) A statutory declaration made by a company's directors under section 155(6) shall contain such particulars of the financial assistance to be given, and of the business of the company of which they are directors, as may be prescribed, and shall identify the person to whom the assistance is to be given.

(1A) A statement made by a company's directors under section 155(6A) shall state—

    (a) the names and addresses of all the directors of the company,

    (b) whether the business of the company is that of a banking company or insurance company or some other business,

    (c) that the company or (as the case may be) a company (naming such company) of which it is the holding company is proposing to give financial assistance in connection with the acquisition of shares in the company or (as the case may be) its holding company (naming that holding company),

    (d) whether the assistance is for the purpose of that acquisition or for reducing or discharging a liability incurred for the purpose of that acquisition,

    (e) the name and address of the person to whom the assistance is to be given (and in the case of a company its registered office),

    (f) the name of the person who has acquired or will acquire the shares and the number and class of the shares acquired or to be acquired,

    (g) the principal terms on which the assistance will be given,

    (h) the form the financial assistance will take (stating the amount of cash or value of any asset to be transferred to the person assisted), and

    (i) the date on which the assistance is to be given.

(2) The declaration under section 155(6) or (as the case may be) statement under section 155(6A) shall state that the directors have formed the opinion, as regards the company's initial situation immediately following the date on which the assistance is proposed to be given, that there will be no ground on which it could then be found to be unable to pay its debts; and either—

    (a) if it is intended to commence the winding up of the company within 12 months of that date, that the company will be able to pay its debts in full within 12 months of the commencement of the winding up, or

    (b) in any other case, that the company will be able to pay its debts as they fall due during the year immediately following that date.

(3)   In forming their opinion for purposes of subsection (2), the directors shall take into account the same liabilities (including contingent and prospective liabilities) as would be relevant under section 122 of the Insolvency Act (winding up by the court) to the question whether the company is unable to pay its debts.

(4)   The directors' statutory declaration or statement shall have annexed to it a report addressed to them by their company's auditors stating that—

    (a)   they have enquired into the state of affairs of the company, and

    (b)   they are not aware of anything to indicate that the opinion expressed by the directors in the declaration or statement as to any of the matters mentioned in subsection (2) of this section is unreasonable in all the circumstances.

(5)   The statutory declaration or statement and auditors' report shall be delivered to the registrar of companies—

    (a)   together with a copy of any special resolution passed by the company under section 155 and delivered to the registrar in compliance with section 380, or

    (b)   where no such resolution is required to be passed, within 15 days after the making of the declaration or statement.

(6)   If a company fails to comply with subsection (5), the company and every officer of it who is in default is liable to a fine and, for continued contravention, to a daily default fine.

(7)   A director of a company who makes a statutory declaration or statement under section 155 without having reasonable grounds for the opinion expressed in it is liable to imprisonment or a fine, or both.

S 156(1)

Particulars of the financial assistance   The legislation does not state how detailed the particulars must be but the prescribed form requires details, inter alia, of the form of assistance and the principal terms on which it is given, see the Companies (Forms) Regulations 1985, SI 1985/854, Sch 3; and Forms 156(6)(a) and 156(6)(b). As long as those essentials as to the form of the assistance and the principal terms are included, the court may be prepared to overlook the omission of other matters: *Re S H & Co (Realisations) 1990 Ltd* [1993] BCLC 1309. However, in this case, Mummery J advised solicitors to err on the side of caution in terms of the amount of detail which they include in the form, in order to avoid any difficulties over non-compliance (at 1318).

S 156(1A)

Electronic communication   This provision was inserted by the Companies Act 1985 (Electronic Communications) Order 2000, SI 2000/3373, art 11(1),(2), as from 22 December 2000. To avoid the uncertainties noted above as to the level of detail required of the particulars of the financial assistance, this provision sets out the various matters which must be included in the directors' statement.

S 156(2),(3)

Directors' opinion   The statutory declaration required places a considerable burden on the directors (including in some instances the directors of the holding company or any intermediate holding company, see s 155(6)) for they are required to state that the company (by which is meant the company giving the financial assistance) 'will be able to pay' its debts in the period specified, which is at least one year and, in the case of sub-s (2)(a), may be longer.

In forming their opinion, the directors are required to take into account contingent and prospective liabilities as required by IA 1986, s 122 and, in effect, by s 123 (definition of inability to pay debts). It is difficult to determine what weight should be given to such liabilities. In *Re a Company (No 006794 of 1983)* [1986] BCLC 261, it was held that when the court was required to 'take into account' contingent and prospective liabilities, this did not mean that the court should merely add them up and strike a balance against assets, but rather that it should take into consideration whether, and if so when, the prospective liabilities are likely to become present liabilities.

The directors must have regard to their obligation to act bona fide in the interests of the company and the background to their decision to give financial assistance and the reasons for it should be set out in detail in the board minutes.

Problems of timing   If the financial assistance is given as part of a take-over of a company following which the current directors are to be replaced, they will not be willing to make a statutory declaration as they have no knowledge as to what the company's position will be following the take-over. This in effect will require the bidder to put off the financial assistance aspect of the transaction until the new board of directors is in place and willing to swear the declaration. This in turn can cause difficulties with banks funding the take-over which will be unwilling to advance the funds until the financial assistance is in place. Essentially, completion of the take-over has to be organised in a way which will enable the new board of the target company to give financial assistance.

Penalties   The penalties for an unreasonable statutory declaration are set out in sub-s (7).

S 156(4)

A private company which is exempt from the obligation to appoint auditors (see s 249A) will need to appoint them for these purposes.

Auditors' report   The auditors are required to support the directors' declaration and the breadth of the obligations imposed on the directors increases the nature (and therefore the costs) of the investigation which the auditors must undertake. The requirement in sub-s (4)(a) extends beyond the nature and purpose of the financial assistance and will required a detailed and substantial review by the auditors.

The reference to 'their company's auditors' should be a reference to the auditors of the company giving the financial assistance as some of the directors swearing the statutory declaration may be directors of the holding company or of an intermediate holding company (see s 155(6)).

Auditors' liability   It is specifically required that the auditors' report be addressed to the company's directors. It is not addressed to the shareholders and the contents of the report reinforce this by concentrating as they do on supporting the directors' declaration. Equally, however, the auditors are aware that the report will go to the general meeting and is of sufficient importance that it must be available for inspection by the members at the meeting at which the resolution is passed, or provided to the members in advance of signature of a written resolution: s 157(4); Sch 15A, para 4. These factors will be important in terms of potential liability in the event of the declaration and report proving to be erroneous, see *Caparo Industries plc v Dickman* [1990] 2 AC 605, HL, and detailed note to s 235.

S 156(5), (6)

Delivery to the registrar   Delivery of these matters to the registrar is required. Care must be taken to ensure the delivery of all the required particulars to the registrar: the fact that a particular form for the statutory declaration is not used will not mean that there is non-compliance with the statutory obligation to deliver the prescribed particulars: *Re NL Electrical* [1994] 1 BCLC 22.

A failure to deliver within the 15 days required will not result in the financial assistance being improperly provided; it is a breach of the duty to register within the appropriate time but the only consequence will be that the penalties imposed by sub-s (6) will apply: *Re NL Electrical* [1994] 1 BCLC 22. As to penalties, see s 730, Sch 24; 'officer in default' is defined in s 730(5).

S 156(7)

The penalties are purely penal, as to which see s 730, Sch 24; 'officer in default' is defined in s 730(5). No civil liability attaches under the Insolvency Act 1986 in the event of insolvency within 12 months of the payment of the financial assistance (cf IA 1986, s 76).

---

157. Special resolution under s 155

(1) A special resolution required by section 155 to be passed by a company approving the giving of financial assistance must be passed on the date on which the directors of that company make the statutory declaration or statement required by that section in connection with the giving of that assistance, or within the week immediately following that date.

(2) Where such a resolution has been passed, an application may be made to the court for the cancellation of the resolution—

    (a) by the holders of not less in the aggregate than 10 per cent in nominal value of the company's issued share capital or any class of it, or

    (b) if the company is not limited by shares, by not less than 10 per cent of the company's members;

but the application shall not be made by a person who has consented to or voted in favour of the resolution.

(3) Subsections (3) to (10) of section 54 (litigation to cancel resolution under section 53) apply to applications under this section as to applications under section 54.

(4) A special resolution passed by a company is not effective for purposes of section 155—

(a) unless the declaration or statement made in compliance with subsection (6) of that section by the directors of the company, together with the auditors' report annexed to it, is available for inspection by members of the company at the meeting at which the resolution is passed,

(b) if it is cancelled by the court on an application under this section.

S 157(1)

The short time frame reflects concerns that the position as reflected in the directors' declaration of solvency can alter quickly and so the resolution relating to the financial assistance should be close in time to the statutory declaration. In practice, the two matters would commonly be dealt with on the same day. See s 158(2), (4) as to other time limits affecting the giving of the financial assistance.

S 157(2)

As to the meaning of issued share capital, see note to s 738; as to the members of a company, see s 22.

S 157(4)(a)

Where a written resolution is used, see the modification to this requirement in Sch 15A, para 4.

158. Time for giving financial assistance under s 155

(1) This section applies as to the time before and after which financial assistance may not be given by a company in pursuance of section 155.

(2) Where a special resolution is required by that section to be passed approving the giving of the assistance, the assistance shall not be given before the expiry of the period of 4 weeks beginning with—

(a) the date on which the special resolution is passed, or

(b) where more than one such resolution is passed, the date on which the last of them is passed,

unless, as respects that resolution (or, if more than one, each of them), every member of the company which passed the resolution who is entitled to vote at general meetings of the company voted in favour of the resolution.

(3) If application for the cancellation of any such resolution is made under section 157, the financial assistance shall not be given before the final determination of the application unless the court otherwise orders.

(4) The assistance shall not be given after the expiry of the period of 8 weeks beginning with—

   (a) the date on which the directors of the company proposing to give the assistance made their statutory declaration or statement under section 155, or

   (b) where that company is a subsidiary and both its directors and the directors of any of its holding companies made such a declaration or statements, the date on which the earliest of the declarations is made,

unless the court, on an application under section 157, otherwise orders.

S 158(2), (3)

Time limits The reference to more than one resolution is a reference to the situation where a holding company and intermediate holding companies need to approve the financial assistance, see s 155(5). The four-week period does not begin to run until the last resolution is passed, unless there is unanimity. See s 381A(3) as to the date of a written resolution.

Unanimity The limitation on proceeding for a period of four weeks is to allow objecting members to apply to the court (s 157(2),(3)) but the financial assistance may be given immediately if the shareholders with voting rights unanimously approved the resolution. In practice, unanimity may be required by a financial institution which is participating in the transaction.

    Where unanimity amongst the shareholders with voting rights prevails, sub-s (2) envisages that financial assistance may be given immediately but if there are non-voting shareholders who may object to the court, it is inadvisable to proceed since, in the event of an application, financial assistance must not be given before the court determines the matter.

S 158(4)

This provision ensures that the directors cannot give financial assistance at a time far distant from the declaration of solvency. Under sub-s (4)(b), the eight-week period runs from the date of the earliest statutory declaration.

CHAPTER VII

REDEEMABLE SHARES; PURCHASE BY A COMPANY OF ITS OWN SHARES

REDEMPTION AND PURCHASE GENERALLY

159. Power to issue redeemable shares

(1)   Subject to the provisions of this Chapter, a company limited by shares or limited by guarantee and having a share capital may, if authorised to do so by its articles, issue shares which are to be redeemed or are liable to be redeemed at the option of the company or the shareholder.

(2)   No redeemable shares may be issued at a time when there are no issued shares of the company which are not redeemable.

(3)   Redeemable shares may not be redeemed unless they are fully paid; and the terms of redemption must provide for payment on redemption.

General note

Opposition to limited companies acquiring their own shares has been an integral element of English law since the decision in *Trevor v Whitworth* (1887) 12 App Cas 409, HL; and the statutory prohibition of such acquisitions can be found in s 143. However, s 143(3) provides that the prohibition does not apply in relation to, inter alia, the redemption or purchase of shares in accordance with this Chapter, ie ss 159–181.

This power to issue redeemable shares of any class was introduced by CA 1981, together with powers enabling companies to purchase their own shares (see s 162 et seq). These powers are designed to complement each other; a company may issue redeemable shares, envisaging from the outset that the shareholder's commitment will be a short term one or at least for a definite period, while the purchase powers enable the company to buy back shares without having to anticipate that eventuality at the time of issue. Having both powers gives companies considerable flexibility, as the issue and redemption of redeemable shares, procedurally, is less complicated than an exercise of the purchase powers.

This provision applies to the purchase of a company's shares as it applies to a redemption of redeemable shares: s 162(2).

S 159(1)

A company limited by guarantee with a share capital can no longer be formed and must therefore have been in existence prior to 22 December 1980: s 1(4).

Authorisation in the articles   As to authorisation in the articles, see Table A, reg 3. Once authorisation is included in the articles, the company may issue redeemable shares by way of an ordinary resolution. It is not possible to convert existing issued shares into redeemable shares other than where the conversion is part of a properly authorised reduction of capital under s 135: see *Re St James' Court Estates Ltd* [1944] Ch 6; *Forth Wines Ltd, Petitioners* [1991] BCC 638, Ct Sess. Details of any allotted redeemable shares must be included in the notes to the company's accounts: Sch 4, para 38(2).

Time of redemption   Redeemable shares may be redeemed at the option of the company or the shareholder and redemption may occur on a fixed date, or over a fixed period, or on the occurrence of various specified events. The consequences of a failure to redeem are dealt with in s 178.

In addition to redemption, it is possible for the company to purchase redeemable shares, ie outside of their scheme of redemption: see s 162(1). This might be useful where the shareholders are happy to agree to a different time-scale than that originally envisaged by the redemption scheme.

S 159(2)

Non-redeemable shares required   The aim of this provision is to prevent the company being left with no shares; and see s 162(3) which provides that a company may not purchase all its non-redeemable shares so leaving only redeemable shares and defeating the purpose of this provision. On the other hand, there is no specified minimum number of non-redeemable shares so one non-redeemable share will suffice in the case of a private company, or two in the case of a public company.

S 159(3)

The requirement that the shares to be redeemed are fully paid reflects the requirements of the doctrine of capital maintenance.

Payment on redemption   This requirement of payment on redemption is thought to require a payment in cash. The authorities establish that in ordinary legislative usage, and in the absence of a special context, the word 'sale' (and, therefore, its correlative 'purchase') denotes an exchange of property for cash and not for any other form of property: see *Re Westminster Property Group plc* [1985] BCLC 188 at 195, CA, [1984] BCLC 459 at 463; *IRC v Littlewoods Mail Order Stores Ltd* [1963] AC 135; *Robshaw Bros Ltd v Mayer* [1957] Ch 125; *Simpson v Connolly* [1953] 2 All ER 474; *J P Coats Ltd v IRC* [1897] 1 QB 778. But see *BDG Roof-Bond Ltd v Douglas* [2000] 1 BCLC 401, where Park J did not agree that the words 'payment on redemption' were limited to payment in money; in his view, a company could pay for an own share purchase by a transfer of assets.

The requirement of payment on redemption precludes the parties agreeing to a deferral of payment.

Payment on redemption (or purchase: s 162(2)) in accordance with the statutory scheme is exempt from the prohibition on companies giving financial assistance for the purchase of their own shares: s 153(3)(d).

159A   Terms and manner of redemption

(1)   Redeemable shares may not be issued unless the following conditions are satisfied as regards the terms and manner of redemption.

(2)   The date on or by which, or dates between which, the shares are to be or may be redeemed must be specified in the company's articles or, if the articles so provide, fixed by the directors, and in the latter case the date or dates must be fixed before the shares are issued.

(3) Any other circumstances in which the shares are to be or may be redeemed must be specified in the company's articles.

(4) The amount payable on redemption must be specified in, or determined in accordance with, the company's articles, and in the latter case the articles must not provide for the amount to be determined by reference to any person's discretion or opinion.

(5) Any other terms and conditions of redemption shall be specified in the company's articles.

(6) Nothing in this section shall be construed as requiring a company to provide in its articles for any matter for which provision is made by this Act.

General note

This section was inserted by CA 1989, s 133 as from a day to be appointed. However, following consultation, the Department of Trade and Industry concluded that the provision should not be commenced and it will be repealed when the next legislative opportunity arises.

160. Financing etc of redemption

(1) Subject to the next subsection and to sections 171 (private companies redeeming or purchasing own shares out of capital) and 178(4)(terms of redemption or purchase enforceable in a winding up)—

    (a) redeemable shares may only be redeemed out of distributable profits of the company or out of the proceeds of a fresh issue of shares made for the purposes of the redemption; and

    (b) any premium payable on redemption must be paid out of distributable profits of the company.

(2) If the redeemable shares were issued at a premium, any premium payable on their redemption may be paid out of the proceeds of a fresh issue of shares made for the purposes of the redemption, up to an amount equal to—

    (a) the aggregate of the premiums received by the company on the issue of the shares redeemed, or

    (b) the current amount of the company's share premium account (including any sum transferred to that account in respect of premiums on the new shares),

whichever is the less; and in that case the amount of the company's share premium account shall be reduced by a sum corresponding (or by sums in the aggregate corresponding) to the amount of any payment made by virtue of this subsection out of the proceeds of the issue of the new shares.

(3) Subject to the following provisions of this Chapter, redemption of shares may be effected on such terms and in such manner as may be provided by the company's articles.

(4)   Shares redeemed under this section shall be treated as cancelled on redemption, and the amount of the company's issued share capital shall be diminished by the nominal value of those shares accordingly; but the redemption of shares by a company is not to be taken as reducing the amount of the company's authorised share capital.

(5)   Without prejudice to subsection (4), where a company is about to redeem shares, it has power to issue shares up to the nominal value of the shares to be redeemed as if those shares had never been issued.

General note

This provision, other than sub-s (3), applies to the purchase of a company's shares as it applies to a redemption of redeemable shares: s 162(2). As to payments apart from the purchase price, see s 168. As to the ability of a private company to redeem or purchase its own shares out of capital, see s 171 et seq.

S 160(1)

Required funds   Use of the specified funds is designed to ensure that there is no erosion of the capital maintenance doctrine and this position is reinforced by the requirement that the company set up a capital redemption reserve: s 170.

Distributable profits   As to the definition of 'distributable profits', see s 181, which refers to the profits out of which the company could lawfully make a distribution within s 263(2). A lawful distribution in that context requires compliance with various additional rules in ss 270–276; in particular, the auditors must state in writing whether any matter in respect to which the company's accounts are qualified is material for determining whether the distribution is lawful: s 271(4). This requirement can be overlooked and, where no auditors' statement to this effect is obtained, a distribution in reliance on those accounts is unlawful for the purposes of s 263(2), so the company does not have distributable profits within s 181 and any purchase by the company of its own shares on that basis is invalid: *BDF Roof-Bond Ltd v Douglas* [2000] 1 BCLC 401.
   A special reserve arising from a properly authorised cancellation of a share premium account is a sum available for distribution under s 263(3) and, therefore, equally available under s 160(1)(a), even though a share premium account itself could not be so utilised: *Quayle Munro Ltd, Petitioners* [1994] 1 BCLC 410, Ct Sess. This would not be a payment out of capital which would be subject to ss 171–177 but a payment out of distributable profits.

Fresh issue   The fresh issue must be one made for the purposes of the redemption so there will be timing issues to consider in that respect.

Premium on redemption   As a general rule, any premium which is payable on redemption must be paid out of the distributable profits of the company, subject to: (1) the exception in sub-s (2) below; and (2) the ability of a private company to redeem or purchase out of capital, see ss 171–177.

S 160(2)

Redemption when issued at a premium   This complex subsection makes a concession to the general rule that any premium payable on redemption must come from distributable profits. The concession applies to cases where the shares to be redeemed at a premium were originally issued at a premium.

In that situation, any premium payable on their redemption may be paid out of the proceeds of a fresh issue of shares made for the purposes of the redemption, subject to set limits. The amount of the proceeds which may be used in this way is restricted to the lesser of the amounts set out in sub-ss (2)(a) and (b). The share premium account is then reduced by a sum corresponding to the amount paid under this subsection from the proceeds of a fresh issue.

This is one of the limited ways (see also s 171(5)) in which the share premium account (see s 130) may be reduced other than under a statutory scheme of reduction under s 135.

S 160(3)

Provision in the articles   There has been confusion as to the matters which must be contained in the articles, in particular as to whether the articles can provide that certain matters, such as the date of redemption and the amount payable on redemption, are to be left to the discretion of the directors. In practice, matters as to pricing are often left to a formula, in the case of a public company, and to valuation by an auditor, in the case of a private company. The key requirement is that sufficient certainty is provided with respect to the terms and manner of redemption so as to protect the interests of the shareholders. The Department of Trade and Industry considered prescribing (in s 159A) the matters to be covered but it was subsequently considered that such prescription was undesirable and that provision has not been brought into force.

This requirement as to the inclusion of these matters in the articles applies only to redemption and not to purchase schemes: s 162(2). Where a company makes a number of issues of redeemable shares, it is necessary to insert provisions as to each issue in the articles.

S 160(4)

Cancellation of shares redeemed   The requirement that the company cancel the shares redeemed thus reducing the company's issued (but not authorised) capital by the nominal amount of the shares redeemed is consistent with the statutory requirement that the company must not be a member of itself: s 143. In devising a scheme, it is important to envisage the impact which cancellation will have on existing voting patterns and on the question of control within the company.

See s 170 as to the capital redemption reserve which must be established so as to ensure that capital is maintained despite the reduction in the company's issued capital.

Where cancellation has the effect of bringing the nominal value of a public company's allotted share capital below the authorised minimum for a public company of £50,000 (see ss 117, 118), the company is not obliged to re-register as a private company under s 53 (cf ss 139, 146(2)(b) and see s 149).

Notification   If a company redeems any redeemable shares, it must within one month after so doing notify the registrar of companies, specifying the shares redeemed: s 122(1)(e); and the registrar must publish the notification in the Gazette: s 711(1)(h); and if any proceeds of a fresh issue were utilised, a return of allotments is required under s 88.

Holding in treasury   The Department of Trade and Industry announced in early 2000 that, following consultation, it had decided that the present law should be amended to allow companies to purchase their own shares and hold them in treasury for resale at a later date although this facility is to be restricted to listed companies. At the time of writing, regulations to implement these changes are still awaited.

S 160(5)

Where the company is a public company, it may be desirable (though not required, it seems) to issue further shares in order to maintain the company's minimum allotted capital at £50,000, being the authorised minimum under s 118.

The company can re-issue shares up to the nominal value of the shares to be redeemed under this provision without increasing the authorised capital at this stage.

The precise timescale of 'about to redeem' is not defined but was defined in 1981, s 45(12) (for stamp duty purposes), as requiring the shares to be redeemed within one month after the issue of the new shares. A court may still find that figure a useful guide as to the appropriate period to allow.

---

161. *(Repealed by FA 1988, s 148, Sch 14, Pt XI, with effect from 22 March 1988.)*

162. Power of company to purchase own shares

(1) Subject to the following provisions of this Chapter, a company limited by shares or limited by guarantee and having a share capital may, if authorised to do so by its articles, purchase its own shares (including any redeemable shares).

(2) Sections 159 to 161 apply to the purchase by a company under this section of its own shares as they apply to the redemption of redeemable shares, save that the terms and manner of purchase need not be determined by the articles as required by section 160(3).

(3) A company may not under this section purchase its shares if as a result of the purchase there would no longer be any member of the company holding shares other than redeemable shares.

General note

In addition to a power to issue redeemable shares of any class, CA 1981 also introduced provisions to enable companies to purchase their own shares.

While the statutory provisions enable a company to purchase its own shares, the company and the members will need to have regard to the taxation implications of so doing. Consideration of the taxation position is beyond the scope of this work.

It is not possible to regard the requirements of this section and s 164 (authority for off-market purchase) as merely procedural and imposed for the benefit only of the current members; accordingly, it is not open to the members unanimously to waive due performance of the statutory requirements: *Re R W Peak (Kings Lynn) Ltd* [1998] 1 BCLC 193; *Wright v Atlas Wright (Europe) Ltd* [1999] 2 BCLC 301 at 315, CA.

S 162(1)

In order for a company to purchase its own shares, it must be authorised to do so by the articles, see Table A, reg 35.

It is possible for a company to purchase redeemable shares, ie outside of their scheme of redemption. This might be useful where the shareholders are happy to agree to a different timescale to that originally envisaged by the redemption scheme.

S 162(2)

The provisions on redemption and purchase complement one another and together provide a degree of flexibility for a company's equity capital structure. The requirements of ss 159–161 (except s 160(3)) with respect to redemption schemes are specifically applied to purchases by this provision and note, in particular, the financing requirements in s 160. The exclusion of s 160(3) means that the terms and manner of purchase need not be set out in the articles.

Any shares purchased must be cancelled (s 160(4)) and the registrar of companies notified of the cancellation under s 122(1)(f).

S 162(3)

Non-redeemable shares   A company cannot issue redeemable shares unless it has other shares which are not redeemable: s 159(2). This provision complements that provision by providing that a company with redeemable and non-redeemable shares cannot opt to purchase back the non-redeemable shares so leaving only redeemable shares and defeating the statutory purpose.

---

163. Definitions of 'off-market' and 'market' purchase

(1)   A purchase by a company of its own shares is 'off-market' if the shares either—

  (a)   are purchased otherwise than on a recognised investment exchange, or

  (b)   are purchased on a recognised investment exchange but are not subject to a marketing arrangement on that investment exchange.

(2)   For this purpose, a company's shares are subject to a marketing arrangement on a recognised investment exchange if either—

  (a)   they are listed under Part IV of the Financial Services Act 1986; or

  (b)   the company has been afforded facilities for dealings in those shares to take place on that investment exchange without prior permission for individual transactions from the authority governing that investment exchange and without limit as to the time during which those facilities are to be available.

(3) A purchase by a company of its own shares is a 'market purchase' if it is a purchase made on a recognised investment exchange, other than a purchase which is an off-market purchase by virtue of subsection (1)(b).

(4) In this section 'recognised investment exchange' means a recognised investment exchange other than an overseas investment exchange within the meaning of the Financial Services Act 1986.

General note

The procedures applicable to purchase schemes vary depending on whether the purchase is an off-market purchase or a market purchase. This section defines those terms although in a somewhat obscure manner. The net effect of the definitions is that:

(1) any private company purchasing its own shares will always make an off-market purchase;

(2) whether a public company makes an off-market purchase or a market purchase depends on whether the purchase takes place on a recognised investment exchange.

S 163(1), (2)

A purchase by a company of its own shares is an off-market purchase where the shares are not purchased on a recognised investment exchange which, for these purposes, means purchases on the London Stock Exchange or on Virt-x Exchange, formerly Tradepoint, see sub-s (4) below.

Subsection (1)(b) also includes purchases on a recognised investment exchange where the shares are not subject to a marketing arrangement on that exchange. This element related to the now abolished Stock Exchange rule 4.2, whereby bargains in unlisted securities could be transacted on the exchange between Stock Exchange member firms but such transactions are no longer possible. Subsection (1)(b) is therefore obsolete; as is sub-s (2).

The key distinction now is whether the purchase occurs on a recognised investment exchange (defined by sub-s (4)), something which can be unclear. Guidance as to market practice is likely to be influential here, as to which see the London Stock Exchange Market Rules, Ch 2, para 2.1, as to the transactions which are on market transactions for those purposes; included are transactions in AIM (Alternative Investment Market) securities.

S 163(3)

A purchase by a company of its own shares is a market purchase if it is a purchase made on a recognised investment exchange; the final clause here is rendered obsolete by the change in Stock Exchange practices noted above.

S 163(4)

A recognised investment exchange is defined by reference to FSA 1986. There are currently six recognised investment exchanges but this provision is limited to a recognised investment exchange where shares may be purchased and which is not an overseas investment exchange. The net result is that the only recognised investment exchanges for these purposes currently are the London Stock Exchange and Virt-x Exchange, formerly Tradepoint (an electronic, order-driven stock exchange for professional securities traders).

164. Authority for off-market purchase

(1)   A company may only make an off-market purchase of its own shares in pursuance of a contract approved in advance in accordance with this section or under section 165 below.

(2)   The terms of the proposed contract must be authorised by a special resolution of the company before the contract is entered into; and the following subsections apply with respect to that authority and to resolutions conferring it.

(3)   Subject to the next subsection, the authority may be varied, revoked or from time to time renewed by special resolution of the company.

(4)   In the case of a public company, the authority conferred by the resolution must specify a date on which the authority is to expire; and in a resolution conferring or renewing authority that date must not be later than 18 months after that on which the resolution is passed.

(5)   A special resolution to confer, vary, revoke or renew authority is not effective if any member of the company holding shares to which the resolution relates exercises the voting rights carried by any of those shares in voting on the resolution and the resolution would not have been passed if he had not done so.

For this purpose—

(a)   a member who holds shares to which the resolution relates is regarded as exercising the voting rights carried by those shares not only if he votes in respect of them on a poll on the question whether the resolution shall be passed, but also if he votes on the resolution otherwise than on a poll;

(b)   notwithstanding anything in the company's articles, any member of the company may demand a poll on that question; and

(c)   a vote and a demand for a poll by a person as proxy for a member are the same respectively as a vote and a demand by the member.

(6)   Such a resolution is not effective for the purposes of this section unless (if the proposed contract is in writing) a copy of the contract or (if not) a written memorandum of its terms is available for inspection by members of the company both—

(a)   at the company's registered office for not less than 15 days ending with the date of the meeting at which the resolution is passed, and

(b)   at the meeting itself.

A memorandum of contract terms so made available must include the names of any members holding shares to which the contract relates; and a copy of the contract so made available must have annexed to it a written memorandum specifying any such names which do not appear in the contract itself.

(7) A company may agree to a variation of an existing contract so approved, but only if the variation is authorised by a special resolution of the company before it is agreed to; and subsections (3) to (6) above apply to the authority for a proposed variation as they apply to the authority for a proposed contract, save that a copy of the original contract or (as the case may require) a memorandum of its terms, together with any variations previously made, must also be available for inspection in accordance with subsection (6).

S 164(1)–(4)

Approval of the contract in advance An 'off-market' purchase is defined by s 163. The general meeting must authorise in advance, by a special resolution, the terms of a specific contract of purchase under this section or a contingent contract under s 165. As the terms of the proposed contract must be authorised, the contract or memorandum must indicate the price to be paid for the shares. Approval of the terms of the contract must be given before, and not at the same time as, the contract is entered into: see *Re R W Peak (Kings Lynn) Ltd* [1998] 1 BCLC 193.

Special resolution As to the requirements with respect to a special resolution, see s 378; delivery to the registrar of companies is required: s 380(1), (4)(a).

Written resolution Private companies may proceed by way of a written resolution signed by or on behalf of all the members who would be entitled to attend and vote at a general meeting: s 381A; and the statutory written resolution procedure is modified when used in relation to a purchase scheme: Sch 15A, para 5(1)(a). In such cases, the member holding shares to which the resolution relates is not for these purposes regarded as a member who is entitled to attend and vote at the general meeting: s 381A, Sch 15A, para 5(2). The vendor's consent to the written resolution is not required and he does not participate in the written process. Where a written resolution is used, therefore, the member is precluded from taking part even if only a small proportion of his shares are the subject of the contract.

    This exclusion of the member affected means that the written resolution procedure could not be used in this context by a single member private company. This can be overcome by the single member holding a meeting for, as the company is not purchasing all of his shares (which is precluded by s 162(3)), he may pass the required resolution at a meeting by exercising the vote attached to his remaining share or shares.

Informal unanimous consent It is not possible to regard the requirements of this section as merely procedural and imposed for the benefit only of the current members; accordingly, it is not open to the members unanimously to waive due compliance with the detailed requirements of this provision (*Re R W Peak (Kings Lynn) Ltd* [1998] 1 BCLC 193; also *Wright v Atlas Wright (Europe) Ltd* [1999] 2 BCLC 301 at 315); although, perhaps, such consent would be sufficient to overcome other elements of the statutory scheme, such as the requirement in sub-s (6) that a memorandum of the terms of the contract for purchase be available for inspection by members ahead of a general meeting to decide on the matter: see *BDG Roof-Bond Ltd v Douglas* [2000] 1 BCLC 401 at 417.

S 164(5)

Voting by the vendor   This provision does not prohibit directly a member whose shares are the subject of the special resolution from voting on the resolution. Instead, it provides that if the votes attached to the affected shares are exercised, whether on a show of hands or a poll, and whether by proxy or by the member, and the resolution would not have been passed if this had not been done, then the resolution is ineffective.

This limitation only affects the votes attached to the shares in question so, on a poll, a vendor may exercise without restraint any votes attached to any other shares which he may hold. These may be sufficient in number to have an impact on the passing of the resolution. In view of the significance of the transaction, any member may demand a poll, notwithstanding any provision in the articles.

As to the identification of those members holding shares to which the contract relates, see sub-s (6).

S 164(6)

Disclosure requirements   The special resolution is not effective if the specified disclosure requirements are not satisfied.

This 15-day disclosure requirement limits the speed with which a general meeting can be called to pass the required special resolution. A private company can overcome the problem by using the written resolution procedure (if unanimity can be achieved) which requires that, instead of the contract or details of the contract being available for inspection for 15 days before the meeting, the documents referred to must be supplied to each member at or before the time when the resolution was supplied to him for signature: Sch 15A, para 5(3).

The contract or memorandum available for inspection must include the names of the members holding shares to which the contract relates. This will identify the voting rights affected by sub-s (5).

S 164(7)

Variation of contract already approved   Changing circumstances may mean that it becomes necessary to vary a contract which has been approved by the general meeting. The variation too has to be approved by special resolution and sub-ss (3)–(6) apply so that the same conditions relating to voting and disclosure apply to the special resolution authorising the variation as applied to the authorisation of the original contract.

In this case, a copy of the original contract together with any variations previously made must be available for inspection by the members. Where a written resolution is used, these documents must be supplied to each member at or before the time when the resolution was supplied to him for signature: Sch 15A, para 5(3).

Payments in consideration of the variation of the contract are governed by s 168.

---

165. Authority for contingent purchase contract

(1)   A contingent purchase contract is a contract entered into by a company and relating to any of its shares—

(a) which does not amount to a contract to purchase those shares, but

(b) under which the company may (subject to any conditions) become entitled or obliged to purchase those shares.

(2)   A company may only make a purchase of its own shares in pursuance of a contingent purchase contract if the contract is approved in advance by a special resolution of the company before the contract is entered into; and subsections (3) to (7) of section 164 apply to the contract and its terms.

General note

A company may make an off-market purchase by approving in advance a specific contract under s 164 or by approving in advance a contingent contract under this provision.

Contingent contracts were included to provide a further element of flexibility. A company might want to enter into contingent agreements, for example, with a view to buying out a particular shareholder at some future date, or when a certain level of profits is achieved. A contingent contract could also be a useful alternative to issuing a new class of redeemable shares.

See s 168 as to payments (apart from the purchase price) made in respect of contingent contracts.

S 165(2)

The company in general meeting must approve in advance the contingent purchase contract by special resolution but it need not subsequently approve the actual purchase. Only one special resolution is needed.

The purchase process with regard to a contingent contract is identical to that outlined in relation to a specific contract and the provisions of s 164(3)–(7) apply. The modifications of s 164(3)–(7) which are necessary where a written resolution is used also apply where a written resolution is used to approve a contingent purchase contract: Sch 15A, para 5(4)(a).

166. Authority for market purchase

(1)   A company shall not make a market purchase of its own shares unless the purchase has first been authorised by the company in general meeting.

(2)   That authority—

(a) may be general for that purpose, or limited to the purchase of shares of any particular class or description, and

(b) may be unconditional or subject to conditions.

(3)   The authority must—

(a) specify the maximum number of shares authorised to be acquired,

(b) determine both the maximum and the minimum prices which may be paid for the shares, and

(c) specify a date on which it is to expire.

(4) The authority may be varied, revoked or from time to time renewed by the company in general meeting, but this is subject to subsection (3) above; and in a resolution to confer or renew authority, the date on which the authority is to expire must not be later than 18 months after that on which the resolution is passed.

(5) A company may under this section make a purchase of its own shares after the expiry of the time limit imposed to comply with subsection (3)(c), if the contract of purchase was concluded before the authority expired and the terms of the authority permitted the company to make a contract of purchase which would or might be executed wholly or partly after its expiration.

(6) A resolution to confer or vary authority under this section may determine either or both the maximum and minimum prices for purchase by—

(a) specifying a particular sum, or

(b) providing a basis or formula for calculating the amount of the price in question without reference to any person's discretion or opinion.

(7) A resolution of a company conferring, varying, revoking or renewing authority under this section is subject to section 380 (resolution to be sent to registrar of companies within 15 days).

S 166(1)–(4), (6)

Authorisation in advance A 'market' purchase is defined in s 163. Authorisation must be sought before any purchase is made. In this instance, the general meeting does not approve a specific contract but authorises the company to purchase shares and this affects the procedure required by the section. For example, there is no question of preventing any potential vendor from voting on the resolution since the authority is not specifically aimed at any particular shares (cf s 164(5)).

Price for purchase The maximum and minimum price which may be paid for the shares must be determined in the authority so as to ensure that the directors are not in a position to enter into transactions at varying prices, depending on their relationship with the vendors; this is subject to the discretion in sub-s (6) as to specifying a particular sum or using a formula.

S 166(7)

Notification This requirement to notify the registrar of companies within 15 days is an exception to the general rule that ordinary resolutions do not have to be notified.

167. Assignment or release of company's right to purchase own shares

(1) The rights of a company under a contract approved under section 164 or 165, or under a contract for a purchase authorised under section 166, are not capable of being assigned.

(2) An agreement by a company to release its rights under a contract approved under section 164 or 165 is void unless the terms of the release agreement are approved in advance by a special resolution of the company before the agreement is entered into; and subsections (3) to (7) of section 164 apply to approval for a proposed release agreement as to authority for a proposed variation of an existing contract.

S 167(1)

Assignment This prohibition on assignment is designed, in conjunction with the requirement that companies cancel any shares purchased (ss 160(4), 162(2)), to ensure that companies are not able to deal or speculate in their own shares.

S 167(2)

Release There may be good commercial reasons for a company to be permitted to give up its right to purchase. Hence a company is allowed to enter into an agreement to release its rights under a specific contract of purchase off-market or a contingent purchase contract.

In recognition of the fact that abuses can occur where companies pay significant sums to be released from their obligations, the requirements imposed by s 164(3)–(7) apply to the release agreement as they apply to authority for a proposed variation of an existing contract. This means, in particular, that the special resolution authorising the release is ineffective unless certain voting and disclosure requirements are adhered to, see s 164(3)–(7), with appropriate modifications where a written resolution is used for the release, see Sch 15A, para 5(4)(b).

Payments with respect to any release are governed by s 168.

168. Payments apart from purchase price to be made out of distributable profits

(1) A payment made by a company in consideration of—

   (a) acquiring any right with respect to the purchase of its own shares in pursuance of a contract approved under section 165, or

   (b) the variation of a contract approved under section 164 or 165, or

   (c) the release of any of the company's obligations with respect to the purchase of any of its own shares under a contract approved under section 164 or 165 or under a contract for a purchase authorised under section 166,

must be made out of the company's distributable profits.

(2) If the requirements of subsection (1) are not satisfied in relation to a contract—

   (a) in a case within paragraph (a) of the subsection, no purchase by the company of its own shares in pursuance of that contract is lawful under this Chapter,

(b) in a case within paragraph (b), no such purchase following the variation is lawful under this Chapter, and

(c) in a case within paragraph (c), the purported release is void.

S 168(1)

This section ensures that certain payments made by the company, apart from the purchase price, are made out of distributable profits (defined in s 181). The intention is to prevent companies evading the requirements as to the funding of the purchase money (see s 160) by making significant payments in addition to the purchase price.

While a private company under s 171 may make a payment in respect of redemption or purchase out of capital, this concession does not extend to the payments specified in this provision. This is clear because, unlike s 160, there is no saving here for purchases out of capital.

S 168(2)

If a purchase is not lawful under this Chapter, s 143(1) will apply and the purchase will be illegal and void under s 143(2).

169. Disclosure by company of purchase of own shares

(1) Within the period of 28 days beginning with the date on which any shares purchased by a company under this Chapter are delivered to it, the company shall deliver to the registrar of companies for registration a return in the prescribed form stating with respect to shares of each class purchased the number and nominal value of those shares and the date on which they were delivered to the company.

(2) In the case of a public company, the return shall also state—

(a) the aggregate amount paid by the company for the shares; and

(b) the maximum and minimum prices paid in respect of shares of each class purchased.

(3) Particulars of shares delivered to the company on different dates and under different contracts may be included in a single return to the registrar; and in such a case the amount required to be stated under subsection (2)(a) is the aggregate amount paid by the company for all the shares to which the return relates.

(4) Where a company enters into a contract approved under section 164 or 165, or a contract for a purchase authorised under section 166, the company shall keep at its registered office—

(a) if the contract is in writing, a copy of it; and

(b) if not, a memorandum of its terms,

from the conclusion of the contract until the end of the period of 10 years beginning with the date on which the purchase of all the shares in pursuance of the contract is completed or (as the case may be) the date on which the contract otherwise determines.

(5)   Every copy and memorandum so required to be kept shall ... be open to inspection without charge—

   (a) by any member of the company, and

   (b) if it is a public company, by any other person.

(6)   If default is made in delivering to the registrar any return required by this section, every officer of the company who is in default is liable to a fine and, for continued contravention, to a daily default fine.

(7)   If default is made in complying with subsection (4), or if an inspection required under subsection (5) is refused, the company and every officer of it who is in default is liable to a fine and, for continued contravention, to a daily default fine.

(8)   In the case of a refusal of an inspection required under subsection (5) of a copy or memorandum, the court may by order compel an immediate inspection of it.

(9)   The obligation of a company under subsection (4) to keep a copy of any contract or (as the case may be) a memorandum of its terms applies to any variation of the contract so long as it applies to the contract.

General note

In view of the departure from the capital maintenance doctrine and the potential significance for members and creditors of any exercise by a company of these powers to purchase its own shares, the company is required to comply with extensive disclosure requirements designed to keep all interested parties informed of purchase transactions.

   Details of shares purchased or redeemed by the company must be included in the directors' report: Sch 7, paras 7–8.

S 169(1)–(3)

Notification   The important date for these purposes is the date of delivery of the shares to the company. There is no definition of 'delivery' in this context but what must be envisaged is the depositing at the company's registered office, or such other place as may be agreed, of the share certificates evidencing title to the shares in question. Where the shares are uncertificated, the equivalent position would appear to be that delivery occurs when the company receives a CREST instruction to change an entry on the register of securities in relation to uncertificated securities: Uncertificated Securities Regulations 1995, SI 1995/3272, reg 23. As to uncertificated securities and CREST, see note to s 182(1)(b), below.

S 169(4)–(5), (9)

As to the registered office, see s 287; the requirement to maintain these records for a period of ten years beginning on the date specified can be overlooked. As to inspection, see the Companies (Inspection and Copying of Registers, Indices and Documents) Regulations 1991, SI 1991/1998.

S 169(6)–(7)

As to penalties, see s 730, Sch 24; 'officer in default' is defined in s 730(5).

S 169(8)

This provision is necessary because, but for the section, it is not clear that there is any right of inspection or that the court has the power to compel inspection: see *Conway v Petronius Clothing Co Ltd* [1978] 1 All ER 185 at 199. The court's power is discretionary: see *Pelling v Families need Fathers Ltd* [2001] All ER (D) 03, (Aug) CA.

170. The capital redemption reserve

(1)   Where under this Chapter shares of a company are redeemed or purchased wholly out of the company's profits, the amount by which the company's issued share capital is diminished in accordance with section 160(4) on cancellation of the shares redeemed or purchased shall be transferred to a reserve, called 'the capital redemption reserve'.

(2)   If the shares are redeemed or purchased wholly or partly out of the proceeds of a fresh issue and the aggregate amount of those proceeds is less than the aggregate nominal value of the shares redeemed or purchased, the amount of the difference shall be transferred to the capital redemption reserve.

(3)   But subsection (2) does not apply if the proceeds of the fresh issue are applied by the company in making a redemption or purchase of its own shares in addition to a payment out of capital under section 171.

(4)   The provisions of this Act relating to the reduction of a company's share capital apply as if the capital redemption reserve were paid-up share capital of the company, except that the reserve may be applied by the company in paying up its unissued shares to be allotted to members of the company as fully paid bonus shares.

General note

One of the concerns with purchase schemes is that they involve the reduction of capital to the possible detriment of the creditors in a manner which is not subject to the controls of the statutory scheme for reduction of capital in ss 135–141. To protect against this possibility, companies exercising the power to redeem or purchase are required to establish a capital redemption reserve under this provision which is one of the company's undistributable reserves (see s 264(3)(b)).

This provision applies to redemption and purchase schemes.

S 170(1)

Wholly out of profits   Capital is maintained with the issued capital reduced and the capital redemption reserve increased by a like amount.

S 170(2)–(3)

Wholly or partly out of the proceeds of a fresh issue A transfer is required to the capital redemption reserve where the proceeds of the new issue are insufficient to replace entirely the nominal value of the old capital which is being redeemed or purchased. This is qualified by sub-s (3), whereby no transfer to the capital redemption reserve is required where the proceeds of the fresh issue are used as part of a scheme by a private company to purchase out of capital under s 171. It is accepted that there will be a reduction of capital in such case

S 170(4)

Nature of the capital redemption reserve The capital redemption reserve, like the share premium account (see s 130), must be treated as if it were paid up share capital and can be used only for restricted purposes in keeping with its role as a mechanism to ensure the maintenance of capital. It is one of the company's undistributable reserves (see s 264(3)(b)) but this provision allows for its use for the allotment of fully paid bonus shares.

The capital redemption reserve is subject to the statutory scheme for reduction of capital (ss 135–141) but it may also be reduced in accordance with s 171(5).

REDEMPTION OR PURCHASE OF OWN SHARES OUT OF CAPITAL (PRIVATE COMPANIES ONLY)

171. Power of private companies to redeem or purchase own shares out of capital

(1) Subject to the following provisions of this Chapter, a private company limited by shares or limited by guarantee and having a share capital may, if so authorised by its articles, make a payment in respect of the redemption or purchase under section 160 or (as the case may be) section 162, of its own shares otherwise than out of its distributable profits or the proceeds of a fresh issue of shares.

(2) References below in this Chapter to payment out of capital are (subject to subsection (6)) to any payment so made, whether or not it would be regarded apart from this section as a payment out of capital.

(3) The payment which may (if authorised in accordance with the following provisions of this Chapter) be made by a company out of capital in respect of the redemption or purchase of its own shares is such an amount as, taken together with—

 (a) any available profits of the company, and

 (b) the proceeds of any fresh issue of shares made for the purposes of the redemption or purchase, is equal to the price of redemption or purchase; and the payment permissible under this subsection is referred to below in this Chapter as the permissible capital payment for the shares.

(4)   Subject to subsection (6), if the permissible capital payment for shares redeemed or purchased is less than their nominal amount, the amount of the difference shall be transferred to the company's capital redemption reserve.

(5)   Subject to subsection (6), if the permissible capital payment is greater than the nominal amount of the shares redeemed or purchased—

  (a)   the amount of any capital redemption reserve, share premium account or fully paid share capital of the company, and

  (b)   any amount representing unrealised profits of the company for the time being standing to the credit of any reserve maintained by the company in accordance with paragraph 34 of Schedule 4 or paragraph 34 of Schedule 8 (revaluation reserve),

may be reduced by a sum not exceeding (or by sums not in the aggregate exceeding) the amount by which the permissible capital payment exceeds the nominal amount of the shares.

(6)   Where the proceeds of a fresh issue are applied by a company in making any redemption or purchase of its own shares in addition to a payment out of capital under this section, the references in subsections (4) and (5) to the permissible capital payment are to be read as referring to the aggregate of that payment and those proceeds.

General note

This section, and the following provisions, permit a private company in certain circumstances to redeem or purchase its own shares out of capital, ie out of assets representing its existing paid-up share capital.

One of the attractions of such a scheme is that it enables companies to reduce capital without the court confirmation which is required under s 137 in reduction schemes. The absence of any court involvement (save where there are objectors under s 176) means that this mechanism can provide a quicker and less expensive route for capital reduction for private companies.

However, ss 171–177 impose detailed requirements, if this method of payment for redemption or purchase is to be used; and the appropriate scheme for purchase, which must necessarily be an off-market purchase (ss 163–164), must also be followed. This does mean that a great number of procedural requirements are involved.

A redemption or purchase by a private company out of capital is not a 'distribution' for the purpose of Part VIII (ss 263–281) and so is not subject to the rules of that Part governing distributions by companies: s 263(2)(b).

S 171(1)–(2)

Authorised by the articles   Private companies must be specifically authorised by their articles to redeem or purchase out of capital and an authority simply to purchase their own shares is insufficient: see Table A, reg 35. Companies limited by guarantee with a share capital may no longer be formed, see s 1(4).

S 171(3)

Permissible capital payment   The company is required to use:

(1)   any available profits, ie profits available for distribution as defined in s 263(3) but determined in this instance in accordance with s 172 rather than ss 270–275 which apply generally: s 172(1) (and see note to that section, below); and

(2)   the proceeds of any fresh issue of shares made for the purposes of the redemption or purchase;

before resorting to capital with the amount then needed being described as the permissible capital payment. This is in order to restrict the use of capital to that which is strictly necessary.

However, if there are no available profits and no fresh issue of shares (and there is no obligation to have a fresh issue), the entire purchase price can come out of capital, subject to the ability of the directors to make the statutory declaration required by s 173(3).

The general rule in s 160(1) that any premium payable on purchase or redemption must be found out of distributable profits is expressly subject to this provision.

S 171(4)–(6)

Capital redemption reserve   These subsections deal with the position governing the capital redemption reserve (see s 170) in cases where there is a payment out of capital. Payments wholly out of profits or out of profits and the proceeds of a fresh issue of shares without using capital are governed by s 170.

Permissible capital payment less than nominal value   Where the permissible capital payment (which for this purpose includes the proceeds of any fresh issue applied for the purposes of the redemption or purchase: sub-s (6)) is less than the nominal amount of the shares redeemed or purchased, the difference must be transferred to the capital redemption reserve. This ensures that the reduction of share capital is limited to the amount of the permissible capital payment.

Permissible capital payment greater than nominal value   Where the permissible capital payment (which for this purpose includes the proceeds of any fresh issue applied for the purposes of the redemption or purchase: sub-s (6)) is greater than the nominal amount of the shares purchased or redeemed, the amount of any of the specified funds may be reduced by a sum not exceeding the amount by which the permissible capital payment (as here defined) exceeds the nominal amount of the shares. This ensures that the aggregate of the share capital and undistributable reserves is reduced by the amount of the permissible capital payment.

This provision confers a discretion on the company which is not obliged to reduce any of these funds but may do so if it chooses; equally there is no order of reduction which must be adhered to. It is unlikely that a company would choose not to make such a reduction as otherwise the balance sheet will not reflect the permissible capital payment; also the funds identified are all funds which otherwise can only be reduced or distributed or utilised in limited circumstances: see s 130 (share premium account); s 170 (capital redemption reserve); s 264(3) (undistributable reserves); Sch 4, para 34 or Sch 8, para 34 (revaluation reserve).

172. Availability of profits for purposes of s 171

(1) The reference in section 171(3)(a) to available profits of the company is to the company's profits which are available for distribution (within the meaning of Part VIII); but the question whether a company has any profits so available and the amount of any such profits are to be determined for purposes of that section in accordance with the following subsections, instead of sections 270 to 275 in that Part.

(2) Subject to the next subsection, that question is to be determined by reference to—

(a) profits, losses, assets and liabilities,

(b) provisions of any of the kinds mentioned in paragraphs 88 and 89 of Schedule 4 (depreciation, diminution in value of assets, retentions to meet liabilities, etc), and

(c) share capital and reserves (including undistributable reserves),

as stated in the relevant accounts for determining the permissible capital payment for shares.

(3) The relevant accounts for this purpose are such accounts, prepared as at any date within the period for determining the amount of the permissible capital payment, as are necessary to enable a reasonable judgment to be made as to the amounts of any of the items mentioned in subsection (2)(a) to (c) above.

(4) For purposes of determining the amount of the permissible capital payment for shares, the amount of the company's available profits (if any) determined in accordance with subsections (2) and (3) is treated as reduced by the amount of any distributions lawfully made by the company after the date of the relevant accounts and before the end of the period for determining the amount of that payment.

(5) The reference in subsection (4) to distributions lawfully made by the company includes—

(a) financial assistance lawfully given out of distributable profits in a case falling within section 154 or 155,

(b) any payment lawfully made by the company in respect of the purchase by it of any shares in the company (except a payment lawfully made otherwise than out of distributable profits), and

(c) a payment of any description specified in section 168(1) lawfully made by the company.

(6) References in this section to the period for determining the amount of the permissible capital payment for shares are to the period of 3 months ending with the date on which the statutory declaration of the directors purporting to specify the amount of that payment is made in accordance with subsection (3) of the section next following.

General note

This section sets out in detail the rules for determining the available profits which, by virtue of s 171(3), must be used before a payment can be made out of capital. It is crucial that the available profits be properly and accurately determined since the figure has a direct bearing on the permissible capital payment under s 171(3). The lower the available profits figure, the greater the amount of the permissible capital payment.

S 172(1)

Available profits Whether the company has any available profits and the amount of such profits is to be determined in accordance with this section and not ss 270–275 which apply generally to the question of distributable profits. The undistributable reserves of a private company would be the share premium account and the capital redemption reserve but a revaluation reserve is not an undistributable reserve for a private company although it is for a public company: s 264(3).

S 172(3), (6)

Relevant accounts Questions as to the amount of the available profits are to be answered not by reference to the company's last annual accounts (as would be required by s 270(3)) but by reference to the relevant accounts prepared as at any date within the period of three months ending with the date on which the directors make their statutory declaration specifying the permissible capital payment as required by s 173(3).

The purpose is to ensure that the accounts have been prepared as recently as possible so that the company has the most up to date information on which to base its decision. The accounts need not be audited although the annual accounts could be used if the appropriate timetable is adhered to. The accounts prepared within the period must be such as are necessary to enable a reasonable judgment to be made as to the amount of any of the items specified in sub-s (2), namely the profits, losses, assets and liabilities, etc.

S 172(4)–(5)

Distributions The amount of the available profits determined under s 172(2) and (3) above is to be reduced by any distributions lawfully made by the company (ie in accordance with Part VIII, ss 263–281) after the date of the accounts and before the end of the three-month period noted above, ie before the date of the directors' statutory declaration required by s 173(3). 'Distributions' in this case will include those payments identified in sub-s (5).

---

173. Conditions for payment out of capital

(1) Subject to any order of the court under section 177, a payment out of capital by a private company for the redemption or purchase of its own shares is not lawful unless the requirements of this and the next two sections are satisfied.

(2) The payment out of capital must be approved by a special resolution of the company.

(3)   The company's directors must make a statutory declaration specifying the amount of the permissible capital payment for the shares in question and stating that, having made full inquiry into the affairs and prospects of the company, they have formed the opinion—

(a)   as regards its initial situation immediately following the date on which the payment out of capital is proposed to be made, that there will be no grounds on which the company could then be found unable to pay its debts, and

(b)   as regards its prospects for the year immediately following that date, that, having regard to their intentions with respect to the management of the company's business during that year and to the amount and character of the financial resources which will in their view be available to the company during that year, the company will be able to continue to carry on business as a going concern (and will accordingly be able to pay its debts as they fall due) throughout that year.

(4)   In forming their opinion for purposes of subsection (3)(a), the directors shall take into account the same liabilities (including prospective and contingent liabilities) as would be relevant under section 122 of the Insolvency Act (winding up by the court) to the question whether a company is unable to pay its debts.

(5)   The directors' statutory declaration must be in the prescribed form and contain such information with respect to the nature of the company's business as may be prescribed, and must in addition have annexed to it a report addressed to the directors by the company's auditors stating that—

(a)   they have inquired into the company's state of affairs; and

(b)   the amount specified in the declaration as the permissible capital payment for the shares in question is in their view properly determined in accordance with sections 171 and 172; and

(c)   they are not aware of anything to indicate that the opinion expressed by the directors in the declaration as to any of the matters mentioned in subsection (3) is unreasonable in all the circumstances.

(6)   A director who makes a declaration under this section without having reasonable grounds for the opinion expressed in the declaration is liable to imprisonment or a fine, or both.

S 173(1)

There must be strict compliance with the procedures applicable to payments out of capital as set out in ss 173–175, subject to any order of the court under s 177 which can only arise in cases where there has been an application by an objecting member or creditor under s 176.

S 173(2)

Special resolution   The payment out of capital must be approved by a special resolution, the detailed requirements regarding which are set out in s 174. As to special resolutions, see s 378; as to the notification of a special resolution to the registrar of companies, see s 380(1), (4)(a); a written resolution may be used by a private company (s 381A); as to the date of a written resolution, see s 381A(3). The date of the resolution is important because various timetable limits run from that time: see ss 174–176.

S 173(3)–(4)

Statutory declaration   See note to s 156(2), above as to a similar statutory declaration in respect to the giving of financial assistance.

The obligations imposed on the directors are quite onerous: they must have 'made full inquiry into the affairs and prospects of the company'. Their opinion must extend to the long-term solvency of the company and its ability to continue to carry on business as a going concern throughout the year immediately following the date on which the payment out of capital is proposed to be made. It would seem that the declaration does commit the directors to ensuring that the company will actually continue as a going concern for that period since their statement must be made 'having regard to their intentions with respect to the management of the company's business during that year'.

If the directors make the statutory declaration and then find that circumstances change so rendering it inaccurate (although the time limits between the declaration and payment are very short to prevent this happening: see s 174(1)), the company should not proceed to purchase the shares. It is protected in such circumstances from an action for damages or specific performance by s 178.

The statutory declaration must be available to the shareholders at the general meeting called to pass the necessary special resolution (s 174(4)); and filed with the registrar of companies (s 175(5)); and available at the registered office for a period after the resolution is passed (s 175(6)).

S 173(5)

Auditors' report   These requirements are similar to those imposed by s 156(4), see the note to that provision, above. It is specifically required that the auditors' report be addressed to the company's directors. It is not addressed to the shareholders and the contents of the report reinforce this by concentrating as they do on supporting the directors' declaration. Equally, however, the auditors are aware that the report will go to the general meeting and is of sufficient importance that it must be available for inspection by the members at the meeting at which the resolution is passed, or provided to the members in advance of signature of a written resolution: s 174(4); Sch 15A, para 6(3). These factors will be important in terms of potential liability in the event of the declaration and report proving to be erroneous, see *Caparo Industries plc v Dickman* [1990] 2 AC 605, HL, and the detailed note to s 235, below.

The auditors' report must be available to the shareholders at the general meeting called to pass the necessary special resolution (s 174(4)); and delivered to the registrar of companies (s 175(5)); and available at the registered office for a period after the resolution is passed (s 175(6)).

S 173(6)

Liabilities of directors and vendors   Dishonesty is not an ingredient of the offence, an opinion which is not based on reasonable grounds will suffice. As to penalties, see s 730, Sch 24.

A more significant penalty, possibly, than this criminal sanction is IA 1986, s 76, which applies where the company is wound up within one year of the date on which the relevant payment out of capital was made, and the aggregate of its assets and the amounts paid by way of contribution is not sufficient for the payment of its debts and liabilities and the expenses of winding up. In those circumstances, the person whose shares were redeemed or purchased and the directors who signed the statutory declaration are liable to contribute to the company's assets.

Directors who can show (and the burden of proof is on them: IA 1986, s 76(2)(b)) that they had reasonable grounds for forming the opinion set out in the declaration are not liable.

Where liability does arise, a person whose shares were redeemed or purchased is liable to contribute an amount not exceeding so much of the redemption or purchase payment as was a payment out of capital.

Any member or director who would be so liable to contribute in the event of a winding up is entitled to petition to have the company wound up under IA 1986, s 122(1)(f) and (g): see s 124(3). This enables persons who are potentially liable under IA 1986, s 76 to take action at an early stage to prevent the company's financial position deteriorating and consequently their potential liability increasing.

174. Procedure for special resolution under s 173

(1)   The resolution required by section 173 must be passed on, or within the week immediately following, the date on which the directors make the statutory declaration required by that section; and the payment out of capital must be made no earlier than 5 nor more than 7 weeks after the date of the resolution.

(2)   The resolution is ineffective if any member of the company holding shares to which the resolution relates exercises the voting rights carried by any of those shares in voting on the resolution and the resolution would not have been passed if he had not done so.

(3)   For purposes of subsection (2), a member who holds such shares is to be regarded as exercising the voting rights carried by them in voting on the resolution not only if he votes in respect of them on a poll on the question whether the resolution shall be passed, but also if he votes on the resolution otherwise than on a poll; and, notwithstanding anything in a company's articles, any member of the company may demand a poll on that question.

(4)   The resolution is ineffective unless the statutory declaration and auditors' report required by the section are available for inspection by members of the company at the meeting at which the resolution is passed.

(5)   For purposes of this section a vote and a demand for a poll by a person as proxy for a member are the same (respectively) as a vote and demand by the member.

General note

This section imposes requirements (similar to those noted in s 164) as regards voting and disclosure which determine the validity of the special resolution required to authorise payment out of capital. It also imposes a strict timetable both for passing the special resolution and for the actual payment out of capital.

S 174(1)

There are two timetable requirements which must be observed.

Resolution within seven days   The payment out of capital must be approved by a special resolution passed on or within the week immediately following the date on which the directors make the statutory declaration required by s 173(3). The standard timetable would be for the directors to make their statutory declaration on the day of the general meeting at which the resolution is passed.

Because of this timetable, it will be necessary to give notice of the general meeting (see s 369) ahead of the making of the statutory declaration, unless consents to short notice have been obtained (see s 369(3)), or a written resolution is used (see s 381A).

Where a written resolution is used, the statutory declaration and auditors' report required by s 173(3), (5) must be circulated to each member: Sch 15A, para 6(3); this may delay matters, using up some of the seven days available. The date of a written resolution is the date when the resolution is signed by or on behalf of the last member to sign: s 381A(3). Therefore, care must be taken to ensure that the statutory declaration and auditors' report have been circulated and that the last member signs the written resolution on, or within seven days of, the declaration being made.

Payment time limits   The actual payment must be no earlier than five weeks in order to allow dissentient creditors and members to object to the court: see s 176. It must be no later than seven weeks after the date of the resolution in case the financial position of the company has altered so negating the value of the statutory declaration and auditors' report.

S 174(2)–(3), (5)

Voting by the vendor   The same limitations on the exercise of voting rights apply as apply in relation to off-market purchases: see note to s 164(5). When a written resolution is used, the vendor's consent to the written resolution is not required and he does not participate in the written process: Sch 15A, para 6.

S 174(4)

Disclosure   The statutory declaration and auditors' report must be available for inspection at the meeting at which the resolution is passed. This can be contrasted with the requirement under s 164 that the contract of purchase in an off-market situation must be available for 15 days prior to the general meeting approving the contract. However, a payment out of capital by a private company will entail an off-market purchase within s 164 in any event, so no time advantage is gained by this relaxation. Where a private company uses a written resolution, the documents must have been supplied to each member at or before the time when the resolution was supplied to him for signature: Sch 15A, para 6(3). This may cause timing difficulties, as noted above.

175. Publicity for proposed payment out of capital

(1)   Within the week immediately following the date of the resolution for payment out of capital the company must cause to be published in the Gazette a notice—

  (a) stating that the company has approved a payment out of capital for the purpose of acquiring its own shares by redemption or purchase or both (as the case may be);

  (b) specifying the amount of the permissible capital payment for the shares in question and the date of the resolution under section 173;

  (c) stating that the statutory declaration of the directors and the auditors' report required by that section are available for inspection at the company's registered office; and

  (d) stating that any creditor of the company may at any time within the 5 weeks immediately following the date of the resolution for payment out of capital apply to the court under section 176 for an order prohibiting the payment.

(2)   Within the week immediately following the date of the resolution the company must also either cause a notice to the same effect as that required by subsection (1) to be published in an appropriate national newspaper or give notice in writing to that effect to each of its creditors.

(3)   'An appropriate national newspaper' means a newspaper circulating throughout England and Wales (in the case of a company registered in England and Wales), and a newspaper circulating throughout Scotland (in the case of a company registered in Scotland).

(4)   References below in this section to the first notice date are to the day on which the company first publishes the notice required by subsection (1) or first publishes or gives the notice required by subsection (2) (whichever is the earlier).

(5)   Not later than the first notice date the company must deliver to the registrar of companies a copy of the statutory declaration of the directors and of the auditors' report required by section 173.

(6)   The statutory declaration and auditors' report—

  (a) shall be kept at the company's registered office throughout the period beginning with the first notice date and ending 5 weeks after the date of the resolution for payment out of capital, and

  (b) shall ... be open to the inspection of any member or creditor of the company without charge.

(7)   If an inspection required under subsection (6) is refused, the company and every officer of it who is in default is liable to a fine and, for continued contravention, to a daily default fine.

(8)   In the case of refusal of an inspection required under subsection (6) of a declaration or report, the court may by order compel an immediate inspection of that declaration or report.

S 175(1)–(3)

Publicity Various matters must be published in a notice in the Gazette (and elsewhere: see sub-s (2)) and these disclosure requirements aim to bring the proposed payment out of capital to the attention, in particular, of creditors who may wish to apply to the court under s 176 for an order cancelling the resolution approving the payment. The obligation to give notice to each creditor under sub-s (2) if the opportunity is not taken to publish a notice in a national newspaper may be quite onerous. Shareholders will be aware of the scheme because of the need to pass a special resolution: see s 173(2).

S 175(6)

Disclosure These documents have already been available to the members at the meeting at which the special resolution authorising payment out of capital was passed (s 174(4)) but this provision offers absent members and creditors the opportunity for inspection for a period of time which is dictated by s 176. As to inspection, see the Companies (Inspection and Copying of Registers, Indices and Documents) Regulations 1991, SI 1991/1998. As to the registered office, see s 287.

S 175(7)

As to penalties, see s 730, Sch 24; 'officer in default' is defined in s 730(5).

S 175(8)

This provision is necessary because, but for the section, it is not clear that there is any right of inspection or that the court has the power to compel inspection: see *Conway v Petronius Clothing Co Ltd* [1978] 1 All ER 185 at 199. The court's power is discretionary: see *Pelling v Families need Fathers Ltd* [2001] All ER (D) 03, (Aug) CA.

176. Objections by company's members or creditors

(1) Where a private company passes a special resolution approving for purposes of this Chapter any payment out of capital for the redemption or purchase of any of its shares—

(a) any member of the company other than one who consented to or voted in favour of the resolution; and

(b) any creditor of the company,

may within 5 weeks of the date on which the resolution was passed apply to the court for cancellation of the resolution.

(2) The application may be made on behalf of the persons entitled to make it by such one or more of their number as they may appoint in writing for the purpose.

(3) If an application is made, the company shall—

(a) forthwith give notice in the prescribed form of that fact to the registrar of companies; and

(b) within 15 days from the making of any order of the court on the hearing of the application, or such longer period as the court may by order direct, deliver an office copy of the order to the registrar.

(4) A company which fails to comply with subsection (3), and any officer of it who is in default, is liable to a fine and for continued contravention, to a daily default fine.

General note

Redemption or purchase out of capital does allow companies essentially to reduce capital without the sanction of the court as required by s 135, hence provision is made for an application by any objecting creditor or a dissenting member to the court to cancel the resolution authorising the payment. There is no provision (cf s 158(3)) preventing the company from acting on the resolution pending the court hearing although, as a matter of practice, the company is unlikely to proceed in view of the possibility that the court may cancel the resolution under s 177(2).

S 176(1), (2)

As to the special resolution required, see s 173(2). No ground for the application is specified and it will be for those objecting to identify for the court the basis on which the resolution is attacked which might include, for example, an impropriety in the voting procedures or the non-disclosure of required information. No minimum debt or shareholding is required of those objecting but the more insignificant the amounts, the less weight is likely to be attached to the objections.

S 176(3)

The obligation to keep the registrar of companies informed lies with the company.

S 176(4)

As to penalties, see s 730, Sch 24; 'officer in default' is defined in s 730(5).

177. Powers of court on application under s 176

(1) On the hearing of an application under section 176 the court may, if it thinks fit, adjourn the proceedings in order that an arrangement may be made to the court's satisfaction for the purchase of the interests of dissentient members or for the protection of dissentient creditors (as the case may be); and the court

315

may give such directions and make such orders as it thinks expedient for facilitating or carrying into effect any such arrangement.

(2)   Without prejudice to its powers under subsection (1), the court shall make an order on such terms and conditions as it thinks fit either confirming or cancelling the resolution; and, if the court confirms the resolution, it may in particular by order alter or extend any date or period of time specified in the resolution or in any provision in this Chapter which applies to the redemption or purchase of shares to which the resolution refers.

(3)   The court's order may, if the court thinks fit, provide for the purchase by the company of the shares of any of its members and for the reduction accordingly of the company's capital, and may make such alterations in the company's memorandum and articles as may be required in consequence of that provision.

(4)   If the court's order requires the company not to make any, or any specified, alteration in its memorandum or articles, the company has not then power without leave of the court to make any such alteration in breach of the requirement.

(5)   An alteration in the memorandum or articles made by virtue of an order under this section, if not made by resolution of the company, is of the same effect as if duly made by resolution; and this Act applies accordingly to the memorandum or articles as so altered.

S 177(1)

In many instances, whether the objector is a member or a creditor, the most satisfactory outcome for both sides may be to end that party's interest in the company by the purchase of their shares or the repayment of their debt, as the case may be. To facilitate this, the court may adjourn the proceedings in order that the parties can come to a suitable arrangement. As to the type of arrangements made for creditors on a reduction of capital, see note to s 136, above.

S 177(2)

The court may extend the time periods applicable, if necessary. For example, the requirement that the payment out of capital must take place not later than seven weeks after the passing of the special resolution (see s 174(1)) might be relaxed.

S 177(3)

This allows for the purchase by the company of the shares and requires that the entire shareholding be purchased; the order may apply to any of the members and is not limited to the shares of the dissenting members although in practice it would be so limited; any purchase under this provision is exempt from the general prohibition on a company purchasing its own shares: s 143(1), (3)(c). Although the wording of this provision is broad, its use may be confined, in practice, to situations where the objecting parties have not reached agreement as envisaged under sub-s (1).

S 177(4), (5)

See note to s 5(6), (7)

SUPPLEMENTARY

178. Effect of company's failure to redeem or purchase

(1) This section has effect where a company has, on or after 15th June 1982,—

 (a) issued shares on terms that they are or are liable to be redeemed, or

 (b) agreed to purchase any of its own shares.

(2) The company is not liable in damages in respect of any failure on its part to redeem or purchase any of the shares.

(3) Subsection (2) is without prejudice to any right of the holder of the shares other than his right to sue the company for damages in respect of its failure; but the court shall not grant an order for specific performance of the terms of redemption or purchase if the company shows that it is unable to meet the costs of redeeming or purchasing the shares in question out of distributable profits.

(4) If the company is wound up and at the commencement of the winding up any of the shares have not been redeemed or purchased, the terms of redemption or purchase may be enforced against the company; and when shares are redeemed or purchased under this subsection, they are treated as cancelled.

(5) However, subsection (4) does not apply if—

 (a) the terms provided for the redemption or purchase to take place at a date later than that of the commencement of the winding up, or

 (b) during the period beginning with the date on which the redemption or purchase was to have taken place and ending with the commencement of the winding up the company could not at any time have lawfully made a distribution equal in value to the price at which the shares were to have been redeemed or purchased.

(6) There shall be paid in priority to any amount which the company is liable under subsection (4) to pay in respect of any shares—

 (a) all other debts and liabilities of the company (other than any due to members in their character as such),

 (b) if other shares carry rights (whether as to capital or as to income) which are preferred to the rights as to capital attaching to the first-mentioned shares, any amount due in satisfaction of those preferred rights;

but, subject to that, any such amount shall be paid in priority to any amounts due to members in satisfaction of their rights (whether as to capital or income) as members.

(7) . . .

S 178(1)–(3)

Limitations on enforcement   The recovery of damages for breach by the company of the contract for the redemption or purchase of its shares is prohibited but this is without prejudice to any other right of the holder of the shares. One possibility is an injunction to restrain the payment of a dividend if this would deprive the company of the funds necessary to pay for redemption or purchase: see *Re Holders Investment Trust Ltd* [1971] 2 All ER 289 at 295.

The section does not prohibit the recovery of damages for breach of another agreement, even though it had some connection to the contract for purchase or redemption and even if the amount recovered for that breach may be equivalent to the damages which would be available (were it not for the statutory prohibition) on a failure to redeem or purchase: *Barclays Bank plc v British and Commonwealth Holdings plc* [1996] 1 BCLC 1 at 27, CA.

Specific performance may still be available but the court cannot order it where the company would have to finance the purchase out of capital; presumably this limitation was imposed because it was thought too damaging to creditors' interests to allow shareholders to obtain payment out of capital in circumstances where the reason for the company's non-performance may be concerns about its financial ability to do so, although it is difficult to envisage that specific performance would be ordered in such circumstances.

S 178(4)

Position on winding up   The ability to enforce the redemption or purchase agreement in these circumstances is subject to sub-ss (5), (6). The effect is to secure priority for these shareholders ahead of a return of capital to the ordinary shareholders. Where the company is insolvent, such limited priority is unlikely to be of any advantage.

If the company is solvent, it is unlikely that it will not have honoured its agreement to redeem or purchase before the commencement of the winding up and, in any event, specific performance may still be available in that case. Where there is a significant surplus for distribution, the shareholders may wish to remain and not be redeemed or purchased but the liquidator may choose to enforce the agreement against them.

The date of the commencement of the winding up is determined in accordance with IA 1986, ss 86, 129.

S 178(5)

Whether the company could lawfully have made a distribution during that period must be determined in accordance with the provisions of Part VIII (ss 263–281). The date of the commencement of the winding up is determined in accordance with IA 1986, ss 86, 129.

S 178(6)

Priority is accorded to creditors of the company and to any shareholders having preferred rights.

179. Power for Secretary of State to modify this Chapter

(1)   The Secretary of State may by regulations made by statutory instrument modify the provisions of this Chapter with respect to any of the following matters—

   (a) the authority required for a purchase by a company of its own shares,

   (b) the authority required for the release by a company of its rights under a contract for the purchase of its own shares or a contract under which the company may (subject to any conditions) become entitled or obliged to purchase its own shares,

   (c) the information to be included in a return delivered by a company to the registrar of companies in accordance with section 169(1),

   (d) the matters to be dealt with in the statutory declaration of the directors under section 173 with a view to indicating their opinion of their company's ability to make a proposed payment out of capital with due regard to its financial situation and prospects, and

   (e) the contents of the auditors' report required by that section to be annexed to that declaration.

(2)   The Secretary of State may also by regulations so made make such provision (including modification of the provisions of this Chapter) as appears to him to be appropriate—

   (a) for wholly or partly relieving companies from the requirement of section 171(3)(a) that any available profits must be taken into account in determining the amount of the permissible capital payment for shares under that section, or

   (b) for permitting a company's share premium account to be applied, to any extent appearing to the Secretary of State to be appropriate, in providing for the premiums payable on redemption or purchase by the company of any of its own shares.

(3)   Regulations under this section—

   (a) may make such further modification of any provisions of this Chapter as appears to the Secretary of State to be reasonably necessary in consequence of any provision made under such regulations by virtue of subsection (1) or (2),

   (b) may make different provision for different cases or classes of case, and

   (c) may contain such further consequential provisions, and such incidental and supplementary provisions, as the Secretary of State thinks fit.

(4)   No regulations shall be made under this section unless a draft of the instrument containing them has been laid before Parliament and approved by resolution of each House.

General note

This section grants sweeping powers to the Secretary of State to amend these provisions subject to affirmative resolution of Parliament. The powers have not been exercised.

180. Transitional cases arising under this Chapter; and savings

(1) Any preference shares issued by a company before 15th June 1982 which could but for the repeal by the Companies Act 1981 of section 58 of the Companies Act 1948 (power to issue redeemable preference shares) have been redeemed under that section are subject to redemption in accordance with the provisions of this Chapter.

(2) In a case to which sections 159 and 160 apply by virtue of this section, any premium payable on redemption may, notwithstanding the repeal by the 1981 Act of any provision of the 1948 Act, be paid out of the share premium account instead of out of profits, or partly out of that account and partly out of profits (but subject to the provisions of this Chapter so far as payment is out of profits).

(3) Any capital redemption reserve fund established before 15th June 1982 by a company for the purposes of section 58 of the Act of 1948 is to be known as the company's capital redemption reserve and be treated as if it had been established for the purposes of section 170 of this Act; and accordingly, a reference in any enactment or in the articles of any company, or in any other instrument, to a company's capital redemption reserve fund is to be construed as a reference to the company's capital redemption reserve.

S 180(2)

Under CA 1948, s 58, the premium on redemption of redeemable preference shares could come from the share premium account or out of profits but s 160(1)(b) requires that any premium on redemption be out of distributable profits. This provision retained the original position for transitional cases and so permitted recourse to the share premium account instead of or in addition to distributable profits.

181. Definitions for Chapter VII

In this Chapter—

    (a) 'distributable profits', in relation to the making of any payment by a company, means those profits out of which it could lawfully make a distribution (within the meaning given by section 263(2)) equal in value to the payment, and

    (b) 'permissible capital payment' means the payment permitted by section 171;

and references to payment out of capital are to be construed in accordance with section 171.

General note

See the note to s 160(1), above as to the application of the provisions of s 263 in this context.

CHAPTER VIII

MISCELLANEOUS PROVISIONS ABOUT SHARES AND DEBENTURES

SHARE AND DEBENTURE CERTIFICATES, TRANSFERS AND WARRANTS

182. Nature, transfer and numbering of shares

(1)   The shares or other interest of any member in a company—

(a)   are personal estate or, in Scotland, moveable property and are not in the nature of real estate or heritage,

(b)   are transferable in manner provided by the company's articles, but subject to the Stock Transfer Act 1963 (which enables securities of certain descriptions to be transferred by a simplified process) and to regulations made under section 207 of the Companies Act 1989 (which enable title to securities to be evidenced and transferred without a written instrument).

(2)   Each share in a company having a share capital shall be distinguished by its appropriate number; except that, if at any time all the issued shares in a company, or all the issued shares in it of a particular class, are fully paid up and rank pari passu for all purposes, none of those shares need thereafter have a distinguishing number so long as it remains fully paid up and ranks pari passu for all purposes with all shares of the same class for the time being issued and fully paid up.

S 182(1)(a)

Nature of a share   A share in a company is a chose in action: *Colonial Bank v Whinney* (1886) 11 App Cas 426, HL. In *Borland's Trustee v Steel Bros & Co Ltd* [1901] 1 Ch 279 at 288, Farwell J defined a share as consisting of the interest of the shareholder in the company measured by a sum of money, for the purpose of liability in the first place, and of interest in the second, but also consisting of a series of covenants entered into by all the shareholders inter se in accordance with, what is now, s 14.

Location   Shares are situated at the place where the register of members (see ss 22, 352) is kept: *A-G v Higgins* (1857) 2 H & N 339; *Brassard v Smith* [1925] AC 371; *International Credit and Investment Co (Overseas) Ltd v Adham* [1994] 1 BCLC 66.

   As to who is a member, see s 22. The reference to 'or other interest of any member' is to accommodate those companies without a share capital where a member will not be a shareholder.

S 182(1)(b)

Right to transfer shares   A shareholder has a prima facie right to transfer his shares and directors have no discretionary powers, independent of the powers given to them by the articles, to refuse to register a transfer: *Re Smith, Knight & Co, Weston's Case* (1868) 4 Ch App 20; *Re Smith & Fawcett Ltd* [1942] 1 All ER 542; listed securities must be freely transferable, see the *Listing Rules*, para 3.15.

A person presenting a share transfer impliedly warrants the authenticity of the transfer and he is required to indemnify the company for any liability it has incurred to a third party (for example, the costs of having to acquire equivalent shares to restore the original holder to his rightful position and to pay accrued dividends): *Sheffield Corpn v Barclay* [1905] AC 392; *Welch v Bank of England* [1955] Ch 508 at 548–549; *Yeung Kai Yung v Hong Kong and Shanghai Banking Corpn* [1981] AC 787; *Royal Bank of Scotland plc v Sandstone Properties Ltd* [1998] 2 BCLC 429.

Restrictions imposed by statute   The right to transfer may be cut down by statute, for example, see s 454(1) (orders imposing restrictions on shares); Trading with the Enemy Act 1939, s 5.

Restrictions in private companies   In practice, it is usual for the articles of private companies to contain a restriction on transfer but any restriction on transfer will be interpreted strictly for the prima facie right to transfer shares 'is not to be cut down by uncertain language or doubtful implications': *Re Smith & Fawcett Ltd* [1942] 1 All ER 542 at 543, per Lord Greene, MR; see also *Stothers v William Steward (Holdings) Ltd* [1994] 2 BCLC 266, CA. The courts will not remedy any defect in the drafting of the restriction: *Delavenne v Broadhurst* [1931] 1 Ch 234; *Roberts v Letter T Estates Ltd* [1961] AC 795, PC; however, a distinction can be drawn between a restriction which the court will not make good and a restriction which is clear but which lacks the necessary machinery to give it business efficacy. In *Tett v Phoenix Property and Investment Co Ltd* [1986] BCLC 149, the Court of Appeal, applying standard contractual principles, implied a term as to notification to give business efficacy to a pre-emption scheme in the articles..

A transfer not in accordance with the articles may, through lapse of time coupled with recognition of the transferee as a shareholder, be incapable of being impeached: *Nisbet v Shepherd* [1994] 1 BCLC 300 at 304.

Common restrictions in the articles   Table A, reg 24 provides that the directors may refuse to register certain transfers such as transfers of partly paid shares to a person of whom they disapprove or transfers of shares on which the company has a lien. This article is narrow in scope and it is commonly replaced by a broader restriction.

A typical provision adopted by private companies is one which contains a pre-emption requirement coupled with an absolute discretion in the directors to refuse to register any transfer of any shares.

For example, a member wishing to sell may be permitted to transfer his shares to an existing member without restriction but where he seeks to transfer to an outsider then a pre-emption provision will come into effect. This would normally require the intending transferor to give notice to the company secretary who must notify the other members that there are shares available for purchase. If the other members make an offer for the shares, the transferor may accept or reject their offer but, if he rejects it, he would be precluded normally from proceeding with the transfer of the shares to an outsider. If the shares are not taken up by the other shareholders, the transferor is usually entitled at that stage to offer his shares to an outside purchaser, subject to the proviso that the directors may refuse to register a transfer in such circumstances. A further refinement can be that on the death of a member, the person becoming entitled to the shares is deemed to have served a transfer notice on the company secretary in respect of all of those shares so bringing the transfer procedure into operation and enabling the shares to be offered to the other members. There are numerous variations on these schemes so the particular company's articles must always be consulted.

Triggering a pre-emption requirement   To trigger a pre-emption provision, it must be established that a shareholder wishes/desires/intends to transfer his shares as required by the wording of the particular article. In the absence of a clear indication that 'transfer' is intended to encompass dealings with the beneficial interest, 'transfer' will be limited to dealings in the legal title to the shares: *Theakston v London Trust plc* [1984] BCLC 390 at 397. This approach means that it is possible to enter into arrangements which fall short of a transfer of the legal title without triggering the pre-emption mechanism. Whether this has been done successfully depends on the conduct of the parties and the actual wording of the articles: see, for example, *Re Macro (Ipswich) Ltd* [1994] 2 BCLC 354; *Theakston v London Trust plc* [1984] BCLC 390; *Safeguard Industrial Investments Ltd v National Westminster Bank Ltd* [1982] 1 All ER 449; *Lyle and Scott Ltd v Scott's Trustees* [1959] 2 All ER 661; *Re Sedgefield Steeplechase Co (1927) Ltd, Scotto v Petch* [2000] 2 BCLC 211; affd (2001) Times, 8 February.

If the parties wish to preclude dealing in the beneficial interest, they must do so expressly: *Safeguard Industrial Investments Ltd v National Westminster Bank Ltd* [1980] 3 All ER 849 at 860, per Vinelott J.

Directors' refusal to register a share transfer   The power vested in the directors to refuse to register any transfer is frequently expressed in the form of the 1948 Table A, Part II, reg 3, which provides that the directors may, in their absolute discretion and without assigning any reason therefor, decline to register any transfer of any share, whether or not it is a fully paid share.

The significance of a refusal by directors to register a transfer is that legal title to shares is transferred only by registration; without registration, the transferee obtains only the beneficial interest: *Société Générale de Paris v Walker* (1886) 11 App Cas 20 at 28; *Roots v Williamson* (1888) 38 Ch D 485 at 493; *Re Copal Varnish Co Ltd* [1917] 2 Ch 349 at 354. Moreover, membership is dependent on registration: s 22(2).

Where the power to refuse registration is drafted as an absolute discretion, there is no limitation on the exercise by directors of that power other than the standard requirement that, as a fiduciary power, it must be exercised bona fide in what they consider – and not what a court may consider – to be in the interests of the company and not for any collateral purpose: *Re Smith & Fawcett Ltd* [1942] 1 All ER 542.

When the provision is drafted in this form, the directors are entitled to refuse to register simply on the basis that the transferee is a stranger: *Charles Forte Investments Ltd v Amanda* [1963] 2 All ER 940; equally, they may refuse to register a transfer to a person who is already a member: *Re Dublin North City Milling Co* [1909] 1 IR 179; cf *Tangney v Clarence Hotels Co* [1933] IR 51, where the power was more limited.

The precise scope of a limited power will vary from company to company. Here too the basic obligation is that the directors must act bona fide in what they consider to be in the interests of the company and not for any collateral purpose. More specifically, they must act within the limits laid down by the provisions in the articles which will be strictly construed: *Re Smith & Fawcett Ltd* [1942] 1 All ER 542.

The power to refuse to register cannot be exercised effectively if there are no validly appointed directors of the company: *Re New Cedos Engineering Co Ltd* [1994] 1 BCLC 797.

An erroneous refusal to register, although based on a bona fide belief that they had the power to refuse, may result exceptionally in the directors being personally liable for the costs of rectification of the share register: *Morgan v Morgan Insurance Brokers Ltd* [1993] BCLC 676.

Reasons and grounds for their decision   Directors cannot be required to give reasons to justify their decision and this is so regardless of whether the discretion to refuse to register is absolute or limited, and regardless of whether the articles specifically state 'without assigning any reason therefor': *Re Coalport China Co* [1895] 2 Ch 404; *Re Gresham Life Assurance Society, ex p Penney* (1872) 8 Ch App 446. But see *Re Hafner, Olhausen v Powderley* [1943] IR 264, where an inference of improper motives was drawn from a refusal to give reasons.

Where there are a number of possible grounds for refusal, as is customary in a limited discretion provision, the directors can be required to state under which branch of the article they have acted: *Duke of Sutherland v British Dominions Land Settlement Corpn Ltd* [1926] Ch 746; unless the articles state that the directors shall not be bound to specify the grounds: *Berry and Stewart v Tottenham Hotspur Football and Athletic Co Ltd* [1935] Ch 718.

Decision on registration to be taken and notified   The directors must actively exercise their discretion and decide to refuse to register a transfer, otherwise the prima facie right to transfer will prevail: *Re Hackney Pavilion Ltd* [1924] 1 Ch 276; *Moodie v W J Shepherd (Bookbinders) Ltd* [1949] 2 All ER 1044; *Re Swaledale Cleaners Ltd* [1968] 3 All ER 619.

The decision must be taken within a reasonable time: *Re Swaledale Cleaners Ltd* [1968] 3 All ER 619; and a reasonable time for these purposes is generally accepted to be within two months of the transfer being lodged with the company. This period is effectively dictated by s 183(5), which requires that notice of rejection be given within two months. Thereafter, the directors will no longer be able to exercise their discretion: *Re Swaledale Cleaners Ltd* [1968] 3 All ER 619; *Re Inverdeck Ltd* [1998] 2 BCLC 242.

Where the directors take a decision to refuse to register a transfer but fail to notify the transferee of the refusal, the failure to notify does not nullify the decision: *Popely v Planarrive Ltd* [1997] 1 BCLC 8. See note to s 183(5), below.

Challenging a refusal to register   Challenging a refusal to register is difficult for the court will presume that the directors did exercise their powers honestly and rightly unless it appears by the document itself, or by a confession on their part, or some other circumstance, that they have not done so: *Re Gresham Life Assurance Society, ex p Penney* (1872) 8 Ch App 446; *Re Coalport China Co* [1895] 2 Ch 404. If anyone alleges to the contrary, the onus is on him to prove it: *Duke of Sutherland v British Dominions Land Settlement Corpn* [1926] Ch 746 at 756; *Re Coalport China Co* [1895] 2 Ch 404; *Charles Forte Investments Ltd v Amanda* [1963] 2 All ER 940.

The possibility of challenging a refusal is greatest where the power to refuse is a limited power: see *Re Bede Steam Shipping Co Ltd* [1917] 1 Ch 123.

The contract of sale   The vendor's obligations are to deliver his share certificate and a duly executed transfer to the purchaser and to do nothing to impede or delay registration: *London Founders' Association Ltd v Clarke* (1888) 20 QBD 576; *Hooper v Herts* [1906] 1 Ch 549. Unless the contract so provides, the vendor does not promise to secure registration and, if the directors do refuse to register the transfer, the purchaser cannot recover the price from the vendor: *Stray v Russell* (1859) 1 E & E 888 at 916; *London Founders' Association Ltd v Clarke* (1888) 20 QBD 576; although the vendor will hold the shares as trustee for the purchaser until registration: *Stevenson v Wilson* 1907 SC 445; *Hawks v McArthur* [1951] 1 All ER 22; *Re Rose* [1952] 1 All ER 1217; *Lyle and Scott Ltd v Scott's Trustees* [1959] 2 All ER 661, HL.

The effect of a specifically enforceable contract for the sale of shares is that the equitable title to the shares passes to the purchaser once the contract is made (whether or not the price has been paid) and legal title passes on completion and registration by the company; but, until payment of the price, the vendor has a lien securing payment and the vendor is entitled, for example, to exercise the votes attached to the shares although any such exercise must be subject to his fiduciary obligations as a trustee for the purchaser: *Musselwhite v Musselwhite & Son Ltd* [1962] 1 All ER 201; *Michaels v Harley House (Marylebone) Ltd* [1999] 1 BCLC 670, CA. The ability to vote is also subject to any contract terms to the contrary, but see *JRRT (Investments) Ltd v Haycraft* [1993] BCLC 401, where the unpaid vendor retained the right to vote despite the contract between the parties providing that the voting rights be transferred to the (defaulting) purchaser. The court interpreted the agreement as based on a presumption that benefits such as this would not be transferred to a party in default.

The Stock Transfer Act 1963   The Stock Transfer Act 1963 provides for a simplified form which may be used with respect to transfers of fully paid shares and which requires the signature of the transferor only. It must show particulars of the consideration, the description and number or amount of the securities and the full name of the registered holder and the full name and address of the transferee.

Where this form is used, it overrides any requirements in the articles but it does not apply in the case of partly paid up shares where the form specified in the articles must be adhered to (see Table A, reg 23, which requires the signature of the transferee).

CREST – electronic transfer   The electronic transfer of securities can occur through a computerised system called CREST operated by CRESTCo, and the provisions of the Companies Act 1985 providing for instruments of transfer and share certificates have had to be amended to accommodate these changes. This has been done by regulations made under CA 1989, s 207: see the Uncertificated Securities Regulations 1995, SI 1995/3272.

S 182(2)

Number   This provision requires shares to be numbered (subject to an exception for fully paid up shares) and the number is usually called the denoting number. The provision as to distinguishing shares by their appropriate number is directory only and its purpose is to enable the title of particular persons to be traced: *Re International Contract Co, Ind's Case* (1872) 7 Ch App 485. No penalty attaches for non-compliance.

183. Transfer and registration

(1)   It is not lawful for a company to register a transfer of shares in or debentures of the company unless a proper instrument of transfer has been delivered to it, or the transfer is an exempt transfer within the Stock Transfer Act 1982 or is in accordance with regulations made under section 207 of the Companies Act 1989.

This applies notwithstanding anything in the company's articles.

(2)   Subsection (1) does not prejudice any power of the company to register as shareholder or debenture holder a person to whom the right to any shares in or debentures of the company has been transmitted by operation of law.

(3)   A transfer of the share or other interest of a deceased member of a company made by his personal representative, although the personal representative is

not himself a member of the company, is as valid as if he had been such a member at the time of the execution of the instrument of transfer.

(4)   On the application of the transferor of any share or interest in a company, the company shall enter in its register of members the name of the transferee in the same manner and subject to the same conditions as if the application for the entry were made by the transferee.

(5)   If a company refuses to register a transfer of shares or debentures, the company shall, within 2 months after the date on which the transfer was lodged with it, send to the transferee notice of the refusal.

(6)   If default is made in complying with subsection (5), the company and every officer of it who is in default is liable to a fine and, for continued contravention, to a daily default fine.

S 183(1)

This provision was introduced in order to prevent the evasion of stamp duty through oral transfers. It applies to the transfer of debentures as well as of shares; 'debenture' is defined in s 744; 'company' is defined in s 735(1).

A company cannot contract out of this provision and an article providing that, on the death of a director, his shares were to be deemed to have passed to his wife if she survived him and requiring her to be registered as the holder of the shares was held to conflict with this section and to be invalid: *Re Greene, Greene v Greene* [1949] 1 All ER 167.

A proper instrument   A 'proper instrument' means no more than an instrument 'appropriate' or 'suitable' for stamping for stamp duty purposes and a document may be a 'proper instrument' even if it omits the consideration since that can be ascertained subsequently for the purpose of stamping: *Nisbet v Shepherd* [1994] 1 BCLC 300. As the purpose of the requirement is an instrument suitable for stamping, it need not be an instrument complying with every formality for transfer required by the articles: *Re Paradise Motor Co Ltd* [1968] 2 All ER 625, CA. The section is not designed to ensure regularity as between transferor and transferee or between them and the company: see *Dempsey v Celtic Football and Athletic Co Ltd* [1993] BCC 514 at 536.

In the absence of any instrument of transfer, an alteration to entries on the register of members (see s 352) results in a change in the legal but not the beneficial ownership of the shares and the new registered holder will hold as bare trustee for the original shareholder: *International Credit and Investment Co (Overseas) Ltd v Adham* [1994] 1 BCLC 66.

Exceptions   Transfers of certain gilt-edged securities (as set out in the Stock Transfer Act 1982, Sch 1) are effective without the need for an instrument in writing. The Uncertificated Securities Regulations 1995, SI 1995/3272, enable title to securities (including shares and debentures) to be evidenced and transferred without a written instrument. See note to s 182(1)(b).

S 183(2)

Transmission   The process of transmission involves a devolution of shares or debentures by law as opposed to a transfer which is by act of the parties, and it occurs on the death or bankruptcy of a member or debenture holder. As transmission is not a transfer of shares or debentures, it does not require a proper instrument of transfer. On death, title to shares or debentures vest in the holder's personal representative; on the appointment of a trustee in bankruptcy, title vests in the trustee.

S 183(3)

Transfers by personal representatives　In the absence of a specific provision in the articles, a personal representative of the deceased is entitled as of right to be registered as the holder of the shares or debentures registered in the name of the deceased: *Scott v Frank F Scott (London) Ltd* [1940] Ch 794. It is unusual, however, for the articles not to make provision for this matter: see Table A, regs 30, 31.

A transfer by a personal representative is treated as if it were an instrument of transfer executed by a member with the result that any provision in the articles affecting transfers by members will come into effect: see *Stothers v William Steward (Holdings) Ltd* [1994] 2 BCLC 266, CA.

S 183(4)

Upon a sale of shares in a company, it is for the transferee to pay the consideration money and get the transfer registered. It is not part of the contract that the transferor will get it registered but this provision is included to assist the transferor where there is a liability on the shares and the transferee has neglected to apply for registration: *Skinner v City of London Marine Insurance Corpn* (1885) 14 QBD 882.

S 183(5)

Notice of refusal to register　Notice of any refusal to register a transfer of shares or debentures must be sent to the transferee but need not be sent to the transferor: *Gustard's Case* (1869) LR 8 Eq 438.

Where directors have a discretion to refuse to register a transfer of shares, they must reach a decision on the transfer within the two-month period. If they fail to do so, they may no longer exercise their discretion: *Re Swaledale Cleaners Ltd* [1968] 3 All ER 619; *Re Inverdeck Ltd* [1998] 2 BCLC 242.

However, where the directors have reached a decision to refuse to register a transfer, a failure to notify the transferee of the refusal within two months does not nullify that decision to refuse registration, although it may be that in some circumstances it would be open to the court to find that the length of the delay in notification and the shareholder's actions, taken on the assumption that he had been registered, were such that the courts would not allow the company to rely on the resolution to refuse to register: *Popely v Planarrive Ltd* [1997] 1 BCLC 8 at 15.

This provision also applies to a refusal to register a transfer through CREST: see the Uncertificated Securities Regulations 1995, SI 1995/3272, reg 23(1), (8)–(9).

S 183(6)

As to penalties, see s 730, Sch 24; 'officer in default' is defined in s 730(5).

184. Certification of transfers

(1)   The certification by a company of any instrument of transfer of any shares in, or debentures of, the company is to be taken as a representation by the company to any person acting on the faith of the certification that there have been produced to the company such documents as on their face show a prima facie title to the shares or debentures in the transferor named in the instrument.

However, the certification is not to be taken as a representation that the transferor has any title to the shares or debentures.

(2)   Where a person acts on the faith of a false certification by a company made negligently, the company is under the same liability to him as if the certification had been made fraudulently.

(3)   For purposes of this section—

    (a)   an instrument of transfer is deemed certificated if it bears the words 'certificate lodged' (or words to the like effect);

    (b)   the certification of an instrument of transfer is deemed made by a company if—

        (i)   the person issuing the instrument is a person authorised to issue certificated instruments of transfer on the company's behalf, and

        (ii)   the certification is signed by a person authorised to certificate transfers on the company's behalf or by an officer or servant either of the company or of a body corporate so authorised;

    (c)   a certification is deemed signed by a person if—

        (i)   it purports to be authenticated by his signature or initials (whether handwritten or not), and

        (ii)   it is not shown that the signature or initials was or were placed there neither by himself nor by a person authorised to use the signature or initials for the purpose of certificating transfers on the company's behalf.

General note

Certification of transfers is needed where a shareholder sells shares included in one certificate to a number of buyers or transfers part of his holdings. As the shareholder cannot hand his certificate to the various buyers, the practice is for him to send his certificate and the executed transfers to the company. The company marks the transfer with the words 'certificate lodged' and this is known as certification. In due course, the company issues new share certificates to the purchasers and to the vendor for the balance, if any, of his holding. The section also applies to transfers of debentures.

S 184(1)

Nature of certification   Certification is no warranty of the transferor's title, nor even of the validity of the documents lodged: *Bishop v Balkis Consolidated Co* (1890) 25 QBD 512. It is simply a representation that documents have been lodged and the documents prima facie show the title of the transferor.

S 184(2)

This provision, which equates negligent and fraudulent certification, reflects a time when actions did not lie for careless or negligent misrepresentation: *Bishop v Balkis Consolidated Co* (1890) 25 QBD 512.

S 184(3)

Certification is deemed made by the company if the requirements of this subsection are met. For sub-s (3)(b)(i), it would seem that actual authority (express or implied) is required and apparent authority would not suffice; sub-s (3)(b)(ii) imposes requirements as to the signing of the certification. There is no requirement that any officer or servant of the company who signs must have been authorised to certificate transfers; 'officer' is defined in s 744.

A third party is assisted in meeting the requirements of sub-s (3)(b)(ii) by the fact that a certificate is deemed signed by a person if the requirements of sub-s (3)(c) are met; and sub-s (3)(c)(ii) places the onus on the company to show that it is not bound by the signature.

185. Duty of company as to issue of certificates

(1) Subject to the following provisions, every company shall—

    (a) within 2 months after the allotment of any of its shares, debentures or debenture stock, and

    (b) within 2 months after the date on which a transfer of any such shares, debentures or debenture stock is lodged with the company,

complete and have ready for delivery the certificates of all shares, the debentures and the certificates of all debenture stock allotted or transferred (unless the conditions of issue of the shares, debentures or debenture stock otherwise provide).

(2) For this purpose, 'transfer' means a transfer duly stamped and otherwise valid, or an exempt transfer within the Stock Transfer Act 1982, and does not include such a transfer as the company is for any reason entitled to refuse to register and does not register.

(3) Subsection (1) does not apply in the case of a transfer to any person where, by virtue of regulations under section 3 of the Stock Transfer Act 1982, he is not entitled to a certificate or other document of or evidencing title in respect of the securities transferred; but if in such a case the transferee—

    (a) subsequently becomes entitled to such a certificate or other document by virtue of any provision of those regulations, and

    (b) gives notice in writing of that fact to the company,

this section has effect as if the reference in subsection (1)(b) to the date of the lodging of the transfer were a reference to the date of the notice.

(4) A company of which shares or debentures are allotted or debenture stock is allotted to a recognised clearing house or a nominee of a recognised clearing

house or of a recognised investment exchange, or with which a transfer is lodged for transferring any shares, debentures or debenture stock of the company to such a clearing house or nominee, is not required, in consequence of the allotment or the lodging of the transfer, to comply with subsection (1); but no person shall be a nominee for the purposes of this section unless he is a person designated for the purposes of this section in the rules of the recognised investment exchange in question.

'Recognised clearing house' means a recognised clearing house within the meaning of the Financial Services Act 1986 acting in relation to a recognised investment exchange and 'recognised investment exchange' has the same meaning as in that Act.

(5)   If default is made in complying with subsection (1), the company and every officer of it who is in default is liable to a fine and, for continued contravention, to a daily default fine.

(6)   If a company on which a notice has been served requiring it to make good any default in complying with subsection (1) fails to make good the default within 10 days after service of the notice, the court may, on the application of the person entitled to have the certificates or the debentures delivered to him, exercise the power of the following subsection.

(7)   The court may make an order directing the company and any officer of it to make good the default within such time as may be specified in the order; and the order may provide that all costs of and incidental to the application shall be borne by the company or by an officer of it responsible for the default.

General note

This section applies to shares, debentures (defined in s 744) and debenture stock. It also applies to the conversion of uncertificated units (ie securities settled within the CREST electronic settlement system) into certificated form: Uncertificated Securities Regulations 1995, SI 1995/3272, reg 26(3). See note to s 182(1).

S 185(1)

Time limit for deliver of certificates   The time limit is within two months of allotment (defined in s 738) or the lodging of a transfer. Where a conversion of uncertificated securities to certificated form is involved, the time limit is determined by the Uncertificated Securities Regulations 1995, SI 1995/3272, reg 26(3).

The time limit applies unless the conditions of issue otherwise provide and public companies making an allotment will not usually issue share certificates until the full issue price has been paid and this will be provided for in the terms of issue. Until such time, the shareholder relies on a letter of allotment. No share certificates may be issued where the securities are allotted or transferred through CREST: see the Uncertificated Securities Regulations 1995, SI 1995/3272, reg 32(2).

A shareholder is entitled to a clean certificate, ie one which does not contain any statement derogatory to his title: *Re W Key & Son Ltd* [1902] 1 Ch 467.

S 185(3)

Certain transfers under the Stock Transfer Act 1982 are exempt from the requirement of a proper instrument of transfer in s 183(1) and they are likewise exempt from the requirement of certificates to the extent stated.

S 185(4)

This provision ensures that where an allotment or transfer of shares or debentures is via a recognised clearing house or a nominee thereof or a nominee of a recognised investment exchange etc which acts as an intermediary between the company and the investors, the company does not have to issue share certificates etc to the intermediary.

S 185(5)–(7)

As to penalties, see s 730, Sch 24; 'officer in default' is defined in s 730(5).

186. Certificate to be evidence of title

(1) A certificate under the common seal of the company specifying any shares held by a member is—

    (a) in England and Wales, prima facie evidence, and

    (b) in Scotland, sufficient evidence unless the contrary is shown,

of his title to the shares.

(2) Without prejudice to subsection (1), as respects Scotland a certificate specifying any shares held by a member and subscribed by the company in accordance with the Requirements of Writing (Scotland) Act 1995 is, unless the contrary is shown, sufficient evidence of his title to the shares.

General note

As to the equivalent provision where uncertificated securities are involved, see the Uncertificated Securities Regulations 1995, SI 1995/3272, reg 20(2); in that case, it is entry on the register of persons holding units of the participating security in an uncertificated form which is the prima facie evidence of title. It is further specifically provided that s 186 does not apply to any document issued with respect to uncertificated shares: see SI 1995/3272, reg 32(3).

S 186(1)

It is no longer necessary for companies to have a common seal and, whether they do or not, a document signed by a director and the secretary of the company, or by two directors of the company, and expressed (in whatever form of words) to be executed by the company has the same effect as if executed under the common seal of the company: s 36A(4).

Accordingly, there is no requirement for share certificates to be sealed and a share certificate issued under a common seal, or executed in accordance with s 36A, or executed under s 40, which allows for an official seal which has the same effect as a common seal, is governed by this section.

The certificate, as against the company, is a statement that the company asserts that the person to whom it is granted is the registered shareholder entitled to the shares included in the certificate: *Re Bahia and San Francisco Rly Co* (1868) LR 3 QB 584; *Balkis Consolidated Co v Tomkinson* [1893] AC 396; and, in the case of a bona fide transferee who has no notice to the contrary, that the amount certified to be paid has been paid: *Burkinshaw v Nicolls* (1878) 3 App Cas 1004, 1027; *Spargo's Case* (1873) 8 Ch App 407 at 410; *Bush's Case* (1874) 9 Ch App 554.

Estoppel not warranty An erroneous certificate does not confer a title to the shares: *Bahia and San Francisco Rly Co* (1868) LR 3 QB 584. Nor is it a warranty of title upon which anyone can sue the company: see *Royal Bank of Scotland plc v Sandstone Properties Ltd* [1998] 2 BCLC 429. However, the company is estopped, as against any person altering his position to his detriment on the faith of the representations contained in the certificate, from denying that the facts are as stated in the certificate: *Balkis Consolidated Co v Tomkinson* [1893] AC 396 at 405. This will include the person to whom the certificate was issued as well as a transferee from that person: *Dixon v Kennaway & Co* [1900] 1 Ch 833.

As against a person who buys shares on the faith of a certificate held by his vendor and pays for them against delivery of such certificate and a duly executed transfer, the company is estopped by the certificate, although obtained by fraud or under mistake, from denying the title of the vendor and is accordingly liable in damages to the purchaser if it refuses to register him as holder of the shares: *Bahia and San Francisco Rly Co* (1868) LR 3 QB 584; *Webb v Herne Bay Comrs* (1870) LR 5 QB 642; *Balkis Consolidated Co v Tomkinson* [1893] AC 396; *Re Ottos Kopje Diamond Mines* [1893] 1 Ch 618; *Dixon v Kennaway & Co* [1900] 1 Ch 833.

As against a vendor of shares who, relying upon the certificate held by himself, enters into contracts for sale of the shares, the company is in like manner estopped from disputing that he is the holder of the shares and the company is liable in damages for declining to register the transfers to the purchasers: *Balkis Consolidated Co v Tomkinson* [1893] AC 396 (vendor had to go into the market and purchase shares to satisfy his purchasers).

Forged certificate A company is not estopped by a forged certificate (ie one to which the company's seal is affixed without proper authority): *Ruben v Great Fingall Consolidated* [1904] 2 KB 712; affd [1906] AC 439, where the seal was affixed without authority by the company secretary who forged the names of the two directors. The court found the document to be a nullity and as such incapable of giving rise to any estoppel. It was followed in *South London Greyhound Racecourses Ltd v Wake* [1931] 1 Ch 496, where a certificate signed by two directors and the company secretary but without authority was held to be a nullity. The approach in these cases has been criticised as erroneous.

The position would be governed by s 36A(6) now, which provides, in favour of a purchaser in good faith for valuable consideration, that a document is deemed to be duly executed by a company if it purports to be signed by a director and the secretary of the company, or by two directors. It is clear that this would cover the situation which arose in *South London Greyhound Racecourses Ltd v Wake* but it is not altogether clear whether 'purports' can be interpreted widely enough to cover the situation in *Ruben* itself, ie where the document is a forgery. It seems it would not do so.

187. Evidence of grant of probate or confirmation as executor

The production to a company of any document which is by law sufficient evidence of probate of the will, or letters of administration of the estate, or confirmation as executor, of a deceased person having been granted to some person shall be accepted by the company as sufficient evidence of the grant.

This has effect notwithstanding anything in the company's articles.

General note

It is assumed that 'by law' means by the law of this country and a company may not recognise an executor or administrator until probate or letters of administration have been obtained in this country: see *Re Commercial Bank Corpn of India and the East, Fernades' Executors' Case* (1870) 5 Ch App 314; and see *New York Breweries Co v A-G* [1899] AC 62, HL.

However, a liquidator is not bound to ignore the claims of persons claiming under a foreign grant and to insist on an English grant being obtained if he is satisfied that the personal representatives would be so entitled. He can proceed to distribute a deceased member's share of the surplus assets to a claimant without the formality of an English grant but he must keep in mind the possibility of becoming liable as an executor de son tort; although he can protect himself by securing a suitable indemnity. If he does not consider that to be sufficient protection, he may wish to insist on the protection of an English grant: *Re Baku Consolidated Oilfields Ltd* [1994] 1 BCLC 173 at 176.

188. Issue and effect of share warrant to bearer

(1)   A company limited by shares may, if so authorised by its articles, issue with respect to any fully paid shares a warrant (a 'share warrant') stating that the bearer of the warrant is entitled to the shares specified in it.

(2)   A share warrant issued under the company's common seal (or, in the case of a company registered in Scotland, subscribed in accordance with the Requirements of Writing (Scotland) Act 1995) entitles the bearer to the shares specified in it; and the shares may be transferred by delivery of the warrant.

(3)   A company which issues a share warrant may, if so authorised by its articles, provide (by coupons or otherwise) for the payment of the future dividends on the shares included in the warrant.

General note

The bearer of a share warrant is a shareholder but not a member because his name is not entered on the register as required by s 22. If the articles so provide, the bearer of a warrant may be deemed to be a member of the company, either to the full extent or for any purposes defined in the articles: s 355(5). As to the recording of share warrants on the register of members, see s 355. If a holder of warrants is to vote at a meeting of the company, the articles usually require that the warrant be deposited beforehand.

Shares held under warrant are not sufficient for the purposes of directors' share qualification requirements: s 291(2).

Any shares with respect to which share warrants to bearer are issued are regarded as forming a separate class of shares for the purposes of the Uncertificated Securities Regulations 1995, see SI 1995/3272, regs 17, 19(6).

S 188(1)

It would appear from this wording that share warrants can only be issued with respect to fully paid shares which have already been issued and which are to be replaced by these share warrants. In other words, it appears that a company cannot issue warrants directly without a prior issue of the shares specified in the warrant. Table A makes no provision for a company to issue share warrants to bearer.

S 188(2)

It is no longer necessary for companies to have a common seal and, whether they do or not, a document signed by a director and the secretary of the company, or by two directors of the company, and expressed (in whatever form of words) to be executed by the company has the same effect as if executed under the common seal of the company: s 36A(4).

Accordingly, a share warrant may be issued under a common seal, or issued in accordance with s 36A, or issued under s 40 which allows for an official seal which has the same effect as a common seal.

A share warrant to bearer is a negotiable instrument: *Webb, Hale & Co v Alexandria Water Co Ltd* (1905) 93 LT 339; and is transferable by delivery of the warrant itself. It does not require a proper instrument of transfer.

189. Offences in connection with share warrants (Scotland)

(1)   If in Scotland a person—

    (a)   with intent to defraud, forges or alters, or offers, utters, disposes of, or puts off, knowing the same to be forged or altered, any share warrant or coupon, or any document purporting to be a share warrant or coupon, issued in pursuance of this Act; or

    (b)   by means of any such forged or altered share warrant, coupon, or document, purporting as aforesaid, demands or endeavours to obtain or receive any share or interest in any company under this Act, or to receive any dividend or money payable in respect thereof, knowing the warrant, coupon, or document to be forged or altered;

he is on conviction thereof liable to imprisonment or a fine, or both.

(2)   If in Scotland a person without lawful authority or excuse (proof whereof lies on him)—

  (a)   engraves or makes on any plate, wood, stone, or other material , any share warrant or coupon purporting to be—

  (i)   a share warrant or coupon issued or made by any particular company in pursuance of this Act; or

  (ii)   a blank share warrant or coupon so issued or made; or

  (iii)   a part of such a share warrant or coupon; or

  (b)   uses any such plate, wood, stone, or other material, for the making or printing of any such share warrant or coupon, or of any such blank share warrant or coupon, or any part thereof respectively; or

  (c)   knowingly has in his custody or possession any such plate, wood, stone, or other material;

he is on conviction thereof liable to imprisonment or a fine, or both.

General note

This section applies to Scotland only.

DEBENTURES

190. Register of debenture holders

(1)   A company registered in England and Wales shall not keep in Scotland any register of holders of debentures of the company or any duplicate of any such register or part of any such register which is kept outside Great Britain.

(2)   A company registered in Scotland shall not keep in England and Wales any such register as above-mentioned.

(3)   Neither a register of holders of debentures of a company nor a duplicate of any such register or part of any such register which is kept outside Great Britain shall be kept in England and Wales (in the case of a company registered in England and Wales) or in Scotland (in the case of a company registered in Scotland) elsewhere than—

  (a)   at the company's registered office; or

  (b)   at any office of the company at which the work of making it up is done; or

(c) if the company arranges with some other person for the making up of the register or duplicate to be undertaken on its behalf by that other person, at the office of that other person at which the work is done.

(4) Where a company keeps (in England and Wales or in Scotland, as the case may be) both such a register and such a duplicate, it shall keep them at the same place.

(5) Every company which keeps any such register or duplicate in England and Wales or Scotland shall send to the registrar of companies notice (in the prescribed form) of the place where the register or duplicate is kept and of any change in that place.

(6) But a company is not bound to send notice under subsection (5) where the register or duplicate has, at all times since it came into existence, been kept at the company's registered office.

General note

This section does not impose an obligation on a company to keep a register of debenture holders but it deals with the location of such a register, if a company chooses to have one. It is normal practice where a series of debentures or debenture stock is issued for the debentures themselves or the trust deed to provide for the registration of holders. If any such register or duplicate is kept elsewhere than at the registered office, the annual return must state where it is kept: s 364(1)(h). Inspection of the register is dealt with in s 191.

The register of debenture holders may be kept otherwise than in a legible form (see s 722, 723); and, in that case, the requirements as to the register are contained in the Companies (Registers and Other Records) Regulations 1985, SI 1985/724, regs 4, 5.

Where the securities are uncertificated, see the Uncertificated Securities Regulations 1995, SI 1995/3272, reg 19(2), (3). See also the register of charges which a company is required to keep at its registered office (s 407); as to the registered office, see s 287.

'Debenture' is broadly defined in s 744 as including debenture stock, bonds and any other securities of a company, whether constituting a charge on the assets of the company or not.

191. Right to inspect register

(1) Every register of holders of debentures of a company shall, except when duly closed ..., be open to the inspection—
(a) of the registered holder of any such debentures or any holder of shares in the company without fee; and
(b) of any other person on payment of such fee as may be prescribed.

(2) Any such registered holder of debentures or holder of shares, or any other person, may require a copy of the register of the holders of debentures of the company or any part of it, on payment of such fee as may be prescribed.

(3) A copy of any trust deed for securing an issue of debentures shall be forwarded to every holder of any such debentures at his request on payment of such fee as may be prescribed.

(4)   If inspection is refused, or a copy is refused or not forwarded, the company and every officer of it who is in default is liable to a fine and, for continued contravention, to a daily default fine.

(5)   Where a company is in default as above-mentioned, the court may by order compel an immediate inspection of the register or direct that the copies required be sent to the person requiring them.

(6)   For purposes of this section, a register is deemed to be duly closed if closed in accordance with provisions contained in the articles or in the debentures or, in the case of debenture stock, in the stock certificates, or in the trust deed or other document securing the debentures or debenture stock, during such period or periods not exceeding in the whole 30 days in any year, as may be therein specified.

(7)   Liability incurred by a company from the making or deletion of an entry in its register of debenture holders, or from a failure to make or delete any such entry, is not enforceable more than 20 years after the date on which the entry was made or deleted or, in the case of any such failure, the failure first occurred.
   This is without prejudice to any lesser period of limitation.

S 191(1)–(3)

These provisions permit inspection of the register of debenture holders by persons other than debenture holders and members of the company and allows debenture holders to obtain a copy of any trust deed; 'debenture' is broadly defined in s 744. As to the inspection of the register, see the Companies (Inspection and Copying of Registers, Indices and Documents) Regulations 1991, SI 1991/1998.

S 191(4), (5)

As to penalties, see s 730, Sch 24; 'officer in default' is defined in s 730(5). The court's power to compel inspection is discretionary: see *Pelling v Families need Fathers Ltd* [2001] All ER (D) 03 (Aug), CA.

S 191(7)

See note to s 352(7), below, which is an identical provision with respect to the register of members.

192. Liability of trustees of debentures

(1)   Subject to this section, any provision contained—

    (a)   in a trust deed for securing an issue of debentures, or

    (b)   in any contract with the holders of debentures secured by a trust deed,

is void in so far as it would have the effect of exempting a trustee of the deed from, or indemnifying him against, liability for breach of trust where he fails to show the degree of care and diligence required of him as trustee, having regard to the provisions of the trust deed conferring on him any powers, authorities or discretions.

(2)   Subsection (1) does not invalidate—

(a)   a release otherwise validly given in respect of anything done or omitted to be done by a trustee before the giving of the release; or

(b)   any provision enabling such a release to be given—

(i)   on the agreement thereto of a majority of not less than three-fourths in value of the debenture holders present and voting in person or, where proxies are permitted, by proxy at a meeting summoned for the purpose, and

(ii)   either with respect to specific acts or omissions or on the trustee dying or ceasing to act.

(3)   Subsection (1) does not operate—

(a)   to invalidate any provision in force on 1st July 1948 so long as any person then entitled to the benefit of that provision or afterwards given the benefit of that provision under the following subsection remains a trustee of the deed in question; or

(b)   to deprive any person of any exemption or right to be indemnified in respect of anything done or omitted to be done by him while any such provision was in force.

(4)   While any trustee of a trust deed remains entitled to the benefit of a provision saved by subsection (3), the benefit of that provision may be given either—

(a)   to all trustees of the deed, present and future; or

(b)   to any named trustees or proposed trustees of it,

by a resolution passed by a majority of not less than three-fourths in value of the debenture holders present in person or, where proxies are permitted, by proxy at a meeting summoned for the purpose in accordance with the provisions of the deed or, if the deed makes no provision for summoning meetings, a meeting summoned for the purpose in any manner approved by the court.

S 192(1)

Limitations on liability   It had become the general practice for debenture trust deeds to contain clauses absolving every trustee from liability for anything but his own wilful neglect or default. This section limits the extent to which such trustees can escape liability for failure to do their duty properly but it is subject to the exceptions in sub-ss (2)–(4).

S 192(2)

Permissible provisions   It is permissible to release a trustee from liability with respect to particular acts or on the trustee dying or ceasing to act. A trustee of a debenture trust deed is entitled to the protection of the Trustee Act 1925, s 30 (trustee answerable only for his own acts) and could benefit from the power of the court to excuse a trustee under the Trustee Act 1925, s 61 (trustee acted honestly and reasonably and ought fairly to be excused).

S 192(3), (4)

Pre-1948 trust deed   Subsection (3) not only preserves the position of trustees in office at the commencement of CA 1948 (1 July 1948), but also exempts all trustees of a deed from the effects of the section as long as any trustee of that deed, who was in office at the commencement of the Act, remains a trustee of the deed. Subsection (4) enables debenture holders to extend the exemption. If it is extended, all the trustees of the deed will have the benefit of the exemption so long as any of them is entitled to it.

The result is that such clauses in force at the commencement of CA 1948 (1 July 1948) can be kept in operation indefinitely but any trust deed which came into operation after the commencement of that Act is subject to this section.

193. Perpetual debentures

A condition contained in debentures, or in a deed for securing debentures, is not invalid by reason only that the debentures are thereby made irredeemable or redeemable only on the happening of a contingency (however remote), or on the expiration of a period (however long), any rule of equity to the contrary notwithstanding.

This applies to debentures whenever issued, and to deeds whenever executed.

General note

'Irredeemable' debentures   This power was introduced by CA 1907, s 14, to give validity to the issuing of debentures or debenture stock where the principal is in terms either not repayable at all in the sense that no date is specified ('perpetual') or only in certain specified and contingent events, eg the company going into winding up or the company giving notice to redeem.

Doubts had been expressed as to the validity of such 'irredeemable' debentures which were regarded as a clog on the equity of redemption (see *Re Southern Brazilian Rio Grande do Sul Rly Co* [1905] 2 Ch 78) and this section was enacted to give them validity.

Clogs on the equity of redemption   The general position is that the doctrine relating to clogs on the equity of redemption applies to the issue of debentures or debenture stock by, or other mortgage transactions of, companies in the same way as to the mortgage transactions of individuals and, semble, to floating charges as much as to any other mortgage securities: *Jarrah Timber and Wood Paving Corpn Ltd v Samuel* [1903] 2 Ch 1, CA; sub nom *Samuel v Jarrah Timber and Wood Paving Corpn Ltd* affd [1904] AC 323, HL; *Kreglinger v New Patagonia Meat and Cold Storage Co Ltd* [1914] AC 25; save where the clog arises from the time frame imposed which, by virtue of this section, is allowed to be perpetual in the case of company debentures.

An ordinary mortgage of land by a company is a debenture for these purposes and could therefore be irredeemable for 40 years without being void as a clog on the equity of redemption: *Knightsbridge Estates Trust v Byrne* [1940] AC 613.

Where debentures were issued on a prospectus which stated that they were to be 'redeemable' within a certain period, North J held that even if the court was entitled to go outside the debentures and look at the prospectus (semble, it was not so entitled), still, on the construction of the prospectus, 'redeemable' meant 'liable to be redeemed' and the company was not bound to redeem within the stated period: *Re Chicago and North West Granaries Co Ltd* [1898] 1 Ch 263. But a covenant to pay 'on or after' a specified date entitles the holders to demand payment after the specified date has arrived: *Re Tewkesbury Gas Co* [1911] 2 Ch 279.

'Debenture' is broadly defined in s 744 as including debenture stock, bonds and any other securities of a company, whether constituting a charge on the assets of the company or not.

194. Power to re-issue redeemed debentures

(1)　Where (at any time) a company has redeemed debentures previously issued, then—

(a)　unless provision to the contrary, whether express or implied, is contained in the articles or in any contract entered into by the company; or

(b)　unless the company has, by passing a resolution to that effect or by some other act, manifested its intention that the debentures shall be cancelled,

the company has, and is deemed always to have had, power to re-issue the debentures, either by re-issuing the same debentures or by issuing other debentures in their place.

(2)　On a re-issue of redeemed debentures, the person entitled to the debentures has, and is deemed always to have had, the same priorities as if the debentures had never been redeemed.

(3)　Where a company has (at any time) deposited any of its debentures to secure advances from time to time on current account or otherwise, the debentures are not deemed to have been redeemed by reason only of the company's account having ceased to be in debit while the debentures remained so deposited.

(4)　The re-issue of a debenture or the issue of another debenture in its place under the power which by this section is given to or deemed to be possessed by a company is to be treated as the issue of a new debenture for purposes of stamp duty; but it is not to be so treated for the purposes of any provision limiting the amount or number of debentures to be issued.

This applies whenever the issue or re-issue was made.

(5)　A person lending money on the security of a debenture re-issued under this section which appears to be duly stamped may give the debenture in evidence in any proceedings for enforcing his security without payment of the stamp duty or any penalty in respect of it, unless he had notice (or, but for his negligence, might have discovered) that the debenture was not duly stamped; but in that case the company is liable to pay the proper stamp duty and penalty.

S 194(1)

Re-issue of redeemed debentures　At common law, a company could not re-issue redeemable debentures conferring the same priority rights as before: *Re W Tasker &*

Sons Ltd [1905] 2 Ch 587; and redeemed or re-purchased debentures were extinguished. This provision allows companies to re-issue debentures, however, unless precluded from doing so in the manner specified. 'Debenture' is broadly defined in s 744 as including debenture stock, bonds and any other securities of a company, whether constituting a charge on the assets of the company or not.

S 194(2)

Same terms apply   This section does not authorise the issue, in the place of redeemed debentures, of debentures different in terms from those which have been redeemed. A company cannot redeem debentures and re-issue them under this section with a different redemption date: *Re Antofagasta (Chili) and Bolivia Rly Co Ltd's Trust Deed v Schroder* [1939] Ch 732 (the section only gives power to revive the original transaction and not to enter into a new and different transaction).

S 194(3)

This provision alters the position from that laid down in *Re Russian Petroleum and Liquid Fuel Co Ltd* [1907] 2 Ch 540, which held that once an overdraft (secured by the deposit of a debenture) was paid off, the debenture was spent and could not be re-charged to other debts incurred by the company.

S 194(4), (5)

Stamp duty on debentures and loan capital was removed by the FA 1971.

---

195. Contract to subscribe for debentures

A contract with a company to take up and pay for debentures of the company may be enforced by an order for specific performance.

General note

An agreement to take up a debenture or pay up money on a debenture is merely a contract to lend money on a particular security. The courts had held that specific performance of such an agreement could not be enforced and the company could not sue for the amount of the debenture or the instalment unpaid thereof but was only entitled to damages for the actual loss caused by the breach: *Re Smelting Corpn* [1915] 1 Ch 472; *South African Territories v Wallington* [1898] AC 309. This provision reverses these decisions and entitles a company to seek specific performance to obtain the money promised to it.

'Debenture' is broadly defined in s 744 as including debenture stock, bonds and any other securities of a company, whether constituting a charge on the assets of the company or not.

196. Payment of debts out of assets subject to floating charge (England and Wales)

(1)   The following applies in the case of a company registered in England and Wales, where debentures of the company are secured by a charge which, as created, was a floating charge.

(2)   If possession is taken, by or on behalf of the holders of any of the debentures, of any property comprised in or subject to the charge, and the company is not at that time in course of being wound up, the company's preferential debts shall be paid out of assets coming to the hands of the person taking possession in priority to any claims for principal or interest in respect of the debentures.

(3)   'Preferential debts' means the categories of debts listed in Schedule 6 to the Insolvency Act; and for the purposes of that Schedule 'the relevant date' is the date of possession being taken as above mentioned.

(4)   Payments made under this section shall be recouped, as far as may be, out of the assets of the company available for payment of general creditors.

General note

Position prior to Insolvency Act reforms   The position prior to the reforms effected by the IA 1986 was that priority was given by statute to preferential debts where either a receiver was appointed on behalf of holders of any debenture secured by a floating charge or possession was taken by or on behalf of those debentures holders of any property comprised in or subject to the charge. An equivalent provision applied on a winding up.

However, this priority for preferential debts over the holders of a debenture secured by a floating charge only existed if the floating charge was still floating at the time when the receiver was appointed or possession was taken or at the moment of winding up: *Re Griffin Hotel Co Ltd* [1940] 4 All ER 324; *Re Christonette International Ltd* [1982] 3 All ER 225; *Re Permanent Houses (Holdings) Ltd* [1988] BCLC 563.

A great deal of drafting effort concentrated therefore on making the floating charge crystallise ahead of a winding up and without the appointment of a receiver for, if the floating charge had so crystallised, then the preference debts had no priority: see *Re Brightlife Ltd* [1986] BCLC 418.

Reforms introduced by The Insolvency Act 1986   The IA 1986 substituted a new s 196 with a view to re-establishing the priority of the preferential debts.

The key change effected by this provision is that a floating charge is now defined as a charge which, *as created*, was a floating charge: s 196(1). The focus shifts from whether or not the charge has crystallised to whether, as created, the charge was a floating charge. If it was, then regardless of whether it has crystallised or not, the preferential debts have priority. The expenses of winding up are also payable out of assets subject to the floating charge (even if it has crystallised before liquidation) but in priority to the preferential debts: see *Re Portbase Clothing Ltd* [1993] BCLC 796 at 812–813; *Re Leyland Daf Ltd, Buchler v Talbot* [2001] 1 BCLC 419.

As has been noted above, this priority arises in three cases:

(1)   where possession is taken by or on behalf of a debenture holder;
(2)   where a receiver is appointed; and
(3)   where the company is in winding up.

Section 196 deals only with the first possibility. The more common situations, where a receiver is appointed or the company is in winding up, are governed by IA 1986, ss 40 and 175(2)(b) respectively.

S 196(1)–(2)

A positive duty   The section imposes a positive duty to pay the preferential creditors in priority to the debenture holders: *Westminster Corpn v Haste* [1950] Ch 442; *IRC v Goldblatt* [1972] 2 All ER 202 (see also *Re Pearl Maintenance Services Ltd, Re Pearl Building Contracts Ltd* [1995] 1 BCLC 449, a case on IA 1986, s 40).

In possession   A debenture holder in possession who fails, with notice of the preferential claims, to comply with this statutory duty is directly liable to the preferential creditors: *IRC v Goldblatt* [1972] 2 All ER 202. This is so whether the debenture holder is in possession as mortgagee or in full ownership in satisfaction of his claim: *IRC v Goldblatt*.

A receiver appointed by a debenture holder, not being the agent of the debenture holder, does not take possession of any goods of the company 'on behalf of' the debenture holder so as to fall within this provision: *Re H & K (Medway) Ltd, Mackay v IRC* [1997] 1 BCLC 545. The position where receivers are appointed is governed by IA 1986, s 40.

Property comprised in the charge   If the charge is partly fixed and partly floating, the priority afforded by this provision applies only to the assets subject to the floating charge and assets comprised in the fixed charge are outside the scope of the section: *Re Lewis Merthyr Consolidated Collieries Ltd* [1929] 1 Ch 498; *Re G L Saunders Ltd* [1986] BCLC 40. If it is agreed by a deed of priority that a fixed charge is to be subject to a floating charge, the situation is distinguishable from that governed by the rule in *Re Lewis Merthyr* and the fixed charge assets, being assets subject to the floating charge, will be available to meet the preferential debts: *Re Portbase Clothing Ltd* [1993] BCLC 796.

In the course of being wound up   A company is in 'the course of being wound up' only after an order for its compulsory winding up has been made or a resolution to wind it up has been passed: *Re Christonette International Ltd* [1982] 3 All ER 225.

Payment in priority to any debentures   The payment to the preferential creditors must be in priority to any claim for principal or interest in respect of any debenture of the company which, as created, was a floating charge, and not just in priority to any claim in respect of the debenture under which possession is taken: *Re H & K (Medway) Ltd, Mackay v IRC* [1997] 1 BCLC 545, 550 (case under IA 1986, s 40 where receiver appointed but IA 1986, s 40 and s 196 should be given the same effect); cf *Griffiths v Yorkshire Bank plc* [1994] 1 WLR 1427, which was not followed in *Re H & K (Medway) Ltd*.

S 196(3)

Preferential status   The debts granted preferential status are itemised in IA 1986, Sch 6, and consist chiefly of certain sums due to the Inland Revenue, to Customs and Excise, and to the Department of Health and Social Security together with certain sums due to employees including wages or salary for services rendered in the four months before winding up (but up to a specified maximum amount per employee) and all accrued holiday remuneration.

S 196(4)

Payments may be recouped   The floating charge may encompass all of the assets of the company so there are no further assets out of which these payments might be recouped but, in so far as there are further assets, the burden of meeting the preferential claims falls on the general creditors of the company.

197. Debentures to bearer (Scotland)

Notwithstanding anything in the statute of the Scots Parliament of 1696, chapter 25, debentures to bearer issued in Scotland are valid and binding according to their terms.

General note

This section applies to Scotland only.

PART VI

DISCLOSURE OF INTERESTS
IN SHARES

General note to this Part

This Part contains two distinct sets of provisions, first, requiring persons with interests in shares in a public company to notify the company of those interests (ss 198–211), and secondly, enabling a company to seek information as to those holding interests in shares in the company (ss 212–219). The intention behind the provisions initially was to enable shareholders and the public generally to know promptly of the acquisition of significant (voting) shareholdings in public companies. More recently, the emphasis has been on facilitating market transparency.

Obligation of disclosure   Turning to the complex provisions requiring the disclosure of interests in shares in a public company, the basic obligation of disclosure falls on a person who knows or becomes aware that he has a material interest in 3% of any class of voting shares of a public company. He must inform the company of his interest within two days and thereafter he must disclose each percentage change in his interests above 3% and if he ceases to hold a 3% interest. For non-material interests, defined in s 199(2A), the threshold is 10%. The interests which must be disclosed are defined in s 208 and are subject to the exemptions in s 209. The interests of family members and companies under his control are attributed to a person as set out in s 203. Provision is also made for the attribution of interests arising under a concert party agreement whereby persons act together to acquire shares in pursuance of an agreement as defined in s 204. The company must enter the information disclosed in a register of interests in shares kept for the purpose which is open to public inspection. Non-compliance with an obligation of disclosure is a criminal offence and, on conviction, the shares in question may be subject to restrictions: see s 210.

Company may require disclosure   Sections 211–219 enable public companies to require any person to disclose the interests which he and any other persons hold in any shares or have held in the preceding three years. This information must also be entered on the register of interests in shares and is open to inspection by the public. Shareholders may require the directors to exercise these powers in certain circumstances. Non-compliance with a request for information is a criminal offence and the shares held by that person may be subject to various restrictions.

Investigations by the Department of Trade and Industry   These provisions are in addition to the powers of the Department of Trade and Industry to investigate the ownership of companies via the appointment of inspectors (s 442) or requests for information (s 444) and to impose restrictions on the shares under Part XV (ss 454–457) if information is not forthcoming. Further provisions requiring the disclosure of interests in shares are contained in the Take-over Code and the Rules Governing Substantial Acquisitions of Shares issued by the Take-over Panel.

INDIVIDUAL AND GROUP ACQUISITIONS

198. Obligation of disclosure: the cases in which it may arise and 'the relevant time'

(1)   Where a person either—

    (a) to his knowledge acquires an interest in shares comprised in a public company's relevant share capital, or ceases to be interested in shares so comprised (whether or not retaining an interest in other shares so comprised), or

    (b) becomes aware that he has acquired an interest in shares so comprised or that he has ceased to be interested in shares so comprised in which he was previously interested,

then in certain circumstances he comes under an obligation ('the obligation of disclosure') to make notification to the company with respect to his interests (if any), in its shares.

(2)   In relation to a public company, 'relevant share capital' means the company's issued share capital of a class carrying rights to vote in all circumstances at general meetings of the company; and it is hereby declared for the avoidance of doubt that—

    (a) where a company's share capital is divided into different classes of shares, references in this Part to a percentage of the nominal value of its relevant share capital are to a percentage of the nominal value of the issued shares comprised in each of the classes taken separately, and

    (b) the temporary suspension of voting rights in respect of shares comprised in issued share capital of a company of any such class does not affect the application of this Part in relation to interests in those or any other shares comprised in that class.

(3)   Where, otherwise than in circumstances within subsection (1), a person—

    (a) is aware at the time when it occurs of any change of circumstances affecting facts relevant to the application of the next following section to an existing interest of his in shares comprised in a company's share capital of any description, or

    (b) otherwise becomes aware of any such facts (whether or not arising from any such change of circumstances),

then in certain circumstances he comes under the obligation of disclosure.

(4)   The existence of the obligation in a particular case depends (in part) on circumstances obtaining before and after whatever is in that case the relevant time; and that is—

    (a) in a case within subsection (1)(a) or (3)(a), the time of the event or change of circumstances there mentioned, and

    (b) in a case within subsection (1)(b) or (3)(b), the time at which the person became aware of the facts in question.

General note

Companies must maintain a register of members (s 352 et seq) but that register relates only to legal ownership and no other interests may be recorded (s 360); and directors must disclose their interests in shares in their own company under s 324 et seq; but these provisions (ss 198–220) ensure disclosure of a wider range of interests in shares in a public company.

S 198(1)

The obligation of disclosure   This provision is triggered by the acquisition or disposal of an interest in voting shares in a public company, whether listed or unlisted; the interests to be notified are defined by s 208, subject to exemptions in s 209; and the thresholds for notification are set out in s 199(2), (4)–(5), see also s 200. The interests of others may be attributed to a person for these purposes: see ss 203, 204.

Knowledge   The obligation of disclosure arises only where a person 'to his knowledge' acquires or ceases to be interested in any shares or 'becomes aware' that he has acquired etc and actual knowledge is required (see also s 199(3)). As to knowledge where the acquisition is made through an agent, see s 210(1). Where the person with a notifiable interest is a company, the company knows it has acquired the interest when it is known to the person who, with the authority of the company, acquired the relevant interest. Such a rule of attribution is necessary if the policy of the Act, namely the immediate disclosure of the identity of those with substantial interests in a public company, is not to be defeated: see *Meridian Global Funds Management Asia Ltd v Securities Commission* [1995] 3 All ER 918, PC.

Manner of disclosure   Notification must be in writing to the company; the particulars required are set out in s 202; and see s 210(2) as to the manner in which this obligation must be fulfilled. The company must maintain a register of interests notified to it (s 211) and this register is open to inspection by any member of the public (s 219).

Penalties   Non-compliance with the obligation of disclosure is a criminal offence (s 210(3)); on conviction, the shares in question may be subject to restrictions: see s 210(5), (5A).

S 198(2)

Relevant share capital   Whether a disclosure obligation arises depends on the percentage of the relevant share capital in which the person has an interest (see s 199). The ascertainment of the relevant share capital figure for the purpose of working out the percentage held can be difficult. Companies are required to include a statement of their authorised and allotted share capital in a note to the accounts (Sch 4, para 38) but that figure does not specifically identify those shares with unrestricted voting rights. In any event, the figure may be affected by subsequent events, eg rights issues, purchases by the company of its own shares, variation of class rights, etc. In cases of doubt, the company secretary should be contacted.

'Issued share capital' is not defined in the legislation, but in *National Westminster Bank plc v IRC* [1995] 1 AC 119 the House of Lords accepted that allotment and entry on the register of members is required for shares to be issued; and see the note to s 738(1), below. It is possible, therefore, that an interest requiring notification will arise following an allotment but will not trigger the obligation of disclosure within sub-s (1) until all of the shares allotted have been registered. This could mean that there is a significant period during which the interest need not be disclosed. The Department of Trade and Industry did consider re-defining share capital so it would apply to allotted rather than issued shares but it found it difficult to devise a scheme which would work in practice.

Convertible securities giving the right to subscribe to the issue of new shares in the company can be ignored in calculating the total relevant share capital since they are not interests in issued share capital.

Classes of shares   Where a company has more than one class of shares with unrestricted voting rights, the test is applied to each class taken separately, so a person with more than 3% of a class must disclose that interest although he only has an interest in a small percentage of the overall share capital of the company. It is not clear that any great purpose is served by this extension to class rights, particularly as voting shares tend to be concentrated in one class of ordinary shares. Voting control in the context of a class of shares might be significant, however, if the company planned to vary those rights and was anxious to ascertain where control lay within the class.

Voting rights   Only interests in shares with full voting rights in all circumstances at a general meeting are relevant and there is no obligation to disclose any interest in non-voting shares. A temporary suspension of voting rights, perhaps under the company's articles or following the exercise by the Secretary of State for Trade and Industry of his powers to impose restrictions on shares under s 445, may be disregarded. Equally, shares which generally do not carry the right to vote, such as preference shares with rights to vote only when dividends are in arrears, need not be included in the calculation even if at the time those shares do carry voting rights.

S 198(3)

Changes in circumstances   Subsection (1) imposes an obligation of disclosure where a person acquires an interest or ceases to be interested through some act of his or of those whose interests are attributed to him. This subsection imposes an obligation of disclosure where there has been no such act but a change in circumstances has altered the person's position. For example, a reduction of capital, a scheme of arrangement or the variation of class rights may affect his interests in any shares. On a change of circumstances, the disclosure obligation only arises where the person knows or becomes aware of the changed circumstances or facts giving rise to the obligation. Non-compliance with the obligation of disclosure is a criminal offence (s 210(3)); on conviction, the shares in question may be subject to restrictions: see s 210(5), (5A).

As to the thresholds which trigger the obligation of disclosure, see s 199(2), (4)–(5); as to the calculation of percentage levels in relation to notifiable interests, see s 200.

S 198(4)

This provision determines the point in time at which the person must consider whether an obligation of disclosure has arisen. See also s 199(3).

199. Interests to be disclosed

(1)　For the purposes of the obligation of disclosure, the interests to be taken into account are those in relevant share capital of the company concerned.

(2)　Where a person is interested in shares comprised in relevant share capital, then—

    (a)　if in some or all of those shares he has interests which are material interests, he has a notifiable interest at any time when the aggregate nominal value of the shares in which those material interests subsist is equal to or more than 3 per cent of the nominal value of that share capital; and

    (b)　he has a notifiable interest at any time when, not having such an interest by virtue of paragraph (a), the aggregate nominal value of the shares in which he has interests (whether or not including material interests) is equal to or more than 10 per cent of the nominal value of the relevant share capital.

(2A)　For the purposes of this Part, a material interest is any interest other than—

    (a)　an interest which a person authorised to manage investments belonging to another has by virtue of having the management of such investments under an agreement in or evidenced in writing;

    (b)　an interest which a person has by virtue of being the operator of—

        (i)　an authorised unit trust scheme;

        (ii)　a recognised scheme; or

        (iii)　a UCITS (as defined in subsection (8));

    (bb)　an interest belonging to an open-ended investment company;

    (c)　an interest in shares in a listed company which, if that company were not listed, would fall to be disregarded by virtue of section 209(10); or

    (d)　an interest of another which a person is taken to have by virtue of the application of section 203 or 205, where the interest of that other person falls within paragraph (a),(b), (bb) or (c).

(3)　All facts relevant to determining whether a person has a notifiable interest at any time (or the percentage level of his interest) are taken to be what he knows the facts to be at that time.

(4)　The obligation of disclosure arises under section 198(1) or (3) where the person has a notifiable interest immediately after the relevant time, but did not have such an interest immediately before that time.

(5)　The obligation also arises under section 198(1)or (3) where—

    (a)　the person had a notifiable interest immediately before the relevant time, but does not have such an interest immediately after it, or

    (b)　he had a notifiable interest immediately before that time, and has such an interest immediately after it, but the percentage levels of his interest immediately before and immediately after that time are not the same.

(6)　For the purposes of subsection (2A), a person is authorised to manage investments belonging to another if—

    (a)　he is an authorised person under Chapter III of Part I of the Financial Services Act 1986 and may manage that other's investments without contravening any prohibition mentioned in subsection (7); or

(b) it is an authorised credit institution which may manage that other's investments without being in breach of its authorisation.

(7) The prohibitions referred to in subsection (6)(a) are—

    (a) any prohibition contained in rules—

        (i) which make provision of a description mentioned in section 48(2)(a) and (b) of the Financial Services Act 1986; and

        (ii) which are made by the Secretary of State, the Treasury, a designated agency, a recognised professional body or a recognised self-regulating organisation; and

    (b) any prohibition imposed under section 65 of that Act.

(8) In this Part 'UCITS' means a collective investment scheme which—

    (a) is constituted in a member State other than the United Kingdom, and

    (b) complies with the conditions necessary for it to enjoy the rights conferred by Council Directive 85/611/EEC co-ordinating the laws, regulations and administrative provisions relating to undertakings for collective investment in transferable securities;

and subsection (8) of section 86 of the Financial Services Act 1986 (meaning of 'constituted in a member State') applies for the purposes of paragraph (a) of this subsection as it applies for the purposes of that section.

General note

This provision reflects amendments made by the Disclosure of Interests in Shares (Amendment) Regulations 1993, SI 1993/1819, which were necessary to implement EC Directive (EEC) 88/627 (OJ L348/62 17.12.88) on the information to be published when a major holding in a listed company is acquired or disposed of (the Major Shareholdings Directive). Member states are entitled to adopt stricter measures than those contained in the directive and Part VI (ss 198–220) is more restrictive in a number of ways than the directive.

S 199(1)

'Relevant share capital' is defined in s 198(2).

S 199(2)

Thresholds This provision provides for two thresholds: (a) 3% applicable, as the general rule, for interests described as material; and (b) 10% for those interests described as non-material interests, defined sub-s (2A).

To be within (b), material interests must be less than 3% ('not having an interest by virtue of para (a)') but the total interests, combining material and non-material, must equal or exceed 10%.

Although the wording is unclear (because of the proviso 'not having an interest by virtue of para (a)'), the intention is that unless and until a person's aggregated interests reach 10%, he is required only to disclose his material interests; at 10%, he comes under an obligation to disclose all of his interests (and see s 202(2), (2A)). So if A has a 2% material interest and a 7% non-material interest in X plc, he is not obliged to notify either interest; if he has a 3% material interest and a 4% non-material interest, he is required only to disclose the material interest; and if he has a 3% material interest and a 7% non-material interest, he is obliged to notify both the 3% and the 7% interest.

S 199(2A)

This provision was amended by the Open-Ended Investment Companies Regulations 2001, SI 2001/1228, reg 84, Sch 7, para 5.

Material and non-material interests   This section defines material interests as being all interests other than the following non-material interests which are subject to the 10% threshold. They are:

(a)   interests of persons authorised to manage investments, as defined in sub-ss (6), (7); such persons by contract may have the power to dispose of the interests and to exercise voting rights and it is important that their interests be disclosed;

(b)   interests of operators of certain collective investment schemes; see definitions, s 220;

(bb)   interests belonging to an open-ended investment company;

(c)   s 209(10) lists those interests in shares in an unlisted public company which are exempt from disclosure but which are required to be disclosed in the case of a listed public company because of the requirements of the Major Shareholdings Directive. To mitigate the increased burden of disclosure in respect of interests in shares in listed companies, it was decided to require disclosure in such cases only to the level required by the Directive which set a threshold of 10%. 'Listed company' is defined in s 220.

(d)   where non-material interests of the types specified in (a), (b), (bb) or (c) are attributed to a person, the person to whom they are attributed can continue to treat them as non-material for these purposes (ie the disclosure threshold will be 10% and not 3%).

There is no netting off provision in the legislation, so various interests acquired and disposed of over, say, a period of a day cannot be netted and the final position disclosed. Instead, each notifiable interest must be disclosed.

S 199(3)

This provision reinforces the point that, for the purposes of s 198(1), (3), the knowledge required is actual knowledge.

S 199(4), (5)

The obligation of disclosure arises, following an acquisition or disposal of an interest within s 198(1) or a change of circumstances within s 198(3), either:

(a)   where a person had no notifiable interest but now has a notifiable interest (ie crosses into the 3% or 10% category, as the case may be);

(b)   where a person had a notifiable interest and now has no such interest (ie had been in the 3% or 10% category and now has fallen below it);

(c)   where a person had a notifiable interest and now still has a notifiable interest but the percentage level had changed (ie over the threshold and position has changed, up or down, by 1% or more). As to how to determine the percentage level, see s 200.

S 199(6)

'Authorised credit institution' is defined in s 220.

200.'Percentage level' in relation to notifiable interests

(1) Subject to the qualifications mentioned below, 'percentage level', in section 199(5)(b), means the percentage figure found by expressing the aggregate nominal value of all the shares comprised in the share capital concerned in which the person has material interests immediately before or (as the case may be) immediately after the relevant time as a percentage of the nominal value of that share capital and rounding that figure down, if it is not a whole number, to the next whole number.

(2) In relation to a notifiable interest which a person has when the aggregate nominal value of the shares in which he is interested is equal to or more than 10 per cent of the nominal value of that relevant share capital, subsection (1) shall have effect as if for the words 'has material interests' there were substituted 'is interested'.

(3) Where the nominal value of the share capital is greater immediately after the relevant time than it was immediately before, the percentage level of the person's interest immediately before (as well as immediately after) that time is determined by reference to the larger amount.

S 200(1),(2)

This provision identifies how to determine the percentage level for the purposes of applying s 199(5)(b), ie for determining whether there has been a change from one percentage level to another which must be disclosed. The 'relevant time' is determined by s 198(4). The percentage is rounded down to the nearest whole number.

S 200(3)

This obscure provision applies where the company increases its nominal capital, for example, by a further allotment of shares. If this is simply an increase in capital without any increase in the person's interests, then by applying the same denominator to his interests before and after the increase, there will be no change in his percentage level requiring any notification from him. On the other hand, if the increase is the result of a rights issue under which he does acquire further interests then he may have a notifable interest, for example, because he falls out of or into a category or because there has been a percentage change.

---

201. *(Repealed by CA 1989, s 212, Sch 24, as from 31 May 1990.)*

202. Particulars to be contained in notification

(1)   Where notification is required by section 198 with respect to a person's interest (if any) in shares comprised in relevant share capital of a public company, the obligation to make the notification must ... be performed within the period of 2 days next following the day on which that obligation arises; and the notification must be in writing to the company.

(2)   The notification must specify the share capital to which it relates, and must also—

- (a) subject to subsections (2A) and (2B), state the number of shares comprised in that share capital in which the person making the notification knows he had material interests immediately after the time when the obligation arose, or
- (b) in a case where the person no longer has a notifiable interest in shares comprised in that share capital, state that he no longer has that interest.

(2A) Where, immediately after the relevant time, the aggregate nominal value of the shares in which the person making the notification is interested is equal to or more than 10 per cent of the nominal value of that relevant share capital, subsection (2)(a) shall have effect as if for the words 'had material interests' there were substituted 'was interested'.

(2B) Nothing in subsection (2) or (2A) requires a notification to state, in relation to any shares, whether the interest of the person making the notification is (or is not) a material interest.

(3)   A notification (other than one stating that a person no longer has a notifiable interest) shall include the following particulars, so far as known to the person making the notification at the date when it is made—

- (a) the identity of each registered holder of shares to which the notification relates and the number of such shares held by each of them, and
- (b) the number of such shares in which the interest of the person giving the notification is such an interest as is mentioned in section 208(5).

(4)   A person who has an interest in shares comprised in a company's relevant share capital, that interest being notifiable, is under obligation to notify the company in writing—

- (a) of any particulars in relation to those shares which are specified in subsection (3), and
- (b) of any change in those particulars,

of which in either case he becomes aware at any time after any interest notification date and before the first occasion following that date on which he comes under any further obligation of disclosure with respect to his interest in shares comprised in that share capital.

An obligation arising under this section must be performed within the period of 2 days next following the day on which it arises.

(5)   The reference in subsection (4) to an interest notification date, in relation to a person's interest in shares comprised in a public company's relevant share capital, is to either of the following—

(a)   the date of any notification made by him with respect to his interest under this Part, and

(b)   where he has failed to make a notification, the date on which the period allowed for making it came to an end.

(6)   A person who at any time has an interest in shares which is notifiable is to be regarded under subsection (4) as continuing to have a notifiable interest in them unless and until he comes under obligation to make a notification stating that he no longer has such an interest in those shares.

S 202(1)

Time and manner of notification   The notification obligation only arises under s 198 when the person knows or becomes aware of the notifiable interest. Notification must be in writing and must be received by the company, it seems, with the time limit. For guidance as to the calculation of the two day period, see s 220(2). An obligation of disclosure is not fulfilled unless there is compliance with s 210(2). The company must maintain a register of interests notified to it (s 211) and this register is open to inspection by any member of the public (s 219).

S 202(2)–(2B)

Content of notification   It is the number of shares in which the person has material interests (if disclosure has been triggered by the 3% threshold) which must be identified, not the percentage of the votes controlled; and if the threshold of 10% has triggered the obligation of disclosure, it is the number of shares in which he is interested (whether those interests are material or non-material) which must be disclosed; and in that case there is no need to distinguish between material and non-material interests. There is no requirement to disclose the date of the event giving rise to the notifiable interest or the date on which the person became aware of that event so it is not always clear whether the person has notified within the two-day period.

S 202(3)

Name of registered holder and number of shares   This information is essential to enable the company to track which shares on the register of members are the subject of the notification or the subject of the options to which the notification relates: see s 208(5). This information need be provided only 'so far as known'.

S 202(4)

Ongoing notification   This provision requires the ongoing notification to the company of information of which the person with the notifiable interest becomes aware with respect to the registered holders and the number of shares held by them and the number of shares in respect of which the person has options, and any changes to those particulars (including any exercise of any options). He is not entitled to wait until a further obligation of disclosure arises (following some change in his notifiable interests) before providing this information.

203. Notification of family and corporate interests

(1)   For purposes of sections 198 to 202, a person is taken to be interested in any shares in which his spouse or any infant child or step-child of his is interested; and 'infant' means, in relation to Scotland, person under the age of 18 years.

(2)   For those purposes, a person is taken to be interested in shares if a body corporate is interested in them and—

    (a) that body or its directors are accustomed to act in accordance with his directions or instructions, or

    (b) he is entitled to exercise or control the exercise of one-third or more of the voting power at general meetings of that body corporate.

(3)   Where a person is entitled to exercise or control the exercise of one-third or more of the voting power at general meetings of a body corporate and that body corporate is entitled to exercise or control the exercise of any of the voting power at general meetings of another body corporate ('the effective voting power') then, for purposes of subsection (2)(b), the effective voting power is taken as exercisable by that person.

(4)   For purposes of subsections (2) and (3), a person is entitled to exercise or control the exercise of voting power if—

    (a) he has a right (whether subject to conditions or not) the exercise of which would make him so entitled, or

he is under an obligation (whether or not so subject) the fulfilment of which would make him so entitled.

General note

Attribution   This is an anti-avoidance provision which requires the interests of the specified persons to be attributed to a person in determining whether he has a notifiable interest. If those whose interests are so attributed have themselves a notifiable interest, they must also notify the company with the result that there may be multiple notifications of the same interests.

As to when a person knows of these attributed interests for the purposes of triggering the obligation of disclosure under ss 198, 199, see s 207.

S 203(2)

Interests of bodies corporate   Of greatest significance is the requirement to attribute interests of other bodies corporate (defined in s 740) which, in practice, will require the interests of subsidiaries to be attributed to the parent company. If the subsidiary's interest is notifiable in its own right, the subsidiary and the parent company must each notify the company which can lead to an element of double counting. In practice, this can be avoided by the parent company indicating in its notification which interests are held by it and which are attributed to it by other persons.

The threshold for control is set at a holding of 33% which is not consistent with the general definition of a subsidiary: see s 736. Setting the threshold at this level increases the number of notifications required.

A parent company only comes under the obligation of disclosure when it knows or becomes aware of the interests to be attributed to it; and s 207 confirms that this is when the parent knows of the other's interests. If the subsidiary does not notify the parent, and with control set at the lower level of 33%, the subsidiary may not always be amenable to assisting the parent, the parent does not come under an obligation of disclosure. There is no obligation under the legislation for a parent company to establish internal systems to obtain or collate information regarding interests held by the group although, as a matter of practice, most large companies will do so.

Subsection (2)(a) covers the situation where the person is a shadow director: see s 741(2); and see *Re TR Technology Investment Trust plc* (1988) 4 BCC 244 at 261.

S 203(3)

The chain of control extends to include companies controlled by a company (again by the exercise or controlling the exercise of 33% of the voting power) which is controlled by the person to whom the interests are attributed.

S 203(4)

Any rights under options, the exercise or fulfilment of which would entitle a person to exercise or control the exercise of voting power, must be taken into account in determining whether a person controls a body corporate under sub-ss (2) or (3). This provision is important in preventing avoidance through purchases of shares by companies not owned by the person under consideration but in respect of which he holds options to acquire a controlling shareholding. This enables the attribution of the interests held by those companies to that person before he exercises the options; likewise, if there is an agreement enabling the shareholders in those companies to require the person to purchase their holdings.

204. Agreement to acquire interests in a particular company

(1) In certain circumstances the obligation of disclosure may arise from an agreement between two or more persons which includes provision for the acquisition by any one or more of them of interests in shares of a particular

public company ('the target company'), being shares comprised in the relevant share capital of that company.

(2)   This section applies to such an agreement if—

(a)   the agreement also includes provisions imposing obligations or restrictions on any one or more of the parties to it with respect to their use, retention or disposal of their interests in that company's shares acquired in pursuance of the agreement (whether or not together with any other interests of theirs in the company's shares to which the agreement relates), and

(b)   any interest in the company's shares is in fact acquired by any of the parties in pursuance of the agreement;

and in relation to such an agreement references below in this section, and in sections 205 and 206, to the target company are to the company which is the target company for that agreement in accordance with this and the previous subsection.

(3)   The reference in subsection (2)(a) to the use of interests in shares in the target company is to the exercise of any rights or of any control or influence arising from those interests (including the right to enter into any agreement for the exercise, or for control of the exercise, of any of those rights by another person).

(4)   Once any interest in shares in the target company has been acquired in pursuance of such an agreement as is mentioned above, this section continues to apply to that agreement irrespective of—

(a)   whether or not any further acquisitions of interests in the company's shares take place in pursuance of the agreement, and

(b)   any change in the persons who are for the time being parties to it, and

(c)   any variation of the agreement,

so long as the agreement continues to include provisions of any description mentioned in subsection (2)(a).

References in this subsection to the agreement include any agreement having effect (whether directly or indirectly) in substitution for the original agreement.

(5)   In this section, and also in references elsewhere in this Part to an agreement to which this section applies, 'agreement' includes any agreement or arrangement; and references in this section to provisions of an agreement—

(a)   accordingly include undertakings, expectations or understandings operative under any arrangement, and

(b)   (without prejudice to the above) also include any provisions, whether express or implied and whether absolute or not.

(6)   However, this section does not apply to an agreement which is not legally binding unless it involves mutuality in the undertakings, expectations or understandings of the parties to it; nor does the section apply to an agreement to underwrite or sub-underwrite any offer of shares in a company, provided the agreement is confined to that purpose and any matters incidental to it.

General note

Concert party agreements   The aim of these provisions (ss 204–206) is to prevent the easy avoidance of the requirements of ss 198, 199 by persons securing interests just below the disclosure threshold and then combining under a concert party agreement to secure control of a company. The term 'concert party' is not used in the legislation which refers to 'persons acting together'. There is no prohibition on the use of a concert party agreement but an obligation to disclose interests arising thereunder.

S 204(1)–(3)

Agreements for the acquisition of interests   An agreement is within this provision and may give rise to an obligation of disclosure *only* if all these conditions are met:

(1)   The agreement makes provision for the acquisition of interests in voting shares in a public company. The requirement that shares be acquired means, for example, that an agreement among existing shareholders as to how they will exercise the voting rights attached to their existing shares, where there is no requirement for any further acquisition of any interests in any shares, is not within the provision.

(2)   The agreement contains provisions as specified in sub-s (2)(a). These provisions must relate to the use, retention or disposal of the interests acquired. This requirement excludes agreements simply to acquire shares which do not impose any of these conditions: see *Re TR Technology Investment Trust plc* (1988) 4 BCC 244 at 248.

(3)   An interest in the particular company's shares is in fact acquired by any of the parties in pursuance of the agreement: *Re Ricardo Group plc* [1989] BCLC 566.

The term 'target company' is defined in the proviso to sub-s (2). The obligation to disclose will only arise if the agreement is within this section and the interests attributed to a party to it under s 205 give rise to a notifiable interest under ss 198, 199.

S 204(4)

Once an agreement is brought within the scope of the section (on the acquisition of any interests in any shares in pursuance of it), the agreement and the parties to it continue to be within the scope of the section (and therefore ss 205, 206 continue to apply) although no further interests are acquired in pursuance of it, the parties change and the agreement itself is varied or even substituted (as long as the agreement contains provisions within sub-s (2)(a)).

S 204(5), (6)

Nature of the agreement   An agreement need not be in writing nor need it have contractual force: sub-s (5). However, the breadth of the definition in sub-s (5) is limited by sub-s (6), which requires the agreement either to be legally binding or to involve mutuality in the undertakings etc of the parties in the sense that they are agreed as to the acquisition of the shares and the mutual restrictions in s 204(2)(a). In *Re TR Technology Investment Trust plc* (1988) 4 BCC 244 at 248, Hoffmann J took the view that 'mutuality' means that the agreement must involve the parties receiving as well as giving undertakings but not that the undertakings must be the same. An agreement providing for one party to provide the funding and the other to acquire the shares would have sufficient mutuality. The reality is that the existence of mutual arrangements, where there is no legally binding agreement, is very difficult to prove.

Underwriting agreements are exempt as long as the agreement is confined to that purpose and matters incidental.

205. Obligation of disclosure arising under s 204

(1)   In the case of an agreement to which section 204 applies, each party to the agreement is taken (for purposes of the obligation of disclosure) to be interested in all shares in the target company in which any other party to it is interested apart from the agreement (whether or not the interest of the other party in question was acquired, or includes any interest which was acquired, in pursuance of the agreement).

(2)   For those purposes, and also for those of the next section, an interest of a party to such an agreement in shares in the target company is an interest apart from the agreement if he is interested in those shares otherwise than by virtue of the application of section 204 and this section in relation to the agreement.

(3)   Accordingly, any such interest of the person (apart from the agreement) includes for those purposes any interest treated as his under section 203 or by the application of section 204 and this section in relation to any other agreement with respect to shares in the target company to which he is a party.

(4)   A notification with respect to his interest in shares in the target company made to that company under this Part by a person who is for the time being a party to an agreement to which section 204 applies shall—

  (a) state that the person making the notification is a party to such an agreement,

  (b) include the names and (so far as known to him) the addresses of the other parties to the agreement, identifying them as such, and

  (c) state whether or not any of the shares to which the notification relates are shares in which he is interested by virtue of section 204 and this section and, if so, the number of those shares.

(5)   Where a person makes a notification to a company under this Part in consequence of ceasing to be interested in any shares of that company by virtue of the fact that he or any other person has ceased to be a party to an agreement to which section 204 applies, the notification shall include a statement that he or that other person has ceased to be a party to the agreement (as the case may require) and also (in the latter case) the name and (if known to him) the address of that other.

S 205(1)–(3)

Multiple interests   A parson who is a party to a concert party agreement and who acquires any shares in pursuance of it is directly interested in those shares; likewise, if purchases are made jointly on behalf of the parties, each has an interest in the shares acquired: s 208(7).

In addition, this provision provides that a person who is a party to a concert party agreement (as defined in s 204(1), (2)) is taken to be interested in all the shares in the target company (defined in s 204(2)) in which every other party to the agreement is interested (sub-s (1)), other than interests of those parties arising from the application of these provisions (this is necessary to avoid multiple counting: see sub-s (2)).

Included in the interests which must be counted are interests attributed to those other parties because of the operation of s 203 (family and corporate interests) as well as any interests arising under any other concert party agreement to which that person is a member.

As to when a person knows of these interests for the purposes of triggering the disclosure obligation under ss 198, 199, see s 207.

S 205(4)

Contents of notification   These requirements are additional to the disclosure obligations in s 202. The identification of the members of the concert party and whether the shares notified are the subject of a concert party agreement helps to eliminate double counting. Where another person is named in this way, the company is obliged to notify him of the fact (see 217(2)), and to inform him of his right to apply to have the entry removed in accordance with s 217.

206. Obligation of persons acting together to keep each other informed

(1)   A person who is a party to an agreement to which section 204 applies is subject to the requirements of this section at any time when—

     (a) the target company is a public company, and he knows it to be so, and

     (b) the shares in that company to which the agreement relates consist of or include shares comprised in relevant share capital of the company, and he knows that to be the case; and

     (c) he knows the facts which make the agreement one to which section 204 applies.

(2)   Such a person is under obligation to notify every other party to the agreement, in writing, of the relevant particulars of his interest (if any) apart from the agreement in shares comprised in relevant share capital of the target company—

     (a) on his first becoming subject to the requirements of this section, and

     (b) on each occurrence after that time while he is still subject to those requirements of any event or circumstances within section 198(1) (as it applies to his case otherwise than by reference to interests treated as his under section 205 as applying to that agreement).

(3)   The relevant particulars to be notified under subsection (2) are—

(a)   the number of shares (if any) comprised in the target company's relevant share capital in which the person giving the notice would be required to state his interest if he were under the wide obligation of disclosure with respect to that interest(apart from the agreement) immediately after the time when the obligation to give notice under subsection (2) arose, and

(b)   the relevant particulars with respect to the registered ownership of those shares, so far as known to him at the date of the notice, and

(c)   except in the circumstances mentioned in subsection (3A), the number of shares (if any) out of the number given under paragraph (a) in which he knows that, immediately after the time when the obligation to give the notice arose, he had interests (apart from the agreement) which were not material interests.

(3A) The circumstance referred to in subsection (3)(c) is that the aggregate nominal value of the shares comprised in relevant share capital in which the person is interested (apart from the agreement) is equal to or more than 10 per cent of the nominal value of the relevant share capital.

(3B) For the purposes of subsection (3)(a) 'the wide obligation of disclosure' means the obligation to disclose the number of shares in which the person concerned has any interest (material or otherwise).

(4)   A person who is for the time being subject to the requirements of this section is also under obligation to notify every other party to the agreement, in writing—

(a)   of any relevant particulars with respect to the registered ownership of any shares comprised in relevant share capital of the target company in which he is interested apart from the agreement, and

(b)   of any change in those particulars,

of which in either case he becomes aware at any time after any interest notification date and before the first occasion following that date on which he becomes subject to any further obligation to give notice under subsection (2) with respect to his interest in shares comprised in that share capital.

(5)   The reference in subsection (4) to an interest notification date, in relation to a person's interest in shares comprised in the target company's relevant share capital, is to either of the following—

(a)   the date of any notice given by him with respect to his interest under subsection (2), and

(b)   where he has failed to give that notice, the date on which the period allowed by this section for giving the notice came to an end.

(6)   A person who is a party to an agreement to which section 204 applies is under an obligation to notify each other party to the agreement, in writing, of his current address—

(a)   on his first becoming subject to the requirements of this section, and

(b)   on any change in his address occurring after that time and while he is still subject to those requirements.

(7)   A reference to the relevant particulars with respect to the registered ownership of shares is to such particulars in relation to those shares as are mentioned in section 202(3)(a) or (b).

(8)   A person's obligation to give any notice required by this section to any other person must be performed within the period of 2 days next following the day on which that obligation arose.

General note

A failure to comply with this notification obligation is a criminal offence: see s 210(3)(c), subject to the defence in sub-s (4). On conviction, the shares involved may be subject to restrictions: see s 210(5), (5A).

Notification under this provision has important consequences for the recipient: see s 207(5). A person is regarded as knowing of the interests of which he has been notified for the purposes of determining whether he knows that he has acquired or ceased to have an interest in shares: s 207(3). This knowledge in turn determines whether he is under an obligation of disclosure under ss 198, 199.

S 206(1)

A person is within this provision if shares have been acquired in pursuance of an agreement which meets the conditions in s 204(1), (2); 'target company' is defined in s 204(2).

S 206(2), (3)

Obligations to other parties to the agreement   The obligation on each party to the agreement is to notify every other party of his 'other' interests in shares in the target once the agreement is entered into and shares acquired; see also the obligation in sub-s (6). This is so even though he does not yet have a notifiable interest to report to the company. Thereafter, there is an obligation to notify them of every acquisition and disposal which would be within s 198(1), ie every change in his interests brought about by his acquiring an interest or ceasing to be interested in any shares in the company.

S 206(3)–(3B)

Particulars to be notified   Disclosure must be of the total number of shares in which he has any interest, material or non-material (sub-s (3)(a)); the 'wide obligation of disclosure' is defined in sub-s (3B). As to the relevant particulars in sub-s (3)(b), see sub-s (7). The requirement in sub-s (3)(a) is to disclose all interests but, under sub-s (3)(c), the person making the disclosure must indicate which interests are not material interests so that the other members of the concert party can take advantage of the 10% threshold, if appropriate. If the person notifying has already passed the 10% threshold, the notification obligation has already been triggered and there is no exemption which the other parties can take advantage of. In that situation, therefore, the information in sub-s (3)(c) is unnecessary (sub-s (3A)).

S 206(4), (5)

Once the person has given any notice required by sub-s (2) (ie either initially or following on from an acquisition or disposal of any interests), there is an ongoing obligation to notify every other party to the agreement of particulars regarding the registered ownership of any shares and of any changes in those particulars of which he becomes aware; the 'relevant particulars' with respect to registered ownership is defined by sub-s (7); the 'interest notification date' is defined by sub-s (5). A person is not entitled to wait until a further obligation of disclosure arises (following some change in his notifiable interests) before providing this information.

S 206(6)

An 'agreement to which s 204 applies' is one which meets the criteria in s 204(1), (2); a person is 'subject to the requirements of this section' when the conditions in sub-s (1) are met.

S 206(8)

See s 220(2) for guidance as to the calculation of the two-day period. If the act of acquiring an interest in shares of the target company (which triggers the obligation under this provision) is sufficient to give rise to a notifiable interest of which the company must be notified, the member of the concert party must notify the other members within two days and also notify the company within two days.

---

207. Interests in shares by attribution

(1)   Where section 198 or 199 refers to a person acquiring an interest in shares or ceasing to be interested in shares, that reference in certain cases includes his becoming or ceasing to be interested in those shares by virtue of another person's interest.

(2)   Such is the case where he becomes or ceases to be interested by virtue of section 203 or (as the case may be) section 205 whether—

(a) by virtue of the fact that the person who is interested in the shares becomes or ceases to be a person whose interests (if any) fall by virtue of either section to be treated as his, or

(b) in consequence of the fact that such a person has become or ceased to be interested in the shares, or

(c) in consequence of the fact that he himself becomes or ceases to be a party to an agreement to which section 204 applies to which the person interested in the shares is for the time being a party, or

(d) in consequence of the fact that an agreement to which both he and that person are parties becomes or ceases to be one to which that section applies.

(3) The person is then to be treated as knowing he has acquired an interest in the shares or (as the case may be) that he has ceased to be interested in them, if and when he knows both—

(a) the relevant facts with respect to the other person's interest in the shares, and

(b) the relevant facts by virtue of which he himself has become or ceased to be interested in them in accordance with section 203 or 205.

(4) He has the knowledge referred to in subsection (3)(a) if he knows (whether contemporaneously or not) either of the subsistence of the other person's interest at any material time or of the fact that the other has become or ceased to be interested in the shares at any such time; and 'material time' is any time at which the other's interests (if any) fall or fell to be treated as his under section 203 or 205.

(5) A person is to be regarded as knowing of the subsistence of another's interest in shares or (as the case may be) that another has become or ceased to be interested in shares if he has been notified under section 206 of facts with respect to the other's interest which indicate that he is or has become or ceased to be interested in the shares (whether on his own account or by virtue of a third party's interest in them).

General note

This provision determines when a person, to whom interests of other persons have been attributed by ss 203, 205, knows of those interests for the purpose of triggering his disclosure obligations under ss 198, 199.

S 207(3)–(4)

Knowledge The knowledge required is actual knowledge both of the interests of that other person in any shares (and knowledge in that context is further defined by sub-ss (4), (5)) and knowledge of the connection to that other person which requires those interests to be attributed. See also s 199(3).

S 207(5)

The effect of notification under s 206 is to deem the recipient to know of another's interests for these purposes.

208. Interests in shares which are to be notified

(1) This section applies, subject to the section next following, in determining for purposes of sections 198 to 202 whether a person has a notifiable interest in shares.

(2)   A reference to an interest in shares is to be read as including an interest of any kind whatsoever in the shares; and accordingly there are to be disregarded any restraints or restrictions to which the exercise of any right attached to the interest is or may be subject.

(3)   Where property is held on trust and an interest in shares is comprised in the property, a beneficiary of the trust who apart from this subsection does not have an interest in the shares is to be taken as having such an interest.

(4)   A person is taken to have an interest in shares if—

   (a)   he enters into a contract for their purchase by him (whether for cash or other consideration), or

   (b)   not being the registered holder, he is entitled to exercise any right conferred by the holding of the shares or is entitled to control the exercise of any such right.

(5)   A person is taken to have an interest in shares if, otherwise than by virtue of having an interest under a trust—

   (a)   he has a right to call for delivery of the shares to himself or to his order, or

   (b)   he has a right to acquire an interest in shares or is under an obligation to take an interest in shares,

whether in any case the right or obligation is conditional or absolute.

(6)   For purposes of subsection (4)(b), a person is entitled to exercise or control the exercise of any right conferred by the holding of shares if he—

   (a)   has a right (whether subject to conditions or not) the exercise of which would make him so entitled, or

   (b)   is under an obligation (whether so subject or not) the fulfilment of which would make him so entitled.

(7)   Persons having a joint interest are taken each of them to have that interest.

(8)   It is immaterial that shares in which a person has an interest are unidentifiable.

S 208(2), (7)

Any interest of any kind, regardless of any restriction or restraints, is included. Joint interests count as an interest of each person.

S 208(3)

Interests of beneficiaries under a trust are included, subject to s 209(1)(a).

S 208(4)

An interest under a contract of purchase is included, although the shares cannot be identified as where the shares are purchased on the Stock Exchange: sub-s (8). The rights in sub-s (4)(b) could arise by contract and might relate to rights to vote, to receive dividends, to dispose of the shares: see further sub-s (6); also s 209(12).

S 208(5)

Interests in options are included. Rights acquired by a take-over bidder when it secures an irrevocable undertaking by a shareholder to accept a take-over offer when made will be notifiable under this provision. A notifiable interest may also arise under ss 428–430 where a bidder, having secured 90% acceptances, may be obliged by the remaining shareholders to acquire their shares, or may exercise his right to acquire their shares. In either case, his or their notification of the exercise of his or their rights under those provisions gives him an interest in those shares for these purposes. Disclosure, in this instance, where the bidder already controls 90% of the company is pointless.

209. Interests to be disregarded

(1)   Subject to subsections (5) and (6), the following interests in shares are disregarded for the purposes of sections 198 to 202—

   (a)   where property is held on trust and an interest in shares is comprised in that property, an interest of a person, being a discretionary interest or an interest in reversion or remainder or an interest of a bare trustee;

   (b)   an interest which a person has by virtue of holding units in—

      (i)   an authorised unit trust scheme;

      (ii)   a recognised scheme; or

      (iii)   a UCITS;

   (c)   an interest of a person which is an exempt security interest within the meaning of subsection (2);

   (d)   an interest which a person has by virtue of his being a beneficiary under a retirement benefits scheme as defined in section 611 of the Income and Corporation Taxes Act 1988;

   (e)   an interest which a person has in shares as a result of the acceptance of a take-over offer made by him (either alone or jointly with one or more other persons) for shares where—

      (i)   the offer is subject to a threshold acceptance condition; and

      (ii)   the threshold acceptance condition is not fulfilled;

   (f)   an interest of a person which is an exempt custodian interest within the meaning of subsection (4);

   (g)   an interest which a person has by virtue of his being a personal representative of any estate;

   (h)   an interest which a person has—

      (i)   by virtue of his being a trustee of an authorised unit trust scheme,

      (ii)   in relation to a recognised scheme or a UCITS, by virtue of his being entrusted with the custody of the property in question (whether or not under a trust) or

    (iii) by virtue of his being a depository, within the meaning of the Open-Ended Investment Companies Regulations 2001, of an open-ended investment company.

(2)   An interest in shares is an exempt security interest for the purposes of subsection (1)(c)—

    (a) if it is held by a person who is—

       (i) a person authorised under Part I of the Banking Act 1987, an authorised credit institution, a person authorised under the law of a member State other than the United Kingdom to accept deposits who would, if he were to accept such deposits in the United Kingdom require authorisation under Part I of that Act, or an authorised insurance undertaking; or

       (ii) a person authorised under the law of a member State to deal in securities or derivatives, who deals in securities or derivatives on a relevant stock exchange or on a relevant investment exchange, whether as a member or otherwise; or

       (iii) a relevant stock exchange, a relevant investment exchange or a recognised clearing house; or

    (b) if it is held by the Bank of England or by the central bank of a member State other than the United Kingdom;

and it is held by way of security only for the purposes of a transaction entered into in the ordinary course of his or its business as such a person.

(3)   For the purposes of subsection (1)(e)—

    (a) 'takeover offer' has the same meaning as in Part XIIIA; and

    (b) 'a threshold acceptance condition' means a condition that acceptances are received in respect of such proportion of the shares for which the take-over offer is made as is specified in or determined in accordance with the terms of the take-over offer.

(4)   For the purposes of subsection (1)(f) an interest of a person is an exempt custodian interest if it is held by him—

    (a) as a custodian (whether under a trust or by a contract); or

    (b) under an arrangement pursuant to which he has issued, or is to issue, depository receipts in respect of the shares concerned.

(5)   An interest referred to in any paragraph of subsection (1) (except for paragraph (c)) is disregarded only if the person referred to in the relevant paragraph or in subsection (4) is not entitled to exercise or control the exercise of voting rights in respect of the shares concerned; and for this purpose he is not so entitled if he is bound (whether by contract or otherwise) not to exercise the voting rights, or not to exercise them otherwise than in accordance with the instructions of another.

(6)   In the case of an interest referred to in paragraph (c) of subsection (1), an interest of a person referred to in subsection (2) is disregarded only if that person—

    (a) is not entitled (within the meaning of subsection (5)) to exercise or control the exercise of voting rights in respect of the shares concerned; or

(b) is so entitled, but has not evidenced any intention to exercise them or control their exercise nor taken any step to do so.

(7) For the purposes of subsections (5) and (6), voting rights which a person is entitled to exercise or of which he is entitled to control the exercise only in certain circumstances shall be taken into account only when the circumstances have arisen and for so long as they continue to obtain.

(8) An interest in shares of a company is also disregarded for the purposes of sections 198 to 202—

(a) if it is held by a market maker in securities or derivatives for the purposes of his business, but

(b) only in so far as it is not used by him for the purpose of intervening in the management of the company.

(9) For the purposes of subsection (8) a person is a market maker in securities or derivatives if—

(a) he is authorised under the law of a member State to deal in securities or derivatives and so deals on a relevant stock exchange or on a relevant investment exchange (whether as a member or otherwise); and

(b) he holds himself out at all normal times as willing to acquire and dispose of securities or derivatives at prices specified by him and in so doing is subject to the rules of that exchange;

and he holds an interest for the purposes of his business if he holds it for the purposes of a business carried on by him as a market maker in a member State.

(9A) Where—

(a) in pursuance of arrangements made with the operator of a relevant system—

(i) securities of a particular aggregate value are on any day transferred by means of that system from a person ('A') to another person ('B');

(ii) the securities are of kinds and amounts determined by the operator-system; and

(iii) the securities, or securities of the same kinds and amounts, are on the following day transferred by means of the relevant system from B to A; and

(b) the securities comprise any shares of a company,

any interest of B in those shares is also disregarded for the purposes of sections 198 to 202.

(9B) For the purposes of subsection (9A)—

(a) any day which, in England and Wales, is a non-business day for the purposes of the Bills of Exchange Act 1882 is disregarded; and

(b) expressions which are used in the Uncertificated Securities Regulations 1995 have the same meanings as in those Regulations.

(10) The following interests in shares in a public company which is not listed are also disregarded for the purposes of sections 198 to 202—

(a) an interest which subsists by virtue of—

   (i) a scheme made under section 24 or 25 of the Charities Act 1993, section 25 of the Charities Act (Northern Ireland) 1964, section 11 of the Trustee Investments Act 1961 or section 42 of the Administration of Justice Act 1982, or

   (ii) the scheme set out in the Schedule to the Church Funds Investment Measure 1958;

(b) an interest of the Church of Scotland General Trustees or of the Church of Scotland Trust in shares held by them or of any other person in shares held by those Trustees or that Trust otherwise than as simple trustees;

(c) an interest for the life of himself or another of a person under a settlement in the case of which the property comprised in the settlement consists of or includes shares, and the conditions mentioned in subsection (11) are satisfied;

(d) . . .

(e) an interest of the Accountant General of the Supreme Court in shares held by him;

(f) an interest of the Public Trustee;

(g) an interest of the Probate Judge subsisting by virtue of section 3 of the Administration of Estates Act (Northern Ireland) 1955.

(11) The conditions referred to in subsection (10)(c) are, in relation to a settlement—

(a) that it is irrevocable, and

(b) that the settlor (within the meaning of section 670 of the Income and Corporation Taxes Act 1988) has no interest in any income arising under, or property comprised in, the settlement.

(12) A person is not by virtue of section 208(4)(b) taken to be interested in shares by reason only that he has been appointed a proxy to vote at a specified meeting of a company or of any class of its members and at any adjournment of that meeting, or has been appointed by a corporation to act as its representative at any meeting of a company or of any class of its members.

(13) In the application of subsection (1)(a) to property held on trust according to the law of Scotland, for the words 'or remainder or an interest of a bare trustee' there shall be substituted 'or in fee or an interest of a simple trustee'.

S 209(1)

Interests to be disregarded   This provision sets out those interests which may be disregarded for the purposes of disclosure.

   All of these exemptions (except (c)) apply only where the person (who would otherwise have a notifiable interest) is not entitled to exercise or control the exercise of voting rights other than to the extent permitted by sub-s (5); although it is sufficient for these purposes if he is not entitled to exercise the voting rights other than in accordance with the instructions of another: see sub-s (5); see also sub-s (7). Category (c) is subject to sub-ss (6), (7).

(a) Exempts certain interests in property held on trust regardless of whether the trust is governed by the law of England and Wales or elsewhere. A bare trustee has no control over the rights attached to any shares which he holds and therefore any interests which he possesses can be disregarded. See also sub-ss (5), (7).

(b) Exempts interests of holders under certain collective investment schemes; see definitions, s 220. Operators of such schemes are required to disclose under s 199(2A) but subject to the 10% threshold. See also sub-ss (5), (7).

(c) Exempts certain security interests as defined in sub-s (2) which applies to persons holding security, whether UK, foreign or EU-based, if duly authorised under the Banking Act etc. It is only security interests held by such defined categories which are exempt; other mortgagees would not be exempt. The key requirement is that the interest must be held 'by way of security interest only' and the transaction must be in the ordinary course of business. See also sub-ss (6), (7).

(d) Exempts interests held by virtue of being a beneficiary of certain types of retirement schemes. See also sub-ss (5), (7).

(e) Exempts interests arising as a result of an acceptance of a take-over offer which is defined by sub-s (3). These interests are excluded because they arise under a conditional offer which may lapse because of insufficient acceptances so any interest in the shares is short-lived. If the offer goes unconditional, the earliest at which it will do so is at the level of a 50% holding and, from then on, acceptances would have to be notified as the offeror increases its percentage holding. As to irrevocable undertakings to accept an offer when made, see note to s 208(5). See also sub-ss (5), (7).

(f) Exempts custodians, see sub-s (4) and definitions, s 220. See also sub-ss (5), (7).

(g) Exemptions for personal representatives. See also sub-ss (5), (7).

(h) Exempts interests of those who are trustees or entrusted with the custody of property of authorised unit trust schemes or certain other types of collective investment schemes: see definitions, s 220. In these cases, the manager of these interests has a notifiable interest under s 199(2A) as the person who exercises the voting power and who has the power of disposal of the interests etc. See also sub-ss (5), (7).

S 209(4)

Custodian interests   This exemption applies whether the custodian relationship is trust or contract based and sub-s (4)(b) ensures that deposit arrangements by companies wishing to have their shares traded as American Depository Receipts do not give rise to notifiable interests on the part of the depository. This exemption is subject to sub-ss (5), (7). 'Depository receipt' is defined in s 220.

S 209(5)

The exemptions in sub-s(1) (with the exception of paragraph *(c)*) only apply where there is no control of voting rights and this provision offers guidance as to the question of voting control.

S 209(6)

This provision provides a concession for holders of security interests with the right to exercise or control the exercise of voting rights. The holder of such a security interest does not loose the exemption simply because he has the voting rights if he has given no indication that he intends to exercise them.

S 209(7)

This provision ensures, for example, that an interest in preference shares (with restricted rights to vote) will be exempt as long as the voting rights have not come into operation.

S 209(8), (9)

This exemption excludes the interests of market makers including those authorised in other member states, subject to a condition that those interests are not used to intervene in the management of the company concerned. 'Management' is not defined for these purposes and it is not clear whether what is meant is interference in the operational policies and activities of the company or whether interference in the composition of the board would suffice to lose the exemption. See definitions in s 220.

S 209(9A), (9B)

See definitions in s 220.

S 209(10), (11)

These provisions ensure that certain pre-existing exemptions are retained for unlisted public companies following the implementation of the EC Directive which necessitated their removal from listed public companies.

S 209(12)

This provision exempts proxy holders appointed for a specified meeting.

---

210. Other provisions about notification under this Part

(1) Where a person authorises another ('the agent') to acquire or dispose of, on his behalf, interests in shares comprised in relevant share capital of a public company, he shall secure that the agent notifies him immediately of acquisitions or disposals effected by the agent which will or may give rise to any obligation of disclosure imposed on him by this Part with respect to his interest in that share capital.

(2)   An obligation of disclosure imposed on a person by any provision of sections 198 to 202 is treated as not being fulfilled unless the notice by means of which it purports to be fulfilled identifies him and gives his address and, in a case where he is a director of the company, is expressed to be given in fulfilment of that obligation.

(3)   A person who—

    (a) fails to fulfil, within the proper period, an obligation of disclosure imposed on him by this Part, or

    (b) in purported fulfilment of any such obligation makes to a company a statement which he knows to be false, or recklessly makes to a company a statement which is false, or

    (c) fails to fulfil, within the proper period, an obligation to give another person a notice required by section 206, or

    (d) fails without reasonable excuse to comply with subsection (1) of this section,

is guilty of an offence and liable to imprisonment or a fine, or both.

(4)   It is a defence for a person charged with an offence under subsection (3)(c) to prove that it was not possible for him to give the notice to the other person required by section 206 within the proper period, and either—

    (a) that it has not since become possible for him to give the notice so required, or

    (b) that he gave the notice as soon after the end of that period as it became possible for him to do so.

(5)   Where a person is convicted of an offence under this section (other than an offence relating to his ceasing to be interested in a company's shares), the Secretary of State may by order direct that the shares in relation to which the offence was committed shall, until further order, be subject to the restrictions of Part XV of this Act; and such an order may be made notwithstanding any power in the company's memorandum or articles enabling the company to impose similar restrictions on those shares.

(5A) If the Secretary of State is satisfied that an order under subsection (5) may unfairly affect the rights of third parties in respect of shares then the Secretary of State, for the purpose of protecting such rights and subject to such terms as he thinks fit, may direct that such acts by such persons or descriptions of persons and for such purposes as may be set out in the order, shall not constitute a breach of the restrictions of Part XV of this Act.

(6)   Sections 732 (restriction on prosecutions) and 733(2) and (3) (liability of directors, etc) apply to offences under this section.

S 210(1)

Acquisitions and disposals by an agent   This is an anti-avoidance provision for otherwise a principal could easily avoid liability by utilising the services of an agent as he, the principal, would lack the knowledge to trigger the disclosure obligation under s 198. As the agent would normally be unaware of the client's overall position, the onus is on the principal to secure that the agent notifies him of any transaction which might give rise to an obligation of disclosure. See sub-s (3)(d) as to the consequences of non-compliance with this provision.

S 210(2)

Required information   This requirement assists the company with the maintenance of the register of interests required by s 211; and, in the case of a director, it distinguishes between his notification under these provisions and under s 324 et seq.

S 210(3), (4)

Penalties   Criminal penalties apply to a failure to fulfil any obligation of disclosure (ie under s 198(1), (3)) including a failure to notify the company of interests arising under a concert party (s 204); a failure of members of the concert party to notify one another of their interests (s 206), subject to the defence in sub-s (4); and the failure of a principal to secure notification from any agent of potentially notifiable interests.
   As to penalties, see s 730, Sch 24.

S 210(5), (5A)

As to the operation of these restrictions on shares, see notes to ss 445, 454–457.

210A. Power to make further provision by regulations

(1)   The Secretary of State may by regulations amend—
   (a) the definition of 'relevant share capital'(section 198(2)),
   (b) the percentage giving rise to a 'notifiable interest'(section 199(2)),
   (c) the periods within which an obligation of disclosure must be fulfilled or a notice must be given (sections 202(1) and (4) and 206(8)),
   (d) the provisions as to what is taken to be an interest in shares (section 208) and what interests are to be disregarded (section 209), and
   (e) the provisions as to company investigations (section 212);

and the regulations may amend, replace or repeal the provisions referred to above and make such other consequential amendments or repeals of provisions of this Part as appear to the Secretary of State to be appropriate.

(2)   The regulations may in any case make different provision for different descriptions of company; and regulations under subsection (1)(b), (c) or (d) may make different provision for different descriptions of person, interest or share capital.

(3)   The regulations may contain such transitional and other supplementary and incidental provisions as appear to the Secretary of State to be appropriate, and may in particular make provision as to the obligations of a person whose interest

in a company's shares becomes or ceases to be notifiable by virtue of the regulations.

(4)   Regulations under this section shall be made by statutory instrument.

(5)   No regulations shall be made under this section unless a draft of the regulations has been laid before and approved by a resolution of each House of Parliament.

General note

The regulations made under this provision and which are reflected in the text are: the Disclosure of Interests in Shares (Amendment) Regulations 1993, SI 1993/1819 which implemented EC Council Directive (EEC) 88/627 (OJ L348/62 17.12.88); the Disclosure of Interests in Shares (Amendment) (No 2) Regulations 1993, SI 1993/2689; the Disclosure of Interests in Shares (Amendment) Regulations 1996, SI 1996/1560.

REGISTRATION AND INVESTIGATION OF SHARE ACQUISITIONS AND DISPOSALS

211. Register of interests in shares

(1)   Every public company shall keep a register for purposes of sections 198 to 202, and whenever the company receives information from a person in consequence of the fulfilment of an obligation imposed on him by any of those sections, it is under obligation to inscribe in the register, against that person's name, that information and the date of the inscription.

(2)   Without prejudice to subsection (1), where a company receives a notification under this Part which includes a statement that the person making the notification, or any other person, has ceased to be a party to an agreement to which section 204 applies, the company is under obligation to record that information against the name of that person in every place where his name appears in the register as a party to that agreement (including any entry relating to him made against another person's name).

(3)   An obligation imposed by subsection (1) or (2) must be fulfilled within the period of 3 days next following the day on which it arises.

(4)   The company is not, by virtue of anything done for the purposes of this section, affected with notice of, or put upon enquiry as to, the rights of any person in relation to any shares.

(5)   The register must be so made up that the entries against the several names entered in it appear in chronological order.

(6)   Unless the register is in such form as to constitute in itself an index, the company shall keep an index of the names entered in the register which shall in respect of each name contain a sufficient indication to enable the information entered against it to be readily found; and the company shall, within 10 days after the date on which a name is entered in the register, make any necessary alteration in the index.

(7)   If the company ceases to be a public company it shall continue to keep the register and any associated index until the end of the period of 6 years beginning with the day next following that on which it ceases to be such a company.

(8)   The register and any associated index—

    (a) shall be kept at the place at which the register required to be kept by the company by section 325 (register of directors' interests) is kept, and

    (b) subject to the next subsection, shall be available for inspection in accordance with section 219 below.

(9)   Neither the register nor any associated index shall be available for inspection in accordance with that section in so far as it contains information with respect to a company for the time being entitled to avail itself of the benefit conferred by section 231(3) (disclosure of shareholdings not required if it would be harmful to company's business).

(10) If default is made in complying with subsection (1) or (2), or with any of subsections (5) to (7), the company and every officer of it who is in default is liable to a fine and, for continued contravention, to a daily default fine.

    Any register kept by a company immediately before 15th June 1982 under section 34 of the Companies Act 1967 shall continue to be kept by the company under and for the purposes of this section.

S 211(1)

Entry on the register   The obligation to maintain this register of interests in shares applies only to public companies. Information may be entered on to the register only when received by the company from a person subject to an obligation of disclosure. The disclosure obligations which must be recorded are the interests of a person in voting shares in a public company which are required to be disclosed by ss 198–202 including family and corporate interests attributed to him and interests arising from a concert party agreement. Information obtained by the company pursuant to s 212 must be maintained in a separate part of the register, see s 213(1). Once an entry is made on the register, the information can only be removed in accordance with ss 217, 218. Inspection of this register is governed by s 219.

S 211(2)

Concert party information   Entries regarding the fact that someone has ceased to be a member of a concert party agreement (as defined by s 204(1), (2)) may need to be made in a number of places as each member of the concert party is required in their individual notifications to identify the other members of the concert party: s 205(4). See also s 217(4), which gives a person redress against the company where the company fails to record this information.

S 211(3)

As to the calculation of the period of days, see s 220(2).

S 211(4)

This provision reinforces the general position as stated in s 360, which is that a company does not have notice of any beneficial interests in its shares.

S 211(8)

Location of the register   This register must be kept with the register of directors' interests in shares in the company and the location of that register is governed by s 325(5), Sch 13, para 25. The usual location would be the registered office, as to which see s 287. The register may be kept otherwise than in a legible form (see ss 722, 723), in which case the provisions as to the place at which it must be kept and the place of inspection are subject to the Companies (Registers and Other Records) Regulations 1985, SI 1985/724.

S 211(10)

As to penalties, see s 730, Sch 24; 'officer in default' is defined in s 730(5).

212. Company investigations

(1)   A public company may by notice in writing require a person whom the company knows or has reasonable cause to believe to be or, at any time during the 3 years immediately preceding the date on which the notice is issued, to have been interested in shares comprised in the company's relevant share capital—

    (a) to confirm that fact or (as the case may be) to indicate whether or not it is the case, and

    (b) where he holds or has during that time held an interest in shares so comprised, to give such further information as may be required in accordance with the following subsection.

(2)   A notice under this section may require the person to whom it is addressed—

    (a) to give particulars of his own past or present interest in shares comprised in relevant share capital of the company (held by him at any time during the 3-year period mentioned in subsection (1)),

  (b)   where the interest is a present interest and any other interest in the shares subsists or, in any case, where another interest in the shares subsisted during that 3-year period at any time when his own interest subsisted, to give (so far as lies within his knowledge) such particulars with respect to that other interest as may be required by the notice,

  (c)   where his interest is a past interest, to give (so far as lies within his knowledge) particulars of the identity of the person who held that interest immediately upon his ceasing to hold it.

(3)   The particulars referred to in subsection (2)(a) and (b) include particulars of the identity of persons interested in the shares in question and of whether persons interested in the same shares are or were parties to any agreement to which section 204 applies or to any agreement or arrangement relating to the exercise of any rights conferred by the holding of the shares.

(4)   A notice under this section shall require any information given in response to the notice to be given in writing within such reasonable time as may be specified in the notice.

(5)   Sections 203 to 205 and 208 apply for the purpose of construing references in this section to persons interested in shares and to interests in shares respectively, as they apply in relation to sections 198 to 201 (but with the omission of any reference to section 209).

(6)   This section applies in relation to a person who has or previously had, or is or was entitled to acquire, a right to subscribe for shares in a public company which would on issue be comprised in relevant share capital of that company as it applies in relation to a person who is or was interested in shares so comprised; and references above in this section to an interest in shares so comprised and to shares so comprised are to be read accordingly in any such case as including respectively any such right and shares which would on issue be so comprised.

General note

This provision is important in practice, as it enables a public company both to conduct routine monitoring of the composition of the registers of members and, in a take-over battle, to monitor would-be bidders and their allies. To assist smaller public companies, the Department of Trade and Industry has produced a model s 212 notice which companies can adapt for their own purposes. Where, despite use of these provisions, a company is dissatisfied with the information which it has obtained, it may try to persuade the Department to exercise its statutory powers to investigate company ownership under ss 442, 444.

S 212(1), (5)

Service of a notice   There is no requirement that the recipient of a s 212 notice be a current or former member or the registered holder; the provision applies to 'any person' and it is common for notices to be served on market makers, banks, commercial nominee companies etc; and a notice may be served on a foreign corporation, even one without a presence here and not carrying on business here: *Re F H Lloyd Holdings plc* [1985] BCLC 293.

As the purpose of these provisions is to give a public company, and ultimately the public at large, a prima facie unqualified right to know who are the real owners of its voting shares, the company is not required to show that it has some real ground for believing that the person interested in the shares may be someone who is seeking to build up a substantial holding in it before invoking the provisions of this section: *Re F H Lloyd Holdings plc* [1985] BCLC 293.

Interested in shares   For the meaning of interests in shares, see sub-s (5), which imports the very broad definition of interests from s 208. It is important to note that this provision is wider in scope than the interests encompassed by ss 198–202, for s 209, which disregards a large number of interests for the purposes of disclosure under those provisions, does not apply here. The interests which must be disclosed include family, corporate and concert party interests as identified by ss 203–205. The extensive definition adopted here is designed 'to counter the limitless ingenuity of persons who prefer to conceal their interests behind trusts and corporate entities': *Re TR Technology Investment Trust plc* [1988] BCLC 256 at 261, per Hoffmann J.

There are no thresholds (cf s 199(2)) and information may be sought from any person whatever the size of the shareholding in which the person is interested. It is possible therefore for the company to obtain information under these provisions which a person is not obliged to disclose under ss 198–202.

The company is entitled to seek information not just as to the true beneficial ownership at the time of the notice but also for the preceding three years, for it may want to know of earlier attempts to acquire an undisclosed stake: see *Re Geers Gross plc* [1987] BCLC 253 at 256; affd [1988] BCLC 140.

S 212(2)

Particulars of past and present interests   This provision enables the company to pursue information through a chain of nominees by requiring each to disclose the person for whom they are acting and any person by whom the interest was acquired subsequent to their interest. Extracting information from a chain of nominees, many of whom may be overseas, may be a protracted business, however, and a person is required to give information regarding other persons' interests only 'so far as lies within his knowledge'.

A company is entitled not only to ask for the names of those interested which are known to the person but also to ask the nature of the interest of those persons. A list of names would not enable the company to discover who was 'the real owner of the shares unless it could ask who were the sharks and who were the minnows': *Re TR Technology Investment Trust plc* [1988] BCLC 256 at 275, per Hoffmann J.

The answers to a s 212 notice must be given to the best of the recipient's knowledge at the date when the reply is given, but the interests must be described as they stood at the date stated in the notice: see *Re Ricardo Group plc (No 2)* [1989] BCLC 766.

It is important that care is taken in drafting the notice to ensure that it asks the right questions of the recipients; questions restricted to the wording of sub-s (2) may not elicit as much information as fuller and more specific questions tailored to the particular situation: see *Re Lonrho plc* [1988] BCLC 53 at 54–55.

S 212(3)

A concert party agreement (as defined by s 204) is within this provision but, more broadly, it extends to 'any agreement or arrangement' relating to the exercise of 'any rights' and not just voting rights. This provision is merely an illustration of the information which may be required but it does not limit the particulars which may be required by the notice under s 212(2)(b): see *Re TR Technology Investment Trust plc* [1988] BCLC 256.

S 212(4)

Reasonable time   There is no guidance in the statutory provisions as to what is a reasonable time for these purposes and it will vary according to the circumstances of the request for information. The period which would be reasonable as part of a routine monitoring of the share register might be quite difference from the period where a take-over bid has been made or is thought to be imminent. The intention was to leave the period flexible to meet these differing requirements.

For recipients, however, there is often a dispute over whether a reasonable period has been given for a response, particularly since information can be sought relating to the previous three years which may take some time to collate. As it is an offence not to respond within the time specified (s 216(3)), the question whether the period allowed is reasonable is a matter of some significance. Likewise, for the company, if the notice given to the recipient is not reasonable then the company has failed to serve a valid notice and cannot seek an order imposing restrictions on the shares under s 216(1).

Persons outside the United Kingdom   Where a widely framed notice is served on a person resident and carrying on business outside the United Kingdom, the addressee should be given time to consult with English lawyers to ascertain the extent of the information that can properly be sought and to answer any points of difficulty relating to the formulation of an answer: *Re Lonrho plc (No 2)* [1989] BCLC 309. In that case, the court rejected counsel's submission that a reasonable period for compliance would have been the period of five days. Vinelott J took the view that in a situation of urgency (ie a possible take-over bid) and with respect to an overseas recipient, it would be exceptional for the company to be required to give more than two clear days' working notice. For a UK recipient, one clear working day would prima facie be a reasonable period.

However, given that the notice will be rendered invalid by an inadequate period, companies should be cautious about setting unduly restrictive periods for responses to s 212 notices.

S 212(6)

'Relevant share capital' is defined in s 198(2): s 220; and comprises the company's issued share capital carrying rights to vote in all circumstances. As such, convertibles giving a right to subscribe to the company's capital are excluded, not being issued share capital. This provision includes such rights for the purposes of these provisions.

213. Registration of interests disclosed under s 212

(1)   Whenever in pursuance of a requirement imposed on a person under section 212 a company receives information to which this section applies relating to shares comprised in its relevant share capital, it is under obligation to enter against the name of the registered holder of those shares, in a separate part of its register of interests in shares—

  (a) the fact that the requirement was imposed and the date on which it was imposed, and

  (b) any information to which this section applies received in pursuance of the requirement.

(2)   This section applies to any information received in pursuance of a requirement imposed by section 212 which relates to the present interests held by any persons in shares comprised in relevant share capital of the company in question.

(3)   Subsections (3) to (10) of section 211 apply in relation to any part of the register maintained in accordance with subsection (1) of this section as they apply in relation to the remainder of the register, reading references to subsection (1) of that section to include subsection (1) of this.

(4)   In the case of a register kept by a company immediately before 15th June 1982 under section 34 of the Companies Act 1967, any part of the register so kept for the purposes of section 27 of the Companies Act 1976 shall continue to be kept by the company under and for the purposes of this section.

General note

Information obtained by the company in exercise of its powers under s 212 must be kept in a distinct area of the register of interests in shares. This part of the register too is open to inspection by all: sub-s (3); see ss 211(8), 219.

S 213(1), (2)

Information received   An entry may only be made when a company receives information pursuant to a s 212 notice and the company is not entitled to add information to the register as to the existence of beneficial interests of which it is aware: *Re TR Technology Investment Trust plc* [1988] BCLC 256. If the company wishes to do so, it must first serve a notice under s 212 asking a person to confirm that he has an interest in any shares. Only if he does so, can the information be entered on the register: *Re TR Technology Investment Trust plc*.

The entry is made against the name of the registered holder, who is not necessarily the person providing the information. Only information relating to present interests is included in the register, although the company is able to seek historical information under s 212. 'Relevant share capital' is defined in s 198(2): s 220. Once an entry is made on the register, the information can only be removed in accordance with ss 217, 218.

214. Company investigation on requisition by members

(1)   A company may be required to exercise its powers under section 212 on the requisition of members of the company holding at the date of the deposit of the requisition not less than one-tenth of such of the paid-up capital of the company as carries at that date the right of voting at general meetings of the company.

(2)   The requisition must—

(a)   state that the requisitionists are requiring the company to exercise its powers under section 212,

(b)   specify the manner in which they require those powers to be exercised, and

(c)   give reasonable grounds for requiring the company to exercise those powers in the manner specified,

and must be signed by the requisitionists and deposited at the company's registered office.

(3)   The requisition may consist of several documents in like form each signed by one or more requisitionists.

(4)   On the deposit of a requisition complying with this section it is the company's duty to exercise its powers under section 212 in the manner specified in the requisition.

(5)   If default is made in complying with subsection (4), the company and every officer of it who is in default is liable to a fine.

S 214(1)

Requisition by members   It is thought desirable that members should have the right to require the company to exercise its rights under s 212 where the board is reluctant to do so of its own initiative, possibly because the directors or their allies are involved in stakebuilding from behind the shelter of nominees. In practice, the provision is rarely, if ever, used. This may be because the threshold of 10% of paid-up capital is quite high, given that the company is a public company with dispersed shareholdings.

S 214(2), (4)

Requirements for requisition   The requisition must identify those persons on whom the notices should be served. Presumably, given the purpose of these provisions, it would be reasonable to require this power to be exercised if the requisitionists can show that there are reasonable grounds for believing that the registered owners are not the true owners. Where there are no reasonable grounds for requiring the exercise of these powers, or any other failure to comply with the requirements of sub-ss (1), (2), the duty imposed by sub-s (4) does not arise.

S 214(5)

As to penalties, see s 730, Sch 24; 'officer in default' is defined in s 730(5).

---

215. Company report to members

(1)   On the conclusion of an investigation carried out by a company in pursuance of a requisition under section 214, it is the company's duty to cause a report of the information received in pursuance of that investigation to be prepared, and the report shall be made available at the company's registered office within a reasonable period after the conclusion of that investigation.

(2)   Where—

   (a) a company undertakes an investigation in pursuance of a requisition under section 214, and

   (b) the investigation is not concluded before the end of 3 months beginning with the date immediately following the date of the deposit of the requisition,

it is the duty of the company to cause to be prepared, in respect of that period and each successive period of 3 months ending before the conclusion of the investigation, an interim report of the information received during that period in pursuance of the investigation. Each such report shall be made available at the company's registered office within a reasonable period after the end of the period to which it relates.

(3)   The period for making any report prepared under this section available as required by subsection (1) or (2) shall not exceed 15 days.

(4)   Such a report shall not include any information with respect to a company entitled to avail itself of the benefit conferred by section 231(3)(disclosure of shareholdings not required if it would be harmful to company's business); but where any such information is omitted, that fact shall be stated in the report.

(5)   The company shall, within 3 days of making any report prepared under this section available at its registered office, notify the requisitionists that the report is so available.

(6)   An investigation carried out by a company in pursuance of a requisition under section 214 is regarded for purposes of this section as concluded when the company has made all such inquiries as are necessary or expedient for the purposes of the requisition and in the case of each such inquiry, either a response has been received by the company or the time allowed for a response has elapsed.

(7)   A report prepared under this section—

   (a) shall be kept at the company's registered office from the day on which it is first available there in accordance with subsection (1) or (2) until the expiration of 6 years beginning with the day next following that day, and

   (b) shall be available for inspection in accordance with section 219 below so long as it is so kept.

(8)   If default is made in complying with subsection (1), (2), (5) or (7)(a), the company and every officer of it who is in default is liable to a fine.

General note

The company's obligations under this provision are to prepare the report, make it available at the registered office where it is open to inspection by all (sub-s (7)(b); s 219); and to notify the requisitionists that it is available (sub-s (5)). As to the registered office, see s 287.

S 215(1), (2)

As to when the report is concluded for these purposes, see sub-s (6); provision is made for interim reports where the investigation is delayed.

S 215(3), (5)

These provisions set time limits for the company's actions to prevent the directors defeating the intention of the requisitionists by unduly delaying any report.

S 215(8)

As to penalties, see s 730, Sch 24; 'officer in default' is defined in s 730(5).

216. Penalty for failure to provide information

(1)   Where notice is served by a company under section 212 on a person who is or was interested in shares of the company and that person fails to give the company any information required by the notice within the time specified in it, the company may apply to the court for an order directing that the shares in question be subject to the restrictions of Part XV of this Act.

(1A) On an application made under subsection (1), the court may make an interim order and any such order may be made unconditionally or on such terms as the court thinks fit.

(1B) If the court is satisfied that an order under subsection (1) may unfairly affect the rights of third parties in respect of shares then the court, for the purpose of protecting such rights and subject to such terms as it thinks fit, may direct that such acts by such persons or descriptions of persons and for such purposes as may be set out in the order, shall not constitute a breach of the restrictions of Part XV of this Act.

(2)   An order under this section may be made by the court notwithstanding any power contained in the applicant company's memorandum or articles

enabling the company itself to impose similar restrictions on the shares in question.

(3)　Subject to the following subsections, a person who fails to comply with a notice under section 212 or who, in purported compliance with such a notice, makes any statement which he knows to be false in a material particular or recklessly makes any statement which is false in a material particular is guilty of an offence and liable to imprisonment or a fine, or both.

Section 733(2) and (3) of this Act (liability of individuals for corporate default) apply to offences under this subsection.

(4)　A person is not guilty of an offence by virtue of failing to comply with a notice under section 212 if he proves that the requirement to give the information was frivolous or vexatious.

(5)　A person is not obliged to comply with a notice under section 212 if he is for the time being exempted by the Secretary of State from the operation of that section; but the Secretary of State shall not grant any such exemption unless—

(a)　he has consulted with the Governor of the Bank of England, and

(b)　he (the Secretary of State) is satisfied that, having regard to any undertaking given by the person in question with respect to any interest held or to be held by him in any shares, there are special reasons why that person should not be subject to the obligations imposed by that section.

General note

Failure to comply with s 212 notice　This provision provides for two sanctions for a failure to comply with a s 212 notice: (1) a criminal penalty (see sub-s (3)); and (2) a freezing order restricting the shares (see sub-s (1)). The ability to impose a criminal penalty, although the offence is rarely prosecuted, is thought invaluable as a deterrent to the giving of false information or refusing to answer. The restrictions which can be imposed essentially prevent the exercise of voting rights and preclude any transfer of the shares or the payment of any dividend in respect of them; see ss 454–457. Such restrictions can be effective in placing financial pressure on the other party but they may be of little effect where there is a beneficial owner who is determined not to disclose his interests and who is prepared to endure the restrictions. He will not be able to exercise his voting power but, equally, no one else can exercise the voting power which he controls and, in some circumstances, that may be equally important.

S 216(1)

Foreign nominees　A 'person' includes a foreign corporation without a presence here and not carrying on business here: *Re F H Lloyd Holdings plc* [1985] BCLC 293. It is possible, therefore, to impose restrictions on foreign nominees; without this power, these provisions could easily be avoided.

Failure to give the required information   The company may seek an order under this provision although the person has not been convicted of a failure to give the required information (cf s 210(5)); but restrictions may be sought only if the company has served a valid notice under s 212(1) and it will not have done so if it failed to allow a reasonable time for a response: *Re Lonrho plc (No 2)* [1989] BCLC 309.

It is an offence to fail to give the information required by the notice within the time specified; and a person 'fails to give the company any information required by the notice' if he does not give a full and truthful answer: *Re TR Technology Investment Trust plc* [1988] BCLC 256. Since a public company has an unqualified right to know the identity of the real owner of the shares, where it is shown that sufficient information has not been provided, the company will prima facie be entitled to a restriction order and there is no need to show that damages would not be an adequate remedy or that the company would suffer loss if the information were not provided: *Re TR Technology Investment Trust plc* [1988] BCLC 256.

Restrictions on shares   The only order which the court may make is one imposing the restrictions in Part XV (ss 454–457) which essentially prevent the exercise of voting rights and preclude any transfer of the shares, or the issue of any further shares in right of them, or the payment of any dividend in respect of them. The court has no discretion to pick and choose as between these restrictions; it must impose all or none of them: *Re Lonrho plc (No 4)* [1990] BCLC 151. To have any restrictions lifted, see s 456.

The restrictions may be imposed on the 'shares in question', which means the shares of the company in which the person is interested and restrictions may be imposed not only in relation to shares in respect of which information is not disclosed but in relation to other holdings in the company in respect of which the person has disclosed his interests: see *Re Lonrho plc* [1988] BCLC 53; *Re Ricardo Group plc (No 2)* [1989] BCLC 766.

Costs   The court may require that the costs of an application by the company under this provision should be paid by those persons on whom s 212 notices were served and whose failure to provide full information caused or contributed to the costs incurred in applying to the court: *Re Bestwood plc* [1989] BCLC 606.

S 216(1A)

Instead of granting an interim order, the court may accept an undertaking from the affected persons not to dispose of the shares or any interest in them pending the full hearing: see *Re Lonrho plc (No 3)* [1989] BCLC 480.

S 216(1B)

Rights of third parties   This provision was inserted by the Companies (Disclosure of Interests in Shares) (Orders imposing restrictions on shares) Regulations 1991, SI 1991/1646, following concerns that third parties were being adversely affected by restrictions; 'unfairly affect' is not defined but would cover the situation, for example, where shares are held by third parties as security. The security holders will want to be able to dispose of the shares to realise their security and, in the meantime, will want to receive such dividends as are paid in order to service the loan repayments.

These relaxations in favour of third parties only affect court orders and do not restrict the ability of the company to impose restrictions which may adversely affect third parties using powers to do so contained in the articles.

S 216(2)

The power of the court to make an order is discretionary. In the past, a factor which would have been of some significance in deciding whether to exercise the discretion would have been the impact of any order on third parties. But the position of third parties can now be addressed by the court within an order: see sub-s (1B).

The court-based procedure provided by this provision can be slow and costly and public companies may prefer to have equivalent provisions in their articles which can be exercised by the board although listed companies are restricted in the range of sanctions which they can impose: see Listing Rules, para 9.43. Provisions in the articles lack the criminal sanctions of the statutory provisions.

S 216(3), (4)

Penalties A 'person' in this provision (unlike ss 212(1), 216(1)) probably does not extend to a foreign corporation with no presence here, on the basis that the criminal law generally does not have extra-territorial effect: *Re F H Lloyd Holdings plc* [1985] BCLC 293.

Although the wording of this provision differs from sub-s (1), it seem that the provision of information which is accurate but not disclosed within the specified period is an offence, for 'a notice under s 212' is a notice of interests in writing within a specified time and late compliance would be a failure to comply with the notice.

As the requirements of s 212(2)(b) and (2)(c) are restricted to matters known to the person ('in so far as it lies within his knowledge'), there is no failure to disclose giving rise to an offence where a person provides no information on the basis that he does not know of any interests – unless that answer is false etc within this provision. Subsection (4) is intended to prevent abusive use of s 212 notices by a company, for example, where there are too many requests within a short period with respect to the same interests where no take-over bid appears imminent.

S 216(5)

Exemption under this provision is likely to be rare and, it is thought, would be limited to those acting for foreign governments, heads of state or members of the British royal family.

217. Removal of entries from register

(1) A company may remove an entry against a person's name from its register of interests in shares if more than 6 years have elapsed since the date of the entry being made, and either—

(a) that entry recorded the fact that the person in question had ceased to have an interest notifiable under this Part in relevant share capital of the company, or

(b) it has been superseded by a later entry made under section 211 against the same person's name;

and in a case within paragraph (a) the company may also remove that person's name from the register.

(2) If a person in pursuance of an obligation imposed on him by any provision of this Part gives to a company the name and address of another person as being interested in shares in the company, the company shall, within 15 days of the date on which it was given that information, notify the other person that he has been so named and shall include in that notification—

(a) particulars of any entry relating to him made, in consequence of its being given that information, by the company in its register of interests in shares, and

(b) a statement informing him of his right to apply to have the entry removed in accordance with the following provisions of this section.

(3) A person who has been notified by a company in pursuance of subsection (2) that an entry relating to him has been made in the company's register of interests in shares may apply in writing to the company for the removal of that entry from the register; and the company shall remove the entry if satisfied that the information in pursuance of which the entry was made was incorrect.

(4) If a person who is identified in a company's register of interests in shares as being a party to an agreement to which section 204 applies (whether by an entry against his own name or by an entry relating to him made against another person's name as mentioned in subsection (2)(a)) ceases to be a party to that agreement, he may apply in writing to the company for the inclusion of that information in the register; and if the company is satisfied that he has ceased to be a party to the agreement, it shall record that information (if not already recorded) in every place where his name appears as a party to that agreement in the register.

(5) If an application under subsection (3) or (4) is refused (in a case within subsection (4), otherwise than on the ground that the information has already been recorded) the applicant may apply to the court for an order directing the company to remove the entry in question from the register or (as the case may be) to include the information in question in the register; and the court may, if it thinks fit, make such an order.

(6) Where a name is removed from a company's register of interests in shares in pursuance of subsection (1) or (3) or an order under subsection (5), the company shall within 14 days of the date of that removal make any necessary alteration in any associated index.

(7) If default is made in complying with subsection (2) or (6), the company and every officer of it who is in default is liable to a fine and, for continued contravention, to a daily default fine.

S 217(1)

The removal of an entry against a person's name, or the removal of a name, can only occur in accordance with this provision which limits removal to the two specified cases. See also s 218.

S 217(2), (3)

Note the obligation on the company to notify the 'other person' of the fact that he has been so named (for example, under s 205(4)) and that an entry with respect to him has been made on the register of interests in shares. He may apply to have the entry removed under sub-s (3); and, if need be, may seek a court order under sub-s (5).

S 217(4)

This provision gives a person the right to require the company to include this information where it has failed to do so in accordance with s 211(2); and, if need be, to seek a court order under sub-s (5).

S 217(7)

As to penalties, see s 730, Sch 24; 'officer in default' is defined in s 730(5).

218. Otherwise, entries not to be removed

(1) Entries in a company's register of interests in shares shall not be deleted except in accordance with section 217.

(2) If an entry is deleted from a company's register of interests in shares in contravention of subsection (1), the company shall restore that entry to the register as soon as is reasonably practicable.

(3) If default is made in complying with subsection (1) or (2), the company and every officer of it who is in default is liable to a fine and, for continued contravention of subsection (2), to a daily default fine.

S 218(3)

As to penalties, see s 730, Sch 24; 'officer in default' is defined in s 730(5).

219. Inspection of register and reports

(1)   Any register of interests in shares and any report which is required by section 215(7) to be available for inspection in accordance with this section shall,... be open to the inspection of any member of the company or of any other person without charge.

(2)   Any such member or other person may require a copy of any such register or report, or any part of it, on payment of such fee as may be prescribed; and the company shall cause any copy so required by a person to be sent to him before the expiration of the period of 10 days beginning with the day next following that on which the requirement is received by the company.

(3)   If an inspection required under this section is refused or a copy so required is not sent within the proper period, the company and every officer of it who is in default is liable to a fine and, for continued contravention, to a daily default fine.

(4)   In the case of a refusal of an inspection required under this section of any register or report, the court may by order compel an immediate inspection of it; and in the case of failure to send a copy required under this section, the court may by order direct that the copy required shall be sent to the person requiring it.

(5)   The Secretary of State may by regulations made by statutory instrument substitute a sum specified in the regulations for the sum for the time being mentioned in subsection (2).

General note

For provisions relating to the inspection of documents, registers and fees under this section, see the Companies (Inspection and Copying of Registers, Indices and Documents) Regulations 1991, SI 1991/1998.

S 219(3)

As to penalties, see s 730, Sch 24; 'officer in default' is defined in s 730(5).

S 219(4)

The court's power is discretionary: see *Pelling v Families need Fathers Ltd* [2001] All ER (D) 03 (Aug), CA.

SUPPLEMENTARY

220. Definitions for Part VI

(1)   In this Part of this Act—

'associated index', in relation to a register, means the index kept in relation to that register in pursuance of section 211(6);

'authorised credit institution' means a credit institution as defined in Article 1 of Directive 2000/12/EC of the European Parliament and of the Council which is authorised to carry on the business of a credit institution by a competent authority of a member State other than the United Kingdom;

'authorised insurance undertaking' means an insurance undertaking which has been authorised in accordance with Article 6 or 23 of Council Directive 73/239/EEC or Article 6 or 27 of Council Directive 79/267/EEC, or is authorised under the law of a member State to carry on insurance business restricted to re-insurance;

'authorised unit trust scheme' has the same meaning as in Chapter VIII of Part I of the Financial Services Act 1986;

'depositary receipt' means a certificate or other record (whether or not in the form of a document)—

(a)   which is issued by or on behalf of a person who holds shares or who holds evidence of the right to receive shares, or has an interest in shares, in a particular company; and

(b)   which evidences or acknowledges that another person is entitled to rights in relation to those shares or shares of the same kind, which shall include the right to receive such shares (or evidence of the right to receive such shares) from the person mentioned in paragraph (a);

'derivatives' means—

(a)   options to acquire or dispose of shares; and

(b)   rights under a contract falling within paragraph 8 of Schedule 1 to the Financial Service Act 1986 (futures), where the property in question is shares;

'designated agency' has the same meaning as in the Financial Services Act 1986;

'listed company' means a company any of the shares in which are officially listed on a relevant stock exchange and 'listed' shall be construed accordingly;

'material interest' shall be construed in accordance with section 199(2A);

'open-ended investment company' has the same meaning as in the Open-Ended Investment Companies Regulations 2001;

'operator', in relation to a collective investment scheme, shall be construed in accordance with section 75(8) of the Financial Services Act 1986;

'recognised clearing house','recognised professional body','recognised scheme', and 'recognised self-regulating organisation' have the same meaning as in the Financial Services Act 1986;

'register of interest in shares' means the register kept in pursuance of section 211 including, except where the context otherwise requires, that part of the register kept in pursuance of section 213;

'relevant investment exchange' means an exchange situated or operating in a member State on which derivatives are traded;

'relevant share capital' has the meaning given by section 198(2);

'relevant stock exchange' means a stock exchange situated or operating in a member State;

'UCITS' has the meaning given by section 199(8);

'units' has the same meaning as in section 75 of the Financial Services Act 1986.

(2)   Where the period allowed by any provision of this Part for fulfilling an obligation is expressed as a number of days, any day that is a Saturday or Sunday or a bank holiday in any part of Great Britain is to be disregarded in reckoning that period.

PART VII

ACCOUNTS AND AUDIT

CHAPTER I

PROVISIONS APPLYING TO COMPANIES GENERALLY

ACCOUNTING RECORDS

221. Duty to keep accounting records

(1)   Every company shall keep accounting records which are sufficient to show and explain the company's transactions and are such as to—

(a)   disclose with reasonable accuracy, at any time, the financial position of the company at that time, and

(b)   enable the directors to ensure that any balance sheet and profit and loss account prepared under this Part complies with the requirements of this Act.

(2)   The accounting records shall in particular contain—

(a)   entries from day to day of all sums of money received and expended by the company, and the matters in respect of which the receipt and expenditure takes place, and

(b)   a record of the assets and liabilities of the company.

(3)   If the company's business involves dealing in goods, the accounting records shall contain—

(a)   statements of stock held by the company at the end of each financial year of the company,

(b)   all statements of stocktakings from which any such statement of stock as is mentioned in paragraph (a) has been or is to be prepared, and

(c)   except in the case of goods sold by way of ordinary retail trade, statements of all goods sold and purchased, showing the goods and the buyers and sellers in sufficient detail to enable all these to be identified.

(4)   A parent company which has a subsidiary undertaking in relation to which the above requirements do not apply shall take reasonable steps to secure that the undertaking keeps such accounting records as to enable the directors of the parent company to ensure that any balance sheet and profit and loss account prepared under this Part complies with the requirements of this Act.

(5)   If a company fails to comply with any provision of this section, every officer of the company who is in default is guilty of an offence unless he shows that he acted honestly and that in the circumstances in which the company's business was carried on the default was excusable.

(6)   A person guilty of an offence under this section is liable to imprisonment or a fine, or both.

General note

The purpose of the requirement to maintain accounting records is to ensure that business decisions are made on proper information and that, if the company fails, the administration of the winding up is facilitated: *Re Firedart Ltd, Official*

Receiver v Fairall [1994] 2 BCLC 340; see also *Secretary of State for Trade and Industry v Arif* [1997] 1 BCLC 34. On winding up, various offences may arise under IA 1986 with respect to the non-production, concealment or destruction of these company records: see IA 1986, ss 206–209.

S 221(1)

Accounting records   The term 'accounting records' is broadly expressed and will encompass, for example, sales invoices, purchase invoices, cheque books, paying-in books and bank statements; and documents do not cease to be accounting records simply because their contents have been summarised or included in another document (such as the final accounts): *DTC (CNC) Ltd v Gary Sargeant & Co* [1996] 1 BCLC 529.

As to where the records must be kept, and for how long, and by whom they may be inspected, see s 222; as to the manner in which the records must be kept and the use of computerised records, see ss 722–723. Where the records are kept otherwise than in a legible form, the provisions as to the place at which they must be kept and the place of inspection are subject to the Companies (Registers and Other Records) Regulations 1985, SI 1985/724, regs 2, 6(5).

Lien on the records   As the requirement to keep the accounting records and to make them available for inspection (under s 222) is a statutory obligation, it is not possible for an accountant (or solicitor) to enforce a lien over the records for the purpose of securing payment for professional services with respect to those accounts: see *DTC (CNC) Ltd v Gary Sargeant & Co* [1996] 1 BCLC 529.

Disclose the financial position   The obligation is to ensure that the accounting records disclose the financial position at any time, meaning that they are up to date to the current time but there is no requirement for immediate updating of records as long as it is done within a reasonable time, and what is a reasonable time would vary depending on the nature and size of the company. The records must disclose the financial position of the company and are not restricted to simply the cash position or the banking records of the company.

All companies   The obligation to keep the records falls on the company and where the company has employed others to maintain its accounting records, it is important to ensure that the company retains legal ownership of the records and that officers and the auditors have access to them at all times.

The provision extends to all companies, public or private, limited by shares, by guarantee or unlimited but excluding any foreign company: s 735; and see sub-s (4) below. The provisions of this Part do not apply to oversea companies; for the accounting and disclosure requirements with respect to such companies, see Part XXIII (ss 690A–703R).

Auditors' report   The auditors, where appointed, must state in their report if they are of the opinion that proper accounting records have not been kept: s 237(2); and where an auditors' report is not required, the directors must acknowledge on the balance sheet their responsibility for ensuring that proper accounting records are kept: s 249B(4), (5).

S 221(2)

Content of accounting records   Small private companies are particularly poor at recording *all* sums received and expended and such records as they maintain are frequently incomplete and so are in breach of the requirements of this provision. The obligation imposed by this provision is not just to keep accounting records but to keep them to the degree of detail specified.

Whether an entry must be made in the accounting records is important in determining whether a company is a dormant company: see s 249AA.

S 221(4)

A 'subsidiary undertaking' (defined in s 258, Sch 10A) may be exempt from the obligation under sub-s (1) because it is not 'a company' within s 735 (for example, a foreign company or a partnership) but this exemption is of limited value since the subsidiary undertaking must still keep sufficient records to enable the directors of the parent company (defined in s 258, Sch 10A) to prepare the required accounts.

S 221(5), (6)

Penalties   This defence is likely to be of limited application, since it is difficult to envisage when the circumstances in which the company's business is being conducted would excuse non-compliance with these requirements. As to penalties, see s 730, Sch 24; 'officer in default' is defined in s 730(5).

Disqualification   A failure to maintain accounting records as required by this provision is a matter to which the court may have regard in determining whether a director of an insolvent company is unfit and should be disqualified: Company Directors Disqualification Act 1986, ss 6–9, Sch 1, para 4(a).

In practice, non-compliance with this requirement is a very common basis for a finding of unfitness warranting disqualification: see *Re Galeforce Pleating Co Ltd* [1999] 2 BCLC 704; *Secretary of State for Trade and Industry v Arif* [1997] 1 BCLC 34; *Re Firedart Ltd, Official Receiver v Fairall* [1994] 2 BCLC 340; *Secretary of State for Trade and Industry v Ettinger, Re Swift 736 Ltd* [1993] BCLC 896; *Re New Generation Engineers Ltd* [1993] BCLC 435.

---

222. Where and for how long records to be kept

(1)   A company's accounting records shall be kept at its registered office or such other place as the directors think fit, and shall at all times be open to inspection by the company's officers.

(2)   If accounting records are kept at a place outside Great Britain, accounts and returns with respect to the business dealt with in the accounting records so kept shall be sent to, and kept at, a place in Great Britain, and shall at all times be open to such inspection.

(3)   The accounts and returns to be sent to Great Britain shall be such as to—

    (a)   disclose with reasonable accuracy the financial position of the business in question at intervals of not more than six months, and

    (b)   enable the directors to ensure that the company's balance sheet and profit and loss account comply with the requirements of this Act.

(4)   If a company fails to comply with any provision of subsections (1) to (3), every officer of the company who is in default is guilty of an offence, and liable to imprisonment or a fine or both, unless he shows that he acted honestly and that in the circumstances in which the company's business was carried on the default was excusable.

(5)   Accounting records which a company is required by section 221 to keep shall be preserved by it—

    (a)   in the case of a private company, for three years from the date on which they are made, and

    (b)   in the case of a public company, for six years from the date on which they are made.

This is subject to any provision contained in rules made under section 411 of the Insolvency Act 1986 (company insolvency rules).

    An officer of a company is guilty of an offence, and liable to imprisonment or a fine or both, if he fails to take all reasonable steps for securing compliance by the company with subsection (5) or intentionally causes any default by the company under that subsection.

S 222(1)

As to the registered office, see s 287; but there is no requirement to maintain these records at that office; 'officer' is defined in s 744; as to the meaning of 'accounting records', see s 221. Where the records are kept in a non-legible form, the provisions as to the place at which they must be kept and the place of inspection is subject to the Companies (Registers and Other Records) Regulations 1985, SI 1985/724.

Access by the directors   This provision does not confer a statutory right of access on a director, it merely implicitly recognises the existence of such a right at common law; and the court will assume that a director is exercising his right of access in the interests of the company, unless the court is satisfied affirmatively that the director's intention is to abuse the confidence reposed in him as a director and to injure the company: *Conway v Petronius Clothing Co Ltd* [1978] 1 All ER 185.

Access by the members   Any right of inspection by members is a matter for the articles and Table A, reg 109 excludes access except where conferred by statute or authorised by the directors or by ordinary resolution of the company: see *Butt v Kelson* [1952] 1 Ch 197. It would seem that, quite apart from this article, the directors could authorise inspection by members simply under their general management powers.

Access by others   The auditors have a right of access to these records at all times (s 389A(1)), and access can be demanded where the company is under investigation by the Department of Trade and Industry: see ss 434, 447.

S 222(2), (3)

This provision permits the maintenance of the records outside Great Britain, and it is not limited to companies whose business is conducted mainly outside of Great Britain; moreover, the information to be sent need only reflect the position as at six months' intervals.

S 222(4)

Penalties   See note to s 221(5); 'officer in default' is defined in s 730(5); as to penalties, see s 730, Sch 24. A failure to comply with this provision is a matter to which the court may have regard in disqualification proceedings: Company Directors Disqualification Act 1986, ss 6–9, Sch 1, para 4(b); and see note to s 221.

S 222(5)

Time periods   In effect, these provisions are minimum periods during which the records must be retained. The company will want to maintain these records for much longer periods for taxation and other purposes (for example, where there is any risk of liability where there is a longer limitation period); 'public company' and 'private company' are defined in s 1(3).

S 222(6)

Penalties   The failure to preserve the records for the required period is an offence in its own right; 'officer' is defined in s 744; as to penalties, see s 730, Sch 24. A failure to comply with this provision is a matter to which the court may have regard in disqualification proceedings: Company Directors Disqualification Act 1986, ss 6–9, Sch 1, para 4(b); and see note to s 221.

A COMPANY'S FINANCIAL YEAR AND ACCOUNTING REFERENCE PERIODS

223. A company's financial year

(1)   A company's 'financial year' is determined as follows.

(2)   Its first financial year begins with the first day of its first accounting reference period and ends with the last day of that period or such other date, not more than seven days before or after the end of that period, as the directors may determine.

(3)   Subsequent financial years begin with the day immediately following the end of the company's previous financial year and end with the last day of its

next accounting reference period or such other date, not more than seven days before or after the end of that period, as the directors may determine.

(4)   In relation to an undertaking which is not a company, references in this Act to its financial year are to any period in respect of which a profit and loss account of the undertaking is required to be made up (by its constitution or by the law under which it is established), whether that period is a year or not.

(5)   The directors of a parent company shall secure that, except where in their opinion there are good reasons against it, the financial year of each of its subsidiary undertakings coincides with the company's own financial year.

S 223(1)

A company's financial year (which need not be a calendar year) is the period for which its accounts must be prepared (see ss 226, 227) and that period is known as the accounting reference period. The length of the accounting reference period is determined by s 224 and it ends on the company's accounting reference date, also determined by that section. The length of the accounting reference period and the financial year are essentially the same, the difference being that the financial year can be lengthened or shortened by seven days, see sub-ss (2), (3).

S 223(2), (3)

A company's first 'accounting reference period' is determined in accordance with s 224(4); and it ends on the accounting reference date determined by s 224(2)–(3A). Subsequent periods are determined in accordance with s 224(5) and, essentially, are successive periods of 12 months, subject to any alteration to the accounting reference date under s 225.

S 223(4)

A 'company' is defined by s 735 essentially as a company registered under this or former Companies Acts and so an undertaking which is 'not a company' would include foreign companies and unincorporated bodies.

S 223(5)

The intention is that having a common financial year will facilitate the preparation of the group accounts generally required by s 227; 'good reasons' for not having the same financial year might relate to the location of an undertaking (for example, if overseas) or the nature of its business (for example, if seasonal); 'parent company' and 'subsidiary undertakings' are defined in s 258, Sch 10A.

224. Accounting reference periods and accounting reference date

(1)   A company's accounting reference periods are determined according to its accounting reference date.

(2)   A company incorporated before 1st April 1996 may, at any time before the end of the period of nine months beginning with the date of its incorporation, by notice in the prescribed form given to the registrar specify its accounting reference date, that is, the date on which its accounting reference period ends in each calendar year.

(3)   Failing such notice,the accounting reference date of such a company is—

(a)   in the case of a company incorporated before 1st April 1990, 31st March;

(b)   in the case of a company incorporated after 1st April 1990, the last day of the month in which the anniversary of its incorporation falls.

(3A) The accounting reference date of a company incorporated on or after 1st April 1996 is the last day of the month in which the anniversary of its incorporation falls.

(4)   A company's first accounting reference period is the period of more than six months, but not more than 18 months, beginning with the date of its incorporation and ending with its accounting reference date.

(5)   Its subsequent accounting reference periods are successive periods of twelve months beginning immediately after the end of the previous accounting reference period and ending with its accounting reference date.

(6)   This section has effect subject to the provisions of section 225 relating to the alteration of accounting reference dates and the consequences of such alteration.

S 224(1), (6)

Accounting reference period   The importance of the accounting reference period is that this is the period in respect of which the accounts must be drawn up (see note to s 223(1), (2), above. The date on which the accounting reference period ends, the accounting reference date, determines the time period for laying the accounts before the members and delivering accounts to the registrar of companies: see s 244.

The requirements of this section are subject to any alteration to the accounting reference date effected under s 225.

S 224(2)–(3), (6)

The dates prescribed here are subject to alteration under s 225.

S 224(3A)–(5)

Subsection (3A) provides for the initial accounting reference date for companies incorporated now. The effect is that the first accounting reference period is more than 12 months but less than 13 months, unless the company changes its accounting reference date. The company has the option of doing so under s 225 in order to have a financial year (see s 223) ending on a date which is administratively convenient and appropriate for its activities. Hence the initial accounting reference period may be as short as six months or as long as 18 months; subsequent periods will be for periods of 12 months (unless the company alters the accounting reference date again, subject to s 225).

S 224(4), (6)

First accounting reference period   This provision appears to require that the first accounts be for a period of at least six months but this is subject to any alteration of the accounting reference date, including the first accounting reference date. If the first accounting reference date is altered then the period from incorporation to that date may be less than six months. The maximum period of 18 months cannot be exceeded: s 225(6) (save where the company is in administration).

The period commences with the date of incorporation not the date of the commencement of business.

225. Alteration of accounting reference date

(1)   A company may by notice in the prescribed form given to the registrar specify a new accounting reference date having effect in relation to—
  (a) the company's current accounting reference period and subsequent periods; or
  (b) the company's previous accounting reference period and subsequent periods.

A company's 'previous accounting reference period' means that immediately preceding its current accounting reference period.

(2)   . . .

(3)   The notice shall state whether the current or previous accounting reference period—
  (a) is to be shortened, so as to come to an end on the first occasion on which the new accounting reference date falls or fell after the beginning of the period, or
  (b) is to be extended, so as to come to an end on the second occasion on which that date falls or fell after the beginning of the period.

(4)   A notice under subsection (1) stating that the current or previous accounting reference period is to be extended is ineffective, except as mentioned below, if given less than five years after the end of an earlier accounting reference period of the company which was extended by virtue of this section.

This subsection does not apply—
  (a) to a notice given by a company which is a subsidiary undertaking or parent undertaking of another EEA undertaking if the new accounting reference date coincides with that of the other EEA undertaking or, where that undertaking is not a company, with the last day of its financial year, or

(b) where an administration order is in force under Part II of the Insolvency Act 1986,

or where the Secretary of State directs that it should not apply, which he may do with respect to a notice which has been given or which may be given.

(5) A notice under subsection (1) may not be given in respect of a previous accounting reference period if the period allowed for laying and delivering accounts and reports in relation to that period has already expired.

(6) An accounting reference period may not in any case, unless an administration order is in force under Part II of the Insolvency Act 1986, be extended so as to exceed 18 months and a notice under this section is ineffective if the current or previous accounting reference period as extended in accordance with the notice would exceed that limit.

(7) In this section 'EEA undertaking' means an undertaking established under the law of any part of the United Kingdom or the law of any other EEA State.

S 225(1)

Notification to the registrar of any alteration   The obligation to notify the registrar of companies of any change to the accounting reference date can be overlooked, with serious consequences. The registrar will refuse to accept accounts made up to a different date from that notified and any delay in re-submitting accounts made up to the proper date runs the risk that the company will incur a late filing penalty (see s 242A). The auditors will qualify any accounts prepared (as the statutory accounts) for a period other than the accounting reference period as determined by the accounting reference date recorded by the registrar of companies.

S 225(3)–(4), (6)

Shortening the accounting reference period   There are no limits to the number of times a company may change its accounting reference date where the effect is to shorten the accounting reference period but where the change has the effect of lengthening that period, there are restrictions on the frequency with which that may be done and, in any event, it cannot generally be lengthened beyond 18 months, see sub-s (6).

Lengthening the accounting reference period   The restriction is that the accounting reference period may not be lengthened unless five years has elapsed since it was last lengthened. However, this restriction does not apply if the company is a parent or subsidiary undertaking (defined s 258, Sch 10A) of an EEA undertaking (defined sub-s (7)) and the alteration is made in order to align dates within the group. As to the financial year of an undertaking which is not a company, see s 223(4).

See s 244(4) as to the period allowed for laying and delivering accounts when the accounting reference period is shortened.

S 225(5)

Altering the accounting reference date in order to avoid a late filing penalty is not an option; the period allowed for laying and delivering accounts is determined by s 244.

ANNUAL ACCOUNTS

226. Duty to prepare individual company accounts

(1) The directors of every company shall prepare for each financial year of the company—

(a) a balance sheet as at the last day of the year, and

(b) a profit and loss account.

Those accounts are referred to in this Part as the company's 'individual accounts'.

(2) The balance sheet shall give a true and fair view of the state of affairs of the company as at the end of the financial year; and the profit and loss account shall give a true and fair view of the profit or loss of the company for the financial year.

(3) A company's individual accounts shall comply with the provisions of Schedule 4 as to the form and content of the balance sheet and profit and loss account and additional information to be provided by way of notes to the accounts.

(4) Where compliance with the provisions of that Schedule, and the other provisions of this Act as to the matters to be included in a company's individual accounts or in notes to those accounts, would not be sufficient to give a true and fair view, the necessary additional information shall be given in the accounts or in a note to them.

(5) If in special circumstances compliance with any of those provisions is inconsistent with the requirement to give a true and fair view, the directors shall depart from that provision to the extent necessary to give a true and fair view.

Particulars of any such departure, the reasons for it and its effect shall be given in a note to the accounts.

General note

In addition to the accounts required by this section, a directors' report must be prepared (s 234), and an auditors' report may be required: see ss 235, 249A, 249AA.

A copy of the accounts must be sent to those entitled (s 238; and for a listed public company, see s 251); and laid before the company in general meeting (s 241), unless the company is a private company which has elected to dispense with the laying of accounts and reports under s 252; and delivered to the registrar of companies: see s 242.

S 226(1)

Obligation of directors of every company   The duty to prepare accounts is an obligation of the directors and the duty is owed to the company and not to individual shareholders: *Devlin v Slough Estates Ltd* [1983] BCLC 497. The obligation applies to every 'company', as defined by s 735 which include companies limited by guarantee and unlimited companies; it also applies to dormant companies (defined s 249AA) which must prepare and deliver accounts even though the definition of dormancy is that the company has had no significant accounting transactions in the relevant period.

The 'financial year' is defined by s 223; references to the balance sheet and profit and loss account include notes to the accounts: see s 261(2). If the company is a parent company, as defined by s 258, Sch 10A, group accounts will normally be required in addition to individual accounts: see ss 227–229, 248.

Non-compliance   The sanctions for non-compliance with this requirement are indirect, in that if accounts are not prepared then, of course, they cannot be delivered to the registrar of companies and a failure to deliver the accounts to the registrar of companies is a criminal offence by each director: s 242(2). The company may also incur penalties for non-delivery under s 242A. The extent of a director's responsibility for any non-compliance with this section or the next is also a matter to which the court may have regard in determining whether a director of an insolvent company is unfit and should be disqualified: Company Directors Disqualification Act 1986, ss 6–9, Sch 1, para 5. As to the liability of each director if accounts are approved which do not comply with the requirements of the Act, see s 233(5).

S 226(2)

A true and fair view   Compliance with accounting standards will normally be necessary for financial statements to give a true and fair view (see Accounting Standards Board, Foreword to Accounting Standards, June 1993 and counsel's opinion annexed thereto). The ASB is the prescribed body with responsibility for determining accounting standards under s 256 and it regards accounting standards as definitive statements of how particular types of transactions and other events should be reflected in financial statements. It also envisages that only in exceptional circumstances would departure from an accounting standard be necessary in order for accounts to give a true and fair view. Ultimately, however, the question whether the accounts do give a true and fair view is a matter of law for the courts to decide.

The auditors' report must state whether, in their opinion, the accounts do give a true and fair view: s 235(2).

S 226(3)

Form and content of individual accounts   In general, individual accounts must comply with Sch 4 but there are a number of exceptions:
    (1)   if the company is a small company (within ss 247, 247A), it may comply with Sch 8 instead of Sch 4 (or with Schs 4 and 8) with respect to the accounts to be prepared for the members (s 246(2)); and with Sch 8A with respect to the accounts to be delivered to the registrar of companies: s 246(5);

(2) if the company is a medium-sized company, it may take advantage of the limited exemptions affecting both the accounts to be prepared for the members (s 246A(2)) and those which must be delivered to the registrar (s 246A(3), and these exemptions permits the aggregation or omission of information required by Sch 4: see s 246A;

(3) if the company is a banking company, it must comply with Sch 9, Pt I: s 255(1);

(4) if the company is an insurance company, it must comply with Sch 9A, Pt I: s 255(2).

As to information which must be contained in notes to the accounts, see ss 231 and 232, Schs 5 and 6; see also s 261(2).

S 226(4)

As the requirement to give a true and fair view is an overriding obligation, it may be necessary on occasion to include additional information in the accounts or notes to ensure that this is the case.

S 226(5)

The true and fair override This provision is the 'true and fair override', which requires the directors to depart from the statutory requirements where necessary to ensure that the accounts give a fair and true view. Further guidance as to its operation can be found in Urgent Issues Task Force (UITF), Abstract 7, True and Fair View Override Disclosures (1992). The UITF is part of the Accounting Standards Body, as to which see note to sub-s (2), above. The standing of UITF Abstracts is such that counsel (see note to sub-s (2), above) was of the opinion that there would be a readiness on the part of the court to accept that compliance with UITF Abstracts is necessary to meet the true and fair requirement.

UITF Abstract 7 stresses that where reliance is placed on the true and fair override under this provision, that fact must be stated clearly and unambiguously in the accounts. The Abstract considers that:

(1) 'particulars of any departure' requires a statement of the treatment which the Act would normally require in the circumstances and a statement of the treatment actually adopted;

(2) 'the reasons for it' requires a statement as to why the treatment prescribed would not give a true and fair view;

(3) 'its effect' requires a description of how the position shown in the accounts is different as a result of the departure, normally with quantification, except where quantification is already evident in the accounts themselves or whenever the effect cannot reasonably be quantified, in which case the directors should explain the circumstances. Furthermore the disclosure required by this Abstract should either be included, or cross referenced, in the note required under Sch 4, para 36A (statement whether accounts have been properly prepared in accordance with applicable accounting standards).

227. Duty to prepare group accounts

(1)   If at the end of a financial year a company is a parent company the directors shall, as well as preparing individual accounts for the year, prepare group accounts.

(2)   Group accounts shall be consolidated accounts comprising—

(a) a consolidated balance sheet dealing with the state of affairs of the parent company and its subsidiary undertakings, and

(b) a consolidated profit and loss account dealing with the profit or loss of the parent company and its subsidiary undertakings.

(3)   The accounts shall give a true and fair view of the state of affairs as at the end of the financial year, and the profit or loss for the financial year, of the undertakings included in the consolidation as a whole, so far as concerns members of the company.

(4)   A company's group accounts shall comply with the provisions of Schedule 4A as to the form and content of the consolidated balance sheet and consolidated profit and loss account and additional information to be provided by way of notes to the accounts.

(5)   Where compliance with the provisions of that Schedule, and the other provisions of this Act, as to the matters to be included in a company's group accounts or in notes to those accounts, would not be sufficient to give a true and fair view, the necessary additional information shall be given in the accounts or in a note to them.

(6)   If in special circumstances compliance with any of those provisions is inconsistent with the requirement to give a true and fair view, the directors shall depart from that provision to the extent necessary to give a true and fair view.

Particulars of any such departure, the reasons for it and its effect shall be given in a note to the accounts.

S 227(1)

Requirement to prepare group accounts   The 'end of the financial year' means at the balance sheet date and the test is whether, at that date, the company is a 'parent company' as defined in s 258, Sch 10A. If it is not, although it did have subsidiary undertakings during the financial year, then group accounts are not required. In addition to preparing group accounts, a parent company must also prepare individual accounts subject to the modifications permitted by s 230.

Exemption from requirement to prepare group accounts   A parent company need not prepare group accounts if it is exempt from so doing under s 228 (parent company included in accounts of larger groups) or s 229(5) (all subsidiaries entitled to be excluded) or if the group qualifies as a small or medium-sized group under s 248.

Disclosure   A copy of the accounts must be sent to those entitled (s 238; and for a listed public company, see s 251); and laid before the company in general meeting (s 241) unless the company is a private company which has elected to dispense with the laying of accounts and reports under s 252; and delivered to the registrar of companies: see s 242.

As to the liability of each director if accounts are approved which do not comply with the requirements of the Act, see s 233(5).

S 227(2)

Consolidated accounts are required and all subsidiary undertakings must be included unless they are within one of the excepted categories in s 229; the term 'subsidiary undertaking' (rather than subsidiary company) requires the inclusion of unincorporated subsidiaries (a requirement of the 7th EC Directive on accounts).

S 227(3)

As to the meaning of a 'true and fair view', see note to s 226(2), above. The inclusion of the phrase 'so far as concerns members of the company' (which is not included in s 226(2)) would seem simply to emphasise that the group accounts are to inform the members of the parent company of the financial position of the group.

S 227(4)

Form and content of group accounts   The form and content required is set out in Sch 4A rather than Sch 4; however, Sch 4A, para 1 requires compliance so far as possible with Sch 4. Banking and insurance groups comply with Sch 9, Pt II and Sch 9A, Pt II, respectively: see s 255A. As to information which must be contained in notes to the accounts, see ss 231 and 232, Schs 5 and 6; see also s 261(2).

S 227(5)

See note to s 226(4). As to the application of this provision to group accounts of banking or insurance groups, see s 255A(6).

S 227(6)

This provides for a true and fair view override with respect to group accounts: see note to s 226(5), above. As to the application of this provision to group accounts of banking or insurance groups, see s 255A(6).

---

228. Exemption for parent companies included in accounts of larger group

(1) A company is exempt from the requirement to prepare group accounts if it is itself a subsidiary undertaking and its immediate parent undertaking is

established under the law of a member State of the European Economic Community, in the following cases—

    (a) where the company is a wholly-owned subsidiary of that parent undertaking;

    (b) where that parent undertaking holds more than 50 per cent of the shares in the company and notice requesting the preparation of group accounts has not been served on the company by shareholders holding in aggregate—

        (i) more than half of the remaining shares in the company, or

        (ii) 5 per cent of the total shares in the company.

Such notice must be served not later than six months after the end of the financial year before that to which it relates.

(2) Exemption is conditional upon compliance with all of the following conditions—

    (a) that the company is included in consolidated accounts for a larger group drawn up to the same date, or to an earlier date in the same financial year, by a parent undertaking established under the law of a member State of the European Economic Community;

    (b) that those accounts are drawn up and audited, and that parent undertaking's annual report is drawn up, according to that law, in accordance with the provisions of the Seventh Directive (83/349/EEC) (where applicable as modified by the provisions of the Bank Accounts Directive (86/635/EEC)or the Insurance Accounts Directive (91/674/EEC));

    (c) that the company discloses in its individual accounts that it is exempt from the obligation to prepare and deliver group accounts;

    (d) that the company states in its individual accounts the name of the parent undertaking which draws up the group accounts referred to above and—

        (i) if it is incorporated outside Great Britain, the country in which it is incorporated,

        (ii) . . ., and

        (iii) if it is unincorporated, the address of its principal place of business;

    (e) that the company delivers to the registrar, within the period allowed for delivering its individual accounts, copies of those group accounts and of the parent undertaking's annual report, together with the auditors' report on them; and

    (f) (subject to section 710B(6) (delivery of certain Welsh documents without a translation)) that if any document comprised in accounts and reports delivered in accordance with paragraph (e) is in a language other than English, there is annexed to the copy of that document delivered a translation of it into English, certified in the prescribed manner to be a correct translation.

(3) The exemption does not apply to a company any of whose securities are listed on a stock exchange in any member State of the European Economic Community.

(4)   Shares held by directors of a company for the purpose of complying with any share qualification requirement shall be disregarded in determining for the purposes of subsection (1)(a) whether the company is a wholly-owned subsidiary.

(5)   For the purposes of subsection (1)(b) shares held by a wholly-owned subsidiary of the parent undertaking, or held on behalf of the parent undertaking or a wholly-owned subsidiary, shall be attributed to the parent undertaking.

(6)   In subsection (3) 'securities' includes—

  (a)   shares and stock,

  (b)   debentures, including debenture stock, loan stock, bonds, certificates of deposit and other instruments creating or acknowledging indebtedness,

  (c)   warrants or other instruments entitling the holder to subscribe for securities falling within paragraph (a) or (b), and

  (d)   certificates or other instruments which confer—

    (i)   property rights in respect of a security falling within paragraph (a), (b) or (c),

    (ii)   any right to acquire, dispose of, underwrite or convert a security, being a right to which the holder would be entitled if he held any such security to which the certificate or other instrument relates, or

    (iii)   a contractual right (other than an option) to acquire any such security otherwise than by subscription.

S 228(1)

This provision exempts parent companies (meeting the prescribed criteria) from the obligation to prepare group accounts under s 227 if they themselves are subsidiary undertakings (defined in s 258, Sch 10A) and their immediate parent undertaking (defined in s 258, Sch 10A) is established in a member state of the EU. The criteria are quite precise; 'wholly-owned subsidiary' is defined in s 736(2) and see sub-s (4); in determining whether the parent company holds more than 50% of the shares, see s 736(5).

  Such companies are still obliged to prepare their individual accounts and to include the information in sub-s (2)(c) and (d) in those accounts. Where a company is exempt from the need to prepare group accounts, although it has subsidiary undertakings, it must give the name and, if incorporated outside Great Britain, the place of incorporation of each subsidiary, in the notes to the parent company's individual accounts and give the reasons why group accounts are not required: s 231, Sch 5, para 1.

S 228(2)

There must be compliance with *all* of the conditions laid down and a failure to meet any requirement will mean that the parent company is obliged to prepare group accounts. The required inclusion is in the consolidated accounts of a larger group drawn up by a parent undertaking which need not be the immediate parent undertaking. As to the meaning of 'principal place of business', see note to s 698(2), below.

S 228(3)

As to the definition of 'securities', see sub-s (6).

---

229. Subsidiary undertakings included in the consolidation

(1)   Subject to the exceptions authorised or required by this section, all the subsidiary undertakings of the parent company shall be included in the consolidation.

(2)   A subsidiary undertaking may be excluded from consolidation if its inclusion is not material for the purpose of giving a true and fair view; but two or more undertakings may be excluded only if they are not material taken together.

(3)   In addition, a subsidiary undertaking may be excluded from consolidation where—

(a)   severe long-term restrictions substantially hinder the exercise of the rights of the parent company over the assets or management of that undertaking, or

(b)   the information necessary for the preparation of group accounts cannot be obtained without disproportionate expense or undue delay, or

(c)   the interest of the parent company is held exclusively with a view to subsequent resale and the undertaking has not previously been included in consolidated group accounts prepared by the parent company.

The reference in paragraph (a) to the rights of the parent company and the reference in paragraph (c) to the interest of the parent company are, respectively, to rights and interests held by or attributed to the company for the purposes of section 258 (definition of 'parent undertaking') in the absence of which it would not be the parent company.

(4)   Where the activities of one or more subsidiary undertakings are so different from those of other undertakings to be included in the consolidation that their inclusion would be incompatible with the obligation to give a true and fair view, those undertakings shall be excluded from consolidation.

   This subsection does not apply merely because some of the undertakings are industrial, some commercial and some provide services, or because they carry on industrial or commercial activities involving different products or provide different services.

(5)   Where all the subsidiary undertakings of a parent company fall within the above exclusions, no group accounts are required.

General note

This provision requires all subsidiary undertakings to be included in the consolidated accounts subject to certain permitted exclusions and, in the case of sub-s (4), a mandatory exclusion.

S 229(1)

'Subsidiary undertaking' and 'parent company' are defined in s 258, Sch 10A.

S 229(2)

Multiple exclusions are only permissible under this heading if, taken together, they are not material.

S 229(3)

This is an optional exclusion. Financial Reporting Standard (FRS) 2, Accounting for Subsidiary Undertakings, issued by the Accounting Standards Board (see note to s 226(2), above) offers some guidance as to when some of these situations might arise:

(1)   Severe long-term restrictions might arise, for example, where the subsidiary is insolvent and under the control of an officer-holder, although not all forms of insolvency proceedings would necessarily involve long-term restrictions (for example, where the subsidiary is in administration): see FRS 2, para 78.

(2)   The interest of the parent company may be held exclusively with a view to resale where that interest has arisen as a result of enforcing a security and the parent company does not intend that the subsidiary should become part of the activities of the group: see FRS 2, para 11. The timeframe for a subsequent re-sale within this provision is normally 12 months and, if the subsidiary has not been sold within that period, it should be included in the consolidated accounts.

S 229(4)

Mandatory exclusion   This exclusion, where applicable, is mandatory. However, the circumstances where the activities are so different that it would be incompatible with the obligation to give a true and fair view would be very exceptional: see FRS 2, para 78.

Accounts for subsidiaries excluded under this provision may need to be appended to the copy of the parent company's annual accounts which are delivered to the registrar of companies: see s 243.

S 229(5)

Where a company takes advantage of this provision so as to be exempt from the requirement to prepare group accounts, it must state, in the notes to its account, with respect to each subsidiary which of the exclusions applies: s 231, Sch 5, Pt 1, para 1(5).

230. Treatment of individual profit and loss account where group accounts prepared

(1) The following provisions apply with respect to the individual profit and loss account of a parent company where—

(a) the company is required to prepare and does prepare group accounts in accordance with this Act, and

(b) the notes to the company's individual balance sheet show the company's profit or loss for the financial year determined in accordance with this Act.

(2) The profit and loss account need not contain the information specified in paragraphs 52 to 57 of Schedule 4 (information supplementing the profit and loss account).

(3) The profit and loss account must be approved in accordance with section 233(1) (approval by board of directors) but may be omitted from the company's annual accounts for the purposes of the other provisions below in this Chapter.

(4) The exemption conferred by this section is conditional upon its being disclosed in the company's annual accounts that the exemption applies.

General note

This exemption allows a parent company (defined in s 258, Sch 10A) which meets the criteria to dispense with the inclusion of a profit and loss account in the company's individual accounts.

S 230(1)

Where a parent company, though exempt from the requirement to prepare group accounts, nevertheless wishes to prepare group accounts, it cannot, it seems, take advantage of this exemption (not meeting the criteria in sub-s (1)(a)) and it must include a profit and loss account in its individual accounts.

S 230(2)–(3)

A parent company must still prepare a profit and loss account (although it may take advantage of sub-s (2) in so doing) and the account must be approved by the directors; and the amount of the company's profit or loss for the year must be included in the notes to the company's balance sheet. However, the effect of sub-s (3) is that the individual profit and loss account need not be sent to the members under s 238, nor laid before the general meeting under s 241, nor delivered to the registrar of companies under s 244.

As to the application of this provision to the group accounts of banking or insurance groups, see s 255A(6)(b).

231. Disclosure required in notes to accounts: related undertakings

(1) The information specified in Schedule 5 shall be given in notes to a company's annual accounts.

(2) Where the company is not required to prepare group accounts, the information specified in Part I of that Schedule shall be given; and where the company is required to prepare group accounts, the information specified in Part II of that Schedule shall be given.

(3) The information required by Schedule 5 need not be disclosed with respect to an undertaking which—

(a) is established under the law of a country outside the United Kingdom, or

(b) carries on business outside the United Kingdom,

if in the opinion of the directors of the company the disclosure would be seriously prejudicial to the business of that undertaking, or to the business of the company or any of its subsidiary undertakings, and the Secretary of State agrees that the information need not be disclosed.

This subsection does not apply in relation to the information required under paragraph 6, 9A, 20 or 28A of that Schedule.

(4) Where advantage is taken of subsection (3), that fact shall be stated in a note to the company's annual accounts.

(5) If the directors of the company are of the opinion that the number of undertakings in respect of which the company is required to disclose information under any provision of Schedule 5 to this Act is such that compliance with that provision would result in information of excessive length being given, the information need only be given in respect of—

(a) the undertakings whose results or financial position, in the opinion of the directors, principally affected the figures shown in the company's annual accounts, and

(b) undertakings excluded from consolidation under section 229(3) or (4).

(6) If advantage is taken of subsection (5)—

(a) there shall be included in the notes to the company's annual accounts a statement that the information is given only with respect to such undertakings as are mentioned in that subsection, and

(b) the full information (both that which is disclosed in the notes to the accounts and that which is not) shall be annexed to the company's next annual return.

For this purpose the 'next annual return' means that next delivered to the registrar after the accounts in question have been approved under section 233.

(7) If a company fails to comply with subsection (6)(b), the company and every officer of it who is in default is liable to a fine and, for continued contravention, to a daily default fine.

General note

Those 'related undertakings' mentioned in the title to this section and with respect to which information must be included in the notes to the accounts are identified by Sch 5. Small companies are exempt from some of the disclosures required by this Schedule: see s 246(6). As to the application of this provision to the group accounts of banking or insurance groups, see s 255B.

S 231(1)–(2)

The requirement that the information specified in Sch 5 be included in the notes to a company's annual accounts applies whether or not the company is required to produce group accounts but there are differing disclosure requirements in each case; 'annual accounts' is defined in s 262(1); see also s 261(2) as to the notes to the annual accounts. Whether a company is required to prepare group accounts is determined by ss 227–229, 248.

S 231(3), (4)

This is a limited exemption which is sought by a very small number of companies each year.

S 231(5)–(6)

Whether or not group accounts are prepared, the notes to a parent company's individual accounts must give:
   (1)   the name of each subsidiary undertaking and, if incorporated outside Great Britain, its place of incorporation: Sch 5, paras 1, 15; subject to the ability to limit the information provided in accordance with sub-s (5); and
   (2)   where the parent company is itself a subsidiary undertaking, it must identify the company, if any, regarded as the company's ultimate holding company: Sch 5, paras 12, 31.

However, the full information on the subsidiaries must be annexed to the next annual return; as to the annual return, see s 363.

S 231(7)

Penalties   The offence here is the failure to annex the full information on the company's subsidiaries to the company's next annual return; as to the annual return, see s 363; as to penalties, see s 730, Sch 24; 'officer in default' is defined in s 730(5).

232. Disclosure required in notes to accounts: emoluments and other benefits of directors and others

(1)　The information specified in Schedule 6 shall be given in notes to a company's annual accounts.

(2)　In that Schedule—

Part I relates to the emoluments of directors (including emoluments waived), pensions of directors and past directors, compensation for loss of office to directors and past directors and sums paid to third parties in respect of directors' services,

Part II relates to loans, quasi-loans and other dealings in favour of directors and connected persons, and

Part III relates to transactions, arrangements and agreements made by the company or a subsidiary undertaking for officers of the company other than directors.

(3)　It is the duty of any director of a company, and any person who is or has at any time in the preceding five years been an officer of the company, to give notice to the company of such matters relating to himself as may be necessary for the purposes of Part I of Schedule 6.

(4)　A person who makes default in complying with subsection (3) commits an offence and is liable to a fine.

General note

Small companies may be exempt from some of the disclosures required by Sch 6: see s 246(6).

S 232(1)

'Annual accounts' is defined in s 262; see also s 261(2) as to the notes to the annual accounts. The information to be disclosed relates to the directors of the reporting company so the notes to any group accounts should only include information on the directors of the parent company and not on the directors of the subsidiaries unless they are directors of the parent company.

S 232(2)

As to the substantive provisions governing the transactions etc which are the subject of these disclosure requirements, see Part X, ss 311–347. Definitions of the terms 'quasi-loans' and 'connected persons' are contained in that Part: see ss 331(3), 346.

S 232(3), (4)

The duty on the director (and officer) to disclose the necessary information (on pain of criminal penalties) applies only with respect to information relating to himself and not to connected persons. As to penalties, see s 730, Sch 24; 'officer' is defined in s 744.

APPROVAL AND SIGNING OF ACCOUNTS

233. Approval and signing of accounts

(1) A company's annual accounts shall be approved by the board of directors and signed on behalf of the board by a director of the company.

(2) The signature shall be on the company's balance sheet.

(3) Every copy of the balance sheet which is laid before the company in general meeting, or which is otherwise circulated, published or issued, shall state the name of the person who signed the balance sheet on behalf of the board.

(4) The copy of the company's balance sheet which is delivered to the registrar shall be signed on behalf of the board by a director of the company.

(5) If annual accounts are approved which do not comply with the requirements of this Act, every director of the company who is party to their approval and who knows that they do not comply or is reckless as to whether they comply is guilty of an offence and liable to a fine.

For this purpose every director of the company at the time the accounts are approved shall be taken to be a party to their approval unless he shows that he took all reasonable steps to prevent their being approved.

(6) If a copy of the balance sheet—

    (a) is laid before the company, or otherwise circulated, published or issued, without the balance sheet having been signed as required by this section or without the required statement of the signatory's name being included, or

    (b) is delivered to the registrar without being signed as required by this section,

the company and every officer of it who is in default is guilty of an offence and liable to a fine.

General note

There are two offences here: (1) board approval of non-compliant annual accounts (sub-s (5)); and (2) non-compliance with signature requirements (sub-s (6)). The extent of a director's responsibility for a failure to comply with the requirements of this section is a matter to which the court may have regard in disqualification proceedings: Company Directors Disqualification Act 1986, ss 6–9, Sch 1, para 4.

S 233(1)–(4)

Accounts approved and signed   By 'annual accounts' is meant the company's individual accounts and any group accounts, if required (s 262(1)) so each must be approved by the board and the balance sheet of the individual accounts must be signed (sub-s (2)) although it is customary for the consolidated balance sheet also to be signed by a director. There is no requirement that all other copies circulated, published etc must be signed but they must always indicate the name of the director who signed on behalf of the board.

Signed copy to the registrar of companies   The copy of the balance sheet which is delivered to the registrar of companies must be signed but not necessarily by the same director who signed under sub-s (1) although, in practice, this would be the case. The registrar of companies will reject accounts which fail to comply with this provision and will return them to the company. The delay which will arise from the need to re-submit a properly signed copy of the balance sheet may result in the company incurring a late filing penalty: see s 242A.

Where a small company delivers abbreviated accounts in accordance with s 246(5)(c) to the registrar of companies, the signature of a director is also required on the balance sheet delivered under those provisions: s 246(7).

A small company taking advantage of the exemptions in s 246 will also require an additional statement as specified in s 246(8) ahead of the signature on the balance sheet: see s 246(8); likewise, a medium-sized company taking advantage of the exemptions in s 246A: see s 246A(4).

A company taking advantage of the exemptions from audit conferred by ss 249A or 249AA must also include certain statements on the balance sheet ahead of the director's signature: see s 249B(4)–(5).

S 233(5)

Liability for non-compliant accounts   The requirements in questions are the requirements as to form and content, as well as the overriding requirement that the accounts give a true and fair view: ss 226, 227. The potential liability applies to every director who is party to the approval of the accounts by the board and not just to the signatory to the accounts. A director who takes all reasonable steps to prevent the accounts being approved is not taken to be a party to their approval and so cannot be guilty of the offence. The requirement that the objecting director took all reasonable steps may require more from him than simply a dissenting view at the board meeting. For example, he may need to show that he raised his concerns earlier with the chairman or, indeed, with the auditors (if auditors are appointed).

Liability under this provision would also arise where the directors approve accounts of an inappropriate nature, as where they claim dormant company status when not entitled, or claim an exemption from audit when not entitled, see ss 249A, 249AA. As to penalties, see s 730, Sch 24; 'officer in default' is defined in s 730(5).

S 233(6)

As to penalties, see s 730, Sch 24; 'officer in default' is defined in s 730(5).

DIRECTORS' REPORT

234. Duty to prepare directors' report

(1)   The directors of a company shall for each financial year prepare a report—

(a)   containing a fair review of the development of the business of the company and its subsidiary undertakings during the financial year and of their position at the end of it, and

(b)   stating the amount (if any) which they recommend should be paid as dividend.

(2)   The report shall state the names of the persons who, at any time during the financial year, were directors of the company, and the principal activities of the company and its subsidiary undertakings in the course of the year and any significant change in those activities in the year.

(3)   The report shall also comply with Schedule 7 as regards the disclosure of the matters mentioned there.

(4)   In Schedule 7—

Part I relates to matters of a general nature, including changes in asset values, directors' shareholdings and other interests and contributions for political and charitable purposes,

Part II relates to the acquisition by a company of its own shares or a charge on them,

Part III relates to the employment, training and advancement of disabled persons,

. . .

Part V relates to the involvement of employees in the affairs, policy and performance of the company.

Part VI relates to the company's policy and practice on the payment of creditors.

(5)   In the case of any failure to comply with the provisions of this Part as to the preparation of a directors' report and the contents of the report, every person who was a director of the company immediately before the end of the period for laying and delivering accounts and reports for the financial year in question is guilty of an offence and liable to a fine.

(6)   In proceedings against a person for an offence under this section it is a defence for him to prove that he took all reasonable steps for securing compliance with the requirements in question.

General note

All companies (defined s 735) must prepare a directors' report but small companies are entitled to omit certain information from the report (see s 246(4), including the information required by s 234(1)(a) and (b)) and small companies need not deliver the report to the registrar of companies: see s 246(5). In that case, the report is solely a matter for the company's shareholders and not for the public record.

A copy of the directors' report must be sent to those entitled (s 238) and laid before the company in general meeting (s 241), unless the company is a private company which has elected to dispense with the laying of accounts and reports under s 252. As to the obligation to deliver the report to the registrar, see s 242, subject to s 246(5).

S 234(1)

Directors' duties　　The duty to prepare a report is an obligation of the directors and the duty is owed to the company and not to individual shareholders: see *Devlin v Slough Estates Ltd* [1983] BCLC 497. It is a matter of judgment for the directors as to the degree of detail necessary to ensure that the report contains a 'fair review'. As to the 'financial year', see s 223; a 'subsidiary undertaking' is defined by s 258, Sch 10A.

If the directors become aware of an error in the report, they may prepare a revised report (s 245(1)); and, as an error as to content is an offence under sub-s (5), it may be advisable to do so. The directors' report is not audited but the auditors must review it for consistency with the accounts: see s 235(3).

S 234(2)

This requirement to identify the principal (ie significant) activities of the company is more useful than the statement of objects in the company's memorandum of association (required by s 2(1)(c)), for this tells the reader what the company is actually doing as opposed to what it might do; any 'significant change' would cover both the addition of new activities and the cessation of existing ones.

S 234(3)–(6)

Form and content　　The form and content of the report is dictated by Sch 7, subject to exemptions for small companies (see s 246(4)), and the information required extends far beyond the financial affairs of the company. A failure to include required information will result in the report being rejected by the registrar of companies and is an offence. The offence covers both a failure to prepare the report and a failure to comply with the requirements as to its contents, subject to the defence in sub-s (6); the period for laying and delivering accounts and reports is determined by s 244. As to penalties, see s 730, Sch 24.

234A. Approval and signing of directors' report

(1)　　The directors' report shall be approved by the board of directors and signed on behalf of the board by a director or the secretary of the company.

(2)　　Every copy of the directors' report which is laid before the company in general meeting, or which is otherwise circulated, published or issued, shall state the name of the person who signed it on behalf of the board.

(3)　　The copy of the directors' report which is delivered to the registrar shall be signed on behalf of the board by a director or the secretary of the company.

(4) If a copy of the directors' report—

(a) is laid before the company, or otherwise circulated, published or issued, without the report having been signed as required by this section or without the required statement of the signatory's name being included, or

(b) is delivered to the registrar without being signed as required by this section,

the company and every officer of it who is in default is guilty of an offence and liable to a fine.

General note

The requirements regarding approval and signing of the directors' report are identical to those with respect to the approval and signing of the annual accounts (see s 233 and notes to that section), above, except that it is possible for the report to be signed either by a director or by the company secretary (cf s 233(1)).

S 234A(4)

As to penalties, see s 730, Sch 24; 'officer in default' is defined in s 730(5).

AUDITORS' REPORT

235. Auditors' report

(1) A company's auditors shall make a report to the company's members on all annual accounts of the company of which copies are to be laid before the company in general meeting during their tenure of office.

(2) The auditors' report shall state whether in the auditors' opinion the annual accounts have been properly prepared in accordance with this Act, and in particular whether a true and fair view is given—

(a) in the case of an individual balance sheet, of the state of affairs of the company as at the end of the financial year,

(b) in the case of an individual profit and loss account, of the profit or loss of the company for the financial year,

(c) in the case of group accounts, of the state of affairs as at the end of the financial year, and the profit or loss for the financial year, of the undertakings included in the consolidation as a whole, so far as concerns members of the company.

(3)   The auditors shall consider whether the information given in the directors' report for the financial year for which the annual accounts are prepared is consistent with those accounts; and if they are of opinion that it is not they shall state that fact in their report.

General note

Every company must appoint an auditor unless exempt by virtue of s 388A: s 384(1); the exempt categories are small and dormant companies (see ss 249A, 249AA). As to the auditors' rights to information, see s 389A(1); as to their rights to attend company meetings, see s 390.

Form and content of report   The form and content of the auditors' report is the subject of extensive guidance by the Auditing Practices Board in the form of SAS (Statement of Auditing Standards) 600, *'Auditors' Reports on Financial Statements'*. In particular, SAS 600 requires that the auditors' report states that the financial statements are the responsibility of the directors (para 3) and there must be a statement that the audit has been planned and performed so as to obtain reasonable reassurance that the financial statements are free from material misstatement, whether caused by fraud, or other irregularity, or error (para 4).

Duty to detect and report fraud   As noted above, an auditor's task is to conduct the audit in a manner which provides reasonable reassurance that material misstatements in financial documents will be detected: see *Barings plc v Coopers & Lybrand* [1997] 1 BCLC 427.

   There are a number of old authorities which establish that an auditor is not an insurer: see *Re London and General Bank Ltd (No 2)* [1895] 2 Ch 673; nor is he required to approach his work with suspicion or with a foregone conclusion that something is wrong; and he is justified, in the absence of suspicions, in believing employees in whom confidence is placed by the company: *Re Kingston Cotton Mill Co (No 2)* [1896] 2 Ch 279; but he should approach his work with an inquiring mind (see Lord Denning in *Fomento (Sterling Area) Ltd v Selsdon Fountain Pen Co Ltd* [1958] 1 WLR 45 at 61); and, once put on inquiry, he is under a duty to get to the bottom of the matter in question: *Re Thomas Gerrard & Son Ltd* [1967] 2 All ER 525. These long-established authorities must be treated with some caution, for the courts are likely to expect higher standards from today's, highly paid, professional auditors, but they do provide some basic pointers as to what is expected of auditors.

   Where a company's auditors discover that a senior employee has been defrauding the company on a massive scale, and that employee is in a position to continue doing so, the auditors would normally have a duty to report the discovery to the management immediately, not merely when rendering their report; and if the management are implicated in the wrongdoing, the auditors would have to report directly to a third party without the management's knowledge or consent. The relevant considerations would include the extent of material gain or loss arising from the fraud, whether it was likely to affect a large number of persons, and the extent to which non-disclosure would enable the fraud or irregularity to be repeated in the future: see *Sasea Finance Ltd v KPMG* [2000] 1 BCLC 236.

   For auditors of insurance companies, banks, building societies etc, there are miscellaneous statutory obligations to report directly to the relevant regulator as well as to the members. These obligations will arise in future under the Financial

Services and Markets Act 2000 (once it is fully in force); and regulations will be made under FSMA 2000, ss 342, 343 prescribing the circumstances in which an auditor must communicate matters to the Financial Services Authority.

S 235(1), (2)

As to those entitled to copies of the auditors' report, see s 238; as to the obligation to deliver the report to the registrar of companies, see s 242; as to the obligation to lay the report before the general meeting, see s 241; as to the reference to laying the report before the members in cases where the company has elected to dispense with laying accounts and reports before the general meeting, see s 252(3);

As to the obligation to prepare individual company accounts, see s 226; as to the obligation to prepare group accounts, see s 227; as to the auditors' duty to investigate, see s 237. Additional requirements as to the information which must be stated in the auditors' report are set out in s 237. Where the auditors' report is qualified (as defined in s 271(3)), further information is required if the company proposes to make a distribution, see s 271.

Primary obligation　When a firm of accountants accepts instructions to audit the accounts of a company for a fiscal year, its primary obligation is within a reasonable time to exercise an appropriate level of skill and care in reporting to the company's members on the accounts of the company, stating, in their opinion, whether the accounts of the company give a true and fair view of the company's financial affairs: see *Sasea Finance Ltd v KPMG* [2000] 1 BCLC 236 at 241.

Duty of care　One of the most contentious issues of recent years has been the extent of any duty of care owed by the company's auditors to the company, the shareholders and others who read and rely on the audited accounts. While there is much case law on the matter involving auditors (and other professionals), the general trend is a reluctance to find that a professional adviser owes a common law duty of care to a non-client: see *Bank of Credit and Commerce International (Overseas) Ltd v Price Waterhouse* [1998] BCC 617 at 636, per Sir Brian Neill; *BDG Roof-Bond v Douglas* [2000] 1 BCLC 401 at 420, per Park J.

The obligations of auditors may arise in contract (a duty to exercise reasonable care and skill in performing their contractual obligations) and in tort; and where obligations exist in contract and tort, there may be limitation advantages in pursuing one rather than the other course of action: see *Henderson v Merrett Syndicates Ltd* [1994] 3 All ER 506, HL.

Two approaches　In tort, a duty of care may arise under two different but interrelated approaches: (i) because of an assumption of responsibility for the task/advice in question; or (ii) because of meeting the threefold test established in *Caparo Industries plc v Dickman* [1990] 1 All ER 568.

An assumption of responsibility for the task/advice in question　This approach involves applying the line of authority as to the assumption of responsibility derived from *Hedley Byrne & Co Ltd v Heller & Partners Ltd* [1963] 2 All ER 575, which assumption rests upon a relationship between the parties, which may be general or specific to the particular transaction, and which may or may not be contractual in nature: *Henderson v Merrett Syndicates Ltd* [1994] 3 All ER 506 at 520, HL, per Lord Goff. Whether there is such an assumption of responsibility is a matter to be considered objectively: *Electra Private Equity Partners v KPMG Peat Marwick* [2001] 1 BCLC 589; and on the issue of assumption of responsibility, see *Henderson v Merrett Syndicates Ltd* [1994] 3 All ER 506 at 518–521; *Williams v Natural Life Health Foods Ltd* [1998] 1 BCLC 689; *Peach Publishing Ltd v Slater & Co* [1998] BCC 139.

Meeting the threefold test established in *Caparo*   Here, there must be a reasonable foreseeability of damage, a relationship of sufficient 'proximity' between the party owing the duty and the party to whom it is owed and the imposition of the duty of care contended for should be just and reasonable in all the circumstances: see *Caparo Industries plc v Dickman* [1990] 1 All ER 568 at 573–574, per Lord Bridge. The 'just and reasonable' consideration is not a distinct requirement where the case falls clearly within the *Hedley Byrne* principle for, in those instances, the assumption of responsibility itself justifies the imposition of liability. It is a necessary component of the *Caparo* approach, however, in order to prevent foreseeability alone giving rise to an indeterminate liability for an indeterminate time to an indeterminate class.

Where the parties have a contractual or 'almost contractual' relationship (for example, a client relationship) and so fall clearly within the *Hedley Byrne* principle, the matter is relatively straightforward: see *Henderson v Merrett Syndicates Ltd* [1994] 3 All ER 506, HL; also *Andrew v Kounnis Freeman* [1999] 2 BCLC 641. Most disputes arise where there is no relationship between the auditor and the claimant but the claimant alleges that the parties are sufficiently proximate to give rise to a duty of care on the part of the auditor, applying the threefold test in *Caparo*.

In *Caparo*, Lord Oliver identified the circumstances which should exist in order to establish the necessary relationship of proximity between the person claiming to be owed the duty (the advisee) and the adviser:

'... (1) the advice is required for a purpose, whether particularly specified or generally described, which is made known, either actually or inferentially, to the adviser at the time the advice is given; (2) the adviser knows, either actually or inferentially, that his advice will be communicated to the advisee, either specifically or as a member of an ascertainable class, in order that it should be used by the advisee for that purpose; (3) it is known, either actually or inferentially, that the advice so communicated is likely to be acted upon by the advisee for that purpose without independent inquiry; and (4) it is so acted upon by the advisee to his detriment.'

([1990] 1 All ER 568 at 589.)

Further guidance was provided by Sir Brian Neill in *Bank of Credit and Commerce International (Overseas) Ltd v Price Waterhouse* [1998] BCC 617 at 634–635, who thought the factors to be taken into account would include:

'(a) the precise relationship between (to use convenient terms) the adviser and the advisee. This may be a general relationship or a special relationship which has come into existence for the purpose of a particular transaction. . . . there may be an important difference between the cases where the adviser and the advisee are dealing at arm's length and cases where they are acting 'on the same side of the fence'.

(b) the precise circumstances in which the advice or information or other material came into existence. Any contract or other relationship with a third party will be relevant.

(c) the precise circumstances in which the advice or information or other material was communicated to the advisee, and for what purpose or purposes,

and whether the communication was made by the adviser or by a third party. It will be necessary to consider the purpose or purposes of the communication both as seen by the adviser and as seen by the advisee, and the degree of reliance which the adviser intended or should reasonably have anticipated would be placed on its accuracy by the advisee, and the reliance in fact placed on it.
(d) the presence or absence of other advisers on whom the advisee would or could rely. ...
(e) the opportunity, if any, given to the adviser to issue a disclaimer.'

Some authorities In considering below the authorities which provide some guidance on when a duty of care arises (many of which have been strike out applications), it is important to bear in mind that:

'... the liability of professional advisers, including auditors, for failure to provide accurate information or correct advice can, truly, be said to be in a state of transition or development. As the House of Lords has pointed out, repeatedly, this is an area in which the law is developing pragmatically and incrementally. It is pre-eminently an area in which the legal result is sensitive to the facts ...'

(*Coulthard v Neville Russell* [1998] 1 BCLC 143 at 155, per Chadwick J.)

Duties to shareholders as a body An auditor's statutory duty to prepare accounts is owed to the body of shareholders as a whole, the purpose for which accounts are prepared and audited being to enable the shareholders as a body to exercise informed control of the company: *Caparo Industries plc v Dickman* [1990] 1 All ER 568.

Duties to individual shareholders Auditors owe no duty of care to a member of the public at large who relies on the audited accounts to buy shares; or to an individual shareholder in the company who wishes to buy more shares in the company, since an individual shareholder is in no better position than a member of the public at large: *Caparo Industries plc v Dickman* [1990] 1 All ER 568; although a duty of care to potential investors may be assumed: see *ADT Ltd v BDO Binder Hamlyn* [1996] BCC 808; also *Electra Private Equity Partners v KPMG Peat Marwick* [2001] 1 BCLC 589.

Auditors owe no duty of care to possible take-over bidders: *Caparo Industries plc v Dickman* [1990] 1 All ER 568; see also *James McNaughton Paper Group Ltd v Hicks Anderson & Co* [1991] BCLC 163. The position may be different where representations are made after an identified bidder has emerged, see *Morgan Crucible Co plc v Hill Samuel Bank Ltd* [1991] BCLC 18; *Galoo Ltd v Bright Grahame Murray* [1994] 2 BCLC 492.

Duties to creditors Auditors owe no duty of care to existing or future creditors who simply extend credit on the strength of the audited accounts: *Al Saudi Banque v Clark Pixley* [1989] 3 All ER 361; *Berg Sons & Co Ltd v Mervyn Hampton Adams* [1993] BCLC 1045.

Duties to regulatory authorities Accountants who carry out specific reporting obligations under a statutory requirement to do so owe a duty of care to the regulatory authority to whom they report: see *Law Society v KPMG Peat Marwick* [2000] 4 All ER 540; likewise, auditors may assume a duty of care to a regulatory authority: see *Andrew v Kounnis Freeman* [1999] 2 BCLC 641.

Duties to a parent company It is arguable that auditors of a subsidiary company may owe a duty of care directly to a parent company arising from the circumstances in which work is done and information is supplied to the parent company and its auditors for the purpose of preparing consolidated group accounts; and that duty would include a duty to conduct their audit in such a way that material misstatements in financial documents would be detected: see *Barings plc v Coopers & Lybrand* [1997] 1 BCLC 427.

Causation   The alleged breach of duty must be the effective or dominant cause of the claimants' loss as opposed to merely the occasion for the loss. In determining that issue, the court applies its common sense to the issue: *Galoo Ltd v Bright Grahame Murray* [1994] 2 BCLC 492 (losses arising from continued trading were not caused, in the sense in which 'caused' is used in law, by a defective audit); cf *Sasea Finance Ltd v KPMG* [2000] 1 BCLC 236 (breach of the duty to 'blow the whistle' on fraudulent and dishonest activities of senior staff arguably caused continued losses brought about by such frauds).

Where the payment of improper dividends is the natural and probable result of the false picture which the auditors have allowed the accounts to present, the auditors are liable for the amount of the dividends: *Re Thomas Gerrard & Son Ltd* [1967] 2 All ER 525 (auditors aware of discrepancies but failed to investigate further); *Re London and General Bank (No 2)* [1895] 2 Ch 673 (auditors omitted information from report to shareholders).

Limiting liability   The ability of auditors to limit their liability with respect to their statutory obligations under the companies legislation is restricted by s 310 but they are entitled to apply to the court for relief under s 727. Audit firms may incorporate as a company with limited liability or they may register as a limited liability partnership under the Limited Liability Partnerships Act 2000.

Special auditors' reports   Where a small or medium-sized company delivers abbreviated accounts (and, in the case of a small company, is not exempt from audit under ss 249A or 249AA), a special auditors' report is required under s 247B; as to the contents of that report, see s 247B(2), (3). Where a public listed company is entitled to send summary financial statements to its members under s 251, the auditors must provide a statement as required by s 251(4)(b).

Duties as accountants   Accountants who advise directors as to how they, as directors, should perform their duties (as opposed to accountants acting as auditors conducting the statutory duties relating to audit) may accept a responsibility for that particular task and so owe a duty of care to those directors: see *Coulthard v Neville Russell* [1998] 1 BCLC 143.

An accountant appointed by the directors of a company to value its shares for the purpose of setting the price at which shares owned by a shareholder were to be compulsorily acquired pursuant to the company's articles, owed a duty of care to the shareholder in the conduct of the valuation: *Killick v PricewaterhouseCoopers* [2001] 1 BCLC 65.

236. Signature of auditors' report

(1)   The auditors' report shall state the names of the auditors and be signed by them.

(2) Every copy of the auditors' report which is laid before the company in general meeting, or which is otherwise circulated, published or issued, shall state the names of the auditors.

(3) The copy of the auditors' report which is delivered to the registrar shall state the names of the auditors and be signed by them.

(4) If a copy of the auditors' report—

(a) is laid before the company, or otherwise circulated, published or issued, without the required statement of the auditors' names, or

(b) is delivered to the registrar without the required statement of the auditors' names or without being signed as required by this section,

the company and every officer of it who is in default is guilty of an offence and liable to a fine.

(5) References in this section to signature by the auditors are, where the office of auditor is held by a body corporate or partnership, to signature in the name of the body corporate or partnership by a person authorised to sign on its behalf.

General note

This provision is similar to s 234A with respect to the signing of the directors' report, see note to that section.

This provision also applies to any special auditors' report under s 247B: s 247B(4).

237. Duties of auditors

(1) A company's auditors shall, in preparing their report, carry out such investigations as will enable them to form an opinion as to—

(a) whether proper accounting records have been kept by the company and proper returns adequate for their audit have been received from branches not visited by them, and

(b) whether the company's individual accounts are in agreement with the accounting records and returns.

(2) If the auditors are of opinion that proper accounting records have not been kept, or that proper returns adequate for their audit have not been received from branches not visited by them, or if the company's individual accounts are not in agreement with the accounting records and returns, the auditors shall state that fact in their report.

(3) If the auditors fail to obtain all the information and explanations which, to the best of their knowledge and belief, are necessary for the purposes of their audit, they shall state that fact in their report.

(4) If the requirements of Schedule 6 (disclosure of information: emoluments and other benefits of directors and others) are not complied with in the annual accounts, the auditors shall include in their report, so far as they are reasonably able to do so, a statement giving the required particulars.

(4A) If the directors of the company have taken advantage of the exemption conferred by section 248 (exemption for small and medium-sized groups from the need to prepare group accounts) and in the auditors' opinion they were not entitled so to do, the auditors shall state that fact in their report.

General note

The specific obligations regarding investigations by the auditors and as to the contents of their report which are imposed by this provision are additional to the general duty to report as required by s 235(2) and to carry out such investigations as are necessary to enable them to report in those terms; see the note to that provision. As to the auditors' rights to information, see s 389A(1); as to their rights to attend company meetings, see s 390.

S 237(1)

The directors are obliged to maintain proper accounting records as required by s 221; 'individual accounts' are defined in s 226.

S 237(2)–(4)

These provisions impose obligations on the auditors to indicate areas of non-compliance by the directors; and, in the case of sub-s (4), an obligation on the auditors to provide the information omitted by the directors.

S 237(4A)

This obligation ensures that directors cannot easily evade their obligation to prepare group accounts under s 227.

Where directors file abbreviated individual accounts, the special auditors' report under s 247B must state that the company is entitled to deliver abbreviated accounts: see s 247B(2).

PUBLICATION OF ACCOUNTS AND REPORTS

238. Persons entitled to receive copies of accounts and reports

(1)   A copy of the company's annual accounts, together with a copy of the directors' report for that financial year and of the auditors' report on those accounts, shall be sent to—

   (a) every member of the company,

   (b) every holder of the company's debentures, and

   (c) every person who is entitled to receive notice of general meetings,

not less than 21 days before the date of the meeting at which copies of those documents are to be laid in accordance with section 241.

(2)   Copies need not be sent—

   (a) to a person who is not entitled to receive notices of general meetings and of whose address the company is unaware, or

   (b) to more than one of the joint holders of shares or debentures none of whom is entitled to receive such notices, or

   (c) in the case of joint holders of shares or debentures some of whom are, and some not, entitled to receive such notices, to those who are not so entitled.

(3)   In the case of a company not having a share capital, copies need not be sent to anyone who is not entitled to receive notices of general meetings of the company.

(4)   If copies are sent less than 21 days before the date of the meeting, they shall, notwithstanding that fact, be deemed to have been duly sent if it is so agreed by all the members entitled to attend and vote at the meeting.

(4A) References in this section to sending to any person copies of a company's annual accounts, of the directors' report and of the auditors' report include references to using electronic communications for sending copies of those documents to such address as may for the time being be notified to the company by that person for that purpose.

(4B) For the purposes of this section copies of those documents are also to be treated as sent to a person where—

   (a) the company and that person have agreed to his having access to the documents on a web site (instead of their being sent to him);

   (b) the documents are documents to which that agreement applies; and

   (c) that person is notified, in a manner for the time being agreed for the purpose between him and the company, of—

      (i)   the publication of the documents on a web site;

      (ii) the address of that web site; and

      (iii) the place on that web site where the documents may be accessed, and how they may be accessed.

(4C) For the purposes of this section documents treated in accordance with subsection (4B) as sent to any person are to be treated as sent to him not less than 21 days before the date of a meeting if, and only if—

   (a) the documents are published on the web site throughout a period beginning at least 21 days before the date of the meeting and ending with the conclusion of the meeting; and

   (b) the notification given for the purposes of paragraph (c) of that subsection is given not less than 21 days before the date of the meeting.

(4D) Nothing in subsection (4C) shall invalidate the proceedings of a meeting where—

(a) any documents that are required to be published as mentioned in paragraph (a) of that subsection are published for a part, but not all, of the period mentioned in that paragraph; and

(b) the failure to publish those documents throughout that period is wholly attributable to circumstances which it would not be reasonable to have expected the company to prevent or avoid.

(4E) A company may, notwithstanding any provision to the contrary in its articles, take advantage of any of subsections (4A) to (4D).

(5) If default is made in complying with this section, the company and every officer of it who is in default is guilty of an offence and liable to a fine.

(6) Where copies are sent out under this section over a period of days, references elsewhere in this Act to the day on which copies are sent out shall be construed as references to the last day of that period.

General note

While every member of a company is entitled to this information, shareholders in a public listed company may agree to receive summary financial statements instead: see s 251. Where a private company elects to dispense with the laying of accounts and reports before the general meeting, there may be additional obligations as to what must be sent to members under this provision: see s 252(3).

In addition to the entitlement established by this provision, s 239 provides that a member or debenture holder may demand a copy of the accounts etc under that provision; equally, copies of the accounts can be obtained by anyone from the public registry, Companies House, although what is delivered to the registrar of companies in the case of small and medium-sized companies may not be the same as the accounts and reports prepared for the members: see exemptions in ss 246, 246A.

S 238(1)–(3)

Documents to be sent   This provision identifies the documents which must be sent (and see below as to electronic communication) and the persons entitled to receive them: (i) the annual accounts, defined by s 262(1) as individual and group accounts, if required (see ss 226, 227); (ii) the directors' report (see s 234); (iii) the auditors' report on the company's accounts (see s 235), unless the company is exempt from the audit requirement under ss 249A(1) or 249AA(1), in which case no auditors' report is required: s 249E(1)(a); where the company is a charity and, though exempt from an audit, a report is required on the accounts from a reporting accountant under s 249A(2), that report must be sent to the members: s 249E(2)(b).

Persons entitled   These documents must be sent to: (a) every member (as determined by s 22); (b) every holder of the company's debentures (defined s 744) ('debenture', in this instance, being used in the sense of a holder of securities rather than a mortgagee of the company's property); and (c) every person entitled to notice of general meetings which, under Table A, reg 38, would include those entitled to a share in consequence of death or bankruptcy and the directors and the auditors. Somewhat superfluous exclusions are contained in sub-ss (2) and (3) for, even if excluded under these provisions, every member and debenture holder is entitled to demand a copy under the next section.

S 238(4)

The time period can be truncated with the consent of all members entitled to attend and vote at the meeting.

S 238(4A)

Electronic communication   This provision, and sub-ss (4B)–(4E), was inserted by the Companies Act 1985 (Electronic Communications) Order 2000, SI 2000/3373, art 12, as from 22 December 2000. The intention is to facilitate the electronic communication of these standard documents by a company to a member where the member has agreed to that method of communication; 'address' for this purpose is defined in s 262.

'Electronic communication' means the same as in the Electronic Communications Act 2000: s 744; 'electronic communication' means a communication transmitted (whether from one person to another, from one device to another or from a person to a device or vice versa): (a) by means of a telecommunication system (within the meaning of the Telecommunications Act 1984); or (b) by other means but while in an electronic form: Electronic Communications Act 2000, s 15.

Thus, these documents may be sent, for example, by fax or email and see sub-s (4B) as to the use of a website for these purposes.

S 238(4B)–(4D)

Documents sent electronically   Documents may be treated as sent to a person when they are published on a website. The company is not restricted to the use of the same web site on every occasion, but it must indicate the address of the site being used in each instance. In order to ensure that a member does not have to monitor a website, the company must notify him in the agreed manner when the documents are published on a web site. There is no requirement that that notification of publication be by electronic communication, it could be by post, but in practice it is likely to be by email.

Documents are treated as sent not less than 21 days before the meeting if, inter alia, the notification of publication under sub-s (4B)(c) is given not less than 21 days before the meeting; the time of that notification of publication must be determined in accordance with the company's articles. As noted above, that notification may be by electronic communication and the company's articles may make no provision as to when such notification is treated as given, in which case the matter might be dealt with as part of the agreement by the company and the member as to the use of electronic communications.

As to the future, Table A has been updated to make provision for the sending and receipt of notices by electronic communication, see regs 111–115 as amended by the Companies Act 1985 (Electronic Communications) Order 2000, SI 2000/3373, art 32(1), Sch 1, as from 22 December 2000 but Table A in that form will only apply to companies which have registered after that date and only in the circumstances set out in s 8 (cf s 369(4F)).

The information must be available on the web site throughout the notice period of 21 days before a meeting, subject to sub-s (4D) which condones any failure to publish which is *wholly* attributable to circumstances which it would not be reasonable to have expected the company to prevent or avoid. In other words, the failure to publish as required throughout the period must be due to some unavoidable failure of the technology rather than, say, a failure by the company to maintain the web site in a proper manner.

S 238(4E)

The articles and electronic communications This provision ensures that provisions in a company's articles (for example, references to sending documents by post) do not prevent a company from taking advantage of these powers. No doubt, when it is convenient to do so, companies will take the opportunity to update their articles to reflect the use of electronic communications. In the meantime, they may use these electronic methods, with the agreement of the individual member, and they do not need to adopt new articles to permit them to do so nor must they take steps to alter existing provisions which are restricted to paper communications. But incidental problems remain, such as noted above regarding the time when a notification of publication is given when the notification is by electronic communication, and best practice would be for companies to alter their articles to ensure that they have made comprehensive provision for all aspects of the use of electronic communications.

S 238(5)

As to penalties, see s 730, Sch 24; 'officer in default' is defined in s 730(5).

239. Right to demand copies of accounts and reports

(1) Any member of a company and any holder of a company's debentures is entitled to be furnished, on demand and without charge, with a copy of the company's last annual accounts and directors' report and a copy of the auditors' report on those accounts.

(2) The entitlement under this section is to a single copy of those documents, but that is in addition to any copy to which a person may be entitled under section 238.

(2A) Any obligation by virtue of subsection (1) to furnish a person with a document may be complied with by using electronic communications for sending that document to such address as may for the time being be notified to the company by that person for that purpose.

(2B) A company may, notwithstanding any provision to the contrary in its articles, take advantage of subsection (2A).

(3) If a demand under this section is not complied with within seven days, the company and every officer of it who is in default is guilty of an offence and liable to a fine and, for continued contravention, to a daily default fine.

(4)   If in proceedings for such an offence the issue arises whether a person had already been furnished with a copy of the relevant document under this section, it is for the defendant to prove that he had.

General note

This provision is generally irrelevant as far as public companies, certainly public listed companies, are concerned as they will provide anyone with copies of their last annual accounts and reports; and many larger companies make this information available on the company web site. The provision may be more useful in a private company although a member is entitled to the accounts and reports in any event under s 238. However, the penalties under sub-s (3) may be helpful in ensuring a speedy response to any request for information.

S 239(1)

Entitlement   The right is to a copy of the company's last annual accounts (including group accounts, where required); 'member' is defined by s 22; 'debentures' is defined by s 744. Where the company is exempt from the audit requirements under ss 249A(1) or 249AA(1), obviously, there is no right to a copy of an auditors' report: s 249E(1)(a); where the company is a charity and, though exempt from an audit, a report is required on the accounts from a reporting accountant under s 249A(2), that report may be demanded under this provision: s 249E(2)(b).

S 239(2A), (2B)

Electronic communication   These provisions were inserted by the Companies Act 1985 (Electronic Communications) Order 2000, SI 2000/3373, art 13, as from 22 December 2000. The company may provide the additional copy by electronic communication where the member has agreed to that method of communication; 'electronic communication' means the same as in the Electronic Communications Act 2000: s 744; and see the note to s 238(4A) below; 'address' for this purpose is defined in s 262. Provisions in a company's articles (for example, references to sending documents by post) do not prevent the company from taking advantage of these powers.

S 239(3)

As to penalties, see s 730, Sch 24; 'officer in default' is defined in s 730(5).

---

240. Requirements in connection with publication of accounts

(1)   If a company publishes any of its statutory accounts, they must be accompanied by the relevant auditors' report under section 235 or, as the case may be, the relevant report made for the purposes of section 249A(2).

(2)   A company which is required to prepare group accounts for a financial year shall not publish its statutory individual accounts for that year without also publishing with them its statutory group accounts.

(3)   If a company publishes non-statutory accounts, it shall publish with them a statement indicating—

    (a)   that they are not the company's statutory accounts,

    (b)   whether statutory accounts dealing with any financial year with which the non-statutory accounts purport to deal have been delivered to the registrar,

    (c)   whether the company's auditors have made a report under section 235 on the statutory accounts for any such financial year and, if no such report has been made, whether the company's reporting accountant has made a report for the purposes of section 249A(2) on the statutory accounts for any financial year, and

    (d)   whether any auditors' report so made was qualified or contained a statement under section 237(2) or (3) (accounting records or returns inadequate, accounts not agreeing with records and returns or failure to obtain necessary information and explanations)or whether any report made for the purposes of section 249A(2) was qualified;

and it shall not publish with the non-statutory accounts any auditors' report under section 235 or any report made for the purposes of section 249A(2).

(4)   For the purposes of this section a company shall be regarded as publishing a document if it publishes, issues or circulates it or otherwise makes it available for public inspection in a manner calculated to invite members of the public generally, or any class of members of the public, to read it.

(5)   References in this section to a company's statutory accounts are to its individual or group accounts for a financial year as required to be delivered to the registrar under section 242; and references to the publication by a company of 'non-statutory accounts' are to the publication of—

    (a)   any balance sheet or profit and loss account relating to, or purporting to deal with, a financial year of the company, or

    (b)   an account in any form purporting to be a balance sheet or profit and loss account for the group consisting of the company and its subsidiary undertakings relating to, or purporting to deal with, a financial year of the company,

otherwise than as part of the company's statutory accounts.

(6)   A company which contravenes any provision of this section, and any officer of it who is in default, is guilty of an offence and liable to a fine.

General note

The operation of this provision is modified in so far as it applies to unlimited companies, see s 254(4); references to the auditors' report under s 235 include as appropriate references to the special auditors' report required in some cases by s 247B: s 247B(5).

S 240(1), (2)

Publication requirements   Where a company chooses to publish (defined sub-s (4)) its statutory accounts, ie those accounts required to be delivered to the registrar of companies (see sub-s (5)), the accounts must be accompanied by the auditors' report (or, if required, that of a reporting accountant under s 249A(2)). Likewise, if a company chooses to publish its individual accounts while required to prepare group accounts, it must publish the group accounts as well. However, a company could publish its group accounts without including its individual accounts.

S 240(3)

Additional statement required   There is a prohibition on the auditors' report appearing with any non-statutory accounts, defined sub-s (5). This is to ensure that investors and others are not faced with two sets of accounts over similar periods, one statutory, one non-statutory, each supported by an auditors' report.

The position becomes more complicated now that companies are publishing financial information on web sites. For example, a company may publish on the same site the audited accounts and reports and additional financial information and there is a risk that those using the site may consider that the auditors' report extends to that additional information as well as the statutory accounts.

S 240(4)

This definition does include material published on a company's web site so care must be taken not to publish non-statutory accounts in that way without complying with sub-s (3).

S 240(5)

Any additional accounts in euros delivered to the registrar of companies under s 242B are statutory accounts for this purpose: s 242B(4).

Definition of non-statutory accounts   The definition of 'non-statutory accounts', because of the requirement that they relate to a financial year, does not extend to preliminary announcements of annual results or interim results published by listed companies which are neither statutory accounts requiring the publication of the auditors' report under sub-s (1) nor non-statutory accounts requiring compliance with sub-s (3). However, where interim results set out the previous year's results (and so purport to deal with a financial year of the company), they could be regarded as non-statutory accounts so requiring compliance with sub-s (3).

The definition of non-statutory accounts varies depending on whether the company is an individual company or a member of a group, sub-s (5)(a) being restricted to balance sheets or profit and loss accounts whereas sub-s (5)(b) applies to any document purporting to be such a document which has the effect of encompassing a greater range of documents.

This provision does not apply to summary financial statements provided under s 251: s 251(7).

S 240(6)

As to penalties, see s 730, Sch 24; 'officer in default' is defined in s 730(5).

LAYING AND DELIVERING OF ACCOUNTS AND REPORTS

241. Accounts and reports to be laid before company in general meeting

(1)   The directors of a company shall in respect of each financial year lay before the company in general meeting copies of the company's annual accounts, the directors' report and the auditors' report on those accounts.

(2)   If the requirements of subsection (1) are not complied with before the end of the period allowed for laying and delivering accounts and reports, every person who immediately before the end of that period was a director of the company is guilty of an offence and liable to a fine and, for continued contravention, to a daily default fine.

(3)   It is a defence for a person charged with such an offence to prove that he took all reasonable steps for securing that those requirements would be complied with before the end of that period.

(4)   It is not a defence to prove that the documents in question were not in fact prepared as required by this Part.

General note

Private companies To facilitate private companies which rarely conduct business through general meetings, a private company may elect by elective resolution (s 379A) to dispense with the requirement imposed by this provision for the laying of the accounts and reports before a general meeting: see s 252.

S 241(1)

The statutory obligation is to lay the accounts etc before the general meeting and there is no requirement that the accounts be debated or approved by that meeting although that is the customary practice; likewise, there is no specific requirement that they be laid before the annual general meeting although that too is the customary practice.

Where the company is exempt from the audit requirements under ss 249A or 249AA, there is, of course, no requirement to lay a copy of the auditors' report: s 249E(1)(b); where the company is a charity and, though exempt from an audit, a report is required on the accounts from a reporting accountant under s 249A(2), that report must be laid under this provision: s 249E(2)(b).

A company's 'annual accounts' are defined by s 262 to include individual accounts and group accounts, if required; as to the directors' report, see s 234; as to the auditors' report, see s 235.

S 241(2)

The period allowed for laying the accounts before the general meeting is determined by s 244; as to penalties, see s 730, Sch 24.

S 241(3), (4)

While there is a defence of having taken all reasonable steps etc, sub-s (4) is intended to rule out the defence that the directors gave instructions to another to prepare accounts, which instructions were not carried out, with the result that no accounts were prepared and therefore cannot be laid: see *Stockdale v Coulson* [1974] 1 WLR 1192.

242. Accounts and reports to be delivered to the registrar

(1)   The directors of a company shall in respect of each financial year deliver to the registrar a copy of the company's annual accounts together with a copy of the directors' report for that year and a copy of the auditors' report on those accounts.

... If any document comprised in those accounts or reports is in a language other than English then, subject to section 710B(6) (delivery of certain Welsh documents without a translation), the directors shall annex to the copy of that document delivered a translation of it into English, certified in the prescribed manner to be a correct translation.

(2)   If the requirements of subsection (1) are not complied with before the end of the period allowed for laying and delivering accounts and reports, every person who immediately before the end of that period was a director of the company is guilty of an offence and liable to a fine and, for continued contravention, to a daily default fine.

(3)   Further, if the directors of the company fail to make good the default within 14 days after the service of a notice on them requiring compliance, the court may on the application of any member or creditor of the company or of the registrar, make an order directing the directors (or any of them) to make good the default within such time as may be specified in the order.

The court's order may provide that all costs of and incidental to the application shall be borne by the directors.

(4)   It is a defence for a person charged with an offence under this section to prove that he took all reasonable steps for securing that the requirements of subsection (1) would be complied with before the end of the period allowed for laying and delivering accounts and reports.

(5)   It is not a defence in any proceedings under this section to prove that the documents in question were not in fact prepared as required by this Part.

General note

Non-compliance with the requirements of this provision is a common basis for a finding of unfitness warranting the disqualification of a director under the Company Directors Disqualification Act 1986: see *Secretary of State for Trade and Industry v Ettinger, Re Swift 736 Ltd* [1993] BCLC 896; *Secretary of State for Trade and Industry v Van Hengel* [1995] 1 BCLC 545.

Any documents delivered to the registrar of companies under this provision must be gazetted by him: s 711(1)(k).

Accounts in sterling   There is no specific requirement that the accounts delivered be in sterling but the requirement that the accounts give a true and fair view of the company's affairs (ss 226, 227) would normally require that they be in sterling. For companies with extensive international activities, or which deal in a commodity commonly denominated in a foreign currency, or whose assets and shareholders reside overseas and to whom dividends are paid in a currency other than sterling, it may be appropriate for their accounts to be in another currency.

S 242(1)

Deliver the accounts   The obligation to deliver these documents to the registrar of companies falls on the company's directors; and, as the obligation is 'to deliver' the accounts, the documents must reach the registrar and it is not sufficient simply to show that they were posted; 'company' is defined in s 735; 'annual accounts' is defined in s 262 and includes group accounts, where required; as to the directors' report, see s 234; as to the auditors' report, see s 235.

Exceptions   The general obligation is to deliver accounts and a directors' report and an auditors' report but there are numerous exceptions which will enable a company to deliver more limited information (while still preparing more extensive information for their members):

(1)   A small company (see ss 247, 247A) may deliver only a balance sheet which complies with the requirements of Sch 8A and takes advantage of the exemptions in s 246(6) and there is no requirement to deliver a profit and loss account or a directors' report: s 246(5). Such accounts are described as 'abbreviated accounts': see s 247B(1)(a).

The position as to whether an auditors' report is required depends on whether the company has taken advantage of the exemption from audit:

(a)   Where a small company entitled to deliver abbreviated accounts is also exempt from the audit requirements under ss 249A(1) or 249AA(1), there is no requirement to deliver a copy of an auditors' report, (s 249E(1)(b)); where the small company is a charity and, though exempt from an audit, a report is required on the accounts from a reporting accountant under s 249A(2), that report must be delivered under this provision: s 249E(2)(b).

    (b)   Where a small company entitled to deliver abbreviated accounts chooses not to take advantage of the exemption from audit conferred by s 249A or s 249AA, it is required to deliver a special auditors' report under s 247B(2) and the audit report under s 235 need not be delivered but items from it may need to be included in the special report under s 247B(2): s 247B(3).

(2)   A small company may deliver full accounts prepared in accordance with s 246(2) (rather than the balance sheet only under s 246(5)), but which take advantage of the exemptions in s 246(3), (4) and (6); and where advantage is taken of the exemption in s 246(6), these accounts too are described as 'abbreviated accounts' (see s 247B(1)(a)); and the position as to whether an auditors' report must be delivered is as set out at paras 1(a) and 1(b) above. A directors' report must be delivered.

(3)   A medium-sized company may deliver accounts which take advantage of the limited exemptions in s 246A(3); in that case, these accounts too are described as 'abbreviated accounts' (see s 247B(1)(a)); and the company is required to deliver a special auditors' report under s 247B(2) instead of the auditor's report under s 235 but items from the auditors' report may need to be included in the special report under s 247B(2): s 247B(3). A directors' report must be delivered.

(4)   A dormant company must deliver accounts to the registrar but it is treated as entitled to the exemptions available to small companies in s 246 as set out above: s 249E(1A).

(5)   An unlimited company (defined s 1(2)(c)) is exempt from the requirement to deliver accounts, a directors' report and an auditors' report if it meets the requirements set out in s 254.

(6)   A parent company which has subsidiary undertakings excluded from the consolidated accounts must append the accounts and auditors' reports relating to the excluded undertakings to the accounts delivered to the registrar in the circumstances set out in s 243.

Language other than English   A translation is required if the accounts etc to be delivered are not in English so, for example, a company which trades exclusively in Russia cannot file its accounts in Russian. Where the company's memorandum of association states that the registered office is in Wales (alone), it is for the registrar of companies to provide a translation (save where the company is a listed public company): see The Companies (Welsh Language Forms and Documents) Regulations 1994, SI 1994/117, regs 4(2), (3).

S 242(2), (4)

Penalties   The offence can either be non-delivery of the required information or a failure to attach the required translation. The period for laying and delivering accounts is determined by s 244. Subject to any defence available under sub-s (4), the offence is committed merely by being a director at the particular time and, as the penalty is a daily default fine, the result could be a substantial penalty; as to penalties, see s 730, Sch 24. It is also likely that the company will incur a penalty under s 242A.

S 242(3)

It would appear that a notice of non-compliance under this provision might be served by a member or creditor or the registrar of companies.

S 242(4), (5)

See note to s 241(4), above.

242A. Civil penalty for failure to deliver accounts

(1)   Where the requirements of section 242(1) are not complied with before the end of the period allowed for laying and delivering accounts and reports, the company is liable to a civil penalty.

This is in addition to any liability of the directors under section 242.

(2)   The amount of the penalty is determined by reference to the length of the period between the end of the period allowed for laying and delivering accounts and reports and the day on which the requirements are complied with, and whether the company is a public or private company, as follows—

Length of period	Public company	Private company
Not more than 3 months	£500	£100
More than 3 months but not more than 6 months	£1,000	£250
More than 6 months but not more than 12 months	£2,000	£500
More than 12 months	£5,000	£1,000

(3)   The penalty may be recovered by the registrar and shall be paid by him into the Consolidated Fund.

(4)   It is not a defence in proceedings under this section to prove that the documents in question were not in fact prepared as required by this Part.

General note

This provision came into effect on 1 July 1992 following concerns about the large numbers of companies which, at that time, had failed to comply with the delivery requirements in s 242. Following the introduction of penalties, the registrar of companies operated a three-day concession system in response to the claim that companies were unfamiliar with the Late Filing Penalties system. Given that the system is now well established, that concession has been withdrawn with respect to accounts delivered late on or after 1 October 2000.

Striking off the register   In addition to the liability imposed by this provision, a company which fails to deliver its accounts and reports to the registrar of companies as required may find that the company is deemed to be defunct and struck off the register under s 652. Restoration of the company to the register (under s 653) will normally be conditional on the company's public record being brought up to date. As the accounts are necessarily late, the company will incur penalties under this provision when bringing its public record up to date for that purpose. The directors may also face prosecution under s 242.

S 242A(1)

The period for laying and delivering accounts is determined by s 244. The liability under this provision falls on the company although the obligation to deliver accounts under s 242(1) is on the directors. The offence is one of strict liability.

S 242A(4)

See note to s 241(4).

242B. Delivery and publication of accounts in ECUs

(1)   The amounts set out in the annual accounts of a company may also be shown in the same accounts translated into ECUs.

(2)   When complying with section 242, the directors of a company may deliver to the registrar an additional copy of the company's annual accounts in which the amounts have been translated into ECUs.

(3)   In both cases—

   (a) the amounts must have been translated at the relevant exchange rate prevailing on the balance sheet date, and

   (b) that rate must be disclosed in the notes to the accounts.

(4)   For the purposes of section 240 any additional copy of the company's annual accounts delivered to the registrar under subsection (2) shall be treated as statutory accounts of the company and, in the case of such a copy, references in section 240 to the auditors' report under section 235 shall be read as references to the auditors' report on the annual accounts of which it is a copy.

(5)   In this section—

   'ECU' means a unit with a value equal to the value of the unit known as the ecu used in the European Monetary System, and

   'relevant exchange rate' means the rate of exchange used for translating the value of the ecu for the purposes of that System.

General note

This provision has been rendered redundant with the replacement of the ecu by the euro. As the euro (unlike the ecu) is a currency, it may be used in any accounts, like any other currency, without requiring special statutory authorisation; see note to s 242, 'Accounts in sterling', above.

---

243. Accounts of subsidiary undertakings to be appended in certain cases

(1)   The following provisions apply where at the end of the financial year a parent company has as a subsidiary undertaking—

  (a)   a body corporate incorporated outside Great Britain which does not have an established place of business in Great Britain, or

  (b)   an unincorporated undertaking,

which is excluded from consolidation in accordance with section 229(4)(undertaking with activities different from the undertakings included in the consolidation).

(2)   There shall be appended to the copy of the company's annual accounts delivered to the registrar in accordance with section 242 a copy of the undertaking's latest individual accounts and, if it is a parent undertaking, its latest group accounts.

   If the accounts appended are required by law to be audited, a copy of the auditors' report shall also be appended.

(3)   The accounts must be for a period ending not more than twelve months before the end of the financial year for which the parent company's accounts are made up.

(4)   ... If any document required to be appended is in a language other than English then, subject to section 710B(6) (delivery of certain Welsh documents without a translation), the directors shall annex to the copy of that document delivered a translation of it into English, certified in the prescribed manner to be a correct translation.

(5)   The above requirements are subject to the following qualifications—

  (a)   an undertaking is not required to prepare for the purposes of this section accounts which would not otherwise be prepared, and if no accounts satisfying the above requirements are prepared none need be appended;

  (b)   a document need not be appended if it would not otherwise be required to be published, or made available for public inspection, anywhere in the world, but in that case the reason for not appending it shall be stated in a note to the company's accounts;

  (c)   where an undertaking and all its subsidiary undertakings are excluded from consolidation in accordance with section 229(4), the accounts of such of the subsidiary undertakings of that undertaking as are included in its consolidated group accounts need not be appended.

(6)   Subsections (2) to (4) of section 242 (penalties,&c in case of default) apply in relation to the requirements of this section as they apply in relation to the requirements of subsection (1) of that section.

S 243(1), (5)

Subsidiary undertaking excluded from consolidation   A parent company is generally required to prepare group accounts reflecting the consolidated position of the parent and its subsidiary undertakings: s 227; but it is possible to exclude certain subsidiary undertakings from those consolidated accounts including subsidiary undertakings whose activities are so different as to render their inclusion incompatible with the obligation to give a true and fair view: s 229(4).

This provision requires that the accounts of such a subsidiary, although it is excluded from the consolidation, be delivered to the registrar of companies under sub-s (2). In practice, it is rare for a subsidiary to be excluded from a consolidation in reliance on s 229(4). It would be exceptional, therefore, for this provision to apply and, even when it does apply, the obligation to append the accounts and reports may be negated by the very wide exceptions in sub-s (5).

A 'parent company' is defined in s 736; 'subsidiary undertaking' in s 258, Sch 10A; and the meaning of an established place of business is considered in the note to s 691, below.

S 243(2)

The requirement is that the accounts and reports be appended to the accounts delivered to the registrar of companies as opposed to the accounts laid before the shareholders so the members would not receive this information. This requirement is subject to the very wide exceptions in sub-s (5).

S 243(4)

Where the company's memorandum of association states that the registered office is in Wales (alone), it is for the registrar of companies to provide a translation (save where the company is a listed public company): see The Companies (Welsh Language Forms and Documents) Regulations 1994, SI 1994/117, regs 4(2)(e), 4(3).

244. Period allowed for laying and delivering accounts and reports

(1)   The period allowed for laying and delivering accounts and reports is—
   (a) for a private company, 10 months after the end of the relevant accounting reference period, and
   (b) for a public company, 7 months after the end of that period.

This is subject to the following provisions of this section.

(2)   If the relevant accounting reference period is the company's first and is a period of more than 12 months, the period allowed is—

    (a)   10 months or 7 months, as the case may be, from the first anniversary of the incorporation of the company, or

    (b)   3 months from the end of the accounting reference period,

whichever last expires.

(3)   Where a company carries on business, or has interests, outside the United Kingdom, the Channel Islands and the Isle of Man, the directors may, in respect of any financial year, give to the registrar before the end of the period allowed by subsection (1) or (2) a notice in the prescribed form—

    (a)   stating that the company so carries on business or has such interests, and

    (b)   claiming a 3 month extension of the period allowed for laying and delivering accounts and reports;

and upon such a notice being given the period is extended accordingly.

(4)   If the relevant accounting period is treated as shortened by virtue of a notice given by the company under section 225 (alteration of accounting reference date), the period allowed for laying and delivering accounts is that applicable in accordance with the above provisions or 3 months from the date of the notice under that section, whichever last expires.

(5)   If for any special reason the Secretary of State thinks fit he may, on an application made before the expiry of the period otherwise allowed, by notice in writing to a company extend that period by such further period as may be specified in the notice.

(6)   In this section 'the relevant accounting reference period' means the accounting reference period by reference to which the financial year for the accounts in question was determined.

S 244(1), (6)

The reference to laying accounts is to laying the accounts before the general meeting under s 241; the reference to delivering accounts is to the obligation to deliver the accounts to the registrar of companies under s 242. The accounting reference period is determined by s 224; and 'the relevant accounting reference period' is determined by sub-s (6). Penalties for late filing with the registrar of companies are set out in s 242A; and the directors may be prosecuted under s 242.

    The Companies House Guidance Booklet on Late Filing Penalties (GBA5) (which is available at www.companies-house.gov.uk) contains the following helpful table as to the dates by which the accounts must be delivered.

End of relevant accounting period (accounting reference date)	Deadline for delivery Private company	Deadline for delivery Public Company
January 31	November 30	August 31
February 28	December 28	September 28

March 31	January 31	October 31
April 30	February 28/29	November 30
May 31	March 31	December 31
June 30	April 30	January 30
July 31	May 31	February 28/29
August 31	June 30	March 31
September 30	July 30	April 30
October 31	August 31	May 31
November 30	September 30	June 30
December 31	October 31	July 31

S 244(2)

This provision applies only to newly incorporated companies where the company's first accounting reference period is longer than 12 months. In that case:

(1)   if the company is a private company, accounts must be delivered within 22 months of incorporation, or three months from the accounting reference date, whichever is the longer;

(2)   if the company is a public company, accounts must be delivered within 19 months of incorporation or three months from the accounting reference date, whichever is the longer.

It is important to appreciate that the periods specified in sub-s (2)(a) run from the first anniversary of incorporation and not from the year end; as to accounting reference periods and the accounting reference date, see s 224.

S 244(3)

Interests outside the United Kingdom   A company with interests overseas is allowed a longer period as of right but it must claim the additional period each year by notice to the registrar as specified.

S 244(5)

Application for extension of time allowed   This important provision can be overlooked which is unfortunate given that civil penalties will arise on late filing. The provision allows for some discretion in the registrar of companies to accommodate companies which can give a 'special reason' why they require a longer period, for example where records have been destroyed by fire or flood. Any application under this provision must be made *before* the time for delivery has expired and there is no room for the exercise of discretion when an application for relief is made after the time for filing has passed.

REVISION OF DEFECTIVE ACCOUNTS AND REPORTS

245. Voluntary revision of annual accounts or directors' report

(1) If it appears to the directors of a company that any annual accounts of the company, or any directors' report, did not comply with the requirements of this Act, they may prepare revised accounts or a revised report.

(2) Where copies of the previous accounts or report have been laid before the company in general meeting or delivered to the registrar, the revisions shall be confined to—

- (a) the correction of those respects in which the previous accounts or report did not comply with the requirements of this Act, and
- (b) the making of any necessary consequential alterations.

(3) The Secretary of State may make provision by regulations as to the application of the provisions of this Act in relation to revised annual accounts or a revised directors' report.

(4) The regulations may, in particular—

- (a) make different provision according to whether the previous accounts or report are replaced or are supplemented by a document indicating the corrections to be made;
- (b) make provision with respect to the functions of the company's auditors or reporting accountant in relation to the revised accounts or report;
- (c) require the directors to take such steps as may be specified in the regulations where the previous accounts or report have been—
    - (i)   sent out to members and others under section 238(1),
    - (ii) laid before the company in general meeting, or
    - (iii) delivered to the registrar,

    or where a summary financial statement based on the previous accounts or report has been sent to members under section 251;
- (d) apply the provisions of this Act (including those creating criminal offences) subject to such additions, exceptions and modifications as are specified in the regulations.

(5) Regulations under this section shall be made by statutory instrument which shall be subject to annulment in pursuance of a resolution of either House of Parliament.

General note

Although there is this statutory power to revise the accounts and reports, the directors are obliged, in any event, to take care not to approve accounts which do not comply with the Act (see s 233(5)); and must not prepare a directors' report which is non-compliant as to its required contents (see s 234(5)): both of these matters are criminal offences.

To appreciate the manner in which this provision and ss 245A–245C operate, see the general note to s 245A, below.

S 245(1), (2)

There is no duty to revise the accounts but, for large companies, there is the risk that the matter might come to the attention of the Financial Reporting Review Panel which can take a company to court to compel revisions under s 245B; problems with smaller companies would be a matter for the Department of Trade and Industry but, with over a million small companies on the register, the risk of the problem coming to light is slight; see general note to s 245A, below.

The power to revise extends to both the annual accounts (including group accounts, if required (s 262(1))) and the directors' report required under s 234; problems are most likely to relate to the accounts.

Nature of the corrections   Once the accounts and report have been laid before the general meeting under s 241 or delivered to the registrar of companies under s 242, corrections can only be made to ensure compliance with the statutory requirements. This limitation is intended to ensure that directors are not able to make changes simply to alter their account of the company's affairs with the benefit of hindsight. The scope for revision is not unduly limited, however, for the 'requirements of the Act' is a broad phrase, extending to the format and content of the accounts and the overriding requirement that they give a true and fair view (see ss 226, 227). The power to revise the accounts is not a power to update them to the time of the revision, instead it is an opportunity to replace or supplement the original accounts.

S 245(3)–(5)

The relevant regulations are the Companies (Revision of Defective Accounts and Reports) Regulations 1990, SI 1990/2570, as amended by SI 1992/3075; SI 1994/1935; SI 1995/2092, and SI 1996/315, which deal with a range of matters, in particular, the requirements as to the content, approval and signature, publication, laying and delivering of the revised accounts and reports. Provision is made for the delivery of the revised accounts to the registrar of companies: see SI 1990/2570, reg 12.

245A. Secretary of State's notice in respect of annual accounts

(1)   Where copies of a company's annual accounts have been sent out under section 238, or a copy of a company's annual accounts has been laid before the company in general meeting or delivered to the registrar, and it appears to the Secretary of State that there is, or may be, a question whether the accounts comply with the requirements of this Act, he may give notice to the directors of the company indicating the respects in which it appears to him that such a question arises, or may arise.

(2)   The notice shall specify a period of not less than one month for the directors to give him an explanation of the accounts or prepare revised accounts.

(3)   If at the end of the specified period, or such longer period as he may allow, it appears to the Secretary of State that no satisfactory explanation of the accounts has been given and that the accounts have not been revised so as to comply with the requirements of this Act, he may if he thinks fit apply to the court.

(4)   The provisions of this section apply equally to revised annual accounts, in which case the references to revised accounts shall be read as references to further revised accounts.

General note

Operation of these provisions   The powers provided by this section (and ss 245B–245C) are operated by the Department of Trade and Industry and the Financial Reporting Review Panel (the Panel) which is authorised for these purposes under s 245C. The division of responsibility agreed between these two bodies is that the Panel deals only with the annual accounts of public and large private companies leaving all other companies subject to review by the Department. The Panel confines its review to annual accounts leaving directors' reports, summary financial statements, interim statements and other matters to the Department under its general responsibility for ensuring compliance with the companies legislation.

The Panel will consider any case brought to its attention which may be by an individual or corporate complaint or, for example, as a result of media comment. The Panel is primarily concerned with non-compliance with accounting standards such that the accounts do not give a true and fair view.

While s 245B envisages an application to the court for an order to compel a company to make revisions, the Panel tries to secure revision by voluntary means and there has been no instance to date where the Panel has found it necessary to go to court. Instead the company will be notified by the Panel of the matter giving rise to concern and meetings and correspondence will follow until the matter is resolved to the satisfaction of the Panel. If no action is required, that will be the end of the matter. Where revisions are required, the directors will exercise their powers voluntarily under s 245 to make revisions (either by a full replacement of the accounts, a supplementary note, or some other acceptable method). Once agreement is reached as to the revision, the Panel will issue a Press Notice to that effect. If revisions are called for, and the original accounts were not qualified by the auditors, the Panel will draw the case to the attention of the auditors' professional body.

For companies subject to review by the Department of Trade and Industry, although it has not published its procedures in this regard, it is likely that a similar approach would be taken and only in egregious cases would the Department seek a court order compelling revisions.

S 245A(1)

The provision applies only to the 'annual accounts' (defined s 262(1) to include group accounts, if required) and not to the directors' report; the 'requirements of the Act' extend to the format and content of the accounts and the overriding requirement that they give a true and fair view: see ss 226, 227. It is not necessarily the case that the auditors will have highlighted a problem by qualifying their report.

S 245A(2), (3)

Initial contact between the Panel and the company is by way of this notice and meetings and correspondence will then follow as agreement is sought on the matter giving rise to concern.

There has been no instance to date where the Panel has found it necessary to go to court with companies accepting the inevitability of revision (although, in some cases, only after extensive consultations) once the Panel has become involved. The court has power to order that the costs of the court application and the expenses incurred by the company in connection with the preparation of revised accounts be borne by such of the directors as were party to the approval of the defective accounts: s 245B(4). Such a power provides an incentive for the directors to settle matters with the Panel rather than risk personal liability at a later hearing.

S 245A(4)

The power to seek revisions extends to revised accounts where the Panel remains unhappy with the revisions. In practice, it would be exceptional for a company not to have reached agreement with the Panel as to the precise revisions which are required so it would be very unusual for the Panel to have to seek further revisions under this power.

245B. Application to court in respect of defective accounts

(1)   An application may be made to the court—

    (a) by the Secretary of State, after having complied with section 245A, or

    (b) by a person authorised by the Secretary of State for the purposes of this section,

for a declaration or declarator that the annual accounts of a company do not comply with the requirements of this Act and for an order requiring the directors of the company to prepare revised accounts.

(2)   Notice of the application, together with a general statement of the matters at issue in the proceedings, shall be given by the applicant to the registrar for registration.

(3)   If the court orders the preparation of revised accounts, it may give directions with respect to—

    (a) the auditing of the accounts,

    (b) the revision of any directors' report or summary financial statement, and

    (c) the taking of steps by the directors to bring the making of the order to the notice of persons likely to rely on the previous accounts,

and such other matters as the court thinks fit.

(4)   If the court finds that the accounts did not comply with the requirements of this Act it may order that all or part of—

(a) the costs (or in Scotland expenses) of and incidental to the application, and

(b) any reasonable expenses incurred by the company in connection with or in consequence of the preparation of revised accounts,

shall be borne by such of the directors as were party to the approval of the defective accounts.

For this purpose every director of the company at the time the accounts were approved shall be taken to have been a party to their approval unless he shows that he took all reasonable steps to prevent their being approved.

(5) Where the court makes an order under subsection (4) it shall have regard to whether the directors party to the approval of the defective accounts knew or ought to have known that the accounts did not comply with the requirements of this Act, and it may exclude one or more directors from the order or order the payment of different amounts by different directors.

(6) On the conclusion of proceedings on an application under this section, the applicant shall give to the registrar for registration an office copy of the court order or, as the case may be, notice that the application has failed or been withdrawn.

(7) The provisions of this section apply equally to revised annual accounts, in which case the references to revised accounts shall be read as references to further revised accounts.

General note

To date, the Financial Reporting Review Panel has not found it necessary to have recourse to this power with respect to public or larger private companies: see general note to s 245A, above.

S 245B(1)

The authorised person is the Financial Reporting Review Panel: see general note to s 245A, and s 245C.

S 245B(4)

The court's power to order the directors personally to carry the costs operates as a powerful incentive for them to agree matters with the Panel rather than run the risk of incurring personal liability at a later hearing.

S 245B(7)

See note to s 245A(4), above.

245C. Other persons authorised to apply to court

(1)   The Secretary of State may authorise for the purposes of section 245B any person appearing to him—

   (a) to have an interest in, and to have satisfactory procedures directed to securing, compliance by companies with the accounting requirements of this Act,

   (b) to have satisfactory procedures for receiving and investigating complaints about the annual accounts of companies, and

   (c) otherwise to be a fit and proper person to be authorised.

(2)   A person may be authorised generally or in respect of particular classes of case, and different persons may be authorised in respect of different classes of case.

(3)   The Secretary of State may refuse to authorise a person if he considers that his authorisation is unnecessary having regard to the fact that there are one or more other persons who have been or are likely to be authorised.

(4)   Authorisation shall be by order made by statutory instrument which shall be subject to annulment in pursuance of a resolution of either House of Parliament.

(5)   Where authorisation is revoked, the revoking order may make such provision as the Secretary of State thinks fit with respect to pending proceedings.

(6)   Neither a person authorised under this section, nor any officer, servant or member of the governing body of such a person, shall be liable in damages for anything done or purporting to be done for the purposes of or in connection with—

   (a) the taking of such steps to discover whether there are grounds for an application to the court,

   (b) the determination whether or not to make such an application, or

   (c) the publication of its reasons for any such decision,

unless the act or omission is shown to have been in bad faith.

S 245C(1)–(4)

The Companies (Defective Accounts) (Authorised Person) Order 1991, SI 1991/13, which came into force on 1 February 1991, authorised the Financial Reporting Review Panel Limited for these purposes. It is the only authorised person under this provision.

S 245C(6)

This provision is a typical exclusion of liability provision which is included to ensure that public or quasi-public bodies of this nature can carry out their statutory functions without risk of being sued, save in cases of bad faith (which would be very difficult to prove).

CHAPTER II

EXEMPTIONS, EXCEPTIONS AND SPECIAL PROVISIONS

SMALL AND MEDIUM-SIZED COMPANIES AND GROUPS

246. Special provisions for small companies

(1)   Subject to section 247A, this section applies where a company qualifies as a small company in relation to a financial year.

(2)   If the company's individual accounts for the year—

    (a) comply with the provisions of Schedule 8, or

    (b) fail to comply with those provisions only in so far as they comply instead with one or more corresponding provisions of Schedule 4,

they need not comply with the provisions or, as the case may be, the remaining provisions of Schedule 4; and where advantage is taken of this subsection, references in section 226 to compliance with the provisions of Schedule 4 shall be construed accordingly.

(3)   The company's individual accounts for the year—

    (a) may give the total of the aggregates required by paragraphs (a), (c) and (d) of paragraph 1(1) of Schedule 6 (emoluments and other benefits etc of directors) instead of giving those aggregates individually; and

    (b) need not give the information required by—

        (i) paragraph 4 of Schedule 5 (financial years of subsidiary undertakings);

        (ii) paragraph 1(2)(b) of Schedule 6 (numbers of directors exercising share options and receiving shares under long term incentive schemes);

        (iii) paragraph 2 of Schedule 6 (details of highest paid director's emoluments etc); or

        (iv) paragraph 7 of Schedule 6 (excess retirement benefits of directors and past directors).

(4)   The directors' report for the year need not give the information required by—

    (a) section 234(1)(a) and (b) (fair review of business and amount to be paid as dividend);

    (b) paragraph 1(2) of Schedule 7 (statement of market value of fixed assets where substantially different from balance sheet amount);

    (c) paragraph 6 of Schedule 7 (miscellaneous disclosures); or

    (d) paragraph 11 of Schedule 7 (employee involvement).

(5)   Notwithstanding anything in section 242(1), the directors of the company need not deliver to the registrar any of the following, namely—

    (a) a copy of the company's profit and loss account for the year;

    (b) a copy of the directors' report for the year; and

    (c) if they deliver a copy of a balance sheet drawn up as at the last day of the year which complies with the requirements of Schedule 8A, a copy of the company's balance sheet drawn up as at that day.

(6)   Neither a copy of the company's accounts for the year delivered to the registrar under section 242(1), nor a copy of a balance sheet delivered to the registrar under subsection (5)(c), need give the information required by—

(a)   paragraph 4 of Schedule 5 (financial years of subsidiary undertakings);

(b)   paragraph 6 of Schedule 5 (shares of company held by subsidiary undertakings);

(c)   Part I of Schedule 6 (directors' and chairman's emoluments, pensions and compensation for loss of office); or

(d)   section 390A(3)(amount of auditors' remuneration).

(7)   The provisions of section 233 as to the signing of the copy of the balance sheet delivered to the registrar apply to a copy of a balance sheet delivered under subsection (5)(c).

(8)   Subject to subsection (9), each of the following, namely—

(a)   accounts prepared in accordance with subsection (2) or (3),

(b)   a report prepared in accordance with subsection (4), and

(c)   a copy of accounts delivered to the registrar in accordance with subsection (5) or (6),

shall contain a statement in a prominent position on the balance sheet, in the report or, as the case may be, on the copy of the balance sheet, above the signature required by section 233, 234A or subsection (7), that they are prepared in accordance with the special provisions of this Part relating to small companies.

(9)   Subsection (8) does not apply where the directors of the company have taken advantage of the exemption from audit conferred by section 249AA (dormant companies).

General note

This confusing provision offers small companies a number of options in terms of the accounts which they must prepare for their members and the accounts to be delivered to the registrar of companies.

S 246(1)

Whether a company qualifies as a small company is determined by s 247, subject to the exclusions in s 247A; as to whether a parent company can qualify as a small company, see s 247A(3); the 'financial year' is determined by s 223.

S 246(2)–(4), (8)

There is an obligation on companies generally to prepare their individual accounts in accordance with Sch 4: s 226(3). This provision permits small companies to prepare their accounts instead in accordance with Sch 8, or part of Sch 8 and part of Sch 4, or, of course, they may be prepared in accordance with Sch 4. Certain information may be aggregated or omitted from the accounts (sub-s (3)) and from the directors' report (sub-s (4)). Any accounts and directors' report prepared under sub-ss (2)–(4) must contain a statement on the balance sheet and report as required by sub-s (8).

S 246(5)–(6), (8)

Small companies need not deliver to the registrar the profit and loss account or directors' report prepared for the members and may instead deliver only the balance sheet and accompanying notes.

With respect to the format, there are two possibilities, either the balance sheet prepared for the members (under Sch 8, or Sch 4 or a combination of both) or a further balance sheet prepared in accordance with Sch 8A (involving some small additional cost). In either case, the company may take advantage of the exemptions in sub-s (6) to omit further information from the balance sheet delivered. The balance sheet delivered must be signed as required by s 233; and contain a statement as required by sub-s (8).

Either type of accounts ie either a balance sheet prepared in accordance with sub-s (5)(c) (complying with Sch 8A) or under sub-s (6) (omitting certain information) are described as 'abbreviated accounts' (s 247B(1)(a)); and abbreviated accounts must be accompanied by a special auditors' report (involving some additional cost) instead of the auditors' report under s 235: s 247B(2), (3); subject to any exemption from audit under ss 249A or 249AA. In practice, a large number of small companies are exempt from the audit requirement and so neither an auditors' report nor a special auditors' report will required. As a consequence, the only information delivered to the registrar of companies will be an abbreviated balance sheet.

246A. Special provisions for medium-sized companies

(1)   Subject to section 247A, this section applies where a company qualifies as a medium-sized company in relation to a financial year.

(2)   The company's individual accounts for the year need not comply with the requirements of paragraph 36A of Schedule 4 (disclosure with respect to compliance with accounting standards).

(3)   The company may deliver to the registrar a copy of the company's accounts for the year—

(a)   which includes a profit and loss account in which the following items listed in the profit and loss account formats set out in Part I of Schedule 4 are combined as one item under the heading 'gross profit or loss'—

Items 1, 2, 3 and 6 in Format 1;

Items 1 to 5 in Format 2;

Items A.1, B.1 and B.2 in Format 3;

Items A.1, A.2 and B.1 to B.4 in Format 4;

(b)   which does not contain the information required by paragraph 55 of Schedule 4 (particulars of turnover).

(4)   A copy of accounts delivered to the registrar in accordance with subsection (3) shall contain a statement in a prominent position on the copy of the balance sheet, above the signature required by section 233, that the accounts are prepared in accordance with the special provisions of this Part relating to medium-sized companies.

General note

The exemptions provided for medium-sized companies are much less extensive than those for small companies in s 246 and such companies must deliver to the registrar a balance sheet, abbreviated profit and loss account, directors' report and a special auditors' report (see sub-s (3)).

S 246A(1)

Whether a company qualifies as a medium-sized company is determined by s 247, subject to the exclusions in s 247A; as to whether a parent company can qualify as a medium-sized company, see s 247A(3); the 'financial year' is determined by s 223.

S 246A(2)

This exemption applies to the individual accounts which are prepared for the members. Paragraph 36A requires a statement in the notes to the accounts as to whether the accounts have been prepared in accordance with the applicable accounting standards and requires particulars of any material departure (and the reasons for it) from those standards. In practice, it is unlikely that a medium-sized company would depart from the applicable standards in any event.

S 246A(3)

This exemption applies only to the accounts delivered to the registrar of companies and this information will have to be included in the accounts prepared for the members. However, some privacy is gained by the exclusion and aggregation of information to the extent permitted.

Where a company takes advantage of this exemption, the accounts then delivered to the registrar are described as 'abbreviated accounts' (s 247B(1)(a)) and, in that case, the company must also deliver a special auditors' report instead of the auditors' report under s 235: s 247B(2), (3). The company still needs to obtain an auditors' report under s 235 for its members, so the requirement to deliver a special auditors' report increases the costs.

S 246A(4)

The balance sheet submitted under this provision must be signed as required by s 233; and there must be a statement on the balance sheet to the effect set out in this sub-section. The registrar of companies will reject accounts which do not contain this statement.

---

247. Qualification of company as small or medium-sized

(1) A company qualifies as small or medium-sized in relation to a financial year if the qualifying conditions are met—

    (a) in the case of the company's first financial year, in that year, and

    (b) in the case of any subsequent financial year, in that year and the preceding year.

(2) A company shall be treated as qualifying as small or medium-sized in relation to a financial year—

    (a) if it so qualified in relation to the previous financial year under subsection (1) above or was treated as so qualifying under paragraph (b) below; or

    (b) if it was treated as so qualifying in relation to the previous year by virtue of paragraph (a) and the qualifying conditions are met in the year in question.

(3) The qualifying conditions are met by a company in a year in which it satisfies two or more of the following requirements—

Small company

1. Turnover	Not more than £2.8 million
2. Balance sheet total	Not more than £1.4 million
3. Number of employees	Not more than 50

Medium-sized company

1. Turnover	Not more than £11.2 million
2. Balance sheet total	Not more than £5.6 million
3. Number of employees	Not more than 250.

(4) For a period which is a company's financial year but not in fact a year the maximum figures for turnover shall be proportionately adjusted.

(5) The balance sheet total means—

    (a) where in the company's accounts Format 1 of the balance sheet formats set out in Part I of Schedule 4 or Part I of Schedule 8 is adopted, the aggregate of the amounts shown in the balance sheet under the headings corresponding to items A to D in that Format, and

    (b) where Format 2 is adopted, the aggregate of the amounts shown under the general heading 'Assets'.

(6) The number of employees means the average number of persons employed by the company in the year (determined on a monthly basis).

That number shall be determined by applying the method of calculation prescribed by paragraph 56(2) and (3) of Schedule 4 for determining the corresponding number required to be stated in a note to the company's accounts.

S 247(1), (2)

The 'financial year' is determined in accordance with s 223. The effect of these provisions is that a company qualifies in the respective categories if it meets the qualifying conditions for that financial year and the preceding year. Subsection (2) offers companies one year of grace where they fail to meet the qualifying conditions.

A company which meets the conditions in Year 1 and Year 2, but fails to do so in Year 3, is still treated as qualifying in Year 3 (sub-s (2)(1)). If in Year 4 the company again meets the qualifying conditions, it is treated as qualifying under sub-s (2)(b) (although not within sub-s (1), as it cannot show that the qualifying conditions were met in two successive financial years). If in Year 4 the company fails to meet the conditions, the company ceases to qualify as a small or medium-sized company and will have to meet the qualifying conditions for two successive years before regaining this status.

S 247(3), (4)

The company must meet two out of the three criteria; as to the 'financial year', see s 223.

247A. Cases in which special provisions do not apply

(1) Nothing in section 246 or 246A shall apply where—

    (a) the company is, or was at any time within the financial year to which the accounts relate—

        (i) a public company,

        (ii) a banking or insurance company, or

        (iii) an authorised person under the Financial Services Act 1986; or

    (b) the company is, or was at any time during that year, a member of an ineligible group.

(2) A group is ineligible if any of its members is—

    (a) a public company or a body corporate which (not being a company) has power under its constitution to offer its shares or debentures to the public and may lawfully exercise that power,

    (b) an authorised institution under the Banking Act 1987,

    (c) an insurance company to which Part II of the Insurance Companies Act 1982 applies, or

    (d) an authorised person under the Financial Services Act 1986.

(3)　A parent company shall not be treated as qualifying as a small company in relation to a financial year unless the group headed by it qualifies as a small group, and shall not be treated as qualifying as a medium-sized company in relation to a financial year unless that group qualifies as a medium-sized group (see section 249).

General note

This provision identifies the exclusions which prevent a company from qualifying as a small or medium-sized company so as to take advantage of the exemptions in ss 246 and 246A respectively.

S 247A(1)

The company must not *at any time* in the financial year have been ineligible; the 'financial year' is determined in accordance with s 223; 'public company' is defined in s 1(2); 'banking company' and 'insurance company' are defined in s 744.

S 247A(3)

A parent company (see s 258, Sch 10A) cannot take advantage of the available exemptions for small and medium-sized companies with respect to its individual accounts unless the group headed by it qualifies as a small or medium-sized group respectively as defined by s 249.

247B. Special auditors' report

(1)　This section applies where—
- (a)　the directors of a company propose to deliver to the registrar copies of accounts ('abbreviated accounts') prepared in accordance with section 246(5) or (6) or 246A(3)('the relevant provision'),
- (b)　the directors have not taken advantage of the exemption from audit conferred by section 249A(1) or (2) or section 249AA,...
- (c)　...

(2)　If abbreviated accounts prepared in accordance with the relevant provision are delivered to the registrar, they shall be accompanied by a copy of a special report of the auditors stating that in their opinion—
- (a)　the company is entitled to deliver abbreviated accounts prepared in accordance with that provision, and
- (b)　the abbreviated accounts to be delivered are properly prepared in accordance with that provision.

(3)　In such a case a copy of the auditors' report under section 235 need not be delivered, but—

(a) if that report was qualified, the special report shall set out that report in full together with any further material necessary to understand the qualification; and

(b) if that report contained a statement under—

  (i) section 237(2) (accounts, records or returns inadequate or accounts not agreeing with records and returns), or

  (ii) section 237(3) (failure to obtain necessary information and explanations),

the special report shall set out that statement in full.

(4) Section 236 (signature of auditors' report) applies to a special report under this section as it applies to a report under section 235.

(5) If abbreviated accounts prepared in accordance with the relevant provision are delivered to the registrar, references in section 240 (requirements in connection with publication of accounts) to the auditors' report under section 235 shall be read as references to the special auditors' report under this section.

S 247B(1)

This provision requires the delivery to the registrar of companies, in certain cases, of a special auditors' report in place of the auditors' report required by s 235. Of course, neither the auditors' report under s 235 nor the special auditors' report under this provision is required where the company is exempt from audit under s 249A or 249AA, as will be the case with many small companies.

The special auditors' report is required where the company delivers 'abbreviated accounts', namely:

  (1) where the company is a small company which delivers to the registrar of companies only a balance sheet prepared in accordance with Sch 8A under s 246(5);

  (2) where the company is a small company which delivers accounts which take advantage of the exemptions in s 246(6);

  (3) where the company is a medium-sized company which delivers accounts which take advantage of the exemptions in s 246A(3).

S 247B(2), (3)

The contents of the special auditors' report can be contrasted with that required for the members under s 235; the main omission is any reference to whether the abbreviated accounts give a true and fair view of the state of affairs. This is necessarily the case, as the omitted matters (permitted by the exemptions) mean that the accounts cannot be said to give a true and fair view. As the auditors' report under s 235 is still required for the members, the company is put to the additional cost of preparing this special auditors' report for delivery to the registrar which may in any event have to contain some or all of the information included in the report prepared under s 235.

248. Exemption for small and medium-sized groups

(1)   A parent company need not prepare group accounts for a financial year in relation to which the group headed by that company qualifies as a small or medium-sized group and is not an ineligible group.

(2)   A group is ineligible if any of its members is—

   (a) a public company or body corporate which (not being a company) has power under its constitution to offer its shares or debentures to the public and may lawfully exercise that power,

   (b) an authorised institution under the Banking Act 1987,

   (c) an insurance company to which Part II of the Insurance Companies Act 1982 applies, or

   (d) an authorised person under the Financial Services Act 1986.

(3), (4)   ...

S 248(1)

This is a valuable exemption where the group qualifies as a small or a medium-sized group (defined in s 249), for the combined effect of ss 246, 246A, 247, 247A and this provision is that a parent company heading a group which qualifies as a small or medium-sized group will be able to take advantage of the exemptions in ss 246 or 246A for its individual accounts and is exempt from the preparation of group accounts (which would normally be required under s 227) by this provision. As a result of this, many quite sizeable groups are not required to prepare group accounts. A 'parent company' is defined by s 258, Sch 10A; the 'financial year' is determined by s 223.

If the directors take advantage of this provision not to prepare group accounts when they are not entitled to do so, the auditors must so state in their report: s 237(4A).

248A. Group accounts prepared by small company

(1)   This section applies where a small company—

   (a) has prepared individual accounts for a financial year in accordance with section 246(2) or (3), and

   (b) is preparing group accounts in respect of the same year.

(2)   If the group accounts—

   (a) comply with the provisions of Schedule 8, or

   (b) fail to comply with those provisions only in so far as they comply instead with one or more corresponding provisions of Schedule 4,

they need not comply with the provisions or, as the case may be, the remaining provisions of Schedule 4; and where advantage is taken of this subsection, references in Schedule 4A to compliance with the provisions of Schedule 4 shall be construed accordingly.

(3)   For the purposes of this section, Schedule 8 shall have effect as if, in each balance sheet format set out in that Schedule, for item B.III there were substituted the following item—

'B.III	Investments
1	Shares in group undertakings
2	Interests in associated undertakings
3	Other participating interests
4	Loans to group undertakings and undertakings in which a participating interest is held
5	Other investments other than loans
6	Others.'

(4)   The group accounts need not give the information required by the provisions specified in section 246(3).

(5)   Group accounts prepared in accordance with this section shall contain a statement in a prominent position on the balance sheet, above the signature required by section 233, that they are prepared in accordance with the special provisions of this Part relating to small companies.

General note

This provision applies only to the preparation of abbreviated group accounts by small companies; the legislation does not permit the delivery of abbreviated group accounts to the registrar of companies.

S 248A(1)–(3)

This provision applies where a small company (defined in s 247, subject to the exclusions in s 247A) does prepare group accounts (ie it is not exempt from the requirement to do so under s 248). Companies generally are obliged to prepare group accounts in accordance with Sch 4A, which in turn requires compliance so far as practicable with Sch 4: s 227(4), Sch 4A, para 1. This provision permits the group accounts in this instance to be prepared instead in accordance with Sch 8 (or part of Sch 8 and part of Sch 4). In addition, certain information may be aggregated or omitted from those accounts to the extent specified in s 246(3).

This provision does not apply to a medium-sized company.

S 248A(5)

This balance sheet statement must not be overlooked.

249. Qualification of group as small or medium-sized

(1) A group qualifies as small or medium-sized in relation to a financial year if the qualifying conditions are met—

    (a) in the case of the parent company's first financial year, in that year, and

    (b) in the case of any subsequent financial year, in that year and the preceding year.

(2) A group shall be treated as qualifying as small or medium-sized in relation to a financial year—

    (a) if it so qualified in relation to the previous financial year under subsection (1) above or was treated as so qualifying under paragraph (b) below; or

    (b) if it was treated as so qualifying in relation to the previous year by virtue of paragraph (a) and the qualifying conditions are met in the year in question.

(3) The qualifying conditions are met by a group in a year in which it satisfies two or more of the following requirements—

Small group

1. Aggregate turnover	Not more than £2.8 million net (or £3.36 million gross)
2. Aggregate balance sheet total	Not more than £1.4 million net (or £1.68 million gross)
3. Aggregate number of employees	Not more than 50

Medium-sized group

1. Aggregate turnover	Not more than £11.2 million net (or £13.44 million gross)
2. Aggregate balance sheet total	Not more than £5.6 million net (or £6.72 million gross)
3. Aggregate number of employees	Not more than 250.

(4) The aggregate figures shall be ascertained by aggregating the relevant figures determined in accordance with section 247 for each member of the group.

In relation to the aggregate figures for turnover and balance sheet total, 'net' means with the set-offs and other adjustments required by Schedule 4A in the case of group accounts and 'gross' means without those set-offs and other adjustments; and a company may satisfy the relevant requirements on the basis of either the net or the gross figure.

(5) The figures for each subsidiary undertaking shall be those included in its accounts for the relevant financial year, that is—

    (a) if its financial year ends with that of the parent company, that financial year, and

(b) if not, its financial year ending last before the end of the financial year of the parent company.

(6)   If those figures cannot be obtained without disproportionate expense or undue delay, the latest available figures shall be taken.

S 249(1), (2)

'Financial year' is determined in accordance with s 223; and a 'parent company' is defined in s 258, Sch 10A.

The effect of these provisions is that a group qualifies in the respective categories if the group meets the qualifying conditions for that financial year and the preceding year. Subsection (2) offers groups one year of grace where they fail to meet the qualifying conditions. A group which meets the conditions in Year 1 and Year 2, but fails to do so in Year 3, is still treated as qualifying in Year 3 (sub-s (2)(1)). If in Year 4 the group meets the qualifying conditions, the group is treated as qualifying under sub-s (2)(b) (although not within sub-s (1), as it cannot show that the qualifying conditions were met in two successive financial years). If in Year 4 the group fails to meet the conditions, it ceases to qualify as a small or medium-sized group and it cannot regain that status until it meets the conditions for two successive years.

S 249(3)

The group must meet two out of the three criteria.

EXEMPTIONS FROM AUDIT FOR CERTAIN CATEGORIES OF SMALL COMPANY

249A. Exemptions from audit

(1)   Subject to section 249B, a company which meets the total exemption conditions set out below in respect of a financial year is exempt from the provisions of this Part relating to the audit of accounts in respect of that year.

(2)   Subject to section 249B, a company which is a charity and which meets the report conditions set out below in respect of a financial year is exempt from the provisions of this Part relating to the audit of accounts in respect of that year if the directors cause a report in respect of the company's individual accounts for that year to be prepared in accordance with section 249C and made to the company's members.

(3)   The total exemption conditions are met by a company in respect of a financial year if—

(a) it qualifies as a small company in relation to that year for the purposes of section 246,

(b) its turnover in that year is not more than £1 million, and

(c) its balance sheet total for that year is not more than £1.4 million.

(3A) In relation to any company which is a charity, subsection (3)(b) shall have effect with the substitution—

(a) for the reference to turnover of a reference to gross income, and

(b) for the reference to £1 million, of a reference to £90,000.

(4) The report conditions are met by a company which is a charity in respect of a financial year if—

(a) it qualifies as a small company in relation to that year for the purposes of section 246,

(b) its gross income in that year is more than £90,000 but not more than £250,000, and

(c) its balance sheet total for that year is not more than £1.4 million.

(5) ...

(6) For a period which is a company's financial year but not in fact a year the maximum figures for turnover or gross income shall be proportionately adjusted.

(6A) A company is entitled to the exemption conferred by subsection (1) or (2) notwithstanding that it falls within paragraph (a) or (b) of section 249AA(1).

(7) In this section—

'balance sheet total' has the meaning given by section 247(5), and

'gross income' means the company's income from all sources, as shown in the company's income and expenditure account.

General note

Following a lengthy debate on the issue, it was finally decided to grant exemption from audit for certain companies in 1994: see the Companies Act 1985 (Audit Exemption) Regulations 1994, SI 1994/1935, which essentially provided that companies with a turnover below £90,000 per annum were able to dispense with the statutory audit. The turnover threshold was subsequently raised to £350,000 by the Companies Act 1985 (Audit Exemption) (Amendment) Regulations 1997, SI 1997/936; and was raised further to £1m by the Companies Act 1985 (Audit Exemption) (Amendment) Regulations 2000, SI 2000/1430, reg 2(1), (2), as from 26 May 2000, in relation to annual accounts and reports in respect of financial years ending two months or more after that date.

While companies within the qualifying conditions set out below are automatically exempt from the requirement for a statutory audit, their directors may find that the Inland Revenue, banks and major customers still require audited accounts from the company. Companies with articles which pre-date the 1985 Table A should also check that the articles do not require them to appoint auditors. The articles can be altered by special resolution: s 9.

S 249A(1), (3), (3A)

Automatic entitlement   No steps need be taken by a company to claim exempt status, it arises automatically if the company is within the thresholds in sub-s (3) or, in the case of a company which is a charity, within sub-s (3) as modified by sub-s (3A). However, although a company may qualify automatically for the exemption from audit, members holding 10% or more of the issued share capital may give notice to the company requiring an audit (see s 249B(2)–(3)); and a company is not entitled to the exemption conferred by these provisions unless its balance sheet contains a statement by the directors as required by s 249B(4). If that statement is omitted, the registrar of companies will reject the accounts.

Those categories of companies which are excluded from exemption are set out in s 249B(1)–(1C), the most significant exclusion being public companies and there are limits on the extent to which members of groups can claim exemption; as to the effect of the exemption, see s 249E(1); the 'financial year' is determined in accordance with s 223; the requirement to appoint an auditor is contained in s 384.

See s 388A as to the time period for the appointment of an auditor when a company ceases to be exempt under this provision from the appointment of an auditor.

S 249A(2), (4)

Charities   For companies which are charities, the threshold for total exemption is set at a gross income not in excess of £90,000, as noted above. Such companies with a gross income of more than £90,000 but less than £250,000 are also exempt from the requirement of an audit but there must be a report in the terms prescribed by s 249C. This is subject to the right of members holding 10% or more of the issued share capital to give notice to the company requiring an audit (see s 249B(2)–(3)); and a company is not entitled to the exemption conferred by these provisions unless the balance sheet contains a statement by the directors as required by s 249B(4).

As to those qualified to act as reporting accountants, see s 249D; as to the effect of the exemption, see s 249E(2). In addition to being sent to the members, this report must be delivered to the registrar of companies: see s 249E(2)(b).

S 249A(6A)

Dormant companies   This provision was inserted in 1997 to clarify that a dormant company might be exempt from audit either under s 250, now repealed, or this provision. With the repeal of s 250, and therefore the repeal of any requirement for a dormant company to pass a special resolution in order to gain exemption from the audit, this provision is superfluous. See s 249AA for the position governing dormant companies.

249AA. Dormant companies

(1)   Subject to section 249B(2) to (5), a company is exempt from the provisions of this Part relating to the audit of accounts in respect of a financial year if—

(a) it has been dormant since its formation, or

(b) it has been dormant since the end of the previous financial year and subsection (2) applies.

(2) This subsection applies if the company—

(a) is entitled in respect of its individual accounts for the financial year in question to prepare accounts in accordance with section 246, or would be so entitled but for the application of section 247A(1)(a)(i) or (b), and

(b) is not required to prepare group accounts for that year.

(3) Subsection (1) does not apply if at any time in the financial year in question the company was—

(a) a banking or insurance company, or

(b) an authorised person for the purposes of the Financial Services Act 1986.

(4) A company is 'dormant' during any period in which it has no significant accounting transaction.

(5) 'Significant accounting transaction' means a transaction which—

(a) is required by section 221 to be entered in the company's accounting records; but

(b) is not a transaction to which subsection (6) or (7) applies.

(6) This subsection applies to a transaction arising from the taking of shares in the company by a subscriber to the memorandum as a result of an undertaking of his in the memorandum.

(7) This subsection applies to a transaction consisting of the payment of—

(a) a fee to the registrar on a change of name under section 28 (change of name),

(b) a fee to the registrar on the re-registration of a company under Part II (re-registration as a means of altering a company's status),

(c) a penalty under section 242A (penalty for failure to deliver accounts), or

(d) a fee to the registrar for the registration of an annual return under Chapter III of Part XI.

General note

Exemption from audit for dormant companies　This provision was inserted by the Companies Act 1985 (Audit Exemption) (Amendment) Regulations 2000, SI 2000/1430, reg 3, as from 26 May 2000, in relation to annual accounts and reports in respect of financial years ending two months or more after that date. It is intended to clarify certain points which had arisen as to the availability of the exemption from audit for dormant companies. It clarifies, in particular, that qualifying dormant companies are entitled to the audit exemption automatically without the need to pass any special resolution (a matter which was unclear in the now repealed s 250).

Reasons for dormancy   A company may be dormant for any number of reasons, for example, it may have been incorporated to protect a name; or was acquired for a particular venture which did not materialise; or was incorporated for sale as an off-the-shelf company by a formation agent.

Extent of the exemptions for dormant companies   The exemption is solely an exemption from the requirements relating to audit.

A dormant company must still prepare accounts to be laid before the general meeting (unless it is a private company which has dispensed with the laying of accounts under s 252), sent to every member (s 238) *and* delivered to the registrar of companies (s 242). However, the effect of dormant status is that such a company will be entitled to prepare accounts in accordance with s 246 (exemptions for small companies) and so will be entitled to deliver abbreviated accounts under s 246(5) (ie only an abbreviated balance sheet in accordance with Sch 8A): s 249E(1A). If the company has been dormant from formation, little information will be required. A standard form balance sheet for companies which have been dormant since formation is available from Companies House to assist such companies in preparing their accounts: see Companies House, Guidance Booklet, *Dormant companies*. A dormant company is still required to complete an annual return: see s 363.

Agents for undisclosed principals   Difficulties have arisen with companies acting as agents for an undisclosed principal. Third parties dealing with such companies (which appear to be trading) have been aggrieved on searching the public record at Companies House to find that such companies have claimed to be dormant.

Now, where directors take advantage of this section to claim dormant status, they must disclose in the notes to the accounts whether the company has acted during the financial year in question as agent for any person (but without requiring them to name the person for whom they acted): Sch 4, para 58A; Sch 8, para 51A; Sch 8A, para 9A. This is intended to improve the transparency of agency companies while continuing to allow such companies to claim dormant status if, under the terms of their agency agreement, they are entitled to it. If the agency company has acquired rights or assumed liabilities which should be reflected in its accounting records under s 221, it cannot claim dormant status.

Whether category still relevant   It is debatable whether there remains any need for dormant status. It was important when dormancy was the only method of claiming exemption from audit but now that companies with a turnover of less than £1m may be automatically exempt from the audit under s 249A, the need for this category is less clear. The remaining advantages would seem to be for public companies (which are excluded from s 249A (exemptions from audit)) and members of groups whose total turnover exceeds the audit threshold (see ss 249A, 249B(1A)-(1C)) and which are ineligible therefore under s 249A.

S 249AA(1)–(3)

Claiming status as dormant   There are two possibilities:
- (1)   a company may have been dormant since its formation or,
- (2)   it can claim dormant status in respect of a financial year, if it has been dormant since the end of the previous financial year. If the company traded from March 1999 to March 2000 but was dormant from March 2000 to

March 2001, it can claim dormant status for the year 2000–01. If any transaction occurred during March 2000–March 2001 which must be entered in the company's accounting records, however, it ceases to be dormant and cannot claim exemption under this provision although it may be entitled to do so under s 249A.

To qualify as a company which has become dormant (rather than one which has been dormant throughout), it must be shown that:

(1)   the company is entitled to prepare individual accounts in accordance with the provisions applicable to small companies (under s 246); or

(2)   the company would be so entitled, were it not for the fact that it is a public company or a member of an ineligible group; and

(3)   the company must not be required to prepare group accounts (see ss 227–229, 248).

The provisions of s 249B(1) which exclude certain categories of companies from exemption under s 249A do not apply to dormant companies but some of those categories are excluded in any event by this provision, for example, banking and insurance companies and persons authorised under FSA 1986 (see sub-s (3)). See note to s 249B(1), below. However, public companies and members of certain groups excluded by s 249B(1)(a) and (f) from claiming exemption under s 249A are not excluded by this provision and may therefore claim dormant status if they fall within the criteria above.

Automatic entitlement to exemption from audit   A dormant company which meets these conditions is automatically entitled to the audit exemption without the need for any special resolution or procedure. However, although a dormant company qualifies automatically for the exemption from audit, members holding 10% or more of the issued share capital may give notice to the company requiring an audit (see s 249B(2)–(3)); and a company is not entitled to the exemption conferred by these provisions unless the balance sheet contains a statement by the directors as required by s 249B(4). If this statement is omitted, the registrar of companies will reject the accounts.

See s 388A as to the time period for the appointment of an auditor when a company ceases to be exempt under this provision from the appointment of an auditor.

S 249AA(4)–(7)

No significant accounting transactions   It is central to the concept of dormancy that the company has no significant accounting transactions in the year which would need to be entered in the company's accounting records. Although 'significant' is used in sub-s (4), the effect of sub-s (5) is that any transaction, however immaterial, which must be entered in the records will prevent the company claiming dormant status.

Subscriber shares and payments to the registrar of companies   Subsections (6) and (7) identify transactions which, although required to be entered in the records, are of such a minor administrative nature that they should not be considered when determining whether a company is dormant. This will resolve the problems which have arisen in the past when companies have lost dormant status because of payments to the registrar of companies in respect of fees or late filing penalties.

Other payments   Apart from the situations covered by sub-ss (6) and (7), there are many other minor transactions such as bank charges, the receipt of interest and administrative expenses incurred by a non-trading company which must be recorded in the records and which will prevent the company from claiming dormant status. Such companies will probably qualify for exemption from audit under s 249A in any event.

249B. Cases where exemptions not available

(1)   Subject to subsections (1A) to (1C), a company is not entitled to the exemption conferred by subsection (1) or (2) of section 249A in respect of a financial year if at any time within that year—

   (a) it was a public company,
   (b) it was a banking or insurance company,
   (c) . . . ,
   (d) it was an authorised person or an appointed representative under the Financial Services Act 1986,
   (e) it was a special register body as defined in section 117(1) of the Trade Union and Labour Relations (Consolidation) Act 1992 or an employers' association as defined in section 122 of that Act, or
   (f) it was a parent company or a subsidiary undertaking.

(1A) A company which, apart from this subsection, would fall within subsection (1)(f) by virtue of its being a subsidiary undertaking for any period within a financial year shall not be treated as so falling if it is dormant (within the meaning of section 249AA) throughout that period.

(1B) A company which, apart from this subsection, would fall within subsection (1)(f) by virtue of its being a parent company or a subsidiary undertaking for any period within a financial year, shall not be treated as so falling if throughout that period it was a member of a group meeting the conditions set out in subsection (1C).

(1C) The conditions referred to in subsection (1B) are—

   (a) that the group qualifies as a small group, in relation to the financial year within which the period falls, for the purposes of section 249 (or if all bodies corporate in such group were companies, would so qualify) and is not, and was not at any time within that year, an ineligible group within the meaning of section 248(2),
   (b) that the group's aggregate turnover in that year (calculated in accordance with section 249) is, where the company referred to in subsection (1B) is a charity, not more than £350,000 net (or £420,000 gross) or, where the company so referred to is not a charity, not more than £1 million net (or £1.2 million gross), and
   (c) that the group's aggregate balance sheet total for that year (calculated in accordance with section 249) is not more than £1.4 million net (or £1.68 million gross).

(2)   Any member or members holding not less in the aggregate than 10 per cent in nominal value of the company's issued share capital or any class of it or, if the company does not have a share capital, not less than 10 per cent in number of the members of the company, may, by notice in writing deposited at the registered office of the company during a financial year but not later than one month before the end of that year, require the company to obtain an audit of its accounts for that year.

(3)   Where a notice has been deposited under subsection (2), the company is not entitled to the exemption conferred by subsection (1) or (2) of section 249A or by subsection (1) of section 249AA in respect of the financial year to which the notice relates.

(4)   A company is not entitled to the exemption conferred by subsection (1) or (2) of section 249A or by subsection (1) of section 249AA unless its balance sheet contains a statement by the directors—

    (a)   to the effect that for the year in question the company was entitled to exemption under subsection (1) or (2) ... of section 249A or subsection (1) of section 249AA,

    (b)   to the effect that members have not required the company to obtain an audit of its accounts for the year in question in accordance with subsection (2) of this section, and

    (c)   to the effect that the directors acknowledge their responsibilities for—

        (i)   ensuring that the company keeps accounting records which comply with section 221, and

        (ii)   preparing accounts which give a true and fair view of the state of affairs of the company as at the end of the financial year and of its profit or loss for the financial year in accordance with the requirements of section 226, and which otherwise comply with the requirements of this Act relating to accounts, so far as applicable to the company.

(5)   The statement required by subsection (4) shall appear in the balance sheet above the signature required by section 233.

S 249B(1)(a)–(e)

These companies cannot claim exemption from audit under s 249A but, if within the criteria, they may claim exemption under s 249AA as dormant companies, except for categories (b) and (d), which are excluded by s 249AA(3). Members of a group of companies will be able to claim dormancy only if they meet the criteria in s 249AA(1).

S 249B(1)(f), (1A)–(1C)

Companies which form part of a group   When the audit exemption for small companies was originally introduced in 1994, companies which formed part of a group were automatically excluded from the exemption. This was felt subsequently to be too restrictive and so, while sub-s (1)(f) states that original position, it is qualified by sub-ss (1A)–(1C), which permit parent companies and subsidiary undertakings to qualify under s 249A for exemption from audit, if certain conditions are met.

Companies which are parent or subsidiary companies may take advantage of the exemption provided the case falls within one of the two qualifications, namely that:

   (1)   the 'subsidiary undertaking' (defined in s 258, Sch 10A) has been dormant (defined in s 249AA) throughout the period;

   (2)   the 'parent company' or 'subsidiary undertaking' (defined in s 258, Sch 10A) are: (a) members of a small group (or it would be a small group if all the bodies corporate in the group were companies within the meaning of s 735 – ie this allows foreign companies to be treated as companies within the group); (b) the group is not an ineligible group (within s 248(2)); and (c) the thresholds have not been exceeded.

To prevent abuse of group structures, the exemption for members of a group has been restricted to groups whose total turnover does not exceed the threshold for individual exemption.

S 249B(2), (3)

It is important to observe the time limits imposed by this provision; as to the registered office, see s 287.

S 249B(4), (5)

This requirement for a statement by the directors to this effect on the balance sheet can be overlooked with the consequence that the company is not entitled to the exemption claimed. In a serious case, the Department could seek revision of the accounts under ss 245, 245A; and the directors, having approved non-compliant accounts, are liable to the penalties imposed by s 233.

249C. The report required for the purposes of section 249A(2)

(1)   The report required for the purposes of section 249A(2) shall be prepared by a person (referred to in this Part as 'the reporting accountant') who is eligible under section 249D.

(2)   The report shall state whether in the opinion of the reporting accountant making it—

   (a)   the accounts of the company for the financial year in question are in agreement with the accounting records kept by the company under section 221, and

   (b)   having regard only to, and on the basis of, the information contained in those accounting records, those accounts have been drawn up in a manner consistent with the provisions of this Act specified in subsection (6), so far as applicable to the company.

(3)   The report shall also state that in the opinion of the reporting accountant, having regard only to, and on the basis of, the information contained in the

accounting records kept by the company under section 221, the company satisfied the requirements of subsection (4) of section 249A ... for the financial year in question, and did not fall within section 249B(1)(a) to (f) at any time within that financial year.

(4)　The report shall state the name of the reporting accountant and be signed by him.

(5)　Where the reporting accountant is a body corporate or partnership, any reference to signature of the report, or any copy of the report, by the reporting accountant is a reference to signature in the name of the body corporate or partnership by a person authorised to sign on its behalf.

(6)　The provisions referred to in subsection (2)(b) are—

(a)　section 226(3) and Schedule 4,

(b)　section 231 and paragraphs 7 to 9A and 13(1),(3) and (4) of Schedule 5, and

(c)　section 232 and Schedule 6,

where appropriate as modified by section 246(2) and (3).

S 249C(1)

This report is required only where the company is a charity and its gross income exceeds £90,000 (so preventing it from claiming a total audit exemption) but its income does not exceed £250,000 when an audit would be required, see s 249A.

249D. The reporting accountant

(1)　The reporting accountant shall be either—

(a)　any member of a body listed in subsection (3) who, under the rules of the body—

(i)　is entitled to engage in public practice, and

(ii)　is not ineligible for appointment as a reporting accountant, or

(b)　any person (whether or not a member of any such body) who—

(i)　is subject to the rules of any such body in seeking appointment or acting as auditor under Chapter V of Part XI, and

(ii)　under those rules, is eligible for appointment as auditor under that Chapter.

(1A) In subsection (1), references to the rules of a body listed in subsection (3) are to the rules (whether or not laid down by the body itself) which the body has power to enforce and which are relevant for the purposes of Part II of the Companies Act 1989 or this section.

This includes rules relating to the admission and expulsion of members of the body, so far as relevant for the purposes of that Part or this section.

(2)　An individual, a body corporate or a partnership may be appointed as a reporting accountant, and section 26 of the Companies Act 1989 (effect of appointment of partnership) shall apply to the appointment as reporting accountant of a partnership constituted under the law of England and Wales or Northern Ireland, or under the law of any other country or territory in which a partnership is not a legal person.

(3)   The bodies referred to in subsections (1) and (1A) are—

(a)   the Institute of Chartered Accountants in England and Wales,

(b)   the Institute of Chartered Accountants of Scotland,

(c)   the Institute of Chartered Accountants in Ireland,

(d)   the Association of Chartered Certified Accountants,

(e)   the Association of Authorised Public Accountants.

(f)   the Association of Accounting Technicians,

(g)   the Association of International Accountants, and

(h)   the Chartered Institute of Management Accountants.

(4)   A person is ineligible for appointment by a company as reporting accountant if he would be ineligible for appointment as an auditor of that company under section 27 of the Companies Act 1989 (ineligibility on ground of lack of independence).

General note

This section identifies those accountants who are entitled to act as reporting accountants for the purposes of s 249A(2).

249E. Effect of exemptions

(1)   Where the directors of a company have taken advantage of the exemption conferred by section 249A(1)or 249AA(1)—

(a)   sections 238 and 239 (right to receive or demand copies of accounts and reports) shall have effect with the omission of references to the auditors' report;

(b)   no copy of an auditors' report need be delivered to the registrar or laid before the company in general meeting;

(c)   subsections (3) to (5) of section 271 (accounts by reference to which distribution to be justified) shall not apply.

(1A) Where the directors of a company have taken advantage of the exemption conferred by section 249AA, then for the purposes of that section the company shall be treated as a company entitled to prepare accounts in accordance with section 246 even though it is a member of an ineligible group.

(2)   Where the directors of a company have taken advantage of the exemption conferred by section 249A(2)—

(a)   subsections (2) to (4) of section 236 (which require copies of the auditors' report to state the names of the auditors) shall have effect with the substitution for references to the auditors and the auditors' report of references to the reporting accountant and the report made for the purposes of section 249A(2) respectively;

(b) sections 238 and 239 (right to receive or demand copies of accounts and reports), section 241 (accounts and reports to be laid before company in general meeting) and section 242 (accounts and reports to be delivered to the registrar) shall have effect with the substitution for references to the auditors' report of references to the report made for the purposes of section 249A(2);

(c) subsections (3) to (5) of section 271 (accounts by reference to which distribution to be justified) shall not apply;

(d) section 389A(1) and (2)(rights to information) shall have effect with the substitution for references to the auditors of references to the reporting accountant.

General note

This section makes the necessary modifications to those provisions throughout the Act which require an auditors' report to be received, or laid, or delivered; sub-s (1) applies in those situations where the company is entitled to a total exemption from the audit requirements and sub-s (2) applies where the company is a charity entitled to provide a report from a reporting accountant.

S 249E(1A)

The wording of this provision, which has been altered from that contained in the now repealed s 250(4)(d), is intended to clarify (although it has not necessarily done so) that a dormant company is entitled to prepare accounts in accordance with all of the exemptions available to small companies in s 246, even though it is a member of an ineligible group.

250. *(Repealed by the Companies Act 1985 (Audit Exemption) (Amendment) Regulations 2000, SI 2000/1430, reg 8(6), as from 26 May 2000, in relation to annual accounts and reports in respect of financial years ending two months or more after that date.)*

LISTED PUBLIC COMPANIES

251. Provision of summary financial statement to shareholders

(1) A public company whose shares or debentures, or any class of whose shares or debentures, are listed need not, in such cases as may be specified by

regulations made by the Secretary of State, and provided any conditions so specified are complied with, send copies of the documents referred to in section 238(1) to entitled persons, but may instead send them a summary financial statement.

In this section—

'entitled persons', in relation to a company, means such of the persons specified in paragraphs (a) to (c) of subsection (1) of section 238 as are or would apart from this section be entitled to be sent copies of those documents relating to the company which are referred to in that subsection; and

'listed' means admitted to the Official List of The International Stock Exchange of the United Kingdom and the Republic of Ireland Limited.

(2) Copies of the documents referred to in section 238(1) shall, however, be sent to any entitled person who wishes to receive them; and the Secretary of State may by regulations make provision as to the manner in which it is to be ascertained (whether before or after he becomes an entitled person) whether an entitled person wishes to receive them.

(2A) References in this section to sending a summary financial statement to an entitled person include references to using electronic communications for sending the statement to such address as may for the time being be notified to the company by that person for that purpose.

(2B) For the purposes of this section a summary financial statement is also to be treated as sent to an entitled person where—

(a) the company and that person have agreed to his having access to summary financial statements on a web site (instead of their being sent to him);

(b) the statement is a statement to which that agreement applies; and

(c) that person is notified, in a manner for the time being agreed for the purpose between him and the company, of—

(i) the publication of the statement on a web site;

(ii) the address of that web site; and

(iii) the place on that web site where the statement may be accessed, and how it may be accessed.

(2C) For the purposes of this section a statement treated in accordance with subsection (2B) as sent to an entitled person is to be treated as sent to him if, and only if—

(a) the statement is published on the web site throughout a period beginning at least 21 days before the date of the meeting at which the accounts and directors' report from which the statement is derived are to be laid and ending with the conclusion of that meeting; and

(b) the notification given for the purposes of paragraph (c) of that subsection is given not less than 21 days before the date of the meeting.

(2D) Nothing in subsection (2C) shall invalidate the proceedings of a meeting where—

(a) any statement that is required to be published as mentioned in paragraph (a) of that subsection is published for a part, but not all, of the period mentioned in that paragraph; and

(b) the failure to publish that statement throughout that period is wholly attributable to circumstances which it would not be reasonable to have expected the company to prevent or avoid.

(2E) A company may, notwithstanding any provision to the contrary in its articles, take advantage of any of subsections (2A) to (2D).

(3) The summary financial statement shall be derived from the company's annual accounts and the directors' report and shall be in such form and contain such information as may be specified by regulations made by the Secretary of State.

(4) Every summary financial statement shall—

(a) state that it is only a summary of information in the company's annual accounts and the directors' report;

(b) contain a statement by the company's auditors of their opinion as to whether the summary financial statement is consistent with those accounts and that report and complies with the requirements of this section and regulations made under it;

(c) state whether the auditors' report on the annual accounts was unqualified or qualified, and if it was qualified set out the report in full together with any further material needed to understand the qualification;

(d) state whether the auditors' report on the annual accounts contained a statement under—

(i) section 237(2) (accounting records or returns inadequate or accounts not agreeing with records and returns), or

(ii) section 237(3) (failure to obtain necessary information and explanations),

and if so, set out the statement in full.

(5) Regulations under this section shall be made by statutory instrument which shall be subject to annulment in pursuance of a resolution of either House of Parliament.

(6) If default is made in complying with this section or regulations made under it, the company and every officer of it who is in default is guilty of an offence and liable to a fine.

(7) Section 240 (requirements in connection with publication of accounts) does not apply in relation to the provision to entitled persons of a summary financial statement in accordance with this section.

General note

This provision (introduced by CA 1989) permits listed public companies to offer summary financial statements to their shareholders (and others) instead of the full annual accounts and reports. This concession enables companies to save costs and provides shareholders with information in a more accessible format.

S 251(1)

A company cannot take advantage of this provision if it is prohibited from so doing by a 'relevant provision' in the memorandum or articles of association or any debenture instrument, see the Companies (Summary Financial Statements) Regulations 1995, SI 1995/2092, reg 3(1).

The reference to the Official List as maintained by The London Stock Exchange Limited is to be read as a reference to the Official List as maintained by the Financial Services Authority, by virtue of the Official Listing of Securities (Change of Competent Authority) Regulations 2000, SI 2000/968, reg 4.

S 251(2), (3), (5)

The use of summary financial statements is governed by the Companies (Summary Financial Statements) Regulations 1995, SI 1995/2092, which lay down detailed rules governing the ascertainment of the shareholders' wishes with regard to the receipt of the annual accounts and reports.

S 251(2A)–(2E)

Electronic communication   These provisions were inserted by the Companies Act 1985 (Electronic Communications) Order 2000, SI 2000/3373, art 14, as from 22 December 2000. The intention is to facilitate the electronic communication of this document by a company to a member where the member has agreed to that method of communication. The provisions are identical to s 238(4A)–(4E) which provide for the electronic communication of the annual accounts and reports to the members, see the note to those provisions.

S 251(4)

The detailed requirements as to the auditors' statement in effect requires a review by the auditors in addition to that required in order to prepare their report under s 235 and therefore involves the company in additional costs.

S 251(6)

As to penalties, see s 730, Sch 24; 'officer in default' is defined in s 730(5).

S 251(7)

This exclusion of s 240 ensures that summary financial statements can be published without having to comply with the various obligations imposed by s 240 with respect to the publication of statutory and non-statutory accounts.

PRIVATE COMPANIES

252. Election to dispense with laying of accounts and reports before general meeting

(1)   A private company may elect (by elective resolution in accordance with section 379A) to dispense with the laying of accounts and reports before the company in general meeting.

(2)   An election has effect in relation to the accounts and reports in respect of the financial year in which the election is made and subsequent financial years.

(3)   Whilst an election is in force, the references in the following provisions of this Act to the laying of accounts before the company in general meeting shall be read as references to the sending of copies of the accounts to members and others under section 238(1)—

(a)   section 235(1)(accounts on which auditors are to report),

(b)   section 270(3) and (4) (accounts by reference to which distributions are justified), and

(c)   section 320(2) (accounts relevant for determining company's net assets for purposes of ascertaining whether approval required for certain transactions);

and the requirement in section 271(4) that the auditors' statement under that provision be laid before the company in general meeting shall be read as a requirement that it be sent to members and others along with the copies of the accounts sent to them under section 238(1).

(4)   If an election under this section ceases to have effect, section 241 applies in relation to the accounts and reports in respect of the financial year in which the election ceases to have effect and subsequent financial years.

General note

This provision (inserted by CA 1989) recognises that, for many private companies, the procedure of laying accounts and reports before a general meeting is a meaningless formality which is usually ignored.

S 252(1)

The requirements as to the laying of accounts and reports are contained in s 241; an elective resolution requires the agreement of all those entitled to attend and vote at the general meeting: s 379A(2).

There are no threshold requirements here and any private company may take advantage of this provision if the shareholders so elect. However, any member or auditor of the company may require that a general meeting be held for the purpose of laying the accounts and reports before the company (see s 253); and any member, by withholding his consent to the elective resolution, may prevent the company from dispensing with this requirement in the first place.

As to the appointment of auditors by a company (which is required to appoint them) which has elected under this provision to dispense with the laying of accounts before the company in general meeting, see ss 384, 385A.

S 252(2), (4)

The election has effect indefinitely unless the elective resolution ceases to have effect, see s 379A(3), (4).

---

253. Right of shareholder to require laying of accounts

(1)   Where an election under section 252 is in force, the copies of the accounts and reports sent out in accordance with section 238(1)—

  (a) shall be sent not less than 28 days before the end of the period allowed for laying and delivering accounts and reports, and

  (b) shall be accompanied, in the case of a member of the company, by a notice informing him of his right to require the laying of the accounts and reports before a general meeting;

and section 238(5) (penalty for default) applies in relation to the above requirements as to the requirements contained in that section.

(2)   Before the end of the period of 28 days beginning with the day on which the accounts and reports are sent out in accordance with section 238(1), any member or auditor of the company may by notice in writing deposited at the registered office of the company require that a general meeting be held for the purpose of laying the accounts and reports before the company.

(2A) The power of a member or auditor under subsection (2) to require the holding of a general meeting is exercisable not only by the deposit of a notice in writing but also by the transmission to the company at such address as may for the time being be specified for the purpose by or on behalf of the company of an electronic communication containing the requirement.

(3)   If the directors do not within 21 days from the date of—

  (a) the deposit of a notice containing a requirement under subsection (2), or

  (b) the receipt of such a requirement contained in an electronic communication, proceed

duly to convene a meeting, the person who required the holding of the meeting may do so himself.

(4)   A meeting so convened shall not be held more than three months from that date and shall be convened in the same manner, as nearly as possible, as that in which meetings are to be convened by directors.

(5)   Where the directors do not duly convene a meeting, any reasonable expenses incurred by reason of that failure by the person who required the

holding of the meeting shall be made good to him by the company, and shall be recouped by the company out of any fees, or other remuneration in respect of their services, due or to become due to such of the directors as were in default.

(6)   The directors shall be deemed not to have duly convened a meeting if they convene a meeting for a date more than 28 days after the date of the notice convening it.

S 253(1)

The period allowed for laying and delivering accounts and reports is determined by s 244; a 'member' is defined by s 22.

S 253(2)

Notice requiring meeting   The right to require the accounts and reports to be laid before the general meeting is given expressly to the auditors as well as the members. This is important as the auditors have the right to be heard at a general meeting on any part of the business which concerns them as auditors: s 390(1)(c). Without this provision, the directors could effectively prevent the auditors from being heard by ensuring that the company dispensed with the laying of the accounts. As to the registered office, see s 287.

S 253(2A)

Electronic communication   This provision was inserted by the Companies Act 1985 (Electronic Communications) Order 2000, SI 2000/3373, art 15(1), (2), as from 22 December 2000; it enables a member to give electronic notice for these purposes where the company is agreeable to such methods of communication being used, as evidenced by the company providing an address for these purposes; 'address' is defined in s 262.

S 253(3)–(6)

See notes to s 368(4)–(8), below, which contain equivalent provisions.

UNLIMITED COMPANIES

254. Exemption from requirement to deliver accounts and reports

(1)   The directors of an unlimited company are not required to deliver accounts and reports to the registrar in respect of a financial year if the following conditions are met.

(2)   The conditions are that at no time during the relevant accounting reference period—

   (a)   has the company been, to its knowledge, a subsidiary undertaking of an undertaking which was then limited, or

   (b)   have there been, to its knowledge, exercisable by or on behalf of two or more undertakings which were then limited, rights which if exercisable by one of them would have made the company a subsidiary undertaking of it, or

   (c)   has the company been a parent company of an undertaking which was then limited.

The references above to an undertaking being limited at a particular time are to an undertaking (under whatever law established) the liability of whose members is at that time limited.

(3)   The exemption conferred by this section does not apply if—

   (a)   the company is a banking or insurance company or the parent company of a banking or insurance group, or

   (b)   the company is a qualifying company within the meaning of the Partnerships and Unlimited Companies (Accounts) Regulations 1993, or

   (c)   if at any time during the relevant accounting period the company carried on business as the promoter of a trading stamp scheme within the Trading Stamps Act 1964.

(4)   Where a company is exempt by virtue of this section from the obligation to deliver accounts, section 240 (requirements in connection with publication of accounts) has effect with the following modifications—

   (a)   in subsection (3)(b) for the words from 'whether statutory accounts' to 'have been delivered to the registrar' substitute 'that the company is exempt from the requirement to deliver statutory accounts', and

   (b)   in subsection (5) for 'as required to be delivered to the registrar under section 242' substitute 'as prepared in accordance with this Part and approved by the board of directors'.

General note

Although this provision exempts unlimited companies within it from the requirement to deliver accounts and reports to the registrar of companies, such companies are obliged to deliver an annual return under s 363.

S 254(1)

The exemption provided by this provision is with respect to the delivery of accounts and reports to the registrar of companies as required by s 242 and an unlimited company must still prepare accounts as required by s 226. The accounts must be sent to every member (s 238) and laid before the general meeting (s 241, unless the company has dispensed with the laying of accounts under s 252). Where appropriate, the company may take advantage of the exemptions available to small companies in s 246. An 'unlimited company' is defined in s 1(2)(b).

In the past, this category of company was particularly useful for those who were unhappy about disclosing their business affairs to the public registry. Now, however, small limited companies are entitled to a large degree of privacy under s 246 so privacy requirements no longer dictate the use of an unlimited company.

S 254(2)

Part of a group of companies   There are limitations on the exemption where the unlimited company is part of a group and falls within any of the three categories prescribed: sub-s (2)(a) and (b) are dependent on the company's knowledge, for the company is not necessarily aware of arrangements between its members which may make it a subsidiary undertaking of another (see s 258, Sch 10A); but a company must know, for the purposes of sub-s (2)(c), if it is a parent company (defined in s 258, Sch 10A).

If the rights of limited companies in an unlimited company aggregated would make the unlimited company a subsidiary of one of them, the unlimited company cannot claim the exemption; as to the rights exercisable which might make a company a subsidiary undertaking, see Sch 10A. As to the determination of the accounting reference period, see s 224.

S 254(3)

As to the definition of 'a banking company', see s 744; likewise, as to the definition of 'an insurance company'; as to the definition of banking or insurance groups, see s 255A(4), (5).

BANKING AND INSURANCE COMPANIES AND GROUPS

255. Special provisions for banking and insurance companies

(1)   A banking company shall prepare its individual accounts in accordance with Part I of Schedule 9 rather than Schedule 4.

(2)   An insurance company shall prepare its individual accounts in accordance with Part I of Schedule 9A rather than Schedule 4.

(3)   Accounts so prepared shall contain a statement that they are prepared in accordance with the special provisions of this Part relating to banking companies or insurance companies, as the case may be.

(4)   In relation to the preparation of individual accounts in accordance with the special provisions of this Part, the references to Schedule 4 in section 226(4)

Section 255   Companies Act 1985

and (5) (relationship between specific requirements and duty to give true and
fair view) shall be read as references to the provisions of Part I of Schedule 9,
in the case of the accounts of banking companies, or to the provisions of
Part I of Schedule 9A, in the case of the accounts of insurance companies.

(5)   ...

General note

Companies generally prepare their individual accounts in accordance with Sch 4:
see s 226, but this and the following provisions make special provision for banking
and insurance companies to reflect their specialist activities.

S 255(1), (2)

As to the definition of 'a banking company', see s 744; likewise, as to the definition
of 'an insurance company'.

255A. Special provisions for banking and insurance groups

(1)   The parent company of a banking group shall prepare group accounts in
accordance with the provisions of this Part as modified by Part II of Schedule 9.

(2)   The parent company of an insurance group shall prepare group accounts
in accordance with the provisions of this Part as modified by Part II of Schedule
9A.

(3)   Accounts so prepared shall contain a statement that they are prepared in
accordance with the special provisions of this Part relating to banking groups
or to insurance groups, as the case may be.

(4)   References in this Part to a banking group are to a group where the parent
company is a banking company or where—

   (a) the parent company's principal subsidiary undertakings are wholly or
       mainly credit institutions, and

   (b) the parent company does not itself carry on any material business apart
       from the acquisition, management and disposal of interests in subsidiary
       undertakings.

(5)   References in this Part to an insurance group are to a group where the parent
company is an insurance company or where—

   (a) the parent company's principal subsidiary undertakings are wholly or
       mainly insurance companies, and

   (b) the parent company does not itself carry on any material business apart
       from the acquisition, management and disposal of interests in subsidiary
       undertakings.

(5A) For the purposes of subsections (4) and (5) above—

(a) a parent company's principal subsidiary undertakings are the subsidiary undertakings of the company whose results or financial position would principally affect the figures shown in the group accounts, and

(b) the management of interests in subsidiary undertakings includes the provision of services to such undertakings.

(6) In relation to the preparation of group accounts in accordance with the special provisions of this Part:

(a) the references to the provisions of Schedule 4A in section 227(5) and (6) (relationship between specific requirements and duty to give true and fair view) shall be read as references to those provisions as modified by Part II of Schedule 9, in the case of the group accounts of a banking group, or Part II of Schedule 9A, in the case of the group accounts of an insurance group; and

(b) the reference to paragraphs 52 to 57 of Schedule 4 in section 230(2)(relief from obligation to comply with those paragraphs where group accounts prepared) shall be read as a reference to 75 to 77, 80 and 81 of Part I of Schedule 9, in the case of the group accounts of a banking group, and as a reference to paragraphs 73, 74, 79 and 80 of Part I of Schedule 9A, in the case of the group accounts of an insurance group ...

General note

Companies generally prepare group accounts in accordance with Sch 8 (see s 227), but this provision makes special provision for banking and insurance companies.

S 255A(4)–(6))

As to the definition of 'a banking company', see s 744; likewise, as to the definition of 'an insurance company'; as to the definition of 'parent company' and 'subsidiary undertakings', see s 258 and Sch 10A.

255B. Modification of disclosure requirements in relation to banking company or group

(1) In relation to a banking company, or the parent company of a banking group, the provisions of Schedule 5 (Disclosure of information: related undertakings) have effect subject to Part III of Schedule 9.

(2) In relation to a banking company, or the holding company of a credit institution, the provisions of Schedule 6 (Disclosure of information: emoluments and other benefits of directors and others) have effect subject to Part IV of Schedule 9.

General note

Companies generally are required to disclose the information specified in Schs 5 and 6 in notes to their accounts (ss 231, 232); this provision modifies the application of those Schedules in the case of banking companies or groups.

S 255B(1)

As to the definition of 'a banking company', see s 744; as to the definition of 'a parent company of a banking group', see s 255A(4); as to the definition of 'a credit institution', see s 262(1); 'holding company' is defined in s 736.

255C. *(Inserted by CA 1989, s 18(1), and repealed by the Companies Act 1985 (Insurance Companies Accounts) Regulations 1993, SI 1993/3246, reg 5(1), Sch 2, para 3, as from 19 December 1993, subject to transitional provisions contained in regs 6, 7 thereof.)*

255D. Power to apply provisions to banking partnerships

(1)   The Secretary of State may by regulations apply to banking partnerships, subject to such exceptions, adaptations and modifications as he considers appropriate, the provisions of this Part applying to banking companies.

(2)   A 'banking partnership' means a partnership which is an authorised institution under the Banking Act 1987.

(3)   Regulations under this section shall be made by statutory instrument.

(4)   No regulations under this section shall be made unless a draft of the instrument containing the regulations has been laid before Parliament and approved by a resolution of each House.

255E.   *(Inserted by the Companies Act 1985 (Welsh Language Accounts) Regulations 1992, SI 1992/1083, reg 2(1),(4), and repealed by the Welsh Language Act 1993, ss 30(1),(5), 35(1), Sch 2, as from 1 February 1994.)*

CHAPTER III

SUPPLEMENTARY PROVISIONS

ACCOUNTING STANDARDS

256. Accounting standards

(1)   In this Part 'accounting standards' means statements of standard accounting practice issued by such body or bodies as may be prescribed by regulations.

(2)   References in this Part to accounting standards applicable to a company's annual accounts are to such standards as are, in accordance with their terms, relevant to the company's circumstances and to the accounts.

(3)   The Secretary of State may make grants to or for the purposes of bodies concerned with—

  (a) issuing accounting standards,

  (b) overseeing and directing the issuing of such standards, or

  (c) investigating departures from such standards or from the accounting requirements of this Act and taking steps to secure compliance with them.

(4)   Regulations under this section may contain such transitional and other supplementary and incidental provisions as appear to the Secretary of State to be appropriate.

General note

The Companies Act does not expressly say that there must be compliance with accounting standards but adherence to such standards follows from the requirement that accounts must give a true and fair view (although, it is accepted that, in exceptional cases, a departure from those standards might be necessary to give such a view): see note to s 226(2).

Sch 4, para 36A requires companies to state in the notes to the accounts as to whether the accounts have been prepared in accordance with the applicable accounting standards and requires particulars of any material departure (and the reasons for it) from those standards. However, a medium-sized company is exempt from compliance with this requirement (s 246A(2)); and there is no such requirement in Sch 8 applicable to the accounts of small companies: s 246(2).

S 256(1)

The Accounting Standards Board Limited, a subsidiary of the Financial Reporting Council, has been prescribed for these purposes: the Accounting Standards (Prescribed Body) Regulations 1990, SI 1990/1667.

POWER TO ALTER ACCOUNTING REQUIREMENTS

257. Power of Secretary of State to alter accounting requirements

(1) The Secretary of State may by regulations made by statutory instrument modify the provisions of this Part.

(2) Regulations which—

    (a) add to the classes of documents required to be prepared, laid before the company in general meeting or delivered to the registrar,

    (b) restrict the classes of company which have the benefit of any exemption, exception or special provision,

    (c) require additional matter to be included in a document of any class, or

    (d) otherwise render the requirements of this Part more onerous,

shall not be made unless a draft of the instrument containing the regulations has been laid before Parliament and approved by a resolution of each House.

(3) Otherwise, a statutory instrument containing regulations under this section shall be subject to annulment in pursuance of a resolution of either House of Parliament.

(4) Regulations under this section may—

    (a) make different provision for different cases or classes of case,

    (b) repeal and re-enact provisions with modifications of form or arrangement, whether or not they are modified in substance,

    (c) make consequential amendments or repeals in other provisions of this Act, or in other enactments, and

    (d) contain such transitional and other incidental and supplementary provisions as the Secretary of State thinks fit.

(5) Any modification by regulations under this section of section 258 or Schedule 10A (parent and subsidiary undertakings) does not apply for the purposes of enactments outside the Companies Acts unless the regulations so provide.

General note

This power has proved very useful and has been used on numerous occasions to modify the provisions of this Part to take account of changes in policy and practice. Note the differing procedures in sub-ss (2) and (3), depending on whether the proposed changes increase the regulatory burden on companies.

PARENT AND SUBSIDIARY UNDERTAKINGS

258. Parent and subsidiary undertakings

(1)   The expressions 'parent undertaking' and 'subsidiary undertaking' in this Part shall be construed as follows; and a 'parent company' means a parent undertaking which is a company.

(2)   An undertaking is a parent undertaking in relation to another undertaking, a subsidiary undertaking, if—

- (a)   it holds a majority of the voting rights in the undertaking, or
- (b)   it is a member of the undertaking and has the right to appoint or remove a majority of its board of directors, or
- (c)   it has the right to exercise a dominant influence over the undertaking—
  - (i)   by virtue of provisions contained in the undertaking's memorandum or articles, or
  - (ii)   by virtue of a control contract, or
- (d)   it is a member of the undertaking and controls alone, pursuant to an agreement with other shareholders or members, a majority of the voting rights in the undertaking.

(3)   For the purposes of subsection (2) an undertaking shall be treated as a member of another undertaking—

- (a)   if any of its subsidiary undertakings is a member of that undertaking, or
- (b)   if any shares in that other undertaking are held by a person acting on behalf of the undertaking or any of its subsidiary undertakings.

(4)   An undertaking is also a parent undertaking in relation to another undertaking, a subsidiary undertaking, if it has a participating interest in the undertaking and—

- (a)   it actually exercises a dominant influence over it, or
- (b)   it and the subsidiary undertaking are managed on a unified basis.

(5)   A parent undertaking shall be treated as the parent undertaking of undertakings in relation to which any of its subsidiary undertakings are, or are to be treated as, parent undertakings; and references to its subsidiary undertakings shall be construed accordingly.

(6)   Schedule 10A contains provisions explaining expressions used in this section and otherwise supplementing this section.

General note

Definition for accounting purposes only   This section operates for the purposes of this Part only, ie for accounting purposes only, and adopts a broader definition of 'parent and subsidiary undertakings' than that of 'parent and subsidiary companies', adopted for general purposes by ss 736, 736A (see notes to those provisions, below). The broader definition for accounting purposes was necessary to meet the requirements of the 7th EC Directive on Company Law (EEC) 83/349 ([1983] OJ L193/1).

This provision is supplemented by the detailed provisions of Schedule 10A.

S 258(1)

Inclusion of undertakings   'Undertaking' is defined in s 259 and encompasses incorporated and unincorporated entities; notwithstanding this, the obligation in s 227 to prepare group accounts falls on a 'parent company' and a parent company can only be an undertaking which is a company, ie within s 735 (essentially, a company incorporated under this or previous companies legislation). If a parent undertaking is not such a company, there is no requirement under this Part to prepare group accounts.

But where the parent company is a company required to prepare group accounts, the extension to 'undertakings' (defined in s 259) means that a body corporate (for example, a foreign company), partnership or unincorporated undertaking may need to be included in the consolidated accounts. This extension to undertakings has significantly reduced the ability of groups to exclude elements of their operations from their consolidated accounts.

S 258(2), (4), (5)

A parent undertaking   An undertaking is a parent undertaking of another undertaking, a subsidiary undertaking, in the following circumstances:

(1)   It holds a majority of the voting rights in the undertaking (defined in s 259) which is not the same necessarily as a majority of the shares in the undertaking, for shares may be non-voting. Sch 10A, para 2 explains what is meant by 'voting rights' in cases where the company has no share capital or the entity is not a company.

(2)   It is a member (as defined in sub-s (3)) and has the right to appoint or remove a majority of the board; see Sch 10A, para 3 for further elaboration on this provision.

(3)   It has a right to exercise a dominant influence either under the constitution or under a control contract; by which is meant, a right to give directions with respect to the operating and financial policies of that other undertaking which its directors are obliged to comply with, whether or not they are for the benefit of that other undertaking: Sch 10A, para 4. Doubt exists as to whether any such right could be permissible in this jurisdiction given the duty of the directors of a subsidiary to act in the best interests of the subsidiary.

(4)   It is a member (as defined in sub-s (3)) and controls, pursuant to an agreement, a majority of the voting rights in the undertaking.

(5)   It has a participating interest (defined in s 260) in an undertaking and actually exercises a dominant influence; an interest of 20% is presumed to be a participating interest unless the contrary is shown: s 260(2).

     This provision has had the greatest impact in terms of requiring the inclusion of entities in the consolidated accounts. Previously, parent companies were able to exclude entities which (because the parent only had a minority interest) were not subsidiaries requiring inclusion. The use of such off-balance sheet vehicles is greatly restricted now by this provision, for an entity in which the parent undertaking only has a minority interest but in respect of which it actually exercises a dominant influence must be included.

No guidance is given as to when a company exercises a dominant influence for these purposes (Sch 10A, para 4 is specifically excluded from application: see para 4(3)) but FRS 2, 'Accounting for Subsidiary Undertakings' (issued by the Accounting Standards Board, see note to s 226(2), above) offers some guidance.

FRS 2, 'Accounting for Subsidiary Undertakings' defines the 'actual exercise of a dominant influence' as the exercise of an influence that achieves the result that the operating and financial policies of the undertaking influenced are set in accordance with the wishes of the holder of the influence and for the benefit of the holder (whether or not the wishes are explicit); the effect of formal and informal agreements must be considered; commercial relationships, such as that of supplier, customer or lender, do not of themselves constitute an actual exercise of dominant influence; influence may be exercised in an interventionist or non-interventionist way; once evidence of the actual exercise of dominant influence is shown to exist, it should be presumed to continue unless the contrary is shown: see paras 69–73.

(6)   It has a participating interest as above and the parent and subsidiary undertaking are managed on a unified basis; this type of operation would be very rare in this jurisdiction.

(7)   A parent company of a subsidiary undertaking which itself has subsidiaries is a parent undertaking of those sub-subsidiaries also.

The reference to 'rights' in these provisions, such as the right to appoint or remove a majority of the directors or the right to exercise a dominant influence, is explained by Sch 10A, paras 5–11. Note, in particular, that rights held by a person in a fiduciary capacity are treated as not held by him (para 6); and that rights held by a nominee for another are treated as held by the other (para 7).

Even if a relationship is not that of a parent and subsidiary undertaking, the parent company still has to give information in the accounts about any significant interests which it has in entities which are not subsidiary undertakings: see Sch 4A, para 20, Sch 5, paras 21, 22 (joint ventures, associated undertakings); Sch 5, para 23 (other significant holdings of parent company or group). This is the case even if the parent company does not prepare group accounts: see Sch 5, para 7 (significant holdings in undertakings other than subsidiary undertakings to be disclosed in notes to the accounts).

S 258(3)

This provision ensures that a parent undertaking cannot avoid being so categorised by having shares held for it by a nominee and such interests are treated as being the direct interests of the parent undertaking; as to the meaning of 'shares' in this context, see s 259(2).

OTHER INTERPRETATION PROVISIONS

259. Meaning of 'undertaking' and related expressions

(1)   In this Part 'undertaking' means—

    (a)   a body corporate or partnership, or

    (b)   an unincorporated association carrying on a trade or business, with or without a view to profit.

(2)   In this Part references to shares—

    (a)   in relation to an undertaking with a share capital, are to allotted shares;

    (b)   in relation to an undertaking with capital but no share capital, are to rights to share in the capital of the undertaking; and

    (c)   in relation to an undertaking without capital, are to interests—

        (i)   conferring any right to share in the profits or liability to contribute to the losses of the undertaking, or

        (ii) giving rise to an obligation to contribute to the debts or expenses of the undertaking in the event of a winding up.

(3)   Other expressions appropriate to companies shall be construed, in relation to an undertaking which is not a company, as references to the corresponding persons, officers, documents or organs, as the case may be, appropriate to undertakings of that description.

This is subject to provision in any specific context providing for the translation of such expressions.

(4)   References in this Part to 'fellow subsidiary undertakings' are to undertakings which are subsidiary undertakings of the same parent undertaking but are not parent undertakings or subsidiary undertakings of each other.

(5)   In this Part 'group undertaking', in relation to an undertaking, means an undertaking which is—

    (a)   a parent undertaking or subsidiary undertaking of that undertaking, or

    (b)   a subsidiary undertaking of any parent undertaking of that undertaking.

S 259(1)

As to the definition of 'body corporate', see s 740; unincorporated entities had to be included in order to meet the requirements of the 7th EC Directive on Company Law (EEC) 83/349 ([1983] OJ L193/1).

S 259(2)

As not all undertakings will be companies with a share capital, references to 'shares' have to be modified to encompass the differing entities which are undertakings for these purposes. As to when shares are allotted, see s 738(1).

260. Participating interests

(1)   In this Part a 'participating interest' means an interest held by an undertaking in the shares of another undertaking which it holds on a long-term basis for the purpose of securing a contribution to its activities by the exercise of control or influence arising from or related to that interest.

(2)   A holding of 20 per cent or more of the shares of an undertaking shall be presumed to be a participating interest unless the contrary is shown.

(3)   The reference in subsection (1) to an interest in shares includes—

    (a)   an interest which is convertible into an interest in shares, and

    (b)   an option to acquire shares or any such interest;

and an interest or option falls within paragraph (a) or (b) notwithstanding that the shares to which it relates are, until the conversion or the exercise of the option, unissued.

(4)   For the purposes of this section an interest held on behalf of an undertaking shall be treated as held by it.

(5)   For the purposes of this section as it applies in relation to the expression 'participating interest' in section 258(4) (definition of 'subsidiary undertaking')—

    (a)   there shall be attributed to an undertaking any interests held by any of its subsidiary undertakings, and

    (b)   the references in subsection (1) to the purpose and activities of an undertaking include the purposes and activities of any of its subsidiary undertakings and of the group as a whole.

(6)   In the balance sheet and profit and loss formats set out in Part I of Schedule 4, Part I of Schedule 8, Schedule 8A, Chapter I of Part I of Schedule 9 and Chapter I of Part I of Schedule 9A, 'participating interest' does not include an interest in a group undertaking.

(7)   For the purposes of this section as it applies in relation to the expression 'participating interest'—

    (a)   in those formats as they apply in relation to group accounts, and

    (b)   in paragraph 20 of Schedule 4A (group accounts: undertakings to be accounted for as associated undertakings),

the references in subsections (1) to (4) to the interest held by, and the purposes and activities of, the undertaking concerned shall be construed as references to the interest held by, and the purposes and activities of, the group (within the meaning of paragraph 1 of that Schedule).

S 260(1)

As to the meaning of 'shares' in this context (given that undertakings need not necessarily have share capital), see s 259(2).

S 260(6)

'Group undertaking' is defined in s 259(5).

261. Notes to the accounts

(1) Information required by this Part to be given in notes to a company's annual accounts may be contained in the accounts or in a separate document annexed to the accounts.

(2) References in this Part to a company's annual accounts, or to a balance sheet or profit and loss account, include notes to the accounts giving information which is required by any provision of this Act, and required or allowed by any such provision to be given in a note to company accounts.

General note

This provision clarifies the position regarding the notes to the accounts.

262. Minor definitions

(1) In this Part—

'address', except in section 228, in relation to electronic communications, includes any number or address used for the purposes of such communications;

'annual accounts' means—

(a) the individual accounts required by section 226, and

(b) any group accounts required by section 227,

(but see also section 230 (treatment of individual profit and loss account where group accounts prepared));

'annual report', in relation to a company, means the directors' report required by section 234;

'balance sheet date' means the date as at which the balance sheet was made up;

'capitalisation', in relation to work or costs, means treating that work or those costs as a fixed asset;

'credit institution' means a credit institution as defined in article 1 of Directive 2000/12/EC of the European Parliament and of the Council of 20 March 2000 relating to the taking up and pursuit of the business of credit institutions, that is to say an undertaking whose business is to receive deposits or other repayable funds from the public and to grant credits for its own account;

...

'fixed assets' means assets of a company which are intended for use on a continuing basis in the company's activities, and 'current assets' means assets not intended for such use;

'group' means a parent undertaking and its subsidiary undertakings;

'included in the consolidation', in relation to group accounts, or 'included in consolidated group accounts', means that the undertaking is included in the accounts by the method of full (and not proportional) consolidation, and references to an undertaking excluded from consolidation shall be construed accordingly;

'purchase price', in relation to an asset of a company or any raw materials or consumables used in the production of such an asset, includes any consideration (whether in cash or otherwise) given by the company in respect of that asset or those materials or consumables, as the case may be;

'qualified', in relation to an auditors' report, means that the report does not state the auditors' unqualified opinion that the accounts have been properly prepared in accordance with this Act or, in the case of an undertaking not required to prepare accounts in accordance with this Act, under any corresponding legislation under which it is required to prepare accounts;

'true and fair view' refers—

(a)   in the case of individual accounts, to the requirement of section 226(2), and

(b)   in the case of group accounts, to the requirement of section 227(3);

'turnover', in relation to a company, means the amounts derived from the provision of goods and services falling within the company's ordinary activities, after deduction of—

(i)   trade discounts,

(ii)   value added tax, and

(iii) any other taxes based on the amounts so derived.

(2)   In the case of an undertaking not trading for profit, any reference in this Part to a profit and loss account is to an income and expenditure account; and references to profit and loss and, in relation to group accounts, to a consolidated profit and loss account shall be construed accordingly.

(3)   References in this Part to 'realised profits' and 'realised losses', in relation to a company's accounts, are to such profits or losses of the company as fall to be treated as realised in accordance with principles generally accepted, at the time when the accounts are prepared, with respect to the determination for accounting purposes of realised profits or losses.

This is without prejudice to—

(a)   the construction of any other expression (where appropriate) by reference to accepted accounting principles or practice, or

(b)   any specific provision for the treatment of profits or losses of any description as realised.

General note

See also s 742.

'**Address**'　This definition was inserted by the Companies Act 1985 (Electronic Communications) Order 2000, SI 2000/3373, art 16(1), as from 22 December 2000; and the reference to any number enables a fax number to be an address for these purposes.

262A. Index of defined expressions

The following Table shows the provisions of this Part defining or otherwise explaining expressions used in this Part (other than expressions used only in the same section or paragraph)—

the 1982 Act (in Schedule 9A)	paragraph 81 of Part I of that Schedule
accounting reference date and accounting reference period	section 224
accounting standards and applicable accounting standards	section 256
address	section 262(1)
annual accounts (generally)	section 262(1)
(includes notes to the accounts)	section 261(2)
annual report	section 262(1)
associated undertaking (in Schedule 4A)	paragraph 20 of that Schedule
balance sheet (includes notes)	section 261(2)
balance sheet date	section 262(1)
.....	
banking group	section 255A(4)
.....	
capitalisation (in relation to work or costs)	section 262(1)
credit institution	section 262(1)
current assets	section 262(1)
.....	
fellow subsidiary undertaking	section 259(4)
financial fixed assets (in Schedule 9)	paragraph 82 of Part I of that Schedule

financial year	section 223
fixed assets	section 262(1)
general business (in Schedule 9A)	paragraph 81 of Part I of that Schedule
group	section 262(1)
group undertaking	section 259(5)
historical cost accounting rules	
—in Schedule 4	paragraph 29 of that Schedule
—in Schedule 8	paragraph 29 of that Schedule
—in Schedule 9	paragraph 39 of Part I of that Schedule
—in Schedule 9A	paragraph 20(1) of Part I of that Schedule
included in the consolidation and related expressions	section 262(1)
individual accounts	section 226(1)
insurance group	section 255A(5)
land of freehold tenure and land of leasehold tenure (in relation to Scotland)	
—in Schedule 4	paragraph 93 of that Schedule
—in Schedule 9	paragraph 86 of Part I of that Schedule
—in Schedule 9A	paragraph 85 of Part I of that Schedule
lease, long lease and short lease	
—in Schedule 4	paragraph 83 of that Schedule
—in Schedule 9	paragraph 82 of Part I of that Schedule
—in Schedule 9A	paragraph 81 of Part I of that Schedule
listed investment	
—in Schedule 4	paragraph 84 of that Schedule
—in Schedule 8	paragraph 54 of that Schedule
—in Schedule 9A	paragraph 81 of Part I of that Schedule
listed security (in Schedule 9)	paragraph 82 of Part I of that Schedule
long term business (in Schedule 9A)	paragraph 81 of Part I of that Schedule
long term fund (in Schedule 9A)	paragraph 81 of Part I of that Schedule

notes to the accounts	section 261(1)
parent undertaking (and parent company)	section 258 and Schedule 10A
participating interest	section 260
pension costs	
—in Schedule 4	paragraph 94(2) of that Schedule
—in Schedule 8	paragraph 59(2) of that Schedule
—in Schedule 9	paragraph 87(b) of Part I of that Schedule
—in Schedule 9A	paragraph 86(b) of Part I of that Schedule
period allowed for laying and delivering accounts and reports	section 244
policy holder (in Schedule 9A)	paragraph 81 of Part I of that Schedule
profit and loss account (includes notes)	section 261(2)
(in relation to a company not trading for profit)	section 262(2)
provision	
—in Schedule 4	paragraphs 88 and 89 of that Schedule
—in Schedule 8	paragraphs 57 and 58 of that Schedule
—in Schedule 9	paragraph 85 of Part I of that Schedule
—in Schedule 9A	paragraph 84 of Part I of that Schedule
provision for unexpired risks (in Schedule 9A)	paragraph 81 of Part I of that Schedule
purchase price	section 262(1)
qualified	section 262(1)
realised losses and realised profits	section 262(3)
repayable on demand (in Schedule 9)	paragraph 82 of Part I of that Schedule
reporting accountant	section 249C(1)
reserve (in Schedule 9A)	paragraph 32 of that Schedule
sale and repurchase transaction (in Schedule 9)	paragraph 82 of Part I of that Schedule

sale and option to resell transaction (in Schedule 9)	paragraph 82 of Part I of Schedule
shares	section 259(2)
social security costs	
—in Schedule 4	paragraph 94(1) and (3) of that Schedule
—in Schedule 8	paragraph 59(1) and (3) of that Schedule
—in Schedule 9	paragraph 87(a) and (c) of Part I of that Schedule
—in Schedule 9A	paragraph 86(a) and (c) of Part I of that Schedule
special provisions for banking and insurance companies and groups	sections 255 and 255A
subsidiary undertaking	section 258 and Schedule 10A
true and fair view	section 262(1)
turnover	section 262(1)
undertaking and related expressions	section 259(1) to (3).

PART VIII

DISTRIBUTION OF PROFITS AND ASSETS

General note to this Part

These provisions, which were introduced by CA 1980, provide the technical framework which determines what is a lawful distribution by a company to its members. The most common form of distribution is a dividend but the provisions extend beyond simple dividend payments. The statutory provisions operate alongside the common law which is expressly retained by s 281 and which remains an essential component in the regulation of improper distributions.

Ultra vires distributions   The fundamental rule is that there can be no return of capital to shareholders other than on a reduction of capital, properly approved, or by the use of some other lawful procedure (for example, a purchase of the company's own shares), or on the winding up of the company: *Trevor v Whitworth* (1887) 12 App Cas 409, HL; see s 263(2). Inherent in that proposition is the rule that dividends may not be paid out of capital: *Re Exchange Banking Co, Flitcroft's Case* (1882) 21 Ch D 519. That common law position is in turn reflected in the statutory statement that there may be no distribution (very broadly defined) of the company's assets to its members except out of profits available for the purpose (s 263(1)); a requirement which does not amount to an obligation to maintain net assets to the value of the share capital and the undistributable reserves although that obligation is imposed on public companies by s 264.

A distribution of the company's assets to its members not out of available profits (other than those excepted by s 263(2)(a)–(d)) in breach of the prohibition on a distribution to the members out of capital is ultra vires, beyond the company's capacity, and void; and it cannot be ratified, not even by the unanimous consent of the shareholders: *Ashbury Railway Carriage and Iron Co Ltd v Riche* (1875) LR 7 HL 653; *Re Exchange Banking Co, Flitcroft's Case* (1882) 21 Ch D 519; *Aveling Barford Ltd v Perion Ltd* [1989] BCLC 626; *Re Halt Garage (1964) Ltd* [1982] 3 All ER 1016; s 35 is irrelevant here since it relates only to acts which are ultra vires by reason of anything in the company's memorandum.

Directors' duties   Directors must act bona fide in the interests of the company as a whole, taking into account the interests of their shareholders and employees (s 309) and, if the company is insolvent or of doubtful solvency, the interests of their creditors. It may be the case that a distribution is technically possible, in that the company has profits available for distribution having regard to the relevant accounts (ss 263(1), 270), but a more prudent course, in the best interests of the company, would be the transfer of sums to reserves rather than their distribution as a dividend.

Directors must exercise care and skill to the objective standard set by IA 1986, s 214, which standard, it is now accepted, is of general application. A director's conduct will be judged against the general knowledge, skill and experience that may reasonably be expected of a person carrying out the same functions as are carried out by that director in relation to the company as well as the general knowledge, skill and experience that that director has: see *Norman v Theodore Goddard* [1991] BCLC 1028 at 1030, 1031; *Re D'Jan of London Ltd* [1994] 1 BCLC 561 at 563. This duty applies in the context of dividend decisions as in any other sphere of management activity: *Bairstow v Queens Moat Houses plc* [2000] 1 BCLC 549.

Application of the statutory provisions and the common law   Section 281 specifically retains the common law and it impacts in a number of ways, as can be seen by considering the position where a distribution by a company to a member or members is challenged. The initial issue would be whether there has been a 'distribution' as defined by s 263(2) which provision is all encompassing and extends to 'every description of distribution of a company's assets to its members, whether in cash or otherwise'; see note to s 263(2), below. If there was no distribution within s 263(2), the issue would be whether the directors had acted in accordance with their duties, including their duties to the creditors when the company is insolvent or of doubtful solvency.

Assuming the transaction was a distribution, the next issue would be whether the company had profits available for distribution as required by this Part; this is a technical matter to be determined by reference to the company's accounts: s 270(1). If the company did not have distributable profits, then the company had no capacity to make a distribution and it would be ultra vires and void. Having caused the company to make an unlawful distribution, the directors would be liable to account to the company for it to the extent discussed in the note to s 277. Recipients of the distribution also could be liable to the extent discussed in that note. The directors may be in breach of their duties to act bona fide in the interests of the company as a whole and to exercise such care and skill as is required.

If the company did have profits available for distribution, then the issue would be whether the directors had acted in accordance with their duties to act bona fide in the interests of the company as a whole and to exercise such care and skill as is required. If the directors acted in breach of either of those obligations then, despite the availability of distributable profits, they and the recipients of any distribution would be liable to the extent discussed in the note to s 277, below.

Redemption or purchase of own shares   The definition of distributable profits in s 263(3) also applies to the redemption and purchase of a company's own shares: ss 160, 181; and a redemption or purchase (other than any excluded under s 263(2)(b)) is a distribution within s 263(1) and subject therefore to the accounting requirements in ss 270–276: see *BDG Roof-Bond v Douglas* [2000] 1 BCLC 401.

Statutory modification for banking and insurance companies   The application of ss 264–275 is modified by Sch 11 with respect to banking and insurance companies which have prepared their accounts in accordance with the special provisions of Part VII (ss 255–255D) relating to such companies: s 279.

LIMITS OF COMPANY'S POWER OF DISTRIBUTION

263. Certain distributions prohibited

(1)   A company shall not make a distribution except out of profits available for the purpose.

(2)   In this Part,'distribution' means every description of distribution of a company's assets to its members, whether in cash or otherwise, except distribution by way of—

    (a)   an issue of shares as fully or partly paid bonus shares,

(b) the redemption or purchase of any of the company's own shares out of capital (including the proceeds of any fresh issue of shares) or out of unrealised profits in accordance with Chapter VII of Part V,

(c) the reduction of share capital by extinguishing or reducing the liability of any of the members on any of the company's shares in respect of share capital not paid up, or by paying off paid up share capital, and

(d) a distribution of assets to members of the company on its winding up.

(3)   For purposes of this Part, a company's profits available for distribution are its accumulated, realised profits, so far as not previously utilised by distribution or capitalisation, less its accumulated, realised losses, so far as not previously written off in a reduction or reorganisation of capital duly made.

This is subject to the provision made by sections 265 and 266 for investment and other companies.

(4)   A company shall not apply an unrealised profit in paying up debentures, or any amounts unpaid on its issued shares.

(5)   Where the directors of a company are, after making all reasonable enquiries, unable to determine whether a particular profit made before 22nd December 1980 is realised or unrealised, they may treat the profit as realised; and where after making such enquiries they are unable to determine whether a particular loss so made is realised or unrealised, they may treat the loss as unrealised.

General note

This provision applies to all distributions of a company's assets to its members, whether in cash or otherwise, and whether the company is public or private, limited or, even, unlimited. The application of this Part to unlimited companies appears somewhat anomalous given, for example, that such companies may reduce capital without the sanction of the court and the fact that the members have an unlimited liability on winding up. Possibly the mischief which is being addressed is uncontrolled distributions to members of such a company who then swiftly part with their assets so that their unlimited status on winding up is of no assistance to the company' creditors.

Additional constraints on public companies are set out in s 264.

Private companies   The most common form of distribution is a dividend, of course, but private companies (which make up 99% of the register of companies) rarely declare dividends. In such companies, the shareholders typically are also the directors and receive a return on their investment in the form of directors' remuneration rather than dividends. Where there are shareholders who are not directors in such companies, the failure to declare dividends can be a source of tension and may, in an appropriate case, merit a petition under s 459: see *Re a company (No 004415 of 1996)* [1997] 1 BCLC 479; *Quinlan v Essex Hinge Co Ltd* [1996] 2 BCLC 417; *Re Sam Weller & Sons Ltd* [1990] BCLC 80.

Any distribution must be justified by reference to the company's accounts: see s 270(1), (5).

S 263(1)

The key issues are: (i) the meaning of a 'distribution' for these purposes; and (ii) the meaning of 'profits available' for these purposes. Issue (i) is addressed in sub-s (2); issue (ii) in sub-s (3).

A distribution in breach of this provision is ultra vires: see *Precision Dippings Ltd v Precision Dippings Marketing Ltd* [1985] BCLC 385; *Re Cleveland Trust plc* [1991] BCLC 424; *Bairstow v Queens Moat Houses plc* [2001] All ER (D) 211 (May), CA, affg [2000] 1 BCLC 549; *Allied Carpets Group plc v Nethercott* [2001] BCC 81; and the general note to this Part, above.

It would seem that a company 'makes' a distribution both when it declares a dividend (at which point it becomes a debt due to the shareholder: *Re Severn and Wye and Severn Bridge Railway Co* [1896] 1 Ch 559) and when it pays that dividend, which may be some time later. There must be distributable profits at both times, therefore, if the directors are to make the distribution. Where the payment of a declared dividend is not made, and winding up intervenes, the position as to the sums due by way of dividend is governed by IA 1986, s 74(2)(f).

S 263(2)

Meaning of 'distribution'   A fuller description of 'distribution' might be any distribution by a company to its members where what the company gives to the members is not matched by what the company receives, ie any transaction other than one for consideration. A company which hires a member to carry out work for it does not make a distribution when paying for those services but the paying of remuneration to a member for non-existent services (see *Re Halt Garage Ltd* [1982] 3 All ER 1016), or the transfer of an asset to a member at a considerable undervalue (see *Aveling Barford Ltd v Perion Ltd* [1989] BCLC 626), or the payment of a dividend, would be a distribution. With the exception of the excluded matters in sub-s (2)(a)–(d), all distributions by a company to its members are within the statutory provisions and can only be made out of distributable profits.

Label is not determinative   The label which the parties give to a transaction is not determinative of whether a distribution for these purposes, requiring available profits, has occurred. In *Aveling Barford Ltd v Perion Ltd* [1989] BCLC 626 the distribution in question was the sale of property by a company (which had no distributable profits) at a considerable undervalue to another entity controlled by the company's sole beneficial shareholder. The problem arose, of course, only because the sale was at a substantial undervalue; had there been full consideration, then there would have been no distribution of assets in the first place. As it was, the transaction was ultra vires and void as an unauthorised return of capital; see also *Ridge Securities Ltd v IRC* [1964] 1 All ER 275. In those instances where the company clearly had no distributable assets, the courts tend not to concern themselves with a consideration of whether there was a distribution and whether the company had distributable profits and instead, as a matter of shorthand, simply apply the common law principle prohibiting a return of capital, directly or indirectly, to the shareholders.

Directors' remuneration need not be paid out of distributable profits but the mere fact that the label of 'director's remuneration' is attached to drawings does not preclude the court from examining their true nature: *Re Halt Garage (1964) Ltd* [1982] 3 All ER 1016. Sums paid to a director in excess of what she was entitled to under the articles for holding office as a director, at a time when the company was insolvent, were a disguised gift of capital or payment of dividends in recognition of her co-proprietorship of the business and as such were ultra vires: *Re Halt Garage (1964) Ltd* [1982] 3 All ER 1016.

The decision in *MacPherson v European Strategic Bureau Ltd* [2000] 2 BCLC 683, illustrates the confusion which can arise on this question of whether there has been a distribution. The shareholders in a company had agreed with the company that there would be a distribution to the shareholders of the gross proceeds of all current contracts held by the company, once certain liabilities had been met and expenses incurred reimbursed. The company was insolvent at the time of the agreement. The company subsequently refused to implement the agreement arguing, inter alia, that the distribution was contrary to s 263.

The Court of Appeal held that the agreement was unenforceable but on other grounds. Chadwick LJ, with whom Peter Gibson J agreed, found that the agreement was contractually binding, being in consideration of services provided and to be provided by the shareholders to the company. It was not therefore a distribution within s 263 and so there was no requirement for distributable profits. However, the directors in entering into such an agreement (which in practice effected an informal winding up of the company without making proper provision for the company's creditors) were in breach of their duty to act bona fide in the interests of the company as a whole; alternatively, Chadwick LJ thought, the agreement was ultra vires the company.

Buxton LJ, while agreeing that the agreement was unenforceable, would have disagreed on the 'distribution' issue, believing that the agreement was not supported by consideration and therefore there was a distribution within s 263. This would have led to a more logical analysis, perhaps, which would be that distributable profits were required but, as the company was insolvent at the time of the agreement, the distribution was ultra vires and void and so unenforceable. Directors, in entering into such an agreement, would be in breach of their duties.

Postscript on *Aveling Barford*   The decision in *Aveling Barford Ltd v Perion Ltd* [1989] BCLC 626, or rather the practical consequences of the decision, has been the subject of much comment by the Law Society Company Law Committee which has made representations on the matter to the Department of Trade and Industry on a number of occasions.

The concern is the impact of the decision on intra-group asset transfers conducted by reference to book value rather than the higher market value, something which may be done for business or tax reasons. As a transfer at book value may have an element of undervalue, the transaction would be a 'distribution' and the company must ensure that it has distributable profits. The result, in the view of the Law Society Committee, is that companies are often required either to abandon a transfer or to structure it in a more complex way (for example, having assets revalued and sold so that the realised profit can be distributed) with an increase in the costs and time involved. The Committee's preference is for an amendment to the statute to make clear that, save where the company has no distributable reserves, transfers of assets at book value should be treated as a nil distribution.

S 263(2)(a)–(d)

Matters which are not distributions   As the specified matters are not distributions for these purposes, there is no need for the company to have profits available for distribution before undertaking the transaction.

Fully paid bonus issues may be funded by the share premium account (s 130(2)) or the capital redemption reserve (s 170(4)), neither of which are distributable otherwise. Likewise, an unrealised profit may be applied in paying up a bonus issue (see s 278, also Table A, reg 110) although it could not otherwise be distributed (see sub-s (3)).

> 'The reason for the lack of legislative concern [with a bonus issue] is that the fund necessary to pay up the shares remains with the company. There is no distribution of company assets to shareholders and creditors' interests are not therefore at risk'.

(*Re Cleveland Trust plc* [1991] BCLC 424 at 432, per Scott J.)

A purchase out of capital may only be made by a private company: see s 171. The effect of this provision is that purchases of a company's own shares other than out of these specified funds is a distribution for the purposes of this Part so, for example, ss 270–276 apply with regard to the relevant accounts: see *BDG Roof-Bond v Douglas* [2000] 1 BCLC 401. The requirement that the purchase etc be 'in accordance with Part V' excludes unlimited companies (to whom Part V does not apply) from this exemption. The result is that an unlimited company wishing to purchase or redeem shares must have distributable profits.

As to a reduction of capital, see s 135.

The requirement in sub-s (2)(d) is a distribution by the company 'on its winding up' and, to be within this exemption, it would not suffice if the members attempted an informal winding up. The provision envisages that the company has utilised one of the formal mechanisms for voluntary or compulsory winding up.

S 263(3)

As to definitions, 'profits and losses' are defined in s 280(3); 'realised profits' and 'realised losses' are defined in s 262(3); s 742; 'capitalisation' is defined in s 280(2).

Accumulated profits and losses   The requirement that profits and losses be measured as accumulated profits or losses prevents a company from considering one accounting period in isolation and declaring a dividend while ignoring previous losses.

Realised profits and losses   Only realised profits may be used, but equally only realised losses have to be taken into account. The meaning of 'realised profits' and 'realised losses' is to be determined in accordance with 'principles generally accepted', a definition which is not too helpful but throws the issue back on accounting practices: s 262(3) applied by s 742. It would seem that the accounting position is that realised profits are primarily those which meet the criterion of 'cash or other assets, the ultimate cash realisation of which can be assessed with reasonable certainty' while all losses should be regarded as realised losses except 'to the extent that the law, accounting standards or Technical Releases provide otherwise': see ICAEW draft Technical Release 25/00 *The Determination of Realised Profits and*

Distributable Profits. Unrealised losses are not ignored, in fact, since the amount available for distribution has to be justified by reference to the company's accounts (s 270(1)); and a public company is subject to s 264, which requires that unrealised losses be taken into account.

Certain provisions offer further guidance as to what is a realised profit: see s 263(5) (treatment of pre-1980 Act profits); s 275(2) (unrealised profit on a revaluation of a fixed asset treated as realised profit in certain circumstances); s 276 (distributions in kind). Likewise, with respect to what is a realised loss: see s 269 (treatment of development costs); s 275(1) (certain provisions treated as realised loss). As to pre-1980 Act losses, see s 263(5) which allows them to be treated as unrealised losses.

A company conducting an unlawful lottery with the result that all contributions by participants are liable to repayment has no profits out of which it might lawfully make a distribution: see *One Life Ltd v Roy* [1996] 2 BCLC 608.

S 263(4)

This is essentially an anti-avoidance provision.

264. Restriction on distribution of assets

(1)   A public company may only make a distribution at any time—

  (a) if at that time the amount of its net assets is not less than the aggregate of its called-up share capital and undistributable reserves, and

  (b) if, and to the extent that, the distribution does not reduce the amount of those assets to less than that aggregate.

This is subject to the provision made by sections 265 and 266 for investment and other companies.

(2)   In subsection (1),'net assets' means the aggregate of the company's assets less the aggregate of its liabilities ('liabilities' to include any provision for liabilities or charges within paragraph 89 of Schedule 4).

(3)   A company's undistributable reserves are—

  (a) the share premium account,

  (b) the capital redemption reserve,

  (c) the amount by which the company's accumulated, unrealised profits, so far as not previously utilised by capitalisation of a description to which this paragraph applies, exceed its accumulated, unrealised losses (so far as not previously written off in a reduction or reorganisation of capital duly made), and

  (d) any other reserve which the company is prohibited from distributing by any enactment (other than one contained in this Part) or by its memorandum or articles;

and paragraph (c) applies to every description of capitalisation except a transfer of profits of the company to its capital redemption reserve on or after 22nd December 1980.

(4)   A public company shall not include any uncalled share capital as an asset in any accounts relevant for purposes of this section.

General note

Any distribution must be justified by reference to the company's accounts: see s 270(1), (5).

S 264(1)

Public companies   The effect of this provision is that a public company must take unrealised losses into account. A 'public company' is defined by s 1(3); 'distribution' by s 263(2); 'called-up share capital' by s 737.

S 264(2), (4)

The inclusion within 'liabilities' of provisions within Sch 4, para 89 will require the inclusion of any amount retained as reasonably necessary for the purpose of providing for any liability or loss which is either likely to be incurred, or certain to be incurred but uncertain as to amount or as to the date on which it will arise. 'Uncalled share capital' (defined in s 737) must not be treated as an asset: sub-s (4).

S 264(3)

Undistributable reserves   As to the share premium account, see s 130; sums released from the share premium account following its cancellation are available for distribution: *Quayle Munro Ltd, Petitioners* [1994] 1 BCLC 410 at 414; subject to any undertakings given to the court which confirmed the reduction of capital. As to the capital redemption reserve, see s 170.

The net accumulated unrealised profit standing to the credit of the revaluation reserve must be treated as undistributable to the extent indicated here, ie the amount by which the unrealised profit (not defined, but see note to s 263(3), above as to what is a realised profit) exceeds the unrealised losses (not defined, but see note to s 263(3), above as to what is a realised loss); 'capitalisation' is defined by s 280(2). For an example of an undistributable reserve within sub-s (3)(d), see s 148(4).

265. Other distributions by investment companies

(1)   Subject to the following provisions of this section, an investment company (defined in section 266) may also make a distribution at any time out of its accumulated, realised revenue profits, so far as not previously utilised by a distribution or capitalisation, less its accumulated revenue losses (whether realised or unrealised), so far as not previously written off in a reduction or reorganisation of capital duly made—

(a)   if at that time the amount of its assets is at least equal to one and a half times the aggregate of its liabilities, and

    (b) if, and to the extent that, the distribution does not reduce that amount to less than one and a half times that aggregate.

(2) In subsection (1)(a),'liabilities' includes any provision for liabilities or charges (within the meaning of paragraph 89 of Schedule 4).

(3) The company shall not include any uncalled share capital as an asset in any accounts relevant for purposes of this section.

(4) An investment company may not make a distribution by virtue of subsection (1) unless—

    (a) its shares are listed on a recognised investment exchange other than an overseas investment within the meaning of the Financial Services Act 1986, and

    (b) during the relevant period it has not—

        (i) distributed any of its capital profits otherwise than by way of the redemption or purchase of any of the company's own shares in accordance with section 160 or 162 in Chapter VII of Part V, or

        (ii) applied any unrealised profits or any capital profits (realised or unrealised) in paying up debentures or amounts unpaid on its issued shares.

(5) The 'relevant period' under subsection (4) is the period beginning with—

    (a) the first day of the accounting reference period immediately preceding that in which the proposed distribution is to be made, or

    (b) where the distribution is to be made in the company's first accounting reference period, the first day of that period,

and ending with the date of the distribution.

(6) An investment company may not make a distribution by virtue of subsection (1) unless the company gave to the registrar of companies the requisite notice (that is, notice under section 266(1)) of the company's intention to carry on business as an investment company—

    (a) before the beginning of the relevant period under subsection (4), or

    (b) in the case of a company incorporated on or after 22nd December 1980, as soon as may have been reasonably practicable after the date of its incorporation.

General note

Any distribution must be justified by reference to the company's accounts: see s 270(1), (5).

S 265(1), (6)

Permitted distributions by investment companies This provision allows for an additional category ('may also make') of permitted distribution by a company which qualifies as an 'investment company'; 'distribution' is defined in s 263(2). Many investment trust companies are within this definition and have notified the registrar of companies as required by sub-s (6).

The effect is to allow investment companies to ignore capital losses, whether realised or unrealised, when making a distribution. An investment trust company which has incurred capital losses on the securities which it holds may still pay a dividend to its shareholders provided they have revenue profits. In fact, such companies must make distributions to meet the requirements of s 266(2)(d) and to retain certain tax advantages. This provision facilitates those distributions by allowing the company to ignore capital losses.

This ability to make a distribution is subject to the safety net of assets equal to one and half times the aggregate of its liabilities; and subject to the requirements of sub-ss (4), (6).

S 265(3)

'Uncalled share capital' is defined by s 737.

S 265(4)

Paragraph (b) was amended by the Companies (Investment Companies) (Distribution of Profits) Regulations 1999, SI 1999/2770: see note to s 266(2A), below.

S 265(5)

The 'accounting reference period' is determined in accordance with s 224.

266. Meaning of 'investment company'

(1) In section 265 'investment company' means a public company which has given notice in the prescribed form (which has not been revoked) to the registrar of companies of its intention to carry on business as an investment company, and has since the date of that notice complied with the requirements specified below.

(2) Those requirements are—

   (a) that the business of the company consists of investing its funds mainly in securities, with the aim of spreading investment risk and giving members of the company the benefit of the results of the management of its funds,

   (b) that none of the company's holdings in companies (other than those which are for the time being in investment companies) represents more than 15 per cent by value of the investing company's investments,

   (c) that subject to subsection (2A), distribution of the company's capital profits is prohibited by its memorandum or articles of association,

(d) that the company has not retained, otherwise than in compliance with this Part, in respect of any accounting reference period more than 15 per cent of the income it derives from securities.

(2A) An investment company need not be prohibited by its memorandum or articles from redeeming or purchasing its own shares in accordance with section 160 or 162 in Chapter VII of Part V out of its capital profits.

(3)   Notice to the registrar of companies under subsection (1) may be revoked at any time by the company on giving notice in the prescribed form to the registrar that it no longer wishes to be an investment company within the meaning of this section; and, on giving such notice, the company ceases to be such a company.

(4)   Subsections (1A) to (3) of section 842 of the Income and Corporation Taxes Act 1988 apply for the purposes of subsection (2)(b) above as for those of subsection (1)(b) of that section.

S 266(2), (4)

Requirement to be an investment company   Whether the holdings meet the requirements of sub-s (2)(b) is determined by criteria in the Income and Corporation Taxes Act 1988: see sub-s (4). By 'capital profits' in sub-s (2)(c) is meant increases in the value of the securities which the investment company holds; these cannot be distributed although dividends earned on those holdings may be and must be to the extent dictated by sub-s (2)(d); this is subject to sub-s (2A). A distribution by an investment company out of capital profits (not being within sub-s (2A)) is ultra vires and a recipient with notice of the facts holds the distribution as a constructive trustee for the company: see *Re Cleveland Trust plc* [1991] BCLC 424. An investment company must distribute up to the amount dictated by sub-s (2)(d) unless it would be an unlawful distribution under this Part.

S 266(2A)

Redemption or purchase out of capital profits   This provision was inserted by the Companies (Investment Companies) (Distribution of Profits) Regulations 1999, SI 1999/2770, following consultation by the Department of Trade and Industry on the question of investment companies using capital profits for the purchase of their own shares. The issue was essentially one of concern to investment trust companies which, as a general rule, seek to come within the definition of an 'investment company' in order to take advantage of s 265(1).

Investment trust companies had been concerned that their share prices were discounted by the market, in part because of the restrictions on distributions which prevented the distribution of capital profits. On the other hand, a general freedom to utilise capital profits would have denied them the benefits of being an 'investment company'. This more limited amendment enables them to use capital profits to repurchase their shares while retaining their status as investment companies able to make distributions under s 265(1).

267. Extension of ss 265, 266 to other companies

(1)　The Secretary of State may by regulations in a statutory instrument extend the provisions of sections 265 and 266 (with or without modifications) to companies whose principal business consists of investing their funds in securities, land or other assets with the aim of spreading investment risk and giving their members the benefit of the results of the management of the assets.

(2)　Regulations under this section—

(a)　may make different provision for different classes of companies and may contain such transitional and supplemental provisions as the Secretary of State considers necessary, and

(b)　shall not be made unless a draft of the statutory instrument containing them has been laid before Parliament and approved by a resolution of each House.

No regulations have been made under this provision.

268. Realised profits of insurance company with long term business

(1)　Where an insurance company to which Part II of the Insurance Companies Act 1982 applies carries on long term business—

(a)　any amount included in the relevant part of the balance sheet of the company which represents a surplus in the fund or funds maintained by it in respect of that business and which has not been allocated to policy holders in accordance with section 30(1) of that Act or carried forward unappropriated as mentioned in section 30(7) of that Act, and

(b)　any deficit in that fund or those funds,

are to be (respectively) treated, for purposes of this Part, as a realised profit and a realised loss; and, subject to this, any profit or loss arising in that business is to be left out of account for those purposes.

(2)　In subsection (1)—

(aa)　the reference to the relevant part of the balance sheet is to that part of the balance sheet which represents Liabilities item A.V (profit and loss account) in the balance sheet format set out in section B of Chapter I of Part I of Schedule 9A,

(a)　the reference to a surplus in any fund or funds of an insurance company is to an excess of the assets representing that fund or those funds over the liabilities of the company attributable to its long term business, as shown by an actuarial investigation, and

(b)　the reference to a deficit in any such fund or funds is to the excess of those liabilities over those assets, as so shown.

(3)　In this section—

(a)　'actuarial investigation' means an investigation to which section 18 of the Insurance Companies Act 1982 (periodic actuarial investigation of company with long term business) applies or which is made in pursuance of a requirement imposed by section 42 of that Act (actuarial investigation required by Secretary of State); and

(b) 'long term business' has the same meaning as in that Act.

General note

This provision elaborates on the definition of 'realised profits' and 'losses' for insurance companies carrying on long term business, ie life and related business.

269. Treatment of development costs

(1) Subject as follows, where development costs are shown as an asset in a company's accounts, any amount shown in respect of those costs is to be treated—

(a) under section 263, as a realised loss, and

(b) under section 265, as a realised revenue loss.

(2) This does not apply to any part of that amount representing an unrealised profit made on revaluation of those costs; nor does it apply if—

(a) there are special circumstances in the company's case justifying the directors in deciding that the amount there mentioned is not to be treated as required by subsection (1), and

(b) the note to the accounts required by paragraph 20 of Schedule 4 paragraph 20 of Schedule 8 (reasons for showing development costs as an asset) states that the amount is not to be so treated and explains the circumstances relied upon to justify the decision of the directors to that effect.

General note

The costs of research may not be treated as assets in any company's balance sheet (Sch 4, para 3(2)); and an amount may only be included in a company's balance sheet in respect of development costs in special circumstances: Sch 4, para 20. The issue is primarily one for accounting practice.

RELEVANT ACCOUNTS

270. Distribution to be justified by reference to company's accounts

(1) This section and sections 271 to 276 below are for determining the question whether a distribution may be made by a company without contravening sections 263, 264 or 265.

(2)   The amount of a distribution which may be made is determined by reference to the following items as stated in the company's accounts—

  (a) profits, losses, assets and liabilities,

  (b) provisions of any of the kinds mentioned in paragraphs 88 and 89 of Schedule 4 (depreciation, diminution in value of assets, retentions to meet liabilities, etc), and

  (c) share capital and reserves (including undistributable reserves).

(3)   Except in a case falling within the next subsection, the company's accounts which are relevant for this purpose are its last annual accounts, that is to say those prepared under Part VII which were laid in respect of the last preceding accounting reference period in respect of which accounts so prepared were laid; and for this purpose accounts are laid if section 241(1) has been complied with in relation to them.

(4)   In the following two cases—

  (a) where the distribution would be found to contravene the relevant section if reference were made only to the company's last annual accounts, or

  (b) where the distribution is proposed to be declared during the company's first accounting reference period, or before any accounts are laid in respect of that period,

the accounts relevant under this section (called 'interim accounts' in the first case, and 'initial accounts' in the second) are those necessary to enable a reasonable judgment to be made as to the amounts of the items mentioned in subsection (2) above.

(5)   The relevant section is treated as contravened in the case of a distribution unless the statutory requirements about the relevant accounts (that is, the requirements of this and the following three sections, as and where applicable) are complied with in relation to that distribution.

S 270(1),(5)

Importance of compliance with accounting requirements   The significance of these provisions is that a failure to comply with these statutory requirements regarding the relevant accounts renders the distribution unlawful even if, in fact, the distribution is out of profits available for the purpose within s 263(1): *Precision Dippings Ltd v Precision Dippings Marketing Ltd* [1985] BCLC 385; *Allied Carpets Group plc v Nethercott* [2001] BCC 81.

In *Bairstow v Queens Moat Houses plc* [2001] All ER (D) 211 (May), CA, affg [2000] 1 BCLC 549 the directors (who were liable in respect of unlawful dividends declared by the company based on accounts which did not meet the requirements of this provision) argued, inter alia, that there was only a technical failure to comply with the legislation since there was a sufficiency of distributable profits in the group although not in the holding company which paid the dividends.

The Court of Appeal held that whether the dividends could in fact have been paid out of distributable profits available in the group was irrelevant to the issue of liability, given the non-compliance by the company with the strict and mandatory requirements of this provision. The fact that the payments might have been made out of distributable profits is something which would go to the issue of relief, not to that of liability (at paras 35–36).

S 270(2)(c)

Items stated in the accounts   'Undistributable reserves' are defined in s 264(3). Matters referred to in the notes to the accounts, not being in the items identified here, do not affect the calculation of the distributable profits save to the extent they are reflected in items stated in the accounts.

S 270(3)

Last annual accounts   The starting point is the company's last 'annual accounts', defined by s 262(1); and a distribution has to be determined by reference to the company's individual accounts, though part of a group: see *Bairstow v Queens Moat Houses plc* [2001] All ER (D) 211 (May), CA, affg [2000] 1 BCLC 549. The 'accounting reference period' is as determined by s 224. As the period allowed for laying accounts is seven or ten months (s 244, depending on whether the company is a public or private company), subsequent developments may have altered the position from that reflected in the accounts. In that case, the common law rule, retained by s 281, requires that the directors take into account subsequent losses in determining the availability of distributable profits: see *Lee v Neuchatel Asphalte Co* (1889) 41 Ch D 1; *Verner v General and Commercial Investment Trust* [1894] 2 Ch 239.

The accounts must have been laid before the general meeting in accordance with s 241(1); for a company which has elected to dispense with laying accounts before the general meeting, the reference here should be read as referring to the sending of the accounts to the members and others: s 252(3)(b).

The accounts must be audited unless the company is exempt from audit under ss 249A, 249B.

S 270(4)

Interim and initial accounts   This provision gives established and newly formed companies additional flexibility by allowing them to justify distributions by reference to either interim or initial accounts. For public companies wishing to rely on either interim or initial accounts in this way, there are additional requirements in ss 272, 273. There are no further requirements with respect to private companies which may use management accounts for this purpose.

271. Requirements for last annual accounts

(1)   If the company's last annual accounts constitute the only accounts relevant under section 270, the statutory requirements in respect of them are as follows.

(2)   The accounts must have been properly prepared in accordance with this Act, or have been so prepared subject only to matters which are not material

for determining, by reference to items mentioned in section 270(2), whether the distribution would contravene the relevant section; and, without prejudice to the foregoing—

  (a) so much of the accounts as consists of a balance sheet must give a true and fair view of the state of the company's affairs as at the balance sheet date, and

  (b) so much of the accounts as consists of a profit and loss account must give a true and fair view of the company's profit or loss for the period in respect of which the accounts were prepared.

(3)   The auditors must have made their report on the accounts under section 235; and the following subsection applies if the report is a qualified report, that is to say, it is not a report without qualification to the effect that in the auditors' opinion the accounts have been properly prepared in accordance with this Act.

(4)   The auditors must in that case also have stated in writing (either at the time of their report or subsequently) whether, in their opinion, the matter in respect of which their report is qualified is material for determining, by reference to items mentioned in section 270(2), whether the distribution would contravene the relevant section; and a copy of the statement must have been laid before the company in general meeting.

(5)   A statement under subsection (4) suffices for purposes of a particular distribution not only if it relates to a distribution which has been proposed but also if it relates to distributions of any description which includes that particular distribution, notwithstanding that at the time of the statement it has not been proposed.

S 271(2)

Accounts properly prepared   This provision gives companies a choice of either accounts properly prepared or accounts properly prepared subject to immaterial exclusions, which would permit the omission of notes to the account which are not relevant to the distribution issue. In determining whether a matter is material, the question would be whether it affected the amount of distributable profits available. As to the requirement that the accounts give a true and fair view, see note to s 226.

  The consequence of the accounts not being properly prepared or not giving a true and fair view is that, applying s 270(5), there will be a breach of ss 263, 264; see *Bairstow v Queens Moat Houses plc* [2001] All ER (D) 211 (May), CA; affg [2000] 1 BCLC 549; *Allied Carpets Group plc v Nethercott* [2001] BCC 81.

  Where a sum was included in a parent company's accounts which the directors knew or ought to have known was an unlawful distribution by a subsidiary company, the result was that the parent company's accounts were not properly prepared and a dividend declared by the parent company was also unlawful: see *Re Cleveland Trust plc* [1991] BCLC 424; s 270(5).

S 271(3)

Auditors' report   Where the company is exempt from audit, these requirements do not apply: s 249E(1)(c), (2)(c).

It would seem from the rather unclear wording of that anything other than a statement that the accounts have been properly prepared is to be treated for these purposes as a qualification. This is not the position under the relevant accounting standards and so there is a difference between the legal position and accounting practice.

S 271(4), (5)

Auditors' statement on any qualification   The auditors' statement is required before the distribution ('would contravene'): *Precision Dippings Ltd v Precision Dippings Marketing Ltd* [1985] BCLC 385, and should be made even if no distribution is presently in mind in order to prevent any subsequent problems. If the auditors' statement relates only to a particular distribution, another statement will be required if the company decides on a further distribution by reference to the same accounts.

In the event of a failure to secure compliance with this requirement, there is a breach of the requirements relating to the relevant accounts amounting to a breach of the relevant section: s 270(5); *Re Cleveland Trust plc* [1991] BCLC 424; and any distribution made is unlawful. The position cannot be remedied by a subsequent statement by the auditors for, as an unlawful distribution, it is ultra vires, beyond the company's capacity and void; and it cannot be ratified, not even by the unanimous consent of the shareholders: *Ashbury Railway Carriage and Iron Co Ltd v Riche* (1875) LR 7 HL 653; *Aveling Barford Ltd v Perion Ltd* [1989] BCLC 626; a fortiori, if the company is insolvent by the time the problem comes to light and the auditors make their statement: *Precision Dippings Ltd v Precision Dippings Marketing Ltd* [1985] BCLC 385. It may be possible for the shareholders to agree to relieve the directors of any liability arising as a result of having caused the company to make an ultra vires distribution but this would depend on the circumstances of the distribution and would not be possible where it amounts to a fraud on the minority: *Cook v Deeks* [1916] 1 AC 554.

As to the reference to laying the statement before the members in cases where the company has elected to dispense with laying accounts and reports before the general meting, see s 252(3).

---

272. Requirements for interim accounts

(1)   The following are the statutory requirements in respect of interim accounts prepared for a proposed distribution by a public company.

(2)   The accounts must have been properly prepared, or have been so prepared subject only to matters which are not material for determining, by reference to items mentioned in section 270(2), whether the proposed distribution would contravene the relevant section.

(3)   'Properly prepared' means that the accounts must comply with section 226 (applying that section and Schedule 4 with such modifications as are necessary because the accounts are prepared otherwise than in respect of an accounting reference period) and any balance sheet comprised in the accounts must have been signed in accordance with section 233; and, without prejudice to the foregoing—

    (a) so much of the accounts as consists of a balance sheet must give a true and fair view of the state of the company's affairs as at the balance sheet date, and

    (b) so much of the accounts as consists of a profit and loss account must give a true and fair view of the company's profit or loss for the period in respect of which the accounts were prepared.

(4) A copy of the accounts must have been delivered to the registrar of companies.

(5) If the accounts are in a language other than English and the second sentence of section 242(1) (translation) does not apply,then, subject to section 710B(6) (delivery of certain Welsh documents without a translation), a translation into English of the accounts, certified in the prescribed manner to be a correct translation, must also have been delivered to the registrar.

S 272(1)

'Interim accounts' for these purposes is defined in s 270(4).

S 272(2), (3)

See note to s 271(2), above; while interim accounts must be 'properly prepared', they need not be audited.

273. Requirements for initial accounts

(1) The following are the statutory requirements in respect of initial accounts prepared for a proposed distribution by a public company.

(2) The accounts must have been properly prepared, or they must have been so prepared subject only to matters which are not material for determining, by reference to items mentioned in section 270(2), whether the proposed distribution would contravene the relevant section.

(3) Section 272(3) applies as respects the meaning of 'properly prepared'.

(4) The company's auditors must have made a report stating whether, in their opinion, the accounts have been properly prepared; and the following subsection applies if their report is a qualified report, that is to say it is not a report without qualification to the effect that in the auditors' opinion the accounts have been so prepared.

(5) The auditors must in that case also have stated in writing whether, in their opinion, the matter in respect of which their report is qualified is material for determining, by reference to items mentioned in section 270(2), whether the distribution would contravene the relevant section.

(6) A copy of the accounts, of the auditors' report under subsection (4) and of the auditors' statement (if any) under subsection (5) must have been delivered to the registrar of companies.

(7)   If the accounts are, or the auditors' report under subsection (4) or their statement (if any) under subsection (5) is, in a language other than English and the second sentence of section 242(1) (translation) does not apply,then, subject to section 710B(6) (delivery of certain Welsh documents without a translation), a translation into English of the accounts, the report or the statement (as the case may be), certified in the prescribed manner to be a correct translation, must also have been delivered to the registrar.

S 273(1)

'Initial accounts' for these purposes is defined in s 270(4). In this instance, the accounts must have been prepared for a proposed distribution, unlike under s 271(5).

S 273(2), (3)

See notes to s 271(2), above.

S 273(4)

See notes to s 271(3)–(5), above.

274. Method of applying s 270 to successive distributions

(1)   For the purpose of determining by reference to particular accounts whether a proposed distribution may be made by a company, section 270 has effect, in a case where one or more distributions have already been made in pursuance of determinations made by reference to those same accounts, as if the amount of the proposed distribution was increased by the amount of the distributions so made.

(2)   Subsection (1) of this section applies (if it would not otherwise do so) to—
   (a)   financial assistance lawfully given by a public company out of its distributable profits in a case where the assistance is required to be so given by section 154,
   (b)   financial assistance lawfully given by a private company out of its distributable profits in a case where the assistance is required to be so given by section 155(2),
   (c)   financial assistance given by a company in contravention of section 151, in a case where the giving of that assistance reduces the company's net assets or increases its net liabilities,
   (d)   a payment made by a company in respect of the purchase by it of shares in the company (except a payment lawfully made otherwise than out of distributable profits), and
   (e)   a payment of any description specified in section 168 (company's purchase of right to acquire its own shares, etc),

being financial assistance given or payment made since the relevant accounts were prepared, as if any such financial assistance or payment were a distribution already made in pursuance of a determination made by reference to those accounts.

(3)　In this section the following definitions apply—

'financial assistance' means the same as in Chapter VI of Part V;

'net assets' has the meaning given by section 154(2)(a); and

'net liabilities', in relation to the giving of financial assistance by a company, means the amount by which the aggregate amount of the company's liabilities (within the meaning of section 154(2)(b)) exceeds the aggregate amount of its assets, taking the amount of the assets and liabilities to be as stated in the company's accounting records immediately before the financial assistance is given.

(4)　Subsections (2) and (3) of this section are deemed to be included in Chapter VII of Part V for purposes of the Secretary of State's power to make regulations under section 179.

S 274(1)

It is permissible to make more than one distribution by reference to the same accounts, provided that the aggregate total of distributions is used when determining whether there are distributable profits for these purposes.

S 274(2)

Where any of the specified events have occurred since the relevant accounts were prepared, they must be taken into account in deciding whether a distribution can be made, ie they are counted as a distribution within sub-s (1). This will have the effect of reducing the profits available for distribution.

275. Treatment of assets in the relevant accounts

(1)　For purposes of sections 263 and 264, a provision of any kind mentioned in paragraphs 88 and 89 of Schedule 4, other than one in respect of a diminution in value of a fixed asset appearing on a revaluation of all the fixed assets of the company, or of all of its fixed assets other than goodwill, is treated as a realised loss.

(2)　If, on the revaluation of a fixed asset, an unrealised profit is shown to have been made and, on or after the revaluation, a sum is written off or retained for depreciation of that asset over a period, then an amount equal to the amount by which that sum exceeds the sum which would have been so written off or retained for the depreciation of that asset over that period, if that profit had not been made, is treated for purposes of sections 263 and 264 as a realised profit made over that period.

(3)   Where there is no record of the original cost of an asset, or a record cannot be obtained without unreasonable expense or delay, then for the purpose of determining whether the company has made a profit or loss in respect of that asset, its cost is taken to be the value ascribed to it in the earliest available record of its value made on or after its acquisition by the company.

(4)   Subject to subsection (6), any consideration by the directors of the value at a particular time of a fixed asset is treated as a revaluation of the asset for the purposes of determining whether any such revaluation of the company's fixed assets as is required for purposes of the exception from subsection (1) has taken place at that time.

(5)   But where any such assets which have not actually been revalued are treated as revalued for those purposes under subsection (4), that exception applies only if the directors are satisfied that their aggregate value at the time in question is not less than the aggregate amount at which they are for the time being stated in the company's accounts.

(6)   Where section 271(2), 272(2) or 273(2) applies to the relevant accounts, subsections (4) and (5) above do not apply for the purpose of determining whether a revaluation of the company's fixed assets affecting the amount of the relevant items (that is, the items mentioned in section 270(2)) as stated in those accounts has taken place, unless it is stated in a note to the accounts—

(a)   that the directors have considered the value at any time of any fixed assets of the company, without actually revaluing those assets,

(b)   that they are satisfied that the aggregate value of those assets at the time in question is or was not less than the aggregate amount at which they are or were for the time being stated in the company's accounts, and

(c)   that the relevant items in question are accordingly stated in the relevant accounts on the basis that a revaluation of the company's fixed assets which by virtue of subsections (4) and (5) included the assets in question took place at that time.

S 275(1), (4)–(6)

Provisions in the accounts   Any provision made in the accounts (including provision for depreciation) must be treated as a realised loss, which has the effect of reducing the profits available for distribution. However, there is an exception where the depreciation arises on a revaluation of all the fixed assets except goodwill and, in that case, the depreciation can be treated as an unrealised loss.

In fact, a revaluation of all the assets is not called for, provided there is compliance with sub-ss (4)–(6). Under these provisions, the directors are not required actually to revalue the fixed assets but they must have considered the value of the fixed assets and be satisfied as required by sub-s (5) and so state in the accounts as required by sub-s (6). The effect is to allow the directors to write down the value of a particular asset without affecting the profits available for distribution. The position is stricter for a public company because of s 264, which requires a public company to take into account any unrealised losses.

As to the definition of 'fixed assets', see ss 262(1), 742.

S 275(2)

This subsection provides for the situation where there is a revaluation of an asset upwards giving an unrealised profit; a proportion of that unrealised profit, to the extent identified here, can be treated as a realised profit.

276. Distributions in kind

Where a company makes a distribution of or including a non-cash asset, and any part of the amount at which that asset is stated in the accounts relevant for the purposes of the distribution in accordance with sections 270 to 275 represents an unrealised profit, that profit is to be treated as a realised profit—

   (a) for the purpose of determining the lawfulness of the distribution in accordance with this Part (whether before or after the distribution takes place), and

   (b) for the purpose of the application of paragraphs 12(a) and 34(3)(a) of Schedule 4 or paragraphs 12(a) and 34(3)(a) of Schedule 8 (only realised profits to be included in or transferred to the profit and loss account) in relation to anything done with a view to or in connection with the making of that distribution.

General note

This provision allows a company which has revalued assets showing an unrealised profit in the accounts to treat that profit as a realised profit where the distribution is one of, or including, a non-cash asset: 'non-cash asset' is defined in s 739. The assets must have been revalued at some point for the accounts to show the unrealised profit but there is no requirement to revalue them prior to making the distribution.

SUPPLEMENTARY

277. Consequences of unlawful distribution

(1)   Where a distribution, or part of one, made by a company to one of its members is made in contravention of this Part and, at the time of the distribution, he knows or has reasonable grounds for believing that it is so made, he is liable to repay it (or that part of it, as the case may be) to the company or (in the case of a distribution made otherwise than in cash) to pay the company a sum equal to the value of the distribution (or part) at that time.

(2)   The above is without prejudice to any obligation imposed apart from this section on a member of a company to repay a distribution unlawfully made to him; but this section does not apply in relation to—

(a) financial assistance given by a company in contravention of section 151, or

(b) any payment made by a company in respect of the redemption or purchase by the company of shares in itself.

(3) Subsection (2) of this section is deemed included in Chapter VII of Part V for purposes of the Secretary of State's power to make regulations under section 179.

General note

This provision provides for the recovery of unlawful dividends from the members of the company. In practice, it is quite unlikely that recovery of the amount received individually would be sought from the members, especially in a public company, for the members are quite unlikely to have any knowledge, actual or constructive, as to the lawfulness or otherwise of the distribution. It is much more likely that full recovery of the loss to the company will be sought from the directors who caused the unlawful dividend to be paid: see *Bairstow v Queens Moat Houses plc* [2001] All ER (D) 211 (May), CA; affg [2000] 1 BCLC 549 (where recovery of the full amount paid to the shareholders in dividends was sought); and *Allied Carpets Group plc v Nethercott* [2001] BCC 81 (where the company limited its claim to the amount of dividends received personally by its ex-managing director).

Directors' liability   It has long been the case that directors who pay a dividend out of capital are liable to repay that dividend where the payment is made with knowledge that the funds of the company are being misappropriated or with knowledge of the facts which establish the misappropriation: *Re Exchange Banking Co, Flitcroft's Case* (1882) 21 Ch D 519; and the Court of Appeal confirmed in *Precision Dippings Ltd v Precision Dippings Marketing Ltd* [1985] BCLC 385 that directors are accountable for dividends whether paid out of capital or in any other circumstances in which under any of the provisions of this Part there are not profits available for distribution (at 389). The fact that the company is still solvent is not a defence to a claim against directors to make good an unlawful distribution: *Bairstow v Queens Moat Houses plc* [2001] All ER (D) 211 (May), CA; affg [2000] 1 BCLC 549.

In *Bairstow v Queens Moat Houses plc* the Court of Appeal rejected an argument that no actionable loss had been caused by the unlawful dividends since dividends could have been declared and paid in a lawful manner (ie by first paying up profits elsewhere in the group to the holding company for distribution). The court found that the directors were guilty of a breach of fiduciary duty in the wrongful disbursement of the company's funds which were in their stewardship, which payments had never been reimbursed to the company, and for which the directors were fully accountable.

Knowledge of the directors   The nature of the knowledge required on the part of the directors was the subject of detailed consideration in *Bairstow v Queens Moat Houses plc* [2000] 1 BCLC 549 at 559, where Nelson J concluded that a director who authorises the payment of an unlawful dividend in breach of his duty as a quasi-trustee, will be liable to repay such dividends:

(1) if he knows that the dividends were unlawful, whether or not that actual knowledge amounts to fraud; or

(2) if he knows the facts that established the impropriety of the payments, even though he was unaware that such impropriety rendered the payment

unlawful (*Re Kingston Cotton Mill Co (No 2)* [1896] 1 Ch 331 at 347 and *Precision Dippings Ltd v Precision Dippings Marketing Ltd* [1985] BCLC 385 at 390) – there is no need to appreciate the law which renders those facts unlawful;

 (3) if he must be taken in all the circumstances to know all the facts which render the payments unlawful (*Precision Dippings Ltd v Precision Dippings Marketing Ltd* [1985] BCLC 385 at 390);

 (4) if he ought to have known, as a reasonably competent and diligent director, that the payments were unlawful (*Norman v Theodore Goddard* [1991] BCLC 1028; *Re D'Jan of London Ltd* [1994] 1 BCLC 561 and IA 1986, s 214).

The Court of Appeal did not comment on this guidance in the appeal in this case: see *Bairstow v Queens Moat Houses plc* [2001] All ER (D) 211 (May).

Knowing assistance and knowing receipt Third parties, including recipients, who dishonestly assist the directors in their breach of duty or who receive trust funds with knowledge of the directors' breach of duty may also be liable as constructive trustees: *Precision Dippings Ltd v Precision Dippings Marketing Ltd* [1985] BCLC 385; *Aveling Barford Ltd v Perion Ltd* [1989] BCLC 626; *Re Cleveland Trust plc* [1991] BCLC 424; see detailed note to s 151(3) on constructive trust liability and the degree of 'knowledge' required.

Burden of proof If a dividend is called into question, the burden lies on the directors to show that it was paid out of profits: *Rance's Case* (1870) 6 Ch App 104 at 123.

Relief from liability On the facts, it may be possible for a director to seek relief from any liability arising under s 727 (or Trustee Act 1925, s 61) where, despite the breach of trust, his conduct does not justify a personal liability: see *Bairstow v Queens Moat Houses plc* [2001] All ER (D) 211 (May), CA; affg [2000] 1 BCLC 549.

S 277(1)

Recovery against members This provision provides a statutory right of recovery against members (see s 22) but it is of limited significance for the reasons given above. The knowledge required is either actual or constructive and it must be of the facts which constitute the contravention, rather than a requirement that the member be aware that such impropriety rendered the payment unlawful: *Re Kingston Cotton Mill Co (No 2)* [1896] 1 Ch 331 at 347; and see *Bairstow v Queens Moat Houses plc* [2000] 1 BCLC 549.

 In *Precision Dippings Ltd v Precision Dippings Marketing Ltd* [1985] BCLC 385, the Court of Appeal preferred to resort to liability at common law (which is preserved by sub-s (2)) rather than rely on this statutory liability.

 For an example of a situation where only part of a distribution was unlawful, see *Re Cleveland Trust plc* [1991] BCLC 424.

S 277(2)

Common law liability Any liability imposed on a member, apart from this provision, would be as a recipient of an ultra vires distribution with knowledge of the directors' breach of trust with the result that he will hold the money on constructive trust for the company: *Precision Dippings Ltd v Precision Dippings Marketing Ltd* [1985] BCLC 385; *Re Cleveland Trust plc* [1991] BCLC 424; *Aveling Barford Ltd v Perion Ltd* [1989] BCLC 626; *Allied Carpets Group plc v Nethercott* [2001] BCC 81; see detailed note to s 151(3) on constructive trust liability and the degree of 'knowledge' required.

Unlawful financial assistance payments and unlawful payments in respect of purchase and redemption are excluded as those transactions are void for illegality and the company cannot enforce those agreements against the members although it may pursue other methods of redress: see notes to ss 151 and 143 respectively.

278. Saving for provision in articles operative before Act of 1980

Where immediately before 22nd December 1980 a company was authorised by a provision of its articles to apply its unrealised profits in paying up in full or in part unissued shares to be allotted to members of the company as fully or partly paid bonus shares, that provision continues (subject to any alteration of the articles) as authority for those profits to be so applied after that date.

General note

This provision is of limited significance now. It was introduced to ensure that companies which had articles in the form of 1948 Table A retained power to capitalise unrealised profits by issuing fully or partly paid bonus shares. It was thought that the statutory changes introduced by CA 1980 cast some doubt on the continuing validity of those provisions.

Most companies will probably have altered their articles by now to adopt 1985 Table A, reg 110 which authorises the capitalisation of unrealised profits by the issue of fully or partly paid bonus shares, as permitted by s 263(2)(a).

279. Distributions by banking or insurance companies

Where a company's accounts relevant for the purposes of this Part are prepared in accordance with the special provisions of Part VII relating to banking or insurance companies, sections 264 to 275 apply with the modifications shown in Schedule 11.

General note

The application of this Part is modified by Sch 11 with respect to banking and insurance companies which have prepared their accounts in accordance with the special provisions of Part VII (ss 255–255D) relating to such companies.

280. Definitions for Part VIII

(1)   The following has effect for the interpretation of this Part.

(2)   'Capitalisation', in relation to a company's profits, means any of the following operations (whenever carried out)—

(a)   applying the profits in wholly or partly paying up unissued shares in the company to be allotted to members of the company as fully or partly paid bonus shares, or

(b)   transferring the profits to capital redemption reserve.

(3)   References to profits and losses of any description are (respectively) to profits and losses of that description made at any time and, except where the context otherwise requires, are (respectively) to revenue and capital profits and revenue and capital losses.

S 280(3)

This provision confirms that it is the accumulated profits and losses which must be considered under s 263(3); as for 'except where the context otherwise requires', see with respect to investment companies: s 265.

---

281. Saving for other restraints on distribution

The provisions of this Part are without prejudice to any enactment or rule of law, or any provision of a company's memorandum or articles, restricting the sums out of which, or the cases in which, a distribution may be made.

General note

See the general note to this Part for a detailed explanation of the relationship between the statutory provisions and the existing common law rules on unlawful distributions which are retained by this provision and which are an essential component in the regulation of improper distributions.

The company's articles may be more restrictive than the statute but this is unlikely now. For a provision in the memorandum of association, see *Re Cleveland Trust plc* [1991] BCLC 424.

PART IX

A COMPANY'S MANAGEMENT; DIRECTORS AND SECRETARIES; THEIR QUALIFICATIONS, DUTIES AND RESPONSIBILITIES

OFFICERS AND REGISTERED OFFICE

282. Directors

(1)   Every company registered on or after 1st November 1929 (other than a private company) shall have at least two directors.

(2)   Every company registered before that date (other than a private company) shall have at least one director.

(3)   Every private company shall have at least one director.

S 282(1)

'Director' is defined in s 741; see the note to that provision as to shadow directors and de facto directors.

Executive directors   A common business distinction, which is not found in the statute, is between executive and non-executive directors. Executive directors are those directors concerned with the actual management of the company. They will have extensive management powers delegated to them by the articles (Table A, reg 72) and will usually have separate service contracts with the company which, together with the articles, will delimit their powers and responsibilities: see *Harold Holdsworth & Co (Wakefield) Ltd v Caddies* [1955] 1 All ER 725.

Non-executive directors   Non-executive directors are more commonly found in larger public companies and have an advisory and supervisory role. The legislation makes no specific provision for non-executive directors and the position is that their duties are the same as those of any other director: see *Dorchester Finance Co Ltd v Stebbing* [1989] BCLC 498.

When considering some duties, such as the duty of care and skill, it will be appropriate, however, to define the obligations of the non-executive director in the context of the role which he has undertaken. The minimum which would be expected of a non-executive director would be that he is informed, and kept informed, of the company's constitution, its board membership, the nature and course of its business, and its financial position from time to time, so that he is in a position to monitor the manner in which the executive directors are conducting its affairs: *Re Kaytech International plc, Secretary of State for Trade and Industry v Kaczer* [1999] 2 BCLC 351 at 407; *Re Westmid Packing Services Ltd* [1998] 2 BCLC 646 at 653.

The responsibility of ensuring that proper accounting records are kept, as required by s 221, is as much a responsibility of the non-executive directors as the executive directors: *Re Kaytech International plc, Secretary of State for Trade and Industry v Kazcer* [1999] 2 BCLC 351 at 410. The degree of competence required by the Act extends at least to a requirement that a non-executive director who is a corporate financier should be prepared to read and understand the statutory accounts and to satisfy himself that transactions between a holding company and its subsidiary are properly reflected in the statutory accounts of the subsidiary: a failure to reach this standard would justify a finding of unfitness for the purposes of disqualification:

Re Continental Assurance Co of London plc, Secretary of State for Trade and Industry v Burrows [1997] 1 BCLC 48.

Appointments   As to the appointment of the first directors, see s 10; thereafter matters are left to the individual company's articles. Where Table A is adopted, appointments are a matter for the general meeting although the board has power to appoint additional directors and to fill casual vacancies, with persons so appointed holding office until the next annual general meeting (regs 73–80); retirement and reappointment too are matters for the articles (regs 73–75) as is resignation and vacation of office (reg 81). It is not the case that a director must necessarily be an individual and a company may be appointed: *Re Bulawayo Market and Offices Co Ltd* [1907] 2 Ch 458.

Where no directors are appointed and the existing directors have died or retired, there must necessarily be at least one de facto director, ie someone must have assumed the position and be acting as such though not formally appointed, unless the company is defunct.

Publicity   Details of the directors must be entered on the company's register of directors and secretaries (s 288) and notified to the registrar of companies (ss 10, 288(2)); and must include the corporate name and registered office of any company holding the office of director: s 289(1)(b). Directors' names must not be included on any business letter (other than in the text or as a signatory) unless the names of every director are included: s 305.

S 282(3)

Although a private company need have only one director, it must also have a company secretary who cannot be the same person: s 283(2); see also s 283(4)(b).

---

283. Secretary

(1)   Every company shall have a secretary.

(2)   A sole director shall not also be secretary.

(3)   Anything required or authorised to be done by or to the secretary may, if the office is vacant or there is for any other reason no secretary capable of acting, be done by or to any assistant or deputy secretary or, if there is no assistant or deputy secretary capable of acting, by or to any officer of the company authorised generally or specially in that behalf by the directors.

(4)   No company shall—

   (a)   have as secretary to the company a corporation the sole director of which is a sole director of the company;

   (b)   have as sole director of the company a corporation the sole director of which is secretary to the company.

S 283(1)–(2)

Appointment of the company secretary   All companies are required to have a company secretary and a company can have more than one, in which case they are joint secretaries and the signature of both will be required on any document requiring the signature of the company secretary, unless the articles otherwise provide. The particulars of the company secretary must be recorded in the register of directors and secretaries: see ss 288, 290. A sole director cannot act as the company secretary so ensuring, in the case of a private company, that there are always two officers.

The appointment and removal of the company secretary is a matter for the directors (Table A, reg 99) and, in the case of a public company, they have a duty to ensure that the secretary possesses certain qualifications: see s 286. A company can be appointed, subject to sub-s (4)(a). As to the appointment of the first company secretary, see s 10.

Duties of the company secretary   The duties of a company secretary are not spelt out in the Act but the courts have accepted that he is no longer a mere clerk but an officer of the company who may have extensive duties and responsibilities: *Panorama Developments (Guildford) Ltd v Fidelis Furnishing Fabrics Ltd* [1971] 3 All ER 16. His responsibilities would include ensuring compliance by the company with the disclosure and filing requirements of the legislation including the maintenance of the statutory registers, the filing of the accounts and annual return with the registrar of companies and the organisation of board and general meetings.

As regards matters concerned with the administration of the company's affairs, the secretary has ostensible authority to contract on the company's behalf: *Panorama Developments (Guildford) Ltd v Fidelis Furnishing Fabrics Ltd* [1971] 3 All ER 16. The duties and responsibilities vary depending on the size and nature of the company and are greatest in listed public companies where the company secretary plays an important role in ensuring high standards of corporate governance. The responsibilities of the company secretary also extend beyond the companies legislation to matters such as health and safety requirements and employment law.

Secretary as an officer of the company   The company secretary is an officer of the company (s 744) and potentially liable under the numerous provisions which impose criminal penalties on the 'officer in default'. A secretary, while merely performing the duties appropriate to the office of secretary, is not concerned in the management of the company or the carrying on the business of the company: *Re Maidstone Buildings Ltd* [1971] 3 All ER 363. However, a person who holds the office of secretary may in some other capacity be concerned in the management of the company's business: *Re Maidstone Buildings Ltd*; and a person purporting to be the company secretary but who devoted himself to matters which went beyond those with which a company secretary is ordinarily concerned, in particular with respect to the company's property and financial interests, was a de facto director and subject to disqualification under the Company Directors Disqualification Act 1986, s 6: see *Re Kaytech International plc, Secretary of State for Trade and Industry v Kaczer* [1999] 2 BCLC 351.

284. Acts done by person in dual capacity

A provision requiring or authorising a thing to be done by or to a director and the secretary is not satisfied by its being done by or to the same person acting both as director and as, or in place of, the secretary.

General note

This provision clarifies the position where there is a person acting as both director and company secretary. For example, where a document requires the signature of a director and the secretary (see s 36A(4)), it will require two signatures and cannot be signed by one individual who combines both roles.

285. Validity of acts of directors

The acts of a director or manager are valid notwithstanding any defect that may afterwards be discovered in his appointment or qualification; and this provision is not excluded by section 292(2) (void resolution to appoint).

General note

See also s 382(4).

Defective appointment   This provision (which is reflected in the wider wording of Table A, reg 92) applies where there has been some technical breach of the requirements regarding appointment, for example, insufficient notice of the meeting at which the appointment was made, with the result that the appointment is defective. The provision validates acts done and assumes that once the defect comes to light, steps will be taken to rectify the position as to the future.

No appointment   However, the section does not validate the acts of someone who has not been appointed at all but who simply purports to fill the office of director: *Morris v Kanssen* [1946] AC 459, HL (a non-appointment includes the case where the term of office of a director has expired, but he nevertheless continues to act as a director, and where the office has been assumed without an appointment). The provisions in the statute and the articles 'being designed as machinery to avoid questions being raised as to the validity of transactions where there has been a slip in the appointment of a director, cannot be utilized for the purpose of ignoring or overriding the substantive provisions relating to such appointment': *Morris v Kanssen* [1946] AC 459 at 472, per Lord Simonds. See also *British Asbestos Co Ltd v Boyd* [1903] 2 Ch 439; *Dawson v African Consolidated Land Trading Co* [1898] 1 Ch 6.

Where there has been a defective appointment, neither the section nor any provision in the articles will assist a party having knowledge of the facts giving rise to the defect or a party who is put on inquiry but does not inquire: see *Re New Cedos Engineering Co Ltd* [1994] 1 BCLC 797 at 812.

The provision also applies to any defect in qualification, meaning share qualification, but such qualification requirements are rare now: see note to s 291, below.

286. Qualifications of company secretaries

(1) It is the duty of the directors of a public company to take all reasonable steps to secure that the secretary (or each joint secretary) of the company is a

person who appears to them to have the requisite knowledge and experience to discharge the functions of secretary of the company and who—

    (a) on 22nd December 1980 held the office of secretary or assistant or deputy secretary of the company; or

    (b) for at least 3 of the 5 years immediately preceding his appointment as secretary held the office of secretary of a company other than a private company; or

    (c) is a member of any of the bodies specified in the following subsection; or

    (d) is a barrister, advocate or solicitor called or admitted in any part of the United Kingdom; or

    (e) is a person who, by virtue of his holding or having held any other position or his being a member of any other body, appears to the directors to be capable of discharging those functions.

(2) The bodies referred to in subsection (1)(c) are—

    (a) the Institute of Chartered Accountants in England and Wales;

    (b) the Institute of Chartered Accountants of Scotland;

    (c) the Chartered Association of Certified Accountants;

    (d) the Institute of Chartered Accountants in Ireland;

    (e) the Institute of Chartered Secretaries and Administrators;

    (f) the Institute of Cost and Management Accountants;

    (g) the Chartered Institute of Public Finance and Accountancy.

General note

This provision, originally introduced by CA 1980, applies only to public companies, defined in s 1(3), and although it seems to restrict the position of company secretary to a limited number of categories, sub-s (1)(e) ensures that there is little restriction on who may be appointed, as long as the person appears to the directors to have the requisite knowledge and experience.

287. Registered office

(1) A company shall at all times have a registered office to which all communications and notices may be addressed.

(2) On incorporation the situation of the company's registered office is that specified in the statement sent to the registrar under section 10.

(3) The company may change the situation of its registered office from time to time by giving notice in the prescribed form to the registrar.

(4) The change takes effect upon the notice being registered by the registrar, but until the end of the period of 14 days beginning with the date on which it is registered a person may validly serve any document on the company at its previous registered office.

(5)   For the purposes of any duty of a company—

   (a) to keep at its registered office, or make available for public inspection there, any register, index or other document, or

   (b) to mention the address of its registered office in any document,

a company which has given notice to the registrar of a change in the situation of its registered office may act on the change as from such date, not more than 14 days after the notice is given, as it may determine.

(6)   Where a company unavoidably ceases to perform at its registered office any such duty as is mentioned in subsection (5)(a) in circumstances in which it was not practicable to give prior notice to the registrar of a change in the situation of its registered office, but—

   (a) resumes performance of that duty at other premises as soon as practicable, and

   (b) gives notice accordingly to the registrar of a change in the situation of its registered office within 14 days of doing so,

it shall not be treated as having failed to comply with that duty.

(7)   In proceedings for an offence of failing to comply with any such duty as is mentioned in subsection (5), it is for the person charged to show that by reason of the matters referred to in that subsection or subsection (6) no offence was committed.

General note

Although the expectation would be that the statutory registers etc would be maintained at the registered office, the legislation in many instances permits the records to be maintained at the registered office or elsewhere; in some cases, the requirement is that information be available at the registered office for a period of years, in others, the requirement is for documents to be available for a short period of time, usually 15 days, before a meeting.

Registers and records to be maintained at the registered office
   •   Register of directors and secretary: s 288.
   •   Minute books of general meetings and records of written resolutions: ss 383, 382A.
   •   Register of company charges (and a copy of the instrument creating the charge): ss 406, 407.

Registers and records to be maintained at the registered office or elsewhere
   •   Register of debenture holders, where maintained: s 190(3).
   •   Accounting records: s 222(1).
   •   Register of members: s 353(1).
   •   Register of directors' interests in shares in own company (at registered office or elsewhere but in that case with the register of members): s 325, Sch 13, para 25.
   •   Register of interests in shares in a public company (at registered office or elsewhere but in any case with the register of directors' interests): s 211(8).

Documents available (ahead of a meeting) for inspection at the registered office
- Contracts (or memorandum of terms, or variations) for off-market purchases of own shares for approval: ss 164(6), (7), 169.
- Statutory declaration by directors and auditors' report where proposed payment for purchase of own shares out of capital: s 175(1), (6).
- Details of directors' contracts of employment extending beyond five years for approval: s 319(5).
- Details of certain transactions by banking companies and credit institutions with directors and connected persons: s 343(4).

Documents available for inspection at the registered office
- Purchase contracts approved under ss 164–166: s 169.
- Report of investigation into share ownership: s 215(7).
- Service contracts of directors (at registered office or elsewhere): s 318.
- Periodic statements of business by insurance companies etc: s 720.

Requisitions, requests and notices to be lodged at the registered office
- Requisition for investigation of share ownership: s 214.
- Request for audit by members: s 249B(2).
- Request for accounts to be laid before members: s 253(2).
- Requisition by members for extraordinary general meeting: s 368(3).
- Requisition by members for circulation of resolutions to members: s 377(1).
- Deposit of auditors' resignation notice: s 392(1).
- Members' notice proposing auditor's appointment be terminated: s 393(1).
- Auditor's notice of circumstances connected with ceasing to hold office: s 394(1).

Service of documents on the company at the registered office
- Registrar of companies may serve notice of intention to strike off: s 652(7).
- Service of documents on a company may be at registered office: s 725.

S 287(1), (2)

All companies This obligation to have a registered office applies to all companies, public and private, limited and unlimited. All business letters and order forms of the company must give the address of the registered office: s 351. Notification of the initial registered office is governed by s 10(6).

A physical location As the Companies House, *Notes for Guidance for Directors and Secretaries* makes clear, the address must be a physical location, not just a post office box, because of the right of persons to inspect certain registers and documents at the registered office and to deliver documents by hand to it.

S 287(3)–(5)

Change must be notified It is essential that the registrar of companies is informed of any change, so that searchers of the public record may obtain accurate information but also so that the registrar is aware of the change. The registrar of companies will communicate only with the address of the registered office and this will be used, for example, for the despatch of the annual return to the company and to send reminders to the company of matters such as filing obligations. Having missed these reminders, because of their being sent to the (now) wrong address, the company may incur late filing penalties and, in the worst cases, may be struck off the register as defunct under s 652. Any change in the situation of the registered office must be gazetted by the registrar (s 711(1)(n)); and is subject to s 42 which limits the company's ability to rely on the alteration until officially notified in the London Gazette.

A company cannot be without a registered office, for until a change is registered by the registrar of companies, the old address continues to be the registered office for the purposes of the Act. As documents may continue to be served on the old address for 14 days following the registration of the change of location, a company needs to have arrangements in place to check for documents at the old address during this period.

The company has some flexibility under sub-s (5) as to when, having given notice, it wishes to act on the change of location and it does not have to await the actual registration of the change by the registrar of companies. This is of practical importance as the company is required to include the address of its registered office on company correspondence, see s 351, and so needs some time to organise the changes.

Within the jurisdiction Companies can only change the situation within the jurisdiction which they have chosen in their memorandum of association, ie within England and Wales, Wales or Scotland as appropriate (see s 2(1)); and freedom of association under the EEC Treaty does not confer on a company incorporated and with its registered office in one member state, the right to transfer its central management and control to another member state: *R v HM Treasury, ex p Daily Mail* [1989] BCLC 206.

Only the company can notify of a change A practical problem which has arisen with this provision is that it only enables the company to change its registered office. Occasionally, a company will move from its registered office without notifying the registrar of companies of any change and the new occupants of those premises will continue to receive mail addressed to the original occupant by the registrar of companies (and any third party relying on the address, as it appears on the public record). It seems that the registrar cannot accept notification by the new occupants that the address is no longer the address of the registered office of the company. Likewise, where a company initially uses a formation agent or professional advisers' address as its registered office and those advisers loose touch with the company: that address remains as the address of the registered office until the company changes it.

Failure to notify No criminal sanction is imposed for a failure to notify the registrar under this provision but criminal liability would arise in most cases under the substantive provisions, for example, for a failure to maintain the register of directors and secretaries at the registered office and provide for its inspection at that location, subject to the defence in sub-s (7).

S 287(6)–(7)

The phrase 'unavoidably ceases to perform', presumably, will require something in the nature of a fire at the premises. The requirement is to resume the obligation 'as soon as practicable' with the onus on the company to establish that it has done so.

288. Register of directors and secretaries

(1)   Every company shall keep at its registered office a register of its directors and secretaries; and the register shall, with respect to the particulars to be contained in it of those persons, comply with sections 289 and 290 below.

(2)   The company shall, within the period of 14 days from the occurrence of—

   (a) any change among its directors or in its secretary, or

   (b) any change in the particulars contained in the register,

send to the registrar of companies a notification in the prescribed form of the change and of the date on which it occurred; and a notification of a person having become a director or secretary, or one of joint secretaries, of the company shall contain a consent, signed by that person, to act in the relevant capacity.

(3)   The register shall ... be open to the inspection of any member of the company without charge and of any other person on payment of such fee as may be prescribed.

(4)   If an inspection required under this section is refused, or if default is made in complying with subsection (1) or (2), the company and every officer of it who is in default is liable to a fine and, for continued contravention, to a daily default fine.

(5)   In the case of a refusal of inspection of the register, the court may by order compel an immediate inspection of it.

(6)   For purposes of this and the next section, a shadow director of a company is deemed a director and officer of it.

(7)   Subsections (3) and (5) are subject to sections 723B.

General note

On incorporation, there must be delivered to the registrar of companies a statement containing the names and particulars of the first directors and the company secretary: s 10, Sch 1. This provision provides that the identical information must be entered on the register maintained by the company.

Register is not definitive   Neither record (ie that maintained by the registrar of companies or the company itself) is definitive as to who is a director (or secretary) of the company, subject to s 13(5): see *POW Services Ltd v Clare* [1995] 2 BCLC 435. First, there may be persons acting whom the company has not notified as being directors to the registrar of companies or entered their particulars in the company's own register but who, in law, are de facto or shadow directors (as to which, see note to s 741, below). Secondly, the names of persons who have in fact resigned as directors may remain on the register, through inadvertence or some other cause, on either or both the public register maintained by the registrar of companies and at the company's registered office.

   The register may be kept otherwise than in a legible form (ss 722, 723) and in that case the provisions as to the place at which the register must be kept and the place of inspection are subject to the Companies (Registers and Other Records) Regulations 1985, SI 1985/724.

S 288(1), (6)

As to the registered office, see s 287; this register must be kept at the registered office unlike other registers which may be located there or elsewhere (eg the register of members); this is subject to s 287(5)–(6). A shadow director (defined in s 741(2)) is unlikely, despite this requirement, to register his directorship.

Alternate directors   It seems that the appointment of an alternate director, at least where the matter is governed by Table A, regs 65–69, must be notified to the registrar of companies and particulars entered on the register. This is because under Table A an alternate is deemed for all purposes to be a director (reg 69) but even this provision is qualified 'save as otherwise provided by the articles'. It would seem that the articles may allow for an alternate but so delimit his role that he is not a director for the purposes of this provision. This would accommodate the situation where there might be numerous brief appointments swiftly followed by the vacating of the post such that registration of the particulars on each occasion would be quite burdensome. However, the difficulty lies in defining the alternate's role in such a way as to ensure that he does not become a director: if he does, then his particulars must be notified to the registrar of companies and entered on the company's register.

S 288(2)

The obligation to notify the registrar of companies falls on the company and not on the appointee; in practice, it is a matter for the company secretary.

The consent of the person appointed must be secured and his signature is required; on resignation, his signature is not required on the notification to the registrar of companies but the signature of a serving officer is, and where there are disputes within the company, particularly a small company, this can be difficult to obtain so preventing any notification to the registrar of companies. The result is that the public record will be inaccurate but the position of the resigning director is not adversely affected by this, assuming that he has truly resigned. He should take such steps as he can, internally, to ensure that his resignation is documented, for example, by formal letters to the board and to the company secretary.

Any change in the company's directors (not the secretary) must be gazetted by the registrar (s 711(1)(c)), and is subject to s 42 which limits the company's ability to rely on the alteration until officially notified in the London Gazette.

The requirement in sub-s (2)(b) to notify changes in the particulars, as well as changes in personnel, can be overlooked.

S 288(3)–(5), (7)

Inspection   The right to inspect the register is subject to any confidentiality orders made under s 723B. For provisions relating to the inspection of documents, registers and fees under this section, see the Companies (Inspection and Copying of Registers, Indices and Documents) Regulations 1991, SI 1991/1998. The provision in sub-s (5) is necessary because, but for the section, it is not clear that there is any right of inspection or that the court has the power to compel inspection: see *Conway v Petronius Clothing Co Ltd* [1978] 1 All ER 185 at 199. The court's power is discretionary: see *Pelling v Families need Fathers Ltd* [2001] All ER (D) (Aug), CA.

Penalties   As to penalties, see s 730, Sch 24; officer in default' is defined in s 730(5).

289. Particulars of directors to be registered under s 288

(1)   Subject to the provisions of this section, the register kept by a company under section 288 shall contain the following particulars with respect to each director—

- (a) in the case of an individual—
  - (i)   his present name,
  - (ii)   any former name,
  - (iii) his usual residential address,
  - (iv)   his nationality,
  - (v)   his business occupation (if any),
  - (vi)   particulars of any other directorships held by him or which have been held by him, and
  - (vii) the date of his birth;
- (b) in the case of a corporation or Scottish firm, its corporate or firm name and registered or principal office.

(2)   In subsection (1)(a)—

- (a) 'name' means a person's Christian name (or other forename) and surname, except that in the case of a peer, or an individual usually known by a title, the title may be stated instead of his Christian name (or other forename) and surname, or in addition to either or both of them; and
- (b) the reference to a former name does not include—
  - (i)   in the case of a peer, or an individual normally known by a British title, the name by which he was known previous to the adoption of or succession to the title, or
  - (ii)   in the case of any person, a former name which was changed or disused before he attained the age of 18 years or which has been changed or disused for 20 years or more, or
  - (iii) in the case of a married woman, the name by which she was known previous to the marriage.

(3)   It is not necessary for the register to contain on any day particulars of a directorship—

- (a) which has not been held by a director at any time during the 5 years preceding that day,
- (b) which is held by a director in a company which—
  - (i)   is dormant or grouped with the company keeping the register, and
  - (ii)   if he also held that directorship for any period during those 5 years, was for the whole of that period either dormant or so grouped,
- (c) which was held by a director for any period during those 5 years in a company which for the whole of that period was either dormant or grouped with the company keeping the register.

(4)   For purposes of subsection (3), 'company' includes any body corporate incorporated in Great Britain; and—

- (a) section 249AA(3) applies as regards whether and when a company is or has been dormant, and

(b) a company is to be regarded as being, or having been, grouped with another at any time if at that time it is or was a company of which the other is or was a wholly-owned subsidiary, or if it is or was a wholly-owned subsidiary of the other or of another company of which that other is or was a wholly-owned subsidiary.

S 289(1)

Residential addresses   The inclusion of residential addresses (sub-s (1)(a)(iii)) (and see s 10, Sch 1) has been criticised in view of increased targeting of company directors by persons such as animal rights activists. The Department of Trade and Industry has obtained powers to make confidentiality orders under s 723B, inserted by the Criminal Justice and Police Act 2001, s 45(1), (2), which will allow the private addresses of directors (or the company secretary) at serious risk of violence or intimidation to be kept on a secure register.

Previous directorships   The requirements in sub-s (1)(a)(vi) are subject to sub-ss (3)–(4) which limits the information to directorships held in the previous five years. The Department of Trade and Industry has indicated that it intends to remove this requirement when a legislative opportunity arises. Information as to other directorships is compiled by the registrar of companies automatically without the need for this additional disclosure and searchers of the public record can obtain a list of directorships held by any individual.

Corporate directors   It is not the case that a director must necessarily be an individual and a company may be appointed: *Re Bulawayo Market and Offices Co Ltd* [1907] 2 Ch 458.

S 289(2)

The provision in sub-s (2)(b)(iii) excludes the need for a married woman to give the name by which she was known previous to *the* (current) marriage; as the requirement under sub-s (1)(a)(ii) is to give 'any' former name, it would seem that where the person has been married more than once, other former names would have to be disclosed.

S 289(4)

The exemption for directorships which are or were held in companies within a group (as defined in sub-s (4)(b)) avoids multiple entries to the registers of the companies across the group and the need to make multiple changes every time any change in the particulars of the individual director is recorded. 'Wholly-owned subsidiary' is defined in s 736.

290. Particulars of secretaries to be registered under s 288

(1)   The register to be kept by a company under section 288 shall contain the following particulars with respect to the secretary or, where there are joint secretaries, with respect to each of them—

(a) in the case of an individual, his present name, any former name and his usual residential address, and

(b) in the case of a corporation or a Scottish firm, its corporate or firm name and registered or principal office.

(2) Where all the partners in a firm are joint secretaries, the name and principal office of the firm may be stated instead of the particulars specified above.

(3) Section 289(2)(a) and (b) apply for the purposes of the obligation under subsection (1)(a) of this section to state the name or former name of an individual.

General note

This provision envisages that a company may have more than one secretary. See the note to s 289(1) as to residential addresses.

PROVISIONS GOVERNING APPOINTMENT OF DIRECTORS

291. Share qualification of directors

(1) It is the duty of every director who is by the company's articles required to hold a specified share qualification, and who is not already qualified, to obtain his qualification within 2 months after his appointment, or such shorter time as may be fixed by the articles.

(2) For the purpose of any provision of the articles requiring a director or manager to hold any specified share qualification, the bearer of a share warrant is not deemed the holder of the shares specified in the warrant.

(3) The office of director of a company is vacated if the director does not within 2 months from the date of his appointment (or within such shorter time as may be fixed by the articles) obtain his qualification, or if after the expiration of that period or shorter time he ceases at any time to hold his qualification.

(4) A person vacating office under this section is incapable of being reappointed to be a director of the company until he has obtained his qualification.

(5) If after the expiration of that period or shorter time any unqualified person acts as a director of the company, he is liable to a fine and, for continued contravention, to a daily default fine.

General note

A share qualification is quite rare now. It was designed to protect the shareholders by ensuring that the directors would act in the interests of the company.

S 291(1)

The two-month period runs from the date of ascertaining the result of the poll electing the director: *Holmes v Keyes* [1958] 2 All ER 129. See also s 285.

S 291(5)

As to penalties, see s 730, Sch 24.

292. Appointment of directors to be voted on individually

(1) At a general meeting of a public company, a motion for the appointment of two or more persons as directors of the company by a single resolution shall not be made, unless a resolution that it shall be so made has first been agreed to by the meeting without any vote being given against it.

(2) A resolution moved in contravention of this section is void, whether or not its being so moved was objected to at the time; but where a resolution so moved is passed, no provision for the automatic reappointment of retiring directors in default of another appointment applies.

(3) For purposes of this section, a motion for approving a person's appointment, or for nominating a person for appointment, is to be treated as a motion for his appointment.

(4) Nothing in this section applies to a resolution altering the company's articles.

S 292(1)

Each proposed director must be voted on individually unless there is unanimous consent to a block resolution. This is to ensure that shareholders can express their disapproval of any particular director without having to reject the entire board.

S 292(2)

Although the appointment is void, s 285 applies to validate the acts of any such director. For an example of provisions in the articles providing for the automatic reappointment of retiring directors, see Table A, reg 75.

S 292(4)

It is not altogether clear what is meant by this provision; it appears to say that a special resolution altering the articles which has the effect of appointing two or more persons as directors of a public company is not void.

293. Age limit for directors

(1)   A company is subject to this section if—

(a) it is a public company, or

(b) being a private company, it is a subsidiary of a public company or of a body corporate registered under the law relating to companies for the time being in force in Northern Ireland as a public company.

(2)   No person is capable of being appointed a director of a company which is subject to this section if at the time of his appointment he has attained the age of 70.

(3)   A director of such a company shall vacate his office at the conclusion of the annual general meeting commencing next after he attains the age of 70; but acts done by a person as director are valid notwithstanding that it is afterwards discovered that his appointment had terminated under this subsection.

(4)   Where a person retires under subsection (3), no provision for the automatic reappointment of retiring directors in default of another appointment applies; and if at the meeting at which he retires the vacancy is not filled, it may be filled as a casual vacancy.

(5)   Nothing in subsections (2) to (4) prevents the appointment of a director at any age, or requires a director to retire at any time, if his appointment is or was made or approved by the company in general meeting; but special notice is required of a resolution appointing or approving the appointment of a director for it to have effect under this subsection, and the notice of the resolution given to the company, and by the company to its members, must state, or have stated, the age of the person to whom it relates.

(6)   A person reappointed director on retiring under subsection (3), or appointed in place of a director so retiring, is to be treated, for the purpose of determining the time at which he or any other director is to retire, as if he had become director on the day on which the retiring director was last appointed before his retirement.

Subject to this, the retirement of a director out of turn under subsection (3) is to be disregarded in determining when any other directors are to retire.

(7)   In the case of a company first registered after the beginning of 1947, this section has effect subject to the provisions of the company's articles; and in the case of a company first registered before the beginning of that year—

(a) this section has effect subject to any alterations of the company's articles made after the beginning of that year; and

(b) if at the beginning of that year the company's articles contained provision for retirement of directors under an age limit, or for preventing or restricting appointments of directors over a given age, this section does not apply to directors to whom that provision applies.

General note

This provision and the next contains over-elaborate provisions to deal with the issue of directors aged 70 and over in public companies or private companies which are subsidiaries of public companies. In any event, it is easy for any company to avoid the application of the provisions through reliance on sub-ss (5) or (7); as such, the provisions are of limited use. There are no age restrictions in relation to directors of private companies which are not subsidiaries of public companies.

S 293(1)

The application of the provision to private companies which are subsidiaries of public companies is sometimes overlooked; 'subsidiary' is defined in s 736.

S 293(2)

The result will be that there is no appointment where the person exceeds the age limit at the time of his appointment and s 285 would not therefore apply. A person who is to be appointed at a time when he has attained the retiring age must give notice to the company of his age under s 294.

S 293(3)

The company will be aware that the director has reached this age as the date of birth of each director is included in the register of directors: see s 289(1)(vii).

S 293(4)

The directors typically have power to fill a casual vacancy: see Table A, reg 79.

S 293(5)

The easiest method of avoiding the operation of this provision is to have the appointment made by an informed general meeting. 'Special notice' requires notice of the resolution to be given to the company at least 28 days before the meeting (s 379(1)), which is pointless in practice since it entails the directors giving notice to the company, ie to themselves.

S 293(7)

The other method of avoiding the operation of this provision is to so provide in the articles.

---

294. Duty of director to disclose his age

(1) A person who is appointed or to his knowledge proposed to be appointed director of a company subject to section 293 at a time when he has attained

any retiring age applicable to him under that section or under the company's articles shall give notice of his age to the company.

(2)   For purposes of this section, a company is deemed subject to section 293 notwithstanding that all or any of the section's provisions are excluded or modified by the company's articles.

(3)   Subsection (1) does not apply in relation to a person's reappointment on the termination of a previous appointment as director of the company.

(4)   A person who—

(a) fails to give notice of his age as required by this section; or

(b) acts as director under any appointment which is invalid or has terminated by reason of his age,

is liable to a fine and, for continued contravention, to a daily default fine.

(5)   For purposes of subsection (4), a person who has acted as director under an appointment which is invalid or has terminated is deemed to have continued so to act throughout the period from the invalid appointment or the date on which the appointment terminated (as the case may be), until the last day on which he is shown to have acted thereunder.

General note

Companies will be aware of the ages of their existing directors as their dates of birth must be entered on the register of directors (s 289(1)(vii)); this provision requires those to be appointed at a time when they have attained the retiring age to notify the company of their age, apparently even if the company has excluded the operation of s 293 through a provision in its articles, see sub-s (2).

S 294(1)

This provision also applies to restrictions in the company's articles (although it is rare for such restrictions to be included) as well as the statutory restriction. The articles could set a lower age, say, 65.

S 294(2)

For these purposes, 'a company subject to s 293' is a public company or a private company which is a subsidiary of a public company regardless of whether it has excluded the operation of the age limit under its articles. This provision appears to impose the obligation on a person to notify the company of his age, even if the company has excluded the operation of s 293.

S 294(4)

As to penalties, see s 730, Sch 24.

295–302 (ss *295–299, 301, 302 repealed by the Company Directors Disqualification Act 1986, s 23(2), Sch 4; s 300 repealed by the Insolvency Act 1985, s 235(3), Sch 10, Pt II.)*

REMOVAL OF DIRECTORS

303. Resolution to remove director

(1)　A company may by ordinary resolution remove a director before the expiration of his period of office, notwithstanding anything in its articles or in any agreement between it and him.

(2)　Special notice is required of a resolution to remove a director under this section or to appoint somebody instead of a director so removed at the meeting at which he is removed.

(3)　A vacancy created by the removal of a director under this section, if not filled at the meeting at which he is removed, may be filled as a casual vacancy.

(4)　A person appointed director in place of a person removed under this section is treated, for the purpose of determining the time at which he or any other director is to retire, as if he had become director on the day on which the person in whose place he is appointed was last appointed a director.

(5)　This section is not to be taken as depriving a person removed under it of compensation or damages payable to him in respect of the termination of his appointment as director or of any appointment terminating with that as director, or as derogating from any power to remove a director which may exist apart from this section.

General note

Practical considerations　This provision provides shareholders with a statutory power to remove any director but reliance on it is constrained by a number of practical considerations: (i) the company's exposure to damages as a result of the exercise of the power, see note to s 303(5); (ii) the damage to a company's reputation, in the case of a larger public company, were it to dismiss a director in the full glare of publicity surrounding a general meeting; and (iii) the possibility, in smaller private companies especially, that the director will seek redress for his removal under s 459 (unfairly prejudicial conduct). Indeed, removal from office is the most common ground of complaint under that section.

Impact of s 459　Essentially, the position under s 459 is that if the parties have come together on the basis of a personal relationship involving mutual trust and confidence and on the basis that all or some of them shall participate in the management of the company, equitable considerations will come into play which may make the exercise by the majority of the statutory power to remove a director unfairly prejudicial conduct, in the absence of an opportunity for that person to sell his interest in the company at a fair price: *O'Neill v Phillips* [1999] 2 BCLC 1. As Lord Hoffmann stressed in that case, the unfairness does not lie in the exclusion but in the exclusion without a reasonable offer (at 16). But see the detailed note to s 459, below, as to the impact which that provision has on the exclusion or removal of directors. In the absence of such equitable considerations, every director is subject to the possibility of removal and has no right to remain in office: *Re Estate Acquisition and Development Ltd* [1995] BCC 338; *Re a Company (No 005685 of 1988), ex p Schwarcz (No 2)* [1989] BCLC 427.

In the past, removal of a director in a small quasi-partnership type company might have warranted winding up the company on the just and equitable ground under IA 1986, s 122(1)(g) (*Ebrahimi v Westbourne Galleries Ltd* [1973] AC 360); but, in recent years, given the availability of more appropriate relief under s 459, this jurisdiction has fallen somewhat into abeyance, a position reinforced by the decision in *Re Guidezone Ltd* [2000] 2 BCLC 321, see note to s 459, below.

S 303(1)

Ordinary resolution　　An ordinary resolution is required, ie a simply majority of the votes cast. In private companies, it is possible to give a director/shareholder weighted votes on any resolution to remove him from the board, a practice permitted by the House of Lords in *Bushell v Faith* [1970] AC 1099. In that case, the articles provided that on a resolution to remove a particular director, the shares which he held would carry three times the number of votes they normally carried. As a consequence, it was impossible for the other shareholders to pass the required ordinary resolution. The House of Lords rejected any argument that such provisions defeated the statutory intention behind s 303. Although the decision has been criticised, provisions of this nature in the articles remain a valid method of entrenchment for directors. A shareholders' agreement as to how to vote on any resolution to remove a particular director would be equally effective: see *Russell v Northern Bank Development Corp* [1992] BCLC 1016.

A private company cannot use a written resolution (s 381A(5), Sch 15A, para 1; and see note to s 381C, below) as the director has a right to be heard at the general meeting under s 304.

'Permanent' directors　　The power to remove a director applies to all directors, even if their positions are described as 'permanent' or 'for life' in the company's articles (this simply means that they are exempt from the requirement for retirement in rotation).

Calling the meeting　　It may be necessary for the shareholders to seek the court's help, under s 371, to call a general meeting in order to exercise their rights to remove a director. This can arise in companies with a limited number of shareholders where minority shareholders refuse to attend meetings, so rendering them inquorate, with a view to preventing the majority of shareholders from exercising their voting powers to remove the minority shareholders from office as directors: see *Re Whitchurch Insurance Consultants Ltd* [1993] BCLC 1359; *Re Opera Photographic Ltd* [1989] BCLC 763; *Re El Sombrero Ltd* [1958] Ch 900.

A shareholder has no right to compel the inclusion of a resolution proposing the removal of a director on the agenda for a general meeting: *Pedley v Inland Waterways*

Assoc Ltd [1977] 1 All ER 209; but will have to rely on s 376 (circulation of members' resolution) or s 368 (extraordinary general meeting on members' requisition).

Provisions in the articles　The statutory power to remove a director is in addition to any provisions in the articles governing removal, for example, see Table A, reg 81. It may be that the articles contain: (i) an identical power vested in the shareholders; or (ii) provisions enabling the directors to terminate the position of any director, for example, by a notice in writing signed by all the directors: see *Lee v Chou Wen Hsien* [1985] BCLC 45.

A director cannot obtain an injunction to prevent the company altering the articles to facilitate his removal as a director: *Shuttleworth v Cox Bros & Co (Maidenhead) Ltd* [1927] 2 KB 9.

S 303(2), (3)

Special notice is defined by s 379. These provisions apply only to removal under this section, as opposed to under an equivalent provision in the articles. Casual vacancies can usually be filled by the directors, see Table A, reg 79.

S 303(5)

Damages payable　The obligation to pay damages is a significant limitation on the exercise of the power to remove a director. This is particularly so when the company attempts to dismiss an executive director with a service contract. To assist shareholders to gauge the possible costs, details of directors' service contracts must be available for inspection at the registered office (s 318) and specific shareholder approval is required of any contract in excess of five years in the circumstances dictated by s 319. If shareholders approve such a lengthy service contract, then they are taken to appreciate that considerable costs will arise if the company seeks to terminate that contract, other than for serious wrongdoing.

Executive position　The articles commonly provide that any appointment of a director to an executive position will terminate if he ceases to be a director (see Table A, reg 84). If a managing director (or any other executive director) is appointed by contract for a fixed term and the company exercises its power to remove him as a director before that term expires, the company will be liable in damages as the courts will imply a term that the company undertakes to do nothing of its own accord (for example, by revoking his appointment as a director) to bring to an end the circumstances necessary to enable a person to act as managing director: *Shindler v Northern Raincoat Co Ltd* [1960] 2 All ER 239; *Southern Foundries (1926) Ltd v Shirlaw* [1940] 2 All ER 445, HL. This position is confirmed by Table A, reg 84, which provides that any appointment of a director to an executive position will terminate if he ceases to be a director but without prejudice to any claim for damages for breach of the contract of service between the director and the company. As with any breach of contract, there is a duty on the innocent party to mitigate his losses, in this case, by seeking alternative employment.

Where a director does not have a service contract and has simply been appointed under the articles, his position can be terminated at any time and he cannot recover any damages: *Read v Astoria Garage (Streatham) Ltd* [1952] Ch 637.

See also Table A, reg 87 and ss 312–316 as to compensation for loss of office.

304. Director's right to protest removal

(1)   On receipt of notice of an intended resolution to remove a director under section 303, the company shall forthwith send a copy of the notice to the director concerned; and he (whether or not a member of the company) is entitled to be heard on the resolution at the meeting.

(2)   Where notice is given of an intended resolution to remove a director under that section, and the director concerned makes with respect to it representations in writing to the company (not exceeding a reasonable length) and requests their notification to members of the company, the company shall, unless the representations are received by it too late for it to do so—

(a) in any notice of the resolution given to members of the company state the fact of the representations having been made; and

(b) send a copy of the representations to every member of the company to whom notice of the meeting is sent (whether before or after receipt of the representations by the company).

(3)   If a copy of the representations is not sent as required by subsection (2) because received too late or because of the company's default, the director may (without prejudice to his right to be heard orally) require that the representations shall be read out at the meeting.

(4)   But copies of the representations need not be sent out and the representations need not be read out at the meeting if, on the application either of the company or of any other person who claims to be aggrieved, the court is satisfied that the rights conferred by this section are being abused to secure needless publicity for defamatory matter.

(5)   The court may order the company's costs on an application under this section to be paid in whole or in part by the director, notwithstanding that he is not a party to the application.

General note

It is unusual for use to be made of this provision. If the company is a public company, removal is rarely a matter for a resolution in general meeting; and if the company is a private company, it is likely that the smaller numbers involved will mean that all members are appraised of the arguments for and against the removal of a particular individual without the need to resort to the formalities prescribed by this provision. Nevertheless, the provision provides a safeguard against removal without the director being able to present his case.

S 304(2)

The director must specifically request that his representations be circulated to the shareholders.

S 304(4)

It is the right of the company or 'any other person' to go to court; but the director is still entitled to be heard and could attempt to repeat any defamatory matter at the general meeting.

See *Jarvis plc v PricewaterhouseCoopers* [2000] 2 BCLC 368 with respect to a company's attempts to prevent an auditor from circulating an equivalent statement under s 392A(7). The court indicated its wariness of attempts by a company to use court proceedings to prevent the dissemination of information of interest to the shareholders. In appropriate circumstances, for example, where a director alleged that he was being removed because of his knowledge of wrongdoing by the remaining directors, the courts would, no doubt, take a similar approach.

OTHER PROVISIONS ABOUT DIRECTORS AND OFFICERS

305. Directors' names on company correspondence, etc

(1)　A company to which this section applies shall not state, in any form, the name of any of its directors (otherwise than in the text or as a signatory) on any business letter on which the company's name appears unless it states on the letter in legible characters [the name of every director of the company.

(2)　This section applies to—

    (a)　every company registered under this Act or under the former Companies Acts (except a company registered before 23rd November 1916); and

    (b)　every company incorporated outside Great Britain which has an established place of business within Great Britain, unless it had established such a place of business before that date.

(3)　If a company makes default in complying with this section, every officer of the company who is in default is liable for each offence to a fine; and for this purpose, where a corporation is an officer of the company, any officer of the corporation is deemed an officer of the company.

(4)　For the purposes of the obligation under subsection (1) to state the name of every director of the company, a person's 'name' means—

    (a)　in the case of an individual, his Christian name (or other forename) and surname; and

    (b)　in the case of a corporation or Scottish firm, its corporate or firm name.

(5)　The initial or a recognised abbreviation of a person's Christian name or other forename may be stated instead of the full Christian name or other forename.

(6)　In the case of a peer, or an individual usually known by a title, the title may be stated instead of his Christian name (or other forename) and surname or in addition to either or both of them.

(7)   In this section 'director' includes a shadow director and the reference in subsection (3) to an 'officer' shall be construed accordingly.

General note

For provisions governing the identification of the company in business letters etc, see ss 348–349, 351.

S 305(2)

For the meaning of 'an established place of business', see note to s 691.

S 305(3)

As to penalties, see s 730, Sch 24; 'officer in default' is defined in s 730(5).

S 305(7)

'Shadow director' is defined in s 741(2); it is unlikely that a shadow director might be named on the company's correspondence when necessary under this provision.

306. Limited company may have directors with unlimited liability

(1)   In the case of a limited company the liability of the directors or managers, or of the managing director, may, if so provided by the memorandum, be unlimited.

(2)   In the case of a limited company in which the liability of a director or manager is unlimited, the directors and any managers of the company and the member who proposes any person for election or appointment to the office of director or manager, shall add to that proposal a statement that the liability of the person holding that office will be unlimited.

(3)   Before the person accepts the office or acts in it, notice in writing that his liability will be unlimited shall be given to him by the following or one of the following persons, namely—

    (a)   the promoters of the company,

    (b)   the directors of the company,

    (c)   any managers of the company,

    (d)   the company secretary.

(4)   If a director, manager or proposer makes default in adding such a statement, or if a promoter, director, manager or secretary makes default in giving the notice required by subsection (3), then—

(a) he is liable to a fine, and

(b) he is also liable for any damage which the person so elected or appointed may sustain from the default;

but the liability of the person elected or appointed is not affected by the default.

General note

This provision is effectively obsolete now.

307. Special resolution making liability of directors unlimited

(1)   A limited company, if so authorised by its articles, may by special resolution alter its memorandum so as to render unlimited the liability of its directors or managers, or of any managing director.

(2)   When such a special resolution is passed, its provisions are as valid as if they had been originally contained in the memorandum.

General note

This provision is effectively obsolete now.

308. Assignment of office by directors

If provision is made by a company's articles, or by any agreement entered into between any person and the company, for empowering a director or manager of the company to assign his office as such to another person, any assignment of office made in pursuance of that provision is (notwithstanding anything to the contrary contained in the provision) of no effect unless and until it is approved by a special resolution of the company.

General note

This provision is primarily of historical interest. It was common once for a retiring director to seek to assign his position, for example, to another member of the family. In modern articles, provision is usually made for the retirement of directors and their reappointment or new appointments, as the case may be, either by the directors or the general meeting, see Table A, regs 73–80. As nominations to the board are usually at the behest of the existing directors (Table A, reg 76(a)), it is possible to ensure that posts remain within a family without any formal assignment as envisaged by this provision.

309. Directors to have regard to interests of employees

(1)   The matters to which the directors of a company are to have regard in the performance of their functions include the interests of the company's employees in general, as well as the interests of its members.

(2)   Accordingly, the duty imposed by this section on the directors is owed by them to the company (and the company alone) and is enforceable in the same way as any other fiduciary duty owed to a company by its directors.

(3)   This section applies to shadow directors as it does to directors.

S 309(1)

Common law position   The common law position was that directors were entitled to take into account employees' interests when it was in the best interests of the company to do so, for example, gratuitous dispositions to the employees to promote loyalty and diligence when the company was a going concern were in the best interests of the company: *Hampson v Price's Patent Candle Co* (1876) 45 LJ Ch 437; but not when the business was being wound up: *Hutton v West Cork Rly Co* (1883) 23 Ch D 654; *Parke v Daily News Ltd* [1962] 2 All ER 929. Provision for employees on the cessation or transfer of business is now governed by s 719.

A declaratory provision   Whether this statutory provision is merely declaratory of that common law position or whether it alters the law significantly by requiring the directors to give equal weight to employees' and shareholders' interests so displacing the members as the embodiment of 'the interests of the company as a whole', is unclear.

   The vague wording of the provision, the lack of guidance as to the respective weight to be given to employees' interests when they conflict with those of the members, and the fact that the provision is not directly enforceable by employees (see sub-s (2)) would suggest that the provision was intended to be merely declaratory of the common law position. As such, the provision may add little to the employees' position. On the other hand, it may be useful for directors who can justify decisions not to the liking of their shareholders by reliance on the duty to the employees under this provision.

Peripheral significance   In keeping with the minimalist nature of the provision, it has been of little significance in the case law, other than peripherally. In *Re Saul D Harrison & Sons plc* [1995] 1 BCLC 14, directors (defending an unfairly prejudicial conduct petition under s 459), justified their decision to continue to run the company (rather than to sell the business and realise the assets for the shareholders) on the basis, inter alia, that they had to have regard to the interests of their 100 employees who were unlikely to find other employment. In *Re Welfab Engineers Ltd* [1990] BCLC 833 the court rejected allegations of misfeasance against directors who sold their business to a purchaser who agreed to keep on the directors and the employees, when a higher price might have been obtained from another purchaser. See also *Fulham Football Club Ltd v Cabra Estates plc* [1994] 1 BCLC 363 at 393.

S 309(2)

Enforcement   Employees as such have no right to enforce this provision, it is a matter for the members. As the duty is owed to the company, the rule in *Foss v*

Harbottle (1843) 2 Hare 461 will come into play and enforcement of the duty will be at the discretion of the directors or the general meeting who are unlikely to be interested in pursuing the matter. A minority shareholder may bring a derivative action on the grounds of fraud on the minority but it is not clear that a breach of this obligation could be so construed. In any event, the obstacles generally to bringing a derivative action are so considerable that it is quite unlikely that any attempt would be made to enforce this provision through that route. It is also unclear whether a breach of the duty might be ratified by the shareholders, given that it is for the benefit of the employees; nor is there any indication of the appropriate remedy which might be awarded in the event of a successful case being brought. These difficulties might suggest that enforcement of the provision was not envisaged.

S 309(3)

'Shadow director' is defined in s 741(2); and a parent company cannot be a shadow director for these purposes: s 741(3).

310. Provisions exempting officers and auditors from liability

(1) This section applies to any provision, whether contained in a company's articles or in any contract with the company or otherwise, for exempting any officer of the company or any person (whether an officer or not) employed by the company as auditor from, or indemnifying him against, any liability which by virtue of any rule of law would otherwise attach to him in respect of any negligence, default, breach of duty or breach of trust of which he may be guilty in relation to the company.

(2) Except as provided by the following subsection, any such provision is void.

(3) This section does not prevent a company—

  (a) from purchasing and maintaining for any such officer or auditor insurance against any such liability, or

  (b) from indemnifying any such officer or auditor against any liability incurred by him—

    (i) in defending any proceedings (whether civil or criminal) in which judgment is given in his favour or he is acquitted, or

    (ii) in connection with any application under section 144(3) or (4) (acquisition of shares by innocent nominee) or section 727 (general power to grant relief in case of honest and reasonable conduct) in which relief is granted to him by the court.

General note

It had been the practice for companies to include in their articles widely drafted exemption clauses relieving their officers from liability arising from breaches of their duties, save in the case of wilful negligence or default: see *Re Brazilian Rubber*

Plantations and Estates Ltd [1911] 1 Ch 425; *Re City Equitable Fire Insurance Co Ltd* [1925] Ch 407. But in 1929 the Greene Committee on Company Law recommended that this practice be prohibited (Cmnd 2657, paras 46–47) and the prohibition was introduced by CA 1929 s 152, now s 310.

Although the company is prohibited to the extent indicated here from relieving an officer etc of any liability in respect of any negligence, default, breach of duty or breach of trust of which he may be guilty in relation to the company, the court has a discretion to do so, on an application from the officer under s 727, see note to that provision, below.

S 310(1), (2)

Scope of the provision   The prohibition on indemnities etc applies only to those given by the company, not by third parties: *Burgoine v Waltham Forest London Borough Council* [1997] 2 BCLC 612. The words 'or otherwise' are to construed eiusdem generis with the preceding words 'whether contained in the company's articles or in any contract with the company', the genus being an arrangement to which the company is a party: *Burgoine v London Borough of Waltham Forest* [1997] 2 BCLC 612 at 627. Despite this approach in *Burgoine*, there remains some uncertainty as to whether a parent company may give indemnities in respect to directors of a subsidiary company and whether a subsidiary may provide an indemnity for a director of a holding company.

The provision which is void is one which exempts or indemnifies in respect of any liability to whomsoever incurred, there being no limitation with respect to liability to the company. However, the prohibition extends only to contractual or similar provisions which exempt or indemnify an officer or auditor against any liability; the provision has no application to the ratification (where permissible) by shareholders of breaches of duty after they occur; and even where the breach of duty has not been or cannot be ratified, the shareholders may choose not to sue: see *Smith v Croft (No 2)* [1987] 3 All ER 909.

Officers and auditors   The exemption or indemnity must be given to an 'officer', defined s 744 (see note to that provision), or an auditor (whether an officer or not). An auditor is not always an officer of the company: he will be if appointed to office as the company's auditor under ss 384, 385 but he will not be if he is simply appointed ad hoc to carry out a limited function: see *Mutual Reinsurance Co Ltd v Peat Marwick Mitchell & Co* [1997] 1 BCLC 1; *R v Shacter* [1960] 1 All ER 61; and see note to s 744, below. It is this provision which has prevented auditors from contracting to limit their liabilities to the company and the shareholders when conducting the statutory audit of the company. The provision does not affect their ability to contract to limit their liabilities with respect to non-audit work not conducted as auditors as when they are acting as reporting accountants conducting due diligence work.

The auditing profession campaigned (unsuccessfully) for the amendment of this provision as part of their attempts to limit claims in negligence against them with respect to company audits. Auditors do now have the option of incorporating as limited liability partnerships (LLPs) under the Limited Liability Partnership Act 2000 but this provision remains in force and will prevent any attempt by the LLP as auditor to contract out of liability as an auditor for breach of duty, negligence, etc.

Relationship with the articles of association   There has been much debate as to whether this section invalidates provisions such as Table A, reg 85, allowing a director to be a party to or interested in a transaction despite a conflict of interest (provided that the director has disclosed the nature and extent of his interest). The issue was addressed in *Movitex Ltd v Bulfield* [1988] BCLC 104, where Vinelott J thought that, given the statutory origins of both provisions, a construction of s 310 must be found which will allow the provisions to co-exist. His analysis (at 120) was that the rule with respect to conflicts of interests is an over-riding principle of equity but not a part of the law defining the duties of directors. On that basis, reg 85 is a modification by the shareholders of a general equitable principle (as they are entitled to do) and does not amount to an exclusion of a duty for the purposes of s 310. Hence there can be no doubt as to the validity of reg 85.

It is clear that this dispensation is of limited utility, restricted as it is to provisions relaxing the rules on conflict of interests. The other obligations of directors, to act in the interests of the company, to exercise care and skill, and to avoid profiting from their position, are correctly classified as duties of the directors which cannot be modified by contractual provisions.

S 310(3)

Insurance cover　This provision was added by CA 1989 and permits the purchase by the company of what is commonly know as D & O liability insurance, providing cover for directors and officers, although the wording of sub-s (3)(a) does not allow the company to meet the cost of any excess on the policy which must be met personally by the officers.

While improving the position of directors and officers, D & O insurance may be costly to obtain and policies may be subject to a variety of exclusions which may still leave directors and officers exposed to considerable liabilities. In addition, there are liabilities which cannot be covered such as those arising from fraudulent and illegal conduct. Disclosure of such purchases by a company originally had to be made in the directors' report but, as the practice is now commonplace, this requirement has been repealed.

It is permissible for the company to purchase such cover for their auditors but it is very rare for a company to do so.

Relief from liability　This provision in sub-s (3)(b) allows for the recovery of costs by officers and auditors when proceedings have been successfully defended or relief successfully obtained from the court (see note to s 727, below). As the company is only entitled to indemnify where the officer is successful in the proceedings, the company should await the outcome of any proceedings before making any payments in this respect. While this may cause practical difficulties for the officer, it is preferable to attempting to recover the payments at a later stage if the officer proves unsuccessful in his defence.

PART X

ENFORCEMENT OF FAIR DEALING BY DIRECTORS

General note to this Part

The provisions of this Part are intended to reinforce the common law rules by regulating to a greater degree certain transactions or arrangements or agreements by directors with their companies which give rise to possible conflicts of interest. In some instances, transactions are prohibited and, in others, the approval of the company in general meeting is required.

Additional disclosure of many of these matters is called for in the notes to the accounts: see s 232, Sch 6; and it is the duty of any director to disclose to the company such matters as may be necessary to ensure that the company can make the necessary disclosures under Sch 6, Pt 1 (directors' emoluments, pensions, compensation for loss of office, etc): see s 232(3).

In addition to the statutory requirements, directors must bear in mind their general obligation to disclose conflicts of interests as required by the articles, see Table A, reg 85, and their overriding duty to act in the best interests of the company. See, for example, *Neptune (Vehicle Washing Equipment) Ltd v Fitzgerald (No 2)* [1995] BCC 1000; *JJ Harrison (Properties) Ltd v Harrison* [2001] 1 BCLC 158.

RESTRICTIONS ON DIRECTORS TAKING FINANCIAL ADVANTAGE

311. Prohibition on tax-free payments to directors

(1) It is not lawful for a company to pay a director remuneration (whether as director or otherwise) free of income tax, or otherwise calculated by reference to or varying with the amount of his income tax, or to or with any rate of income tax.

(2) Any provision contained in a company's articles, or in any contract, or in any resolution of a company or a company's directors, for payment to a director of remuneration as above mentioned has effect as if it provided for payment, as a gross sum subject to income tax, of the net sum for which it actually provides.

S 311(1)

The provision is limited to payments to a director but extends to payments to him whether in his capacity as a director or any other capacity such as an employee.

If a company were to pay a director remuneration free of income tax, the amount of tax paid by the company would itself be taxable as a benefit received by the director so no advantage would be gained by this manoeuvre. Any sums paid by the company would have to be disclosed in the company's annual accounts as a benefit received by the director: Sch 6, para 1(3)(a).

The requirement that remuneration should not be calculated by reference to the amount of the director's income tax is unenforceable, as directors will frequently have regard to what their take-home pay will be when negotiating the gross amount of their remuneration.

S 311(2)

The net sum stated in the articles or contract or resolution is treated as the gross sum payable which would then be subject to tax, so reducing in fact the amount received by the director. This is a positive disincentive to breach of the provision.

312. Payment to director for loss of office, etc

It is not lawful for a company to make to a director of the company any payment by way of compensation for loss of office, or as consideration for or in connection with his retirement from office, without particulars of the proposed payment (including its amount) being disclosed to members of the company and the proposal being approved by the company.

General note

Payments to directors These provisions (ss 312–314) are designed to cover a variety of payments to directors, namely:

(1)   payments to the directors by the company on loss of office or on retirement (s 312);

(2)   such payments by any person on the transfer of the whole or part of the undertaking or property of the company (s 313); and

(3)   such payments by any person on certain types of take-over occurring (s 314).

However, the range of exceptions to the provisions (noted below) mean that they are of limited importance.

Publicity Details of directors' service contracts must be available for inspection by any member (s 318); limits are imposed on the duration of directors' contracts of employment without the approval of the general meeting (s 319), and details of directors' remuneration and compensation for loss of office must be included in notes to the company's accounts (s 232(1) and Sch 6, Pt 1); although details of compensation for loss of office are presented as an aggregate figure for compensation paid to all directors without the figures being broken down as between individual directors: Sch 6, Pt 1, para 8.

Disclosure and approval The key to a lawful payment within this provision is prior disclosure and approval by the members of the company. Disclosure must be to all the members of the company (ie of whatever class and whether voting or not) (see *Re Duomatic Ltd* [1969] 2 Ch 365: those who cannot vote may nevertheless influence those who can), and the approval required in advance is by an ordinary resolution. If the company is a charity in England and Wales, any approval for the purpose of this provision is ineffective without the prior written consent of the Charity Commissioners: Charities Act 1993, s 66(1), (2)(a).

Payments included   The provision covers payments *by* the company *to* a director of the company. It does not cover payments by a subsidiary company to a director of a parent company in connection with his loss of office; nor does it cover payments to a connected person of such a director although such circuitous payments are not very likely in practice and may in any event be open to challenge as not being in the best interests of the company.

The decision in *Taupo*   Many of the difficulties which surround the interpretation of this provision arise from the decision of the Privy Council in *Taupo Totara Timber Co Ltd v Rowe* [1977] 3 All ER 123, involving an identical provision in the New Zealand legislation.

The interpretation of the provision adopted by the Privy Council was that:

(1)   The provision applies only to payments for loss of office *as a director* of the company and does not extent to payments for loss of other offices (such as that of managing director or company secretary).

Strictly speaking, this point was obiter in *Taupo* but there is support for this interpretation of the provision in the Jenkins Committee Report in 1962 (Report of the Company Law Committee, Cmnd 1749, para 93) and in *Lander v Premier Pict Petroleum Ltd* [1998] BCC 248 (CS,OH). If this interpretation is correct, however, it significantly reduces the scope of the section. It would also render s 316(3) (payments by way of damages for breach of contract do not need shareholder approval) of limited significance if payments to those in executive positions are beyond the scope of the provision in any event.

The better view, it is thought, is that the provision extends to payments for loss of any office held by the director, such as a position as a managing director or as the company secretary.

(2)   The provision does not apply to payments which the company is legally bound to make.

This interpretation of the provision is generally accepted as correct although the effect of it is to narrow the scope of the provision considerably. Disclosure and approval is required for gratuitous, uncovenanted, payments only and not for payments which the company is legally bound to make.

Such payments would include pre-determined payments due under a contract (so-called 'golden parachutes') as well as payments, for example, arising on a quantum meruit for services rendered. In *Taupo Totara Timber Co Ltd v Rowe* [1977] 3 All ER 123 the contract entitled a director to five times his annual salary in the event of a change of control of the company; and in *Lander v Premier Pict Petroleum Ltd* [1998] BCC 248 (CS,OH), the contract entitled a director to three times his annual salary on a change of control. Shareholder approval was not required in either case. Predetermined payment clauses must be carefully drafted as liquidated damages clauses to prevent the court construing them as unenforceable penalty provisions: *Dunlop Pneumatic Tyre Co Ltd v New Garage and Motor Co Ltd* [1915] AC 79.

Payments exempted   Bona fide payments by way of damages for breach of contract are specifically excluded, as are bona fide payments by way of pension in respect of past services (s 316(3)); and see that section for the meaning of 'pension'.

Damages for breach of contract should be subject, in theory, to the requirement on the part of the departing director to mitigate his loss by obtaining alternative employment but this element in the calculation of damages often appears to be missing. The amounts paid may not then be bona fide damages, strictly speaking, and may in fact be sums which should be within s 312 (and so require approval) rather than sums which are exempt by virtue of s 316(3); but this is difficult to establish.

An unlawful payment   As the payment is rendered unlawful by a failure to secure prior approval, subsequent ratification is not possible. There is no provision here to the effect of s 313(2) but the recipient of any payment remains liable to account for it to the company and those directors responsible for authorising the unlawful payment are also liable to indemnify the company against any loss arising: see *Re Duomatic Ltd* [1969] 2 Ch 365.

Relationship with s 320 (substantial property transactions)   A debatable issue is whether payments to directors of compensation for loss of office or in connection with retirement from office which do not require approval under s 312 (or ss 313, 314) would nevertheless require shareholder approval under s 320 (substantial property transactions involving the acquisition of a non-cash asset). While the majority of compensation payments involve a payment of cash to a director and so clearly would not be within s 320, the breadth of the definition of a non-cash asset (see s 739) is such that, arguably, some compensation packages could be subject to s 320. See the Law Commission Consultation Paper: *Company Directors: Regulating Conflicts of Interests and Formulating a Statement of Duties* (CP No 153, 1998), para 4.35. However, it is arguable that ss 312–316 are intended to provide a comprehensive code on compensation packages and such payments should not then be subject to scrutiny under other provisions such as s 320. There is some first instance support for this approach, see *Lander v Premier Pict Petroleum Ltd* [1998] BCC 248 (CS,OH). The Law Commission has recommended that s 320 be clarified to exclude compensation payments from that provision.

313. Company approval for property transfer

(1) It is not lawful, in connection with the transfer of the whole or any part of the undertaking or property of a company, for any payment to be made to a director of the company by way of compensation for loss of office, or as consideration for or in connection with his retirement from office, unless particulars of the proposed payment (including its amount) have been disclosed to members of the company and the proposal approved by the company.

(2) Where a payment unlawful under this section is made to a director, the amount received is deemed to be received by him in trust for the company.

S 313(1)

Disclosure and approval   Disclosure of the proposed payment must be made to all the members, of whatever class and whether voting or not, and the approval required in advance is by an ordinary resolution. If the company is a charity in England and Wales, any approval for the purpose of this provision is ineffective without the prior written consent of the Charity Commissioners: Charities Act 1993, s 66(1), (2)(b). As the payment is rendered unlawful by a failure to secure prior approval, subsequent ratification is not possible.

Payments included   This provision covers payments *by* any person *to* a director of the company; and 'payment' is more broadly defined under ss 313–315 than under s 312. Disguised payments, as where a director receives a sum for any shares which he holds in the company in excess of the price available to other holders of like shares at that time, are included in the definition: s 316(2)(a); and payments with respect to offices other than that of director would be within s 316(2)(b). In either case, the payment is deemed to be a payment by way of compensation for loss of office or on retirement.

Payments exempted   Bona fide payments by way of damages for breach of contract are specifically excluded, as are bona fide payments by way of pension in respect of past services: s 316(3); as are payments which the company is legally obliged to make: *Taupo Totara Timber Co Ltd v Rowe* [1977] 3 All ER 123, PC; and see note to s 312.

S 313(2)

See the anti-avoidance provisions included in s 316(1); and note also s 316(4).

314. Director's duty of disclosure on takeover, etc

(1) This section applies where, in connection with the transfer to any persons of all or any of the shares in a company, being a transfer resulting from—

    (a) an offer made to the general body of shareholders; or

    (b) an offer made by or on behalf of some other body corporate with a view to the company becoming its subsidiary or a subsidiary of its holding company; or

    (c) an offer made by or on behalf of an individual with a view to his obtaining the right to exercise or control the exercise of not less than one-third of the voting power at any general meeting of the company; or

    (d) any other offer which is conditional on acceptance to a given extent,

a payment is to be made to a director of the company by way of compensation for loss of office, or as consideration for or in connection with his retirement from office.

(2) It is in those circumstances the director's duty to take all reasonable steps to secure that particulars of the proposed payment (including its amount) are included in or sent with any notice of the offer made for their shares which is given to any shareholders.

(3) If—

    (a) the director fails to take those steps, or

   (b) any person who has been properly required by the director to include those particulars in or send them with the notice required by subsection (2) fails to do so,

he is liable to a fine.

S 314(1)

Payments included   This provision covers payments *by* any person *to* a director of the company and 'payment' is more broadly defined under ss 313–315 than under s 312. Disguised payments, as where a director receives a sum for any shares which he holds in the company in excess of the price available to other holders of like shares at that time, are included in the definition (s 316(2)(a)); and payments with respect to offices other than that of director would be within s 316(2)(b). In either case, the payment is deemed to be a payment by way of compensation for loss of office or on retirement.

   The provision only applies to the curious list of offers identified in this subsection which do not embrace all methods of take-overs and, in particular, do not extend to take-overs effected by a scheme of arrangement under s 425 which involve a cancellation of shares rather than an offer for shares.

Payments exempted   Bona fide payments by way of damages for breach of contract are specifically excluded, as are bona fide payments by way of pension in respect of past services (s 316(3)); as are payments which the company is legally obliged to make: *Taupo Totara Timber Co Ltd v Rowe* [1977] 3 All ER 123, PC; and see note to s 312.

S 314(2)

Disclosure and approval   The disclosure required is disclosure in the take-over documentation. There initially appears to be no requirement of shareholder approval but this can be found in s 315(1)(b).

S 314(3)

Penalties   The failure to disclose in this case is made a criminal offence, a penalty which applies to persons other than the company director such as the company secretary or a professional adviser. As to penalties, see s 730, Sch 23. The civil consequences of non-compliance are set out in s 315.

---

315. Consequences of non-compliance with s 314

(1) If in the case of any such payment to a director as is mentioned in section 314(1)—

   (a) his duty under that section is not complied with, or

   (b) the making of the proposed payment is not, before the transfer of any shares in pursuance of the offer, approved by a meeting (summoned for the purpose) of the holders of the shares to which the offer relates and of other holders of shares of the same class as any of those shares,

any sum received by the director on account of the payment is deemed to have been received by him in trust for persons who have sold their shares as a result of the offer made; and the expenses incurred by him in distributing that sum amongst those persons shall be borne by him and not retained out of that sum.

(2) Where—

   (a) the shareholders referred to in subsection (1)(b) are not all the members of the company, and

   (b) no provision is made by the articles for summoning or regulating the meeting referred to in that paragraph,

the provisions of this Act and of the company's articles relating to general meetings of the company apply (for that purpose) to the meeting either without modification or with such modifications as the Secretary of State on the application of any person concerned may direct for the purpose of adapting them to the circumstances of the meeting.

(3) If at a meeting summoned for the purpose of approving any payment as required by subsection (1)(b) a quorum is not present and, after the meeting has been adjourned to a later date, a quorum is again not present, the payment is deemed for the purposes of that subsection to have been approved.

General note

There might appear to be an overlap between s 312 (payment to director for loss of office etc) and ss 314–315 (payments as compensation for loss of office to a director in connection with a take-over). As the remedies are different (s 312 would result in a remedy for the company, s 315 giving relief to the shareholders of the offeree company), it is important to determine which section applies. It seems clear that ss 314, 315 should prevail as the more specific provision and as giving the more appropriate remedy in the circumstances. A remedy for the company would allow the offeror company (post take-over) to recoup the money paid.

S 315(1)

Disclosure and approval   In addition to the requirement in s 314 to disclose details of the payment in a circular to the shareholders, a meeting of the shareholders to whom the offer relates and of others holding shares of that class (ie shares held by the offeror and therefore not shares to which the offer relates) must approve of the payment before the transfer of any shares in pursuance of the offer. The notice of the meeting must indicate that this is the business to be conducted. There is no restriction on the offeror and his associates voting at that meeting in respect of any shares in the offeree company which they already hold.

   Approval in advance is required and ratification is not possible as, in the absence of approval, the director holds the payment on a statutory trust for the offeree shareholders who have accepted the offer. See also s 316(1), (4).

S 315(2)

This subsection makes provision for the class meetings arising from sub-s (1).

---

316. Provisions supplementing ss 312–315

(1) Where in proceedings for the recovery of any payment as having, by virtue of section 313(2) or 315(1) been received by any person in trust, it is shown that—

    (a) the payment was made in pursuance of any arrangement entered into as part of the agreement for the transfer in question, or within one year before or two years after that agreement or the offer leading to it; and

    (b) the company or any person to whom the transfer was made was privy to that arrangement,

payment is deemed, except in so far as the contrary is shown, to be one to which the provisions mentioned above in this subsection apply.

(2) If in connection with any such transfer as is mentioned in any of sections 313 to 315—

    (a) the price to be paid to a director of the company whose office is to be abolished or who is to retire from office for any shares in the company held by him is in excess of the price which could at the time have been obtained by other holders of the like shares; or

    (b) any valuable consideration is given to any such director,

the excess or the money value of the consideration (as the case may be) is deemed for the purposes of that section to have been a payment made to him by way of compensation for loss of office or as consideration for or in connection with his retirement from office.

(3) References in sections 312 to 315 to payments made to a director by way of compensation for loss of office or as consideration for or in connection with his retirement from office, do not include any bona fide payment by way of damages for breach of contract or by way of pension in respect of past services.

'Pension' here includes any superannuation allowance, superannuation gratuity or similar payment.

(4) Nothing in sections 313 to 315 prejudices the operation of any rule of law requiring disclosure to be made with respect to such payments as are there mentioned, or with respect to any other like payments made or to be made to a company's directors.

S 316(1)

This is an anti-avoidance provision designed to catch side arrangements entered into as part of the agreement for the transfer of the company's undertaking or property or shares or entered into either one year before or two years after the agreement in question. In these cases, the payment will be deemed to be subject to the statutory trust imposed by the specified provisions, unless the contrary is shown.

S 316(2)

This provision extends the definition of payments for the purpose of those sections; see note to s 313(1). This provision does not apply to s 312.

S 316(3)

Bona fide damages or pension payments   This provision is a significant limitation on the scope of ss 312–315; see note to s 312 above. There is no express requirement that the pension payment be a legal entitlement but if this provision extends to gratuitous pension payments and exempts such payments from disclosure and approval, this is a major loophole in the provisions.

In addition to damages for breach of contract, it is common for a settlement with a departing director to include a payment in respect of his release of any entitlement to compensation for unfair dismissal or redundancy under employment law, but such payments are not specifically encompassed by s 316(3) and therefore approval of these payments would seem to be required.

S 316(4)

This provision retains the general requirement to disclose conflicts of interests, see s 317; Table A, reg 85.

317. Directors to disclose interest in contracts

(1) It is the duty of a director of a company who is in any way, whether directly or indirectly, interested in a contract or proposed contract with the company to declare the nature of his interest at a meeting of the directors of the company.

(2) In the case of a proposed contract, the declaration shall be made—

    (a) at the meeting of the directors at which the question of entering into the contract is first taken into consideration; or

    (b) if the director was not at the date of that meeting interested in the proposed contract, at the next meeting of the directors held after he became so interested;

and, in a case where the director becomes interested in a contract after it is made, the declaration shall be made at the first meeting of the directors held after he becomes so interested.

(3) For purposes of this section, a general notice given to the directors of a company by a director to the effect that—

    (a) he is a member of a specified company or firm and is to be regarded as interested in any contract which may, after the date of the notice, be made with that company or firm; or

(b) he is to be regarded as interested in any contract which may after the date of the notice be made with a specified person who is connected with him (within the meaning of section 346 below),

is deemed a sufficient declaration of interest in relation to any such contract.

(4) However, no such notice is of effect unless either it is given at a meeting of the directors or the director takes reasonable steps to secure that it is brought up and read at the next meeting of the directors after it is given.

(5) A reference in this section to a contract includes any transaction or arrangement (whether or not constituting a contract) made or entered into on or after 22nd December 1980.

(6) For purposes of this section, a transaction or arrangement of a kind described in section 330 (prohibition of loans, quasi-loans etc to directors) made by a company for a director of the company or a person connected with such a director is treated (if it would not otherwise be so treated, and whether or not it is prohibited by that section) as a transaction or arrangement in which that director is interested.

(7) A director who fails to comply with this section is liable to a fine.

(8) This section applies to a shadow director as it applies to a director, except that a shadow director shall declare his interest, not at a meeting of the directors, but by a notice in writing to the directors which is either—

(a) a specific notice given before the date of the meeting at which, if he had been a director, the declaration would be required by subsection (2) to be made; or

(b) a notice which under subsection (3) falls to be treated as a sufficient declaration of that interest (or would fall to be so treated apart from subsection (4)).

(9) Nothing in this section prejudices the operation of any rule of law restricting directors of a company from having an interest in contracts with the company.

General note

The equitable principle   It is a long-established principle of equity, preserved by s 317(9), that where directors place themselves in a position where their duties and their personal interests conflict, any transaction arising therefrom is voidable at the instance of the company, without the court enquiring into the fairness or otherwise of the transaction: *Aberdeen Rly Co v Blaikie Bros* (1854) 1 Macq 461. The company has a choice whether to affirm or avoid the contract but the right to avoid the transaction will be lost if: (1) the company delays unduly before rescinding; or (2) restitutio in integrum becomes impossible; or (3) the rights of bona fide third parties intervene: *Hely-Hutchinson v Brayhead Ltd* [1967] 3 All ER 98. In addition to setting aside the transaction, the company can call upon the director to account for any profit which he has made.

Informed consent of the members   However, a director may enter into a transaction in which he has a conflict of interest with the informed consent of the shareholders in general meeting. In practice, instead of requiring the approval in general meeting on each occasion of conflict, it is common for a company, by its articles, to permit directors to be interested in transactions or arrangements with the company or in which the company is otherwise interested, provided they disclose the nature and extent of any interest to the board, see Table A, reg 85.

Relationship between statute and articles   The relationship between the statutory requirement of disclosure in this section and Table A, reg 85, was addressed by the Court of Appeal in *Hely-Hutchinson v Brayhead Ltd* [1967] 3 All ER 98, which concluded that the section merely creates a statutory duty of disclosure and imposes a fine for non-compliance. Accordingly, a breach of the statutory provision, or indeed compliance with it, has no effect on the issue of the validity of a contract entered into in disregard of the no-conflict rule.

That issue is determined by whether the articles have relaxed the self-dealing rule and whether there has been strict compliance with the articles. Hence Table A, reg 85, or its equivalent, is the key provision in terms of avoiding the full rigour of the equitable rules on conflicts of interest and s 317 is a mere statutory disclosure provision. This approach was endorsed by Lord Goff in *Guinness plc v Saunders* [1990] 1 All ER 652 at 665.

Duty to act bona fide   In addition to the statutory requirements, and the obligations arising under the articles, directors must bear in mind their overriding duty to act in the best interests of the company. See, for example, *Neptune (Vehicle Washing Equipment) Ltd v Fitzgerald (No 2)* [1995] BCC 1000; *JJ Harrison (Properties) Ltd v Harrison* [2001] 1 BCLC 158.

S 317(1), (5)

Disclosure of an interest   There is no de minimis financial threshold and disclosure is required of any interest, however small in financial terms. On the other hand, the nature of the interest which requires disclosure must be real and substantial and not merely theoretical and insubstantial and a minimal financial interest would have a bearing on that issue: *Re Dominion International Group plc (No 2)* [1996] 1 BCLC 572 at 597; *Boulting v Association of Cinematograph, Television and Allied Technicians* [1963] 1 All ER 716.

Disclosure is required whether it is a direct or an indirect interest – a formula broad enough to include the interests of persons connected with the director. The wording of the provision on this point lacks clarity but that contracts by the company with a connected person may be matters in which a director is indirectly interested is confirmed by s 317(3)(b) (which allows a director to give a general notice of such interests). See also s 317(6).

There is no exemption of interests of which the director has no knowledge and of which it would be unreasonable to expect him to have any knowledge, which would particularly be the case with respect to indirect interests; cf Table A, reg 86(b).

The definition of 'contract' is expanded by s 317(5) to include any transaction or arrangement, but it is only interests in contracts or proposed contracts (so defined) *with* the company which must be disclosed.

Disclosure to the board and not a committee   Disclosure must be to the board at a board meeting and disclosure to a committee of directors would be insufficient for these purposes: see *Guinness plc v Saunders* [1988] BCLC 607 at 611, CA. The matter must then be minuted as required by s 382. The timing of the disclosure is dealt with by s 317(2). Note also Sch 6, paras 15(c), 16(c), which require disclosure in the notes to the accounts of particulars of transactions and arrangements in which a director had, directly or indirectly, a material interest (defined in Sch 6, para 17(2)).

Full and frank disclosure   The disclosure required is full and frank disclosure as to the nature of the transaction so that the other directors or director can see what the director's interest is and how far it extends: *Movitex Ltd v Bulfield* [1988] BCLC 104 at 121; *Imperial Mercantile Credit Association v Coleman* (1873) LR 6 HL 189 at 205; and see *JJ Harrison (Properties) Ltd v Harrison* [2001] 1 BCLC 158. See also s 317(3).

Even if all directors aware   Disclosure at a board meeting may be required even though all of the directors are aware informally of the conflict of interest but there are conflicting views on this point. In *Lee Panavision Ltd v Lee Lighting Ltd* [1992] BCLC 22, Dillon LJ noted, obiter, that he would have been loath to regard a technical non-declaration of an interest in this way as having an adverse affect on any agreement (at 33). The non-disclosure in question was a failure to disclose formally at a board meeting a conflict which was known to and common to all the directors. In *Runciman v Walter Runciman plc* [1992] BCLC 1084, Simon Brown J queried, obiter, whether in all commonsense a formal declaration of interest is required where all the board would have been aware of the conflict (at 1095). In this case, the interest in question was the interest of a director in his own service contract which had been varied by the board. See also *MacPherson v European Strategic Bureau Ltd* [1999] 2 BCLC 203 at 219 (support, obiter, for the approach in *Runciman*). It seems that such a technical default would not in general constitute grounds for finding a director to be unfit for the purpose of disqualification: *Re Dominion International Group plc (No 2)* [1996] 1 BCLC 572 at 600.

On the other hand, in *Guinness plc v Saunders* [1988] BCLC 607, Fox LJ thought that regardless of the knowledge of all, the matter still should be the subject of a positive consideration of the board as a body (at 612); and see *Neptune (Vehicle Washing Equipment) Ltd v Fitzgerald* [1995] 1 BCLC 352 for a strict interpretation of the requirement of disclosure.

As an evidential matter, it may be difficult to establish the full extent and nature of the knowledge of the directors in the absence of a formal disclosure. Given the uncertainties, and the importance of disclosure for the purposes of Table A, reg 85, it is advisable to make a formal declaration.

Disclosure when sole director   Disclosure is required under the section even in the case of a sole director: *Neptune (Vehicle Washing Equipment) Ltd v Fitzgerald* [1995] 1 BCLC 352. In this case, Lightman J considered the objects of disclosure to be the following, namely: that all the directors should know or be reminded of the interest of any director; that the making of the declaration should be the occasion for a statutory pause for thought about the existence of the conflict of interest and the duty to prefer the interests of the company; and that the disclosure or reminder should be a distinct happening at a meeting and be recorded in the minutes (at 359). It followed that, even in the case of a sole director, a formal disclosure of the conflict of interest must take place.

As to the manner of disclosure where the director is a sole director, this could be by recording the matter in the minutes where the director has met alone or, if the meeting is attended by others, then the declaration should be made aloud in their presence and recorded in the minutes: [1995] 1 BCLC 352 at 360.

Not everyone would agree with this approach. In *Movitex Ltd v Bulfield* [1988] BCLC 104, Vinelott J doubted, obiter, whether disclosure can sensibly occur where there is only one director since, in his view, 'disclosure imports the concept of informing someone of something of which he would not otherwise be aware' (at 116). In *Neptune (Vehicle Washing Equipment) Ltd v Fitzgerald (No 2)* [1995] BCC 1000, the court applied Lightman J's approach while having 'doubts about its correctness' (at 1003). A better approach might be to require that disclosure by a sole director should be to the shareholders in general meeting as the only other body which can exclude the equitable rule against self-dealing: see *Neptune (Vehicle Washing Equipment) Ltd v Fitzgerald (No 2)* [1995] BCC 1000 at 1003.

S 317(2)

The Jenkins Committee (Report of the Company Law Committee, Cmnd 1749, 1962, para 95) had considered that the requirement of disclosure only applies to contracts brought before the board of directors which interpretation arises from the wording of sub-s (2) and which would considerably narrow the provision, as in larger companies many contracts are not discussed at board level. But in *Neptune (Vehicle Washing Equipment) Ltd v Fitzgerald* [1995] 1 BCLC 352, Lightman J declined to accept such a narrow interpretation of the provision pointing out that the requirement in s 317(1) is perfectly general and extends to contracts whether or not considered or resolved upon at a meeting of directors (at 359). To do otherwise would 'enable the statutory obligation to be sidestepped by avoiding consideration and decisions on such contracts at directors' meetings and emasculate the statutory policy and protection' (at 359).

S 317(3), (4)

This provision deems two types of general notices to be a sufficient declaration of interest for the purposes of s 317(1). The timing of such notices is dealt with by sub-s (4). A shadow director can utilise this procedure: see s 317(8)(b).

The notice required by sub-s (3)(a) does not require that a director indicate the nature and extent of the interest; nor does it require further disclosure as changes occur in that interest. The provision is limited, however, to interests arising out of membership (by the director) of a company or a firm and an interest arising in any other way could not be the subject of a general notice, unless it fell within sub-s (3)(b). A general notice of a director's interest in any contract which the company may make with a connected person is permitted by sub-s (3)(b).

S 317(6)

This provision deems any transaction or arrangement within s 330, whether prohibited or not, and whether with a director or a connected person, to be within s 317(1) and therefore it must be disclosed by the director.

S 317(7)

As noted above, the provision merely creates a statutory duty of disclosure and imposes a fine for non-compliance: *Hely-Hutchinson v Brayhead Ltd* [1967] 3 All ER 98. As to penalties, see s 730, Sch 24.

S 317(8)

'Shadow director' is defined in s 741(2). In reality, given that many shadow directors wish to conceal their relationship with their companies, it is unlikely that a shadow director will comply with this requirement for written disclosure of a conflict of interests.

Where a declaration of interest is made by a shadow director, the declaration is deemed to form part of the proceedings of the relevant board meeting (s 382(3)) and must be minuted and will then benefit from the deemed validity conferred by s 382(4).

S 317(9)

As noted above, the statutory provision merely creates a statutory duty of disclosure and imposes a fine for non-compliance (*Hely-Hutchinson v Brayhead Ltd* [1967] 3 All ER 98), and it has no effect on the issue of the validity of a transaction entered into in disregard of the equitable principles governing conflicts of interests. This matter must be determined by the application of those equitable principles which are retained by this provision. Their application in turn may be modified by the articles as in Table A, reg 85.

318. Directors' service contracts to be open to inspection

(1) Subject to the following provisions, every company shall keep at an appropriate place—

    (a) in the case of each director whose contract of service with the company is in writing, a copy of that contract;

    (b) in the case of each director whose contract of service with the company is not in writing, a written memorandum setting out its terms; and

    (c) in the case of each director who is employed under a contract of service with a subsidiary of the company, a copy of that contract or, if it is not in writing, a written memorandum setting out its terms.

(2) All copies and memoranda kept by a company in pursuance of subsection (1) shall be kept at the same place.

(3) The following are appropriate places for the purposes of subsection (1)—

    (a) the company's registered office;

    (b) the place where its register of members is kept (if other than its registered office);

    (c) its principal place of business, provided that is situated in that part of Great Britain in which the company is registered.

(4) Every company shall send notice in the prescribed form to the registrar of companies of the place where copies and memoranda are kept in compliance with subsection (1), and of any change in that place, save in a case in which they have at all times been kept at the company's registered office.

(5) Subsection (1) does not apply to a director's contract of service with the company or with a subsidiary of it if that contract required him to work wholly

or mainly outside the United Kingdom; but the company shall keep a memorandum—

    (a) in the case of a contract of service with the company, giving the director's name and setting out the provisions of the contract relating to its duration;

    (b) in the case of a contract of service with a subsidiary, giving the director's name and the name and place of incorporation of the subsidiary, and setting out the provisions of the contract relating to its duration,

at the same place as copies and memoranda are kept by the company in pursuance of subsection (1).

(6) A shadow director is treated for purposes of this section as a director.

(7) Every copy and memorandum required by subsection (1) or (5) to be kept shall … be open to inspection of any member of the company without charge.

(8) If—

    (a) default is made in complying with subsection (1) or (5), or

    (b) an inspection required under subsection (7) is refused, or

    (c) default is made for 14 days in complying with subsection (4),

the company and every officer of it who is in default is liable to a fine and, for continued contravention, to a daily default fine.

(9) In the case of a refusal of an inspection required under subsection (7) of a copy or memorandum, the court may by order compel an immediate inspection of it.

(10) Subsections (1) and (5) apply to a variation of a director's contract of service as they apply to the contract.

(11) This section does not require that there be kept a copy of, or memorandum setting out the terms of, a contract (or its variation) at a time when the unexpired portion of the term for which the contract is to be in force is less than 12 months, or at a time at which the contract can, within the next ensuing 12 months, be terminated by the company without payment of compensation.

S 318(1), (6), (10)

Disclosure required   This provision applies only to contracts of service and any variation thereof (sub-s (10)); and it is not clear whether an increase in salary which is automatic on the application of a formula amounts to a variation for these purposes and would require disclosure. This provision does not apply to contracts for services; nor does it extend to the standard letters of appointment commonly used for the appointment of non-executive directors.

   The disclosure required is of the contract or a memorandum of its terms. Collateral documentation (which might contain information, for example, on benefits to be received by the director and which would be of interest to the shareholders) need not be disclosed. The disclosure requirement in sub-s (1)(c) can be overlooked. Note s 318(5) and (11) below, which offer some scope for avoiding the reach of this section.

This provision applies to 'shadow directors' as defined in s 741(2). In reality, given that many shadow directors wish to conceal their relationship with their companies, it is unlikely that a shadow director will comply with this requirement for disclosure.

S 318(3), (4)

Place of inspection   If the information is kept otherwise than at the registered office, then the location of that other place must be notified to the registrar of companies. As to the company's registered office, see s 287; as to the register of members, see s 352; as to the meaning of 'principal place of business', see note to s 698(2), below.

S 318(5), (11)

Avoidance   The disclosure requirements imposed by sub-s (5) are minimal and are thought to be open to abuse. There is uncertainty as to the meaning of 'mainly outside the UK' with directors seeking to take advantage of the provision where they worked outside the UK initially or at stages in the contract even though they now work within the UK. Subsection (11) also provides scope for avoiding the reach of the section with directors accepting rolling contracts of less than one year in duration in order to avoid disclosure.

S 318(7), (9)

Inspection by members only   As to the manner of inspection, see the Companies (Inspection and Copying of Registers, Indices and Documents) Regulations 1991, SI 1991/1998. The provision in sub-s (9) is necessary because, but for the section, it is not clear that there is any right of inspection or that the court has the power to compel inspection: see *Conway v Petronius Clothing Co Ltd* [1978] 1 All ER 185 at 199. The court's power is discretionary: see *Pelling v Families need Fathers Ltd* [2001] All ER (D) 03 (Aug), CA.

S 318(8)

Penalties   As to penalties, see s 730, Sch 24; 'officer who is in default' is defined in s 730(5).

---

319. Director's contract of employment for more than 5 years

(1) This section applies in respect of any term of an agreement whereby a director's employment with the company of which he is a director or, where he is the director of a holding company, his employment within the group is to continue, or may be continued, otherwise than at the instance of the company (whether under the original agreement or under a new agreement entered into in pursuance of it), for a period of more than 5 years during which the employment—

    (a) cannot be terminated by the company by notice; or

    (b) can be so terminated only in specified circumstances.

(2) In any case where—

    (a) a person is or is to be employed with a company under an agreement which cannot be terminated by the company by notice or can be so terminated only in specified circumstances; and

    (b) more than 6 months before the expiration of the period for which he is or is to be so employed, the company enters into a further agreement (otherwise than in pursuance of a right conferred by or under the original agreement on the other party to it) under which he is to be employed with the company or, where he is a director of a holding company, within the group,

this section applies as if to the period for which he is to be employed under that further agreement there were added a further period equal to the unexpired period of the original agreement.

(3) A company shall not incorporate in an agreement such a term as is mentioned in subsection (1), unless the term is first approved by a resolution of the company in general meeting and, in the case of a director of a holding company, by a resolution of that company in general meeting.

(4) No approval is required to be given under this section by any body corporate unless it is a company within the meaning of this Act, or is registered under section 680, or if it is a wholly-owned subsidiary of any body corporate, wherever incorporated.

(5) A resolution of a company approving such a term as is mentioned in subsection (1) shall not be passed at a general meeting of the company unless a written memorandum setting out the proposed agreement incorporating the term is available for inspection by members of the company both—

    (a) at the company's registered office for not less than 15 days ending with the date of the meeting; and

    (b) at the meeting itself.

(6) A term incorporated in an agreement in contravention of this section is, to the extent that it contravenes the section, void; and that agreement and, in a case where subsection (2) applies, the original agreement are deemed to contain a term entitling the company to terminate it at any time by the giving of reasonable notice.

(7) In this section—

    (a) 'employment' includes employment under a contract for services; and

    (b) 'group', in relation to a director of a holding company, means the group which consists of that company and its subsidiaries;

and for purposes of this section a shadow director is treated as a director.

General note

Lengthy service agreements can be a source of abuse by making it too expensive for a company to remove a director. This section attempts to limit the duration of such contracts to a five-year period (where the company's power to terminate the contract is restricted) while allowing the shareholders to approve longer arrangements if thought appropriate.

S 319(1)

Agreements requiring approval   The section only regulates agreements in excess of a five-year period which cannot be terminated by notice and so it will not cover a contract which, while of six years duration, can be terminated by the company on 12 months' notice. The provision does not address this issue of the duration of notice which can be extensive and therefore equally costly (see *Runciman v Walter Runciman plc* [1992] BCLC 1084, where the period of notice was five years long). Such provisions as to notice are controlled by the directors' obligation to act bona fide in the interests of the company as a whole: see *Runciman v Walter Runciman plc* [1992] BCLC 1084.

The provision applies to any agreement including agreements not directly with the director but with a company controlled by him. It is not limited to employment as a director but extends to any employment including under a contract for services (s 319(7)(a)) and including, where the company is a group, any employment within the group. It is immaterial whether the agreement is subject to a foreign law: s 347.

S 319(2)

Aggregation of periods   This provisions requires the aggregation of periods in certain circumstances so that the provision cannot be avoided by a string of contracts. However, the rather obscure wording of the provision does offer scope for avoidance. In particular, the provision requires that the unexpired portion of the original contract be added to the new contract but this will not arise if there is no unexpired portion of the original contract as where the first contract (for four years, say) is replaced after 12 months with another which in turn is replaced after 12 months and so on. These rolling contracts are not within the scope of the provision and are widely used in practice to avoid the requirements of this section.

Equally, this provision does not apply if the contract has less than six months to run, at which point a new contract can be entered into without any aggregation at all.

S 319(3)–(5)

Approval by ordinary resolution   What is required is approval by way of an ordinary resolution in general meeting and, if the director is a director of the holding company, the consent of the general meeing of the holding company is also required. Where the company is a wholly-owned subsidiary (defined in s 736(2)), only the consent of the holding company is required. A 'company' is defined in s 735; a company registered under s 680 is a company not formed under the companies legislation (such as a deed of settlement company or a company formed by private Act of Parliament or letters patent) but which has registered under it. If the company is a charity in England and Wales, any approval for the purpose of this provision is ineffective without the prior written consent of the Charity Commissioners: Charities Act 1993, s 66(1), (2)(c).

If the company is a private company, approval may be sought by way of a statutory written resolution (s 381A), in which case the operation of sub-s (5) is modified as provided by Sch 15A, para 7.

Informal unanimous assent   Applying the *Duomatic* principle (see general note to Part XI, Ch IV, s 366 et seq, below), the informal unanimous consent of the shareholders will suffice for these purposes: *Wright v Atlas Wright (Europe) Ltd* [1999] 2 BCLC 301, CA. In that case, the agreement at issue was one whereby a retired director was made president of the company for life with no provision for termination of the agreement by the company. No approval had been sought under this provision but the sole shareholder of the company at the time was fully informed and assented to the agreement. On a subsequent change of control at the company, it was alleged that the term of the agreement as to indefinite duration was void under sub-s (6) for non-compliance with sub-ss (3) and (5).

The Court of Appeal held that there was no statutory purpose underlying sub-ss (3) and (5) other than for the benefit and protection of the shareholders of the company. The requirement of sub-s (3) taken alone was unarguably amenable to the *Duomatic* principle. Subsection (5) was simply designed to ensure the opportunity for fully informed consent of the shareholders and was thus amenable to waiver by the class for whose protection it was designed (at 315).

S 319(6)

Where shareholder approval is required and not obtained, the provision invalidates the term of the agreement as to the duration and replaces it with a term entitling the company to terminate the agreement at any time by giving notice.

S 319(7)

'Shadow director' is defined in s 741(2); and a parent company cannot be a shadow director for these purposes: s 741(3).

320. Substantial property transactions involving directors, etc

(1) With the exceptions provided by the section next following, a company shall not enter into an arrangement—

   (a) whereby a director of the company or its holding company, or a person connected with such a director, acquires or is to acquire one or more non-cash assets of the requisite value from the company; or

   (b) whereby the company acquires or is to acquire one or more non-cash assets of the requisite value from such a director or a person so connected,

unless the arrangement is first approved by a resolution of the company in general meeting and, if the director or connected person is a director of its holding company or a person connected with such a director, by a resolution in general meeting of the holding company.

(2) For this purpose a non-cash asset is of the requisite value if at the time the arrangement in question is entered into its value is not less than £2,000 but (subject to that) exceeds £100,000 or 10 per cent of the company's asset value, that is—

    (a) except in a case falling within paragraph (b) below, the value of the company's net assets determined by reference to the accounts prepared and laid under Part VII in respect of the last preceding financial year in respect of which such accounts were so laid; and

    (b) where no accounts have been so prepared and laid before that time, the amount of the company's called-up share capital.

(3) For purposes of this section and sections 321 and 322, a shadow director is treated as a director.

General note

The possibility of self-dealing when directors acquire assets from, or sell assets to, their companies is obvious. As Carnwath J stated in *British Racing Drivers' Club Ltd v Hextall Erskine & Co* [1997] 1 BCLC 182 at 198, the danger is that their judgment may be distorted by conflicts of interests and loyalties, even in cases where there is no actual dishonesty. The purpose of this statutory provision, he noted, is to provide the members of a company with an opportunity to check on any potential abuse of position by directors and to allow the matter to be more widely considered and a more objective decision reached.

S 320(1)

This provision is subject to the exceptions in s 321.

'Arrangements' The section is broadly drafted with 'arrangement' being deliberately chosen with a view to catching a range of transactions other than a direct contract between the specified parties. For example, it would encompass any scheme whereby an asset was first transferred to a third party and subsequently to a director or a connected person but not any bona fide transaction which ultimately had this outcome. It also encompasses agreements or understandings having no contractual effect: see *Re Duckwari plc (No 2), Duckwari plc v Offerventure Ltd (No 2)* [1998] 2 BCLC 315 at 319.

    The section covers arrangements whereby a director or connected person (defined in s 346) acquires a non-cash asset but also where the company acquires a non-cash asset from a director or a person connected with a director, as abuses can arise under either type of transaction. 'Non-cash asset' is defined very broadly in s 739 and extends to transactions which might not otherwise appear to be substantial property transactions as those words would be commonly understood; see the note to that provision and sub-s (2), below. It is immaterial that the arrangement is subject to a foreign law: s 347.

    As to the possible overlap between this provision and ss 312–314 (payments for loss of office etc), see the note to s 312, above; also *Lander v Premier Pict Petroleum Ltd* [1998] BCC 248 (CS,OH) (rejecting an argument that directors' service agreements are within s 320).

Thresholds   Approval is required (subject to the exceptions in s 321) once the requisite thresholds are passed without there being any issue of whether an acquisition is at an overvalue or an undervalue. It is the fact of the conflict of interest which gives rise to the need for approval and it is not necessary for the transaction to be unfair: see *Re Duckwari plc (No 2), Duckwari plc v Offerventure Ltd (No 2)* [1998] 2 BCLC 315 at 323.

Approval by the members   The requirement of approval is subject to the exceptions in s 321; and, as an arrangement entered into in contravention of this provision is voidable, the company may affirm the arrangement, see s 322(2)(c).

The approval required is of the company in general meeting *and* where the director is a director of the holding company (defined in s 736) or a person connected with such a director (defined in s 346), the approval of the holding company in general meeting is also required, a requirement which can be overlooked. For an example of the importance of securing the approval of the holding company where necessary, see *British Racing Drivers' Club Ltd v Hextall Erskine & Co* [1997] 1 BCLC 182. The consequences of a failure to secure approval are set out in s 322.

Prior approval must be obtained which can delay a transaction. The prohibition on the company entering into an arrangement within the provision means that, as the provision stands, a company cannot enter into a conditional contract to buy or sell an asset subject to approval by the shareholders.

The requirement is for approval of the arrangement and while this does not require the approval of every last detail, the shareholders must have had the central aspects of the arrangement before them including evidence of the price: see *Demite Ltd v Protec Health Ltd* [1998] BCC 638 at 649.

If the company is a charity in England and Wales, any approval for the purpose of this provision is ineffective without the prior written consent of the Charity Commissioners: Charities Act 1993, s 66(1), (2)(d).

Ordinary resolution   Approval is by a resolution in general meeting although a private company may use the statutory written resolution procedure under s 381A.

Whether the informal unanimous consent of the shareholders would suffice, applying the *Duomatic* principle (see general note to Part XI, Ch IV, s 366 below), was thought debatable: see *Demite Ltd v Protec Health Ltd* [1998] BCC 638 at 648. However, the issue must be approached now in the light of the decision by the Court of Appeal in *Wright v Atlas Wright (Europe) Ltd* [1999] 2 BCLC 301, which concluded that the extent to which statutory requirements can be overridden by informal consent must be answered by considering the purpose and underlying rationale of the particular statutory formality in question.

The purpose of s 320 being the protection of the shareholders (as noted in *Re Duckwari plc (No 2), Duckwari plc v Offerventure Ltd (No 2)* [1998] 2 BCLC 315 at 324; and in *British Racing Drivers' Club Ltd v Hextall Erskine & Co* [1997] 1 BCLC 182), applying *Wright v Atlas Wright (Europe) Ltd* [1999] 2 BCLC 301, CA, it is amenable to waiver by the class for whose protection it is designed.

Creditors who might have an interest in these transactions (but only if the company goes into liquidation shortly thereafter) are protected by the provisions in IA 1986, ss 238–246 (adjustments of prior transactions).

Voting by the interested director   The section does not prohibit the interested director from voting as a shareholder in favour of the arrangement at the general meeting: see *North-West Transportation Co Ltd v Beatty* (1887) 12 App Cas 589 at 593, PC; *Northern Counties Securities Ltd v Jackson & Steeple Ltd* [1974] 2 All ER 625.

Directors may not vote, however, to make a present of corporate assets to themselves: *Cook v Deeks* [1916] 1 AC 554.

Other requirements The approval required under this provision is in addition to complying with the requirements laid down in the company's articles for excluding the no-conflict rule (see Table A, reg 85); and there must be compliance with the statutory requirement for disclosure of interests to the board of directors (s 317); and, in entering into any such transaction, the directors must have regard to their duty to act in the best interests of the company. The transaction must also be disclosed in the notes to the company's accounts: s 232, Sch 6, Pt II, para 15(c).

S 320(2)

Non-cash assets Where it is alleged that there is a contravention of the statutory provision, the onus is on the person alleging the contravention to prove that the value of the non-cash asset exceeds the requisite value: *Niltan Carson Ltd v Hawthorne* [1988] BCLC 298. 'Non-cash asset' is defined in s 739.

In *Re Duckwari plc, Duckwari plc v Offerventure Ltd* [1997] 2 BCLC 713, O Ltd had contracted to purchase a property and had paid the deposit. An agreement was reached between O Ltd and D plc to let D plc take over O's rights and liabilities under the contract and O directed the vendor to convey the property direct to D plc. All the shares in O Ltd were owned by C and his wife. C was a director of D plc.

The court found that D plc had entered into an arrangement whereby it acquired a non-cash asset of the requisite value from O Ltd which was connected with a director of D (C). The agreement therefore contravened sub-s (1)(b).

Millett LJ noted that the non-cash asset in this case could be described in either of two ways with equal accuracy: it was the benefit of O's rights under the contract of purchase to call for the conveyance of the legal estate in the property on payment of the balance of the purchase price; or it could be categorised as the benefit of O's beneficial interest in the property which was subject to the unpaid vendor's lien for the balance. Either was a non-cash asset as defined in s 739(1).

As to the reference to laying the accounts before the members in cases where the company has elected to dispense with laying accounts and reports before the general meeting, see s 252(3); as to the definition of 'called-up share capital', see s 737.

The value of the non-cash asset In a Scottish case, the court held that the 'value' of the non-cash asset for the purpose of establishing whether the case falls within this provision must be determined, having regard to the statutory purposes, in the context of the particular transaction or arrangement. For example, where land being acquired by a director from the company was adjacent to land which the director already owned, the value of the land should be determined in the light of that additional circumstance: see *Micro Leisure Ltd v Country Properties and Developments Ltd (No 2)* [2000] BCC 872.

S 320(3)

'Shadow director' is defined in s 741(2); and a parent company cannot be a shadow director for these purposes: s 741(3).

321. Exceptions from s 320

(1) No approval is required to be given under section 320 by any body corporate unless it is a company within the meaning of this Act or registered under section 680 or, if it is a wholly-owned subsidiary of any body corporate, wherever incorporated.

(2) Section 320(1) does not apply to an arrangement for the acquisition of a non-cash asset—

    (a) if the asset is to be acquired by a holding company from any of its wholly-owned subsidiaries or from a holding company by any of its wholly-owned subsidiaries, or by one wholly-owned subsidiary of a holding company from another wholly-owned subsidiary of that same holding company, or

    (b) if the arrangement is entered into by a company which is being wound up, unless the winding up is a members' voluntary winding up.

(3) Section 320(1)(a) does not apply to an arrangement whereby a person is to acquire an asset from a company of which he is a member, if the arrangement is made with that person in his character as a member.

(4) Section 320(1) does not apply to a transaction on a recognised investment exchange which is effected by a director, or a person connected with him, through the agency of a person who in relation to the transaction acts as an independent broker.

For this purpose an 'independent broker' means—

    (a) in relation to a transaction on behalf of a director, a person who independently of the director selects the person with whom the transaction is to be effected, and

    (b) in relation to a transaction on behalf of a person connected with a director, a person who independently of that person or the director selects the person with whom the transaction is to be effected;

and 'recognised', in relation to an investment exchange, means recognised under the Financial Services Act 1986.

S 321(1)

A 'company' within the meaning of CA 1985 means any company formed and registered under this and previous companies legislation so excluding foreign registered companies: see s 735. A company registered under s 680 is a company not formed under the companies legislation (such as a deed of settlement company or a company formed by private Act of Parliament or letters patent) but which has registered under it.

No approval of the members of a company is required if the company is a wholly-owned subsidiary (defined in s 736); in that case, only the consent of the members of the holding company (defined in s 736) is required.

S 321(2)(a)

Acquisitions within groups   The particular problem which this exception was designed to address was the situation where a director's control of the holding company meant, as a consequence of the elaborate definition of connected person in ss 346(2)(b), (4), (5) and (8), that the holding company and each subsidiary company in a group was a connected person of the director with the consequence that transactions between the subsidiaries and with the holding company would be transactions with a person connected with a director of the holding company and require approval by the holding company.

This was thought to be much too cumbersome given the volume of subsidiary-to-subsidiary and subsidiary-to-holding company business which occurs hence the exemption for transactions between wholly-owned subsidiaries and with holding companies.

S 321(2)(b)

Arrangements on winding up   Approval is not required if the arrangement is entered into by a company which is being wound up, since in a winding up, the liquidator will represent the company's interests and ensure an arm's length transaction with a director or connected person. If transactions of this nature with directors were prohibited, a liquidator might be unduly hampered in the execution of his duties.

This exception does not apply if the winding up is a members' voluntary winding up (ie a solvent winding up), as a risk of self dealing remains because of the possibility of the directors in that case ensuring the appointment of their nominee as liquidator.

Only liquidators   This exception applies only to liquidators and does not extend to receivers or administrative receivers contracting on behalf of the company: *Demite Ltd v Protec Health Ltd* [1998] BCC 638 (company could invoke the provision to invalidate a sale of assets by an administrative receiver to a company connected to one of its directors). Park J notes that the problems here could be overcome by having the debenture holder rather than the receiver effect the sale, or possibly by having the court direct the sale under IA 1986, s 35(2): see [1998] BCC 638 at 647. The same problem arise with sales in this manner by administrators. Compliance with s 320 is therefore required in these cases, unless reliance can be placed on any of the other exceptions.

S 321(3)

This exemption is designed to ensure that persons might participate in bonus issues or rights issue (shares being a non-cash asset) in their capacity as members without falling within s 320.

S 321(4)

This exception was added by CA 1989, s 145, Sch 19, para 8 and was intended to exempt transactions in securities which might otherwise fall within this provision (being between a company and a director or connected person). The exemption arises if the transaction is effected on a recognised investment exchange through an independent broker so that the director or the connected person has no role in selecting the counterparty.

322. Liabilities arising from contravention of s 320

(1) An arrangement entered into by a company in contravention of section 320, and any transaction entered into in pursuance of the arrangement (whether by the company or any other person) is voidable at the instance of the company unless one or more of the conditions specified in the next subsection is satisfied.

(2) Those conditions are that—

    (a)   restitution of any money or other asset which is the subject-matter of the arrangement or transaction is no longer possible or the company has been indemnified in pursuance of this section by any other person for the loss or damage suffered by it; or

    (b)   any rights acquired bona fide for value and without actual notice of the contravention by any person who is not a party to the arrangement or transaction would be affected by its avoidance; or

    (c)   the arrangement is, within a reasonable period, affirmed by the company in general meeting and, if it is an arrangement for the transfer of an asset to or by a director of its holding company or a person who is connected with such a director, is so affirmed with the approval of the holding company given by a resolution in general meeting.

(3) If an arrangement is entered into with a company by a director of the company or its holding company or a person connected with him in contravention of section 320, that director and the person so connected, and any other director of the company who authorised the arrangement or any transaction entered into in pursuance of such an arrangement, is liable—

    (a)   to account to the company for any gain which he has made directly or indirectly by the arrangement or transaction, and

    (b)   (jointly and severally with any other person liable under this subsection) to indemnify the company for any loss or damage resulting from the arrangement or transaction.

(4) Subsection (3) is without prejudice to any liability imposed otherwise than by that subsection, and is subject to the following two subsections; and the liability under subsection (3) arises whether or not the arrangement or transaction entered into has been avoided in pursuance of subsection (1).

(5) If an arrangement is entered into by a company and a person connected with a director of the company or its holding company in contravention of section 320, that director is not liable under subsection (3) if he shows that he took all reasonable steps to secure the company's compliance with that section.

(6) In any case, a person so connected and any such other director as is mentioned in subsection (3) is not so liable if he shows that, at the time the arrangement was entered into, he did not know the relevant circumstances constituting the contravention.

S 322(1)

Arrangements voidable   The arrangement *and* any linked transaction is voidable (subject to s 322(2)) at the instance of the company only. See *Re Duckwari plc (No 2)*,

Duckwari plc v Offerventure Ltd (No 2) [1998] 2 BCLC 315, the facts of which were noted in the text to s 320(2): the arrangement between the connected person (O Ltd) and the company (D plc), together with the contract of purchase into which the company (D plc) entered with a third party pursuant to that agreement, were voidable.

S 322(2)

Right to avoid can be lost   The effect of sub-s (2)(a) is that, even if restitution is still possible, the contract is not voidable if the company has been indemnified in respect of any loss. It follows that the indemnity (which is payable under s 322(3)) must be such as to place the company in the position it would have been in had rescission been ordered: see *Re Duckwari plc (No 2), Duckwari plc v Offerventure Ltd (No 2)* [1998] 2 BCLC 315 at 324. Subsection (2)(b) provides the standard protection for third party rights, while sub-s (2)(c) makes provision for the arrangement to be affirmed within a reasonable time of the arrangement having been entered into in contravention of s 320.

There is no provision for lapse of time as a factor which prevents the exercise of the right of rescission, although it is inherent in each element of the section. In *Demite Ltd v Protec Health Ltd* [1998] BCC 638, Park J refused to permit reliance on it as a separate ground defeating the company's right to avoid the arrangement in the absence of any specific provision to that effect.

S 322(3)

Liability of directors and connected persons   This provision identifies those persons to whom liability attaches which includes any directors who authorised the transaction although not party to it. Note the exceptions in s 322(5), (6), below.

Account for any gain   This requirement will arise in respect of any breach of s 320(1)(a) where the director or a connected person acquires an asset from the company. In *Re Duckwari plc (No 2), Duckwari plc v Offerventure Ltd (No 2)* [1998] 2 BCLC 315 at 324, it was accepted that the gain must be measured at the date of the judgment and not at the date of the arrangement.

Indemnify for any loss or damage   This requirement will arise in respect of any breach of s 320(1)(b) where the company acquires an asset from a director or a connected person. The full scope of the liability under this provision was addressed extensively in two Court of Appeal hearings: *Re Duckwari plc (No 2), Duckwari plc v Offerventure Ltd (No 2)* [1998] 2 BCLC 315; *Re Duckwari plc (No 3), Duckwari plc v Offerventure Ltd (No 3)* [1999] 1 BCLC 168 from which the following propositions can be deduced:

(1)   The loss recoverable is the difference between the cost of the acquisition and the amount realised on the sale of the asset and not the difference between the cost of the acquisition and the market value of the acquisition at that date. This means that those liable will be responsible for any depreciation in value of the asset subsequent to its acquisition by the company.

(2)   The basis of recovery under sub-s (3) is equitable and it is not a common law claim for damages hence liability is strict, and no question of foreseeability or remoteness, in particular, a foreseeability of a depreciation

in value, arises as it would at common law.

(3)   The loss or damage recoverable is limited to that resulting from the breach of s 320(1)(b), namely the acquisition itself, and does not extend to the means by which the acquisition is brought about. Liability does not extend therefore to the bank costs incurred by a company when it borrows the funds with which to proceed with the acquisition.

S 322(4)

Liability imposed otherwise   This provision preserves any liability under the general law such as a director's liability for breach of duty and a third party's liabilities for participation in a breach of duty or receipt of company property, as to which, see note to s 151(3), above.

Liability regardless of avoidance   Liability can arise although the company has not avoided the transaction. Given the wording of this subsection, it would seem that affirmation of the transaction (under s 322(2)(b)) would not relieve the parties of their liabilities under s 322(3) unless, when affirming the transaction, the company chooses also to relieve those persons of their liabilities.

S 322(5), (6)

Defences   Where the transaction is with a connected person, this provision exempts from liability the director with whom the person is connected if he can show that he took all reasonable steps to ensure the *company's* compliance with s 320.

It is quite difficult to imagine what such steps might involve. It might apply where the director has provided the company secretary, or chief executive, with a list of connected persons where approval would be required and those officers have failed to consult that information when entering into the transaction. If, as would often be the case, the matter is not considered at board level, then the director may be quite unaware of the transaction and has done all that he can reasonably be expected to have done to ensure that shareholder approval is sought. A similar defence is contained in s 341(4).

Subsection (6) offers a defence to a director who authorised the transaction and a connected person liable under sub-s (3) where they can show that they did not have actual knowledge of the relevant circumstances which brought the transaction within s 320. This would cover the case where they are unaware of the facts giving rise to the connection. A similar defence is contained in s 341(5).

322A. Invalidity of certain transactions involving directors, etc

(1) This section applies where a company enters into a transaction to which the parties include—

(a)   a director of the company or of its holding company, or

(b)   a person connected with such a director or a company with whom such a director is associated, and the board of directors, in connection with the transaction, exceed any limitation on their powers under the company's constitution.

(2) The transaction is voidable at the instance of the company.

(3) Whether or not it is avoided, any such party to the transaction as is mentioned in subsection (1)(a) or (b), and any director of the company who authorised the transaction, is liable—

    (a) to account to the company for any gain which he has made directly or indirectly by the transaction, and

    (b) to indemnify the company for any loss or damage resulting from the transaction.

(4) Nothing in the above provisions shall be construed as excluding the operation of any other enactment or rule of law by virtue of which the transaction may be called in question or any liability to the company may arise.

(5) The transaction ceases to be voidable if—

    (a) restitution of any money or other asset which was the subject-matter of the transaction is no longer possible, or

    (b) the company is indemnified for any loss or damage resulting from the transaction, or

    (c) rights acquired bona fide for value and without actual notice of the directors' exceeding their powers by a person who is not party to the transaction would be affected by the avoidance, or

    (d) the transaction is ratified by the company in general meeting, by ordinary or special resolution or otherwise as the case may require.

(6) A person other than a director of the company is not liable under subsection (3) if he shows that at the time the transaction was entered into he did not know that the directors were exceeding their powers.

(7) This section does not affect the operation of section 35A in relation to any party to the transaction not within subsection (1)(a) or (b).

But where a transaction is voidable by virtue of this section and valid by virtue of that section in favour of such a person, the court may, on the application of that person or of the company, make such order affirming, severing or setting aside the transaction, on such terms, as appear to the court to be just.

(8) In this section 'transaction' includes any act; and the reference in subsection (1) to limitations under the company's constitution includes limitations deriving—

    (a) from a resolution of the company in general meeting or a meeting of any class of shareholders, or

    (b) from any agreement between the members of the company or of any class of shareholders.

S 322A(1), (2)

Invalidity of certain transactions   This provision relates to ss 35 and 35A, which validate transactions by a company beyond the company's capacity and/or in excess of the powers of the board of directors. Where one of the parties to such a transaction is an 'insider' of the company to the extent identified in sub-s (1)(a) and (b), it is thought inappropriate that they should avail of the protection afforded by ss 35 and 35A and so the transaction is voidable at the instance of the company. 'Company' is defined in s 735; 'holding company' in s 736; 'connected person' in s 346(2),(3); a company is associated with a director in the circumstances set out in s 346(4); and 'transaction' is defined in s 322A(8).

S 322A(3), (6)

As to the extent of any liability (which applies whether or not the transaction is avoided), see note to s 322(3), (4), above. A defence for persons other than a director of the company is provided in sub-s (6).

S 322A(4)

This provision preserves any liability under the general law such as a director's liability for breach of duty and a third party's liability for participation in a breach of duty or receipt of company property.

S 322A(5)

The right to avoid the transaction is lost in circumstances which are very similar to those set out in s 322(2): see the note to that provision, above.

Ratifying the transaction   The type of resolution required to ratify the transaction depends on whether the transaction is beyond the company's capacity, in which case a special resolution is required (s 35(3)), or, whether the transaction is in excess of the board's authority, in which case an ordinary resolution is required. It is not clear why the provision states 'or otherwise' unless it is a reference to the fact that a private company may use a statutory written resolution (s 381A) or it may be a reference to the possibility of ratification through the application of the *Duomatic* principle (informal unanimous consent), as to which see the general note to Part XI, Ch IV, s 366 et seq, below.

Where a company is a charity, the ratification of a transaction to which this section applies is ineffective without the prior written consent of the Charity Commissioners: Charities Act 1993, s 65(4).

S 322A(7)

Transaction valid and voidable   As noted above, the transaction may be valid under ss 35 and 35A while voidable under this provision. Where that position arises, the court is to have a free hand in deciding whether to affirm, sever or set aside the transaction on such terms as appear just.

An example of the problems which can arise can be seen in *Re Torvale Group Ltd* [1999] 2 BCLC 605, where the court was faced with debentures which had been issued by a company to trustees of a retirement benefits scheme in circumstances where there was a possibility that limitations under the company's constitution (requiring the consent of a third party to the issue of the debentures) had not been observed. One of the five trustees was a director of the company and it was argued that the issue of the debentures was within s 322A and voidable (assuming that it could be established that the consent of the third party to their issue had not been obtained).

Neuberger J looked at all the circumstances surrounding the issue of the debentures and found that at the time the company was in great need of funds, the terms of the loans secured by the debentures were reasonable, the director trustee had received no personal benefit from the transaction and the breach of the constitution was an oversight. On those facts, he had no difficulty in concluding that he ought, despite the transaction being voidable, to affirm the transaction.

S 322A(8)

The definition of 'transaction' is not limited to acquisitions of, say, non-cash assets as s 320 is; the reference to limitations under the company's constitution refers back to s 35A(3).

322B. Contracts with sole members who are directors

(1) Subject to subsection (2), where a private company limited by shares or by guarantee having only one member enters into a contract with the sole member of the company and the sole member is also a director of the company, the company shall, unless the contract is in writing, ensure that the terms of the contract are either set out in a written memorandum or are recorded in the minutes of the first meeting of the directors of the company following the making of the contract.

(2) Subsection (1) shall not apply to contracts entered into in the ordinary course of the company's business.

(3) For the purposes of this section a sole member who is a shadow director is treated as a director.

(4) If a company fails to comply with subsection (1), the company and every officer of it who is in default is liable to a fine.

(5) Subject to subsection (6), nothing in this section shall be construed as excluding the operation of any other enactment or rule of law applying to contracts between a company and a director of that company.

(6) Failure to comply with subsection (1) with respect to a contract shall not affect the validity of that contract.

S 322B(1)–(3)

Contracts to be recorded   The effect of this provision is that a contract between a single member company (see s 1(3)(a)) and a director who is that sole member must be: (1) in writing; or (2) recorded in a written memorandum; or (3) recorded in the minutes of a directors' meeting, with the exception of any contracts entered into in the ordinary course of *that* company's business. The director need not be a sole director, the key issue is whether he is the sole member. 'Shadow director' is defined in s 741(2); and a parent company cannot be a shadow director for these purposes: s 741(3).

S 322B(4)–(6)

Penalties The consequence of non-compliance with these requirements is that the company and every officer in default suffers the penalties in sub-s (4): as to which, see s 730, Sch 24; 'officer who is in default' is defined in s 730(5). The validity of the transaction is a matter for the general law on directors' conflicts of interest.

SHARE DEALINGS BY DIRECTORS AND THEIR FAMILIES

323. Prohibition on directors dealing in share options

(1) It is an offence for a director of a company to buy—

   (a) a right to call for delivery at a specified price and within a specified time of a specified number of relevant shares or a specified amount of relevant debentures; or

   (b) a right to make delivery at a specified price and within a specified time of a specified number of relevant shares or a specified amount of relevant debentures; or

   (c) a right (as he may elect) to call for delivery at a specified price and within a specified time or to make delivery at a specified price and within a specified time of a specified number of relevant shares or a specified amount of relevant debentures.

(2) A person guilty of an offence under subsection (1) is liable to imprisonment or a fine, or both.

(3) In subsection (1)—

   (a) 'relevant shares', in relation to a director of a company, means shares in the company or in any other body corporate, being the company's subsidiary or holding company, or a subsidiary of the company's holding company, being shares as respects which there has been granted a listing on a stock exchange (whether in Great Britain or elsewhere);

   (b) 'relevant debentures', in relation to a director of a company, means debentures of the company or of any other body corporate, being the company's subsidiary or holding company or a subsidiary of the company's holding company, being debentures as respects which there has been granted such a listing; and

   (c) 'price' includes any consideration other than money.

(4) This section applies to a shadow director as to a director.

(5) This section is not to be taken as penalising a person who buys a right to subscribe for shares in, or debentures of, a body corporate or buys debentures of a body corporate that confer upon the holder of them a right to subscribe for, or to convert the debentures (in whole or in part) into, shares of that body.

General note

This section prohibits options dealings in certain listed shares and debentures by directors (and their families: s 327). Any suspected contravention of this prohibition may be the subject of an investigation under s 446.

This provision belongs more naturally in the statutory provisions dealing with the regulation of insider dealing (Criminal Justice Act 1993 (CJA 1993), Part V). Indeed the Law Commission has taken the view that these sections have been effectively superseded by the requirements of the CJA 1993 and the Listing Rules Model Code on directors' dealings in securities and should be repealed (Law Commission Report *Company Directors: Regulating Conflicts of Interests and Formulating a Statement of Duties*: Law Com No 261, September 1999, paras 11.3–11.7).

S 323(1), (3), (4)

The prohibition is on a director (and his family: see s 327) dealing in call options (the right to buy at a pre-determined price); put options (the right to sell at a pre-determined price); and double options (the right to buy or sell). In each case, the dealings must be in listed shares or debentures (defined in s 744) of the company or a group company; and whether listed in Great Britain or elsewhere. The prohibitions are extended to 'shadow directors', as defined in s 741(2).

The offence is committed whether the dealing takes place on or off-market and the prohibition applies to dealings whether or not the director (or his family) are in possession of unpublished price sensitive information (and therefore it is broader in its application than CJA 1993). As such, it reflects the statutory concern with conflicts of interest rather than the use of unpublished price sensitive information.

S 323(2)

As to penalties, see s 730, Sch 24. The section makes no provision for the civil consequences of a breach of the prohibition. On the one hand, it might be argued that any contract entered into in breach of the section is illegal and therefore void; alternatively, it might be argued that the wording of the provision indicates clearly that the purpose of the section is to attach a penalty to the person of the director and says nothing about the validity of the contract which is unaffected. This approach is probably justified given the difficulties which might arise in the markets were such transactions to be void.

S 323(5)

The prohibition does not extend to options to subscribe for shares or debentures.

324. Duty of director to disclose shareholdings in own company

(1) A person who becomes a director of a company and at the time when he does so is interested in shares in, or debentures of, the company or any other body corporate, being the company's subsidiary or holding company or a subsidiary of the company's holding company, is under obligation to notify the company in writing—

    (a) of the subsistence of his interests at that time; and

    (b) of the number of shares of each class in, and the amount of debentures of each class of, the company or other such body corporate in which each interest of his subsists at that time.

(2) A director of a company is under obligation to notify the company in writing of the occurrence, while he is a director, of any of the following events—

    (a) any event in consequence of whose occurrence he becomes, or ceases to be, interested in shares in, or debentures of, the company or any other body corporate, being the company's subsidiary or holding company or a subsidiary of the company's holding company;

    (b) the entering into by him of a contract to sell any such shares or debentures;

    (c) the assignment by him of a right granted to him by the company to subscribe for shares in, or debentures of, the company; and

    (d) the grant to him by another body corporate, being the company's subsidiary or holding company or a subsidiary of the company's holding company, of a right to subscribe for shares in, or debentures of, that other body corporate, the exercise of such a right granted to him and the assignment by him of such a right so granted;

and notification to the company must state the number or amount, and class, of shares or debentures involved.

(3) Schedule 13 has effect in connection with subsections (1) and (2) above; and of that Schedule—

    (a) Part I contains rules for the interpretation of, and otherwise in relation to, those subsections and applies in determining, for purposes of those subsections, whether a person has an interest in shares or debentures;

    (b) Part II applies with respect to the periods within which obligations imposed by the subsections must be fulfilled; and

    (c) Part III specifies certain circumstances in which obligations arising from subsection (2) are to be treated as not discharged;

and subsections (1) and (2) are subject to any exceptions for which provision may be made by regulations made by the Secretary of State by statutory instrument.

(4) Subsection (2) does not require the notification by a person of the occurrence of an event whose occurrence comes to his knowledge after he has ceased to be a director.

(5) An obligation imposed by this section is treated as not discharged unless the notice by means of which it purports to be discharged is expressed to be given in fulfilment of that obligation.

(6) This section applies to shadow directors as to directors; but nothing in it operates so as to impose an obligation with respect to shares in a body corporate which is the wholly-owned subsidiary of another body corporate.

(7) A person who—

- (a) fails to discharge, within the proper period, an obligation to which he is subject under subsection (1) or (2), or
- (b) in purported discharge of an obligation to which he is so subject, makes to the company a statement which he knows to be false, or recklessly makes to it a statement which is false,

is guilty of an offence and liable to imprisonment or a fine, or both.

(8) Section 732 (restriction on prosecutions) applies to an offence under this section.

General note

This section requires directors (and shadow directors) to disclose details of their interests in shares and debentures of the company and the group. This requirement of disclosure applies to public and private companies. Any suspected contravention of these provisions may be the subject of an investigation under s 446.

S 324(1)

Interests held on appointment   The interests in shares or debentures which must be disclosed are set out in the complex provisions of Sch 13, Pt 1; subject to the exceptions provided by the Companies (Disclosure of Directors' Interests) (Exceptions) Regulations 1985, SI 1985/802 (see text to s 324(3), below); and the exemptions provided by sub-ss (4), (6). The interests of spouses and children are attributed to the director by s 328.

The information to be disclosed is set out in the provision and see s 324(5). Sch 7, paras 2–2B requires information regarding directors' interests to be included also in the directors' report or alternatively in a note to the annual accounts.

Time limits   The time limit within which this disclosure obligation must be met is governed by Sch 13, Pt II, para 14 (essentially, within five days of the director knowing of the interest requiring disclosure).

S 324(2)

Events giving rise to a change in interests   While s 324(1) is designed to record the director's interests on appointment, this provision provides for changes in those interests thereafter – hence the emphasis on 'events' which give rise to some change in position. There is no de minimis threshold and any change in the director's interests, however small, must be notified. For example, if a director elects to receive scrip dividends then, on every dividend payment, the director's interests in the company's shares will change to a small extent which must be notified.

The requirement in sub-s (2)(d) only relates to options granted by other group companies and not by the company itself, there being little sense in requiring a director to notify his company of something which the company has granted to him. However, the company must include such options in the register to be maintained by it under s 325.

The information which must be disclosed is set out in the provision but the obligation to notify is not discharged if the information prescribed by Sch 13, Pt III has not been included in the notification: see s 324(3)(c). See also s 324(5).

Time limits The time limit within which this disclosure obligation must be met is governed by Sch 13, Pt II, para 15. Essentially, disclosure must be made within five days of the event giving rise to the disclosure obligation, but see the detailed wording of para 15, as the time period depends on the director's knowledge of the event occurring and of the fact that it gives rise to an obligation to disclose.

S 324(3)

Exceptions to the disclosure requirements The Companies (Disclosure of Directors' Interests) (Exceptions) Regulations 1985, SI 1985/802, exclude the following interests from the disclosure requirements of s 324(1) and (2):

(1)   interests in shares or debentures of any person in his capacity as trustee or personal representative of any trust or estate jointly with the Public Trustee;

(2)   interests in shares in, or debentures of, a society registered under the Industrial and Provident Societies Act 1965;

(3)   interests in shares or debentures of a person in his capacity as trustee of, or as beneficiary under, a trust relating exclusively to certain retirement benefits schemes or superannuation funds;

(4)   interests in shares in a body corporate which arise solely on account of any limitation imposed by the memorandum or articles of association of the body corporate on a person's right to dispose of a share such as a pre-emption right on a transfer of any member's shares (reg 2).

A director of a wholly-owned subsidiary company where the holding company is incorporated outside Great Britain is not required to notify the company of interests in shares in, or debentures of, that body corporate or any other body corporate so incorporated (reg 3).

A director who is a director of a wholly-owned subsidiary and of the holding company (which is itself required to keep a register under s 325) is not obliged to notify his interests to the wholly-owned subsidiary but only to the holding company (reg 3).

S 324(5)

Notification must indicate that it is in purported compliance with the section. The disclosure can then be measured against the requirements of Sch 13, Pt III. This also avoids any confusion as to whether the director is complying with these provisions or with the disclosure obligations in Pt VI (ss 198–220).

S 324(6)

'Shadow director' is defined in s 741(2). There is no obligation of disclosure on the part of a director or shadow director of any interest in shares which he might have in a wholly-owned subsidiary since in that case the interest must be held as a nominee. This exemption does not apply to debentures in the subsidiary.

S 324(7)

Penalties   The penalties fall on the director as the person obliged to disclose and not on the family members whose interests are attributed to him. As to penalties, see s 730, Sch 24.

---

325. Register of directors' interests notified under s 324

(1) Every company shall keep a register for the purposes of section 324.

(2) Whenever a company receives information from a director given in fulfilment of an obligation imposed on him by that section, it is under obligation to enter in the register, against the director's name, the information received and the date of the entry.

(3) The company is also under obligation, whenever it grants to a director a right to subscribe for shares in, or debentures of, the company to enter in the register against his name—

    (a) the date on which the right is granted,

    (b) the period during which, or time at which, it is exercisable,

    (c) the consideration for the grant (or, if there is no consideration, that fact), and

    (d) the description of shares or debentures involved and the number or amount of them, and the price to be paid for them (or the consideration, if otherwise than in money).

(4) Whenever such a right as is mentioned above is exercised by a director, the company is under obligation to enter in the register against his name that fact (identifying the right), the number or amount of shares or debentures in respect of which it is exercised and, if they were registered in his name, that fact and, if not, the name or names of the person or persons in whose name or names they were registered, together (if they were registered in the names of two persons or more) with the number or amount of the shares or debentures registered in the name of each of them.

(5) Part IV of Schedule 13 has effect with respect to the register to be kept under this section, to the way in which entries in it are to be made, to the right of inspection, and generally.

(6) For purposes of this section, a shadow director is deemed a director.

S 325(1), (5)

The detailed rules as to the maintenance of this register are contained in Sch 13, Pt IV. Where the register is kept otherwise than in a legible form (see ss 722, 723), see also the Companies (Registers and Other Records) Regulations 1985, SI 1985/724, regs 3, 6(4).

The register is open to inspection by any person: see Sch 13, Pt IV, para 25. As to inspection, see the Companies (Inspection and Copying of Registers, Indices and Documents) Regulations 1991, SI 1991/1998.

S 325(2)

This provision applies to information notified to the company by the director which will include information on the interests of spouses and infant children attributed to him by s 328.

Sch 13, Pt IV, para 22 imposes a time limit of three days (beginning with the day after the director notifies the company) for the inclusion of this information in the register.

S 325(3), (4)

This information is not notified by the director to the company and so does not fall within sub-s (2), hence the obligation on the company to include it in the register. The time limit on its inclusion is as under sub-s (2): Sch 13, Pt IV, para 22.

S 325(6)

'Shadow director' is defined in s 741(2).

326. Sanctions for non-compliance

(1) The following applies with respect to defaults in complying with, and to contraventions of, section 325 and Part IV of Schedule 13.

(2) If default is made in complying with any of the following provisions—

(a) section 325(1),(2),(3) or (4), or

(b) Schedule 13, paragraph 21, 22 or 28,

the company and every officer of it who is in default is liable to a fine and, for continued contravention, to a daily default fine.

(3) If an inspection of the register required under paragraph 25 of the Schedule is refused, or a copy required under paragraph 26 is not sent within the proper period, the company and every officer of it who is in default is liable to a fine and, for continued contravention, to a daily default fine.

(4) If default is made for 14 days in complying with paragraph 27 of the Schedule (notice to registrar of where register is kept), the company and every officer of it who is in default is liable to a fine and, for continued contravention, to a daily default fine.

(5) If default is made in complying with paragraph 29 of the Schedule (register to be produced at annual general meeting), the company and every officer of it who is in default is liable to a fine.

(6) In the case of a refusal of an inspection of the register required under paragraph 25 of the Schedule, the court may by order compel an immediate inspection of it; and in the case of failure to send within the proper period a copy required under paragraph 26, the court may by order direct that the copy be sent to the person requiring it.

General note

These sanctions relate to various failures with respect to the maintenance, inspection etc of the company's register of interests. As to penalties, see s 730, Sch 24: 'officer who is in default' is defined in s 730(5).

S 326(6)

This provision is necessary because, but for the section, it is not clear that there is any right of inspection or that the court has the power to compel inspection: see *Conway v Petronius Clothing Co Ltd* [1978] 1 All ER 185 at 199. The court's power is discretionary: see *Pelling v Families need Fathers Ltd* [2001] All ER (D) 01 (Aug), CA.

327. Extension of s 323 to spouses and children

(1) Section 323 applies to—
  (a) the wife or husband of a director of a company (not being herself or himself a director of it), and
  (b) an infant son or infant daughter of a director (not being himself or herself a director of the company),

as it applies to the director; but it is a defence for a person charged by virtue of this section with an offence under section 323 to prove that he (she) had no reason to believe that his (her) spouse or, as the case may be, parent was a director of the company in question.

(2) For purposes of this section—
  (a) 'son' includes step-son, and 'daughter' includes step-daughter ('parent' being construed accordingly),
  (b) 'infant' means, in relation to Scotland, person under the age of 18 years, and
  (c) a shadow director of a company is deemed a director of it.

General note

This provision extends to directors' spouses and children the prohibitions on dealing in options in listed shares and debentures of the company or a group company which are set out in s 323.

608

S 327(1)

Where the spouse or child is a director of the company, they fall within s 323 in any event.

The application of s 323 to family members means that they may be guilty of an offence under that provision, subject to the defence provided here. It is difficult to envisage the circumstances when this defence might arise except, perhaps, where the spouse or parent was a shadow director.

S 327(2)(c)

'Shadow director' is defined in s 741(2).

---

328. Extension of s 324 to spouses and children

(1) For the purposes of section 324—

    (a) an interest of the wife or husband of a director of a company (not being herself or himself a director of it) in shares or debentures is to be treated as the director's interest; and

    (b) the same applies to an interest of an infant son or infant daughter of a director of a company (not being himself or herself a director of it) in shares or debentures.

(2) For those purposes—

    (a) a contract, assignment or right of subscription entered into, exercised or made by, or a grant made to, the wife or husband of a director of a company (not being herself or himself a director of it) is to be treated as having been entered into, exercised or made by, or (as the case may be) as having been made to, the director; and

    (b) the same applies to a contract, assignment or right of subscription entered into, exercised or made by, or grant made to, an infant son or infant daughter of a director of a company (not being himself or herself a director of it).

(3) A director of a company is under obligation to notify the company in writing of the occurrence while he or she is a director, of either of the following events, namely—

    (a) the grant by the company to his (her) spouse, or to his or her infant son or infant daughter, of a right to subscribe for shares in, or debentures of, the company; and

    (b) the exercise by his (her) spouse or by his or her infant son or infant daughter of such a right granted by the company to the wife, husband, son or daughter.

(4) In a notice given to the company under subsection (3) there shall be stated—

    (a) in the case of the grant of a right, the like information as is required by section 324 to be stated by the director on the grant to him by another body corporate of a right to subscribe for shares in, or debentures of, that other body corporate; and

(b) in the case of the exercise of a right, the like information as is required by that section to be stated by the director on the exercise of a right granted to him by another body corporate to subscribe for shares in, or debentures of, that other body corporate.

(5) An obligation imposed by subsection (3) on a director must be fulfilled by him before the end of 5 days beginning with the day following that on which the occurrence of the event giving rise to it comes to his knowledge; but in reckoning that period of days there is disregarded any Saturday or Sunday, and any day which is a bank holiday in any part of Great Britain.

(6) A person who—

(a) fails to fulfil, within the proper period, an obligation to which he is subject under subsection (3), or

(b) in purported fulfilment of such an obligation, makes to a company a statement which he knows to be false, or recklessly makes to a company a statement which is false,

is guilty of an offence and liable to imprisonment or a fine, or both.

(7) The rules set out in Part I of Schedule 13 have effect for the interpretation of, and otherwise in relation to, subsections (1) and (2); and subsections (5),(6) and (8) of section 324 apply with any requisite modification.

(8) In this section, 'son' includes step-son, 'daughter' includes step-daughter, and 'infant' means, in relation to Scotland, person under the age of 18 years.

(9) For purposes of section 325, an obligation imposed on a director by this section is to be treated as if imposed by section 324.

General note

This provision is linked to s 324, which requires directors and shadow directors to disclose to the company any interests which they have in shares or debentures of the company or any group company. For the purpose of that requirement, the interests of a spouse and children are attributed by this provision to the director.

S 328(1)

Where the spouse or child is a director of the company, they fall within s 324 in any event.

S 328(2)

These transactions by a spouse or infant child are treated as if they were transactions by the director and so will fall within s 324(2), altering his interests in the company and requiring notification.

S 328(3)

While a director is not obliged to notify the company of any options granted by the company to him (s 324(2)(d)), this provision requires him to notify the company of any grant of, or any exercise of, any option to subscribe for shares in or debentures of the company granted by the company to a spouse or infant child. The timing requirements for this notification are set out in s 328(5).

S 328(4)

As to the required information, see s 324(2) and Sch 13, Pt III, para 19.

S 328(6)

As to penalties, see s 730, Sch 24.

S 328(7)

What amounts to an interest in shares and debentures for these purposes is determined by Sch 13, Pt I, subject to the exceptions provided by the Companies (Disclosure of Directors' Interests) (Exceptions) Regulations 1985, SI 1985/802: see note to s 324(3), above.

S 328(9)

This obliges the company to include any information received from the director regarding a spouse or a child's interests in the company's register of interests maintained under s 325.

329. Duty to notify stock exchange of matters notified under preceding sections

(1) Whenever a company whose shares or debentures are listed on a recognised investment exchange other than an overseas investment exchange within the meaning of the Financial Services Act 1986 is notified of any matter by a director in consequence of the fulfilment of an obligation imposed by section 324 or 328, and that matter relates to shares or debentures so listed, the company is under obligation to notify that investment exchange of that matter; and the investment exchange may publish, in such manner as it may determine, any information received by it under this subsection.

(2) An obligation imposed by subsection (1) must be fulfilled before the end of the day next following that on which it arises; but there is disregarded for this purpose a day which is a Saturday or a Sunday or a bank holiday in any part of Great Britain.

(3) If default is made in complying with this section, the company and every officer of it who is in default is guilty of an offence and liable to a fine and, for continued contravention, to a daily default fine.

Section 732 (restriction on prosecutions) applies to an offence under this section.

S 329(1)

A company, having been notified by a director of his interests arising under s 324 or s 328, is obliged in turn to notify any recognised investment exchange (RIE) on which the shares or debentures are listed (other than an overseas RIE). The section does appear to require that notification be made to each RIE on which the shares or debentures are listed.

This notification requirement, limited as it is to information which the director is obliged to notify to the company, does not extend to information which by virtue of s 325 (3), (4), the company is obliged to include in the register of interests, namely the grant of, and the exercise of, options to subscribe for any shares in or debentures of the company.

S 329(3)

As to penalties, see s 730, Sch 24; 'officer who is in default' is defined in s 730(5).

RESTRICTIONS ON A COMPANY'S POWER TO MAKE LOANS, ETC, TO DIRECTORS AND PERSONS CONNECTED WITH THEM

330. General restriction on loans etc to directors and persons connected with them

(1) The prohibitions listed below in this section are subject to the exceptions in sections 332 to 338.

(2) A company shall not—

(a) make a loan to a director of the company or of its holding company;

(b) enter into any guarantee or provide any security in connection with a loan made by any person to such a director.

(3) A relevant company shall not—

(a) make a quasi-loan to a director of the company or of its holding company;

(b) make a loan or a quasi-loan to a person connected with such a director;

(c) enter into a guarantee or provide any security in connection with a loan or quasi-loan made by any other person for such a director or a person so connected.

(4) A relevant company shall not—

    (a) enter into a credit transaction as creditor for such a director or a person so connected;

    (b) enter into any guarantee or provide any security in connection with a credit transaction made by any other person for such a director or a person so connected.

(5) For purposes of sections 330 to 346, a shadow director is treated as a director.

(6) A company shall not arrange for the assignment to it, or the assumption by it, of any rights, obligations or liabilities under a transaction which, if it had been entered into by the company, would have contravened subsection (2),(3) or (4); but for the purposes of sections 330 to 347 the transaction is to be treated as having been entered into on the date of the arrangement.

(7) A company shall not take part in any arrangement whereby—

    (a) another person enters into a transaction which, if it had been entered into by the company, would have contravened any of subsections (2),(3),(4) or (6); and

    (b) that other person, in pursuance of the arrangement, has obtained or is to obtain any benefit from the company or its holding company or a subsidiary of the company or its holding company.

General note

Any transaction or arrangement of the kind described in this provision (loan, quasi-loan, credit transactions etc) made by a company for a director of the company or a person connected with such a director, whether prohibited or not, is treated as a transaction or arrangement in which that director is interested and it must be disclosed at a meeting of the directors of the company: s 317(1), (6).

Details of such transactions, whether prohibited or not, must also be included in the notes to the company's accounts (s 232, Sch 6, Pts II, III), which are modified for transactions by banks or certain credit institutions: see ss 343–344, Sch 9, Pt IV, para 2. See also s 237(4).

It is immaterial for the purposes of ss 330–343 that the transaction or arrangement is subject to a foreign law: s 347.

S 330(1)

There are a large number of exceptions to the prohibitions set out in this provision. Each stands alone and it may be possible to bring a transaction within more than one exception.

S 330(2)

Loans and related transactions   'Loan' is not defined, but see *Champagne Perrier-Jouet SA v HH Finch Ltd* [1982] 3 All ER 713 at 717: a loan is a sum of money lent for a time to be returned in money or money's worth. The essence of a loan is that the money outstanding is to be repaid and sometimes it can be difficult to ascertain whether money paid to a director is an advance on salary or, in fact, a loan. Loans to directors of subsidiary companies are not affected provided that the director is not also a director of the holding company. 'Company' is defined in s 735; 'holding company' in s 736; 'guarantee' in s 331(2).

For exceptions to these prohibitions, see s 334 (small amounts); s 337 (funding of director's expenditure on duty to company); s 338 (loan or quasi-loan by money-lending company).

S 330(3)

Relevant companies   A 'relevant company' is a public company or a company which is part of a group which contains a public company: s 331(6). There is no prohibition on private companies, which are not relevant companies, making loans to persons connected with the directors or entering into quasi-loan transactions. 'Quasi-loan' is defined in s 331(3); 'connected persons' in s 346; 'guarantee' in s 331(2). See also s 331(9)(a), (c).

For exceptions to these prohibitions, see s 332 (short term quasi-loans); s 333 (inter-company loans in same group); s 336(a) (transactions at behest of holding company); s 337 (funding of director's expenditure on duty to company); s 338 (loan or quasi-loan by money-lending company).

S 330(4)

Credit transactions   These prohibitions apply only to relevant companies (defined in s 331(6)); 'credit transaction' is defined in s 331(7); see also s 331(9)(b) and (c).

For exceptions to these prohibitions, see s 335 (minor and business transactions); s 336(b) (transactions at behest of holding company); s 337 (funding of director's expenditure on duty to company).

S 330(5)

'Shadow director' is defined in s 741(2); and a parent company cannot be a shadow director for these purposes: s 741(3).

S 330(6)

Assignments   This subsection (and the next) are anti-avoidance provisions designed to cover indirect arrangements. This provision is intended to prevent the company taking over obligations (either on an assignment or by assuming the liabilities, for example, of a guarantor) under a transaction which the company could not have entered into in the first place. The closing phrase of the provision means that for the purpose of calculating the value of the transaction, the value is taken as at the date of the company entering into the arrangement for the assignment or assumption of liabilities.

S 330(7)

Back-to-back arrangements   The arrangement envisaged by this provision is one where a third party enters into a transaction with a director or connected person which the company could not enter into and pursuant to the arrangement the third party obtains or is to obtain some benefit from the company or the group. For example, the company places funds on deposit with a bank in return for the bank making a loan to a director or a connected person. These arrangements are frequently referred to as back-to-back arrangements. The benefit obtained by the third party must be an integral part of an arrangement whereby the third party entered into the prohibited transaction with the director or connected person. The company itself is not, and does not become, a party to what would be a prohibited transaction with the director or connected person.

331. Definitions for ss 330 ff

(1) The following subsections apply for the interpretation of sections 330 to 346.

(2) 'Guarantee' includes indemnity, and cognate expressions are to be construed accordingly.

(3) A quasi-loan is a transaction under which one party ('the creditor') agrees to pay, or pays otherwise than in pursuance of an agreement, a sum for another ('the borrower') or agrees to reimburse, or reimburses otherwise than in pursuance of an agreement, expenditure incurred by another party for another ('the borrower')—

    (a) on terms that the borrower (or a person on his behalf) will reimburse the creditor; or

    (b) in circumstances giving rise to a liability on the borrower to reimburse the creditor.

(4) Any reference to the person to whom a quasi-loan is made is a reference to the borrower; and the liabilities of a borrower under a quasi-loan include the liabilities of any person who has agreed to reimburse the creditor on behalf of the borrower.

(5) …

(6) 'Relevant company' means a company which—

    (a) is a public company, or

    (b) is a subsidiary of a public company, or

    (c) is a subsidiary of a company which has as another subsidiary a public company, or

    (d) has a subsidiary which is a public company.

(7) A credit transaction is a transaction under which one party ('the creditor')—

    (a) supplies any goods or sells any land under a hire-purchase agreement or a conditional sale agreement;

    (b) leases or hires any land or goods in return for periodical payments;

   (c) otherwise disposes of land or supplies goods or services on the understanding that payment (whether in a lump sum or instalments or by way of periodical payments or otherwise) is to be deferred.

(8) 'Services' means anything other than goods or land.

(9) A transaction or arrangement is made 'for' a person if—

   (a) in the case of a loan or quasi-loan, it is made to him;

   (b) in the case of a credit transaction, he is the person to whom goods or services are supplied, or land is sold or otherwise disposed of, under the transaction;

   (c) in the case of a guarantee or security, it is entered into or provided in connection with a loan or quasi-loan made to him or a credit transaction made for him;

   (d) in the case of an arrangement within subsection (6) or (7) of section 330, the transaction to which the arrangement relates was made for him; and

   (e) in the case of any other transaction or arrangement for the supply or transfer of, or of any interest in, goods, land or services, he is the person to whom the goods, land or services (or the interest) are supplied or transferred.

(10) 'Conditional sale agreement' means the same as in the Consumer Credit Act 1974.

S 331(2)

Guarantee and indemnity   An indemnity is an independent contract by one party to keep the other harmless against loss but a contract of guarantee is a contract to answer for the debt, default or miscarriage of another who is to be primarily liable: see *Yeoman Credit Ltd v Latter* [1961] 2 All ER 294 at 296.

S 331(3), (4)

Quasi-loan   The essence of a quasi-loan is that the company (the creditor) pays a debt for the director or connected person (the borrower) or reimburses expenditure incurred by a third party for the borrower with the borrower being obliged to reimburse the company later. The common example of this category is the company credit card to which the director charges personal expenditure which is initially paid by the company subject to reimbursement later by the director; see s 332(1). The quasi-loan is made to the director or connected person and not to the third party to whom payment is made.

S 331(6)

The prohibitions applicable to a relevant company are set out in s 330(3), (4), (6) and (7). It is important to appreciate that a private company can be a relevant company; 'subsidiary' is defined in s 736.

S 331(7)

Credit transactions The essence of a credit transaction is the supply of goods or services (defined in sub-s (8)) or land on a deferred payment basis. These are transactions by the company with a director or connected person.

S 331(9)

This provision determines for whom a transaction is made which is important to the calculation of relevant amounts under s 339.

332. Short-term quasi-loans

(1) Subsection (3) of section 330 does not prohibit a company ('the creditor') from making a quasi-loan to one of its directors or to a director of its holding company if—

    (a) the quasi-loan contains a term requiring the director or a person on his behalf to reimburse the creditor his expenditure within 2 months of its being incurred; and

    (b) the aggregate of the amount of that quasi-loan and of the amount outstanding under each relevant quasi-loan does not exceed £5,000.

(2) A quasi-loan is relevant for this purpose if it was made to the director by virtue of this section by the creditor or its subsidiary or, where the director is a director of the creditor's holding company, any other subsidiary of that company; and 'the amount outstanding' is the amount of the outstanding liabilities of the person to whom the quasi-loan was made.

S 332(1)

This exception applies only to directors and shadow directors and does not extend to persons connected with such a director: see also s 331(4).

The short time period and low financial limit make this exception of limited practical significance. The provision would permit a director to charge a company credit card with personal expenditure which is then paid off by him when the credit card bill is presented.

The aggregate in this case is determined in accordance with s 332(2) rather than s 339 which applies to the other exceptions.

S 332(2)

In determining whether the monetary limit has been reached, it is necessary to take into account each quasi-loan made under this exception to the director by any of the specified companies. As to the person to whom a quasi-loan is made, see s 331(4).

333. Inter-company loans in same group

In the case of a relevant company which is a member of a group of companies (meaning a holding company and its subsidiaries), paragraphs (b) and (c) of section 330(3) do not prohibit the company from—

   (a) making a loan or quasi-loan to another member of that group; or

   (b) entering into a guarantee or providing any security in connection with a loan or quasi-loan made by any person to another member of the group,

by reason only that a director of one member of the group is associated with another.

General note

This exception, which is without financial limit, is necessary because a company (A) within a group may be a connected person of a director of another company (B) in the group with the result that a loan by company B to company A will amount to a prohibited loan by company B to a person connected with a director of company B.

As the problem arises because of the connected person definition, the exception is necessarily limited to relevant companies (defined in s 331(6)) since it is only in the case of such companies that transactions with connected persons are prohibited (see s 330(3)(b)).

A director is associated with a body corporate in the circumstances set out in s 346(4).

334. Loans of small amounts

Without prejudice to any other provision of sections 332 to 338, paragraph (a) of section 330(2) does not prohibit a company from making a loan to a director of the company or of its holding company if the aggregate of the relevant amounts does not exceed £5,000.

General note

This exception applies only to loans and only to loans made to a director and not to a person connected with a director; the 'relevant amounts' are determined in accordance with s 339.

335. Minor and business transactions

(1) Section 330(4) does not prohibit a company from entering into a transaction for a person if the aggregate of the relevant amounts does not exceed £10,000.

(2) Section 330(4) does not prohibit a company from entering into a transaction for a person if—

    (a) the transaction is entered into by the company in the ordinary course of its business; and

    (b) the value of the transaction is not greater, and the terms on which it is entered into are no more favourable, in respect of the person for whom the transaction is made, than that or those which it is reasonable to expect the company to have offered to or in respect of a person of the same financial standing but unconnected with the company.

S 335(1)

Minor credit transactions   This exception relates to credit transactions (and guarantees and the provision of security in respect of such transactions) entered into by a relevant company (as defined in s 331(6)). 'Credit transaction' is defined in s 331(7); and a credit transaction *for* a person is defined in s 331(9)(b) and (c); the 'relevant amounts' are determined in accordance with s 339.

S 335(2)(a)

Credit transactions in the ordinary course of business   This exception relates to credit transactions (and guarantees and the provision of security in respect of such transactions) entered into by a relevant company (as defined in s 331(6)) provided the two specified conditions are met. 'Credit transaction' is defined in s 331(7) and a credit transaction *for* a person is defined in s 331(9)(b) and (c). As to the value of the transaction, see s 340(6).

The transaction must be in the ordinary course of the *company's* business. It may be difficult in a particular instance to be certain that a particular scheme is 'no more favourable' etc, other than when a financial services company is involved.

336. Transactions at behest of holding company

The following transactions are excepted from the prohibitions of section 330—

    (a) a loan or quasi-loan by a company to its holding company, or a company entering into a guarantee or providing any security in connection with a loan or quasi-loan made by any person to its holding company;

    (b) a company entering into a credit transaction as creditor for its holding company, or entering into a guarantee or providing any security in connection with a credit transaction made by any other person for its holding company.

General note

This provision is designed to allow subsidiary companies in a group to give loans etc to the holding company (defined s 736) which might otherwise be prohibited because the holding company may be a connected person of the donor company. As the problem arises because of the connected person definition (see s 346 and, in particular, s 346(2)(b)), the exception is limited to relevant companies (defined s 331(6)) since it is only in the case of such companies that transactions with connected persons are prohibited (see s 330). 'Quasi-loan' is defined in s 331(3); 'guarantee' in s 331(2); and 'credit transaction' in s 331(7).

    This exception in favour of holding companies (defined s 736) is without financial limit.

337. Funding of director's expenditure on duty to company

(1) A company is not prohibited by section 330 from doing anything to provide a director with funds to meet expenditure incurred or to be incurred by him for the purposes of the company or for the purpose of enabling him properly to perform his duties as an officer of the company.

(2) Nor does the section prohibit a company from doing any thing to enable a director to avoid incurring such expenditure.

(3) Subsections (1) and (2) apply only if one of the following conditions is satisfied—

    (a) the thing in question is done with prior approval of the company given at a general meeting at which there are disclosed all the matters mentioned in the next subsection;

    (b) that thing is done on condition that, if the approval of the company is not so given at or before the next annual general meeting, the loan is to be repaid, or any other liability arising under any such transaction discharged, within 6 months from the conclusion of that meeting;

but those subsections do not authorise a relevant company to enter into any transaction if the aggregate of the relevant amounts exceeds £20,000.

(4) The matters to be disclosed under subsection (3)(a) are—

    (a) the purpose of the expenditure incurred or to be incurred, or which would otherwise be incurred, by the director,

    (b) the amount of the funds to be provided by the company, and

    (c) the extent of the company's liability under any transaction which is or is connected with the thing in question.

S 337(1)

This exception only applies to directors including directors of the holding company and cannot be used to justify payments to connected persons. The meaning of 'the purposes of the company' and 'properly to perform his duties as an officer' is uncertain but would exclude purely personal expenses.

S 337(3)

Shareholder approval may be sought before or after the funds are provided with the risk that if subsequent approval is not forthcoming, then repayment is required within six months. A statutory written resolution may be used in which case the information required by s 337(4) must be available to the shareholders before they sign: s 381A, Sch 15A, para 8.

Where the company is a charity in England and Wales, any approval given by the company is ineffective without the prior written consent of the Charity Commissioners: Charities Act 1993, s 66(1), (2)(e).

A monetary limit is imposed on 'relevant companies', as defined in s 331(6); the 'relevant amounts' are determined in accordance with s 339.

338. Loan or quasi-loan by money-lending company

(1) There is excepted from the prohibitions in section 330—

    (a) a loan or quasi-loan made by a money-lending company to any person; or

    (b) a money-lending company entering into a guarantee in connection with any other loan or quasi-loan.

(2) 'Money-lending company' means a company whose ordinary business includes the making of loans or quasi-loans, or the giving of guarantees in connection with loans or quasi-loans.

(3) Subsection (1) applies only if both the following conditions are satisfied—

    (a) the loan or quasi-loan in question is made by the company, or it enters into the guarantee, in the ordinary course of the company's business; and

    (b) the amount of the loan or quasi-loan, or the amount guaranteed, is not greater, and the terms of the loan, quasi-loan or guarantee are not more favourable, in the case of the person to whom the loan or quasi-loan is made or in respect of whom the guarantee is entered into, than that or those which it is reasonable to expect that company to have offered to or in respect of a person of the same financial standing but unconnected with the company.

(4) But subsection (1) does not authorise a relevant company (unless it is a banking company) to enter into any transaction if the aggregate of the relevant amounts exceeds £100,000.

(5) In determining that aggregate, a company which a director does not control is deemed not to be connected with him.

(6) The condition specified in subsection (3)(b) does not of itself prevent a company from making a loan to one of its directors or a director of its holding company—

(a) for the purpose of facilitating the purchase, for use as that director's only or main residence, of the whole or part of any dwelling-house together with any land to be occupied and enjoyed with it;

(b) for the purpose of improving a dwelling-house or part of a dwelling-house so used or any land occupied and enjoyed with it;

(c) in substitution for any loan made by any person and falling within paragraph (a) or (b) of this subsection,

if loans of that description are ordinarily made by the company to its employees and on terms no less favourable than those on which the transaction in question is made, and the aggregate of the relevant amounts does not exceed £100,000.

S 338(1)

Exceptions for money-lending companies   Given the nature of their business, it was thought necessary to exempt money-lending companies from these prohibitions but a monetary limit is placed on relevant companies (defined in s 331(6)) other than banking companies (defined in s 744). The result is that money-lending companies which are not relevant companies are not subject to any financial limits; neither are money-lending companies which are banking companies; while money-lending companies which are relevant companies but are not banking companies are subject to the financial limits in sub-s (4).

The exceptions cover loans, quasi-loans (defined in s 331(3)) and guarantees (defined in s 331(2)) but do not extend to credit transactions (defined in s 331(7)) or the provision of security; the 'relevant amounts' are determined in accordance with s 339.

S 338(3)

Conditions which must be satisfied   The transaction must be entered into in the ordinary course of that company's business. The 'not more favourable than' formula is easier to apply here than s 335(2) given that the company's ordinary business is the making of loans etc.

S 338(4), (5)

Relevant companies   A money-lending company which is a relevant company but not a banking company is restricted to transactions where the aggregate of the relevant amounts as determined by s 339 does not exceed £100,000.

In determining that aggregate under s 339, account is taken of transactions by a director and any connected persons (as defined in s 346) which includes companies with which the director is associated. Subsection (5) excludes such companies from the calculation for the purpose of sub-s (4) where the director does not control the company (and a director is deemed to control a company in the circumstances set out in s 346(5)).

S 338(6)

Home loans   This exception, peculiar to money-lending companies, allows them to make favourable house purchase/improvement loans to their directors (but not to connected persons) if the specified conditions are met. It only applies to loans and not to quasi-loans or guarantees. The aggregate of relevant amounts is determined in accordance with s 339 and see, in particular, s 339(4).

339. 'Relevant amounts' for purposes of ss 334 ff

(1) This section has effect for defining the 'relevant amounts' to be aggregated under sections 334, 335(1), 337(3) and 338(4); and in relation to any proposed transaction or arrangement and the question whether it falls within one or other of the exceptions provided by those sections, 'the relevant exception' is that exception; but where the relevant exception is the one provided by section 334 (loan of small amount), references in this section to a person connected with a director are to be disregarded.

(2) Subject as follows, the relevant amounts in relation to a proposed transaction or arrangement are—

    (a) the value of the proposed transaction or arrangement,

    (b) the value of any existing arrangement which—

        (i)   falls within subsection (6) or (7) of section 330, and

        (ii)   also falls within subsection (3) of this section, and

        (iii) was entered into by virtue of the relevant exception by the company or by a subsidiary of the company or, where the proposed transaction or arrangement is to be made for a director of its holding company or a person connected with such a director, by that holding company or any of its subsidiaries;

    (c) the amount outstanding under any other transaction—

        (i)   falling within subsection (3) below, and

        (ii)   made by virtue of the relevant exception, and

        (iii) made by the company or by a subsidiary of the company or, where the proposed transaction or arrangement is to be made for a director of its holding company or a person connected with such a director, by that holding company or any of its subsidiaries.

(3) A transaction falls within this subsection if it was made—

    (a) for the director for whom the proposed transaction or arrangement is to be made, or for any person connected with that director; or

    (b) where the proposed transaction or arrangement is to be made for a person connected with a director of a company, for that director or any person connected with him;

and an arrangement also falls within this subsection if it relates to a transaction which does so.

(4) But where the proposed transaction falls within section 338 and is one which a banking company proposes to enter into under subsection (6) of that section

(housing loans, etc), any other transaction or arrangement which apart from this subsection would fall within subsection (3) of this section does not do so unless it was entered into in pursuance of section 338(6).

(5) A transaction entered into by a company which is (at the time of that transaction being entered into) a subsidiary of the company which is to make the proposed transaction, or is a subsidiary of that company's holding company, does not fall within subsection (3) if at the time when the question arises (that is to say, the question whether the proposed transaction or arrangement falls within any relevant exception), it no longer is such a subsidiary.

(6) Values for purposes of subsection (2) of this section are to be determined in accordance with the section next following; and 'the amount outstanding' for purposes of subsection (2)(c) above is the value of the transaction less any amount by which that value has been reduced.

General note

These provisions defining the relevant amounts to be aggregated are designed to prevent attempts to circumvent the legislation by breaking up a transaction into a number of smaller transactions.

S 339(1)

Each of the specified sections provides an exception to the prohibitions contained in s 330 subject to a financial limit. The purpose of this provision is to determine the aggregate of the relevant amounts for the purposes of those financial limits.

S 339(2)

Amounts to be aggregated   This provision identifies the amounts which have to be aggregated which are:
- (a) the value of the proposed transaction or arrangement (value being determined by s 340);
- (b) the value (determined by s 340) of any existing arrangement which is: (i) within the prohibitions in s 330(6) and (7) (assignment and assumption of liabilities and back-to-back arrangements); (ii) made for the specified parties (see sub-s (3)); and (iii) entered into under the self-same exception by any of the specified companies (and note the exclusion of former subsidiaries in sub-s (5)); and
- (c) the amount outstanding (defined sub-s (6)) of any existing transaction or arrangement entered into under the self-same exception made for the specified parties (see sub-s (3)) and by any of the specified companies.

S 339(3)

A transaction is made 'for' a person in the circumstances set out in s 331(9); 'connected person' is defined in s 346.

Where the proposed use of the exception in question is for a director, then transactions for the director or any person connected with the director are counted in applying s 339(2); subject to the proviso in s 339(1) which excludes transactions for a connected person when aggregating amounts for the purpose of s 334.

Where the proposed use of the exception in question is for a connected person, then transactions for the director with whom the person is connected or for any person connected with the director are counted when applying sub-s (2); subject to the proviso in sub-s (1) which excludes transactions for a connected person when aggregating amounts for the purpose of s 334.

S 339(4)

Home loans   Under s 338(6), a money-lending company may make house purchase/improvement loans where the aggregate of the relevant amounts does not exceed £100,000. This provision states that in calculating the aggregate of the relevant amounts under s 339(2), any other transaction or arrangement need not be aggregated unless it is a transaction entered into with a director in pursuance of s 338(6). In other words, only existing house purchase/improvement loans to the director need to be aggregated when proposing to make a further house loan to that director. This provision is limited to proposed transactions by a banking company, defined s 744.

S 339(5)

This provision excludes from the aggregation transactions by former subsidiary companies.

S 339(6)

By taking into account any reduction in liabilities, this provision ensures that only sums actually owing at the time the proposed transaction is being considered are taken into account.

---

340. 'Value' of transactions and arrangements

(1) This section has effect for determining the value of a transaction or arrangement for purposes of sections 330 to 339.

(2) The value of a loan is the amount of its principal.

(3) The value of a quasi-loan is the amount, or maximum amount, which the person to whom the quasi-loan is made is liable to reimburse the creditor.

(4) The value of a guarantee or security is the amount guaranteed or secured.

(5) The value of an arrangement to which section 330(6) or (7) applies is the value of the transaction to which the arrangement relates less any amount by

which the liabilities under the arrangement or transaction of the person for whom the transaction was made have been reduced.

(6) The value of a transaction or arrangement not falling within subsections (2) to (5) above is the price which it is reasonable to expect could be obtained for the goods, land or services to which the transaction or arrangement relates if they had been supplied (at the time the transaction or arrangement is entered into) in the ordinary course of business and on the same terms (apart from price) as they have been supplied, or are to be supplied, under the transaction or arrangement in question.

(7) For purposes of this section, the value of a transaction or arrangement which is not capable of being expressed as a specific sum of money (because the amount of any liability arising under the transaction or arrangement is unascertainable, or for any other reason), whether or not any liability under the transaction or arrangement has been reduced, is deemed to exceed £100,000.

General note

The value of each transaction is intended to be the measure of the company's resources tied up in favour of the director or connected person.

S 340(3)

'Quasi-loan' is defined in s 331(3) and the person to whom a quasi-loan is made is defined by s 331(4).

S 340(5)

The value of the arrangement etc is necessary for the purpose of aggregation under s 339(2) and is the amount outstanding. The person for whom the transaction was made is determined by s 331(9).

S 340(6)

This determines the value of a credit transaction (see s 330(4)) and looks for the objective value (which it is reasonable to expect) which could be obtained for the goods, land or services.

S 340(7)

By deeming the value to exceed £100,000, this ensures that the transaction cannot be within any of the exceptions provided. This might encourage the parties not to assert that the value is unquantifiable.

341. Civil remedies for breach of s 330

(1) If a company enters into a transaction or arrangement in contravention of section 330, the transaction or arrangement is voidable at the instance of the company unless—

- (a) restitution of any money or any other asset which is the subject matter of the arrangement or transaction is no longer possible, or the company has been indemnified in pursuance of subsection (2)(b) below for the loss or damage suffered by it, or
- (b) any rights acquired bona fide for value and without actual notice of the contravention by a person other than the person for whom the transaction or arrangement was made would be affected by its avoidance.

(2) Where an arrangement or transaction is made by a company for a director of the company or its holding company or a person connected with such a director in contravention of section 330, that director and the person so connected and any other director of the company who authorised the transaction or arrangement (whether or not it has been avoided in pursuance of subsection (1)) is liable—

- (a) to account to the company for any gain which he has made directly or indirectly by the arrangement or transaction; and
- (b) (jointly and severally with any other person liable under this subsection) to indemnify the company for any loss or damage resulting from the arrangement or transaction.

(3) Subsection (2) is without prejudice to any liability imposed otherwise than by that subsection, but is subject to the next two subsections.

(4) Where an arrangement or transaction is entered into by a company and a person connected with a director of the company or its holding company in contravention of section 330, that director is not liable under subsection (2) of this section if he shows that he took all reasonable steps to secure the company's compliance with that section.

(5) In any case, a person so connected and any such other director as is mentioned in subsection (2) is not so liable if he shows that, at the time the arrangement or transaction was entered into, he did not know the relevant circumstances constituting the contravention.

General note

See the detailed notes to s 322, above, where there is an identical scheme of liability, save that there is no question of the right to rescind being lost here by affirmation of the transaction (as is provided for by s 322(2)(c)) as contravention of s 330 attracts the criminal penalties set out in s 342.

S 341(1)

See *Tait Consibee (Oxford) Ltd v Tait* [1997] 2 BCLC 349 (company avoided loan prohibited by s 330 when it sent a letter demanding repayment).

342. Criminal penalties for breach of s 330

(1) A director of a relevant company who authorises or permits the company to enter into a transaction or arrangement knowing or having reasonable cause to believe that the company was thereby contravening section 330 is guilty of an offence.

(2) A relevant company which enters into a transaction or arrangement for one of its directors or for a director of its holding company in contravention of section 330 is guilty of an offence.

(3) A person who procures a relevant company to enter into a transaction or arrangement knowing or having reasonable cause to believe that the company was thereby contravening section 330 is guilty of an offence.

(4) A person guilty of an offence under this section is liable to imprisonment or a fine, or both.

(5) A relevant company is not guilty of an offence under subsection (2) if it shows that, at the time the transaction or arrangement was entered into, it did not know the relevant circumstances.

General note

Criminal penalties have been imposed in respect of breaches of the provisions by relevant companies (defined in s 331(6)), their directors and others. This reflects the much tougher line taken in respect of those companies where there has been most abuse of the loan provisions in the past. Given the complexity of the provisions, it would be very difficult to establish the requisite mens rea for the purpose of a prosecution and, not surprisingly, it appears that no prosecutions have ever been brought under these provisions.

S 342(2)

A defence is available to the company under s 342(5).

S 342(3)

This provision would encompass a connected person.

S 342(4)

As to penalties, see s 730, Sch 24.

343. Record of transactions not disclosed in company accounts

(1) The following provisions of this section—

    (a) apply in the case of a company which is a banking company, or is the holding company of a credit institution, and

    (b) are subject to the exceptions provided by section 344.

(2) Where such a company takes advantage of the provisions of paragraph 2 of Part IV of Schedule 9 in relation to a financial year, that company shall keep a register containing a copy of every transaction, arrangement or agreement of which particulars would, but for that paragraph, be required to be disclosed in the company's accounts or group accounts for that financial year and for each financial year in the preceding 10 in relation to which the company has taken advantage of the provisions of that paragraph.

(3) In the case of a transaction, arrangement or agreement which is not in writing, there shall be contained in the register a written memorandum setting out its terms.

(4) Where such a company takes advantage of the provisions of paragraph 2 of Part IV of Schedule 9 in relation to the last complete financial year preceding its annual general meeting, that company shall before that meeting make available at its registered office for not less than 15 days ending with the date of the meeting a statement containing the particulars of transactions, arrangements and agreements which the company would, but for that paragraph, be required to disclose in its accounts or group accounts for that financial year.

(5) The statement shall be so made available for inspection by members of the company; and such a statement shall also be made available for their inspection at the annual general meeting.

(6) It is the duty of the company's auditors to examine the statement before it is made available to members of the company and to make a report to the members on it; and the report shall be annexed to the statement before it is made so available.

(7) The auditors' report shall state whether in their opinion the statement contains the particulars required by subsection (4); and, where their opinion is that it does not, they shall include in the report, so far as they are reasonably able to do so, a statement giving the required particulars.

(8) If a company fails to comply with any provision of subsections (2) to (5), every person who at the time of the failure is a director of it is guilty of an offence and liable to a fine; but—

    (a) it is a defence in proceedings against a person for this offence to prove that he took all reasonable steps for securing compliance with the subsection concerned, and

    (b) a person is not guilty of the offence by virtue only of being a shadow director of the company.

(9) For purposes of the application of this section to loans and quasi-loans made by a company to persons connected with a person who at any time is a director of the company or of its holding company, a company which a person does not control is not connected with him.

S 343(1)

Special provision for financial institutions   Companies generally have to include details of loans, quasi-loans and other dealings in favour of directors and connected persons in the notes to the company's accounts: s 232, Sch 6, Pts II, III, but it was thought that such a disclosure obligation would be unduly onerous when applied to transactions between certain financial institutions and their directors or persons connected with them, hence this provision and the next makes special provision for such transactions.

A 'banking company' is defined in s 744. There is no definition of credit institution for the purposes of this Part but it is defined in ss 262(1) and 699A(3) for other purposes, which definition must apply here also.

S 343(2), (3)

A register   Instead of disclosure in the notes to the company's accounts (see text to Sch 9, Pt IV), the company must maintain a register of the transactions, subject to the de minimis exception in s 344(1).

S 343(4), (5)

A statement to the members   This requirement to make a statement available to the members etc is subject to the de minimis exception in s 344(1) and to the exemption in s 344(2). The information which must be disclosed in the statement is set out in Sch 6, Pt II, paras 22–23.

S 343(6), (7)

These provisions set out the auditors' obligations with regard to the statement of transactions.

S 343(8)

'Shadow director' is defined in s 741(2). As to penalties, see s 730, Sch 24.

S 343(9)

'Connected persons' is defined in s 346 and the category includes companies with which the director is associated. This subsection excludes such companies from the category of connected person for the purposes of this provision where the director does not control the company (and a director is deemed to control a company in the circumstances set out in s 346(5)).

344. Exceptions from s 343

(1) Section 343 does not apply in relation to—

   (a) transactions or arrangements made or subsisting during a financial year by a company or by a subsidiary of a company for a person who was at any time during that year a director of the company or of its holding company or was connected with such a director, or

   (b) an agreement made or subsisting during that year to enter into such a transaction or arrangement,

if the aggregate of the values of each transaction or arrangement made for that person, and of each agreement for such a transaction or arrangement, less the amount (if any) by which the value of those transactions, arrangements and agreements has been reduced, did not exceed £2,000 at any time during the financial year.

   For purposes of this subsection, values are to be determined as under section 340.

(2) Section 343(4) and (5) do not apply to a banking company which is the wholly-owned subsidiary of a company incorporated in the United Kingdom.

S 344(1)

Small transactions are exempted from the disclosure obligations of s 343. A transaction is made *for* a person in the circumstances set out in s 331(9).

S 344(2)

A 'banking company' is defined in s 744; 'wholly-owned subsidiary' is defined in s 736.

SUPPLEMENTARY

345. Power to increase financial limits

(1) The Secretary of State may by order in a statutory instrument substitute for any sum of money specified in this Part a larger sum specified in the order.

(2) An order under this section is subject to annulment in pursuance of a resolution of either House of Parliament.

(3) Such an order does not have effect in relation to anything done or not done before its coming into force; and accordingly, proceedings in respect of any liability (whether civil or criminal) incurred before that time may be continued or instituted as if the order had not been made.

General note

This power has been exercised on one occasion: see the Companies (Fair Dealing by Directors) (Increase in Financial Limits) Order 1990, SI 1990/1393 – the increases in financial limits so authorised are reflected in the text.

346. 'Connected persons', etc

(1) This section has effect with respect to references in this Part to a person being 'connected' with a director of a company, and to a director being 'associated with' or 'controlling' a body corporate.

(2) A person is connected with a director of a company if, but only if, he (not being himself a director of it) is—

    (a) that director's spouse, child or step-child; or

    (b) except where the context otherwise requires, a body corporate with which the director is associated; or

    (c) a person acting in his capacity as trustee of any trust the beneficiaries of which include—

       (i) the director, his spouse or any children or step-children of his, or

       (ii) a body corporate with which he is associated,

    or of a trust whose terms confer a power on the trustees that may be exercised for the benefit of the director, his spouse, or any children or step-children of his, or any such body corporate; or

    (d) a person acting in his capacity as partner of that director or of any person who, by virtue of paragraph (a), (b) or (c) of this subsection, is connected with that director; or

    (e) a Scottish firm in which—

       (i) that director is a partner,

       (ii) a partner is a person who, by virtue of paragraph (a), (b) or (c) above, is connected with that director, or

       (iii) a partner is a Scottish firm in which that director is a partner or in which there is a partner who, by virtue of paragraph (a), (b) or (c) above, is connected with that director.

(3) In subsection (2)—

    (a) a reference to the child or step-child of any person includes an illegitimate child of his, but does not include any person who has attained the age of 18; and

    (b) paragraph (c) does not apply to a person acting in his capacity as trustee under an employees' share scheme or a pension scheme.

(4) A director of a company is associated with a body corporate if, but only if, he and the persons connected with him, together—

    (a) are interested in shares comprised in the equity share capital of that body corporate of a nominal value equal to at least one-fifth of that share capital; or

(b) are entitled to exercise or control the exercise of more than one-fifth of the voting power at any general meeting of that body.

(5) A director of a company is deemed to control a body corporate if, but only if—

    (a) he or any person connected with him is interested in any part of the equity share capital of that body or is entitled to exercise or control the exercise of any part of the voting power at any general meeting of that body; and

    (b) that director, the persons connected with him and the other directors of that company, together, are interested in more than one-half of that share capital or are entitled to exercise or control the exercise of more than one-half of that voting power.

(6) For purposes of subsections (4) and (5)—

    (a) a body corporate with which a director is associated is not to be treated as connected with that director unless it is also connected with him by virtue of subsection (2)(c) or (d); and

    (b) a trustee of a trust the beneficiaries of which include (or may include) a body corporate with which a director is associated is not to be treated as connected with a director by reason only of that fact.

(7) The rules set out in Part I of Schedule 13 apply for the purposes of subsections (4) and (5).

(8) References in those subsections to voting power the exercise of which is controlled by a director include voting power whose exercise is controlled by a body corporate controlled by him; but this is without prejudice to other provisions of subsections (4) and (5).

S 346(2)(a)

See the definition of child or step-child in s 346(3)(a).

S 346(2)(b)

The complex definition of what is an associated body corporate is contained in s 346(4)–(8); a 'body corporate' is defined in s 740.

S 346(2)(c)

See the definition of child or step-child in s 346(3)(a); and note the exclusion in s 346(3)(b).

S 346(3)

As to the definition of an 'employees' share scheme', see s 743.

S 346(4)–(8)

Associated with a body corporate   The interests of the director and persons
connected with him (as defined in s 346(2)) are aggregated for these purposes.
This is subject to sub-s (6) which provides that certain connected persons are not
to be so treated for this purpose. The tests in sub-s (4)(a) and (b) are alternative
tests.

An 'interest in shares' as required by sub-s (4)(a) is determined in accordance
with Sch 13, Pt I (sub-s (7)); 'equity share capital' is defined in s 744. When
considering for the purposes of sub-s (4)(b) whether a director is entitled to
exercise or control the exercise of voting power, there must be included any
voting power the exercise of which is controlled by a body corporate controlled
by the director (sub-s (8)). Whether a body corporate is controlled by him is
determined by sub-s (5).

S 346(5)

Deemed control of a body corporate   When considering whether a director is
entitled to exercise or control the exercise of voting power for the purposes of
s 346(4), there must be included any voting power the exercise of which is
controlled by a body corporate controlled by the director (s 346(8)). Whether a
body corporate is controlled by him is determined by this provision.

The tests in sub-s (5)(a) and (b) must be satisfied in this case. The requirement
in sub-s (5)(a) is that the director *or* any person connected with him be interested
or entitled etc. This is subject to s 346(6), which provides that certain connected
persons are not to be so treated for this purpose. An interest in equity share capital
is determined in accordance with Sch 13, Pt I (s 346(7)); 'equity share capital' is
defined in s 744.

The aggregation required by sub-s (5)(b) is of the director's interests, those of
connected persons (subject to s 346(6)) *and* the interests of the other directors of
that company. An 'interest' is determined in accordance with Sch 13, Pt I
(s 346(7)); 'equity share capital' is defined in s 744.

S 346(6)

Certain connected persons excluded   As noted above, sub-ss (4) and (5) require
that account be taken of the interests etc of persons connected with a director.
However, in order to draw some limits to the category of connected person, this
provision excludes (for the purposes of those subsections), any body corporate
with which the director is associated (which would otherwise have to be counted
because of s 346(2)(b)) unless the company in question falls within sub-s (2)(c)
or (d) (a corporate trustee or corporate partner in certain circumstances).

Equally, for the purposes of those subsections, it is not necessary to count a trustee
as a connected person in the circumstances set out in sub-s (6)(b).

347. Transactions under foreign law

For purposes of sections 319 to 322 and 330 to 343, it is immaterial whether the law which (apart from this Act) governs any arrangement or transaction is the law of the United Kingdom, or of a part of it, or not.

General note

This provision is designed to stop the parties attempting to contract out of the specified sections by choosing a foreign law to govern the transaction or arrangement.

PART XA

CONTROL OF POLITICAL DONATIONS

347A. Introductory provisions

(1)   This Part has effect for controlling—

(a)   contributions and other donations made by companies to registered parties and other EU political organisations; and

(b)   EU political expenditure incurred by companies.

(2)   The following provisions have effect for the purposes of this Part, but subsections (4) and (7) have effect subject to section 347B.

(3)   'Director' includes shadow director.

(4)   'Donation', in relation to an organisation, means anything that would constitute a donation for the purposes of Part IV of the Political Parties, Elections and Referendums Act 2000 in accordance with sections 50 to 52 of that Act (references in those sections to a registered party being read as applying equally to an organisation which is not such a party); and—

(a)   subsections (3) to (8) of section 50 of that Act shall apply, with any necessary modifications, for the purpose of determining whether something is a donation to an organisation for the purposes of this Part as they apply for the purpose of determining whether something is a donation to a registered party for the purposes of Part IV of that Act; and

(b)   section 53 of that Act shall similarly apply for the purpose of determining, for the purposes of this Part, the value of any donation.

(5)   'EU political expenditure', in relation to a company, means any expenditure incurred by the company—

(a)   in respect of the preparation, publication or dissemination of any advertising or any other promotional or publicity material—

(i)   of whatever nature, and

(ii)   however published or otherwise disseminated,

which, at the time of publication or dissemination, is capable of being reasonably regarded as intended to affect public support for any EU political organisation, or

(b)   in respect of any activities on the part of the company such as are mentioned in subsection (7)(b) or (c).

(6)   'EU political organisation' means—

(a)   a registered party; or

(b)   any other organisation to which subsection (7) applies.

(7)   This subsection applies to an organisation if—

(a)   it is a political party which carries on, or proposes to carry on, activities for the purpose of or in connection with the participation of the party in any election or elections to public office held in a member State other than the United Kingdom;

(b)   it carries on, or proposes to carry on, activities which are capable of being reasonably regarded as intended to affect public support for—

(i)   any registered party,

(ii)   any other political party within paragraph (a), or

(iii) independent candidates at any election or elections of the kind mentioned in that paragraph; or

(c) it carries on, or proposes to carry on, activities which are capable of being reasonably regarded as intended to influence voters in relation to any national or regional referendum held under the law of any member State.

(8)   'Organisation' includes any body corporate and any combination of persons or other unincorporated association.

(9)   'Registered party' means a party registered under Part II of the Political Parties, Elections and Referendums Act 2000.

(10)   'The relevant time', in relation to any donation or expenditure made or incurred by a company or subsidiary undertaking, means—

(a) the time when the donation or expenditure is made or incurred; or

(b) if earlier, the time when any contract is entered into by the company or undertaking in pursuance of which the donation or expenditure is made or incurred.

(11)   'Subsidiary undertaking' has the same meaning as in Part VII.

General note

This provision was inserted, together with the preceding cross-heading and ss 347B–347K (Pt XA) by the Political Parties, Elections and Referendums Act 2000, s 139(1), Sch 19, as from 16 February 2001: Political Parties, Elections and Referendums Act 2000 (Commencement No 1 and Transitional Provisions) Order 2001, SI 2001/222.

See also Sch 7 (directors' report), paras 3–5 inserted by the Political Parties, Elections and Referendums Act 2000, s 140, as from 16 February 2001: Political Parties, Elections and Referendums Act 2000 (Commencement No 1 and Transitional Provisions) Order 2001, SI 2001/222. These provisions set out the matters as to donations etc which must be included in the directors' report.

S 347A(1)

Scope of these provisions   This Part is directed to controlling (through the need for prior authorisation: see s 347C) these two distinct matters.

Contributions and donations to registered parties and other EU political organisations   The term 'donation' is defined in sub-s (4), unhelpfully, by reference to the Political Parties, Elections and Referendums Act 2000, ss 50–52 (which provisions include any gift of money or other property, any sponsorship or subscriptions paid, any loans other than on commercial terms and the provision of property, services or facilities other than on commercial terms, but which exclude any donations where the value does not exceed £200); 'registered party' is defined in sub-s (9).

The extension of the provision to any 'EU political organisation' results in legislation of the widest possible scope. That term is defined very broadly in sub-ss (6)–(8), going beyond political parties to all types of organisations carrying on, or proposing to carry on, activities capable of being reasonably regarded as intended to affect public support for parties, candidates etc and to organisations carrying on etc activities capable of being reasonably regarded as intended to influence voters in any national or regional referendum in any member state.

There is an exemption from the need for prior authorisation in this instance for sums not exceeding £5,000: see s 347B(4)–(7).

EU political expenditure   This term is defined in the broadest possible way in sub-s (5). An exemption from the need for prior authorisation in this instance may be conferred by order: see s 347B(8)–(11).

Payment by a company   In each case, the payment must be by a company, ie a company formed and registered in Great Britain under this and previous companies legislation: s 735.

Given the breadth of the definitions in this provision, the controls imposed by s 347C, and the potential personal liabilities of directors under s 347F, it must be likely that the effect of this Part will be to curb all contributions and donations and expenditure by companies on any activities which might conceivably fall within these sections. Of course, that may well have been Parliament's intention in enacting these provisions in this form. It will still be possible for controlling shareholders and directors who wish to make these payments to make them personally rather than through a company.

S 347A(3)

As to shadow directors, see s 741(2).

S 347A(4)

'Donation'   This definition is subject to s 347B(1) which excludes subscriptions to EU trade associations from the definition of 'donation'.

S 347A(5)

'EU political expenditure'   Such is the width of this definition that it encompasses companies involved in news media and so an immediate exemption had to be made for such companies: see note to s 347B(8), below.

S 347A(6)–(9)

'EU political organisation'   This definition of an 'EU political organisation' is subject to s 347B(3) which excludes an all-party parliamentary group, as there defined, from being classified as such an organisation for these purposes.

S 347A(10), (11)

As to the definition of 'subsidiary undertaking', see s 258, Sch 10A.

347B. Exemptions

(1)   Section 347A(4) does not extend to a subscription paid to an EU trade association for membership of the association, and accordingly such a payment is not a donation to the association for the purposes of this Part.

(2)   In subsection (1)—

'EU trade association' means any organisation formed for the purpose of furthering the trade interests—

(a)   of its members, or

(b)   of persons represented by its members,

which carries on its activities wholly or mainly in one or more of the member States;

'subscription', in relation to a trade association, does not include any payment to the association to the extent that it is made for the purpose of financing any particular activity of the association.

(3)   Section 347A(7) does not apply to any all-party parliamentary group composed of members of one or both of the Houses of Parliament (or of such members and other persons), and accordingly any such group is not an EU political organisation for the purposes of this Part.

(4)   For the purposes of this Part—

(a)   a company does not need to be authorised as mentioned in section 347C(1) or section 347D(2) or (3), and

(b)   a subsidiary undertaking does not need to be authorised as mentioned in section 347E(2),

in connection with any donation or donations to any EU political organisation or organisations made in a particular qualifying period, except to the extent (if any) that the amount or aggregate amount of any such donation or donations made in that period exceeds £5,000.

(5)   The restrictions imposed by sections 347C(1), 347D(2) and (3) and 347E(2) accordingly have effect subject to subsection (4); and, where a resolution is passed for the purposes of any of those provisions, any amount of donations in relation to which, by virtue of subsection (4), no authorisation is needed shall accordingly not count towards the sum specified in the resolution.

(6)   In subsection (4) 'qualifying period' means—

(a)   the period of 12 months beginning with the relevant date for the company or (in the case of a subsidiary undertaking) the parent company; and

(b)   each succeeding period of twelve months.

(7)   For the purposes of subsection (6) the relevant date for a company is—

(a)   if an annual general meeting of the company is held within the period of 12 months beginning with the date of the coming into force of this section, the date of that meeting; and

(b)   otherwise, the date immediately following the end of that period.

(8)   For the purposes of this Part—

(a) a company does not need to be authorised as mentioned in section 347C(1) or section 347D(2) or (3), and

(b) a subsidiary undertaking does not need to be authorised as mentioned in section 347E(2),

in connection with any EU political expenditure in relation to which an exemption is conferred on the company or (as the case may be) subsidiary undertaking by virtue of an order made by the Secretary of State by statutory instrument.

(9)   The restrictions imposed by sections 347C(1), 347D(2) and (3) and 347E(2) accordingly have effect subject to subsection (8); and, where a resolution is passed for the purposes of any of those provisions, any amount of EU political expenditure in relation to which, by virtue of subsection (8), no authorisation is needed shall accordingly not count towards the sum specified in the resolution.

(10) An order under subsection (8) may confer an exemption for the purposes of that subsection in relation to—

(a) companies or subsidiary undertakings of any description or category specified in the order, or

(b) expenditure of any description or category so specified (whether framed by reference to goods, services or other matters in respect of which such expenditure is incurred or otherwise),

or both.

(11) An order shall not be made under subsection (8) unless a draft of the statutory instrument containing the order has been laid before and approved by each House of Parliament.

S 347B(1)–(3)

Limited exemptions   These provisions offer two exemptions of limited significance:
(1)   subscriptions paid to an EU trade association do not amount to a 'donation' for these purposes; and
(2)   an all-party parliamentary group, as defined in sub-s (3), is not an 'EU political organisation' for these purposes.

S 347B(4)–(7)

Small donations   Authorisation for donations (as defined in s 347A(4)) to EU political organisations (as defined in s 347A(6)–(8)) is not required unless the donation or aggregate amount of the donations exceeds £5,000 in the particular qualifying period. This period is defined in sub-ss (6), (7) and, essentially, means successive periods of 12 months commencing from the date of the company's first annual general meeting after 16 February 2001 (the date the section came into force) or 17 February 2002, whichever is earlier.

As to the meaning of 'company', see s 735; as to the meaning of 'subsidiary undertaking', see ss 347A(11), 258, Sch 10A.

S 347B(8)–(11)

Exemption by order for EU political expenditure   Authorisation is not required for EU political expenditure (as defined by s 347A(5)) where an exemption is conferred by order; and see The Companies (EU Political Expenditure) Exemption Order 2001, SI 2001/445.

This Order exempts from the need for approval any company or subsidiary undertaking whose ordinary course of business includes, or is proposed to include, the preparation, publication or dissemination to the public, or any part of the public, of material relating to news and public and political affairs and events and to views, opinion and comment on the news and on public and political affairs and events.

As to the meaning of 'company', see s 735; as to the meaning of 'subsidiary undertaking', see ss 347A(11), 258, Sch 10.

347C. Prohibition on donations and political expenditure by companies

(1)   A company must not—

(a)   make any donation to any registered party or to any other EU political organisation, or

(b)   incur any EU political expenditure,

unless the donation or expenditure is authorised by virtue of an approval resolution passed by the company in general meeting before the relevant time.

This subsection has effect subject to section 347D(3).

(2)   For the purposes of this section an approval resolution is a qualifying resolution which authorises the company to do either (or both) of the following, namely—

(a)   make donations to EU political organisations not exceeding in total a sum specified in the resolution, or

(b)   incur EU political expenditure not exceeding in total a sum so specified,

during the requisite period beginning with the date of the resolution.

(3)   In subsection (2)—

(a)   'qualifying resolution' means an ordinary resolution or, if the directors so determine or the articles so require—

(i)   a special resolution, or

(ii)   a resolution passed by any percentage of the members greater than that required for an ordinary resolution;

(b)   'the requisite period' means four years or such shorter period as the directors may determine or the articles may require;

and the directors may make a determination for the purposes of paragraph (a) or (b) above except where any provision of the articles operates to prevent them from doing so.

(4)   The resolution must be expressed in general terms conforming with subsection (2), and accordingly may not purport to authorise particular donations or expenditure.

(5)   Where a company makes any donation or incurs any expenditure in contravention of subsection (1), no ratification or other approval made or given by the company or its members after the relevant time is capable of operating to nullify that contravention.

(6)   Nothing in this section enables a company to be authorised to do anything that it could not lawfully do apart from this section.

S 347C(1)

Prior authorisation required   Where the donation or expenditure is within this provision and not within the exemptions provided by s 347B(4) (£5,000 threshold) or s 347B(8) (exemption by order), authorisation by the company in general meeting in the form of an 'approval resolution' is required.

This authorisation must be obtained before the donation is made or expenditure incurred, or before the company is contractually bound to make the donation or incur the expenditure, if earlier (the 'relevant time'): see s 347A(10). 'Donation' is defined in s 347A(4), subject to s 347B(1); 'registered party' is defined in s 347A(9); 'EU political organisation' is defined in s 347A(6), subject to s 347B(3); and 'EU political expenditure' is defined in s 347A(5).

Where the company which must seek authorisation is a wholly-owned subsidiary, see s 347D(3); where the company which must seek authorisation is a subsidiary but not a wholly-owned subsidiary, see s 347D(2).

As to the consequences where a company has made any donation or incurred any expenditure in contravention of this provision, see s 347F.

S 347C(2)–(4)

An approval resolution   These provisions set out detailed requirements as to the 'approval resolution' and a failure to adhere to these requirements will mean a contravention of the section attracting the penalties imposed by s 347F; subsequent ratification is not possible (sub-s (5)). A private company may use a written resolution: s 381A.

The resolution:

(1)   may relate to donations or political expenditure or both;

(2)   must not identify specific donations or expenditure, but must seek authorisation for a global amount over the requisite period. That period cannot exceed four years beginning with the date of the resolution. A shorter period may be specified at the determination of the directors (unless prevented from doing so by the articles) or as required by the articles, and larger public companies are likely to seek authority on an annual basis rather than for a lengthier period of time;

(3)   may be an ordinary resolution. A special resolution or a resolution 'by any percentage of the members greater than that required for an ordinary resolution' may be required at the determination of the directors (unless

prevented from doing so by the articles) or as required by the articles. There is no equivalent provision elsewhere in the legislation for the latter type of resolution. It may be that the intention here was to allow for a majority which is more than a simple majority and less than the 75% majority required by a special resolution. However, this is not what the wording says and a resolution requiring, for example, a 90% majority could be specified.

Donations which are within the £5,000 threshold in a qualifying period do not count towards the sum specified in the resolution (s 347B(5)); nor do sums exempted by order under s 347B(8): s 347B(9).

S 347C(5)

No ratification   This provision imposes a comprehensive prohibition on ratification or 'other approval' (for example, by informal unanimous consent) after the relevant time (defined in s 347A(10)). The consequences of an unauthorised payment are set out in s 347F.

S 347C(6)

Authorisation ineffective in certain cases   A company may have provisions in its memorandum of association or articles prohibiting political donations and the company cannot override those provisions by seeking authorisation under this section. Equally, other legal requirements, for example, in the Political Parties, Elections and Referendums Act 2000, cannot be overridden by an authorisation under this section.

347D. Special rules for subsidiaries

(1)   This section applies where a company is a subsidiary of another company ('the holding company').

(2)   Where the subsidiary is not a wholly-owned subsidiary of the holding company—

(a) it must not make any donation or incur any expenditure to which subsection (1) of section 347C applies unless the donation or expenditure is authorised by virtue of a subsidiary approval resolution passed by the holding company in general meeting before the relevant time; and

(b) this requirement applies in addition to that imposed by that subsection.

(3)   Where the subsidiary is a wholly-owned subsidiary of the holding company—

(a) it must not make any donation or incur any expenditure to which subsection (1) of section 347C applies unless the donation or expenditure is authorised by virtue of a subsidiary approval resolution passed by the holding company in general meeting before the relevant time; and

(b) this requirement applies in place of that imposed by that subsection.

(4) For the purposes of this section a subsidiary approval resolution is a qualifying resolution of the holding company which authorises the subsidiary to do either (or both) of the following, namely—

(a) make donations to EU political organisations not exceeding in total a sum specified in the resolution, or

(b) incur EU political expenditure not exceeding in total a sum so specified,

during the requisite period beginning with the date of the resolution.

(5) Subsection (3) of section 347C shall apply for the purposes of subsection (4) above as it applies for the purposes of subsection (2) of that section.

(6) The resolution must be expressed in general terms conforming with subsection (4), and accordingly may not purport to authorise particular donations or expenditure.

(7) The resolution may not relate to donations or expenditure by more than one subsidiary.

(8) Where a subsidiary makes any donation or incurs any expenditure in contravention of subsection (2) or (3), no ratification or other approval made or given by the holding company or its members after the relevant time is capable of operating to nullify that contravention.

(9) Nothing in this section enables a company to be authorised to do anything that it could not lawfully do apart from this section.

S 347D(1)

'Company' is defined in s 735; 'subsidiary' is defined in s 736.

S 347D(2)–(7)

As to whether the donation or expenditure is one for which authorisation is required, see the note to s 347C(1), above.

If authorisation is required, the procedure imposed by these provisions varies depending on whether or not the subsidiary is a wholly-owned subsidiary.

Company is not a wholly-owned subsidiary   If the company which is to make the donation or incur the expenditure is not a wholly–owned subsidiary, a subsidiary approval resolution is required of the holding company under this provision *and* an approval resolution is required of the subsidiary under s 347C.

Company is a wholly-owned subsidiary   If the company which is to make the donation or incur the expenditure is a wholly-owned subsidiary, a subsidiary approval resolution is required *only* of the holding company under this provision and the subsidiary does not require an approval resolution under s 347C.

Subsidiary approval resolution   As to the subsidiary approval resolution required of the holding company, these provisions mirror those in s 347C(2)–(4) as to the contents and nature of an approval resolution: see the notes to those provisions, above. An additional point to note here is the requirement for separate resolutions for donations or expenditure by each subsidiary. As to the relevant time, see s 347A(10).

Donations which are within the £5,000 threshold in a qualifying period do not count towards the sum specified in the subsidiary approval resolution (s 347B(5)); nor do sums exempted by order under s 347B(8) (s 347B(9)).

As to the consequences where a company has made any donation or incurred any expenditure in contravention of this provision, see s 347F.

S 347D(8), (9)

See notes to s 347C(5), (6), above.

347E. Special rule for parent company of non-GB subsidiary undertaking

(1)   This section applies where a company ('the parent company') has a subsidiary undertaking which is incorporated or otherwise established outside Great Britain.

(2)   The parent company shall take all such steps as are reasonably open to it to secure that the subsidiary undertaking does not make any donation or incur any expenditure to which subsection (1) of section 347C applies except to the extent that the donation or expenditure is authorised by virtue of a subsidiary approval resolution passed by the parent company in general meeting before the relevant time.

(3)   For the purposes of this section a subsidiary approval resolution is a qualifying resolution of the parent company which authorises the subsidiary undertaking to do either (or both) of the following, namely—

(a)   make donations to EU political organisations not exceeding in total a sum specified in the resolution, or

(b)   incur EU political expenditure not exceeding in total a sum so specified,

during the requisite period beginning with the date of the resolution.

(4)   Subsection (3) of section 347C shall apply for the purposes of subsection (3) above as it applies for the purposes of subsection (2) of that section.

(5)   The resolution must be expressed in general terms conforming with subsection (3), and accordingly may not purport to authorise particular donations or expenditure.

(6)   The resolution may not relate to donations or expenditure by more than one subsidiary undertaking.

(7)   Where a subsidiary undertaking makes any donation or incurs any expenditure which (to any extent) is not authorised as mentioned in subsection (2), no ratification or other approval made or given by the parent company or its members after the relevant time is capable of operating to authorise that donation or expenditure.

General note

The legislation attempts to prevent evasion by donations or expenditure through non-GB subsidiary undertakings by imposing obligations on the GB parent company and its directors to ensure any donation or expenditure is made only with the authorisation of the parent company.

S 347E(1)

'Company' is defined in s 735; 'subsidiary undertaking' is defined in s 258, Sch 10A (s 347A(11)); and that definition is not limited to bodies corporate, nor is this provision restricted to wholly-owned subsidiary undertakings.

S 347E(2)–(6)

As to whether the donation or expenditure is one for which authorisation is required, see the note to s 347C(1), above.

Subsidiary approval resolution   As to the subsidiary approval resolution required of the parent company, these provisions mirror those in s 347C(2)–(4) as to the contents and nature of an approval resolution: see the notes to those provisions, above. An additional point to note here is the requirement for separate resolutions for donations or expenditure by each subsidiary undertaking. As to the relevant time, see s 347A(10).

Donations which are within the £5,000 threshold in a qualifying period do not count towards the sum specified in the subsidiary approval resolution (s 347B(5)); nor do sums exempted by order under s 347B(8) (s 347B(9)).

Obligations of the parent company   The obligation in this case on the parent company is to take *all* such steps as are *reasonably* open to it to ensure no unauthorised donations are made or expenditure incurred. It is not clear what is envisaged by this requirement, and the steps which are reasonably open to the parent will depend on the degree of control which the parent company has of the subsidiary undertaking.

Given the potential personal liability which the directors of the parent company may incur in the event of a breach of these provisions (see s 347G), it will be of considerable importance to have in place information and control mechanisms as between the parent company and the non-GB subsidiary undertaking which are sufficient to prevent unauthorised donations or expenditure of this nature.

S 347E(7)

See note to s 347C(5).

347F. Remedies for breach of prohibitions on company donations etc

(1)   This section applies where a company has made any donation or incurred any expenditure in contravention of any of the provisions of sections 347C and 347D.

(2)   Every person who was a director of the company at the relevant time is liable to pay the company—

    (a) the amount of the donation or expenditure made or incurred in contravention of the provisions in question; and

    (b) damages in respect of any loss or damage sustained by the company as a result of the donation or expenditure having been made or incurred in contravention of those provisions.

(3)   Every such person is also liable to pay the company interest on the amount mentioned in subsection (2)(a) in respect of the period—

    (a) beginning with the date when the donation or expenditure was made or incurred, and

    (b) ending with the date when that amount is paid to the company by any such person;

and such interest shall be payable at such rate as the Secretary of State may prescribe by regulations.

(4)   Where two or more persons are subject to a particular liability arising by virtue of any provision of this section, each of those persons is jointly and severally liable.

(5)   Where only part of any donation or expenditure was made or incurred in contravention of any of the provisions of sections 347C and 347D, this section applies only to so much of it as was so made or incurred.

(6)   Where—

    (a) this section applies as mentioned in subsection (1), and

    (b) the company in question is a subsidiary of another company ('the holding company'),

then (subject to subsection (7)) subsections (2) to (5) shall, in connection with the donation or expenditure made or incurred by the subsidiary, apply in relation to the holding company as they apply in relation to the subsidiary.

(7)   Those subsections do not apply in relation to the holding company if—

    (a) the subsidiary is not a wholly-owned subsidiary of the holding company; and

    (b) the donation or expenditure was authorised by such a resolution of the holding company as is mentioned in section 347D(2)(a).

(8)   Nothing in section 727 shall apply in relation to any liability of any person arising under this section.

General note

The intention here is to ensure that the obligations imposed on directors by this Part are obligations owed to the company and in respect of which the company may obtain recompense; provision is made additionally for shareholders to enforce the directors' liability under this provision by derivative action: see s 347I.

S 347F(2)–(5), (8)

Directors' liabilities   These provisions impose joint and several liability on the directors (including shadow directors, see s 347A(3)) who were in office at the time the donation was made or the expenditure incurred etc (see s 347A(10) as to the relevant time) in contravention of s 347C, s 347D (see notes to those provisions, above).
   The liability is to pay to the company which has made the donation etc:
   (1)   the amount of the donation or expenditure;
   (2)   damages in respect of any loss sustained etc as a result of the donation or expenditure – this potentially allows for the recovery of indirect losses such as the loss of customers, damage to goodwill, and damage to reputation although it would be difficult to establish and to quantify such losses; and
   (3)   interest.

Any director liable under these provisions is precluded from seeking relief from the court under s 727 (see note to that provision, below), although more limited relief is provided by s 347H.

S 347F(6)–(8)

Liabilities where payments by subsidiaries   These provisions apply the liabilities noted above to a number of different situations. As different rules apply to donations etc made by wholly-owned subsidiaries and by non-wholly-owned subsidiaries (see s 347D(3) and (2) respectively), this results in a number of permutations as to liabilities under these provisions.

Wholly-owned subsidiary   Where there is a contravention as defined in sub-s (1) by a wholly-owned subsidiary, the liability imposed on directors as outlined above applies to the directors of the holding company and to the directors of the subsidiary.

Subsidiary is not a wholly-owned subsidiary   Where the subsidiary is not a wholly-owned subsidiary, a resolution of the holding company and of the subsidiary company is required (s 347D(2)) and so there are two possible breaches here:
   (1)   the holding company has not authorised the donation or expenditure but the subsidiary company has authorised it: in that case, the liability imposed on directors as outlined above applies to the directors of the holding company and to the directors of the subsidiary;
   (2)   the holding company has authorised the donation or expenditure but the subsidiary company has not authorised it: in that case, liability attaches only to the directors of the subsidiary.

Any director liable under these provisions is precluded from seeking relief from the court under s 727 (see note to that provision, below), although more limited relief is provided by s 347H.

347G. Remedy for unauthorised donation or expenditure by non-GB subsidiary

(1) This section applies where—

   (a) a company ('the parent company') has a subsidiary undertaking falling within subsection (1) of section 347E;

   (b) the subsidiary undertaking has made any donation or incurred any expenditure to which subsection (1) of section 347C applies; and

   (c) the parent company has, in relation to that donation or expenditure, failed to discharge its duty under subsection (2) of section 347E to take all such steps as are mentioned in that subsection.

(2) Subsections (2) to (4) of section 347F shall, in connection with the donation or expenditure made or incurred by the subsidiary undertaking, apply in relation to the holding company as if—

   (a) it were a company falling within subsection (1) of that section, and

   (b) the donation or expenditure had been made or incurred by it in contravention of section 347C or 347D.

(3) Where only part of the donation or expenditure was not authorised as mentioned in section 347E(2), those subsections shall so apply only to that part of it.

(4) Section 347F(8) applies to any liability of any person arising under section 347F by virtue of this section.

S 347G(1)

Application   This provision applies to a parent company which has a non-GB subsidiary undertaking which has made an unauthorised donation or expenditure in contravention of s 347C(1) (see note to that provision, above) and the parent company has failed to take all of the steps required of it by s 347E(2); see generally the note to s 347E, above.

S 347G(2), (3)

Directors' liabilities   The result of the parent company falling within sub-s (1) above is that it is treated as a company within s 347F(1), ie as a company in contravention of ss 347C, 347D, which results in the directors of the parent company being liable to the extent provided by s 347F(2)–(4) (see notes to those provisions, above). Provision is made additionally for shareholders to enforce the directors' liability under this provision by derivative action: see s 347I.

S 347G(4)

See note to s 347F(8).

347H. Exemption of directors from liability in respect of unauthorised donation or expenditure

(1) Where proceedings are brought against a director or former director of a company in respect of any liability arising under section 347F(2)(a) in connection with a donation or expenditure made or incurred by the company, it shall be a defence for that person to show that—

    (a) the unauthorised amount has been repaid to the company, together with any interest on that amount due under section 347F(3);

    (b) that repayment has been approved by the company in general meeting; and

    (c) in the notice of the relevant resolution submitted to that meeting full disclosure was made—

        (i) of the circumstances in which the donation or expenditure was made or incurred in contravention of section 347C or 347D, and

        (ii) of the circumstances in which, and the person or persons by whom, the repayment was made.

(2) Where proceedings are brought against a director or former director of a holding company in respect of any liability arising under section 347F(2)(a) in connection with a donation or expenditure made or incurred by a subsidiary of the company, it shall be a defence for that person to show that—

    (a) the unauthorised amount has been repaid either to the subsidiary or to the holding company, together with any interest on that amount due under section 347F(3);

    (b) that repayment has been approved—

        (i) (if made to the subsidiary) by both the subsidiary and the holding company in general meeting, or

        (ii) (if made to the holding company) by the holding company in general meeting; and

    (c) in the notice of the relevant resolution submitted to each of those meetings or (as the case may be) to that meeting, full disclosure was made—

        (i) of the circumstances in which the donation or expenditure was made in contravention of section 347D, and

        (ii) of the circumstances in which, and the person or persons by whom, the repayment was made.

(3) If the subsidiary is a wholly-owned subsidiary of the holding company, it is not necessary for the purposes of subsection (2) to show (where the repayment was made to the subsidiary) that the repayment has been approved by the subsidiary, and paragraphs (b) and (c) of that subsection shall apply accordingly.

(4) Where proceedings are brought against a director or former director of a holding company in respect of any liability arising under section 347F(2)(a) in connection with a donation or expenditure made or incurred by a subsidiary of the company which is not a wholly-owned subsidiary, then (subject to subsection (5)) it shall be a defence for that person to show that—

    (a) proceedings have been instituted by the subsidiary against all or any of its directors in respect of the unauthorised amount; and

    (b) those proceedings are being pursued with due diligence by the subsidiary.

(5) A person may not avail himself of the defence provided by subsection (4) except with the leave of the court; and on an application for leave under this subsection the court may make such order as it thinks fit, including an order adjourning, or sanctioning the continuation of, the proceedings against the applicant on such terms and conditions as it thinks fit.

(6) Where proceedings are brought against a director or former director of a company in respect of any liability arising under section 347F(2)(a) (as applied by virtue of section 347G) in connection with a donation or expenditure made or incurred by a subsidiary undertaking of the company, it shall be a defence for that person to show that—

    (a) the unauthorised amount has been repaid to the subsidiary undertaking, together with any interest on that amount due under section 347F(3) (as so applied);

    (b) that repayment has been approved by the company in general meeting; and

    (c) in the notice of the relevant resolution submitted to that meeting full disclosure was made—

        (i) of the circumstances in which the donation or expenditure was made without having been authorised as mentioned in section 347E(2), and

        (ii) of the circumstances in which, and the person or persons by whom, the repayment was made.

(7) In this section 'the unauthorised amount', in relation to any donation or expenditure, means the amount of the donation or expenditure—

    (a) which was made or incurred in contravention of section 347C or 347D, or

    (b) which was not authorised as mentioned in section 347E(2),

as the case may be.

S 347H(1)

Defences for directors when company in breach   This provision provides a defence for a director (defined s 347A(3)) or former director liable as a result of a contravention by the company of any of the provisions of ss 347C and 347D. The conditions which must be met are quite onerous in that not only must there be a repayment of the entire amount plus interest, but that repayment must have been approved by the company in general meeting following full disclosure of the circumstances of the payment and repayment. The unauthorised amount is defined in sub-s (7).

S 347H(2)–(5)

Defences for directors of holding company   These provision provide defences for a director (defined s 347A(3)) or former director of a holding company liable as a result of a contravention by a subsidiary company of any of the provisions of ss 347C, 347D.

Generally, the directors of a holding company can be liable in two instances, see notes to s 347F(6)–(8), above:

(1)   where the contravention is by a wholly-owned subsidiary. In this case, the defence in sub-s (2) is available; the repayment may be to the holding company or the subsidiary company (see definitions in s 736); and no resolution of the subsidiary company is required if the repayment is made to it (sub-s (3)). As to the nature of the defence, see the comment to sub-s (1), above;

(2)   where the contravention is by a subsidiary which is not wholly-owned and the donation or expenditure has not been authorised by the holding company. In this case, the defence in sub-s (2) is available but the repayment, presumably, must be made to the subsidiary and so sub-s (2)(b)(i) applies; it will also be possible to rely on the defence under sub-s (4) but only with the leave of the court: sub-s (5).

S 347H(6)

Defences when breach by non-GB subsidiary undertaking   This provision provides a defence for a director (defined s 347A(3)) or former director of a parent company liable as a result of a contravention by a non-GB subsidiary undertaking of any of the provisions of s 347C: see ss 347E, 347G. As to the nature of the defence, see the comment to sub-s (1). The repayment must be to the subsidiary undertaking, but the approval of the repayment must be by the parent company.

347I. Enforcement of directors' liabilities by shareholder action

(1)   Any liability of any person under section 347F or 347G as a director or former director of a company is (in addition to being enforceable by proceedings brought by the company) enforceable by proceedings brought under this section in the name of the company by an authorised group of members of the company.

(2)   For the purposes of this section 'authorised group', in relation to the members of a company, means any such combination of members as is specified in section 54(2)(a), (b) or (c).

(3)   An authorised group of members of a company may not bring proceedings under this section unless—

(a)   the group has given written notice to the company stating—

(i)   the cause of action and a summary of the facts on which the proceedings are to be based,

(ii)   the names and addresses of the members of the company comprising the group, and

(iii) the grounds on which it is alleged that those members constitute an authorised group; and

(b)   not less than 28 days have elapsed between the date of the giving of the notice to the company and the institution of the proceedings.

(4)   Where such a notice is given to a company, any director may apply to the court within the period of 28 days beginning with the date of the giving of

the notice for an order directing that the proposed proceedings are not to be instituted.

(5)   An application under subsection (4) may be made on one or more of the following grounds—

   (a) that the unauthorised amount within the meaning of section 347H has been repaid to the company or subsidiary undertaking as mentioned in subsection (1), (2), (4) or (6) of that section (as the case may be) and the other conditions mentioned in that subsection were satisfied with respect to that repayment;

   (b) that proceedings to enforce the liability have been instituted by the company and are being pursued with due diligence by the company;

   (c) that the members proposing to institute proceedings under this section do not constitute an authorised group.

(6)   Where such an application is made on the ground mentioned in subsection (5)(b), the court may make such order as it thinks fit; and such an order may, as an alternative to directing that the proposed proceedings under this section are not to be instituted, direct—

   (a) that those proceedings may be instituted on such terms and conditions as the court thinks fit;

   (b) that the proceedings instituted by the company are to be discontinued;

   (c) that the proceedings instituted by the company may be continued on such terms and conditions as the court thinks fit.

(7)   If proceedings are brought under this section by an authorised group of members of a company, the group shall owe the same duties to the company in relation to the bringing of those proceedings on behalf of the company as would be owed by the directors of the company if the proceedings were being brought by the company itself; but no proceedings to enforce any duty owed by virtue of this subsection shall be brought by the company except with the leave of the court.

(8)   Proceedings brought under this section may not be discontinued or settled by the group except with the leave of the court; and the court may grant leave under this subsection on such terms as it thinks fit.

S 347I(1)

A derivative action   This provision enables an authorised group of members to bring a derivative action on behalf of the company to enforce the liability of the directors arising under s 347F (remedies for breach of the prohibitions on company donations etc) or s 347G (remedy for unauthorised donations or expenditure by non-GB subsidiary undertaking).

S 347I(2)

An authorised group of members   Those entitled to bring the proceedings are defined by reference to s 54(2) (those entitled to challenge the re-registration of a public company as a private company). No shareholders other than those so defined will be able to bring a shareholder action.

In practice, it is difficult to imagine that any shareholders would want to bring proceedings: they may have difficulty obtaining the information on which to bring a case (and see s 347K); any benefit obtained is solely for the company; the shareholders are not entitled as of right to their costs from the company; and they may be liable for costs: see s 347J.

S 347I(3)–(8)

These provisions set out very definite criteria as to when proceedings may be brought and how they may be discontinued or settled etc.

347J. Costs of shareholder action

(1)   This section applies in relation to proceedings brought under section 347I by an authorised group of members of a company ('the group').

(2)   The group may apply to the court for an order directing the company to indemnify the group in respect of costs incurred or to be incurred by the group in connection with the proceedings; and on such an application the court may make such an order on such terms as it thinks fit.

(3)   The group shall not be entitled to be paid any such costs out of the assets of the company except by virtue of such an order.

(4)   If—
   (a) the company is awarded costs in connection with the proceedings or it is agreed that costs incurred by the company in connection with the proceedings should be paid by any defendant, and
   (b) no order has been made with respect to the proceedings under subsection (2),

the costs shall be paid to the group.

(5)   If—
   (a) any defendant is awarded costs in connection with the proceedings or it is agreed that any defendant should be paid costs incurred by him in connection with the proceedings, and
   (b) no order has been made with respect to the proceedings under subsection (2),

the costs shall be paid by the group.

(6)   In the application of this section to Scotland references to costs are to expenses and references to any defendant are to any defender.

S 347J(2)

Court order required   In practice, this is likely to be the key provision, since the company is prohibited by sub-s (3) from paying the costs incurred or to be incurred out of the company's assets without a court order. If a group fails to secure a court order under this provision, they are unlikely to want to proceed with the action, particularly in the light of sub-s (5); as to the discontinuance of proceedings, see s 347I(8).

347K. Information for purposes of shareholder action

(1) Where any proceedings have been instituted under section 347I by an authorised group within the meaning of that section, the group is entitled to require the company to provide the group with all information relating to the subject matter of the proceedings which is in the company's possession or under its control or which is reasonably obtainable by it.

(2) If the company, having been required by the group to provide the information referred to in subsection (1), refuses to provide the group with all or any of the information, the court may, on an application made by the group, make an order directing—

     (a) the company, and

     (b) any of its officers or employees specified in the application,

to provide the group with the information in question in such form and by such means as the court may direct.

General note

It was essential to make some provision of this nature to enable a group to obtain the information necessary to exercise its rights under s 347I, but the wording only allows them to seek the assistance of this provision where proceedings 'have been instituted'. In effect, they must institute proceedings on the basis of their own knowledge and then seek to exercise this power in order to determine, inter alia, whether to continue the proceedings.

PART XI

COMPANY ADMINISTRATION AND PROCEDURE

CHAPTER I

COMPANY IDENTIFICATION

.

348. Company name to appear outside place of business

(1)   Every company shall paint or affix, and keep painted or affixed, its name on the outside of every office or place in which its business is carried on, in a conspicuous position and in letters easily legible.

(2)   If a company does not paint or affix its name as required above, the company and every officer of it who is in default is liable to a fine; and if a company does not keep its name painted or affixed as so required, the company and every officer of it who is in default is liable to a fine and, for continued contravention, to a daily default fine.

General note

A company which trades under a business name must also comply with the requirements of the Business Names Act 1985.

S 348(1)

Company must display name   The obligation to display the name falls on the 'company', defined in s 735; the company's name must include the statutory designations ('public limited company' or 'limited'), or their permitted abbreviations (see ss 25, 27(2)), or the Welsh equivalents, if so entitled (see s 25). A company which is exempt from the requirement to include 'limited' in its title under s 30 is also exempt from this requirement: s 30(7).

The name must be displayed *outside* every office or place in which the company's business is carried on, which is defined in s 744 as including a share transfer or share registration office, activities which are typically conducted at the company's registered office. Even if the company has a registered office at which share transfer or registration is not carried on, being dealt with elsewhere, the registered office is still a place at which the business of the company is carried on, given that provision must be made for the maintenance of various records there (and some can only be maintained there) and for their inspection: see note to s 287, above. The provision is not limited to the places at which the company's trading or commercial activities are carried on but applies to any place at which the business of the company is carried on, and the conduct of its administrative affairs is part of its business.

Current problems   This provision, which dates back to the early part of the last century, may have worked well originally, but its application to some modern practices is problematic. Many family companies, for example, carry on business from the family home, which should display the company's name but probably does not, in breach of this provision, although the risk of prosecution is slim. Likewise, where the company uses a formation agent or its accountants or solicitors as its registered office, or where a larger company uses the services of a registration agent, those premises are places in which the business of the company is carried on and the provision requires that the company affix its name to those premises in a conspicuous position etc. Of course, this is frequently overlooked or ignored, or compliance is impractical, as where formation agents act as the registered office of a company for a relatively short period of time or registration agents act for a very large number of companies. Such businesses may instead maintain a list of companies for which they act as registered office in prominent display in the reception of the building, but this is not in compliance with this section and the company would remain in breach.

S 348(2)

As to penalties, see s 730, Sch 24, below. 'Officer in default' is defined in s 730(5).

349. Company's name to appear in its correspondence, etc

(1) Every company shall have its name mentioned in legible characters—
   (a) in all business letters of the company,
   (b) in all its notices and other official publications,
   (c) in all bills of exchange, promissory notes, endorsements, cheques and orders for money or goods purporting to be signed by or on behalf of the company, and
   (d) in all its bills of parcels, invoices, receipts and letters of credit.

(2) If a company fails to comply with subsection (1) it is liable to a fine.

(3) If an officer of a company or a person on its behalf—
   (a) issues or authorises the issue of any business letter of the company, or any notice or other official publication of the company, in which the company's name is not mentioned as required by subsection (1), or
   (b) issues or authorises the issue of any bill of parcels, invoice, receipt or letter of credit of the company in which its name is not so mentioned,

he is liable to a fine.

(4) If an officer of a company or a person on its behalf signs or authorises to be signed on behalf of the company any bill of exchange, promissory note, endorsement, cheque or order for money or goods in which the company's name is not mentioned as required by subsection (1), he is liable to a fine; and he is further personally liable to the holder of the bill of exchange, promissory note, cheque or order for money or goods for the amount of it (unless it is duly paid by the company).

General note

Potential personal liability   This provision is of considerable practical importance as company officers may find themselves personally liable in the circumstances prescribed by sub-s (4) if the company's name is not stated as required; and the omission can be something very simple such as the failure to include 'Ltd' or 'p.l.c'.

The financial penalty may be significant in a particular case and the provision has been criticised as an excessive penalty for what is no more than an administrative error; but the courts have taken the view that this outcome must have been apparent to Parliament when the provision was first created: see *Rafsanjan Pistachio*

Producers Co-operative v Reiss [1990] BCLC 352 at 363 (company name omitted entirely from cheques, director personally liable); and a provision to this effect has been in the companies legislation for many decades.

Statutory requirements　As to the requirements to publish the company's name outside any place of business, see s 348, above; see further requirements as to publicity in s 351, below. A company which is exempt from the requirement to include 'limited' in its title under s 30 is also exempt from these requirements relating to the publication of its name: s 30(7). A company which trades under a business name must also comply with the requirements of the Business Names Act 1985.

　The wording of this section is unchanged from that in CA 1948, s 108, to which some of the cases refer.

S 349(1)

By name is meant the registered corporate name; the fact that the company has another name under the Business Names Act 1985 is irrelevant to the application of this provision: *Maxform SpA v Mariani & Goodville Ltd* [1981] 2 Lloyd's Rep 54. The company's name must include the statutory designations ('public limited company' or 'limited') or their permitted abbreviations: see ss 25, 27(2), above. The requirement that the corporate name appear in all business letters would include in all business e-mails, being simply letters sent by electronic communication.

S 349(2)

As to penalties, see s 730, Sch 24. The only consequence for the company is a fine; and a company in breach of this requirement is not prevented from suing to protect its goodwill by restraining a company trading under a similar name: *HE Randall Ltd v British and American Shoe Co Ltd* [1902] 2 Ch 354. More significant liabilities arise for officers under sub-s (4).

S 349(3)

Criminal liability under this provision attaches to breaches of sub-s (1)(a), (b) and (d); liability for breach of (c) is the subject of sub-s (4). As to penalties, see s 730, Sch 24, below; 'officer' is defined in s 744.

S 349(4)

This provision imposes liability on an officer of a company or a person acting on its behalf, but the liability falls mainly on the officers of the company, for any other person acting on its behalf will have been authorised by the officers so to act.

　Where the liability arises from the authorised signature of another, the officer is not liable unless the authority given is not merely to sign the document but to sign on a document which does not contain the company's name as required; although that authority may be inferred and it may not always be necessary to find a specific authorisation to use a specific incorrect form: *John Wilkes (Footwear) Ltd v Lee*

International (Footwear) Ltd [1985] BCLC 444 (action brought against director who authorised the transaction as well as the director who signed the order form).

It may be that the requirement that the officer 'signs or authorises to be signed on behalf of the company' requires that there must be some affixing of the company's name to the instrument by writing under hand and not by a stamp or some printed name: see *Oshkosh B'gosh Inc v Dan Marbel Inc Ltd* [1989] BCLC 507 at 512.

The provision does not require that the misdescription be a material one: *Atkin v Wardle* (1889) 58 LJQB 377; *Durham Fancy Goods v Michael Jackson (Fancy Goods)* [1968] 2 All ER 987; but see *Jenice Ltd v Dan* [1993] BCLC 1349.

Abbreviations   The company's name includes the statutory designations 'limited' and 'public limited company' and the permitted abbreviations of those designations (see ss 25, 27(2), above). It is vital therefore that these designations (or the Welsh equivalents, if so entitled (see s 25)) are not omitted: see *Lindholst & Co A/S v Fowler* [1988] BCLC 166 ('Ltd' omitted, director personally liable); *Blum v OCP Repartition SA* [1988] BCLC 170 ('Limited' omitted, director liable); *Novaknit Hellas SA v Kumar Bros International Ltd* [1998] CLC 971 ('Limited' omitted, directors liable).

Where there is an accepted abbreviation of a word which is treated as equivalent to that word, and where there is no other word which is abbreviated to that particular abbreviation, and where there is no question of the registrar of companies accepting for registration two companies, both of which have the same name, except that one contains the full word and the other the abbreviated word, then in those circumstances there is absolutely no possibility of any confusion arising by reason of the abbreviation, and use of the abbreviation is permissible: *Banque de l'Indochine et de Suez SA v Euroseas Group Finance Co Ltd* [1981] 3 All ER 198 at 202. Hence 'Co' is an acceptable abbreviation of 'Company': *Banque de l'Indochine et de Suez SA v Euroseas Group Finance Co Ltd* [1981] 3 All ER 198; likewise, semble, 'and' and an ampersand: see *Banque de l'Indochine et de Suez SA v Euroseas Group Finance Co Ltd*.

However, the abbreviation of a word in the company's name to an initial is unacceptable; and a bill of exchange accepted in the name of 'M Jackson (Fancy Goods) Ltd' was in breach of the provision when the company's name was Michael Jackson (Fancy Goods) Ltd: *Durham Fancy Goods v Michael Jackson (Fancy Goods)* [1968] 2 All ER 987.

Omissions   The omission of an ampersand so that L & R Agencies Ltd was written as L R Agencies Ltd is a breach of the provision: *Hendon v Adelman* (1973) 117 Sol Jo 631; see also *Rafsanjan Pistachio Producers Co-operative v Reiss* [1990] BCLC 352 (company name omitted entirely from cheques, director personally liable).

Spelling or typographical errors   Where the name is mentioned but there is a spelling or typographical error which could not mislead anyone either as to the fact that the company is a limited company or as to the identify of the company, then the officer should not be liable: *Jenice Ltd v Dan* [1993] BCLC 1349 ('Primkeen' printed on company's cheques instead of 'Primekeen').

Rectification and estoppel   Rectification of cheques etc to reflect the intention of the parties that the cheque should be a company cheque is not possible, for the purpose of the rectification is not to reflect the true bargain between the parties but to enable an officer to escape the liability imposed by s 349 and to deprive the recipient of the benefit of the statutory liability imposed upon the signatory: *Rafsanjan Pistachio Producers Co-operative v Reiss* [1990] BCLC 352; *Blum v OCP Repartition SA* [1988] BCLC 170.

In *Durham Fancy Goods v Michael Jackson (Fancy Goods)* [1968] 2 All ER 987 a bill of exchange was accepted by the company's officers in the incorrect name of M Jackson (Fancy Goods) Ltd. The officers were personally liable but the court found that the claimant was estopped by its own conduct from enforcing that liability (the claimants induced the error by prescribing the form of words required for acceptance). Outside of those exceptional circumstances, the courts are reluctant to accept an argument based on estoppel: see *Lindholst & Co A/S v Fowler* [1988] BCLC 166 (no words prescribed, it was for the officers to accept the bill of exchange in the proper form prescribed by statute; directors who signed were liable); see also *Blum v OCP Repartition SA* [1988] BCLC 170 at 175; *Rafsanjan Pistachio Producers Co-operative v Reiss* [1990] BCLC 352 at 358–360.

Liability   The position of an officer who is personally liable under this provision is not one which was identical in its legal consequences with the liability of a guarantor or surety under a contract of guarantee: *British Airways Board v Parish* [1979] 2 Lloyd's Rep 361.

An officer found liable under this provision is able to seek an indemnity from the company but, in practice, this remedy will be worthless as the third party will only have sued the officer because the company is in insolvent liquidation.

The fact that the recipient of the dishonoured cheques has obtained judgment against the company with respect to them (but has been unable to recover on that judgment) does not preclude the recipient from pursuing the officer for personal liability, since the remedies are concurrent, the only limit being that the third party cannot recover twice: *Maxform SpA v Mariani and Goodville Ltd* [1981] 2 Lloyd's Rep 54.

Whether a document is a bill of exchange or promissory note must be determined in accordance with the specialist meaning of those terms contained in the Bills of Exchange Act 1882, as amended.

350. Company seal

(1)   A company which has a common seal shall have its name engraved in legible characters on the seal; and if it fails to comply with this subsection it is liable to a fine.

(2)   If an officer of a company or a person on its behalf uses or authorises the use of any seal purporting to be a seal of the company on which its name is not engraved as required by subsection (1), he is liable to a fine.

S 350(1)

A company seal is no longer required (s 36A(3)); but where the company retains a seal, then it must meet these requirements; use of the permitted abbreviations of the statutory designations (see ss 25, 27(2), above) or the Welsh equivalents, if so entitled (see s 25, above) is permissible. Although the point is not free from difficulty, it seems that a company which chooses to have a seal may only have one seal subject to the express statutory provision for a seal for use abroad and a seal for securities purposes: see ss 39, 40, above. A company which is exempt from the requirement to include 'limited' in its title under s 30 is also exempt from the requirements of this provision: s 30(7).

As to penalties, see s 730, Sch 24, below.

S 350(2)

'Officer' is defined in s 744; the only penalty provided is a fine and it would seem that no further consequence is envisaged, ie the use of a seal where the name is not legible will not affect the validity of the document: see *HE Randall Ltd v British and American Shoe Co Ltd* [1902] 2 Ch 354; and see note to s 349(2) above. But the point is not free from difficulty.

As to penalties, see s 730, Sch 24, below.

351. Particulars in correspondence etc

(1)   Every company shall have the following particulars mentioned in legible characters in all business letters and order forms of the company, that is to say—

  (a) the company's place of registration and the number with which it is registered,

  (b) the address of its registered office,

  (c) in the case of an investment company (as defined in section 266), the fact that it is such a company, and

  (d) in the case of a limited company exempt from the obligation to use the word 'limited' as part of its name, the fact that it is a limited company.

(2)   If in the case of a company having a share capital there is on the stationery used for any such letters, or on the company's order forms, a reference to the amount of share capital, the reference must be to paid-up share capital.

(3), (4)   ...

(5)   As to contraventions of this section, the following applies—

  (a) if a company fails to comply with subsection (1) or (2), it is liable to a fine,

  (b) if an officer of a company or a person on its behalf issues or authorises the issue of any business letter or order form not complying with those subsections, he is liable to a fine,...

  (c) ...

S 351(1)

As to the registered office, see s 287, above; and note s 287(5). As to the exemption from the use of the word 'limited', see s 30, above; such exempt companies are subject to the requirements of this provision although exempt from the requirements of ss 348–350: s 30(7). As to alterations to the company's registered number, see s 705(4), below.

S 351(2)

This provision is obsolete as it is unheard of now for a company to include details of its share capital in this way.

S 351(5)

'Officer' is defined in s 744. As to penalties, see s 730, Sch 24, below.

CHAPTER II

REGISTER OF MEMBERS

352. Obligation to keep and enter up register

(1)   Every company shall keep a register of its members and enter in it the particulars required by this section.

(2)   There shall be entered in the register—
  (a) the names and addresses of the members;
  (b) the date on which each person was registered as a member; and
  (c) the date at which any person ceased to be a member.

(3)   The following applies in the case of a company having a share capital—
  (a) with the names and addresses of the members there shall be entered a statement—
    (i)   of the shares held by each member, distinguishing each share by its number (so long as the share has a number) and, where the company has more than one class of issued shares, by its class, and
    (ii) of the amount paid or agreed to be considered as paid on the shares of each member;
  (b) where the company has converted any of its shares into stock and given notice of the conversion to the registrar of companies, the register shall show the amount and class of stock held by each member, instead of the amount of shares and the particulars relating to shares specified in paragraph (a).

(4)   In the case of a company which does not have a share capital but has more than one class of members, there shall be entered in the register, with the names and addresses of the members, the class to which each member belongs.

(5)   If a company makes default in complying with this section, the company and every officer of it who is in default is liable to a fine and, for continued contravention, to a daily default fine.

(6)   An entry relating to a former member of the company may be removed from the register after the expiration of 20 years from the date on which he ceased to be a member.

(7)   Liability incurred by a company from the making or deletion of an entry in its register of members, or from a failure to make or delete any such entry, is not enforceable more than 20 years after the date on which the entry was made or deleted or, in the case of any such failure, the failure first occurred.
    This is without prejudice to any lesser period of limitation.

General note

As to the application of ss 352–362 to securities which are subject to settlement through CREST, the computerised settlement system, see generally the Uncertificated Securities Regulations 1995, SI 1995/3272, regs 19–25.

S 352(1)–(3)

The register   Entry on the register is essential to membership in all cases save that of subscribers to the memorandum, see s 22, above. In addition to the maintenance of this register by the company, information as to the membership of the company must be provided in the annual return each year to the registrar of companies: see ss 362–365, below.

As to the status of the register of members, see s 361, below. Inspection of the register is governed by s 356; and see the Companies (Inspection and Copying of Registers, Indices and Documents) Regulations 1991, SI 1991/1998. The register may be maintained otherwise than in a legible form, see ss 722, 723, below.

The company may also maintain an overseas branch register (see s 362, below) which is deemed to be part of the company's register of members: Sch 14, Pt II, para 2(1); copies of entries in the overseas branch register must be transmitted to the registered office as soon as may be after the entry is made and a duplicate of the overseas branch register must be kept with the principal register: Sch 14, Pt II, para 4.

Time limits   No time limit is set for the entry of information on the register, but any person aggrieved by a delay in entering or removing a name may apply to the court for the register to be rectified under s 359. For smaller companies, a court would probably regard a period in excess of two months to be unacceptable, by analogy with the two-month limit on the directors' power to refuse to register a transfer of shares (see s 183(5), above); for larger companies, a much shorter period would probably be required.

Information to be entered   The addresses to be entered must be those provided by the members, not an address inserted by the company: see *POW Services Ltd v Clare* [1995] 2 BCLC 435 at 451 (addresses inserted as c/o the company's offices); the date of entry on the register as a member and the date of ceasing to be a member may prove significant with regard to voting and dividend rights.

A company which is participating in CREST (the computerised securities settlement system operated by CRESTCo) must enter on the register of members in respect of any class of shares which are capable of settlement through CREST, how many shares each member holds in uncertificated and certificated form respectively: the Uncertificated Securities Regulations 1995, SI 1995/3272, reg 19(1). Breach of this provision attracts the sanctions provided for by sub-s (5) below: SI 1995/3272, reg 19(4).

Lien on the register   As the requirement to keep the register of members and make it available for inspection (s 356) is a statutory obligation, it is not possible for a solicitor (or accountant) to enforce a lien over the register: see *Re Capital Fire Insurance Association* (1883) 24 Ch D 408; *Re Anglo-Maltese Hydraulic Dock Co Ltd* (1885) 54 LJ Ch 730. A receiver appointed under a debenture which encompasses all of the property of the company is not entitled to retain the register of members which must be delivered to the liquidator: *Engel v South Metropolitan Brewing And Bottling Co* [1892] 1 Ch 442.

S 352(3), (4)

Classes of members   The composition of the classes of shareholders or members, as the case may be, must be ascertainable from the register. This information will facilitate, for example, those members and shareholders who need to approach other members of a class for their support for a particular matter and will help identify where control lies within a class.

S 352(5)

Penalties   As to penalties, see s 730, Sch 24, below; 'officer in default' is defined in s 730(5). In addition to these penalties, the extent of a director's responsibility for the failure by the company to comply with this provision is a matter to which the court must have regard in disqualification proceedings under the Company Directors Disqualification Act 1986: ss 6–9, Sch 1, para 4(d).

S 352(7)

This provision gives a company statutory immunity from liability with respect to entries on the register after 20 years but without prejudice to any shorter limitation period which may preclude a claim at an earlier date.

352A. Statement that company has only one member

(1)   If the number of members of a private company limited by shares or by guarantee falls to one there shall upon the occurrence of that event be entered in the company's register of members with the name and address of the sole member—

   (i)   a statement that the company has only one member, and

   (ii)   the date on which the company became a company having only one member.

(2)   If the membership of a private company limited by shares or by guarantee increases from one to two or more members there shall upon the occurrence of that event be entered in the company's register of members, with the name and address of the person who was formerly the sole member, a statement that the company has ceased to have only one member together with the date on which that event occurred.

(3)   If a company makes default in complying with this section, the company and every officer of it who is in default is liable to a fine and, for continued contravention, to a daily default fine.

General note

This provision was inserted by the Companies (Single Member Private Limited Companies) Regulations 1992, SI 1992/1699, which implemented the 12th Council Directive on Company Law ((EEC) 89/667) on single-member private limited liability companies: see [1989] OJ L395/40.

As to other provisions dealing with single member companies, see:

- s 1(3A) (mode of forming incorporated company);
- s 24 (minimum membership for carrying on business);
- s 322B (contracts with sole members who are directors);
- s 370A (quorum at meetings of sole member); and
- s 382B (recording of decisions by sole member).

S 352A(3)

As to penalties, see s 730, Sch 24, below; 'officer in default' is defined in s 730(5).

353. Location of register

(1) A company's register of members shall be kept at its registered office, except that—

    (a) if the work of making it up is done at another office of the company, it may be kept there; and

    (b) if the company arranges with some other person for the making up of the register to be undertaken on its behalf by that other, it may be kept at the office of the other at which the work is done;

but it must not be kept, in the case of a company registered in England and Wales, at any place elsewhere than in England and Wales or, in the case of a company registered in Scotland, at any place elsewhere than in Scotland.

(2) Subject as follows, every company shall send notice in the prescribed form to the registrar of companies of the place where its register of members is kept, and of any change in that place.

(3) The notice need not be sent if the register has, at all times since it came into existence (or, in the case of a register in existence on 1st July 1948, at all times since then) been kept at the company's registered office.

(4) If a company makes default for 14 days in complying with subsection (2), the company and every officer of it who is in default is liable to a fine and, for continued contravention, to a daily default fine.

S 353(1)

Location of the register   There is no obligation to keep the register of members at the registered office (as to which, see s 287) but it must be kept within England and Wales or Scotland, as the case may be. Where the register is kept otherwise than in a legible form (as permitted by ss 722, 723), the company is not required to keep the register at any place specified in the Act: the Companies (Registers and Other Records) Regulations 1985, SI 1985/724, reg 2(3)(a), which raises the question as to the location of the register in such cases. The Regulations go on, in effect, to equate the place of inspection of the register (which must be within the place of incorporation) with the place where the register is kept, and that may be an appropriate solution for the purposes of determining the location of any register kept otherwise than in a legible form.

Situation of the shares   As a general rule, shares are situated at the place where they can effectively be dealt with. In the ordinary way, this will be where the register of members is located, entry on the register being required for membership of the company (s 22). For companies incorporated in England and Wales or Scotland, the register must be kept within the place of incorporation with the result that the lex situs is the law of the place of incorporation: *A-G v Higgins* (1857) 2 H & N 339; *Brassard v Smith* [1925] AC 371. Where the shares are negotiable, for example, bearer warrants, the position may be different, with the lex situs being where the pieces of paper constituting the negotiable instruments are at the time of transfer: see *Macmillan Inc v Bishopsgate Investment Trust plc (No 3)* [1996] 1 All ER 585 at 602, 608; *Re Harvard Securities Ltd, Holland v Newbury* [1997] 2 BCLC 369.

Maintenance and inspection of the register   The register need not be maintained by the company, but may be maintained by another person, as is common in the case of large companies; where that other person defaults, see s 357, below. Where the register is kept at the office of a person other than the company, and that person fails to maintain a duplicate of an overseas branch register with the principal register as required by Sch 14, para 4(1)(b), that person is liable to the same penalty as if he were an officer of the company who was in default: Sch 14, para 4(3). As to inspection of the register, see s 356, below.

S 353(2)

Notice of location or place of inspection   This notice of where the register is kept is not required if the register is kept otherwise than in a legible form (Companies (Registers and Other Records) Regulations 1985, SI 1985/724, reg 2(3)(b)); but the company must instead send a notice of the place of inspection of the register to the registrar of companies (reg 3(1), (2)); and if that place of inspection is a place other than the registered office, the address of the place of inspection must be included in the annual return: reg 3(4).

S 353(4)

Penalties   'Officer in default' is defined in s 730(5). As to penalties, see s 730, Sch 24, below; see also s 357 where the default is that of an agent of the company.
    In addition to these penalties, the extent of a director's responsibility for the failure by the company to comply with this provision is a matter to which the court must have regard in disqualification proceedings under the Company Directors Disqualification Act 1986: ss 6–9, Sch 1, para 4(e).

354. Index of members

(1)   Every company having more than 50 members shall, unless the register of members is in such a form as to constitute in itself an index, keep an index of the names of the members of the company and shall, within 14 days after the

date on which any alteration is made in the register of members, make any necessary alteration in the index.

(2)   The index shall in respect of each member contain a sufficient indication to enable the account of that member in the register to be readily found.

(3)   The index shall be at all times kept at the same place as the register of members.

(4)   If default is made in complying with this section, the company and every officer of it who is in default is liable to a fine and, for continued contravention, to a daily default fine.

General note

For provisions relating to the inspection of the index, see the Companies (Inspection and Copying of Registers, Indices and Documents) Regulations 1991, SI 1991/1998.

S 354(3)

As to the location of the register of members, see s 353, above. Where the index is kept otherwise than in legible form (as permitted by ss 722, 723), the company is not required to keep the index at any place specified in this provision (Companies (Registers and Other Records) Regulations 1985, SI 1985/724, reg 2(3)(a)); but the company must allow inspection of any such index at the places specified in SI 1985/724, Sch 2, Pt I: reg 2(2).

S 354(4)

As to penalties, see s 730, Sch 24, below; 'officer in default' is defined in s 730(5). As to default by another person, see s 357, below.

355. Entries in register in relation to share warrants

(1)   On the issue of a share warrant the company shall strike out of its register of members the name of the member then entered in it as holding the shares specified in the warrant as if he had ceased to be a member, and shall enter in the register the following particulars, namely—

(a)   the fact of the issue of the warrant;

(b)   a statement of the shares included in the warrant, distinguishing each share by its number so long as the share has a number; and

(c)   the date of the issue of the warrant.

(2)   Subject to the company's articles, the bearer of a share warrant is entitled, on surrendering it for cancellation, to have his name entered as a member in the register of members.

(3)   The company is responsible for any loss incurred by any person by reason of the company entering in the register the name of a bearer of a share warrant in respect of the shares specified in it without the warrant being surrendered and cancelled.

(4)   Until the warrant is surrendered, the particulars specified in subsection (1) are deemed to be those required by this Act to be entered in the register of members; and, on the surrender, the date of the surrender must be entered.

(5)   Except as provided by section 291(2) (director's share qualification), the bearer of a share warrant may, if the articles of the company so provide, be deemed a member of the company within the meaning of this Act, either to the full extent or for any purposes defined in the articles.

General note

As to share warrants, see note to s 188, above.

S 355(1)

The wording of this provision suggests (as does s 188) that a company can only issue share warrants to bearer by converting existing shares, hence the need to delete the information as to the existing member and replace it with the information required by this provision.

S 355(5)

The holder of a warrant is not a member of the company, for his name has not been entered on the register as required by s 22, but the articles may deem him to be a member (for example, to allow attendance at general meetings).

356. Inspection of register and index

(1)   Except when the register of members is closed under the provisions of this Act, the register and the index of members' names shall ... be open to the inspection of any member of the company without charge, and of any other person on payment of such fee as may be prescribed.

(2)   ...

(3)   Any member of the company or other person may require a copy of the register, or of any part of it, on payment of such fee as may be prescribed; and the company shall cause any copy so required by a person to be sent to him within 10 days beginning with the day next following that on which the requirement is received by the company.

(4)   ...

(5)   If an inspection required under this section is refused, or if a copy so required is not sent within the proper period, the company and every officer of it who is in default is liable in respect of each offence to a fine.

(6)   In the case of such refusal or default, the court may by order compel an immediate inspection of the register and index, or direct that the copies required be sent to the persons requiring them.

General note

For provisions relating to the inspection of documents, registers and fees under this section, see the Companies (Inspection and Copying of Registers, Indices and Documents) Regulations 1991, SI 1991/1998.

S 356(1)

As to closure of the register, see s 358, below. Where the register is kept otherwise than in a legible form (as permitted by ss 722, 723), the place of inspection is determined by the Companies (Registers and Other Records) Regulations 1985, SI 1985/724, reg 3, Sch 2, Pt I; and notice of that place must be given to the registrar of companies (reg 3(1)); if that place of inspection is different from the registered office of the company, the address of that place must be included in the annual return: reg 3(4).

Inspection by any person   It is sometimes overlooked, especially by private companies, that the register is open to inspection by any person. A person seeking to inspect the register cannot be required to give their reasons for wanting to do so: *Holland v Dickson* (1888) 37 Ch D 669. Once the company has gone into liquidation, the right of inspection ceases: *Re Kent Coalfields Syndicate Ltd* [1898] 1 QB 754; but the court has power to permit inspection by creditors and contributories under IA 1986, s 155.

S 356(3)

The entitlement is to require a copy rather than to make a copy; and the ability to require a copy of the entire register is open to abuse, as where businesses acquire the register for marketing purposes.

S 356(5)

'Officer in default' is defined in s 730(5); as to penalties, see s 730, Sch 24; as to default by another person, see s 357.

S 356(6)

This provision is necessary because, but for the section, it is not clear that there is any right of inspection or that the court has the power to compel inspection: see *Conway v Petronius Clothing Co Ltd* [1978] 1 All ER 185 at 199. The use of the word 'may' indicates that the court's power is discretionary; whether the power will be exercised depends upon the relevant considerations affecting the power in the light of the facts: *Pelling v Families need Fathers Ltd* [2001] All ER (D) 03 (Aug), CA.

357. Non-compliance with ss 353, 354, 356: agent's default

Where under section 353(1)(b), the register of members is kept at the office of some person other than the company, and by reason of any default of his the company fails to comply with—

section 353(2) (notice to registrar),

section 354(3) (index to be kept with register), or

section 356 (inspection),

or with any requirement of this Act as to the production of the register, that other person is liable to the same penalties as if he were an officer of the company who was in default, and the power of the court under section 356(6) extends to the making of orders against that other and his officers and servants.

General note

This liability of the agent is additional to that of the company, which retains primary responsibility for these statutory obligations.

Where the register of members is kept otherwise in a legible form by a person other than the company and that person defaults on the obligations as to the inspection of that register and notification to the registrar of companies as to the place at which it may be inspected, this provision applies with respect to such failures: Companies (Registers and Other Records) Regulations 1985, SI 1985/724, reg 6(2).

As to penalties, see s 730, Sch 24; 'officer in default' is defined in s 730(5).

358. Power to close register

A company may, on giving notice by advertisement in a newspaper circulating in the district in which the company's registered office is situated, close the register of members for any time or times not exceeding in the whole 30 days in each year.

General note

Closing the register may be convenient where the company wishes to determine the members' entitlement to dividends or to an issue of new shares but companies may find it easier to determine entitlement by reference to those on the register on a fixed 'record' date. This avoids the need to close the register for any period of time.

For uncertificated securities dealt with through CREST, the register cannot be closed without the consent of the operator of the system: see the Uncertificated Securities Regulations 1995, SI 1995/3272, reg 22.

359. Power of court to rectify register

(1)　If—

　(a)　the name of any person is, without sufficient cause, entered in or omitted from a company's register of members, or

　(b)　default is made or unnecessary delay takes place in entering on the register the fact of any person having ceased to be a member,

the person aggrieved, or any member of the company, or the company, may apply to the court for rectification of the register.

(2)　The court may either refuse the application or may order rectification of the register and payment by the company of any damages sustained by any party aggrieved.

(3)　On such an application the court may decide any question relating to the title of a person who is a party to the application to have his name entered in or omitted from the register, whether the question arises between members or alleged members, or between members or alleged members on the one hand and the company on the other hand, and generally may decide any question necessary or expedient to be decided for rectification of the register.

(4)　In the case of a company required by this Act to send a list of its members to the registrar of companies, the court, when making an order for rectification of the register, shall by its order direct notice of the rectification to be given to the registrar.

General note

As to the rectification of a register in relation to uncertificated units of a security, see the Uncertificated Securities Regulations 1995, SI 1995/3272, reg 21. As to the rectification of an overseas branch register (where one is kept), see s 362, Sch 14, Pt II, para 3.

S 359(1)

Jurisdiction　This provision determines the court's jurisdiction to hear the case; the jurisdiction to rectify the register is exclusive to the jurisdiction where the register is kept: see *Re Fagin's Bookshop plc* [1992] BCLC 118. As to the location of the register, see s 353, above; in effect, for companies incorporated in England and Wales, it is the place of incorporation.

A summary remedy　The section provides a summary remedy and this procedure is inappropriate, therefore, if the dispute as to the entitlement to the shares can only be resolved by oral evidence and cross-examination: *Re Hoicrest Ltd* [2000] 1 BCLC 194; or if rectification would prejudice persons not party to the proceedings: see *Re R W Peak (Kings Lynn) Ltd* [1998] 1 BCLC 193.

　　The provision applies whether the dispute is between the company and the members or the members and the members: see sub-s (3). There is a clear distinction between sub-s (1)(a) and (b) and there is no necessity under sub-s (1)(a) to show any wrongdoing by the company, and any question of omission from, or entry on, the register without sufficient cause can be raised: *Re Diamond Rock Boring Co Ltd, ex p Shaw* (1877) 2 QBD 463; see also *Re Fagin's Bookshop plc* [1992] BCLC 118.

The proper respondents to an application to rectify the register are the company and the registered holder or holders of the shares whose registration is in question, if not the applicant; and the directors should not be joined unless a costs order is sought against them personally: *Morgan v Morgan Insurance Brokers Ltd* [1993] BCLC 676.

Any shareholder wishing to challenge an entry in the register must act promptly: *Re Scottish Petroleum Co* (1883) 23 Ch D 413, CA; *First National Reinsurance Co v Greenfield* [1921] 2 KB 260; and see *Re R W Peak (Kings Lynn) Ltd* [1998] 1 BCLC 193 at 206.

Company in winding up   Rectification is available although the company has gone into winding up: *Re Sussex Brick Co* [1904] 1 Ch 598; *Reese River Silver Mining Co v Smith* (1869) LR 4 HL 64; see also IA 1986, s 148.

Court's discretion   In ordering rectification, whether the company is in liquidation or not, the court has power, in a proper case, to fix a particular date at which the registration shall become operative, even to the extent of making it retrospective; but subject, if necessary, to conditions protecting the rights of third parties: *Re Sussex Brick Co* [1904] 1 Ch 598.

The court may refuse to exercise its discretion in the light of the circumstances in which and the purpose for which the relief is sought: *Re Piccadilly Radio plc* [1989] BCLC 683 (rectification refused; the applicants had no interest in the shares and were searching for a means to disenfranchise opposition at a general meeting).

Irregular/improper allotments   The power to rectify has been exercised where there has been an irregularity as to an allotment of shares: see *Re Cleveland Trust plc* [1991] BCLC 424 (register rectified by deletion of bonus shares after bonus issue mistakenly made); *Re Thundercrest Ltd* [1995] 1 BCLC 117 (register rectified by cancellation of allotment to two members who were also directors when the third member of the company, to their knowledge, had not received a provisional letter of allotment of those shares to him, a letter which was in any event defective as it allowed insufficient time for acceptance); *Re Transatlantic Life Assurance Co Ltd* [1979] 3 All ER 352 (register rectified after allotment in breach of exchange controls then applicable).

The wording of the provision is also wide enough to empower the court to order rectification by deleting a reference to some only of a registered holder's shares, even thought the rectification does not involve the entire deletion of the name of a registered holder: *Re Transatlantic Life Assurance Co Ltd* [1979] 3 All ER 352.

Transfers of shares   Many of the cases involve situations where a transfer of shares has been improperly registered or registration has been improperly refused: see *International Credit and Investment Co (Overseas) Ltd v Adham* [1994] 1 BCLC 66 (rectification ordered to restore status quo where no proper share transfers were executed, merely entries made in share register purporting to deprive the true owner of his entire holding); *Re New Cedos Engineering Co Ltd* [1994] 1 BCLC 797 (rectification ordered where, on their true construction, a right to be registered existed under the articles); *Stothers v William Steward (Holdings) Ltd* [1994] 2 BCLC 266 (rectification ordered where directors purported to refuse registration which power, on the true construction of the articles, they did not possess); see also *Re Inverdeck Ltd* [1998] 2 BCLC 242. If the directors have properly exercised their discretion under the articles to refuse to register a transfer, then there is no basis on which rectification can be sought, see *Popely v Planarrive Ltd* [1997] 1 BCLC 8.

Rectification by the directors   The directors of a company may rectify the register of members without any application to the court if there is no dispute about the matter and it is plain that an entry or omission is mistaken: *Reese River Silver Mining Co v Smith* (1869) LR 4 HL 64 at 74, 81; *Re Poole Firebrick and Blue Clay Co, Hartley's Case* (1875) 10 Ch App 157; *First National Reinsurance Co v Greenfield* [1921] 2 KB 260 at 279, 280; see also *Michaels v Harley House (Marylebone) Ltd* [1997] 2 BCLC 166 at 174. But ordinarily, the protection of the court's order is essential to any rectification by the removal of the name of a registered holder of shares: *Re Derham and Allen Ltd* [1946] Ch 31 at 36.

S 359(2)

Rectification and damages   The damages are designed to put the applicant in the proper position. If a name is entered in error, any money paid should be repaid with interest: see *Karberg's Case* [1892] 3 Ch 1. If a name is omitted in error, the holder when properly registered would be entitled to the dividends paid in the intervening period (plus interest): see *Sri Lanka Omnibus Co Ltd v L A Perera* [1952] AC 76. See also *Lloyd v Popely* [2000] 1 BCLC 19. It seems that the court may award damages under this provision only if it also orders rectification: see *Re Ottos Kopje Diamond Mines Ltd* [1893] 1 Ch 618.

S 359(3)

Once the court has jurisdiction under sub-s (1) to hear an application, then the court has a very wide discretion under this provision to decide any question relating to the title of a party to be registered as a member although the court will not make an order which would require a company or its board to register a transfer of shares without delivery to it of a proper instrument of transfer in contravention of s 183: see *Re Hoicrest Ltd* [2000] 1 BCLC 194 at 199, CA.

S 359(4)

As to the companies required to send a list of their members to the registrar of companies, see s 364A, below.

360. Trusts not to be entered on register in England and Wales

No notice of any trust, expressed, implied or constructive, shall be entered on the register, or be receivable by the registrar, in the case of companies registered in England and Wales.

General note

This provision ensures that a company registered in England and Wales is not concerned with trusts over its shares: *Société Générale de Paris v Walker* (1885) 11 App Cas 20. A company usually expands on the statutory position by a provision in its articles encompassing all equitable interests, however arising: see Table A, reg 5.

The register then will be limited to the legal owners, who may well be nominees. A public company may obtain information as to the beneficial owners of its shares either by relying on the disclosure requirements imposed by ss 198 – 210 or by exercising the company's power to investigate the ownership of its shares under s 212. The Department of Trade and Industry also retains power under ss 442 and 444 to investigate share ownership.

As to the equivalent provision with respect to holdings of uncertificated units, see the Uncertificated Securities Regulations 1995, SI 1995/3272, reg 19(7).

361. Register to be evidence

The register of members is prima facie evidence of any matters which are by this Act directed or authorised to be inserted in it.

General note

That the register is prima facie but not conclusive evidence of any matters directed or authorised to be inserted in it is clear from the Act itself which makes provision for its rectification: *Reese River Silver Mining Co v Smith* (1869) LR 4 HL 64 at 80, per Lord Cairns; see also *Re Briton Medical and General Life Association* (1888) 39 Ch D 61 at 72, per Stirling J.

The position with respect to the register is the same where the holder is registered as a holder of uncertificated units: Uncertificated Securities Regulations 1995, SI 1995/3272, reg 20, subject to reg 23(7) (purported registration of transfer of title to an uncertificated unit otherwise than in accordance with reg 23 of no effect).

362. Overseas branch registers

(1)   A company having a share capital whose objects comprise the transaction of business in any of the countries or territories specified in Part I of Schedule 14 to this Act may cause to be kept in any such country or territory in which it transacts business a branch register of members resident in that country or territory.

(2)   Such a branch register is to be known as an 'overseas branch register'; and—

(a)   any dominion register kept by a company under section 119 of the Companies Act 1948 is to become known as an overseas branch register of the company;

    (b) where any Act or instrument (including in particular a company's articles) refers to a company's dominion register, that reference is to be read (unless the context otherwise requires) as being to an overseas branch register kept under this section; and

    (c) references to a colonial register occurring in articles registered before 1st November 1929 are to be read as referring to an overseas branch register.

(3)   Part II of Schedule 14 has effect with respect to overseas branch registers kept under this section; and Part III of the Schedule enables corresponding facilities in Great Britain to be accorded to companies incorporated in other parts of the world.

(4)   The Foreign Jurisdiction Act 1890 has effect as if subsection (1) of this section, and Part II of Schedule 14, were included among the enactments which by virtue of section 5 of that Act may be applied by Order in Council to foreign countries in which for the time being Her Majesty has jurisdiction.

(5)   Her Majesty may by Order in Council direct that subsection (1) above and Part II of Schedule 14 shall extend, with such exceptions, modifications or adaptations (if any) as may be specified in the Order, to any territories under Her Majesty's protection to which those provisions cannot be extended under the Foreign Jurisdiction Act 1890.

General note

For general provisions with respect to overseas branch registers, see Sch 14, below.

An overseas branch register is deemed to be part of the company's register of members (Sch 14, Pt II, para 2(1)); and copies of entries in the overseas branch register must be transmitted to the registered office as soon as may be after the entry is made, and a duplicate of the overseas branch register must be kept with the principal register: Sch 14, Pt II, para 4. However, the Uncertificated Securities Regulations 1995, SI 1995/3272, provide that the holders of uncertificated shares must not be entered on an overseas branch register: reg 19(6). The effect is that uncertificated holdings must be entered on the principal register only.

S 362(1)

The register may be maintained otherwise than in a legible form (as permitted by ss 722, 723) and, in that case, the company is not required to keep the register at any place specified in this provision: Companies (Registers and Other Records) Regulations 1985, SI 1985/724, reg 2(1), (3)(a). But the company must allow inspection of any such register at the places specified in SI 1985/724, Sch 2, Pt I: reg 2(2) (in fact, at any place where the register could be kept under sub-s (1)); and the company must notify the registrar of the place of inspection: reg 3(1), (2).

CHAPTER III

ANNUAL RETURN

363. Duty to deliver annual returns

(1)   Every company shall deliver to the registrar successive annual returns each of which is made up to a date not later than the date which is from time to time the company's 'return date', that is—

    (a) the anniversary of the company's incorporation, or

    (b) if the company's last return delivered in accordance with this Chapter was made up to a different date, the anniversary of that date.

(2)   Each return shall—

    (a) be in the prescribed form,

    (b) contain the information required by or under the following provisions of this Chapter, and

    (c) be signed by a director or the secretary of the company;

and it shall be delivered to the registrar within 28 days after the date to which it is made up.

(3)   If a company fails to deliver an annual return in accordance with this Chapter before the end of the period of 28 days after a return date, the company is guilty of an offence and liable to a fine and, in the case of continued contravention, to a daily default fine.

The contravention continues until such time as an annual return made up to that return date and complying with the requirements of subsection (2) (except as to date of delivery) is delivered by the company to the registrar.

(4)   Where a company is guilty of an offence under subsection (3), every director or secretary of the company is similarly liable unless he shows that he took all reasonable steps to avoid the commission or continuation of the offence.

(5)   The references in this section to a return being delivered 'in accordance with this Chapter' are—

    (a) in relation to a return made on or after 1st October 1990, to a return with respect to which all the requirements of subsection (2) are complied with;

    (b) in relation to a return made before 1st October 1990, to a return with respect to which the formal and substantive requirements of this Chapter as it then had effect were complied with, whether or not the return was delivered in time.

General note

The annual return is now a 'shuttle' return, with the registrar of companies pre-printing much of the information required and asking companies simply to amend, sign and return with the required fee, currently £15. The shuttle form usually is sent out about two weeks before the return date, see sub-s (1) below; equally, a company can bring forward its annual return date by requesting a shuttle form at any time from the registrar of companies.

S 363(1)

All companies   The requirement to deliver an annual return applies to all companies, public and private, limited by shares, limited by guarantee (although the information required may differ in some respects) and unlimited; and it applies quite independently of any accounting exemptions or obligations. A dormant company (see s 249AA) must deliver an annual return. 'Company' is defined by s 735 as a company formed and registered under this Act so excluding oversea companies from these requirements; as to disclosure by such companies, see Pt XXIII. As noted above, a company may alter its return date to an earlier date simply by requesting a shuttle annual return form from the registrar of companies. It may be convenient to do this in order to align the return dates of companies within a group.

S 363(2)–(4)

Delivery of the return   The requirement that the return is signed (by a director or the secretary) is often overlooked; the time limit for delivery is within 28 days of the return date identified in sub-s (1), so the maximum period between annual returns is 13 months. 'Director' includes shadow director, except for the purposes of signing the annual return: s 365(3).

Penalties   As to penalties, see s 730, Sch 24, below. Non-compliance, in addition to attracting penalties under this provision, may result in the company being regarded as defunct and struck off the register under s 652. Furthermore, the extent of a director's responsibility for the failure by the company to comply with this provision is a matter to which the court must have regard in disqualification proceedings under the Company Directors Disqualification Act 1986: ss 6–9, Sch 1, para 4(f).

364. Contents of annual return: general

(1)   Every annual return shall state the date to which it is made up and shall contain the following information—
  (a) the address of the company's registered office;
  (b) the type of company it is and its principal business activities;
  (c) the name and address of the company secretary;
  (d) the name and address of every director of the company;
  (e) in the case of each individual director—
      (i)   his nationality, date of birth and business occupation,...
      (ii)   ... ;
  (f)   ... ;
  (g) if the register of members is not kept at the company's registered office, the address of the place where it is kept;
  (h) if any register of debenture holders (or a duplicate of any such register or a part of it) is not kept at the company's registered office, the address of the place where it is kept;

(i)   ... .

(2)   The information as to the company's type shall be given by reference to the classification scheme prescribed for the purposes of this section.

(3)   The information as to the company's principal business activities may be given by reference to one or more categories of any prescribed system of classifying business activities.

(4)   A person's 'name' and 'address' mean, respectively—

  (a)   in the case of an individual, his Christian name (or other forename) and surname and his usual residential address;

  (b)   in the case of a corporation or Scottish firm, its corporate or firm name and its registered or principal office.

(5)   In the case of a peer, or an individual usually known by a title, the title may be stated instead of his Christian name (or other forename) and surname or in addition to either or both of them.

(6)   Where all the partners in a firm are joint secretaries, the name and principal office of the firm may be stated instead of the names and addresses of the partners.

S 364(1)

Information required   The requirement to state the date as to which the return is made up is often overlooked. The information provided under the various headings below must match the information which is currently on the public register so, for example, a company cannot use the occasion of submitting its annual return to alter the address of its registered office or to notify a change of directors. Such events must be notified as required by the provisions governing those procedures, in this case, ss 287 and 288 respectively.

As to the registered office, see s 287, above; as to the type of company and its business activities, see sub-ss (2), (3). 'Director' includes shadow director (s 365(3)) although shadow directors are unlikely to comply with this requirement; particulars of other directorships held are no longer required.

Where the register of members is kept otherwise than in a legible form, this provision does not apply (Companies (Registers and Other Records) Regulations 1985, SI 1985/724, reg 2(3)(c)); but notice of the place of inspection of the register must be provided by a notice to the registrar and, if that place of inspection is other than at the registered office, the address of that place of inspection must be included in the annual return: reg 3(4).

Where the register of debenture holders is kept otherwise than in a legible form, this provision does not apply (Companies (Registers and Other Records) Regulations 1985, SI 1985/724, reg 4(4)(c)), but notice of the place of inspection of the register must be provided by a notice to the registrar and, if the place of inspection is other than the registered office, the address of that place of inspection must be included in the annual return: reg 5(3).

A company which is entitled to exclude certain information concerning related undertakings from its accounts may need to annex that information to the next annual return: see s 231(6)(b). Failure to do so when required is a criminal offence: s 231(7).

S 364(2), (3)

The prescribed classification scheme for these purposes is set out in the Companies (Forms Amendment No 2 and Company's Type and Principal Business Activities) Regulations 1990, SI 1990/1766, as amended by SI 1996/1105.

364A. Contents of annual return: particulars of share capital and shareholders

(1)   The annual return of a company having a share capital shall contain the following information with respect to its share capital and members.

(2)   The return shall state the total number of issued shares of the company at the date to which the return is made up and the aggregate nominal value of those shares.

(3)   The return shall state with respect to each class of shares in the company—

(a)   the nature of the class, and

(b)   the total number and aggregate nominal value of issued shares of that class at the date to which the return is made up.

(4)   The return shall contain a list of the names and addresses of every person who—

(a)   is a member of the company on the date to which the return is made up, or

(b)   has ceased to be a member of the company since the date to which the last return was made up (or, in the case of the first return, since the incorporation of the company);

and if the names are not arranged in alphabetical order the return shall have annexed to it an index sufficient to enable the name of any person in the list to be easily found.

(5)   The return shall also state—

(a)   the number of shares of each class held by each member of the company at the date to which the return is made up, and

(b)   the number of shares of each class transferred since the date to which the last return was made up (or, in the case of the first return, since the incorporation of the company) by each member or person who has ceased to be a member, and the dates of registration of the transfers.

(6)   The return may, if either of the two immediately preceding returns has given the full particulars required by subsections (4) and (5), give only such particulars as relate to persons ceasing to be or becoming members since the date of the last return and to shares transferred since that date.

(7)   Subsections (4) and (5) do not require the inclusion of particulars entered in an overseas branch register if copies of those entries have not been received at the company's registered office by the date to which the return is made up.

   Those particulars shall be included in the company's next annual return after they are received.

(8)   Where the company has converted any of its shares into stock, the return shall give the corresponding information in relation to that stock, stating the amount of stock instead of the number or nominal value of shares.

S 364A(1)

The information required by this provision is not required of a company limited by guarantee which, since 22 December 1980, cannot be formed with a share capital s 1(4); the information will be required of such companies formed prior to that date and having a share capital.

S 364A(2)

The requirement is the total of the issued share capital, not the total of the authorised or nominal capital.

S 364A(4)–(6)

Details of the membership   The annual return can be a useful source of information on matters of share transfers and the date of registration of those transfers although it is no substitute for the register of members which would usually be more up to date. Using the public registry enables searchers to obtain the information discretely without having to approach the company with a request to inspect the register of members under s 356.

Full list of members   A full list of members is only required in the first annual return following incorporation and then every third year; in the intervening two years, the company need only provide information on those who become members, or cease to be members, or any share transfers. Large companies are able to provide their lists of members to the registrar of companies in a variety of formats, including on CD-ROM; for such companies, it is often easier to provide a full list of members every year rather than attempt to track changes in the intervening two years.

S 364A(7)

There is unlikely to be any delay in the transmission of information from the branch register to the registered office since the requirement is that copies of such entries must be transmitted as soon as may be after the entries are made: Sch 14, para 4.

365. Supplementary provisions: regulations and interpretation

(1)   The Secretary of State may by regulations make further provision as to the information to be given in a company's annual return, which may amend or repeal the provisions of sections 364 and 364A.

(2)   Regulations under this section shall be made by statutory instrument which shall be subject to annulment in pursuance of a resolution of either House of Parliament.

(3)   For the purposes of this Chapter, except section 363(2)(c)(signature of annual return), a shadow director shall be deemed to be a director.

General note

See the Companies (Contents of Annual Return) Regulations 1999, SI 1999/2322, which amended s 364(1) prescribing the contents of the annual return.

CHAPTER IV

MEETINGS AND RESOLUTIONS

General note to this Chapter

Meetings are an integral part of the decision-making process in any company, and for listed public companies, general meetings of shareholders are significant occasions in the corporate calendar, not least for the media attention which they attract. The importance of company meetings in the overall legal structure is recognised by the legislation which lays down the basic framework governing meetings while permitting much of the detail to be contained in the company's articles of association. In most cases, the legislative provisions are permissive and a company may adapt the provisions to its particular requirements in the articles.

Smaller companies, given that many have only two members, frequently either hold meetings on short notice (see s 369, below) or dispense with the formalities of meetings and resolutions altogether and act on an informal basis, a practice recognised by the elective regime introduced by the CA 1989. The elective regime allows shareholders in private companies to elect unanimously to opt out of certain provisions of the Companies Act, such as the requirement to hold an annual general meeting: see s 379A, below.

The legislation also makes provision for written resolutions of private companies (s 381A), as may the company's articles (see Table A, reg 53), in the case of both public and private companies (although the need for unanimity necessarily limits the utility of written resolutions in public companies).

The Duomatic principle   While members can act through passing resolutions at general meetings and by using written resolutions in a private company, in addition, the courts have recognised that: '... the unanimous consent of all shareholders who have a right to attend and vote at a general meeting of the company can override formal (including statutory) requirements in relation to the passing of resolutions at such meetings (for convenience called the *Re Duomatic* principle) ...' (*Wright v Atlas Wright (Europe) Ltd* [1999] 2 BCLC 301 at 307, CA, per Potter LJ).

The *Duomatic* principle operates on the basis that assent is tantamount to a resolution of a properly convened general meeting: '... where it can be shown that all shareholders who have a right to attend and vote at a general meeting of the company assent to some matter which a general meeting of the company could carry into effect, that assent is as binding as a resolution in general meeting would be.' (*Re Duomatic Ltd* [1969] 1 All ER 161 at 168, per Buckley J; *Parker & Cooper Ltd v Reading* [1926] Ch 975; *Re Oxted Motor Co Ltd* [1921] 3 KB 32; *Re Express Engineering Works Ltd* [1920] 1 Ch 466). It is an illustration of the principle that all the corporators of the company acting together may do anything which is intra vires the company: see *Cane v Jones* [1981] 1 All ER 533 at 539.

The *Duomatic* principle may override requirements of the articles (see *Re Duomatic Ltd* [1969] 1 All ER 161) or the statute (see *Wright v Atlas Wright (Europe) Ltd* [1999] 2 BCLC 301, CA) and it applies also where the consent required is of a particular group of shareholders rather than all the shareholders of the company: *Re Torvale Group Ltd* [1999] 2 BCLC 605 (informal unanimous consent of a class sufficed where a requirement of class consent had been imposed for the protection of the class). Informal decisions of this nature must be notified to the registrar of companies in accordance with s 380(4)(c) and (4)(d).

Assent by the shareholders for these purposes may be given formally or informally (ie without any meeting); it need not be in writing and it need not be given simultaneously, but at different times: *Parker & Cooper Ltd v Reading* [1926] Ch 975. The assent may be tacit, in the form of acquiescence by the shareholders with knowledge of the matter, rather than express: see *Re Torvale Group Ltd* [1999] 2 BCLC 605; *Re Bailey Hay & Co Ltd* [1971] 3 All ER 693. However, the persons assenting must be competent to effect the act to which they have assented: *Re New Cedos Engineering Co Ltd* [1994] 1 BCLC 797; and see *Wright v Atlas Wright (Europe) Ltd* [1999] 2 BCLC 301 at 314–315, CA.

There is uncertainty as to the application of the principle where those members entitled to attend and vote at a meeting have assented unanimously but a person entitled to notice of the meeting (but not entitled to attend and vote) has not received notice, see *Re Duomatic Ltd* [1969] 1 All ER 161 at 168–169. On the one hand, to allow the principle to prevail is to treat the right to receive notice of meetings as valueless but, on the other hand, if assent is tantamount to a resolution of a properly convened meeting and a resolution could have been passed without the assent of this person, then the absence of notice to him should not affect the application of the principle. The Court of Appeal in *Wright v Atlas Wright (Europe) Ltd* [1999] 2 BCLC 301, CA, also choose most recently to formulate the principle in terms of those 'entitled to attend and vote' (at 307).

Formalities required by statute   A particular issue of concern and uncertainty has been the extent to which '… formalities required by statute as apparent preconditions for the efficacy of company arrangements can or cannot in general be brushed aside by reference to *Duomatic* … ' (*Re R W Peak (Kings Lynn) Ltd* [1998] 1 BCLC 193 at 201, per Lindsay J). In other words, where the statute lays down a detailed scheme as to how to proceed with a transaction, the issue is whether informal unanimous consent of the members to the transaction validates the transaction despite the failure of the company to adhere to the statutory scheme. Some fine distinctions on this issue have appeared in the cases.

Conflicting approaches   In *Cane v Jones* [1981] 1 All ER 533, for example, the court permitted an alteration of the articles by way of informal unanimous consent although s 9 requires a special resolution; and in *Re Home Treat Ltd* [1991] BCLC 705 the court permitted an alteration of the objects clause in the memorandum of association by way of informal unanimous consent, although s 4 requires a special resolution.

However, in *Re R W Peak (Kings Lynn) Ltd* [1998] 1 BCLC 193, the court did not accept that the informal unanimous consent of the members could operate to excuse non-compliance with the detailed requirements of s 164 (terms of proposed contract for purchase of own shares to be authorised by special resolution before the contract is entered into); although, perhaps, such consent would be sufficient to overcome other elements of the statutory scheme for a purchase by the company of its own shares, such as the requirement in s 164(6) that a memorandum of the terms of the contract for purchase be available for inspection by members ahead of a general meeting to decide on the matter: see *BDG Roof-Bond Ltd v Douglas* [2000] 1 BCLC 401 at 417.

The *Duomatic* principle did not apply in *Precision Dippings Ltd v Precision Dippings Marketing Ltd* [1985] BCLC 385 where there was a failure to comply with the statutory procedures governing auditors' reports when the company proposed to make a distribution on the strength of qualified accounts; nor in *Re S H & Co (Realisations) 1990 Ltd* [1993] BCLC 1309 where there was a failure to comply with the statutory scheme governing the giving of financial assistance by a company for the purchase of its own shares.

Guidance from the Court of Appeal   Guidance is provided on this issue now by the Court of Appeal in *Wright v Atlas Wright (Europe) Ltd* [1999] 2 BCLC 301, which distinguished *Re R W Peak (Kings Lynn) Ltd* [1998] 1 BCLC 193 and concluded that the extent to which statutory requirements can be overridden by informal consent must be answered by considering the purpose and underlying rationale of the particular statutory formality in question.

On the facts in the *Wright* case, the purpose of the statutory provision in question, s 319 (shareholders' approval of director's service contract in excess of five years) did not extend beyond the benefit and protection of the shareholders of the company. It was therefore amenable to waiver by the class for whose protection it was designed in circumstances where it was clear that they were fully informed.

The limit to the *Duomatic* principle, then, is that it cannot apply to statutory provisions whose purpose and rationale extends beyond the protection of the class which has purported to waive the provision.

Unfortunately, the Court of Appeal did not identify those statutory provisions which would be regarded as of a wider remit, other than to note that it was logical in *Re R W Peak (Kings Lynn) Ltd* [1998] 1 BCLC 193 not to apply the *Duomatic* principle, when it would have undermined the clear statutory purpose of s 164(2) and s 164(5) as well as the broader policy considerations of the provisions dealing with purchase of a company's own shares. Clearly, the purpose and rationale of many, though not necessarily all, of the provisions governing the purchase by a company of its own shares extends beyond the protection of the current registered holders of the shares.

Equally, the decisions in *Precision Dippings Ltd v Precision Dippings Marketing Ltd* [1985] BCLC 385 (distributions) and *Re S H & Co (Realisations) 1990 Ltd* [1993] BCLC 1309 (financial assistance) are correct as the statutory provisions at issue in those cases are aimed, in part at least, at creditor protection and compliance with them could not therefore be waived by the members, even unanimously; a point confirmed, with respect to the need for compliance with s 270 (distributions to be justified by reference to company's accounts) in *Bairstow v Queens Moat Houses plc* [2001] All ER (D) 211 (May): the strict and mandatory mature of s 270 was fatal to any argument based on *Duomatic* (see para 36). Equally, applying *Wright,* it would seem that, just as a written resolution cannot be used by a private company to remove a director under s 303 or an auditor under s 391 (s 381A(7), Sch 15A, para (1)), neither can the *Duomatic* principle operate in those instances in view of the rights conferred by those provisions on the director and auditor to be removed, ie on persons other than the class purporting to waive the statutory requirements.

Validity of decisions made   There are then a range of ways in which shareholders may reach decisions and when considering whether the correct procedural steps have been taken, it is necessary to consider:

(1)   whether the decision was taken by a resolution at a meeting properly convened and conducted; this method has the advantage of certainty and finality and ensures that there can be no challenge to a decision on procedural grounds (assuming that the proper procedures regarding calling the meeting, notice etc have been observed) but it may be slow and cumbersome;

(2)   whether, if the company is a private company, the decision was taken by a written resolution of all the members in accordance with s 381A; here, at least there will be a definite record of the decision reached and of the assent of all the corporators. As to the use of written resolution procedures set out in the company's articles, see notes to ss 381A, 381C, below.

(3)   whether, if there has been an apparent failure to adhere to procedures, it is possible to rely on the *Duomatic* principle to rectify the position, subject to the need for unanimity and the limits to the principle as explained in *Wright v Atlas Wright (Europe) Ltd* [1999] 2 BCLC 301, CA.

366. Annual general meeting

(1) Every company shall in each year hold a general meeting as its annual general meeting in addition to any other meetings in that year, and shall specify the meeting as such in the notices calling it.

(2) However, so long as a company holds its first annual general meeting within 18 months of its incorporation, it need not hold it in the year of its incorporation or in the following year.

(3) Not more than 15 months shall elapse between the date of one annual general meeting of a company and that of the next.

(4) If default is made in holding a meeting in accordance with this section, the company and every officer of it who is in default is liable to a fine.

General note

Calling the meeting   Convening the annual general meeting is a matter for the directors (see Table A, reg 37); meetings of members other than the annual general meeting are called extraordinary general meetings and may also be convened by the directors: see Table A, regs 36, 37. The Secretary of State for Trade and Industry may call or direct the calling of an annual general meeting where the company defaults (s 367(1)); and the court may convene an annual general meeting under s 371. Private companies may elect to dispense with annual general meetings: s 366A.

Business of the meeting   The legislation does not dictate the business of an annual general meeting but the typical business of such a meeting includes:
- (1)   laying the annual accounts, the directors' report and the auditors' report before the meeting (s 241);
- (2)   re-electing retiring directors and electing new directors (Table A, reg 73);
- (3)   appointing an auditor, if required to do so (see s 384, below), and setting the auditor's remuneration (s 390A) although in practice that issue is often delegated to the board; and
- (4)   declaring a dividend (Table A, reg 102).

The 1948 Table A (reg 52) treated the items listed above as 'ordinary business' and everything else as 'special business', but this distinction does not appear in the 1985 Table A. The meeting is not restricted to a consideration of these matters alone and other matters may be dealt with, provided proper notice of any other business has been given. As to notice of resolutions, see ss 376, 378–379A, below. Public companies typically will include resolutions relating to the allotment of shares (s 80) and disapplying the statutory pre-emption rights (s 95). There is no statutory requirement that members be allowed to put questions to the board at the meeting, although that is standard practice.

Notice required   As to the length of notice required for an annual general meeting and as to the contents and service of that notice, see ss 369, 370.

Documents to be available at the annual general meeting   The register of directors' interests in shares and debentures must be available at the annual general meeting: ss 324–325, Sch 13, para 29. Details of certain transactions by banking companies and credit institutions with directors and connected persons must be available for inspection by the members at the annual general meeting: s 343(5).

Location of a meeting   The rationale behind the requirement for meetings is that the members are able to attend in person so as to debate and vote on matters affecting the company, but it is not necessary for all the members physically to be present in the same room: *Byng v London Life Association Ltd* [1989] BCLC 400, CA. A valid meeting can be held using overflow rooms, provided that all due steps are taken to direct those unable to get into the main meeting into the overflow rooms, and that there are adequate audio-visual links to enable those in all the rooms to see and hear what is going on in the other rooms: *Byng v London Life Association Ltd* [1989] BCLC 400, CA. Clearly as *Byng* shows, multiple linked rooms are acceptable and, if they are, there seems no reason why that accommodation need be in the same building, as was the case in *Byng*.

Use of technology   The key question in terms of the use of technology is whether it can achieve the same result as persons physically present in one place. If it can, it should not matter whether those persons are in the same building, same town, or indeed the same country (assuming there is no prohibition in the articles on meetings being held overseas and there are none in Table A). However, with multiple locations including overseas locations, there may be jurisdictional difficulties in determining just where the meeting took place, which may be important in certain contexts. Issues concerning authentication and registration of those attending would also need to be addressed if multiple locations are used.

Another issue is whether a general meeting can be conducted entirely by conference telephone call without any visual link. If the essence of a meeting is to vote and to participate in the debate, it would seem that there is no need for a visual link, although in *Byng* Browne-Wilkinson V-C seemed to emphasise the need 'to see and be seen, to hear and to be heard' (at 406). Certainly, for large public companies where visual presentations are now a common element of the annual general meeting, a visual link would seem essential. The position may be different in smaller companies.

Whatever about the visual element, communication must be instantaneous in the sense that there is an immediate opportunity to respond and participate in the debate. For example, a 'meeting' cannot be held by fax, given that it offers no possibility of participating in a debate, although fax technology facilitates the passing of written resolutions which do away with the need for a meeting in the first place.

E-mail clearly is not an acceptable method of conducting a meeting at present, as it too fails the test of 'to see and be seen, to hear and be heard', although an issue for the future is whether the articles, especially in smaller companies, might allow for a 'meeting' through this medium.

Defamation   A fair and accurate report of proceedings at a general meeting of a UK public company; and a fair and accurate copy of or extract from any document circulated to members of a UK public company – (a) by or with the authority of the board of directors of the company, (b) by the auditors of the company, or (c) by any member of the company in pursuance of a right conferred by any statutory provision; and a fair and accurate copy of or extract from any document circulated to members of a UK public company which relates to the appointment, resignation, retirement or dismissal of directors of the company is privileged, subject to explanation or contradiction: Defamation Act 1996, s 15, Sch 1, Pt II, para 13; see also para 14.

S 366(1), (3)

Timing requirements   The notice calling the annual general meeting must specify that it is an annual general meeting. There are two timing requirements:

(1)   a meeting in each calendar year; and

(2)   not more than 15 months apart – this second element is necessary to stop companies stretching the period between meetings effectively to two years by calling a meeting, for example, in January 2002 and then in December 2003.

In exercising their power to call a meeting, the directors must act in good faith (*Cannon v Trask* (1875) LR 20 Eq 669), which precludes calling the meeting for unsuitable dates, such as Christmas Day, or for unsuitable locations. It might be necessary in some circumstances to call a meeting for a bank holiday or a Sunday, but in most cases it would not be reasonable. The meeting must be called for a reasonable time and what would be a reasonable time would depend on the circumstances. The best practice is to hold the meeting on a working day during normal business hours.

S 366(2)

The first annual general meeting   A longer time-scale is permitted with respect to the first annual general meeting and the timing of it will be linked to the preparation of the first accounts. The accounting requirements are as follows:

(1)   the first period for which the accounts must be made up must not exceed 18 months (s 224(4));

(2)   a private company is allowed a maximum period of 22 months (a public company is allowed 21 months) from the date of incorporation in which to lay its first accounts before the general meeting (s 244(2)); and

(3)   the requirement is to lay the accounts before a general meeting, not necessarily the annual general meeting (s 241).

The meeting requirements are that the first annual general meeting must be held within 18 months. It follows that the first set of accounts need not be laid before the first annual general meeting (given that a company has 22 months (or 21) in which to do so), but if they are not so laid, the company would have to call another general meeting in order to lay the accounts before the meeting. In practice, the preparation of the first accounts will be timed to ensure that they can be laid before the first annual general meeting.

Private companies may dispense, in any event, with the laying of accounts before a general meeting: ss 252, 379A(1)(b).

S 366(4)

As to penalties, see s 730, Sch 24; 'officer in default' is defined in s 730(5).

Repeated failures to hold annual general meetings may amount to unfairly prejudicial conduct under s 459: see *Re a company (No 00789 of 1987), ex p Shooter* [1990] BCLC 384.

366A. Election by private company to dispense with annual general meetings

(1) A private company may elect (by elective resolution in accordance with section 379A) to dispense with the holding of annual general meetings.

(2) An election has effect for the year in which it is made and subsequent years, but does not affect any liability already incurred by reason of default in holding an annual general meeting.

(3) In any year in which an annual general meeting would be required to be held but for the election, and in which no such meeting has been held, any member of the company may, by notice to the company not later than three months before the end of the year, require the holding of an annual general meeting in that year.

(3A) The power of a member under subsection (3) to require the holding of an annual general meeting is exercisable not only by the giving of a notice but also by the transmission to the company at such address as may for the time being be specified for the purpose by or on behalf of the company of an electronic communication containing the requirement.

(4)   If such a notice is given or electronic communication is transmitted, the provisions of section 366(1) and (4) apply with respect to the calling of the meeting and the consequences of default.

(5) If the election ceases to have effect, the company is not obliged under section 366 to hold an annual general meeting in that year if, when the election ceases to have effect, less than three months of the year remains.

    This does not affect any obligation of the company to hold an annual general meeting in that year in pursuance of a notice given or electronic communication transmitted under subsection (3).

(5A) In this section, 'address' includes any number or address used for the purposes of electronic communications.

General note

The elective regime was introduced by the Companies Act 1989 to reduce the burden on private companies of complying with formalities such as annual general meetings.

S 366A(1)

An elective resolution to this effect requires the agreement of all the members entitled to attend and vote: s 379A(2)(b).

S 366A(2)–(3A)

Duration of election   The election to dispense with annual general meetings will be effective indefinitely unless revoked by an ordinary resolution (see s 379A(3));

or the company is re-registered as a public company (s 379A(4)); but it can be interrupted by any member requiring the holding of an annual general meeting for that year, which may be done by notice or by an electronic communication (defined in s 744 and see note to s 369(4A), below) to the company where the company has specified an address (as defined in sub-s (5A)) for this purpose. There are no threshold requirements regarding size of shareholding, voting strength or length of membership affecting this right of a member to require a meeting.

Once the meeting requested has been held, the election resumes operation unless the opportunity was taken to revoke it.

An election to dispense with annual general meetings does not operate retrospectively to cure a past failure to hold an annual general meeting, which is an offence under s 366(4).

S 366A(4)

Requirement to hold a meeting   Once a member gives notice, the company must hold an annual general meeting in accordance with s 366(1), ie in that calendar year, and the notice calling the meeting must specify that it is an annual general meeting and a failure to comply will attract the sanctions of s 366(4).

However, there is no time requirement with regard to the holding of the meeting so if, in January, a member gives notice requiring an annual general meeting to be held, there would be due compliance with the provision if the directors then called the meeting for December of that year. The absence of any requirement to call the meeting, say, within 21 days of the member's request for a date no later than 28 days from the notice convening the meeting (along the lines of s 368) rather undermines the effectiveness of this provision.

S 366A(5)

If the elective resolution is revoked when less than three months of the year remain, there is no need to hold a meeting in that calendar year, but thereafter the obligation in s 366(1) would require a meeting in the next year.

The proviso at the end of this subsection is designed to prevent a company from defeating the member's right to require a meeting under sub-s (3), by the company revoking the elective resolution (after the member has requested a meeting) with less than three months remaining and then asserting its right under sub-s (5) not to hold a meeting in that year.

367. Secretary of State's power to call meeting in default

(1) If default is made in holding a meeting in accordance with section 366, the Secretary of State may, on the application of any member of the company, call, or direct the calling of, a general meeting of the company and give such ancillary or consequential directions as he thinks expedient, including directions modifying or supplementing, in relation to the calling, holding and conduct of the meeting, the operation of the company's articles.

(2) The directions that may be given under subsection (1) include a direction that one member of the company present in person or by proxy shall be deemed to constitute a meeting.

(3) If default is made in complying with directions of the Secretary of State under subsection (1), the company and every officer of it who is in default is liable to a fine.

(4) A general meeting held under this section shall, subject to any directions of the Secretary of State, be deemed to be an annual general meeting of the company; but, where a meeting so held is not held in the year in which the default in holding the company's annual general meeting occurred, the meeting so held shall not be treated as the annual general meeting for the year in which it is held unless at that meeting the company resolves that it be so treated.

(5) Where a company so resolves, a copy of the resolution shall, within 15 days after its passing, be forwarded to the registrar of companies and recorded by him; and if default is made in complying with this subsection, the company and every officer of it who is in default is liable to a fine and, for continued contravention, to a daily default fine.

General note

It is very unusual for the Secretary of State to exercise this power; resort is more frequently had to the broader power of the court to call a meeting under s 371.

S 367(3)

As to penalties, see s 730, Sch 24, below; 'officer in default' is defined in s 730(5).

S 367(4), (5)

If necessary, the general meeting can resolve that the meeting called at the direction of the Secretary of State is the annual general meeting for the year in default and for the current year. Exceptionally, this ordinary resolution must be filed with the registrar of companies. As to penalties, see s 730, Sch 24, below; 'officer in default' is defined in s 730(5).

368. Extraordinary general meeting on members' requisition

(1) The directors of a company shall, on a members' requisition, forthwith proceed duly to convene an extraordinary general meeting of the company.

This applies notwithstanding anything in the company's articles.

(2) A members' requisition is a requisition of—

    (a) members of the company holding at the date of the deposit of the requisition not less than one-tenth of such of the paid-up capital of the company as at that date carries the right of voting at general meetings of the company; or

(b) in the case of a company not having a share capital, members of it representing not less than one-tenth of the total voting rights of all the members having at the date of deposit of the requisition a right to vote at general meetings.

(3) The requisition must state the objects of the meeting, and must be signed by the requisitionists and deposited at the registered office of the company, and may consist of several documents in like form each signed by one or more requisitionists.

(4) If the directors do not within 21 days from the date of the deposit of the requisition proceed duly to convene a meeting, the requisitionists, or any of them representing more than one half of the total voting rights of all of them, may themselves convene a meeting, but any meeting so convened shall not be held after the expiration of 3 months from that date.

(5) A meeting convened under this section by requisitionists shall be convened in the same manner, as nearly as possible, as that in which meetings are to be convened by directors.

(6) Any reasonable expenses incurred by the requisitionists by reason of the failure of the directors duly to convene a meeting shall be repaid to the requisitionists by the company, and any sum so repaid shall be retained by the company out of any sums due or to become due from the company by way of fees or other remuneration in respect of their services to such of the directors as were in default.

(7) In the case of a meeting at which a resolution is to be proposed as a special resolution, the directors are deemed not to have duly convened the meeting if they do not give the notice required for special resolutions by section 378(2).

(8) The directors are deemed not to have duly convened a meeting if they convene a meeting for a date more than 28 days after the date of the notice convening the meeting.

General note

All general meetings other than the annual general meeting are called extraordinary general meetings: see Table A, reg 36. There are no requirements as to the business to be conducted at such a meeting. An extraordinary general meeting may be convened by the directors of their own volition at any time: see Table A, reg 37; but this statutory provision requires the directors to convene a meeting; as does s 142 (duty of directors on serious loss of capital); and s 392A (rights of resigning auditors).

S 368(1)

Duty to convene an extraordinary general meeting   The articles cannot override this right of the members to requisition an extraordinary general meeting; equally, there is nothing to stop the articles providing more generous rights than the statutory

706

provision. 'Forthwith' means as soon as practicable: see *Re Windward Islands Enterprises (UK) Ltd* [1983] BCLC 293 at 295.

The obligation to convene the meeting can only arise if the requisition is valid and where it is ineffective because of a defect in its form then, despite the requirements of sub-s (2) having been met, the directors are not obliged to call a meeting: *Rose v McGivern* [1998] 2 BCLC 593.

S 368(2)

Thresholds for a requisition   There is no minimum period during which the shares or membership must have been held. The threshold in sub-s (2)(a) is difficult to meet for shareholders in a public company: cf s 376(2).

What is required is a members' requisition, ie a requisition by more than one member, so a member holding almost 77% of the shares cannot requisition a meeting without first transferring a share to a nominee: see *Morgan v Morgan Insurance Brokers Ltd* [1993] BCLC 676.

S 368(3)

Contents of a requisition   Care must be taken in drafting the requisition, for a meeting convened on requisition cannot transact any business other than that covered by the terms of the requisition (*Ball v Metal Industries Ltd* 1957 SC 315) together with any resolutions which the directors might put forward and of which due notice has been given: see *Rose v McGivern* [1998] 2 BCLC 593.

Care must be taken also in terms of the amount of detail which is included in the requisition. On the one hand, there is the obligation to state the objects of the meeting, although the courts will accept a requisition to consider the working and general management of the company without setting out particular resolutions: *Isle of Wight Rly Co v Tahourdin* (1883) 25 Ch D 320; *Fruit and Vegetable Growers' Association Ltd v Kekewich* [1912] 2 Ch 52. However, if the requisition is expressly stated to be for the purpose of passing specific resolutions, then care must be taken to ensure that such resolutions would be effective and valid for, if they are invalid, the directors have no obligation to call the meeting, there being no point in having a meeting to pass ineffective resolutions: *Rose v McGivern* [1998] 2 BCLC 593.

Where part of the requisition is invalid and part valid, there seems no reason why the directors should not be required to call the meeting for a consideration of the valid element: *Isle of Wight Rly Co v Tahourdin* (1883) 25 Ch D 320. 'In like form' does not mean in identical form: *Fruit and Vegetable Growers Association Ltd v Kekewich* [1912] 2 Ch 52. As to the registered office, see s 287.

S 368(4), (5)

Consequences of non-compliance by the directors   The requisitionists are given greater leeway than the directors and are allowed three months from the date of the deposit of the requisition in which to call the meeting, a concession which reflects their (likely) inexperience in calling meetings. The meeting must be duly convened and the formalities observed as if the directors were calling the meeting so, for example, the appropriate notice (see s 369, below) must be given.

There are no criminal penalties where the directors fail to convene the members' meeting. The only consequence of non-compliance is that this triggers the right of the members to convene the meeting and, potentially, a liability on the part of the directors for the requisitionists' expenses under sub-s (6). Alternatively, the requisitionists could seek an order from the court that the directors call the meeting: see *Rose v McGivern* [1998] 2 BCLC 593.

S 368(6)

It is difficult to imagine that the directors will pursue themselves for any sum paid by the company to the requisitionists unless, of course, the purpose of the extraordinary general meeting is to appoint a new board which might pursue the matter. In reality, liability under this provision is a remote possibility.

S 368(7)

If the extraordinary general meeting is to be called for the purpose of passing a special resolution, the directors cannot summon it on less than 21-days' notice as required for a special resolution by s 378(2). This deemed non-compliance will trigger sub-s (4) and allow the requisitionists to convene the meeting.

S 368(8)

Time limits This provision was added by CA 1989, s 145, Sch 19, para 9, following complaints that directors would call a meeting within 21 days as required by sub-s (4), but would do so for a date a considerable distance in the future: see *McGuinness v Bremner plc* [1988] BCLC 673 (directors convened meeting for seven months after the date of the requisition). This practice had the effect of blocking the requisitionists' right under sub-s (4) to call the meeting themselves while postponing the actual meeting for a long time.

The timetable required then by this provision is:
- starting with the date of deposit of the requisition at the registered office of the company – the directors must proceed to convene a meeting within 21 days; and it must be convened for a date no more than 28 days after the date of the notice convening the meeting;
- if the meeting is to consider a special resolution, the meeting must be called in a way which allows 21 days' notice to be given;
- there is a maximum 49 days therefore between the date of deposit of the requisition and the date of meeting, where the meeting is to be convened by the directors;
- Table A, reg 37 which would allow eight weeks is superceded by these statutory provisions;
- if the directors do not act, the requisitionists can convene a meeting within 3 months of the date of deposit of the requisition.

Finally, if the articles require, for example, 60 days' notice of any proposal for the appointment of a director, the requisitionists must be careful not to requisition their meeting under s 368 until sufficient time has elapsed under the articles to allow both sets of timing requirements to be met: see *Rose v McGivern* [1998] 2 BCLC 593 at 611.

369. Length of notice for calling meetings

(1) A provision of a company's articles is void in so far as it provides for the calling of a meeting of the company (other than an adjourned meeting) by a shorter notice than—

(a) in the case of the annual general meeting, 21 days' notice in writing; and

(b) in the case of a meeting other than an annual general meeting or a meeting for the passing of a special resolution—

(i) 7 days' notice in writing in the case of an unlimited company, and

(ii) otherwise, 14 days' notice in writing.

(2) Save in so far as the articles of a company make other provision in that behalf (not being a provision avoided by subsection (1)), a meeting of the company (other than an adjourned meeting) may be called—

(a) in the case of the annual general meeting, by 21 days' notice in writing; and

(b) in the case of a meeting other than an annual general meeting or a meeting for the passing of a special resolution—

(i) by 7 days' notice in writing in the case of an unlimited company, and

(ii) otherwise, 14 days' notice in writing.

(3) Notwithstanding that a meeting is called by shorter notice than that specified in subsection (2) or in the company's articles (as the case may be), it is deemed to have been duly called if it is so agreed—

(a) in the case of a meeting called as the annual general meeting, by all the members entitled to attend and vote at it; and

(b) otherwise, by the requisite majority.

(4) The requisite majority for this purpose is a majority in number of the members having a right to attend and vote at the meeting, being a majority—

(a) together holding not less than 95 per cent in nominal value of the shares giving a right to attend and vote at the meeting; or

(b) in the case of a company not having a share capital, together representing not less than 95 per cent of the total voting rights at that meeting of all the members.

A private company may elect (by elective resolution in accordance with section 379A) that the above provisions shall have effect in relation to the company as if for the references to 95 per cent there were substituted references to such lesser percentage, but not less than 90 per cent, as may be specified in the resolution or subsequently determined by the company in general meeting.

(4A) For the purposes of this section the cases in which notice in writing of a meeting is to be taken as given to a person include any case in which notice of the meeting is sent using electronic communications to such address as may for the time being be notified by that person to the company for that purpose.

(4B) For the purposes of this section a notice in writing of a meeting is also to be treated as given to a person where—

    (a) the company and that person have agreed that notices of meetings required to be given to that person may instead be accessed by him on a web site;

    (b) the meeting is a meeting to which that agreement applies;

    (c) that person is notified, in a manner for the time being agreed between him and the company for the purpose, of—

        (i)   the publication of the notice on a web site;

        (ii) the address of that web site; and

        (iii) the place on that web site where the notice may be accessed, and how it may be accessed;

        and

    (d) the notice continues to be published on that web site throughout the period beginning with the giving of that notification and ending with the conclusion of the meeting;

and for the purposes of this section a notice treated in accordance with this subsection as given to any person is to be treated as so given at the time of the notification mentioned in paragraph (c).

(4C) A notification given for the purposes of subsection (4B)(c) must—

    (a) state that it concerns a notice of a company meeting served in accordance with this Act,

    (b) specify the place, date and time of the meeting, and

    (c) state whether the meeting is to be an annual or extraordinary general meeting.

(4D) Nothing in subsection (4B) shall invalidate the proceedings of a meeting where—

    (a) any notice that is required to be published as mentioned in paragraph (d) of that subsection is published for a part, but not all, of the period mentioned in that paragraph; and

    (b) the failure to publish that notice throughout that period is wholly attributable to circumstances which it would not be reasonable to have expected the company to prevent or avoid.

(4E) A company may, notwithstanding any provision to the contrary in a company's articles, take advantage of any of subsections (4A) to (4D).

(4F) In so far as the articles of the company do not provide for notices and notifications to be served using electronic communications, the provisions of Table A (as for the time being in force) as to such service shall apply.

(4G) In this section, 'address' includes any number or address used for the purposes of electronic communications.

General note

Many of the provisions regarding meetings will be found in the articles of association (see Table A, regs 36–53) but this section imposes certain minimum requirements as to the length of notice for calling a meeting. As to the contents of the notice, see s 370; and as for notice requirements for resolutions, see ss 376, 378–379A.

S 369(1), (2)

Specified periods of notice   It is possible for the company's articles to specify longer notice periods, but a provision in the articles which provides for shorter periods than those specified here is void. As to those entitled to notice and the contents of the notice, see ss 366(1), above and 370, below; as to the time when notice is given and received, see Table A, regs 111–116, below. The requirement is 21 or 14 or 7 calendar days, there being no restriction to business or working days; and the periods of notice prescribed must be clear both of the day of service and of the day of the meeting: *Re Hector Whaling Ltd* [1936] Ch 208; and see Table A, regs 1, 38. The requirement is notice in writing, but this may be by electronic communication: see sub-s (4A).

Failure to give required notice   Failure to give timely notice will invalidate the meeting and nullify the proceedings: *Smyth v Darley* (1849) 2 HL Cas 789; as will a failure to give notice to all those entitled: *Musselwhite v C H Musselwhite & Son Ltd* [1962] Ch 964; and the transaction of business at a meeting which has not been correctly notified is invalid: *Re Bridport Old Brewery Co* (1867) LR 2 Ch App 191.

However, it is possible to cure procedural defects by reliance on the *Duomatic* principle, see the general note to this Chapter, above. See also s 382(4): a general meeting is deemed duly convened and held, until the contrary is proved, where minutes are made of the meeting in accordance with that section.

Notice of adjourned meetings   These notice requirements do not apply to adjourned meetings, as to which, see Table A, reg 45; if adjourned for less than 14 days, no notice is required; if adjourned for 14 or more, then at least 7 days' clear notice must be given.

S 369(3), (4)

Short notice   It is clear from the majorities required to secure short notice that it is of limited use to a public company or indeed a private company with any significant number of shareholders. Indeed, the thresholds set are very high even for a private company with a few shareholders because of the need for a majority in number as well as voting control which, on particular facts, might in effect require unanimity. Where voting control is assured but not a majority in number, this may be achieved by transfers to nominees (assuming there are no restrictions on transfer): see, for example, *Re Ransomes plc* [1999] 1 BCLC 775 at 779–780.

For a private company with a few shareholders who are also the directors, it is possible at the end of a board meeting for all the shareholders then to consent to short notice and immediately hold an annual general meeting, and they may so constitute themselves without any formalities (see *Re Express Engineering Works Ltd* [1920] 1 Ch 466), although, to avoid subsequent difficulties, it is best if the consent to short notice is in writing and signed by the members. A private company can elect, in any event, to dispense with annual general meetings: see s 366A. Once the requisite majorities are agreeable to short notice, there is no minimum period and it can be as brief as the members choose.

S 369(4A)

Notice by electronic communication This provision, and sub-ss (4B)-(4G), were inserted by the Companies Act 1985 (Electronic Communications) Order 2000, SI 2000/3373, art 18, as from 22 December 2000; it allows a company to give notice of meetings by electronic communication to a member where the member has agreed to that method of communication. 'Address' is defined in sub-s (4G).

'Electronic communication' means the same as in the Electronic Communications Act 2000, s 744; where it is defined as a communication transmitted (whether from one person to another, from one device to another or from a person to a device or vice versa): (a) by means of a telecommunication system (within the meaning of the Telecommunications Act 1984); or (b) by other means but while in an electronic form: Electronic Communications Act 2000, s 15.

Thus, notice in writing of a meeting is treated as given where, for example, notice of the meeting is given by fax or e-mail; see sub-s (4B) as to the use of a web site for these purposes.

S 369(4B)–(4D)

Notice on a web site Notice in writing may be treated as given to a person where there is agreement that notices of meetings may be accessed on a web site.

Notification of publication on a web site In order to ensure that a member does not have to monitor a web site, the company must notify him in the agreed manner of the publication of a notice of a meeting on a web site. There is no requirement that that notification of publication be by electronic communication, it could be by post, but in practice it is likely to be by e-mail. Certain basic matters must be included in that notification to ensure that the member appreciates the nature of the meeting which is being called without being required to go to the web site. The company is not restricted to the use of the same web site on every occasion, but it must indicate the address of the web site being used in each instance.

Where the notice of the meeting is posted on a web site, notice is treated as given at the time of the notification to the member of the publication of the notice of the meeting on a web site (so the 21 days etc must be calculated from this date). As to the time when that notification is treated as given, see the company's articles and Table A, reg 115. However, if the company uses electronic communication for that notification, there is a danger that its articles will make no provision for serving notices and notifications by electronic communication: this lacunae is dealt with by sub-s (4F) below.

Availability on the web site The notice of the meeting must be available on the web site throughout the period beginning with the notification of the publication of the notice on a web site and ending with the conclusion of the meeting, subject to sub-s (4D) which condones any failure to publish the notice which is *wholly* attributable to circumstances which it would not be reasonable to have expected the company to prevent or avoid. In other words, the failure to publish as required throughout the period must be due to some unavoidable failure of the technology rather than, say, a failure by the company to maintain the web site in a proper manner.

S 369(4E)–(4F)

Electronic communication and provisions in the articles   Subsection (4E) ensures that provisions in a company's articles (for example, references to notices in writing) do not prevent the company from taking advantage of these powers. No doubt, when it is convenient to do so, companies will take the opportunity to update their articles to reflect the use of electronic communications; in the meantime, they may use these electronic methods, with the agreement of the individual member, and they do not need to adopt new articles to permit them to do so, nor must they take steps to alter existing provisions which are restricted to paper communications.

However, while companies may utilise these provisions and are not affected by provisions to the contrary in their articles, there is a lacunae in that the company's existing articles will not provide for the service and receipt of notice by electronic communications. These statutory provisions treating notification by electronic communication to be notice in writing operate only for the purposes of this statutory provision and do not apply to the company's articles. Practical difficulties could therefore arise where a company uses these powers without updating its articles.

The solution provided is that, where the articles make no provision for notices or notifications to be served using electronic communications, Table A as for the time being in force, exceptionally, applies; this is exceptional for the practice of the Act is that companies are subject to Table A as in force at the time of registration: see note to s 8(2). The application is limited to those provisions of Table A as apply to service by electronic communication: see Table A, regs 111–115, as amended by the Companies Act 1985 (Electronic Communications) Order 2000, SI 2000/3373, art 32(1), Sch 1, as from 22 December 2000.

370. General provisions as to meetings and votes

(1) The following provisions have effect in so far as the articles of the company do not make other provision in that behalf.

(2) Notice of the meeting of a company shall be served on every member of it in the manner in which notices are required to be served by Table A (as for the time being in force).

(3) Two or more members holding not less than one-tenth of the issued share capital or, if the company does not have a share capital, not less than 5 per cent in number of the members of the company may call a meeting.

(4) Two members personally present are a quorum.

(5) Any member elected by the members present at a meeting may be chairman of it.

(6) In the case of a company originally having a share capital, every member has one vote in respect of each share or each £10 of stock held by him; and in any other case every member has one vote.

S 370(1)

Default provisions   These provisions are default provisions which apply only in the absence of provisions in the articles. In practice, these matters are invariably provided for in the articles.

S 370(2)

Notice to whom   There are a variety of persons entitled to notice:
(1)   all the members: Table A, reg 38; but this will depend on the terms of issue of any shares. For example, it is frequently the case that preference shareholders are not entitled to receive notice or to attend and vote at an annual general meeting unless the meeting is to consider a matter directly pertaining to them. Notice to holders of warrants will usually be by way of advertisement in a national newspaper;
(2)   all persons entitled to a share in consequence of the death or bankruptcy of a member: Table A, reg 38 (but see reg 31 as to the rights of such persons – they are not entitled to attend and vote at the meeting, but notice will alert them as to matters before the shareholders);
(3)   the directors: Table A, reg 38;
(4)   the auditors: Table A, reg 38; s 390.

Where there are joint holders of a share, notice must be given to each holder save that Table A, reg 112 provides that all notices must be given to the joint holder whose name stands first in the register of members in respect of the joint holding and notice so given is sufficient notice to all the joint holders.

Manner of service of notice   The manner of service is a matter for the articles, see Table A, regs 111–116. In the absence of contrary provision, it is the provisions of the current Table A, exceptionally, which apply; exceptionally, for the practice of the Act is that companies are subject to Table A as in force at the time of registration: see note to s 8(2).

Contents of notice   The notice must specify the time and place of the meeting and the general nature of the business to be transacted: Table A, reg 38. If the meeting is the annual general meeting, the notice must so specify (s 366(1)), and it must state that a proxy may be appointed: see s 372(3). The practice is to list the standard items of business (see note to s 366) and to set out in greater detail all other matters such as resolutions. For example, if a special or extraordinary resolution is to be proposed, then the full text of the resolution must be set out (see note to s 378); and even if the resolution is an ordinary resolution, it may be advantageous to set it out in full so as to avoid complications later as to whether adequate notice was given; although the court will take a more generous approach to such resolutions: see *Betts v McNaghten* [1910] 1 Ch 430. Where the resolution is technical in nature, an explanation of its nature and effect should be included.

The importance of this level of detail (even in an ordinary resolution) is that, to be valid, the notice must disclose all relevant facts so that a member can exercise an informed business judgment as to whether or not he ought to attend the meeting: *Tiessen v Henderson* [1899] 1 Ch 861. The need to make full disclosure of all relevant facts may mean in a particular case that the directors should disclose their own voting intentions on a particular matter.

Particular attention must be given to full and frank notice of any resolution involving a pecuniary advantage to a director: *Baillie v Oriental Telephone and Electric Co Ltd* [1915] 1 Ch 503; *Normandy v Ind Coope & Co Ltd* [1908] 1 Ch 84; *Tiessen v Henderson* [1899] 1 Ch 861; *Kaye v Croydon Tramways* [1898] 1 Ch 358.

If the notice is misleading, the court can restrain the holding of the meeting (*Jackson v Munster Bank* (1884) 13 LR Ir 118); and the transaction of business at a meeting which has not been correctly notified is invalid and resolutions improperly notified are not duly passed: *Baillie v Oriental Telephone and Electric Co Ltd* [1915] 1 Ch 503; *Normandy v Ind Coope & Co Ltd* [1908] 1 Ch 84; *Kaye v Croydon Tramways* [1898] 1 Ch 358.

As to notice of resolutions, see ss 376, 378–379A.

Failure to give notice   The importance of notice, at common law, is that an omission to give notice to even one person entitled to attend invalidates the meeting and nullifies its proceedings: *Smyth v Darley* (1849) 2 HL Cas 789; *John v Rees* [1969] 2 All ER 274.

Accidental omission of notice   However, Table A, reg 39 provides that the accidental omission to give notice of a meeting to, or the non-receipt of notice of a meeting by, any person entitled to receive notice shall not invalidate the proceedings at that meeting. Failure to give notice because of an error of law on the part of directors, for example, where they were under the erroneous impression that the petitioner had ceased to be a member of the company, does not fall within that provision: *Musselwhite v C H Musselwhite & Son Ltd* [1962] Ch 964. Once it is shown that some members have not been given notice, the onus is on those claiming that the meeting was valid to show an accidental omission: see *POW Services Ltd v Clare* [1995] 2 BCLC 435 at 450.

S 370(3)

It is highly unusual for this provision not to be overridden by the articles. For example, Table A, reg 37 provides that it is for the directors to call meetings, with the members restricted to situations where there are not sufficient directors within the UK to call a meeting or situations where they can exercise their powers to requisition a meeting under s 368.

S 370(4)

Quorum requirements   Table A, reg 40 is less restrictive than this provision as it does not require the two members to be personally present. Any resolution passed at a meeting which is inquorate is void: *Re Cambrian Peat, Fuel and Charcoal Ltd, De La Mott's and Turner's Case* (1875) 31 LT 773; *Re Romford Canal Co, Pocock's Claims* (1883) 24 Ch D 85.

The articles may provide that a quorum is only required initially (*Re Hartley Baird Ltd* [1955] Ch 143); but Table A, reg 41 provides that the quorum must be present throughout the meeting such that the meeting is adjourned if the number falls below the quorum required.

A meeting of one member   As a general rule, one member cannot form a meeting, not even if he holds proxies for other members: *Sharp v Dawes* (1876) 2 QBD 26; *Re Sanitary Carbon* Co (1877) WN 223; *Re London Flats Ltd* [1969] 2 All ER 744.

However, there are exceptions:

(1)   if there is one only shareholder in a class of shareholders, the assent of that shareholder is the equivalent of a meeting of the class: *East v Bennett Bros Ltd* [1911] 1 Ch 163; *Re RMCA Reinsurance Ltd* [1994] BCC 378;

(2)   if the company is a single member private company, then notwithstanding anything to the contrary in the articles, one member present in person or by proxy will be a quorum: s 370A;

(3)   where the Secretary of State convenes an annual general meeting under s 367 or the court convenes a meeting under s 371, in either case a direction may be given that one member present in person or by proxy may be deemed to constitute a meeting: ss 367(2), 371(2).

S 370(5)

Chairman of the meeting   The articles invariably provide that the chairman of the board of directors or, in his absence, some other director nominated by the directors, is to act as chairman of a general meeting: see Table A, reg 42. Under Table A, the members' power to appoint a chairman only comes into effect where no director can be found to take the role, see reg 43. As to a chairman's casting vote, see Table A, reg 50.

S 370(6)

Voting rights of the members   Voting rights are dealt with under the articles which typically provide that:

(1)   on a show of hands, every member shall have one vote; and

(2)   on a poll, every member shall have one vote for every share of which he is the holder (see Table A, reg 54).

The terms of issue of a class of shares may restrict the voting rights of the class, as is often the case with preference shareholders, who may be restricted to voting on matters of direct concern to them. Equally, the articles may increase the votes; see *Bushell v Faith* [1969] 1 All ER 1002 where it was provided that on a resolution being proposed at any general meeting of the company for removal from office of any director, any shares held by that director would on a poll in respect of such resolution carry the right to three votes per share.

No member may vote his shares unless all moneys presently payable by him in respect of the shares have been paid up (Table A, reg 57); as shares are generally fully paid now, this provision is of limited significance.

Anyone who wishes to challenge the qualification of any voter must do so at the meeting or adjourned meeting where the vote objected to is given or tendered and the chairman's decision on this matter is final and conclusive: Table A, reg 58; save where there is doubt as to the validity of the chairman's appointment: *Re Bradford Investments Ltd* [1991] BCLC 224.

Limitations on a member's right to vote   In addition to procedural constraints on voting, there are a number of common law principles constraining the exercise of the right to vote.

In general, in exercising their right to vote, shareholders are not trustees for the company or for one another and they may act in accordance with their personal wishes and prejudices: *Pender v Lushington* (1877) 6 Ch D 70; *Menier v Hooper's Telegraph Works* (1874) 9 Ch App 350; *North-West Transportation Co Ltd v Beatty* (1887) 12 App Cas 589, PC; *Burland v Earle* [1902] AC 83.

There is a range of wrongs, essentially covering illegal and fraudulent transactions, which are unratifiable by the shareholders, whether by a majority or unanimously, and in those cases the votes cast by the shareholders for ratification are ineffective: *Burland v Earle* [1902] AC 83; *Menier v Hooper's Telegraph Works* (1874) 9 Ch App 350. But where the wrong is ratifiable, any shareholder has a right to vote on the matter: *North-West Transportation Co Ltd v Beatty* (1887) 12 App Cas 589.

In addition, shareholders are subject to ill-defined obligations, in the context of alteration of articles, to act bona fide for the benefit of the company as a whole (*Allen v Gold Reefs of West Africa Ltd* [1900] 1 Ch 656 and see note to s 9) and, in the context of class meetings, to act in the interests of that class of shareholders as a whole: *Re Holders Investment Trust Ltd* [1971] 2 All ER 289 and see note to s 125.

370A. Quorum at meetings of the sole member

Notwithstanding any provision to the contrary in the articles of a private company limited by shares or by guarantee having only one member, one member present in person or by proxy shall be a quorum.

General note

This provision is a necessary consequence of allowing single member private companies: see s 1(3A). For the method of recording decisions made at a meeting of one, see s 382B.

371. Power of court to order meeting

(1) If for any reason it is impracticable to call a meeting of a company in any manner in which meetings of that company may be called, or to conduct the meeting in manner prescribed by the articles or this Act, the court may, either of its own motion or on the application—

(a) of any director of the company, or

(b) of any member of the company who would be entitled to vote at the meeting,

order a meeting to be called, held and conducted in any manner the court thinks fit.

(2) Where such an order is made, the court may give such ancillary or consequential directions as it thinks expedient; and these may include a direction that one member of the company present in person or by proxy be deemed to constitute a meeting.

(3) A meeting called, held and conducted in accordance with an order under subsection (1) is deemed for all purposes a meeting of the company duly called, held and conducted.

General note

This discretionary jurisdiction relates only to general meetings. There is no discretion to call a board meeting, although the net result of calling a general meeting may be that a new board is appointed and board meetings then follow.

S 371(1)

Application by any member   An application under this provision may be made by any member without any threshold requirements beyond the requirement that they be entitled to vote at the meeting, but no provision is made for an application by a personal representative of a member which means that resort cannot be had to the provision by a personal representative where disputes have arisen following the death of a member.

Court to call meeting   The assistance of the court might be sought where a company finds itself without directors able to convene a meeting, or there is uncertainty as to who are the members, or the members are overseas and the company is unable to serve notice on them (see Dillon LJ in *Harman v BML Group Ltd* [1994] 2 BCLC 674 at 677); or, unusually, because of the potential for violence: *Re British Union for the Abolition of Vivisection* [1995] 2 BCLC 1 (impractical to call general meeting of all 9,000 members when previous meeting had degenerated into near riot and had been stopped by the police). 'Impractical' raises the question whether, in the particular circumstances of the case, the desired meeting of the company could, as a practical matter, take place: *Re El Sombrero Ltd* [1958] Ch 900.

Inquorate meetings   The courts are often asked to exercise their discretion under this provision to resolve the situation which arises where minority shareholders refuse to attend meetings, so rendering them inquorate, with a view to preventing the majority of shareholders from exercising their voting powers on a particular issue, such as the removal of the minority shareholders from office as directors: see *Re Whitchurch Insurance Consultants Ltd* [1993] BCLC 1359; *Re Opera Photographic Ltd* [1989] BCLC 763; *Re El Sombrero Ltd* [1958] Ch 900. To fail to exercise the discretion in such a case would be to confer on the minority a right of veto not commensurate with their shareholding: *Re HR Paul & Son Ltd* (1974) 118 Sol Jo 166.
  The court will not exercise its discretion, however:
    (1)   if the quorum requirement was imposed originally as a class right for the protection of the holder of shares of that class: *Harman v BML Group Ltd* [1994] 2 BCLC 674, CA;
    (2)   if there is deadlock in a 50–50 company: *Ross v Telford* [1998] 1 BCLC 82 – such potential deadlock must be taken to have been imposed with the consent and for the protection of the two equal shareholders. The statutory provision is designed to solve procedural difficulties, but not to shift the balance of power within a company.

Relationship with s 459   The mere fact that a petition alleging unfairly prejudicial conduct has been presented under s 459 does not automatically oust the court's jurisdiction under s 371, but it may be a relevant factor: *Harman v BML Group Ltd* [1994] 2 BCLC 674, CA; *Re Whitchurch Insurance Consultants Ltd* [1993] BCLC 1359; cf *Re Sticky Fingers Restaurant Ltd* [1992] BCLC 84.

S 371(2)

For an example of very unusual directions, see *Re British Union for the Abolition of Vivisection* [1995] 2 BCLC 1, including a direction for postal voting although the company's constitution made no such provision.

---

372. Proxies

(1) Any member of a company entitled to attend and vote at a meeting of it is entitled to appoint another person (whether a member or not) as his proxy to attend and vote instead of him; and in the case of a private company a proxy appointed to attend and vote instead of a member has also the same right as the member to speak at the meeting.

(2) But, unless the articles otherwise provide—

    (a) subsection (1) does not apply in the case of a company not having a share capital; and

    (b) a member of a private company is not entitled to appoint more than one proxy to attend on the same occasion; and

    (c) a proxy is not entitled to vote except on a poll.

(2A) The appointment of a proxy may, notwithstanding any provision to the contrary in a company's articles, be contained in an electronic communication sent to such address as may be notified by or on behalf of the company for that purpose.

(2B) In so far as the articles of the company do not make other provision in that behalf, the appointment of a proxy may be contained in an electronic communication in accordance with the provisions of Table A (as for the time being in force).

(3) In the case of a company having a share capital, in every notice calling a meeting of the company there shall appear with reasonable prominence a statement that a member entitled to attend and vote is entitled to appoint a proxy or, where that is allowed, one or more proxies to attend and vote instead of him, and that a proxy need not also be a member.

(4) If default is made in complying with subsection (3) as respects any meeting, every officer of the company who is in default is liable to a fine.

(5) A provision contained in a company's articles is void in so far as it would have the effect of requiring the appointment of a proxy or any document necessary to show the validity of, or otherwise relating to, the appointment of a proxy, to be received by the company or any other person more than 48 hours before a meeting or adjourned meeting in order that the appointment may be effective.

(6) If for the purpose of any meeting of a company invitations to appoint as proxy a person or one of a number of persons specified in the invitations are issued at the company's expense to some only of the members entitled to be sent a notice of the meeting and to vote at it by proxy, then every officer of the

company who knowingly and wilfully authorises or permits their issue in that manner is liable to a fine.

However, an officer is not so liable by reason only of the issue to a member at his request ... of a form of appointment naming the proxy, or of a list of persons willing to act as proxy, if the form or list is available on request ... to every member entitled to vote at the meeting by proxy.

(6A) In this section,'address' includes any number or address used for the purposes of electronic communications.

(7) This section applies to meetings of any class of members of a company as it applies to general meetings of the company.

General note

A person is not taken to be interested in any shares or debentures of a company for the purposes of s 324 (disclosure by directors of shareholdings in own company) by reason only of his appointment as a proxy: Sch 13, para 3(3)(a).

S 372(1)

Proxies are instruments executed by a voting member of a company in favour of another person, enabling that person to exercise the member's rights to attend and vote at a meeting of the company.

Appointment of a proxy   The right to appoint a proxy is a statutory right, in the case of a company with a share capital, which is not dependent on the articles of the company, but the extent of the rights of the person appointed as a proxy will depend to some extent on the provisions of the articles: see sub-s (2). It might appear that a proxy must be an individual, as the provision envisages that the proxy himself will attend and vote, but the provision does allow for the appointment of 'any person', so there is no reason why a company might not act as a proxy and appoint an individual to carry out the task.

The instrument appointing a proxy may be in writing or it may be contained in an electronic communication (see sub-s (2A)) and it may be a general proxy (allowing the proxy to vote as he chooses) or a two-way proxy (ie cast in a form which requires the proxy holder to cast his principal's vote either for or against a resolution). For examples, see Table A, regs 60, 61; as to the need to notify the company of the appointment, see Table A, reg 63.

Duration of proxy   The authority given by a proxy is valid until it has been revoked in writing and notice of the revocation is received by the company before the commencement of the meeting or the taking of a poll: Table A, reg 63. Even where a proxy has been given and has not been revoked, the member may still attend and vote in person on a poll, in which case the proxy cannot be used: *Cousins v International Brick Co Ltd* [1931] 2 Ch 90, CA.

Attend and speak   By implication, a proxy at a meeting of a public company can attend and vote (on a poll, sub-s (2)(c)), but cannot speak at the meeting although, in practice, the chairman of a meeting of a public company may be prepared to allow a proxy to speak, provided there are no objections from the members.

S 372(2)

Table A does make provision for multiple proxies in private companies: see reg 59. This can be useful if the shareholder is representing numerous beneficial interests.

Voting by a proxy   Unless the articles otherwise provide, a proxy cannot vote on a show of hands (and Table A makes no provision for a proxy to vote on a show of hands) and this applies whether the company is a private or a public company; but a proxy can vote on a poll, and a proxy has the same right to demand a poll as a member: s 373(2).

What is unresolved is whether a proxy, once appointed, must vote and whether he must vote in accordance with his instructions: see *Re Dorman, Long & Co Ltd* [1934] Ch 635; *Second Consolidated Trust Ltd v Ceylon Amalgamated Tea and Rubber Estates Ltd* [1943] 2 All ER 567 at 570; *Oliver v Dalgleish* [1963] 1 WLR 1274. While the courts might be reluctant to hold a proxy to what is, in most cases, a gratuitous obligation, the courts might draw the line at allowing a proxy to vote contrary to the specific instructions given to him: see *Second Consolidated Trust Ltd v Ceylon Amalgamated Tea and Rubber Estates Ltd* [1943] 2 All ER 567 at 570.

S 372(2A)

Electronic communication   This provision was inserted by the Companies Act 1985 (Electronic Communications) Order 2000, SI 2000/3373, art 19(1), (2), as from 22 December 2000 to facilitate the appointment of proxies by electronic communication where the company is agreeable to appointments being made in this way and has provided an address for this purpose; 'electronic communication' means the same as in the Electronic Communications Act 2000: s 744, and see note to s 369(4A); 'address' is defined in sub-s (6A) to allow for the use of fax or e-mail, hence number or address.

This provision applies notwithstanding any provision in the company's articles, such as a requirement that an instrument appointing a proxy be in writing.

S 372(2B)

Electronic communication and provisions in the articles   While companies may utilise sub-s (2A) above without being affected by provisions to the contrary in their articles, there is a lacunae in that the company's existing articles will not provide for practical matters, such as the manner in which an appointment contained in an electronic communication must be deposited with the company ahead of a meeting. Practical difficulties could therefore arise where a company uses these powers without updating its articles; at the same time, Parliament did not want to put every company to the trouble of having to alter its articles.

The statutory solution is to provide that, where the articles do not make other provision, Table A as for the time being in force, exceptionally, applies; this is exceptional for the practice of the Act is that companies are subject to Table A as in force at the time of registration: see note to s 8(2). The application is limited to those provisions of Table A as apply to the appointment of a proxy by electronic communication: see Table A, regs 60-63, as amended by the Companies Act 1985 (Electronic Communications) Order 2000, SI 2000/3373, art 32(1), Sch 1, as from 22 December 2000.

S 372(4)

As to penalties, see s 730, Sch 24; 'officer in default' is defined in s 730(5).

S 372(6)

Company funds may be used to send out proxies (*Peel v London and North Western Rly Co* [1907] 1 Ch 5, CA); but the company may not send out invitations to appoint a proxy to some only of the shareholders. As to penalties, see s 730, Sch 24; 'officer in default' is defined in s 730(5).

S 372(7)

As to class meetings, see s 125.

373. Right to demand a poll

(1) A provision contained in a company's articles is void in so far as it would have the effect either—

    (a) of excluding the right to demand a poll at a general meeting on any question other than the election of the chairman of the meeting or the adjournment of the meeting; or

    (b) of making ineffective a demand for a poll on any such question which is made either—

        (i) by not less than 5 members having the right to vote at the meeting; or

        (ii) by a member or members representing not less than one-tenth of the total voting rights of all the members having the right to vote at the meeting; or

        (iii) by a member or members holding shares in the company conferring a right to vote at the meeting, being shares on which an aggregate sum has been paid up equal to not less than one-tenth of the total sum paid up on all the shares conferring that right.

(2) The appointment of a proxy to vote at a meeting of a company is deemed also to confer authority to demand or join in demanding a poll; and for the purposes of subsection (1) a demand by a person as proxy for a member is the same as a demand by the member.

General note

Initial voting at a meeting may be on a show of hands (one vote per person), but a poll (reflecting the voting rights per share) may be necessary for an accurate reflection of the true position in the company. As to voting on a poll, see s 374. A resolution adopted on a poll takes effect from the date when the result of the poll is ascertained: *Holmes v Lord Keyes* [1959] Ch 199, CA.

Demand by members   A member has a right at common law to demand a poll (*R v Wimbledon Local Board* (1882) 8 QBD 459); this right is subject to any provisions in the articles and this statutory provision imposes limits on the extent to which the articles can exclude or render ineffective a demand for a poll.

Demand by the chairman   The power of the chairman to demand a poll is subject to an obligation to exercise it in furtherance of his general duty, ie in such a way as to give effect to the real sense of the meeting: *Second Consolidated Trust Ltd v Ceylon Amalgamated Tea and Rubber Estates Ltd* [1943] 2 All ER 567. If no poll is demanded, and the chairman is satisfied that he need not demand one, the chairman's decision as to whether a resolution is carried or lost on a show of hands and an entry to that effect in the minute book, is conclusive: see Table A, reg 47; *Re Horbury Bridge, Coal, Iron and Waggon Co* (1879) 11 Ch D 109, CA.

S 373(1)(a)

The articles commonly provide for a poll on the election of the chairman or the adjournment of the meeting: see Table A, reg 51.

S 373(1)(b)

The articles cannot impose any greater restrictions on the right to demand a poll than a minimum of five members or the holders of 10% of the voting rights or of the paid up capital. Table A, reg 46 provides that a poll can be demanded by the chairman, or by two members having the right to vote at the meeting (so it is more liberal than the statutory provision), or by a member or members holding a one-tenth interest of the type specified in sub-s (1)(b)(ii) or (iii). In private companies, this provision is commonly altered to allow one member to demand a poll, so ensuring that the majority shareholder can exercise voting control.

   See also s 164(5)(b) which allows one member to demand a poll, and s 125(6)(b) which allows one member of a class to demand a poll, in certain circumstances.

374. Voting on a poll

On a poll taken at a meeting of a company or a meeting of any class of members of a company, a member entitled to more than one vote need not, if he votes, use all his votes or cast all the votes he uses in the same way.

General note

This provision recognises that a person may hold shares in more than one capacity as where he holds shares both individually and on behalf of a third party or parties. As to class meetings, see s 125.

375. Representation of corporations at meetings

(1) A corporation, whether or not a company within the meaning of this Act, may—

(a) if it is a member of another corporation, being such a company, by resolution of its directors or other governing body authorise such person as it thinks fit to act as its representative at any meeting of the company or at any meeting of any class of members of the company;

(b) if it is a creditor (including a holder of debentures) of another corporation, being such a company, by resolution of its directors or other governing body authorise such person as it thinks fit to act as its representative at any meeting of creditors of the company held in pursuance of this Act or of rules made under it, or in pursuance of the provisions contained in any debenture or trust deed, as the case may be.

(2) A person so authorised is entitled to exercise the same powers on behalf of the corporation which he represents as that corporation could exercise if it were an individual shareholder, creditor or debenture-holder of the other company.

General note

This section is designed to enable a corporation owning shares in a company to be in the same situation for the purpose of meetings of that company as it would be if it were an individual: *Hillman v Crystal Bowl Amusements Ltd* [1973] 1 All ER 379.

A person is not taken to be interested in any shares or debentures of a company for the purposes of s 324 (disclosure by directors of shareholdings in own company) by reason only of his appointment as a corporate representative: Sch 13, para 3(3)(b).

S 375(1)

Corporation is personally present   A corporate shareholder present through a corporate representative is personally present and therefore such a representative can vote on a show of hands, for he is not a proxy; and, in the case of a public company, he can speak at the general meeting, and he can be counted in any quorum requirement which requires members to be personally present: *Hillman v Crystal Bowl Amusements Ltd* [1973] 1 All ER 379.

Only one corporate representative   Only one representative of the corporation is permitted under this provision, which can be inconvenient where the corporation is acting for a number of beneficial owners, as is commonly the case with the growth of corporate nominee services. One possible solution to that difficulty is to appoint multiple proxies although the position of proxies is not identical in all respects to that of a member personally present: see note to s 372, above.

There is some uncertainty as to whether the company can insist on a corporate representative producing evidence of his authority to act as a representative; as a matter of good practice, whatever the legal position, the representative should be able to produce a copy of the resolution authorising his appointment.

This provision applies to class meetings, meetings of creditors and debenture holders. As to the meaning of 'company', see s 735 and as to 'this Act', see s 735A(1).

RESOLUTIONS

376. Circulation of members' resolutions

(1) Subject to the section next following, it is the duty of a company, on the requisition in writing of such number of members as is specified below and (unless the company otherwise resolves) at the expense of the requisitionists—

(a) to give to members of the company entitled to receive notice of the next annual general meeting notice of any resolution which may properly be moved and is intended to be moved at that meeting;

(b) to circulate to members entitled to have notice of any general meeting sent to them any statement of not more than 1,000 words with respect to the matter referred to in any proposed resolution or the business to be dealt with at that meeting.

(2) The number of members necessary for a requisition under subsection (1) is—

(a) any number representing not less than one-twentieth of the total voting rights of all the members having at the date of the requisition a right to vote at the meeting to which the requisition relates; or

(b) not less than 100 members holding shares in the company on which there has been paid up an average sum, per member, of not less than £100.

(3) Notice of any such resolution shall be given, and any such statement shall be circulated, to members of the company entitled to have notice of the meeting sent to them, by serving a copy of the resolution or statement on each such member in any manner permitted for service of notice of the meeting.

(4) Notice of any such resolution shall be given to any other member of the company by giving notice of the general effect of the resolution in any manner permitted for giving him notice of meetings of the company.

(5) For compliance with subsections (3) and (4), the copy must be served, or notice of the effect of the resolution be given (as the case may be) in the same manner and (so far as practicable) at the same time as notice of the meeting; and, where it is not practicable for it to be served or given at the same time, it must be served or given as soon as practicable thereafter.

(6) The business which may be dealt with at an annual general meeting includes any resolution of which notice is given in accordance with this section; and for purposes of this subsection notice is deemed to have been so given notwithstanding the accidental omission, in giving it, of one or more members. This has effect notwithstanding anything in the company's articles.

(7) In the event of default in complying with this section, every officer of the company who is in default is liable to a fine.

_____

General note

Unless a member can rely on this provision or a provision in the company's articles, he has no right to compel the inclusion of a resolution on the agenda of a meeting of the company: *Pedley v Inland Waterways Association Ltd* [1977] 1 All ER 209.

A member may requisition a meeting under s 368, and this provision for the circulation of members' resolutions and statements is seen as another important aspect of shareholder protection, although the protection is more theoretical than real as the provision is rarely used. These rights are of greatest potential significance, perhaps, in public companies where members may want to use these provisions to promote discussion and to gain media attention. A problem, however, is the question of costs, which are the responsibility of the requisitionists unless the company decides otherwise. Some companies may be prepared to carry the costs, provided the requisitionists supply the material in time for it to be included in the mailing of the company's annual accounts and reports.

S 376(1)

Resolutions and statements   There are two distinct rights here:
- (a)   the right to give notice of any resolution what is to be put to the next annual general meeting; and/or
- (b)   a right to circulate any statement regarding any such proposed resolution or any business to be dealt with at that meeting (ie at that next annual general meeting).

There is some uncertainty as to whether sub-s (1)(b) permits the circulation of statements at any general meeting, but the phrase 'entitled to have notice of any general meeting sent to them' in sub-s (1)(b) simply defines the members to whom the statement must be circulated and does not broaden the scope of the provision beyond annual general meetings: see *Rose v McGivern* [1998] 2 BCLC 593 at 603.

Even if the thresholds set out in sub-s (2) are met, there is no obligation to call the meeting unless the requirements of s 377 are met; and those requirements may pose further problems for the requisitionists.

S 376(2)

Thresholds   There is no minimum period of time for which these shares must have been held. The threshold in sub-s (2)(a) is especially high for shareholders in public companies, although sub-s (2)(b) sets a more modest target. These thresholds are different from those in s 368, which determine whether shareholders can requisition an extraordinary general meeting.

S 376(5), (6)

These provisions impose requirements as to the manner and timing of notice and provide the statutory authority for the consideration of this members' resolution at the annual general meeting.

S 376(7)

As to penalties, see s 730, Sch 24; 'officer in default' is defined in s 730(5).

377. In certain cases, compliance with s 376 not required

(1) A company is not bound under section 376 to give notice of a resolution or to circulate a statement unless—

    (a) a copy of the requisition signed by the requisitionists (or two or more copies which between them contain the signatures of all the requisitionists) is deposited at the registered office of the company—

        (i) in the case of a requisition requiring notice of a resolution, not less than 6 weeks before the meeting, and

        (ii) otherwise, not less than one week before the meeting; and

    (b) there is deposited or tendered with the requisition a sum reasonably sufficient to meet the company's expenses in giving effect to it.

(2) But if, after a copy of a requisition requiring notice of a resolution has been deposited at the company's registered office, an annual general meeting is called for a date 6 weeks or less after the copy has been deposited, the copy (though not deposited within the time required by subsection (1)) is deemed properly deposited for the purposes of that subsection.

(3) The company is also not bound under section 376 to circulate a statement if, on the application either of the company or of any other person who claims to be aggrieved, the court is satisfied that the rights conferred by that section are being abused to secure needless publicity for defamatory matter; and the court may order the company's costs on such an application to be paid in whole or in part by the requisitionists, notwithstanding that they are not parties to the application.

S 377(1)

Time limits   There are difficulties of timing here, for the shareholders may only have decided to try to circulate a resolution after they have received the annual accounts and reports. Typically, these documents will have been sent out with a notice convening the annual general meeting, usually for a date six to eight weeks later. It could be quite difficult, therefore, to deposit a copy of the requisition requiring notice of a resolution six weeks ahead of the meeting; the time scale is more generous with respect to a requisition for the circulation of a statement.

S 377(2)

This provision is designed to stop the company frustrating the requisitionists by calling the annual general meeting promptly after the requisitionists have shown their hand, such that the six weeks requirement in sub-s (1) cannot be met.

S 377(3)

A criticism of this provision is that it limits the court's intervention to situations where the provision is being abused to secure needless publicity for defamatory matter and does not impose other requirements, such as a test of relevance to the company's business. Directors argue that such an approach would help exclude lobbying groups seeking wider platforms for their views on issues which, perhaps, have only a marginal relevance to the company's main activities.

378. Extraordinary and special resolutions

(1) A resolution is an extraordinary resolution when it has been passed by a majority of not less than three-fourths of such members as (being entitled to do so) vote in person or, where proxies are allowed, by proxy, at a general meeting of which notice specifying the intention to propose the resolution as an extraordinary resolution has been duly given.

(2) A resolution is a special resolution when it has been passed by such a majority as is required for the passing of an extraordinary resolution and at a general meeting of which not less than 21 days' notice, specifying the intention to propose the resolution as a special resolution, has been duly given.

(3) If it is so agreed by a majority in number of the members having the right to attend and vote at such a meeting, being a majority—

    (a) together holding not less than 95 per cent in nominal value of the shares giving that right; or

    (b) in the case of a company not having a share capital, together representing not less than 95 per cent of the total voting rights at that meeting of all the members,

a resolution may be proposed and passed as a special resolution at a meeting of which less than 21 days' notice has been given.

    A private company may elect (by elective resolution in accordance with section 379A) that the above provisions shall have effect in relation to the company as if for the references to 95 per cent there were substituted references to such lesser percentage, but not less than 90 per cent, as may be specified in the resolution or subsequently determined by the company in general meeting.

(4) At any meeting at which an extraordinary resolution or a special resolution is submitted to be passed, a declaration by the chairman that the resolution is carried is, unless a poll is demanded, conclusive evidence of the fact without proof of the number or proportion of the votes recorded in favour of or against the resolution.

(5) In computing the majority on a poll demanded on the question that an extraordinary resolution or a special resolution be passed, reference is to be had to the number of votes cast for and against the resolution.

(6) For purposes of this section, notice of a meeting is deemed duly given, and the meeting duly held, when the notice is given and the meeting held in the manner provided by this Act or the company's articles.

General note

No specific statutory provision is made for an ordinary resolution which is passed by a simple majority of those voting and which is used whenever the statute or articles require a power to be exercised by the company in general meeting. All extraordinary and special resolutions must be notified to the registrar of companies whereas only certain ordinary resolutions must be so notified: s 380. In addition to resolutions, decisions may be reached by way of informal unanimous consent, see the general note to this Chapter preceding s 366.

Consequences of improper notice　While s 369 provides for the period of notice required for a meeting, this provision imposes obligations as to the notice required of certain resolutions and a company must take care to give proper notice of the contents of the resolution, for a resolution of which inadequate notice is given is invalid and not binding on the company: *Baillie v Oriental Telephone and Electric Co Ltd* [1915] 1 Ch 503; *Normandy v Ind Coope & Co Ltd* [1908] 1 Ch 84; *Tiessen v Henderson* [1899] 1 Ch 861.

S 378(1)

Period of notice　No special period of notice is prescribed for an extraordinary resolution and so the period of notice required will depend upon whether the meeting is an annual general meeting (21 days) or an extraordinary general meeting (14 days): s 369. An extraordinary resolution can be passed by written resolution: s 381A(6).

Requirement for extraordinary resolution　Extraordinary resolutions are something of an oddity and, it would seem, of little utility, save perhaps in the case of IA 1986, s 84(1)(c) (voluntary winding up): see below. The main distinction between an extraordinary resolution and a special resolution is that the period of notice required for an extraordinary resolution can be shorter than that required for a special resolution (21 days), but since short notice of a special resolution is possible, this distinction is of little significance.

Extraordinary resolutions are not commonly required save occasionally by the company's articles (see Table A, reg 117); or by statute. An extraordinary resolution is required for certain variations of class rights (s 125(2)(b)); to wind up the company voluntarily (IA 1986, s 84(1)(c), and the shorter notice required than for a special resolution may be important in this context); and to sanction the exercise by a liquidator of certain powers in a members' voluntary winding up: IA 1986, s 165(2)(a).

Amendments　Amendments to an extraordinary resolution are only permitted if they do not alter the substance of the resolution as notified to the shareholders: *Re Moorgate Mercantile Holdings Ltd* [1980] 1 All ER 40, discussed below.

S 378(2)

A special resolution can be passed by written resolution: s 381A(6).

Requirement for a special resolution　A special resolution is required by the legislation on a number of occasions including:

(1)   on an alteration of objects (s 4);

(2)   on an alteration of articles (s 9);

(3)   on a change of name (s 28);

(4)   on the re-registration of a public company as a private company (s 53);

(5)   on disapplying the statutory pre-emption rights (s 95);

(6)   on a reduction of share capital (s 135);

(7)   where a private company gives financial assistance for the purchase of its own shares (s 155(4));

(8)   on the occasion of an off-market purchase of a company's own shares (s 164(4)); and

(9)   on a resolution to wind up the company voluntarily (IA 1986, s 84(1)(b)).

Notice of a special resolution   The nature of the notice required to propose a special resolution was considered in depth in *Re Moorgate Mercantile Holdings Ltd* [1980] 1 All ER 40 where Slade J laid down the following propositions:

- The notice must identify the intended resolution by specifying either the text or the entire substance of the resolution which it is intended to propose; and nothing is achieved by the addition of such words as 'with such amendments and alterations as shall be determined on at such meeting'. In practice, the text of the resolution should be set out in full.

- If the resolution is to be validly passed, it must be the same resolution as that identified in the preceding notice, so an amendment to the previously circulated text of a special resolution can be put to and voted on at a meeting only if the amendment involves no departure from the substance of the circulated text. Amendments are limited, therefore, to the correction of grammatical or clerical errors or to reducing the words to more formal language.

- In deciding whether there is complete identity between the substance of a resolution as passed and the substance of an intended resolution as notified, there is no room for the court to apply the de minimis principle or a limit of tolerance. The substance must be identical.

- The above propositions may be subject to modification where all the members, or a class of members, of a company unanimously agree to waive their rights to notice, applying the *Duomatic* principle: see the general note to this Chapter which precedes s 366.

The justification, Slade J thought, for such a strict approach was that special resolutions are used in special situations where the resolutions are likely either to affect the company's constitution or to have an important effect on its future (although he had in mind the limited circumstances in which such resolutions were required under the CA 1948). Shareholders therefore require clear and precise notice of the substance of the resolution.

Amendments   The difficulty with the restrictions on amendments (see above) is that the chairman may be uncertain whether the substance of the resolution has remained the same and whether he can put it to the meeting. If he is unsure, he may choose to adjourn the proceedings to allow notice to be given of the proposed (amended) resolution. The shareholders could then agree to short notice (s 378(3)) and proceed to consider the amended resolution.

Ordinary resolutions   The same considerations do not apply to ordinary resolutions, where there is greater scope for amendment (*Betts v MacNaghten* [1910] 1 Ch 430);

although this too is subject to the overriding requirement that the notice must disclose all relevant facts so that a member can exercise an informed business judgment as to whether or not he ought to attend the meeting: *Tiessen v Henderson* [1899] 1 Ch 861. If amendments change the resolution too significantly from what was originally notified, there is a danger that proper notice has not been given and the resolution is invalid.

Where the ordinary resolution is one of which special notice is required (see s 379), it is likely that, as far as permitting amendments is concerned, the courts would treat such a resolution in the same manner as a special resolution.

S 378(3)

The requirement is for a majority in number as well as voting thresholds; see notes to s 369(3), (4).

Those consenting to the passing of a special resolution on short notice must appreciate that it is being passed on short notice: *Re Pearce, Duff & Co Ltd* [1960] 3 All ER 222. As to elective resolutions, see s 379A.

S 378(4)

It is only a declaration that a resolution is carried which is conclusive and it is only conclusive where no poll is demanded. Table A, reg 47 is to similar effect, but it is wider, not being limited to extraordinary and special resolutions, nor solely to resolutions which are carried; but it does require in addition that the declaration of the chairman be entered in the minutes: see also s 382(4).

This declaration of the chairman is open to challenge where the declaration shows on its face that it is invalid: *Re Hadleigh Castle Gold Mines Ltd* [1900] 2 Ch 419; *Re Caratal (New) Mines Ltd* [1902] 2 Ch 498.

S 378(5)

In other words, in calculating the voting percentages, no account is taken of those abstaining from voting.

---

379. Resolution requiring special notice

(1) Where by any provision of this Act special notice is required of a resolution, the resolution is not effective unless notice of the intention to move it has been given to the company at least 28 days before the meeting at which it is moved.

(2) The company shall give its members notice of any such resolution at the same time and in the same manner as it gives notice of the meeting or, if that is not practicable, shall give them notice either by advertisement in a newspaper having an appropriate circulation or in any other mode allowed by the company's articles, at least 21 days before the meeting.

(3) If, after notice of the intention to move such a resolution has been given to the company, a meeting is called for a date 28 days or less after the notice has

been given, the notice is deemed properly given, though not given within the time required.

General note

The special notice of any ordinary resolution within this provision must be given *to* the company at least 28 days before the meeting. The provision is somewhat peculiar in that in most instances the proposed resolution will have been initiated by the company (ie the board) and therefore the requirement is to give notice to the company by the company. The company's articles may also make provision for special notice, see Table A, reg 76.

Using a written resolution   It is unclear whether this requirement for special notice can be side-stepped by a private company using a written resolution under s 381A. It seems that a written resolution without any special notice is effective, for the provisions governing written resolutions were added to the Act in the knowledge of the existence of the restrictions imposed by this provision. Section 381A(1) specifically states that a written resolution may be passed without *any* previous notice (to anyone) having been given; and Sch 15A, para 1 specifically identifies the two situations when a written resolution may not be used. The position would have been clearer, however, had this section been amended to state that it has no application where a written resolution is used.

S 379(1)

When special notice is required   Special notice is required of the following resolutions:
- (1) for the appointment to a public company of a director over 70 years of age (s 293(5));
- (2) for the removal of a director (s 303(2));
- (3) to fill a casual vacancy in the office of auditor or to re-appoint as auditor a retiring auditor who was appointed to a casual vacancy (s 388(3));
- (4) for the removal of an auditor before the expiry of his term of office or the appointment as auditor of a person other than the retiring auditor (s 391A(1)).

The intention of Parliament in enacting this provision is to ensure that, with regard to matters of such importance, all concerned have at least 21 days' notice; and, for this reason, short notice of a resolution requiring special notice is not possible: *Pedley v Inland Waterways Association Ltd* [1977] 1 All ER 209 at 217.

S 379(2)

The requirement that the company 'shall give its members notice' does not confer on an individual member the right to compel the inclusion of a resolution (of which he has given special notice) on the agenda of a company meeting. If a member is to get a resolution on the agenda, he must rely on s 376 or a provision in the articles of association: *Pedley v Inland Waterways Association Ltd* [1977] 1 All ER 209. This wording simply means that members have the right to receive notice of any resolution for which special notice is needed and duly given, and which is to form part of the agenda to be dealt with at the relevant meeting. To interpret it more broadly would be to confer rights on shareholders more extensive than those granted by s 376, which cannot have been the intention of Parliament: *Pedley v Inland Waterways Association Ltd* [1977] 1 All ER 209.

S 379(3)

This is to prevent the company from rendering the resolution ineffective by convening the meeting to take place in less than 28 days.

379A. Elective resolution of private company

(1) An election by a private company for the purposes of—

(a) section 80A (election as to duration of authority to allot shares),

(b) section 252 (election to dispense with laying of accounts and reports before general meeting),

(c) section 366A (election to dispense with holding of annual general meeting),

(d) section 369(4) or 378(3) (election as to majority required to authorise short notice of meeting), or

(e) section 386 (election to dispense with appointment of auditors annually),

shall be made by resolution of the company in general meeting in accordance with this section.

Such a resolution is referred to in this Act as an 'elective resolution'.

(2) An elective resolution is not effective unless—

(a) at least 21 days' notice in writing is given of the meeting, stating that an elective resolution is to be proposed and stating the terms of the resolution, and

(b) the resolution is agreed to at the meeting, in person or by proxy, by all the members entitled to attend and vote at the meeting.

(2A) An elective resolution is effective notwithstanding the fact that less than 21 days' notice in writing of the meeting is given if all the members entitled to attend and vote at the meeting so agree.

(2B) For the purposes of this section, notice in writing of the meeting is to be taken as given to a person where notice of the meeting is sent using electronic communications to such address as may for the time being be notified by that person to the company for that purpose.

(2C) For the purposes of this section a notice in writing of the meeting is also to be treated as given to a person where—

(a) the company and that person have agreed that notices of meetings required to be given to that person may instead be accessed by him on a web site;

(b) the meeting is a meeting to which that agreement applies;

(c) that person is notified, in a manner for the time being agreed between him and the company for the purpose, of—

(i) the publication of the notice on a web site;

(ii) the address of that web site; and

(iii) the place on that web site where the notice may be accessed, and how it may be accessed; and

(d) the notice continues to be published on that web site throughout the period beginning with the giving of that notification and ending with the conclusion of the meeting;

and for the purposes of this section a notice treated in accordance with this subsection as given to any person is to be treated as so given at the time of the notification mentioned in paragraph (c).

(2D) A notification given for the purposes of subsection (2C)(c) must—

(a) state that it concerns a notice of a company meeting at which an elective resolution is to be proposed, and

(b) specify the place, date and time of the meeting.

(2E) Nothing in subsection (2C) shall invalidate the proceedings of a meeting where—

(a) any notice that is required to be published as mentioned in paragraph (d) of that subsection is published for a part, but not all, of the period mentioned in that paragraph; and

(b) the failure to publish that notice throughout that period is wholly attributable to circumstances which it would not be reasonable to have expected the company to prevent or avoid.

(2F) In so far as the articles of the company do not provide for notices and notifications to be served using electronic communications, the provisions of Table A (as for the time being in force) as to such service shall apply.

(3) The company may revoke an elective resolution by passing an ordinary resolution to that effect.

(4) An elective resolution shall cease to have effect if the company is re-registered as a public company.

(5) An elective resolution may be passed or revoked in accordance with this section, and the provisions referred to in subsections (1) and (2B) to (2E) have effect, notwithstanding any contrary provision in the company's articles of association.

(5A) In this section, 'address' includes any number or address used for the purposes of electronic communications.

General note

The CA 1989 made provision for elective resolutions whereby private companies might opt out of the provisions of the companies legislation specified in s 379A. Elective resolutions must be registered under s 380.

S 379A(1)

Elective resolutions   An elective resolution may refer to all or any of the provisions specified; and it must be agreed to at a meeting, subject to the ability of a private company to use a written resolution instead, see s 381A(6).

S 379A(2)

Notice of the terms of the resolution   As the terms of the resolution must be notified, it is clear that the restrictive approach adopted to amendments of special and extraordinary resolutions will also apply here: see s 378(2). If the resolution is to be validly passed, it must be the same resolution as that identified in the preceding notice: *Re Moorgate Mercantile Holdings Ltd* [1980] 1 All ER 40, and see note to s 378(2), above.

The provision applies to all private companies, but the requirement of unanimity will restrict its use and the agreement required is that of all of those entitled to attend and vote as opposed to those present and voting.

S 379A(2A)

Short notice is possible where all the shareholders so agree; and an elective resolution may be passed by written resolution without notice under s 381A.

S 379A(2B)

Notice by electronic communication   This provision, and sub-ss (2C)–(2F), (5A) were inserted by the Companies Act 1985 (Electronic Communications) Order 2000, SI 2000/3373, art 21, as from 22 December 2000; it allows a company to give notice of a meeting (at which an elective resolution is to be proposed) by electronic communication to a member where the member has agreed to that method of communication; 'address' is defined in sub-s (5A).

'Electronic communication' means the same as in the Electronic Communications Act 2000: s 744; where it is defined as a communication transmitted (whether from one person to another, from one device to another or from a person to a device or vice versa): (a) by means of a telecommunication system (within the meaning of the Telecommunications Act 1984); or (b) by other means but while in an electronic form: Electronic Communications Act 2000, s 15.

Thus, notice in writing of a meeting is treated as given where, for example, notice of the meeting is given by fax or e-mail, and see sub-s (2C) as to the use of a web site for these purposes.

S 379A(2C)–(2E)

Notice on a web site   Notice in writing may be treated as given to a person where there is agreement that notices of meetings may be accessed on a web site.

Notification of publication on a web site   In order to ensure that a member does not have to monitor a web site, the company must notify him in the agreed manner of the publication of a notice of a meeting on a web site. There is no requirement that that notification of publication be by electronic communication; it could be by post, but in practice it is likely to be by e-mail. Certain basic matters must be included in that notification to ensure that the member appreciates the nature of the meeting which is being called without being required to go to the web site. The company is not restricted to the use of the same web site on every occasion, but it must indicate the address of the site being used in each instance.

Where the notice of the meeting is published on a web site, notice is treated as given at the time of this notification to the member of the publication of the notice on a web site (so the 21 days must be calculated from this date). As to the time when that notification is treated as given, see the company's articles. However, if the company uses electronic communication for that notification, there is a danger that its articles will make no provision for serving notices and notifications by electronic communication: this lacunae is dealt with by sub-s (2F), below.

Availability on the web site   The notice must be available on the web site throughout the period beginning with the notification of the publication of the notice on a web site and ending with the conclusion of the meeting, subject to sub-s (2E) which condones any failure to publish the notice which is *wholly* attributable to circumstances which it would not be reasonable to have expected the company to prevent or avoid. In other words, the failure to publish as required throughout the period must be due to some unavoidable failure of the technology rather than, say, a failure by the company to maintain the web site in a proper manner.

S 379A(2F), (5)

Provisions in the articles   Sub-section (5) ensures that provisions in a company's articles (for example, references to notices in writing) do not prevent the company from taking advantage of these powers. No doubt, when it is convenient to do so, companies will take the opportunity to update their articles to reflect the use of electronic communications; in the meantime, they may use these electronic methods, with the agreement of the individual member, and they do not need to adopt new articles to permit them to do so, nor must they take steps to alter existing provisions which are restricted to paper communications.

However, while companies may utilise these provisions and are not affected by provisions to the contrary in their articles, there is a lacunae in that the company's existing articles will not provide for the service and receipt of notice by electronic communications. These provisions treating notification by electronic communication to be notice in writing operate only for the purposes of this statutory provision and do not apply to the company's articles. Practical difficulties could therefore arise where a company uses these powers without updating its articles.

The solution provided in sub-s (2F) is that, where the articles make no provision for notices or notifications to be served using electronic communications, Table A as for the time being in force, exceptionally, applies; this is exceptional for the practice of the Act is that companies are subject to Table A as in force at the time of registration: see note to s 8(2). The application is limited to those provisions of Table A as apply to service by electronic communication: see Table A, regs 111–115, as amended by the Companies Act 1985 (Electronic Communications) Order 2000, SI 2000/3373, art 32(1), Sch 1, as from 22 December 2000.

S 379A(3), (4)

Revoking elective resolutions   The terminology of these two provisions is slightly confusing, with sub-s (3) referring to the resolution being revoked (when it necessarily ceases to have effect) and sub-s (4) referring to a resolution 'ceasing to have effect' when the company re-registers as a public company.

As other provisions in the Act refer to an election under this provision 'ceasing to have effect' (see, for example, ss 80A(7), 252(4), 366A(5)) which will encompass sub-ss (3) and (4), it would have been preferable if the language of sub-ss (3) and (4) could have been consistent with that terminology.

---

380. Registration, etc of resolutions and agreements

(1) A copy of every resolution or agreement to which this section applies shall, within 15 days after it is passed or made, be forwarded to the registrar of companies and recorded by him; and it must be either a printed copy or else a copy in some other form approved by the registrar.

(2) Where articles have been registered, a copy of every such resolution or agreement for the time being in force shall be embodied in or annexed to every copy of the articles issued after the passing of the resolution or the making of the agreement.

(3) Where articles have not been registered, a printed copy of every such resolution or agreement shall be forwarded to any member at his request on payment of 5 pence or such less sum as the company may direct.

(4) This section applies to—

   (a) special resolutions;

   (b) extraordinary resolutions;

   (bb) an elective resolution or a resolution revoking such a resolution;

   (c) resolutions or agreements which have been agreed to by all the members of a company but which, if not so agreed to, would not have been effective for their purpose unless (as the case may be) they had been passed as special resolutions or as extraordinary resolutions;

   (d) resolutions or agreements which have been agreed to by all the members of some class of shareholders but which, if not so agreed to, would not have been effective for their purpose unless they had been passed by some particular majority or otherwise in some particular manner, and all resolutions or agreements which effectively bind all the members of any class of shareholders though not agreed to by all those members;

   (e) a resolution passed by the directors of a company in compliance with a direction under section 31(2) (change of name on Secretary of State's direction);

   (f) a resolution of a company to give, vary, revoke or renew an authority to the directors for the purposes of section 80 (allotment of relevant securities);

(g) a resolution of the directors passed under section 147(2) (alteration of memorandum on company ceasing to be a public company, following acquisition of its own shares);

(h) a resolution conferring, varying, revoking or renewing authority under section 166 (market purchase of company's own shares);

(j) a resolution for voluntary winding up, passed under section 84(1)(a) of the Insolvency Act;

(k) a resolution passed by the directors of an old public company, under section 2(1) of the Consequential Provisions Act, that the company should be re-registered as a public company.

(l) a resolution of the directors passed by virtue of regulation 16(2) of the Uncertificated Securities Regulations 1995 (which allow title to a company's shares to be evidenced and transferred without written instrument); and

(m) a resolution of a company passed by virtue of regulation 16(6) of the Uncertificated Securities Regulations 1995 (which prevents or reverses a resolution of the directors under regulation 16(2) of those Regulations).

(5) If a company fails to comply with subsection (1), the company and every officer of it who is in default is liable to a fine and, for continued contravention, to a daily default fine.

(6) If a company fails to comply with subsection (2) or (3), the company and every officer of it who is in default is liable to a fine.

(7) For purposes of subsections (5) and (6), a liquidator of a company is deemed an officer of it.

General note

Written resolutions must be forwarded to the registrar   Written resolutions are treated as if they were resolutions passed at a meeting of the company or a class of shareholders (s 381A(4)) and, therefore, if within the categories specified in this section, they too must be notified to the registrar of companies.

Other provisions which require resolutions to be notified to the registrar of companies are: s 367(5) which requires an ordinary resolution to be registered where the Secretary of State has ordered a company to call an annual general meeting and the company has resolved to combine that meeting with its annual general meeting for the current year; s 111(2) which requires the registration of an ordinary resolution under s 104(4)(c) authorising the transfer of a non-cash asset to a public company in the initial period; and s 123(3) which requires the registration of an ordinary resolution authorising an increase in share capital.

S 380(1)

As to when a resolution is passed when a meeting is adjourned, see s 381.

Conditional resolutions   Problems can arise where a company passes a resolution which is conditional on certain other events occurring (for example, a name change conditional on the completion of the acquisition of some business). As this provision imposes a 15-day limit, the resolution may have to be delivered to the registrar of companies at a time when the condition is not then satisfied. On delivery, the registrar of companies may act on the resolution without appreciating that the condition has not been satisfied and so proceed, for example, to take the steps required by s 28(6), ie to change the name and issue a certificate of incorporation in the new name. To avoid these problems, companies should take care either to complete all steps within the 15 days allowed for delivery of the resolution, so that the condition is satisfied by the time of delivery, or to make clear on the face of the document when submitting it to the registrar of companies that the condition has not been satisfied.

S 380(2)

This requirement (which is very broadly defined) is frequently overlooked, especially in smaller companies. Articles need not be registered: see ss 7, 8.

S 380(4)

As to special and extraordinary resolutions, see s 378; as to elective resolutions, see s 379A.

Uncertain scope   The exact application of sub-ss (4)(c) and (d) is somewhat unclear but it seems that they would cover resolutions which for some reason, such as inadequate notice, do not amount to valid special or extraordinary resolutions, or class resolutions, but which are valid and binding because of the application of the *Duomatic* principle (see the general note to this Chapter which precedes s 366, above), ie because of the agreement of all of the members of the company (sub-s (4)(c)) or of the class (sub-s (4)(d)). The fact that decisions reached by such informal unanimous assent must be notified can be overlooked. Note the requirement to register all resolutions or agreements binding all members of any class though not agreed to by all those members (ie where a majority consent to the variation or abrogation of class rights under s 125).

     A further uncertainty is with respect to shareholder agreements. It seems clear that a shareholders' agreement would not require registration under this provision, unless it was possible to treat an agreement in a particular instance as, say, an informal alteration of the articles which alteration would require registration: see *Harman v BML Group Ltd* [1994] 2 BCLC 674 at 678; *Cane v Jones* [1981] 1 All ER 533.

Resolutions of directors   The provisions in sub-ss (4)(e), (g), (k), and (l) are unusual in that they refer to resolutions of the directors.

Ordinary resolutions   The provisions in sub-s (4)(f), (h), (j), and (m) relate to ordinary resolutions of the company dealing with matters of such significance that registration is required: and see the general note to this section, above.

Certain resolutions within this provision must be gazetted by the registrar of companies: see s 711(1)(l).

S 380(5),(6)

Non-compliance   Non-registration under this provision has no effect on the validity of the resolution or agreement which has not been notified (subject to the limited matters within s 42 which cannot be relied on as against a third party where they have not been officially notified as required; and official notification can only take place if the registrar has received notice). The only penalty is a criminal sanction attached to the company and the officer in default: as to penalties, see s 730, Sch 24; 'officer in default' is defined in s 730(5). Of course, the absence of registration may cause evidential problems at a later date.

381. Resolution passed at adjourned meeting

Where a resolution is passed at an adjourned meeting of—

    (a) a company;

    (b) the holders of any class of shares in a company;

    (c) the directors of a company;

the resolution is for all purposes to be treated as having been passed on the date on which it was in fact passed, and is not to be deemed passed on any earlier date.

General note

This provision is of broad application, applying to class and board meetings as well as general meetings; on the adjournment of general meetings, see Table A, reg 45. The significance of this provision is that the time limit for filing resolutions under s 380 with the registrar of companies starts from a later date.

WRITTEN RESOLUTIONS OF PRIVATE COMPANIES

381A. Written resolutions of private companies

(1) Anything which in the case of a private company may be done—

    (a) by resolution of the company in general meeting, or

    (b) by resolution of a meeting of any class of members of the company, may be done, without a meeting and without any previous notice being required, by resolution in writing signed by or on behalf of all the members of the company who at the date of the resolution would be entitled to attend and vote at such meeting.

(2) The signatures need not be on a single document provided each is on a document which accurately states the terms of the resolution.

(3) The date of the resolution means when the resolution is signed by or on behalf of the last member to sign.

(4) A resolution agreed to in accordance with this section has effect as if passed—

  (a) by the company in general meeting, or

  (b) by a meeting of the relevant class of members of the company,

as the case may be; and any reference in any enactment to a meeting at which a resolution is passed or to members voting in favour of a resolution shall be construed accordingly.

(5) Any reference in any enactment to the date of passing of a resolution is, in relation to a resolution agreed to in accordance with this section, a reference to the date of the resolution, …

(6) A resolution may be agreed to in accordance with this section which would otherwise be required to be passed as a special, extraordinary or elective resolution; and any reference in any enactment to a special, extraordinary or elective resolution includes such a resolution.

(7) This section has effect subject to the exceptions specified in Part I of Schedule 15A; and in relation to certain descriptions of resolution under this section the procedural requirements of this Act have effect with the adaptations specified in Part II of that Schedule.

General note

This provision is designed to expedite matters for private companies, especially small private companies, and allows them to substitute a written resolution for any type of resolution required by the statute, subject to the exceptions in s 381A(7). As to the recording of such resolutions, see s 382A.

  This provision is in addition to any provision for written resolutions which the company may have in its articles: s 381C; see Table A, reg 53.

S 381A(1)

Written resolutions   The provision applies to all private companies, although the unanimity requirement will limit its utility in larger companies. It is sometimes overlooked that the mechanism is available for use in class meetings as well as general meetings.

Unanimity   No meeting is required, and no notice need be given, but the resolution must be signed by the member or on his behalf and the consent of all members entitled to attend and vote (as opposed to those actually voting) is required. The requirement of unanimity means that any shareholder, even one with a minuscule holding who will be outvoted at a meeting, can prevent the company proceeding in this way and require a meeting to be held to outvote him. While the wording states that no notice is required, it is not altogether clear whether a written resolution could be used where special notice is required under s 379, but it seems that it can: see the note to that provision.

S 381A(2)

Multiple documents   This provision expedites matters by enabling the resolution to go to each member at the same time without any need to circulate a single document among all the members. The requirement that the document accurately states the terms of the resolution will preclude any amendment of the terms after some of the members have signed and, in that case, a new resolution would have to be circulated.

S 381A(3), (5)

Date of the resolution   These provisions clarify the position as to the date of the resolution. It is important when signing that each member also dates his signature so as to identify the date of the last signature.

S 381A(4)

Notification to the registrar   As a written resolution is the same as a resolution passed at a meeting, it will have to be forwarded to the registrar of companies under s 380 when the resolution falls within the categories of resolution there specified.

S 381A(6)

Statutory requirements   This provision specifically addresses the doubts expressed in *Re Barry Artists Ltd* [1985] BCLC 283 as to whether a written resolution might be used where the statute expressly provided for a special resolution.

However, this only removes those doubts if the statutory written resolution procedure is used ('in accordance with this section') as opposed to any written resolution procedure which the company may have in its articles: see note to s 381C.

S 381A(7)

Statutory exclusions   The statutory written resolution procedure does not apply to—
    (1)   a resolution under s 303 removing a director before the expiration of his period of office, or
    (2)   a resolution under s 391 removing an auditor before the expiration of his term of office: Sch 15A, para 1.

In these cases, where the powers under those statutory provisions are to be utilised, such directors and auditors have a statutory right to make representations at a general meeting, (ss 304, 390(1), 391(4)). For the same reasons, a written resolution procedure provided by the articles would be ineffective where a company purported to exercise its powers under s 303 or s 391 to remove a director or auditor.

Statutory modifications   Certain schemes in the legislation require documents to be available for inspection by shareholders at a general meeting. Obviously, such schemes must be adapted if a written resolution is to be used. Sch 15A, Pt II, modifies the schemes dealing with:

(1)   the disapplication of pre-emption rights (s 95);

(2)   the giving of financial assistance for share purchase (s 155);

(3)   an off-market or contingent purchases of own shares (ss 164, 165, 167);

(4)   the redemption or purchase of own shares out of capital (s 173);

(5)   the approval of directors' service contracts (s 319); and

(6)   the funding of directors' expenditure in performing their duties, s 337.

The additional requirement in such cases is that copies of such documents as would otherwise be available at a general meeting must be circulated to the members at or before the time when the resolution is supplied for signature. The unanimous voting requirement is also modified since some shareholders entitled to vote are not permitted to do so with respect to certain transactions: see Sch 15A, paras 5, 6.

This provision, therefore, disapplies the statutory written resolution procedure in two cases and modifies its operation in respect of the specified provisions. As these constraints only apply where the statutory written resolution procedure is used, it might be thought that, to avoid these additional complications, a company should utilise the written resolution procedure under its articles: see s 381C. However, this may be ill-advised in view of the doubts expressed in *Re Barry Artists Ltd* [1985] BCLC 283 as to the effectiveness of written resolutions effected under the articles in the face of specific statutory requirements, in that case, the requirement for a special resolution.

A decision taken by written resolution which fails to meet the statutory requirements because, for example, information was not circulated ahead of the signing of the resolution as required, might still be validated under the *Duomatic* principle: see the general note to this Chapter which precedes s 366.

381B. Duty to notify auditors of proposed written resolution

(1) If a director or secretary of a company—

(a)   knows that it is proposed to seek agreement to a resolution in accordance with section 381A, and

(b)   knows the terms of the resolution,

he shall, if the company has auditors, secure that a copy of the resolution is sent to them, or that they are otherwise notified of its contents, at or before the time the resolution is supplied to a member for signature.

(2) A person who fails to comply with subsection (1) is liable to a fine.

(3) In any proceedings for an offence under this section it is a defence for the accused to prove—

(a)   that the circumstances were such that it was not practicable for him to comply with subsection (1), or

(b)   that he believed on reasonable grounds that a copy of the resolution had been sent to the company's auditors or that they had otherwise been informed of its contents.

(4) Nothing in this section affects the validity of any resolution.

General note

This provision, as substituted by the Deregulation (Resolutions of Private Companies) Order 1996, SI 1996/1471, replaced an even more cumbersome mechanism which gave the auditors a significant role in the written resolution procedure. The current provision has reduced the obligation to one of mere notification, but its utility too must be questioned.

S 381B(1)

Notification to the auditors   The obligation falls on a director or the company secretary but the requirement to notify the auditors only arises under the statutory written resolution procedure and does not arise if the company opts to use any written resolution procedure in its articles (see Table A, reg 53), but see the note to s 381C.

The provision specifically states that it only applies if the company has auditors, so clarifying the position for the very large number of private companies which are exempt from the requirement to appoint auditors: see s 388A.

S 381B(2)

As to penalties, see s 730, Sch 24.

S 381B(3)

It would not be practicable to comply, for example, when a written resolution is agreed to immediately by all the members present together and so there is no period when the auditors might be notified of it.

S 381B(4)

Notification (or not) to the auditors has no effect on the validity of the resolution, so there is no need for the company to await a response from the auditors or for any set period of time to pass before proceeding with or acting on the resolution.

381C. Written resolutions: supplementary provisions

(1) Sections 381A and 381B have effect notwithstanding any provision of the company's memorandum or articles, but do not prejudice any power conferred by any such provision.

(2) Nothing in those sections affects any enactment or rule of law as to—

    (a) things done otherwise than by passing a resolution, or

    (b) cases in which a resolution is treated as having been passed, or a person is precluded from alleging that a resolution has not been duly passed.

S 381C(1)

This provision clarifies the relationship between the statutory provisions governing written resolutions and the provisions on written resolutions which companies commonly have in their articles (see Table A, reg 53); although the need for unanimity necessarily limits the utility of written resolutions in public companies.

The result is that a private company may utilise either the statutory procedure or the procedure provided for in its own articles, but there seems to be no advantage now in utilising the procedure under the articles (particularly in the light of the amendments to s 381B) and the statutory procedure avoids any difficulties arising from the decision in *Re Barry Artists Ltd* [1985] BCLC 283: see note to s 381A(6), (7). As the statutory provision applies only to private companies, public companies will have to rely on a provision in their articles, in so far as it is practical for them to use a written resolution. In that case, the decision in *Re Barry Artists Ltd* [1985] BCLC 283 remains relevant; see note to s 381A(6).

S 381C(2)

This provision shows that the procedure for written resolutions is not intended to affect the operation of the *Duomatic* principle (see the general note to this Chapter which precedes s 366): see *Wright v Atlas Wright (Europe) Ltd* [1999] 2 BCLC 301 at 311.

RECORDS OF PROCEEDINGS

382. Minutes of meetings

(1) Every company shall cause minutes of all proceedings of general meetings, all proceedings at meetings of its directors and, where there are managers, all proceedings at meetings of its managers to be entered in books kept for that purpose.

(2) Any such minute, if purporting to be signed by the chairman of the meeting at which the proceedings were had, or by the chairman of the next succeeding meeting, is evidence of the proceedings.

(3) Where a shadow director by means of a notice required by section 317(8) declares an interest in a contract or proposed contract, this section applies—

   (a) if it is a specific notice under paragraph (a) of that subsection, as if the declaration had been made at the meeting there referred to, and

   (b) otherwise, as if it had been made at the meeting of the directors next following the giving of the notice;

and the making of the declaration is in either case deemed to form part of the proceedings at the meeting.

(4) Where minutes have been made in accordance with this section of the proceedings at any general meeting of the company or meeting of directors or managers, then, until the contrary is proved, the meeting is deemed duly held and convened, and all proceedings had at the meeting to have been duly had; and all appointments of directors, managers or liquidators are deemed valid.

(5) If a company fails to comply with subsection (1), the company and every officer of it who is in default is liable to a fine and, for continued contravention, to a daily default fine.

S 382(1)

Despite the requirement that minutes be entered in 'books', minutes need not be kept in any particular form and may be recorded in any other manner, including a non-legible form, ie on computer: ss 722, 723. Where a bound book is not used, adequate precautions must be taken against falsification: s 722. As to the inspection of minutes, see s 383. The minute books of general meetings must be kept at the registered office, but there is no such requirement for other minute books: s 383.

S 382(2), (4)

Minutes are evidence, but only prima facie evidence, of the proceedings. The extent of the presumptions in sub-s (4) should be noted, including a presumption that appointments are valid. The burden of challenging the record is on those wishing to do so. This provision will only apply when there is (i) a minute and (ii) a minute entered in the company minute book; and it only provides that what is minuted is evidence, not that the minutes are conclusive: see *POW Services Ltd v Clare* [1995] 2 BCLC 435 at 444. See also s 285 and Table A, reg 92.

S 382(3)

'Shadow director' is defined in s 741(2).

S 382(5)

As to penalties, see s 730, Sch 24; 'officer in default' is defined in s 730(5).

382A. Recording of written resolutions

(1) Where a written resolution is agreed to in accordance with section 381A which has effect as if agreed by the company in general meeting, the company shall cause a record of the resolution (and of the signatures) to be entered in a book in the same way as minutes of proceedings of a general meeting of the company.

(2) Any such record, if purporting to be signed by a director of the company or by the company secretary, is evidence of the proceedings in agreeing to the resolution; and where a record is made in accordance with this section, then, until the contrary is proved, the requirements of this Act with respect to those proceedings shall be deemed to be complied with.

(3) Section 382(5) (penalties) applies in relation to a failure to comply with subsection (1) above as it applies in relation to a failure to comply with subsection (1) of that section; and section 383 (inspection of minute books) applies in relation to a record made in accordance with this section as it applies in relation to the minutes of a general meeting.

S 382A(1)

As to the minutes of general meetings, see s 382. While there is no requirement to minute a written resolution under Table A, reg 53, good practice is to do so.

S 382A(2)

This provision is the equivalent provision to s 382(2), (4).

S 382A(3)

This makes clear that the right to inspect the minutes extends to the record of written resolutions.

382B. Recording of decisions by the sole member

(1) Where a private company limited by shares or by guarantee has only one member and he takes any decision which may be taken by the company in general meeting and which has effect as if agreed by the company in general meeting, he shall (unless that decision is taken by way of a written resolution) provide the company with a written record of that decision.

(2) If the sole member fails to comply with subsection (1) he shall be liable to a fine.

(3) Failure by the sole member to comply with section (1) shall not affect the validity of any decision referred to in that subsection.

S 382B(1)

For single-member companies, see s 1(3A). It is clear from this provision that there are two methods by which a single member company can take formal decisions, either by written resolution (whether under the statutory provision, s 381A, or under the company's articles) or by way of a decision, as if at a meeting, recorded in this fashion.

S 382B(2)

As to penalties, see s 730, Sch 24.

---

383. Inspection of minute books

(1) The books containing the minutes of proceedings of any general meeting of a company held on or after 1st November 1929 shall be kept at the company's registered office, and shall … be open to the inspection of any member without charge.

(2) …

(3) Any member shall be entitled on payment of such fee as may be prescribed to be furnished, within 7 days after he has made a request in that behalf to the company, with a copy of any such minutes as are referred to above, …

(4) If an inspection required under this section is refused or if a copy required under this section is not sent within the proper time, the company and every officer of it who is in default is liable in respect of each offence to a fine.

(5) In the case of any such refusal or default, the court may by order compel an immediate inspection of the books in respect of all proceedings of general meetings, or direct that the copies required be sent to the persons requiring them.

General note

This provision also applies to the inspection and copying of records of written resolutions: s 382A(3). For provisions relating to the inspection of documents, registers and fees under this section, see the Companies (Inspection and Copying of Registers, Indices and Documents) Regulations 1991, SI 1991/1998.

Lien on the minute books   As the requirement to keep minute books and, in this case, the requirement to make the minute book of general meetings available for inspection, is a statutory obligation, it is not possible for a solicitor (or accountant) to enforce a lien over these books: see *Re Capital Fire Insurance Association* (1883) 24 Ch D 408; *Re Anglo-Maltese Hydraulic Dock Co Ltd* (1885) 54 LJ Ch 730.

Inspection of board minutes by a director   A director has a right at common law to inspect the minutes of board meetings and to be accompanied by a professional adviser: *McCusker v McRae* 1966 SC 253.

S 383(1)

Inspection of minutes by a member   This provision applies to any general meeting and not just the annual general meeting. Inspection is limited to any member which would seem to require inspection in person rather than by an agent, such as his solicitor. No provision is made for inspection by any member of the public. A member has no right to inspect the minutes of a board meeting. However, some resolutions of the directors must be registered with the registrar of companies under s 380. As to the registered office, see s 287.

S 383(3)

A person inspecting the minutes is entitled to copy any information by means of taking notes or transcribing the information: Companies (Inspection and Copying of Registers, Indices and Documents) Regulations 1991, SI 1991/1998, reg 3(2)(b).

S 383(4)

As to penalties, see s 730, Sch 24; 'officer in default' is defined in s 730(5).

S 383(5)

This provision is necessary because, but for the section, it is not clear that there is any right of inspection or that the court has the power to compel inspection: see *Conway v Petronius Clothing Co Ltd* [1978] 1 All ER 185 at 199. The court's power is discretionary, see *Pelling v Families need Fathers Ltd* [2001] All ER (D) 03 (Aug), CA.

CHAPTER V

AUDITORS

APPOINTMENT OF AUDITORS

384. Duty to appoint auditors

(1)   Every company shall appoint an auditor or auditors in accordance with this Chapter.

   This is subject to section 388A (certain companies exempt from obligation to appoint auditors).

(2)   Auditors shall be appointed in accordance with section 385 (appointment at general meeting at which accounts are laid), except in the case of a private company which has elected to dispense with the laying of accounts in which case the appointment shall be made in accordance with section 385A.

(3)   References in this Chapter to the end of the time for appointing auditors are to the end of the time within which an appointment must be made under section 385(2) or 385A(2), according to whichever of those sections applies.

(4)   Sections 385 and 385A have effect subject to section 386 under which a private company may elect to dispense with the obligation to appoint auditors annually.

General note

Auditors (who may be individuals or firms) must be appropriately qualified, members of recognised supervisory bodies and sufficiently independent, as prescribed by CA 1989, ss 24–27.

S 384(1)

The obligation applies to every company, public and private, limited and unlimited, subject to the exemptions permitted by s 388A for small and dormant companies within ss 249A and 249AA.

Officers of the company   Auditors may or may not be officers of the company: see definition in s 744 and note to that provision, below. If they are appointed under this and the following provision as auditors to the company, they will be officers of the company for the periods for which they are appointed: *Mutual Reinsurance Co Ltd v Peat Marwick Mitchell & Co* [1997] 1 BCLC 1; *Re London and General Bank* [1895] 2 Ch 166; *Re Kingston Cotton Mill Co* [1896] 1 Ch 6. However, if auditors are merely retained to conduct and carry out an audit function, without being appointed as auditors, they will not be officers: *Mutual Reinsurance Co Ltd v Peat Marwick Mitchell & Co* [1997] 1 BCLC 1.

385. Appointment at general meeting at which accounts laid

(1)   This section applies to every public company and to a private company which has not elected to dispense with the laying of accounts.

(2)   The company shall, at each general meeting at which accounts are laid, appoint an auditor or auditors to hold office from the conclusion of that meeting until the conclusion of the next general meeting at which accounts are laid.

(3)   The first auditors of the company may be appointed by the directors at any time before the first general meeting of the company at which accounts are laid; and auditors so appointed shall hold office until the conclusion of that meeting.

(4)   If the directors fail to exercise their powers under subsection (3), the powers may be exercised by the company in general meeting.

S 385(1)

A private company may dispense with the laying of accounts in accordance with s 252.

S 385(2), (3)

The powers of appointment are vested in the shareholders (save in the case of the initial appointment), but the reality is that the auditors will be selected by the directors and their appointment endorsed by the shareholders. Where the auditors are appointed by the general meeting, a private company may use a written resolution (s 381A); and notice of the resolution must be given to an existing auditor: s 381B.

The period between appointments is measured as the period between general meetings at which the accounts are laid, which period may be longer than a year: see s 244. The appointment runs from the conclusion of the meeting at which they are appointed to the conclusion of the next meeting at which they may or may not be reappointed. As to the position if the auditor resigns, see s 392(2).

Where the appointment by the general meeting is to reappoint as auditor a retiring auditor who was appointed by the directors to fill a casual vacancy, special notice is required: see s 388(3).

385A. Appointment by private company which is not obliged to lay accounts

(1)   This section applies to a private company which has elected in accordance with section 252 to dispense with the laying of accounts before the company in general meeting.

(2)   Auditors shall be appointed by the company in general meeting before the end of the period of 28 days beginning with the day on which copies of the company's annual accounts for the previous financial year are sent to members

under section 238 or, if notice is given under section 253(2) requiring the laying of the accounts before the company in general meeting, the conclusion of that meeting.

Auditors so appointed shall hold office from the end of that period or, as the case may be, the conclusion of that meeting until the end of the time for appointing auditors for the next financial year.

(3) The first auditors of the company may be appointed by the directors at any time before—

    (a) the end of the period of 28 days beginning with the day on which copies of the company's first annual accounts are sent to members under section 238, or

    (b) if notice is given under section 253(2) requiring the laying of the accounts before the company in general meeting, the beginning of that meeting;

and auditors so appointed shall hold office until the end of that period or, as the case may be, the conclusion of that meeting.

(4) If the directors fail to exercise their powers under subsection (3), the powers may be exercised by the company in general meeting.

(5) Auditors holding office when the election is made shall, unless the company in general meeting determines otherwise, continue to hold office until the end of the time for appointing auditors for the next financial year; and auditors holding office when an election ceases to have effect shall continue to hold office until the conclusion of the next general meeting of the company at which accounts are laid.

————————————————————————

S 385A(1)

An elective resolution requires unanimity: see s 379A(2).

S 385A(2), (3)

These somewhat obscure provisions determine the time for appointing auditors where a private company has dispensed with the laying of accounts before the general meeting. Essentially, the requirement is for the company in general meeting to appoint the auditors for the subsequent year within 28 days of the circulation of the accounts of the previous financial year.

Appointment of the first auditors   If the auditors to be appointed are the first auditors, the appointment may be made by the directors for the period specified in sub-s (3); thereafter appointments are by the company in general meeting under sub-s (2).

The wording in sub-s (3) is ambiguous as it appears to permit the appointment to take place after the accounts have been sent out to the members under s 238. However, the first annual accounts to be sent out under s 238 must include an auditors' report, and therefore the auditors would need to be appointed at an earlier time.

In practice, a company taking advantage of the dispensation from laying accounts is also likely to be exempt from the audit requirement under ss 249A or 249AA, so this confusion as to the time within which the first auditors must be appointed will be irrelevant. If the company is not exempt, it is likely that the directors will have appointed the company's auditors early in the first financial year, regardless of the wording of sub-s (3).

Dispensing with annual appointment   A further point to note is that a company which has dispensed with the laying of accounts will probably also have dispensed (under s 386) with the appointment annually of auditors; otherwise the benefits of having dispensed with the laying of accounts are negated by the requirement for the company in general meeting to appoint the auditors.

386. Election by private company to dispense with annual appointment

(1)   A private company may elect (by elective resolution in accordance with section 379A) to dispense with the obligation to appoint auditors annually.

(2)   When such an election is in force the company's auditors shall be deemed to be re-appointed for each succeeding financial year on the expiry of the time for appointing auditors for that year, unless—

   (a)   the directors of the company have taken advantage of the exemption conferred by section 249A or 249AA, or

   (b)   a resolution has been passed under section 393 to the effect that their appointment should be brought to an end.

(3)   If the election ceases to be in force, the auditors then holding office shall continue to hold office—

   (a)   where section 385 then applies, until the conclusion of the next general meeting of the company at which accounts are laid;

   (b)   where section 385A then applies, until the end of the time for appointing auditors for the next financial year under that section.

(4)   No account shall be taken of any loss of the opportunity of further deemed re-appointment under this section in ascertaining the amount of any compensation or damages payable to an auditor on his ceasing to hold office for any reason.

S 386(1)

An elective resolution requires unanimity: see s 379A(2). Many private companies will in any event be exempt from the obligation to appoint auditors under s 388A.

S 386(2)(b)

The time at which the existing auditors are deemed reappointed ('the expiry of the time for appointing auditors') is determined by s 384(3). Any member may deposit a notice at the registered office proposing that the appointment of the auditors (which would otherwise be deemed to continue under this provision) be brought to an end: s 393.

S 386(3)

As to when an election ceases to be in force, see note to s 379A(3), (4), above.

S 386(4)

This provision ensures that a company which elects to dispense with the annual reappointment of auditors and is therefore deemed to have reappointed the auditors each year, should not face increased damages (because of that election) on the auditors ceasing to hold office.

387. Appointment by Secretary of State in default of appointment by company

(1)   If in any case no auditors are appointed, re-appointed or deemed to be re-appointed before the end of the time for appointing auditors, the Secretary of State may appoint a person to fill the vacancy.

(2)   In such a case the company shall within one week of the end of the time for appointing auditors give notice to the Secretary of State of his power having become exercisable.

If a company fails to give the notice required by this subsection, the company and every officer of it who is in default is guilty of an offence and liable to a fine and, for continued contravention, to a daily default fine.

General note

It is rare for this power to be exercised.

S 387(2)

The time period for notice to the Secretary of State is very short: the 'end of the time for appointing auditors' is determined by s 384(3). As to penalties, see s 730, Sch 24; 'officer in default' is defined in s 730(5).

388. Filling of casual vacancies

(1)   The directors, or the company in general meeting, may fill a casual vacancy in the office of auditor.

(2)   While such a vacancy continues, any surviving or continuing auditor or auditors may continue to act.

(3)   Special notice is required for a resolution at a general meeting of a company—

(a) filling a casual vacancy in the office of auditor, or

(b) re-appointing as auditor a retiring auditor who was appointed by the directors to fill a casual vacancy.

(4)   On receipt of notice of such an intended resolution the company shall forthwith send a copy of it—

(a) to the person proposed to be appointed, and

(b) if the casual vacancy was caused by the resignation of an auditor, to the auditor who resigned.

General note

As it is permissible (and common) to appoint a firm as the company's auditors, the possibility of a casual vacancy arising is limited. A casual vacancy is defined as 'any vacancy not occurring by effluxion of time, that is any vacancy occurring by death, resignation or bankruptcy': *York Tramways Co v Willows* (1882) 8 QBD 685 at 694, per Lord Coleridge CJ.

S 388(1)

In practice, the filling of a casual vacancy would be a matter for the directors, not least because if it is a matter for the general meeting, special notice is required under sub-s (3).

S 388(3)

Special notice As to special notice, see s 379. A private company may use a written resolution requiring no notice under s 381A, but notice of the written resolution must be given to any surviving or continuing auditor under s 381B at or before the time the resolution is supplied to the members for signature.

388A. Certain companies exempt from obligation to appoint auditors

(1)   A company which by virtue of section 249A (certain categories of small company) or section 249AA (dormant companies) is exempt from the provisions of Part VII relating to the audit of accounts is also exempt from the obligation to appoint auditors.

(2)   The following provisions apply if a company which has been exempt from those provisions ceases to be so exempt.

(3)   Where section 385 applies (appointment at general meeting at which accounts are laid), the directors may appoint auditors at any time before the next meeting of the company at which accounts are to be laid; and auditors so appointed shall hold office until the conclusion of that meeting.

(4)   Where section 385A applies (appointment by private company not obliged to lay accounts), the directors may appoint auditors at any time before—

(a)   the end of the period of 28 days beginning with the day on which copies of the company's annual accounts are next sent to members under section 238, or

(b)   if notice is given under section 253(2) requiring the laying of the accounts before the company in general meeting, the beginning of that meeting;

and auditors so appointed shall hold office until the end of that period or, as the case may be, the conclusion of that meeting.

(5)   If the directors fail to exercise their powers under subsection (3) or (4), the powers may be exercised by the company in general meeting.

General note

See notes to ss 249A and 249AA, above.

S 388A(3), (4)

The general position as stated in s 385 is that the appointment of auditors is made at a general meeting at which the accounts are laid. Where an audit exemption ceases to apply and auditors must be appointed, the auditors should be appointed at the next general meeting at which the accounts are laid. As those accounts may relate to the period in which the exemption was lost and require auditing, it is not possible to wait until that date in order to appoint, hence subs-s (3) allows for an earlier appointment of auditors by the directors.

The period in sub-s (4) for private companies which have elected not to lay their accounts before the general meeting mirrors the requirements of s 385A(3): see note to that provision. In either case, it is for the directors to appoint.

389. (*Repealed by CA 1989, s 212, Sch 24, as from 1 October 1991.*)

RIGHTS OF AUDITORS

389A. Rights to information

(1) The auditors of a company have a right of access at all times to the company's books, accounts and vouchers, and are entitled to require from the company's officers such information and explanations as they think necessary for the performance of their duties as auditors.

(2) An officer of a company commits an offence if he knowingly or recklessly makes to the company's auditors a statement (whether written or oral) which—

(a) conveys or purports to convey any information or explanations which the auditors require, or are entitled to require, as auditors of the company, and

(b) is misleading, false or deceptive in a material particular.

A person guilty of an offence under this subsection is liable to imprisonment or a fine, or both.

(3) A subsidiary undertaking which is a body corporate incorporated in Great Britain, and the auditors of such an undertaking, shall give to the auditors of any parent company of the undertaking such information and explanations as they may reasonably require for the purposes of their duties as auditors of that company.

If a subsidiary undertaking fails to comply with this subsection, the undertaking and every officer of it who is in default is guilty of an offence and liable to a fine; and if an auditor fails without reasonable excuse to comply with this subsection he is guilty of an offence and liable to a fine.

(4) A parent company having a subsidiary undertaking which is not a body corporate incorporated in Great Britain shall, if required by its auditors to do so, take all such steps as are reasonably open to it to obtain from the subsidiary undertaking such information and explanations as they may reasonably require for the purposes of their duties as auditors of that company.

If a parent company fails to comply with this subsection, the company and every officer of it who is in default is guilty of an offence and liable to a fine.

(5) Section 734 (criminal proceedings against unincorporated bodies) applies to an offence under subsection (3).

S 389A(1)

Right of access to information A company has no power to make regulations precluding its auditors from availing themselves of all the information to which they are entitled under the companies legislation: *Newton v Birmingham Small Arms Co Ltd* [1906] 2 Ch 378.

S 389A(2)

Misleading information to auditors   The potential criminal liability of officers (only) is a useful weapon in the hands of auditors faced with unco-operative directors; 'officer' is defined in s 744; as to penalties, see s 730, Sch 24. The most effective sanction, though, is the obligation on the auditors, where they fail to obtain all the information and explanations which they believe necessary for the purposes of the audit, to state that fact in their report: s 237(3).

S 389A(3), (4)

Information from subsidiary undertakings   These provisions place obligations on subsidiary undertakings and their auditors to assists the auditors of the parent company (who may need the information, for example, to prepare group accounts under s 227); and place an obligation on a parent company with an overseas subsidiary to assist the parent company's auditors with obtaining information regarding the subsidiary. 'Parent company' and 'subsidiary undertaking' are defined by s 258, Sch 10A: s 742. 'Body corporate' is defined by s 740. As to penalties, see s 730, Sch 24. 'Officer in default' is defined in s 730(5).

390. Right to attend company meetings, &c

(1)   A company's auditors are entitled—

   (a)   to receive all notices of, and other communications relating to, any general meeting which a member of the company is entitled to receive;

   (b)   to attend any general meeting of the company; and

   (c)   to be heard at any general meeting which they attend on any part of the business of the meeting which concerns them as auditors.

(1A) Subsections (4A) to (4G) of section 369 (electronic communication of notices of meetings) apply for the purpose of determining whether notice of a meeting is received by the company's auditors as they apply in determining whether such a notice is given to any person.

(2)   In relation to a written resolution proposed to be agreed to by a private company in accordance with section 381A, the company's auditors are entitled—

   (a)   to receive all such communications relating to the resolution as, by virtue of any provision of Schedule 15A, are required to be supplied to a member of the company,

   (b)–(d)   ...

(3)   The right to attend or be heard at a meeting is exercisable in the case of a body corporate or partnership by an individual authorised by it in writing to act as its representative at the meeting.

General note

See s 391(4) as to the application of this provision to an auditor who has been removed from office; and s 392A(8) as to its application to an auditor who has resigned.

S 390(1)

Right to notices, to attend and to be heard   This provision applies to any general meeting and not simply the annual general meeting. However, private companies may dispense with the laying of accounts before the company in general meeting (s 252) so curtailing the opportunities for auditors to be heard under sub-s (1)(c). Hence the statutory right of an auditor to give notice under s 253(2) requiring that the accounts be laid, so preserving their right to be heard under this provision. The auditors are not restricted to matters relating to the accounts and are entitled to be heard on 'any part of the business of the meeting which concerns them as auditors' but, obviously, the accounts are the most likely item on which the auditors would wish to exercise this right to be heard.

Position of retiring auditor   As appointment as the company's auditors runs from the conclusion of the meeting at which they are appointed to the conclusion of the next meeting (s 385(2)), a retiring auditor who is not being reappointed may still attend the meeting at which another auditor is to be appointed, for the retiring auditor holds office until the end of the meeting. This ensures that the retiring auditor can be heard, and he may wish to be heard as to the reasons relating to his failure to secure reappointment.

S 390(2)

Auditors are entitled to notice of written resolutions under s 381B and this provision entitles them to any additional information which must be supplied to members in connection with such a resolution under Sch 15A; as to written resolutions, see s 381A, Sch 15A.

REMUNERATION OF AUDITORS

390A. Remuneration of auditors

(1)   The remuneration of auditors appointed by the company in general meeting shall be fixed by the company in general meeting or in such manner as the company in general meeting may determine.

(2)   The remuneration of auditors appointed by the directors or the Secretary of State shall be fixed by the directors or the Secretary of State, as the case may be.

(3)   There shall be stated in a note to the company's annual accounts the amount of the remuneration of the company's auditors in their capacity as such.

(4)   For the purposes of this section 'remuneration' includes sums paid in respect of expenses.

(5)   This section applies in relation to benefits in kind as to payments in cash, and in relation to any such benefit references to its amount are to its estimated money value.
    The nature of any such benefit shall also be disclosed.

S 390A(1), (2)

In keeping with the intention that the shareholders should appoint the auditors (see ss 384-385A), this provision requires that they should also fix the auditors' remuneration or provide for the manner in which it is to be fixed. In many instances, the matter will be left to the directors to determine. Appointment by the Secretary of State may arise exceptionally under s 387. As to the appointment of auditors, see ss 385–388A.

S 390A(3)

Small companies are entitled to omit this information from the accounts which they deliver to the registrar of companies: s 246(6). Group accounts must contain this information for the group: Sch 4A, para 1(1).

390B. Remuneration of auditors or their associates for non-audit work

(1)   The Secretary of State may make provision by regulations for securing the disclosure of the amount of any remuneration received or receivable by a company's auditors or their associates in respect of services other than those of auditors in their capacity as such.

(2)   The regulations may—
    (a)   provide that 'remuneration' includes sums paid in respect of expenses,
    (b)   apply in relation to benefits in kind as to payments in cash, and in relation to any such benefit require disclosure of its nature and its estimated money value,
    (c)   define 'associate' in relation to an auditor,
    (d)   require the disclosure of remuneration in respect of services rendered to associated undertakings of the company, and
    (e)   define 'associated undertaking' for that purpose.

(3)   The regulations may require the auditors to disclose the relevant information in their report or require the relevant information to be disclosed in a note to

the company's accounts and require the auditors to supply the directors of the company with such information as is necessary to enable that disclosure to be made.

(4)　The regulations may make different provision for different cases.

(5)　Regulations under this section shall be made by statutory instrument which shall be subject to annulment in pursuance of a resolution of either House of Parliament.

General note

Auditors increasingly provide companies, especially larger companies, with an extensive range of services other than audit, for example, tax consultancy, information technology and management services. These services are often much more valuable to the audit firm (in terms of profit generation) than the audit itself and there are concerns as to the conflicts of interest which this creates. The provisions of this section are intended to bring an element of transparency to these arrangements so that users of company accounts and reports are at least informed as to the extent of the relationship between the auditors and the company.

S 390B(1)

The regulations are the Companies Act 1985 (Disclosure of Remuneration for Non-Audit Work) Regulations 1991, SI 1991/2128, as amended by SI 1995/1520.

S 390B(2)

'Associate' is defined in SI 1991/2128, regs 2, 3, 7; 'associated undertaking' is defined in reg 2.

S 390B(3)

The information must be disclosed in the notes to the accounts: SI 1991/2128, reg 5.

S 390B(4)

A limited exemption is provided for companies which qualify as small or medium-sized companies by virtue of s 247; they are not required to give the specified information in the notes to the annual accounts of the company relating to a financial year in respect of which the company is entitled to the exemptions mentioned in s 246 (special provisions for small companies): SI 1991/2128, reg 4. This exemption applies both to the accounts prepared for the members and those delivered to the registrar of companies.

REMOVAL, RESIGNATION, &C OF AUDITORS

391. Removal of auditors

(1)   A company may by ordinary resolution at any time remove an auditor from office, notwithstanding anything in any agreement between it and him.

(2)   Where a resolution removing an auditor is passed at a general meeting of a company, the company shall within 14 days give notice of that fact in the prescribed form to the registrar.

If a company fails to give the notice required by this subsection, the company and every officer of it who is in default is guilty of an offence and liable to a fine and, for continued contravention, to a daily default fine.

(3)   Nothing in this section shall be taken as depriving a person removed under it of compensation or damages payable to him in respect of the termination of his appointment as auditor or of any appointment terminating with that as auditor.

(4)   An auditor of a company who has been removed has, notwithstanding his removal, the rights conferred by section 390 in relation to any general meeting of the company—

(a)   at which his term of office would otherwise have expired, or

(b)   at which it is proposed to fill the vacancy caused by his removal.

In such a case the references in that section to matters concerning the auditors as auditors shall be construed as references to matters concerning him as a former auditor.

S 391(1), (3)

This provision is similar to the power which the company in general meeting has to remove a director under s 303 and, just as that power is rarely exercised (outside of small companies), so too this power would rarely be exercised by the company in general meeting. It is more likely that following a disagreement with the board, an auditor would resign rather than be removed under this provision. If the company, unusually, does attempt to remove the auditors by a resolution in general meeting, then the requirements of s 391A must be observed.

A private company cannot use a written resolution to remove an auditor under this provision: s 381A(7), Sch 15A, para 1.

S 391(2)

As to penalties, see s 730, Sch 24; 'officer in default' is defined in s 730(5).

S 391(4)

This provision preserves the auditor's rights under s 390 to attend and be heard at the relevant general meeting.

391A. Rights of auditors who are removed or not re-appointed

(1)   Special notice is required for a resolution at a general meeting of a company—

   (a) removing an auditor before the expiration of his term of office, or

   (b) appointing as auditor a person other than a retiring auditor.

(2)   On receipt of notice of such an intended resolution the company shall forthwith send a copy of it to the person proposed to be removed or, as the case may be, to the person proposed to be appointed and to the retiring auditor.

(3)   The auditor proposed to be removed or (as the case may be) the retiring auditor may make with respect to the intended resolution representations in writing to the company (not exceeding a reasonable length) and request their notification to members of the company.

(4)   The company shall (unless the representations are received by it too late for it to do so)—

   (a) in any notice of the resolution given to members of the company, state the fact of the representations having been made, and

   (b) send a copy of the representations to every member of the company to whom notice of the meeting is or has been sent.

(5)   If a copy of any such representations is not sent out as required because received too late or because of the company's default, the auditor may (without prejudice to his right to be heard orally) require that the representations be read out at the meeting.

(6)   Copies of the representations need not be sent out and the representations need not be read at the meeting if, on the application either of the company or of any other person claiming to be aggrieved, the court is satisfied that the rights conferred by this section are being abused to secure needless publicity for defamatory matter; and the court may order the company's costs on the application to be paid in whole or in part by the auditor, notwithstanding that he is not a party to the application.

S 391A(1)

As to special notice, see s 379.

Removing an auditor   As for sub-s (1)(a), a written resolution cannot be used by a private company: s 381A(7), Sch 15A, para 1, and so, for all companies, a meeting must be held and the formalities of this provision observed.

Failing to reappoint   As for sub-s (1)(b), a private company may use a written resolution so avoiding the need for special notice and the other requirements of this provision. The retiring auditor is entitled to notice of the written resolution under s 381B, but loses the protection of this provision and, obviously, the ability to use s 390 to be heard by the members at a general meeting. The retiring auditor must submit a statement as required by s 394, however, of any circumstances connected with his ceasing to hold office which he considers should be brought to the attention of the members or creditors of the company and the company must either circulate that statement or apply to the court: see s 394. Appointing new auditors by written resolution, therefore, will not enable the directors to gag any retiring auditor.

S 391A(2)–(6)

See notes to equivalent provisions in s 304(2)–(5), above.

392. Resignation of auditors

(1)   An auditor of a company may resign his office by depositing a notice in writing to that effect at the company's registered office.

The notice is not effective unless it is accompanied by the statement required by section 394.

(2)   An effective notice of resignation operates to bring the auditor's term of office to an end as of the date on which the notice is deposited or on such later date as may be specified in it.

(3)   The company shall within 14 days of the deposit of a notice of resignation send a copy of the notice to the registrar of companies.

If default is made in complying with this subsection, the company and every officer of it who is in default is guilty of an offence and liable to a fine and, for continued contravention, a daily default fine.

S 392(1), (3)

Notice of resignation and statement   The statement required by s 394 should not be included within the notice of resignation but should be set out in a separate document as envisaged by this provision and s 394(2). The reason being that if the company decides to challenge the statement under s 394(3) and the two documents have been combined, then the company will not be able to send a copy of the notice of resignation to the registrar as required by sub-s (3).

If the statement is one which the resigning auditor considers should be brought to the attention of members or creditors of the company, see s 392A.

As to penalties, see s 730, Sch 24; 'officer in default' is defined in s 730(5).

392A. Rights of resigning auditors

(1)   This section applies where an auditor's notice of resignation is accompanied by a statement of circumstances which he considers should be brought to the attention of members or creditors of the company.

(2)   He may deposit with the notice a signed requisition calling on the directors of the company forthwith duly to convene an extraordinary general meeting of

the company for the purpose of receiving and considering such explanation of the circumstances connected with his resignation as he may wish to place before the meeting.

(3) He may request the company to circulate to its members—

    (a) before the meeting convened on his requisition, or

    (b) before any general meeting at which his term of office would otherwise have expired or at which it is proposed to fill the vacancy caused by his resignation,

a statement in writing (not exceeding a reasonable length) of the circumstances connected with his resignation.

(4) The company shall (unless the statement is received too late for it to comply)—

    (a) in any notice of the meeting given to members of the company, state the fact of the statement having been made, and

    (b) send a copy of the statement to every member of the company to whom notice of the meeting is or has been sent.

(5) If the directors do not within 21 days from the date of the deposit of a requisition under this section proceed duly to convene a meeting for a day not more than 28 days after the date on which the notice convening the meeting is given, every director who failed to take all reasonable steps to secure that a meeting was convened as mentioned above is guilty of an offence and liable to a fine.

(6) If a copy of the statement mentioned above is not sent out as required because received too late or because of the company's default, the auditor may (without prejudice to his right to be heard orally) require that the statement be read out at the meeting.

(7) Copies of a statement need not be sent out and the statement need not be read out at the meeting if, on the application either of the company or of any other person who claims to be aggrieved, the court is satisfied that the rights conferred by this section are being abused to secure needless publicity for defamatory matter; and the court may order the company's costs on such an application to be paid in whole or in part by the auditor, notwithstanding that he is not a party to the application.

(8) An auditor who has resigned has, notwithstanding his resignation, the rights conferred by section 390 in relation to any such general meeting of the company as is mentioned in subsection (3)(a) or (b).

In such a case the references in that section to matters concerning the auditors as auditors shall be construed as references to matters concerning him as a former auditor.

S 392A(1)

The statement in question is that required by s 394.

S 392A(2), (3), (5)

Convening a meeting These provisions give the resigning auditor the option of requiring the convening of an extraordinary general meeting and/or the circulation of a statement of the circumstances connected with his resignation (ie a different statement to that required under s 394, although the content would be similar). The intention behind the provision is to protect an auditor where his resignation is involuntary and he has been effectively forced out by the directors. In practice, a resigning auditor who has been forced out is likely to rely simply on his right under s 394 to have his statement under that provision circulated to the members and creditors and copied to the registrar of companies. It would be unusual for a resigning auditor to invoke these provisions.

As to the procedure, see the notes to the equivalent provisions in s 368(4), (8). Where there is non-compliance by the directors with the obligation to convene a meeting, the auditor may not convene the meeting himself (cf the members' position under s 368); but, given that every director faces potential criminal liability for non-compliance, it is unlikely that the auditor will face any difficulty in having the meeting convened.

S 392A(4), (6), (7)

See notes to the equivalent provisions in s 304(2)–(5); also note to s 394(6), (7).

S 392A(8)

In any event, the auditor retains his rights under s 390 to attend and be heard at the appropriate general meeting, so his inability to require that the general meeting be convened (see sub-s (5)) may not be that significant, except in cases where the relevant general meeting is some time away.

---

393. Termination of appointment of auditors not appointed annually

(1)   When an election is in force under section 386 (election by private company to dispense with annual appointment), any member of the company may deposit notice in writing at the company's registered office proposing that the appointment of the company's auditors be brought to an end.

No member may deposit more than one such notice in any financial year of the company.

(2)   If such a notice is deposited it is the duty of the directors—

   (a)   to convene a general meeting of the company for a date not more than 28 days after the date on which the notice was given, and

   (b)   to propose at the meeting a resolution in a form enabling the company to decide whether the appointment of the company's auditors should be brought to an end.

(3)   If the decision of the company at the meeting is that the appointment of the auditors should be brought to an end, the auditors shall not be deemed to be re-appointed when next they would be and, if the notice was deposited within the period immediately following the distribution of accounts, any deemed re-appointment for the financial year following that to which those accounts relate which has already occurred shall cease to have effect.

The period immediately following the distribution of accounts means the period beginning with the day on which copies of the company's annual accounts are sent to members of the company under section 238 and ending 14 days after that day.

(4)   If the directors do not within 14 days from the date of the deposit of the notice proceed duly to convene a meeting, the member who deposited the notice (or, if there was more than one, any of them) may himself convene the meeting; but any meeting so convened shall not be held after the expiration of three months from that date.

(5)   A meeting convened under this section by a member shall be convened in the same manner, as nearly as possible, as that in which meetings are to be convened by directors.

(6)   Any reasonable expenses incurred by a member by reason of the failure of the directors duly to convene a meeting shall be made good to him by the company; and any such sums shall be recouped by the company from such of the directors as were in default out of any sums payable, or to become payable, by the company by way of fees or other remuneration in respect of their services.

(7)   This section has effect notwithstanding anything in any agreement between the company and its auditors; and no compensation or damages shall be payable by reason of the auditors' appointment being terminated under this section.

S 393(1)

The effect of electing to dispense with annual reappointment of auditors is that they are deemed reappointed each year: s 386(2); hence the need for this provision whereby any member can attempt to bring that situation to an end by requiring a meeting to be held and the issue to be debated.

S 393(2)

The duty on the directors is not just to call the meeting but to propose the resolution, for members as such have no right to place resolutions before the meeting save in limited circumstances, see note to s 376.

S 393(3)

This provision determines when a deemed reappointment under s 386 ceases to have effect.

S 393(4)–(6)

See notes to the equivalent provisions in s 368(4)–(6), above.

S 393(7)

See note to s 386(4), above.

---

394. Statement by person ceasing to hold office as auditor

(1) Where an auditor ceases for any reason to hold office, he shall deposit at the company's registered office a statement of any circumstances connected with his ceasing to hold office which he considers should be brought to the attention of the members or creditors of the company or, if he considers that there are no such circumstances, a statement that there are none.

(2) In the case of resignation, the statement shall be deposited along with the notice of resignation; in the case of failure to seek re-appointment, the statement shall be deposited not less than 14 days before the end of the time allowed for next appointing auditors; in any other case, the statement shall be deposited not later than the end of the period of 14 days beginning with the date on which he ceases to hold office.

(3) If the statement is of circumstances which the auditor considers should be brought to the attention of the members or creditors of the company, the company shall within 14 days of the deposit of the statement either—

    (a) send a copy of it to every person who under section 238 is entitled to be sent copies of the accounts, or

    (b) apply to the court.

(4) The company shall if it applies to the court notify the auditor of the application.

(5) Unless the auditor receives notice of such an application before the end of the period of 21 days beginning with the day on which he deposited the statement, he shall within a further seven days send a copy of the statement to the registrar.

(6) If the court is satisfied that the auditor is using the statement to secure needless publicity for defamatory matter—

    (a) it shall direct that copies of the statement need not be sent out, and

    (b) it may further order the company's costs on the application to be paid in whole or in part by the auditor, notwithstanding that he is not a party to the application;

and the company shall within 14 days of the court's decision send to the persons mentioned in subsection (3)(a) a statement setting out the effect of the order.

(7) If the court is not so satisfied, the company shall within 14 days of the court's decision—

    (a) send copies of the statement to the persons mentioned in subsection (3)(a), and

    (b) notify the auditor of the court's decision;

and the auditor shall within seven days of receiving such notice send a copy of the statement to the registrar.

S 394(1)

Statement on ceasing to hold office   The statement required by this provision is required whenever an auditor ceases for any reason to hold office so this would encompass when the auditor resigns, or is removed, or when there is a failure to reappoint a retiring auditor; and a statement is required even if there are no circumstances which should be brought to the attention of the members or creditors. The importance of this obligation is reflected in the criminal penalties imposed by s 394A for non-compliance.

The auditor must exercise his judgment and, uninfluenced by any collateral considerations, make up his own mind as to whether there are circumstances which need to be brought to the attention of the mentioned parties; and the court will presume that the auditors are acting in faithful discharge of their duty and not in pursuit of any private or collateral interest, unless the contrary is shown: *Jarvis plc v PricewaterhouseCoopers* [2000] 2 BCLC 368.

As to the rights of a resigning auditor whose statement he considers should be brought to the attention of the mentioned parties, see s 392A.

S 394(2)

Time limits   This provision identifies the appropriate time-frame which depends on the circumstances which have resulted in the auditor ceasing to hold office; the 'end of the time allowed for next appointing auditors' is determined by s 384(3).

S 394(3)-(5)

Circulation to members or application to court   The company's options on receiving a statement which the auditor considers should be brought to the attention of the mentioned parties are: (1) to circulate the statement; or (2) to apply to the court. The company must decide within 21 days for, if the auditor has not received notice of a court application by the end of the specified period, he is under a duty within seven days to send a copy of the statement to the registrar of companies where it will be placed on the public record.

If the company does apply to the court, this will have two consequences: (1) the company is not required to circulate the statement to the members etc; and (2) the auditor cannot send a copy to the registrar of companies.

Application to the court   In *Jarvis plc v PricewaterhouseCoopers* [2000] 2 BCLC 368, Lightman J noted that the opportunity afforded to companies to delay the dissemination of statements by commencing proceedings is susceptible of abuse by the unscrupulous. He emphasised that 'the court must be alert to question whether the decisions taken to commence and subsequently to continue the proceedings were made in good faith and not for some ulterior purpose, for example to put pressure on the auditor or prevent the statement being disseminated at an inconvenient time or to obtain a breathing period to prepare a counter or response to the statement. If an ulterior purpose is found to underlie the decision making, again the court may be expected to express its disapproval vigorously by appropriate orders against those responsible' (at 377).

In this case, the company, having applied to the court, discontinued the proceedings three months later, without explanation and just 24 hours before the court hearing.

It then circulated the statement to the members etc the next day. The court noted that the three-month delay had been used to enable the company's new auditors to prepare accounts and the company to prepare a circular to shareholders concerning the resignation of the former auditors which was then circulated with the former auditors' statement. The court found that the company had made serious allegations against the auditors which had to be withdrawn as the auditors had acted with total propriety and so the proceedings were bound to fail. The company was ordered to pay the costs on an indemnity basis.

S 394(6), (7)

Bad faith   The requirement that the auditors are 'using the statement to secure needless publicity', focuses on the purpose or motive behind the making of the statement and will require an allegation of bad faith: *Jarvis plc v PricewaterhouseCoopers* [2000] 2 BCLC 368.

Court order   A court order is necessary under sub-s (6) upholding the charge of impropriety against the auditors and the court must then direct what is to occur but a court order is not required under sub-s (7) since the section itself dictates what is to occur (ie the statement must be circulated and a copy sent to the registrar of companies). All that sub-s (7) contemplates is that the proceedings are brought to an end without the court being 'so satisfied' and it does not matter whether they are brought to an end by a final judgment, an order striking out the proceedings or a discontinuance: *Jarvis plc v PricewaterhouseCoopers* [2000] 2 BCLC 368.

394A. Offences of failing to comply with s 394

(1)   If a person ceasing to hold office as auditor fails to comply with section 394 he is guilty of an offence and liable to a fine.

(2)   In proceedings for an offence under subsection (1) it is a defence for the person charged to show that he took all reasonable steps and exercised all due diligence to avoid the commission of the offence.

(3)   Sections 733 (liability of individuals for corporate default) and 734 (criminal proceedings against unincorporated bodies) apply to an offence under subsection (1).

(4)   If a company makes default in complying with section 394, the company and every officer of it who is in default is guilty of an offence and liable to a fine and, for continued contravention, to a daily default fine.

S 394A(4)

As to penalties, see s 730, Sch 24; 'officer in default' is defined in s 730(5).

PART XII

REGISTRATION OF CHARGES

CHAPTER I

REGISTRATION OF CHARGES (ENGLAND AND WALES)

General note to this Chapter

Security for a debt   As Nourse LJ noted in *Re New Bullas Trading Ltd* [1994] 1 BCLC 485 at 487: 'He who lends money to a trading company neither wishes nor expects it to become insolvent ... But against an evil day he wants the best security the company can give him consistently with its ability to trade meanwhile.'

By security is meant that, in addition to the ability to sue the debtor for the discharge of the obligation, the creditor wants to look to some property in which the debtor has an interest in order to enforce the discharge of the debtor's obligation to the creditor (see *Bristol Airport plc v Powdrill* [1990] 2 All ER 493 at 502), or to look to some third party who has guaranteed the obligations of the debtor.

There are four main types of consensual security – the mortgage, the charge, the pledge and lien (see *Re Cosslett (Contractors) Ltd* [1999] 1 BCLC 205 at 216) – with registration under s 395 being required only of mortgages and charges. As a consequence, many of the cases concern disputes as to whether or not the security is of a type which requires registration. These are complex issues and, as the Diamond Report noted, the law is: 'too fragmented, treating transactions essentially similar in nature in very different ways and complicating the legal issues quite unnecessarily' (DTI, *A Review of Security Interests in Property*, Prof A Diamond, 1989, para 1.8). The result is to compel the parties and their advisers to draw up complex agreements, and many of the cases turn on the construction of a particular debenture, with much court time being devoted to a review of the actual wording of the charging clause.

Documentation   It is clear that some of the problems in this area could be avoided by greater initial attention to the documentation. A debenture may be derived from a variety of precedents without being reviewed for internal consistency and to ensure that it has given effect to the parties' wishes. There may be clauses which contradict one another; the language may be unnecessarily vague, for example, providing for a legal charge when, strictly speaking (and with one statutory exception), there are no legal charges, only equitable ones. A debenture may use terms appropriate to a charge on book debts but the charge is over machinery (see *Re Cimex Tissues Ltd* [1995] 1 BCLC 409 at 417 ('general standard of drafting of the debenture indicates that little care was taken in adapting it to the circumstances of the case')); or a debenture may provide for something described as a charge on floating assets (when in fact the parties wished to create a fixed charge): see *Re G E Tunbridge Ltd* [1995] 1 BCLC 34.

The legal characterisation of the transaction   In deciding into which category a transaction falls, the courts adopt a two-step approach. The first is to determine whether the documents are a sham intended to mask the true agreement of the parties, in which case the court must attempt to discover the nature of the real transaction. Secondly, where the documents are genuine, then the proper legal characterisation of the transaction is a matter of construction of the documents: see *Orion Finance Ltd v Crown Financial Management Ltd* [1996] 2 BCLC 78 at 84; *Re ASRS Establishment Ltd* [2000] 2 BCLC 631.

The terms which the parties have used to describe the transaction are not necessarily determinative. For example, if they describe a charge as fixed when it is in fact floating, then 'their ill-chosen language must yield to the substance': *Orion Finance Ltd v Crown Financial Management Ltd* [1996] 2 BCLC 78 at 84, per Millett LJ. See also *Welsh Development Agency v Export Finance Co Ltd* [1992] BCLC 148; *Re Cimex Tissues Ltd* [1995] 1 BCLC 409 at 415.

The nature of the security must be determined at the time when it is created: *Paul & Frank Ltd v Discount Bank (Overseas) Ltd* [1966] 2 All ER 922 at 927.

Fixed and floating charges   Of course, lenders want not just security for the debt owed by the company, but also security in priority to the claims of other creditors on insolvency. In particular, lenders prefer to take fixed charges as floating charges rank behind the statutory preferential creditors (IA 1986, ss 40(2), 175(2)(b); see also s 196(2)), which reduces the chances of the floating charge holder recouping the full amount due to him. As to whether a charge is a fixed or a floating charge, see the note to s 396(1)(f).

In addition to the issue of priority over preferential creditors, there are a number of other circumstances where the distinction between fixed and floating charges will be important:

(1)   it may affect whether registration is required under s 395 – all floating charges must be registered but fixed charges need only be registered if they are over one of the specified classes of assets in s 396 (admittedly s 396 encompasses practically all charges);

(2)   it may affect the chargee's priority as against subsequent charges;

(3)   it may affect the mechanics of enforcement;

(4)   floating charges only are subject to challenge under IA 1986, s 245 (avoidance of certain floating charges);

(5)   the costs of liquidation come out of the assets of the company which for these purposes include assets subject to a floating charge, so liquidation expenses must be paid out of the floating charge assets in priority to the claims of a chargee: *Re Leyland Daf Ltd, Buchler v Talbot* [2001] 1 BCLC 419; *Re Portbase Clothing Ltd* [1993] BCLC 796.

(6)   an administrator can dispose of the property subject to the floating charge without the consent of the chargee; if the charge is fixed, the consent of the court is required: IA 1986, s 15.

However, there are still advantages to having a floating charge, especially, as is commonly the case, when it is taken in addition to fixed charges. While a floating charge is ranked after the preferential creditors, it does rank ahead of the unsecured creditors; and a person entitled to appoint an administrative receiver under a floating charge is able to block an administration order (IA 1986, ss 9(3), 29(2)).

Much of the litigation involves disputes between secured creditors, frequently banks, and the preferential creditors, frequently the Inland Revenue, as to whether a charge is fixed or floating in order to determine the respective priorities between them.

The modern form of debenture aims to give the lender a fixed charge over assets (such as land and fixtures) that the company does not need to deal with in the ordinary course of business and a floating charge over those that it does (such as stock and work in progress): see *Re New Bullas Trading Ltd* [1994] 1 BCLC 485 at 487. To enhance further their position, lenders have attempted to create fixed charges over an increasing range of assets, such as book debts: see the note to s 396(1)(e).

Vulnerable transactions   Security granted too close to insolvency may be open to challenge under provisions relating to preferences (IA 1986, s 239); and, in the case of floating charges, under IA 1986, s 245 (avoidance of certain floating charges).

Specialist registers   Charges on assets such as land, ships, aircraft, patents and trademarks will require registration in other specialist registries in addition to registration with the registrar of companies, and it is important not to overlook the invalidation which could arise from a failure to register in those locations.

Scotland   Distinctive provisions on charges by companies registered in Scotland are provided by ss 410–424 and are beyond the scope of this work.

Reform   Significant reforms of the registration requirements of this Part were included in CA 1989, Pt IV, but those provisions were never brought into force and will not now be brought into force. They are not reproduced in this work.

395. Certain charges void if not registered

(1) Subject to the provisions of this Chapter, a charge created by a company registered in England and Wales and being a charge to which this section applies is, so far as any security on the company's property or undertaking is conferred by the charge, void against the liquidator or administrator and any creditor of the company, unless the prescribed particulars of the charge together with the instrument (if any) by which the charge is created or evidenced, are delivered to or received by the registrar of companies for registration in the manner required by this Chapter within 21 days after the date of the charge's creation.

(2) Subsection (1) is without prejudice to any contract or obligation for repayment of the money secured by the charge; and when a charge becomes void under this section, the money secured by it immediately becomes payable.

General note

The object of registration is not to provide a comprehensive account of all of a company's charges but to warn unsuspecting creditors that the debtor company has charged its assets: see *Re Welsh Irish Ferries Ltd* [1985] BCLC 327 at 332. The register of charges is publicly available (see s 401) so enabling creditors taking security to appreciate to what extent the assets are already encumbered; and it can assist unsecured creditors in appreciating the extent to which the assets are earmarked for other creditors in the event of insolvency.

S 395(1), (2)

Charges created by a company   This provision is limited to charges of the type specified in s 396 *created* by a company registered in England and Wales. As the charge must be created by the company, security interests arising by law, such as liens and pledges, are excluded from the registration requirements. Registration is required even if the property charged is situated abroad (see s 398); and charges existing on property acquired by the company must also be registered: see s 400. As to charges comprising property in Scotland or Northern Ireland, see s 398(4). These provisions concerning registration do not apply to unregistered companies (defined in s 718). As to the registration of charges on property in England and Wales created by overseas companies: see s 409.

There is some uncertainty as to whether charges created by a company acting as a trustee over property which is trust property are registrable; on a strict application of this provision, it would seem that they are, being charges created by the company over property in respect of which the company is the legal owner. The registrar of companies will accept particulars of such charges for registration and the chargor should indicate clearly on those particulars that it is acting as a trustee charging trust property.

Charge and mortgage   'Charge' includes mortgage: s 396(4). A mortgage may be legal or equitable and all types of property, personal and real, may be mortgaged and charged. Since the Law of Property Act 1925, the form of legal mortgage of an estate in fee simple may be by a charge by deed expressed to be by way of legal mortgage and, for various reasons, the charge by deed has become the standard form of mortgage so that the terms 'mortgage' and 'charge' have become interchangeable. With that statutory exception, all charges are equitable.

While the terms 'mortgage' and 'charge' have become interchangeable, there are important differences between them both practically (with respect to remedies and the manner of redemption) and conceptually. A mortgage involves the conveyance of property subject to a right of redemption whereas: '... the essence of an equitable charge is that, without any conveyance or assignment to the chargee, specific property of the chargor is expressly or constructively appropriated to or made answerable for the payment of a debt, and the chargee is given the right to resort to the property for the purpose of having it realised and applied in or towards payment of the debt'(*Re Charge Card Services Ltd* [1987] BCLC 17 at 40, per Millett J). A mere right to retain possession of an asset and to make use of it for a particular purpose does not create such a proprietary interest and does not constitute a charge: *Re Cosslett (Contractors) Ltd* [1999] 1 BCLC 205 at 215.

There are two types of charge, a fixed charge and a floating charge. The nature of the distinction between these charges, and the significance of that distinction, are discussed in the note to s 396(1)(f), below, and in the general note to this Chapter.

Charge or sale   It is often difficult to determine whether a transaction is one of sale or security and the court will look at the totality of the relationship to determine whether the relationship between the parties amounts to a debtor-creditor relationship or a vendor-purchaser relationship: see *Orion Finance Ltd v Crown Financial Management Ltd* [1996] 2 BCLC 78; *Welsh Development Agency v Export Finance Co Ltd* [1992] BCLC 148; *Re Curtain Dream plc* [1990] BCLC 925; and, in particular, *Re George Inglefield Ltd* [1933] Ch 1 at 27–28.

Charge or lien   Essentially, a lien is a right to retain possession of goods pending payment of a debt, the goods having come into the creditor's possession not for the purpose of security but for some other purpose such as repair or storage. The distinction between the possessory lien and a charge can be explained as follows:

> 'the most essential distinction ... is that a true possessory lien depends entirely on possession and is lost with the loss of possession. A charge, on the other hand, exists independent of possession and confers an interest in the property which carries with it a right to resort to the property (as opposed to merely detaining it) to satisfy or discharge some obligation secured by the charge.'
> (*Waitomo Wools (NZ) Ltd v Nelsons (NZ) Ltd* [1974] 1 NZLR 484 at 490, per Richmond J, NZCA.)

A lien is not registrable, even if coupled with a contractual power of sale of the goods to pay any moneys due: *Re Hamlet International plc, Trident International Ltd v Barlow* [1999] 2 BCLC 506, aff'g [1998] 2 BCLC 164. That power of sale, being a purely personal right dependent on continued possession under the lien, does not convert the lien into an equitable charge: *Re Hamlet International plc*, above.

If a security described as a lien is, in fact, a charge, it must be registered: see *Re Welsh Irish Ferries Ltd* [1985] BCLC 327, and discussion in note to s 396(1)(e), below.

Charge or pledge   A pledge is a possessory security which allows the pledgee to retain possession of goods until the debt incurred by the pledgor is repaid. As such, it does not amount to a charge or mortgage of the goods and does not require registration: see *Wrightson v McArthur and Hutchisons (1919) Ltd* [1921] 2 KB 807. If a security described as a pledge, on a proper analysis, is shown to be a floating charge, it will require registration: *Mercantile Bank of India Ltd v Chartered Bank of India, Australia and China* [1937] 1 All ER 231.

Charge or retention of title   In many cases involving retention or reservation of title clauses (used by suppliers when supplying goods on credit), the courts have concluded that the contractual terms have gone further than retaining title in goods supplied. Instead, the purchaser has granted the seller, as security for the unpaid purchase price, a floating charge on goods manufactured from the goods supplied or on book debts derived from their sale. As such, these charges must be registered (s 396(1)(f)): see *Compaq Computers Ltd v Abercorn Group Ltd* [1993] BCLC 602 and authorities listed there (at 611); *Modelboard Ltd v Outer Box Ltd* [1993] BCLC 623.

Particulars of the charge and the instrument   The requirement is to deliver the particulars of the charge and the *original* charge instrument, if any (subject to s 398); and there would normally be an instrument, although the legislation clearly encompasses an oral charge. This obligation to deliver the original instrument can cause problems of timing when registration is also required at one of the specialist registries: see general note to this Chapter. An 'instrument' for these purposes includes any written document, whether formal or informal, under which any right or liability, whether legal or equitable, exists: see *R v Registrar of Companies, ex p Central Bank of India* [1985] BCLC 465 at 481, 488.

The particulars required are set out in prescribed forms (Forms 395, 397, 400, prescribed by SI 1985/854, as amended) which must be signed and dated: see Companies House, Guidance Booklet, *Company Charges and Mortgages*. A registration fee of £10 is payable: Companies (Fees) (Amendment) Regulations 1998, SI 1998/3088, reg 3. A failure to provide the correct registered number of the company creating the charge does not constitute a failure to comply with this provision so as to attract the statutory invalidity; the company's registered number is a detail which the applicant for registration is required to complete on the forms, but it could not fairly be described as a 'particular of the charge'; it was a particular of the mortgagor: *Grove v Advantage Healthcare (T10) Ltd* [2000] 1 BCLC 661.

There is no provision on the form for the registration of restrictive clauses or negative pledges, ie covenants which limit the ability of the chargor to deal with the charged assets, in particular, to create additional securities ranking pari passu with or in priority to the current charge, although chargees sometimes include them. Third parties cannot be affected by constructive notice of such extra-statutory material: see *Siebe Gorman & Co Ltd v Barclays Bank Ltd* [1979] 2 Lloyd's Rep 142 at 159-160. See note below as to priority between charges.

Following delivery of the prescribed particulars and the original instrument of charge, the registrar will check the accuracy of the particulars against the charge instrument. The original instrument is then returned to the presenter together with a certificate of registration, and an entry is made on the register of charges: see s 401.

A copy of the instrument of charge must be available at the company's registered office for inspection by any creditor or member: see ss 406, 408(1).

Delivered to or received by the registrar within 21 days   The requirement is one of delivery to the registrar of companies and it is delivery of the prescribed particulars within the required time-frame which saves a charge from invalidity, regardless of when the registrar completes the formalities of registration: see *NV Slavenburg's Bank NV v Intercontinental Natural Resources Ltd* [1980] 1 All ER 955 at 963; *National Provincial and Union Bank of England v Charnley* [1924] 1 KB 431 at 447. As to who may register the charge, see s 399.

The period permitted is 21 calendar days and commences from the date after the date of creation, ie the date of the execution of the charge. The problem which this period creates is that anyone searching the register of charges with respect to the company (see s 401), and finding that there are no charges, cannot be sure that there are not charges which have been created but have not yet been registered. Searchers of the register must not rely therefore on the absence of charges and must ask the company to confirm that no other charges have been created which have yet to be registered. The 21-day period is extended where the charge is created outside the UK over property situated outside the UK: see s 398.

If, because of errors in the particulars provided, the registrar is required to return the forms to the presenter for correction, resubmission must occur within the 21-day limit. If the registrar improperly rejects a form, for example, because of doubts as to whether the charge is within s 396, the charge is not invalidated as delivery will have occurred within the 21-day period.

21-day period has elapsed   Where a charge has not been registered and the 21-day period has elapsed so attracting the invalidity provided for by this provision, there are a number of options open to the company and the chargee:

(1)   an application may be made to the court for registration out of time under s 404 – this step should be taken without delay once the failure to register is discovered;

(2)   the chargee may attempt to remedy the situation without recourse to the court, by getting another charge executed by the company and registered before any third party intervenes – a process which may be fraught with difficulties: see *Re Telomatic Ltd* [1994] 1 BCLC 90.

This approach is a risky strategy for, if it fails, the court may look unfavourably on an application under s 404: see *Victoria Housing Estates Ltd v Ashpurton Estates Ltd* [1982] 3 All ER 665 at 677 (the court should look askance at a chargee who deliberately defers his application in order to see which way the wind is going to blow). A further risk with a new charge is that if the company goes into insolvent liquidation or administration shortly thereafter, the new charge may be open to challenge as a vulnerable transaction under IA 1986, ss 239, 245.

(3)   The chargee can seek immediate repayment of the sum secured, since the statutory invalidity only bites against a liquidator, administrator or any creditor, see below. This ability to demand immediate repayment of the entire amount may assist him in obtaining a new charge from the company.

Void against the liquidator or administrator and any creditor   The statutory invalidity occurs automatically on the expiry of the 21-day period, but it is a limited invalidity: 'it makes void a security; not the debt, not the cause of action, but the security, and not as against everybody, not as against the company grantor, but against the liquidator, [and now an administrator] and against any creditor': *Re Monolithic Building Company* [1915] 1 Ch 643 at 667, per Phillimore LJ; and *Smith (administrator of Cosslett (Contractors) Ltd) v Bridgend County Borough Council* [2000] 1 BCLC 775 at 790–791 (a contract between a company which had gone into administration and a council which included an unregistered charge in favour of the council remained a good contract at all material times as between the company and the council – only the charge was void as against the administrator).

The result is that, on a winding up or administration, the liquidator or administrator may deal with the company's assets free from any security created by the charge in question: see *Re Cosslett (Contractors) Ltd* [1999] 1 BCLC 205 at 218–219 but see *Smith (administrator of Cosslett (Contractors) Ltd) v Bridgend County Borough Council* [2000] 1 BCLC 775 as to the difficulties which the administrator encountered in that case in attempting to take advantage of the statutory invalidity. 'Liquidator' primarily means a liquidator in an English winding up but, as the section is applied to overseas companies by s 409, it can extend to a liquidator in a foreign liquidation: see *NV Slavenburg's Bank NV v Intercontinental Natural Resources Ltd* [1980] 1 All ER 955.

As the money has become immediately repayable, a creditor can enforce the debt secured by the unregistered charge at any time before a liquidator or administrator is appointed and, if he succeeds in securing repayment, the charge is spent before liquidation or administration and there is nothing for the statutory provision to bite on: *Mercantile Bank of India Ltd v Chartered Bank of India, Australia and China* [1937] 1 All ER 231; *Re Row Dal Construction Pty Ltd* [1966] VR 249 at 258; *NV Slavenburg's Bank NV v Intercontinental Natural Resources Ltd* [1980] 1 All ER 955.

The invalidity also extends to 'any creditor' but, where the company has not gone into liquidation or administration, this effectively means any secured creditor and an unsecured creditor cannot prevent payment being made to the unregistered chargee. The reason being that, prior to liquidation or administration, the chargor may pay such of its creditors as it chooses, including the unregistered chargee, unless there is a creditor who has acquired a proprietary right to or an interest in the subject matter of the unregistered charge, such as a secured creditor or a judgment creditor levying execution against the company's assets: see *Re Ehrmann Bros Ltd* [1906] 2 Ch 697 at 708; *Re Telomatic Ltd* [1994] 1 BCLC 90 at 95; *Victoria Housing Estates Ltd v Ashpurton Estates Ltd* [1982] 3 All ER 665 at 670–671. However, once a petition has been presented for winding up (and now administration), the statutory invalidity in respect of any creditor takes effect: see *R v Registrar of Companies, ex p Central Bank of India* [1985] BCLC 465 at 471, 472. This position is recognised in effect by the '*Joplin*' and '*Charles*' provisos commonly attached to orders for late registration: see note to s 404; *Victoria Housing Estates Ltd v Ashpurton Estates Ltd* [1982] 3 All ER 665 at 670–671.

The fact that a subsequent secured creditor took with notice of the existence of the unregistered charge does not prevent that subsequent creditor from relying on the statutory invalidity: *Re Monolithic Building Co* [1915] 1 Ch 643.

On liquidation or administration, an individual creditor has no locus standi to invoke this section and seek a declaration against a chargee that a particular charge is void for non-registration; that is a matter for the liquidator or administrator: see *Re Ayala Holdings Ltd* [1993] BCLC 256.

Priority as between charges   Registration required under this Chapter does not determine priorities as between successive chargees, save to the extent arising as a result of the statutory invalidity affecting an unregistered charge.

Priority issues are determined at common law with the basic rules being that legal interests prevail over equitable, fixed charges over floating charges, and where the equities are equal, then the first in time prevails. The position is then complicated by issues of notice and, in particular, the application of the doctrine of constructive notice. Anyone dealing with a company is deemed under the doctrine of constructive notice to have notice of its public documents, which includes the memorandum and articles of association, which doctrine was extended, obiter, by *Wilson v Kelland* [1910] 2 Ch 306 to the register of charges, but only to the extent that there is constructive notice of the existence of a registered charge but not of any special provisions contained in the charge; and see *Siebe Gorman & Co Ltd v Barclays Bank Ltd* [1979] 2 Lloyd's Rep 142 at 160. See generally Gough *Company Charges* (2nd edn, 1996) Ch 23.

396. Charges which have to be registered

(1) Section 395 applies to the following charges—

    (a) a charge for the purpose of securing any issue of debentures,

    (b) a charge on uncalled share capital of the company,

    (c) a charge created or evidenced by an instrument which, if executed by an individual, would require registration as a bill of sale,

    (d) a charge on land (wherever situated) or any interest in it, but not including a charge for any rent or other periodical sum issuing out of the land,

    (e) a charge on book debts of the company,

    (f) a floating charge on the company's undertaking or property,

    (g) a charge on calls made but not paid,

    (h) a charge on a ship or aircraft, or any share in a ship,

    (j) a charge on goodwill, or on any intellectual property.

(2) Where a negotiable instrument has been given to secure the payment of any book debts of a company, the deposit of the instrument for the purpose of securing an advance to the company is not, for purposes of section 395, to be treated as a charge on those book debts.

(3) The holding of debentures entitling the holder to a charge on land is not for purposes of this section deemed to be an interest in land.

(3A) The following are 'intellectual property' for the purposes of this section—

    (a) any patent, trade mark, ... registered design, copyright or design right;

    (b) any licence under or in respect of any such right.

(4) In this Chapter, 'charge' includes mortgage.

General note

Only charges covered by this provision have to be registered, but the list includes most forms of company property over which security might be given: for example, immovable property (a charge on land (sub-s (1)(d))); tangible movable property (a charge on ships or aircraft (sub-s (1)(h)), or on goods (sub-s (1)(c))); and intangible property (a charge on book debts (sub-s (1)(e)); or on goodwill, patents, trademarks, copyright (sub-s (1)(j))). There is an overlap between a number of the categories so, for example, a charge could be registrable because it falls within sub-ss (1)(e) or (f). Equally, notwithstanding the scope of the provision, some charges are not registrable, such as a fixed charge on a credit balance at a bank (assuming it does not amount to a book debt: see discussion below under sub-s (1)(e)); or a fixed charge on shares; or a fixed charge on an insurance policy (see *Paul & Frank Ltd v Discount Bank (Overseas) Ltd* [1966] 2 All ER 922).

S 396(1)(a)

Any issue of debentures   It is unclear whether this provision requires the registration of a charge securing a single debenture. The better view is that it refers to the issue of a series of debentures (and this view has been taken on equivalent provisions in New Zealand and Australia). The issue of a single debenture secured by a charge will in any event fall under another heading such as a charge over land or a floating charge. As to registration of a charge securing an issue of debentures, see s 397.

S 396(1)(b),(g)

It is rare now for a company to have uncalled share capital (defined in s 737(2)) but where it does, any charge over it must be registered.

S 396(1)(c)

This category of charges that require registration is defined by reference to the obscure legislation governing the registration of non-possessory securities over goods, evidenced in writing, under the Bills of Sale Acts 1878 and 1882. An excellent treatment of this legislation can be found in Halsbury's Laws of England, vol 4(1), *Bills of Sale*.

S 396(1)(e)

Book debts   There is no agreed definition of book debts ('an imprecise expression': *Re ASRS Establishment Ltd* [2000] 2 BCLC 631 at 641, per Robert Walker LJ) but essentially it encompasses debts connected with and arising in the course of trade or business, due or growing due to the proprietor of that business and entered or commonly entered in the books: see *Paul & Frank Ltd v Discount Bank (Overseas) Ltd* [1966] 2 All ER 922 at 925-926; *Independent Automatic Sales Ltd v Knowles and Foster* [1962] 3 All ER 27 at 34; *Shipley v Marshall* (1863) 143 ER 567.

Bank balances   Sums standing to a company's credit in a bank account are not within a charge on 'book debts' granted by the company: *Northern Bank Ltd v Ross* [1991] BCLC 504 at 508; *Re Brightlife Ltd* [1986] BCLC 418 at 422; but such funds, although not encompassed by a charge on book debts, can be the subject of a charge, even a charge in favour of the bank which is the debtor of the company with respect to that asset: *Re Bank of Credit and Commerce International SA (No 8)* [1998] 1 BCLC 68, doubting dicta to the contrary expressed in *Re Charge Card Services Ltd (No 2)* [1987] BCLC 17. Whether such charges over bank deposits require registration was left open by Lord Hoffmann in *Re Bank of Credit and Commerce International SA (No 8)* [1998] 1 BCLC 68 at 77, although he drew attention to the decision in *Northern Bank Ltd v Ross* [1991] BCLC 504 where Lord Hutton suggested that there would not be an obligation to register such charges. Nevertheless, the cautious practice is to register such charges and the registrar of companies will accept them for registration.

Substance of the transaction   As the parties' description is not determinative of the issue, describing something as a lien does not obviate the need for registration if the security provided is, in fact, a charge on book debts: see *Re Welsh Irish Ferries Ltd* [1985] BCLC 327 (a lien on sub-freights created by a charterer (the company) in favour of a shipowner amounted to an assignment of book debts by way of security to the shipowner and as such was an equitable charge requiring registration). But the better view is that a lien on sub-freights is not a charge at all: see *Agnew v IRC (Re Brumark Investments Ltd)* [2001] UKPC 28, [2001] All ER (D) 21 (Jun), PC, para 39.

Where there is an absolute assignment of the debt rather than an assignment by way of security, there is no charge requiring registration under this provision: see *Ashby, Warner & Co Ltd v Simmons* [1936] 2 All ER 697 (absolute assignment); *Re Kent and Sussex Sawmills Ltd* [1947] Ch 177 (assignment by way of security); and the true nature of the assignment is primarily a matter of construction of the documentation.

Factoring and discounting book debts   It is well established that factoring or block discounting amounts to a sale of book debts, rather than a charge on book debts, even though under the relevant agreement the purchaser of the debts is given recourse against the vendor in the event of default in payment of the debt by the debtor: *Welsh Development Agency v Export Finance Co Ltd* [1992] BCLC 148 at 154; see *Re George Inglefield Ltd* [1932] All ER Rep 244; *Olds Discount Co Ltd v John Playfair Ltd* [1938] 3 All ER 275; and *Olds Discount Co Ltd v Cohen* [1938] 3 All ER 281n, endorsed by the House of Lords in *Lloyds and Scottish Finance Ltd v Cyril Lord Carpets Sales Ltd* [1992] BCLC 609.

A fixed charge on book debts   Prior to the decision in *Siebe Gorman & Co Ltd v Barclays Bank Ltd* [1979] 2 Lloyds Rep 142, it was thought that any charge over book debts, being a fluctuating class of assets used by the company in the ordinary course of business, must of necessity be a floating charge (as to the distinction between fixed and floating charges, see the note to sub-s (1)(f), below). However, in the *Siebe Gorman* case, it was established that it is possible for a company to give a fixed charge over its book debts provided that there are express restrictions on the company's freedom to deal with those assets. Restrictions are typically imposed through a provision that the chargor must pay all monies received in respect of such book debts into a designated bank account and is not able to withdraw, charge or assign those sums to any other person without the prior consent of the chargee. See also *Re Keenan Bros Ltd* [1986] BCLC 242 (segregation of funds such that they were unusable by the chargor save with the consent of the chargee indicated a fixed charge).

The key requirement to render a charge on book debts a fixed charge is a restriction on the freedom of the chargor to use the charged assets, which are instead under the control of the chargee; where this element has been lacking or inadequate, the courts have found the charge to be floating. See, for example, *Re Brightlife Ltd* [1986] BCLC 418 (although there were some restrictions on the debtor company, it retained the freedom to collect in the debts and pay the proceeds into its bank account and use them in the ordinary course of business: the charge was a floating charge); *Re Pearl Maintenance Ltd* [1995] 1 BCLC 449 (no restrictions on the freedom of the chargor to realise the book debts and to use the proceeds in the ordinary course of business: the charge was a floating charge although described as fixed); *Royal Trust Bank v National Westminster Bank plc* [1996] 2 BCLC 682 (failure to require and control a designated account: charge was a floating charge); *Re Westmaze Ltd* [1999] BCC 441 (failure to require separate account: charge was a floating charge); *Re Double S Printers Ltd* [1999] 1 BCLC 220 (chargee had no control over the debts or the proceeds: charge was a floating charge); *Re ASRS Establishment Ltd* [2000] 2 BCLC 631 (charge on escrow account fell within charge on 'debts and other claims' which was designated as a fixed charge but chargor was free to use the proceeds of the escrow account in the ordinary course of business: the charge was a floating charge); and see *Agnew v IRC (Re Brumark Investments Ltd)* [2001] UKPC 28, [2001] All ER (D) 21 (Jun), PC, discussed in detail below.

A case which is incompatible with this line of reasoning is *Re Atlantic Computer Systems plc* [1991] BCLC 606 at 625, CA (charge on rental income was fixed although the chargor retained the ability to use the rentals in the ordinary course of business), which was followed by *Re Atlantic Medical Ltd* [1993] BCLC 386. Both decisions have been the subject of much critical comment: see Goode (1994) 110 LQR 592; Zacaroli (1997) Insolv Int 41; and must be considered doubtful authorities in the light of *Agnew v IRC (Re Brumark Investments Ltd)* [2001] UKPC 28, [2001] All ER (D) 21 (Jun), PC.

It will be appreciated that, save where the chargee is a clearing bank (as in *Siebe Gorman & Co Ltd v Barclays Bank Ltd* [1979] 2 Lloyd's Rep 142 or *Re Keenan Bros Ltd* [1986] BCLC 242), it may be difficult to impose the level of control over the proceeds necessary for the charge to be classified as a fixed charge without paralysing the company's activities. However, it is not impossible: see *William Gaskell Group Ltd v Highley* [1994] 1 BCLC 197. See also *Chalk v Kahn* [2000] 2 BCLC 361 (chargor to collect and pay proceedings into designated account which was not with the chargee but another bank, chargee had no control over the chargor's dealings with money in that account: the charge was a floating charge although described as fixed).

Book debts and the proceeds of book debts – *New Bullas* to *Brumark*   Having established in *Siebe Gorman & Co Ltd v Barclays Bank Ltd* [1979] 2 Lloyds Rep 142 that a fixed charge on book debts was possible, a further drafting refinement appeared in *Re New Bullas Trading Ltd* [1994] 1 BCLC 485, CA, where the debenture provided for a fixed charge on book debts whilst uncollected and a floating charge on realisation.

The Court of Appeal accepted that the draftsman had deliberately and conscientiously set out to create two charges; that it was for the parties to reach agreement as to the type of security required; and that there was no authority or principle in law that preventing them from agreeing as they had. The charge was fixed while the debts remained uncollected and the proceeds were subject to a floating charge once realised.

This decision was controversial, it not having been the practice previously to regard the debt and the proceeds as divisible, and much (but not all) of the commentary on the case was hostile: see Goode, 'Charges Over Book Debts: A Missed Opportunity' (1994) 110 LQR 592; Berg, 'Charges Over Book Debts: A Reply' (1995) JBL 433; Worthington, 'Fixed Charges Over Book Debts and Other Receivables' (1997) 113 LQR 562. Subsequent cases emphasised that the *New Bullas* case turned on the unusual and specific wording of the debenture: see *Re Pearl Maintenance Services Ltd* [1995] 1 BCLC 449 at 454; *Re Westmaze Ltd* [1999] BCC 441 at 444; *Re ASRS Establishment Ltd* [2000] 2 BCLC 631 at 642; *Chalk v Kahn* [2000] 2 BCLC 361 at 366.

The Court of Appeal in New Zealand, on a similarly worded debenture, then declined to follow the approach in *New Bullas*: *Re Brumark Investments Ltd, IRC v Agnew* [2000] 1 BCLC 353, although the judgment of Gault J in *Brumark* was not without its own problems and inconsistencies (see '*New Bullas* in New Zealand: Round Two' (2000) 116 LQR 211). The New Zealand court held that where the chargor was free to collect the book debts, thus extinguishing them, and was free to deal with the proceeds in the normal course of its business, the charged book debts were not sufficiently under the control of the chargee to make the charge a fixed charge. There was no basis for distinguishing between dealing with charged assets by way of disposal to third parties and dealing by collection. Gault J concluded: '... we cannot see how the debate on whether book debts and their proceeds constitute separate security interests offers any new aid in determining whether a particular charge is fixed or floating' (at 364).

On appeal, the Privy Council has confirmed the decision by the New Zealand Court of Appeal that the charge was a floating charge and has concluded that *New Bullas* was wrongly decided: *Agnew v IRC (Re Brumark Investments Ltd)* [2001] UKPC 28, [2001] All ER (D) 21 (Jun), PC.

Technically of course, decisions of the Privy Council are only of persuasive authority but made up as it was of five Law Lords (Lords Bingham, Nicholls, Hoffmann, Hobhouse and Millett), it is highly unlikely that this decision will not be followed by the English courts.

Lord Millett, who delivered the judgment, emphasised that the hallmark of the floating charge is a company's freedom to deal with charged assets without the consent of the holder of the charge (para 13). The question is whether the charged assets are intended to be under the control of the company or of the charge holder. The fact that the company may be prohibited from assigning, factoring or charging the asset to anyone else is not sufficient to make a charge a fixed charge if the company retains the freedom to collect the asset in the ordinary course of business for its own benefit (para 36).

It is possible to create a charge on book debts as a fixed charge and it is sufficient for such purposes to prohibit the company from realising the debts itself, whether by assignment or collection. Moreover, it is not inconsistent with the fixed nature of a charge on book debts for the holder of the charge to appoint the company as its agent to collect the debts for its account and on its behalf. In *Re Keenan Bros Ltd* [1986] BCLC 242, this was effected by means of a requirement that funds collected by the company were to be paid into a blocked account with the charge holder. As the debts are not available to the company as a source of its cash flow, such an arrangement is inconsistent with the charge being a floating charge. However, the account must be operated in practice as a blocked account and the appearance of a restraint without its practical operation will be disregarded by the court when categorising the charge as a matter of law (para 48).

On the facts in *Brumark*, the company's freedom to deal with the charged assets (by collecting the proceeds of the book debts) without the consent of the holder of the charge was characteristic of a floating charge; furthermore, the company was free to deal with the proceeds of the uncollected book debts for its own benefit which was inconsistent with the nature of a fixed charge; the charge was a floating charge.

On the one asset/two assets controversy, there was acceptance of the view that the debt and its proceeds are two separate assets; however, Lord Millett noted that the proceeds represent the entire value of the debt so 'any attempt to separate the ownership of the debts from the ownership of their proceeds, even if conceptually possible, makes no commercial sense.' (para 46). In general, it would seem then that a charge on book debts will be a charge on the indivisible asset, making no distinction between the uncollected book debts and the proceeds, while leaving the door open to the draftsman to treat it as two assets where he can perceive some advantage in so doing.

S 396(1)(f)

The floating charge need not be on the whole undertaking nor on the whole property of the company: *Re Yorkshire Woolcombers Association* [1903] 2 Ch 284 at 298, per Cozens-Hardy LJ; and see *Re Cimex Tissues Ltd* [1995] 1 BCLC 409 at 420.

Fixed and floating charges   The distinction between fixed and floating charges was explained by Lord Macnaghten in *Illingworth v Houldsworth* [1904] AC 355 at 358 as follows:

> 'A specific charge ... is one that without more fastens on ascertained and definite property or property capable of being ascertained or defined. A floating charge, on the other hand, is ambulatory and shifting in its nature, hovering over and so to speak floating with the property which it is intended to affect until some event occurs or some act is done which causes it to settle and fasten on the subject of the charge within its reach and grasp.'

The importance of the distinction is explained in the general note to this Chapter, which precedes s 395.

A floating charge is an equitable invention, first recognised by the Court of Appeal in *Re Panama, New Zealand & Australian Royal Mail Co* (1878) LR 5 Ch App 318. The classic description of a floating charge is that:

(1)   it is a charge on a class of assets of a company present and future;

(2)   that class is one which, in the ordinary course of the business of the company, would be changing from time to time; and

(3)   by the charge it is contemplated that, until some future step is taken by or on behalf of those interested in the charge, the company may carry on its business in the ordinary way: *Re Yorkshire Woolcombers Association* [1903] 2 Ch 284 at 295, per Romer LJ (although Romer LJ did not say that all three elements must be present in order for the charge to be floating).

The attraction of a floating charge is this freedom it gives to the chargor company to continue to deal with the assets in the ordinary course of business so avoiding the 'restricting (and in some cases, paralysing) effect on the use of the assets of the company resulting from a fixed charge': *Re Keenan Bros Ltd* [1986] BCLC 242 at 245, per Walsh J. It is this third charcteristic, the ability to carry on business in the ordinary way, without the consent of the charge holder, which is the hallmark of a floating charge and secures to distinguish it from a fixed charge: *Agnew v IRC (Re Brumark Investments Ltd)* [2001] UKPC 28, [2001] All ER (D) 21 (Jun), PC, para 13.

In determining whether a charge is fixed or floating, the court will consider whether, on the true construction of the debenture, the charge possesses the characteristics of a fixed or a floating charge and the parties' description of the charge is not determinative: *Re Westmaze Ltd* [1999] BCC 441; *Royal Trust Bank plc v National Westminster Bank plc* [1996] 2 BCLC 682; *Re Brightlife Ltd* [1986] BCLC 418; *Re Armagh Shoes Ltd* [1984] BCLC 405. The court will engage in a two-stage process. Initially, the court must construe the charge instrument – not to discover whether the parties intended to create a fixed or floating charge (that is a matter of law) but to discover the nature of the rights and obligations which the parties intended to grant each other in respect of the charged assets. Having identified the rights and obligations so granted, the charge must then be classified as a matter of law. If the rights granted are inconsistent with the nature of a fixed charge, the charge cannot be a fixed charge, however the parties choose to describe it: *Agnew v IRC (Re Brumark Investments Ltd)* [2001] UKPC 28, [2001] All ER (D) 21 (Jun), PC.

Freedom to deal with the assets in the ordinary course of business The first two elements identified by Romer LJ, noted above, are usually easily established, but much debate can arise as to whether restrictions have been imposed on the chargor's freedom to deal with the assets in the ordinary course of business so as to negate the third element and render the charge a fixed charge with the assets effectively under the control of the chargee. Much of that debate has taken place in the context of charges on book debts and is considered in detail in the note to sub-s (1)(e) above; see also *Re CCG International Enterprises Ltd* [1993] BCLC 1428.

However, there may be some restrictions on the chargor's freedom to deal with the assets without rendering the charge a fixed charge. For example, any well drafted floating charge will restrict the ability of the chargor to create further charges, as Millett LJ noted in *Re Cosslett (Contractors) Ltd* [1999] 1 BCLC 205 at 217; and see *Re Brightlife Ltd* [1986] BCLC 418 at 422, per Hoffmann J (a prohibition against factoring debts was not sufficient to convert what was otherwise a floating charge on book debts into a fixed charge); and *Re G E Tunbridge Ltd* [1995] 1 BCLC 34 at 39 (a restriction on the sale of certain assets did not convert a charge which was otherwise floating into a fixed charge). Conversely, it seems that a charge can be a fixed charge although the chargor has some limited power to deal with the assets but the extent to which the licence to deal is compatible with a fixed charge will depend on the circumstances and the nature of the charged property: see *Re Cimex Tissues Ltd* [1995] 1 BCLC 409 at 420–421 (asset charged was machinery).

Power to create further securities The freedom of the chargor to deal with the assets in the ordinary course of business includes a freedom to create further fixed charges ranking in priority to the floating charge: *Wheatley v Silkstone Haigh Moor Coal Co* (1885) 29 Ch D 715; but the courts have restricted the ability to create subsequent floating charges. A second floating charge over all of the property comprised in the first charge and ranking pari passu with or in priority to that charge is incompatible with the first charge and ranks subject to it: *Re Benjamin Cope & Sons Ltd* [1914] 1 Ch 800. However, a subsequent floating charge can rank pari passu with or in priority to the first floating charge where the first floating charge permits of such a charge and the second charge is over part only of the assets comprised in the original charge: *Re Automatic Bottle Makers Ltd* [1926] Ch 412.

The possibility of granting subsequent charges over the assets within the reach of the floating charge has resulted in the practice of including negative pledges prohibiting the chargor from creating further charges ranking pari passu with or in priority to the current charge, but these clauses cannot bind a subsequent chargee for value without notice. Details of these clauses are sometimes included by chargees in the particulars delivered to the registrar (see note to s 395(1)) although they are not amongst the prescribed particulars and third parties cannot be affected by constructive notice of such extra-statutory material: see *Siebe Gorman & Co Ltd v Barclays Bank Ltd* [1979] 2 Lloyd's Rep 142 at 159–160.

397. Formalities of registration (debentures)

(1) Where a series of debentures containing, or giving by reference to another instrument, any charge to the benefit of which the debenture holders of that series are entitled pari passu is created by a company, it is for purposes of section 395 sufficient if there are delivered to or received by the registrar, within 21 days after the execution of the deed containing the charge (or, if there is no

such deed, after the execution of any debentures of the series), the following particulars in the prescribed form—

    (a) the total amount secured by the whole series, and

    (b) the dates of the resolutions authorising the issue of the series and the date of the covering deed (if any) by which the security is created or defined, and

    (c) a general description of the property charged, and

    (d) the names of the trustees (if any) for the debenture holders,

together with the deed containing the charge or, if there is no such deed, one of the debentures of the series:

    Provided that there shall be sent to the registrar of companies, for entry in the register, particulars in the prescribed form of the date and amount of each issue of debentures of the series, but any omission to do this does not affect the validity of any of those debentures.

(2) Where any commission, allowance or discount has been paid or made either directly or indirectly by a company to a person in consideration of his—

    (a) subscribing or agreeing to subscribe, whether absolutely or conditionally, for debentures of the company, or

    (b) procuring or agreeing to procure subscriptions, whether absolute or conditional, for such debentures,

the particulars required to be sent for registration under section 395 shall include particulars as to the amount or rate per cent of the commission, discount or allowance so paid or made, but omission to do this does not affect the validity of the debentures issued.

(3) The deposit of debentures as security for a debt of the company is not, for the purposes of subsection (2), treated as the issue of the debentures at a discount.

S 397(1)

A series of debentures   This provision reduces the burden in terms of the information to be registered where there is the issue of a series of debentures. It is sufficient to send the required particulars and the trust deed or one of the debentures in the series. There is no need to repeat the process every time any of the debentures are issued although, on each issue, the date and the amount of the issue should be notified, but this is a mere disclosure requirement.

398. Verification of charge on property outside United Kingdom

(1) In the case of a charge created out of the United Kingdom comprising property situated outside the United Kingdom, the delivery to and the receipt by the registrar of companies of a copy (verified in the prescribed manner) of the instrument by which the charge is created or evidenced has the same effect for purposes of sections 395 to 398 as the delivery and receipt of the instrument itself.

(2) In that case, 21 days after the date on which the instrument or copy could, in due course of post (and if despatched with due diligence), have been received in the United Kingdom are substituted for the 21 days mentioned in section 395(1) (or as the case may be, section 397(1)) as the time within which the particulars and instrument or copy are to be delivered to the registrar.

(3) Where a charge is created in the United Kingdom but comprises property outside the United Kingdom, the instrument creating or purporting to create the charge may be sent for registration under section 395 notwithstanding that further proceedings may be necessary to make the charge valid or effectual according to the law of the country in which the property is situated.

(4) Where a charge comprises property situated in Scotland or Northern Ireland and registration in the country where the property is situated is necessary to make the charge valid or effectual according to the law of that country, the delivery to and receipt by the registrar of a copy (verified in the prescribed manner) of the instrument by which the charge is created or evidenced, together with a certificate in the prescribed form stating that the charge was presented for registration in Scotland or Northern Ireland (as the case may be) on the date on which it was so presented has, for purposes of sections 395 to 398, the same effect as the delivery and receipt of the instrument itself.

S 398(1)

A copy of the instrument is permitted in this instance, cf s 395.

S 398(2)

This provision does not prescribe an extended period but provides for a calculation to be made as to when a copy could, in due course of post, have been received in the UK, and the result is uncertainty as to how long a period might be permissible.

399. Company's duty to register charges it creates

(1) It is a company's duty to send to the registrar of companies for registration the particulars of every charge created by the company and of the issues of debentures of a series requiring registration under sections 395 to 398; but registration of any such charge may be effected on the application of any person interested in it.

(2) Where registration is effected on the application of some person other than the company, that person is entitled to recover from the company the amount of any fees properly paid by him to the registrar on the registration.

(3) If a company fails to comply with subsection (1), then, unless the registration has been effected on the application of some other person, the company and every officer of it who is in default is liable to a fine and, for continued contravention, to a daily default fine.

S 399(1), (2)

It is the company's duty to deliver the particulars and the charge instrument to the registrar of companies and an incentive to do so is provided by s 395(2). In practice, because of the consequences of non-delivery in s 395(1), the majority of registrations are undertaken by the chargee. The registration fee payable to the registrar of companies is £10.

S 399(3)

As to penalties, see s 730, Sch 24; 'officer in default' is defined in s 730(5). In practice, prosecutions for breach of this provision are never brought.

400. Charges existing on property acquired

(1) This section applies where a company registered in England and Wales acquires property which is subject to a charge of any such kind as would, if it had been created by the company after the acquisition of the property, have been required to be registered under this Chapter.

(2) The company shall cause the prescribed particulars of the charge, together with a copy (certified in the prescribed manner to be a correct copy) of the instrument (if any) by which the charge was created or is evidenced, to be delivered to the registrar of companies for registration in manner required by this Chapter within 21 days after the date on which the acquisition is completed.

(3) However, if the property is situated and the charge was created outside Great Britain, 21 days after the date on which the copy of the instrument could in due course of post, and if despatched with due diligence, have been received in the United Kingdom is substituted for the 21 days above-mentioned as the time within which the particulars and copy of the instrument are to be delivered to the registrar.

(4) If default is made in complying with this section, the company and every officer of it who is in default is liable to a fine and, for continued contravention, to a daily default fine.

S 400(1)

See s 396 as to the charges which require registration.

S 400(2)–(4)

Consequences of non-registration   A failure to register as required by this provision does not attract the statutory invalidity of s 395 but merely a fine under this provision; there is no need therefore to obtain a court order for late registration. 'Officer in default' is defined in s 730(5). A fee of £10 is payable on registration.

401. Register of charges to be kept by registrar of companies

(1) The registrar of companies shall keep, with respect to each company, a register in the prescribed form of all the charges requiring registration under this Chapter; and he shall enter in the register with respect to such charges the following particulars—

    (a) in the case of a charge to the benefit of which the holders of a series of debentures are entitled, the particulars specified in section 397(1),

    (b) in the case of any other charge—

        (i)   if it is a charge created by the company, the date of its creation, and if it is a charge which was existing on property acquired by the company, the date of the acquisition of the property, and

        (ii) the amount secured by the charge, and

        (iii) short particulars of the property charged, and

        (iv) the persons entitled to the charge.

(2) The registrar shall give a certificate of the registration of any charge registered in pursuance of this Chapter, stating the amount secured by the charge. The certificate—

    (a) shall be either signed by the registrar, or authenticated by his official seal, and

    (b) is conclusive evidence that the requirements of this Chapter as to registration have been satisfied.

(3) The register kept in pursuance of this section shall be open to inspection by any person.

General note

As to the company's register of charges which must be maintained at the registered office, see s 407.

S 401(1)

Entry on the register   In practice, the registrar of companies maintains the information delivered as to charges in two formats: first, the prescribed forms once submitted are filed on the company's public record; secondly, the registrar, as required by this provision, maintains a register of charges for each company, which involves the registrar extracting a summary of those particulars, as specified by sub-ss (1)(a) and (b), for entry on the register. Any memoranda of satisfaction filed by the company will also be entered on the register (see s 403); as will the appointment of a receiver or manager: see s 405. A copy of the instrument of charge is not retained by the registrar but must be available at the company's registered office for inspection by any creditor or member of the company: see ss 406, 408(1). As to constructive notice of the register of charges, see *Wilson v Kelland* [1910] 2 Ch 306 and the note to s 395(1), above.

Error   See *Grove v Advantage Healthcare (T10) Ltd* [2000] 1 BCLC 661 where an error as to a company's registered number resulted in a charge being entered on the file of Company A when the charge had been created by Company B. Lightman J (at 665) noted that such an error could prejudice third parties and he speculated as to the possible liability in that situation of the registrar (who did not pick up that the company name and the number on the particulars provided did not tally) and of the party who misinformed the registrar as to the registered number.

Variations in the terms   There is no procedure whereby subsequent variations in the terms of the charge, for example, an increase in the secured monies or a variation of priorities as between chargees, can be registered. Of course, if the effect of the variations are that an entirely new charge is created, it must be registered as required by s 395.

S 401(2)

The amount secured by the charge will be stated on the certificate as either: all monies due, or to become due from the company to the chargee, under the terms of the instrument creating or evidencing the charge; or all monies due, or to become due from the company to the chargee, on any account whatsoever.

S 401(2)(b)

Conclusive evidence   The wording of this provision precludes evidence being adduced to challenge the correctness of the registrar's decision to register a charge in all judicial proceedings, including an application for judicial review, save on the application of the Attorney General: *R v Registrar of Companies, ex p Central Bank of India* [1985] BCLC 465. Once the certificate has been issued, the courts will refuse to go into any question as to whether or not the requirements regarding registration have been complied with: *R v Registrar of Companies, ex p Central Bank of India* [1985] BCLC 465; *Re C L Nye Ltd* [1970] 3 All ER 1061; *Re Yolland Husson and Birkett Ltd* [1908] 1 Ch 152. See also the note to s 13(7).

Even if in error   The certificate is conclusive as to compliance with the registration requirements even if it is inaccurate (*Re Mechanisations (Eaglescliffe) Ltd* [1966] Ch 20 (amount secured wrongly stated), and even if it shows the wrong date of creation of the charge, so that the charge may not have been delivered within the 21-day period: *Re C L Nye Ltd* [1970] 3 All ER 1061.

     The conclusiveness of the certificate is unaffected even where it is issued in reliance on a court order granting an extension of time under s 404 which order is subsequently overruled on appeal: *Exeter Trust Ltd v Screenways Ltd* [1991] BCLC 888, CA (the order is beyond recall once registration has been effected in reliance on the granted extension of time and the validity of the registration is not dependent on the continued existence of the order extending time. However, the order in this case did not contain, as it ought to have contained, a '*Re Charles*' proviso which would have affected the position: see the note to s 404(1)).

As to registration   The conclusiveness of the certificate relates only to the issue of registration and does not confer validity on a charge which is invalid for reasons other than lack of registration, such as fraud: see *R v Registrar of Companies, ex p Central Bank of India* [1985] BCLC 465 at 491.

S 401(3)

This provision is included for the avoidance of doubt. As to the inspection of the register of charges maintained by the company, see ss 407, 408.

402. Endorsement of certificate on debentures

(1) The company shall cause a copy of every certificate of registration given under section 401 to be endorsed on every debenture or certificate of debenture stock which is issued by the company, and the payment of which is secured by the charge so registered.

(2) But this does not require a company to cause a certificate of registration of any charge so given to be endorsed on any debenture or certificate of debenture stock issued by the company before the charge was created.

(3) If a person knowingly and wilfully authorises or permits the delivery of a debenture or certificate of debenture stock which under this section is required to have endorsed on it a copy of a certificate of registration, without the copy being so endorsed upon it, he is liable (without prejudice to any other liability) to a fine.

General note

This provision is cumbersome and was found by the Jenkins Committee, as long ago as 1962, to serve no useful purpose. Its repeal was recommended but never implemented.

S 402(3)

As to penalties, see s 730, Sch 24.

403. Entries of satisfaction and release

(1) Subject to subsection (1A), the registrar of companies, on receipt of a statutory declaration in the prescribed form verifying, with respect to a registered charge,—

    (a) that the debt for which the charge was given has been paid or satisfied in whole or in part, or

    (b) that part of the property or undertaking charged has been released from the charge or has ceased to form part of the company's property or undertaking,

may enter on the register a memorandum of satisfaction in whole or in part, or of the fact that part of the property or undertaking has been released from the charge or has ceased to form part of the company's property or undertaking (as the case may be).

(1A) The registrar of companies may make any such entry as is mentioned in subsection (1) where, instead of receiving such a statutory declaration as is mentioned in that subsection, he receives a statement by a director, secretary, administrator or administrative receiver of the company which is contained in an electronic communication and that statement—

(a) verifies the matters set out in paragraph (a) or (b) of that subsection,

(b) contains a description of the charge,

(c) states the date of creation of the charge and the date of its registration under this Chapter,

(d) states the name and address of the chargee or, in the case of a debenture, trustee, and

(e) where paragraph (b) of subsection (1) applies, contains short particulars of the property or undertaking which has been released from the charge, or which has ceased to form part of the company's property or undertaking (as the case may be).

(2) Where the registrar enters a memorandum of satisfaction in whole, he shall if required furnish the company with a copy of it.

(2A) Any person who makes a false statement under subsection (1A) which he knows to be false or does not believe to be true is liable to imprisonment or a fine, or both.

S 403(1)

No obligation　There is no statutory requirement to notify the registrar of companies of the satisfaction or release of any charge, but companies that want to clear debts off their public record will make a statutory declaration or statement to this effect.

The wording allows for a statutory declaration or statement in the specified circumstances, but not where all of the property is released without paying off any of the debt. The provision does not indicate who should make the statutory declaration but the prescribed forms require it to be made either by a director, the company secretary, an administrator or administrative receiver; in other words, the consent of the chargee is not required.

S 403(1A), (2A)

Statement by electronic communication　This provision was inserted by the Companies Act 1985 (Electronic Communications) Order 2000, SI 2000/3373, art 22(1), (2), as from 22 December 2000; and it facilitates the acceptance by the registrar of companies of electronic statements as to certain matters in the same manner as he accepts statutory declarations as to those matters. The provision goes on to spell out the various matters which must be included in the statement and which reflect the contents of the prescribed forms under sub-s (1). As to the delivery of documents to the registrar using electronic communications, see s 707B.

The intention in sub-s (2A) is to provide the same penalties for false statements as is provided by the Perjury Act 1911 for false statutory declarations; as to penalties, see s 730, Sch 24.

404. Rectification of register of charges

(1) The following applies if the court is satisfied that the omission to register a charge within the time required by this Chapter or that the omission or mis-statement of any particular with respect to any such charge or in a memorandum of satisfaction was accidental, or due to inadvertence or to some other sufficient cause, or is not of a nature to prejudice the position of creditors or shareholders of the company, or that on other grounds it is just and equitable to grant relief.

(2) The court may, on the application of the company or a person interested, and on such terms and conditions as seem to the court just and expedient, order that the time for registration shall be extended or, as the case may be, that the omission or mis-statement shall be rectified.

S 404(1)

Given that the certificate issued by the registrar of companies is conclusive despite errors (see note to s 401(2)(b)), it is not surprising that applications under this provision to correct omissions or mis-statements are rare and the great majority of applications are cases where there has been a failure to register, with the result that the charge is void to the extent specified by s 395(1): see the note to that provision, above.

Grounds for application　There are five separate grounds on which the court might exercise its discretion and the final 'just and equitable' category allows for any reason, whether specified in the section or not, to be put forward; see *Re Braemar Investments Ltd* [1988] BCLC 556 at 561. If none of the grounds are made out, the discretion does not arise: *Re Telomatic Ltd* [1994] 1 BCLC 90; and, even if the discretion does arise, the court may decide not to exercise it as where the application is made only after long delay: *Re Telomatic Ltd* [1994] 1 BCLC 90; *Victoria Housing Estates Ltd v Ashpurton Estates Ltd* [1982] 3 All ER 665. But, in general, the practice of the court is to exercise the power to extend the period for registration, subject to the provisos noted below.

Imminent liquidation　The fact that the liquidation of the company is imminent is a relevant factor for the court to consider but it is not an absolute bar to an order for registration: *Re Braemar Investments Ltd* [1988] BCLC 556; *Victoria Housing Estates Ltd v Ashpurton Estates Ltd* [1982] 3 All ER 665. As long as the '*Joplin*' and '*Re Charles*' provisos, noted below, are included, the discretion should be exercised in favour of registration; the only circumstance in which the granting of permission would not be appropriate is if the judge is satisfied that an application, following liquidation, to set aside the extension of time would be bound to succeed: *Barclays Bank plc v Stuart Landon Ltd* [2001] All ER (D) 266 (Jan), CA.

　It is the settled practice of the court not to make an order extending the time for registration after the commencement of the winding up: *Victoria Housing Estates Ltd v Ashpurton Estates Ltd* [1982] 3 All ER 665; see also *Barclays Bank plc v Stuart Landon Ltd* [2001] All ER (D) 266 (Jan), CA; although there may be wholly exceptional cases where it would do so, as in *Re R M Arnold & Co Ltd* [1984] BCLC 535.

The '*Joplin*' proviso　Where the court grants an extension to the time permitted for registration of a charge, it will do so subject to the '*Joplin*' proviso – that registration is without prejudice to any rights acquired between the date of creation of the charge and the date of its actual registration: *Re Joplin Brewery Co Ltd* [1902] 1 Ch 79 (as modified following the decision in *Watson v Duff Morgan & Vermont (Holdings) Ltd* [1974] 1 All ER 794); and see *Victoria Housing Estates Ltd v Ashpurton Estates Ltd* [1982] 3 All ER 665 at 670 for the history of this proviso. That proviso will apply even if the intervening creditors have actual notice of the unregistered charge: see *Re Telomatic Ltd* [1994] 1 BCLC 90 at 97. Its application may be modified, however, where an intervening charge was registered by the company's directors in their own favour: *Re Fablehill Ltd* [1991] BCLC 830 (it would be inequitable to protect such persons against the unregistered chargee).

The '*Re Charles*' proviso   Where the court grants an extension of time notwithstanding the imminence of liquidation, it will do so subject to the '*Joplin*' proviso and subject to the proviso in *Re L H Charles & Co Ltd* [1935] WN 15 allowing the company, through any liquidator subsequently appointed, to apply within a specified period (for example, 42 days) after the commencement of the winding up to discharge the order granting an extension of time and containing an undertaking by the applicant for late registration to abide by any order which the court may make.

The '*Re Charles*' proviso is designed to protect the interests of the unsecured creditors in the liquidation who will lose out if late registration is allowed: see *Re Braemar Investments Ltd* [1988] BCLC 556 at 559; *Re Chantry House Developments plc* [1990] BCLC 813. On an application by the liquidator, it is not inevitable that the order granting the extension of time will be set aside: see *Barclays Bank plc v Stuart Landon Ltd* [2001] All ER (D) 266 (Jan), CA.

The undertaking by the applicant for late registration to abide by any subsequent order is necessary to overcome the conclusiveness of the certificate granted by the registrar of companies under s 401. By the time the liquidator is in a position to challenge the extension order, the charge will have been registered pursuant to that order and the registrar will have issued the conclusive certificate under s 401 (see note to that provision). Without this undertaking, the applicant for the extension would be able to stand on that certificate as against the liquidator. The result of the undertaking is that the charge is registered pursuant to the extension order but the finality of the relief obtained by that order will not be settled until the court determines the matter on a subsequent application by the liquidator: see *Re Chantry House Developments Ltd* [1990] BCLC 813 at 822, per Scott J.

See *Exeter Trust Ltd v Screenways Ltd* [1991] BCLC 888, CA, where late registration effected in reliance on the granted extension of time was conclusive and could not be challenged by the liquidator as the order in that case did not contain, as it ought to have contained, a '*Re Charles*' proviso.

The court will omit the '*Re Charles*' proviso where there is an affidavit from an officer of the chargor stating that winding up proceedings are not pending against the chargor.

S 404(2)

The application for an extension of time may be made by the company (including an overseas company within s 409) or the chargee. The jurisdiction of the court is limited to the options specified and does not extend to making an order deleting a registration nor is there any inherent power of rectification outside of this provision: see *Exeter Trust Ltd v Screenways Ltd* [1991] BCLC 888 at 894–895.

405. Registration of enforcement of security

(1) If a person obtains an order for the appointment of a receiver or manager of a company's property, or appoints such a receiver or manager under powers contained in an instrument, he shall within 7 days of the order or of the appointment under those powers, give notice of the fact to the registrar of companies; and the registrar shall enter the fact in the register of charges.

(2) Where a person appointed receiver or manager of a company's property under powers contained in an instrument ceases to act as such receiver or manager, he shall, on so ceasing, give the registrar notice to that effect, and the registrar shall enter the fact in the register of charges.

(3) A notice under this section shall be in the prescribed form.

(4) If a person makes default in complying with the requirements of this section, he is liable to a fine and, for continued contravention, to a daily default fine.

S 405(1)

The appointment of a receiver or manager whether by court order or under an instrument must be notified and entered on the public register.

S 405(4)

As to penalties, see s 730, Sch 24.

406. Companies to keep copies of instruments creating charges

(1) Every company shall cause a copy of every instrument creating a charge requiring registration under this Chapter to be kept at its registered office.

(2) In the case of a series of uniform debentures, a copy of one debenture of the series is sufficient.

S 406(1)

No copy of the instrument of charge is kept on the public record by the registrar of companies, so it is important that the company is obliged to keep a copy at the registered office which is available for inspection in accordance with s 408. As to the registered office, see s 287.

407. Company's register of charges

(1) Every limited company shall keep at its registered office a register of charges and enter in it all charges specifically affecting property of the

company and all floating charges on the company's undertaking or any of its property.

(2) The entry shall in each case give a short description of the property charged, the amount of the charge and, except in the case of securities to bearer, the names of the persons entitled to it.

(3) If an officer of the company knowingly and wilfully authorises or permits the omission of an entry required to be made in pursuance of this section, he is liable to a fine.

S 407(1)

All charges   This provision requires the company to maintain a register of all charges, whether or not registrable under this Chapter; inspection is governed by s 408. If all charges are included, this will include, for example, very short-term fixed charges over shares; in practice, these requirements as to the inclusion of all charges are probably flouted and, in the case of small companies, the obligation to maintain this register is probably widely ignored.

Information not invalidity   This register is for information purposes only and a failure to enter a charge on the company's register has no effect on the validity of the charge: *Wright v Horton* (1887) 12 App Cas 371. Given the lack of sanction, the need for this register has been questioned.

The register may be kept otherwise than in a legible form (ss 722, 723) and, in that case, the provisions as to the place at which it must be kept and the place of inspection (see s 408) are subject to the Companies (Registers and Other Records) Regulations 1985, SI 1985/724.

S 407(3)

As to penalties, see s 730, Sch 24.

408. Right to inspect instruments which create charges, etc

(1) The copies of instruments creating any charge requiring registration under this Chapter with the registrar of companies, and the register of charges kept in pursuance of section 407, shall be open during business hours (but subject to such reasonable restrictions as the company in general meeting may impose, so that not less than 2 hours in each day be allowed for inspection) to the inspection of any creditor or member of the company without fee.

(2) The register of charges shall also be open to the inspection of any other person on payment of such fee, not exceeding 5 pence, for each inspection, as the company may prescribe.

(3) If inspection of the copies referred to, or of the register, is refused, every officer of the company who is in default is liable to a fine and, for continued contravention, to a daily default fine.

(4) If such a refusal occurs in relation to a company registered in England and Wales, the court may by order compel an immediate inspection of the copies or register.

S 408(1)

Only creditors and members can inspect copies of the instrument itself; and it is only copies of charges requiring registration (see ss 395, 396, 400, 409) which must be made available. In practice, any prospective creditor can ask the company to see copies of existing charges and it is a business decision whether to allow them to do so.

S 408(2)

Where the records are kept in a non-legible form, the provisions as to the place at which they must be kept and the place of inspection is subject to the Companies (Registers and Other Records) Regulations 1985, SI 1985/724.

S 408(3)

As to penalties, see s 730, Sch 24.

S 408(4)

This provision is necessary because, but for the section, it is not clear that there is any right of inspection or that the court has the power to compel inspection: see *Conway v Petronius Clothing Co Ltd* [1978] 1 All ER 185 at 199. The court's power is discretionary, see *Pelling v Families need Fathers Ltd* [2001] All ER (D) 03 (Aug), CA.

409. Charges on property in England and Wales created by overseas company

(1) This Chapter extends to charges on property in England and Wales which are created, and to charges on property in England and Wales which is acquired, by a company (whether a company within the meaning of this Act or not) incorporated outside Great Britain which has an established place of business in England and Wales.

(2) In relation to such a company, sections 406 and 407 apply with the substitution, for the reference to the company's registered office, of a reference to its principal place of business in England and Wales.

S 409(1)

Application of the provision   This provision applies the registration requirements of this Chapter to an overseas company in respect of: (i) charges on property in

England and Wales created by the company; and (ii) charges on property in England and Wales acquired by the company. The date at which it must be determined whether the section applies is the date of creation of the charge or the date on which property is acquired which falls within the section: see *Re Oriel Ltd* [1985] BCLC 343. The requirement to register charges created on property in England and Wales is not confined to a charge on property existing in England at the time when the charge was created but extends to a charge on future property in England: *NV Slavenburg's Bank NV v Intercontinental Natural Resources Ltd* [1980] 1 All ER 955.

An established place of business   To be within the provision, the overseas company must have an established place of business in England and Wales, a term also used in Pt XXIII (oversea companies) and see the note to s 691 for a detailed consideration of its scope. Essentially, there must be some more or less permanent location associated with the company within England and Wales and from which habitually, or with some degree of regularity, business is conducted: *Re Oriel Ltd* [1985] BCLC 343 at 347; *Cleveland Museum of Art v Capricorn Art International SA* [1990] BCLC 546.

Provisions applicable   The effect of being within the provision is to apply the provisions of this Chapter to such charges so a failure to register will attract the invalidity imposed by s 395(1) (see, for example, *Re Oriel Ltd* [1985] BCLC 343; *NV Slavenburg's Bank NV v Intercontinental Natural Resources Ltd* [1980] 1 All ER 955); the company is entitled to apply to the court for late registration under s 404; and it is obliged to maintain a register of charges (s 407) at its principal place of business.

Slavenburg filings   An overseas company with an established place of business in England and Wales must register any of its charges which fall within sub-s (1), whether or not the company has registered as required under Pt XXIII (oversea companies): *NV Slavenburg's Bank NV v Intercontinental Natural Resources Ltd* [1980] 1 All ER 955 (the operation of this provision is not dependent on registration under that Part).

This decision in the *Slavenburg* case produces a 'curious state of affairs', as Sir Robert Megarry V-C described it in *Re Alton Corpn* [1985] BCLC 27 at 33–34. The practice is that overseas companies, although they have not registered under Pt XXIII, deliver the prescribed particulars and charging instrument to the registrar of companies as required by s 395. The registrar makes a note of the documents sent and then returns them to the sender with a standard letter as proof of delivery to the registrar. This delivery to the registrar protects the charge from the statutory invalidity imposed by s 395(1). The details cannot be entered on to the company's record (the company has no record as it has not registered under Pt XXIII) so instead the details are entered on a special *Slavenburg* file: see Companies House, *Guidance Notes, Company Charges and Mortgages*. There is a fee of £10 for registering every *Slavenburg* charge: The Companies (Fees) (Amendment) Regulations 1998, SI 1998/3088, reg 3.

Many of the companies which register on the *Slavenburg* register do so from an excess of caution. They believe that they do not have an established place of business in England and Wales and are therefore neither within Pt XXIII nor this provision. However, they are concerned that a court could decide to the contrary at a later date whereupon they would find that they should have registered any charges within this provision. To avoid any risk of invalidity under s 395, therefore, they register their charges on the *Slavenburg* register in the manner indicated.

S 409(2)

As to the meaning of 'principal place of business', see note to s 698(2), below.

CHAPTER II

REGISTRATION OF CHARGES (SCOTLAND)

General note to this Chapter

Significant reforms of the registration requirements of this Chapter were included in CA 1989, Pt IV but those provisions were never brought into force and will not now be brought into force. They are not reproduced in this work.

410. Charges void unless registered

(1)   The following provisions of this Chapter have effect for the purpose of securing the registration in Scotland of charges created by companies.

(2)   Every charge created by a company, being a charge to which this section applies, is, so far as any security on the company's property or any part of it is conferred by the charge, void against the liquidator or administrator and any creditor of the company unless the prescribed particulars of the charge, together with a copy (certified in the prescribed manner to be a correct copy) of the instrument (if any) by which the charge is created or evidenced, are delivered to or received by the registrar of companies for registration in the manner required by this Chapter within 21 days after the date of the creation of the charge.

(3)   Subsection (2) is without prejudice to any contract or obligation for repayment of the money secured by the charge; and when a charge becomes void under this section the money secured by it immediately becomes payable.

(4)   This section applies to the following charges—
   (a) a charge on land wherever situated, or any interest in such land (not including a charge for any rent, ground annual or other periodical sum payable in respect of the land, but including a charge created by a heritable security within the meaning of section 9(8) of the Conveyancing and Feudal Reform (Scotland) Act 1970),
   (b) a security over the uncalled share capital of the company,
   (c) a security over incorporeal moveable property of any of the following categories—
      (i)   the book debts of the company,
      (ii)   calls made but not paid,
      (iii) goodwill,
      (iv)   a patent or a licence under a patent,
      (v)   a trademark,
      (vi)   a copyright or a licence under a copyright,
      (vii) a registered design or a licence in respect of such a design,
      (viii) a design right or a licence under a design right,
   (d) a security over a ship or aircraft or any share in a ship, and
   (e) a floating charge.

(5)   In this Chapter 'company'(except in section 424) means an incorporated company registered in Scotland;'registrar of companies' means the registrar or other officer performing under this Act the duty of registration of companies in Scotland; and references to the date of creation of a charge are—

   (a) in the case of a floating charge, the date on which the instrument creating the floating charge was executed by the company creating the charge, and

   (b) in any other case, the date on which the right of the person entitled to the benefit of the charge was constituted as a real right.

General note

This provision applies to Scotland only and is outside the scope of this work.

411. Charges on property outside United Kingdom

(1) In the case of a charge created out of the United Kingdom comprising property situated outside the United Kingdom, the period of 21 days after the date on which the copy of the instrument creating it could (in due course of post, and if despatched with due diligence) have been received in the United Kingdom is substituted for the period of 21 days after the date of the creation of the charge as the time within which, under section 410(2), the particulars and copy are to be delivered to the registrar.

(2) Where a charge is created in the United Kingdom but comprises property outside the United Kingdom, the copy of the instrument creating or purporting to create the charge may be sent for registration under section 410 notwithstanding that further proceedings may be necessary to make the charge valid or effectual according to the law of the country in which the property is situated.

General note

This provision applies to Scotland only and is outside the scope of this work.

412. Negotiable instrument to secure book debts

Where a negotiable instrument has been given to secure the payment of any book debts of a company, the deposit of the instrument for the purpose of securing an advance to the company is not, for purposes of section 410, to be treated as a charge on those book debts.

General note

This provision applies to Scotland only and is outside the scope of this work.

413. Charges associated with debentures

(1)   The holding of debentures entitling the holder to a charge on land is not, for the purposes of section 410, deemed to be an interest in land.

(2)   Where a series of debentures containing, or giving by reference to any other instrument, any charge to the benefit of which the debenture-holders of that series are entitled pari passu, is created by a company, it is sufficient for purposes of section 410 if there are delivered to or received by the registrar of companies within 21 days after the execution of the deed containing the charge or if there is no such deed, after the execution of any debentures of the series, the following particulars in the prescribed form—

  (a) the total amount secured by the whole series,
  (b) the dates of the resolutions authorising the issue of the series and the date of the covering deed (if any) by which the security is created or defined,
  (c) a general description of the property charged,
  (d) the names of the trustees (if any) for the debenture holders, and
  (e) in the case of a floating charge, a statement of any provisions of the charge and of any instrument relating to it which prohibit or restrict or regulate the power of the company to grant further securities ranking in priority to, or pari passu with, the floating charge, or which vary or otherwise regulate the order of ranking of the floating charge in relation to subsisting securities,

together with a copy of the deed containing the charge or, if there is no such deed, of one of the debentures of the series:

Provided that where more than one issue is made of debentures in the series, there shall be sent to the registrar of companies for entry in the register particulars (in the prescribed form) of the date and amount of each issue of debentures of the series, but any omission to do this does not affect the validity of any of those debentures.

(3)   Where any commission, allowance or discount has been paid or made, either directly or indirectly, by a company to any person in consideration of his subscribing or agreeing to subscribe, whether absolutely or conditionally, for any debentures of the company, or procuring or agreeing to procure subscriptions (whether absolute or conditional) for any such debentures, the particulars required to be sent for registration under section 410 include particulars as to the amount or rate per cent of the commission, discount or allowance so paid or made; but any omission to do this does not affect the validity of the debentures issued.

The deposit of any debentures as security for any debt of the company is not, for purposes of this subsection, treated as the issue of the debentures at a discount.

General note

This provision applies to Scotland only and is outside the scope of this work.

414. Charge by way of ex facie absolute disposition, etc

(1)   For the avoidance of doubt, it is hereby declared that, in the case of a charge created by way of an ex facie absolute disposition or assignation qualified by a back letter or other agreement, or by a standard security qualified by an agreement, compliance with section 410(2) does not of itself render the charge unavailable as security for indebtedness incurred after the date of compliance.

(2)   Where the amount secured by a charge so created is purported to be increased by a further back letter or agreement, a further charge is held to have been created by the ex facie absolute disposition or assignation or (as the case may be) by the standard security, as qualified by the further back letter or agreement; and the provisions of this Chapter apply to the further charge as if—

    (a) references in this Chapter (other than in this section) to the charge were references to the further charge, and

    (b) references to the date of the creation of the charge were references to the date on which the further back letter or agreement was executed.

General note

This provision applies to Scotland only and is outside the scope of this work.

415. Company's duty to register charges created by it

(1)   It is a company's duty to send to the registrar of companies for registration the particulars of every charge created by the company and of the issues of debentures of a series requiring registration under sections 410 to 414; but registration of any such charge may be effected on the application of any person interested in it.

(2)   Where registration is effected on the application of some person other than the company, that person is entitled to recover from the company the amount of any fees properly paid by him to the registrar on the registration.

(3)   If a company makes default in sending to the registrar for registration the particulars of any charge created by the company or of the issues of debentures of a series requiring registration as above mentioned, then, unless the registration has been effected on the application of some other person, the company and every officer of it who is in default is liable to a fine and, for continued contravention, to a daily default fine.

General note

This provision applies to Scotland only and is outside the scope of this work.

416. Duty to register charges existing on property acquired

(1)   Where a company acquires any property which is subject to a charge of any kind as would, if it had been created by the company after the acquisition of the property, have been required to be registered under this Chapter, the company shall cause the prescribed particulars of the charge, together with a copy (certified in the prescribed manner to be a correct copy) of the instrument (if any) by which the charge was created or is evidenced, to be delivered to the registrar of companies for registration in the manner required by this Chapter within 21 days after the date on which the transaction was settled.

(2)   If, however, the property is situated and the charge was created outside Great Britain, 21 days after the date on which the copy of the instrument could (in due course of post, and if despatched with due diligence) have been received in the United Kingdom are substituted for 21 days after the settlement of the transaction as the time within which the particulars and the copy of the instrument are to be delivered to the registrar.

(3)   If default is made in complying with this section, the company and every officer of it who is in default is liable to a fine and, for continued contravention, to a daily default fine.

General note

This provision applies to Scotland only and is outside the scope of this work.

417. Register of charges to be kept by registrar of companies

(1)   The registrar of companies shall keep, with respect to each company, a register in the prescribed form of all the charges requiring registration under this Chapter, and shall enter in the register with respect to such charges the particulars specified below.

(2)   In the case of a charge to the benefit of which the holders of a series of debentures are entitled, there shall be entered in the register the particulars specified in section 413(2).

(3)   In the case of any other charge there shall be entered—
   (a)   if it is a charge created by the company, the date of its creation, and if it was a charge existing on property acquired by the company, the date of the acquisition of the property,
   (b)   the amount secured by the charge,
   (c)   short particulars of the property charged,
   (d)   the persons entitled to the charge, and
   (e)   in the case of a floating charge, a statement of any of the provisions of the charge and of any instrument relating to it which prohibit or restrict or regulate the company's power to grant further securities ranking in priority to, or pari passu with, the floating charge, or which

vary or otherwise regulate the order of ranking of the floating charge in relation to subsisting securities.

(4)   The register kept in pursuance of this section shall be open to inspection by any person.

General note

This provision applies to Scotland only and is outside the scope of this work.

418. Certificate of registration to be issued

(1)   The registrar of companies shall give a certificate of the registration of any charge registered in pursuance of this Chapter.

(2)   The certificate—

(a)   shall be either signed by the registrar, or authenticated by his official seal,

(b)   shall state the name of the company and the person first-named in the charge among those entitled to the benefit of the charge (or, in the case of a series of debentures, the name of the holder of the first such debenture to be issued) and the amount secured by the charge, and

(c)   is conclusive evidence that the requirements of this Chapter as to registration have been complied with.

General note

This provision applies to Scotland only and is outside the scope of this work.

419. Entries of satisfaction and relief

(1)   Subject to subsections (1A) and (1B), the registrar of companies, on application being made to him in the prescribed form, and on receipt of a statutory declaration in the prescribed form verifying, with respect to any registered charge—

(a)   that the debt for which the charge was given has been paid or satisfied in whole or in part, or

(b)   that part of the property charged has been released from the charge or has ceased to form part of the company's property,

may enter on the register a memorandum of satisfaction (in whole or in part) regarding that fact.

(1A) On an application being made to him in the prescribed form, the registrar of companies may make any such entry as is mentioned in subsection (1) where, instead of receiving such a statutory declaration as is mentioned in that subsection, he receives a statement by a director, secretary, liquidator, receiver or administrator of the company which is contained in an electronic communication and that statement—

    (a) verifies the matters set out in paragraph (a) or (b) of that subsection,

    (b) contains a description of the charge,

    (c) states the date of creation of the charge and the date of its registration under this Chapter,

    (d) states the name and address of the chargee or, in the case of a debenture, trustee, and

    (e) where paragraph (b) of subsection (1) applies, contains short particulars of the property which has been released from the charge, or which has ceased to form part of the company's property (as the case may be).

(1B) Where the statement under subsection (1A) concerns the satisfaction of a floating charge, then there shall be delivered to the registrar a further statement which—

    (a) is made by the creditor entitled to the benefit of the floating charge or a person authorised to act on his behalf;

    (b) is incorporated into, or logically associated with, the electronic communication containing the statement; and

    (c) certifies that the particulars contained in the statement are correct.

(2)   Where the registrar enters a memorandum of satisfaction in whole, he shall, if required, furnish the company with a copy of the memorandum.

(3)   Without prejudice to the registrar's duty under this section to require to be satisfied as above mentioned, he shall not be so satisfied unless—

    (a) the creditor entitled to the benefit of the floating charge, or a person authorised to do so on his behalf, certifies as correct the particulars submitted to the registrar with respect to the entry on the register of a memorandum under this section, or

    (b) the court, on being satisfied that such certification cannot readily be obtained, directs him accordingly.

(4)   Nothing in this section requires the company to submit particulars with respect to the entry in the register of a memorandum of satisfaction where the company, having created a floating charge over all or any part of its property, disposes of part of the property subject to the floating charge.

(5)   A memorandum or certification required for the purposes of this section shall be in such form as may be prescribed.

(5A) Any person who makes a false statement under subsection (1A) or (1B) which he knows to be false or does not believe to be true is liable to imprisonment or a fine, or both.

————————————————————

General note

This provision applies to Scotland only and is outside the scope of this work.

420. Rectification of register

The court, on being satisfied that the omission to register a charge within the time required by this Act or that the omission or mis-statement of any particular with respect to any such charge or in a memorandum of satisfaction was accidental, or due to inadvertence or to some other sufficient cause, or is not of a nature to prejudice the position of creditors or shareholders of the company, or that it is on other grounds just and equitable to grant relief, may, on the application of the company or any person interested, and on such terms and conditions as seem to the court just and expedient, order that the time for registration shall be extended or (as the case may be) that the omission or mis-statement shall be rectified.

General note

This provision applies to Scotland only and is outside the scope of this work.

421. Copies of instruments creating charges to be kept by company

(1) Every company shall cause a copy of every instrument creating a charge requiring registration under this Chapter to be kept at the company's registered office.

(2) In the case of a series of uniform debentures, a copy of one debenture of the series is sufficient.

General note

This provision applies to Scotland only and is outside the scope of this work.

422. Company's register of charges

(1) Every company shall keep at its registered office a register of charges and enter in it all charges specifically affecting property of the company, and all floating charges on any property of the company.

(2) There shall be given in each case a short description of the property charged, the amount of the charge and, except in the case of securities to bearer, the names of the persons entitled to it.

(3) If an officer of the company knowingly and wilfully authorises or permits the omission of an entry required to be made in pursuance of this section, he is liable to a fine.

General note

This provision applies to Scotland only and is outside the scope of this work.

423. Right to inspect copies of instruments, and company's register

(1) The copies of instruments creating charges requiring registration under this Chapter with the registrar of companies, and the register of charges kept in pursuance of section 422, shall be open during business hours (but subject to such reasonable restrictions as the company in general meeting may impose, so that not less than 2 hours in each day be allowed for inspection) to the inspection of any creditor or member of the company without fee.

(2) The register of charges shall be open to the inspection of any other person on payment of such fee, not exceeding 5 pence for each inspection, as the company may prescribe.

(3) If inspection of the copies or register is refused, every officer of the company who is in default is liable to a fine and, for continued contravention, to a daily default fine.

(4) If such a refusal occurs in relation to a company, the court may by order compel an immediate inspection of the copies or register.

General note

This provision applies to Scotland only and is outside the scope of this work.

424. Extension of Chapter II

(1) This Chapter extends to charges on property in Scotland which are created, and to charges on property in Scotland which is acquired, by a

company incorporated outside Great Britain which has a place of business in Scotland.

(2)　In relation to such a company, sections 421 and 422 apply with the substitution, for the reference to the company's registered office, of a reference to its principal place of business in Scotland.

General note

This provision applies to Scotland only and is outside the scope of this work.

PART XIII

ARRANGEMENTS AND RECONSTRUCTIONS

425. Power of company to compromise with creditors and members

(1)   Where a compromise or arrangement is proposed between a company and its creditors, or any class of them, or between the company and its members, or any class of them, the court may on the application of the company or any creditor or member of it or, in the case of a company being wound up, or an administration order being in force in relation to a company, of the liquidator or administrator, order a meeting of the creditors or class of creditors, or of the members of the company or class of members (as the case may be), to be summoned in such manner as the court directs.

(2)   If a majority in number representing three-fourths in value of the creditors or class of creditors or members or class of members (as the case may be), present and voting either in person or by proxy at the meeting, agree to any compromise or arrangement, the compromise or arrangement, if sanctioned by the court, is binding on all creditors or the class of creditors or on the members or class of members (as the case may be), and also on the company or, in the case of a company in the course of being wound up, on the liquidator and contributories of the company.

(3)   The court's order under subsection (2) has no effect until an office copy of it has been delivered to the registrar of companies for registration; and a copy of every such order shall be annexed to every copy of the company's memorandum issued after the order has been made or, in the case of a company not having a memorandum, of every copy so issued of the instrument constituting the company or defining its constitution.

(4)   If a company makes default in complying with subsection (3), the company and every officer of it who is in default is liable to a fine.

(5)   An order under subsection (1) pronounced in Scotland by the judge acting as vacation judge in pursuance of section 4 of the Administration of Justice (Scotland) Act 1933 is not subject to review, reduction, suspension or stay of execution.

(6)   In this section and the next—

  (a) 'company' means any company liable to be wound up under this Act, and

  (b) 'arrangement' includes a reorganisation of the company's share capital by the consolidation of shares of different classes or by the division of shares into shares of different classes, or by both of those methods.

General note

Methods of reorganisation   This provision allows for a wide range of re-organisations, reconstructions and arrangements, whether solely within a company or as a mechanism for an agreed merger or demerger (agreed because the co-operation of the board of the target company will be needed for the application to the court and for calling the various meetings required under the section). A typical scheme of arrangement effecting a transfer of control would provide for the cancellation of the shares in the target company and the capitalisation of the reserve arising on the cancellation of those shares to be used to pay up new shares in the target to be allotted, credited as fully paid, to the bidder as consideration for the allotment of shares in the bidder company to the shareholders of the target company (and see notes to ss 103(3), 130(2)).

Equally, a reconstruction or takeover can be effected by 'a takeover offer' within ss 428–430F which enables the offeror in certain circumstances to acquire compulsorily the shares of dissenting shareholders. Reconstructions may also be effected under the Insolvency Act 1986, s 110, which provides (on a voluntary winding up) for the transfer or sale of a business to another company. As far as compositions with creditors are concerned, use may be made of the provisions governing company voluntary arrangements under IA 1986, Pt I.

Each scheme has its advantages and disadvantages, and which is most appropriate will depend on the context in which the scheme is being used. For example, a s 425 scheme requires a majority in number and 75% in value and court approval while a ss 428–430F take-over offer requires a higher majority (90%) but the offeror is then entitled to compulsorily acquire the minority. A scheme under IA 1986, s 110 requires a 75% majority and there is no need for court approval, but provision must be made for cash payments to dissenting shareholders. Company voluntary arrangements under IA 1986, Pt I, for their part, do not require the sanction of the court. Where a scheme properly falls under IA 1986, s 110, that section must be complied with and cannot be evaded by calling the arrangement a scheme within s 425: see *Re Anglo-Continental Supply Co Ltd* [1922] 2 Ch 723.

In *Re National Bank Ltd* [1966] 1 All ER 1006 the question arose as to whether, if a s 425 scheme involves the compulsory elimination of minority shareholders, the court should impose a 90% acceptance level as a condition for approving the scheme and require, in effect, the company to proceed under s 428 et seq rather than under s 425. Plowman J rejected the argument (see [1966] 1 All ER 1006 at 1013) stating that:

' . . . the two sections, section [425] and [ss 428–430F] involve quite different considerations and different approaches. Under section [425] an arrangement can only be sanctioned if the question of its fairness has first been submitted to the court. Under [ss 428–430F], on the other hand, the matter may never come to the court at all. If it does come to the court, then the onus is cast on the dissenting minority to demonstrate the unfairness of the scheme. There are, therefore, good reasons for requiring a smaller majority in favour of a scheme under section [425] than the majority which is required under [ss 428–430F] if the minority is to be expropriated.'

The approach taken in *Re National Bank* [1966] 1 All ER 1006 was approved by Jonathan Parker J in *Re BTR plc* [1999] 2 BCLC 675 at 684, with whom the Court of Appeal agreed: '. . . Parliament clearly intended that s 425 should be available as a means of effecting a binding compromise between a company and its members and that it should be available as an alternate to the route under ss 428 and 429' ([2000] 1 BCLC 740 at 747, per Chadwick LJ). In so far as Templeman J suggested to the contrary in *Re Hellenic & General Trust Ltd* [1975] 3 All ER 382, that case must be regarded as of doubtful validity on this point.

When the scheme being proposed is for the purposes of, or in connection with, a reconstruction or amalgamation of any company or companies and under the scheme, the whole or part of the undertaking or property of one or more of the companies is to be transferred to another company, the court has extensive powers under s 427 to make such ancillary orders as are necessary. Certain mergers and divisions of public companies effected under ss 425–427 are subject to the additional requirements of s 427A and Sch 15B. Nothing in s 125(2)–(5) (variation of class rights) derogates from the court's powers under this provision: s 126.

As to the history of this provision, see the useful account in *Re Savoy Hotel Ltd* [1981] 3 All ER 646 at 651–652.

S 425(1)

Three stages There are three stages to the procedure under s 425:
 (1)   the application to the court for an order convening the meeting(s);
 (2)   the holding of the meeting(s) for approval by the requisite majority; and
 (3)   the application to the court for the sanctioning of the scheme under sub-s (2): see *Re Hawk Insurance Co* [2001] All ER (D) 289 (Feb); *Re BTR plc* [2000] 1 BCLC 740 at 742.

The provision applies to any compromise or arrangement proposed between a company (see sub-s (6)) and its members or its creditors, or any class of members or creditors.

'Compromise or arrangement' The court's approach has been to interpret the words 'compromise or arrangement' broadly so as to enable a wide variety of different types of arrangement to be put forward: see *Re Savoy Hotel Ltd* [1981] 3 All ER 646; *Singer Manufacturing Co v Robinow* 1971 SC 11. The word 'compromise' implies some element of accommodation on each side and 'arrangement' similarly implies some element of give and take; they are not apt to describe a total surrender of the rights of one side: *Re NFU Development Trust* [1973] 1 All ER 135 at 140, per Brightman J; 'the object of the section is not confiscation' – *Re Alabama, New Orleans, Texas and Pacific Junction Rly Co* [1891] 1 Ch 213 at 243, per Bowen LJ, CA; and a scheme can be 'an arrangement' without being 'a compromise': see *Re Guardian Assurance Co* [1917] 1 Ch 431. See also sub-s (6)(b) as to what is included in 'arrangement'.

A wide variety of schemes may be proposed under the provision including:
 •   a scheme to effect a merger (see *Re BTR plc* [1999] 2 BCLC 675, [2000] 1 BCLC 740);
 •   a scheme to effect an alteration of a memorandum of association which cannot be effected under ss 4, 17, 28, 121 (see *Re RAC Motoring Services Ltd* [2000] 1 BCLC 307);
 •   a scheme to effect the run-off and winding up of an insurance company (see *Re Osiris Insurance Ltd* [1999] 1 BCLC 182; *Kempe v Ambassador Insurance Co* [1998] 1 BCLC 234, PC);
 •   a scheme to allow for the variation of the rights of creditors on a winding up, for example, to exclude the operation of the *pari passu* rule (*Re Trix Ltd* [1970] 3 All ER 397; and see *Re Bank of Credit and Commerce International SA (No 3)* [1993] BCLC 1490, aff'g [1993] BCLC 106);
 •   a scheme to achieve a reduction of capital where shareholders of the same class are to be treated differently (see *Re Robert Stephen Holdings Ltd* [1968] 1 WLR 522);
 •   a scheme to allow for an alteration of class rights which cannot be effected under s 125;
 •   a scheme to reorganise the company's share capital (see sub-s (6)(b)).

Schemes of arrangement and reductions of capital It is common for schemes of arrangement to include a scheme for a reduction of capital and in that case, in addition to applying to the court to sanction the scheme as required by this provision, it will be necessary to ask the court to confirm the proposed reduction of capital consequent upon that scheme of arrangement, as required by s 137 (see, for example, *Re BTR plc* [1999] 2 BCLC 675, [2000] 1 BCLC 740).

'Members' and 'creditors' The scheme must be one 'proposed between' a company and its members or creditors, as the case may be, and the court has no jurisdiction to sanction an arrangement regarding the members of a company which does not have the company's approval, either through its board or by a majority of the members in general meeting: *Re Savoy Hotel Ltd* [1981] 3 All ER 646 (court rejected an application by a member for the convening of meetings as required by this provision). The term 'creditor' is defined broadly to include all persons having any pecuniary claims against the company, so including actual and contingent creditors: *Re Midland Coal, Coke and Iron Co, Craig's Claim* [1895] 1 Ch 267; and see *Re Cancol Ltd* [1996] 1 BCLC 100.

A company may proceed with a scheme without regard to the wishes of a class of shareholders or creditors with no real interest in the assets of the company: *Re Oceanic Steam Navigation Co Ltd* [1938] 3 All ER 740 at 742, per Simonds J; *Re Tea Corpn Ltd* [1904] 1 Ch 12 (approval of ordinary shareholders not required when funds insufficient to pay preference shareholders in full); see *Re British and Commonwealth Holdings plc (No 3)* [1992] BCLC 322 (subordinated creditors could be excluded and their approval of the scheme was not required as the deficiency in the company was such that they had no interest in the assets); see also *Re Maxwell Communications Corpn plc (No 2)* [1994] 1 BCLC 1.

Classes of members or creditors The definition of a class for these purposes, which has been followed in numerous authorities, is that a class consists of 'those persons whose rights are not so dissimilar as to make it impossible for them to consult together with a view to their common interest': *Sovereign Life Assurance Co v Dodd* [1892] 2 QB 573 at 583, CA, per Bowen LJ (holders of matured insurance policies constituted a different class from holders of unmatured policies); cf *Re Osiris Insurance Ltd* [1999] 1 BCLC 182 (only one meeting required where the scheme proposed applied to all former policyholders, even if those holders had different types of insurance). For these purposes, partly-paid shares and fully-paid shares are different classes requiring separate meetings: *Re United Provident Assurance Co Ltd* [1910] 2 Ch 477. Where there are differing classes, a class meeting can be called although there is only one person within the class (*Re RMCA Reinsurance Ltd* [1994] BCC 378); and there are no territorial restrictions on where the meetings might be held (*Re RMCA Reinsurance Ltd*, above).

In *Re Hellenic & General Trust Ltd* [1975] 3 All ER 382 Templeman J held that the bidder and those associated with him (for example, a wholly owned subsidiary) constituted a separate class from the other ordinary shareholders in a target company and so a single class meeting composed of those interests and the remaining ordinary shareholders was improperly constituted and the court would refuse to sanction the scheme. The practice thereafter was to ensure the exclusion of such interests from the class meeting to approve the scheme. However, considerable doubt as to the correctness of this approach has now arisen as a result of the decision in *Re BTR plc* [1999] 2 BCLC 675.

Rights not interests A number of recent cases have attempted to bring a degree of pragmatic restatement to the test, noted above, in *Sovereign Life Assurance Co v Dodd* [1892] 2 QB 573 at 583, CA, per Bowen LJ, while accepting that the test laid down there is settled law.

In *Re BTR plc* [1999] 2 BCLC 675 the court was asked by an objecting shareholder not to sanction a scheme on the basis that more than one meeting of members should have been held given that the members considering the scheme had differing interests. For example, some of the shareholders already held shares in the bidder company and their interests might therefore be different from other shareholders.

The court held that whether or not a separate class meeting needed to be held depended on whether the shares had different *rights* attached to them, as opposed to whether the shareholders had different *interests*: see [1999] 2 BCLC 675 at 682, per Jonathan Parker J, with whom the Court of Appeal agreed ([2000] 1 BCLC 740). A requirement to hold different meetings for those with different interests would render the statutory scheme under s 425 unworkable.

Reliance was placed in *Re BTR plc* [1999] 2 BCLC 675 on dicta by Nazareth J in the High Court of Hong Kong in *Re Industrial Equity (Pacific) Ltd* [1991] 2 HKLR 614 where he said (at 625):

'Is every different interest to constitute a different class? Clearly not, but where then is the line to be drawn? The difficulties in identifying shareholders with such interests ... could raise in terms of practicality virtually insuperable difficulties. It is determination by reference to *rights* of shareholders that meets such difficulties, while leaving any conflict of interest which may result in a minority being overborne or coerced to be dealt with by the courts when their sanction is sought.'

Indeed, in *Re BTR* itself even the objecting shareholder could not identify the number of classes with different interests in respect of which meetings might have to be held. In *Re Anglo American Insurance Ltd* [2001] 1 BCLC 755, Neuberger J agreed that, unless a practical approach is adopted, there is a danger that 'one could end up with virtually as many classes as there are members of a particular group' (at 764).

This approach in *Re BTR plc* [1999] 2 BCLC 675 casts significant doubt on the decision in *Re Hellenic & General Trust Ltd* [1975] 3 All ER 382. Jonathan Parker J (implicitly) and Nazareth J (explicitly) were critical of the approach in *Hellenic* and were anxious to confine its ratio very strictly to its facts (see [1999] 2 BCLC 675 at 682). As Nazareth J emphasised, the issue of conflicting interests should be considered by the court at the sanction stage and not at the stage of determining the composition of the classes.

This emphasis on rights has been endorsed by the Court of Appeal in *Re Hawk Insurance Co* [2001] All ER (D) 289 (Feb) where Chadwick LJ stated that the correct approach (to the test in *Sovereign Life Assurance*) is to ask 'are the rights of those who are to be affected by the scheme proposed such that the scheme can be seen as a single arrangement or ought it to be regarded, on a true analysis, as a number of linked arrangements'. If the latter, then applying Lord Justice Bowen's test, the parties must have separate meetings, if the former, then the rights are sufficiently similar that the parties should be required to consult together with a view to their common interest, lest by ordering separate meetings, the court gives a veto to a minority group (at paras 32–33).

Protection for the aggrieved shareholder The protection for any shareholder who feels aggrieved at the composition of the meeting lies in the requirement that the court must sanction a scheme: *Re BTR plc* [1999] 2 BCLC 675 at 680, [2000] 1 BCLC 740. As Chadwick LJ noted 'Parliament has recognised that it is for the court ... to hold the ring between different interests; and to decline to sanction a scheme if satisfied that members having one interest have sought to take advantage over those having another.' ([2000] 1 BCLC 740 at 748). See also *Re Hawk Insurance Co* [2001] All ER (D) 289 (Feb), para 33, CA.

Company must identify classes The net effect is that the onus is still on the company to ensure that the meetings are properly constituted according to the *rights* of the members or creditors, as the case may be, and the court will not sanction a scheme where separate meetings have not been held for those with different substantive rights. But a class is not wrongly composed simply because it contains within it persons with differing interests, for the review of the significance of those differing interests will be a matter for the court in deciding whether to sanction the scheme under s 425(2).

There remains a risk that the company may not correctly identify the classes for which separate meetings are required and so, at the later stage, it will find that the court will not sanction the scheme. In *Re Hawk Insurance Co Ltd* [2001] All ER (D) 289 (Feb), Chadwick LJ, while noting that this method of proceeding has been the practice of the court for the past 65 years or more, said that he wanted to draw attention to the position because of the delay and expense which it leads to and because he thought that the existing practice merits re-examination (paras 18, 22). While his concerns are understandable, requiring the court to determine the classes would mean that stage one will become longer and more expensive, possibly even requiring additional parties to be represented before the court on the initial application, an approach which may be equally undesirable.

Classes cannot be identified Where the complexity of the company's affairs prevents the identification of the relevant classes so that it is impractical to direct that a meeting or a series of meeting be held, it will not be possible to proceed with a scheme of arrangement under s 425: see *Re Bank of Credit and Commerce International SA (No 3)* [1993] BCLC 1490.

S 425(2)

Majority in number and 75% in value The approval required is that of a majority in number representing 75% in value of those present and voting either in person or by proxy at the meeting. For an example of the calculation required, see *Re BTR plc* [1999] 2 BCLC 675 at 679. As to the calculation of the required majority in a company limited by guarantee without a share capital, see *Re NFU Development Trust* [1973] 1 All ER 135. Each class affected by the scheme must approve the scheme. The Company Law Committee of the Law Society has drawn attention to the difficulties which the requirement of a 'majority in number' creates when modern practice is for substantial holdings to be held by a small number of nominees.

The sanction of the court The courts have frequently endorsed the following statement in *Buckley on the Companies Acts* which explains the role of the court in these terms:

'In exercising its power of sanction the court will see, first, that the provisions of the statute have been complied with, second, that the class was fairly represented by those who attended the meeting and that the statutory majority are acting bona fide and are not coercing the minority in order to promote interests adverse to those of the class whom they purport to represent, and thirdly, that the arrangement is such as an intelligent and honest man, a member of the class concerned and acting in respect of his interest, might reasonably approve.

The court does not sit merely to see that the majority are acting bona fide and thereupon to register the decision of the meeting, but, at the same time, the court will be slow to differ from the meeting, unless either the class has not been properly consulted, or the meeting has not considered the matter with a view to the interests of the class which it is empowered to bind, or some blot is found in the scheme.' ((14th edn, 1981) vol 1, at pp 473–474.)

This statement was approved by Plowman J in *Re National Bank Ltd* [1966] 1 All ER 1006 at 1012, and has subsequently been cited and applied by the courts on numerous occasions: see *Re Allied Domecq plc* [2000] 1 BCLC 134 at 142; *Re RAC Motoring Services Ltd* [2000] 1 BCLC 307 at 321; *Re BTR plc* [1999] 2 BCLC 675 at 680; *Re Osiris Insurance Ltd* [1999] 1 BCLC 182 at 188. It is based, in turn, on a long line of authorities which have considered this matter, including: *Re Dorman, Long & Co Ltd, South Durham Steel and Iron Co Ltd* [1934] Ch 635; *Re English, Scottish and Australian Chartered Bank* [1893] 3 Ch 385; and *Re Alabama, New Orleans, Texas and Pacific Junction Rly Co* [1891] 1 Ch 213, CA.

The court's discretion The court has a discretion whether to confirm the scheme, and it is not limited to rubber-stamping the decision of the meeting: see *Re BTR plc* [1999] 2 BCLC 675 at 680, [2000] 2 BCLC 740 at 747; and also *Re Hawk Insurance Co* [2001] All ER (D) 289 (Feb), para 33. The protection for an aggrieved party lies in the fact that the court may refuse to sanction the scheme if it is satisfied that the class meeting was incorrectly composed or was unrepresentative, or those voting at the meeting had voted to promote a special interest which differed from the interest of the ordinary independent and objective shareholder: *Re BTR plc* [1999] 2 BCLC 675, [2000] 1 BCLC 740; *Re Hawk Insurance Co* [2001] All ER (D) 289 (Feb), para 33; and also *Re Allied Domecq plc* [2000] 1 BCLC 134.

The court can approve a scheme which is to be binding after liquidation; and can approve a scheme, exceptionally, which involves a departure from the rules as to mutual credit and set-off in the Insolvency Rules 1986, SI 1986/1925, r 4.90: *Re Anglo American Insurance Ltd* [2001] 1 BCLC 755.

The court's approval may be subject to undertakings: as to the types of undertakings which might be required, see *Re Osiris Insurance Ltd* [1999] 1 BCLC 182; *Re Allied Domecq plc* [2000] 1 BCLC 134.

For an example of a case where the court did refuse to sanction a scheme although it had been approved by the requisite majority, see *Re NFU Development Trust* [1973] 1 All ER 135 (the scheme properly examined was a scheme which no member voting in the interests of the members as a whole could reasonably approve).

Effect of the court order Once sanctioned, the scheme is binding on all creditors or the class of creditors or on the members or class of members (as the case may be), and also on the company or, in the case of a company in the course of being wound up, on the liquidator and contributories of the company; as to the meaning of 'contributory', see IA 1986, s 79.

S 425(3)

Delivery to the registrar The court order becomes effective upon a copy of the court order being delivered to the registrar of companies for registration; if the scheme involves a reduction of capital, the resolution for reducing share capital does not become effective until the requirements of s 138(2) are met, which may delay matters. Any order under this provision in respect of a compromise or arrangement to which s 427A(1) applies must be gazetted by the registrar: s 711(1)(t).

Any agreement entered into pursuant to the court's order is binding, even though it might otherwise be ultra vires and void, unless steps are taken to have the order set aside or rescinded by some valid judicial process: see *Barclays Bank plc v British & Commonwealth Holdings plc* [1996] 1 BCLC 1; *Fletcher v Royal Automobile Club Ltd* [2000] 1 BCLC 331.

While a scheme requires the approval of the court, it does not as a consequence become an order of the court and therefore the court has no jurisdiction to make an alteration to the substance of the scheme: *Kempe v Ambassador Insurance Co* [1998] 1 BCLC 234, PC.

Financial assistance The prohibition on financial assistance in s 151 does not prohibit anything done in pursuance of an order of the court under this provision (s 153(3)(e)); and this concession can be of considerable practical value although, as the order will relate only to the company, the concession cannot be used to enable subsidiaries of the company to provide financial assistance.

S 425(4)

As to penalties, see s 730, Sch 24; 'officer in default' is defined in s 730(5).

S 425(6)

This is a wider definition of 'company' than is used generally in the Act (see s 735) and ensures the application of schemes of arrangement under this provision to companies incorporated abroad; however, orders under s 427 do not apply to such companies: see s 427(6). As to the meaning of 'this Act', see s 735A(1).

426. Information as to compromise to be circulated

(1)   The following applies where a meeting of creditors or any class of creditors, or of members or any class of members, is summoned under section 425.

(2)   With every notice summoning the meeting which is sent to a creditor or member there shall be sent also a statement explaining the effect of the compromise or arrangement and in particular stating any material interests of the directors of the company (whether as directors or as members or as creditors of the company or otherwise) and the effect on those interests of the compromise or arrangement, in so far as it is different from the effect on the like interests of other persons.

(3)   In every notice summoning the meeting which is given by advertisement there shall be included either such a statement as above-mentioned or a notification of the place at which, and the manner in which, creditors or members entitled to attend the meeting may obtain copies of the statement.

(4)   Where the compromise or arrangement affects the rights of debenture holders of the company, the statement shall give the like explanation as respects the trustees of any deed for securing the issue of the debentures as it is required to give as respects the company's directors.

(5)　Where a notice given by advertisement includes a notification that copies of a statement explaining the effect of the compromise or arrangement proposed can be obtained by creditors or members entitled to attend the meeting, every such creditor or member shall, on making application in the manner indicated by the notice, be furnished by the company free of charge with a copy of the statement.

(6)　If a company makes default in complying with any requirement of this section, the company and every officer of it who is in default is liable to a fine; and for this purpose a liquidator or administrator of the company and a trustee of a deed for securing the issue of debentures of the company is deemed an officer of it.

However, a person is not liable under this subsection if he shows that the default was due to the refusal of another person, being a director or trustee for debenture holders, to supply the necessary particulars of his interests.

(7)　It is the duty of any director of the company, and of any trustee for its debenture holders, to give notice to the company of such matters relating to himself as may be necessary for purposes of this section; and any person who makes default in complying with this subsection is liable to a fine.

S 426(2), (4)

Information to be disclosed　An explanation of the 'effect' of the proposed scheme requires an explanation of how the scheme will affect the shareholder or creditor commercially: *Re Heron International NV* [1994] 1 BCLC 667. The circular (and any subsequent circulars) must set out the scheme and its purpose adequately and accurately so that persons who are entitled to vote on it may do so in a properly informed manner, but the extent of the information required will depend on the facts of the particular case: see *Re Heron International NV* [1994] 1 BCLC 667; *Re Allied Domecq plc* [2000] 1 BCLC 134. It is necessary to assess the adequacy of the notice convening the meeting in the light of the circular accompanying it: *Re RAC Motoring Services Ltd* [2000] 1 BCLC 307.

Information omitted or unclear　If information is omitted or is unclear, the court may still sanction the scheme if satisfied that a reasonable shareholder would not have altered his decision as to how to vote in the light of the information: see *Re Heron International NV* [1994] 1 BCLC 667; *Re Allied Domecq plc* [2000] 1 BCLC 134; *Re Jessel Trust Ltd* [1985] BCLC 119; *Re Minster Assets plc* [1985] BCLC 200. But if the information would have affected the shareholder's decision as to how to cast his vote, the court will not sanction the scheme: see *Re Jessel Trust Ltd* [1985] BCLC 119.

Subsequent changes　All changes of circumstances (and not simply changes to the directors' or trustees' material interests) which are material in the sense that a reasonable shareholder would be likely to be affected in his voting by the new facts, which become known to the board between a circular and the holding of a scheme meeting, ought to be disclosed to the persons entitled to vote: *Re M B Group Ltd* [1989] BCLC 672; *Re Jessel Trust Ltd* [1985] BCLC 119; *Re Minster Assets plc* [1985] BCLC 200.

Where the shareholders had been informed that the company was to dispose of an asset to A but, by the time that the court's sanction was sought, the scheme was to dispose of the asset to B, the shareholders were sufficiently well informed as to the nature of the transaction to allow the court to confirm the disposal, although to a different party, since the information circulated envisaged a disposal and was not dependent on a disposal to A: *Re Allied Domecq plc* [2000] 1 BCLC 134.

S 426(6), (7)

As to penalties, see s 730, Sch 24; 'officer in default' is defined in s 730(5).

427. Provisions for facilitating company reconstruction or amalgamation

(1)   The following applies where application is made to the court under section 425 for the sanctioning of a compromise or arrangement proposed between a company and any such persons as are mentioned in that section.

(2)   If it is shown—

    (a)   that the compromise or arrangement has been proposed for the purposes of, or in connection with, a scheme for the reconstruction of any company or companies, or the amalgamation of any two or more companies, and

    (b)   that under the scheme the whole or any part of the undertaking or the property of any company concerned in the scheme ('a transferor company') is to be transferred to another company ('the transferee company'),

the court may, either by the order sanctioning the compromise or arrangement or by any subsequent order, make provision for all or any of the following matters.

(3)   The matters for which the court's order may make provision are—

    (a)   the transfer to the transferee company of the whole or any part of the undertaking and of the property or liabilities of any transferor company,

    (b)   the allotting or appropriation by the transferee company of any shares, debentures, policies or other like interests in that company which under the compromise or arrangement are to be allotted or appropriated by that company to or for any person,

    (c)   the continuation by or against the transferee company of any legal proceedings pending by or against any transferor company,

    (d)   the dissolution, without winding up, of any transferor company,

    (e)   the provision to be made for any persons who, within such time and in such manner as the court directs, dissent from the compromise or arrangement,

    (f)   such incidental, consequential and supplemental matters as are necessary to secure that the reconstruction or amalgamation is fully and effectively carried out.

(4)   If an order under this section provides for the transfer of property or liabilities, then—

(a) that property is by virtue of the order transferred to, and vests in, the transferee company, and

(b) those liabilities are, by virtue of the order, transferred to and become liabilities of that company;

and property (if the order so directs) vests freed from any charge which is by virtue of the compromise or arrangement to cease to have effect.

(5)   Where an order is made under this section, every company in relation to which the order is made shall cause an office copy of the order to be delivered to the registrar of companies for registration within 7 days after its making; and if default is made in complying with this subsection, the company and every officer of it who is in default is liable to a fine and, for continued contravention, to a daily default fine.

(6)   In this section the expression 'property' includes property, rights and powers of every description; the expression 'liabilities' includes duties and 'company' includes only a company as defined in section 735(1).

General note

Nothing in s 125(2)–(5) derogates from the court's powers under this provision: s 126.

S 427(2)

The section is very widely drafted, applying as it does to any scheme 'for the purposes of or in connection with' a reconstruction or amalgamation etc; 'company' is defined as in s 735, so limiting these ancillary powers of the court to companies formed and registered under the companies legislation or its predecessors. In fact, it is rare for a transfer of the undertaking or property as envisaged by this provision to occur and mergers proceed more commonly on the basis of a transfer of shares.

S 427(3), (4), (6)

The court can transfer by virtue of the order (ie without formal conveyances) not only the whole or any part of a company's undertaking or property (broadly defined, sub-s (6)) but also its liabilities: sub-s (3)(a). Creditors could, of course, agree to be transferred and, if appropriate meetings of creditors are held, a majority in number representing 75% in value could bind them all. But in cases where the company is solvent and there is no risk to creditors, the court will not require meetings of creditors to be held but will transfer the liabilities by court order. See also sub-s (4).

Only property which is transferable by the parties may be transferred under this provision, and personal obligations cannot be so transferred: see *Re Skinner* [1958] 3 All ER 273; *Re L Hotel Co Ltd and Langham Hotel Co Ltd* [1946] 1 All ER 319. The former rule, that contracts of employment could not be transferred (*Nokes v Doncaster Amalgamated Collieries Ltd* [1940] AC 1014, HL), is now reversed for they are automatically transferred when the undertaking or part thereof is transferred, whether the transfer is effected by sale or by some other disposition or by operation of law: Transfer of Undertakings (Protection of Employment) Regulations 1981, SI 1981/1794, as amended.

S 427(3)(b)–(f)

This method of proceeding greatly facilitates those reconstructions and amalgamations within the provision. It enables the company to obtain authorisation by court order for a large number of matters rather than having to seek authority from the shareholders etc for each specific element of the arrangement.

S 427(5)

As to penalties, see s 730, Sch 24; 'officer in default' is defined in s 730(5). If the scheme is subject to s 427A, any order under s 427 must be gazetted by the registrar: s 711(1)(t).

427A. Application of ss 425–427 to mergers and divisions of public companies

(1) Where—

    (a) a compromise or arrangement is proposed between a public company and any such persons as are mentioned in section 425(1) for the purposes of, or in connection with, a scheme for the reconstruction of any company or companies or the amalgamation of any two or more companies,

    (b) the circumstances are as specified in any of the Cases described in subsection (2), and

    (c) the consideration for the transfer or each of the transfers envisaged in the Case in question is to be shares in the transferee company or any of the transferee companies receivable by members of the transferor company or transferor companies, with or without any cash payment to members,

sections 425 to 427 shall, as regards that compromise or arrangement, have effect subject to the provisions of this section and Schedule 15B.

(2) The Cases referred to in subsection (1) are as follows—

Case 1

Where under the scheme the undertaking, property and liabilities of the company in respect of which the compromise or arrangement in question is proposed are to be transferred to another public company, other than one formed for the purpose of, or in connection with, the scheme.

Case 2

Where under the scheme the undertaking, property and liabilities of each of two or more public companies concerned in the scheme, including the company in respect of which the compromise or arrangement in question is proposed, are to be transferred to a company (whether or not a public company) formed for the purpose of, or in connection with, the scheme.

Case 3

Where under the scheme the undertaking, property and liabilities of the company in respect of which the compromise or arrangement in question is proposed are to be divided among and transferred to two or more companies each of which is either—

    (a) a public company, or

    (b) a company (whether or not a public company) formed for the purposes of, or in connection with, the scheme.

(3)   Before sanctioning any compromise or arrangement under section 425(2) the court may, on the application of any pre-existing transferee company or any member or creditor of it or, an administration order being in force in relation to the company, the administrator, order a meeting of the members of the company or any class of them or of the creditors of the company or any class of them to be summoned in such manner as the court directs.

(4)   This section does not apply where the company in respect of which the compromise or arrangement is proposed is being wound up.

(5)   This section does not apply to compromise or arrangements in respect of which an application has been made to the court for an order under section 425(1) before 1st January 1988.

(6)   Where section 427 would apply in the case of a scheme but for the fact that the transferee company or any of the transferee companies is a company within the meaning of Article 3 of the Companies (Northern Ireland) Order 1986 (and thus not within the definition of 'company' in subsection (6) of section 427), section 427 shall apply notwithstanding that fact.

(7)   In the case of a scheme mentioned in subsection (1), for a company within the meaning of Article 3 of the Companies (Northern Ireland) Order 1986, the reference in section 427(5) to the registrar of companies shall have effect as a reference to the registrar as defined in Article 2 of that Order.

(8)   In this section and Schedule 15B—

    'transferor company' means a company whose undertaking, property and liabilities are to be transferred by means of a transfer envisaged in any of the Cases specified in subsection (2);

    'transferee company' means a company to which a transfer envisaged in any of those Cases is to be made;

    'pre-existing transferee company' means a transferee company other than one formed for the purpose of, or in connection with, the scheme;

    'compromise or arrangement' means a compromise or arrangement to which subsection (1) applies;

    'the scheme' means the scheme mentioned in subsection (1)(a);

    'company' includes only a company as defined in section 735(1) except that, in the case of a transferee company, it also includes a company as defined in Article 3 of the Companies (Northern Ireland) Order 1986 (referred to in these definitions as a 'Northern Ireland company');

'public company' means, in relation to a transferee company which is a Northern Ireland company, a public company within the meaning of Article 12 of the Companies (Northern Ireland) Order 1986;

'the registrar of companies' means, in relation to a transferee company which is a Northern Ireland company, the registrar as defined in Article 2 of the Companies (Northern Ireland) Order 1986;

'the Gazette' means, in relation to a transferee company which is a Northern Ireland company, the Belfast Gazette;

'Case 1 Scheme','Case 2 Scheme' and 'Case 3 Scheme' mean a scheme of the kind described in Cases 1, 2 and 3 of subsection (2) respectively;

'property' and 'liabilities' have the same meaning as in section 427.

General note

Mergers and divisions of public companies Certain compromises or arrangements involving the merger or division of public companies are subject to further detailed requirements set out in Sch 15B (such as the approval of the scheme by each class of members of the transferee company involved, as well as by those in the transferor company) before the court can sanction the scheme. The draft terms of the merger or division must be delivered to the registrar of companies, a notice confirming this must be placed in the Gazette, a directors' report and an expert's report on the draft terms of the merger are required and various documents must be available for inspection prior to the meetings. This provision imposes considerable additional obligations therefore in respect of the three cases which fall within it. In practice, it is rarely used, as transfers of shares are more commonly used to effect a merger or division in this jurisdiction than a transfer of the undertaking or property.

The provision was inserted by the Companies (Mergers and Divisions) Regulations 1987, SI 1987/1991, implementing the Third Company Law Directive (EEC 78/855, OJ 1978 L 295) and the Sixth Company Law Directive (EEC 82/891, OJ 1982 L 378).

PART XIIIA

TAKEOVER OFFERS

428. Takeover offers

(1)   In this Part of this Act 'takeover offer' means an offer to acquire all the shares, or all the shares of any class or classes, in a company (other than shares which at the date of the offer are already held by the offeror), being an offer on terms which are the same in relation to all the shares to which the offer relates or, where those shares include shares of different classes, in relation to all the shares of each class.

(2)   In subsection (1) 'shares' means shares which have been allotted on the date of the offer but a takeover offer may include among the shares to which it relates all or any shares that are subsequently allotted before a date specified in or determined in accordance with the terms of the offer.

(3)   The terms offered in relation to any shares shall for the purposes of this section be treated as being the same in relation to all the shares or, as the case may be, all the shares of a class to which the offer relates notwithstanding any variation permitted by subsection (4).

(4)   A variation is permitted by this subsection where—

(a) the law of a country or territory outside the United Kingdom precludes an offer of consideration in the form or any of the forms specified in the terms in question or precludes it except after compliance by the offeror with conditions with which he is unable to comply or which he regards as unduly onerous; and

(b) the variation is such that the persons to whom an offer of consideration in that form is precluded are able to receive consideration otherwise than in that form but of substantially equivalent value.

(5)   The reference in subsection (1) to shares already held by the offeror includes a reference to shares which he has contracted to acquire but that shall not be construed as including shares which are the subject of a contract binding the holder to accept the offer when it is made, being a contract entered into by the holder either for no consideration and under seal or for no consideration other than a promise by the offeror to make the offer.

(6)   In the application of subsection (5) to Scotland the words 'and under seal' shall be omitted.

(7)   Where the terms of an offer make provision for their revision and for acceptances on the previous terms to be treated as acceptances on the revised terms, the revision shall not be regarded for the purposes of this Part of this Act as the making of a fresh offer and references in this Part of this Act to the date of the offer shall accordingly be construed as references to the date on which the original offer was made.

(8)   In this Part of this Act 'the offeror' means, subject to section 430D, the person making a takeover offer and 'the company' means the company whose shares are the subject of the offer.

General note

Regulation of take-overs Take-overs of public companies (and certain private companies) generally are subject to the Take-over Code and only limited provision for take-overs, most notably through the provisions of this Part, is made in the companies legislation. For other provisions with particular relevance to take-overs, see s 151 et seq (financial assistance); s 198 et seq (disclosure of interests in shares in public companies); ss 314, 315 (compensation for directors on loss of office); ss 425–427A (schemes of arrangement).

The statutory scheme The purpose of these provisions is to facilitate the acquisition by an offeror of 100% of the shares in a target company so enabling the offeror to operate the subsidiary as a wholly-owned subsidiary without regard to minority shareholders. Equally, the provisions facilitate the exit of minority shareholders from a target company so enabling such shareholders to avoid the problems arising from being locked into a company under new control.

This provision, and ss 429–430F, were substituted for the original ss 428–430 by FSA 1986, s 172(1), Sch 12 as from 30 April 1987; although the provisions were then modified, the basic concept of this Part, that those making a bid for the shares in a company retain the right compulsorily to acquire the remaining shares if acceptances exceed 90%, is unaltered and the old authorities remain relevant: see *Re Chez Nico (Restaurants) Ltd* [1992] BCLC 192 at 201, per Browne-Wilkinson V-C. Given that these provisions allow for the compulsory acquisition of property, the terms upon which that right is exercisable ought to be defined with some strictness, and the statutory requirements must be strictly complied with: *Re Chez Nico (Restaurants) Ltd* [1992] BCLC 192 at 203; *Re Carlton Holdings Ltd* [1971] 2 All ER 1082 at 1088.

S 428(1), (2)

As to the modification of these provisions where the takeover offer is made by two or more persons jointly, see 430D.

A takeover offer To be 'a takeover offer' within this provision, the bidder must make an offer and not merely an invitation to treat: see *Re Chez Nico (Restaurants) Ltd* [1992] BCLC 192. No formalities are prescribed as to the manner in which the offer must be made.

The use of the word 'offer' should be taken to mean a process by which the offeror puts himself in a position in which, by making a sufficiently widely distributed and notified offer or offers, anyone with the relevant shares can provide him with an acceptance and give rise to a contract to buy and sell the shares; it follows that the mere fact that the offer is not communicated to a particular shareholder is not fatal to the process involving 'a takeover offer' for these purpose: *Re Joseph Holt plc, Winpar Holdings Ltd v Joseph Holt Group plc* [2000] 44 LS Gaz R 44; affd sub nom *Winpar Holdings Ltd v Joseph Holt Group plc* [2001] All ER (D) 165 (May), CA (for regulatory reasons, an offer was not communicated in Australia to Australian shareholders of an English company, but it was still a takeover offer within this provision).

An offer for shares The offer must be for shares, as defined in sub-s (2). The offer may be limited to shares allotted on the date of the offer, or the terms of the offer may include shares allotted (for example, on the exercise of outstanding options) before a cut-off date specified in the offer. In practice, the offer will have to extend to shares allotted subsequently to the offer if 100% control is to be achieved. The power compulsorily to acquire shares under s 429 only applies to 'shares to which the offer relates' so if shares allotted subsequently are excluded from the offer, they cannot be the subject of compulsory acquisition under s 429, and the offeror cannot achieve 100% control.

To avoid any uncertainty as to whether 90% acceptances have been achieved (for example, when there is still a possibility of shares being allotted on the exercise of options), the offeror may wait until the cut-off date specified in the offer has passed before serving any notices under s 429. Alternatively, the offeror might proceed to issue notices under s 429 (as 90% has been achieved) and such notices are valid but if there is some further allotments and the offeror falls below 90% no further notices may be issued until 90% is achieved again.

Convertible securities are treated by s 430F as being within the category of 'shares' for which the offer is to be made; they will constitute a separate class of shares, so an offeror will need to make an offer to that class. As and when the shares are converted, they become shares of the class to which they belong and count in that class with respect to the 90% acceptances.

All the shares The offer must be to acquire *all* the shares in the company or the class, other than those already held by the offeror at the date of the offer (and see sub-s (5)) or held or contracted to be acquired by any associate: see s 430E(1), (4). The effect is that such shares (of the offeror and associates) cannot count in calculating the acceptances secured for the purposes of s 429, subject to an exception for shares acquired or contracted to be acquired during the offer period at prices at or below the offer price which can be so counted: ss 429(8), 430E(2).

An offer can be for all the shares in a company, although it is not communicated to certain classes of shareholders for regulatory reasons: *Re Joseph Holt plc, Winpar Holdings Ltd v Joseph Holt Group plc* [2000] 44 LS Gaz R 44, sub nom *Winpar Holdings Ltd v Joseph Holt Group plc* [2001] All ER (D) 165 (May), CA (for regulatory reasons, an offer was not communicated to Australian residents holding ordinary shares in an English company although such shareholders could still accept the offer, if they became aware of it. It was held that this was an offer for all the ordinary shares in the company so as to be within this provision). Note the unease expressed by the Court of Appeal in this case as to this standard practice of not directly communicating a takeover offer to certain classes of shareholders for regulatory reasons: see [2001] All ER (D) 165 (May), para 41.

In a company The target of the takeover offer must be a company, defined in s 735; the provision applies therefore to offers to acquire shares in any company formed and registered under the Companies Act and its predecessors, whether it be a public or a private company although takeover offers for private companies are rare. The offeror need not be a company (see sub-s (8)), although it commonly will be; joint offerors are accommodated by s 430D.

The date of the offer The date of the offer is not defined in the legislation but is generally treated as the date when the offer documentation is posted (as opposed to the date when the offer is announced).

S 428(3), (4)

Same terms for all the shares The offer must be on the same terms for all the shares of the same class, subject to sub-ss (3), (4) which allow for variations as to the consideration offered in order to accommodate overseas shareholders etc, but on the basis that the consideration offered must be of 'substantially equivalent value'.

S 428(5)

Shares excluded from the offer It was noted in sub-s (1) that shares held by the offeror are excluded from the takeover offer; as are shares held or contracted to be acquired by associates, see s 430E(1), (4). This provision in turn excludes shares which the offeror has contracted to acquire which cannot be counted towards the 90% acceptances required by s 429; an exception is made for shares subject to irrevocable undertakings arising in the circumstances specified which will count towards the 90% acceptances required.

Contracted to acquire With respect to shares which the offeror has contracted to acquire, there is some uncertainty as to whether this includes conditional as well as unconditional contracts, the argument being that as Parliament had seen fit to specify the arrangements which can count towards the required acceptances, other conditional contracts must be excluded. To exclude from the calculation only those shares which the offeror has contracted unconditionally to acquire might be considered too favourable to the offeror and provide him with too much assistance in securing the 90% threshold required for compulsory acquisition under s 429. It seems that the more restrictive interpretation is generally accepted and shares which the offeror holds or has contracted, conditionally or unconditionally, to acquire are excluded from the calculation.

Irrevocable undertakings Shares which are the subject of the irrevocable undertakings specified can be counted towards the required 90% threshold under s 429; however, the undertaking must have been entered into by the holder of the shares (rather than the beneficial owner) and the agreement of the holder may be difficult to secure in the time available, where shares are held by professional nominees. The provision is also specific as to the consideration which may be provided.

S 428(7)

Revised offers A revised offer is not a fresh offer as long as the original offer allowed for revision and for acceptance of the previous terms to be treated as acceptance of the revised terms. If the original offer does not allow for revision, a revised offer in effect requires the process to be started again with the acceptances already received not counting towards the 90% acceptances required by s 429: see *Re Chez Nico (Restaurants) Ltd* [1992] BCLC 192.

429. Right of offeror to buy out minority shareholders

(1) If, in a case in which a takeover offer does not relate to shares of different classes, the offeror has by virtue of acceptances of the offer acquired or contracted to acquire not less than nine-tenths in value of the shares to which the offer relates he may give notice to the holder of any shares to which the offer relates which the offeror has not acquired or contracted to acquire that he desires to acquire those shares.

(2) If, in a case in which a takeover offer relates to shares of different classes, the offeror has by virtue of acceptances of the offer acquired or contracted to acquire not less than nine-tenths in value of the shares of any class to which the offer relates, he may give notice to the holder of any shares of that class which the offeror has not acquired or contracted to acquire that he desires to acquire those shares.

(3) No notice shall be given under subsection (1) or (2) unless the offeror has acquired or contracted to acquire the shares necessary to satisfy the minimum specified in that subsection before the end of the period of four months beginning

with the date of the offer; and no such notice shall be given after the end of the period of two months beginning with the date on which he has acquired or contracted to acquire shares which satisfy that minimum.

(4) Any notice under this section shall be given in the prescribed manner; and when the offeror gives the first notice in relation to an offer he shall send a copy of it to the company together with a statutory declaration by him in the prescribed form stating that the conditions for the giving of the notice are satisfied.

(5) Where the offeror is a company (whether or not a company within the meaning of this Act) the statutory declaration shall be signed by a director.

(6) Any person who fails to send a copy of a notice or a statutory declaration as required by subsection (4) or makes such a declaration for the purposes of that subsection knowing it to be false or without having reasonable grounds for believing it to be true shall be liable to imprisonment or a fine, or both, and for continued failure to send the copy or declaration, to a daily default fine.

(7) If any person is charged with an offence for failing to send a copy of a notice as required by subsection (4) it is a defence for him to prove that he took reasonable steps for securing compliance with that subsection.

(8) Where during the period within which a takeover offer can be accepted the offeror acquires or contracts to acquire any of the shares to which the offer relates but otherwise than by virtue of acceptances of the offer, then, if—

  (a) the value of the consideration for which they are acquired or contracted to be acquired ('the acquisition consideration') does not at that time exceed the value of the consideration specified in the terms of the offer; or

  (b) those terms are subsequently revised so that when the revision is announced the value of the acquisition consideration, at the time mentioned in paragraph (a) above, no longer exceeds the value of the consideration specified in those terms,

the offeror shall be treated for the purposes of this section as having acquired or contracted to acquire those shares by virtue of acceptances of the offer; but in any other case those shares shall be treated as excluded from those to which the offer relates.

General note

As to the modification of these provisions where the takeover offer is made by two or more persons jointly, see 430D.

  These provisions for the compulsory acquisition of the dissentient's shares are subject to the right of the recipient of the notice to apply to the court under s 430C which may allow or disallow the acquisition or specify terms different from those in the offer.

S 429(1), (2)

Notice of acquisition As to the effect of a notice under this provision, see s 430; the holder is able to apply to the court for relief under s 430C.

Acceptances of the offer It is 'acceptances of the offer' (as defined in s 428(1)) which must be counted, including deemed acceptances under sub-s (8); the phrase 'contacted to acquire' in this context must be limited to unconditional contracts. As to the position where shareholders cannot be traced so making it difficult to secure the necessary 90% acceptances, see s 430C(5).

Shares to which the offer relates As to the 'shares to which the offer relates', see s 428(2). Shares which are not shares to which the offer relates cannot be acquired under this provision. The fact that a takeover offer has not been communicated (for regulatory reasons) to a shareholder or shareholders does not prevent the offer being an offer for all the shares in the company for the purposes of s 428(1); it follows that a notice under this provision may be served on such shareholders as holders of 'shares to which the offer relates': *Re Joseph Holt plc, Winpar Holdings Ltd v Joseph Holt Group plc* [2000] 44 LS Gaz R 44, sub nom *Winpar Holdings Ltd v Joseph Holt Group plc* [2001] All ER (D) 165 (May), CA.

Under sub-s (1), and contrast the wording with that in s 430A(1), the right of the offeror to buy out the minority only arises in the case of an offer which 'does not relate to shares of different classes' (ie an offer for all the shares of the company or for all the shares of a particular class) where he has acquired 90% acceptances of the shares to which the offer relates. Under sub-s (2), where the takeover offer relates to different classes, the right of the offeror to buy out the minority arises on a class-by-class basis as 90% acceptances of a class are achieved.

S 429(3)

Time limits Two important time limits are set by this provision:
(1)   the offeror must secure acceptances by holders of 90% in value of the shares to which the offer relates within four months of the date of the offer if he is to utilise these powers;
(2)   once the offeror has secured such acceptances, he only has two months from the date when he reached the 90% threshold to notify dissentient shareholders that he wishes to exercise his powers under this provision to acquire their shares.

In practice, it can be difficult to meet the time limits in (1), particularly where regulatory consents are required; and (2) presents difficulties if the shares in question are allotted more than two months after the 90% threshold is reached (on the exercise of an option, for example) – in that case, those shares cannot be the subject of a notice for compulsory acquisition.

As to the date of the offer, see the note to s 428(1), above.

S 429(4)

Notice to the holder The prescribed form is Form 429(4); where the notice is given by a company, the form must be signed by a director or the secretary or by an authorised agent: see *Re Chez Nico (Restaurants) Ltd* [1992] BCLC 192.

Notice to the company A copy of the first notice for compulsory acquisition under this provision is sent to the company at the time when the notice is sent to the holder, presumably to alert the company that the process is in train, as various steps will be required of the company at a later stage under s 430(6)–(11); thereafter, notices need only be sent to the company in accordance with s 430(5).

These provisions as to the sending of these documents to the company are directory rather than mandatory and so a failure to adhere to these requirements is not fatal to an otherwise valid notice under this provision (see *Re Chez Nico (Restaurants) Ltd* [1992] BCLC 192); although the position may be different if the six-week time period in s 430(5) is exceeded: see *Re Chez Nico (Restaurants) Ltd* [1992] BCLC 192 at 206. As to the statutory declaration where there are joint offerors, see s 430D(3).

S 429(6), (7)

As to penalties, see s 730, Sch 24.

S 429(8)

This provision enables the offeror and associates (see s 430E(2)) to continue to acquire shares in the target company in the market during the period of the offer and for such purchases to count towards the 90% threshold. If such purchases did not count towards the 90% threshold, these ongoing purchases would make it more difficult to secure a 90% acceptance of the actual offer.

No shares may be acquired at a higher price than the offer price unless the offeror is prepared to increase the price for all shareholders. It can be difficult where the shares are acquired for a non-cash consideration to be sure, without an independent valuation, that the 'acquisition consideration' does not exceed the value of the terms of the offer.

---

430. Effect of notice under s 429

(1)   The following provisions shall, subject to section 430C, have effect where a notice is given in respect of any shares under section 429.

(2)   The offeror shall be entitled and bound to acquire those shares on the terms of the offer.

(3)   Where the terms of an offer are such as to give the holder of any shares a choice of consideration the notice shall give particulars of the choice and state—

(a)   that the holder of the shares may within six weeks from the date of the notice indicate his choice by a written communication sent to the offeror at an address specified in the notice; and

(b)   which consideration specified in the offer is to be taken as applying in default of his indicating a choice as aforesaid;

and the terms of the offer mentioned in subsection (2) shall be determined accordingly.

(4)   Subsection (3) applies whether or not any time-limit or other conditions applicable to the choice under the terms of the offer can still be complied with; and if the consideration chosen by the holder of the shares—

(a)   is not cash and the offeror is no longer able to provide it; or

(b)   was to have been provided by a third party who is no longer bound or able to provide it, the consideration shall be taken to consist of an amount of cash payable by the offeror which at the date of the notice is equivalent to the chosen consideration.

(5)   At the end of six weeks from the date of the notice the offeror shall forthwith—

(a) send a copy of the notice to the company; and

(b) pay or transfer to the company the consideration for the shares to which the notice relates.

(6)   If the shares to which the notice relates are registered the copy of the notice sent to the company under subsection (5)(a) shall be accompanied by an instrument of transfer executed on behalf of the shareholder by a person appointed by the offeror; and on receipt of that instrument the company shall register the offeror as the holder of those shares.

(7)   If the shares to which the notice relates are transferable by the delivery of warrants or other instruments the copy of the notice sent to the company under subsection (5)(a) shall be accompanied by a statement to that effect; and the company shall on receipt of the statement issue the offeror with warrants or other instruments in respect of the shares and those already in issue in respect of the shares shall become void.

(8)   Where the consideration referred to in paragraph (b) of subsection (5) consists of shares or securities to be allotted by the offeror the reference in that paragraph to the transfer of the consideration shall be construed as a reference to the allotment of the shares or securities to the company.

(9)   Any sum received by a company under paragraph (b) of subsection (5) and any other consideration received under that paragraph shall be held by the company on trust for the person entitled to the shares in respect of which the sum or other consideration was received.

(10) Any sum received by a company under paragraph (b) of subsection (5), and any dividend or other sum accruing from any other consideration received by a company under that paragraph, shall be paid into a separate bank account, being an account the balance on which bears interest at an appropriate rate and can be withdrawn by such notice (if any) as is appropriate.

(11) Where after reasonable enquiry made at such intervals as are reasonable the person entitled to any consideration held on trust by virtue of subsection (9) cannot be found and twelve years have elapsed since the consideration was received or the company is wound up the consideration (together with any interest, dividend or other benefit that has accrued from it) shall be paid into court.

(12) In relation to a company registered in Scotland, subsections (13) and (14) shall apply in place of subsection (11).

(13) Where after reasonable enquiry made at such intervals as are reasonable the person entitled to any consideration held on trust by virtue of subsection (9) cannot be found and twelve years have elapsed since the consideration was received or the company is wound up—

(a) the trust shall terminate;

(b) the company or, as the case may be, the liquidator shall sell any consideration other than cash and any benefit other than cash that has accrued from the consideration; and

(c) a sum representing—

    (i)   the consideration so far as it is cash;

    (ii) the proceeds of any sale under paragraph (b) above; and

    (iii) any interest, dividend or other benefit that has accrued from the consideration,

shall be deposited in the name of the Accountant of Court in a bank account such as is referred to in subsection (10) and the receipt for the deposit shall be transmitted to the Accountant of Court.

(14) Section 58 of the Bankruptcy (Scotland) Act 1985 (so far as consistent with this Act) shall apply with any necessary modifications to sums deposited under subsection (13) as that section applies to sums deposited under section 57(1)(a) of that Act.

(15) The expenses of any such enquiry as is mentioned in subsection (11) or (13) may be defrayed out of the money or other property held on trust for the person or persons to whom the enquiry relates.

General note

As to the modification of these provisions where the takeover offer is made by two or more persons jointly, see 430D.

S 430(1)

Right to apply to the court These provisions for the compulsory acquisition of the dissentient's shares are subject to the right of the recipient of the notice to apply to the court under s 430C, which may allow or disallow the acquisition or specify terms different from those in the offer.

S 430(2)

Since the acquisition is not pursuant to the offer, there is nothing to stop the shareholder and the offeror agreeing to different terms (cf s 430B(2) where this is explicitly provided for) but the statute protects the minority by specifying the default terms.

S 430(3)–(4)

Terms of the offer It was established in *Re Carlton Holdings Ltd* [1971] 2 All ER 1082 that the dissentient shareholder must be treated no less favourably than an accepting shareholder. These provisions give effect to that decision by requiring that the offer to the dissentient shareholder must be on the terms available when the offer was made, even if under the terms of the offer those payment terms (for example, a cash alternative) have lapsed. Where a non-cash consideration is no longer available, the offeror can offer the cash equivalent (see sub-s (4)). But the requirement to maintain a cash alternative under this section, if one was originally offered, is the most onerous requirement. However, it is a requirement which the offeror will bear in mind in deciding whether to exercise these powers under this section.

The equivalent provision contained in s 430B(3), (4) (which apply where the minority shareholder opts to be bought out by the offeror) is more onerous in that, in that situation, the offeror has no choice as to the exercise of this power and will be unable to gauge how many shareholders may utilise this facility so as to anticipate the resources required to meet the terms of the offer.

S 430(5)–(8)

The process These provisions deal with the mechanics of the compulsory acquisition process and require the company to register the offeror as the holder of the shares. As to the position where the notice relates to any uncertificated securities, see the Uncertificated Securities Regulations 1995, SI 1995/3272, reg 35. As to the position with respect to these powers where a shareholder subject to an acquisition notice applies to the court, see s 430C(2).

S 430(9)

The money held on trust is thus ring-fenced from the company's creditors.

S 430(11)

It can be inconvenient for the company to retain these funds but the funds may be transferred to the court after 12 years, subject to there having been reasonable enquiries etc, which typically would be made through newspaper advertisements.

430A. Right of minority shareholder to be bought out by offeror

(1) If a takeover offer relates to all the shares in a company and at any time before the end of the period within which the offer can be accepted—

    (a) the offeror has by virtue of acceptances of the offer acquired or contracted to acquire some (but not all) of the shares to which the offer relates; and

    (b) those shares, with or without any other shares in the company which he has acquired or contracted to acquire, amount to not less than nine-tenths in value of all the shares in the company,

the holder of any shares to which the offer relates who has not accepted the offer may by a written communication addressed to the offeror require him to acquire those shares.

(2) If a takeover offer relates to shares of any class or classes and at any time before the end of the period within which the offer can be accepted—

    (a) the offeror has by virtue of acceptances of the offer acquired or contracted to acquire some (but not all) of the shares of any class to which the offer relates; and

(b) those shares, with or without any other shares of that class which he has acquired or contracted to acquire, amount to not less than nine-tenths in value of all the shares of that class,

the holder of any shares of that class who has not accepted the offer may by a written communication addressed to the offeror require him to acquire those shares.

(3) Within one month of the time specified in subsection (1) or, as the case may be, subsection (2) the offeror shall give any shareholder who has not accepted the offer notice in the prescribed manner of the rights that are exercisable by him under that subsection; and if the notice is given before the end of the period mentioned in that subsection it shall state that the offer is still open for acceptance.

(4) A notice under subsection (3) may specify a period for the exercise of the rights conferred by this section and in that event the rights shall not be exercisable after the end of that period; but no such period shall end less than three months after the end of the period within which the offer can be accepted.

(5) Subsection (3) does not apply if the offeror has given the shareholder a notice in respect of the shares in question under section 429.

(6) If the offeror fails to comply with subsection (3) he and, if the offeror is a company, every officer of the company who is in default or to whose neglect the failure is attributable, shall be liable to a fine and for continued contravention, to a daily default fine.

(7) If an offeror other than a company is charged with an offence for failing to comply with subsection (3) it is a defence for him to prove that he took all reasonable steps for securing compliance with that subsection.

General note

Where the holder of any shares exercises his rights under this provision, an application can be made to the court under s 430C, either by the holder or the offeror, to determine the terms on which the offeror must acquire the shares: s 430C(3). A holder so applying is protected against costs to the extent specified in s 430C(4).

As to the modification of these provisions where the takeover offer is made by two or more persons jointly, see 430D.

S 430A(1), (2)

A 'takeover offer' is defined in s 428(1); the period within which the offer can be accepted is determined by the terms of the offer.

Shares in a company or in a class Where the takeover offer is for all the shares in the company, shareholders in a class will be unable to exercise these powers where 90% acceptances of the class have been achieved but 90% acceptances of all the shares have not; if, on the other hand, the offer relates to any class or classes of shares but not to all the shares, then as soon as the offeror has secured 90% acceptances of any class to which the offer relates, any non-assenting shareholder in that class may exercise his rights under this provision.

The 90% threshold The threshold for exercise by the minority shareholder of his right to be bought out is lower than that imposed on an offeror which wishes to exercise the powers of compulsory purchase provided by s 429 (90% acceptances excluding shares already held or contracted to be acquired by the offeror and its associates). Under this provision, it is possible to count shares held or contracted to be acquired by the offeror (and associates: see s 430E(3)) other than in pursuance of the offer so making it easier to establish that the 90% threshold has been reached. The only question is whether the offeror holds 90% or more, not how it acquired the shares; indeed, the minority shareholder may be able to exercise his rights under this provision while an offeror may find, because of the different method of calculating the thresholds, that it never acquires the powers of acquisition under s 429.

As to the offeror's obligations to bring these provisions to the attention of the shareholder and the time frame for the exercise of these rights, see sub-ss (3)–(5).

S 430A(3)–(5)

Notification obligations The offeror must notify the holder of his rights under these provisions and therefore the offeror must monitor whether it has reached the 90% threshold under this provision as well as the (different) 90% threshold under s 429. There is no requirement on the offeror to so notify if the offeror has already given notice to the shareholder of the exercise of its rights under s 429 but equally the offeror may have to give notice under this provision before it sends out any notices under s 429.

The notice must be sent within 1 month of the end of the period within which the offer can be accepted; equally, the notice may be sent at a time when the offer is still open for acceptance (90% acceptances having been secured although the time period for the offer has not lapsed), in which case, this fact must be drawn to the shareholder's attention. This enables the shareholder to decide at that stage to accept the offer rather than be put to the trouble of exercising his rights under this provision.

Subsection (4) imposes a minimum period which the offeror must allow for the exercise of these rights but imposes no conditions as to the time scale within which the acquisition of the shares must be completed (*cf.* s 430(5)).

S 430A(6), (7)

As to penalties, see s 730, Sch 24; 'officer in default' is defined by s 730(5).

430B. Effect of requirement under s 430A

(1)   The following provisions shall, subject to section 430C, have effect where a shareholder exercises his rights in respect of any shares under section 430A.

(2)   The offeror shall be entitled and bound to acquire those shares on the terms of the offer or on such other terms as may be agreed.

(3) Where the terms of an offer are such as to give the holder of shares a choice of consideration the holder of the shares may indicate his choice when requiring the offeror to acquire them and the notice given to the holder under section 430A(3)—

  (a) shall give particulars of the choice and of the rights conferred by this subsection; and

  (b) may state which consideration specified in the offer is to be taken as applying in default of his indicating a choice;

and the terms of the offer mentioned in subsection (2) shall be determined accordingly.

(4) Subsection (3) applies whether or not any time-limit or other conditions applicable to the choice under the terms of the offer can still be complied with; and if the consideration chosen by the holder of the shares—

  (a) is not cash and the offeror is no longer able to provide it; or

  (b) was to have been provided by a third party who is no longer bound or able to provide it,

the consideration shall be taken to consist of an amount of cash payable by the offeror which at the date when the holder of the shares requires the offeror to acquire them is equivalent to the chosen consideration.

General note

As to the modification of these provisions where the takeover offer is made by two or more persons jointly, see 430D.

S 430B(3), (4)

This provision compels the offeror to make available to the shareholder the consideration which was provided by the terms of the offer; see notes to the equivalent provisions in s 430(3), (4).

430C. Applications to the court

(1) Where a notice is given under section 429 to the holder of any shares the court may, on an application made by him within six weeks from the date on which the notice was given—

  (a) order that the offeror shall not be entitled and bound to acquire the shares; or

  (b) specify terms of acquisition different from those of the offer.

(2) If an application to the court under subsection (1) is pending at the end of the period mentioned in subsection (5) of section 430 that subsection shall not have effect until the application has been disposed of.

(3)   Where the holder of any shares exercises his rights under section 430A the court may, on an application made by him or the offeror, order that the terms on which the offeror is entitled and bound to acquire the shares shall be such as the court thinks fit.

(4)   No order for costs or expenses shall be made against a shareholder making an application under subsection (1) or (3) unless the court considers—

> (a) that the application was unnecessary, improper or vexatious; or
>
> (b) that there has been unreasonable delay in making the application or unreasonable conduct on his part in conducting the proceedings on the application.

(5)   Where a takeover offer has not been accepted to the extent necessary for entitling the offeror to give notices under subsection (1) or (2) of section 429 the court may, on the application of the offeror, make an order authorising him to give notices under that subsection if satisfied—

> (a) that the offeror has after reasonable enquiry been unable to trace one or more of the persons holding shares to which the offer relates;
>
> (b) that the shares which the offeror has acquired or contracted to acquire by virtue of acceptances of the offer, together with the shares held by the person or persons mentioned n paragraph (a), amount to not less than the minimum specified in that subsection; and
>
> (c) that the consideration offered is fair and reasonable;

but the court shall not make an order under this subsection unless it considers that it is just and equitable to do so having regard, in particular, to the number of shareholders who have been traced but who have not accepted the offer.

General note

As to the modification of these provisions where the takeover offer is made by two or more persons jointly, see 430D(7).

S 430C(1)

Application to the court – compulsory acquisition The holder has six weeks from the date on which the notice for compulsory purchase was given under s 429 to apply to the court; where he does so apply, the effect is to suspend the offeror's ability to proceed with the compulsory purchase of any shares, see note to sub-s (2).

The holder is not obliged to notify the offeror of his application which can cause difficulties where it is lodged very close to the end of the period and the offeror proceeds to act under s 430(5) unaware that his powers to do so have been suspended under sub-s (2).

Powers of the court The court's powers enable it: (i) to prevent the compulsory acquisition taking place; or (ii) to allow it to proceed but on terms different from those of the offer.

It is unclear as to whether the court in its order is limited to making an order with respect to the applicant's shares (as appears to be the case) or whether it can make an order of general application with respect to all shares which may be the subject of a s 429 notice by the offeror. To some extent, the point may be academic since an offeror is unlikely to attempt to deal with other shareholders in a manner different to that of the applicant.

Approach of the court   The courts have been unsympathetic generally when faced with challenges to the procedure by minority shareholders and are much swayed by the fact that 90% of the shareholders think the scheme is proper.

Onus on dissenters   The onus is on the dissenters, therefore, to establish affirmatively that compulsory purchase would be unfair: *Re Grierson, Oldham and Adams Ltd* [1967] 1 All ER 192; *Re Sussex Brick Co Ltd* [1960] 1 All ER 772n; *Re Press Caps Ltd* [1949] 1 All ER 1013; *Re Hoare & Co Ltd* (1933) 150 LT 374. It is not enough for the dissentient shareholder to show that the scheme is open to criticism or capable of improvement: *Re Grierson, Oldham and Adams Ltd* [1967] 1 All ER 192; *Re Sussex Brick Co Ltd* [1960] 1 All ER 772n. The test is whether the offer is fair to the shareholders as a body without reference to the particular circumstances of the applicant to the court: *Re Grierson, Oldham and Adams Ltd* [1967] 1 All ER 192; where the shares are quoted on the Stock Exchange and the offer price is above the market price, that is cogent evidence of the fairness of the offer: *Re Grierson, Oldham and Adams Ltd* [1967] 1 All ER 192; see also *Re Press Caps Ltd* [1949] 1 All ER 1013.

   The onus of proof might be discharged if the dissentients are able to establish that the directors of the target company had misled the acceptors so that the 90% acceptances secured is not such an influential factor as would otherwise be the case: see *Gething v Kilner* [1972] 1 All ER 1166; *Re Lifecare International plc* [1990] BCLC 222 at 224. A substantial failure by an offeror to comply with the Take-over Code's provisions as to disclosure would be a major factor against permitting the compulsory acquisition of the non-assenting shareholders' shares: see *Re Chez Nico (Restaurants) Ltd* [1992] BCLC 192 at 209.

   The onus of proof is reversed when those accepting the offer are in effect the offerors: see *Re Bugle Press Ltd* [1960] 3 All ER 791, CA, where the 90% acceptances came from two persons who owned all the shares in the offeror company. The court held that, in the exceptional circumstances, the onus of proof was on them to show positively that the offer was fair rather than on the dissenter to show the offer was unfair. This approach was endorsed in *Re Chez Nico (Restaurants) Ltd* [1992] BCLC 192 at 207.

S 430C(2)

Mechanism suspended   Although the wording of the provision is somewhat ambiguous, the effect of any application under sub-s (1) is to suspend the mechanism for compulsory purchase which is contained in s 430(5) with respect to all shares and not simply the shares of the applicant. This must be the case as the consequence of the application may be a determination that the scheme is unfair and therefore the company should not be able to proceed with it with respect to other shareholders when the very issue is before the court.

S 430C(3)

Application to the court – holder seeking to be bought out   The protection of the court is not restricted to those subject to compulsory purchase but extends to those who seek to be bought out under s 430A. In this case, the court is restricted to making an order as to terms and it cannot block the minority's right to exit.

S 430C(4)

This provision offers the shareholders valuable protection against costs.

S 430C(5)

Untraceable shareholders This provision assists an offeror who is finding it difficult to secure 90% acceptances and there are a number of untraceable shareholders. The court will authorised the serving of notices under s 429 notwithstanding that, in this instance, 90% acceptances have not been achieved, if certain conditions are met, and subject to the final proviso as to the number of holders who have not accepted the offer.

430D. Joint offers

(1)   A takeover offer may be made by two or more persons jointly and in that event this Part of this Act has effect with the following modifications.

(2)   The conditions for the exercise of the r ghts conferred by sections 429 and 430A shall be satisfied by the joint offerors acquiring or contracting to acquire the necessary shares jointly (as respects acquisitions by virtue of acceptances of the offer) and either jointly or separately (in other cases); and, subject to the following provisions, the rights and obligations of the offeror under those sections and sections 430 and 430B shall be respectively joint rights and joint and several obligations of the joint offerors.

(3)   It shall be a sufficient compliance with any provision of those sections requiring or authorising a notice or other document to be given or sent by or to the joint offerors that it is given or sent by or to any of them; but the statutory declaration required by section 429(4) shall be made by all of them and, in the case of a joint offeror being a company, signed by a director of that company.

(4)   In sections 428, 430(8) and 430E references to the offeror shall be construed as references to the joint offerors or any of them.

(5)   In section 430(6) and (7) references to the offeror shall be construed as references to the joint offerors or such of them as they may determine.

(6)   In sections 430(4)(a) and 430B(4)(a) references to the offeror being no longer able to provide the relevant consideration shall be construed as references to none of the joint offerors being able to do so.

(7)   In section 430C references to the offeror shall be construed as references to the joint offerors except that any application under subsection (3) or (5) may be made by any of them and the reference in subsection (5)(a) to the offeror having been unable to trace one or more of the persons holding shares shall be construed as a reference to none of the offerors having been able to do so.

General note

This provision clarifies the position with respect to joint offers following the restrictive effect of the decision of the Privy Council in *Blue Metal Industries Ltd v Dilley* [1970] AC 827 (the Australian statutory scheme (akin to the then English provisions) did not apply to a scheme involving the transfer of shares in a company to two other companies jointly but only applied to a scheme or contract involving the transfer of shares to another company alone).

430E. Associates

(1)   The requirement in section 428(1) that a takeover offer must extend to all the shares, or all the shares of any class or classes, in a company shall be regarded as satisfied notwithstanding that the offer does not extend to shares which associates of the offeror hold or have contracted to acquire; but, subject to subsection (2), shares which any such associate holds or has contracted to acquire, whether at the time when the offer is made or subsequently, shall be disregarded for the purposes of any reference in this Part of this Act to the shares to which a takeover offer relates.

(2)   Where during the period within which a takeover offer can be accepted any associate of the offeror acquires or contracts to acquire any of the shares to which the offer relates, then, if the condition specified in subsection (8)(a) or (b) of section 429 is satisfied as respects those shares they shall be treated for the purposes of that section as shares to which the offer relates.

(3)   In section 430A(1)(b) and (2)(b) the reference to shares which the offeror has acquired or contracted to acquire shall include a reference to shares which any associate of his has acquired or contracted to acquire.

(4)   In this section 'associate', in relation to an offeror means—

    (a)   a nominee of the offeror;

    (b)   a holding company, subsidiary or fellow subsidiary of the offeror or a nominee of such a holding company, subsidiary or fellow subsidiary;

    (c)   a body corporate in which the offeror is substantially interested; or

    (d)   any person who is, or is a nominee of, a party to an agreement with the offeror for the acquisition of, or of an interest in, the shares which are the subject of the takeover offer, being an agreement which includes provisions imposing obligations or restrictions such as are mentioned in section 204(2)(a).

(5)   For the purposes of subsection (4)(b) a company is a fellow subsidiary of another body corporate if both are subsidiaries of the same body corporate but neither is a subsidiary of the other.

(6)   For the purposes of subsection (4)(c) an offeror has a substantial interest in a body corporate if—

    (a)   that body or its directors are accustomed to act in accordance with his directions or instructions; or

    (b) he is entitled to exercise or control the exercise of one-third or more of the voting power at general meetings of that body.

(7) Subsections (5) and (6) of section 204 shall apply to subsection (4)(d) above as they apply to that section and subsections (3) and (4) of section 203 shall apply for the purposes of subsection (6) above as they apply for the purposes of subsection (2)(b) of that section.

(8) Where the offeror is an individual his associates shall also include his spouse and any minor child or step-child of his.

General note

As to the modification of these provisions where the takeover offer is made by two or more persons jointly, see 430D(4).

S 430E(1), (2)

The effect of this provision is that an offer can be a takeover offer for all the shares within s 428(1) even though it is, naturally, not extended to shares held etc by the offeror's associates; equally, given that the offer is not extended to shares held or contracted to be acquired by such associates, such shares cannot count towards the 90% acceptances required by s 429; save to the extent permitted by s 429(8).

S 430E(4)–(6)

These provisions provide an elaborate and expansive definition of those treated as 'associates' for these purposes; 'holding company' and 'subsidiary' are defined in s 736; 'fellow subsidiary' is defined in sub-s (5); those party to an agreement of the type mentioned in s 204(2)(a) (a concert party) are also treated as associates for these purposes.

430F. Convertible securities

(1) For the purposes of this Part of this Act securities of a company shall be treated as shares in the company if they are convertible into or entitle the holder to subscribe for such shares; and references to the holder of shares or a shareholder shall be construed accordingly.

(2) Subsection (1) shall not be construed as requiring any securities to be treated—

    (a) as shares of the same class as those into which they are convertible or for which the holder is entitled to subscribe; or

    (b) as shares of the same class as other securities by reason only that the shares into which they are convertible or for which the holder is entitled to subscribe are of the same class.

General note

This provision clarifies the position with respect to convertible securities, see note to s 428(1), (2).

PART XIV

INVESTIGATION OF COMPANIES AND THEIR AFFAIRS; REQUISITION OF DOCUMENTS

General note to this Part

The investigation powers available to the Department of Trade and Industry under this Part exist alongside an array of investigation powers available to liquidators and other office-holders under the Insolvency Act 1986 and to bodies such as the Serious Fraud Office, the Financial Services Authority and the police. Investigations under this Part apply to any registered company, any unregistered company (to the extent indicated by s 718 and Sch 22) and to overseas companies (to the extent indicated by s 453). In addition, the Secretary of State may exercise similar powers to assist an overseas regulatory authority under CA 1989, ss 82–91.

This Part provides for a variety of types of investigation but it does not dictate the consequences of an investigation. Where wrongdoing is discovered, it is probable that the Secretary of State for Trade and Industry will consider one or more of the following options:

(i) criminal prosecutions, typically proceedings might be brought against directors and officers for matters such as fraudulent trading, theft and conspiracy to defraud;

(ii) the winding up of the company under IA 1986, s 124A, on public interest grounds;

(iii) the disqualification of the directors involved under the Company Directors Disqualification Act 1986, s 8.

The information secured by an investigation may be disclosed (see ss 449, 451A) to other regulatory and professional bodies who, in turn, may initiate action in response to it. Finally, it is possible for the Secretary of State to commence a civil action on behalf of the company under s 438 and to petition the court for relief on behalf of the members under Part XVII (ss 459–461): s 460; in practice, these powers are never exercised.

APPOINTMENT AND FUNCTIONS OF INSPECTORS

431. Investigation of a company on its own application or that of its members

(1) The Secretary of State may appoint one or more competent inspectors to investigate the affairs of a company and to report on them in such manner as he may direct.

(2) The appointment may be made—

(a) in the case of a company having a share capital, on the application either of not less than 200 members or of members holding not less than one-tenth of the shares issued,

(b) in the case of a company not having a share capital, on the application of not less than one-fifth in number of the persons on the company's register of members, and

(c) in any case, on application of the company.

(3)   The application shall be supported by such evidence as the Secretary of State may require for the purpose of showing that the applicant or applicants have good reason for requiring the investigation.

(4)   The Secretary of State may, before appointing inspectors, require the applicant or applicants to give security, to an amount not exceeding £5,000, or such other sum as he may by order specify, for payment of the costs of the investigation.

An order under this subsection shall be made by statutory instrument subject to annulment in pursuance of a resolution of either House of Parliament.

General note

The Secretary of State for Trade and Industry is obliged to appoint inspectors only in the exceptional instance where the court by order declares that a company's affairs ought to be investigated by inspectors: s 432(1). Otherwise, appointment is at the discretion of the Secretary of State under this or, in practice, under the following provision. This provision does not apply to overseas companies, see s 453(1A)(a).

Application for appointment   This provision allows for an appointment following an application by one of the specified parties but it is rarely, if ever, used. The applicants must establish 'good reason' for the investigation and may be required to provide security for costs. Where they have good reason for wanting an investigation (which in practice would require circumstances similar to those identified in s 432(2)), they are much more likely to put that information to the Secretary of State and await an appointment on his initiative under s 432 so avoiding any potential liability for the costs of the investigation under s 439(5).

Where an application for an appointment under this provision is refused, it seems that the applicants could seek a court order requiring an appointment under s 432(1).

432. Other company investigations

(1)   The Secretary of State shall appoint one or more competent inspectors to investigate the affairs of a company and report on them in such manner as he directs, if the court by order declares that its affairs ought to be so investigated.

(2)   The Secretary of State may make such an appointment if it appears to him that there are circumstances suggesting—

(a) that the company's affairs are being or have been conducted with intent to defraud its creditors or the creditors of any other person, or otherwise for a fraudulent or unlawful purpose, or in a manner which is unfairly prejudicial to some part of its members, or

(b) that any actual or proposed act or omission of the company (including an act or omission on its behalf) is or would be so prejudicial, or that the company was formed for any fraudulent or unlawful purpose, or

(c) that persons concerned with the company's formation or the management of its affairs have in connection therewith been guilty of fraud, misfeasance or other misconduct towards it or towards its members, or

(d) that the company's members have not been given all the information with respect to its affairs which they might reasonably expect.

(2A) Inspectors may be appointed under subsection (2) on terms that any report they may make is not for publication; and in such a case, the provisions of section 437(3)(availability and publication of inspectors' reports) do not apply.

(3) Subsections (1) and (2) are without prejudice to the powers of the Secretary of State under section 431; and the power conferred by subsection (2) is exercisable with respect to a body corporate notwithstanding that it is in course of being voluntarily wound up.

(4) The reference in subsection (2)(a) to a company's members includes any person who is not a member but to whom shares in the company have been transferred or transmitted by operation of law.

General note

The Department of Trade and Industry receives a large number of requests for investigations of companies each year, the majority of which come from the public but a considerable number are generated from within the Department itself and complaints may also originate from other Government and regulatory agencies.

A large number of these requests will be rejected at the stage of initial vetting. Of those cases that are formally considered, only about 20% (in the region of 210–250 cases each year) will be accepted for investigation. The vast majority of these cases will be the subject of a confidential fact-finding investigation under s 447 rather than an inspection under this provision. The appointment of inspectors is exceptional with only four appointments between 1992 and 2000, in part, no doubt, because of the huge costs involved. It follows that the appointment of inspectors under this provision is reserved, in practice, for cases where the issues are complex, there are (usually) multi-million pound losses and a significant public interest in ascertaining what has occurred.

S 432(1)

Court may order investigation   It would appear that no court has ever exercised, or been asked to exercise, this power to require an investigation of a company's affairs. If the purpose is to provide an avenue of redress for those refused an appointment of inspectors under s 431, the provision might be contained more appropriately in that section.

S 432(2)

The decision to appoint   The Secretary of State must reach his decision to appoint inspectors in good faith but it is not incumbent upon him to disclose the material he has before him or the reasons for the inquiry: *Norwest Holst Ltd v Secretary of State for Trade and Industry* [1978] 3 All ER 280, CA; nor is he required to desist from making an appointment because it may involve investigating fraudulent or criminal activity which could be investigated also by the police or the Serious Fraud Office: see *Re London United Investments plc* [1992] 2 All ER 842, CA. The investigation powers in the companies legislation are separate from, even if they overlap with, the investigation powers of other bodies: see *Re London United Investments plc* [1992] 2 All ER 842 at 849, CA.

The grounds on which to appoint   The grounds provided by this provision cover every eventuality although some are unlikely to justify an appointment. For example, if the conduct complained of is unfairly prejudicial to some part of the members, the members complaining have a direct civil remedy under s 459 and there is unlikely to be any public interest justifying the appointment of inspectors under this provision.

The reference to the company's 'affairs' is unambiguous and the words must be given their natural meaning of the business affairs of the company, which includes its goodwill, its profit and loss, its contracts and investments and assets, including its shareholding in and ability to control a subsidiary or sub-subsidiary, and the affairs of a company do not cease to be its affairs upon the appointment of a receiver and manager: *R v Board of Trade, ex p St Martins Preserving Co Ltd* [1964] 2 All ER 561. The practice of the Department of Trade and Industry is that where there has been the appointment of an Official Receiver, liquidator, administrative receiver or administrator, the first point of contact should be with the person so appointed. They have a duty to investigate the conduct of the company's officers and to prepare a report for the Department. However, the DTI may still start an investigation in appropriate cases, except where the Official Receiver has been appointed (the OR has a statutory duty to investigate the affairs of a company which is being compulsorily wound up: IA 1986, s 132).

An investigation of a company's affairs may extend to the affairs of other bodies corporate to the extent permitted by s 433; these powers may also be exercised with respect to overseas companies, see s 453.

The wording of sub-s (2)(a) reflects the provisions on fraudulent trading (s 458) and unfairly prejudicial conduct (s 459); the term 'or other misconduct' in sub-s (2)(c) should be interpreted ejusdem generis with fraud and misfeasance so as to exclude negligence: see *SBA Properties Ltd v Cradock* [1967] 2 All ER 610; sub-s (2)(d) permits an appointment where the members have received their statutory reports and accounts but, nevertheless, the Secretary of State is of the view that the company's members have not been given all the information with respect to its affairs (for example, with respect to a takeover) which they might reasonably expect. For an example of an appointment on this basis, see *Maxwell v Department of Trade & Industry* [1974] 2 All ER 122.

The persons appointed   It is common practice for a senior barrister, a Queen's Counsel, and an accountant to be appointed as joint inspectors.

Position on appointment   There is no formal notification to the company of the fact of the appointment and the inspectors will simply present themselves at the company's premises, with written authorisation, and possibly a search warrant under s 448.

S 432(2A)

No publication of report   Although the Department has a discretion generally as to whether to publish inspectors' reports under s 437, this provision was inserted by the CA 1989, s 55, to enable the Department to rule out any possibility of publication from the outset. This approach may be appropriate where it is anticipated that criminal proceedings are likely which would in any event delay the possibility of publication. Any subsequent proceedings will bring the matters which have occurred into the public domain without the necessity of publishing the report.

Where an appointment is made on this basis, it is Departmental practice not to announce the appointment; it is not clear if this policy of not announcing appointments extends to not including such cases in the published statistics.

433. Inspectors' powers during investigation

(1)   If inspectors appointed under section 431 or 432 to investigate the affairs of a company think it necessary for the purposes of their investigation to investigate also the affairs of another body corporate which is or at any relevant time has been the company's subsidiary or holding company, or a subsidiary of its holding company or a holding company of its subsidiary, they have power to do so; and they shall report on the affairs of the other body corporate so far as they think that the results of their investigation of its affairs are relevant to the investigation of the affairs of the company first mentioned above.

(2)   ...

General note

This provision enables inspectors to investigate companies within (or which were within) a group as the need arises without the Secretary of State having to make a separate appointment for each company.

S 433(1)

While the initial appointment must be with respect to a 'company', as defined by s 735, this power extends to any 'body corporate', as defined by s 740, which includes an overseas company; as to the definitions of 'subsidiary' and 'holding company', see s 736.

This ability to investigate the affairs of other bodies corporate is restricted to situations where the inspectors think it 'necessary for the purposes of their investigation' of the first company; and their report on the affairs of these additional companies must be limited to matters which are relevant to the main investigation.

434. Production of documents and evidence to inspectors

(1)   When inspectors are appointed under section 431 or 432, it is the duty of all officers and agents of the company, and of all officers and agents of any other body corporate whose affairs are investigated under section 433(1)—

(a) to produce to the inspectors all documents of or relating to the company or, as the case may be, the other body corporate which are in their custody or power,

(b) to attend before the inspectors when required to do so, and

(c) otherwise to give the inspectors all assistance in connection with the investigation which they are reasonably able to give.

(2) If the inspectors consider that an officer or agent of the company or other body corporate, or any other person, is or may be in possession of information relating to a matter which they believe to be relevant to the investigation, they may require him—

(a) to produce to them any documents in his custody or power relating to that matter,

(b) to attend before them, and

(c) otherwise to give them all assistance in connection with the investigation which he is reasonably able to give;

and it is that person's duty to comply with the requirement.

(3) An inspector may for the purposes of the investigation examine any person on oath, and may administer an oath accordingly.

(4) In this section a reference to officers or to agents includes past, as well as present, officers or agents (as the case may be); and 'agents', in relation to a company or other body corporate, includes its bankers and solicitors and persons employed by it as auditors, whether these persons are or are not officers of the company or other body corporate.

(5) An answer given by a person to a question put to him in exercise of powers conferred by this section (whether as it has effect in relation to an investigation under any of sections 431 to 433, or as applied by any other section in this Part) may be used in evidence against him.

(5A) However, in criminal proceedings in which that person is charged with an offence to which this subsection applies—

(a) no evidence relating to the answer may be adduced, and

(b) no question relating to it may be asked,

by or on behalf of the prosecution, unless evidence relating to it is adduced, or a question relating to it is asked, in the proceedings by or on behalf of that person.

(5B) Subsection (5A) applies to any offence other than—

(a) an offence under section 2 or 5 of the Perjury Act 1911 (false statements made on oath otherwise than in judicial proceedings or made otherwise than on oath); or

(b) an offence under section 44(1) or (2) of the Criminal Law (Consolidation) (Scotland) Act 1995 (false statements made on oath or otherwise than on oath).

(6) In this section 'documents' includes information recorded in any form; and, in relation to information recorded otherwise than in legible form, the power to require its production includes power to require the production of a copy of the information in legible form [, or in a form from which it can readily be produced in visible and legible form.].

General note

European Convention on Human Rights   This provision provides sweeping powers for inspectors appointed under ss 431, 432 and it is here that the impact of the Human Rights Act 1998 may be felt as these statutory powers must now be considered against the need to ensure compatibility with the European Convention on Human Rights which has been incorporated into domestic law by that statute. However, the European Court of Human Rights has already drawn an important distinction between the investigation process – the stage at which the inspectors are involved – and any action which is subsequently taken on account of that investigation.

In *Fayed v United Kingdom* (1994) 18 EHRR 393 the court concluded that the proceedings conducted by the inspectors do not involve the determination of a criminal charge within the meaning of article 6(1) of the Convention (set out below); and that to subject such preparatory investigations to the guarantees of judicial procedure set forth in art 6(1) would unduly hamper the effective regulation in the public interest of complex financial and commercial activities (at 428). This view was endorsed subsequently by the European Court in *Saunders v United Kingdom* [1998] 1 BCLC 362 at 378; and *IJL, GMR, AKP v United Kingdom* (2000) Times, 13 October ECHR; and see *R v Hertfordshire County Council, ex p Green Environmental Industries Ltd* [2000] 1 All ER 773, HL (the European jurisprudence under art 6(1) is firmly anchored to the fairness of the trial and is not concerned with extra-judicial activities).

The application of art 6(1) to any action taken subsequent to the investigation, such as criminal prosecutions or disqualification proceedings, is considered below. Other Convention provisions, such as the right to privacy under article 8, may have some application (for example, to the requirement to disclose documents under s 447 and the provision of search warrants under s 448) but such rights tend to be much less absolute than those provided by article 6. Article 8, for example, is subject to a qualification which permits interference with that right in accordance with law and 'in so far as is necessary … for the prevention of disorder or crime … or for the protection of the rights and freedoms of others'; and see *DC, HS and AD v United Kingdom* [2000] BCC 710, ECHR; *WGS and MSLS v United Kingdom* [2000] BCC 719, ECHR, where the European Court of Human Rights acknowledges the importance in modern economic life of public confidence in limited companies.

Article 6 Right to a fair trial

   1.   In the determination of his civil rights and obligations or of any criminal charge against him, everyone is entitled to a fair and public hearing within a reasonable time by an independent and impartial tribunal established by law. Judgment shall be pronounced publicly but the press and public may be excluded from all or part of the trial in the interests of morals, public order or national security in a democratic society, where the interests of juveniles or the protection of the private life of the parties so require, or to the extent strictly necessary in the opinion of the court in special circumstances where publicity would prejudice the interests of justice.

   2.   Everyone charged with a criminal offence shall be presumed innocent until proved guilty according to law.

   3.   Everyone charged with a criminal offence has the following minimum rights:

       a.   to be informed promptly, in a language which he understands and in detail, of the nature and cause of the accusation against him;

    b.   to have adequate time and facilities for the preparation of his defence;

    c.   to defend himself in person or through legal assistance of his own choosing or, if he has not sufficient means to pay for legal assistance, to be given it free when the interests of justice so require;

    d.   to examine or have examined witnesses against him and to obtain the attendance and examination of witnesses on his behalf under the same conditions as witnesses against him;

    e.   to have the free assistance of an interpreter if he cannot understand or speak the language used in court.

S 434(1)–(4)

The powers in sub-ss (1) and (2) are essentially the same and it is convenient to consider them together but it should be noted that sub-s (2) is broader than sub-s (1) in that it is not restricted to an officer or agent of the company or other body corporate but extends the powers of the inspectors to 'any other person'. In addition, it allows the inspectors to seek 'any information relating to a matter which they believe to be relevant to the investigation'.

There is no specific requirement to answer the inspectors' questions although non-compliance may be certified to the court under s 436. The requirement to answer questions is inherent, however, in the obligation to give all assistance as the witness is reasonably able to give.

'Officer' is defined in s 744 and amplified by sub-s (4); 'agents' is defined in sub-s (4); 'documents' is defined in sub-s (6); 'company' is defined in s 735; 'body corporate' is defined in s 740. The inclusion of bankers and solicitors in the categories of persons who must assist (sub-s (4)) is subject to s 452 (legal professional privilege and bank confidentiality). As to the consequences of non-compliance with this section, see s 436. As to the disclosure of information obtained under this provision, see s 451A.

General conduct of an investigation   Inspectors are masters of their own procedures and the responsibility for the conduct of the investigation is theirs alone; their functions are administrative and not judicial: *Re Pergamon Press Ltd* [1970] 3 All ER 535, CA; *Maxwell v Department of Trade and Industry* [1974] 2 All ER 122. The exercise is one solely of fact-finding and their report when completed is not determinative of any issue.

All proceedings before the inspectors are conducted in private: *Re Pergamon Press Ltd* [1970] 3 All ER 535, CA; see also *Hearts of Oak Assurance Co Ltd v A-G* [1932] AC 392; and the inspectors may be accompanied by anyone whose presence is reasonably necessary to enable them properly to carry out their duties: *Re Gaumont-British Picture Corpn Ltd* [1940] 2 All ER 415. Witnesses may be accompanied by their legal advisers (although there may, it seems, be some advantage to being unrepresented, see *Re an inquiry into Mirror Group Newspapers plc* [1999] 1 BCLC 690). Inspectors are not required to caution witnesses under the Police and Criminal Evidence Act 1984, s 67(9), as they are not investigating offences for these purposes: *R v Seelig* [1991] BCLC 869.

Dealing with witnesses   There are generally three stages with respect to each witness (see *British and Commonwealth Holdings plc v Barclays de Zoete Wedd Ltd* [1999] 1 BCLC 86 at 93):

(1)   the interview with the inspectors;
(2)   witnesses are given the opportunity to correct any mistake in their evidence, or any misleading impression given, and to add to their evidence, where they think it appropriate, after receiving a transcript of their evidence;
(3)   witnesses are notified of any provisional criticisms and are given the opportunity to make further submissions.

The formal interview may be preceded by written statements, informal interviews and possibly advance notice of the questions. Once formally interviewed, a transcript will be created and the witness cannot object to the presence of a shorthand writer for such purpose: *Re Gaumont-British Picture Corp Ltd* [1940] 2 All ER 415. If the interview is informal, the interviewer would provide the witness with notes of the interview.

Inspectors need not provide a witness with transcripts of witness statements against him nor will a witness be allowed to cross-examine other witnesses: *Maxwell v Department of Trade & Industry* [1974] 2 All ER 122. A transcript of his own evidence will normally be supplied to the witness at an appropriate time during the course of the inquiry. It will usually be supplied to him in confidence, as to which, see below.

Inspectors must act fairly   In carrying out the investigation, the basic requirement is that the inspectors must act fairly and give people an opportunity to respond before criticising them in their report: *Re Pergamon Press Ltd* [1970] 3 All ER 535, CA. If they are minded to criticise a person, they must put to him the substance of the evidence against him and their intended criticisms and give him an opportunity to respond, either at an interview or further interview or in writing, if he so wishes: see *Re Pergamon Press Ltd* [1970] 3 All ER 535; *Maxwell v Department of Trade and Industry* [1974] 2 All ER 122, CA. There is no requirement, however, to provide a witness with extracts from the draft report: *Maxwell v Department of Trade & Industry* [1974] 2 All ER 122.

Demands on witnesses   Inspectors cannot place demands on persons that are unreasonable, whether as to the time they have to expend or the expense they have to incur in preparation for the questions or in any other respect: *Re an inquiry into Mirror Group Newspapers plc* [1999] 1 BCLC 690. In this case, Sir Richard Scott, V-C, explained that:

'The reasonableness and proportionality of inspectors' demands may depend upon the purpose of the inquiry and the nature of the office in the company held by the particular witness. Inspectors appointed, for example, to inquire into what has become of company assets that have gone missing can reasonably, in my view, place a heavy burden of assistance on directors of the company whose duty it was to manage and preserve those assets. All the circumstances must, in my judgment, be taken into account in deciding whether or not assistance which a person is, in an absolute sense, able to give is also assistance which he is *reasonably* able to give. But if, in all the circumstances, the demands made on the person go beyond what he is *reasonably* able to give, his failure to comply with the demands will not be a breach of his statutory duty and should not be treated as a contempt of court' (at 709).

The absence of legal representation may have a bearing on what is an unreasonable demand, see *Re an inquiry into Mirror Group Newspapers plc* [1999] 1 BCLC 690.

Confidentiality undertakings   As a matter of discretion, inspectors may seek confidentiality undertakings from those interviewed but, as there is no express statutory power entitling the inspectors to require witnesses to sign a confidentiality undertaking, a refusal to sign such an undertaking will not represent a failure on the part of an ex-director of a company to give the inspectors any assistance he was reasonably able to give: *Re an inquiry into Mirror Group Newspapers plc* [1999] 1 BCLC 690.

Inspectors owe no duty to the witness as to the use for the purposes of their statutory inquiry to which they may put the information or documents obtained from that person so, for example, they may present that information and documents to another witness. However, the person to whom they present the information or documents may be put on notice of their confidential character. This notice will not inhibit the second witness from making use of the information and documents for the purpose of answering the inspectors' questions (for example, by consulting lawyers and others) but he must not disclose their contents for a purpose unconnected with the purposes for which the documents have been supplied to him: see *Re an inquiry into Mirror Group Newspapers plc* [1999] 1 BCLC 690 at 706–707, per Sir Richard Scott V-C.

Use of transcripts in subsequent proceedings   Witnesses should be aware that the information which they give to the inspectors may be admissible, and its disclosure sought, in a variety of subsequent proceedings. In general, evidence given by a witness to inspectors, whether or not under oath, is admissible in civil proceedings: see *London & County Securities Ltd v Nicholson* [1980] 3 All ER 861 (transcripts of statements to inspectors by auditors of insolvent company were admissible in civil proceedings brought by a liquidator against the auditors for negligence).

Transcripts may be disclosed to various parties under the powers set out in ss 449 and 451A and may be relied on by the Secretary of State in disqualification proceedings: *R v Secretary of State for Trade and Industry, ex p McCormick* [1998] BCC 379; and in winding up proceedings under IA 1986, s 124A.

Disclosure of transcripts of evidence given by persons to inspectors may be ordered in civil litigation where necessary to dispose fairly of the matter, subject to the right of witnesses to object to the production of all or part of the transcripts and the exclusion of any material subject to a public interest immunity certificate by a relevant minister or secretary of state: *British and Commonwealth Holdings plc v Barclays de Zoete Wedd Ltd* [1999] 1 BCLC 86; *Soden v Burns* [1996] 2 BCLC 636.

The inspectors' own notes, drafts, internal materials etc are not admissible nor subject to disclosure in any proceedings: *Re Astra Holdings plc, Secretary of State for Trade and Industry v Anderson* [1998] 2 BCLC 44. Disclosure of a side letter to a report would be ordered, as necessary to the fair conduct of the proceedings, when the inspectors expressed the view in the letter that the conduct of a director considered in the report was not such as to justify the conclusion that the director was unfit to be concerned in the management of a company: *Re Astra Holdings plc*.

As to the admissibility of the inspectors' report in any proceedings, see s 441.

S 434(5)

The right of silence when faced with inspectors' questions   Until the decision of the European Court of Human Rights in *Saunders v United Kingdom* [1998] 1 BCLC 362, the courts had consistently held that these statutory provisions governing investigations impliedly excluded the common law privilege against self-incrimination so that those subject to investigation were not able to rely on that privilege as entitling them to refuse to answer the inspectors' questions: *R v Saunders* [1996] 1 Cr App Rep 463, CA; *Re London United Investments plc* [1992] 2 All ER 842;

R v Seelig [1991] 4 All ER 429. Such answers might then be used in evidence against the witness, as provided by this subsection.

Saunders, former chief executive of Guinness plc, had been convicted of various offences arising from the take-over of Distillers plc by Guinness in the mid-1980s and that conviction was upheld on appeal. At trial, the prosecution relied heavily on the transcripts of interviews between Saunders and inspectors appointed to investigate the affairs of the company under s 432(2).

Saunders brought a case against the UK Government under the European Convention on Human Rights challenging the use of such evidence in criminal proceedings on the grounds that it was a breach of the due process provisions (article 6) of the European Convention on Human Rights. Article 6 is set out above in the general note to this section.

The European Court of Human Rights found that aspects of the trial did depart from the basic principles of fair procedure. The unfairness arose from the use in the criminal trial of information disclosed by Saunders when questioned by inspectors. He had been compelled to answer their questions, there being no right of silence in such circumstances, and was in effect compelled to incriminate himself. This was a violation of art 6(1) of the European Convention on Human Rights which provides that in the determination of any criminal charge, everyone is entitled to a fair hearing by an independent and impartial tribunal. The public interest in combating fraud could not be invoked to justify the use of answers compulsorily obtained in a non-judicial investigation to incriminate him at his trial.

Limits to Saunders case   It is important to appreciate the limits of the decision in the *Saunders* case which is under increasing scrutiny in the courts; for example, the Privy Council has indicated dissatisfaction with the decision and the lack of clarity in the judgment on the question as to whether the right to silence and the right not to incriminate oneself are absolute rights: see *Brown v Stott* [2001] 2 All ER 97.

Compelled evidence in criminal proceedings   The decision in *Saunders v UK* [1998] 1 BCLC 362 is restricted to invalidating the use of compelled evidence obtained by inspectors in criminal proceedings; it follows that only a limited amendment to the section has been necessary to bring the statute into line with the requirements of the European Convention, see sub-ss (5A), (5B).

Statements not documents   In the *Saunders* case, the European court emphasised that the right not to incriminate oneself is primarily concerned with respecting the right of an accused person to remain silent. It does not extend to the use in criminal proceedings of material which may be obtained from the accused through the use of compulsory powers but which has an existence independent of the will of the suspect such as, inter alia, documents acquired pursuant to a warrant (as well as breath, blood and urine samples and bodily tissue for the purpose of DNA testing).

This issue has been addressed further by the Court of Appeal in *A-G's Reference (No 7 of 2000)* (2001) Times, 12 April. The issue before the court was whether the use in criminal proceedings of documents obtained by compulsion backed by contempt sanctions violated Article 6 of the European Convention of Human Rights. Applying *Saunders*, the court concluded that there is a clear distinction between statements made and other material independent of the making of a statement; such material is admissible and does not amount to a violation of article 6 of the European Convention; subject always to the trial judge's discretion to exclude evidence under s 78 of the Police and Criminal Evidence Act 1984.

Derivative or secondary evidence   There remains some uncertainty as to the extent to which derivative or secondary evidence to which the prosecution is led by the compelled evidence is admissible: see *R v Hertfordshire County Council, ex p Green Environmental Industries Ltd* [2000] 1 All ER 773 where Lord Hoffmann noted that there was no difficulty with such evidence as a matter of English law (at 780) although Lord Cooke was concerned at the unsatisfactory nature of the European jurisprudence on this matter (at 784).

Disqualification proceedings   The decision in *Saunders* has not prevented the use of compelled evidence against a director in disqualification proceedings as such proceedings are not criminal proceedings, see *R v Secretary of State for Trade and Industry, ex p McCormick* [1998] BCC 379; *EDC v United Kingdom* [1998] BCC 370; *DC, HS and AD v United Kingdom* [2000] BCC 710. As to whether the conduct of disqualification proceedings infringes a director's right to a fair trial under art 6(1) of the European Convention on Human Rights, that is a matter to be considered in the round by the trial judge having regard to all the relevant factors including the degrees of coercion involved in different investigative procedures under the IA 1986 and CA 1985: *Re Westminster Property Management Ltd, Official Receiver v Stern* [2000] 2 BCLC 396; *WGS and MSLS v United Kingdom* [2000] BCC 719, ECHR; see also *R v Secretary of State for Trade and Industry, ex p McCormick* [1998] BCC 379.

Extra-judicial activities   It is established that European jurisprudence under art 6(1) of the European Convention on Human Rights is firmly anchored to the fairness of the trial and is not concerned with extra-judicial activities (see general note above and *R v Hertfordshire County Council, ex p Green Environmental Industries Ltd* [2000] 1 All ER 773, HL). It remains the case therefore that, under this section, witnesses may be compelled to answer questions put to them by the inspectors or face the penalties imposed by s 436.

S 434(5A)–(5B)

Subsections (5A) and (5B) were inserted by the Youth Justice and Criminal Evidence Act 1999, s 59, Sch 3, paras 4, 5, as from 14 April 2000, in order to address the decision of the European Court of Human Rights in *Saunders v United Kingdom* [1998] 1 BCLC 362, discussed above. The effect of these provisions is to ensure that compelled evidence in the form of statements by the accused cannot be used against the accused in any subsequent criminal trial save where the offence itself arises from any statement made (sub-s (5B)). The amendment is limited to statements made and does not extend to the admission of documents in such proceedings, see note above on this point.

S 434(6)

Words in square brackets inserted by the Criminal Justice and Police Act 2001, s 70, Sch 2, Pt 2, para 17, as from a day to be appointed.

---

435. *(Repealed by CA 1989, s 212, Sch 24, as from 21 February 1990.)*

436. Obstruction of inspectors treated as contempt of court

(1) If any person—

    (a) fails to comply with section 434(1)(a) or (c),

(b) refuses to comply with a requirement under section 434(1)(b) or (2), or

(c) refuses to answer any question put to him by the inspectors for the purposes of the investigation,

the inspectors may certify that fact in writing to the court.

(3) The court may thereupon enquire into the case; and, after hearing any witnesses who may be produced against or on behalf of the alleged offender and after hearing any statement which may be offered in defence, the court may punish the offender in like manner as if he had been guilty of contempt of the court.

General note

Subsection (1) of this provision was substituted for the original sub-ss (1), and (2), by the CA 1989, s 56(6), hence the absence of any sub-s (2) to this provision.

S 436(1)

Unreasonable demands   Whether there has been a failure to comply with the requirements of the inspectors will depend on the nature of the refusal, for the witness is only required to provide such assistance as he is reasonably able to give (s 434). If, in all the circumstances, the demands for assistance made on a person go beyond what he is reasonably able to give, his failure to comply with the demands will not be a breach of his statutory duty and will not be treated as a contempt of court: *Re an inquiry into Mirror Group Newspapers plc* [1999] 1 BCLC 690.

Unreasonable refusals   A refusal by the Secretary of State to give assurances that disqualification proceedings would not be brought cannot possibly justify the refusal of an ex-director to answer inspectors' questions: see *Re an inquiry into Mirror Group Newspapers plc* [1999] 1 BCLC 690 at 711. It is not reasonable to refuse to answer questions put by the inspector on the ground that he, the inspector, has brought in a shorthand writer to take a note of the evidence: *Re Gaumont-British Picture Corporation Ltd* [1940] Ch 506.

S 436(3)

Court must determine   This provision makes clear that it is not a case simply of referring the matter to the court for the court to impose an appropriate penalty; the court is required to hear the case, enquiring into the matter and hearing witnesses for and against the defendant and giving the defendant an opportunity to put his defence; it must not act as a rubber stamp to support the view of the inspectors: see *Re an Inquiry under the Company Securities (Insider Dealing) Act 1985* [1988] 1 All ER 203 at 210, HL (concerning similar provisions governing investigations into insider dealing); *McClelland, Pope and Langley Ltd v Howard* [1968] 1 All ER 569n. This requirement provides an important element of procedural fairness.

European Convention on Human Rights   A question which arises is whether this power to penalise someone for non-compliance with the inspectors under s 434 is compatible with the European Convention on Human Rights and, in particular, with article 6 of the Convention which entitles persons to due process in the determination of their civil rights or of any criminal charge. Article 6 is set out above in the general note to s 434.

The European Court of Human Rights has already identified the limits to the application of art 6(1) in this context – it is anchored to the fairness of the trial and is not concerned with extra-judicial activities – and it will not affect, it seems, the ability to impose a penalty for non-compliance with the inspectors' inquiries (see general note to s 434 and *R v Hertfordshire County Council, ex p Green Environmental Industries Ltd* [2000] 1 All ER 773, HL; also *Abas v Netherlands* [1997] EHRLR 418). The important factor is that the imposition of a penalty is not a matter for the inspectors but for the courts following a fair hearing.

The individual faced with a request to assist the inspectors has two options: (i) to refuse to assist which refusal will attract certification under this provision and the possibility of the imposition of a penalty by the court after a fair hearing; (ii) in order to avoid such a consequence, the witness may assist under compulsion and such compelled statements cannot be used against him in any subsequent criminal trial; although documents obtained by compulsion may be relied on, derivative evidence may be obtained and statements obtained by compulsion may be relied on in disqualification proceedings: see the detailed note to s 434.

Penalties The penalties for contempt of court include the imposition of a fine or imprisonment for up to two years, see the Contempt of Court Act 1981.

437. Inspectors' reports

(1) The inspectors may, and if so directed by the Secretary of State shall, make interim reports to the Secretary of State, and on the conclusion of their investigation shall make a final report to him.

Any such report shall be written or printed, as the Secretary of State directs.

(1A) Any persons who have been appointed under section 431 or 432 may at any time and, if the Secretary of State directs them to do so, shall inform him of any matters coming to their knowledge as a result of their investigations.

(1B) If it appears to the Secretary of State that matters have come to light in the course of the inspectors' investigation which suggest that a criminal offence has been committed, and those matters have been referred to the appropriate prosecuting authority, he may direct the inspectors to take no further steps in the investigation or to take only such further steps as are specified in the direction.

(1C) Where an investigation is the subject of a direction under subsection (1B), the inspectors shall make a final report to the Secretary of State only where—

    (a) they were appointed under section 432(1)(appointment in pursuance of an order of the court), or

    (b) the Secretary of State directs them to do so.

(2) If the inspectors were appointed under section 432 in pursuance of an order of the court, the Secretary of State shall furnish a copy of any report of theirs to the court.

(3) In any case the Secretary of State may, if he thinks fit—

    (a) forward a copy of any report made by the inspectors to the company's registered office,

(b) furnish a copy on request and on payment of the prescribed fee to—

   (i)   any member of the company or other body corporate which is the subject of the report,

   (ii) any person whose conduct is referred to in the report,

   (iii) the auditors of that company or body corporate,

   (iv) the applicants for the investigation,

   (v)   any other person whose financial interests appear to the Secretary of State to be affected by the matters dealt with in the report, whether as a creditor of the company or body corporate, or otherwise, and

(c) cause any such report to be printed and published.

S 437(1)

Interim reports are optional but the inspectors must make a final report (subject to sub-s (1C)); whether that report is published is essentially a discretionary matter for the Secretary of State under sub-s (3).

S 437(1A)–(1C)

Steps to expedite matters   Inspections have often attracted criticism for the length of time and costs involved and these provisions were introduced by CA 1989 to speed up the process and avoid unproductive inquiries and unnecessary reports. The ability of the Secretary of State to obtain information from the inspectors under sub-s (1A) avoids the need for a formal interim report under sub-s (1). For an example of the exercise of this power to call for information, see *Re an inquiry into Mirror Group Newspapers plc* [1999] 1 BCLC 690 at 693. Under sub-s (1B), the Secretary of State may direct no further steps are taken etc (in which case no final report is required, subject to sub-s (1C)), but there is no obligation on him to call off the investigation simply because matters have been referred to a prosecuting authority although in practice he may well do so.

S 437(3)

Discretion to publish   The publication of inspectors' reports is a discretionary matter for the Secretary of State (subject to sub-s (2)). In exercising his discretion as to whether to publish the report, the Secretary of State is required to act in the public interest after taking such advice as he considers appropriate: *Lonrho plc v Secretary of State for Trade and Industry* [1989] 2 All ER 609. The general approach of the Department is to publish reports with respect to public companies, as being matters of public interest, but publication may be delayed in order not to prejudice further inquiries or possible criminal proceedings.

Inspectors may be appointed on the basis that their report will not be published, in which case this provision does not apply: s 432(2A); and where the report follows an investigation of company ownership under s 442, provision is made for part of the report to be withheld from publication in certain cases, see s 443(3).

Manner of publication　Subsection (3)(a) allows for publication to the company only while sub-s (3)(b) allows specific categories of persons to request a copy; in practice, the Secretary of State will publish either the entire report under sub-s (3)(c) or not publish the report at all.

Qualified privilege　The report when published is subject to qualified privilege and neither the Department of Trade and Industry nor the inspectors may be sued for defamation, other than on proof of express malice: as to which, see *Horrocks v Lowe* [1975] AC 135 at 149, per Lord Diplock.

European Convention on Human Rights　The reports are frequently highly critical of named individuals but the European Court of Human Rights has rejected a claim that publishing such critical reports without allowing the individuals concerned to vindicate their position in a court of law is a breach of the due process provisions of the European Convention on Human Rights: *Fayed v United Kingdom* (1994) 18 EHRR 393. The court found that investigations were carried out in the public interest to ensure the proper conduct of the affairs of public companies. The investigation process itself did not involve any adjudication and the procedure adopted was surrounded by considerable safeguards to ensure fair procedures. The court also thought that directors of large companies must tolerate wider limits of acceptable criticisms than private individuals: (1994) 18 EHRR 393 at 433.

438. Power to bring civil proceedings on company's behalf

(1)　If from any report made or information obtained under this Part it appears to the Secretary of State that any civil proceedings ought in the public interest to be brought by any body corporate, he may himself bring such proceedings in the name and on behalf of the body corporate.

(2)　The Secretary of State shall indemnify the body corporate against any costs or expenses incurred by it in or in connection with proceedings brought under this section.

General note

While a power of this nature has been exercised in the past (see *SBA Properties Ltd v Cradock* [1967] 2 All ER 610, action brought under CA 1948, s 169(4), which contained a similar power), it is very unlikely now that a case would arise where it would be considered appropriate for the Secretary of State, in the public interest, to bring civil proceedings on behalf of the company. If any civil proceedings are to follow an investigation, they are likely to be commenced by an administrator or liquidator.

This provision does not apply to overseas companies, see s 453(1A)(b).

439. Expenses of investigating a company's affairs

(1)　The expenses of an investigation under any of the powers conferred by this Part shall be defrayed in the first instance by the Secretary of State, but he may recover those expenses from the persons liable in accordance with this section.

There shall be treated as expenses of the investigation, in particular, such reasonable sums as the Secretary of State may determine in respect of general staff costs and overheads.

(2) A person who is convicted on a prosecution instituted as a result of the investigation, or is ordered to pay the whole or any part of the costs of proceedings brought under section 438, may in the same proceedings be ordered to pay those expenses to such extent as may be specified in the order.

(3) A body corporate in whose name proceedings are brought under that section is liable to the amount or value of any sums or property recovered by it as a result of those proceedings; and any amount for which a body corporate is liable under this subsection is a first charge on the sums or property recovered.

(4) A body corporate dealt with by an inspectors' report, where the inspectors were appointed otherwise than of the Secretary of State's own motion, is liable except where it was the applicant for the investigation, and except so far as the Secretary of State otherwise directs.

(5) Where inspectors were appointed—

    (a) under section 431, or

    (b) on an application under section 442(3),

the applicant or applicants for the investigation is or are liable to such extent (if any) as the Secretary of State may direct.

(6) The report of inspectors appointed otherwise than of the Secretary of State's own motion may, if they think fit, and shall if the Secretary of State so directs, include a recommendation as to the directions (if any) which they think appropriate, in the light of their investigation, to be given under subsection (4) or (5) of this section.

(7) For purposes of this section, any costs or expenses incurred by the Secretary of State in or in connection with proceedings brought under section 438 (including expenses incurred under subsection (2) of it) are to be treated as expenses of the investigation giving rise to the proceedings.

(8) Any liability to repay the Secretary of State imposed by subsections (2) and (3) above is (subject to satisfaction of his right to repayment) a liability also to indemnify all persons against liability under subsections (4) and (5); and any such liability imposed by subsection (2) is (subject as mentioned above) a liability also to indemnify all persons against liability under subsection (3).

(9) A person liable under any one of those subsections is entitled to contribution from any other person liable under the same subsection, according to the amount of their respective liabilities under it.

(10) Expenses to be defrayed by the Secretary of State under this section shall, so far as not recovered under it, be paid out of money provided by Parliament.

General note

These powers to recover the costs of an investigation were introduced by CA 1989, s 59, but appear never to have been used; note, in particular, sub-s (2).

440. *(Repealed by CA 1989, ss 60(1), 212, Sch 24, as from 21 February 1990.)*

441. Inspectors' report to be evidence

(1)　A copy of any report of inspectors appointed under this Part, certified by the Secretary of State to be a true copy, is admissible in any legal proceedings as evidence of the opinion of the inspectors in relation to any matter contained in the report and, in proceedings on an application under section 8 of the Company Directors Disqualification Act 1986, as evidence of any fact stated therein.

(2)　A document purporting to be such a certificate as is mentioned above shall be received in evidence and be deemed to be such a certificate, unless the contrary is proved.

S 441(1)

Limited admissibility　This provision provides for limited admissibility of the inspectors' report; it is not a blanket provision allowing the report to be used in all cases as evidence: see *Savings and Investment Bank Ltd v Gasco Investments (Netherlands) BV* [1984] 1 All ER 296 at 305; and the report is not evidence as to any fact but only as to the opinion of the inspectors, save in disqualification proceedings as specified.

Winding up petition　The report is admissible to support a winding up petition by the Secretary of State on public interest grounds under IA 1986, s 124A, where the court will take the report, if not challenged, into account in deciding whether it is just and equitable that the company should be wound up: see *Savings and Investment Bank Ltd v Gasco Investments (Netherlands) BV* [1984] 1 All ER 296; *Re St Piran Ltd* [1981] 3 All ER 270; *Re Armvent Ltd* [1975] 3 All ER 441; a contributory may likewise rely on an inspectors' report to support a winding up petition: *Re St Piran Ltd* [1981] 3 All ER 270.

OTHER POWERS OF INVESTIGATION AVAILABLE TO THE SECRETARY OF STATE

442. Power to investigate company ownership

(1)　Where it appears to the Secretary of State that there is good reason to do so, he may appoint one or more competent inspectors to investigate and report on the membership of any company, and otherwise with respect to the company, for the purpose of determining the true persons who are or have been financially interested in the success or failure (real or apparent) of the company or able to control or materially to influence its policy.

(2)   The appointment of inspectors under this section may define the scope of their investigation (whether as respects the matter or the period to which it is to extend or otherwise) and in particular may limit the investigation to matters connected with particular shares or debentures.

(3)   If an application for investigation under this section with respect to particular shares or debentures of a company is made to the Secretary of State by members of the company, and the number of applicants or the amount of shares held by them is not less than that required for an application for the appointment of inspectors under section 431(2)(a) or (b), then, subject to the following provisions, the Secretary of State shall appoint inspectors to conduct the investigation applied for.

(3A) The Secretary of State shall not appoint inspectors if he is satisfied that the application is vexatious; and where inspectors are appointed their terms of appointment shall exclude any matter in so far as the Secretary of State is satisfied that it is unreasonable for it to be investigated.

(3B) The Secretary of State may, before appointing inspectors, require the applicant or applicants to give security, to an amount not exceeding £5,000, or such other sum as he may by order specify, for payment of the costs of the investigation.

An order under this subsection shall be made by statutory instrument which shall be subject to annulment in pursuance of a resolution of either House of Parliament.

(3C) If on an application under subsection (3) it appears to the Secretary of State that the powers conferred by section 444 are sufficient for the purposes of investigating the matters which inspectors would be appointed to investigate, he may instead conduct the investigation under that section.

(4)   Subject to the terms of their appointment, the inspectors' powers extend to the investigation of any circumstances suggesting the existence of an arrangement or understanding which, though not legally binding, is or was observed or likely to be observed in practice and which is relevant to the purposes of the investigation.

General note

Sections 442–446 envisage two types of investigation of company ownership, either by appointing inspectors under this provision (similar to appointments under s 432) or by using departmental officials under s 444 (similar to powers under s 447). These provisions do not apply to overseas companies, see s 453(1A)(c), (d).

Given the potential scope of any investigation under sub-s (1), an appointment under this provision could equally be accommodated within s 432. The advantage in proceeding under this provision rather than s 432 is that a failure to obtain information under this provision (or s 444) enables the Secretary of State to impose restrictions on the transfer etc of the shares in question: see ss 445, 454–457.

In practice, use of these powers is exceptional, with no appointments under s 442 in the past five years and only one investigation under s 444 in that period. This decline in the use of these provisions reflects changing practices and structures. The powers had been used mainly to investigate the existence of concert parties (see sub-s (4)) in the run up to a take-over and to consider allegations of insider dealing; the disclosure provisions of Part VI have reduced significantly the possibility of the former practice while investigations of insider dealing are dealt with by powers under Part XI of the Financial Services and Markets Act 2000.

S 442(1)

Appointment of inspectors   As to the requirement that there be a 'good reason' for an investigation, see note to s 447(2). The ability of the Secretary of State to appoint inspectors under this provision reinforces the powers granted to a public company to serve a s 212 notice requiring any person who is or has been interested in its share capital to disclose the nature and extent of that interest, see notes to that provision. That provision enables a public company to monitor the composition of its register of members. Where, despite that power, a company is dissatisfied with the information which it has obtained, it may try to persuade the Secretary of State to exercise these statutory powers to investigate the ownership of the company.

As to the disclosure of information obtained under this provision, see s 451A; as to the protection of legal professional privilege and bank confidentiality, see s 452.

S 442(3)–(3C)

Application by members   Members of a company, provided they are sufficient in number to meet the statutory thresholds in relation to inspections (see s 431(2)), can require the Secretary of State to appoint inspectors to investigate the membership subject to the requirements of sub-ss (3A)–(3C), including the possibility of being required to give security for costs. As to the definition of 'debentures', see s 744.

---

443. Provisions applicable on investigation under s 442

(1)   For purposes of an investigation under section 442, sections 433(1), 434, 436 and 437 apply with the necessary modifications of references to the affairs of the company or to those of any other body corporate, subject however to the following subsections.

(2)   Those sections apply to—

    (a)   all persons who are or have been, or whom the inspector has reasonable cause to believe to be or have been, financially interested in the success or failure or the apparent success or failure of the company or any other body corporate whose membership is investigated with that of the company, or able to control or materially influence its policy (including persons concerned only on behalf of others), and

    (b)   any other person whom the inspector has reasonable cause to believe possesses information relevant to the investigation,

as they apply in relation to officers and agents of the company or the other body corporate (as the case may be).

(3)   If the Secretary of State is of opinion that there is good reason for not divulging any part of a report made by virtue of section 442 and this section, he may under

section 437 disclose the report with the omission of that part; and he may cause to be kept by the registrar of companies a copy of the report with that part omitted or, in the case of any other such report, a copy of the whole report.

(4)   ...

S 443(1)

The specified provisions relate to the conduct of an inspection (ss 433, 434), the obstruction of the inspectors (s 436) and the publication of any report (s 437); see the notes to those sections. Sections 448 (search warrants); 450 (destroying documents) and 452 (legal professional privilege and bankers' confidentiality) also apply.

S 443(3)

The omission of part of the report might arise in circumstances where s 216(5) would apply, see the note to that provision.

444. Power to obtain information as to those interested in shares, etc

(1)   If it appears to the Secretary of State that there is good reason to investigate the ownership of any shares in or debentures of a company and that it is unnecessary to appoint inspectors for the purpose, he may require any person whom he has reasonable cause to believe to have or to be able to obtain any information as to the present and past interests in those shares or debentures and the names and addresses of the persons interested and of any persons who act or have acted on their behalf in relation to the shares or debentures to give any such information to the Secretary of State.

(2)   For this purpose a person is deemed to have an interest in shares or debentures if he has any right to acquire or dispose of them or of any interest in them, or to vote in respect of them, or if his consent is necessary for the exercise of any of the rights of other persons interested in them, or if other persons interested in them can be required, or are accustomed, to exercise their rights in accordance with his instructions.

(3)   A person who fails to give information required of him under this section, or who in giving such information makes any statement which he knows to be false in a material particular, or recklessly makes any statement which is false in a material particular, is liable to imprisonment or a fine, or both.

General note

See the general note to s 442. These powers, which do not apply to overseas companies, see s 453(1A)(c), have been used on only one occasion in the past five years.

S 444(1)

Investigation without inspectors   This provision enables the Secretary of State when it appears that there is 'good reason' (as to which, see s 447(2)) for investigating the ownership of any company to dispense with the costly appointment of inspectors under s 442 and to use departmental officials instead. The power to investigate extends in this instance to 'any person' who has or 'is able to obtain' any information with respect to a present or past interest in the shares (as broadly defined by sub-s (2)); 'debentures' is defined in s 744. There is no provision for the publication of any report of an investigation carried out under this provision.

As to the disclosure of information obtained under this provision, see s 451A; as to the protection of legal professional privilege and bank confidentiality, see s 452; as to the imposition of restrictions on any shares, see s 445.

S 444(3)

As to penalties, see s 730, Sch 24.

445. Power to impose restrictions on shares and debentures

(1)   If in connection with an investigation under either section 442 or 444 it appears to the Secretary of State that there is difficulty in finding out the relevant facts about any shares (whether issued or to be issued), he may by order direct that the shares shall until further order be subject to the restrictions of Part XV of this Act.

(1A) If the Secretary of State is satisfied that an order under subsection (1) may unfairly affect the rights of third parties in respect of shares then the Secretary of State, for the purpose of protecting such rights and subject to such terms as he thinks fit, may direct that such acts by such persons or descriptions of persons and for such purposes as may be set out in the order, shall not constitute a breach of the restrictions of Part XV of this Act.

(2)   This section, and Part XV in its application to orders under it, apply in relation to debentures as in relation to shares save that subsection (1A) shall not so apply.

S 445(1)

Freezing orders   One of the most important provisions relating to investigations of membership (whether by inspectors under s 442 or departmental investigators under s 444) is the power given to the Secretary of State to impose the restrictions of Part XV, ss 454–457, commonly known as freezing orders, where there is difficulty in finding out the relevant facts about any shares.

A freezing order involves restrictions on the payment of dividends on the affected shares; on the transfer of such shares; on the exercise of voting rights attached to the shares; and on the acceptance of any rights issue or take-over offer with respect to the affected shares, see generally notes to ss 454–457.

S 445(1A)

This provision was inserted by the Companies (Disclosure of Interests in Shares)(Orders imposing restrictions on shares) Regulations 1991, SI 1991/1646, made under CA 1989, s 135, following concerns that freezing orders could unfairly affect third parties.

S 445(2)

The ability to impose restrictions under s 445 applies to debentures as well as shares; as to the meaning of 'debentures', see s 744.

446. Investigation of share dealings

(1)   If it appears to the Secretary of State that there are circumstances suggesting that contraventions may have occurred, in relation to a company's shares or debentures, of section 323 or 324 (taken with Schedule 13), or of subsections (3) to (5) of section 328 (restrictions on share dealings by directors and their families; obligation of director to disclose shareholding in his own company), he may appoint one or more competent inspectors to carry out such investigations as are requisite to establish whether or not such contraventions have occurred and to report the result of their investigations to him.

(2)   The appointment of inspectors under this section may limit the period to which their investigation is to extend or confine it to shares or debentures of a particular class, or both.

(3)   For purposes of an investigation under this section, sections 434 to 437 apply—

    (a) with the substitution, for references to any other body corporate whose affairs are investigated under section 433(1), of a reference to any other body corporate which is, or has at any relevant time been, the company's subsidiary or holding company, or a subsidiary of its holding company,...

    (b) ...

(4)   Sections 434 to 436 apply under the preceding subsection—

    (a) to any individual who is an authorised person within the meaning of the Financial Services Act 1986;

    (b) to any individual who holds a permission granted under paragraph 23 of Schedule 1 to that Act;

    (c) to any officer (whether past or present) of a body corporate which is such an authorised person or holds such a permission;

    (d) to any partner (whether past or present) in a partnership which is such an authorised person or holds such a permission;

    (e) to any member of the governing body or officer (in either case whether past or present) of an unincorporated association which is such an authorised person or holds such a permission;

as they apply to officers of the company or of the other body corporate.

(5)–(7)…

General note

This provision enables the Secretary of State to appoint inspectors to investigate share dealings and non-disclosure of dealings by directors and their families where the circumstances appear to suggest a breach of the requirements of ss 323–328. Section 323 prohibits option dealings in certain listed shares and debentures by directors (and their families, s 327); s 324 requires directors (and shadow directors) to disclose details of their interests in shares and debentures of the company and the group and the interests of spouses and children are attributed to the director by s 328.

Appointments under this provision are rare with the last appointment being in 1992/93.

As to the general powers of inspectors, see s 434; as to the disclosure of information obtained under this provision, see s 451A; as to the protection of legal professional privilege and bank confidentiality, see s 452.

This provision does not apply to overseas companies, see s 453(1A)(d).

REQUISITION AND SEIZURE OF BOOKS AND PAPERS

447. Secretary of State's power to require production of documents

(1) …

(2) The Secretary of State may at any time, if he thinks there is good reason to do so, give directions to a company requiring it, at such time and place as may be specified in the directions, to produce such documents as may be so specified.

(3) The Secretary of State may at any time, if he thinks there is good reason to do so, authorise an officer of his or any other competent person, on producing (if so required) evidence of his authority, to require a company to produce to him (the officer or other person) forthwith any documents which he (the officer or other person) may specify.

(4) Where by virtue of subsection (2) or (3) the Secretary of State or an officer of his or other person has power to require the production of documents from a company, he or the officer or other person has the like power to require production of those documents from any person who appears to him or the officer or other person to be in possession of them; but where any such person claims a lien on documents produced by him, the production is without prejudice to the lien.

(5) The power under this section to require a company or other person to produce documents includes power—

> (a) if the documents are produced—

    (i)   to take copies of them or extracts from them, and

    (ii) to require that person, or any other person who is a present or past officer of, or is or was at any time employed by, the company in question, to provide an explanation of any of them;

  (b) if the documents are not produced, to require the person who was required to produce them to state, to the best of his knowledge and belief, where they are.

(6)   If the requirement to produce documents or provide an explanation or make a statement is not complied with, the company or other person on whom the requirement was so imposed is guilty of an offence and liable to a fine.

Sections 732 (restriction on prosecutions), 733 (liability of individuals for corporate default) and 734 (criminal proceedings against unincorporated bodies) apply to this offence.

(7)   However, where a person is charged with an offence under subsection (6) in respect of a requirement to produce any documents, it is a defence to prove that they were not in his possession or under his control and that it was not reasonably practicable for him to comply with the requirement.

(8)   A statement made by a person in compliance with such a requirement may be used in evidence against him.

(8A) However, in criminal proceedings in which that person is charged with an offence to which this subsection applies—

  (a) no evidence relating to the statement may be adduced, and

  (b) no question relating to it may be asked,

by or on behalf of the prosecution, unless evidence relating to it is adduced, or a question relating to it is asked, in the proceedings by or on behalf of that person.

(8B) Subsection (8A) applies to any offence other than—

  (a) an offence under subsection (6) or section 451;

  (b) an offence under section 5 of the Perjury Act 1911 (false statements made otherwise than on oath); or

  (c) an offence under section 44(2) of the Criminal Law (Consolidation) (Scotland) Act 1995 (false statements made otherwise than on oath).

(9)   In this section 'documents' includes information recorded in any form; and, in relation to information recorded otherwise than in legible form, the power to require its production includes power to require the production of a copy of it in legible form [, or in a form from which it can readily be produced in visible and legible form].

General note

Discrete fact-finding inquiries Investigations under this provision are not announced by the Department of Trade and Industry; no reports are published and the use of any information obtained is strictly controlled by s 449. These powers enable the Department to embark on discrete and speedy fact-finding investigations with minimum fuss and publicity. The private nature of the investigation ensures that the company concerned is not the subject of adverse speculation before an investigation has determined whether any wrongdoing has actually occurred.

Section 721 is an equivalent provision dealing with the production and inspection of books or papers where an offence relating to the management of the company's affairs is suspected but it appears to be obsolete now given the extensive powers available under this provision; and the Secretary of State no longer relies upon that section.

Results of an investigation   Where an investigation under this provision does uncover wrongdoing, the options open to the Secretary of State include petitioning to have the company wound up under IA 1986, s 124A; bringing disqualification proceedings against the directors under the Company Directors Disqualification Act 1986, s 8; and possible prosecutions for offences such as fraudulent trading, theft and conspiracy to defraud.

European Convention on Human Rights   As to the due process requirements (art 6) of the European Convention on Human Rights and its application to investigation powers, including the powers provided by this section, see the detailed note to s 434.

This provision applies to overseas companies, see s 453.

S 447(2)–(4)

Good reason for investigation   There is no statutory definition of 'good reason' for these purposes, it suffices simply that the Department has concerns and has formed the prima facie view that there may be an undesirable situation in relation to a company which requires investigation but the power to appoint must not be abused or used for any ulterior motive: see *R v Secretary of State for Trade, ex p Perestrello* [1980] 3 All ER 28. Any of the matters specified in s 432(2) might be present although not on a scale which would justify the appointment of inspectors under that provision.

Production of documents   Sub-s (2) allows for the possibility of an advance request to the company (defined s 735) for documents (defined sub-s (9)) while sub-s (3) enables their production to be demanded 'forthwith', a power which will be necessary where there are concerns that, given advance notice, documents might be removed or altered. In practice, this latter power is commonly relied on by investigators. In addition to seeking documents from the company, sub-s (4) enables their production to be sought from any person who appears to be in possession of them, so the scope of the provision is extremely broad. However, the Secretary of State must be careful about making demands which are too broad and become unreasonable, see *R v Secretary of State for Trade, ex p Perestrello* [1980] 3 All ER 28.

Departmental officials   Investigations of this nature are usually carried out by the Secretary of State's own officials but this provision permits these powers to be exercised, in addition, by 'any other competent person' which enables the Department to use external investigators, usually from accountancy firms, when appropriate to do so.

S 447(5)

Production and explanation   This provision is of critical importance to the operation of s 447 investigations for it provides not only for the production and copying of documents but for an explanation of the documents; and it is an offence under sub-s (6) to fail to produce the documents or provide an explanation; and an offence under s 451 to provide a false explanation.

The scope of sub-s (5)(a)(ii) was considered by the Court of Appeal in *A-G's Reference (No 2 of 1998)* [1999] BCC 590 which examined in detail what is meant by an 'explanation of' a document for these purposes. An explanation of a document is not simply an exposition of its literal or grammatical meaning in the narrow or restricted sense. An explanation of a document (or of anything else) is that which makes it possible for a person to understand its significance in the context in which it appears.

An investigator may ask questions about the contents of a document which are designed not only to enable him to consider the context in which the document came into existence but any transaction referred to in it and any other matters which would enable him to understand the significance of the document for the purposes of his investigations. He is entitled to ask questions about subjects referred to in the document and other matters arising out of and properly connected with those subjects. How far questioning about the relationship of a document with other documents should extend and whether it should include an explanation of discrepancies will depend on how closely the documents and explanations are connected. Ultimately, the question is one of degree under the general limitation that the questions must be reasonably necessary to enable the examiner to decide whether the reasons which led the Secretary of State to authorise the enquiry in the first place have any foundation (at 598–599).

As to the protection of documents on the grounds of legal professional privilege and bank confidentiality, see s 452(2) and (3); as to the publication or disclosure of the information obtained under this provision, see s 449.

Use of information obtained   There is no provision comparable to s 441 dealing with the admissibility of the findings of an investigation in subsequent proceedings (a report not being required under this provision). When applying to the court subsequent to a s 447 investigation, the practice is for the officer appointed under s 447 to swear an affidavit exhibiting the documents which he obtained and summarising the information provided to him: see *Secretary of State for Trade and Industry v Ashcroft* [1997] 3 All ER 86 at 91.

Information obtained under s 447, though hearsay, may be used to support a petition for the winding up of the company on the grounds that it is just and equitable to do so under IA 1986, s 124A; and the information is also impliedly admissible in disqualification proceedings under the Company Directors Disqualification Act 1986, s 8 (disqualification following an investigation): *Re Rex Williams Leisure plc* [1994] 2 BCLC 555; *Re Barings plc (No 2), Secretary of State for Trade and Industry v Baker* [1998] 1 BCLC 590; and in proceedings under the Company Directors Disqualification Act 1986, s 7 (unfit directors of insolvent companies): *Secretary of State for Trade and Industry v Ashcroft* [1997] 3 All ER 86. When that evidence is challenged by direct evidence from the respondent, the Secretary of State must then back up the case with direct evidence dealing with the points which are challenged or run the risk of loosing the action: see *Re Barings plc (No 2), Secretary of State for Trade and Industry v Baker* [1998] 1 BCLC 590 at 596; *Re Rex Williams Leisure plc* [1994] 2 BCLC 555 at 568; see also *Re Walter L Jacob & Co Ltd* [1989] BCLC 345.

S 447(6)–(7)

Penalties   As to penalties, see s 730, Sch 24. Sub-s (7) provides a valuable defence against, in effect, unreasonable demands for documents and the approach to that provision would, no doubt, be similar to that adopted in relation to s 436: see *Re an inquiry into Mirror Group Newspapers plc* [1999] 1 BCLC 690.

As to the question whether this power to penalise someone for non-compliance with an investigation is compatible with the European Convention on Human Rights and, in particular, with article 6 of the Convention which entitles persons to due process in the determination of their civil rights or of any criminal charge, see the note to s 436. Sub-s (7) makes clear that the court will have to inquire as to the nature of the refusal before imposing a penalty.

See also s 451 which imposes a penalty for the provision of false information in purported compliance with a requirement under this section.

S 447(8)–(8B)

Use of compelled evidence   The effect of sub-s (8) is to permit the use of compelled statements against a person in subsequent proceedings including, at first sight, criminal proceedings and excluding the common law privilege against self-incrimination. However, the position on the use of compelled statements in criminal trials is restricted by the decision of the European Court of Human Rights in *Saunders v United Kingdom* [1998] 1 BCLC 362, which is discussed in detail in the note to s 434; see in particular the note as to the limits to the *Saunders* case and the distinction drawn between statements made by the accused and documents produced under compulsion.

In response to that decision, this provision has been amended by the insertion of sub-s (8A) and (8B) by the Youth Justice and Criminal Evidence Act 1999, s 59, Sch 3, paras 4, 6, as from 14 April 2000. The effect is to preclude reliance on such statements made by a person in any subsequent criminal proceedings. Subsection (8B)(a) necessarily allows for evidence as to the statement made to be brought in prosecutions under sub-s (6) or s 451 since the offence in those cases arises from the statement made, or not made, as the case may be.

S 447(9)

Words in square brackets inserted by the Criminal Justice and Police Act 2001, s 70, Sch 2, Pt 2, para 17, as from a day to be appointed.

448. Entry and search of premises

(1)   A justice of the peace may issue a warrant under this section if satisfied on information on oath given by or on behalf of the Secretary of State, or by a person appointed or authorised to exercise powers under this Part, that there are reasonable grounds for believing that there are on any premises documents whose production has been required under this Part and which have not been produced in compliance with the requirement.

(2)   A justice of the peace may also issue a warrant under this section if satisfied on information on oath given by or on behalf of the Secretary of State, or by a person appointed or authorised to exercise powers under this Part—

(a)   that there are reasonable grounds for believing that an offence has been committed for which the penalty on conviction on indictment is imprisonment for a term of not less than two years and that there are on any premises documents relating to whether the offence has been committed,

   (b) that the Secretary of State, or the person so appointed or authorised, has power to require the production of the documents under this Part, and

   (c) that there are reasonable grounds for believing that if production was so required the documents would not be produced but would be removed from the premises, hidden, tampered with or destroyed.

(3) A warrant under this section shall authorise a constable, together with any other person named in it and any other constables—

   (a) to enter the premises specified in the information, using such force as is reasonably necessary for the purpose;

   (b) to search the premises and take possession of any documents appearing to be such documents as are mentioned in subsection (1) or (2), as the case may be, or to take, in relation to any such documents, any other steps which may appear to be necessary for preserving them or preventing interference with them;

   (c) to take copies of any such documents; and

   (d) to require any person named in the warrant to provide an explanation of them or to state where they may be found.

(4) If in the case of a warrant under subsection (2) the justice of the peace is satisfied on information on oath that there are reasonable grounds for believing that there are also on the premises other documents relevant to the investigation, the warrant shall also authorise the actions mentioned in subsection (3) to be taken in relation to such documents.

(5) A warrant under this section shall continue in force until the end of the period of one month beginning with the day on which it is issued.

(6) Any documents of which possession is taken under this section may be retained—

   (a) for a period of three months; or

   (b) if within that period proceedings to which the documents are relevant are commenced against any person for any criminal offence, until the conclusion of those proceedings.

(7) Any person who intentionally obstructs the exercise of any rights conferred by a warrant issued under this section or fails without reasonable excuse to comply with any requirement imposed in accordance with subsection (3)(d) is guilty of an offence and liable to a fine.

Sections 732 (restriction on prosecutions), 733 (liability of individuals for corporate default) and 734 (criminal proceedings against unincorporated bodies) apply to this offence.

(8) For the purposes of sections 449 and 451A (provision for security of information) documents obtained under this section shall be treated as if they had been obtained under the provision of this Part under which their production was or, as the case may be, could have been required.

(9) In the application of this section to Scotland for the references to a justice of the peace substitute references to a justice of the peace or a sheriff, and for the references to information on oath substitute references to evidence on oath.

(10) In this section 'document' includes information recorded in any form.

S 448(1), (2)

The documents (defined sub-s (10)) sought may be on 'any premises'; and the provision is not restricted to the premises of the company being investigated or of any of its directors. This very broad power is curtailed only by the need for 'reasonable grounds' before a warrant will be issued. These powers enable a search warrant to be obtained for the purposes of inspections or investigations, ie it is not limited to requests for documents under s 447.

Under sub-s (1), an attempt to obtain the documents will have been made and have failed; in practice, to prevent documents being destroyed or altered, a warrant is likely to be sought in advance under sub-s (2).

As to the difficulties involved where some of the documents concerned may be subject to legal professional privilege, see s 452(1), (2) and *R v Chesterfield Justices, ex p Bramley* [2000] 1 All ER 411.

S 448(7)

As to penalties, see s 730, Sch 24.

449. Provision for security of information obtained

(1)   No information or document relating to a company which has been obtained under section 447 ... shall, without the previous consent in writing of that company, be published or disclosed, except to a competent authority, unless the publication or disclosure is required—

(a) with a view to the institution of or otherwise for the purposes of criminal proceedings;

(ba) with a view to the institution of, or otherwise for the purposes of, any proceedings on an application under section 6, 7 or 8 of the Company Directors Disqualification Act 1986;

(c) for the purposes of enabling or assisting any inspector appointed under this Part, or under section 94 or 177 of the Financial Services Act 1986, to discharge his functions;

(cc) for the purpose of enabling or assisting any person authorised to exercise powers or appointed under section 43A or 44 of the Insurance Companies Act 1982, section 447 of this Act, section 106 of the Financial Services Act 1986 or section 84 of the Companies Act 1989 to discharge his functions;

(d) for the purpose of enabling or assisting the Secretary of State or the Treasury to exercise any of their functions under this Act, the insider dealing legislation, the Prevention of Fraud (Investments) Act 1958, the Insurance Companies Act 1982, the Insolvency Act 1986, the Company Directors Disqualification Act 1986,the Financial Services Act 1986 or Part II, III or VII of the Companies Act 1989,

(dd) for the purpose of enabling or assisting the Department of Economic Development for Northern Ireland to exercise any powers conferred on it by the enactments relating to companies or insolvency or for the purpose of enabling or assisting any inspector appointed by it under the enactments relating to companies to discharge his functions

(de) for the purpose of enabling or assisting the Chief Registrar of friendly societies or the Assistant Registrar of Friendly Societies for Scotland to discharge his functions under the enactments relating to friendly societies;

(df) for the purpose of enabling or assisting the Friendly Societies Commission to discharge its functions under the Financial Services Act 1986;

(dg) for the purpose of enabling or assisting the Occupational Pensions Regulatory Authority to discharge their functions under the Pension Schemes Act 1993 or the Pensions Act 1995 or any enactment in force in Northern Ireland corresponding to either of them;

(e) ...

(f) for the purpose of enabling or assisting the Bank of England to discharge its functions,

(fa) for the purpose of enabling or assisting the Financial Services Authority to discharge—

(i) any functions under the Financial Services Act 1986, other than as a designated agency within the meaning of that Act,

(ii) its functions under the Banking Act 1987, or

(iii) its functions under section 171 of the Companies Act 1989,

(g) for the purpose of enabling or assisting the Deposit Protection Board to discharge its functions under that Act,

(h) for any purpose mentioned in section 180(1)(b),(e),(h),or (n) of the Financial Services Act 1986,

(hh) for the purpose of enabling or assisting a body established by order under section 46 of the Companies Act 1989 to discharge its functions under Part II of that Act, or of enabling or assisting a recognised supervisory or qualifying body within the meaning of that Part to discharge its functions as such;

(i) for the purpose of enabling or assisting the Industrial Assurance Commissioner or the Industrial Assurance Commissioner for Northern Ireland to discharge his functions under the enactments relating to industrial assurance,

(j) ...

(k) for the purpose of enabling or assisting an official receiver to discharge his functions under the enactments relating to insolvency or for the purpose of enabling or assisting a body which is for the time being a recognised professional body for the purposes of section 391 of the Insolvency Act 1986 to discharge its functions as such,

(l) with a view to the institution of, or otherwise for the purposes of, any disciplinary proceedings relating to the exercise by a solicitor, auditor, accountant, valuer or actuary of his professional duties,

(ll) with a view to the institution of, or otherwise for the purposes of, any disciplinary proceedings relating to the discharge by a public servant of his duties;

(m) for the purpose of enabling or assisting an overseas regulatory authority to exercise its regulatory functions.

(1A) In subsection (1)—

(a) in paragraph (ll) 'public servant' means an officer or servant of the Crown or of any public or other authority for the time being designated for the purposes of that paragraph by the Secretary of State by order made by statutory instrument; and

(b) in paragraph (m) 'overseas regulatory authority' and 'regulatory functions' have the same meaning as in section 82 of the Companies Act 1989.

(1B) Subject to subsection (1C), subsection (1) shall not preclude publication or disclosure for the purpose of enabling or assisting any public or other authority for the time being designated for the purposes of this subsection by the Secretary of State by an order in a statutory instrument to discharge any functions which are specified in the order.

(1C) An order under subsection (1B) designating an authority for the purpose of that subsection may—

(a) impose conditions subject to which the publications or disclosure of any information or document is permitted by that subsection; and

(b) otherwise restrict the circumstances in which that subsection permits publication or disclosure.

(1D) Subsection (1) shall not preclude the publication or disclosure of any such information as is mentioned in section 180(5) of the Financial Services Act 1986 by any person who by virtue of that section is not precluded by section 179 of that Act from disclosing it.

(2) A person who publishes or discloses any information or document in contravention of this section is guilty of an offence and liable to imprisonment or a fine, or both.

Sections 732 (restriction on prosecutions), 733 (liability of individuals for corporate default) and 734 (criminal proceedings against unincorporated bodies) apply to this offence.

(3) For the purposes of this section each of the following is a competent authority—

(a) the Secretary of State,

(b) an inspector appointed under this Part or under section 94 or 177 of the Financial Services Act 1986,

(c) any person authorised to exercise powers under section 44 of the Insurance Companies Act 1982, section 447 of this Act, section 106 of the Financial Services Act 1986 or section 84 of the Companies Act 1989,

(d) the Department of Economic Development in Northern Ireland,

(e) the Treasury,

(f) the Bank of England,

(g) the Lord Advocate,

(h) the Director of Public Prosecutions, and the Director of Public

Prosecutions for Northern Ireland,

(ha) the Financial Services Authority, other than in its capacity as a designated agency within the meaning of the Financial Services Act 1986,

(i) any designated agency or transferee body within the meaning of the Financial Services Act 1986, and any body administering a scheme under section 54 of or paragraph 18 of Schedule 11 to that Act (schemes for compensation of investors),

(j) the Chief Registrar of friendly societies ...,

(jj) the Friendly Societies Commission

(k) the Industrial Assurance Commissioner ...,

(l) any constable,

(m) any procurator fiscal,

(n) the Scottish Ministers.

(3A) Any information which may by virtue of this section be disclosed to a competent authority may be disclosed to any officer or servant of the authority.

(4) A statutory instrument containing an order under subsection (1A)(a) or (1B) is subject to annulment in pursuance of a resolution of either House of Parliament.

S 449(1)–(1D)

The wording of this provision obscures the fact that information or documents obtained under these powers may be published or disclosed in a number of ways:

(1) with the previous consent in writing of the company to which it relates, something which is unlikely to occur;

(2) for one of the numerous purposes set out in sub-s (1)(a)–(1)(m), a list of gateways which is in need of updating as many of the references are to legislation and bodies which have been replaced. Essentially, disclosure is permitted for the purposes of the main statutes, and to all the main regulatory bodies, in this area including inspectors appointed under other provisions, the Bank of England, the Financial Services Authority and overseas regulatory bodies. Disclosure is most commonly sought for the purposes of prosecution and disqualification under sub-s (1)(a) and sub-s (1)(ba).

(3) to a competent authority, as listed in sub-s (3).

(4) for the purpose of enabling or assisting any public or other authority so designated by statutory instrument, under sub-s (1B), to discharge its functions. A number of bodies have been designated including the Insolvency Practitioners Tribunal; the Occupational Pensions Regulatory Authority; the Panel on Take-overs and Mergers, the Director General of Fair Trading; the Competition Commission, the Charity Commissioners; the Financial Reporting Review Panel Ltd; and the National Lottery Commission. Some of the designations are restricted for particular purposes (sub-ss(1B), (1C)). The Orders currently in force are the Companies (Disclosure of Information) (Designated Authorities) Order

1988, SI 1988/1334; Financial Services (Disclosure of Information) (Designated Authorities) (No 2) Order 1987, SI 1987/859; (No 3) Order 1987, SI 1987/1141; (No 5) Order 1989, SI 1989/940; (No 6) Order 1989, SI 1989/2009; (No 7) Order 1993, SI 1993/1826; (No 8) Order 1994, SI 1994/340.

(5)   The disclosure permitted by sub-s (1D) will be rendered obsolete by the coming into force of the Financial Services and Markets Act 2000.

S 449(2)

As to penalties, see s 730, Sch 24.

---

450. Punishment for destroying, mutilating etc company documents

(1)   An officer of a company, or of an insurance company to which Part II of the Insurance Companies Act 1982 applies, who—

   (a) destroys, mutilates or falsifies, or is privy to the destruction, mutilation or falsification of a document affecting or relating to the company's property or affairs, or

   (b) makes, or is privy to the making of, a false entry in such a document,

is guilty of an offence, unless he proves that he had no intention to conceal the state of affairs of the company or to defeat the law.

(2)   Such a person as above mentioned who fraudulently either parts with, alters or makes an omission in any such document or is privy to fraudulent parting with, fraudulent altering or fraudulent making of an omission in, any such document, is guilty of an offence.

(3)   A person guilty of an offence under this section is liable to imprisonment or a fine, or both.

(4)   Sections 732 (restriction on prosecutions), 733 (liability of individuals for corporate default) and 734 (criminal proceedings against unincorporated bodies) apply to an offence under this section.

(5)   In this section 'document' includes information recorded in any form.

S 450(1)

An 'officer' of the company is defined in s 744; as to the meaning of 'document', see sub-s (5).

S 450(3)

As to penalties, see s 730, Sch 24.

---

451. Punishment for furnishing false information

A person who, in purported compliance with a requirement imposed under section 447 to provide an explanation or make a statement, provides or makes an explanation or statement which he knows to be false in a material particular or recklessly provides or makes an explanation or statement which is so false, is guilty of an offence and liable to imprisonment or a fine, or both.

Sections 732 (restriction on prosecutions), 733 (liability of individuals for corporate default) and 734 (criminal proceedings against unincorporated bodies) apply to this offence.

General note

As to the nature of the obligation to provide an explanation, see note to s 447(5); as to the right to penalise a person for non-compliance with s 447, see note to s 447(6); as to penalties, see s 730, Sch 24.

451A. Disclosure of information by Secretary of State or inspector

(1) This section applies to information obtained under sections 434 to 446.

(2) The Secretary of State may, if he thinks fit—

   (a) disclose any information to which this section applies to any person to whom, or for any purpose for which, disclosure is permitted under section 449, or

   (b) authorise or require an inspector appointed under this Part to disclose such information to any such person or for any such purpose.

(3) Information to which this section applies may also be disclosed by an inspector appointed under this Part to—

   (a) another inspector appointed under this Part or an inspector appointed under section 94 or 177 of the Financial Services Act 1986, or

   (b) a person authorised to exercise powers or appointed under section 43A or 44 of the Insurance Companies Act 1982, section 447 of this Act, section 106 of the Financial Services Act 1986 or section 84 of the Companies Act 1989.

(4) Any information which may by virtue of subsection (3) be disclosed to any person may be disclosed to any officer or servant of that person.

(5) The Secretary of State may, if he thinks fit, disclose any information obtained under section 444 to—

   (a) the company whose ownership was the subject of the investigation,

   (b) any member of the company,

   (c) any person whose conduct was investigated in the course of the investigation,

   (d) the auditors of the company, or

(e) any person whose financial interests appear to the Secretary of State to be affected by matters covered by the investigation.

General note

This provision applies s 449 (which permits disclosure of information obtained from s 447 investigations) to inspectors operating under ss 434, 442 and 446 and investigators under s 444.

SUPPLEMENTARY

452. Privileged information

(1) Nothing in sections 431 to 446 requires the disclosure to the Secretary of State or to an inspector appointed by him—

(a) by any person of information which he would in an action in the High Court or the Court of Session be entitled to refuse to disclose on grounds of legal professional privilege except, if he is a lawyer, the name and address of his client,

(b) ...

(1A) Nothing in sections 434, 443 or 446 requires a person (except as mentioned in subsection (1B) below) to disclose information or produce documents in respect of which he owes an obligation of confidence by virtue of carrying on the business of banking unless—

(a) the person to whom the obligation of confidence is owed is the company or other body corporate under investigation,

(b) the person to whom the obligation of confidence is owed consents to the disclosure or production, or

(c) the making of the requirement is authorised by the Secretary of State.

(1B) Subsection (1A) does not apply where the person owing the obligation of confidence is the company or other body corporate under investigation under section 431, 432 or 433.

(2) Nothing in sections 447 to 451 compels the production by any person of a document which he would in an action in the High Court or the Court of Session be entitled to refuse to produce on grounds of legal professional privilege, or authorises the taking of possession of any such document which is in the person's possession.

(3) The Secretary of State shall not under section 447 require, or authorise an officer of his or other person to require, the production by a person carrying on the business of banking of a document relating to the affairs of a customer of his unless either it appears to the Secretary of State that it is necessary to do so for the purpose of investigating the affairs of the first-mentioned person, or the

customer is a person on whom a requirement has been imposed under that section, or under section 43A or 44(2) to (4) of the Insurance Companies Act 1982 (provision corresponding to section 447).

S 452(1), (2)

Legal professional privilege   These provisions enable persons to refuse to disclose information to inspectors appointed under ss 432, 442 and 446 and to investigators under s 444, and to refuse to produce documents to investigators under s 447, on the grounds of legal professional privilege. Essentially, legal professional privilege protects oral and written communications between legal advisers and clients, made in confidence, for the purpose of obtaining or giving legal advice. As to the difficulties in executing a search **ent where some of the documents seized may be subject to legal professional privilege, see *R v Chesterfield Justices, ex p Bramley* [2000] 1 All ER 411.

S 452(1A), (1B), (3)

Banking confidentiality   The protection afforded to banking information is limited; in particular, there is no protection for information or documents under these provisions where the person to whom the obligation is owed is the person being investigated or the bank itself is being investigated.

453. Investigation of oversea companies

(1)   The provisions of this Part apply to bodies corporate incorporated outside Great Britain which are carrying on business in Great Britain, or have at any time carried on business there, as they apply to companies under this Act; but subject to the following exceptions, adaptations and modifications.

(1A) The following provisions do not apply to such bodies—

    (a)   section 431 (investigation on application of company or its members),

    (b)   section 438 (power to bring civil proceedings on the company's behalf),

    (c)   sections 442 to 445 (investigation of company ownership and power to obtain information as to those interested in shares,&c), and

    (d)   section 446 (investigation of share dealings).

(1B) The other provisions of this Part apply to such bodies subject to such adaptations and modifications as may be specified by regulations made by the Secretary of State.

(2)   Regulations under this section shall be made by statutory instrument subject to annulment in pursuance of a resolution of either House of Parliament.

S 453(1), (1A)

While sub-s (1A) excludes the operation of a number of provisions of this Part with respect to oversea companies, the main inspection powers under s 432 and investigation powers under s 447 do apply to such companies.

Definition of oversea companies   The definition of oversea companies for the purposes of this provision differs from the categorisations adopted with respect to oversea companies generally by Part XXIII. That Part provides two regimes depending on whether the oversea company has established a place of business or a branch here. The requirement under this provision is simply that the oversea company is 'carrying on business' here which embraces a wider range of conduct and would extend to companies conducting business on an occasional basis or using agents where their presence does not involve having a branch or establishing a place of business.

PART XV

ORDERS IMPOSING RESTRICTIONS ON SHARES (SECTIONS 210, 216, 445)

454. Consequence of order imposing restrictions

(1) So long as any shares are directed to be subject to the restrictions of this Part then, subject to any directions made in relation to an order pursuant to sections 210(5A), 216(1B), 445(1A) or 456(1A) or subject in the case of an interim order pursuant to section 216(1A) to the terms of that order—

- (a) any transfer of those shares or, in the case of unissued shares, any transfer of the right to be issued with them, and any issue of them, is void;
- (b) no voting rights are exercisable in respect of the shares;
- (c) no further shares shall be issued in right of them or in pursuance of any offer made to their holder; and
- (d) except in a liquidation, no payment shall be made of any sums due from the company on the shares, whether in respect of capital or otherwise.

(2) Where shares are subject to the restrictions of subsection (1)(a), any agreement to transfer the shares or, in the case of unissued shares, the right to be issued with them is void (except such agreement or right as may be made or exercised under the terms of directions made by the Secretary of State or the court under section 210(5A), 216(1B), 445(1A), 456(1A) or of an interim order made under section 216(1A) or an agreement to transfer the shares on the making of an order under section 456(3)(b) below).

(3) Where shares are subject to the restrictions of subsection (1)(c) or (d), an agreement to transfer any right to be issued with other shares in right of those shares, or to receive any payment on them (otherwise than in a liquidation) is void (except such agreement or right as may be made or exercised under the terms of directions made by the Secretary of State or the court under sections 210(5A), 216(1B), 445(1A), 456(1A) or of an interim order made under section 216(1A) or an agreement to transfer any such right on the transfer of the shares on the making of an order under section 456(3)(b) below).

General note

As to the circumstances in which an order imposing restrictions may be made, see s 210, 216, 445.

Restriction orders under Part XV are granted as a sanction to compel the provision of information to which the company is entitled under the specified provisions but such orders are not to be used as weapons to gain a temporary advantage over an opponent in a contested takeover bid: see *Re Ricardo Group plc* [1989] BCLC 566.

Position of third parties The operation of Part XV was modified by regulations made under the CA 1989, s 135(4), the Companies (Disclosure of Interests in Shares) (Orders imposing restrictions on shares) Regulations 1991, SI 1991/1646, in order to prevent any restrictions imposed from unfairly affecting third parties, such as chargees with security interests in the shares in question. Such chargees would wish to retain the ability to realise their security and to continue receiving dividends to service the loans, see *Re Lonrho plc (No 3)* [1989] BCLC 480.

This Part, in its application to orders made under s 445, applies to debentures as well as shares: see s 445(2).

S 454(1)

The order imposing the restrictions should specify, if possible, the precise shares which are the subject of the restrictions: see *Re Ricardo Group plc* [1989] BCLC 566 at 578; an order directing that the shares be subject to restrictions may be made by the Secretary of State under ss 210 and 445 and by the court under s 216.

Any order imposing restrictions, despite some ambiguity in the wording of sub-s (2) and (3), must impose all of the restrictions in sub-s (1): see *Re Lonrho plc (No 4)* [1990] BCLC 151; subject to any modifications made to prevent third parties from being unfairly affected.

The words 'payment ... of any sums due from the company' in sub-s (1)(d) are not limited to payment of dividends or of capital on a reduction of capital or on redemption of shares but extend to any payment in respect of the shares: *Re Ashbourne Investments Ltd* [1978] 2 All ER 418.

S 454(2), (3)

These anti-avoidance provisions extend the reach of sub-s (1)(a), (c) and (d) to certain agreements.

---

455. Punishment for attempted evasion of restrictions

(1)   Subject to the terms of any directions made under sections 210(5A), 216(1B), 445(1A) or 456 or of an interim order made under section 216(1A) a person is liable to a fine if he—

   (a)   exercises or purports to exercise any right to dispose of any shares which, to his knowledge, are for the time being subject to the restrictions of this Part or of any right to be issued with any such shares, or

   (b)   votes in respect of any such shares (whether as holder or proxy), or appoints a proxy to vote in respect of them, or

   (c)   being the holder of any such shares, fails to notify of their being subject to those restrictions any person whom he does not know to be aware of that fact but does know to be entitled (apart from the restrictions) to vote in respect of those shares whether as holder or as proxy, or

   (d)   being the holder of any such shares, or being entitled to any right to be issued with other shares in right of them, or to receive any payment on them (otherwise than in a liquidation), enters into any agreement which is void under section 454(2) or (3).

(2)   Subject to the terms of any directions made under sections 210(5A), 216(1B), 445(1A) or 456 or of an interim order made under section 216(1A) if shares in a company are issued in contravention of the restrictions, the company and every officer of it who is in default is liable to a fine.

(3)   Section 732 (restriction on prosecutions) applies to an offence under this section.

S 455(1), (2)

This provision is subject to any directions under the specified provisions which might be made in order to protect a third party.

S 455(2)

As to penalties, see s 730, Sch 24; 'officer in default' is defined in s 730(5).

456. Relaxation and removal of restrictions

(1)   Where shares in a company are by order made subject to the restrictions of this Part, application may be made to the court for an order directing that the shares be no longer so subject.

(1A) Where the court is satisfied that an order subjecting the shares to the restrictions of this Part unfairly affects the rights of third parties in respect of shares then the court, for the purpose of protecting such rights and subject to such terms as it thinks fit and in addition to any order it may make under subsection (1), may direct on an application made under that subsection that such acts by such persons or descriptions of persons and for such purposes, as may be set out in the order, shall not constitute a breach of the restrictions of Part XV of this Act.

Subsection (3) does not apply to an order made under this subsection.

(2)   If the order applying the restrictions was made by the Secretary of State, or he has refused to make an order disapplying them, the application may be made by any person aggrieved; and if the order was made by the court under section 216 (non-disclosure of share holding), it may be made by any such person or by the company.

(3)   Subject as follows, an order of the court or the Secretary of State directing that shares shall cease to be subject to the restrictions may be made only if—

    (a)   the court or (as the case may be) the Secretary of State is satisfied that the relevant facts about the shares have been disclosed to the company and no unfair advantage has accrued to any person as a result of the earlier failure to make that disclosure, or

    (b)   the shares are to be transferred for valuable consideration and the court (in any case) or the Secretary of State (if the order was made under section 210 or 445) approves the transfer.

(4)   Without prejudice to the power of the court to give directions under subsection (1A), where shares in a company are subject to the restrictions, the court may on application order the shares to be sold, subject to the court's

approval as to the sale, and may also direct that the shares shall cease to be subject to the restrictions.

An application to the court under this subsection may be made by the Secretary of State (unless the restrictions were imposed by court order under section 216), or by the company.

(5) Where an order has been made under subsection (4), the court may on application make such further order relating to the sale or transfer of the shares as it thinks fit.

An application to the court under this subsection may be made—

(a) by the Secretary of State (unless the restrictions on the shares were imposed by court order under section 216), or

(b) by the company, or

(c) by the person appointed by or in pursuance of the order to effect the sale, or

(d) by any person interested in the shares.

(6) An order (whether of the Secretary of State or the court) directing that shares shall cease to be subject to the restrictions of this Part, if it is—

(a) expressed to be made with a view to permitting a transfer of the shares, or

(b) made under subsection (4) of this section,

may continue the restrictions mentioned in paragraphs (c) and (d) of section 454(1), either in whole or in part, so far as they relate to any right acquired or offer made before the transfer.

(7) Subsection (3) does not apply to an order directing that shares shall cease to be subject to any restrictions which have been continued in force in relation to those shares under subsection (6).

General note

This somewhat convoluted provision identifies various methods by which restrictions imposed by the Secretary of State or the court may be relaxed or removed.

Restrictions imposed by the Secretary of State   Where the restrictions were imposed by the Secretary of State by order under ss 210 and 445, he may remove those restrictions by further order, subject to sub-s (3); and see sub-s (6). Alternatively, any aggrieved party may go to the court to seek their removal (and he will be compelled to go to court where the Secretary of State refuses to remove the restrictions) and the court's discretion is subject to sub-s (3).

Restrictions imposed by the court   Where the restrictions were imposed by the court under s 216, an application has to be made to the court for their removal and the court's discretion is subject to sub-s (3).

Application for the shares to be sold   Another possibility is that an application may be made to the court by the Secretary of State or the company (ie by the persons who imposed or sought the imposition of the restrictions in the first place) for an order directing that the shares be sold and that application is governed by sub-s (4).

S 456(1A)

This provision was inserted by the Companies (Disclosure of Interests in Shares) (Orders imposing restrictions on shares) Regulations 1991, SI 1991/1646, made under CA 1989, s 134(5), to protect third parties. The court in lifting restrictions to assist third parties is not constrained by the requirements of sub-s (3).

S 456(2)

Where the Secretary of State has imposed the restrictions (under either s 210 or s 445), any aggrieved person may apply to the court; the application in most cases would be by the registered holder of the shares but it could be by the beneficial owners who have come forward.

Where the court has imposed the restrictions under s 216 (following an application by the company), any aggrieved party or the company can apply to have the restrictions lifted.

S 456(3), (6)

Lifting the restrictions   The restrictions may be lifted in two circumstances: (i) because the information has been disclosed (sub-s (3)(a)) or (ii) because the shares are to be transferred for valuable consideration (sub-s (3)(b)).

Subsection (3)(a) empowers the court to free shares subject to a restriction but it does not require it to do so, and it may not do so where it appears that the person applying to have a restriction lifted has not disclosed information reasonably required in relation to other shares of the company: see *Re Lonrho plc* [1988] BCLC 53.

Although sub-s (3)(b) does not specifically state that the information must have been disclosed etc, the court must approve the fact of the transfer as well as the terms and in deciding whether to approve the fact of the transfer, the court can take into account any failure to disclose the relevant facts about the shares: see *Re Geers Gross plc* [1988] BCLC 140.

The wording of this provision ('transferred for valuable consideration') was inserted by CA 1989, s 145, Sch 19, para 10(1) in place of the previous requirement ('the share are to be sold') which the court had interpreted in *Re Westminster Property Group plc* [1985] BCLC 188 as requiring that the shares be sold for cash so that the court could not approve a transfer of shares for a non-cash consideration; the current wording would permit the court now to approve such a transfer.

The requirements of sub-s (3) only apply to the final order of the court and not to orders made at an interlocutory stage although the sub-section shows the type of circumstances requiring the maintenance of any restriction: see *Re T R Technology Investment Trust plc* [1988] BCLC 256.

If the order under this provision is expressed to be made with a view to permitting the transfer of the shares, sub-s (6) applies.

S 456(4)–(7)

Application for the shares to be sold   This provision entitles the Secretary of State (where the restrictions have been imposed by his order) or the company (where the restrictions were imposed by the court on the application of the company under s 216) to seek an order directing that the shares be sold. See s 457(3) as to the costs of the application.

In this case, the application is not concerned with freeing the shares from the restrictions, rather the parties who imposed or sought the imposition of the restrictions are seeking to exert maximum pressure on those interested in the shares by selling them. The sale must be for a cash consideration: *Re Westminster Property Group plc* [1985] BCLC 188. See s 457 which makes further provision with respect to any sale of the shares.

In *Re Westminster Property Group plc* [1985] BCLC 188, the court doubted whether an order under this provision could, or should, be made where the shares in question were the subject of a pre-existing contract entered into prior to the restrictions being imposed, save with the consent of the contracting parties or in other very exceptional circumstances. In such a case, the proper procedure would be to apply for the restrictions to be lifted under sub-s (3)(b), ie to have the court approve the transfer of the shares.

The effect of sub-s (6) is that, if the sale is ordered under sub-s (4), the restrictions of s 454(1)(c), (d) with regard to accrued rights to additional shares or payments could be continued while permitting the transfer of the shares. The operation of the provision can be seen in *Re Ashbourne Investments Ltd* [1978] 2 All ER 418 where shares subject to a restriction were freed from the restrictions to enable a take-over bidder to secure 100% control but subject to the continuation of the restrictions to the extent permitted by sub-s (6). The effect was that the shares of a holder who had not disclosed his identity were ordered to be transferred to the bidder but the continuation of restrictions under sub-s (6) meant that the holder was unable to receive the payment of the take-over price for the shares (being a sum due on the shares under s 454(1)(d)) which would be held on account for him. A relaxation or removal of those continued restrictions is not subject to sub-s (3): sub-s (7).

457. Further provisions on sale by court order of restricted shares

(1)   Where shares are sold in pursuance of an order of the court under section 456(4) the proceeds of sale, less the costs of the sale, shall be paid into court for the benefit of the persons who are beneficially interested in the shares; and any such person may apply to the court for the whole or part of those proceeds to be paid to him.

(2)   On application under subsection (1) the court shall (subject as provided below) order the payment to the applicant of the whole of the proceeds of sale together with any interest thereon or, if any other person had a beneficial interest in the shares at the time of their sale, such proportion of those proceeds and interest as is equal to the proportion which the value of the applicant's interest in the shares bears to the total value of the shares.

(3)   On granting an application for an order under section 456(4) or (5) the court may order that the applicant's costs be paid out of the proceeds of sale; and if that order is made, the applicant is entitled to payment of his costs out of those proceeds before any person interested in the shares in question receives any part of those proceeds.

General note

See note to s 456(4) with respect to court ordered sales of shares.

S 457(1), (3)

It is for those beneficially interested in the shares to apply to the court for payment of the proceeds of sale; to allow the registered holder to apply would defeat the purpose of imposing restrictions in the first place. A further sanction, in effect, is the ability of the court under sub-s (3) to order that the applicant for the order for sale of the shares may recover his costs out of the proceeds of sale and ahead of any claim by the beneficial owner.

PART XVI

FRAUDULENT TRADING BY A COMPANY

458. Punishment for fraudulent trading

If any business of a company is carried on with intent to defraud creditors of the company or creditors of any other person, or for any fraudulent purpose, every person who was knowingly a party to the carrying on of the business in that manner is liable to imprisonment or a fine, or both.

This applies whether or not the company has been, or is in the course of being, wound up.

General note

Criminal and civil liability   There are two aspects to fraudulent trading: (1) the criminal offence contained in this provision; and (2) an identically worded provision imposing a civil liability in IA 1986, s 213. That provision enables a liquidator, when the company is in the course of winding up, to apply to the court for a declaration that any persons knowingly party to the carrying on of the business with an intent to defraud in this manner are liable to make such contribution to the company's assets as the court thinks proper. IA 1986, s 213 has been rendered redundant by IA 1986, s 214 (wrongful trading) which enables a liquidator to seek a similar declaration but without any need to establish any dishonest intent. As the sections apply to the same persons and are expressed in identical terms, authorities on s 458 can be applied to s 213 and vice versa.

As to possible disqualification for fraudulent trading, see Company Directors Disqualification Act 1986, ss 4, 10.

Carrying on any business   The requirement that the company 'carry on any business' is not necessarily synonymous with actively carrying on trade and the collection of assets acquired in the course of business and the distribution of the proceeds of those assets in the discharge of business liabilities can constitute the carrying on of any business for these purposes: *Re Sarflax Ltd* [1979] 1 All ER 529; equally, a single transaction designed to defraud a single creditor will suffice for these purposes: *Re Gerald Cooper Chemicals Ltd* [1978] 2 All ER 49; see also *R v Lockwood* [1986] Crim LR 244, CA. The company must be a 'company' within the meaning in s 735 – essentially a company formed and registered under this and previous Companies Acts so it will not extend to an oversea company carrying on business in this way in this jurisdiction.

Defraud creditors or others   The central requirement is that the business of the company has been carried on with intent to defraud creditors of the company, or creditors of any other person, or for any fraudulent purpose. The word 'creditor', in its ordinary meaning, denotes one to whom money is owed; whether that debt can presently be sued for is immaterial: *R v Smith* [1996] 2 BCLC 109, CA. The provision is not limited to defrauding creditors and the expression 'for any fraudulent purpose' is not to be construed ejusdem generis with the preceding clauses but can encompass any fraudulent trading (see *R v Kemp* [1988] QB 645, CA); including, for example, defrauding HM Customs and Excise: see *Re L Todd Swanscomb Ltd* [1990] BCLC 454.

Some examples   Offences of fraudulent trading cover a wide spectrum of matters. At one extreme, there may have been deliberate reckless trading on a large scale aimed at a rapid return, with no genuine intention to discharge the company's debts. At the other extreme, there may have been a properly funded business which ran into financial difficulties out of which the directors attempt to trade in order to save their own and their employees' jobs, but reach a point where they become reckless as to the reality: see *R v Smith and Palk* [1997] 2 Cr App R (S) 167, CA. Probably the most typical illustrations of fraudulent trading involve companies obtaining payments from customers for goods knowing they cannot supply the goods and will not repay the money (see *Re Gerald Cooper Chemicals Ltd* [1978] 2 All ER 49); and companies incurring debts at a time when the directors have no good reason for thinking that funds will be available to pay those debts when they became due or shortly thereafter: see *R v Grantham* [1984] 3 All ER 166, CA; see also *Re a company (No 001418 of 1988)* [1991] BCLC 197.

Dishonesty   Dishonesty is an essential ingredient of the offence: *R v Cox, R v Hodges* [1983] BCLC 169. It is not enough to show that the company has continued to trade while insolvent (although such conduct may give rise to liability for wrongful trading, see IA 1986, s 214), the conduct must '... involve actual dishonesty, involving, according to current notions of fair trading among commercial men, real moral blame': *Re Patrick and Lyon Ltd* [1933] Ch 786 at 790, per Maugham J. In considering dishonesty for the purposes of fraudulent trading, it is correct to apply the *Ghosh* test which is of general application: *R v Lockwood* [1986] Crim LR 244, CA; *R v Ghosh* [1982] 2 All ER 689.

Dishonesty will clearly be made out when directors allow a company to incur credit when they have no reason to think the creditors will ever be paid: *Re William C Leitch Bros Ltd* [1932] 2 Ch 71. Equally, it is dishonest to continue to incur debts at a time when the directors have no good reason for thinking that funds will be available to pay those debts when they became due or shortly thereafter: *R v Grantham* [1984] 3 All ER 166, CA; see also *Re a company (No 001418 of 1988)* [1991] BCLC 197.

It is not per se fraudulent for a debtor, knowing or having good grounds to suspect that he cannot pay all his creditors in full, to pay some but not the others; the bare fact of a preference, without more, is not sufficient to constitute fraudulent trading for these purposes: *Re Sarflax Ltd* [1979] 1 All ER 529.

Persons party to the carrying on of the business   The provision is designed to include those exercising a controlling or managerial function over a company, or those who are 'running the business' (*R v Miles* [1992] Crim LR 657); and it encompasses, clearly, the company's directors as persons who are knowingly party to the carrying on of the business in this way. It must be shown that the person took some positive steps in the carrying on of the company's business in a fraudulent manner; and a person performing the duties appropriate to the office of secretary is not within the provision although a person who holds the office of secretary may in some other capacity be concerned in the management of the company's business: see *Re Maidstone Buildings Provisions Ltd* [1971] 3 All ER 363 at 368. An employee of the company merely carrying out orders is not a person who is a party to the carrying on of the business (*R v Miles* [1992] Crim LR 657); but someone who orchestrates, organises or can seize control of the business concerned would be within the provision: *Re BCCI, Banque Arabe v Morris* [2001] 1 BCLC 263.

The provision is not limited, however, to those who perform a managerial or controlling role within the company concerned or who actually direct or manage the business. It extends to third parties who are not employed by the company at all; and a company which is involved in, and assists and benefits from, the offending business, or the business carried on in an offending way, and does so knowingly and, therefore dishonestly, does fall or at least can fall within the provision: *Re BCCI, Banque Arabe v Morris* [2001] 1 BCLC 263.

A creditor is party to the carrying on of a business with intent to defraud creditors if he accepts money which he knows full well has in fact been procured by carrying on the business with intent to defraud creditors for the very purpose of making the payment: *Re Gerald Cooper Chemicals Ltd* [1978] 2 All ER 49; and see *Re Augustus Barnett & Son Ltd* [1986] BCLC 170 at 173.

No need for winding up   CA 1981, s 96 amended the provision, as reflected in the final sentence, to remove a bar which had previously existed which required the company to be in winding up before criminal proceedings could be instituted.

Penalties   As to penalties, see s 730, Sch 24.

PART XVII
PROTECTION OF COMPANY'S MEMBERS AGAINST UNFAIR PREJUDICE

459. Order on application of company member

(1)   A member of a company may apply to the court by petition for an order under this Part on the ground that the company's affairs are being or have been conducted in a manner which is unfairly prejudicial to the interests of its members generally or of some part of its members (including at least himself) or that any actual or proposed act or omission of the company (including an act or omission on its behalf) is or would be so prejudicial.

(2)   The provisions of this Part apply to a person who is not a member of a company but to whom shares in the company have been transferred or transmitted by operation of law, as those provisions apply to a member of the company; and references to a member or members are to be construed accordingly.

(3)   In this section (and so far as applicable for the purposes of this section, in section 461(2)) 'company' means any company within the meaning of this Act or any company which is not such a company but is a statutory water company within the meaning of the Statutory Water Companies Act 1991.

General note

This provision, introduced by CA 1980, s 75 and subsequently amended by CA 1989, s 145, Sch 19, para 11, is intended essentially to provide a remedy for minority shareholders whose interests are unfairly prejudiced by the manner in which the company's affairs are being conducted.

The section provides a broad discretionary jurisdiction which has given rise to a great deal of litigation, much of it characterised by lengthy examinations of a company's history and the personal relationships between the shareholders in an attempt to establish whether there has been conduct which is unfairly prejudicial to the petitioner's interests. Where unfairly prejudicial conduct is established, the remedy most commonly sought is an order under s 461(2)(d) that the petitioner's shares be bought by the respondents. That issue too has been the subject of lengthy hearings as to who should conduct the valuation and the basis of the valuation.

Case management   In the light of the nature of this litigation, the case management powers under the Civil Procedure Rules 1998, SI 1998/3132, will have a significant role to play to enable petitions to come on for trial efficiently, quickly and as inexpensively as possible: see *North Holdings Ltd v Southern Tropics Ltd* [1999] 2 BCLC 625 at 638. The duty on the court to manage cases actively and on the parties to agree as much as possible with a view to avoiding the necessity of going to court was emphasised in *Re Rotadata Ltd* [2000] 1 BCLC 122, where Neuberger J thought that there would be a great deal to be said for the registrar to consider giving directions requiring the parties and/or their advisers to meet with a view to narrowing the issues, identifying what issues are really important, what issues are really in dispute, how those issues are to be resolved or proved, and resolving and narrowing any other matters which in the context of the particular petition could reasonably be expected to be narrowed (at 127). See too *West v Blanchet* [2000] 1 BCLC 795 at 798.

S 459(1), (2)

Petition by a member   As to membership of a company, see s 22. The definition of member is extended by sub-s (2) to include those to whom shares have been transferred or transmitted by operation of law. For these purposes, 'transferred' requires at least that a proper instrument of transfer should have been executed and delivered to the transferee or the company and an agreement to transfer is insufficient: *Re Quickdome Ltd* [1988] BCLC 370; *Re a Company (No 00316 of 1986)* [1986] BCLC 391. Transmission by operation of law will occur on death or bankruptcy so permitting petitions by personal representatives or a trustee in bankruptcy. The existence of an alleged constructive trust over shares does not amount to a transmission by operation of law: *Re a Company (No 007828 of 1985)* (1985) 2 BCC 98, 951.

While the section does not preclude a petition by a majority shareholder, the court would normally expect such a petitioner to exercise its control as a majority shareholder to terminate any unfairly prejudicial conduct which is occurring (for example, by altering the composition of the board) and not to seek court assistance: *Re Legal Costs Negotiators Ltd* [1999] 2 BCLC 171, CA; see also *Re Baltic Real Estate Ltd (No 2)* [1993] BCLC 503.

Respondents   The company is made a respondent to the petition as a matter of course: Companies (Unfair Prejudice Applications) Proceedings Rules 1986, SI 1986/2000, r 4(1). The company may be affected by the petition in a number of ways, the disclosure of documents may be called for and the company may be affected by the relief ordered, such as an order that the company purchase the petitioner's shares: see *Re a Company (No 004502 of 1988), ex p Johnson* [1992] BCLC 701 at 703.

While the company may passively participate in a s 459 petition to the extent noted above, and properly incur costs in so doing, a company's active participation in a petition normally cannot be justified, it being a dispute amongst shareholders. While there is no rule that necessarily and in all cases active participation and expenditure is improper, there is a heavy onus on a company which has so actively participated or has so incurred costs to satisfy the court with evidence of the necessity or expedience in the particular case: *Re a Company (No 001126 of 1992)* [1994] 2 BCLC 146.

As a matter of practice, in a small private company every member ought to be joined as a respondent, although in certain circumstances, such as where the rights of the members would not be affected by any order made, it might be appropriate not to join all the members: *Re a Company (No 007281 of 1986)* [1987] BCLC 593.

Petition to the court   The procedure in the case of s 459 petitions is governed by the Companies (Unfair Prejudice Applications) Proceedings Rules 1986, SI 1986/2000. The court in this instance means the court having jurisdiction to wind up the company (s 744); which in turn is determined by IA 1986, s 117, as the High Court or, in some circumstances, the County Court.

There can be no advertisement of the petition without a court direction to that effect: Companies (Unfair Prejudice Applications) Proceedings Rules 1986, SI 1986/2000, r 5(c); and where the court has not made any direction, any notification to a third party of the existence of the petition is a breach of the spirit of the rules and an abuse of process of the Companies Court. In deciding the appropriate response to such abuse, the court will consider a number of factors. Where the abuse is serious, as where the notification was for some improper purpose such as to bring pressure to bear on the company, the court will be very ready to strike out the petition: see *Re a Company (No 002015 of 1996)* [1997] 2 BCLC 1 at 24.

Interlocutory relief   The court has jurisdiction to grant interlocutory relief, especially if it is to maintain the status quo or to ensure that the relief that might ultimately be granted is not rendered nugatory: *Re X Ltd* (2001) Times, 5 June, Ch D.

Clean hands   There is no independent requirement that it should be just and equitable to grant relief or that the petitioner should come with clean hands:

Re London School of Electronics Ltd [1985] BCLC 273. However, the conduct of the petitioner may be relevant in a number of ways: as where the conduct complained of is found to be prejudicial but not unfair in the light of the petitioner's conduct: *Re R A Noble & Sons (Clothing) Ltd* [1983] BCLC 273 (exclusion from participation not unfair in view of the petitioner's disinterest in the business); or it may affect the relief granted by the court: *Re London School of Electronics Ltd* [1985] BCLC 273.

Company's affairs are being or have been conducted   The conduct complained of must relate to the conduct of the affairs of the company. The section is concerned with acts done by the company or those authorised to act as its organs and a remedy is not available where the conduct complained of is merely that of an individual shareholder acting in a personal capacity: *Re Legal Costs Negotiators Ltd* [1999] 2 BCLC 171; see also *Re Saul D Harrison & Sons* plc [1995] 1 BCLC 14, CA; *Re a Company (No 005685 of 1988), ex p Schwarcz (No 2)* [1989] BCLC 427 at 437. See *Re Unisoft Group Ltd (No 3)* [1994] 1 BCLC 609 (allegations concerning the activities of shareholders and an alleged breach of a shareholders' agreement do not constitute conduct of the affairs of the company); *Re Leeds United Holdings plc* [1996] 2 BCLC 545 (a dispute as to an agreement between shareholders over the sale of their shares does not relate to the company's affairs); *Arrow Nominees Inc v Blackledge* [2000] 2 BCLC 167 (allegations, even if established, related to majority's conduct as a supplier or lender to the company and did not relate to the conduct of the company's affairs by the majority).

Past conduct is clearly encompassed, even if remedied by the date of the petition or the date of the hearing: *Re Kenyon Swansea Ltd* [1987] BCLC 514; but only if the conduct could recur: *Re Legal Costs Negotiators Ltd* [1999] 2 BCLC 171. If the remedying of the unfairness is carried out in such a way that the objectionable conduct cannot recur, there is no scope for the court to give relief under s 461 in respect of the matter complained of and the petition may be struck out: *Re Legal Costs Negotiators Ltd* [1999] 2 BCLC 171 at 196; *Re Hailey Group Ltd* [1993] BCLC 459. Of course, with respect to past conduct, unreasonably delay in pursuing the petition may bar relief: *Re a Company (No 005134 of 1986), ex p Harries* [1989] BCLC 383.

Threatened future conduct is included: *Re Kenyon Swansea Ltd* [1987] BCLC 514; *Re a Company (No 00314 of 1989), ex p Estate Acquisition and Development Ltd* [1991] BCLC 154. But the petition must not be premature: see *Re Astec (BSR) plc* [1998] 2 BCLC 556 at 577–578; *Re a Company (No 005685 of 1988), ex p Schwarcz (No 2)* [1989] BCLC 427 at 451.

The interests of the members as members   The focus of the provision is on conduct which is unfairly prejudicial to the interests of the members as members: *Re a Company (No 004475 of 1982)* [1983] 2 All ER 36 at 44; *Re a Company (No 005685 of 1988), ex p Schwarcz (No 2)* [1989] BCLC 427; *Re a Company (No 00314 of 1989), ex p Estate Acquisition and Development Ltd* [1991] BCLC 154; as opposed to any other interests which the member might possess: see *Re a Company (No 003843 of 1986)* [1987] BCLC 562 (petitioner complained in capacity as a creditor or consultant pursuant to a contract with the company); *Re J E Cade & Son Ltd* [1992] BCLC 213 (petitioner protecting his interests as a freeholder of a farm, not as a member of the company); *Re Unisoft Group Ltd (No 3)* [1994] 1 BCLC 609 at 626 (allegations concerned relationship of the parties as landlord and tenant).

However, the requirement that the prejudice must be suffered as a member must not be too narrowly or technically construed: *O'Neill v Phillips* [1999] 2 BCLC 1 at 15; *R & H Electric Ltd v Haden Bill Electrical Ltd* [1995] 2 BCLC 280. Where the terms on which a person became or continues as a member include his participation in the management of the company, his removal as a director is a prejudice suffered in his capacity as a member: *O'Neill v Phillips* [1999] 2 BCLC 1 at 14.

Conduct which is unfairly prejudicial to those interests   The question whether the company's affairs are being or have been conducted in a manner which is unfairly prejudicial to the interests of the members must be judged on an objective basis: *Re Macro (Ipswich) Ltd* [1994] 2 BCLC 354 at 404; *Re Little Olympian Each-Ways Ltd (No 3)* [1995] 1 BCLC 636; *Re R A Noble & Sons (Clothing) Ltd* [1983] BCLC 273.

There are two elements to the requirement of unfair prejudice: the conduct complained of must be prejudicial in the sense of causing prejudice or harm to the relevant interest of the members or some part of the members and also unfairly so: conduct may be unfair without being prejudicial; or prejudicial without being unfair and it is not sufficient if the conduct satisfies only one of these tests: *Re Saul D Harrison & Sons plc* [1995] 1 BCLC 14, CA; *Re a Company (No 005685 of 1988), ex p Schwarcz (No 2)* [1989] BCLC 427 at 437; *Re R A Noble & Sons (Clothing) Ltd* [1983] BCLC 273; *Nicholas v Soundcraft Electronics Ltd* [1993] BCLC 360.

The decision in *O'Neill v Phillips*   The nature of the conduct required to establish the court's jurisdiction under s 459 was reviewed by the House of Lords in *O'Neill v Phillips* [1999] 2 BCLC 1, where Lord Hoffmann emphasised that the central criterion is fairness but it is fairness in the context of a commercial relationship carried on by persons within a company, as he had previously noted in *Re Saul D Harrison & Sons plc* [1995] 1 BCLC 14 at 17.

A member will not ordinarily be entitled to complain of unfairness, therefore, unless there has been:

(1)   a breach of the terms on which he had agreed that the affairs of the company should be conducted (ie an abuse by directors of their powers or an infringement of the member's rights under the constitution or the companies legislation); or

(2)   a use of the rules in a manner which equity would regard as contrary to good faith (ie where equitable considerations have arisen which make it unfair for those conducting the affairs of the company to rely upon their strict legal powers).

This decision has been criticised as unduly narrowing the scope of the provision but it is consistent with the line of authorities in this area since the landmark decision in *Ebrahimi v Westbourne Galleries Ltd* [1973] AC 360 and see, more recently, *Re Saul D Harrison & Sons plc* [1995] 1 BCLC 14. What the decision has done is to reject the concept of 'legitimate expectations' as a basis on which these petitions might be brought. That term had been used originally as a shorthand for the concept encompassed by (2) above, but those roots to that term had come to be ignored such that the concept of 'legitimate expectations' had begun erroneously to take on a life of its own and was relied on increasingly by parties as the basis for their petition under s 459. It is that expansion to the scope of the section which is decisively and correctly rejected by the House of Lords in *O'Neill v Phillips* [1999] 2 BCLC 1.

The first ground – a breach of the terms   The first ground identified in *O'Neill* is that there has been some breach of the terms on which the affairs of the company should be conducted – ie an abuse by directors of their powers or an infringement of the member's rights under the constitution or the companies legislation.

The starting point is to ask whether the conduct of which the member complains is in accordance with the articles and the powers which the members have entrusted to the board. If it is, a petitioner cannot complain; even if it is not, it may not necessarily be unfairly prejudicial. For example, trivial or technical infringements of the articles will not give rise to relief: *Re Saul D Harrison & Sons plc* [1995] 1 BCLC 14; nor will breaches of directors' duties which do not result in any unfair prejudice: *Re BSB Holdings Ltd (No 2)* [1996] 1 BCLC 155; *Re Blackwood Hodge plc* [1997] 2 BCLC 650.

Some illustrations   The following examples illustrate the types of complaint which may amount to unfairly prejudicial conduct on this basis:

(1)   **Diversion of corporate property** and misapplication of the company's assets by those in control of the company's affairs for their own benefit: see *Re Brenfield Squash Racquets Club* [1996] 2 BCLC 184; *Re Little Olympian Each-Ways Ltd (No 3)* [1995] 1 BCLC 636; *Re Full Cup International Trading Ltd* [1995] BCC 682, aff'd *sub nom Antoniades v Wong* [1997] 2 BCLC 419, CA; *Re Elgindata Ltd* [1991] BCLC 959.

(2)   **Abuse of power** including allotments, or proposed, allotments of shares for an improper purpose and improper calls on shares: see *Re a Company (No 005134 of 1986), ex p Harries* [1989] BCLC 383; *Re Hailey Group Ltd* [1993] BCLC 459; *Re Regional Airports Ltd* [1999] 2 BCLC 30.

(3)   **Mismanagement** – The court will normally be very reluctant to accept that managerial decisions can amount to unfairly prejudicial conduct: see *Re Elgindata Ltd* [1991] BCLC 959 at 993–994; *Re Saul D Harrison & Sons plc* [1995] 1 BCLC 14, CA; although it did so in *Re Macro (Ipswich) Ltd* [1994] 2 BCLC 354, where it was possible to identify acts of serious mismanagement repeated over many years causing actual financial loss to the company.

(4)   **Breach of the members' statutory rights**, such as repeated failures to hold annual general meetings and to lay accounts before the members (see *Re a Company (No 00789 of 1987), ex p Shooter* [1990] BCLC 384), or breach of the statutory pre-emption requirements: see *Re a Company (No 005134 of 1986), ex p Harries* [1989] BCLC 383.

Frequently, the court will be faced with complaints on a number of these grounds and, in addition to the specific complaints, the court will look at the cumulative effect of the conduct complained of.

The second ground – equitable considerations have arisen   The second ground identified in *O'Neill v Phillips* [1999] 2 BCLC 1 on which a petition might be based, is that there has been a use of the rules in a manner which equity would regard as contrary to good faith – ie where equitable considerations have arisen which make it unfair for those conducting the affairs of the company to rely upon their strict legal powers. An initial issue, then, is to identify the circumstances in which equitable considerations will come into play.

The type of company which will typically give rise to such equitable constraints on the exercise of legal powers will be a company which has one, or probably more, of the characteristics identified by Lord Wilberforce in *Ebrahimi v Westbourne Galleries Ltd* [1972] 2 All ER 492 at 500, namely:

(1)   an association formed or continued on the basis of a personal relationship involving mutual confidence;

(2)   an agreement, or understanding, that all or some (for there may be 'sleeping' members) of the shareholders shall participate in the conduct of the business; and

(3)   restrictions on the transfers of shares so that a member cannot take his stake and go elsewhere.

These companies are commonly described as quasi-partnerships (despite Lord Wilberforce urging caution as to the use of that term) and such quasi-partnerships are based on understandings between the members reached when they entered into the association as well as later promises, by word or conduct (which need not be legally binding promises), as to how the affairs of the company are to be conducted: see *O'Neill v Phillips* [1999] 2 BCLC 1 at 10–11; *Re Guidezone Ltd* [2000] 2 BCLC 321 at 356. Equity will hold the majority to that agreement, promise or understanding, assuming the minority has acted in reliance on it: see *Re Guidezone Ltd* [2000] 2 BCLC 321 at 356.

It is important to appreciate, as Lord Wilberforce stressed in *Ebrahimi*, that the case for giving effect to equitable considerations must be made in each instance and it is not sufficient simply to assert that the company is small or private, for in many such companies the basis of the association is purely commercial and the relationship will be adequately and exhaustively laid down in the articles. However, a petitioner is not prevented from asserting that the relationship has these characteristics, simply because his shareholding is small: see *Quinlan v Essex Hinge Co Ltd* [1996] 2 BCLC 417.

It is also important to appreciate that, over time, the parties' relationship may change, moving from a purely commercial relationship to one where equitable considerations come into play: see *O'Neill v Phillips* [1999] 2 BCLC 1 at 12; or, vice versa, moving from a quasi-partnership type company to a more commercial footing: see *Re a Company (No 005134 of 1986), ex p Harries* [1989] BCLC 383.

Some illustrations   The following examples illustrate circumstances in which equitable considerations have come into play (the company possessing the characteristics identified above), so constraining the exercise by the majority of the specified legal powers.

(1)   **Removal from office**   The situation where equitable considerations most commonly arise to restrict the exercise of legal rights is where the majority shareholder seeks to remove the minority shareholder from his position as a director and to exclude him from the management of the company, the parties having come together on the basis that all or some of them shall participate in the management of the company: see *Quinlan v Essex Hinge Co Ltd* [1996] 2 BCLC 417; *Re Guidezone Ltd* [2000] 2 BCLC 321; *Brownlow v G H Marshall Ltd* [2000] 2 BCLC 655.

If that is the basis on which the parties have come together, then the exercise by the majority of the statutory power to remove a director will amount to unfairly prejudicial conduct in the absence of an opportunity for that person to sell his interest in the company at a fair price: *O'Neill v Phillips* [1999] 2 BCLC 1. As Lord Hoffmann stressed (at 16) the unfairness does not lie in the exclusion but in the exclusion without a reasonable offer: 'If the respondent to the petition has plainly made a reasonable offer, then the exclusion as such will not be unfairly prejudicial and he will be entitled to have the petition struck out.' What is a reasonable offer for these purposes is discussed in detail below.

In the absence of such equitable considerations, every director is subject to the possibility of removal and has no right to remain in office: *Re Estate Acquisition & Development Ltd* [1995] BCC 338; *Re a Company (No 005134 of 1986), ex p Harries* [1989] BCLC 383; *Re a Company (No 005685 of 1988), ex p Schwarcz (No 2)* [1989] BCLC 427; *Re Blue Arrow plc* [1987] BCLC 585.

(2)   **Alteration of the articles**   In the absence of equitable considerations restraining the exercise of the rights of the majority, a change in the articles of association is one of the ordinary incidents to which a member of a company

cannot validly object: *Re Estate Acquisition & Development Ltd* [1995] BCC 338 at 352. However, equitable considerations might restrict such a power where the proposed alteration would affect the basis on which the parties have come together in the company: *Re Kenyon Swansea Ltd* [1987] BCLC 514. In this situation, the passing of a resolution by the shareholders in general meeting of the company is an act of the company in the conduct of its affairs: see *Re Astec (BSR) plc* [1998] 2 BCLC 556 at 575.

It is doubtful if an alteration which involved the adoption of provisions of Table A (see s 8) could ever be unfairly prejudicial conduct to the members' interests for these purposes: *Re Estate Acquisition & Development Ltd* [1995] BCC 338 at 351.

(3) **Non-payment of dividends** It is arguable that a failure to maintain a reasonable level of dividend payment while paying significant benefits to the majority shareholders (often in the form of director's fees) may be unfairly prejudicial. It might be argued that the parties had come together on the basis that all would participate in the profits of the business such that the non-payment of dividends or the payment of an unjustifiably low rate of dividend is inequitable when coupled with significant benefits to the majority: see *Re a company (No 004415 of 1996)* [1997] 1 BCLC 479; *Quinlan v Essex Hinge Co Ltd* [1996] 2 BCLC 417; *Re Sam Weller & Sons Ltd* [1990] BCLC 80.

(4) **Destruction of the basis of association** Lord Hoffmann in *O'Neill v Phillips* [1999] 2 BCLC 1 at 11 noted that unfairness can arise from the majority using its legal powers to maintain the association in circumstances to which the minority can reasonably say it did not agree. There may be some event which puts an end to the basis on which the parties entered into association with each other, making it unfair that one shareholder should insist on the continuance of the association. In those circumstances, he thought, such a case could be said to come within s 459: see also *Re Guidezone Ltd* [2000] 2 BCLC 321, and the note as to the relationship between s 459 and winding up on the just and equitable ground, below.

Frequently, the court will be faced with complaints on a number of these grounds and, in addition to the specific complaints, it will look at the cumulative effect of the conduct complained of.

A reasonable offer As noted above, Lord Hoffmann emphasised in *O'Neill v Phillips* [1999] 2 BCLC 1 that the unfairness in cases of exclusion lies in the failure of those responsible for the breakdown in the relations between the parties to make a reasonable offer to purchase the petitioner's shares (at 16). The crucial issue then is what is a reasonable offer and on this Lord Hoffmann provided the following guidance in *O'Neill v Phillips* [1999] 2 BCLC 1 at 16–17, although the issue did not arise there as, on the facts, there was no unfairly prejudicial conduct.

(1) The offer must be to purchase the shares at a fair value. This will ordinarily be a value representing an equivalent proportion of the total issued share capital, that is, without a discount for its being a minority holding.

(2) The value, if not agreed, should be determined by a competent expert.

(3) The offer should be to have the value determined by the expert as an expert. It is not required that the offer should provide for the full machinery of arbitration or the half-way house of an expert who gives reasons. The objective should be economy and expedition, even if this carries the possibility of a rough edge for one side or the other (and both parties in this respect take the same risk) compared with a more elaborate procedure.

(4)   The offer should provide for equality of arms between the parties. Both should have the same right of access to information about the company which bears upon the value of the shares and both should have the right to make submissions to the expert.

(5)   When the offer is made after a lengthy period of litigation, it cannot serve as an independent ground for dismissing the petition, on the assumption that it was otherwise well founded, without an offer of costs. But this does not mean that payment of costs need always be offered. If there is a breakdown in relations between the parties, the majority shareholder should be given a reasonable opportunity to make an offer (which may include time to explore the question of how to raise finance) before he becomes obliged to pay costs.

In considering the reasonableness of competing offers made by two equal shareholders to buy out the other, the court must decide which of the offerors had a realistic prospect, a reasonable likelihood, of being able to pay the price likely to be decided upon by an independent expert valuer: *West v Blanchet* [2000] 1 BCLC 795.

Exit provisions in the articles   The articles may make provision for the 'exit' of a shareholder but whether the petitioner is obliged to go that route rather than seek redress under this provision will depend on whether that route provides for a fair offer: *Re a Company (No 00330 of 1991), ex p Holden* [1991] BCLC 597 (it is not always reasonable to insist that a member exit via the articles). Whether the machinery provided by the articles is reasonable will be considered now against the background of the guidance (discussed above) given in *O'Neill v Phillips* [1999] 2 BCLC 1 as to what is a reasonable offer in these cases. An example of an offer which was not sufficient to remove any potential unfairly prejudicial conduct can be seen in *North Holdings Ltd v Southern Tropics Ltd* [1999] 2 BCLC 625 where the issue of valuation raised serious questions of law which it was not appropriate to leave to a valuer; in that instance, the petition would not be struck out. See also *Nugent v Benfield Greig Group plc* [2001] All ER (D) 166 (Mar), CA, (values not independent).

The court will strike out a petition if the offer provided by the articles gives the petitioner all the relief that he could realistically expect to obtain on the petition and it would therefore be an abuse to continue with the litigation: *Re a Company (No 00836 of 1995)* [1996] 2 BCLC 192 (the majority shareholder had made a pro rata offer to buy out the minority on a valuation to be provided by an independent accountant); see also *Re Rotadata Ltd* [2000] 1 BCLC 122 at 132–133.

Companies which are not quasi-partnerships   The application of the statutory remedy is not confined to cases where the company is a quasi-partnership; see *Re a Company (No 00314 of 1989), ex p Estate Acquisition & Development Ltd* [1991] BCLC 154 at 161. However, where the company is not a quasi-partnership, the parties' entire relationship is limited to the company's constitution and the legislation, leaving no scope for equitable considerations to arise. Therefore, the petitioner will be restricted to bringing his case on the grounds of a breach of the terms on which the company's affairs should be run, ie some breach of the directors' fiduciary duties, the terms of the articles or the companies legislation: *Re Saul D Harrison & Sons plc* [1995] 1 BCLC 14; *Re Estate Acquisition & Development Ltd* [1995] BCC 338; see also *CAS (Nominees) Ltd v Nottingham Forest FC plc* [2001] All ER (D) 49 (Apr), Ch D.

This will be the position with private companies which are not quasi-partnerships: see *Re Posgate & Denby (Agencies) Ltd* [1987] BCLC 8; *Re Elgindata Ltd* [1991] BCLC 959; and public companies: see *Re Saul D Harrison & Sons plc* [1995] 1 BCLC 14; *Re a Company (No 005685 of 1988), ex p Schwarz (No 2)* [1989] BCLC 427; and, a fortiori, if the company is a listed public company: *Re Astec (BSR) plc* [1998] 2 BCLC 556; *Re Tottenham Hotspur plc* [1994] 1 BCLC 655; *Re Blue Arrow plc* [1987] BCLC 585.

Relationship with derivative actions   In many of the cases, the unfairly prejudicial conduct is such that the petitioner could have brought a derivative action with respect to the alleged conduct (for example, misappropriation of corporate assets by the directors) but this does not preclude him seeking relief under the unfairly prejudicial provision: *Re a Company (No 005287 of 1985)* [1986] BCLC 68; *Re Little Olympian Each-Ways Ltd* [1995] 1 BCLC 636 at 665. In practice, it will be preferable to bring a s 459 petition, as this will result in a direct personal remedy for the petitioner rather than a remedy for the benefit of the company which would be the outcome of a successful derivative action.

Relationship with winding up petitions   For some time, it had been common practice to petition under s 459 and, in the alternative, for winding up on the just and equitable ground under IA 1986, s 122(1)(g). A Practice Direction then made clear that a petitioner should not seek relief under s 459 and winding up, unless winding up was the relief which the petitioner preferred or it was thought that it may be the only relief to which he is entitled: Practice Direction: Applications under the Companies Act 1985 and the Insurance Companies Act 1982, para 9(1), 19 April 1999, see [1999] BCC 741; *Re a Company (No 004415 of 1996)* [1997] 1 BCLC 479. It was important tactically to adopt the correct approach for if the petitioner failed to petition for winding up and the court ultimately considered that winding up was the only appropriate remedy, the court could not so order under s 461 and it was necessary to amend the petition to seek winding up: see *Re Full Cup International Trading Ltd* [1995] BCC 682 at 694.

However, the position as to petitioning for winding up in the alternative has been affected by the decision in *O'Neill v Phillips* [1999] 2 BCLC 1, as applied in *Re Guidezone Ltd* [2000] 2 BCLC 321. It will be recalled that in *O'Neill v Phillips* [1999] 2 BCLC 1, Lord Hoffmann's view was that unfairness can arise from the majority using its legal powers to maintain the association in circumstances to which the minority can reasonably say it did not agree.

These issues have been explored further in *Re Guidezone Ltd* [2000] 2 BCLC 321 where Jonathan Parker J held that the jurisdiction to make a winding-up order on the just and equitable ground under IA 1986, s 122(1)(g) was not wider than the jurisdiction to grant relief under s 459. Accordingly, if the conduct by the majority relied on by the petitioner was not unfair for the purposes of s 459, it could not found a case for a winding-up order on the just and equitable ground. The result is that a failure to establish a case under s 459 will necessarily mean failure to secure a winding-up order under IA 1986, s 122(1)(g). It follows that the circumstances which would justify a winding up order would equally justify relief under s 459. Given a choice of remedy, the petitioner would usually seek a buy-out order at a pro rata price under s 461 and would not wish to obtain a winding-up order. The net effect must be that the circumstances in which it makes sense to seek a winding-up order on the just and equitable ground as an alternative to relief under s 459 must be limited indeed.

S 459(3)

A member of a company   As to any company 'within the meaning of this Act', see s 735.

460. Order on application of Secretary of State

(1) If in the case of any company—

    (a) the Secretary of State has received a report under section 437, or exercised his powers under section 447 or 448 of this Act or section 43A or 44(2) to (6) of the Insurance Companies Act 1982 ..., and

    (b) it appears to him that the company's affairs are being or have been conducted in a manner which is unfairly prejudicial to the interests of its members generally or of some part of its members, or that any actual or proposed act or omission of the company (including an act or omission on its behalf) is or would be so prejudicial,

he may himself (in addition to or instead of presenting a petition ... for the winding up of the company) apply to the court by petition for an order under this Part.

(2) In this section (and, so far as applicable for its purposes, in the section next following) 'company' means any body corporate which is liable to be wound up under this Act.

General note

This power has never been exercised and the Secretary of State for Trade and Industry would not normally consider there to be sufficient public interest to initiate a petition under this provision.

461. Provisions as to petitions and orders under this Part

(1) If the court is satisfied that a petition under this Part is well founded, it may make such order as it thinks fit for giving relief in respect of the matters complained of.

(2) Without prejudice to the generality of subsection (1), the court's order may—

    (a) regulate the conduct of the company's affairs in the future,

    (b) require the company to refrain from doing or continuing an act complained of by the petitioner or to do an act which the petitioner has complained it has omitted to do,

    (c) authorise civil proceedings to be brought in the name and on behalf of the company by such person or persons and on such terms as the court may direct,

    (d) provide for the purchase of the shares of any members of the company by other members or by the company itself and, in the case of a purchase by the company itself, the reduction of the company's capital accordingly.

(3) If an order under this Part requires the company not to make any, or any specified, alteration in the memorandum or articles, the company does not then have power without leave of the court to make any such alteration in breach of that requirement.

(4) Any alteration in the company's memorandum or articles made by virtue of an order under this Part is of the same effect as if duly made by resolution of

the company, and the provisions of this Act apply to the memorandum or articles as so altered accordingly.

(5)   An office copy of an order under this Part altering, or giving leave to alter, a company's memorandum or articles shall, within 14 days from the making of the order or such longer period as the court may allow, be delivered by the company to the registrar of companies for registration; and if a company makes default in complying with this subsection, the company and every officer of it who is in default is liable to a fine and, for continued contravention, to a daily default fine.

(6)   The power under section 411 of the Insolvency Act to make rules shall, so far as it relates to a winding-up petition, apply for the purposes of a petition under this Part.

General note

There is no power under this provision, despite its apparent width, for the court to order the winding up of the company. If, therefore, the petitioner either requires such a remedy or is concerned that such may be the only appropriate remedy, it is necessary to petition specifically for such relief: see *Re Full Cup International Trading Ltd* [1995] BCC 682 at 694; but see the note to s 459 as to the relationship between relief under these provisions and winding up on the just and equitable ground.

Nothing in s 125(2)–(5) requiring consent to a variation or abrogation of class rights affects the court's powers under this provision: s 126.

S 461(1)

Petition is well founded   There must be a finding of unfair prejudice before the court can make any order for relief: *Re a Company (No 004175 of 1986)* [1987] BCLC 574; *Re a Company (No 004502 of 1988), ex p Johnson* [1992] BCLC 701. It follows that there is no jurisdiction to make interim orders for payment in anticipation of a purchase order at the full hearing: *Re a Company (No 004175 of 1986)* [1987] BCLC 574. In all cases, the petitioner should clearly state in his petition the precise relief to which he considers himself entitled: *Re J E Cade & Son Ltd* [1992] BCLC 213 at 223, in addition to seeking such other order as the court thinks fit.

Relief ordered   The court may order relief against another company to whom assets have been diverted in a manner unfairly prejudicial to the interests of the petitioner: *Re Little Olympian Each-Ways Ltd (No 3)* [1995] 1 BCLC 636. Where the unfairly prejudicial conduct involves the diversion of corporate assets, the court may make an order in favour of the company under this provision: *Lowe v Fahey* [1996] 1 BCLC 262, and it may make an order against members, former members and directors as well as third parties participating in the wrongful diversion of corporate assets. However, on such facts, it would not necessarily allow the case to proceed by petition as opposed to by derivative action: *Lowe v Fahey* [1996] 1 BCLC 262.

Where it is appropriate to order relief, that relief need not be directed solely towards remedying the particular things that have happened and the provision enables the court to ensure that, for the future, the affairs of the company will be properly run: see *Re Hailey Group Ltd* [1993] BCLC 459; *Re a Company (No 00789 of 1987), ex p Shooter* [1990] BCLC 384 at 394.

Relief may be refused   The court's discretion as to the relief it may order extends to the refusal of specific relief where the court is unable to devise relief which would constitute an appropriate remedy or where some other course of action (such as winding up) seems to be preferable: see *Re Full Cup International Trading Ltd* [1995] BCC 682; aff'd sub nom *Antoniades v Wong* [1997] 2 BCLC 419, CA (no relief which would meet the justice of the case and which would be more advantageous than a winding up was capable of being devised).

S 461(2)(a)

As to future conduct   See *R & H Electric Ltd v Haden Bill Electrical Ltd* [1995] 2 BCLC 280, where the court ordered, inter alia, that the petitioner should cease to be chairman and a director, that his shares be purchased by the majority shareholders and that the company repay as soon as possible loans made to it by the petitioner.

S 461(2)(b)

Obligation to act   See *McGuinness v Bremner plc* [1988] BCLC 673 (directors delayed in convening meeting: court ordered extraordinary general meeting to be held on set date). This case prompted an alteration to the statutory provisions on extraordinary general meetings so as to enable the shareholders to call the meeting themselves where the directors fail to do so: see s 368(4).

S 461(2)(c)

Authorise civil proceedings   This provision was designed to extend the causes of action open to a minority shareholder by allowing him to petition under s 459 for permission to commence a derivative action. In practice, this relief is rarely sought and has never been ordered. It is highly unlikely that any successful petitioner who is then in a position to obtain a direct personal remedy would want to proceed to commence a derivative action on behalf of the company.

S 461(2)(d)

Purchase orders   The most commonly sought relief is a purchase order requiring the respondents to purchase the shares of the petitioner so enabling the petitioner to recover his investment and depart from the company. Quite exceptionally, the court may order the majority shareholder to sell to the petitioner: see *Re Brenfield Squash Racquets Club Ltd* [1996] 2 BCLC 184; *Re a Company (No 00789 of 1987), ex p Shooter* [1990] BCLC 384. Where the shareholdings are equal, the court may order the member responsible for the unfairly prejudicial conduct to sell his shares to the petitioner: see *Re Planet Organic Ltd* [2000] 1 BCLC 366.

The purchase order must relate, it appears, to the entire holding and may provide for the purchase by the respondents (as is commonly the case) or by the company; and where the company is required to purchase the shares, such a purchase is exempt from the prohibition on a company acquiring its own shares: s 143(3)(a).

Case management   The valuation of the petitioner's shares under a purchase order can be a contentious issue which contributes considerably to the length and complexity of s 459 proceedings. As discussed in the general note to s 459 above, the expectation is that the case management powers under the Civil Procedure Rules 1998, SI 1998/3132 will have a significant role to play in expediting these petitions, and this will include with respect to valuation issues: see *North Holdings Ltd v Southern Tropics Ltd* [1999] 2 BCLC 625 at 639. Furthermore, the lead given in *O'Neill v Phillips* [1999] 2 BCLC 1 as to the importance of a reasonable offer in securing the striking out of a petition, should encourage parties to resolve these matters without the expensive assistance of the court.

The basis of valuation   The overall approach of the courts to the question of valuation was established in *Re Bird Precision Bellows Ltd* [1984] 3 All ER 444; aff'd [1985] 3 All ER 523, CA, which has been followed in numerous cases.

(1)   It is axiomatic that the price fixed by the court must be fair.

(2)   There is no rule that the shares have to be bought on a pro rata basis but nor is there a general rule that they have to be bought on a discounted basis to reflect the fact that they are a minority holding. It all depends on the circumstances of the case and, in general, the court would distinguish between two types of shareholding in small private companies.

(3)   Where the sale is of a holding acquired in what is essentially a quasi-partnership and the sale is being forced on the holder because of the unfairly prejudicial manner in which the majority have conducted the affairs of the company then, as a general rule, the correct course would be to fix the price pro rata according to the value of the shares as a whole and without any discount: see, for example, *Quinlan v Essex Hinge Co Ltd* [1996] 2 BCLC 417. This would be the only fair method of compensating an unwilling vendor of the equivalent of a partnership share.

(4)   In other cases, for example, where a minority shareholding is acquired as an investment, different considerations apply and the price fixed will normally be discounted to reflect the fact that it is a minority holding; a fortiori, where the company has never been a quasi-partnership or has ceased to be one: see *Re Elgindata Ltd* [1991] BCLC 959; *Re a Company (No 005134 of 1986), ex p Harries* [1989] BCLC 383; see also *Re Planet Organic Ltd* [2000] 1 BCLC 366 (preference shareholders were investors and should be bought out at a discount).

The date of valuation   As the value of the shares may fluctuate throughout the period in question, the choice of the date of valuation will be of great importance to the parties. Here, too, there is no general rule, only an overriding requirement to do what is fair in the circumstances: *Re Bird Precision Bellows Ltd* [1984] 3 All ER 444; aff'd [1985] 3 All ER 523, CA.

Commonly, the shares will be valued at the date of the order for purchase, as that is the time when the unfairly prejudicial conduct is brought to an end: see *Re Elgindata Ltd* [1991] BCLC 959; *Re Ghyll Beck Driving Range Ltd* [1993] BCLC 1126; *Re a Company (No 005134 of 1986), ex p Harries* [1989] BCLC 383. But fairness, in the circumstances of a particular case, may require that the valuation may be directed to take place earlier, for example, at the date of the petition: see *Re London School of Electronics Ltd* [1985] BCLC 273 (otherwise the petitioner might be able to take advantage of improvements in the company's business for which he was not responsible); *Re Cumana Ltd* [1986] BCLC 430, CA; or even at a date before the petition: see *R & H Electric Ltd v Haden Bill Electrical Ltd* [1995] 2 BCLC 280.

Further guidance on these issues was forthcoming recently from the Court of Appeal in *Profinance Trust SA v Gladstone* [2001] 30 LS Gaz R 37. As to the appropriate date for valuation, the starting point in the court's view was that, prima facie, an interest in a going concern should be valued as at the date on which it was ordered to be purchased, subject to the overriding requirement that the valuation should be fair on the facts of the particular case. While recognising this as a starting point, the court accepted that there are many cases in which fairness (to one side or the other) requires the court to take another date and it offered the following examples (at para 61):

(1)   where a company has been deprived of its business, an early valuation date (and compensating adjustments) may be required in fairness to the claimant;

(2)   where a company has been reconstructed or its business has changed significantly, so that it has a new economic identity, an early valuation date may be required in fairness to one or both parties;

(3)   where a minority shareholder has a petition on foot and there is a general fall in the market, the court may in fairness to the claimant have the shares valued at an early date, especially if it strongly disapproves of the majority shareholder's prejudicial conduct.

However, the Court of Appeal emphasised that a claimant is not entitled to a one-way bet, and the court will not direct an early valuation date simply to give the claimant the most advantageous exit from the company, especially where severe prejudice has not been made out. Moreover, all these points may be heavily influenced by the parties' conduct in making and accepting or rejecting offers either before or during the course of the proceedings, in accordance with the decision of the House of Lord in *O'Neill v Phillips* [1999] 2 BCLC 1.

A purchase order made when the company is insolvent is tantamount to a fine but there may be circumstances in which, despite the company's insolvency at the time of the hearing, the court would feel it necessary to impose an obligation to purchase the petitioner's shares: *Re Hailey Group Ltd* [1993] BCLC 459. It might be appropriate, for example, where the unfairly prejudicial conduct had prevented the petitioner from selling his shares at a proper price prior to the onset of insolvency or where the purchase order was sought at a time when the company was solvent: see *Re Hailey Group Ltd* [1993] BCLC 459 at 473 (purchase order refused: it was sought only at the eleventh hour).

Interest   Interest is not generally payable on the purchase price of the shares: *Re Bird Precision Bellows Ltd* [1984] 3 All ER 444; aff'd [1985] 3 All ER 523, CA; *Re Planet Organic Ltd* [2000] 1 BCLC 366. However, the Court of Appeal has recently confirmed that it is not beyond the power of the court to make an order for the equivalent of interest, though it is a power which should be exercised with great caution. It might arise where the date for valuation of the shares was very early and the petitioner argued that it should be augmented by interest but he would have to persuade the court by evidence that this was the only way, or the best way, to a fair result: *Profinance Trust SA v Gladstone* [2001] 30 LS Gaz R 37.

S 461(3)–(5)

See notes to s 5(6)–(7), above; as to penalties, see s 730, Sch 24; 'officer in default' is defined in s 730(5).

S 461(6)

The current rules are the Companies (Unfair Prejudice Applications) Proceedings Rules 1986, SI 1986/2000.

PART XVIII
FLOATING CHARGES AND
RECEIVERS (SCOTLAND)

CHAPTER I

FLOATING CHARGES

462. Power of incorporated company to create floating charge

(1)   It is competent under the law of Scotland for an incorporated company (whether a company within the meaning of this Act or not), for the purpose of securing any debt or other obligation (including a cautionary obligation) incurred or to be incurred by, or binding upon, the company or any other person, to create in favour of the creditor in the debt or obligation a charge, in this Part referred to as a floating charge, over all or any part of the property (including uncalled capital) which may from time to time be comprised in its property and undertaking.

(2)   ...

(4)   References in this Part to the instrument by which a floating charge was created are, in the case of a floating charge created by words in a bond or other written acknowledgment, references to the bond or, as the case may be, the other written acknowledgment.

(5)   Subject to this Act, a floating charge has effect in accordance with this Part and Part III of the Insolvency Act 1986 in relation to any heritable property in Scotland to which it relates, notwithstanding that the instrument creating it is not recorded in the Register of Sasines or, as appropriate, registered in accordance with the Land Registration (Scotland) Act 1979.

NOTES

Sub-s (2): repealed by the Law Reform (Miscellaneous Provisions) (Scotland) Act 1990, s 74(1),(2), Sch 8, para 33(6), Sch 9, as from 1 December 1990.

Sub-s (3): repealed by the Requirements of Writing (Scotland) Act 1995, s 14(2), Sch 5, as from 1 August 1995.

General note

This provision applies to Scotland only and is outside the scope of this work.

463. Effect of floating charge on winding up

(1)   Where a company goes into liquidation within the meaning of section 247(2) of the Insolvency Act 1986, a floating charge created by the company attaches to the property then comprised in the company's property and undertaking or, as the case may be, in part of that property and undertaking, but does so subject to the rights of any person who—

(a) has effectually executed diligence on the property or any part of it; or

(b) holds a fixed security over the property or any part of it ranking in priority to the floating charge; or

(c) holds over the property or any part of it another floating charge so ranking.

(2)   The provisions of Part IV of the Insolvency Act (except section 185) have effect in relation to a floating charge, subject to subsection (1), as if the charge were a fixed security over the property to which it has attached in respect of the principal of the debt or obligation to which it relates and any interest due or to become due thereon.

(3)   Nothing in this section derogates from the provisions of sections 53(7) and 54(6) of the Insolvency Act (attachment of floating charge on appointment of receiver), or prejudices the operation of sections 175 and 176 of that Act (payment of preferential debts in winding up).

(4)   ... interest accrues, in respect of a floating charge which after 16th November 1972 attaches to the property of the company, until payment of the sum due under the charge is made.

NOTES

Sub-s (4): words omitted repealed by the Insolvency Act 1986, s 438, Sch 12, as from 29 December 1986.

General note

This provision applies to Scotland only and is outside the scope of this work.

464. Ranking of floating charges

(1)　Subject to subsection (2), the instrument creating a floating charge over all or any part of the company's property under section 462 may contain—

- (a)　provisions prohibiting or restricting the creation of any fixed security or any other floating charge having priority over, or ranking pari passu with, the floating charge; or
- (b)　with the consent of the holder of any subsisting floating charge or fixed security which would be adversely affected provisions regulating the order in which the floating charge shall rank with any other subsisting or future floating charges or fixed securities over that property or any part of it.

(1A) Where an instrument creating a floating charge contains any such provision as is mentioned in subsection (1)(a), that provision shall be effective to confer priority on the floating charge over any fixed security or floating charge created after the date of the instrument.

(2)　Where all or any part of the property of a company is subject both to a floating charge and to a fixed security arising by operation of law, the fixed security has priority over the floating charge.

(3)　The order of ranking of the floating charges with any other subsisting or future floating charges or fixed securities over all or any part of the company's property is determined in accordance with the provisions of subsections (4) and (5) except where it is determined in accordance with any provision such as is mentioned in paragraph (a) or (b) of subsection (1).

(4)　Subject to the provisions of this section—

- (a)　a fixed security, the right to which has been constituted as a real right before a floating charge has attached to all or any part of the property of the company, has priority of ranking over the floating charge;
- (b)　floating charges rank with one another according to the time of registration in accordance with Chapter II of Part XII;
- (c)　floating charges which have been received by the registrar for registration by the same postal delivery rank with one another equally.

(5)　Where the holder of a floating charge over all or any part of the company's property which has been registered in accordance with Chapter II of Part XII has received intimation in writing of the subsequent registration in accordance with that Chapter of another floating charge over the same property or any part thereof, the preference in ranking of the first-mentioned floating charge is restricted to security for—

- (a)　the holder's present advances;
- (b)　future advances which he may be required to make under the instrument creating the floating charge or under any ancillary document;
- (c)　interest due or to become due on all such advances; ...

(d) any expenses or outlays which may reasonably be incurred by the holder ; and

(e) (in the case of a floating charge to secure a contingent liability other than a liability arising under any further advances made from time to time) the maximum sum to which that contingent liability is capable of amounting whether or not it is contractually limited.

(6) This section is subject to Part XII and to sections 175 and 176 of the Insolvency Act (preferential debts in winding up).

NOTES

Sub-s (5): word omitted from para (c) repealed by CA 1989, s 212, Sch 24, as from 3 July 1995; sub-s (6): words in square brackets inserted by CA 1989, s 140(2), (7), as from a day to be appointed.

General note

This provision applies to Scotland only and is outside the scope of this work.

465. Continued effect of certain charges validated by Act of 1972

(1) Any floating charge which—

(a) purported to subsist as a floating charge on 17th November 1972, and

(b) if it had been created on or after that date, would have been validly created by virtue of the Companies (Floating Charges and Receivers)(Scotland) Act 1972,

is deemed to have subsisted as a valid floating charge as from the date of its creation.

(2) Any provision which—

(a) is contained in an instrument creating a floating charge or in any ancillary document executed prior to, and still subsisting at, the commencement of that Act,

(b) relates to the ranking of charges, and

(c) if it had been made after the commencement of that Act, would have been a valid provision,

is deemed to have been a valid provision as from the date of its making.

General note

This provision applies to Scotland only and is outside the scope of this work.

466. Alteration of floating charges

(1) The instrument creating a floating charge under section 462 or any ancillary document may be altered by the execution of an instrument of alteration by the company, the holder of the charge and the holder of any other charge (including a fixed security) which would be adversely affected by the alteration.

(2) Without prejudice to any enactment or rule of law regarding the execution of documents, such an instrument of alteration is validly executed if it is executed—

(a) ...

(b) where trustees for debenture-holders are acting under and in accordance with a trust deed, by those trustees; or

(c) where, in the case of a series of secured debentures, no such trustees are acting, by or on behalf of—

(i) a majority in nominal value of those present or represented by proxy and voting at a meeting of debenture-holders at which the holders of at least one-third in nominal value of the outstanding debentures of the series are present or so represented; or

(ii) where no such meeting is held, the holders of at least one-half in nominal value of the outstanding debentures of the series; ...

(d) ...

(3) Section 464 applies to an instrument of alteration under this section as it applies to an instrument creating a floating charge.

(4) Subject to the next subsection, section 410(2) and (3) and section 420 apply to an instrument of alteration under this section which—

(a) prohibits or restricts the creation of any fixed security or any other floating charge having priority over, or ranking pari passu with, the floating charge; or

(b) varies, or otherwise regulates the order of, the ranking of the floating charge in relation to fixed securities or to other floating charges; or

(c) releases property from the floating charge; or

(d) increases the amount secured by the floating charge.

(5) Section 410(2) and (3) and section 420 apply to an instrument of alteration falling under subsection (4) of this section as if references in the said sections to a charge were references to an alteration to a floating charge, and as if in section 410(2) and (3)—

(a) references to the creation of a charge were references to the execution of such alteration; and

(b) for the words from the beginning of subsection (2) to the word 'applies' there were substituted the words 'Every alteration to a floating charge created by a company'.

(6) Any reference (however expressed) in any enactment, including this Act, to a floating charge is, for the purposes of this section and unless the context otherwise requires, to be construed as including a reference to the floating charge as altered by an instrument of alteration falling under subsection (4) of this section.

NOTES

Sub-s (2) words omitted repealed, by CA 1989, ss 130(7), 212, Sch 17, para 9, Sch 24, as from 31 July 1990. Sub-ss (4)–(6) were to be repealed and amended by CA 1989, ss 140(8), 212, Sch 24, as from a day to be appointed but these reforms have never been implemented.

General note

This provision applies to Scotland only and is outside the scope of this work.

467.–485. *((Ch II) Repealed by the IA 1986, s 438, Sch 12, as from 29 December 1986.)*

CHAPTER III

GENERAL

486. Interpretation for Part XVIII generally

(1)   In this Part, unless the context otherwise requires, the following expressions have the following meanings respectively assigned to them, that is to say—

'ancillary document' means—

(a)   a document which relates to the floating charge and which was executed by the debtor or creditor in the charge before the registration of the charge in accordance with Chapter II of Part XII; or

(b)   an instrument of alteration such as is mentioned in section 466 in this Part;

'company', ... means an incorporated company (whether a company within the meaning of this Act or not);

'fixed security', in relation to any property of a company, means any security, other than a floating charge or a charge having the nature of a floating charge, which on the winding up of the company in Scotland would be treated as an effective security over that property, and (without prejudice to that generality) includes a security over that property, being a heritable security within the meaning of section 9(8) of the Conveyancing and Feudal Reform (Scotland) Act 1970;

...

'Register of Sasines' means the appropriate division of the General Register of Sasines.

NOTES

Words omitted repealed by the Insolvency Act 1986, s 438, Sch 12, as from 29 December 1986.

General note

This provision applies to Scotland only and is outside the scope of this work.

487. Extent of Part XVIII

This Part extends to Scotland only.

488.–500. *((Pt XIX) Repealed by the Insolvency Act 1986, s 438, Sch 12, as from 29 December 1986.)*

PART XX

WINDING UP OF COMPANIES REGISTERED UNDER THIS ACT OR THE FORMER COMPANIES ACTS

501.–650. *((Chs I–V) Repealed by the Insolvency Act 1986, s 438, Sch 12, as from 29 December 1986.)*

CHAPTER VI

MATTERS ARISING SUBSEQUENT TO WINDING UP

651. Power of court to declare dissolution of company void

(1)   Where a company has been dissolved, the court may ..., on an application made for the purpose by the liquidator of the company or by any other person appearing to the court to be interested, make an order, on such terms as the court thinks fit, declaring the dissolution to have been void.

(2)   Thereupon such proceedings may be taken as might have been taken if the company had not been dissolved.

(3)   It is the duty of the person on whose application the order was made, within 7 days after its making (or such further time as the court may allow), to deliver to the registrar of companies for registration an office copy of the order.

If the person fails to do so, he is liable to a fine and, for continued contravention, to a daily default fine.

(4)   Subject to the following provisions, an application under this section may not be made after the end of the period of two years from the date of the dissolution of the company.

(5)   An application for the purpose of bringing proceedings against the company—

  (a) for damages in respect of personal injuries (including any sum claimed by virtue of section 1(2)(c) of the Law Reform (Miscellaneous Provisions) Act 1934 (funeral expenses)), or

  (b) for damages under the Fatal Accidents Act 1976 or the Damages (Scotland) Act 1976,

may be made at any time; but no order shall be made on such an application if it appears to the court that the proceedings would fail by virtue of any enactment as to the time within which proceedings must be brought.

(6)   Nothing in subsection (5) affects the power of the court on making an order under this section to direct that the period between the dissolution of the company and the making of the order shall not count for the purposes of any such enactment.

(7)   In subsection (5)(a) 'personal injuries' includes any disease and any impairment of a person's physical or mental condition.

General note

The provisions of this section were amended by CA 1989, s 141 which came into force on 16 November 1989. The amendments were not applicable to any company which had been dissolved more than two years before the commencement of CA 1989, s 141: CA 1989, s 141(5). However, an exception was made for applications under s 651(5), as amended (proceedings for personal injury etc), which may be made in respect of a company which was dissolved before the commencement of the section, provided it had not been dissolved more than twenty years before the commencement: CA 1989, s 141(4).

S 651(1), (2)

Dissolution following liquidation A company is dissolved automatically three months after the registration by the registrar of companies of the liquidator's final return (in the case of voluntary winding up) under IA 1986, s 201(1), (2); or the final notice of the liquidator or Official Receiver (in the case of compulsory winding up) under IA 1986, s 205(1), (2); or the Official Receiver's application for early dissolution under IA 1986, s 202(2), (5); unless deferment is sought: IA 1986, ss 201(3), 205(3).

The purpose of the application Ordinarily, the purpose of an application under s 651 is to enable the liquidator to distribute an overlooked asset (including where the liquidator was aware of the asset but unaware that it had any realisable value) or to enable a creditor to make a claim which he has not previously made: *Stanhope Pension Trust Ltd v Registrar of Companies* [1994] 1 BCLC 628 at 632, per Hoffmann LJ; *Re Oakleague Ltd* [1995] 2 BCLC 624. Provided that the application for restoration falls within the general legislative purpose, as described above, the company will be restored and whether the restoration does anyone any good or not is a matter to be decided by another tribunal in the future: *Re Oakleague Ltd* [1995] 2 BCLC 624.

In most cases, there will be no point in a creditor seeking restoration in order to pursue a claim against the company, as the available assets will have been distributed on the liquidation and that distribution cannot now be altered. Hence, the need for there to be an asset which has been overlooked; see *Stanhope Pension Trust Ltd v Registrar of Companies* [1994] 1 BCLC 628 (potential indemnity from solvent company in same group as dissolved company); *Re Oakleague Ltd* [1995] 2 BCLC 624 (potentially valuable claim for damages for defective goods supplied to dissolved company). Alternatively, the purpose of the application may be secure a judgment against the company which can be enforced against its insurers under the Third Parties (Rights against Insurers) Act 1930.

Relationship between this provision and s 653 Applications under this provision are not restricted to a dissolution which has followed a liquidation and an application may also be made where the company has been dissolved as a result of being struck off the register under s 652, notwithstanding the fact that s 653 provides for applications to the court for restoration in such cases: *Re Townreach Ltd (No 002081 of 1994)* [1995] Ch 28; *Re Thompson & Riches Ltd* [1981] 2 All ER 477; *Re Test Holdings (Clifton) Ltd* [1969] 3 All ER 517; *Re M Belmont & Co Ltd* [1951] 2 All ER 898. Presumably, on a similar basis, an application might be made where the company has been struck off under s 652A. In theory, it may be desirable to apply under s 651 rather than s 653 because the category of persons who may apply under the former provision (any person appearing to the court to be interested) is wider than the specified categories (member, creditor etc) under s 653, although in effect the court interprets each provision as applying to any person appearing to be interested. On the other hand, an application cannot be made under s 653 for the restoration of a company which has been dissolved following liquidation.

Applicants The interest of an applicant in having the company revived does not have to be firmly established or highly likely to prevail, provided that it is not 'merely shadowy': *Re Wood and Martin (Bricklaying Contractors) Ltd* [1971] 1 All ER 732 at 736, per Megarry J, approved in *Stanhope Pension Trust Ltd v Registrar of Companies* [1994] 1 BCLC 628 at 635.

Where a company has been struck off by the registrar of companies under s 652 but, being unaware of this, the company proceeds to winding up, the so-called liquidator appointed under that process cannot apply under this provision as the 'liquidator' because, on the true construction of the provision, the expression must mean a liquidator validly appointed before the dissolution of the company. However, he may apply as a 'person appearing to the court to be interested': *Re Wood and Martin (Bricklaying Contractors) Ltd* [1971] 1 All ER 732.

The Secretary of State for Trade and Industry is a person 'appearing to be interested' for these purposes, his interest lying in the proper exercise of his statutory duties with respect to the regulation and supervision of companies: *Re Townreach Ltd (No 002081 of 1994)* [1995] Ch 28 (restoration sought to commence an investigation of one company and to consider disqualification proceedings with respect to the directors of another).

Respondents   The typical respondents to the application under s 651 are the registrar of companies, who appears by counsel instructed by the Treasury Solicitor, who has no interest other than in securing the registrar's costs, and, possibly, the former liquidator who on the dissolution being declared void may be appointed, under IA 1986, s 108(1), as liquidator of the company as restored.

It is customary in cases where the application is for the purpose of pursuing an action for damages for personal injuries for the company's insurers to be joined as a party to the action as the intention is to secure a judgment against the company which can be enforced against its insurers under the Third Parties (Rights against Insurers) Act 1930; see *Re Workvale Ltd* [1991] BCLC 528.

In general, as the making of an order does not determine any claim against the company or a third party, there should be no joinder of third parties, save where the order will directly affect the rights of a third party: see *Stanhope Pension Trust Ltd v Registrar of Companies* [1994] 1 BCLC 628 at 635–636; also *Re Servers of Blind League* [1960] 2 All ER 298. A third party who merely wants to say that the applicant has no claim against the company or that any proceedings by the revived company against him has no prospect of success should not be entitled to intervene. RSC Ord 15, r 6(2)(b)(i) enabled a party to be added where 'necessary' for the determination of the matter etc, while the CPR, r 19.1(2), changes the wording to the less onerous 'if it is desirable' but the change in the wording is unlikely to make any difference to the court's approach to this issue: see *Re Blenheim Leisure (Restaurants) Ltd* [2000] BCC 554.

Powers of the court   The court's power to make an order is discretionary and, though apparently unrestricted, must be limited to the statutory purposes for which it is conferred: see *Stanhope Pension Trust Ltd v Registrar of Companies* [1994] 1 BCLC 628 at 631. The order may be on 'such terms as the court thinks fit' and the court may need to give directions as to the company's name, where a company with the same name has been registered in the period between dissolution and restoration. The registrar of companies will also want undertakings by the company to bring the public record up to date on restoration and the order will give directions as to these requirements also.

A section 651 (limitation) direction   In exercise of its jurisdiction to make the order declaring the dissolution to have been void on 'such terms as the court thinks fit', the court can adjust the limitation consequences of the declaration so as to produce a just result in the circumstances of a particular case: *Smith v White Knight Laundry Ltd* [2001] All ER(D) 152 (May). This decision of the Court of Appeal has brought considerably clarity to the position on this issue.

Prior to this decision, there had been uncertainty as to whether the court could make such limitation directions under s 651(1). The uncertainty arose because of the ambiguous wording of s 651(6), which might be interpreted as limiting the court's powers to make such limitation directions to cases within s 651(5). That interpretation was supported by *Re Mixhurst plc* [1994] 2 BCLC 19 but it was rejected in *Re Townreach Ltd (No 002081 of 1994)* [1995] Ch 28, with the result that there was some uncertainty as to the true position.

The Court of Appeal in *Smith v White Knight Laundry Ltd* [2001] All ER(D) 152 (May) has resolved the issue. The power of the court to make what the court described as 'a section 651 direction' (para 5), ie a direction that the period from dissolution to the date of the order should not count for limitation purposes, is to be found in sub-s (1); sub-s (6) does not in terms confer such a power but merely provides that nothing in sub-s (5) shall affect that power (para 49).

As a matter of general practice, where a restoration order is sought by a prospective claimant in a personal injuries action, a section 651 direction should not normally be made unless notice of the application has first been given to all those parties who may be expected to oppose the making of such a direction, including the company's insurers: *Smith v White Knight Laundry Ltd* [2001] All ER(D) 152 (May), CA, para 60.

Company recreated   The effect of an order declaring the dissolution to have been void is that the corporate existence of the company is restored as from the date of the dissolution: see *Smith v White Knight Laundry Ltd* [2001] All ER(D) 152 (May), CA, paras 52–53. As the dissolution is void ab initio, any property which purported to have vested in the Crown under s 654 (bona vacantia) never so vested and no order for the re-vesting of such property in the company is necessary: *Re C W Dixon Ltd* [1947] 1 All ER 279; as to the position if the asset has been disposed of, see s 655.

However, there is a distinction between the corporate existence of the company which is restored as from the date of the dissolution and proceedings which have taken place during the period of dissolution, for the purported acts of a dissolved, and hence non-existent company, are not validated by the subsequent avoidance of the dissolution: *Morris v Harris* [1927] AC 252; *Smith v White Knight Laundry Ltd* [2001] All ER(D) 152 (May), CA, paras 52–53; as sub-s (2) makes clear. The dissolution of a company causes proceedings against it to go not into abeyance but to come to a permanent end: *Foster Yates & Thom Ltd v H W Edgehill Equipment Ltd* (1978) 122 Sol Jo 860; *Morris v Harris* [1927] AC 252; and see *Re Philip Powis Ltd* [1998] 1 BCLC 440 at 444, [1997] 2 BCLC 481; cf s 653.

New proceedings against the company and limitation problems   Having restored the company to the register, new proceedings must be commenced. Such proceedings may be statute-barred under the Limitation Act 1980 but that problem may be overcome either by the court making a section 651 direction, ie a direction that the period from dissolution to the date of the order should not count for limitation purposes, or by an application to the court under the Limitation Act 1980 s 33 (discretionary exclusion of limitation period in actions for personal injuries or death).

In the exercise of the discretion conferred by sub-s (1), the court must bear in mind that where the applicant for a restoration order is a prospective claimant in a personal injuries action in circumstances where the claim would otherwise be statute-barred, the effect of making a section 651 direction will be the same as granting the applicant relief under the Limitation Act 1980, s 33: *Smith v White Knight Laundry Ltd* [2001] All ER(D) 152 (May), CA, para 50; and see the note to sub-s (5), below.

S 651(3)

As to penalties, see s 730, Sch 24.

S 651(4)

Time limits for application – any case   An application under this provision within this time limit may be for any purpose and is not restricted to the purposes of bringing proceedings for personal injuries, as is the case under sub-s (5). Where an application is made within two years of dissolution, the proviso to sub-s (5) has no direct application to the court's consideration of the application although whether any action would be statute-barred is a matter for the court in the exercise of its general discretion under sub-s (1): *Re Philip Powis Ltd* [1998] 1 BCLC 440; and see the note above as to limitation directions by the court when exercising its powers under sub-s (1).

S 651(5)

Time limit for application – personal injuries   This provision was inserted by CA 1989 in order to address the consequences of the decision in *Bradley v Eagle Star Insurance Co Ltd* [1989] BCLC 469, HL, which had established that a claimant against a dissolved company for personal injury damages had to obtain a judgment against the company first in order to establish the company's right to be indemnified by its insurers. A necessary first step, then, is to obtain the restoration of the company and there is no time limit to an application for restoration for the purposes of bringing these specified proceedings; see also the general note to this section, above.

Proceedings must not be statute-barred   An application in this case is subject to the proviso, however, that no order may be made if it appears to the court that the prospective proceedings would be statute-barred; and it is for the applicant to satisfy the court that the proceedings would not be statute-barred: *Re Workvale Ltd (No 2)* [1992] BCLC 544, CA. This approach is understandable for, if the proceedings are statute-barred, the only permissible purpose of the application is unattainable and to restore the company would be pointless: see *Re Philip Powis Ltd* [1998] 1 BCLC 440 at 445.

Relationship with Limitation Act 1980, s 33   However, if there is an arguable case that the proceedings would not be statute-barred, because an application under the Limitation Act 1980, s 33 (discretionary exclusion of limitation period in actions for personal injuries or death) might be successful, then it could not be predicated that the proceedings would fail; consequently an order declaring the dissolution to have been void might, in the court's discretion, be made: *Re Workvale Ltd (No 2)* [1992] BCLC 544, CA; *Re Philip Powis Ltd* [1998] 1 BCLC 440, CA.

In that situation, it may not be necessary to bring an application under the Limitation Act 1980, s 33 because the court can achieve the same outcome by way of a section 651 direction under this provision: see *Smith v White Knight Laundry Ltd* [2001] All ER(D) 152 (May), CA, para 50.

Where the case is one where the primary limitation period had not expired at the time of the dissolution (although it has since expired), notice has been given to all those parties who may be expected to opposing the making of a section 651 direction, including the company's insurers, all the evidence which the parties would wish to adduce on the Limitation Act 1980, s 33 application is before the court and the court is satisfied that an application under the Limitation Act 1980, s 33 would be bound to succeed, the court may make a section 651 direction so that the applicants may use the remaining period of the primary limitation period in which to commence proceedings and thereby avoid an unnecessary section 33 application: see *Re Workvale Ltd (No 2)* [1992] BCLC 544 at 552-553; *Smith v White Knight Laundry Ltd* [2001] All ER(D) 152 (May), CA, para 60. If the primary limitation period has expired, so that a section 651 direction will not assist, or if any of the other elements are not present (for example, the insurers are not represented), the applicant must be left to seek relief under the Limitation Act 1980, s 33: *Re Workvale Ltd (No 2)* [1992] BCLC 544 at 552–553; *Smith v White Knight Laundry Ltd* [2001] All ER (D) 152 (May), CA, para 61.

S 651(6)

Limitation direction The purpose of a limitation direction in these terms is to ensure that new proceedings, commenced once the dissolution is declared to have been void, are not statute-barred; and it does this by ignoring, for limitation purposes, the period between the date of dissolution and the date of the order.

As noted above, there had been uncertainty as to whether the wording of this provision prevented the court from making a limitation direction in cases other than those within sub-s (5). That interpretation was supported by *Re Mixhurst plc* [1994] 2 BCLC 19 but it was rejected in *Re Townreach Ltd (No 002081 of 1994)* [1995] Ch 28, with the result that there was some uncertainty as to the true position.

The Court of Appeal in *Smith v White Knight Laundry Ltd* [2001] All ER (D) 152 (May) has resolved the issue. The power of the court to make a section 651 direction, ie a direction that the period from dissolution to the date of the order should not count for limitation purposes, is to be found in sub-s (1); sub-s (6) does not in terms confer such a power but merely provides that nothing in sub-s (5) shall affect that power (para 49).

---

652. Registrar may strike defunct company off register

(1) If the registrar of companies has reasonable cause to believe that a company is not carrying on business or in operation, he may send to the company by post a letter inquiring whether the company is carrying on business or in operation.

(2) If the registrar does not within one month of sending the letter receive any answer to it, he shall within 14 days after the expiration of that month send to the company by post a registered letter referring to the first letter, and stating that no answer to it has been received, and that if an answer is not received to the second letter within one month from its date, a notice will be published in the Gazette with a view to striking the company's name off the register.

(3) If the registrar either receives an answer to the effect that the company is not carrying on business or in operation, or does not within one month after sending the second letter receive any answer, he may publish in the Gazette, and send to the company by post, a notice that at the expiration of 3 months

from the date of that notice the name of the company mentioned in it will, unless cause is shown to the contrary, be struck off the register and the company will be dissolved.

(4) If, in a case where a company is being wound up, the registrar has reasonable cause to believe either that no liquidator is acting, or that the affairs of the company are fully wound up, and the returns required to be made by the liquidator have not been made for a period of 6 consecutive months, the registrar shall publish in the Gazette and send to the company or the liquidator (if any) a like notice as is provided in subsection (3).

(5) At the expiration of the time mentioned in the notice the registrar may, unless cause to the contrary is previously shown by the company, strike its name off the register, and shall publish notice of this in the Gazette; and on the publication of that notice in the Gazette the company is dissolved.

(6) However—

    (a) the liability (if any) of every director, managing officer and member of the company continues and may be enforced as if the company had not been dissolved, and

    (b) nothing in subsection (5) affects the power of the court to wind up a company the name of which has been struck off the register.

(7) A notice to be sent to a liquidator under this section may be addressed to him at his last known place of business; and a letter or notice to be sent under this section to a company may be addressed to the company at its registered office or, if no office has been registered, to the care of some officer of the company.

If there is no officer of the company whose name and address are known to the registrar of companies, the letter or notice may be sent to each of the persons who subscribed the memorandum, addressed to him at the address mentioned in the memorandum.

General note

Circumstances giving rise to striking off   This provision provides for two situations when the registrar of companies may strike companies of the register: (1) where a company is not carrying on business or in operation; and (2) where a company is being wound up but there is no liquidator or the relevant returns which would lead to the dissolution of the company (see general note to s 651, above) have not been made. This power is used extensively and 119,400 companies were struck off the register under this provision and s 652A in 1999–2000: DTI Companies in 1999–2000, Table C1.

A company which is solvent and which has paid off all its creditors may find it easier and cheaper to be struck off in this fashion rather than to terminate its activities through a formal winding up. The company must have paid off its creditors for otherwise they will object to the striking off or subsequently seek the restoration of the company under ss 651 or 653. It must also be the case that there is no surplus remaining for the members, for any assets remaining at the time of striking off are deemed to be bona vacantia under s 654 and fall into the ownership of the Crown.

Striking off may be attractive also for companies which are hopelessly insolvent such that no creditor has any incentive to object to the striking off or to seek restoration; in that case, the advantage for the directors is that the company is struck off without going through a formal procedure which would have required an office-holder to report to the Secretary of State (under the Company Directors Disqualification Act 1986, s 7) as to whether they are unfit to be concerned with the management of a company. Where a company has been struck off but requires investigation, or there are grounds for commencing disqualification proceedings, the Secretary of State may apply for restoration of the company, see *Re Townreach Ltd (No 002081 of 1994)* [1995] Ch 28; and that application may be under either s 651 or s 653(2D).

Where proceedings are commenced by a company which has been struck off under this provision, the proper procedure for the court will generally be to stay the proceedings pending an application to have the company restored to the register under the following section: *Steans Fashions Ltd v Legal and General Assurance Society Ltd* [1995] 1 BCLC 332, CA.

S 652(1)–(3), (7)

'Reasonable cause'   The 'reasonable cause' for believing that a company is not carrying on business or in operation is the company's failure to file its accounts and annual returns and the fact that mail from the registrar of companies to the company has been returned; 'company' is defined in s 735.

Procedure and timetable for striking off   There are three steps before the company is dissolved, offering ample opportunity over a period of months for those associated with the company to respond and prevent the striking off, if they so wish. The steps involved are:

(1) an initial letter of inquiry to the company (sub-s (1));
(2) a registered letter to the company warning of striking off (sub-s (2)); and
(3) a notice in the Gazette and to the company warning of striking off in three months' time unless cause is shown to the contrary (sub-s (3)); and it is open to anyone to show cause why the company should not be struck off.

If there is no response from the company, it will be struck off and dissolved. This outcome may be what those running the company wanted, as discussed in the general note to this section, and it is cheaper (and easier) not to respond and to allow dissolution to occur in this way than it is to apply, in the case of a private company, to be struck off under s 652A.

Company unaware of striking off   However, striking off may occur without the company being aware of it, as where the company has moved premises without notifying the registrar of a current address with the result that the warning letters and notices were sent to the 'old' registered office. The company is in breach of its obligations under s 287 to notify the registrar of a change of address of registered office, of course, and so can scarcely complain of this outcome.

If the company is in fact trading and wishes to continue to do so, then being struck off will be very inconvenient, not least because its property is deemed to be bona vacantia and vests in the Crown (see s 654) and a court order is required to restore the company to the register under ss 651 or 653.

S 652(4)–(5), (7)

Typically, where a company has gone through a formal winding up process, the company is dissolved automatically three months after the registration by the registrar of companies of the liquidator's final return (in the case of voluntary winding up) under IA 1986, s 201(1), (2); or the final notice of the liquidator or Official Receiver (in the case of compulsory winding up) under IA 1986, s 205(1), (2).

This provision allows the registrar of companies (following appropriate notice, see sub-s (4)) to strike off and dissolve a company which has commenced a formal liquidation but, either for want of a liquidator or an absence of returns, the liquidation has not led to dissolution in the normal way. Again, the striking off will not proceed if cause is shown to the contrary.

S 652(6)

Directors' liabilities　　This provision ensures that striking off will not advantage the directors and members with respect to any liability to which individually they may be subject, for example, where a director is liable to account to the company for a profit which he has made.

Winding up　　The court retains the power to wind up a company even though it has already been dissolved through being struck off. This course may be necessary where there is a liability to the company to be enforced or wrongdoing has come to light which needs to be investigated and these issues can be pursued through the appointment of the Official Receiver to wind up the company. Despite the wording of sub-s (6)(b), the practice in such a case, following *Re Cambridge Coffee Room Association Ltd* [1952] 1 All ER 112n, is to seek a restoration order initially followed by the grant of a winding up order; see note to s 654(2) as to the desirability of proceeding in that way, below.

652A. Registrar may strike private company off register on application

(1)　On application by a private company, the registrar of companies may strike the company's name off the register.

(2)　An application by a company under this section shall—

　(a)　be made on its behalf by its directors or by a majority of them,

　(b)　be in the prescribed form, and

　(c)　contain the prescribed information.

(3)　The registrar shall not strike a company off under this section until after the expiration of 3 months from the publication by him in the Gazette of a notice—

　(a)　stating that he may exercise his power under this section in relation to the company, and

　(b)　inviting any person to show cause why he should not do so.

(4)   Where the registrar strikes a company off under this section, he shall publish notice of that fact in the Gazette.

(5)   On the publication in the Gazette of a notice under subsection (4), the company to which the notice relates is dissolved.

(6)   However, the liability (if any) of every director, managing officer and member of the company continues and may be enforced as if the company had not been dissolved.

(7)   Nothing in this section affects the power of the court to wind up a company the name of which has been struck off the register.

General note

This provision, together with ss 652B–652F, was inserted by the Deregulation and Contracting Out Act 1994, s 13(1), Sch 5, paras 1, 2, as from 1 July 1995 to facilitate those companies which wish to be removed from the register; and 66,000 companies used this method of striking off in 1999/2000: DTI *Companies in 1999–2000,* Table G1.

Reasons for the application   A company may wish to be struck off for a variety of reasons: the company may be dormant; the company may have been formed to protect a name and this is no longer required; the company may have been formed for a particular project which has ended and no further activity is contemplated; the company may be a subsidiary for which a group of companies has no further use. As noted above, it may be preferable to await striking off under s 652 (at no cost) rather than to take the initiative under this provision which, in addition to the requirement of a fee, imposes obligations (on pain of criminal sanctions, see s 652E) with respect to notification etc which can be onerous and costly.

S 652A(1), (2)

Application by the company   The application must be by the company, not by individual directors or members, and accompanied by the appropriate fee, currently £10. The company must be a private company, whether limited by shares or by guarantee, although a public company could re-register as private (see ss 53–55) if it particularly wanted to take advantage of this procedure. Again, in that case, it is probably easier to await striking off under s 652. An application can only be made if the company is within the criteria set out in s 652B and criminal penalties attach to improper applications under s 652F.

It is important to appreciate that, in effect, a three month period of inactivity prior to making the application is required: see s 652B(1).

S 652A(3)

Position of objectors   Any person may show cause why the company should not be struck off; typically it will be an unsatisfied creditor or, occasionally, a disgruntled member in a small company dispute. Notice in the Gazette is unlikely, given the nature of that publication, to attract objections which are more likely to arise as a result of the individual notifications of the application which must be made under s 652B(6).

The Companies House Guidance Booklet, *Strike-off, Dissolution and Restoration*, indicates that objections must be in writing and sent to the registrar of companies with any supporting evidence, such as copies of invoices that may prove the company is trading. The Guidance Booklet suggests that the reasons for objecting might include that the company has broken any of the conditions of its application during the three-month period before the application or afterwards (see ss 652B, 652C); the directors have not informed interested parties under s 652B(6); any of the declarations on the application form are false; some form of action is being taken, or is pending, to recover any money owed (such as a winding-up petition or action in a small claims court); other legal action is being taken against the company; or the directors have wrongfully traded or committed a tax fraud or some other offence.

S 652A(4), (5)

These provisions determine the date of dissolution; and any remaining property will then become bona vacantia: see s 654.

S 652A(6), (7)

See note to s 652(6), above.

652B. Duties in connection with making application under section 652A

(1) A person shall not make an application under section 652A on behalf of a company if, at any time in the previous 3 months, the company has—

    (a) changed its name,

    (b) traded or otherwise carried on business,

    (c) made a disposal for value of property or rights which, immediately before ceasing to trade or otherwise carry on business, it held for the purpose of disposal for gain in the normal course of trading or otherwise carrying on business, or

    (d) engaged in any other activity, except one which is—

        (i) necessary or expedient for the purpose of making an application under section 652A, or deciding whether to do so,

        (ii) necessary or expedient for the purpose of concluding the affairs of the company,

        (iii) necessary or expedient for the purpose of complying with any statutory requirement, or

        (iv) specified by the Secretary of State by order for the purposes of this sub-paragraph.

(2) For the purposes of subsection (1), a company shall not be treated as trading or otherwise carrying on business by virtue only of the fact that it makes a

payment in respect of a liability incurred in the course of trading or otherwise carrying on business.

(3)   A person shall not make an application under section 652A on behalf of a company at a time when any of the following is the case—

  (a) an application has been made to the court under section 425 on behalf of the company for the sanctioning of a compromise or arrangement and the matter has not been finally concluded;

  (b) a voluntary arrangement in relation to the company has been proposed under Part I of the Insolvency Act 1986 and the matter has not been finally concluded;

  (c) an administration order in relation to the company is in force under Part II of that Act or a petition for such an order has been presented and not finally dealt with or withdrawn;

  (d) the company is being wound up under Part IV of that Act, whether voluntarily or by the court, or a petition under that Part for the winding up of the company by the court has been presented and not finally dealt with or withdrawn;

  (e) there is a receiver or manager of the company's property;

  (f) the company's estate is being administered by a judicial factor.

(4)   For the purposes of subsection (3)(a), the matter is finally concluded if—

  (a) the application has been withdrawn,

  (b) the application has been finally dealt with without a compromise or arrangement being sanctioned by the court, or

  (c) a compromise or arrangement has been sanctioned by the court and has, together with anything required to be done under any provision made in relation to the matter by order of the court, been fully carried out.

(5)   For the purposes of subsection (3)(b), the matter is finally concluded if—

  (a) no meetings are to be summoned under section 3 of the Insolvency Act 1986,

  (b) meetings summoned under that section fail to approve the arrangement with no, or the same, modifications,

  (c) an arrangement approved by meetings summoned under that section, or in consequence of a direction under section 6(4)(b) of that Act, has been fully implemented, or

  (d) the court makes an order under subsection (5) of section 6 of that Act revoking approval given at previous meetings and, if the court gives any directions under subsection (6) of that section, the company has done whatever it is required to do under those directions.

(6)   A person who makes an application under section 652A on behalf of a company shall secure that a copy of the application is given, within 7 days from the day on which the application is made, to every person who, at any time on that day, is—

  (a) a member of the company,

  (b) an employee of the company,

  (c) a creditor of the company,

(d) a director of the company,

(e) a manager or trustee of any pension fund established for the benefit of employees of the company, or

(f) a person of a description specified for the purposes of this paragraph by regulations made by the Secretary of State.

(7) Subsection (6) shall not require a copy of the application to be given to a director who is a party to the application.

(8) The duty imposed by subsection (6) shall cease to apply if the application is withdrawn before the end of the period for giving the copy application.

(9) The Secretary of State may by order amend subsection (1) for the purpose of altering the period in relation to which the doing of the things mentioned in paragraphs (a) to (d) of that subsection is relevant.

General note

This provision sets out the conditions which must be met before an application for striking off can be made; the following provision deals with the position between the date of the application and the final determination or withdrawal of the application.

Breach of the various duties imposed by this section is an offence: s 652E(1), subject to the defences provided by that provision.

S 652B(1), (2)

Conditions which must be met before application   The effect of this provision is that the company must have ceased all activities (other than the payment of its debts, sub-s (2), and any activities permitted by sub-s (1)(d)(i)–(iv)) three months prior to the application; 'disposal' includes part disposal, see s 652D(7) and note that the prohibition is on disposals which would otherwise be for gain in the normal course of trading. If any of the activities included in sub-s (1) subsequently occur, the application must be withdrawn, see s 652C(4).

Three months prior to the application   It is important to appreciate that this period of three months relates to the time before the application; it is not a case of applying and then ceasing activity while waiting to be dissolved. In view of the fact that criminal penalties attach to an application in breach of these requirements (see s 652E(1), subject to the defence in s 652E(3)), if there is any doubt as to the level of activity in the relevant period, it may be best to delay the application to ensure that there is a 'clear' period of three months.

A notifiable person, defined s 653(2C), may apply to the court for the restoration of the company's name to the register and the court may so order if satisfied, inter alia, that the application was in breach of sub-s (1): s 653(2B)(b).

S 652B(3)–(5)

Other proceedings under way or proposed   The effect of sub-s (3) is to rule out an attempt by the company to exit from the register and be dissolved via strike off

959

proceedings while other proceedings, mainly driven by creditors, may be underway or have been proposed with respect to the company.

An application in breach of these requirements is an offence under s 652E(1), subject to the defence in s 652E(3).

A notifiable person, defined s 653(2C), may apply to the court for the restoration of the company's name to the register and the court may so order if satisfied, inter alia, that the application was in breach of sub-s (3): s 653(2B)(b).

S 652B(6)

Persons who must be notified of application   These persons must be notified (subject to sub-s (8)) so as to enable them to object to the striking off if they so wish: see s 652A(3)(b) and the note to that provision, above. As notifiable persons, they may also apply to the court to have the company's name restored to the register under s 653: s 653(2B), (2C). The term 'creditor' includes contingent or prospective creditors (s 652D(8)), so the obligation to notify every creditor may be difficult; even with respect to known creditors, the obligations as to notice may be onerous: see s 652D(4). Of course, a company will only use this procedure if it has no assets left (in view of the fact that any property on dissolution is deemed to be bona vacantia: s 654) so it may seem unlikely that a creditor might want to object but see notes to ss 651 and 653 as to the circumstances in which creditors may seek restoration of dissolved companies.

Directors who have not signed the application must receive a copy in case they are unaware of what their colleagues are proposing; as to how notification is 'given' to any of the notifiable persons, see s 652D(1)–(4).

Penalties   It is an offence not to comply with these requirements as to notification (s 652E(1), subject to the defence in s 652E(4)), and there is a further offence, for which no defence is provided and for which the penalties are increased, where the failure to comply was done with the intention of concealing the making of the application in question: see s 652E(2) and Sch 24.

A person to whom notice is given under this provision is a notifiable person entitled to make an application for the company's name to be restored to the register under s 653: and the court may so order if satisfied, inter alia, that the application was in breach of sub-s (6): s 653(2B)(a).

S 652B(7)

An application is withdrawn by notice in the prescribed form to the registrar of companies: see s 652D(6).

S 652B(9)

No orders have been made under this provision.

652C. Directors' duties following application under section 652A

(1)   Subsection (2) applies in relation to any time after the day on which a company makes an application under section 652A and before the day on which the application is finally dealt with or withdrawn.

(2)   A person who is a director of the company at the end of a day on which a person other than himself becomes—

(a)   a member of the company,

(b)   an employee of the company,

(c)   a creditor of the company,

(d)   a director of the company,

(e)   a manager or trustee of any pension fund established for the benefit of employees of the company, or

(f)   a person of a description specified for the purposes of this paragraph by regulations made by the Secretary of State,

shall secure that a copy of the application is given to that person within 7 days from that day.

(3)   The duty imposed by subsection (2) shall cease to apply if the application is finally dealt with or withdrawn before the end of the period for giving the copy application.

(4)   Subsection (5) applies where, at any time on or after the day on which a company makes an application under section 652A and before the day on which the application is finally dealt with or withdrawn—

(a)   the company—

(i)   changes its name,

(ii)   trades or otherwise carries on business,

(iii)   makes a disposal for value of any property or rights other than those which it was necessary or expedient for it to hold for the purpose of making, or proceeding with, an application under section 652A, or

(iv)   engages in any other activity, except one to which subsection (6) applies;

(b)   an application is made to the court under section 425 on behalf of the company for the sanctioning of a compromise or arrangement;

(c)   a voluntary arrangement in relation to the company is proposed under Part I of the Insolvency Act 1986;

(d)   a petition is presented for the making of an administration order under Part II of that Act in relation to the company;

(e)   there arise any of the circumstances in which, under section 84(1) of that Act, the company may be voluntarily wound up;

(f)   a petition is presented for the winding up of the company by the court under Part IV of that Act;

(g)   a receiver or manager of the company's property is appointed; or

(h)   a judicial factor is appointed to administer the company's estate.

(5)   A person who, at the end of a day on which an event mentioned in any of paragraphs (a) to (h) of subsection (4) occurs, is a director of the company shall secure that the company's application is withdrawn forthwith.

(6)   This subsection applies to any activity which is—

  (a) necessary or expedient for the purpose of making, or proceeding with, an application under section 652A,

  (b) necessary or expedient for the purpose of concluding affairs of the company which are outstanding because of what has been necessary or expedient for the purpose of making, or proceeding with, such an application,

  (c) necessary or expedient for the purpose of complying with any statutory requirement, or

  (d) specified by the Secretary of State by order for the purposes of this subsection.

(7)   For the purposes of subsection (4)(a), a company shall not be treated as trading or otherwise carrying on business by virtue only of the fact that it makes a payment in respect of a liability incurred in the course of trading or otherwise carrying on business.

General note

Breach of the various duties imposed by this section is an offence: s 652E, subject to the defences provided by that provision.

S 652C(1)

Period between application and determination or withdrawal   This provision governs the period between the application for striking off and the final determination of that application or its withdrawal (as to the withdrawal of the application, see s 652D(6)).

S 652C(2)

Notification obligations   The effect of this oddly worded provision is to require a director, subject to sub-s (3), to give a copy of the application for striking off to any person who in this period becomes involved with the company in any of the guises specified; 'creditor' includes contingent or prospective creditors: s 652D(8); as to how a copy of the application is 'given', see s 652D(1)–(4).

Penalties   It is an offence not to comply with these requirements as to notification (s 652E(1), subject to the defence in s 652E(5)), and there is a further offence, for which no defence is provided and for which the penalties are increased, where the failure to comply was done with the intention of concealing the making of the application in question: see s 652E(2) and Sch 24.

   A person to whom notice is given under this provision is a notifiable person (see s 653(2C)) entitled to make an application for the company's name to be restored to the register under s 653: and the court may so order if satisfied, inter alia, that the application was in breach of this subsection: s 653(2B)(a).

S 652C(3)

An application is withdrawn by notice in the prescribed form to the registrar of companies: see s 652D(6).

S 652C(4)–(7)

Circumstances requiring withdrawal of application   These provisions mirror the provisions of s 652B(1), (3) which limit the circumstances in which an application for striking off can be made. This provision provides that the occurrence of any of those circumstances (other than the continued payment of the company's debts, sub-s (7)) in the period between the application and its final determination requires that the application be withdrawn (s 652C(4)), and the obligation to do so is placed on each director: see s 652C(5). It is an offence not to comply with this requirement to withdraw the application: s 652E(1), subject to the defence in s 652E(5). As to the withdrawal of an application, see s 652D(6).

Disposals of assets   The restriction on disposals (which includes part disposal: see s 652D(7)) is wider than that in s 652B(1)(c). There may be no disposals of assets of any sort other than those retained for the purposes of the application for striking off, for example, office premises.

The combined effect of s 652B(1) and these provisions is that all assets held for the purpose of disposal for gain in the normal course of trading etc must have been disposed of more than three months before the application; any other assets not within that classification, for example, premises and equipment, must be disposed of no later than in the three months prior to the application; and, finally, between the application and its determination, the company may only dispose of assets retained for the purpose of the application, for example, office premises.

In practice, given the criminal penalties, and the fact that the application must be withdrawn if any prohibited disposal takes place, it is best to ensure that all assets other than any necessary for the purpose of the application have been disposed of more than three months before the application. This will also ensure that no assets are overlooked which would then fall into bona vacantia under s 654.

652D. Sections 652B and 652C: supplementary provisions

(1)   For the purposes of sections 652B(6) and 652C(2), a document shall be treated as given to a person if it is delivered to him or left at his proper address or sent by post to him at that address.

(2)   For the purposes of subsection (1) and section 7 of the Interpretation Act 1978 (which relates to the service of documents by post) in its application to that subsection, the proper address of any person shall be his last known address, except that—

    (a) in the case of a body corporate, other than one to which subsection (3) applies, it shall be the address of its registered or principal office,

    (b) in the case of a partnership, other than one to which subsection (3) applies, it shall be the address of its principal office, and

    (c) in the case of a body corporate or partnership to which subsection (3) applies, it shall be the address of its principal office in the United Kingdom.

(3)   This subsection applies to a body corporate or partnership which—

    (a) is incorporated or formed under the law of a country or territory outside the United Kingdom, and

    (b) has a place of business in the United Kingdom.

(4)   Where a creditor of the company has more than one place of business, subsection (1) shall have effect, so far as concerns the giving of a document to him, as if for the words from 'delivered' to the end there were substituted 'left, or sent by post to him, at each place of business of his with which the company has had dealings in relation to a matter by virtue of which he is a creditor of the company.'

(5)   Any power to make an order or regulations under section 652B or 652C shall—

    (a) include power to make different provision for different cases or classes of case,

    (b) include power to make such transitional provisions as the Secretary of State considers appropriate, and

    (c) be exercisable by statutory instrument subject to annulment in pursuance of a resolution of either House of Parliament.

(6)   For the purposes of sections 652B and 652C, an application under section 652A is withdrawn if notice of withdrawal in the prescribed form is given to the registrar of companies.

(7)   In sections 652B and 652C, 'disposal' includes part disposal.

(8)   In sections 652B and 652C and this section, 'creditor' includes a contingent or prospective creditor.

General note

This provision makes no reference to the company's own articles and any provisions which might be contained therein as to the giving of notice, for example, to the members. Given that the section is part of a comprehensive block of sections (ss 652A–652F) added by CA 1989 to provide for the entire procedure for applications for striking off, this would seem to preclude any reliance on the company's own articles in this regard.

S 652D(4)

The obligation to give notice at 'each place of business' is potentially onerous, depending on the nature of the company's dealings with a particular creditor.

652E. Sections 652B and 652C: enforcement

(1)   A person who breaches or fails to perform a duty imposed on him by section 652B or 652C is guilty of an offence and liable to a fine.

(2)   A person who fails to perform a duty imposed on him by section 652B(6) or 652C(2) with the intention of concealing the making of the application in question from the person concerned is guilty of an offence and liable to imprisonment or a fine, or both.

(3)   In any proceedings for an offence under subsection (1) consisting of breach of a duty imposed by section 652B(1) or (3), it shall be a defence for the accused to prove that he did not know, and could not reasonably have known, of the existence of the facts which led to the breach.

(4)   In any proceedings for an offence under subsection (1) consisting of failure to perform the duty imposed by section 652B(6), it shall be a defence for the accused to prove that he took all reasonable steps to perform the duty.

(5)   In any proceedings for an offence under subsection (1) consisting of failure to perform a duty imposed by section 652C(2) or (5), it shall be a defence for the accused to prove—

    (a) that at the time of the failure he was not aware of the fact that the company had made an application under section 652A, or

    (b) that he took all reasonable steps to perform the duty.

General note

As to penalties, see s 730, Sch 24; note sub-s(2) which imposes more onerous penalties on breaches with the intention of concealing an application and the defences provided by sub-ss(3)-(5) are not applicable to that offence.

652F. Other offences connected with section 652A

(1)   Where a company makes an application under section 652A, any person who, in connection with the application, knowingly or recklessly furnishes any information to the registrar of companies which is false or misleading in a material particular is guilty of an offence and liable to a fine.

(2)   Any person who knowingly or recklessly makes an application to the registrar of companies which purports to be an application under section 652A, but which is not, is guilty of an offence and liable to a fine.

General note

There are two offences here: under sub-s (1), there is a legitimate application (ie by a company and within the requirements of s 652A) but false information etc is provided in connection with the application; in sub-s (2), the application is false (ie either by someone other than the company and/or not within the requirements of s 652A). As to penalties, see s 730, Sch 24.

653. Objection to striking off by person aggrieved

(1)   Subsection (2) applies if a company or any member or creditor of it feels aggrieved by the company having been struck off the register under section 652.

(2)   The court, on an application by the company or the member or creditor made before the expiration of 20 years from publication in the Gazette of notice under section 652, may, if satisfied that the company was at the time of the striking off carrying on business or in operation, or otherwise that it is just that the company be restored to the register, order the company's name to be restored.

(2A) Subsections (2B) and (2D) apply if a company has been struck off the register under section 652A.

(2B) The court, on an application by a notifiable person made before the expiration of 20 years from publication in the Gazette of notice under section 652A(4), may, if satisfied—

- (a) that any duty under section 652B or 652C with respect to the giving to that person of a copy of the company's application under section 652A was not performed,
- (b) that the making of the company's application under section 652A involved a breach of duty under section 652B(1) or (3), or
- (c) that it is for some other reason just to do so,

order the company's name to be restored to the register.

(2C) In subsection (2B),'notifiable person' means a person to whom a copy of the company's application under section 652A was required to be given under section 652B or 652C.

(2D) The court, on an application by the Secretary of State made before the expiration of 20 years from publication in the Gazette of notice under section 652A(4), may, if satisfied that it is in the public interest to do so, order the company's name to be restored.

(3)   On an office copy of an order under subsection (2),(2B) or (2D) being delivered to the registrar of companies for registration the company to which the order relates is deemed to have continued in existence as if its name had not been struck off; and the court may by the order give such directions and make such provisions as seem just for placing the company and all other persons in the same position (as nearly as may be) as if the company's name had not been struck off.

General note

This provision has no application to companies which have been dissolved following liquidation, restoration in those cases is governed by s 651.

S 653(1), (2)

Applicants and respondents   This provision involves a statutory fiction whereby the non-existent company is deemed to exist, but solely for the purpose of applying under this provision; in practice, the court usually requires that another person, whether a member or creditor, join in the application so as to ensure that a person against whom orders can effectively be made (for example, for costs if the petition fails) is party to the proceedings: see *Re AGA Estate Agencies Ltd* [1986] BCLC 346 at 348.

'Member' includes a personal representative of a member although not on the register of shareholders at the time: *Re Bayswater Trading Co Ltd* [1970] 1 All ER 608. 'Creditor' for these purposes includes prospective and contingent creditors; it is not necessary for the applicant creditor to have an existing cause of action at the time when the company was struck off the register, it suffices that the company was then subject to a liability, whether contingent or prospective, which a creditor might need to enforce: *City of Westminster Assurance Co Ltd v Registrar of Companies* [1997] BCC 960 at 963; *Re Harvest Lane Motor Bodies Ltd* [1969] 1 Ch 457. See also the Scottish case *Conti v Ueberseebank AG* [2000] BCC 172 (Ct of Sess, OH), where the court held that the date when the grievance must exist is the date of the application and, in determining whether there is a grievance, one is not necessarily limited to a consideration of the situation as it was at the date of striking off.

The practice had been that on an application for restoration, a person other than the applicant and the registrar of companies could not be joined as a party (see *Re Portrafram Ltd* [1986] BCLC 533); but in *Re Blenheim Leisure (Restaurants) Ltd* [2000] BCC 554, the Court of Appeal, by a majority, decided that third parties could be joined where the order for restoration would directly affect their rights (following *Stanhope Pension Trust Ltd v Registrar of Companies* [1994] 1 BCLC 628, with respect to applications for restoration under s 651, see note to that section, above); see also *Re Jayham Ltd* [1995] 2 BCLC 455; and it does not matter that the right directly affected arose post-striking off: *Re Blenheim Leisure (Restaurants) Ltd* [2000] BCC 554. In *Blenheim*, the party seeking to be joined in the proceedings was a landlord who in effect had regained possession of premises leased to the company by virtue of the dissolution and who was therefore opposed to restoration which would restore the company's possession of the premises.

The court's discretion   The court has a discretion to order restoration either because the registrar of companies was incorrect in believing that the company was not carrying on business or in operation or on the basis that it is just that the company be restored. Whether a company was carrying on business or in operation must be considered by reference to the time of dissolution. If, at the time of dissolution, the company was carrying on any activity at all, the court's power to restore is brought into play; it is only if, at that time, the company was completely dormant, that the court's jurisdiction is not made out: see *Re Priceland Ltd, Waltham Forest London BC v Registrar of Companies* [1997] 1 BCLC 467 at 472.

Exercising the court's discretion against restoration should be the exception, not the rule: see *Re Priceland Ltd, Waltham Forest London Borough Council v Registrar of Companies* [1997] 1 BCLC 467. While not suggesting that an application is a formality, the practice of the court is to make the order under this provision if a real advantage will accrue to the contributories or creditors of the company from its revival and if all defaults are remedied, the costs of the registrar of companies are provided for and the Treasury Solicitor has stated that no objection is taken on behalf of the Crown in right of bona vacantia: see *Steans Fashions Ltd v Legal and General Assurance Society Ltd* [1995] 1 BCLC 332 at 335–336, CA.

The approach of the court under s 651, that the interest of an applicant in having the company revived does not have to be firmly established or highly likely to prevail, provided that it is not 'merely shadowy' *(Re Wood and Martin (Bricklaying Contractors) Ltd* [1971] 1 All ER 732 at 736, per Megarry J, approved in *Stanhope Pension Trust Ltd v Registrar of Companies* [1994] 1 BCLC 628 at 635), is equally applicable to proceedings under this provision: see *Re Blenheim Leisure (Restaurants) Ltd (No 2)* [2000] BCC 821 at 829–830. A member seeking restoration need not establish that, if restored, the company will on the balance of probabilities be solvent; if he can establish that the company has some real prospect of being valuable then, the right course is to restore the company and let any other arguments be dealt with in another court: see *Re Blenheim Leisure (Restaurants) Ltd (No 2)* [2000] BCC 821 at 836.

The fact that the benefit sought might be described as collateral does not take the application outside the scope of the section which is intended to provide a remedy for a person who has a claim, whether against the company or against a third party, such as the company's insurer or guarantor, which remedy can only be enforced if the company is restored to the register: *City of Westminster Assurance Co Ltd v Registrar of Companies* [1997] BCC 960 (application by landlord to have company restored in order to enforce guarantee given by the company's holding company was not outside the scope of the section).

S 653(2A)–(2C)

These provisions apply where the company was struck off following an application by the company under s 652A; the applicant here is any 'notifiable person' defined by sub-s (2C). A director who signs the application to strike off cannot apply to have the company restored: see sub-s (2C); s 652B(7); and *Re Blenheim Leisure (Restaurants) Ltd (No 2)* [2000] BCC 821 at 829 (cf *Conti v Ueberseebank AG* [2000] BCC 172 (Ct of Sess, OH), an application under s 653(1)).

Whether it is just to order restoration will depend on the circumstances of the case including the nature of the application to remove the company's name from the register, the reasons for the application to restore and the subsequent events which have happened including intervening substantive rights which have arisen since dissolution: *Re Blenheim Leisure (Restaurants) Ltd* [2000] BCC 554.

S 653(2D)

Application by the Secretary of State This provision was inserted by the Deregulation and Contracting Out Act 1994, s 13(1), Sch 5, paras 1, 3(1),(3), as from 1 July 1995 to close the loophole which had been exposed by *Re Townreach Ltd (No 002081 of 1994)* [1995] Ch 28, namely that the Secretary of State, despite his statutory duties with respect to the regulation and supervision of companies, was not a person then entitled to seek restoration of a company struck off by the registrar of companies under this provision.

S 653(3)

Company deemed to have continued in existence An order made under this provision restoring a company to the register is effective to validate retrospectively all acts done in the name or on behalf of the company during the period between its dissolution and the restoration of its name to the register: *Top Creative Ltd v St Albans District Council* [2000] 2 BCLC 379, CA; *Tyman's Ltd v Craven* [1952] 1 All ER 613. The proviso to this subsection enables the court (consistently with justice) to achieve to the fullest extent the 'as you were position' of the company: *Tyman's Ltd v Craven* [1952] 1 All ER 613 at 618–619. In *Top Creative Ltd v St Albans District Council* [2000] 2 BCLC 379 an action commenced by the company prior to dissolution was revived on the company being restored to the register and steps taken by the officers of the company on the company's behalf while it was dissolved become the acts of the company by virtue of the resuscitating properties of this section (at 387).

Assets remained in ownership of the company   As the company is deemed never to have been removed from the register, any assets which vested in the Crown as bona vacantia are deemed not have so vested with the result that no revesting order is required. It follows that a disclaimer by the Crown of a lease to which it has become entitled by virtue of bona vacantia is treated as never having happened so that the restoration of the company results also in the restoration of the company's lease, assuming that it has not been forfeited in the interim; and when the lease is restored, any liability of sureties under the lease with respect to the period between the dissolution and restoration is also restored: see *Allied Dunbar Assurance plc v Fowle* [1994] 2 BCLC 197.

Directions must support the statutory fiction   Any directions given under this provision must support and not negative the statutory fiction that the company has never been removed from the register; and it is not right to insert, as a condition of restoration, a clause to preserve the position as if the company had been struck off: *Re Lindsey Bowman Ltd* [1969] 3 All ER 601; *Re Priceland Ltd, Waltham Forest London Borough Council v Registrar of Companies* [1997] 1 BCLC 467; see also *Re Blenheim Leisure (Restaurants) Ltd (No 2)* [2000] BCC 821 at 831.

Where a company has been struck off and dissolved due to a failure to file accounts, it is common practice to require an undertaking to comply with the statutory filing obligations on restoration, or, as had been done more recently, to order restoration in principle but directing that the restoration order should not be drawn up and delivered to the registrar of companies until there had been compliance. Undertakings as to the company's name may also be sought, where another company with the same name has been registered in the intervening period. Depending on the purpose for which restoration was sought, it may be appropriate to seek an undertaking that if the company is insolvent and fails in the purpose for which it is restored, the directors will petition for winding up: see *Re Blenheim Leisure (Restaurants) Ltd (No 2)* [2000] BCC 821 at 836–837. In *Shire Court Residents Ltd v Registrar of Companies* [1995] BCC 821 the court imposed a condition that a lease held by the company to be restored should take effect subject to three new sub-leases which had been granted while the company had been dissolved.

In *Re Blenheim Leisure (Restaurants) Ltd (No 2)* (1999) Times, 26 October, Ch D, the dissolved company's former landlord asked the court to impose as a condition on any restoration, that the company would pay the £180,000 in rent which it owed. The court considered that its power to impose conditions for the benefit of a particular party when exercising its jurisdiction to restore a company to the register should be limited, and not regarded as an opportunity for parties who were neither the company nor the registrar of companies to obtain benefits by way of conditions save in exceptional circumstances. However, in the wholly exceptional facts of that case, the court thought it would be right to impose the condition sought.

654. Property of dissolved company to be bona vacantia

(1)   When a company is dissolved, all property and rights whatsoever vested in or held on trust for the company immediately before its dissolution (including leasehold property, but not including property held by the company on trust for any other person) are deemed to be bona vacantia and—

  (a)   accordingly belong to the Crown, or to the Duchy of Lancaster or to the Duke of Cornwall for the time being (as the case may be), and

  (b)   vest and may be dealt with in the same manner as other bona vacantia accruing to the Crown, to the Duchy of Lancaster or to the Duke of Cornwall.

(2)   Except as provided by the section next following, the above has effect subject and without prejudice to any order made by the court under section 651 or 653.

S 654(1)

Whether the property belongs to the Duchy of Lancaster or the Duchy of Cornwall under this provision depends on whether the registered office of the company is in Lancashire or in Cornwall. As to a disclaimer of any property so vesting and the effect of any such disclaimer, see ss 656, 657.

Property of the company   If the property is held on trust by the company, on dissolution the legal title and the trusteeship is in the Crown and it is not a case of bona vacantia; the initial dispute in such cases is whether the property is held on trust or owned by the company, see for example, *Neville v Wilson* [1996] 2 BCLC 310; *Orwin v A-G* [1998] 2 BCLC 693.

   A waste management licence granted under the Environmental Protection Act 1990 and held by a company which is dissolved is not 'property' in the sense in which property is used in this provision such that it vests in the Crown as bona vacantia under this provision; rather the licence ceases to exists on dissolution: *Re Wilmott Trading Ltd (Nos 1 and 2)* [1999] 2 BCLC 541; but see also *Re Celtic Extraction Ltd* [1999] 2 BCLC 555.

S 654(2)

As to the automatic re-vesting of the property in the company on the dissolution being declared void or on the court's order that the company's name be restored to the register, see notes to s 651(1),(2), s 653(3), respectively.

   As this subsection appears to require an order under s 651 or s 653, it seems that this re-vesting would not arise on a compulsory winding up order being made (as permitted by s 652(6)) which is not preceded by an order for the restoration of the company: see *Re Cambridge Coffee Room Association Ltd* [1952] 1 All ER 112n.

655. Effect on s 654 of company's revival after dissolution

(1)   The person in whom any property or right is vested by section 654 may dispose of, or of an interest in, that property or right notwithstanding that an order may be made under section 651 or 653.

(2)   Where such an order is made—

(a) it does not affect the disposition (but without prejudice to the order so far as it relates to any other property or right previously vested in or held on trust for the company), and

(b) the Crown or, as the case may be, the Duke of Cornwall shall pay to the company an amount equal to—

(i)   the amount of any consideration received for the property or right, or interest therein, or

(ii)   the value of any such consideration at the time of the disposition,

or, if no consideration was received, an amount equal to the value of the property, right or interest disposed of, as at the date of the disposition.

(3)   Where a liability accrues under subsection (2) in respect of any property or right which, before the order under section 651 or 653 was made, had accrued as bona vacantia to the Duchy of Lancaster, the Attorney General of the Duchy shall represent Her Majesty in any proceedings arising in connection with that liability.

(4)   Where a liability accrues under subsection (2) in respect of any property or right which, before the order under section 651 or 653 was made, had accrued as bona vacantia to the Duchy of Cornwall, such persons as the Duke of Cornwall (or other possessor for the time being of the Duchy) may appoint shall represent the Duke (or other possessor) in any proceedings arising out of that liability.

(5)   This section applies in relation to the disposition of any property, right or interest on or after 22nd December 1981, whether the company concerned was dissolved before, on or after that day.

S 655(1), (2)

The Crown may dispose of the property which has vested in it as bona vacantia subject to the payment of the amount due to the company in the event of it being restored by virtue of an order under s 651 or s 653.

656. Crown disclaimer of property vesting as bona vacantia

(1)   Where property vests in the Crown under section 654, the Crown's title to it under that section may be disclaimed by a notice signed by the Crown representative, that is to say the Treasury Solicitor, or, in relation to property in Scotland, the Queen's and Lord Treasurer's Remembrancer.

(2)   The right to execute a notice of disclaimer under this section may be waived by or on behalf of the Crown either expressly or by taking possession or other act evincing that intention.

(3)   A notice of disclaimer under this section is of no effect unless it is executed—

- (a) within 12 months of the date on which the vesting of the property under section 654 came to the notice of the Crown representative, or
- (b) if an application in writing is made to the Crown representative by any person interested in the property requiring him to decide whether he will or will not disclaim, within a period of 3 months after the receipt of the application or such further period as may be allowed by the court which would have had jurisdiction to wind up the company if it had not been dissolved.

(4)   A statement in a notice of disclaimer of any property under this section that the vesting of it came to the notice of the Crown representative on a specified date, or that no such application as above mentioned was received by him with respect to the property before a specified date, is sufficient evidence of the fact stated, until the contrary is proved.

(5)   A notice of disclaimer under this section shall be delivered to the registrar of companies and retained and registered by him; and copies of it shall be published in the Gazette and sent to any persons who have given the Crown representative notice that they claim to be interested in the property.

(6)   This section applies to property vested in the Duchy of Lancaster or the Duke of Cornwall under section 654 as if for references to the Crown and the Crown representative there were respectively substituted references to the Duchy of Lancaster and to the Solicitor to that Duchy, or to the Duke of Cornwall and to the Solicitor to the Duchy of Cornwall, as the case may be.

General note

As to the effect of a disclaimer under this provision, see s 657.

S 656(3)

The Crown has to make its mind up as to a disclaimer within 12 months of the vesting of the property coming to the notice of the Crown representative; or within three months of an application by an interested party which enables such parties to expedite a decision on the matter.

657. Effect of Crown disclaimer under s 656

(1)   Where notice of disclaimer is executed under section 656 as respects any property, that property is deemed not to have vested in the Crown under section 654.

(2)   As regards property in England and Wales, section 178(4) and sections 179 to 182 of the Insolvency Act shall apply as if the property had been disclaimed by the liquidator under the said section 91 immediately before the dissolution of the company.

(3)   As regards property in Scotland, the following 4 subsections apply.

(4)   The Crown's disclaimer operates to determine, as from the date of the disclaimer, the rights, interests and liabilities of the company, and the property of the company, in or in respect of the property disclaimed; but it does not (except so far as is necessary for the purpose of releasing the company and its property from liability) affect the rights or liabilities of any other person.

(5)   The court may, on application by a person who either claims an interest in disclaimed property or is under a liability not discharged by this Act in respect of disclaimed property, and on hearing such persons as it thinks fit, make an order for the vesting of the property in or its delivery to any persons entitled to it, or to whom it may seem just that the property should be delivered by way of compensation for such liability, or a trustee for him, and on such terms as the court thinks just.

(6)   On such a vesting order being made, the property comprised in it vests accordingly in the person named in that behalf in the order, without conveyance or assignation for that purpose.

(7)   Part II of Schedule 20 has effect for the protection of third parties where the property disclaimed is held under a lease.

General note

Reference in s 657(2) to 'said section 91': it is thought that this reference should have been altered by IA 1986 to a reference to IA 1986, ss 178–180.

S 657(1), (2)

The disclaimer by the Crown is to be treated as if it were a disclaimer by a liquidator immediately before the dissolution of the company within IA 1986, s 178, thus bringing into operation s 178(4) and IA 1986, ss 179–182 but this subsection does not require the Crown disclaimer to be treated for all purposes as if it were a liquidator's disclaimer, for the language used is very narrow and it does not deem there to have been a liquidation or provide that leases and other contractual arrangements should have effect as if the Crown disclaimer were a disclaimer by the liquidator: *Re Yarmarine (IW) Ltd* [1992] BCLC 276; *Re No 1 London Ltd* [1991] BCLC 501.

Where a company is restored to the register under s 653, any assets which vested in the Crown as bona vacantia are deemed not have so vested with the result that no revesting order is required. It follows that a disclaimer by the Crown of a lease to which it has become entitled by virtue of bona vacantia is treated as never having occurred so that the restoration of the company results also in the restoration of the company's lease, assuming that it has not been forfeited in the interim; and when the lease is restored, any liability of sureties under the lease with respect to the period between the dissolution and restoration is also restored: see *Allied Dunbar Assurance plc v Fowle* [1994] 2 BCLC 197.

658. Liability for rentcharge on company's land after dissolution

(1)   Section 180 of the Insolvency Act shall apply to land in England and Wales which by operation of law vests subject to a rentcharge in the Crown or any other person on the dissolution of a company as it applies to land so vesting on a disclaimer under that section.

(2)   In this section 'company' includes any body corporate.

General note

The effect of this provision is to ensure that the Crown is not subject to any liability when land subject to a rentcharge vests in the Crown as bona vacantia; IA 1986, s 180 imposes liability only where the Crown takes possession or control of the land or enters into occupation of it.

659.–674. *((Pt XX, Chapter VII, Pt XXI) Repealed by the Insolvency Act 1986, s 438, Sch 12, as from 29 December 1986.)*

PART XXII

BODIES CORPORATE SUBJECT, OR
BECOMING SUBJECT, TO THIS ACT
(OTHERWISE THAN BY ORIGINAL
FORMATION UNDER PART I)

COMPANIES FORMED OR REGISTERED UNDER FORMER COMPANIES ACTS

675. Companies formed and registered under former Companies Acts

(1)   In its application to existing companies, this Act applies in the same manner—

    (a)   in the case of a limited company (other than a company limited by guarantee) as if the company had been formed and registered under Part I of this Act as a company limited by shares,

    (b)   in the case of a company limited by guarantee, as if the company had been formed and registered under that Part as a company limited by guarantee, and

    (c)   in the case of a company other than a limited company, as if the company had been formed and registered under that Part as an unlimited company.

(2)   But reference, express or implied, to the date of registration is to be read as the date at which the company was registered under the Joint Stock Companies Acts, the Companies Act 1862, the Companies (Consolidation) Act 1908, the Companies Act 1929, or the Companies Act 1948.

General note

These provisions (ss 675–678) ensure, subject to the exclusion provided for by s 679, that companies formed and registered under earlier legislation, or registered but not formed under earlier legislation, etc are subject to the provisions of this Act. As to the meaning of 'this Act', see s 735A(1).

676. Companies registered but not formed under former Companies Acts

(1)   This Act applies to every company registered but not formed under the Joint Stock Companies Acts, the Companies Act 1862, the Companies (Consolidation) Act 1908, the Companies Act 1929, or the Companies Act 1948, in the same manner as it is in Chapter II of this Part declared to apply to companies registered but not formed under this Act.

(2)   But reference, express or implied, to the date of registration is to be read as referring to the date at which the company was registered under the Joint Stock Companies Acts, the Companies Act 1862, the Companies (Consolidation) Act 1908, the Companies Act 1929, or the Companies Act 1948.

General note

See the note to s 675, above and note the exclusion in s 679, below; as to the meaning of 'this Act', see s 735A(1).

677. Companies re-registered with altered status under former Companies Acts

(1)   This Act applies to every unlimited company registered or re-registered as limited in pursuance of the Companies Act 1879, section 57 of the Companies (Consolidation) Act 1908, section 16 of the Companies Act 1929, section 16 of the Companies Act 1948 or section 44 of the Companies Act 1967 as it (this Act) applies to an unlimited company re-registered as limited in pursuance of Part II of this Act.

(2)   But reference, express or implied, to the date of registration or re-registration is to be read as referring to the date at which the company was registered or re-registered as a limited company under the relevant enactment.

General note

See the note to s 675 and note the exclusion in s 679; as to the meaning of 'this Act', see s 735A(1).

678. Companies registered under Joint Stock Companies Acts

(1)   A company registered under the Joint Stock Companies Acts may cause its shares to be transferred in manner hitherto in use, or in such other manner as the company may direct.

(2)   The power of altering articles under section 9 of this Act extends, in the case of an unlimited company formed and registered under the Joint Stock Companies Acts, to altering any regulations relating to the amount of capital or to its distribution into shares, notwithstanding that those regulations are contained in the memorandum.

General note

This provision is of limited practical significance now; note the exclusion in s 679.

679. Northern Ireland and Irish companies

Nothing in sections 675 to 678 applies to companies registered in Northern Ireland or the Republic of Ireland.

General note

This provision makes clear that the fact that companies registered in the jurisdictions mentioned may have been formed and registered under the statutes specified in ss 675–678 does not bring them within the scope of this Act.

COMPANIES NOT FORMED UNDER COMPANIES LEGISLATION, BUT AUTHORISED TO REGISTER

680. Companies capable of being registered under this Chapter

(1)   With the exceptions and subject to the provisions contained in this section and the next—

   (a) any company consisting of two or more members, which was in existence on 2nd November 1862, including any company registered under the Joint Stock Companies Acts, and

   (b) any company formed after that date (whether before or after the commencement of this Act), in pursuance of any Act of Parliament (other than this Act), or of letters patent, or being otherwise duly constituted according to law, and consisting of two or more members,

may at any time, on making application in the prescribed form, register under this Act as an unlimited company, or as a company limited by shares, or as a company limited by guarantee; and the registration is not invalid by reason that it has taken place with a view to the company's being wound up.

(1A) A company shall not be prevented from registering under this Act as a private company limited by shares or guarantee solely because it has only one member.

(2)   A company registered in any part of the United Kingdom under the Companies Act 1862, the Companies (Consolidation) Act 1908, the Companies Act 1929 or the Companies Act 1948 shall not register under this section.

(3)   A company having the liability of its members limited by Act of Parliament or letters patent, and not being a joint stock company, shall not register under this section.

(4)   A company having the liability of its members limited by Act of Parliament or letters patent shall not register in pursuance of this section as an unlimited company or as a company limited by guarantee.

(5)   A company that is not a joint stock company shall not register under this section as a company limited by shares.

General note

Detailed provisions supplementing these registration provisions are contained in Sch 21, which deals with the vesting of property, the savings for existing liabilities, the continuation of existing actions, the status of the company following registration, and other connected matters: s 689.

S 680(1)

Facility to register under this Act   This provision, subject to the exceptions set out, facilitates the registration under CA 1985 of 'old' companies. Where the company seeks registration as a public company, s 685 imposes additional requirements. Registration may be sought in order to avail of the modern legislation. The alternative is to wind up the company and then incorporate afresh as a registered company.

The categories which can avail of the facility are limited to those specified, ie deed of settlement companies in existence on 2 November 1862 including any company registered under the Joint Stock Companies Acts (defined, s 735(3)) and companies formed thereafter by private Act of Parliament or by letters patent. The words 'or otherwise duly constituted' must be interpreted ejusdem generis with the preceding categories and so is limited to companies constituted in some manner analogous to those classes of companies: *R v Joint Stock Companies Registrar* [1891] 2 QB 598 at 612, per Fry LJ. This would include companies incorporated by royal charter.

Reason for registering Such companies can register even if only to avail of the provisions with regard to the winding up of registered companies. In the absence of registration under this provision, such companies (with the exception of companies registered under the Joint Stock Companies Acts: see IA 1986, s 73(1)) would have to be wound up as unregistered companies under IA 1986, s 220, which companies cannot be wound up voluntarily: IA 1986, s 221(4).

Once registered under s 680, all the provisions of CA 1985 (subject to some limited exceptions) apply to the company, and to its members, contributories and creditors, in the same manner in all respects as if it had been formed under the Act: Sch 21, para 6 (but note that Table A does not apply unless adopted by special resolution: para 6(2)).

S 680(1A)

As to single member private companies, see s 1(3A).

S 680(2)

Such companies are treated as companies under the CA 1985 (s 735(1)) and do not require registration under this provision.

S 680(3)

A statutory company or a company formed by letters patent with limited liability which does not meet the requirements of the definition of a joint stock company in s 683 (essentially a requirement to have share capital and membership based on share ownership) cannot register under these provisions.

S 680(4)

A statutory company or a company formed by letters patent with limited liability and a share capital is prevented from registering as an unlimited company (defined s 1(2)(c)) or as a company limited by guarantee (defined s 1(2)(b)) and can only register as a company limited by shares (defined s 1(2)(a)).

S 680(5)

The effect of the requirements of sub-s (1) and the exclusions contained in sub-s (3) is that a company which is to be registered under this provision which is a company without a share capital cannot register as a company limited by shares but may do so as an unlimited company (defined s 1(2)(c)) or as a company limited by guarantee (defined s 1(2)(b)).

681. Procedural requirements for registration

(1)　A company shall not register under section 680 without the assent of a majority of such of its members as are present in person or by proxy (in cases where proxies are allowed) at a general meeting summoned for the purpose.

(2)　Where a company not having the liability of its members limited by Act of Parliament or letters patent is about to register as a limited company, the majority required to assent as required by subsection (1) shall consist of not less than three-fourths of the members present in person or by proxy at the meeting.

(3)　In computing any majority under this section when a poll is demanded, regard is to be had to the number of votes to which each member is entitled according to the company's regulations.

(4)　Where a company is about to register (under section 680) as a company limited by guarantee, the assent to its being so registered shall be accompanied by a resolution declaring that each member undertakes to contribute to the company's assets, in the event of its being wound up while he is a member, or within one year after he ceases to be a member, for payment of the company's debts and liabilities contracted before he ceased to be a member, and of the costs and expenses of winding up and for the adjustment of the rights of the contributories among themselves, such amount as may be required, not exceeding a specified amount.

(5)　Before a company is registered under section 680, it shall deliver to the registrar of companies—

    (a)　a statement that the registered office of the company is to be situated in England and Wales, or in Wales, or in Scotland (as the case may be),

    (b)　a statement specifying the intended situation of the company's registered office after registration, and

    (c)　in an appropriate case, if the company wishes to be registered with the Welsh equivalent of 'public limited company' or, as the case may be, 'limited' as the last words or word of its name, a statement to that effect.

(6)　Any statement delivered to the registrar under subsection (5) shall be made in the prescribed form.

S 681(1), (2)

Assent of members required　A simple majority of members suffices other than as provided by sub-s (2).

S 681(4)

As to a company limited by guarantee, see s 1(2)(b). This statement (as would be the case if the company had been formed and registered under this Act – see s 2(4)) is treated as included in the memorandum of association of the company: see Sch 21, para 5(2). There is no indication of the nature of the resolution which is required, which presumably is dictated by sub-ss (1), (2)

S 681(5)

Documents to be delivered to the registrar of companies   These requirements match those required on formation as a registered company (see ss 2(1)(b), 10(6), 25); and they apply to any company seeking registration under s 680. As to the company's name, see also s 687. The statement in sub-s (5)(a) (as would be the case if the company had been formed and registered under this Act – see s 2(1)(b)) is treated as included in the memorandum of association of the company: see Sch 21, para 5(2).

Where the company seeking registration is a joint stock company as defined in s 683, there are additional delivery requirements regarding the company's name, members, constitution and capital (if it is to be a limited company) in s 684; and, where registration as a public company is sought, in s 685.

Where the company seeking registration is not a joint stock company as defined in s 683, there are additional delivery requirements regarding the company's name, officers, constitution and amount of guarantee (if the company is to be limited by guarantee) in s 686.

The information delivered to the registrar of companies must be verified by a statutory declaration: see s 686(2).

682. Change of name on registration

(1) Where the name of a company seeking registration under section 680 is a name by which it is precluded from registration by section 26 of this Act, either because it falls within subsection (1) of that section or, if it falls within subsection (2), because the Secretary of State would not approve the company's being registered with that name, the company may change its name with effect from the date on which it is registered under this Chapter.

(2) A change of name under this section requires the like assent of the company's members as is required by section 681 for registration.

General note

Section 26(1) prohibits the use of certain company names while s 26(2) prohibits the use of certain other names except with the consent of the Secretary of State for Trade and Industry, so if the existing name of a company which is to be registered under s 680 infringes these requirements then, by the majority specified by s 681, it may change its name under this provision, which takes effect from registration. As to the company's name, see also s 687.

683. Definition of 'joint stock company'

(1)   For purposes of this Chapter, as far as relates to registration of companies as companies limited by shares, 'joint stock company' means a company—

(a)   having a permanent paid-up or nominal share capital of fixed amount divided into shares, also of fixed amount, or held and transferable as stock, or divided and held partly in one way and partly in the other, and

(b)   formed on the principle of having for its members the holders of those shares or that stock, and no other persons.

(2)   Such a company when registered with limited liability under this Act is deemed a company limited by shares.

General note

See the note to s 680, above.

684. Requirements for registration by joint stock companies

(1)   Before the registration under section 680 of a joint stock company, there shall be delivered to the registrar of companies the following documents—

(a)   a statement in the prescribed form specifying the name with which the company is proposed to be registered,

(b)   a list in the prescribed form showing the names and addresses of all persons who on a day named in the list (not more than 28 clear days before the day of registration) were members of the company, with the addition of the shares or stock held by them respectively (distinguishing, in cases where the shares are numbered, each share by its number), and

(c)   a copy of any Act of Parliament, royal charter, letters patent, deed of settlement, contract of copartnery or other instrument constituting or regulating the company.

(2)   If the company is intended to be registered as a limited company, there shall also be delivered to the registrar of companies a statement in the prescribed form specifying the following particulars—

(a)   the nominal share capital of the company and the number of shares into which it is divided, or the amount of stock of which it consists, and

(b)   the number of shares taken and the amount paid on each share.

S 684(1)

Additional requirements   These requirements are in addition to those in s 681(5) and relate to the company's name (see also s 682), its membership and constitution; and in the case of a limited company, its share capital. As regards the name of the company, this will be subject to the constraints imposed by s 26: see Sch 21, para 6(1). The information delivered to the registrar of companies must be verified by a statutory declaration: see s 686(2).

S 684(2)

The statement as to capital (as would be the case if the company had been formed and registered under this Act – see s 2(5)) is treated as included in the memorandum of association of the company: see Sch 21, para 5(2).

---

685. Registration of joint stock company as public company

(1)   A joint stock company applying to be registered under section 680 as a company limited by shares may, subject to—

(a) satisfying the conditions set out in section 44(2)(a) and (b) (where applicable) and section 45(2) to (4) as applied by this section, and

(b) complying with subsection (4) below,

apply to be so registered as a public company.

(2)   Sections 44 and 45 apply for this purpose as in the case of a private company applying to be re-registered under section 43, but as if a reference to the special resolution required by section 43 were to the joint stock company's resolution that it be a public company.

(3)   The resolution may change the company's name by deleting the word 'company' or the words 'and company', or its or their equivalent in Welsh ('cwmni', 'a'r cwmni'), including any abbreviation of them.

(4)   The joint stock company's application shall be made in the form prescribed for the purpose, and shall be delivered to the registrar of companies together with the following documents (as well as those required by section 684), namely—

(a) a copy of the resolution that the company be a public company,

(b) a copy of a written statement by an accountant with the appropriate qualifications that in his opinion a relevant balance sheet shows that at the balance sheet date the amount of the company's net assets was not less than the aggregate of its called up share capital and undistributable reserves,

(c) a copy of the relevant balance sheet, together with a copy of an unqualified report (by an accountant with such qualifications) in relation to that balance sheet,

(d) a copy of any valuation report prepared under section 44(2)(b) as applied by this section, and

(e) subject to subsection (4A), a statutory declaration in the prescribed form by a director or secretary of the company—

    (i) that the conditions set out in section 44(2)(a) and (b) (where applicable) and section 45(2) to (4) have been satisfied, and

    (ii) that, between the balance sheet date referred to in paragraph (b) of this subsection and the joint stock company's application, there has been no change in the company's financial position that has resulted in the amount of its net assets becoming less than the aggregate of its called up share capital and undistributable reserves.

(4A) In place of the statutory declaration referred to in paragraph (e) of subsection (4), there may be delivered to the registrar of companies using electronic communications a statement made by a director or secretary of the company as to the matters set out in sub-paragraphs (i) and (ii) of that paragraph.

(5) The registrar may accept a declaration under subsection (4)(e) or statement under subsection (4A) as sufficient evidence that the conditions referred to in that paragraph have been satisfied

(6) In this section—

'accountant with the appropriate qualifications' means a person who would be eligible for appointment as the company's auditor, if it were a company registered under this Act,

'relevant balance sheet' means a balance sheet prepared as at a date not more than 7 months before the joint stock company's application to be registered as a public company limited by shares, and

'undistributable reserves' has the meaning given by section 264(3);

and section 46 applies (with necessary modifications) for the interpretation of the reference in subsection (4)(c) above to an unqualified report by the accountant.

(6A) Any person who makes a false statement under subsection (4A) which he knows to be false or does not believe to be true is liable to imprisonment or a fine, or both.

General note

This provision mirrors, with appropriate modifications, the procedure in s 43ff governing re-registration of a private company as a public company: see the notes to those provisions.

S 685(1), (2)

A joint stock company is defined in s 683. Such a company seeking registration as a public company is subject to the rules governing minimum share capital, payment for shares and the valuation of non-cash consideration for shares, which are applied by ss 44 and 45 to private companies seeking to re-register as public companies: see the notes to those provisions.

S 685(3)

See the note to s 43(5). The name of the company must end with the words 'public limited company' or p.l.c. or the Welsh equivalent: s 687(2).

S 685(4)

These requirements are similar to those in s 43(3): see the notes to that provision; the nature of the resolution required is dictated by s 681(1), (2); as to an 'accountant with the appropriate qualifications', see sub-s (6); as to 'an unqualified report' for the purposes of sub-s (4)(c), see sub-s (6).

S 685(4A)

Electronic communication　This provision was inserted by the Companies Act 1985 (Electronic Communications) Order 2000, SI 2000/3373, art 24(1), (3), as from 22 December 2000; it facilitates the acceptance by the registrar of companies of electronic statements as to certain matters in the same manner as he accepts statutory declarations as to those matters. As to the delivery of documents to the registrar using electronic communications, see s 707B.

S 685(5)

By 'sufficient evidence' it is meant that the registrar of companies can proceed on this basis unless the contrary is shown.

S 685(6)

Eligibility for appointment as a company auditor is governed by CA 1989, Pt II.

S 685(6A)

Penalties　This provision was inserted by the Companies Act 1985 (Electronic Communications) Order 2000, SI 2000/3373, art 24(1), (5), as from 22 December 2000; as to penalties, see s 730, Sch 24; the intention is to provide the same penalties for false statements as is provided by the Perjury Act 1911 for false statutory declarations.

686. Other requirements for registration

(1)　Before the registration in pursuance of this Chapter of any company (not being a joint stock company), there shall be delivered to the registrar of companies—

　　(a)　a statement in the prescribed form specifying the name with which the company is proposed to be registered,

(b) a list showing with respect to each director or manager of the company—

   (i)   in the case of an individual, his name, address, occupation and date of birth,

   (ii) in the case of a corporation or Scottish firm, its corporate or firm name and registered or principal office,

(c) a copy of any Act of Parliament, letters patent, deed of settlement, contract of copartnery or other instrument constituting or regulating the company, and

(d) in the case of a company intended to be registered as a company limited by guarantee, a copy of the resolution declaring the amount of the guarantee.

(1A) For the purposes of subsection (1)(b)(i) a person's 'name' means his Christian name (or other forename) and surname, except that in the case of a peer, or an individual usually known by a title, the title may be stated instead of his Christian name (or other forename) and surname or in addition to either or both of them.

(2)   Subject to subsection (2A), the lists of members and directors and any other particulars relating to the company which are required by this Chapter to be delivered to the registrar shall be verified by a statutory declaration in the prescribed form made by any two or more directors or other principal officers of the company.

(2A) In place of the statutory declaration referred to in subsection (2), there may be delivered to the registrar of companies using electronic communications a statement made by any two or more directors or other principal officers of the company verifying the matters set out in that subsection.

 (3) The registrar may require such evidence as he thinks necessary for the purpose of satisfying himself whether a company proposing to be registered is or is not a joint stock company as defined by section 683.

(3A) Any person who makes a false statement under subsection (2A) which he knows to be false or does not believe to be true is liable to imprisonment or a fine, or both.

General note

A company which is not a joint stock company as defined by s 683 cannot be registered as a company limited by shares (s 680(5)) so the only options are to register as an unlimited company or as a company limited by guarantee.

S 686(1)

As to the requirements regarding the name of the company, see s 687; the choice of name is subject to the constraints in s 26: Sch 21, para 6(1).

S 686(2A)

Electronic communication This provision was inserted by the Companies Act 1985 (Electronic Communications) Order 2000, SI 2000/3373, art 25(1), (3), as from 22 December 2000; it facilitates the acceptance by the registrar of companies of electronic statements as to certain matters in the same manner as he accepts statutory declarations as to those matters. As to the delivery of documents to the registrar using electronic communications, see s 707B.

S 686(3)

As the registration options and requirements vary depending on whether the company is or is not a joint stock company (see ss 680, 684–686), the matter is left to the decision of the registrar of companies having considered such evidence as he may require.

S 686(3A)

Penalties This provision was inserted by the Companies Act 1985 (Electronic Communications) Order 2000, SI 2000/3373, art 25(1), (4), as from 22 December 2000; as to penalties, see s 730, Sch 24; the intention is to provide the same penalties for false statements as is provided by the Perjury Act 1911 for false statutory declarations.

687. Name of company registering

(1) The following applies with respect to the name of a company registering under this Chapter (whether a joint stock company or not).

(2) If the company is to be registered as a public company, its name must end with the words 'public limited company' or, if it is stated that the company's registered office is to be situated in Wales, with those words or their equivalent in Welsh ('cwmni cyfyngedig chyoeddus'); and those words or that equivalent may not be preceded by the word 'limited' or its equivalent in Welsh ('cyfyngedig').

(3) In the case of a company limited by shares or by guarantee (not being a public company), the name must have 'limited' as its last word (or, if the company's registered office is to be situated in Wales, 'cyfyngedig'); but this is subject to section 30 (exempting a company, in certain circumstances, from having 'limited' as part of the name).

(4) If the company is registered with limited liability, then any additions to the company's name set out in the statements delivered under section 684(1)(a) or 686(1)(a) shall form and be registered as the last part of the company's name.

General note

See the note to s 25, above.

---

688. Certificate of registration under this Chapter

(1)   On compliance with the requirements of this Chapter with respect to registration, the registrar of companies shall give a certificate (which may be signed by him, or authenticated by his official seal) that the company applying for registration is incorporated as a company under this Act and, in the case of a limited company, that it is limited.

(2)   On the issue of the certificate, the company shall be so incorporated; and a banking company in Scotland so incorporated is deemed a bank incorporated, constituted or established by or under Act of Parliament.

(3)   The certificate is conclusive evidence that the requirements of this Chapter in respect of registration, and of matters precedent and incidental to it, have been complied with.

(4)   Where on an application by a joint stock company to register as a public company limited by shares the registrar of companies is satisfied that the company may be registered as a public company so limited, the certificate of incorporation given under this section shall state that the company is a public company; and that statement is conclusive evidence that the requirements of section 685 have been complied with and that the company is a public company so limited.

General note

As to the certificate of registration, see the note to s 13, above, which is the equivalent provision with respect to companies formed and registered under this Act.

---

689. Effect of registration

Schedule 21 to this Act has effect with respect to the consequences of registration under this Chapter, the vesting of property, savings for existing liabilities, continuation of existing actions, status of the company following registration, and other connected matters.

General note

Of particular importance is para 6 of this Schedule which, following registration, applies all the provisions of CA 1985 (subject to some limited exceptions) to the company, and to its members, contributories and creditors, in the same manner in all respects as if it had been formed under the Act.

690. Power to substitute memorandum and articles for deed of settlement

(1) Subject as follows, a company registered in pursuance of this Chapter may by special resolution alter the form of its constitution by substituting a memorandum and articles for a deed of settlement.

(2) The provisions of sections 4 to 6 of this Act with respect to applications to the court for cancellation of alterations of the objects of a company and matters consequential on the passing of resolutions for such alterations (so far as applicable) apply, but with the following modifications—

(a) there is substituted for the printed copy of the altered memorandum required to be delivered to the registrar of companies a printed copy of the substituted memorandum and articles, and

(b) on the delivery to the registrar of the substituted memorandum and articles or the date when the alteration is no longer liable to be cancelled by order of the court (whichever is the later)—

(i) the substituted memorandum and articles apply to the company in the same manner as if it were a company registered under Part I with that memorandum and those articles, and

(ii) the company's deed of settlement ceases to apply to the company.

(3) An alteration under this section may be made either with or without alteration of the company's objects.

(4) In this section 'deed of settlement' includes any contract of copartnery or other instrument constituting or regulating the company, not being an Act of Parliament, a royal charter or letters patent.

General note

This provision facilitates the modernisation of the company's constitution by entitling (but not requiring) the substitution of a memorandum and articles of association for the deed of settlement (defined in sub-s(4)) so that the company's constitutional structure is the same as if the company was formed and registered under this Act. Where the company does not substitute a memorandum and articles in this way, Sch 21, para 5, treats the existing constitution of the company as if the requirements applicable to a memorandum of association were contained in a memorandum and the residue are treated as the articles.

PART XXIII

OVERSEA COMPANIES

CHAPTER I

REGISTRATION, ETC

690A. Branch registration under the Eleventh Company Law Directive (89/666/EEC)

(1)   This section applies to any limited company which—

(a) is incorporated outside the United Kingdom and Gibraltar, and

(b) has a branch in Great Britain.

(2)   Schedule 21A to this Act (Branch registration under the Eleventh Company Law Directive (89/666/EEC)) shall have effect in relation to any company to which this section applies.

General note

Branch registration   This provision was inserted by the Oversea Companies and Credit and Financial Institutions (Branch Disclosure) Regulations 1992, SI 1992/ 3179 as from 1 January 1993. These Regulations gave effect to the requirements of the Eleventh Company Law Directive (89/666/EEC) OJ 1989 L395/36 (disclosure requirements in respect of branches opened in a member state by certain types of company governed by the law of another state) and the Bank Branches Directive (89/117/EEC) OJ 1989 L44/40 (obligations of branches established in a member state of credit institutions and financial institutions having their head offices outside that member state regarding the publication of annual accounting documents). The intention was, through disclosure, to protect third parties dealing with companies incorporated abroad and to ensure that companies could not avoid disclosure requirements by operating through a branch rather than a subsidiary company.

Two regimes   Prior to the implementation of the Eleventh Directive, oversea companies which established a place of business in Great Britain were subject to the registration and disclosure requirements imposed by s 691. The implementation of the Directive resulted in the creation of a branch regime under s 690A and Sch 21A alongside that place of business regime. Each regime is based on some degree of physical presence within the jurisdiction so companies trading into the jurisdiction but over the Internet without any physical presence here are not subject to either regime.

S 690A(1)

A limited company   It is not clear how the term 'limited company' is to be interpreted, ie whether from the domestic perspective or from the perspective of the state of incorporation. The latter interpretation is preferable since the intention behind the registration and disclosure requirements is to protect third parties dealing with limited companies incorporated elsewhere. The domestic classification of companies is irrelevant; what matters is whether the entity is a company with limited liability in its home jurisdiction; a point reinforced by Sch 21A which requires the company to disclose its legal form (para 2(1)(b)).

An unlimited company incorporated abroad cannot register under the branch regime and, if it is to be registered under this Part, can only be registered under s 691, assuming that it has established a place of business in Great Britain.

Incorporated outside the United Kingdom and Gibraltar   Although the legislation derives from an EEC Directive, it applies to all companies incorporated elsewhere than in the United Kingdom and Gibraltar and regardless of whether they are incorporated in member states of the European Union, although the disclosure requirements may vary depending on whether or not the company is incorporated in a member state.

Branch in Great Britain   To be within the branch regime, a company must be a limited company (cf s 691) incorporated other than in the United Kingdom or Gibraltar and it must have a branch in Great Britain (ie not in Northern Ireland or Gibraltar). Where such a company has a branch in Northern Ireland or Gibraltar, registration is governed by the legislation applicable to companies in those jurisdictions; if such a company also has a branch in Great Britain then registration under this provision will be required: see below as to multiple branches. A Northern Ireland company with a branch in Great Britain cannot register under this provision but can do so under the place of business regime: see s 691.

Meaning of 'branch'   Central to registration under this provision and Sch 21A is the determination that a company incorporated abroad has a branch in Great Britain, but the term 'branch' is not defined in the Eleventh Directive. The legislation provides limited guidance on this issue: s 698(2) defines a branch by reference to the Directive and is therefore of limited use; s 699A(3) offers some guidance as to the characteristics of a branch, but in the limited context of credit and financial institutions.

A branch, as a more permanent establishment, will always include the lesser presence of a place of business, but a place of business will not always amount to a branch. The conduct of merely ancillary activities, such as administrative, marketing or promotional activities, would not suffice to constitute a branch but would suffice for the purposes of being a place of business under s 691.

For the purposes of the Brussels Convention on the Enforcement of Judgments in Civil and Commercial Matters, the European Court of Justice has ruled that:

> 'the concept of a branch, agency or other establishment implies a place of business with an appearance of permanency, and which has a management and which is materially equipped to negotiate business with third parties so that the latter, although knowing that there will if necessary be a legal link with the parent body, the head office of which is abroad, does not have to deal directly with such parent body but may transact business at the place of business of the branch.' (Case 33/78 *Etablissements Somafer SA v Saar-Ferngas AG* [1978] ECR 2183 at 2192.)

It is likely that a similar interpretation would apply to 'branch' for the purposes of the Eleventh Directive.

As to transition between the branch and place of business regimes, see s 692A; as to publicity requirements for branches, see s 693; as to the rules governing names, see s 694; as to the service of documents on branches, see s 694A; as to the registrar to whom documents must be delivered, see s 695A; as to the notification of the closure of a branch, see s 695A(3); as to the requirement to deliver accounts to the registrar, see s 699AA and Sch 21D; as to the notifications required of winding up and other insolvency procedures, see ss 703O–703R.

S 690A(2)

Registration requirements   Schedule 21A sets out the detailed registration requirements applicable to a company subject to the branch registration requirements. A registration fee, currently £20, is also payable. As to the consequences of non-compliance with these requirements, see s 697(3).

Compliance with the registration requirements is required within one month of having opened a branch in a part of Great Britain (Sch 21A, para 1(1)). The particulars required relate to the company (para 2) and the branch (para 3) and the documents required include the company's constitution (para 5). In addition, if the company is one which is required by its parent law to prepare, have audited and disclose accounts, then a copy of the latest accounting documents to have been publicly disclosed in the country of incorporation must be delivered (paras 2, 6). This requirement for accounting documents on initial registration can be contrasted with the position for a company within the place of business regime which is not required to deliver its accounts on registration. An ongoing obligation on a branch to file accounts is imposed by s 699AA and Sch 21D.

Multiple branches   A company may have more than one branch, for example, to cover different activities or to pursue the same activity under separate managements acting independently of one another. Equally, a company may operate from a variety of physical locations but, if they are under the same management (see *Somafer,* noted above, 'where there is a management'), then there is only one branch. Where a company does have more than one branch, registration of each branch is required (and this may mean registration with the registrar for England and Wales and with the registrar for Scotland – see s 695A(2)) but some allowance is made in the registration and disclosure requirements to prevent the unnecessary duplication of information: see Sch 21A, paras 1(2), 1(3), 2(6). See s 698(2)(a) as to the situation of a branch when it consists of a number of places of business in more than one part of the United Kingdom.

An oversea company does not become a company registered in England and Wales by virtue of compliance with the branch registration requirements of this section and Sch 21A: *Sea Assets Ltd v PT Garuda Indonesia* [2000] 4 All ER 371.

The registrar of companies is required to maintain a register of branches registered by companies under this provision: see s 705A.

690B. Scope of sections 691 and 692

Sections 691 and 692 shall not apply to any limited company which—

(a) is incorporated outside the United Kingdom and Gibraltar, and

(b) has a branch in the United Kingdom.

General note

Purpose of the provision   This provision disapplies ss 691 and 692 in certain cases to ensure that a company which is subject to the branch regime is not subject also to the place of business regime. For example, a company incorporated outside the United Kingdom and Gibraltar with a branch in Scotland and a place of business in England is subject only to branch registration in Scotland.

This provision is subject to s 692A(3), which preserves the application of the place of business regime to companies which were within that regime but which are switching to the branch regime, until such companies have notified the relevant registrar of companies (ie for England and Wales or for Scotland) of their now being a branch.

A branch in the United Kingdom   The wording of sub-s (1)(b) is not the same as in s 690A(1)(b), which limits the branch regime to companies with a branch in Great Britain. This provision disapplies ss 691 and 692 with respect to companies with a branch in the United Kingdom. The effect of this is that a company incorporated abroad with a branch in Northern Ireland (and therefore not subject to the branch regime under s 690A) and with a place of business in Great Britain does not fall into the place of business regime under s 691 but remains subject to the branch registration requirements under the legislation applicable to Northern Ireland.

Extent of the exclusion   The exclusion effected by this provision is solely of ss 691 and 692 and the remaining provisions of this Part do apply to branches, either expressly or because they apply to 'oversea companies', a term defined in s 744 as companies incorporated outside Great Britain with an established place of business in Great Britain. As a branch will always encompass a place of business (see note to s 690A(1), above), a company registered under the branch regime will necessarily fall within the definition of an 'oversea company'. Hence any provision applicable to an oversea company applies to a company registered under the branch regime unless the provision expressly (as is the case with ss 691, 692) or by implication is not applicable to such companies.

691. Documents to be delivered to registrar

(1)   When a company incorporated outside Great Britain establishes a place of business in Great Britain, it shall within one month of doing so deliver to the registrar of companies for registration—

(a)   a certified copy of the charter, statutes or memorandum and articles of the company or other instrument constituting or defining the company's constitution, and, if the instrument is not written in the English language, a certified translation of it; and

(b)   a return in the prescribed form containing—

(i)   a list of the company's directors and secretary, containing the particulars specified in the next subsection,

(ii)   a list of the names and addresses of some one or more persons resident in Great Britain authorised to accept on the company's behalf service of process and any notices required to be served on it,

(iii)   a list of the documents delivered in compliance with paragraph (a) of this subsection, and

(iv)   subject to subsection (3A), a statutory declaration (made by a director or secretary of the company or by any person whose name and address are given in the list required by sub-paragraph (ii)), stating the date on which the company's place of business in Great Britain was established.

(2)   The list referred to in subsection (1)(b)(i) shall contain the following particulars with respect to each director—

(a)   in the case of an individual—

(i)   his name,

    (ii)   any former name,

    (iii) his usual residential address,

    (iv) his nationality,

    (v)   his business occupation (if any),

    (vi) if he has no business occupation but holds other directorships, particulars of them, and

    (vii) his date of birth;

  (b) in the case of a corporation or Scottish firm, its corporate or firm name and registered or principal office.

(3)   The list referred to in subsection (1)(b)(i) shall contain the following particulars with respect to the secretary (or, where there are joint secretaries, with respect to each of them)—

  (a) in the case of an individual, his name, any former name and his usual residential address;

  (b) in the case of a corporation or Scottish firm, its corporate or firm name and registered or principal office.

Where all the partners in a firm are joint secretaries of the company, the name and principal office of the firm may be stated instead of the particulars required by paragraph (a).

(3A) In place of the statutory declaration referred to in sub-paragraph (iv) of paragraph (b) of subsection (1), there may be delivered to the registrar of companies using electronic communications a statement made by any person by whom the declaration could have been made stating the date on which the company's place of business in Great Britain was established.

(4)   In subsections (2)(a) and (3)(a) above—

  (a) 'name' means a person's Christian name (or other forename) and surname, except that in the case of a peer, or an individual usually known by a title, the title may be stated instead of his Christian name (or other forename) and surname, or in addition to either or both of them; and

  (b) the reference to a former name does not include—

    (i)   in the case of a peer, or an individual normally known by a British title, the name by which he was known previous to the adoption of or succession to the title, or

    (ii) in the case of any person, a former name which was changed or disused before he attained the age of 18 years or which has been changed or disused for 20 years or more, or

    (iii) in the case of a married woman, the name by which she was known previous to the marriage.

(4A) Any person who makes a false statement under subsection (3A) which he knows to be false or does not believe to be true is liable to imprisonment or a fine, or both.

General note

As to companies incorporated in the Channel Islands and the Isle of Man which establish a place of business in Great Britain, see s 699.

S 691(1)

Companies within the provision   This section applies: (i) to a company, whether limited or unlimited (cf s 690A); (ii) incorporated outside Great Britain (it will apply therefore to a company incorporated in Northern Ireland); (iii) which establishes a place of business in Great Britain.

The provision does not extend to any limited company incorporated outside the United Kingdom and Gibraltar which has a branch in the United Kingdom (s 690B); such companies are subject to the branch regime under s 690A (or the equivalent Northern Ireland provisions in respect of companies with a branch solely in Northern Ireland).

An established place of business   The key issue is whether the company has a branch (see discussion in the note to s 690A, above) or has established a place of business. The statute is of limited assistance on the issue, unhelpfully providing that a place of business includes a share transfer or share registration office (s 744) but the courts have provided guidance as to 'a place of business' on a number of occasions.

A company establishes a place of business within Great Britain if it carries on part of its business activities within the jurisdiction and it is not necessary for those activities to be either a substantial part of or more than incidental to the main objects of the company: *South India Shipping Corpn Ltd v Export-Import Bank of Korea* [1985] 2 All ER 219, CA (bank had premises and staff and conducted research and public relations activities but not banking activities: it had established a place of business).

There must be some more or less permanent location associated with the company within England and Wales and from which habitually, or with some degree of regularity, business is conducted: *Cleveland Museum of Art v Capricorn Art International SA* [1990] BCLC 546. A physical or visible indication that the company has a connection with particular premises is not essential, although the absence of any such indicator is a factor to be taken into account: see *Cleveland Museum of Art v Capricorn Art International SA* [1990] BCLC 546; *Re Oriel Ltd* [1985] BCLC 343.

The same phrase appears with respect to the registration of charges by oversea companies (see s 409(1)) and, in that context, Oliver LJ thought that 'established':

'... connotes not only the setting-up of a place of business at a specific location, but a degree of permanence or recognisability as being a location of the company's business ... The concept ... is of some more or less permanent location, not necessarily owned or even leased by the company, but at least associated with the company and from which habitually or with some degree of regularity business is conducted' (*Re Oriel Ltd* [1985] BCLC 343 at 347.)

Delivery of documents   As to the registrar of companies to whom the information must be delivered, see s 696. The particulars to be disclosed relate to the company and not to the place of business; it follows that regardless of how many places of business a company has, only one registration is required, unless the places of business are in both England and Wales and in Scotland, in which case registration with the registrar for each jurisdiction is required: see s 696(2), below.

As to the meaning of 'certified copy', see s 698(1). Details of the methods of certification are given on Form 691; 'director' and 'secretary' are also defined in s 698(1). Any changes to the documents and the particulars must be notified to the appropriate registrar in accordance with s 692; as to the consequences of non-compliance with the requirements of this section, see s 697(1), below; as to when a company ceases to have a place of business such that the obligation to deliver documents to the registrar ceases, see s 696(4).

As to the service of documents on a company registered under the place of business regime, see s 695, below.

S 691(2)–(4)

Particulars required   The particulars which must be provided are almost identical to the information which must be provided to the registrar of companies by domestic companies (see s 10(2), Sch 1) and included by such companies on the register of directors and secretaries: see the notes to s 289, above.

The distinction between companies registering under this regime and under the branch regime is that there is no requirement here to provide the company's latest disclosed accounts on the initial registration: see note to s 690A(2), above. Ongoing accounting disclosure by a company registered under this regime is governed by s 700.

S 691(3A), (4A)

Electronic communication   These provisions were inserted by the Companies Act 1985 (Electronic Communications) Order 2000, SI 2000/3373, art 26(1), (3), (4) as from 22 December 2000 to facilitate the acceptance by the registrar of companies of electronic statements as to certain matters in the same manner as he accepts statutory declarations as to those matters. As to the delivery of documents to the registrar using electronic communications, see s 707B; as to penalties, see s 730, Sch 24; the intention is to provide the same penalties for false statements as is provided by the Perjury Act 1911 for false statutory declarations.

---

692. Registration of altered particulars

(1)   If any alteration is made in—

    (a) the charter, statutes, or memorandum and articles of an oversea company or any such instrument as is mentioned above, or

    (b) the directors or secretary of an oversea company or the particulars contained in the list of the directors and secretary, or

    (c) the names or addresses of the persons authorised to accept service on behalf of an oversea company,

the company shall, within the time specified below, deliver to the registrar of companies for registration a return containing the prescribed particulars of the alteration.

(2)   If any change is made in the corporate name of an oversea company, the company shall, within the time specified below, deliver to the registrar of companies for registration a return containing the prescribed particulars of the change.

(3)   The time for delivery of the returns required by subsections (1) and (2) is—

    (a)   in the case of an alteration to which subsection (1)(c) applies, 21 days after the making of the alteration, and

    (b)   otherwise, 21 days after the date on which notice of the alteration or change in question could have been received in Great Britain in due course of post (if despatched with due diligence).

General note

These requirements are designed to ensure that the information provided by oversea companies under s 691 remains up to date on pain of the penalties imposed by s 697(1). This provision does not apply to any limited company which is incorporated outside the United Kingdom and Gibraltar and has a branch in the United Kingdom: s 690B.

S 692(1)(c), (3)(a)

Any change in the address of the persons on whom service may be effected is required within the set period rather than the more generous period permitted for other notifications by sub-s (3)(b).

692A. Change in registration regime

(1)   Where a company ceases to be a company to which section 690A applies and, immediately after ceasing to be such a company—

    (a)   continues to have in Great Britain a place of business which it had immediately before ceasing to be such a company, and

    (b)   does not have a branch in Northern Ireland,

it shall be treated for the purposes of section 691 as having established the place of business on the date when it ceased to be a company to which section 690A applies.

(2)   Where a limited company incorporated outside the United Kingdom and Gibraltar—

    (a)   ceases to have a branch in Northern Ireland, and

    (b)   both immediately before and immediately after ceasing to do so, has a place of business, but not a branch, in Great Britain,

it shall be treated for the purposes of section 691 as having established the place of business on the date when it ceased to have a branch in Northern Ireland.

(3)   Where a company—

(a)   becomes a company to which section 690A applies,

(b)   immediately after becoming such a company, has in a part of Great Britain an established place of business but no branch, and

(c)   immediately before becoming such a company, had an established place of business in that part,

sections 691 and 692 shall, in relation to that part, continue to apply to the company (notwithstanding section 690B) until such time as it gives notice to the registrar for that part that it is a company to which that section applies.

(4)   Schedule 21B to this Act (transitional provisions in relation to change in registration regime) shall have effect.

General note

These complex provisions deal with the transition from one regime to the other, ie from a branch to a place of business and vice versa. The provisions are complicated by the fact that companies incorporated outside the United Kingdom and Gibraltar which have a branch in Northern Ireland are excluded from the branch regime by virtue of s 690A and from the place of business regime by the operation of s 690B.

S 692A(1)

From a branch to a place of business   This provision applies where a company which was registered under the branch regime (ie it had a branch in Great Britain) ceases to be subject to the branch regime but continues to operate a place of business in Great Britain and does not have a branch in Northern Ireland. In this instance, the company is treated as having established a place of business as of the date specified in the provision so that the company has one month from that date to file the necessary information under s 691. If the company has a branch in Northern Ireland, it is subject to the registration regime under the Northern Ireland provisions and is excluded from the place of business regime by s 690B.

S 692A(2)

From a branch in Northern Ireland to a place of business in Great Britain   This provision applies where a company (as defined) had a branch in Northern Ireland (which would have been registered under the relevant Northern Ireland provisions and not under s 690A) and which ceases to be so registered but had and continues to have a place of business (but not a branch) in Great Britain. In that case, the company must register under s 691 within one month of the date specified.

S 692A(3)

Becomes a branch and has place of business in another part of Great Britain   This provision deals with the scenario where a company becomes subject to the branch regime, having a branch in Great Britain (for example, in England), but immediately before and after becoming such a company had and has an established place of business (but no branch) in another part of Great Britain (for example, in Scotland). In that case, the place of business regime continues to apply to the company in relation to Scotland until it gives notice to the registrar of companies for Scotland that it is now subject to the branch regime and therefore the place of business regime has no further application in view of s 690B. As noted, s 690B precludes a company which is subject to the branch regime also being subject to the place of business regime.

As to the meaning of 'registrar for that part', see s 695A.

S 692A(4)

Schedule 21B attempts to facilitate a transfer from one regime to another by allowing constitutional documents and particulars of directors and secretary already filed by the company with that registrar to be used for the purposes of the new registration.

693. Obligation to state name and other particulars

(1) Every oversea company shall—

    (a) *in every prospectus inviting subscriptions for its shares or debentures in Great Britain, state the country in which the company is incorporated;*

    (b) conspicuously exhibit on every place where it carries on business in Great Britain the company's name and the country in which it is incorporated,

    (c) cause the company's name and the country in which it is incorporated to be stated in legible characters in all bill-heads and letter paper, and in all notices and other official publications of the company, and

    (d) if the liability of the members of the company is limited, cause notice of that fact to be stated in legible characters *in every such prospectus as above mentioned and* in all bill-heads, letter paper, notices and other official publications of the company in Great Britain, and to be affixed on every place where it carries on its business.

(2) Every company to which section 690A applies shall, in the case of each branch of the company registered under paragraph 1 of Schedule 21A, cause the following particulars to be stated in legible characters in all letter paper and order forms used in carrying on the business of the branch—

    (a) the place of registration of the branch, and

    (b) the registered number of the branch.

(3) Every company to which section 690A applies, which is not incorporated in a Member State and which is required by the law of the country in which it is incorporated to be registered shall, in the case of each branch of the company registered under paragraph 1 of Schedule 21A, cause the following particulars to be stated in legible characters in all letter paper and order forms used in carrying on the business of the branch—

(a) the identity of the registry in which the company is registered in its country of incorporation, and

(b) the number with which it is registered.

(4) Every company to which section 690A applies and which is not incorporated in a Member State shall, in the case of each branch of the company registered under paragraph 1 of Schedule 21A, cause the following particulars to be stated in legible characters in all letter paper and order forms used in carrying on the business of the branch—

(a) the legal form of the company,

(b) the location of its head office, and

(c) if applicable, the fact that it is being wound up.

General note

Publicity requirements for all oversea companies   As noted, 'oversea company' is defined in s 744 in such a way that it includes companies registered under the branch regime as well as those registered under the place of business regime (see note to s 690B) with the result that the provisions of sub-s (1) apply to all companies subject to either regime. In addition, all companies which are registered under the branch regime must comply with the requirements of sub-s (2) in respect of each branch. In addition, companies which are registered under the branch regime and which are not incorporated in a state within the European Economic Area (see the European Economic Area Act 1993, s 2) must comply with the requirements of sub-ss (3) and (4) in the case of each branch registered under Sch 21A.

As to the consequences of non-compliance with these requirements, see s 697(1).

S 693(1)

The precise status of the words in italics in sub-s (1)(a) and (d) is difficult to ascertain. The words in italics were to be repealed by Financial Services Act 1986, s 212(3), Sch 17, Pt 1, which has been only partially commenced through numerous statutory instruments: see SI 1986/2246; 1998/740; 1988/1960; 1988/2285. By these instruments, the italicised words are repealed to the extent that they apply to any investment which is listed, or to any prior offering for subscription for units in a recognised scheme or for units in an open-ended investment company, but the provisions do not appear to have been repealed for all purposes. Any prospectus offering shares to the public governed by the Public Offers of Securities Regulations 1995, SI 1995/1537 will require this information in any event while any recognised prospectus (ie approved in another member state) is deemed to comply with these requirements: see SI 1995/1536, Sch 4, Pt III, para 12.

The remainder of this subsection imposes publicity obligations very similar to those imposed on companies formed and registered under this Act: see the notes to ss 348, 349, above.

S 693(2)

As to changes to the branch number, see s 705A(5).

---

694. Regulation of oversea companies in respect of their names

(1)   If it appears to the Secretary of State that the corporate name of an oversea company is a name by which the company, had it been formed under this Act, would on the relevant date (determined in accordance with subsections (3A) and (3B)) have been precluded from being registered by section 26 either—

    (a) because it falls within subsection (1) of that section, or

    (b) if it falls within subsection (2) of that section, because the Secretary of State would not approve the company's being registered with that name,

the Secretary of State may serve a notice on the company, stating why the name would not have been registered.

(2)   If the corporate name of an oversea company is in the Secretary of State's opinion too like a name appearing on the relevant date in the index of names kept by the registrar of companies under section 714 or which should have appeared in that index on that date, or is the same as a name which should have so appeared, the Secretary of State may serve a notice on the company specifying the name in the index which the company's name is too like or which is the same as the company's name.

(3)   No notice shall be served on a company under subsection (1) or (2) later than 12 months after the relevant date, ...

(3A) For the purposes of subsections (1) to (3), the relevant date, in relation to a company, is the date on which it has complied with paragraph 1 of Schedule 21A or section 691(1) or, if there is more than one such date, the first date on which it has complied with that paragraph or that subsection since becoming an oversea company.

(3B) But where the company's corporate name has changed since the date ascertained in accordance with subsection (3A), the relevant date is the date on which the company has, in respect of the change or, if more than one, the latest change, complied with paragraph 7(1) of Schedule 21A or section 692(2), as the case may be.

(4)   An oversea company on which a notice is served under subsection (1) or (2)—

    (a) may deliver to the registrar of companies for registration a statement in the prescribed form specifying a name approved by the Secretary of State other than its corporate name under which it proposes to carry on business in Great Britain, and

    (b) may, after that name has been registered, at any time deliver to the registrar for registration a statement in the prescribed form specifying a name approved by the Secretary of State (other than its corporate name) in substitution for the name previously registered.

(5)   The name by which an oversea company is for the time being registered under subsection (4) is, for all purposes of the law applying in Great Britain (including this Act and the Business Names Act 1985), deemed to be the company's corporate name; but—

   (a)   this does not affect references to the corporate name in this section, or any rights or obligations of the company, or render defective any legal proceedings by or against the company, and

   (b)   any legal proceedings that might have been continued or commenced against the company by its corporate name or its name previously registered under this section may be continued or commenced against it by its name for the time being so registered.

(6)   An oversea company on which a notice is served under subsection (1) or (2) shall not at any time after the expiration of 2 months from the service of that notice (or such longer period as may be specified in that notice) carry on business in Great Britain under its corporate name.

Nothing in this subsection, or in section 697(2)(which imposes penalties for its contravention) invalidates any transaction entered into by the company.

(7)   The Secretary of State may withdraw a notice served under subsection (1) or (2) at any time before the end of the period mentioned in subsection (6); and that subsection does not apply to a company served with a notice which has been withdrawn.

General note

As to the obligation to notify the registrar of any change of name, see s 692(2), (3); and Sch 21A, para 7.

S 694(1), (2)

Service of notice regarding company name   This provision requires an oversea company (defined s 744 and see the note to s 690B, above) to comply with the regulations governing company names in the same manner as a company registered under this Act. Section 26(1) identifies certain names which are prohibited, while s 26(2) provides that certain names require the consent of the Secretary of State for Trade and Industry (or a designated body): see also the note to s 29, above. The Secretary of State may also direct a company to change its name if it is the same or 'too like' the name of an existing company: s 28(2).

Under this provision, the Secretary of State cannot direct an oversea company to change its name but see sub-s (6) as to the consequence of service of a notice under these provisions.

S 694(3)–(3B)

Time period for notice   The date from which the 12-month period runs depends upon whether the problem arose on the first registration of the branch or place of business or following from the notification of a change of name. The 12-month period does not start afresh if the company changes, say, from the branch regime to the place of business regime, but runs from the time of first registration.

S 694(4)–(5)

These provisions facilitate the adoption of a name other than the company's corporate name in these circumstances without impinging on any rights or obligations of the company.

S 694(6)

If an oversea company fails to nominate an approved name under sub-s (4) to replace the corporate name in response to the notice served under sub-s (1) or (2), there is no power to direct the company to change its name, but the company is prohibited (subject to sub-s (7)) from the continuance of business in Great Britain under the corporate name. Breach of the prohibition attracts criminal penalties under s 697(2).

694A. Service of documents: companies to which section 690A applies

(1)   This section applies to any company to which section 690A applies.

(2)   Any process or notice required to be served on a company to which this section applies in respect of the carrying on of the business of a branch registered by it under paragraph 1 of Schedule 21A is sufficiently served if—

    (a) addressed to any person whose name has, in respect of the branch, been delivered to the registrar as a person falling within paragraph 3(e) of that Schedule, and

    (b) left at or sent by post to the address for that person which has been so delivered.

(3)   Where—

    (a) a company to which this section applies makes default, in respect of a branch, in delivering to the registrar the particulars mentioned in paragraph 3(e) of Schedule 21A, or

    (b) all the persons whose names have, in respect of a branch, been delivered to the registrar as persons falling within paragraph 3(e) of that Schedule are dead or have ceased to reside in Great Britain, or refuse to accept service on the company's behalf, or for any reason cannot be served,

a document may be served on the company in respect of the carrying on of the business of the branch by leaving it at, or sending it by post to, any place of business established by the company in Great Britain.

(4)   Where a company to which this section applies has more than one branch in Great Britain, any notice or process required to be served on the company which is not required to be served in respect of the carrying on of the business

of one branch rather than another shall be treated for the purposes of this section as required to be served in respect of the carrying on of the business of each of its branches.

General note

Service permitted under CPR   An oversea company may be served by any method permitted under the Civil Procedure Rules 1998 (SI 1998/3132), Pt 6, as an alternative to the methods of service set out in this provision: CPR, r 6.2(2). Service at any place of business of the company within the jurisdiction is therefore permissible: CPR, r 6.5(6).

S 694A(1)

This provision applies only to limited companies incorporated outside the United Kingdom and Gibraltar which have a branch in Great Britain.

S 694A(2), (3)

Permissive modes of service under this provision   The modes of service provided by these provisions are permissive and not mandatory: *Sea Assets Ltd v PT Garuda Indonesia* [2000] 4 All ER 371; see also *Saab v Saudi American Bank* [1999] 2 BCLC 462, CA.

Connection with business of branch   Any process or notice served on a branch does not have to relate in substance to the carrying on of the branch's business; rather it is sufficient that the process is partly in respect of the carrying on of its business, unless the connection between the process and the carrying on of the business is de minimis, ie of so little significance that it should be disregarded: *Saab v Saudi American Bank* [1999] 2 BCLC 462, CA. The Court of Appeal in so finding thought that such an approach to the section reduced to a minimum the anomaly existing between a company with a branch in Great Britain and a company with a mere place of business in Great Britain, which could be served with process even though there was no link at all between that process and the place of business (see s 695). Clarke LJ noted that it may be that the intention of the alternative rules for service under CPR, r 6.5(6), noted above, was to address this anomaly and in effect to restore the position to what it was before s 694A was enacted, namely that process can be served on a foreign company with a place of business in the jurisdiction without the necessity for establishing any link between the process and the business being conducted in that place: see *Saab v Saudi American Bank* [1999] 2 BCLC 462 at 466, 468.

695. Service of documents on oversea company

(1)   Any process or notice required to be served on an oversea company to which section 691 applies is sufficiently served if addressed to any person whose name has been delivered to the registrar under preceding sections in this Part and left at or sent by post to the address which has been so delivered.

(2) However—

    (a) where such a company makes default in delivering to the registrar the name and address of a person resident in Great Britain who is authorised to accept on behalf of the company service of process or notices, or

    (b) if at any time all the persons whose names and addresses have been so delivered are dead or have ceased so to reside, or refuse to accept service on the company's behalf, or for any reason cannot be served,

a document may be served on the company by leaving it at, or sending it by post to, any place of business established by the company in Great Britain.

General note

Service permitted under CPR   In *Boocock v Hilton International Co* [1993] 4 All ER 19 the court had held that this section provided a complete code for the service of documents on an oversea company, but this position has been altered by the Civil Procedure Rules 1998 (SI 1998/3132) which provide that an oversea company may be served by any method permitted under CPR, Pt 6 as an alternative to the methods of service set out in this provision: CPR, r 6.2(2). Service at any place of business of the company within the jurisdiction is therefore permissible: CPR, r 6.5(6).

S 695(1)

A claim may be validly served on an oversea company in the manner provided by this section notwithstanding that the company has ceased to have an established place of business in Great Britain, which fact has been notified to and recorded by the registrar of companies: *Rome v Punjab National Bank (No 2)* [1990] 1 All ER 58. The Court of Appeal in this instance felt that any injustice resulting from such service on an oversea company which, for example, had long since left the jurisdiction may always be remedied by a stay of proceedings under the inherent jurisdiction of the court.

S 695(2)

As to whether the company has a place of business, see note to s 691, above. There is no need to establish any link between the proceedings and the place of business at which service is effected.

695A. Registrar to whom documents to be delivered: companies to which section 690A applies

(1) References to the registrar, in relation to a company to which section 690A applies, (except references in Schedule 21C) ... shall be construed in accordance with the following provisions.

(2)   The documents which a company is required to deliver to the registrar shall be delivered—

(a) to the registrar for England and Wales, if required to be delivered in respect of a branch in England and Wales; and

(b) to the registrar for Scotland, if required to be delivered in respect of a branch in Scotland.

(3)   If a company closes a branch in a part of Great Britain, it shall forthwith give notice of that fact to the registrar for that part; and from the date on which notice is so given it is no longer obliged to deliver documents to that registrar in respect of that branch.

(4)   In subsection (3) above, the reference to closing a branch in either part of Great Britain includes a reference to a branch ceasing to be situated in that part on becoming situated elsewhere.

S 695A(1)

This provision applies only to companies which are subject to the branch regime. The words omitted from the text were inserted into the provision by the CA 1989 and SI 1992/3179 but never brought into force and they are not reproduced here.

As to the consequences of breach of these requirements, see s 697(3).

S 695A(2)

See s 698(2)(a) as to the position when a branch consists of a number of places of business in more than one part of the United Kingdom.

S 695A(3)

The onus is on the company to notify the appropriate registrar and, until it does so notify, it remains subject to the disclosure obligations of this Part and potentially liable to criminal penalties for non-compliance under s 697.

Any notice under this provision must be gazetted by the registrar of companies: s 711(1)(w).

696. Office where documents to be filed

(1)   Any document which an oversea company to which section 691 applies is required to deliver to the registrar of companies shall be delivered to the registrar at the registration office in England and Wales or Scotland, according to where the company has established a place of business.

(2)   If the company has established a place of business both in England and Wales and in Scotland, the document shall be delivered at the registration office both in England and Wales and in Scotland.

(3) References in this Part (except references in Schedule 21C) to the registrar of companies, in relation to a company to which section 691 applies, are to be construed in accordance with the above subsections.

(4) If an oversea company to which section 691 applies ceases to have a place of business in either part of Great Britain, it shall forthwith give notice of that fact to the registrar of companies for that part; and as from the date on which notice is so given the obligation of the company to deliver any document to the registrar ceases.

General note

This provision was to have been substituted by CA 1989, s 145, Sch 19, para 13, but the substitution has never been brought into force and it is not reproduced here.

As to the consequences of breach of the requirements of this section, see s 697(1).

S 696(1)

This provision applies to companies subject to the place of business regime; as to whether a company has established a place of business, see note to s 691, above.

S 696(2)

It is important to appreciate the need to deliver the required documents to both the registrar for England and Wales and the registrar for Scotland, particularly in view of the penalties for non-compliance under s 697(1).

S 696(4)

The onus is on the company to notify the appropriate registrar and, until it does so notify, it remains subject to the disclosure obligations of this Part and potentially liable to criminal penalties for non-compliance under s 697.

697. Penalties for non-compliance

(1) If an oversea company fails to comply with any of sections 691 to 693 and 696, the company, and every officer or agent of the company who knowingly and wilfully authorises or permits the default, is liable to a fine and, in the case of a continuing offence, to a daily default fine for continued contravention.

(2) If an oversea company contravenes section 694(6), the company and every officer or agent of it who knowingly and wilfully authorises or permits the contravention is guilty of an offence and liable to a fine and, for continued contravention, to a daily default fine.

(3)   If an oversea company fails to comply with section 695A or Schedule 21A, the company, and every officer or agent of the company who knowingly and wilfully authorises or permits the default, is liable to a fine and, in the case of a continuing offence, to a daily default fine for continued contravention.

General note

While this provision imposes criminal liability with respect to these offences, the officers and agents in default will probably be outside the jurisdiction and beyond the reach of these penalties.

As to penalties, see s 730, Sch 24.

S 697(1)

This provision applies to an 'oversea company' as defined in s 744 and see the note to s 690B, above. The effect is that the provision applies to companies subject to the branch regime and to the place of business regime. However, ss 691 and 692 do not apply to companies subject to the branch regime (s 690B), therefore, the potential penalties imposed by this provision could only apply with respect to such companies where there is a breach of s 693.

S 697(2)

The contravention relates to the continuance of business in Great Britain under a corporate name which has been the subject of a notice by the Secretary of State for Trade and Industry under s 694(1).

S 697(3)

This provision relates to companies subject to the branch registration regime.

698. Definitions ...

(1)   For purposes of this Chapter—

      'certified' means certified in the prescribed manner to be a true copy or a correct translation;

   'director', in relation to an oversea company, includes shadow director; and

   'secretary' includes any person occupying the position of secretary by whatever name called.

(2)   For the purposes of this Part (except section 699A and Schedule 21C)—

   (a) where a branch comprises places of business in more than one part of the United Kingdom the branch shall be treated as being situated in that part of the United Kingdom where its principal place of business is situated; and

(b) 'branch' means a branch within the meaning of the Council Directive concerning disclosure requirements in respect of branches opened in a Member State by certain types of company governed by the law of another State (the Eleventh Company Law Directive, 89/666/EEC).

S 698(2)(a)

This provision deals with the situation where there is only one branch but multiple places of business and it is necessary to determine in which part of the United Kingdom the branch is situated, as this will determine the registrar to whom the documents must be sent under s 695A(2).

As to the meaning of 'principal place of business', this is taken to refer to the place where the general superintendence and management of the company are carried out: *Palmer v Caledonian Rly Co* [1892] 1 QB 823, CA. One has to consider the centre from which instructions are given, and from which control is exercised on behalf of the company over the employees of and the business of the company: *The Polzeath* [1916] P 241 at 245. The word 'principal' does not mean 'main', but 'chief' or 'most important' and the principal place of business does not necessarily mean the place where most of the business is carried out: see *The Rewia* [1991] 2 Lloyd's Rep 325 at 334–335, CA.

S 698(2)(b)

See note to s 690A(1), above, as to the meaning of 'branch'. The Eleventh Directive does not contain a definition of 'branch' so this provision is of limited assistance.

699. Channel Islands and Isle of Man companies

(1)   With the exceptions specified in subsection (3) below, the provisions of this Act requiring documents to be forwarded or delivered to or filed with the registrar of companies and applying to companies formed and registered under Part I apply also (if they would not otherwise) to an oversea company to which section 691 applies incorporated in the Channel Islands or the Isle of Man.

(2)   Those provisions apply to such a company—

(a) if it has established a place of business in England and Wales, as if it were registered in England and Wales,

(b) if it has established a place of business in Scotland, as if it were registered in Scotland, and

(c) if it has established a place of business both in England and Wales and in Scotland, as if it were registered in both England and Wales and Scotland, with such modifications as may be necessary and, in particular, apply in a similar way to documents relating to things done outside Great Britain as if they had been done in Great Britain.

(3) The exceptions are—

section 6(1) (resolution altering company's objects),

section 18 (alteration of memorandum or articles by statute or statutory instrument),

section 242(1) (directors' duty to file accounts),

section 288(2) (notice to registrar of change of directors or secretary), and

section 380 (copies of certain resolutions and agreements to be sent to registrar within 15 days), so far as applicable to a resolution altering a company's memorandum or articles.

General note

A place of business   This provision subjects companies incorporated in the Channel Islands and the Isle of Man which establish a place of business in England and Wales and/or Scotland to the same disclosure and filing obligations with respect to the registrar of companies as domestic companies; as to the meaning of 'this Act': see s 735A(1), below. This somewhat anomalous position is subject to the exceptions in sub-s (3), the most important of which is an exemption from the obligation to deliver annual accounts, but there is no such exemption with respect to the annual return: see ss 363–365, above.

A branch   A Channel Island or Isle of Man company which establishes a branch will be subject to the branch regime under s 690A and Sch 21A in the normal way.

DELIVERY OF ACCOUNTS AND REPORTS

699A. Credit and financial institutions to which the Bank Branches Directive (89/117/EEC) applies

(1) This section applies to any credit or financial institution—

(a) which is incorporated or otherwise formed outside the United Kingdom and Gibraltar,

(b) whose head office is outside the United Kingdom and Gibraltar, and

(c) which has a branch in Great Britain.

(2) Schedule 21C (delivery of accounts and reports) shall have effect in relation to any institution to which this section applies.

(3) In this section—

'branch', in relation to a credit or financial institution, means a place of business which forms a legally dependent part of the institution and which conducts directly all or some of the operations inherent in its business;

'credit institution' means a credit institution as defined in article 1 of Directive 2000/12/EC of the European Parliament and of the Council of 20 March 2000 relating to the taking up and pursuit of the business of credit institutions, that is to say an undertaking whose business is to receive deposits or other repayable funds from the public and to grant credits for its own account;

'financial institution' means a financial institution within the meaning of Article 1 of the Council Directive on the obligations of branches established in a Member State of credit and financial institutions having their head offices outside that Member State regarding the publication of annual accounting documents (the Bank Branches Directive, 89/117/EEC); and

'undertaking' has the same meaning as in Part VII.

General note

This provision was inserted by the Oversea Companies and Credit and Financial Institutions (Branch Disclosure) Regulations 1992, SI 1992/3179 as from 1 January 1993 to give effect to the Bank Branches Directive (89/117/EEC) OJ 1989 L44/40 (obligations of branches established in a member state of credit institutions and financial institutions having their head offices outside that member state regarding the publication of annual accounting documents).

S 699A(1), (2)

Schedule 21C makes provision for the registration of the accounts and reports required by the Bank Branches Directive. In this case, the requirements extend to unincorporated bodies with the result that an unincorporated body must deliver these documents to the registrar of companies, even though it is not required to register under the branch regime under s 690A nor under the place of business regime under s 691.

699AA. Companies to which the Eleventh Company Law Directive applies

(1)   This section applies to any limited company which—

   (a)   is incorporated outside the United Kingdom and Gibraltar,

   (b)   has a branch in Great Britain, and

   (c)   is not an institution to which section 699A applies.

(2)   Schedule 21D to this Act (delivery of accounts and reports) shall have effect in relation to any company to which this section applies.

General note

Accounting disclosure requirements   This provision applies to branches (other than branches of credit and financial institutions) the accounting disclosure requirements set out in Sch 21D; companies which have established a place of business are subject to the accounting disclosure requirements set out in ss 700–703.

S 699AA(2)

Two regimes   Schedule 21D provides for two regimes:
   (1)   if a company is required by the law of the place of incorporation to prepare, have audited and publicly disclose its accounts then, in respect of each branch, it must deliver all the documents (individual accounts, groups accounts, directors and auditors' reports) disclosed in accordance with that parent law, modified as permitted by that law, within three months of the date of disclosure in accordance with that law (paras 2, 4).

   For companies incorporated within the EU and subject to the requirements of the 4th and 7th Directives, the effect will be to require the delivery of full accounts, subject to whatever modifications (as permitted by the Directives) have been adopted by their parent law. For companies not incorporated within the EU, the position will vary from country to country and, in some cases, the parent law may require the disclosure of minimal information. The entitlement to disclose here only what is disclosed in the country of incorporation may encourage a certain amount of forum shopping.

   (2)   if a company is not required by the law of the place of incorporation to prepare, have audited and publicly disclose its accounts, it must deliver accounts prepared in accordance with s 700 (paras 7, 8).

699B. Scope of sections 700 to 703

Sections 700 to 703 shall not apply to any institution to which section 699A applies or to any limited company which is incorporated outside the United Kingdom and Gibraltar and has a branch in the United Kingdom.

General note

Companies not subject to ss 700–703   The effect of this provision is that ss 700–703 do not apply: (i) to credit or financial institutions within s 699A; (ii) to companies which have registered branches under s 690A (but see Sch 21D, paras 7 and 8 noted below); (iii) to companies incorporated outside the United Kingdom and Gibraltar with a branch in Northern Ireland. The wording here is 'branch in the United Kingdom' as opposed to 'branch in Great Britain' (s 690A), the reason for the exclusion being that such companies are subject to the branch registration requirements in Northern Ireland.

Companies which are subject to ss 700–703   These provisions do apply to companies registered under the place of business regime under s 691. Moreover, some companies which have branches in Great Britain, namely companies which are not required by the law of their country of incorporation to prepare, have audited and publicly disclose their accounts, are required to prepare their accounts as if they were companies to which s 700 applies: see Sch 21D, paras 7, 8 and note to s 699AA, above.

700. Preparation of accounts and reports by oversea companies

(1) Every oversea company shall in respect of each financial year of the company prepare the like accounts and directors' report, and cause to be prepared such an auditors' report, as would be required if the company were formed and registered under this Act.

(2) The Secretary of State may by order—

    (a) modify the requirements referred to in subsection (1) for the purpose of their application to oversea companies;

    (b) exempt an oversea company from those requirements or from such of them as may be specified in the order.

(3) An order may make different provision for different cases or classes of case and may contain such incidental and supplementary provisions as the Secretary of State thinks fit.

(4) An order under this section shall be made by statutory instrument which shall be subject to annulment in pursuance of a resolution of either House of Parliament.

General note

This section does not apply to such oversea companies as are excluded by s 699B, and see the note to that provision as to the application and exclusion of this provision.

S 700(1), (2)

Modified accounts required   This section imposes on the companies within it the same obligations with respect to accounts as if the company was formed and registered under the Act. However, that requirement is then substantially modified by the Oversea Companies (Accounts) (Modifications and Exemptions) Order 1990, SI 1990/440, to which reference should be made for the detailed requirements with respect to s 700 accounts, as they are known.

The effect of these modifications is that the accounts are prepared in accordance with the somewhat outdated requirements of Sch 9 of the CA 1985 (as it applied to special category companies, being banking, shipping and insurance companies) prior to the amendment of that Schedule by the CA 1989. Amongst the features of s 700 accounts, the following might be noted: there are no prescribed formats for the balance sheet and the profit and loss account; there is no requirement to disclose turnover or details of the directors' remuneration and other transactions; no directors or auditors' reports are required; and it is unclear whether the accounts must meet UK (or any other) accounting standards. The resulting accounts will be less than comprehensive and, at best, will simply give some impression of the financial standing of the company.

As to the obligation to deliver the accounts, see s 702, below; the penalties for non-compliance are set out in s 703.

701. Oversea company's financial year and accounting reference periods

(1)   Sections 223 to 225 (financial year and accounting reference periods) apply to an oversea company, subject to the following modifications.

(2)   For the references to the incorporation of the company substitute references to the company establishing a place of business in Great Britain.

(3)   Omit section 225(4) (restriction on frequency with which current accounting reference period may be extended).

S 701(1), (2)

The date of establishment of a place of business in Great Britain is regarded as equivalent to the date of incorporation for a company registered and formed under this Act and ss 223–225 then apply: see notes to those provisions.

S 701(3)

Oversea companies are subject to the same limitation on the length of an extended accounting reference period as a company formed and registered under this Act following the application of ss 223–225 above (see s 225(6)), save that there are no restrictions on the frequency with which an oversea company can extend the period (cf s 225(4)).

702. Delivery to registrar of accounts and reports of oversea company

(1)   An oversea company shall in respect of each financial year of the company deliver to the registrar copies of the accounts and reports prepared in accordance with section 700.

If any document comprised in those accounts or reports is in a language other than English, the directors shall annex to the copy delivered a translation of it into English, certified in the prescribed manner to be a correct translation.

(2)   In relation to an oversea company the period allowed for delivering accounts and reports is 13 months after the end of the relevant accounting reference period.

This is subject to the following provisions of this section.

(3)   If the relevant accounting reference period is the company's first and is a period of more than 12 months, the period allowed is 13 months from the first anniversary of the company's establishing a place of business in Great Britain.

(4)   If the relevant accounting period is treated as shortened by virtue of a notice given by the company under section 225 (alteration of accounting reference date), the period allowed is that applicable in accordance with the above provisions or three months from the date of the notice under that section, whichever last expires.

(5)   If for any special reason the Secretary of State thinks fit he may, on an application made before the expiry of the period otherwise allowed, by notice in writing to an oversea company extend that period by such further period as may be specified in the notice.

(6)   In this section 'the relevant accounting reference period' means the accounting reference period by reference to which the financial year for the accounts in question was determined.

General note

This section does not apply to such oversea companies as are excluded by s 699B, and see the note to that provision as to the application and exclusion of this provision.

This provision reflects, with appropriate modifications, the requirements of ss 242 and 244 for companies formed and registered under this Act: see the notes to those provisions.

S 702(1)

As to the consequences of non-compliance with this provision, see s 703.

703. Penalty for non-compliance

(1)   If the requirements of section 702(1) are not complied with before the end of the period allowed for delivering accounts and reports, or if the accounts

and reports delivered do not comply with the requirements of this Act, the company and every person who immediately before the end of that period was a director of the company is guilty of an offence and liable to a fine and, for continued contravention, to a daily default fine.

(2) It is a defence for a person charged with such an offence to prove that he took all reasonable steps for securing that the requirements in question would be complied with.

(3) It is not a defence in relation to a failure to deliver copies to the registrar to prove that the documents in question were not in fact prepared as required by this Act.

S 703(1)

As to penalties, see s 730 and Sch 24.

S 703(3)

See note to s 242(5).

CHAPTER III

REGISTRATION OF CHARGES

General note

Sections 703A–703N were inserted by CA 1989, s 105, Sch 15, as from a day to be appointed. However, the provisions were never brought into force and the Department of Trade and Industry has made clear that the provisions will not now be brought into force. They are not reproduced in this work.

As to the current requirements imposed on oversea companies to register charges, see s 409.

CHAPTER IV

WINDING UP ETC

703O. Scope of Chapter

This Chapter applies to any company to which section 690A applies.

General note

These provisions, ss 703O–703R, were inserted by the Oversea Companies and Credit and Financial Institutions (Branch Disclosure) Regulations 1992, SI 1992/3179 as from 1 January 1993.

Branch regime only   These provisions apply only to companies subject to the branch regime established by s 690A. There are no equivalent disclosure provisions with respect to companies subject to the place of business regime under s 691, in respect of whom no information as to winding up or other insolvency proceedings is required. The only requirement is notification when the company ceases to have a place of business: see s 696(4).

703P. Particulars to be delivered: winding up

(1)   Subject to subsection (8), where a company to which this Chapter applies is being wound up, it shall deliver to the registrar for registration a return in the prescribed form containing the following particulars—

    (a)   the name of the company;

    (b)   whether the company is being wound up by an order of a court and, if so, the name and address of the court and the date of the order;

    (c)   if the company is not being so wound up, as a result of what action the winding up has commenced;

    (d)   whether the winding up has been instigated by—

        (i)   the company's members;

        (ii)   the company's creditors; or

        (iii)   some other person or persons,

    and, in the case of (iii) the identity of that person or those persons shall be given; and

    (e)   the date on which the winding up became or will become effective.

(2)   The period allowed for delivery of a return under subsection (1) above is 14 days from the date on which the winding up begins.

(3)   Subject to subsection (8), a person appointed to be the liquidator of a company to which this Chapter applies shall deliver to the registrar for registration a return in the prescribed form containing the following particulars—

    (a)   his name and address,

    (b)   the date of his appointment, and

    (c)   a description of such of his powers, if any, as are derived otherwise than from the general law or the company's constitution.

(4) The period allowed for delivery of a return under subsection (3) above is 14 days from the date of the liquidator's appointment.

(5) Subject to subsection (8), the liquidator of a company to which this Chapter applies shall deliver to the registrar for registration a return in the prescribed form upon the occurrence of the following events—

    (a) the termination of the winding up of the company, and

    (b) the company ceasing to be registered, in circumstances where ceasing to be registered is an event of legal significance.

The following particulars shall be given—

    (i) in the case of (a), the name of the company and the date on which the winding up terminated; and

    (ii) in the case of (b), the name of the company and the date on which the company ceased to be registered.

(6) The period allowed for delivery of a return under subsection (5) is 14 days from the date of the event concerned.

(7) The obligation to deliver a return under subsection (1), (3) or (5) above shall apply in respect of each branch which the company has in Great Britain (though where the company has more than one branch in a part of Great Britain a return which gives the branch numbers of two or more such branches is to be regarded as a return in respect of each branch whose number is given).

(8) No return is required under subsection (1), (3) or (5) above in respect of a winding up under Part V of the Insolvency Act 1986.

S 703P(1)

The companies to which this Chapter applies are identified in s 703O. As to penalties for non-compliance with this provision, see s 703R(1), (3).

Any return delivered under this provision must be gazetted by the registrar of companies: s 711(1)(z).

S 703P(3), (5)

As to penalties for non-compliance with this provision, see s 703R(2), (3).

S 703P(8)

Part V of the Insolvency Act 1986 provides for the winding up of unregistered companies and an oversea company with a place of business in Great Britain (which encompasses a company with a branch in Great Britain) may be wound up under, and subject to the disclosure requirements of, that Part so obviating any need for disclosure under this Part.

703Q. Particulars to be delivered to the registrar: insolvency proceedings etc

(1)   Where a company to which this Chapter applies becomes subject to any of the following proceedings (other than proceedings for the winding up of the company), that is to say, insolvency proceedings or an arrangement or composition or any analogous proceedings, it shall deliver to the registrar for registration a return in the prescribed form containing the following particulars—

- (a) the name of the company;
- (b) whether the proceedings are by order of a court and, if so, the name and address of the court and the date of the order;
- (c) if the proceedings are not by order of a court, as a result of what action the proceedings have been commenced;
- (d) whether the proceedings have been instigated by—
    - (i)   the company's members;
    - (ii)   the company's creditors; or
    - (iii) some other person or persons,

and, in the case of (iii) the identity of that person or those persons shall be given; and

- (e) the date on which the proceedings became or will become effective.

(2)   Where a company to which this Chapter applies ceases to be subject to any of the proceedings mentioned in subsection (1) it shall deliver to the registrar for registration a return in the prescribed form containing the following particulars—

- (a) the name of the company; and
- (b) the date on which it ceased to be subject to the proceedings.

(3)   The period allowed for delivery of a return under subsection (1) or (2) is 14 days from the date on which the company becomes subject, or (as the case may be) ceases to be subject to the proceedings concerned.

(4)   The obligation to deliver a return under subsection (1) or (2) shall apply in respect of each branch which the company has in Great Britain (though where the company has more than one branch in a part of Great Britain a return which gives the branch numbers of two or more such branches is to be regarded as a return in respect of each branch whose number is given).

S 703Q(1),(2)

As to penalties for non-compliance with this provision, see s 703R(1) and (3).

703R. Penalty for non-compliance

(1)   If a company fails to comply with section 703P(1) or 703Q(1) or (2) within the period allowed for compliance, it, and every person who immediately before

the end of that period was a director of it, is guilty of an offence and liable to a fine and, for continued contravention, to a daily default fine.

(2)   If a liquidator fails to comply with section 703P(3) or (5) within the period allowed for compliance, he is guilty of an offence and liable to a fine and, for continued contravention, to a daily default fine.

(3)   It is a defence for a person charged with an offence under this section to prove that he took all reasonable steps for securing compliance with the requirements concerned.

General note

As to penalties, see s 730, Sch 24.

PART XXIV

THE REGISTRAR OF COMPANIES, HIS FUNCTIONS AND OFFICES

704. Registration offices

(1)   For the purposes of the registration of companies under the Companies Acts, there shall continue to be offices in England and Wales and in Scotland, at such places as the Secretary of State thinks fit.

(2)   The Secretary of State may appoint such registrars, assistant registrars, clerks and servants as he thinks necessary for that purpose, and may make regulations with respect to their duties, and may remove any persons so appointed.

(3)   The salaries of the persons so appointed continue to be fixed by the Secretary of State, with the concurrence of the Treasury, and shall be paid out of money provided by Parliament.

(4)   The Secretary of State may direct a seal or seals to be prepared for the authentication of documents required for or in connection with the registration of companies; and any seal so prepared is referred to in this Act as the registrar's official seal.

(5)   Wherever any act is by the Companies Acts directed to be done to or by the registrar of companies, it shall (until the Secretary of State otherwise directs) be done to or by the existing registrar of companies in England and Wales or in Scotland (as the case may be), or to or by such person as the Secretary of State may for the time being authorise.

(6)   In the event of the Secretary of State altering the constitution of the existing registration offices or any of them, any such act shall be done to or by such officer and at such place with reference to the local situation of the registered offices of the companies to be registered as the Secretary of State may appoint.

(7)   Subsection (8) below applies where by virtue of an order made under section 69 of the Deregulation and Contracting Out Act 1994 a person is authorised by the registrar of companies to accept delivery of any class of documents which are under any provision of the Companies Acts to be delivered to the registrar.

(8)   If—

(a)   the registrar directs that documents of that class shall be delivered to a specified address of the authorised person; and

(b)   the direction is printed and made available to the public (with or without payment),

any document of that class which is delivered to an address other than the specified address shall be treated for the purposes of those Acts as not having been delivered.

General note

The main offices of the registrar of companies are at Cardiff (Companies House, Crown Way, Cardiff CF14 3UZ), London and Edinburgh, with regional centres at Birmingham, Leeds, Manchester and Glasgow: see the web site www.companieshouse.gov.uk.

S 704(5)

As to the meaning of the 'Companies Acts' for these purposes, see ss 735A(2), 735B.

S 704(7), (8)

These provisions were added by the Deregulation and Contracting Out Act 1994, s 76, Sch 16, para 8 as from 3 January 1995 with a view to facilitating the contracting out of the services of the registrar of companies; in general, contracting out has taken place only on a limited scale.

---

705. Companies' registered numbers

(1)   The registrar shall allocate to every company a number, which shall be known as the company's registered number.

(2)   Companies' registered numbers shall be in such form, consisting of one or more sequences of figures or letters, as the registrar may from time to time determine.

(3)   The registrar may upon adopting a new form of registered number make such changes of existing registered numbers as appear to him necessary.

(4)   A change of a company's registered number has effect from the date on which the company is notified by the registrar of the change; but for a period of three years beginning with the date on which that notification is sent by the registrar the requirement of section 351(1)(a) as to the use of the company's registered number on business letters and order forms is satisfied by the use of either the old number or the new.

(5)   In this section 'company' includes—

(za) any oversea company which has complied with paragraph 1 of Schedule 21A other than a company which appears to the registrar not to have a branch in Great Britain;

(a)   any oversea company which has complied with section 691 (delivery of statutes to registrar, &c), other than a company which appears to the registrar not to have a place of business in Great Britain; and

(b)   any body to which any provision of this Act applies by virtue of section 718 (unregistered companies).

General note

By the Contracting Out (Functions in Relation to the Registration of Companies) Order 1995, SI 1995/1013, art 3, Sch 1, para 3 the functions of the registrar of companies in relation to England and Wales conferred by or under this section and ss 705A–707, 709, 710, 710A may be exercised by, or by employees of, such person (if any) as may be authorised in that behalf by the registrar of companies; in general, contracting out has taken place only on a limited scale.

S 705(1), (5)

The definition of 'company' in s 735 is expanded by sub-s (5) to include oversea companies with a branch or a place of business in Great Britain and unregistered companies, so ensuring that these companies also have a registered number.

705A. Registration of branches of oversea companies

(1) For each company to which section 690A applies the registrar, shall keep, in such form as he thinks fit, a register of the branches registered by the company under paragraph 1 of Schedule 21A.

(2) The registrar shall allocate to every branch registered by him under this section a number, which shall be known as the branch's registered number.

(3) Branches' registered numbers shall be in such form, consisting of one or more sequences of figures or letters, as the registrar may from time to time determine.

(4) The registrar may upon adopting a new form of registered number make such changes of existing registered numbers as appear to him necessary.

(5) A change of a branch's registered number has effect from the date on which the company is notified by the registrar of the change; but for a period of three years beginning with the date on which that notification is sent by the registrar the requirement of section 693(2) as to the use of the branch's registered number on business letters and order forms is satisfied by the use of either the old number or the new.

(6) Where an oversea company to which section 690A applies files particulars, in any circumstances permitted by this Act, by—

   (i) adopting particulars already filed in respect of another branch; or

   (ii) including in one document particulars which are to relate to two or more branches,

the registrar shall ensure that the particulars concerned become part of the registered particulars of each branch concerned.

General note

This provision was inserted by the Oversea Companies and Credit and Financial Institutions (Branch Disclosure) Regulations 1992, SI 1992/3179, reg 3(2) as from 1 January 1993. Companies in respect of which s 690A applies are oversea companies which have a branch in Great Britain, hence the need to make provision for a register of branches: see notes to s 690A and Sch 21A.

706. Delivery to the registrar of documents in legible form

(1) This section applies to the delivery to the registrar under any provision of the Companies Acts of documents in legible form.

(2) The document must—

    (a) state in a prominent position the registered number of the company to which it relates and, if the document is delivered under sections 695A(3), 703P or 703Q or Schedules 21A or 21D the registered number of the branch to which it relates,

    (b) satisfy any requirements prescribed by regulations for the purposes of this section, and

    (c) conform to such requirements as the registrar may specify for the purpose of enabling him to copy the document.

(3) If a document is delivered to the registrar which does not comply with the requirements of this section, he may serve on the person by whom the document was delivered (or, if there are two or more such persons, on any of them) a notice indicating the respect in which the document does not comply.

(4) Where the registrar serves such a notice, then, unless a replacement document—

    (a) is delivered to him within 14 days after the service of the notice, and

    (b) complies with the requirements of this section (or section 707B) or is not rejected by him for failure to comply with those requirements,

the original document shall be deemed not to have been delivered to him.

But for the purposes of any enactment imposing a penalty for failure to deliver, so far as it imposes a penalty for continued contravention, no account shall be taken of the period between the delivery of the original document and the end of the period of 14 days after service of the registrar's notice.

(5) Regulations made for the purposes of this section may make different provision with respect to different descriptions of document.

S 706(1)

The term 'legible' means capable of being read with the naked eye: s 715A(1). As to the meaning of the 'Companies Acts' for these purposes, see ss 735A(2), 735B.

S 706(3)

The ability to serve a notice under this provision, giving rise to a period of 14 days in which to re-present the document in the correct manner under sub-s (4), is limited to case where there has been a failure to comply with the requirements of sub-s (2); and essentially applies to cases where the information is delivered but in a format which means it will not copy easily or cannot be scanned for the purposes of putting the information on the public record, as is the case, for example, with glossy annual account documents. See the Companies House Guidance Booklet, *Directors and Secretaries Guide* for further information as to the quality of documents required by the registrar.

707. *(Repealed by the Companies Act 1985 (Electronic Communications) Order 2000, SI 2000/3373, art 31(4) as from 22 December 2000.)*

707A. The keeping of company records by the registrar

(1)   The information contained in a document delivered to the registrar under the Companies Acts may be recorded and kept by him in any form he thinks fit, provided it is possible to inspect the information and to produce a copy of it in legible form.

This is sufficient compliance with any duty of his to keep, file or register the document.

(2)   The originals of documents delivered to the registrar in legible form shall be kept by him for ten years, after which they may be destroyed.

(3)   Where a company has been dissolved, the registrar may, at any time after the expiration of two years from the date of the dissolution, direct that any records in his custody relating to the company may be removed to the Public Record Office; and records in respect of which such a direction is given shall be disposed of in accordance with the enactments relating to that Office and the rules made under them.

This subsection does not extend to Scotland.

(4)   In subsection (3) 'company' includes a company provisionally or completely registered under the Joint Stock Companies Act 1844.

S 707A(1)

As to the meaning of the 'Companies Acts' for these purposes, see ss 735A(2), 735B.

S 707A(3)

The period of two years reflects the fact that, in general, an application for restoration of a company which has been removed from the register on dissolution must be made within two years: see s 651(4), (5).

707B. Delivery to the registrar using electronic communications

(1)   Electronic communications may be used for the delivery of any document to the registrar under any provision of the Companies Acts (including delivery of a document in the prescribed form), provided that such delivery is in such form and manner as is directed by the registrar.

(2)   Where the document is required under any provision of the Companies Acts to be signed or sealed, it shall instead be authenticated in such manner as is directed by the registrar.

(3)   The document must contain in a prominent position—

    (a)   the name and registered number of the company to which it relates, or

    (b)   if the document is delivered under Part XXIII, the registered number of the branch or place of business of the company to which it relates.

(4)   If a document is delivered to the registrar which does not comply with the requirements imposed by or under this section, he may serve on the person by whom

the document was delivered (or, if there are two or more such persons, on any of them) a notice indicating the respect in which the document does not comply.

(5)   Where the registrar serves such a notice, then unless a replacement document—

    (a) is delivered to him within 14 days after the service of the notice, and

    (b) complies with the requirements of this section (or section 706) or is not rejected by him for failure to comply with those requirements,

the original document shall be deemed not to have been delivered to him.

But for the purposes of any enactment imposing a penalty for failure to deliver, so far as it imposes a penalty for continued contravention, no account shall be taken of the period between the delivery of the original document and the end of the period of 14 days after service of the registrar's notice.

(6)   In this section references to the delivery of a document include references to the forwarding, lodging, registering, sending or submission of a document and to the giving of a notice, and cognate expressions are to be construed accordingly.

General note

This provision was inserted by the Companies Act 1985 (Electronic Communications) Order 2000, SI 2000/3373, art 27 as from 22 December 2000. It replaced the previous s 707 which had provided for delivery of documents in a non-legible form (as defined in s 715A). Permitting delivery by any method of electronic communication gives the registrar maximum flexibility in utilising modern technology.

S 707B(1)

As to the meaning of the 'Companies Acts' for these purposes, see s 735A(2).

S 707B(4), (5)

See notes to s 706(3), (4), above.

708. Fees payable to registrar

(1)   The Secretary of State may by regulations made by statutory instrument require the payment to the registrar of companies of such fees as may be specified in the regulations in respect of—

    (a) the performance by the registrar of such functions under the Companies Acts as may be so specified, including the receipt by him of any document which under those Acts is required to be delivered to him,

    (b) the inspection of documents ... kept by him under those Acts.

(2)   A statutory instrument containing regulations under this section requiring the payment of a fee in respect of a matter for which no fee was previously payable, or increasing a fee, shall be laid before Parliament after being made and shall cease to have effect at the end of the period of 28 days beginning with the day on which the regulations were made (but without prejudice to anything previously done under the regulations or to the making of further regulations) unless in that period the regulations are approved by resolution of each House of Parliament.

In reckoning that period of 28 days no account is to be taken of any time during which Parliament is dissolved or prorogued or during which both Houses are adjourned for more than 4 days.

(3)   A statutory instrument containing regulations under this section, where subsection (2) does not apply, is subject to annulment in pursuance of a resolution of either House of Parliament.

(4)   Fees paid to the registrar under the Companies Acts shall be paid into the Consolidated Fund.

(5)   It is hereby declared that the registrar may charge a fee for any services provided by him otherwise than in pursuance of an obligation imposed on him by law.

General note

The Secretary of State for Trade and Industry makes provision from time to time for fees payable both by companies on delivering various documents to the registrar of companies and on searchers accessing the public record; full details of the current fees are available on the Companies House web site: www.companieshouse.gov.uk. The First Company Law Directive (EEC) 68/151 gives the public the right to obtain copies of all documents or particulars filed by companies for no more than the administrative costs of providing the copies (art 3).

S 708(1), (4)

As to the meaning of the 'Companies Acts' for these purposes, see ss 735A(2), 735B.

709. Inspection, &c of records kept by the registrar

(1)   [Subject to section 723B,] any person may inspect any records kept by the registrar for the purposes of the Companies Acts and may require—

  (a) a copy, in such form as the registrar considers appropriate, of any information contained in those records, or

  (b) a certified copy of, or extract from, any such record.

(2)   The right of inspection extends to the originals of documents delivered to the registrar in legible form only where the record kept by the registrar of the contents of the document is illegible or unavailable.

(3)   A copy of or extract from a record kept at any of the offices for the registration of companies in England and Wales or Scotland, certified in writing by the registrar (whose official position it is unnecessary to prove) to be an accurate record of the contents of any document delivered to him under the Companies Acts, is in all legal proceedings admissible in evidence as of equal validity with the original document and as evidence of any fact stated therein of which direct oral evidence would be admissible.

...

(4)   Copies of or extracts from records furnished by the registrar may, instead of being certified by him in writing to be an accurate record, be sealed with his official seal.

(5)   No process for compelling the production of a record kept by the registrar shall issue from any court except with the leave of the court; and any such process shall bear on it a statement that it is issued with the leave of the court.

General note

The words in square brackets in sub-s (1) were inserted by the Criminal Justice and Police Act 2001, s 45(1), (4), as from 18 June 2001 (for the purpose of making regulations or orders) and as from a day to be appointed otherwise. The words omitted in sub-s (3) were repealed by the Youth Justice and Criminal Evidence Act 1999, s 67, Sch 6 as from 14 April 2000.

S 709(1)–(3)

Subject to s 723B (and see note to that provision), the register is a public register, but the registrar of companies is not required to allow access to the originals of documents delivered. As to the meaning of the 'Companies Acts' for these purposes, see ss 735A(2), 735B.

710. Certificate of incorporation

Any person may require a certificate of the incorporation of a company, signed by the registrar or authenticated by his official seal.

General note

As to the certificate of incorporation, see s 13.

710A. Provision and authentication by registrar of documents in non-legible form

(1)   Any requirement of the Companies Acts as to the supply by the registrar of a document may, if the registrar thinks fit, be satisfied by the communication

by the registrar of the requisite information in any non-legible form prescribed for the purposes of this section by regulations or approved by him.

(2)   Where the document is required to be signed by him or sealed with his official seal, it shall instead be authenticated in such manner as may be prescribed by regulations or approved by the registrar.

S 710A(1)

As to the meaning of 'non-legible' form, see s 715A; as to the meaning of the 'Companies Acts' for these purposes, see ss 735A(2), 735B.

710B. Documents relating to Welsh companies

(1)   This section applies to any document which—
- (a) is delivered to the registrar under this Act or the Insolvency Act 1986, and
- (b) relates to a company (whether already registered or to be registered) whose memorandum states that its registered office is to be situated in Wales.

(2)   A document to which this section applies may be in Welsh but, subject to subsection (3), shall on delivery to the registrar be accompanied by a certified translation into English.

(3)   The requirement for a translation imposed by subsection (2) shall not apply—
- (a) to documents of such descriptions as may be prescribed for the purposes of this paragraph, or
- (b) to documents in a form prescribed in Welsh (or partly in Welsh and partly in English) by virtue of section 26 of the Welsh Language Act 1993.

(4)   Where by virtue of subsection (3) the registrar receives a document in Welsh without a certified translation into English, he shall, if that document is to be available for inspection, himself obtain such a translation; and that translation shall be treated as delivered to him in accordance with the same provision as the original.

(5)   A company whose memorandum states that its registered office is to be situated in Wales may deliver to the registrar a certified translation into Welsh of any document in English which relates to the company and which is or has been delivered to the registrar.

(6)   The provisions within subsection (7) (which require certified translations into English of certain documents delivered to the registrar) shall not apply where a translation is required by subsection (2) or would be required but for subsection (3).

(7)   The provisions within this subsection are section 228(2)(f), the second sentence of section 242(1), sections 243(4), 272(5) and 273(7) and paragraph 7(3) of Part II of Schedule 9.

(8)   In this section 'certified translation' means a translation certified in the prescribed manner to be a correct translation.

General note

This provision was inserted by the Welsh Language Act 1993, s 30(1), (6). If a company's memorandum states that its registered office is to be in Wales, the memorandum and articles may be delivered to the registrar of companies in Welsh without a certified translation into English: see The Companies (Welsh Language Forms) Regulations 1994, SI 1994/117, as amended by SIs 1994/727, 1994/734. The most commonly used statutory forms have been prescribed in Welsh for companies with their registered office situated in Wales: see www.companieshouse.gov.uk.

711. Public notice by registrar of receipt and issue of certain documents

(1)   The registrar of companies shall cause to be published in the Gazette notice of the issue or receipt by him of documents of any of the following descriptions (stating in the notice the name of the company, the description of document and the date of issue or receipt)—

    (a)   any certificate of incorporation of a company,

    (b)   any document making or evidencing an alteration in a company's memorandum or articles,

    (c)   any notification of a change among the directors of a company,

    (d)   any copy of a resolution of a public company which gives, varies, revokes or renews an authority for the purposes of section 80 (allotment of relevant securities),

    (e)   any copy of a special resolution of a public company passed under section 95(1), (2) or (3) (disapplication of pre-emption rights),

    (f)   any report under section 103 or 104 as to the value of a non-cash asset,

    (g)   any statutory declaration or statement delivered under section 117 (public company share capital requirements),

    (h)   any notification (given under section 122) of the redemption of shares,

    (j)   any statement or notice delivered by a public company under section 128 (registration of particulars of special rights),

    (k)   any documents delivered by a company under section 242(1) (accounts and reports),

    (l)   a copy of any resolution or agreement to which section 380 applies and which—

        (i)   states the rights attached to any shares in a public company, other than shares which are in all respects uniform (for purposes of section 128) with shares previously allotted, or

        (ii)   varies rights attached to any shares in a public company, or

     (iii) assigns a name or other designation, or a new name or designation, to any class of shares in a public company,

(m) any return of allotments of a public company,

(n) any notice of a change in the situation of a company's registered office,

(p) any copy of a winding-up order in respect of a company,

(q) any order for the dissolution of a company on a winding up,

(r) any return by a liquidator of the final meeting of a company on a winding up,

(s) any copy of a draft of the terms of a scheme delivered to the registrar of companies under paragraph 2(1) of Schedule 15A,

(t) any copy of an order under section 425(2) or section 427 in respect of a compromise or arrangement to which section 427A(1) applies,

(u) any return delivered under paragraph 1, 7 or 8 of Schedule 21A (branch registration),

(v) any document delivered under paragraph 1 or 8 of that Schedule,

(w) any notice under section 695A(3) of the closure of a branch,

(x) any document delivered under Schedule 21C (accounts and reports of foreign credit and financial institutions),

(y) any document delivered under Schedule 21D (accounts and reports of oversea companies subject to branch registration, other than credit and financial institutions),

(z) any return delivered under section 703P (particulars of winding up of oversea companies subject to branch registration).

(2) In section 42 'official notification' means—

(a) in relation to anything stated in a document of any of the above descriptions, the notification of that document in the Gazette under this section, and

(b) in relation to the appointment of a liquidator in a voluntary winding up, the notification of it in the Gazette under section 109 of the Insolvency Act;

and 'officially notified' is to be construed accordingly.

General note

This provision imposes obligations on the registrar to publish various matters in the Gazette, ie the London or Edinburgh Gazette (see s 744), as the case may be. In this way, searchers are alerted to information about particular companies appearing on the public record. In practice, of course, the Gazette is an inaccessible official publication as far as the public are concerned and notification in this way is of value only to commercial searchers such as banks and credit reference agencies.

Notification in the Gazette gives effect to the First Company Law Directive (EEC) 68/15 of 9 March 1968, [1968] OJ 41, which requires member states to publish certain information regarding companies in 'the national gazette' (art 3(4)).

A company cannot rely as against other persons on notifications under sub-s (1)(b), (c), (n), (p), or an appointment notified by a liquidator in a voluntary winding up under sub-s (2)(b), until they are officially notified in this way: s 42; see the note to that provision.

S 711(1)(q)

This provision is obsolete: orders for dissolution were required under former s 568, which has been repealed.

S 711(1)(s)

This provision appears superfluous and in error; the reference to Sch 15A should read Sch 15B and, in any event, para 2(1)(b) of that Schedule requires the registrar to publish in the Gazette notice of receipt by him of a copy of the draft terms of a merger.

711A. *(Exclusion of deemed notice)*

General note

This provision was inserted by CA 1989, s 142(1) as from a day to be appointed, but it has never been brought into force and there is no expectation that it will be brought into force. The text is not reproduced here.

712. *(Repealed by CA 1989, ss 127(3), 212, Sch 24 as from 1 July 1991.)*

713. Enforcement of company's duty to make returns

(1)   If a company, having made default in complying with any provision of the Companies Acts which requires it to deliver a document to the registrar of companies, or to give notice to him of any matter, fails to make good the default within 14 days after the service of a notice on the company requiring it to do so, the court may, on an application made to it by any member or creditor of the company or by the registrar of companies, make an order directing the company and any officer of it to make good the default within such time as may be specified in the order.

(2)   The court's order may provide that all costs of and incidental to the application shall be borne by the company or by any officers of it responsible for the default.

(3)   Nothing in this section prejudices the operation of any enactment imposing penalties on a company or its officers in respect of any such default as is mentioned above.

General note

In practice, little use is made of this provision; the registrar of companies is more likely, for example, to rely on the imposition of late filing penalties under s 242A and criminal penalties under s 242 to ensure compliance with the requirement to deliver accounts and reports than to resort to this provision. As to the meaning of the 'Companies Acts' for these purposes, see ss 735A(2), 735B.

714. Registrar's index of company and corporate names

(1)   The registrar of companies shall keep an index of the names of the following bodies—

(a) companies as defined by this Act,

(aa) companies incorporated outside the United Kingdom and Gibraltar which have complied with paragraph 1 of Schedule 21A and which do not appear to the registrar of companies not to have a branch in Great Britain,

(b) companies incorporated outside Great Britain which have complied with section 691 and which do not appear to the registrar of companies not to have a place of business in Great Britain,

(c) incorporated and unincorporated bodies to which any provision of this Act applies by virtue of section 718 (unregistered companies),

(d) limited partnerships registered under the Limited Partnerships Act 1907,

(da) limited liability partnerships incorporated under the Limited Liability Partnerships Act 2000,

(e) companies within the meaning of the Companies Act (Northern Ireland) 1960,

(f) companies incorporated outside Northern Ireland which have complied with section 356 of that Act (which corresponds with section 691 of this Act), and which do not appear to the registrar not to have a place of business in Northern Ireland, and

(g) societies registered under the Industrial and Provident Societies Act 1965 or the Industrial and Provident Societies Act (Northern Ireland) 1969.

(2)   The Secretary of State may by order in a statutory instrument vary subsection (1) by the addition or deletion of any class of body, except any within paragraph (a) or (b) of the subsection, whether incorporated or unincorporated; and any such statutory instrument is subject to annulment in pursuance of a resolution of either House of Parliament.

General note

The index of names is central to the registrar's powers to regulate company names contained in ss 25–34, in particular, the prohibition on names which are the same as those appearing on the index (s 26(1)(c)); and the power to give a direction to change a name which is the same as or too like an existing name on the index (s 28(2)). See notes to ss 25–34, above.

S 714(1)

The categories are mainly self-explanatory but note that they extend beyond companies formed and registered under this Act; the result is to extend the scope of ss 26(1)(c) and 28(2).

715. *(Repealed by CA 1989, ss 127(3), 212, Sch 24 as from 1 July 1991.)*

715A. Interpretation

(1)   In this Part—

'document' includes information recorded in any form; and

'legible', in the context of documents in legible or non-legible form, means capable of being read with the naked eye.

(2)   References in this Part to delivering a document include sending, forwarding, producing or (in the case of a notice) giving it.

General note

As to the delivery of documents to the registrar of companies in legible form and by electronic communication, see ss 706 and 707B, above.

PART XXV

MISCELLANEOUS AND SUPPLEMENTARY PROVISIONS

716. Prohibition of partnerships with more than 20 members

(1)   No company, association or partnership consisting of more than 20 persons shall be formed for the purpose of carrying on any business that has for its object the acquisition of gain by the company, association or partnership, or by its individual members, unless it is registered as a company under this Act, [is incorporated by virtue of regulations made under section 262 of the Financial Services and Markets Act 2000], or is formed in pursuance of some other Act of Parliament, or of letters patent.

(2)   However, this does not prohibit the formation—

    (a) for the purpose of carrying on practice as solicitors, of a partnership consisting of persons each of whom is a solicitor;

    (b) for the purpose of carrying on practice as accountants, of a partnership which is eligible for appointment as a company auditor under section 25 of the Companies Act 1989;

    (c) for the purpose of carrying on business as members of a recognised stock exchange, of a partnership consisting of persons each of whom is a member of that stock exchange;

    (d) for any purpose prescribed by regulations (which may include a purpose mentioned above), of a partnership of a description so prescribed;

    ...

    (e) of an open-ended investment company within the meaning of the Open-Ended Investment Companies Regulations 2001.

(3)   In subsection (2)(a) 'solicitor'—

    (a) in relation to England and Wales, means solicitor of the Supreme Court, and

    (b) in relation to Scotland, means a person enrolled or deemed enrolled as a solicitor in pursuance of the Solicitors (Scotland) Act 1980.

(4)   In subsection (2)(c) 'recognised stock exchange' means—

    (a) The International Stock Exchange of the United Kingdom and the Republic of Ireland Limited, and

    (b) any other stock exchange for the time being recognised for the purposes of this section by the Secretary of State by order made by statutory instrument.

(5)   Subsection (1) does not apply in relation to any body of persons for the time being approved for the purposes of the Marine and Aviation Insurance (War Risks) Act 1952 by the Secretary of State, being a body the objects of which are or include the carrying on of business by way of the re-insurance of risks which may be re-insured under any agreement for the purpose mentioned in section 1(1)(b) of that Act.

NOTES

Subsection (2)(e) substituted by the Open-Ended Investment Companies Regulations 2001, SI 2001/1228, reg 84, Sch 7, para 7, as from a day to be appointed.

Subsection (1): words in square brackets inserted by the Financial Services and Markets Act 2000, s 263 as from a day to be appointed.

General note

This provision dates back to the earliest companies legislation in 1844. The intention then was to curb large numbers of persons forming an unincorporated deed of settlement company as the large and fluctuating numbers made it impossible to secure judgment and enforcement against the members. Today, the provision is widely regarded as an anachronism and the Department of Trade and Industry is considering the removal of the 20-partner limit.

S 716(1), (2)

The position is that sub-s (1) imposes a limit of 20 persons on a partnership but a very large number of partnerships are exempt from the operation of this limitation either directly under sub-s (2) or by regulations made under that section: see the Partnerships (Unrestricted Size) No 4 Regulations 1970, SI 1970/1319, as amended by SI 1992/1438; and subsequent 'unrestricted size' regulations, Nos 5–17, SI 1982/530, SI 1990/1581; SI 1990/1969; SI 1991/2729; SI 1992/1028; SI 1992/1439, SI 1994/644; SI 1997/1937; SI 1999/2464; SI 2000/486; SI 2000/2711; SI 2001/1389; SI 2001/2422.

717. Limited partnerships: limit on number of members

(1)   So much of the Limited Partnerships Act 1907 as provides that a limited partnership shall not consist of more than 20 persons does not apply—

  (a) to a partnership carrying on practice as solicitors and consisting of persons each of whom is a solicitor,

  (b) to a partnership carrying on practice as accountants which is eligible for appointment as a company auditor under section 25 of the Companies Act 1989,

  (c) to a partnership carrying on business as members of a recognised stock exchange and consisting of persons each of whom is a member of that exchange,

  (d) to a partnership carrying on business of any description prescribed by regulations (which may include a business of any description mentioned above), of a partnership of a description so prescribed.

  ...

(2)   In subsection (1)(a) 'solicitor'—

  (a) in relation to England and Wales, means solicitor of the Supreme Court, and

  (b) in relation to Scotland, means a person enrolled or deemed enrolled as a solicitor in pursuance of the Solicitors (Scotland) Act 1980.

(3)   In subsection (1)(c) 'recognised stock exchange' means—

  (a) The International Stock Exchange of the United Kingdom and the Republic of Ireland Limited, and

  (b) any other stock exchange for the time being recognised for the purposes of this section by the Secretary of State by order made by statutory instrument.

General note

This provision is intended to have the same effect as s 716; again, the limit of 20 persons is subject to the exemptions in sub-s (1) and the regulations made under it: see the Limited Partnerships (Unrestricted Size) No 1 Regulations 1971, SI 1971/782; the Limited Partnerships (Unrestricted Size) No 2 Regulations 1990, SI 1990/1580; the Limited Partnerships (Unrestricted Size) No 3 Regulations 1992, SI 1992/1027.

---

718. Unregistered companies

(1)   The provisions of this Act specified in the first column of Schedule 22 (relating respectively to the matters specified in the second column of the Schedule) apply to all bodies corporate incorporated in and having a principal place of business in Great Britain, other than those mentioned in subsection (2) below, as if they were companies registered under this Act, but subject to any limitations mentioned in relation to those provisions respectively in the third column and to such adaptations and modifications (if any) as may be specified by regulations made by the Secretary of State.

(2)   Those provisions of this Act do not apply by virtue of this section to any of the following—

    (a)   any body incorporated by or registered under any public general Act of Parliament,

    (b)   any body not formed for the purpose of carrying on a business which has for its object the acquisition of gain by the body or its individual members,

    (c)   any body for the time being exempted by direction of the Secretary of State (or before him by the Board of Trade).

    (d)   any open-ended investment company within the meaning of the Open-Ended Investment Companies Regulations 2001.

(3)   Where against any provision of this Act specified in the first column of Schedule 22 there appears in the third column the entry 'Subject to section 718(3)', it means that the provision is to apply by virtue of this section so far only as may be specified by regulations made by the Secretary of State and to such bodies corporate as may be so specified.

(4)   The provisions specified in the first column of the Schedule also apply in like manner in relation to any unincorporated body of persons entitled by virtue of letters patent to any of the privileges conferred by the Chartered Companies Act 1837 and not registered under any other public general Act of Parliament, but subject to the like exceptions as are provided for in the case of bodies corporate by paragraphs (b) and (c) of subsection (2).

(5)   This section does not repeal or revoke in whole or in part any enactment, royal charter or other instrument constituting or regulating any body in relation to which those provisions are applied by virtue of this section, or restrict the power of Her Majesty to grant a charter in lieu or supplementary to any such charter as above mentioned; but, in relation to any such body, the operation of any such enactment, charter or instrument is suspended in so far as it is inconsistent with any of those provisions as they apply for the time being to that body.

(6) The power to make regulations conferred by this section (whether regulations under subsection (1) or subsection (3)) is exercisable by statutory instrument subject to annulment in pursuance of a resolution of either House of Parliament.

NOTES

Subsection (2)(d) substituted by the Open-Ended Investment Companies Regulations 2001, SI 2001/1228, reg 84, Sch 7, para 8, as from a day to be appointed.

S 718(1), (3), (4)

Companies within this category   This provision is necessary to sweep into the legislation any remaining deed of settlement companies, companies formed by letters patent and companies formed by private Act of Parliament.

As these companies do not indicate their status as unregistered companies in any way, it is difficult to know whether many of them remain, particularly since they have the option of re-registering under ss 680–690 and moving to the status of companies formed and registered under this Act.

Subject only to limited elements of the legislation   This provision subjects all bodies incorporated in and having a principal place of business in Great Britain, not falling within sub-s (2), to such provisions of this Act as are specified in Sch 22. See the Companies (Unregistered Companies) Regulations 1985, SI 1985/680, as amended by SI 1990/438, SI 1990/1394, SI 1990/2571, and SI 2001/86 as to the provisions of the Act which are applicable to these unregistered companies.

Many important provisions, such as those relating to distributions (s 263ff), registration of charges (s 395ff) and minority protection (s 459), are not applicable to unregistered companies and persons dealing with such companies may be unaware of this fact. As to the meaning of 'principal place of business', see note to s 698(2), above.

S 718(2)

The provisions of the statute do not apply to these exempted categories.

719. Power of company to provide for employees on cessation or transfer of business

(1) The powers of a company include (if they would not otherwise do so apart from this section) power to make the following provision for the benefit of persons employed or formerly employed by the company or any of its subsidiaries, that is to say, provision in connection with the cessation or the transfer to any person of the whole or part of the undertaking of the company or that subsidiary.

(2) The power conferred by subsection (1) is exercisable notwithstanding that its exercise is not in the best interests of the company.

(3) The power which a company may exercise by virtue only of subsection (1) shall only be exercised by the company if sanctioned—

(a) in a case not falling within paragraph (b) or (c) below, by an ordinary resolution of the company, or

(b) if so authorised by the memorandum or articles, a resolution of the directors, or

(c) if the memorandum or articles require the exercise of the power to be sanctioned by a resolution of the company of some other description for which more than a simple majority of the members voting is necessary, with the sanction of a resolution of that description;

and in any case after compliance with any other requirements of the memorandum or articles applicable to its exercise.

(4) Any payment which may be made by a company under this section may, if made before the commencement of any winding up of the company, be made out of profits of the company which are available for dividend.

General note

This provision was introduced by the Companies Act 1980, s 74, and it was intended to reverse the decision in *Parke v Daily News Ltd* [1962] 2 All ER 929 which had held that payments to former employees on the cessation of business were ultra vires and not in the best interests of the company.

The issue of ultra vires is addressed by sub-s (1) while sub-s (2) provides that the payments made under sub-s (1) may be made notwithstanding that the exercise of this power is not in the best interests of the company (ie because there is no reason to secure the goodwill of the employees when the business has been transferred). The provision is probably of limited practical significance in view of the fact that, under sub-s (3), any payment can only be made if approved by the shareholders, either by resolution or by the inclusion of a power to this effect in the memorandum or articles of association; and shareholders may not feel generous on this issue.

Where the company goes into winding up, the liquidator has power (subject to various conditions) to make any payment which the company has, prior to the commencement of the winding up, decided to make under this provision: IA 1986, s 187(1); equally, the decision to make such provision may be made after the commencement of the winding up (see IA 1986, s 187(2)).

S 719(1)

The power to make provision as envisaged by this sub-section may be exercised for the benefit of employees in a subsidiary; employees and former employees, but not their families, are within the class of beneficiary; the payments must be 'in connection with' the cessation etc, so the timing of the payment would be important. The transaction must involve a 'cessation or transfer' of the whole or part of the undertaking, but there is no requirement that the company go into winding up.

S 719(2)–(4)

All three subsections are constrained by sub-s (1), so it is only an exercise of the power conferred by sub-s (1) which is protected by sub-s (2); and which requires the authorisation set out in sub-s (3) and the funds specified by sub-s (4). Any other provision for employees or former employees, not arising as an exercise of a power conferred by sub-s (1), is not subject to these provisions but will have to be considered in the light of ss 35, 35A, and the directors' duty to act bona fide in the interests of the company as a whole. Sub-s (4), although apparently permissive, means that payments may only be made out of profits available for dividend, as to which see the notes to s 263ff, above; and see IA 1986, s 187(3) as to the source of payment on a winding up.

720. Certain companies to publish periodical statement

(1)   Every company, being an insurance company or a deposit, provident or benefit society, shall before it commences business, and also on the first Monday in February and the first Tuesday in August in every year during which it carries on business, make a statement in the form set out in Schedule 23, or as near to it as circumstances admit.

(2)   A copy of the statement shall be put up in a conspicuous place in the company's registered office, and in every branch office or place where the business of the company is carried on.

(3)   Every member and every creditor of the company is entitled to a copy of the statement, on payment of a sum not exceeding 2½ pence.

(4)   If default is made in complying with this section, the company and every officer of it who is in default is liable to a fine and, for continued contravention, to a daily default fine.

(5)   For purposes of this Act, a company which carries on the business of insurance in common with any other business or businesses is deemed an insurance company.

(6)   In the case of an insurance company to which Part II of the Insurance Companies Act 1982 applies, this section does not apply if the company complies with provisions of that Act as to the accounts and balance sheet to be prepared annually and deposited by such a company.

(7)   The Secretary of State may, by regulations in a statutory instrument (subject to annulment in pursuance of a resolution of either House of Parliament), alter the form in Schedule 23.

General note

By virtue of the Insurance Companies (Third Insurance Directives) Regulations 1994, SI 1994/1696, reg 68(1), Sch 8, Pt I, para 9(6) this section does not apply in the case of an EC company if the company complies with provisions of law of its home state as to the accounts and balance sheets to be prepared annually and deposited with the supervisory authority in that state by such a company. See also sub-s (6).

S 720(1)

This provision which derives from the CA 1948 and requires the companies specified to make available periodical statements of this nature is somewhat anachronistic in the light of the extensive substantive legislation now applicable to such entities in their own right. Moreover, it is doubtful if members and creditors regard it as a particularly valuable disclosure obligation. See Sch 23.

S 720(4)

As to penalties, see s 730, Sch 24.

721. Production and inspection of books where offence suspected

(1) The following applies if on an application made—

    (a) in England and Wales, to a judge of the High Court by the Director of Public Prosecutions, the Secretary of State or a chief officer of police, or

    (b) in Scotland, to one of the Lords Commissioners of Justiciary by the Lord Advocate,

there is shown to be reasonable cause to believe that any person has, while an officer of a company, committed an offence in connection with the management of the company's affairs and that evidence of the commission of the offence is to be found in any books or papers of or under the control of the company.

(2) An order may be made—

    (a) authorising any person named in it to inspect the books or papers in question, or any of them, for the purpose of investigating and obtaining evidence of the offence, or

    (b) requiring the secretary of the company or such other officer of it as may be named in the order to produce the books or papers (or any of them) to a person named in the order at a place so named.

(3) The above applies also in relation to any books or papers of a person carrying on the business of banking so far as they relate to the company's affairs, as it applies to any books or papers of or under the control of the company, except that no such order as is referred to in subsection (2)(b) shall be made by virtue of this subsection.

(4) The decision of a judge of the High Court or of any of the Lords Commissioners of Justiciary on an application under this section is not appealable.

General note

It appears that this provision is obsolete, with the Secretary of State for Trade and Industry preferring to exercise his powers under s 447, while any other named person entitled to make use of this provision is likely to refer the matter to the Department of Trade and Industry for action under s 447.

S 721(4)

As a result of this express provision, the Court of Appeal has no jurisdiction to entertain an appeal and no distinction is to be drawn as between appeals on matters of fact and matters of law: *Re Racal Communications Ltd* [1981] AC 374, HL.

722. Form of company registers, etc

(1)   Any register, index, minute book or accounting records required by the Companies Acts to be kept by a company may be kept either by making entries in bound books or by recording the matters in question in any other manner.

(2)   Where any such register, index, minute book or accounting record is not kept by making entries in a bound book, but by some other means, adequate precautions shall be taken for guarding against falsification and facilitating its discovery.

(3)   If default is made in complying with subsection (2), the company and every officer of it who is in default is liable to a fine and, for continued contravention, to a daily default fine.

S 722(1)

See also s 723.

S 722(3)

As to penalties, see s 730, Sch 24.

723. Use of computers for company records

(1)   The power conferred on a company by section 722(1) to keep a register or other record by recording the matters in question otherwise than by making entries in bound books includes power to keep the register or other record by recording those matters otherwise than in a legible form, so long as the recording is capable of being reproduced in a legible form.

(2)   Any provision of an instrument made by a company before 12th February 1979 which requires a register of holders of the company's debentures to be kept in a legible form is to be read as requiring the register to be kept in a legible or non-legible form.

(3)   If any such register or other record of a company as is mentioned in section 722(1), or a register of holders of a company's debentures, is kept by the company by recording the matters in question otherwise than in a legible form, any duty imposed on the company by this Act to allow inspection of, or to furnish a copy of, the register or other record or any part of it is to be treated as a duty to allow inspection of, or to furnish, a reproduction of the recording or of the relevant part of it in a legible form.

(4)   The Secretary of State may by regulations in a statutory instrument make such provision in addition to subsection (3) as he considers appropriate in connection with such registers or other records as are mentioned in that subsection, and are kept as so mentioned; and the regulations may make modifications of provisions of this Act relating to such registers or other records.

(5)   A statutory instrument under subsection (4) is subject to annulment in pursuance of a resolution of either House of Parliament.

General note

See the Companies (Registers and other Records) Regulations 1985, SI 1985/724.

723A. Obligations of company as to inspections of registers, &c

(1)   The Secretary of State may make provision by regulations as to the obligations of a company which is required by any provision of this Act—

    (a)   to make available for inspection any register, index or document, or

    (b)   to provide copies of any such register, index or document, or part of it;

and a company which fails to comply with the regulations shall be deemed to have refused inspection or, as the case may be, to have failed to provide a copy.

(2)   The regulations may make provision as to the time, duration and manner of inspection, including the circumstances in which and extent to which the copying of information is permitted in the course of inspection.

(3)   The regulations may define what may be required of the company as regards the nature, extent and manner of extracting or presenting any information for the purposes of inspection or the provision of copies.

(4)   Where there is a power to charge a fee, the regulations may make provision as to the amount of the fee and the basis of its calculation.

(5)   Regulations under this section may make different provision for different classes of case.

(6)   Nothing in any provision of this Act or in the regulations shall be construed as preventing a company from affording more extensive facilities than are required by the regulations or, where a fee may be charged, from charging a lesser fee than that prescribed or no fee at all.

(7)   Regulations under this section shall be made by statutory instrument which shall be subject to annulment in pursuance of a resolution of either House of Parliament.

General note

See the Companies (Inspection and Copying of Registers, Indices and Documents) Regulations 1991, SI 1991/1998; and sub-s (1) as to the consequences of non-compliance with the Regulations.

723B. Confidentiality orders

(1)   Subject to the provisions of this section, an individual may make an application under this section to the Secretary of State where the condition in subsection (2) is satisfied.

(2)   That condition is that the individual—

(a)   is or proposes to become a director, secretary or permanent representative of a relevant company; and

(b)   considers that the availability for inspection by members of the public of particulars of his usual residential address creates, or (if an order is not made under this section) is likely to create, a serious risk that he or a person who lives with him will be subjected to violence or intimidation.

(3)   Where, on an application made by an individual under this section, the Secretary of State is satisfied that the availability for inspection by members of the public of particulars of the individual's usual residential address creates, or (if an order is not made under this section) is likely to create, a serious risk that the individual, or a person who lives with him, will be subjected to violence or intimidation, he shall make an order under this section ('a confidentiality order') in relation to him.

(4)   Otherwise, he shall dismiss the application.

(5)   An application under this section shall specify, in relation to each company of which the individual is a director, secretary or permanent representative, an address satisfying such conditions as may be prescribed.

(6)   The Secretary of State shall give the applicant notice of his decision under subsection (3) or (4); and a notice under this subsection shall be given within the prescribed period after the making of the decision and contain such information as may be prescribed.

(7)   Regulations may make provision about applications for confidentiality orders; and the regulations may in particular—

(a)   require the payment, on the making of an application, of such fees as may be specified in the regulations;

(b)   make provision about the form and manner in which applications are to be made;

(c)   provide that applications shall contain such information, and be accompanied by such evidence, as the Secretary of State may from time to time direct.

(8)   Regulations may make provision—

(a)   about the manner in which determinations are to be made under subsection (3) or (4);

(b)   for questions to be referred to such persons as the Secretary of State thinks fit for the purposes of such determinations;

(c)   about the review of such determinations;

(d)   about the period for which confidentiality orders shall remain in force and the renewal of confidentiality orders.

(9)   The Secretary of State may at any time revoke a confidentiality order if he is satisfied that such conditions as may be prescribed are satisfied.

(10) Regulations may make provision about the manner in which a determination under subsection (9) is to be made and notified to the individual concerned.

NOTES
Commencement: 18 June 2001 (for the purpose of making regulations or orders); to be appointed (remaining purposes).
Inserted by the Criminal Justice and Police Act 2001, s 45(1),(2), as from 18 June 2001 (for the purpose of making regulations or orders) and as from a day to be appointed otherwise.

General note

This provision, together with ss 723C–723F, was inserted by the Criminal Justice and Police Act 2001, as noted above, in order to restrict public access to the usual residential addresses of directors (and others, see sub-s (2)(a)) at serious risk of violence or intimidation. These provisions provide the framework for the scheme, the details of which will be set out in regulations which have not been laid at the time of writing.

Essentially, the scheme envisaged is one whereby directors etc of relevant companies (which includes overseas companies: see s 723D(1)(b)) who consider that they fall within the criteria in sub-s (2) may apply to the Secretary of State for Trade and Industry for a confidentiality order; the effect of which is spelt out in s 723C. Generally, the effect will be to prevent public inspection of particulars delivered to the registrar of companies of the person's usual residential address; to remove this information from the annual return; and to remove this information from the company's own register of directors and secretaries to a protected part of that register. The regulations will make provision for those persons, such as the police, who may inspect the particulars held by the registrar as to the person's usual residential address.

The confidentiality order will only remove particulars as to a person's usual residential address in documents delivered to the registrar after a confidentiality order comes into force (s 723C(1)(a)), so it will not be possible to require the registrar of companies to remove addresses from the existing records at Companies House.

723C. Effect of confidentiality orders

(1)　At any time when a confidentiality order is in force in relation to an individual—

(a)　section 709(1) shall not apply to so much of any record kept by the registrar as contains information which is recorded as particulars of the individual's usual residential address that were contained in a document delivered to the registrar after the order came into force;

(b)　section 364 shall have effect in relation to each affected company of which the individual is a director or secretary as if the reference in subsection (4)(a) of that section to the individual's usual residential address were a reference to the address for the time being specified by the individual in relation to that company under section 723B(5) or subsection (7) below.

(2)　Regulations may make provision about the inspection and copying of confidential records, and such provision may include—

(a)　provision as to the persons by whom, and the circumstances in which, confidential records may be inspected or copies taken of such records;

(b)　provision under which the registrar may be required to provide certified copies of, or of extracts from, such records.

1069

(3)   Provision under subsection (2) may include provision—

    (a) for persons of a prescribed description to be entitled to apply to the court for authority to inspect or take copies of confidential records;

    (b) as to the criteria to be used by the court in determining whether an authorisation should be given.

(4)   Regulations may make provision for restricting the persons to whom, and the purposes for which, relevant information may be disclosed.

(5)   In subsection (4)'relevant information' means information, relating to the usual residential address of an individual in relation to whom a confidentiality order is in force, which has been obtained in prescribed circumstances.

(6)   Regulations may—

    (a) provide that, where a confidentiality order is in force in relation to an individual who is a director or secretary of a company, subsections (3) and (5) of section 288 shall not apply in relation to so much of the register kept by the company under that section as contains particulars of the usual residential address of that individual ('the protected part of the register'); and

    (b) make provision as to the persons by whom the protected part of the register may be inspected and the conditions (which may include conditions as to the payment of a fee) on which they may inspect it.

(7)   Regulations may make provision—

    (a) requiring any individual in relation to whom a confidentiality order is in force to specify in the prescribed manner, in relation to each company of which he becomes a director, secretary or permanent representative at a time when the order is in force, an address satisfying such conditions as may be prescribed;

    (b) as to the manner in which the address specified in relation to a company under section 723B(5) or this subsection may be changed.

(8)   A company is an affected company for the purposes of subsection (1) if—

    (a) it is required to deliver annual returns in accordance with section 363; and

    (b) the individual has specified an address in relation to it under section 723B(5) or subsection (7) above.

General note

See general note to s 723B, above.

723D. Construction of sections 723B and 723C

(1)   In section 723B 'relevant company' means—

    (a) a company formed and registered under this Act or an existing company; or

    (b) an overseas company.

(2)   For the purposes of sections 723B and 723C, an individual is a permanent representative of a company if—

(a) the company is a company to which section 690A applies; and

(b) he is authorised to represent the company as a permanent representative of the company for the business of one or more of its branches in Great Britain.

(3)   In section 723C 'confidential records' means so much of any records kept by the registrar for the purposes of the Companies Acts as contains information—

(a) which relates to an individual in relation to whom a confidentiality order is in force; and

(b) is recorded as particulars of the individual's usual residential address that were contained in a document delivered to the registrar after the order came into force.

(4)   In sections 723B and 723C—

"confidentiality order" means an order under section 723B;

"the court" means such court as may be specified in regulations;

"director" and "secretary", in relation to an overseas company, have the same meanings as in Chapter 1 of Part 23 of this Act;

"document" has the same meaning as in Part 24 of this Act;

"prescribed" means prescribed by regulations.

(5)   Section 715A(2) applies in relation to sections 723B and 723C as it applies in relation to Part 24 of this Act.

(6)   Regulations may provide that in determining for the purposes of sections 723B and 723C whether a document has been delivered after the coming into force of a confidentiality order, any document delivered to the registrar after the latest time permitted for the delivery of that document shall be deemed to have been delivered at that time.

(7)   For the purposes of section 723B(2)(a) and subsection (2) above it is immaterial whether or not the company in question has already been incorporated or become a relevant company or a company to which section 690A applies at the time of the application under section 723B.

(8)   For the purposes of section 723C(1) and subsection (3) above, it is immaterial whether the record in question consists in the original document concerned.

General note

See general note to s 723B, above.

723E. Sections 723B and 723C: offences

(1)   Regulations may provide—

(a) that any person who in an application under section 723B makes a statement which he knows to be false in a material particular, or recklessly makes a statement which is false in a material particular, shall be guilty of an offence;

(b) that any person who discloses information in contravention of regulations under section 723C(4) shall be guilty of an offence.

(2)   Regulations may provide that a person guilty of an offence under subsection (1) shall be liable—

    (a) on conviction on indictment, to imprisonment for a term not exceeding two years, or to a fine, or to both; and

    (b) on summary conviction, to imprisonment for a term not exceeding six months, or to a fine not exceeding the statutory maximum, or to both.

General note

See general note to s 723B, above.

723F. Regulations under sections 723B to 723E

(1)   In sections 723B to 723E 'regulations' means regulations made by the Secretary of State.

(2)   Any power of the Secretary of State to make regulations under any of those sections shall be exercisable by statutory instrument.

(3)   Regulations under sections 723B to 723E—

    (a) may make different provision for different cases;

    (b) may contain such incidental, supplemental, consequential and transitional provision, as the Secretary of State thinks fit.

(4)   The provision that may be made by virtue of subsection (3)(b) includes provision repealing or modifying any enactment.

(5)   No regulations shall be made under any of sections 723B to 723E unless a draft of the instrument containing them has been laid before Parliament and approved by a resolution of each House.

General note

See general note to s 723B, above.

724. *(Repealed by the Insolvency Act 1986, s 438, Sch 12, as from 29 December 1986.)*

725. Service of documents

(1)   A document may be served on a company by leaving it at, or sending it by post to, the company's registered office.

(2)   Where a company registered in Scotland carries on business in England and Wales, the process of any court in England and Wales may be served on the

company by leaving it at, or sending it by post to, the company's principal place of business in England and Wales, addressed to the manager or other head officer in England and Wales of the company.

(3)   Where process is served on a company under subsection (2), the person issuing out the process shall send a copy of it by post to the company's registered office.

General note

Service under the CPR   A company may be served by any method permitted under the Civil Procedure Rules 1998, SI 1998/3132, Pt 6 as an alternative to the methods of service set out in this provision: CPR r 6.2(2); and see CPR Practice Direction, Pt 6 – Service.

The following methods of service of a document are permitted: (a) personal service, ie by leaving the document with a person holding a senior position within the company: CPR, r 6.4(4); (b) first class post; (c) leaving the document at a place specified by CPR, r 6.5 which for a company registered in England and Wales is the principal office of the company (which need not be the registered office) or any place of business of the company within the jurisdiction which has a real connection with the claim (CPR, r 6.2(1)).

Provision is also made for service using a document exchange or by fax or other means of electronic communication in accordance with CPR Practice Direction, Pt 6 – Service: CPR, r 6.2(1). In addition, where it appears to the court that there is a good reason to authorise service by a method not permitted by the CPR, the court may make an order permitting service by an alternative method: CPR, r 6.8.

S 725(1)

'Company' is defined in s 735 and essentially means companies formed and registered under this and former companies legislation; as to service on oversea companies, see ss 694A and 695 and the notes to those provisions.

In the case of service by post, service is deemed to be effected by properly addressing, pre-paying and posting a letter containing the document and, unless the contrary is proved, to have been effected at the time at which the letter would be delivered in the ordinary course of post: Interpretation Act 1978, s 7. Registered or ordinary post may be used: *TO Supplies (London) Ltd v Jerry Creighton Ltd* [1951] 2 All ER 992.

As to the company's registered office, see s 287; a change of registered office must be notified to the registrar of companies: s 287(3); and receipt of that notice must be gazetted by the registrar: s 711(1)(n). A change in the situation of the registered office is one of the matters which must be officially notified in this way if the company is to rely on it against other persons who do not know of the change: see s 42 and the note to that provision.

Any change to the registered office does not take effect until registered by the registrar, but until the end of the period of 14 days beginning with the date on which it is registered a person may validly serve any document on the company at its previous registered office: s 287(4).

S 725(2)

As to the meaning of 'principal place of business', see note to s 698(2), above.

726. Costs and expenses in actions by certain limited companies

(1) Where in England and Wales a limited company is plaintiff in an action or other legal proceeding, the court having jurisdiction in the matter may, if it appears by credible testimony that there is reason to believe that the company will be unable to pay the defendant's costs if successful in his defence, require sufficient security to be given for those costs, and may stay all proceedings until the security is given.

(2) Where in Scotland a limited company is pursuer in an action or other legal proceeding, the court having jurisdiction in the matter may, if it appears by credible testimony that there is reason to believe that the company will be unable to pay the defender's expenses if successful in his defence, order the company to find caution and sist the proceedings until caution is found.

S 726(1)

Security for costs – certain companies 'Company' is defined in s 735 and essentially means companies formed and registered under this and former companies legislation; in this instance, the category is restricted to limited companies. For security for costs with respect to oversea companies ordinarily resident out of the jurisdiction, see CPR, Sch 1; RSC, Ord 23; for security for costs with respect to a company incorporated in and resident in Northern Ireland, see *DSQ Property Co Ltd v Lotus Cars Ltd* [1987] BCLC 60; *Re Dynaspan (UK) Ltd* [1995] 1 BCLC 536; for companies incorporated in and resident in the Isle of Man, see *Greenwich Ltd v National Westminster Bank plc* [1999] 2 Lloyd's Rep 308.

A plaintiff in an action or other legal proceeding 'Plaintiff' in this context is not to be taken as a person conventionally described as a plaintiff (now claimant) alone, but as pointing to a person who has invoked the jurisdiction of the court by whatever method of commencing a claim he has chosen, including proceedings commenced by petition: *Re Unisoft Group Ltd, Saunderson Holdings Ltd v Unisoft Group Ltd* [1993] BCLC 1292, CA; or an arbitration, see *Smith v UIC Insurance Co Ltd* [2001] BCC 11; but it does not include a defendant which has made an interim application: *C T Bowring & Co (Insurance) Ltd v Corsi & Partners Ltd* [1995] 1 BCLC 148, CA.

Making a counterclaim An impecunious company which makes a counterclaim which is more than a mere formulation of its defence can be ordered to give security for the plaintiff's costs of the counterclaim: *Neck v Taylor* [1893] 1 QB 560. The question is whether in the particular case the counterclaim is a cross-action or operates as a defence, that is to say merely operates as a defence: *Hutchison Telephone (UK) Ltd v Ultimate Response Ltd* [1993] BCLC 307 at 313, per Dillon LJ. An application for an enforcement of a cross-undertaking in damages is a mere matter of defence and not an action or other legal proceeding for which security for costs can be sought: *C T Bowring & Co (Insurance) Ltd v Corsi & Partners Ltd* [1995] 1 BCLC 148, CA.

Credible testimony The section looks forward to a time at which the action has been heard, the plaintiff has failed and the defendant has had an order for costs in his favour. If there is credible testimony at the time of the application that the company will, in such events, then be unable to pay such costs, security can be required. But a present inability or difficulty on the company's part to put up some security is not proof of the particular inability to pay costs which the provision requires: *Paper Properties Ltd* *v Jay Benning & Co* [1995] 1 BCLC 172; see also *Europa Holdings Ltd v Circle Industries (UK) plc* [1993] BCLC 320, CA.

An exercise of discretion   The relevant principles which guide the court in the exercise of its discretion were set out at length by Peter Gibson LJ in *Keary Developments Ltd v Tarmac Construction Ltd* [1995] 2 BCLC 395, CA, the key elements of which (at 400–403) are extracted below:

'1. As was established ... in *Sir Lindsay Parkinson & Co Ltd v Triplan Ltd* [1973] 2 All ER 273, the court has a complete discretion whether to order security, and accordingly it will act in the light of all the relevant circumstances.

2. The possibility or probability that the plaintiff company will be deterred from pursuing its claim by an order for security is not without more a sufficient reason for not ordering security (see *Okotcha v Voest Alpine Intertrading GmbH* [1993] BCLC 474 at 479, per Bingham LJ, with whom Steyn LJ agreed). By making the exercise of discretion under s 726(1) conditional on it being shown that the company is one likely to be unable to pay costs awarded against it, Parliament must have envisaged that the order might be made in respect of a plaintiff company that would find difficulty in providing security (see *Pearson v Naydler* [1977] 3 All ER 531 at 536–537, per Megarry V-C).

3. The court must carry out a balancing exercise. On the one hand it must weigh the injustice to the plaintiff if prevented from pursuing a proper claim by an order for security. Against that, it must weigh the injustice to the defendant if no security is ordered and at the trial the plaintiff's claim fails and the defendant finds himself unable to recover from the plaintiff the costs which have been incurred by him in his defence of the claim.

The court will properly be concerned not to allow the power to order security to be used as an instrument of oppression, such as by stifling a genuine claim by an indigent company against a more prosperous company, particularly when the failure to meet that claim might in itself have been a material cause of the plaintiff's impecuniosity (see *Farrer v Lacy, Hartland & Co* (1885) 28 Ch D 482 at 485 per Bowen LJ). But it will also be concerned not to be so reluctant to order security that it becomes a weapon whereby the impecunious company can use its inability to pay costs as a means of putting unfair pressure on the more prosperous company (see *Pearson v Naydler* [1977] 3 All ER 531 at 537).

4. In considering all the circumstances, the court will have regard to the plaintiff company's prospects of success. But it should not go into the merits in detail unless it can clearly be demonstrated that there is a high degree of probability of success or failure (see *Porzelack KG v Porzelack (UK) Ltd* [1987] 1 All ER 1074 at 1077 per Browne-Wilkinson V-C). In this context it is relevant to take account of the conduct of the litigation thus far, including any open offer or payment into court, indicative as it may be of the plaintiff's prospects of success. But the court will also be aware of the possibility that an offer or payment may be made in acknowledgment not so much of the prospects of success but of the nuisance value of a claim.

5. The court in considering the amount of security that might be ordered will bear in mind that it can order any amount up to the full amount claimed by way of security, provided that it is more than a simply nominal amount; it is not bound to make an order of a substantial amount (see *Roburn Construction Ltd v William Irwin (South) & Co Ltd* [1991] BCC 726).

6. Before the court refuses to order security on the ground that it would unfairly stifle a valid claim, the court must be satisfied that, in all the circumstances, it is probable that the claim would be stifled. There may be cases

where this can properly be inferred without direct evidence (see *Trident International Freight Services Ltd v Manchester Ship Canal Co* [1990] BCLC 263) ... such a case is likely to be a far rarer one than those cases in which the court will require evidence from the plaintiff to make good any assertion that the claim would probably be stifled by an order for security for costs.

The court should consider not only whether the plaintiff company can provide security out of its own resources to continue the litigation, but also whether it can raise the amount needed from its directors, shareholders or other backers or interested persons. As this is likely to be peculiarly within the knowledge of the plaintiff company, it is for the plaintiff to satisfy the court that it would be prevented by an order for security from continuing the litigation (see *Flender Werft AG v Aegean Maritime Ltd* [1990] 2 Lloyd's Rep 27) ...

7. The lateness of the application for security is a circumstance which can properly be taken into account ... But what weight, if any, this factor should have and in which direction it should weigh must depend upon matters such as whether blame for the lateness of the application is to be placed at the door of the defendant or at that of the plaintiff. It is proper to take into account the fact that costs have already been incurred by the plaintiff without there being an order for security. Nevertheless it is appropriate for the court to have regard to what costs may yet be incurred.'

Company in liquidation   The provision by its wording applies to limited companies, whether or not in liquidation. As Millett LJ noted in *Metalloy Supplies Ltd v MA(UK)Ltd* [1997] 1 BCLC 165, a liquidator of an insolvent company may bring proceedings in his own name, in which case he is personally liable for the costs in the ordinary way, though he may be entitled to an indemnity out of the assets of the company; but if he brings the proceedings in the name of the company, the company is the real plaintiff (at 172). A defendant worried about such an impecunious plaintiff may apply for an order for security for costs under this provision in the usual way.

An issue for consideration then will be whether the court should exercise its discretion in favour of making an order for security in view of the protection afforded to a successful defendant by any costs order which he might obtain. It is a well-established principle that any order for costs made against a company in liquidation is payable out of the net assets in the hands of the liquidator, in priority to other claims, including that of the liquidator for his own costs: *Norglen Ltd v Reeds Rains Prudential Ltd* [1998] 1 All ER 218 at 232, per Lord Hoffmann; *Re Movitex Ltd* [1990] BCLC 785; *Re Pacific Coast Syndicate Ltd* [1913] 2 Ch 26; *Re London Metallurgical Co* [1895] 1 Ch 758; *Re Staffordshire Gas and Coke Co* [1893] 3 Ch 523. See also *Smith v UIC Insurance Co Ltd* [2001] BCC 11 where the court was prepared to extend this principle to proceedings brought by provisional liquidators.

A successful defendant will be protected by the operation of this principle, therefore, without a need for an order for security, assuming that the company has sufficient net assets remaining to meet the costs order. Where there are unlikely to be free assets available to meet any order, the defendant may wish to seek security under this provision.

On appeal   An order requiring security paid in to remain in court pending an appeal is not a circumvention of the section since if the plaintiff's action succeeded at first instance and failed on appeal, it would still be the defendant's costs of trial that might need to be provided for: *Stabilad Ltd v Stephens & Carter Ltd* [1998] 4 All ER 129.

727. Power of court to grant relief in certain cases

(1) If in any proceedings for negligence, default, breach of duty or breach of trust against an officer of a company or a person employed by a company as auditor (whether he is or is not an officer of the company) it appears to the court hearing the case that that officer or person is or may be liable in respect of the negligence, default, breach of duty or breach of trust, but that he has acted honestly and reasonably, and that having regard to all the circumstances of the case (including those connected with his appointment) he ought fairly to be excused for the negligence, default, breach of duty or breach of trust, that court may relieve him, either wholly or partly, from his liability on such terms as it thinks fit.

(2) If any such officer or person as above-mentioned has reason to apprehend that any claim will or might be made against him in respect of any negligence, default, breach of duty or breach of trust, he may apply to the court for relief; and the court on the application has the same power to relieve him as under this section it would have had if it had been a court before which proceedings against that person for negligence, default, breach of duty or breach of trust had been brought.

(3) Where a case to which subsection (1) applies is being tried by a judge with a jury, the judge, after hearing the evidence, may, if he is satisfied that the defendant or defender ought in pursuance of that subsection to be relieved either in whole or in part from the liability sought to be enforced against him, withdraw the case in whole or in part from the jury and forthwith direct judgment to be entered for the defendant or defender on such terms as to costs or otherwise as the judge may think proper.

General note

This provision offers protection to officers and auditors in a manner similar to that afforded to trustees under the Trustee Act 1925, s 61. A company may indemnify any officer or auditor from any liability incurred in connection with a successful application under this provision: see s 310(3)(b)(ii). It is not necessary for a party to plead specially s 727 and the section may be raised if the parties so wish for the first time at trial: *Re Kirbys Coaches Ltd* [1991] BCLC 414.

S 727(1)

Proceedings against an officer   Although the section is expressed in wide language, the only proceedings for which relief may be claimed are proceedings against an officer or auditor (typically against a director), by, on behalf of or for the benefit of his company for breach of his duty to the company as a director, or penal proceedings against a director for a breach of the Companies Act: *Customs and Excise Comrs v Hedon Alpha Ltd* [1981] 2 All ER 697, CA. The provision does not apply to claims by a stranger to the company against a director to enforce a civil liability, eg a debt: *Customs and Excise Comrs v Hedon Alpha Ltd* [1981] 2 All ER 697, CA.

An administrator appointed under IA 1986, Pt II, is an 'officer of the company' for these purposes and entitled to seek the protection of the provision: *Re Home Treat Ltd* [1991] BCLC 705. As to when an auditor 'is or is not an officer of the company', see the note to s 744, below.

Acted honestly and reasonably   It is for the court, in the exercise of its discretion, to consider whether a director, though at fault, has not behaved so to justify a personal liability, but the burden of proving and establishing honesty and reasonableness is on those who ask for relief: *Bairstow v Queens Moat Houses plc* [2001] All ER (D) 211 (May), CA. There were suggestions in some instances that the provision enables the court to consider the matter from an essentially subjective point of view: see *Bairstow v Queens Moat Houses plc* [2000] 1 BCLC 549 at 561, 572; *Re Produce Marketing Consortium Ltd* [1989] BCLC 513 at 518. But the Court of Appeal has rejected such an approach as regards reasonableness and questioned whether it could be right as regards honesty: *Bairstow v Queens Moat Houses plc* [2001] All ER (D) 211 (May), CA (at para 58).

Acting reasonably for these purposes requires acting in the way in which a man of affairs dealing with his own affairs with reasonable care and circumspection could reasonably be expected to act in such a case: *Re Duomatic Ltd* [1969] 2 Ch 365 at 377, per Buckley J. For example, it may be unreasonable to fail to take legal advice on a particular matter: see *Re Duomatic Ltd* [1969] 2 Ch 365.

Conduct may be reasonable for the purposes of this provision despite amounting to lack of reasonable care at common law: *Re D'Jan of London Ltd* [1994] 1 BCLC 561 at 564, per Hoffmann LJ. In this case, a director, though guilty of negligence in completing an insurance proposal for the company's premises in a way which invalidated the policy, had acted honestly and reasonably and ought fairly to be excused; his negligence was not gross but the 'kind of thing which could happen to any busy man' (at 564).

Relief not available   Relief under this provision is not available with respect to wrongful trading: *Re Produce Marketing Consortium Ltd* [1989] 3 All ER 1; see also *Re Brian D Pierson (Contractors) Ltd* [2001] 1 BCLC 275 at 309. In *Produce Marketing,* Knox J decided that this provision and IA 1986, s 214 (wrongful trading) were mutually exclusive in that if the court imposed liability for wrongful trading, it did so as a result of an objective assessment of the conduct of the director in question and a conclusion that he had failed to take every step to minimise loss to creditors. Having reached those conclusions, it was not open to the court then to re-assess the director's conduct subjectively for the purpose of relieving him of liability.

Relief is not available under this provision where the directors are liable under s 347F (remedies for breach of prohibitions on company donations) or s 347G (unauthorised expenditure or donation by non-GB subsidiary): ss 347F(8), 347G(4); but see s 347H.

See also *Re Duckwari plc (No 2)* [1997] 2 BCLC 729, [1998] 2 BCLC 315, where the court was invited to consider whether this provision and s 322 (liability for breach of provision governing substantial property transactions) were mutually exclusive. It was not necessary to decide the point but the courts indicated their reluctance to accept such a restriction of the scope of this provision: see [1997] 2 BCLC 729 at 737, [1998] 2 BCLC 315 at 325.

Exercising a discretion   The following examples provide some illustration of the approach taken by the court to claims for relief under this provision:

- a director was not entitled to relief where he incurred liability as a result of a one-sided substantial property transaction with the company in contravention of s 320: see *Re Duckwari plc* [1998] 2 BCLC 315 at 326 (the arrangement provided that the director was to bear no loss);
- a director in receipt of £5.2m under a void contract with the company was not entitled to relief: see *Guinness plc v Saunders* [1990] 1 All ER 652, HL;
- a director who had acted in his own interests in procuring the payment to him by the company of £100,000 was not entitled to relief: see *Neptune (Vehicle Washing Equipment) Ltd v Fitzgerald (No 2)* [1995] BCC 1000;

- directors who negligently failed to carry out their duties and signed blank cheques so allowing another director to misapply £400,000 were not entitled to relief: see *Dorchester Finance Ltd v Stebbing* [1989] BCLC 498;
- a director who took large amounts of uninsured jewellery on board a ferry in a canvas holdall which was stolen had acted honestly but not reasonably – he was grossly negligent and was not entitled to relief: *Re Simmon Box (Diamonds) Ltd* [2000] BCC 275;
- relief was refused with respect to dividends paid on the basis of accounts which the directors knew overstated the company's profits: *Bairstow v Queens Moat Houses plc* [2001] All ER (D) 211 (May), CA;
- the court may be prepared to grant relief to less involved family directors on the grounds of their honest and reasonable reliance on the other directors: see *Re Simmon Box (Diamonds) Ltd* [2000] BCC 275 at 288 (son reliant on his father) (rev'd on other grounds, and reported as *Cohen v Selby* [2001] 1 BCLC 176, CA); *Re Brian D Pierson (Contractors) Ltd* [2001] 1 BCLC 275 at 301 (wife reliant on husband).

S 727(2)

This provision allows an officer etc to bring an application for relief in anticipation of a claim being made; see, for example, *Re Home Treat Ltd* [1991] BCLC 705 (administrators seeking relief against any future claim against them).

728. Enforcement of High Court orders

Orders made by the High Court under this Act may be enforced in the same manner as orders made in an action pending in that court.

General note

As to the meaning of 'this Act', see s 735A(1).

729. Annual report by Secretary of State

The Secretary of State shall cause a general annual report of matters within the Companies Acts to be prepared and laid before both Houses of Parliament.

General note

As to the meaning of the 'Companies Acts' for these purposes, see s 735A(2).

730. Punishment of offences

(1) Schedule 24 to this Act has effect with respect to the way in which offences under this Act are punishable on conviction.

(2)　In relation to an offence under a provision of this Act specified in the first column of the Schedule (the general nature of the offence being described in the second column), the third column shows whether the offence is punishable on conviction on indictment, or on summary conviction, or either in the one way or the other.

(3)　The fourth column of the Schedule shows, in relation to an offence, the maximum punishment by way of fine or imprisonment under this Act which may be imposed on a person convicted of the offence in the way specified in relation to it in the third column (that is to say, on indictment or summarily), a reference to a period of years or months being to a term of imprisonment of that duration.

(4)　The fifth column shows (in relation to an offence for which there is an entry in that column) that a person convicted of the offence after continued contravention is liable to a daily default fine; that is to say, he is liable on a second or subsequent summary conviction of the offence to the fine specified in that column for each day on which the contravention is continued (instead of the penalty specified for the offence in the fourth column of the Schedule).

(5)　For the purpose of any enactment in the Companies Acts which provides that an officer of a company or other body who is in default is liable to a fine or penalty, the expression 'officer who is in default' means any officer of the company or other body who knowingly and wilfully authorises or permits the default, refusal or contravention mentioned in the enactment.

S 730(5)

Many of the offences provided by this Act impose liability on the company and any 'officer in default'; the definition of this term in this provision ensures that liability can only arise where the requisite mens rea can be established and negligence will be insufficient; 'officer' is defined in s 744.

731. Summary proceedings

(1)　Summary proceedings for any offence under the Companies Acts may (without prejudice to any jurisdiction exercisable apart from this subsection) be taken against a body corporate at any place at which the body has a place of business, and against any other person at any place at which he is for the time being.

(2)　Notwithstanding anything in section 127(1) of the Magistrates' Courts Act 1980, an information relating to an offence under the Companies Acts which is triable by a magistrates' court in England and Wales may be so tried if it is laid at any time within 3 years after the commission of the offence and within 12 months after the date on which evidence sufficient in the opinion of the Director of Public Prosecutions or the Secretary of State (as the case may be) to justify the proceedings comes to his knowledge.

(3)　Summary proceedings in Scotland for an offence under the Companies Acts shall not be commenced after the expiration of 3 years from the commission of the offence.

　　Subject to this (and notwithstanding anything in section 136 of the Criminal Procedure (Scotland) Act 1995), such proceedings may (in Scotland) be commenced at any time within 12 months after the date on which evidence sufficient in the Lord Advocate's opinion to justify the proceedings came to his knowledge or, where such evidence was reported to him by the Secretary of State, within 12 months after the date on which it came to the knowledge of the latter; and subsection (3) of that section applies for the purpose of this subsection as it applies for the purpose of that section.

(4) For purposes of this section, a certificate of the Director of Public Prosecutions, the Lord Advocate or the Secretary of State (as the case may be) as to the date on which such evidence as is referred to above came to his knowledge is conclusive evidence.

S 731(1)

As to the definition of 'body corporate', see s 740.

S 731(2)

The time limit provided by this provision applies solely to offences triable only summarily and not to offences which are triable either on indictment or summarily: *R v Thames Magistrates' Court, ex p Horgan* [1998] 2 BCLC 91.

732. Prosecution by public authorities

(1) In respect of an offence under any of sections 210, 324, 329, 447 to 451 and 455, proceedings shall not, in England and Wales, be instituted except by or with the consent of the appropriate authority.

(2) That authority is—

(a) for an offence under any of sections 210, 324 and 329, the Secretary of State or the Director of Public Prosecutions,

(b) for an offence under any of sections 447 to 451, either one of those two persons or the Industrial Assurance Commissioner, and

(c) for an offence under section 455, the Secretary of State.

(3) Where proceedings are instituted under the Companies Acts against any person by the Director of Public Prosecutions or by or on behalf of the Secretary of State or the Lord Advocate, nothing in those Acts is to be taken to require any person to disclose any information which he is entitled to refuse to disclose on grounds of legal professional privilege.

S 732(3)

As to the meaning of the 'Companies Acts' for these purposes, see s 735A(2).

733. Offences by bodies corporate

(1) The following applies to offences under any of sections 210, 216(3) ..., 394A(1) and 447 to 451.

(2) Where a body corporate is guilty of such an offence and it is proved that the offence occurred with the consent or connivance of, or was attributable to any neglect on the part of any director, manager, secretary or other similar officer of

the body, or any person who was purporting to act in any such capacity, he as well as the body corporate is guilty of that offence and is liable to be proceeded against and punished accordingly.

(3)   Where the affairs of a body corporate are managed by its members, ... subsection (2) above applies in relation to the acts and defaults of a member in connection with his functions of management as if he were a director of the body corporate.

(4)   In this section 'director', in relation to an offence under any of sections 447 to 451, includes a shadow director.

S 733(2)

As to the definition of 'body corporate', see s 740; a de facto director would be included in the category of 'any person who was purporting to act': see note to s 741, below; also *Re Lo-Line Electric Motors Ltd* [1988] BCLC 698 at 706.

734. Criminal proceedings against unincorporated bodies

(1)   Proceedings for an offence alleged to have been committed under section 389A(3) or section 394A(1) or any of sections 447 to 451 by an unincorporated body shall be brought in the name of that body (and not in that of any of its members), and for the purposes of any such proceedings, any rules of court relating to the service of documents apply as if that body were a corporation.

(2)   A fine imposed on an unincorporated body on its conviction of such an offence shall be paid out of the funds of that body.

(3)   In a case in which an unincorporated body is charged in England and Wales with such an offence, section 33 of the Criminal Justice Act 1925 and Schedule 3 to the Magistrates' Courts Act 1980 (procedure on charge of an offence against a corporation) have effect in like manner as in the case of a corporation so charged.

(4)   In relation to proceedings on indictment in Scotland for such an offence alleged to have been committed by an unincorporated body, section 70 of the Criminal Procedure (Scotland) Act 1995 (proceedings on indictment against bodies corporate) has effect as if that body were a body corporate.

(5)   Where such an offence committed by a partnership is proved to have been committed with the consent or connivance of, or to be attributable to any neglect on the part of, a partner, he as well as the partnership is guilty of the offence and liable to be proceeded against and punished accordingly.

(6)   Where such an offence committed by an unincorporated body (other than a partnership) is proved to have been committed with the consent or connivance of, or to be attributable to any neglect on the part of, any officer of the body or any member of its governing body, he as well as the body is guilty of the offence and liable to be proceeded against and punished accordingly.

General note

This provision allows for proceedings in respect of certain provisions to be brought against unincorporated bodies as if they were bodies corporate.

PART XXVI

INTERPRETATION

735. 'Company', etc

(1)   In this Act—

(a)   'company' means a company formed and registered under this Act, or an existing company;

(b)   'existing company' means a company formed and registered under the former Companies Acts, but does not include a company registered under the Joint Stock Companies Acts, the Companies Act 1862 or the Companies (Consolidation) Act 1908 in what was then Ireland;

(c)   'the former Companies Acts' means the Joint Stock Companies Acts, the Companies Act 1862, the Companies (Consolidation) Act 1908, the Companies Act 1929 and the Companies Acts 1948 to 1983.

(2)   'Public company' and 'private company' have the meanings given by section 1(3).

(3)   'The Joint Stock Companies Acts' means the Joint Stock Companies Act 1856, the Joint Stock Companies Acts 1856, 1857, the Joint Stock Banking Companies Act 1857 and the Act to enable Joint Stock Banking Companies to be formed on the principle of limited liability, or any one or more of those Acts (as the case may require), but does not include the Joint Stock Companies Act 1844.

(4)   The definitions in this section apply unless the contrary intention appears.

S 735(1)

'Company'   This provision, which is subject to sub-s (4), treats as companies for the purposes of this Act, all companies formed and registered under this or former Companies Acts. The effect is to exclude from the operation of provisions applicable to any 'company', any foreign registered company (including companies formed and registered in Northern Ireland, the Isle of Man, the Channel Islands and Gibraltar). The definition of 'body corporate' (see s 740) is not so limited so a provision applicable to a body corporate has a wider reach that one applicable to a 'company'. Foreign registered companies may fall within the scope of Pt XXIII (oversea companies) and, as such, subject to the provisions of this Act to the extent dictated by that Part.

S 735(4)

A contrary intention   The prima facie definition in sub-s (1) gives way where a contrary intention appears. In *Re International Bulk Commodities Ltd* [1992] BCLC 1074, Mummery J thought that a 'contrary intention' may be express or may appear from the subject and purpose of the statutory provisions under review. This approach was doubted in *Re Devon and Somerset Farmers Ltd* [1994] 1 BCLC 99 where the court did not think that the context and purpose of a provision can be sufficient to amount to a 'contrary intention' so as to override sub-s (1); something more is required for that purpose. See also *Rover International Ltd v Canon Film Sales Ltd* [1987] BCLC 540 at 543–544. Certainly the fact that Parliament has on occasion expressly expanded the primary definition in sub-s (1) (see, for example, IA 1986, s 388(4); Company Directors Disqualification Act 1986, s 22(2)(b)) would suggest that where this has not been done, the primary definition prevails. On the other hand, on that approach, sub-s (4) is superfluous; compare also the wording here and that adopted in s 745 ('except where otherwise expressly provided') when Parliament was anxious to allow only an express contrary provision to prevail.

735A. Relationship of this Act to Insolvency Act

(1) In this Act 'the Insolvency Act' means the Insolvency Act 1986; and in the following provisions of this Act, namely, sections 375(1)(b), 425(6)(a), ... 460(2), 675, 676, 677, 699(1), 728 and Schedule 21, paragraph 6(1), the words 'this Act' are to be read as including Parts I to VII of that Act, sections 411, 413, 414, 416 and 417 in Part XV of that Act, and also the Company Directors Disqualification Act 1986.

(2) In sections 704(5), (7) and (8), 706(1), 707B(1), 707A(1), 708(1)(a) and (4), 709(1) and (3), 710A, 713(1), 729 and 732(3) references to the Companies Acts include Parts I to VII of the Insolvency Act, sections 411, 413, 414, 416 and 417 in Part XV of that Act, and also the Company Directors Disqualification Act 1986.

(3) Subsections (1) and (2) apply unless the contrary intention appears.

General note

The effect of this provision is to import some of the provisions of the Insolvency Act 1986 and all of the Company Directors Disqualification Act 1986 into certain provisions of this Act.

S 735A(3)

As to the meaning of a 'contrary intention' for these purposes, see the note to s 735(4), above.

735B. Relationship of this Act to Parts IV and V of the Financial Services Act 1986

In sections 704(5), (7) and (8), 706(1), 707(1), 707A(1), 708(1)(a) and (4), 709(1) and (3), 710A and 713(1) references to the Companies Acts include Parts IV and V of the Financial Services Act 1986.

General note

See the Public Offers of Securities Regulations 1995, SI 1995/1537, of which regs 4(2) and 10(1) are regarded as provisions of the Companies Acts for the purposes of the provisions mentioned in this section: reg 22.

736.'Subsidiary', 'holding company' and 'wholly-owned subsidiary'

(1)   A company is a 'subsidiary' of another company, its 'holding company', if that other company—

(a)   holds a majority of the voting rights in it, or

(b)   is a member of it and has the right to appoint or remove a majority of its board of directors, or

(c)   is a member of it and controls alone, pursuant to an agreement with other shareholders or members, a majority of the voting rights in it,

or if it is a subsidiary of a company which is itself a subsidiary of that other company.

(2)   A company is a 'wholly-owned subsidiary' of another company if it has no members except that other and that other's wholly-owned subsidiaries or persons acting on behalf of that other or its wholly-owned subsidiaries.

(3)   In this section 'company' includes any body corporate.

General note

This provision, together with s 736A, was substituted for the original s 736 by CA 1989, s 144(1), subject to transitional provisions in CA 1989, Sch 18; see also CA 1989, s 144(2) (references in any enactment to these definitions to be read as references to the definitions in the section as substituted). The original section is set out after s 736A, below.

Similar definitions   This definition is in similar but narrower terms to the definitions of parent and subsidiary undertakings contained in s 258 for accounting purposes (see notes to that provision) which were introduced to give effect to the 7th EC Directive on Company Law (EEC) 83/349, OJ 1983 L193/1). The main difference between the provisions is that this definition requires that both the holding company and the subsidiary company be a company (which includes a body corporate, defined s 740) whereas the accounting definitions extend to parent and subsidiary undertakings and an undertaking need not be a body corporate: see s 259(1).

S 736(1)

This provision identifies three mechanisms by which a company may be a subsidiary and provides that sub-subsidiaries are also subsidiaries of the 'top' holding company. The meaning of each of the categories is expanded on in s 736A.

The requirement in sub-s (1)(a) is that the holding company holds a majority of the voting rights in the subsidiary company rather than a majority of the shares, for shares may be non-voting; as to what is meant by 'voting rights' in this context, see s 736A(2); as to when rights are held by a company, see s 736A(5)–(11); the requirement in sub-s (1)(c) is the control of voting rights rather than the holding of them.

For the purposes of sub-s (1)(b), the holding company must be a member (as defined in s 22) of the subsidiary and must have the right to appoint or remove a majority of the board; but this does not necessarily mean a majority in number of the directors: see s 736A(3).

736A. Provisions supplementing s 736

(1)   The provisions of this section explain expressions used in section 736 and otherwise supplement that section.

(2)   In section 736(1)(a) and (c) the references to the voting rights in a company are to the rights conferred on shareholders in respect of their shares or, in the case of a company not having a share capital, on members, to vote at general meetings of the company on all, or substantially all, matters.

(3)   In section 736(1)(b) the reference to the right to appoint or remove a majority of the board of directors is to the right to appoint or remove directors holding a majority of the voting rights at meetings of the board on all, or substantially all, matters; and for the purposes of that provision—

    (a)   a company shall be treated as having the right to appoint to a directorship if—

        (i)   a person's appointment to it follows necessarily from his appointment as director of the company, or

        (ii)   the directorship is held by the company itself; and

    (b)   a right to appoint or remove which is exercisable only with the consent or concurrence of another person shall be left out of account unless no other person has a right to appoint or, as the case may be, remove in relation to that directorship.

(4)   Rights which are exercisable only in certain circumstances shall be taken into account only—

    (a)   when the circumstances have arisen, and for so long as they continue to obtain, or

    (b)   when the circumstances are within the control of the person having the rights;

and rights which are normally exercisable but are temporarily incapable of exercise shall continue to be taken into account.

(5)   Rights held by a person in a fiduciary capacity shall be treated as not held by him.

(6)   Rights held by a person as nominee for another shall be treated as held by the other; and rights shall be regarded as held as nominee for another if they are exercisable only on his instructions or with his consent or concurrence.

(7)   Rights attached to shares held by way of security shall be treated as held by the person providing the security—

(a)   where apart from the right to exercise them for the purpose of preserving the value of the security, or of realising it, the rights are exercisable only in accordance with his instructions;

(b)   where the shares are held in connection with the granting of loans as part of normal business activities and apart from the right to exercise them for the purpose of preserving the value of the security, or of realising it, the rights are exercisable only in his interests.

(8)   Rights shall be treated as held by a company if they are held by any of its subsidiaries; and nothing in subsection (6) or (7) shall be construed as requiring rights held by a company to be treated as held by any of its subsidiaries.

(9)   For the purposes of subsection (7) rights shall be treated as being exercisable in accordance with the instructions or in the interests of a company if they are exercisable in accordance with the instructions of or, as the case may be, in the interests of—

(a)   any subsidiary or holding company of that company, or

(b)   any subsidiary of a holding company of that company.

(10) The voting rights in a company shall be reduced by any rights held by the company itself.

(11) References in any provision of subsections (5) to (10) to rights held by a person include rights falling to be treated as held by him by virtue of any other provision of those subsections but not rights which by virtue of any such provision are to be treated as not held by him.

(12) In this section 'company' includes any body corporate.

General note

This provision mirrors to some extent the provisions of Sch 10A which elaborates in a similar manner on the definition of parent and subsidiary undertaking for the purposes of s 258: see the notes to that provision, above.

S 736A(2)

See sub-s (10).

S 736A(4)

This provision ensures, for example, that an interest in preference shares (with restricted rights to vote) will be taken into account only if the voting rights are exercisable; voting rights might be temporarily incapable of exercise where, for example, an order imposing restrictions on the shares is in force: see note to s 454(1), above.

S 736A(5)

A registered shareholder who is the vendor under an uncompleted but specifically enforceable contract for the sale of his shares is a fiduciary for these purposes: *Michaels v Harley House (Marylebone) Ltd* [1999] 1 BCLC 670 (shares registered to a corporate vendor in this position, and the voting rights attached, were treated as not held by the corporate vendor, therefore, for the purpose of determining whether the company in which the shares were held was a subsidiary company).

S 736A(7)–(9)

Rights held by way of security are deemed held by the chargee where the rights are exercisable only in accordance with his instructions or only in his interests, as broadly defined by sub-s (9).

UNAMENDED

'736. 'Holding company','subsidiary' and 'wholly-owned subsidiary'

(1)   For the purposes of this Act, a company is deemed to be a subsidiary of another if (but only if)—
- (a)   that other either—
    - (i)   is a member of it and controls the composition of its board of directors, or
    - (ii)   holds more than half in nominal value of its equity share capital, or
- (b)   the first-mentioned company is a subsidiary of any company which is that other's subsidiary.

The above is subject to subsection (4) below in this section.

(2)   For purposes of subsection (1), the composition of a company's board of directors is deemed to be controlled by another company if (but only if) that other company by the exercise of some power exercisable by it without the consent or concurrence of any other person can appoint or remove the holders of all or a majority of the directorships.

(3)   For purposes of this last provision, the other company is deemed to have power to appoint to a directorship with respect to which any of the following conditions is satisfied—
- (a)   that a person cannot be appointed to it without the exercise in his favour by the other company of such a power as is mentioned above, or
- (b)   that a person's appointment to the directorship follows necessarily from his appointment as director of the other company, or
- (c)   that the directorship is held by the other company itself or by a subsidiary of it.

(4) In determining whether one company is a subsidiary of another—

    (a) any shares held or power exercisable by the other in a fiduciary capacity are to be treated as not held or exercisable by it,

    (b) subject to the two following paragraphs, any shares held or power exercisable—

        (i) by any person as nominee for the other (except where the other is concerned only in a fiduciary capacity), or

        (ii) by, or by a nominee for, a subsidiary of the other (not being a subsidiary which is concerned only in a fiduciary capacity),

are to be treated as held or exercisable by the other,

    (c) any shares held or power exercisable by any person by virtue of the provisions of any debentures of the first-mentioned company or of a trust deed for securing any issue of such debentures are to be disregarded,

    (d) any shares held or power exercisable by, or by a nominee for, the other or its subsidiary (not being held or exercisable as mentioned in paragraph (c)) are to be treated as not held or exercisable by the other if the ordinary business of the other or its subsidiary (as the case may be) includes the lending of money and the shares are held or the power is exercisable as above mentioned by way of security only for the purposes of a transaction entered into in the ordinary course of that business.

(5) For purposes of this Act—

    (a) a company is deemed to be another's holding company if (but only if) the other is its subsidiary, and

    (b) a body corporate is deemed the wholly-owned subsidiary of another if it has no members except that other and that other's wholly-owned subsidiaries and its or their nominees.

(6) In this section 'company' includes any body corporate.'

General note

This provision is the original s 736 as contained in the unamended CA 1985, ie as unamended by the CA 1989. It is reproduced here because of its continuing application for certain purposes. Note, in particular, CA 1989, s 144(6) which ensures that references to these terms ('holding company' etc) in documents which preceded the amendments in 1989 (which came into effect on 1 November 1990) are to be interpreted in accordance with the unamended s 736.

736B. Power to amend ss 736 and 736A

(1) The Secretary of State may by regulations amend sections 736 and 736A so as to alter the meaning of the expressions 'holding company', 'subsidiary' or 'wholly-owned subsidiary'.

(2)   The regulations may make different provision for different cases or classes of case and may contain such incidental and supplementary provisions as the Secretary of State thinks fit.

(3)   Regulations under this section shall be made by statutory instrument which shall be subject to annulment in pursuance of a resolution of either House of Parliament.

(4)   Any amendment made by regulations under this section does not apply for the purposes of enactments outside the Companies Acts unless the regulations so provide.

(5)   So much of section 23(3) of the Interpretation Act 1978 as applies section 17(2)(a) of that Act (effect of repeal and re-enactment) to deeds, instruments and documents other than enactments shall not apply in relation to any repeal and re-enactment effected by regulations made under this section.

General note

No regulations have been made under this provision.

737. 'Called-up share capital'

(1)   In this Act, 'called-up share capital', in relation to a company, means so much of its share capital as equals the aggregate amount of the calls made on its shares (whether or not those calls have been paid), together with any share capital paid up without being called and any share capital to be paid on a specified future date under the articles, the terms of allotment of the relevant shares or any other arrangements for payment of those shares.

(2)   'Uncalled share capital' is to be construed accordingly.

(3)   The definitions in this section apply unless the contrary intention appears.

S 737(1)

'Called-up share capital'   It may be noted that 'called-up share capital' includes share capital which is not paid and not the subject of any call but which is due on a specified future date. This definition is relevant, in particular, to s 43(3) (re-registration of private company as public); s 142 (duty of directors on serious loss of capital); s 264 (restriction on distribution of assets) and s 320(2) (substantial property transactions).

S 737(2)

'Uncalled share capital'   This definition is relevant, in particular, to s 120 (reserve liability of limited company); s 124 (reserve capital of unlimited company); s 264 (restriction on distribution of assets); s 265 (other distributions by investment companies) and s 396 (charges requiring registration).

738.'Allotment' and 'paid up'

(1)   In relation to an allotment of shares in a company, the shares are to be taken for the purposes of this Act to be allotted when a person acquires the unconditional right to be included in the company's register of members in respect of those shares.

(2)   For purposes of this Act, a share in a company is deemed paid up (as to its nominal value or any premium on it) in cash, or allotted for cash, if the consideration for the allotment or payment up is cash received by the company, or is a cheque received by it in good faith which the directors have no reason for suspecting will not be paid, or is a release of a liability of the company for a liquidated sum, or is an undertaking to pay cash to the company at a future date.

(3)   In relation to the allotment or payment up of any shares in a company, references in this Act (except sections 89 to 94) to consideration other than cash and to the payment up of shares and premiums on shares otherwise than in cash include the payment of, or any undertaking to pay, cash to any person other than the company.

(4)   For the purpose of determining whether a share is or is to be allotted for cash, or paid up in cash, 'cash' includes foreign currency.

S 738(1)

Allotted and issued share capital   This provision offers a definition of an allotment of shares but there is no definition in the legislation as to the issue of shares. Some guidance on the matter comes from the decision of the House of Lords in *National Westminster Bank plc v IRC* [1994] 2 BCLC 239, a case which concerned the meaning of the 'issue' of shares in the context of a taxation statute. By a 3–2 majority (affirming the majority decision of the Court of Appeal, see [1994] 2 BCLC 30) it was held that the term 'issue' means something distinct from allotment and imports that some subsequent act has been done whereby the title of the allottee has been completed. The allotment, notified to the purchaser, creates an enforceable contract for the issue of the shares; the shares are issued when the process is completed by entry on the register of members.

While all their Lordships were agreed that the word 'issue' is a word which is capable of different meanings according to its context, it appears that the majority were of the view that this definition of 'issue' was applicable in the general context of the companies legislation as well as in the taxation statute under review. Equally, Lord Jauncey, while dissenting on the proper interpretation of 'issue' in the context of the taxation statute, was willing to concede that something more than allotment by the directors followed by notification thereof to the applicant may be required to constitute 'issue' for the purposes of the Companies Act: see [1994] 2 BCLC 239 at 256; see also *Re Ambrose Lake Tin and Copper Co, Clarke's Case* (1878) 8 Ch D 635, CA; *Oswald Tillotson Ltd v IRC* [1933] 1 KB 134 (sending an applicant for shares a renounceable letter of allotment does not amount, at that stage, to an issue of the shares to the applicant); and see *National Westminster Bank plc v IRC* [1994] 2 BCLC 30 at 48–49, per Dillon LJ.

S 738(2)–(4)

Paid up in cash or allotted for cash   These provisions define when shares are deemed paid up in cash or allotted for cash, which definitions are relevant to a number of provisions, for example, shares taken by subscribers to the memorandum of association of a public company must be paid up in cash (s 106); and where a public company proposes to allot shares as fully or partly paid up otherwise than in cash, that consideration must be independently valued: s 103.

There are four possible methods of payment which are treated as cash:

Cash received by the company   Shares allotted for, or paid up in, a foreign currency are allotted for or paid up in cash: sub-s (4). To be allotted for or paid up in cash, the cash must be received by the company. If cash is paid to any other person, it amounts to an allotment for a non-cash consideration by the company, see sub-s (3); but this interpretation of a non-cash consideration does not apply to ss 89–94 and, in particular, to s 89(4) (rights issue not required in the case of a non-cash consideration). The effect is to prevent a company from avoiding the requirements for a rights issue by having the cash paid to another person.

Cheque received by the company   The company must have received the cheque in good faith and the directors must have no reason for suspecting that it will not be paid, as will invariably be the case, for why would the directors accept a cheque which they suspect will not be paid.

The release of a liability of the company for a liquidated sum   This provision allows for the easy avoidance of provisions requiring any non-cash consideration to be valued. An individual sells an asset to the company so creating a bona fide debt in money payable immediately by the company to him for a stated amount. The company allots fully paid shares to him and an equal debt immediately payable by him to the company arises. In full payment of that debt, the company is released from the liability to pay the stated sum. The transaction is no longer an allotment of shares for a non-cash consideration but an allotment of shares for cash: *Re Harmony and Montague Tin and Copper Mining Co, Spargo's Case* (1873) 8 Ch App 407. It is not necessary, moreover, that the formality should be gone through of the money being handed over by the company and then paid back to the company by the allottee. If the two demands are set off against each other, the shares have been paid for in cash (at 412).

If the company never comes under a liability to pay a specified sum, however, the shares cannot be said to be allotted for the release of a liability for a liquidated sum; there must be a liability on the part of the company to pay in cash which is then satisfied by the substitution of an allotment of shares but the court will be alert to the mere artificial resort to two documents instead of one: see *Re Bradford Investments plc (No 2)* [1991] BCLC 688 at 695.

An undertaking to pay cash to the company at a future date   This element of the definition is open to abuse as the shares will be treated as paid up in cash at the time of the allotment, although it may be many years before the company receives the cash, and by the time the company or, more likely, a liquidator seeks the cash, the allottee, and therefore the undertaking, may be worthless. There is no time limit set in the provision as to this undertaking (cf s 102 which prohibits public companies from accepting undertakings regarding non-cash consideration which are not to be performed within five years).

This issue has been the subject of some discussion by the registrar of companies, who has pointed out that the Companies Act allows him to satisfy himself that the relevant amount has been paid up on the company's shares in accordance with s 101(1) and to withhold a certificate under s 47(1) or s 117(2) unless so satisfied (see *Legal Interpretation and Policy*, The Register, Winter 2000). The registrar went on to indicate in that publication that he would not generally accept an undertaking to pay at some future unspecified date as meeting the requirements under those provisions for capital to be paid up. The Company Law Committee of the Law Society, while querying the assumption of an inquisitorial role by the registrar, supports the registrar's interpretation that an undertaking is not sufficient for these purposes if it is open-ended, but it is sufficient if it is expressed as an undertaking to pay no later than a specified date (see Company Law Committee Memorandum, *Companies House: Legal Interpretation and Policy*, May 2000, No 398).

An assignment to the company of a debt due to the allottee is not an undertaking to pay cash at a future date for these purposes: see *System Control plc v Munro Corporate plc* [1990] BCLC 659.

739.'Non-cash asset'

(1)   In this Act 'non-cash asset' means any property or interest in property other than cash; and for this purpose 'cash' includes foreign currency.

(2)   A reference to the transfer or acquisition of a non-cash asset includes the creation or extinction of an estate or interest in, or a right over, any property and also the discharge of any person's liability, other than a liability for a liquidated sum.

General note

This definition is relevant, in particular, to s 104 (transfer to public company of non-cash asset in initial period); s 152(1)(b) (financial assistance definitions); s 276 (distributions in kind) and ss 320–321 (substantial property transactions); and see the notes to those provisions, above.

S 739(1)

'Non-cash asset'   See the Scottish case *Lander v Premier Pict Petroleum Ltd* [1998] BCC 248, (CS,OH) where the court held that payments under a service agreement to be made to a director in the event of a change of control, being rights to cash payments to be made in part to the director and in part to his pension fund, did not amount to a non-cash asset for these purposes so as to fall within s 320 (substantial property transaction) and require the approval of the company in general meeting. See also the note to s 312, above, on this point.

S 739(2)

Transfer or acquisition of a non-cash asset   Having defined a 'non-cash asset' in sub-s (1), this provision more specifically defines the 'transfer of' a non-cash asset, which is relevant to s 104, and the 'acquisition of' a non-cash asset, which is relevant to s 320.

Where company A (of which C was a director) took over the benefit of a contract entered into by company B (of which C was a director) to acquire a particular property, what company A acquired was either the benefit of the purchase contract or company B's beneficial interest in the property; either is a non-cash asset within this definition: see *Re Duckwari plc, Duckwari plc v Offerventure Ltd (No 1)* [1997] 2 BCLC 713 at 724–725.

The Company Law Committee of the Law Society has criticised the breadth of this definition and the uncertainty which it causes, particularly in the context of triggering the need for approval under s 320. For example, it may be that it extends to the granting of an option over shares: see *Lander v Premier Pict Petroleum Ltd* [1998] BCC 248 at 254 (CS,OH).

Rights arising from a profit-sharing agreement between a company and a connected person pursuant to the development of certain lands did not amount to an acquisition of a non-cash asset and did not fall within sub-s (2) because the rights were not concerned with any right over property: see *Micro Leisure Ltd v County Properties & Developments Ltd* 1999 SLT 1307 (Ct of Sess, OH).

740.'Body corporate' and 'corporation'

References in this Act to a body corporate or to a corporation do not include a corporation sole, but include a company incorporated elsewhere than in Great Britain.

Such references to a body corporate do not include a Scottish firm.

General note

The scope of the companies legislation is restricted primarily to companies formed and registered under this and former Companies Acts (s 735). However, it is common to find a provision (see, for example, ss 23, 259, 346, 433, 733, 736) applying to 'a body corporate' thus including within the reach of the particular provision companies incorporated elsewhere than in Great Britain, including companies incorporated in Northern Ireland, Gibraltar, the Isle of Man and the Channel Islands.

741. 'Director' and 'shadow director'

(1)   In this Act 'director' includes any person occupying the position of director, by whatever name called.

(2)   In relation to a company,'shadow director' means a person in accordance with whose directions or instructions the directors of the company are accustomed to act.

However, a person is not deemed a shadow director by reason only that the directors act on advice given by him in a professional capacity.

(3)   For the purposes of the following provisions of this Act, namely—

section 309 (directors' duty to have regard to interests of employees),

section 319 (directors' long-term contracts of employment),

sections 320 to 322 (substantial property transactions involving directors),...

section 322B (contracts with sole members who are directors), and

sections 330 to 346 (general restrictions on power of companies to make loans, etc, to directors and others connected with them),

(being provisions under which shadow directors are treated as directors), a body corporate is not to be treated as a shadow director of any of its subsidiary companies by reason only that the directors of the subsidiary are accustomed to act in accordance with its directions or instructions.

S 741(1)

Nomenclature   The words 'by whatever name called' show that: 'the subsection is dealing with nomenclature; for example, where the company's articles provide that the conduct of the company is committed to "governors" or "managers" ': *Re Lo-Line Electric Motors Ltd* [1988] BCLC 698 at 706, per Browne-Wilkinson V-C. Such persons, despite their titles, may well be directors and, equally, a person may be described as 'sales and marketing director' or even 'deputy managing director' without occupying the position of director: see *Secretary of State for Trade and Industry v Tjolle* [1998] 1 BCLC 333 at 345.

The title is not the issue and instead the courts must decide who is a 'director' for the purpose of the various statutory provisions. The definition provided here can be found also in IA 1986, s 251 and in the Company Directors Disqualification Act 1986, s 22(4) (extended to include shadow directors) and it is in the context of disqualification proceedings that much of the litigation concerning this definition has arisen.

Disqualification proceedings may be brought against a 'director', as defined in this manner, and the courts frequently face an application for the disqualification of a person not formally or validly appointed as a director (so not a de jure director) but who, it is alleged, is a de facto director. As to the appointment of de jure directors, whether executive or non-executive, see the note to s 282.

De facto directors   The crucial issue in determining whether someone is a de facto director is whether the individual in question has assumed the status and functions of a company director so as to make himself responsible as if he were a de jure director: *Re Kaytech International plc, Secretary of State for Trade and Industry v Kaczer* [1999] 2 BCLC 351, CA; see also *Secretary of State for Trade and Industry v Tjolle* [1998] 1 BCLC 333 at 343–344; *Re Hydrodam (Corby) Ltd* [1994] 2 BCLC 180 at 183.

There is no single test which can be applied and what is involved is very much a question of degree. The court takes into account all the relevant factors, including at least whether or not there was a holding out by the company of the individual as a director, whether the individual used the title, whether the individual had proper information (eg management accounts) on which to base decisions, and whether the individual had to make major decisions and so on. Taking all these factors into account, the question is whether the individual was part of the corporate governing structure: *Secretary of State for Trade and Industry v Tjolle* [1998] 1 BCLC 333 at 343–344. This approach was endorsed by the Court of Appeal in *Re Kaytech International plc, Secretary of State for Trade and Industry v Kaczer* [1999] 2 BCLC 351 at 423. It follows that someone who had no, or only peripheral, knowledge of matters of vital company concern (for example, its financial state) and had no right, legal or de facto, to access to such matters is not to be regarded by the law as in substance a director: *Secretary of State for Trade and Industry v Tjolle* [1998] 1 BCLC 333 at 343–344.

The list of factors to be considered is not exhaustive and there is no requirement for all of the elements to be present: *Re Kaytech International plc, Secretary of State for Trade and Industry v Kaczer* [1999] 2 BCLC 351 at 423–424, CA; see also *Re Richborough Furniture Ltd* [1996] 1 BCLC 507; *Re Moorgate Metals Ltd* [1995] 1 BCLC 503. In deciding whether an individual is a de facto director, the court must consider his conduct in the round and reach a conclusion as to whether or not the respondent in fact assumed the role of a director of the company, notwithstanding that he had not been formally appointed as such: *Secretary of State for Trade and Industry v Jones* [1999] BCC 336 at 349, per Jonathan Parker J.

It is often unclear whether what the person did was referable to an assumed directorship or to some other capacity such as manager, shareholder or consultant (see *Re Richborough Furniture Ltd* [1996] 1 BCLC 507); and there can be no justification for holding persons liable for misfeasance or disqualification unless they truly were in a position to exercise the powers and discharge the functions of a director: *Secretary of State for Trade and Industry v Tjolle* [1998] 1 BCLC 333 at 343–344. It is for the Secretary of State for Trade and Industry to establish his case on the balance of probabilities: see *Secretary of State for Trade and Industry v Jones* [1999] BCC 336 at 340.

Some illustrations   The cases below provide some illustration of the nature of the inquiries before the court, but the outcome depends, of course, on the weight of the evidence available with respect to the individual's involvement with the company:

- an individual deeply and openly involved in the company's affairs, who devoted himself to the company's financial and property interests and who dealt with creditors, suppliers and the company's professional advisers, was not merely a consultant or company secretary, but a de facto director: *Re Kaytech International plc, Secretary of State for Trade and Industry v Kaczer* [1999] 2 BCLC 351, CA;
- an undischarged bankrupt who was instrumental in the incorporation of the business, who shared management with the de jure director, who had equal remuneration with him, and who was consulted on everything and could trade without limit, was a de facto director: *Re Moorgate Metals Ltd* [1995] 1 BCLC 503;
- an individual who dealt directly with the creditors and the company's biggest customer and who was a signatory on the bank mandate was a de facto director: *Secretary of State for Trade and Industry v Jones* [1999] BCC 336;
- where there are no validly appointed directors, the person actually conducting the company's affairs must be a de facto director: see *Re Lo-Line Electric Motors Ltd* [1988] BCLC 698.

On the other hand:

- a business consultant providing computer and other management services to a furniture-making company was not a de facto director, despite his having undertaken extensive negotiations with creditors and having performed some of the functions of a finance director: *Re Richborough Furniture Ltd* [1996] 1 BCLC 507;

- a manager employed by a holiday company who had a variety of titles including 'sales and marketing director' and even, for a period, 'deputy managing director', who sometimes attended board meetings, but who was never involved in any financial matters and had no access to the company accounts, was not a de facto director: *Secretary of State for Trade and Industry v Tjolle* [1998] 1 BCLC 333 at 343–344;

- where there was no clear or unequivocal reference or indication that a person was acting as a director rather than as a manager or as a compliant and dutiful wife in a company jointly owned with her husband, that person was not a de facto director: *Re Red Label Fashions Ltd* [1999] BCC 308.

A substantial shareholder in a small company who wishes to take an active part in the running of the affairs of the company in order to protect his investment, must be careful that in so doing he may not be constituting himself a de facto director of the company: see *Secretary of State for Trade and Industry v Jones* [1999] BCC 336 at 349–350.

Once a person has assumed the position of a director, it is a question of fact as to how long that directorship can be taken to continue: see *Secretary of State for Trade and Industry v Laing* [1996] 2 BCLC 324.

Obligations of de facto directors   It is not the case that once someone is a de facto director, all of the provisions of CA 1985 then apply: 'the word 'director' [in a section] is capable of including de facto directors but may not do so. The meaning of 'director' varies according to the context in which it is to be found.': *Re Lo-Line Electric Motors Ltd* [1988] BCLC 698 at 706, per Browne-Wilkinson VC.

Where provisions are essentially protective, the courts will extend their scope to de facto directors to ensure that the intention of Parliament is not defeated, hence de facto directors may be liable under IA 1986, s 214 for wrongful trading (*Re Hydrodam (Corby) Ltd* [1994] 2 BCLC 180 at 182); and may be the subject of disqualification proceedings: *Re Lo-Line Electric Motors Ltd* [1988] BCLC 698.

However, a person acting as a director but not duly appointed to that office is not liable under a penal enactment imposing liability on 'a director of the company': *Dean v Hiesler* [1942] 2 All ER 340. Where a penal liability is involved, the statute must be construed strictly and, if Parliament intended to extend a penal provision to a de facto director, the expectation would be that the phrase 'or any person purporting to act as a director', or some such provision, would be included in the statute as, for example, is done in s 733; see also *Re Lo-Line Electric Motors Ltd* [1988] BCLC 698 at 706.

The extent of the fiduciary obligations of a de facto director has not been authoritatively established but there is obiter support in *Re Hydrodam (Corby) Ltd* [1994] 2 BCLC 180, for the view that, having assumed the office of director, the de facto director is then subject to the responsibilities attaching to that office which would include the fiduciary obligations of a director (at 182); and a de facto director has been held liable for breach of the common law duties of care and skill of a director: see *Re Simmon Box (Diamonds) Ltd* [2000] BCC 275 at 286 (appealed on other grounds and reported as *Cohen v Selby* [2001] 1 BCLC 176).

De facto directors and shadow directors   As to the relationship between de facto directors and shadow directors, see note below.

S 741(2)

Provisions applicable to shadow directors   A large number of provisions of the CA 1985 and the IA 1986 impose obligations or liabilities on directors which are then expressly extended to shadow directors, usually by a provision to that effect as the last sub-section of the provision.

In the companies legislation, the provisions in question are mainly contained in Pt X dealing with the enforcement of fair dealing by directors, see, for example, ss 317(8), 318(6), 319(7), 320(3), 322B(3). This extension of these provisions is designed to prevent the easy evasion of the legislation by persons who control companies but who take care not to be appointed to the board. In many cases, such persons could not be appointed because they are already the subject of disqualification orders under the Company Directors Disqualification Act 1986 or they are undischarged bankrupts prohibited from acting as company directors except with the leave of the court: Company Directors Disqualification Act 1986, s 11.

Definition of shadow director   The definition of 'shadow director' provided here is common to IA 1986, s 251 and the Company Directors Disqualification Act 1986, s 22(5); a 'company' is defined in s 735.

Extensive guidance as to what constitutes a person a shadow director for these purposes has been provided by the Court of Appeal in *Secretary of State for Trade and Industry v Deverell* [2000] 2 BCLC 133. In this case, Morritt LJ (with whom Potter LJ and Morison J agreed) set out the following propositions (at 144–145):

'(1) The definition of a shadow director is to be construed in the normal way to give effect to the parliamentary intention ascertainable from the mischief to be dealt with and the words used ...

(2) The purpose of the legislation is to identify those, other than professional advisers, with real influence in the corporate affairs of the company. But it is not necessary that such influence should be exercised over the whole field of its corporate activities ...

(3) Whether any particular communication from the alleged shadow director, whether by words or conduct, is to be classified as a direction or instruction must be objectively ascertained by the court in the light of all the evidence. In that connection I do not accept that it is necessary to prove the understanding or expectation of either giver or receiver. In many, if not most, cases it will suffice to prove the communication and its consequence ... Certainly the label attached by either or both parties then or thereafter cannot be more than a factor in considering whether the communication came within the statutory description of direction or instruction.

(4) Non-professional advice may come within that statutory description. The proviso excepting advice given in a professional capacity appears to assume that advice generally is or may be included. Moreover the concepts of 'direction' and 'instruction' do not exclude the concept of 'advice' for all three share the common feature of 'guidance'.

(5) It will, no doubt, be sufficient to show that in the face of 'directions or instructions' from the alleged shadow director the properly appointed directors or some of them cast themselves in a subservient role or surrendered their respective discretions. But I do not consider that it is necessary to do so in all cases.... Such a requirement would be to put a gloss on the statutory requirement that the board are 'accustomed to act in accordance with' such directions or instructions ...'

Morritt LJ went on (at 145–146) to caution against the tendency (in previous cases) to use epithets or descriptions as where the board is described as 'the cat's paw, puppet or dancer to the tune of the shadow director' (see, for example, *Re Unisoft Group Ltd (No 3)* [1994] 1 BCLC 609 at 620). Such terms may be misleading, for they imply a degree of control both of quality and extent over the corporate field in excess of what the statutory definition requires. Equally, he noted that, in his opinion, lurking in the shadows may occur but it is not an essential ingredient to the recognition of the shadow director.

As noted above, the issue as to whether someone is a shadow director has been pursued generally in the context of disqualification proceedings against persons who for various reasons (for example, bankruptcy) have not sought appointment to the board. There have also been occasional (and unsuccessful) attempts to identify, for example, major creditors (see *Re PFTZM Ltd, Jourdain v Paul* [1995] 2 BCLC 354), banks (see *Re a Company (No 005009 of 1987), ex p Copp* [1989] BCLC 13) and parent companies (*Re Hydrodam (Corby) Ltd* [1994] 2 BCLC 180) as shadow directors in the hope of finding a deep pocket to meet potential liabilities for wrongful trading under IA 1986, s 214. Where a body corporate is a director of another company, it does not follow that its own directors must ipso facto be shadow directors of that other company: *Re Hydrodam (Corby) Ltd* [1994] 2 BCLC 180; and see the exemption for holding companies in sub-s (3).

Obligations of shadow directors   As already noted, shadow directors are subject to a range of statutory provisions which are expressly stated to apply to them, in both the CA 1985 and the IA 1986. Equally, the Company Directors Disqualification Act 1986 ss 6–9 (disqualification on the grounds of unfitness) are expressly applied to shadow directors. In the light of that established statutory practice and applying the usual rules of interpretation, a provision which does not so provide does not apply to shadow directors.

As to the general fiduciary duties attaching to directors, there appears to be general acceptance, although the issue has not been explicitly addressed by the courts, that having chosen so to act, shadow directors are subject to fiduciary duties: see *Yukong Line Ltd of Korea v Rendsburg Investments Corpn of Liberia* [1998] 2 BCLC 485 at 502; also *Re Simmon Box (Diamonds) Ltd* [2000] BCC 275 at 286.

Relationship between de facto or shadow directors   In *Re Hydrodam (Corby) Ltd* [1994] 2 BCLC 180, Millet J had suggested that the terms, de facto and shadow directors, did not overlap, that they were alternative categories, and in most and perhaps all cases they were mutually exclusive (at 183); an approach which was expressly approved in *Secretary of State for Trade and Industry v Laing* [1996] 2 BCLC 324.

In *Re Kaytech International plc, Secretary of State for Trade and Industry v Kaczer* [1999] 2 BCLC 351 Robert Walker LJ was less emphatic about the matter, noting that:

'the two concepts do have at least this much in common, that an individual who was not a de jure director is alleged to have exercised real influence (otherwise than as a professional adviser) in the corporate governance of a company. Sometimes that influence may be concealed and sometimes it may be open. Sometimes it may be something of a mixture ...' (at 424).

Certainly, a person cannot be both a de facto and a shadow director at the same time, but a person who was a shadow director may become a de facto director and vice versa.

S 741(3)

Holding company as shadow director   It is possible for a holding company to be classed as a shadow director of a subsidiary company where the holding company is a person in accordance with whose directions or instructions the directors of the subsidiary company are accustomed to act: see *Re Hydrodam (Corby)Ltd* [1994] 2 BCLC 180. This provision ensures that a holding company cannot be so classified for the purposes of the specified sections of the companies legislation.

With the exception of s 309, the specified provisions relate essentially to transactions which a company might enter into with a director, including a shadow director. Without this exemption, group transactions between a subsidiary and a holding company would be classed as a transaction between the subsidiary company and a shadow director because of the holding company's ability to control the manner in which the directors of the subsidiary are accustomed to act; in which case the transaction would be subject to the controls imposed by those sections. These controls essentially revolve around disclosure to, and the approval of, the subsidiary's shareholders but, as the transaction is with the subsidiary's controlling shareholder, such approval would be superfluous in these cases.

'Body corporate' is defined in s 740; 'subsidiary company' is defined in s 736.

742. Expressions used in connection with accounts

(1)   In this Act, unless a contrary intention appears, the following expressions have the same meaning as in Part VII (accounts)—

'annual accounts',

'accounting reference date' and 'accounting reference period',

'balance sheet' and 'balance sheet date',

'current assets',

'financial year', in relation to a company,

'fixed assets',

'parent company' and 'parent undertaking',

'profit and loss account', and

'subsidiary undertaking'.

(2)   References in this Act to 'realised profits' and 'realised losses', in relation to a company's accounts, shall be construed in accordance with section 262(3).

(2A) References in this Act to sending or sending out copies of any of the documents referred to in section 238(1) include sending or sending out such copies in accordance with section 238(4A) or (4B).

General note

For the index of definitions in Pt VII, see s 262A; as to a 'contrary intention', see note to s 735(4), above.

743.'Employees' share scheme'

For purposes of this Act, an employees' share scheme is a scheme for encouraging or facilitating the holding of shares or debentures in a company by or for the benefit of—

    (a) the bona fide employees or former employees of the company, the company's subsidiary or holding company or a subsidiary of the company's holding company, or

    (b) the wives, husbands, widows, widowers or children or step-children under the age of 18 of such employees or former employees.

General note

This definition is relevant, in particular, to s 80(2) (authority to allot capital); ss 89(5), 94(4), (5) (pre-emption rights); ss 101(2), 117(4) (share capital) and s 153(4) (financial assistance). 'Debenture' is defined in s 744; 'company' in s 735, 'subsidiary' and 'holding company' in s 736.

743A. Meaning of 'office copy' in Scotland

References in this Act to an office copy of a court order shall be construed, as respects Scotland, as references to a certified copy interlocutor.

744. Expressions used generally in this Act

In this Act, unless the contrary intention appears, the following definitions apply—

    'agent' does not include a person's counsel acting as such;

    ...

    'articles' means, in relation to a company, its articles of association, as originally framed or as altered by resolution, including (so far as applicable to the company) regulations contained in or annexed to any enactment relating to companies passed before this Act, as altered by or under any such enactment;

    [...]

    'authorised minimum' has the meaning given by section 118;

    'bank holiday' means a holiday under the Banking and Financial Dealings Act 1971;

    'banking company' means a company which is authorised under the Banking Act 1987;

    'books and papers' and 'books or papers' include accounts, deeds, writings and documents;

    'communication' means the same as in the Electronic Communications Act 2000;

'the Companies Acts' means this Act, the insider dealing legislation and the Consequential Provisions Act;

'the Consequential Provisions Act' means the Companies Consolidation (Consequential Provisions) Act 1985;

'the court', in relation to a company, means the court having jurisdiction to wind up the company;

'debenture' includes debenture stock, bonds and any other securities of a company, whether constituting a charge on the assets of the company or not;

'document' includes summons, notice, order, and other legal process, and registers;

'EEA State' means a State which is a Contracting Party to the Agreement on the European Economic Area signed at Oporto on 2nd May 1992 as adjusted by the Protocol signed at Brussels on 17th March 1993.

'electronic communication' means the same as in the Electronic Communications Act 2000;

'equity share capital' means, in relation to a company, its issued share capital excluding any part of that capital which, neither as respects dividends nor as respects capital, carries any right to participate beyond a specified amount in a distribution;

'expert' has the meaning given by section 62;

'floating charge' includes a floating charge within the meaning given by section 462;

'the Gazette' means, as respects companies registered in England and Wales, the London Gazette and, as respects companies registered in Scotland, the Edinburgh Gazette;

...

'hire-purchase agreement' has the same meaning as in the Consumer Credit Act 1974;

'the insider dealing legislation' means Part V of the Criminal Justice Act 1993 (insider dealing).

'insurance company' means the same as in the Insurance Companies Act 1982;

'joint stock company' has the meaning given by section 683;

'memorandum', in relation to a company, means its memorandum of association, as originally framed or as altered in pursuance of any enactment;

'number', in relation to shares, includes amount, where the context admits of the reference to shares being construed to include stock;

'officer', in relation to a body corporate, includes a director, manager or secretary;

'official seal', in relation to the registrar of companies, means a seal prepared under section 704(4) for the authentication of documents required for or in connection with the registration of companies;

'oversea company' means—

(a) a company incorporated elsewhere than in Great Britain which, after the commencement of this Act, establishes a place of business in Great Britain, and

(b)   a company so incorporated which has, before that commencement, established a place of business and continues to have an established place of business in Great Britain at that commencement;

'place of business' includes a share transfer or share registration office;

'prescribed' means—

(a)   as respects provisions of this Act relating to winding up, prescribed by general rules ..., and

(b)   otherwise, prescribed by statutory instrument made by the Secretary of State;

'prospectus' means any prospectus, notice, circular, advertisement, or other invitation, offering to the public for subscription or purchase any shares in or debentures of a company;

'prospectus issued generally' means a prospectus issued to persons who are not existing members of the company or holders of its debentures;

...

'the registrar of companies' and 'the registrar' mean the registrar or other officer performing under this Act the duty of registration of companies in England and Wales or in Scotland, as the case may require;

'share' means share in the share capital of a company, and includes stock (except where a distinction between shares and stock is express or implied); and

'undistributable reserves' has the meaning given by section 264(3).

General note

Definitions 'authorised minimum', 'expert', 'floating charge', 'joint stock company' and 'undistributable reserves' repealed by CA 1989, s 212, Sch 24, as from a day to be appointed.

Definitions 'communication' and 'electronic communication' inserted by the Companies Act 1985 (Electronic Communications) Order 2000, SI 2000/3373, art 29 as from 22 December 2000.

Definition 'prospectus issued generally' repealed by FSA 1986, s 212(3), Sch 17, Pt I to the extent specified in SI 1988/740.

These definitions apply, 'unless the contrary intention appears', as to the meaning of which, see the note to s 735(4), above.

'Debenture'   The word 'debenture' has no precise meaning: *Knightsbridge Estates Trust Ltd v Byrne* [1940] 2 All ER 401 at 405–406. It is used throughout the Act in numerous sections and often in more than one sense. A debenture includes a document which either creates a debt or acknowledges it: *Levy v Abercorris Slate & Slab Co* (1887) 37 Ch D 260 at 264, per Chitty J. The term will include mortgage debentures, which are charges on property and debentures which are bonds: see *British India Steam Navigation Co v IRC* (1881) 7 QBD 165 at 172–173, per Lindley, J; and see *Re S H & Co (Realisations) Ltd* [1993] BCLC 1309 at 1317 (a debenture does not necessarily mean a document which creates a charge, let alone a particular type of charge over any particular type of asset).

Auditors as 'officers' An auditor appointed to the office of auditor under ss 384, 385 is an officer of the company, whereas an auditor appointed ad hoc for a limited purpose is not, and there is no distinction in this regard between provisions imposing civil or criminal liability: *Mutual Reinsurance Co Ltd v Peat Marwick Mitchell & Co* [1997] 1 BCLC 1; *R v Shacter* [1960] 1 All ER 61; *Re Western Counties Steam Bakeries and Milling Co* [1897] 1 Ch 617; *Re Kingston Cotton Mill Co* [1896] 1 Ch 6; *Re London and General Bank* [1895] 2 Ch 166. This ability of an auditor to be an officer in some cases but not in others explains the reference in s 727 (power of court to grant relief in certain cases) to 'whether he [an auditor] is or is not an officer of the company': see also s 310(1). See also *R v Shacter* [1960] 1 All ER 61.

Bankers etc as 'officers' As the position of officer is dependent on being appointed to or holding or filling an office of the company, prima facie, the company's bankers are not officers of the company (see *Re Imperial Land Company of Marseilles* (1870) LR 10 Eq 298) nor are the company's solicitors providing professional services in the ordinary way (see *Re Great Western Forest of Dean Coal Consumers Co, Carter's Case* (1886) 31 Ch D 496) but an administrator appointed under IA 1986, Pt II was held to be an officer of the company in *Re Home Treat Ltd* [1991] BCLC 705.

Shadow and de facto directors as 'officers' It seems that a shadow director (see s 741(2)) does not fall within 'director' in this definition and so is not an officer. When a provision in this legislation is extended to a shadow director, it is done by express inclusion and there is no such express provision here. See also, for example, IA 1986, ss 206(3), 210(3), 211(2) where this definition of officers applies (by virtue of IA 1986, s 251), but the term is then expressly extended to shadow directors, so confirming that the draftsman did not believe that the existing definition of 'officer' encompasses a shadow director.

A de facto director (see s 741(1)) would be within the definition as an officer is someone who occupies a post with rights and duties annexed to it and a de facto director has assumed such a position: see *Re Western Counties Steam Bakeries and Milling Co* [1897] 1 Ch 617 at 627.

'Oversea company' As to oversea companies, see Pt XXIII.

744A. Index of defined expressions

The following Table shows provisions defining or otherwise explaining expressions for the purposes of this Act generally—

accounting reference date, accounting reference period	sections 224 and 742(1)
acquisition (in relation to a non-cash asset)	section 739(2)

agent	section 744
allotment (and related expressions)	section 738
annual accounts	sections 261(2), 262(1) and 742(1)
annual general meeting	section 366
annual return	section 363
articles	section 744
authorised minimum	section 118
balance sheet and balance sheet date	sections 261(2), 262(1) and 742(1)
bank holiday	section 744
banking company	section 744
body corporate	section 740
books and papers, books or papers	section 744
called-up share capital	section 737(1)
capital redemption reserve	section 170(1)
the Companies Acts	section 744
communication	section 744
companies charges register	section 397
company	section 735(1)
The Consequential Provisions Act	section 744
corporation	section 740

The court (in relation to a company)	section 744
current assets	sections 262(1) and 742(1)
debenture	section 744
director	section 741(1)
document	section 744
EEA State	section 744
elective resolution	section 379A
electronic communication	section 744
employees' share scheme	section 743
equity share capital	section 744
existing company	section 735(1)
extraordinary general meeting	section 368
extraordinary resolution	section 378(1)
financial year (of a company)	sections 223 and 742(1)
fixed assets	sections 262(1) and 742(1)
floating charge (in Scotland)	section 462
the former Companies Acts	section 735(1)
the Gazette	section 744
hire-purchase agreement	section 744
holding company	section 736

the insider dealing legislation	section 744
the Insolvency Act	section 735A(1)
insurance company	section 744
the Joint Stock Companies Acts	section 735(3)
limited company	section 1(2)
member (of a company)	section 22
memorandum (in relation to a company)	section 744
non-cash asset	section 739(1)
number (in relation to shares)	section 744
office copy (in relation to a court order in Scotland)	section 743A
officer (in relation to a body corporate)	section 744
official seal (in relation to the register of companies)	section 744
oversea company	section 744
overseas branch register	section 362
paid up (and related expressions)	section 738
parent company and parent undertaking	sections 258 and 742(1)
place of business	section 744
prescribed	section 744
private company	section 1(3)

profit and loss account	sections 261(2), 262(1) and 742(1)
prospectus	section 744
public company	section 1(3)
realised profits or losses	sections 262(3) and 742(2)
registered number (of a company)	section 705(1)
registered office (of a company)	section 287
registrar and registrar of companies	section 744
resolution for reducing share capital	section 135(3)
shadow director	section 741(2) and (3)
share	section 744
share premium account	section 130(1)
share warrant	section 188
special notice (in relation to a resolution)	section 379
special resolution	section 378(2)
subsidiary	section 736
subsidiary undertaking	sections 258 and 742(1)
transfer (in relation to a non-cash asset)	section 739(2)
uncalled share capital	section 737(2)
undistributable reserves	section 264(3)
unlimited company	section 1(2)

unregistered company   section 718

wholly-owned subsidiary   section 736(2).

PART XXVII

FINAL PROVISIONS

745. Northern Ireland

(1)   Except where otherwise expressly provided, nothing in this Act (except provisions relating expressly to companies registered or incorporated in Northern Ireland or outside Great Britain) applies to or in relation to companies so registered or incorporated.

(2)   Subject to any such provision, and to any express provision as to extent, this Act does not extend to Northern Ireland.

746. Commencement

... this Act comes into force on 1st July 1985.

747. Citation

This Act may be cited as the Companies Act 1985.

SCHEDULES

SCHEDULE 1

PARTICULARS OF DIRECTORS ETC TO BE CONTAINED IN STATEMENT UNDER SECTION 10

Section 10

Directors

1. Subject as provided below, the statement under section 10(2) shall contain the following particulars with respect to each person named as director—

    (a) in the case of an individual, his present name, any former name, his usual residential address, his nationality, his business occupation (if any), particulars of any other directorships held by him, or which have been held by him and his date of birth;

    (b) in the case of a corporation or Scottish firm, its corporate or firm name and registered or principal office.

2.—(1) It is not necessary for the statement to contain particulars of a directorship—

    (a) which has not been held by a director at any time during the 5 years preceding the date on which the statement is delivered to the registrar,

    (b) which is held by a director in a company which—

        (i) is dormant or grouped with the company delivering the statement, and

        (ii) if he also held that directorship for any period during those 5 years, was for the whole of that period either dormant or so grouped,

    (c) which was held by a director for any period during those 5 years in a company which for the whole of that period was either dormant or grouped with the company delivering the statement.

(2) For these purposes, 'company' includes any body corporate incorporated in Great Britain; and—

    (a) section 249AA(3) applies as regards whether and when a company is or has been 'dormant', and

    (b) a company is treated as being or having been at any time grouped with another company if at that time it is or was a company of which that other is or was a wholly-owned subsidiary, or if it is or was a wholly-owned subsidiary of the other or of another company of which that other is or was a wholly-owned subsidiary.

Secretaries

3.—(1) The statement shall contain the following particulars with respect to the person named as secretary or, where there are to be joint secretaries, with respect to each person named as one of them—

    (a) in the case of an individual, his present name, any former name and his usual residential address,

    (b) in the case of a corporation or a Scottish firm, its corporate or firm name and registered or principal office.

(2) However, if all the partners in a firm are joint secretaries, the name and principal office of the firm may be stated instead of the particulars otherwise required by this paragraph.

Interpretation

4. In paragraphs 1(a) and 3(1)(a) above—

    (a) 'name' means a person's Christian name (or other forename) and surname, except that in the case of a peer, or an individual usually known by a title, the title may be stated instead of his Christian name (or other forename) and surname or in addition to either or both of them; and

    (b) the reference to a former name does not include—

        (i) in the case of a peer, or an individual normally known by a British title, the name by which he was known previous to the adoption of or succession to the title, or

        (ii) in the case of any person, a former name which was changed or disused before he attained the age of 18 years or which has been changed or disused for 20 years or more, or

        (iii) in the case of a married woman, the name by which she was known previous to the marriage.

General note

The particulars of the directors and the company secretary as set out in this Schedule, which must be provided to the registrar of companies under s 10, are the same as those which must be included on the company's own register of directors and secretaries which is required by s 288: see notes to ss 288–290, above. Any changes among the directors or in its secretary or any change in the particulars contained in the register must be notified to the registrar of companies within 14 days: see s 288(2).

Equivalent particulars must be provided to the registrar of companies in respect of directors and secretaries of companies incorporated outside Great Britain (see s 691) save that there is no requirement to give information as to past directorships. As to the position concerning residential addresses, see the note to s 723B.

SCHEDULE 2

INTERPRETATION OF REFERENCES TO 'BENEFICIAL INTEREST'

Sections 23, 145, 146, 148

PART I

REFERENCES IN SECTIONS 23, 145, 146 AND 148

Residual interests under pension and employees' share schemes

1.—(1) Where shares in a company are held on trust for the purposes of a pension scheme or an employees' share scheme, there is to be disregarded any residual interest which has not vested in possession, being an interest of the company or, as this paragraph applies for the purposes of section 23(2) ... of any subsidiary of the company.

(2) In this paragraph,'a residual interest' means a right of the company or subsidiary in question ('the residual beneficiary') to receive any of the trust property in the event of—

    (a) all the liabilities arising under the scheme having been satisfied or provided for, or

    (b) the residual beneficiary ceasing to participate in the scheme, or

    (c) the trust property at any time exceeding what is necessary for satisfying the liabilities arising or expected to arise under the scheme.

(3) In sub-paragraph (2), references to a right include a right dependent on the exercise of a discretion vested by the scheme in the trustee or any other person; and references to liabilities arising under a scheme include liabilities that have resulted or may result from the exercise of any such discretion.

(4) For purposes of this paragraph, a residual interest vests in possession—

    (a) in a case within (a) of sub-paragraph (2), on the occurrence of the event there mentioned, whether or not the amount of the property receivable pursuant to the right mentioned in that sub-paragraph is then ascertained, and

1117

    (b) in a case within (b) or (c) of that sub-paragraph, when the residual beneficiary becomes entitled to require the trustee to transfer to that beneficiary any of the property receivable pursuant to that right.

(5) ...

2.—(1) The following has effect as regards the operation of sections ... 144, 145 and 146 to 149 in cases where a residual interest vests in possession.

(2) ...

(3) Where by virtue of paragraph 1 of this Schedule any shares are exempt from section 144 or 145 at the time when they are issued or acquired but the residual interest in question vests in possession before they are disposed of or fully paid up, those sections apply to the shares as if they had been issued or acquired on the date on which that interest vests in possession.

(4) Where by virtue of paragraph 1 any shares are exempt from sections 146 to 149 at the time when they are acquired but the residual interest in question vests in possession before they are disposed of, those sections apply to the shares as if they had been acquired on the date on which that interest vests in possession.

(5) The above sub-paragraphs apply irrespective of the date on which the residual interest vests or vested in possession; but where the date on which it vested was before 26th July 1983 (the passing of the Companies (Beneficial Interests) Act 1983), they have effect as if the vesting had occurred on that date.

Employer's charges and other rights of recovery

3.—(1) Where shares in a company are held on trust, there are to be disregarded—

    (a) if the trust is for the purposes of a pension scheme, any such rights as are mentioned in the following sub-paragraph, and

    (b) if the trust is for the purposes of an employees' share scheme, any such rights as are mentioned in (a) of the sub-paragraph,

being rights of the company or, as this paragraph applies for the purposes of section 23(2) ... of any subsidiary of the company.

(2) The rights referred to are—

    (a) any charge or lien on, or set-off against, any benefit or other right or interest under the scheme for the purpose of enabling the employer or former employer of a member of the scheme to obtain the discharge of a monetary obligation due to him from the member, and

    (b) any right to receive from the trustee of the scheme, or as trustee of the scheme to retain, an amount that can be recovered or retained under section 61 of the Pension Schemes Act 1993 (deduction of contributions equivalent premium from refund of scheme contributions) or otherwise as reimbursement or partial reimbursement for any contributions equivalent premium paid in connection with the scheme under Part III of that Act.

(3) ...

Trustee's right to expenses, remuneration, indemnity, etc

4.—(1) Where a company is a trustee ..., there are to be disregarded any rights which the company has in its capacity as trustee including, in particular, any right to recover its expenses or be remunerated out of the trust property and any right to be indemnified out of that property for any liability incurred by reason of any act or omission of the company in the performance of its duties as trustee.

(2) As this paragraph applies for the purposes of section 23(2)..., sub-paragraph (1) has effect as if references to a company included any body corporate which is a subsidiary of a company.

(3) As respects sections 145, 146 and 148, sub-paragraph (1) above applies where a company is a personal representative as it applies where a company is a trustee.

Supplementary

5.—(1) The following applies for the interpretation of this Part of this Schedule.

(2) 'Pension scheme' means any scheme for the provision of benefits consisting of or including relevant benefits for or in respect of employees or former employees; and 'relevant benefits' means any pension, lump sum, gratuity or other like benefit given or to be given on retirement or on death or in anticipation of retirement or, in connection with past service, after retirement or death.

(3) In sub-paragraph (2) of this paragraph, and in paragraph 3(2)(a), 'employer' and 'employee' are to be read as if a director of a company were employed by it.

PART II

REFERENCES IN SCHEDULE 5

Residual interests under pension and employees' share schemes

6.—(1) Where shares in an undertaking are held on trust for the purposes of a pension scheme or an employees' share scheme, there shall be disregarded any residual interest which has not vested in possession, being an interest of the undertaking or any of its subsidiary undertakings.

(2) In this paragraph a 'residual interest' means a right of the undertaking in question (the 'residual beneficiary') to receive any of the trust property in the event of—

    (a) all the liabilities arising under the scheme having been satisfied or provided for, or

(b) the residual beneficiary ceasing to participate in the scheme, or

(c) the trust property at any time exceeding what is necessary for satisfying the liabilities arising or expected to arise under the scheme.

(3) In sub-paragraph (2) references to a right include a right dependent on the exercise of a discretion vested by the scheme in the trustee or any other person; and references to liabilities arising under a scheme include liabilities that have resulted or may result from the exercise of any such discretion.

(4) For the purposes of this paragraph a residual interest vests in possession—

(a) in a case within sub-paragraph (2)(a), on the occurrence of the event there mentioned, whether or not the amount of the property receivable pursuant to the right mentioned in that sub-paragraph is then ascertained;

(b) in a case within sub-paragraph (2)(b) or (c), when the residual beneficiary becomes entitled to require the trustee to transfer to that beneficiary any of the property receivable pursuant to that right.

Employer's charges and other rights of recovery

7.—(1) Where shares in an undertaking are held on trust, there shall be disregarded—

(a) if the trust is for the purposes of a pension scheme, any such rights as are mentioned in sub-paragraph (2) below;

(b) if the trust is for the purposes of an employees' share scheme, any such rights as are mentioned in paragraph (a) of that sub-paragraph,

being rights of the undertaking or any of its subsidiary undertakings.

(2) The rights referred to are—

(a) any charge or lien on, or set-off against, any benefit or other right or interest under the scheme for the purpose of enabling the employer or former employer of a member of the scheme to obtain the discharge of a monetary obligation due to him from the member, and

(b) any right to receive from the trustee of the scheme, or as trustee of the scheme to retain, an amount that can be recovered or retained under section 61 of the Pension Schemes Act 1993 (deduction of contributions equivalent premium from refund of scheme contributions) or otherwise as reimbursement or partial reimbursement for any contributions equivalent premium paid in connection with the scheme under Chapter III of Part III of that Act.

Trustee's right to expenses, remuneration, indemnity, &c

8. Where an undertaking is a trustee, there shall be disregarded any rights which the undertaking has in its capacity as trustee including, in particular, any right to recover its expenses or be remunerated out of the trust property and any right to be indemnified out of that property for any liability incurred by reason of any act or omission of the undertaking in the performance of its duties as trustee.

Supplementary

9.—(1) The following applies for the interpretation of this Part of this Schedule.

(2) 'Undertaking' and 'shares', in relation to an undertaking, have the same meaning as in Part VII.

(3) This Part of this Schedule applies in relation to debentures as it applies in relation to shares.

(4) 'Pension scheme' means any scheme for the provision of benefits consisting of or including relevant benefits for or in respect of employees or former employees; and 'relevant benefits' means any pension, lump sum, gratuity or other like benefit given or to be given on retirement or on death or in anticipation of retirement or, in connection with past service, after retirement or death.

(5) In sub-paragraph (4) of this paragraph and in paragraph 7(2) 'employee' and 'employer' shall be read as if a director of an undertaking were employed by it.

Part I

This Part provides that residual rights of the company, not vested in possession, arising from a pension scheme (defined para 5) or employees' share scheme (defined s 743) are disregarded in determining whether a company is beneficially interested in any shares for the purposes of the specified provisions; as are rights arising with respect to employers' charges and other rights of recovery under any such scheme; and rights of the company in its capacity as a trustee and a personal representative: see paras 1, 3–5.

Where s 146 requires that certain shares be cancelled within a specified period, para 2 determines when that period commences where the company's interest has arisen as a result of certain residual rights vesting in possession.

Part II

This Part provides definitions necessary for the purposes of Sch 5, see Sch 5, paras 6(4), 20(4).

Schedule 3 repealed by FSA 1986, section 212(3), Schedule 17, Part I save that paragraph 2 is retained for the purposes of section 83(1)(a), see SI 1995/1538, art 2(9)(ii).

SCHEDULE 3

MANDATORY CONTENTS OF PROSPECTUS

...

2. Where shares are offered to the public for subscription, the prospectus must give particulars as to—

   (a) the minimum amount which, in the opinion of the directors, must be raised by the issue of those shares in order to provide the sums (or, if any part of them is to be defrayed in any other manner, the balance of the sums) required to be provided in respect of each of the following—

      (i) the purchase price of any property purchased or to be purchased which is to be defrayed in whole or in part out of the proceeds of the issue,

      (ii) any preliminary expenses payable by the company, and any commission so payable to any person in consideration of his agreeing to subscribe for, or of his procuring or agreeing to procure subscriptions for, any shares in the company,

      (iii) the repayment of any money borrowed by the company in respect of any of the foregoing matters,

      (iv) working capital, and

   (b) the amounts to be provided in respect of the matters above mentioned otherwise than out of the proceeds of the issue and sources out of which those amounts are to be provided.

...

General note

See the note to CA 1985, s 83(1)(a), above.

SCHEDULE 4

FORM AND CONTENT OF COMPANY ACCOUNTS

PART I

GENERAL RULES AND FORMATS

Section A
General Rules

1.—(1) Subject to the following provisions of this Schedule—

    (a) every balance sheet of a company shall show the items listed in either of the balance sheet formats set out below in section B of this Part; and

    (b) every profit and loss account of a company shall show the items listed in any one of the profit and loss account formats so set out;

in either case in the order and under the headings and sub-headings given in the format adopted.

(2) Sub-paragraph (1) above is not to be read as requiring the heading or sub-heading for any item to be distinguished by any letter or number assigned to that item in the format adopted.

2.—(1) Where in accordance with paragraph 1 a company's balance sheet or profit and loss account for any financial year has been prepared by reference to one of the formats set out in section B below, the directors of the company shall adopt the same format in preparing the accounts for subsequent financial years of the company unless in their opinion there are special reasons for a change.

(2) Particulars of any change in the format adopted in preparing a company's balance sheet or profit and loss account in accordance with paragraph 1 shall be disclosed, and the reasons for the change shall be explained, in a note to the accounts in which the new format is first adopted.

3.—(1) Any item required in accordance with paragraph 1 to be shown in a company's balance sheet or profit and loss account may be shown in greater detail than required by the format adopted.

(2) A company's balance sheet or profit and loss account may include an item representing or covering the amount of any asset or liability, income or expenditure not otherwise covered by any of the items listed in the format adopted, but the following shall not be treated as assets in any company's balance sheet—

    (a) preliminary expenses;

    (b) expenses of and commission on any issue of shares or debentures; and

    (c) costs of research.

(3) In preparing a company's balance sheet or profit and loss account the directors of the company shall adapt the arrangement and headings and sub-headings otherwise required by paragraph 1 in respect of items to which an Arabic number is assigned in the format adopted, in any case where the special nature of the company's business requires such adaptation.

(4) Items to which Arabic numbers are assigned in any of the formats set out in section B below may be combined in a company's accounts for any financial year if either—

    (a) their individual amounts are not material to assessing the state of affairs or profit or loss of the company for that year; or

    (b) the combination facilitates that assessment;

but in a case within paragraph (b) the individual amounts of any items so combined shall be disclosed in a note to the accounts.

(5) Subject to paragraph 4(3) below, a heading or sub-heading corresponding to an item listed in the format adopted in preparing a company's balance sheet or profit and loss account shall not be included if there is no amount to be shown for that item in respect of the financial year to which the balance sheet or profit and loss account relates.

(6) Every profit and loss account of a company shall show the amount of the company's profit or loss on ordinary activities before taxation.

(7) Every profit and loss account of a company shall show separately as additional items—

    (a) any amount set aside or proposed to be set aside to, or withdrawn or proposed to be withdrawn from, reserves; ...

    (b) the aggregate amount of any dividends paid and proposed;

    (c) if it is not shown in the notes to the accounts, the aggregate amount of any dividends proposed.

4.—(1) In respect of every item shown in a company's balance sheet or profit and loss account the corresponding amount for the financial year immediately preceding that to which the balance sheet or profit and loss account relates shall also be shown.

(2) Where that corresponding amount is not comparable with the amount to be shown for the item in question in respect of the financial year to which the balance sheet or profit and loss account relates, the former amount shall be adjusted and particulars of the adjustment and the reasons for it shall be disclosed in a note to the accounts.

(3) Paragraph 3(5) does not apply in any case where an amount can be shown for the item in question in respect of the financial year immediately preceding that to which the balance sheet or profit and loss account relates, and that amount shall be shown under the heading or sub-heading required by paragraph 1 for that item.

5. Amounts in respect of items representing assets or income may not be set off against amounts in respect of items representing liabilities or expenditure (as the case may be), or vice versa.

Section B
The required formats for accounts

Preliminary

6. References in this Part of this Schedule to the items listed in any of the formats set out below are to those items read together with any of the notes following the formats which apply to any of those items, and the requirement imposed by paragraph 1 to show the items listed in any such format in the order adopted in the format is subject to any provision in those notes for alternative positions for any particular items.

7. A number in brackets following any item in any of the formats set out below is a reference to the note of that number in the notes following the formats.

8. In the notes following the formats—

    (a)   the heading of each note gives the required heading or sub-heading for the item to which it applies and a reference to any letters and numbers assigned to that item in the formats set out below (taking a reference in the case of Format 2 of the balance sheet formats to the item listed under 'Assets' or under 'Liabilities' as the case may require); and

    (b)   references to a numbered format are to the balance sheet format or (as the case may require) to the profit and loss account format of that number set out below.

Balance sheet formats

Format 1

  A.   Called up share capital not paid (*1*)

  B.   Fixed assets

      I   Intangible assets

         1.   Development costs

         2.   Concessions, patents, licences, trade marks and similar rights and assets (*2*)

      3.   Goodwill (*3*)

      4.   Payments on account

  II   Tangible assets

      1.   Land and buildings

      2.   Plant and machinery

      3.   Fixtures, fittings, tools and equipment

      4.   Payments on account and assets in course of construction

  III Investments

      1.   Shares in group undertakings

      2.   Loans to group undertakings

      3.   Participating interests

      4.   Loans to undertakings in which the company has a participating interest

      5.   Other investments other than loans

      6.   Other loans

      7.   Own shares (*4*)

C.   Current assets

  I   Stocks

      1.   Raw materials and consumables

      2.   Work in progress

      3.   Finished goods and goods for resale

      4.   Payments on account

  II   Debtors (*5*)

      1.   Trade debtors

      2.   Amounts owed by group undertakings

      3.   Amounts owed by undertakings in which the company has a participating interest

      4.   Other debtors

      5.   Called up share capital not paid (*1*)

      6.   Prepayments and accrued income (*6*)

  III Investments

      1.   Shares in group undertakings

      2.   Own shares (*4*)

      3.   Other investments

  IV Cash at bank and in hand

D.   Prepayments and accrued income (*6*)

E.   Creditors: amounts falling due within one year

      1.   Debenture loans (*7*)

      2.   Bank loans and overdrafts

      3.   Payments received on account (*8*)

      4.   Trade creditors

      5.   Bills of exchange payable

6.   Amounts owed to group undertakings
7.   Amounts owed to undertakings in which the company has a participating interest
8.   Other creditors including taxation and social security (*9*)
9.   Accruals and deferred income (*10*)

F.   Net current assets (liabilities) (*11*)

G.   Total assets less current liabilities

H.   Creditors: amounts falling due after more than one year

1.   Debenture loans (*7*)
2.   Bank loans and overdrafts
3.   Payments received on account (*8*)
4.   Trade creditors
5.   Bills of exchange payable
6.   Amounts owed to group undertakings
7.   Amounts owed to undertakings in which the company has a participating interest
8.   Other creditors including taxation and social security (*9*)
9.   Accruals and deferred income (*10*)

I.   Provisions for liabilities and charges

1.   Pensions and similar obligations
2.   Taxation, including deferred taxation
3.   Other provisions

J.   Accruals and deferred income (*10*)

K.   Capital and reserves

I   Called up share capital (*12*)
II   Share premium account
III   Revaluation reserve
IV   Other reserves

1.   Capital redemption reserve
2.   Reserve for own shares
3.   Reserves provided for by the articles of association
4.   Other reserves

V   Profit and loss account

Balance sheet formats

Format 2

ASSETS

A.   Called up share capital not paid (*1*)

B. Fixed assets
    I   Intangible assets
        1.   Development costs
        2.   Concessions, patents, licences, trade marks and similar rights and assets (2)
        3.   Goodwill (3)
        4.   Payments on account
    II   Tangible assets
        1.   Land and buildings
        2.   Plant and machinery
        3.   Fixtures, fittings, tools and equipment
        4.   Payments on account and assets in course of construction
    III Investments
        1.   Shares in group undertakings
        2.   Loans to group undertakings
        3.   Participating interests
        4.   Loans to undertakings in which the company has a participating interest
        5.   Other investments other than loans
        6.   Other loans
        7.   Own shares (4)
C. Current assets
    I   Stocks
        1.   Raw materials and consumables
        2.   Work in progress
        3.   Finished goods and goods for resale
        4.   Payments on account
    II   Debtors (5)
        1.   Trade debtors
        2.   Amounts owed by group undertakings
        3.   Amounts owed by undertakings in which the company has a participating interest
        4.   Other debtors
        5.   Called up share capital not paid (1)
        6.   Prepayments and accrued income (6)
    III Investments
        1.   Shares in group undertakings
        2.   Own shares (4)
        3.   Other investments
    IV Cash at bank and in hand
D. Prepayments and accrued income (6)

LIABILITIES

A. Capital and reserves

    I   Called up share capital *(12)*

    II   Share premium account

    III Revaluation reserve

    IV Other reserves

        1.   Capital redemption reserve

        2.   Reserve for own shares

        3.   Reserves provided for by the articles of association

        4.   Other reserves

    V   Profit and loss account

B. Provisions for liabilities and charges

        1.   Pensions and similar obligations

        2.   Taxation including deferred taxation

        3.   Other provisions

C. Creditors *(13)*

        1.   Debenture loans *(7)*

        2.   Bank loans and overdrafts

        3.   Payments received on account *(8)*

        4.   Trade creditors

        5.   Bills of exchange payable

        6.   Amounts owed to group undertakings

        7.   Amounts owed to undertakings in which the company has a participating interest

        8.   Other creditors including taxation and social security *(9)*

        9.   Accruals and deferred income *(10)*

D. Accruals and deferred income *(10)*

Notes on the balance sheet formats

(1) Called up share capital not paid

(Formats 1 and 2, items A and C.II.5.)

This item may be shown in either of the two positions given in Formats 1 and 2.

(2) Concessions, patents, licences, trade marks and similar rights and assets

(Formats 1 and 2, item B.I.2.)

Amounts in respect of assets shall only be included in a company's balance sheet under this item if either—

    (a) the assets were acquired for valuable consideration and are not required to be shown under goodwill; or

(b)   the assets in question were created by the company itself.

(3) Goodwill

(Formats 1 and 2, item B.I.3.)

Amounts representing goodwill shall only be included to the extent that the goodwill was acquired for valuable consideration.

(4) Own shares

(Formats 1 and 2, items B.III.7 and C.III.2.)

The nominal value of the shares held shall be shown separately.

(5) Debtors

(Formats 1 and 2, items C.II.1 to 6.)

The amount falling due after more than one year shall be shown separately for each item included under debtors.

(6) Prepayments and accrued income

(Formats 1 and 2, items C.II.6 and D.)

This item may be shown in either of the two positions given in Formats 1 and 2.

(7) Debenture loans

(Format 1, items E.1 and H.1 and Format 2, item C.1.)

The amount of any convertible loans shall be shown separately.

(8) Payments received on account

(Format 1, items E.3 and H.3 and Format 2, item C.3.)

Payments received on account of orders shall be shown for each of these items in so far as they are not shown as deductions from stocks.

(9) Other creditors including taxation and social security

(Format 1, items E.8 and H.8 and Format 2, item C.8.)

The amount for creditors in respect of taxation and social security shall be shown separately from the amount for other creditors.

(10) Accruals and deferred income

(Format 1, items E.9, H.9 and J and Format 2, items C.9 and D.)

The two positions given for this item in Format 1 at E.9 and H.9 are an alternative to the position at J, but if the item is not shown in a position corresponding to that at J it may be shown in either or both of the other two positions (as the case may require).

The two positions given for this item in Format 2 are alternatives.

(11) Net current assets (liabilities)

(Format 1, item F.)

In determining the amount to be shown for this item any amounts shown under 'prepayments and accrued income' shall be taken into account wherever shown.

(12) Called up share capital

(Format 1, item K.I and Format 2, item A.I.)

The amount of allotted share capital and the amount of called up share capital which has been paid up shall be shown separately.

(13) Creditors

(Format 2, items C.1 to 9.)

Amounts falling due within one year and after one year shall be shown separately for each of these items and for the aggregate of all of these items.

Profit and loss account formats

Format 1

(see note (17) below)

1. Turnover
2. Cost of sales *(14)*
3. Gross profit or loss
4. Distribution costs *(14)*
5. Administrative expenses *(14)*
6. Other operating income
7. Income from shares in group undertakings
8. Income from participating interests
9. Income from other fixed asset investments *(15)*
10. Other interest receivable and similar income *(15)*
11. Amounts written off investments
12. Interest payable and similar charges *(16)*
13. Tax on profit or loss on ordinary activities
14. Profit or loss on ordinary activities after taxation

15. Extraordinary income

16. Extraordinary charges

17. Extraordinary profit or loss

18. Tax on extraordinary profit or loss

19. Other taxes not shown under the above items

20. Profit or loss for the financial year

Profit and loss account formats

Format 2

1. Turnover

2. Change in stocks of finished goods and in work in progress

3. Own work capitalised

4. Other operating income

5.   (a) Raw materials and consumables
     (b) Other external charges

6. Staff costs—
     (a) wages and salaries
     (b) social security costs
     (c) other pension costs

7.   (a) Depreciation and other amounts written off tangible and intangible fixed assets
     (b) Exceptional amounts written off current assets

8. Other operating charges

9. Income from shares in group undertakings

10. Income from participating interests

11. Income from other fixed asset investments (*15*)

12. Other interest receivable and similar income (*15*)

13. Amounts written off investments

14. Interest payable and similar charges (*16*)

15. Tax on profit or loss on ordinary activities

16. Profit or loss on ordinary activities after taxation

17. Extraordinary income

18. Extraordinary charges

19. Extraordinary profit or loss

20. Tax on extraordinary profit or loss

21. Other taxes not shown under the above items

22. Profit or loss for the financial year

Profit and loss account formats

Format 3

(see note (17) below)

A. Charges

    1.   Cost of sales *(14)*

    2.   Distribution costs *(14)*

    3.   Administrative expenses *(14)*

    4.   Amounts written off investments

    5.   Interest payable and similar charges *(16)*

    6.   Tax on profit or loss on ordinary activities

    7.   Profit or loss on ordinary activities after taxation

    8.   Extraordinary charges

    9.   Tax on extraordinary profit or loss

    10. Other taxes not shown under the above items

    11. Profit or loss for the financial year

B. Income

    1.   Turnover

    2.   Other operating income

    3.   Income from shares in group undertakings

    4.   Income from participating interests

    5.   Income from other fixed asset investments *(15)*

    6.   Other interest receivable and similar income *(15)*

    7.   Profit or loss on ordinary activities after taxation

    8.   Extraordinary income

    9.   Profit or loss for the financial year

Profit and loss account formats

Format 4

A. Charges

   1.   Reduction in stocks of finished goods and in work in progress

   2.   (a) Raw materials and consumables

          (b) Other external charges

   3.   Staff costs—

          (a) wages and salaries

          (b) social security costs

          (c) other pension costs

   4.   (a) Depreciation and other amounts written off tangible and intangible fixed assets

          (b) Exceptional amounts written off current assets

   5.   Other operating charges

   6.   Amounts written off investments

   7.   Interest payable and similar charges *(16)*

   8.   Tax on profit or loss on ordinary activities

   9.   Profit or loss on ordinary activities after taxation

  10. Extraordinary charges

  11. Tax on extraordinary profit or loss

  12. Other taxes not shown under the above items

  13. Profit or loss for the financial year

B. Income

   1.   Turnover

   2.   Increase in stocks of finished goods and in work in progress

   3.   Own work capitalised

   4.   Other operating income

   5.   Income from shares in group undertakings

   6.   Income from participating interests

   7.   Income from other fixed asset investments *(15)*

   8.   Other interest receivable and similar income *(15)*

   9.   Profit or loss on ordinary activities after taxation

  10. Extraordinary income

  11. Profit or loss for the financial year

Notes on the profit and loss account formats

(14) Cost of sales: distribution costs: administrative expenses

(Format 1, items 2, 4 and 5 and Format 3, items A.1, 2 and 3.)

These items shall be stated after taking into account any necessary provisions for depreciation or diminution in value of assets.

(15) Income from other fixed asset investments: other interest receivable and similar income

(Format 1, items 9 and 10: Format 2, items 11 and 12: Format 3, items B.5 and 6: Format 4, items B.7 and 8.)

Income and interest derived from group undertakings shall be shown separately from income and interest derived from other sources.

(16) Interest payable and similar charges

(Format 1, item 12: Format 2, item 14: Format 3, item A.5: Format 4, item A.7.)

The amount payable to group undertakings shall be shown separately.

(17) Formats 1 and 3

The amount of any provisions for depreciation and diminution in value of tangible and intangible fixed assets falling to be shown under items 7(a) and A.4(a) respectively in Formats 2 and 4 shall be disclosed in a note to the accounts in any case where the profit and loss account is prepared by reference to Format 1 or Format 3.

PART II

ACCOUNTING PRINCIPLES AND RULES

Section A
Accounting Principles

Preliminary

9. Subject to paragraph 15 below, the amounts to be included in respect of all items shown in a company's accounts shall be determined in accordance with the principles set out in paragraphs 10 to 14.

Accounting principles

10. The company shall be presumed to be carrying on business as a going concern.

11. Accounting policies shall be applied consistently within the same accounts as from one financial year to the next.

12. The amount of any item shall be determined on a prudent basis, and in particular—

    (a) only profits realised at the balance sheet date shall be included in the profit and loss account; and

    (b) all liabilities and losses which have arisen or are likely to arise in respect of the financial year to which the accounts relate or a previous financial year shall be taken into account, including those which only become apparent between the balance sheet date and the date on which it is signed on behalf of the board of directors in pursuance of section 233 of this Act.

13. All income and charges relating to the financial year to which the accounts relate shall be taken into account, without regard to the date of receipt or payment.

14. In determining the aggregate amount of any item the amount of each individual asset or liability that falls to be taken into account shall be determined separately.

Departure from the accounting principles

15. If it appears to the directors of a company that there are special reasons for departing from any of the principles stated above in preparing the company's accounts in respect of any financial year they may do so, but particulars of the departure, the reasons for it and its effect shall be given in a note to the accounts.

Section B
Historical cost accounting rules

Preliminary

16. Subject to section C of this Part of this Schedule, the amounts to be included in respect of all items shown in a company's accounts shall be determined in accordance with the rules set out in paragraphs 17 to 28.

Fixed assets

General rules

17. Subject to any provision for depreciation or diminution in value made in accordance with paragraph 18 or 19 the amount to be included in respect of any fixed asset shall be its purchase price or production cost.

18. In the case of any fixed asset which has a limited useful economic life, the amount of—

(a) its purchase price or production cost; or

(b) where it is estimated that any such asset will have a residual value at the end of the period of its useful economic life, its purchase price or production cost less that estimated residual value;

shall be reduced by provisions for depreciation calculated to write off that amount systematically over the period of the asset's useful economic life.

19.—(1) Where a fixed asset investment of a description falling to be included under item B.III of either of the balance sheet formats set out in Part I of this Schedule has diminished in value provisions for diminution in value may be made in respect of it and the amount to be included in respect of it may be reduced accordingly; and any such provisions which are not shown in the profit and loss account shall be disclosed (either separately or in aggregate) in a note to the accounts.

(2) Provisions for diminution in value shall be made in respect of any fixed asset which has diminished in value if the reduction in its value is expected to be permanent (whether its useful economic life is limited or not), and the amount to be included in respect of it shall be reduced accordingly; and any such provisions which are not shown in the profit and loss account shall be disclosed (either separately or in aggregate) in a note to the accounts.

(3) Where the reasons for which any provision was made in accordance with sub-paragraph (1) or (2) have ceased to apply to any extent, that provision shall be written back to the extent that it is no longer necessary; and any amounts written back in accordance with this sub-paragraph which are not shown in the profit and loss account shall be disclosed (either separately or in aggregate) in a note to the accounts.

Rules for determining particular fixed asset items

20.—(1) Notwithstanding that an item in respect of 'development costs' is included under 'fixed assets' in the balance sheet formats set out in Part I of this Schedule, an amount may only be included in a company's balance sheet in respect of development costs in special circumstances.

(2) If any amount is included in a company's balance sheet in respect of development costs the following information shall be given in a note to the accounts—

(a) the period over which the amount of those costs originally capitalised is being or is to be written off; and

(b) the reasons for capitalising the development costs in question.

21.—(1) The application of paragraphs 17 to 19 in relation to goodwill (in any case where goodwill is treated as an asset) is subject to the following provisions of this paragraph.

(2) Subject to sub-paragraph (3) below, the amount of the consideration for any goodwill acquired by a company shall be reduced by provisions for depreciation calculated to write off that amount systematically over a period chosen by the directors of the company.

(3) The period chosen shall not exceed the useful economic life of the goodwill in question.

(4) In any case where any goodwill acquired by a company is shown or included as an asset in the company's balance sheet the period chosen for writing off the consideration for that goodwill and the reasons for choosing that period shall be disclosed in a note to the accounts.

Current assets

22. Subject to paragraph 23, the amount to be included in respect of any current asset shall be its purchase price or production cost.

23.—(1) If the net realisable value of any current asset is lower than its purchase price or production cost the amount to be included in respect of that asset shall be the net realisable value.

(2) Where the reasons for which any provision for diminution in value was made in accordance with sub-paragraph (1) have ceased to apply to any extent, that provision shall be written back to the extent that it is no longer necessary.

Miscellaneous and supplementary provisions

Excess of money owed over value received as an asset item

24.—(1) Where the amount repayable on any debt owed by a company is greater than the value of the consideration received in the transaction giving rise to the debt, the amount of the difference may be treated as an asset.

(2) Where any such amount is so treated—

    (a)   it shall be written off by reasonable amounts each year and must be completely written off before repayment of the debt; and

    (b)   if the current amount is not shown as a separate item in the company's balance sheet it must be disclosed in a note to the accounts.

Assets included at a fixed amount

25.—(1) Subject to the following sub-paragraph, assets which fall to be included—

    (a)   amongst the fixed assets of a company under the item 'tangible assets'; or

    (b)   amongst the current assets of a company under the item 'raw materials and consumables';

may be included at a fixed quantity and value.

(2) Sub-paragraph (1) applies to assets of a kind which are constantly being replaced, where—

    (a)   their overall value is not material to assessing the company's state of affairs; and

(b) their quantity, value and composition are not subject to material variation.

Determination of purchase price or production cost

26.—(1) The purchase price of an asset shall be determined by adding to the actual price paid any expenses incidental to its acquisition.

(2) The production cost of an asset shall be determined by adding to the purchase price of the raw materials and consumables used the amount of the costs incurred by the company which are directly attributable to the production of that asset.

(3) In addition, there may be included in the production cost of an asset—

(a) a reasonable proportion of the costs incurred by the company which are only indirectly attributable to the production of that asset, but only to the extent that they relate to the period of production; and

(b) interest on capital borrowed to finance the production of that asset, to the extent that it accrues in respect of the period of production;

provided, however, in a case within paragraph (b) above, that the inclusion of the interest in determining the cost of that asset and the amount of the interest so included is disclosed in a note to the accounts.

(4) In the case of current assets distribution costs may not be included in production costs.

27.—(1) Subject to the qualification mentioned below, the purchase price or production cost of—

(a) any assets which fall to be included under any item shown in a company's balance sheet under the general item 'stocks'; and

(b) any assets which are fungible assets (including investments);

may be determined by the application of any of the methods mentioned in sub-paragraph (2) below in relation to any such assets of the same class.

The method chosen must be one which appears to the directors to be appropriate in the circumstances of the company.

(2) Those methods are—

(a) the method known as 'first in, first out' (FIFO);

(b) the method known as 'last in, first out' (LIFO);

(c) a weighted average price; and

(d) any other method similar to any of the methods mentioned above.

(3) Where in the case of any company—

(a) the purchase price or production cost of assets falling to be included under any item shown in the company's balance sheet has been determined by the application of any method permitted by this paragraph; and

(b) the amount shown in respect of that item differs materially from the relevant alternative amount given below in this paragraph;

the amount of that difference shall be disclosed in a note to the accounts.

(4) Subject to sub-paragraph (5) below, for the purposes of sub-paragraph (3)(b) above, the relevant alternative amount, in relation to any item shown in a company's balance sheet, is the amount which would have been shown in respect of that item if assets of any class included under that item at an amount determined by any method permitted by this paragraph had instead been included at their replacement cost as at the balance sheet date.

(5) The relevant alternative amount may be determined by reference to the most recent actual purchase price or production cost before the balance sheet date of assets of any class included under the item in question instead of by reference to their replacement cost as at that date, but only if the former appears to the directors of the company to constitute the more appropriate standard of comparison in the case of assets of that class.

(6) For the purposes of this paragraph, assets of any description shall be regarded as fungible if assets of that description are substantially indistinguishable one from another.

Substitution of original stated amount where price or cost unknown

28. Where there is no record of the purchase price or production cost of any asset of a company or of any price, expenses or costs relevant for determining its purchase price or production cost in accordance with paragraph 26, or any such record cannot be obtained without unreasonable expense or delay, its purchase price or production cost shall be taken for the purposes of paragraphs 17 to 23 to be the value ascribed to it in the earliest available record of its value made on or after its acquisition or production by the company.

Section C
Alternative accounting rules

Preliminary

29.—(1) The rules set out in section B are referred to below in this Schedule as the historical cost accounting rules.

(2) Those rules, with the omission of paragraphs 16, 21 and 25 to 28, are referred to below in this Part of this Schedule as the depreciation rules; and references below in this Schedule to the historical cost accounting rules do not include the depreciation rules as they apply by virtue of paragraph 32.

30. Subject to paragraphs 32 to 34, the amounts to be included in respect of assets of any description mentioned in paragraph 31 may be determined on any basis so mentioned.

Alternative accounting rules

31.—(1) Intangible fixed assets, other than goodwill, may be included at their current cost.

(2) Tangible fixed assets may be included at a market value determined as at the date of their last valuation or at their current cost.

(3) Investments of any description falling to be included under item B.III of either of the balance sheet formats set out in Part I of this Schedule may be included either—

    (a) at a market value determined as at the date of their last valuation; or

    (b) at a value determined on any basis which appears to the directors to be appropriate in the circumstances of the company;

but in the latter case particulars of the method of valuation adopted and of the reasons for adopting it shall be disclosed in a note to the accounts.

(4) Investments of any description falling to be included under item C.III of either of the balance sheet formats set out in Part I of this Schedule may be included at their current cost.

(5) Stocks may be included at their current cost.

Application of the depreciation rules

32.—(1) Where the value of any asset of a company is determined on any basis mentioned in paragraph 31, that value shall be, or (as the case may require) be the starting point for determining, the amount to be included in respect of that asset in the company's accounts, instead of its purchase price or production cost or any value previously so determined for that asset; and the depreciation rules shall apply accordingly in relation to any such asset with the substitution for any reference to its purchase price or production cost of a reference to the value most recently determined for that asset on any basis mentioned in paragraph 31.

(2) The amount of any provision for depreciation required in the case of any fixed asset by paragraph 18 or 19 as it applies by virtue of sub-paragraph (1) is referred to below in this paragraph as the adjusted amount, and the amount of any provision which would be required by that paragraph in the case of that asset according to the historical cost accounting rules is referred to as the historical cost amount.

(3) Where sub-paragraph (1) applies in the case of any fixed asset the amount of any provision for depreciation in respect of that asset—

    (a) included in any item shown in the profit and loss account in respect of amounts written off assets of the description in question; or

    (b) taken into account in stating any item so shown which is required by note (*14*) of the notes on the profit and loss account formats set out in Part I of this Schedule to be stated after taking into account any necessary provisions for depreciation or diminution in value of assets included under it;

may be the historical cost amount instead of the adjusted amount, provided that the amount of any difference between the two is shown separately in the profit and loss account or in a note to the accounts.

Additional information to be provided in case of departure from historical cost accounting rules

33.—(1) This paragraph applies where the amounts to be included in respect of assets covered by any items shown in a company's accounts have been determined on any basis mentioned in paragraph 31.

(2) The items affected and the basis of valuation adopted in determining the amounts of the assets in question in the case of each such item shall be disclosed in a note to the accounts.

(3) In the case of each balance sheet item affected (except stocks) either—

    (a) the comparable amounts determined according to the historical cost accounting rules; or

    (b) the differences between those amounts and the corresponding amounts actually shown in the balance sheet in respect of that item;

shall be shown separately in the balance sheet or in a note to the accounts.

(4) In sub-paragraph (3) above, references in relation to any item to the comparable amounts determined as there mentioned are references to—

    (a) the aggregate amount which would be required to be shown in respect of that item if the amounts to be included in respect of all the assets covered by that item were determined according to the historical cost accounting rules; and

    (b) the aggregate amount of the cumulative provisions for depreciation or diminution in value which would be permitted or required in determining those amounts according to those rules.

Revaluation reserve

34.—(1) With respect to any determination of the value of an asset of a company on any basis mentioned in paragraph 31, the amount of any profit or loss arising from that determination (after allowing, where appropriate, for any provisions for depreciation or diminution in value made otherwise than by reference to the value so determined and any adjustments of any such provisions made in the light of that determination) shall be credited or (as the case may be) debited to a separate reserve ('the revaluation reserve').

(2) The amount of the revaluation reserve shall be shown in the company's balance sheet under a separate sub-heading in the position given for the item 'revaluation reserve' in Format 1 or 2 of the balance sheet formats set out in Part I of this Schedule, but need not be shown under that name.

(3) An amount may be transferred

    (a) from the revaluation reserve—

        (i) to the profit and loss account, if the amount was previously charged to that account or represents realised profit, or

(ii) on capitalisation,

(b) to or from the revaluation reserve in respect of the taxation relating to any profit or loss credited or debited to the reserve;

and the revaluation reserve shall be reduced to the extent that the amounts transferred to it are no longer necessary for the purposes of the valuation method used.

(3A) In sub-paragraph (3)(a)(ii) 'capitalisation', in relation to an amount standing to the credit of the revaluation reserve, means applying it in wholly or partly paying up unissued shares in the company to be allotted to members of the company as fully or partly paid shares.

(3B) The revaluation reserve shall not be reduced except as mentioned in this paragraph.

(4) The treatment for taxation purposes of amounts credited or debited to the revaluation reserve shall be disclosed in a note to the accounts.

PART III
NOTES TO THE ACCOUNTS

Preliminary

35. Any information required in the case of any company by the following provisions of this Part of this Schedule shall (if not given in the company's accounts) be given by way of a note to those accounts.

Disclosure of accounting policies

36. The accounting policies adopted by the company in determining the amounts to be included in respect of items shown in the balance sheet and in determining the profit or loss of the company shall be stated (including such policies with respect to the depreciation and diminution in value of assets).

36A. It shall be stated whether the accounts have been prepared in accordance with applicable accounting standards and particulars of any material departure from those standards and the reasons for it shall be given.

Information supplementing the balance sheet

37. Paragraphs 38 to 51 require information which either supplements the information given with respect to any particular items shown in the balance sheet or is otherwise relevant to assessing the company's state of affairs in the light of the information so given.

Share capital and debentures

38.—(1) The following information shall be given with respect to the company's share capital—

    (a) the authorised share capital; and

    (b) where shares of more than one class have been allotted, the number and aggregate nominal value of shares of each class allotted.

(2) In the case of any part of the allotted share capital that consists of redeemable shares, the following information shall be given—

    (a) the earliest and latest dates on which the company has power to redeem those shares;

    (b) whether those shares must be redeemed in any event or are liable to be redeemed at the option of the company or of the shareholder; and

    (c) whether any (and, if so, what) premium is payable on redemption.

39. If the company has allotted any shares during the financial year, the following information shall be given—

    (a) ...

    (b) the classes of shares allotted; and

    (c) as respects each class of shares, the number allotted, their aggregate nominal value, and the consideration received by the company for the allotment.

40.—(1) With respect to any contingent right to the allotment of shares in the company the following particulars shall be given—

    (a) the number, description and amount of the shares in relation to which the right is exercisable;

    (b) the period during which it is exercisable; and

    (c) the price to be paid for the shares allotted.

(2) In sub-paragraph (1) above 'contingent right to the allotment of shares' means any option to subscribe for shares and any other right to require the allotment of shares to any person whether arising on the conversion into shares of securities of any other description or otherwise.

41.—(1) If the company has issued any debentures during the financial year to which the accounts relate, the following information shall be given—

    (a) ...

    (b) the classes of debentures issued; and

    (c) as respects each class of debentures, the amount issued and the consideration received by the company for the issue.

(2) ...

(3) Where any of the company's debentures are held by a nominee of or trustee for the company, the nominal amount of the debentures and the amount at which they are stated in the accounting records kept by the company in accordance with section 221 of this Act shall be stated.

Fixed assets

42.—(1) In respect of each item which is or would but for paragraph 3(4)(b) be shown under the general item 'fixed assets' in the company's balance sheet the following information shall be given—

- (a) the appropriate amounts in respect of that item as at the date of the beginning of the financial year and as at the balance sheet date respectively;
- (b) the effect on any amount shown in the balance sheet in respect of that item of—
    - (i) any revision of the amount in respect of any assets included under that item made during that year on any basis mentioned in paragraph 31;
    - (ii) acquisitions during that year of any assets;
    - (iii) disposals during that year of any assets; and
    - (iv) any transfers of assets of the company to and from that item during that year.

(2) The reference in sub-paragraph (1)(a) to the appropriate amounts in respect of any item as at any date there mentioned is a reference to amounts representing the aggregate amounts determined, as at that date, in respect of assets falling to be included under that item on either of the following bases, that is to say—

- (a) on the basis of purchase price or production cost (determined in accordance with paragraphs 26 and 27); or
- (b) on any basis mentioned in paragraph 31,

(leaving out of account in either case any provisions for depreciation or diminution in value).

(3) In respect of each item within sub-paragraph (1)—

- (a) the cumulative amount of provisions for depreciation or diminution in value of assets included under that item as at each date mentioned in sub-paragraph (1)(a);
- (b) the amount of any such provisions made in respect of the financial year;
- (c) the amount of any adjustments made in respect of any such provisions during that year in consequence of the disposal of any assets; and
- (d) the amount of any other adjustments made in respect of any such provisions during that year;

shall also be stated.

43. Where any fixed assets of the company (other than listed investments) are included under any item shown in the company's balance sheet at an amount determined on any basis mentioned in paragraph 31, the following information shall be given—

- (a) the years (so far as they are known to the directors) in which the assets were severally valued and the several values; and
- (b) in the case of assets that have been valued during the financial year, the names of the persons who valued them or particulars of their qualifications for doing so and (whichever is stated) the bases of valuation used by them.

44. In relation to any amount which is or would but for paragraph 3(4)(b) be shown in respect of the item 'land and buildings' in the company's balance sheet there shall be stated—

  (a) how much of that amount is ascribable to land of freehold tenure and how much to land of leasehold tenure; and

  (b) how much of the amount ascribable to land of leasehold tenure is ascribable to land held on long lease and how much to land held on short lease.

Investments

45.—(1) In respect of the amount of each item which is or would but for paragraph 3(4)(b) be shown in the company's balance sheet under the general item 'investments'(whether as fixed assets or as current assets) there shall be stated—

  (a) how much of that amount is ascribable to listed investments; ...

  (b) ...

(2) Where the amount of any listed investments is stated for any item in accordance with sub-paragraph (1)(a), the following amounts shall also be stated—

  (a) the aggregate market value of those investments where it differs from the amount so stated; and

  (b) both the market value and the stock exchange value of any investments of which the former value is, for the purposes of the accounts, taken as being higher than the latter.

Reserves and provisions

46.—(1) Where any amount is transferred—

  (a) to or from any reserves; or

  (b) to any provisions for liabilities and charges; or

  (c) from any provision for liabilities and charges otherwise than for the purpose for which the provision was established;

and the reserves or provisions are or would but for paragraph 3(4)(b) be shown as separate items in the company's balance sheet, the information mentioned in the following sub-paragraph shall be given in respect of the aggregate of reserves or provisions included in the same item.

(2) That information is—

  (a) the amount of the reserves or provisions as at the date of the beginning of the financial year and as at the balance sheet date respectively;

  (b) any amounts transferred to or from the reserves or provisions during that year; and

  (c) the source and application respectively of any amounts so transferred.

(3) Particulars shall be given of each provision included in the item 'other provisions' in the company's balance sheet in any case where the amount of that provision is material.

Provision for taxation

47. The amount of any provision for deferred taxation shall be stated separately from the amount of any provision for other taxation.

Details of indebtedness

48.—(1) In respect of each item shown under 'creditors' in the company's balance sheet there shall be stated the aggregate of the following amounts, that is to say—

   (a)   the amount of any debts included under that item which are payable or repayable otherwise than by instalments and fall due for payment or repayment after the end of the period of five years beginning with the day next following the end of the financial year; and

   (b)   in the case of any debts so included which are payable or repayable by instalments, the amount of any instalments which fall due for payment after the end of that period.

(2) Subject to sub-paragraph (3), in relation to each debt falling to be taken into account under sub-paragraph (1), the terms of payment or repayment and the rate of any interest payable on the debt shall be stated.

(3) If the number of debts is such that, in the opinion of the directors, compliance with sub-paragraph (2) would result in a statement of excessive length, it shall be sufficient to give a general indication of the terms of payment or repayment and the rates of any interest payable on the debts.

(4) In respect of each item shown under 'creditors' in the company's balance sheet there shall be stated—

   (a)   the aggregate amount of any debts included under that item in respect of which any security has been given by the company; and

   (b)   an indication of the nature of the securities so given.

(5) References above in this paragraph to an item shown under 'creditors' in the company's balance sheet include references, where amounts falling due to creditors within one year and after more than one year are distinguished in the balance sheet—

   (a)   in a case within sub-paragraph (1), to an item shown under the latter of those categories; and

   (b)   in a case within sub-paragraph (4), to an item shown under either of those categories;

and references to items shown under 'creditors' include references to items which would but for paragraph 3(4)(b) be shown under that heading.

49. If any fixed cumulative dividends on the company's shares are in arrear, there shall be stated—

   (a)   the amount of the arrears; and

   (b)   the period for which the dividends or, if there is more than one class, each class of them are in arrear.

Guarantees and other financial commitments

50.—(1) Particulars shall be given of any charge on the assets of the company to secure the liabilities of any other person, including, where practicable, the amount secured.

(2) The following information shall be given with respect to any other contingent liability not provided for—

    (a) the amount or estimated amount of that liability;

    (b) its legal nature; and

    (c) whether any valuable security has been provided by the company in connection with that liability and if so, what.

(3) There shall be stated, where practicable—

    (a) the aggregate amount or estimated amount of contracts for capital expenditure, so far as not provided for;...

    (b) ...

(4) Particulars shall be given of—

    (a) any pension commitments included under any provision shown in the company's balance sheet; and

    (b) any such commitments for which no provision has been made;

and where any such commitment relates wholly or partly to pensions payable to past directors of the company separate particulars shall be given of that commitment so far as it relates to such pensions.

(5) Particulars shall also be given of any other financial commitments which—

    (a) have not been provided for; and

    (b) are relevant to assessing the company's state of affairs.

(6) ...

Miscellaneous matters

51.—(1) Particulars shall be given of any case where the purchase price or production cost of any asset is for the first time determined under paragraph 28.

(2) Where any outstanding loans made under the authority of section 153(4)(b),(bb) or (c) or section 155 of this Act (various cases of financial assistance by a company for purchase of its own shares) are included under any item shown in the company's balance sheet, the aggregate amount of those loans shall be disclosed for each item in question.

(3) ...

Information supplementing the profit and loss account

52. Paragraphs 53 to 57 require information which either supplements the information given with respect to any particular items shown in the profit and loss account or otherwise provides particulars of income or expenditure of the company or of circumstances affecting the items shown in the profit and loss account.

Separate statement of certain items of income and expenditure

53.—(1) Subject to the following provisions of this paragraph, each of the amounts mentioned below shall be stated.

(2) The amount of the interest on or any similar charges in respect of—

    (a) bank loans and overdrafts, ...; and

    (b) loans of any other kind made to the company.

This sub-paragraph does not apply to interest or charges on loans to the company from group undertakings, but, with that exception, it applies to interest or charges on all loans, whether made on the security of debentures or not.

(3)–(7) ...

Particulars of tax

54.—(1) ...

(2) Particulars shall be given of any special circumstances which affect liability in respect of taxation of profits, income or capital gains for the financial year or liability in respect of taxation of profits, income or capital gains for succeeding financial years.

(3) The following amounts shall be stated—

    (a) the amount of the charge for United Kingdom corporation tax;

    (b) if that amount would have been greater but for relief from double taxation, the amount which it would have been but for such relief;

    (c) the amount of the charge for United Kingdom income tax; and

    (d) the amount of the charge for taxation imposed outside the United Kingdom of profits, income and (so far as charged to revenue) capital gains.

These amounts shall be stated separately in respect of each of the amounts which is or would but for paragraph 3(4)(b) be shown under the following items in the profit and loss account, that is to say 'tax on profit or loss on ordinary activities' and 'tax on extraordinary profit or loss'.

Particulars of turnover

55.—(1) If in the course of the financial year the company has carried on business of two or more classes that, in the opinion of the directors, differ substantially from each other, there shall be stated in respect of each class (describing it)—

    (a) the amount of the turnover attributable to that class; ...

    (b) ...

(2) If in the course of the financial year the company has supplied markets that, in the opinion of the directors, differ substantially from each other, the amount of the turnover attributable to each such market shall also be stated.

    In this paragraph 'market' means a market delimited by geographical bounds.

(3) In analysing for the purposes of this paragraph the source (in terms of business or in terms of market) of turnover ..., the directors of the company shall have regard to the manner in which the company's activities are organised.

(4) For the purposes of this paragraph—

    (a) classes of business which, in the opinion of the directors, do not differ substantially from each other shall be treated as one class; and

    (b) markets which, in the opinion of the directors, do not differ substantially from each other shall be treated as one market;

and any amounts properly attributable to one class of business or (as the case may be) to one market which are not material may be included in the amount stated in respect of another.

(5) Where in the opinion of the directors the disclosure of any information required by this paragraph would be seriously prejudicial to the interests of the company, that information need not be disclosed, but the fact that any such information has not been disclosed must be stated.

Particulars of staff

56.—(1) The following information shall be given with respect to the employees of the company—

    (a) the average number of persons employed by the company in the financial year; and

    (b) the average number of persons so employed within each category of persons employed by the company.

(2) The average number required by sub-paragraph (1)(a) or (b) shall be determined by dividing the relevant annual number by the number of months in the financial year.

(3) The relevant annual number shall be determined by ascertaining for each month in the financial year—

    (a) for the purposes of sub-paragraph (1)(a), the number of persons employed under contracts of service by the company in that month (whether throughout the month or not);

    (b) for the purposes of sub-paragraph (1)(b), the number of persons in the category in question of persons so employed;

and, in either case, adding together all the monthly numbers.

(4) In respect of all persons employed by the company during the financial year who are taken into account in determining the relevant annual number for the purposes of sub-paragraph (1)(a) there shall also be stated the aggregate amounts respectively of—

    (a) wages and salaries paid or payable in respect of that year to those persons;

    (b) social security costs incurred by the company on their behalf; and

    (c) other pension costs so incurred;

save in so far as those amounts or any of them are stated in the profit and loss account.

(5) The categories of persons employed by the company by reference to which the number required to be disclosed by sub-paragraph (1)(b) is to be determined shall be such as the directors may select, having regard to the manner in which the company's activities are organised.

Miscellaneous matters

57.—(1) Where any amount relating to any preceding financial year is included in any item in the profit and loss account, the effect shall be stated.

(2) Particulars shall be given of any extraordinary income or charges arising in the financial year.

(3) The effect shall be stated of any transactions that are exceptional by virtue of size or incidence though they fall within the ordinary activities of the company.

[General]

58.—(1) Where sums originally denominated in foreign currencies have been brought into account under any items shown in the balance sheet or profit and loss account, the basis on which those sums have been translated into sterling shall be stated.

(2) Subject to the following sub-paragraph, in respect of every item stated in a note to the accounts the corresponding amount for the financial year immediately preceding that to which the accounts relate shall also be stated and where the corresponding amount is not comparable, it shall be adjusted and particulars of the adjustment and the reasons for it shall be given.

(3) Sub-paragraph (2) does not apply in relation to any amounts stated by virtue of any of the following provisions of this Act—

    (a) paragraph 13 of Schedule 4A (details of accounting treatment of acquisitions),

    (b) paragraphs 2, 8(3), 16, 21(1)(d), 22(4) and (5), 24(3) and (4) and 27(3) and (4) of Schedule 5 (shareholdings in other undertakings),

    (c) Parts II and III of Schedule 6 (loans and other dealings in favour of directors and others), and

    (d) paragraphs 42 and 46 above (fixed assets and reserves and provisions).

[Dormant companies acting as agents]

58A. Where the directors of a company take advantage of the exemption conferred by section 249AA, and the company has during the financial year in question acted as an agent for any person, the fact that it has so acted must be stated.

PART IV
SPECIAL PROVISIONS WHERE COMPANY IS A PARENT COMPANY OR SUBSIDIARY UNDERTAKING

Company's own accounts

59. ...

Guarantees and other financial commitments in favour of group undertakings

59A. Commitments within any of sub-paragraphs (1) to (5) of paragraph 50 (guarantees and other financial commitments) which are undertaken on behalf of or for the benefit of—

    (a) any parent undertaking or fellow subsidiary undertaking, or

    (b) any subsidiary undertaking of the company,

shall be stated separately from the other commitments within that sub-paragraph, and commitments within paragraph (a) shall also be stated separately from those within paragraph (b).

60.–70. ...

PART V
SPECIAL PROVISIONS WHERE THE COMPANY IS AN INVESTMENT COMPANY

71.—(1) Paragraph 34 does not apply to the amount of any profit or loss arising from a determination of the value of any investments of an investment company on any basis mentioned in paragraph 31(3).

(2) Any provisions made by virtue of paragraph 19(1) or (2) in the case of an investment company in respect of any fixed asset investments need not be charged to the company's profit and loss account provided they are either—

    (a) charged against any reserve account to which any amount excluded by sub-paragraph (1) from the requirements of paragraph 34 has been credited; or

    (b) shown as a separate item in the company's balance sheet under the sub-heading 'other reserves'.

(3) For the purposes of this paragraph, as it applies in relation to any company, 'fixed asset investment' means any asset falling to be included under any item shown in the company's balance sheet under the subdivision 'investments' under the general item 'fixed assets'.

72.—(1) Any distribution made by an investment company which reduces the amount of its net assets to less than the aggregate of its called-up share capital and undistributable reserves shall be disclosed in a note to the company's accounts.

(2) For purposes of this paragraph, a company's net assets are the aggregate of its assets less the aggregate of its liabilities (including any provision for liabilities or charges within paragraph 89); and 'undistributable reserves' has the meaning given by section 264(3) of this Act.

73. A company shall be treated as an investment company for the purposes of this Part of this Schedule in relation to any financial year of the company if—

    (a) during the whole of that year it was an investment company as defined by section 266 of this Act, and

    (b) it was not at any time during that year prohibited under section 265(4) of this Act (no distribution where capital profits have been distributed, etc) from making a distribution by virtue of that section.

74. ...

75. *((Part VI) Repealed by CA 1989, section 212, Schedule 24, as from 1 April 1990.)*

PART VII
INTERPRETATION OF SCHEDULE

76. The following paragraphs apply for the purposes of this Schedule and its interpretation.

Historical cost accounting rules

77.–81. ...

82. References to the historical cost accounting rules shall be read in accordance with paragraph 29.

Leases

83.—(1) 'Long lease' means a lease in the case of which the portion of the term for which it was granted remaining unexpired at the end of the financial year is not less than 50 years.

(2) 'Short lease' means a lease which is not a long lease.

(3) 'Lease' includes an agreement for a lease.

Listed investments

84. 'Listed investment' means an investment as respects which there has been granted a listing on a recognised investment exchange other than an overseas investment exchange within the meaning of the Financial Services Act 1986 or on any stock exchange of repute outside Great Britain.

Loans

85. A loan is treated as falling due for repayment, and an instalment of a loan is treated as falling due for payment, on the earliest date on which the lender could require repayment or (as the case may be) payment, if he exercised all options and rights available to him.

Materiality

86. Amounts which in the particular context of any provision of this Schedule are not material may be disregarded for the purposes of that provision.

Notes to the accounts

87. ...

Provisions

88.—(1) References to provisions for depreciation or diminution in value of assets are to any amount written off by way of providing for depreciation or diminution in value of assets.

(2) Any reference in the profit and loss account formats set out in Part I of this Schedule to the depreciation of, or amounts written off, assets of any description is to any provision for depreciation or diminution in value of assets of that description.

89. References to provisions for liabilities or charges are to any amount retained as reasonably necessary for the purpose of providing for any liability or loss which is either likely to be incurred, or certain to be incurred but uncertain as to amount or as to the date on which it will arise.

90.–92. ...

Scots land tenure

93. In the application of this Schedule to Scotland, 'land of freehold tenure' means land in respect of which the company *is the proprietor of the dominium utile or, in the case of land not held on feudal tenure,* is the owner; 'land of leasehold tenure' means land of which the company is the tenant under a lease; *and the reference to ground-rents, rates and other outgoings includes feu-duty and ground annual.*

Staff costs

94.—(1) 'Social security costs' means any contributions by the company to any state social security or pension scheme, fund or arrangement.

(2) 'Pension costs' includes any costs incurred by the company in respect of any pension scheme established for the purpose of providing pensions for persons currently or formerly employed by the company, any sums set aside for the future payment of pensions directly by the company to current or former employees and any pensions paid directly to such persons without having first been set aside.

(3) Any amount stated in respect of the item 'social security costs' or in respect of the item 'wages and salaries' in the company's profit and loss account shall be determined by reference to payments made or costs incurred in respect of all persons employed by the company during the financial year who are taken into account in determining the relevant annual number for the purposes of paragraph 56(1)(a).

95. ...

General note

This Schedule determines the form and content of individual accounts required by s 226 and offers a choice of one of two formats for the balance sheet and one of four formats for the profit and loss account. Balance sheet format 1 and profit and loss account formats 1 and 2 are commonly adopted. Once adopted, companies should adopt the same format in subsequent years unless there are special reasons to change: see para 2(1); and any item required to be shown may be shown in greater detail than required by the format adopted: para 3.

However, many companies (such as small companies, banking and insurance companies) are not subject to Sch 4 and may draw up their accounts in accordance with another Schedule (see the note to CA 1985, s 226(3)); and additional information may be required or, in exceptional cases, a departure from the Schedule permitted, in view of the overriding requirement that the accounts give a true and fair view, see notes to s 226(4)–(5).

Paragraph 36A   This provision was inserted by CA 1989 to require companies to draw attention to the extent to which they have departed from applicable accounting standards. See note to s 226(5), above.

Paragraph 58A   See note to s 249AA, above.

Paragraph 93   Words in italics repealed by the Abolition Feudal Tenure etc (Scotland) Act 2000, s 76(1), (2), Sch 12, Pt 1, para 46(1), (5), Sch B, Pt 1, as from a day to be appointed.

SCHEDULE 4A

FORM AND CONTENT OF GROUP ACCOUNTS

Section 227

General rules

1.—(1) Group accounts shall comply so far as practicable with the provisions of section 390A(3) (amount of auditors' remuneration) and Schedule 4 (form and content of company accounts) as if the undertakings included in the consolidation ('the group') were a single company.

(2) ...

(3) Where the parent company is treated as an investment company for the purposes of Part V of that Schedule (special provisions for investment companies) the group shall be similarly treated.

2.—(1) The consolidated balance sheet and profit and loss account shall incorporate in full the information contained in the individual accounts of the undertakings included in the consolidation, subject to the adjustments authorised or required by the following provisions of this Schedule and to such other adjustments (if any) as may be appropriate in accordance with generally accepted accounting principles or practice.

(2) If the financial year of a subsidiary undertaking included in the consolidation does not end with that of the parent company, the group accounts shall be made up—

    (a) from the accounts of the subsidiary undertaking for its financial year last ending before the end of the parent company's financial year, provided that year ended no more than three months before that of the parent company, or

    (b) from interim accounts prepared by the subsidiary undertaking as at the end of the parent company's financial year.

3.—(1) Where assets and liabilities to be included in the group accounts have been valued or otherwise determined by undertakings according to accounting rules differing from those used for the group accounts, the values or amounts shall be adjusted so as to accord with the rules used for the group accounts.

(2) If it appears to the directors of the parent company that there are special reasons for departing from sub-paragraph (1) they may do so, but particulars of any such departure, the reasons for it and its effect shall be given in a note to the accounts.

(3) The adjustments referred to in this paragraph need not be made if they are not material for the purpose of giving a true and fair view.

4. Any differences of accounting rules as between a parent company's individual accounts for a financial year and its group accounts shall be disclosed in a note to the latter accounts and the reasons for the difference given.

5. Amounts which in the particular context of any provision of this Schedule are not material may be disregarded for the purposes of that provision.

Elimination of group transactions

6.—(1) Debts and claims between undertakings included in the consolidation, and income and expenditure relating to transactions between such undertakings, shall be eliminated in preparing the group accounts.

(2) Where profits and losses resulting from transactions between undertakings included in the consolidation are included in the book value of assets, they shall be eliminated in preparing the group accounts.

(3) The elimination required by sub-paragraph (2) may be effected in proportion to the group's interest in the shares of the undertakings.

(4) Sub-paragraphs (1) and (2) need not be complied with if the amounts concerned are not material for the purpose of giving a true and fair view.

Acquisition and merger accounting

7.—(1) The following provisions apply where an undertaking becomes a subsidiary undertaking of the parent company.

(2) That event is referred to in those provisions as an 'acquisition', and references to the 'undertaking acquired' shall be construed accordingly.

8. An acquisition shall be accounted for by the acquisition method of accounting unless the conditions for accounting for it as a merger are met and the merger method of accounting is adopted.

9.—(1) The acquisition method of accounting is as follows.

(2) The identifiable assets and liabilities of the undertaking acquired shall be included in the consolidated balance sheet at their fair values as at the date of acquisition.

In this paragraph the 'identifiable' assets or liabilities of the undertaking acquired means the assets or liabilities which are capable of being disposed of or discharged separately, without disposing of a business of the undertaking.

(3) The income and expenditure of the undertaking acquired shall be brought into the group accounts only as from the date of the acquisition.

(4) There shall be set off against the acquisition cost of the interest in the shares of the undertaking held by the parent company and its subsidiary undertakings the interest of the parent company and its subsidiary undertakings in the adjusted capital and reserves of the undertaking acquired.

For this purpose—

> 'the acquisition cost' means the amount of any cash consideration and the fair value of any other consideration, together with such amount (if any) in respect of fees and other expenses of the acquisition as the company may determine, and

> 'the adjusted capital and reserves' of the undertaking acquired means its capital and reserves at the date of the acquisition after adjusting the identifiable assets and liabilities of the undertaking to fair values as at that date.

(5) The resulting amount if positive shall be treated as goodwill, and if negative as a negative consolidation difference.

10.—(1) The conditions for accounting for an acquisition as a merger are—

> (a) that at least 90 per cent of the nominal value of the relevant shares in the undertaking acquired is held by or on behalf of the parent company and its subsidiary undertakings,

> (b) that the proportion referred to in paragraph (a) was attained pursuant to an arrangement providing for the issue of equity shares by the parent company or one or more of its subsidiary undertakings,

> (c) that the fair value of any consideration other than the issue of equity shares given pursuant to the arrangement by the parent company and its subsidiary undertakings did not exceed 10 per cent of the nominal value of the equity shares issued, and

> (d) that adoption of the merger method of accounting accords with generally accepted accounting principles or practice.

(2) The reference in sub-paragraph (1)(a) to the 'relevant shares' in an undertaking acquired is to those carrying unrestricted rights to participate both in distributions and in the assets of the undertaking upon liquidation.

11.—(1) The merger method of accounting is as follows.

(2) The assets and liabilities of the undertaking acquired shall be brought into the group accounts at the figures at which they stand in the undertaking's accounts, subject to any adjustment authorised or required by this Schedule.

(3) The income and expenditure of the undertaking acquired shall be included in the group accounts for the entire financial year, including the period before the acquisition.

(4) The group accounts shall show corresponding amounts relating to the previous financial year as if the undertaking acquired had been included in the consolidation throughout that year.

(5) There shall be set off against the aggregate of—

> (a) the appropriate amount in respect of qualifying shares issued by the parent company or its subsidiary undertakings in consideration for the acquisition of shares in the undertaking acquired, and

> (b) the fair value of any other consideration for the acquisition of shares in the undertaking acquired, determined as at the date when those shares were acquired,

the nominal value of the issued share capital of the undertaking acquired held by the parent company and its subsidiary undertakings.

(6) The resulting amount shall be shown as an adjustment to the consolidated reserves.

(7) In sub-paragraph (5)(a) 'qualifying shares' means—

    (a) shares in relation to which section 131 (merger relief) applies, in respect of which the appropriate amount is the nominal value; or

    (b) shares in relation to which section 132 (relief in respect of group reconstructions) applies, in respect of which the appropriate amount is the nominal value together with any minimum premium value within the meaning of that section.

12.—(1) Where a group is acquired, paragraphs 9 to 11 apply with the following adaptations.

(2) References to shares of the undertaking acquired shall be construed as references to shares of the parent undertaking of the group.

(3) Other references to the undertaking acquired shall be construed as references to the group; and references to the assets and liabilities, income and expenditure and capital and reserves of the undertaking acquired shall be construed as references to the assets and liabilities, income and expenditure and capital and reserves of the group after making the set-offs and other adjustments required by this Schedule in the case of group accounts.

13.—(1) The following information with respect to acquisitions taking place in the financial year shall be given in a note to the accounts.

(2) There shall be stated—

    (a) the name of the undertaking acquired or, where a group was acquired, the name of the parent undertaking of that group, and

    (b) whether the acquisition has been accounted for by the acquisition or the merger method of accounting;

and in relation to an acquisition which significantly affects the figures shown in the group accounts, the following further information shall be given.

(3) The composition and fair value of the consideration for the acquisition given by the parent company and its subsidiary undertakings shall be stated.

(4) ...

(5) Where the acquisition method of accounting has been adopted, the book values immediately prior to the acquisition, and the fair values at the date of acquisition, of each class of assets and liabilities of the undertaking or group acquired shall be stated in tabular form, including a statement of the amount of any goodwill or negative consolidation difference arising on the acquisition, together with an explanation of any significant adjustments made.

(6) Where the merger method of accounting has been adopted, an explanation shall be given of any significant adjustments made in relation to the amounts of the assets and liabilities of the undertaking or group acquired, together with a statement of any resulting adjustment to the consolidated reserves (including the re-statement of opening consolidated reserves).

(7) In ascertaining for the purposes of sub-paragraph ..., (5) or (6) the profit or loss of a group, the book values and fair values of assets and liabilities of a

group or the amount of the assets and liabilities of a group, the set-offs and other adjustments required by this Schedule in the case of group accounts shall be made.

14.—(1) There shall also be stated in a note to the accounts the cumulative amount of goodwill resulting from acquisitions in that and earlier financial years which has been written off otherwise than in the consolidated profit and loss account for that or any earlier financial year.

(2) That figure shall be shown net of any goodwill attributable to subsidiary undertakings or businesses disposed of prior to the balance sheet date.

15. Where during the financial year there has been a disposal of an undertaking or group which significantly affects the figures shown in the group accounts, there shall be stated in a note to the accounts—

>   (a)   the name of that undertaking or, as the case may be, of the parent undertaking of that group, and

>   (b)   the extent to which the profit or loss shown in the group accounts is attributable to profit or loss of that undertaking or group.

16. The information required by paragraph 13, 14 or 15 above need not be disclosed with respect to an undertaking which—

>   (a)   is established under the law of a country outside the United Kingdom, or

>   (b)   carries on business outside the United Kingdom,

if in the opinion of the directors of the parent company the disclosure would be seriously prejudicial to the business of that undertaking or to the business of the parent company or any of its subsidiary undertakings and the Secretary of State agrees that the information should not be disclosed.

Minority interests

17.—(1) The formats set out in Schedule 4 have effect in relation to group accounts with the following additions.

(2)   In the Balance Sheet Formats a further item headed 'Minority interests' shall be added—

>   (a)   in Format 1, either after item J or at the end (after item K), and

>   (b)   in Format 2, under the general heading 'LIABILITIES', between items A and B;

and under that item shall be shown the amount of capital and reserves attributable to shares in subsidiary undertakings included in the consolidation held by or on behalf of persons other than the parent company and its subsidiary undertakings.

(3) In the Profit and Loss Account Formats a further item headed 'Minority interests' shall be added—

>   (a)   in Format 1, between items 14 and 15,

>   (b)   in Format 2, between items 16 and 17,

>   (c)   in Format 3, between items 7 and 8 in both sections A and B, and

>   (d)   in Format 4, between items 9 and 10 in both sections A and B;

and under that item shall be shown the amount of any profit or loss on ordinary activities attributable to shares in subsidiary undertakings included in the consolidation held by or on behalf of persons other than the parent company and its subsidiary undertakings.

(4) In the Profit and Loss Account Formats a further item headed 'Minority interests' shall be added—

    (a) in Format 1, between items 18 and 19,

    (b) in Format 2, between items 20 and 21,

    (c) in Format 3, between items 9 and 10 in section A and between items 8 and 9 in section B, and

    (d) in Format 4, between items 11 and 12 in section A and between items 10 and 11 in section B;

and under that item shall be shown the amount of any profit or loss on extraordinary activities attributable to shares in subsidiary undertakings included in the consolidation held by or on behalf of persons other than the parent company and its subsidiary undertakings.

(5) For the purposes of paragraph 3(3) and (4) of Schedule 4 (power to adapt or combine items)—

    (a) the additional item required by sub-paragraph (2) above shall be treated as one to which a letter is assigned, and

    (b) the additional items required by sub-paragraphs (3) and (4) above shall be treated as ones to which an Arabic number is assigned.

Interests in subsidiary undertakings excluded from consolidation

18. The interest of the group in subsidiary undertakings excluded from consolidation under section 229(4) (undertakings with activities different from those of undertakings included in the consolidation), and the amount of profit or loss attributable to such an interest, shall be shown in the consolidated balance sheet or, as the case may be, in the consolidated profit and loss account by the equity method of accounting (including dealing with any goodwill arising in accordance with paragraphs 17 to 19 and 21 of Schedule 4).

Joint ventures

19.—(1) Where an undertaking included in the consolidation manages another undertaking jointly with one or more undertakings not included in the consolidation, that other undertaking ('the joint venture') may, if it is not—

    (a) a body corporate, or

    (b) a subsidiary undertaking of the parent company,

be dealt with in the group accounts by the method of proportional consolidation.

(2) The provisions of this Schedule relating to the preparation of consolidated accounts apply, with any necessary modifications, to proportional consolidation under this paragraph.

Associated undertakings

20.—(1) An 'associated undertaking' means an undertaking in which an undertaking included in the consolidation has a participating interest and over whose operating and financial policy it exercises a significant influence, and which is not—

    (a) a subsidiary undertaking of the parent company, or

    (b) a joint venture dealt with in accordance with paragraph 19.

(2) Where an undertaking holds 20 per cent or more of the voting rights in another undertaking, it shall be presumed to exercise such an influence over it unless the contrary is shown.

(3) The voting rights in an undertaking means the rights conferred on shareholders in respect of their shares or, in the case of an undertaking not having a share capital, on members, to vote at general meetings of the undertaking on all, or substantially all, matters.

(4) The provisions of paragraphs 5 to 11 of Schedule 10A (rights to be taken into account and attribution of rights) apply in determining for the purposes of this paragraph whether an undertaking holds 20 per cent or more of the voting rights in another undertaking.

21.—(1) The formats set out in Schedule 4 have effect in relation to group accounts with the following modifications.

(2) In the Balance Sheet Formats the items headed 'Participating interests', that is—

    (a) in Format 1, item B.III.3, and

    (b) in Format 2, item B.III.3 under the heading 'ASSETS',

    shall be replaced by two items,'Interests in associated undertakings' and 'Other participating interests'.

(3) In the Profit and Loss Account Formats, the items headed 'Income from participating interests', that is—

    (a) in Format 1, item 8,

    (b) in Format 2, item 10,

    (c) in Format 3, item B.4, and

    (d) in Format 4, item B.6,

shall be replaced by two items, 'Income from interests in associated undertakings' and 'Income from other participating interests'.

22.—(1) The interest of an undertaking in an associated undertaking, and the amount of profit or loss attributable to such an interest, shall be shown by the equity method of accounting (including dealing with any goodwill arising in accordance with paragraphs 17 to 19 and 21 of Schedule 4).

(2) Where the associated undertaking is itself a parent undertaking, the net assets and profits or losses to be taken into account are those of the parent and its subsidiary undertakings (after making any consolidation adjustments).

(3) The equity method of accounting need not be applied if the amounts in question are not material for the purpose of giving a true and fair view.

General note

This Schedule determines the form and content of group accounts required by s 227; companies are exempt from the need to prepare group accounts in the circumstances set out in ss 228–229, 248. See notes to those provisions. In fact, para 1(1) requires that group accounts comply so far as practicable with the provisions of Sch 4 (form and content of company accounts) as if the undertakings included in the consolidation ('the group') were a single company. Additional information may be required or, in exceptional cases, a departure from the Schedule permitted, in view of the overriding requirement that the accounts give a true and fair view: see notes to s 227(5), (6), above.

SCHEDULE 5

DISCLOSURE OF INFORMATION: RELATED UNDERTAKINGS

Section 231

PART I
COMPANIES NOT REQUIRED TO PREPARE GROUP ACCOUNTS

Subsidiary undertakings

1.—(1) The following information shall be given where at the end of the financial year the company has subsidiary undertakings.

(2) The name of each subsidiary undertaking shall be stated.

(3) There shall be stated with respect to each subsidiary undertaking—
- (a) if it is incorporated outside Great Britain, the country in which it is incorporated;
- (b) ...
- (c) if it is unincorporated, the address of its principal place of business.

(4) The reason why the company is not required to prepare group accounts shall be stated.

(5) If the reason is that all the subsidiary undertakings of the company fall within the exclusions provided for in section 229, it shall be stated with respect to each subsidiary undertaking which of those exclusions applies.

Holdings in subsidiary undertakings

2.—(1) There shall be stated in relation to shares of each class held by the company in a subsidiary undertaking—
- (a) the identity of the class, and
- (b) the proportion of the nominal value of the shares of that class represented by those shares.

(2) The shares held by or on behalf of the company itself shall be distinguished from those attributed to the company which are held by or on behalf of a subsidiary undertaking.

Financial information about subsidiary undertakings

3.—(1) There shall be disclosed with respect to each subsidiary undertaking—
- (a) the aggregate amount of its capital and reserves as at the end of its relevant financial year, and
- (b) its profit or loss for that year.

(2) That information need not be given if the company is exempt by virtue of section 228 from the requirement to prepare group accounts (parent company included in accounts of larger group).

(2A) That information need not be given if the company's investment in the subsidiary undertaking is included in the company's accounts by way of the equity method of valuation.

(3) That information need not be given if—
- (a) the subsidiary undertaking is not required by any provision of this Act to deliver a copy of its balance sheet for its relevant financial year and does not otherwise publish that balance sheet in Great Britain or elsewhere, and
- (b) the company's holding is less than 50 per cent of the nominal value of the shares in the undertaking.

(4) Information otherwise required by this paragraph need not be given if it is not material.

(5) For the purposes of this paragraph the 'relevant financial year' of a subsidiary undertaking is—
- (a) if its financial year ends with that of the company, that year, and
- (b) if not, its financial year ending last before the end of the company's financial year.

Financial years of subsidiary undertakings

4. Where—
- (a) disclosure is made under paragraph 3(1) with respect to a subsidiary undertaking, and
- (b) that undertaking's financial year does not end with that of the company,

there shall be stated in relation to that undertaking the date on which its last financial year ended (last before the end of the company's financial year).

Further information about subsidiary undertakings

5. ...

Shares and debentures of company held by subsidiary undertakings

6.—(1) The number, description and amount of the shares in ... the company held by or on behalf of its subsidiary undertakings shall be disclosed.

(2) Sub-paragraph (1) does not apply in relation to shares ... in the case of which the subsidiary undertaking is concerned as personal representative or, subject as follows, as trustee.

(3) The exception for shares ... in relation to which the subsidiary undertaking is concerned as trustee does not apply if the company, or any subsidiary undertaking of the company, is beneficially interested under the trust, otherwise than by way of security only for the purposes of a transaction entered into by it in the ordinary course of a business which includes the lending of money.

(4) Schedule 2 to this Act has effect for the interpretation of the reference in sub-paragraph (3) to a beneficial interest under a trust.

Significant holdings in undertakings other than subsidiary undertakings

7.—(1) The information required by paragraphs 8 and 9 shall be given where at the end of the financial year the company has a significant holding in an undertaking which is not a subsidiary undertaking of the company.

(2) A holding is significant for this purpose if—

    (a) it amounts to 20 per cent or more of the nominal value of any class of shares in the undertaking, or

    (b) the amount of the holding (as stated or included in the company's accounts) exceeds one-fifth of the amount (as so stated) of the company's assets.

8.—(1) The name of the undertaking shall be stated.

(2) There shall be stated—

    (a) if the undertaking is incorporated outside Great Britain, the country in which it is incorporated;

    (b) ...

    (c) if it is unincorporated, the address of its principal place of business.

(3) There shall also be stated—

    (a) the identity of each class of shares in the undertaking held by the company, and

    (b) the proportion of the nominal value of the shares of that class represented by those shares.

9.—(1) ... there shall also be stated—

    (a) the aggregate amount of the capital and reserves of the undertaking as at the end of its relevant financial year, and

    (b) its profit or loss for that year.

(2) That information need not be given if—

    (a) the company is exempt by virtue of section 228 from the requirement to prepare group accounts (parent company included in accounts of larger group), and

    (b) the investment of the company in all undertakings in which it has such a holding as is mentioned in sub-paragraph (1) is shown, in aggregate, in the notes to the accounts by way of the equity method of valuation.

(3) That information need not be given in respect of an undertaking if—

    (a) the undertaking is not required by any provision of this Act to deliver a copy of its balance sheet for its relevant financial year and does not otherwise publish that balance sheet in Great Britain or elsewhere, and

    (b) the company's holding is less than 50 per cent of the nominal value of the shares in the undertaking.

(4) Information otherwise required by this paragraph need not be given if it is not material.

(5) For the purposes of this paragraph the 'relevant financial year' of an undertaking is—

    (a) if its financial year ends with that of the company, that year, and

    (b) if not, its financial year ending last before the end of the company's financial year.

Membership of certain undertakings

9A.—(1) The information required by this paragraph shall be given where at the end of the financial year the company is a member of a qualifying undertaking.

(2) There shall be stated—

    (a) the name and legal form of the undertaking, and

    (b) the address of the undertaking's registered office (whether in or outside Great Britain) or, if it does not have such an office, its head office (whether in or outside Great Britain).

(3) Where the undertaking is a qualifying partnership there shall also be stated either—

    (a) that a copy of the latest accounts of the undertaking has been or is to be appended to the copy of the company's accounts sent to the registrar under section 242 of this Act, or

    (b) the name of at least one body corporate (which may be the company) in whose group accounts the undertaking has been or is to be dealt with on a consolidated basis.

(4) Information otherwise required by sub-paragraph (2) above need not be given if it is not material.

(5) Information otherwise required by sub-paragraph (3)(b) above need not be given if the notes to the company's accounts disclose that advantage has been taken of the exemption conferred by regulation 7 of the Partnerships and Unlimited Companies (Accounts) Regulations 1993.

(6) In this paragraph—

    'dealt with on a consolidated basis', 'member', 'qualifying company' and 'qualifying partnership' have the same meanings as in the Partnerships and Unlimited Companies (Accounts) Regulations 1993;

    'qualifying undertaking' means a qualifying partnership or a qualifying company.

10. ...

Parent undertaking drawing up accounts for larger group

11.—(1) Where the company is a subsidiary undertaking, the following information shall be given with respect to the parent undertaking of—

    (a) the largest group of undertakings for which group accounts are drawn up and of which the company is a member, and

    (b) the smallest such group of undertakings.

(2) The name of the parent undertaking shall be stated.

(3) There shall be stated—

    (a) if the undertaking is incorporated outside Great Britain, the country in which it is incorporated;

    (b) ...

    (c) if it is unincorporated, the address of its principal place of business.

(4) If copies of the group accounts referred to in sub-paragraph (1) are available to the public, there shall also be stated the addresses from which copies of the accounts can be obtained.

Identification of ultimate parent company

12.—(1) Where the company is a subsidiary undertaking, the following information shall be given with respect to the company (if any) regarded by the directors as being the company's ultimate parent company.

(2) The name of that company shall be stated.

(3) If known to the directors, there shall be stated—

(a) if that company is incorporated outside Great Britain, the country in which it is incorporated;

(b) ...

(4) In this paragraph 'company' includes any body corporate.

Constructions of references to shares held by company

13.—(1) References in this Part of this Schedule to shares held by a company shall be construed as follows.

(2) For the purposes of paragraphs 2 to 4 (information about subsidiary undertakings)—

    (a) there shall be attributed to the company any shares held by a subsidiary undertaking, or by a person acting on behalf of the company or a subsidiary undertaking; but

    (b) there shall be treated as not held by the company any shares held on behalf of a person other than the company or a subsidiary undertaking.

(3) For the purposes of paragraphs 7 to 9 (information about undertakings other than subsidiary undertakings)—

    (a) there shall be attributed to the company shares held on its behalf by any person; but

    (b) there shall be treated as not held by a company shares held on behalf of a person other than the company.

(4) For the purposes of any of those provisions, shares held by way of security shall be treated as held by the person providing the security—

    (a) where apart from the right to exercise them for the purpose of preserving the value of the security, or of realising it, the rights attached to the shares are exercisable only in accordance with his instructions, and

    (b) where the shares are held in connection with the granting of loans as part of normal business activities and apart from the right to exercise them for the purpose of preserving the value of the security, or of realising it, the rights attached to the shares are exercisable only in his interests.

PART II
COMPANIES REQUIRED TO PREPARE GROUP ACCOUNTS

Introductory

14. In this Part of this Schedule 'the group' means the group consisting of the parent company and its subsidiary undertakings.

Subsidiary undertakings

15.—(1) The following information shall be given with respect to the undertakings which are subsidiary undertakings of the parent company at the end of the financial year.

(2) The name of each undertaking shall be stated.

(3) There shall be stated—

    (a) if the undertaking is incorporated outside Great Britain, the country in which it is incorporated;

    (b) ...

    (c) if it is unincorporated, the address of its principal place of business.

(4) It shall also be stated whether the subsidiary undertaking is included in the consolidation and, if it is not, the reasons for excluding it from consolidation shall be given.

(5) It shall be stated with respect to each subsidiary undertaking by virtue of which of the conditions specified in section 258(2) or (4) it is a subsidiary undertaking of its immediate parent undertaking.

That information need not be given if the relevant condition is that specified in subsection (2)(a) of that section (holding of a majority of the voting rights) and the immediate parent undertaking holds the same proportion of the shares in the undertaking as it holds voting rights.

Holdings in subsidiary undertakings

16.—(1) The following information shall be given with respect to the shares of a subsidiary undertaking held—

    (a) by the parent company, and

    (b) by the group;

and the information under paragraphs (a) and (b) shall (if different) be shown separately.

(2) There shall be stated—

    (a) the identity of each class of shares held, and

    (b) the proportion of the nominal value of the shares of that class represented by those shares.

Financial information about subsidiary undertakings not included in the consolidation

17.—(1) There shall be shown with respect to each subsidiary undertaking not included in the consolidation—

    (a) the aggregate amount of its capital and reserves as at the end of its relevant financial year, and

    (b) its profit or loss for that year.

(2) That information need not be given if the group's investment in the undertaking is included in the accounts by way of the equity method of valuation or if—

    (a) the undertaking is not required by any provision of this Act to deliver a copy of its balance sheet for its relevant financial year and does not otherwise publish that balance sheet in Great Britain or elsewhere, and

    (b) the holding of the group is less than 50 per cent of the nominal value of the shares in the undertaking.

(3) Information otherwise required by this paragraph need not be given if it is not material.

(4) For the purposes of this paragraph the 'relevant financial year' of a subsidiary undertaking is—

    (a) if its financial year ends with that of the company, that year, and

    (b) if not, its financial year ending last before the end of the company's financial year.

18. ...

19. ...

Shares and debentures of company held by subsidiary undertakings

20.—(1) The number, description and amount of the shares in ... the company held by or on behalf of its subsidiary undertakings shall be disclosed.

(2) Sub-paragraph (1) does not apply in relation to shares ... in the case of which the subsidiary undertaking is concerned as personal representative or, subject as follows, as trustee.

(3) The exception for shares ... in relation to which the subsidiary undertaking is concerned as trustee does not apply if the company or any of its subsidiary undertakings is beneficially interested under the trust, otherwise than by way of security only for the purposes of a transaction entered into by it in the ordinary course of a business which includes the lending of money.

(4) Schedule 2 to this Act has effect for the interpretation of the reference in sub-paragraph (3) to a beneficial interest under a trust.

Joint ventures

21.—(1) The following information shall be given where an undertaking is dealt with in the consolidated accounts by the method of proportional consolidation in accordance with paragraph 19 of Schedule 4A (joint ventures)—

(a) the name of the undertaking;

(b) the address of the principal place of business of the undertaking;

(c) the factors on which joint management of the undertaking is based; and

(d) the proportion of the capital of the undertaking held by undertakings included in the consolidation.

(2) Where the financial year of the undertaking did not end with that of the company, there shall be stated the date on which a financial year of the undertaking last ended before that date.

Associated undertakings

22.—(1) The following information shall be given where an undertaking included in the consolidation has an interest in an associated undertaking.

(2) The name of the associated undertaking shall be stated.

(3) There shall be stated—

(a) if the undertaking is incorporated outside Great Britain, the country in which it is incorporated;

(b) ...

(c) if it is unincorporated, the address of its principal place of business.

(4) The following information shall be given with respect to the shares of the undertaking held—

(a) by the parent company, and

(b) by the group;

and the information under paragraphs (a) and (b) shall be shown separately.

(5) There shall be stated—

(a) the identity of each class of shares held, and

(b) the proportion of the nominal value of the shares of that class represented by those shares.

(6) In this paragraph 'associated undertaking' has the meaning given by paragraph 20 of Schedule 4A; and the information required by this paragraph shall be given notwithstanding that paragraph 22(3) of that Schedule (materiality) applies in relation to the accounts themselves.

Other significant holdings of parent company or group

23.—(1) The information required by paragraphs 24 and 25 shall be given where at the end of the financial year the parent company has a significant holding in an undertaking which is not one of its subsidiary undertakings and does not fall within paragraph 21 (joint ventures) or paragraph 22 (associated undertakings).

(2) A holding is significant for this purpose if—

    (a) it amounts to 20 per cent or more of the nominal value of any class of shares in the undertaking, or

    (b) the amount of the holding (as stated or included in the company's individual accounts) exceeds one-fifth of the amount of its assets (as so stated).

24.—(1) The name of the undertaking shall be stated.

(2) There shall be stated—

    (a) if the undertaking is incorporated outside Great Britain, the country in which it is incorporated;

    (b) ...

    (c) if it is unincorporated, the address of its principal place of business.

(3) The following information shall be given with respect to the shares of the undertaking held by the parent company.

(4) There shall be stated—

    (a) the identity of each class of shares held, and

    (b) the proportion of the nominal value of the shares of that class represented by those shares.

25.—(1) ... there shall also be stated—

    (a) the aggregate amount of the capital and reserves of the undertaking as at the end of its relevant financial year, and

    (b) its profit or loss for that year.

(2) That information need not be given in respect of an undertaking if—

    (a) the undertaking is not required by any provision of this Act to deliver a copy of its balance sheet for its relevant financial year and does not otherwise publish that balance sheet in Great Britain or elsewhere, and

    (b) the company's holding is less than 50 per cent of the nominal value of the shares in the undertaking.

(3) Information otherwise required by this paragraph need not be given if it is not material.

(4) For the purposes of this paragraph the 'relevant financial year' of an undertaking is—

    (a) if its financial year ends with that of the company, that year, and

    (b) if not, its financial year ending last before the end of the company's financial year.

26.—(1) The information required by paragraphs 27 and 28 shall be given where at the end of the financial year the group has a significant holding in an undertaking which is not a subsidiary undertaking of the parent company and does not fall within paragraph 21 (joint ventures) or paragraph 22 (associated undertakings).

(2) A holding is significant for this purpose if—

    (a) it amounts to 20 per cent or more of the nominal value of any class of shares in the undertaking, or

(b) the amount of the holding (as stated or included in the group accounts) exceeds one-fifth of the amount of the group's assets (as so stated).

27.—(1) The name of the undertaking shall be stated.

(2) There shall be stated—

(a) if the undertaking is incorporated outside Great Britain, the country in which it is incorporated;

(b) ...

(c) if it is unincorporated, the address of its principal place of business.

(3) The following information shall be given with respect to the shares of the undertaking held by the group.

(4) There shall be stated—

(a) the identity of each class of shares held, and

(b) the proportion of the nominal value of the shares of that class represented by those shares.

28.—(1) ... there shall also be stated—

(a) the aggregate amount of the capital and reserves of the undertaking as at the end of its relevant financial year, and

(b) its profit or loss for that year.

(2) That information need not be given if—

(a) the undertaking is not required by any provision of this Act to deliver a copy of its balance sheet for its relevant financial year and does not otherwise publish that balance sheet in Great Britain or elsewhere, and

(b) the holding of the group is less than 50 per cent of the nominal value of the shares in the undertaking.

(3) Information otherwise required by this paragraph need not be given if it is not material.

(4) For the purposes of this paragraph the 'relevant financial year' of an outside undertaking is—

(a) if its financial year ends with that of the parent company, that year, and

(b) if not, its financial year ending last before the end of the parent company's financial year.

Parent company's or group's membership of certain undertakings

28A.—(1) The information required by this paragraph shall be given where at the end of the financial year the parent company or group is a member of a qualifying undertaking.

(2) There shall be stated—

(a) the name and legal form of the undertaking, and

    (b) the address of the undertaking's registered office (whether in or outside Great Britain) or, if it does not have such an office, its head office (whether in or outside Great Britain).

(3) Where the undertaking is a qualifying partnership there shall also be stated either—

    (a) that a copy of the latest accounts of the undertaking has been or is to be appended to the copy of the company's accounts sent to the registrar under section 242 of this Act, or

    (b) the name of at least one body corporate (which may be the company) in whose group accounts the undertaking has been or is to be dealt with on a consolidated basis.

(4) Information otherwise required by sub-paragraph (2) above need not be given if it is not material.

(5) Information otherwise required by sub-paragraph (3)(b) above need not be given if the notes to the company's accounts disclose that advantage has been taken of the exemption conferred by regulation 7 of the Partnerships and Unlimited Companies (Accounts) Regulations 1993.

(6) In this paragraph—

    'dealt with on a consolidated basis', 'member', 'qualifying company' and 'qualifying partnership' have the same meanings as in the Partnerships and Unlimited Companies (Accounts) Regulations 1993;

    'qualifying undertaking' means a qualifying partnership or a qualifying company.

29. ...

Parent undertaking drawing up accounts for larger group

30.—(1) Where the parent company is itself a subsidiary undertaking, the following information shall be given with respect to that parent undertaking of the company which heads—

    (a) the largest group of undertakings for which group accounts are drawn up and of which that company is a member, and

    (b) the smallest such group of undertakings.

(2) The name of the parent undertaking shall be stated.

(3) There shall be stated—

    (a) if the undertaking is incorporated outside Great Britain, the country in which it is incorporated;

    (b) ...

    (c) if it is unincorporated, the address of its principal place of business.

(4) If copies of the group accounts referred to in sub-paragraph (1) are available to the public, there shall also be stated the addresses from which copies of the accounts can be obtained.

Identification of ultimate parent company

31.—(1) Where the parent company is itself a subsidiary undertaking, the following information shall be given with respect to the company (if any) regarded by the directors as being that company's ultimate parent company.

(2) The name of that company shall be stated.

(3) If known to the directors, there shall be stated—

    (a) if that company is incorporated outside Great Britain, the country in which it is incorporated;

    (b) ...

(4) In this paragraph 'company' includes any body corporate.

Construction of references to shares held by parent company or group

32.—(1) References in this Part of this Schedule to shares held by the parent company or the group shall be construed as follows.

(2) For the purposes of paragraphs 16, 22(4) and (5) and 23 to 25 (information about holdings in subsidiary and other undertakings)—

    (a) there shall be attributed to the parent company shares held on its behalf by any person; but

    (b) there shall be treated as not held by the parent company shares held on behalf of a person other than the company.

(3) References to shares held by the group are to any shares held by or on behalf of the parent company or any of its subsidiary undertakings; but there shall be treated as not held by the group any shares held on behalf of a person other than the parent company or any of its subsidiary undertakings.

(4) Shares held by way of security shall be treated as held by the person providing the security—

    (a) where apart from the right to exercise them for the purpose of preserving the value of the security, or of realising it, the rights attached to the shares are exercisable only in accordance with his instructions, and

    (b) where the shares are held in connection with the granting of loans as part of normal business activities and apart from the right to exercise them for the purpose of preserving the value of the security, or of realising it, the rights attached to the shares are exercisable only in his interests.

General note

See s 231, which requires this information to be given in notes to the accounts subject to certain exemptions in s 231(3)–(6) (for example, where the information would be of excessive length). There are also exemptions for small companies within s 246, both as regards the information to be provided to the members and the information to be delivered to the registrar of companies: see s 246(3), (6). The provisions of the Schedule, so far as they apply to a banking company or the parent company of a banking group, have effect subject to Sch 9, Pt III: s 255B.

The intention is that a company should disclose the information needed to identify the extent and nature of the group of which the company is a part and information regarding other significant holdings which it has which do not give rise to a group relationship (joint ventures and associated undertakings etc).

There are differences as to the information to be provided, depending on whether the company has to prepare group accounts; as to the definition of parent and subsidiary undertakings, see s 258, Sch 10A; as to the requirement to prepare group accounts, see ss 227–229, 248.

The basic information which must be provided, regardless of whether group accounts have been prepared, includes:

(1) the name of each subsidiary undertaking and, if incorporated outside Great Britain, the place of incorporation (paras 1, 15);

(2) the percentage of each class of shares in the subsidiary held by the company (paras 2, 16);

(3) where the company is a subsidiary, the name of the company, if any, regarded by the directors as the ultimate parent company (paras 12, 31).

Where the company omits the information required because of excessive length, under s 231(5), note in particular the obligation which then arises under s 231(6).

SCHEDULE 6

DISCLOSURE OF INFORMATION: EMOLUMENTS AND OTHER BENEFITS OF DIRECTORS AND OTHERS

Section 232

PART I
CHAIRMAN'S AND DIRECTORS' EMOLUMENTS, PENSIONS AND COMPENSATION FOR LOSS OF OFFICE

Aggregate amount of directors' emoluments etc

1.—(1) Subject to sub-paragraph (2), the following shall be shown, namely—

    (a) the aggregate amount of emoluments paid to or receivable by directors in respect of qualifying services;

    (b) the aggregate of the amount of gains made by directors on the exercise of share options;

    (c) the aggregate of the following, namely—

        (i) the amount of money paid to or receivable by directors under long term incentive schemes in respect of qualifying services; and

        (ii) the net value of assets (other than money and share options) received or receivable by directors under such schemes in respect of such services;

    (d) the aggregate value of any company contributions paid, or treated as paid, to a pension scheme in respect of directors' qualifying services, being contributions by reference to which the rate or amount of any money purchase benefits that may become payable will be calculated; and

    (e) in the case of each of the following, namely—

        (i) money purchase schemes; and

        (ii) defined benefit schemes,

the number of directors (if any) to whom retirement benefits are accruing under such schemes in respect of qualifying services.

(2) In the case of a company which is not a listed company—

    (a) sub-paragraph (1) shall have effect as if paragraph (b) were omitted and, in paragraph (c)(ii), 'assets' did not include shares; and

    (b) the number of each of the following (if any) shall be shown, namely—

        (i) the directors who exercised share options; and

        (ii) the directors in respect of whose qualifying services shares were received or receivable under long term incentive schemes.

(3) In this paragraph 'emoluments' of a director—

    (a) includes salary, fees and bonuses, sums paid by way of expenses allowance (so far as they are chargeable to United Kingdom income tax) and, subject to paragraph (b), the estimated money value of any other benefits received by him otherwise than in cash; but

    (b) does not include any of the following, namely—

        (i) the value of any share options granted to him or the amount of any gains made on the exercise of any such options;

        (ii) any company contributions paid, or treated as paid, in respect of him under any pension scheme or any benefits to which he is entitled under any such scheme; or

        (iii) any money or other assets paid to or received or receivable by him under any long term incentive scheme.

(4) In this paragraph 'long term incentive scheme' means any agreement or arrangement under which money or other assets may become receivable by a director and which includes one or more qualifying conditions with respect to service or performance which cannot be fulfilled within a single financial year; and for this purpose the following shall be disregarded, namely—

    (a) bonuses the amount of which falls to be determined by reference to service or performance within a single financial year;

    (b) compensation for loss of office, payments for breach of contract and other termination payments; and

    (c) retirement benefits.

(5) In this paragraph—

    'amount', in relation to a gain made on the exercise of a share option, means the difference between—

        (a) the market price of the shares on the day on which the option was exercised; and

        (b) the price actually paid for the shares;

    'company contributions', in relation to a pension scheme and a director, means any payments (including insurance premiums) made, or treated as made, to the scheme in respect of the director by a person other than the director;

    'defined benefits' means retirement benefits payable under a pension scheme which are not money purchase benefits;

    'defined benefit scheme', in relation to a director, means a pension scheme which is not a money purchase scheme;

    'listed company' means a company—

(a) whose securities have been admitted to the Official List of the Stock Exchange in accordance with the provisions of Part IV of the Financial Services Act 1986; or

(b) dealings in whose securities are permitted on any exchange which is an approved exchange for the purposes of that Part;

'money purchase benefits', in relation to a director, means retirement benefits payable under a pension scheme the rate or amount of which is calculated by reference to payments made, or treated as made, by the director or by any other person in respect of the director and which are not average salary benefits;

'money purchase scheme', in relation to a director, means a pension scheme under which all of the benefits that may become payable to or in respect of the director are money purchase benefits;

'net value', in relation to any assets received or receivable by a director, means value after deducting any money paid or other value given by the director in respect of those assets;

'qualifying services', in relation to any person, means his services as a director of the company, and his services while director of the company—

(a) as director of any of its subsidiary undertakings; or

(b) otherwise in connection with the management of the affairs of the company or any of its subsidiary undertakings;

'shares' means shares (whether allotted or not) in the company, or any undertaking which is a group undertaking in relation to the company, and includes a share warrant as defined by section 188(1);

'share option' means a right to acquire shares;

'value', in relation to shares received or receivable by a director on any day, means the market price of the shares on that day.

(6) For the purposes of this paragraph—

(a) any information, other than the aggregate amount of gains made by directors on the exercise of share options, shall be treated as shown if it is capable of being readily ascertained from other information which is shown; and

(b) emoluments paid or receivable or share options granted in respect of a person's accepting office as a director shall be treated as emoluments paid or receivable or share options granted in respect of his services as a director.

(7) Where a pension scheme provides for any benefits that may become payable to or in respect of any director to be whichever are the greater of—

(a) money purchase benefits as determined by or under the scheme; and

(b) defined benefits as so determined,

the company may assume for the purposes of this paragraph that those benefits will be money purchase benefits, or defined benefits, according to whichever appears more likely at the end of the financial year.

(8) For the purpose of determining whether a pension scheme is a money purchase or defined benefit scheme, any death in service benefits provided for by the scheme shall be disregarded.

Details of highest paid director's emoluments etc

2.—(1) Where the aggregates shown under paragraph 1(1)(a), (b) and (c) total £200,000 or more, the following shall be shown, namely—

    (a) so much of the total of those aggregates as is attributable to the highest paid director; and

    (b) so much of the aggregate mentioned in paragraph 1(1)(d) as is so attributable.

(2) Where sub-paragraph (1) applies and the highest paid director has performed qualifying services during the financial year by reference to which the rate or amount of any defined benefits that may become payable will be calculated, there shall also be shown—

    (a) the amount at the end of the year of his accrued pension; and

    (b) where applicable, the amount at the end of the year of his accrued lump sum.

(3) Subject to sub-paragraph (4), where sub-paragraph (1) applies in the case of a company which is not a listed company, there shall also be shown—

    (a) whether the highest paid director exercised any share options; and

    (b) whether any shares were received or receivable by that director in respect of qualifying services under a long term incentive scheme.

(4) Where the highest paid director has not been involved in any of the transactions specified in sub-paragraph (3), that fact need not be stated.

(5) In this paragraph—

    'accrued pension' and 'accrued lump sum', in relation to any pension scheme and any director, mean respectively the amount of the annual pension, and the amount of the lump sum, which would be payable under the scheme on his attaining normal pension age if—

        (a) he had left the company's service at the end of the financial year;

        (b) there were no increase in the general level of prices in Great Britain during the period beginning with the end of that year and ending with his attaining that age;

        (c) no question arose of any commutation of the pension or inverse commutation of the lump sum; and

        (d) any amounts attributable to voluntary contributions paid by the director to the scheme, and any money purchase benefits which would be payable under the scheme, were disregarded;

    'the highest paid director' means the director to whom is attributable the greatest part of the total of the aggregates shown under paragraph 1(1)(a), (b) and (c);

    'normal pension age', in relation to any pension scheme and any director, means the age at which the director will first become entitled to receive a full pension on retirement of an amount determined without reduction to take account of its payment before a later age (but disregarding any entitlement to pension upon retirement in the event of illness, incapacity or redundancy).

(6) Sub-paragraphs (4) to (8) of paragraph 1 apply for the purposes of this paragraph as they apply for the purposes of that paragraph.

Excess retirement benefits of directors and past directors

7.—(1) Subject to sub-paragraph (2), there shall be shown the aggregate amount of—

    (a) so much of retirement benefits paid to or receivable by directors under pension schemes; and

    (b) so much of retirement benefits paid to or receivable by past directors under such schemes,

as (in each case) is in excess of the retirement benefits to which they were respectively entitled on the date on which the benefits first became payable or 31st March 1997, whichever is the later.

(2) Amounts paid or receivable under a pension scheme need not be included in the aggregate amount if—

    (a) the funding of the scheme was such that the amounts were or, as the case may be, could have been paid without recourse to additional contributions; and

    (b) amounts were paid to or receivable by all pensioner members of the scheme on the same basis;

and in this sub-paragraph 'pensioner member', in relation to a pension scheme, means any person who is entitled to the present payment of retirement benefits under the scheme.

(3) In this paragraph—

    (a) references to retirement benefits include benefits otherwise than in cash; and

    (b) in relation to so much of retirement benefits as consists of a benefit otherwise than in cash, references to their amount are to the estimated money value of the benefit;

and the nature of any such benefit shall also be disclosed.

Compensation to directors for loss of office

8.—(1) There shall be shown the aggregate amount of any compensation to directors or past directors in respect of loss of office.

(2) This amount includes compensation received or receivable by a director or past director for—

    (a) loss of office as director of the company, or

    (b) loss, while director of the company or on or in connection with his ceasing to be a director of it, of—

        (i) any other office in connection with the management of the company's affairs, or

(ii) any office as director or otherwise in connection with the management of the affairs of any subsidiary undertaking of the company;

...

(3) References to compensation include benefits otherwise than in cash; and in relation to such compensation references to its amount are to the estimated money value of the benefit.

The nature of any such compensation shall be disclosed

(4) In this paragraph, references to compensation for loss of office include the following, namely—

(a) compensation in consideration for, or in connection with, a person's retirement from office; and

(b) where such a retirement is occasioned by a breach of the person's contract with the company or with a subsidiary undertaking of the company—

(i) payments made by way of damages for the breach; or

(ii) payments made by way of settlement or compromise of any claim in respect of the breach.

(5) Sub-paragraph (6)(a) of paragraph 1 applies for the purposes of this paragraph as it applies for the purposes of that paragraph.

Sums paid to third parties in respect of directors' services

9.—(1) There shall be shown the aggregate amount of any consideration paid to or receivable by third parties for making available the services of any person—

(a) as a director of the company, or

(b) while director of the company—

(i) as director of any of its subsidiary undertakings, or

(ii) otherwise in connection with the management of the affairs of the company or any of its subsidiary undertakings.

(2) The reference to consideration includes benefits otherwise than in cash; and in relation to such consideration the reference to its amount is to the estimated money value of the benefit.

The nature of any such consideration shall be disclosed.

(3) The reference to third parties is to persons other than—

(a) the director himself or a person connected with him or body corporate controlled by him, and

(b) the company or any of its subsidiary undertakings.

Supplementary

10.—(1) The following applies with respect to the amounts to be shown under this Part of this Schedule.

(2) The amount in each case includes all relevant sums paid by or receivable from—

    (a) the company; and

    (b) the company's subsidiary undertakings; and

    (c) any other person,

except sums to be accounted for to the company or any of its subsidiary undertakings or, by virtue of sections 314 and 315 of this Act (duty of directors to make disclosure on company takeover; consequence of non-compliance), to past or present members of the company or any of its subsidiaries or any class of those members.

(3) ...

(4) References to amounts paid to or receivable by a person include amounts paid to or receivable by a person connected with him or a body corporate controlled by him (but not so as to require an amount to be counted twice).

11.—(1) The amounts to be shown for any financial year under this Part of this Schedule are the sums receivable in respect of that year (whenever paid) or, in the case of sums not receivable in respect of a period, the sums paid during that year.

(2) But where—

    (a) any sums are not shown in a note to the accounts for the relevant financial year on the ground that the person receiving them is liable to account for them as mentioned in paragraph 10(2), but the liability is thereafter wholly or partly released or is not enforced within a period of 2 years; or

    (b) any sums paid by way of expenses allowance are charged to United Kingdom income tax after the end of the relevant financial year,

those sums shall, to the extent to which the liability is released or not enforced or they are charged as mentioned above (as the case may be), be shown in a note to the first accounts in which it is practicable to show them and shall be distinguished from the amounts to be shown apart from this provision.

12. Where it is necessary to do so for the purpose of making any distinction required by the preceding paragraphs in an amount to be shown in compliance with this Part of this Schedule, the directors may apportion any payments between the matters in respect of which these have been paid or are receivable in such manner as they think appropriate.

Interpretation

13.—(1) The following applies for the interpretation of this Part of this Schedule.

(2) A reference to a subsidiary undertaking of the company—

    (a) in relation to a person who is or was, while a director of the company, a director also, by virtue of the company's nomination (direct or indirect) of any other undertaking, includes (subject to the following sub-paragraph) that undertaking, whether or not it is or was in fact a subsidiary undertaking of the company, and

(b) for the purposes of paragraphs 1 to 7 ... is to an undertaking which is a subsidiary undertaking at the time the services were rendered, and for the purposes of paragraph 8 to a subsidiary undertaking immediately before the loss of office as director.

(3) The following definitions apply—

(a) 'pension scheme' has the meaning assigned to 'retirement benefits scheme' by section 611 of the Income and Corporation Taxes Act 1988;

(b) 'retirement benefits' has the meaning assigned to relevant benefits by section 612(1) of that Act.

(4) References in this Part of this Schedule to a person being 'connected' with a director, and to a director 'controlling' a body corporate, shall be construed in accordance with section 346.

Supplementary

14. This Part of this Schedule requires information to be given only so far as it is contained in the company's books and papers or the company has the right to obtain it from the persons concerned.

PART II
LOANS, QUASI-LOANS AND OTHER DEALINGS IN FAVOUR OF DIRECTORS

15. The group accounts of a holding company, or if it is not required to prepare group accounts its individual accounts, shall contain the particulars required by this Schedule of—

(a) any transaction or arrangement of a kind described in section 330 entered into by the company or by a subsidiary of the company for a person who at any time during the financial year was a director of the company or its holding company, or was connected with such a director;

(b) an agreement by the company or by a subsidiary of the company to enter into any such transaction or arrangement for a person who was at any time during the financial year a director of the company or its holding company, or was connected with such a director; and

(c) any other transaction or arrangement with the company or a subsidiary of it in which a person who at any time during the financial year was a director of the company or its holding company had, directly or indirectly, a material interest.

16. The accounts prepared by a company other than a holding company shall contain the particulars required by this Schedule of—

(a) any transaction or arrangement of a kind described in section 330 entered into by the company for a person who at any time during the financial year was a director of it or of its holding company or was connected with such a director;

(b) an agreement by the company to enter into any such transaction or arrangement for a person who at any time during the financial year was a director of the company or its holding company or was connected with such a director; and

(c) any other transaction or arrangement with the company in which a person who at any time during the financial year was a director of the company or of its holding company had, directly or indirectly, a material interest.

17.—(1) For purposes of paragraphs 15(c) and 16(c), a transaction or arrangement between a company and a director of it or of its holding company, or a person connected with such a director, is to be treated (if it would not otherwise be so) as a transaction, arrangement or agreement in which that director is interested.

(2) An interest in such a transaction or arrangement is not 'material' for purposes of those sub-paragraphs if in the board's opinion it is not so; but this is without prejudice to the question whether or not such an interest is material in a case where the board have not considered the matter.

'The board' here means the directors of the company preparing the accounts, or a majority of those directors, but excluding in either case the director whose interest it is.

.....

18. Paragraphs 15 and 16 do not apply in relation to the following transactions, arrangements and agreements—

(a) a transaction, arrangement or agreement between one company and another in which a director of the former or of its subsidiary or holding company is interested only by virtue of his being a director of the latter;

(b) a contract of service between a company and one of its directors or a director of its holding company, or between a director of a company and any of that company's subsidiaries;

(c) a transaction, arrangement or agreement which was not entered into during the financial year and which did not subsist at any time during that year.

19. Paragraphs 15 and 16 apply whether or not—

(a) the transaction or arrangement was prohibited by section 330;

(b) the person for whom it was made was a director of the company or was connected with a director of it at the time it was made;

(c) in the case of a transaction or arrangement made by a company which at any time during a financial year is a subsidiary of another company, it was a subsidiary of that other company at the time the transaction or arrangement was made.

20. Neither paragraph 15(c) nor paragraph 16(c) applies in relation to any transaction or arrangement if—

(a) each party to the transaction or arrangement which is a member of the same group of companies (meaning a holding company and its subsidiaries) as the company entered into the transaction or arrangement in the ordinary course of business, and

(b) the terms of the transaction or arrangement are not less favourable to any such party than it would be reasonable to expect if the interest mentioned in that sub-paragraph had not been an interest of a person who was a director of the company or of its holding company.

21. Neither paragraph 15(c) nor paragraph 16(c) applies in relation to any transaction or arrangement if—

(a) the company is a member of a group of companies (meaning a holding company and its subsidiaries), and

(b) either the company is a wholly-owned subsidiary or no body corporate (other than the company or a subsidiary of the company) which is a member of the group of companies which includes the company's ultimate holding company was a party to the transaction or arrangement, and

(c) the director in question was at some time during the relevant period associated with the company, and

(d) the material interest of the director in question in the transaction or arrangement would not have arisen if he had not been associated with the company at any time during the relevant period.

The particulars required by this Part

22.—(1) Subject to the next paragraph, the particulars required by this Part are those of the principal terms of the transaction, arrangement or agreement.

(2) Without prejudice to the generality of sub-paragraph (1), the following particulars are required—

(a) a statement of the fact either that the transaction, arrangement or agreement was made or subsisted (as the case may be) during the financial year;

(b) the name of the person for whom it was made and, where that person is or was connected with a director of the company or of its holding company, the name of that director;

(c) in a case where paragraph 15(c) or 16(c) applies, the name of the director with the material interest and the nature of that interest;

(d) in the case of a loan or an agreement for a loan or an arrangement within section 330(6) or (7) of this Act relating to a loan—

(i) the amount of the liability of the person to whom the loan was or was agreed to be made, in respect of principal and interest, at the beginning and at the end of the financial year;

(ii) the maximum amount of that liability during that year;

(iii) the amount of any interest which, having fallen due, has not been paid; and

(iv) the amount of any provision (within the meaning of Schedule 4 to this Act) made in respect of any failure or anticipated failure by the borrower to repay the whole or part of the loan or to pay the whole or part of any interest on it;

(e) in the case of a guarantee or security or an arrangement within section 330(6) relating to a guarantee or security—

   (i) the amount for which the company (or its subsidiary) was liable under the guarantee or in respect of the security both at the beginning and at the end of the financial year;

   (ii) the maximum amount for which the company (or its subsidiary) may become so liable; and

   (iii) any amount paid and any liability incurred by the company (or its subsidiary) for the purpose of fulfilling the guarantee or discharging the security (including any loss incurred by reason of the enforcement of the guarantee or security); and

(f) in the case of any transaction, arrangement or agreement other than those mentioned in sub-paragraphs (d) and (e), the value of the transaction or arrangement or (as the case may be) the value of the transaction or arrangement to which the agreement relates.

23. In paragraph 22(2) above, sub-paragraphs (c) to (f) do not apply in the case of a loan or quasi-loan made or agreed to be made by a company to or for a body corporate which is either—

(a) a body corporate of which that company is a wholly-owned subsidiary, or

(b) a wholly-owned subsidiary of a body corporate of which that company is a wholly-owned subsidiary, or

(c) a wholly-owned subsidiary of that company,

if particulars of that loan, quasi-loan or agreement for it would not have been required to be included in that company's annual accounts if the first-mentioned body corporate had not been associated with a director of that company at any time during the relevant period.

Excluded transactions

24.—(1) In relation to a company's accounts for a financial year, compliance with this Part is not required in the case of transactions of a kind mentioned in the following sub-paragraph which are made by the company or a subsidiary of it for a person who at any time during that financial year was a director of the company or of its holding company, or was connected with such a director, if the aggregate of the values of each transaction, arrangement or agreement so made for that director or any person connected with him, less the amount (if any) by which the liabilities of the person for whom the transaction or arrangement was made has been reduced, did not at any time during the financial year exceed £5,000.

(2) The transactions in question are—

(a) credit transactions,

(b) guarantees provided or securities entered into in connection with credit transactions,

   (c) arrangements within subsection (6) or (7) of section 330 relating to credit transactions,

   (d) agreements to enter into credit transactions.

25. In relation to a company's accounts for a financial year, compliance with this Part is not required by virtue of paragraph 15(c) or 16(c) in the case of any transaction or arrangement with a company or any of its subsidiaries in which a director of the company or its holding company had, directly or indirectly, a material interest if—

   (a) the value of each transaction or arrangement within paragraph 15(c) or 16(c) (as the case may be) in which that director had (directly or indirectly) a material interest and which was made after the commencement of the financial year with the company or any of its subsidiaries, and

   (b) the value of each such transaction or arrangement which was made before the commencement of the financial year less the amount (if any) by which the liabilities of the person for whom the transaction or arrangement was made have been reduced,

did not at any time during the financial year exceed in the aggregate £1,000 or, if more, did not exceed £5,000 or 1 per cent of the value of the net assets of the company preparing the accounts in question as at the end of the financial year, whichever is the less.

For this purpose a company's net assets are the aggregate of its assets, less the aggregate of its liabilities ('liabilities' to include any provision for liabilities or charges within paragraph 89 of Schedule 4).

26. Section 345 of this Act (power of Secretary of State to alter sums by statutory instrument subject to negative resolution in Parliament) applies as if the money sums specified in paragraph 24 or 25 above were specified in Part X.

Interpretation

27.—(1) The following provisions of this Act apply for purposes of this Part of this Schedule—

   (a) section 331(2), ... and (7), as regards the meaning of 'guarantee', ... and 'credit transaction';

   (b) section 331(9), as to the interpretation of references to a transaction or arrangement being made 'for' a person;

   (c) section 340, in assigning values to transactions and arrangements, and

   (d) section 346, as to the interpretation of references to a person being 'connected with' a director of a company.

(2) In this Part of this Schedule 'director' includes a shadow director.

PART III
OTHER TRANSACTIONS, ARRANGEMENTS AND AGREEMENTS

28. This Part of this Schedule applies in relation to the following classes of transactions, arrangements and agreements—

    (a) loans, guarantees and securities relating to loans, arrangements of a kind described in subsection (6) or (7) of section 330 of this Act relating to loans and agreements to enter into any of the foregoing transactions and arrangements;

    (b) quasi-loans, guarantees and securities relating to quasi-loans, arrangements of a kind described in either of those subsections relating to quasi-loans and agreements to enter into any of the foregoing transactions and arrangements;

    (c) credit transactions, guarantees and securities relating to credit transactions, arrangements of a kind described in either of those subsections relating to credit transactions and agreements to enter into any of the foregoing transactions and arrangements.

29.—(1) To comply with this Part of this Schedule, the accounts must contain a statement, in relation to transactions, arrangements and agreements made by the company or a subsidiary of it for persons who at any time during the financial year were officers of the company (but not directors or shadow directors), of—

    (a) the aggregate amounts outstanding at the end of the financial year under transactions, arrangements and agreements within sub-paragraphs (a), (b) and (c) respectively of paragraph 28 above, and

    (b) the numbers of officers for whom the transactions, arrangements and agreements falling within each of those sub-paragraphs were made.

(2) This paragraph does not apply to transactions, arrangements and agreements made by the company or any of its subsidiaries for an officer of the company if the aggregate amount outstanding at the end of the financial year under the transactions, arrangements and agreements so made for that officer does not exceed £2,500.

(3) Section 345 of this Act (power of Secretary of State to alter money sums by statutory instrument subject to negative resolution in Parliament) applies as if the money sum specified above in this paragraph were specified in Part X.

30. The following provisions of this Act apply for purposes of this Part—

    (a) section 331(2),(3), ... and (7), as regards the meaning of 'guarantee', 'quasi-loan', ... and 'credit transaction', and

    (b) section 331(9), as to the interpretation of references to a transaction or arrangement being made 'for' a person;

and 'amount outstanding' means the amount of the outstanding liabilities of the person for whom the transaction, arrangement or agreement was made or, in the case of a guarantee or security, the amount guaranteed or secured.

General note

The complex provisions of this Schedule supplement Pt X which deals with the enforcement of fair dealing by directors. The information required by the Schedule must be given in a note to the company's accounts: s 232(1); and a duty is imposed on a director and officer to provide the information relating to himself required under Pt I: s 232(3); but no such obligation is imposed with respect to the information required under Pts II and III. The auditors must include the information required by this Schedule in their report, so far as they are reasonably able to do so, if it is not properly contained in the notes to the accounts: s 237(4). Approval of accounts which are not in compliance with the requirements of the Act is a criminal offence: see s 233(5).

Parts II and III of the Schedule are modified, in relation to banking companies and holding companies of credit institutions, by s 255B(2) and Sch 9, Pt IV.

Part I   Chairman's and directors' emoluments, pensions and compensation for loss of office   The legislation requires the disclosure of the aggregate of directors' emoluments and the emoluments of the highest paid director but it does not require the disclosure of individual directors' emoluments. Where a company qualifies as a small company in relation to a financial year, it may take advantage of the exemptions from disclosure as required by this Part to the extent specified in s 246(3), (6). Note also the exemption from disclosure in paras 10(2), 11(2).

Paragraph 1   Companies are required to show, separately, the aggregate amounts under the five headings below. Emoluments paid or receivable or share options granted in respect of a person's accepting office as a director are treated as emoluments paid or receivable or share options granted in respect of his services as a director (para 1(6)(b)), so ensuring that 'golden handshakes', in whatever form, must be disclosed.

However, a company need not show any information, other than that relating to share options, if it is readily ascertainable from other information which is shown in the accounts (para 1(6)(a)); that paragraph applies to disclosure under para 1 (aggregate amount of directors' emoluments); para 2 (details of highest paid director's emoluments); para 8 (compensation to directors for loss of office). It is not certain what is meant by 'readily ascertainable', but presumably it should require little effort on the part of the user of the company's accounts to extract the information in question.

(1)   **The aggregate amount of the directors' emoluments in respect of qualifying services.**

'Emoluments' is defined in para 1(3) in a non-exclusive manner so any other matter which would amount to an emolument must be disclosed although not specified here. Salary, fees and bonuses are included whether or not there is a contractual entitlement to the amount paid. The provision is designed to catch all other cash and non-cash payments and there may be difficulties in determining the estimated money value of a non-cash benefit such as accommodation or indemnity insurance. The appropriate value in each case is the market value of the benefit provided.

The proviso 'so far as those sums are chargeable to UK income tax' exempts from disclosure sums which the Inland Revenue would regard as pure reimbursement of direct expenses.

'Qualifying services' is defined in para 1(5) so as to require the inclusion (as emoluments of the director) of any sums payable for his services as a director of the company and his services, while a director, as a director of any subsidiary undertaking (as defined in para 13(2)) and, even more broadly still, to include payments otherwise in connection with the management of the affairs of the company or any of its subsidiary undertakings. Amounts paid to or received by a director are defined in para 10(4) to include payments to connected persons or a body corporate which is controlled by the director.

(2)　**The aggregate amount of gains made by directors on the exercise of share options.**

A 'share option' is defined in para 1(5) as a right to acquire 'shares' which in turn is defined in a way which would include an option scheme whether it involves existing shares purchased by the company or newly issued shares and covering any shares in the company or in an undertaking which is a group undertaking (defined s 259(5)).

It is the gain on the exercise of the option which must be disclosed so it is not necessary to consider whether the director has sold or retained the shares. Equally, any gain which arises when retained shares are subsequently sold is irrelevant. The amount of the gain is defined by para 1(5).

These provisions apply to listed companies as defined in para 1(5) and the reference to the Official List as maintained by the Stock Exchange is to be read as a reference to the Official List as maintained by the Financial Services Authority, by virtue of the Official Listing of Securities (Change of Competent Authority) Regulations 2000, SI 2000/968, reg 4.

Where the company is not a listed company, para 1(2)(b) applies. As it is difficult to identify the gains made on share options in unlisted companies, such companies are exempt from the requirement to show options gains by directors under para 1(1)(b) and the value of any shares receivable by them under long term incentive schemes. Instead, such companies must show the number of directors who exercised share options and who received or became entitled to shares under long term incentive schemes.

(3)　**The aggregate amount of money or other assets (other than share options) paid to or received by directors under long term incentive schemes in respect of qualifying services.**

'Long term incentive scheme' is defined in para 1(4). 'Qualifying services' is defined in para 1(5) so as to require the inclusion of any sums payable for the director's services for the company or for a subsidiary undertaking (as defined broadly in para 13(2)). Amounts paid to or received by a director are defined in para 10(4) to include payments to connected persons or a body corporate which is controlled by the director. 'Net value' in relation to assets received or receivable is defined in para 1(5).

(4)　**The aggregate value of company contributions paid in respect of directors to pension schemes where those contributions are in respect of money purchase benefits.**

'Company contributions' is defined in para 1(5) and covers payments made, or treated as made, as where the company takes a pension holiday.

(5)　**The number of directors who are accruing benefits under, respectively, money purchase pension schemes and defined benefit pension schemes.**

These terms are defined in para 1(5).

Paragraph 2   This paragraph (substituted for the original paras 2–6 by SI 1997/570, reg 3(1)) fixes the aggregated emoluments threshold (above which disclosure in respect of the highest paid director is required) at £200,000. The 'highest paid director' is defined in para 2(5) and it is irrelevant whether or not he is UK-based. In determining whether the threshold is passed, it is necessary to aggregate the amounts for emoluments and gains made from share options and long-term incentive schemes. Companies which fall below this threshold provide only the information required by para 1.

The information which must be disclosed where the company falls within this paragraph is specified in para 2(1), with additional disclosure possibly required under paras 2(2) and 2(3). The amount of the highest paid director's accrued retirement benefits, if he is a member of a defined benefit scheme, other than money-purchase benefits or benefits arising from voluntary contributions by that director (see definitions, paras 2(4), 1(5)), must be disclosed: para 2(2). Where the company is unlisted (see note to para 1 on definition of listed companies), the specified information concerning the exercise of share options is required: para 2(3). Golden handshakes must be disclosed: para 2(6), and see para (1)(6)(b). Information required by this paragraph need not be shown if it is readily ascertainable from other information which is shown in the accounts (para 1(6)(a), and see the note to para 1).

Paragraph 7   The effect of this paragraph is to require companies to disclose discretionary increases in the amount of retirement benefits paid to directors or past directors in excess of the amounts to which they were entitled when the benefits became payable unless those excess benefits were paid to all members of the relevant scheme on the same basis and were paid without recourse to additional contributions.

Paragraph 8   This paragraph requires disclosure of the aggregate amount of any compensation for loss of office which must include:

(1)   the sums specified in para 8(2) extending to other offices and loss of position within a subsidiary undertaking (as defined broadly in para 13(2));

(2)   the nature and estimated value of any non-cash benefit; and

(3)   payments in respect of retirement or breach of contract (cf s 316(3)).

Information required by this paragraph need not be shown if it is readily ascertainable from other information which is shown in the accounts (para 1(6)(a), and see the note to para 1).

Paragraph 9   This is an anti-avoidance provision and will apply, for example, where a director's services are provided by a consultancy company.

Paragraph 10   This anti-avoidance provision requires the inclusion of amounts paid whether by the company or by a subsidiary undertaking (as defined broadly in para 13(2)) or any other person; subject to an exception which is discussed in the note to para 11(2), below.

Subparagraph (4) likewise is a anti-avoidance measure, and requires that amounts paid to or receivable by a director include amounts paid to connected persons or a body corporate controlled by the director (defined s 346: para 13(4)); subject to appropriate safeguards against double counting.

Paragraph 11   Subparagraph (1) clarifies when information must be included in the accounts for a financial year. For example, where a contract provides for a bonus for the year 2000/01, then the information must be included in the accounts for that year, even if the bonus may not be actually paid until 2001/02. Likewise, some payments may not be referable to a given period, as where a bonus is payable according to share price performance, in which case disclosure is required in the year when payment is made.

Subparagraph (2) and para 10(2) exempts from disclosure as emoluments sums paid to the director which he is liable to repay to the company, but if the circumstances specified in para 11(2)(a) or (b) arise, the amounts involved must be disclosed and distinguished from other amounts received.

Paragraph 14   As to the definition of 'books and papers', see s 744.

Part II   Loans, quasi-loans and other dealings in favour of directors   This Part requires the disclosure (subject to exemptions) of details of various transactions in the notes to the accounts, whether those accounts are group accounts or individual accounts, as circumstances require; and the disclosure provisions are not restricted to public or relevant companies (as defined in s 331(6)). 'Holding company' is defined in s 736; 'director' in this Part includes shadow director: para 27(2). Part II is modified, in relation to banking companies and holding companies of credit institutions, by s 255B(2) and Sch 9, Pt IV.

The corresponding amount, if any, for the financial year immediately preceding need not be included in the notes to the accounts, see Sch 4, para 58(2), (3)(c); Sch 8, para 51(2), (3)(c); Sch 8A, para 9(2), (3)(c); Sch 9, para 47(2), (3)(d); Sch 9A, para 54(2), (3)(d).

Paragraphs 15(a), (b), 16(a), (b)   The disclosure required is of transactions etc entered into by the company or a subsidiary (defined s 736) and it must be for a director of the company, a director of the holding company, or a person connected with such a director (defined s 346: para 27(1)(d)). Whether a transaction is 'for' a person is determined by s 331(9): para 27(1)(b). The transaction or agreement must have been entered into during the financial year in question or have been subsisting during the financial year (see para 18(c)); and it must be of a kind described in s 330 (loans, quasi-loans, credit transactions, assignments etc and back-to-back arrangements: see note to s 330), subject to para 19. The transactions excluded from these disclosure requirement are those within paras 18 and 24.

Paragraphs 15(c), 16(c)   These provisions are the most difficult to apply, covering as they do 'any other transaction or arrangement' (ie not limited to transactions within s 330), subject to para 19. The transaction must with the company or a subsidiary; and it must be one in which a director of the company or of its holding company has an interest (defined to include the interests of connected persons: para 17(1)); and that interest must be a material interest (defined in para 17(2)). The transactions excluded from these disclosure requirement are those within paras 18, 20, 21, and 25.

Paragraph 17   This provision applies only to cases where disclosure is dictated by the director having a material interest. Subparagraph (1) is obscurely worded, but aggregates the interests of connected persons with the director's interests for the purposes of paras 15(c), 16(c) (ie when deciding whether a director has a material interest). Subparagraph (2) provides that the decision of the board as to whether an interest is material is a subjective one. If the board reaches its decision bona fide and it is not such that no reasonable board could have come to it, then the decision cannot be challenged.

No guidance is given as to the meaning of 'material' and this has proved a contentious issue. One view is that the matter must be relevant to the users of the accounts; another that the director's interest must be substantial in relation to the individual transaction. The Law Commission noted that the wording appears to require that materiality be measured by reference to the extent of a director's interest in the transaction and it recommended that the term should be defined as something which is material either in relation to the director or in relation to the company: *Company Directors: Regulating Conflicts of Interests and Formulating a Statement of Duties* (Law Com No 261, 1999, para 13.8).

The Department of Trade and Industry in an earlier consultation paper had suggested that an interest should be material unless disclosure would be of no significance to the company's members or creditors: DTI *Amendments to Schedule 6 of the Companies Act 1985: Disclosure by Companies of Dealings in favour of Directors, A Consultative Document,* 1991.

Paragraph 18   This provision excludes a number of transactions from the disclosure requirements of this Part, namely, transactions etc where the interest arises only by virtue of the director holding common directorships (para 18(a)); contracts of service (although contracts of service are available for inspection under s 318) (para 18(b)); and transactions which have not been entered into during the financial year nor subsist during the year (para 18(c)).

Paragraph 19   Disclosure under this Part is required whether or not the transaction is prohibited by s 330, so a transaction within the exceptions to that provision must still be disclosed, as must a transaction by a private company which is exempt from many of the prohibitions in s 330 (para 19(a)). Disclosure is required even if the person for whom the transaction was made was not a director or was not a connected person at the time of the transaction (para 19(b)). Likewise, if the company making the transaction or arrangement is a subsidiary at some point in the financial year, it does not matter that it was not a subsidiary at the time of the transaction or arrangement (para 19(c)).

Paragraph 20   The drafting of this provision has given rise to uncertainty. On one interpretation it is argued that the exemption from disclosure only applies if each party to the transaction is a member of the same group, although it seems that the intention behind the provision was that it should exempt any transaction in which a director has a material interest if the transaction was at arm's length in the ordinary course of business. While that may have been the intention, it does not appear to be reflected in the wording and therefore the exemption extends to intra-group transactions only. It can also be difficult to judge whether the criteria in para 20(b) have been met.

Paragraph 21   This obscurely worded provision is intended to exclude from disclosure under this Part any transaction between members of a group of companies which would have been required to be disclosed only because of a director being associated with the contracting companies, provided that there is no minority interest in the reporting company.

Paragraph 22   Subparagraph (1) imposes a general obligation to give the principal terms of the relevant transaction etc. Subparagraph (2) sets out the details what are required. The disclosure required with respect to quasi-loans and credit transactions is governed by sub-para 2(f), which requires the value of the transaction to be disclosed, and s 340 applies to ascertain that value: para 27(1)(c).

Paragraph 23   This provision eliminates the need to disclose some of the detailed information set out in para 22 above with respect to intra-group transactions in which a director is interested only by reason of his association with the holding company. The transaction must be made to or for a holding company, or a wholly-owned subsidiary of the holding company, or a wholly-owned subsidiary of the company entering into the transaction. This exemption applies only to loans and quasi-loans and it does not apply to guarantees or credit transactions.

Paragraph 24   There is no exemption under this provision for loans or quasi-loans. Credit transactions and guarantees are defined in s 331: para 27(1)(a).

Paragraph 25   This de minimis exemption applies to transactions in which a director has a material interest.

Part III   Other transactions, arrangements and agreements   This Part requires details of certain transactions between a company and its officers (defined in s 744, but subject to para 29(1) below) to be disclosed in the notes to the accounts. Part III of the Schedule is modified, in relation to banking companies and holding companies of credit institutions, by s 255B(2) and Sch 9, Pt IV.

Paragraph 28   This provision identifies the transactions of which disclosure is required and it is limited to transactions within the ambit of s 330 (see note to para 15(a), above). There is no requirement here, as there is in Pt II, of the disclosure of transactions outside of s 330 in which an officer has a material interest.

Paragraph 29   This provision requires the disclosure of transactions between a holding company and its subsidiaries with officers of the holding company but it does not require the disclosure of transactions between subsidiaries and their officers. There is a de minimis provision in sub-para (2). The information to be disclosed is much abbreviated when compared with that required by para 22 above.

SCHEDULE 7

MATTERS TO BE DEALT WITH IN DIRECTORS' REPORT

Section 234

PART I
MATTERS OF A GENERAL NATURE

Asset values

1.—(1) ...

(2) If, in the case of such of the fixed assets of the company or of any of its subsidiary undertakings as consist in interests in land, their market value (as at the end of the financial year) differs substantially from the amount at which they are included in the balance sheet, and the difference is, in the directors' opinion, of such significance as to require that the attention of members of the company or of holders of its debentures should be drawn to it, the report shall indicate the difference with such degree of precision as is practicable.

Directors' interests

2.—(1) The information required by paragraphs 2A and 2B shall be given in the directors' report, or by way of notes to the company's annual accounts, with respect to each person who at the end of the financial year was a director of the company.

(2) In those paragraphs—

    (a) 'the register' means the register of directors' interests kept by the company under section 325; and

    (b) references to a body corporate being in the same group as the company are to its being a subsidiary or holding company, or another subsidiary of a holding company, of the company.

2A.—(1) It shall be stated with respect to each director whether, according to the register, he was at the end of the financial year interested in shares in or debentures of the company or any other body corporate in the same group.

(2) If he was so interested, there shall be stated the number of shares in and amount of debentures of each body (specifying it) in which, according to the register, he was then interested.

(3) If a director was interested at the end of the financial year in shares in or debentures of the company or any other body corporate in the same group—

- (a) it shall also be stated whether, according to the register, he was at the beginning of the financial year (or, if he was not then a director, when he became one) interested in shares in or debentures of the company or any other body corporate in the same group, and

- (b) if he was so interested, there shall be stated the number of shares in and amount of debentures of each body (specifying it) in which, according to the register, he was then interested.

(4) In this paragraph references to an interest in shares or debentures have the same meaning as in section 324; and references to the interest of a director include any interest falling to be treated as his for the purposes of that section.

(5) The reference above to the time when a person became a director is, in the case of a person who became a director on more than one occasion, to the time when he first became a director.

2B.—(1) It shall be stated with respect to each director whether, according to the register, any right to subscribe for shares in or debentures of the company or another body corporate in the same group was during the financial year granted to, or exercised by, the director or a member of his immediate family.

(2) If any such right was granted to, or exercised by, any such person during the financial year, there shall be stated the number of shares in and amount of debentures of each body (specifying it) in respect of which, according to the register, the right was granted or exercised.

(3) A director's 'immediate family' means his or her spouse and infant children; and for this purpose 'children' includes step-children, and 'infant', in relation to Scotland, means pupil or minor.

(4) The reference above to a member of the director's immediate family does not include a person who is himself or herself a director of the company.

Political donations and expenditure

3.—(1) If—

- (a) the company (not being the wholly-owned subsidiary of a company incorporated in Great Britain) has in the financial year—

  - (i) made any donation to any registered party or to any other EU political organisation, or

  - (ii) incurred any EU political expenditure, and

(b) the amount of the donation or expenditure, or (as the case may be) the aggregate amount of all donations and expenditure falling within paragraph (a), exceeded £200,

the directors' report for the year shall contain the particulars specified in sub-paragraph (2).

(2) Those particulars are—

     (a) as respects donations falling within sub-paragraph (1)(a)(i)—

         (i) the name of each registered party or other organisation to whom any such donation has been made, and

         (ii) the total amount given to that party or organisation by way of such donations in the financial year; and

     (b) as respects expenditure falling within sub-paragraph (1)(a)(ii), the total amount incurred by way of such expenditure in the financial year.

(3) If—

     (a) at the end of the financial year the company has subsidiaries which have, in that year, made any donations or incurred any such expenditure as is mentioned in sub-paragraph (1)(a), and

     (b) it is not itself the wholly-owned subsidiary of a company incorporated in Great Britain,

the directors' report for the year is not, by virtue of sub-paragraph (1), required to contain the particulars specified in sub-paragraph (2); but, if the total amount of any such donations or expenditure (or both) made or incurred in that year by the company and the subsidiaries between them exceeds £200, the directors' report for the year shall contain those particulars in relation to each body by whom any such donation or expenditure has been made or incurred.

(4) Any expression used in this paragraph which is also used in Part XA of this Act has the same meaning as in that Part.

4.—(1) If the company (not being the wholly-owned subsidiary of a company incorporated in Great Britain) has in the financial year made any contribution to a non-EU political party, the directors' report for the year shall contain—

     (a) a statement of the amount of the contribution, or

     (b) (if it has made two or more such contributions in the year) a statement of the total amount of the contributions.

(2) If—

     (a) at the end of the financial year the company has subsidiaries which have, in that year, made any such contributions as are mentioned in sub-paragraph (1), and

     (b) it is not itself the wholly-owned subsidiary of a company incorporated in Great Britain,

the directors' report for the year is not, by virtue of sub-paragraph (1), required to contain any such statement as is there mentioned, but it shall instead contain a statement of the total amount of the contributions made in the year by the company and the subsidiaries between them.

(3) In this paragraph 'contribution', in relation to an organisation, means—

(a) any gift of money to the organisation (whether made directly or indirectly);

(b) any subscription or other fee paid for affiliation to, or membership of, the organisation; or

(c) any money spent (otherwise than by the organisation or a person acting on its behalf) in paying any expenses incurred directly or indirectly by the organisation.

(4) In this paragraph 'non-EU political party' means any political party which carries on, or proposes to carry on, its activities wholly outside the member States.

Charitable donations

5.—(1) If—

(a) the company (not being the wholly-owned subsidiary of a company incorporated in Great Britain) has in the financial year given money for charitable purposes, and

(b) the money given exceeded £200 in amount,

the directors' report for the year shall contain, in the case of each of the purposes for which money has been given, a statement of the amount of money given for that purpose.

(2) If—

(a) at the end of the financial year the company has subsidiaries which have, in that year, given money for charitable purposes, and

(b) it is not itself the wholly-owned subsidiary of a company incorporated in Great Britain,

sub-paragraph (1) does not apply to the company; but, if the amount given in that year for charitable purposes by the company and the subsidiaries between them exceeds £200, the directors' report for the year shall contain, in the case of each of the purposes for which money has been given by the company and the subsidiaries between them, a statement of the amount of money given for that purpose.

(3) Money given for charitable purposes to a person who, when it was given, was ordinarily resident outside the United Kingdom is to be left out of account for the purposes of this paragraph.

(4) For the purposes of this paragraph 'charitable purposes' means purposes which are exclusively charitable, and as respects Scotland 'charitable' is to be construed as if it were contained in the Income Tax Acts.

Miscellaneous

6. The directors' report shall contain—

(a) particulars of any important events affecting the company or any of its subsidiary undertakings which have occurred since the end of the financial year,

  (b) an indication of likely future developments in the business of the company and of its subsidiary undertakings, ...

  (c) an indication of the activities (if any) of the company and its subsidiary undertakings in the field of research and development, and

  (d) (unless the company is an unlimited company) an indication of the existence of branches (as defined in section 698(2)) of the company outside the United Kingdom.

PART II
DISCLOSURE REQUIRED BY COMPANY ACQUIRING ITS OWN SHARES, ETC

7. This Part of this Schedule applies where shares in a company—

  (a) are purchased by the company or are acquired by it by forfeiture or surrender in lieu of forfeiture, or in pursuance of section 143(3) of this Act (acquisition of own shares by company limited by shares), or

  (b) are acquired by another person in circumstances where paragraph (c) or (d) of section 146(1) applies (acquisition by company's nominee, or by another with company financial assistance, the company having a beneficial interest), or

  (c) are made subject to a lien or other charge taken (whether expressly or otherwise) by the company and permitted by section 150(2) or (4), or section 6(3) of the Consequential Provisions Act (exceptions from general rule against a company having a lien or charge on its own shares).

8. The directors' report with respect to a financial year shall state—

  (a) the number and nominal value of the shares so purchased, the aggregate amount of the consideration paid by the company for such shares and the reasons for their purchase;

  (b) the number and nominal value of the shares so acquired by the company, acquired by another person in such circumstances and so charged respectively during the financial year;

  (c) the maximum number and nominal value of shares which, having been so acquired by the company, acquired by another person in such circumstances or so charged (whether or not during that year) are held at any time by the company or that other person during that year;

  (d) the number and nominal value of the shares so acquired by the company, acquired by another person in such circumstances or so charged (whether or not during that year) which are disposed of by the company or that other person or cancelled by the company during that year;

  (e) where the number and nominal value of the shares of any particular description are stated in pursuance of any of the preceding sub-paragraphs, the percentage of the called-up share capital which shares of that description represent;

(f) where any of the shares have been so charged the amount of the charge in each case; and

(g) where any of the shares have been disposed of by the company or the person who acquired them in such circumstances for money or money's worth the amount or value of the consideration in each case.

PART III
DISCLOSURE CONCERNING EMPLOYMENT, ETC, OF DISABLED PERSONS

9.—(1) This Part of this Schedule applies to the directors' report where the average number of persons employed by the company in each week during the financial year exceeded 250.

(2) That average number is the quotient derived by dividing, by the number of weeks in the financial year, the number derived by ascertaining, in relation to each of those weeks, the number of persons who, under contracts of service, were employed in the week (whether throughout it or not) by the company, and adding up the numbers ascertained.

(3) The directors' report shall in that case contain a statement describing such policy as the company has applied during the financial year—

(a) for giving full and fair consideration to applications for employment by the company made by disabled persons, having regard to their particular aptitudes and abilities,

(b) for continuing the employment of, and for arranging appropriate training for, employees of the company who have become disabled persons during the period when they were employed by the company, and

(c) otherwise for the training, career development and promotion of disabled persons employed by the company.

(4) In this Part—

(a) 'employment' means employment other than employment to work wholly or mainly outside the United Kingdom, and 'employed' and 'employee' shall be construed accordingly; and

(b) 'disabled person' means the same as in the Disability Discrimination Act 1995.

10. *((Part IV) repealed, in relation to any financial year ending on or after 2 February 1996, by the Companies Act 1985 (Miscellaneous Accounting Amendments) Regulations 1996, SI 1996/189, regulations 14(4)(c), 16(1).)*

PART V
EMPLOYEE INVOLVEMENT

11.—(1) This Part of this Schedule applies to the directors' report where the average number of persons employed by the company in each week during the financial year exceeded 250.

(2) That average number is the quotient derived by dividing by the number of weeks in the financial year the number derived by ascertaining, in relation to each of those weeks, the number of persons who, under contracts of service, were employed in the week (whether throughout it or not) by the company, and adding up the numbers ascertained.

(3) The directors' report shall in that case contain a statement describing the action that has been taken during the financial year to introduce, maintain or develop arrangements aimed at—

    (a) providing employees systematically with information on matters of concern to them as employees,

    (b) consulting employees or their representatives on a regular basis so that the views of employees can be taken into account in making decisions which are likely to affect their interests,

    (c) encouraging the involvement of employees in the company's performance through an employees' share scheme or by some other means,

    (d) achieving a common awareness on the part of all employees of the financial and economic factors affecting the performance of the company.

(4) In sub-paragraph (3) 'employee' does not include a person employed to work wholly or mainly outside the United Kingdom; and for the purposes of sub-paragraph (2) no regard is to be had to such a person.

PART VI
POLICY AND PRACTICE ON PAYMENT OF CREDITORS

12.—(1) This Part of this Schedule applies to the directors' report for a financial year if—

    (a) the company was at any time within the year a public company, or

    (b) the company did not qualify as small or medium-sized in relation to the year by virtue of section 247 and was at any time within the year a member of a group of which the parent company was a public company.

(2) The report shall state, with respect to the next following financial year—

    (a) whether in respect of some or all of its suppliers it is the company's policy to follow any code or standard on payment practice and, if so, the name of the code or standard and the place where information about, and copies of, the code or standard can be obtained,

(b) whether in respect of some or all of its suppliers it is the company's policy—

    (i) to settle the terms of payment with those suppliers when agreeing the terms of each transaction,

    (ii) to ensure that those suppliers are made aware of the terms of payment, and

    (iii) to abide by the terms of payment,

(c) where the company's policy is not as mentioned in paragraph (a) or (b) in respect of some or all of its suppliers, what its policy is with respect to the payment of those suppliers;

and if the company's policy is different for different suppliers or classes of suppliers, the report shall identify the suppliers to which the different policies apply.

In this sub-paragraph references to the company's suppliers are references to persons who are or may become its suppliers.

(3) The report shall also state the number of days which bears to the number of days in the financial year the same proportion as X bears to Y where—

    X = the aggregate of the amounts which were owed to trade creditors at the end of the year; and

    Y = the aggregate of the amounts in which the company was invoiced by suppliers during the year.

(4) For the purposes of sub-paragraphs (2) and (3) a person is a supplier of the company at any time if—

(a) at that time, he is owed an amount in respect of goods or services supplied, and

(b) that amount would be included under the heading corresponding to item E.4 (trade creditors) in Format 1 if—

    (i) the company's accounts fell to be prepared as at that time,

    (ii) those accounts were prepared in accordance with Schedule 4, and

    (iii) that Format were adopted.

(5) For the purpose of sub-paragraph (3), the aggregate of the amounts which at the end of the financial year were owed to trade creditors shall be taken to be—

(a) where in the company's accounts Format 1 of the balance sheet formats set out in Part I of Schedule 4 is adopted, the amount shown under the heading corresponding to item E.4 (trade creditors) in that Format,

(b) where Format 2 is adopted, the amount which, under the heading corresponding to item C.4 (trade creditors) in that Format, is shown as falling due within one year, and

(c) where the company's accounts are prepared in accordance with Schedule 9 or 9A, the amount which would be shown under the heading corresponding to item E.4 (trade creditors) in Format 1 if the company's accounts were prepared in accordance with Schedule 4 and that Format were adopted.

General note

This Schedule, together with s 234, dictates the contents of the directors' report required of all companies; see note to s 234, above. Small companies within s 246 may omit from the report the information specified in s 246(4), subject to the requirement to state the fact of that exemption on the balance sheet: s 246(8). A small company need not deliver the directors' report to the registrar of companies, see s 246(5).

Paragraph 1(2)   No definition is provided as to what is a 'substantial' difference of such 'significance' that it should be brought to the attention of the members and the question will have be resolved by the directors and their professional advisers.

Paragraphs 2–2B   These provisions reflect the requirements of ss 324–329, Sch 13 on the disclosure of directors' interests in shares and debentures of the company and group companies. See notes to those sections. This information may be disclosed in the directors' report or contained in the notes to the accounts. The opening and closing position each year must be given so that readers can see clearly the pattern of a director's dealings over the year. The information required here does not extend to disclosure of the price at which the options were exercised, unlike s 325(3) and Sch 13, Pt III.

Paragraphs 3–5   These provisions were substituted by the Political Parties, Elections and Referendums Act 2000, s 140, as from 16 February 2001; Political Parties, Elections and Referendums Act 2000 (Commencement No 1 and Transitional Provisions) Order 2001, SI 2001/222; para 5, as to charitable donations, simply restates the existing position in a more accessible format. Paragraphs 3 and 4 provide respectively for donations and political expenditure in the United Kingdom and European Union and contributions to political parties in the rest of the world.

Paragraph 3   As to controls on donations and political expenditure of this nature, see ss 347A–347K, inserted by the Political Parties, Elections and Referendums Act 2000, s 139(1), Sch 19, as from 16 February 2001; Political Parties, Elections and Referendums Act 2000 (Commencement No 1 and Transitional Provisions) Order 2001, SI 2001/222. The definitions of 'registered party', 'EU political organisation', and 'EU political expenditure' are contained in s 347A; 'wholly-owned subsidiary' is defined in s 736.

Paragraph 4   This provision provides for a reduced level of disclosure with respect to contributions to non-European Union political parties, as defined broadly in para 4(4); only a single aggregate figure for the contributions is required (although there is no monetary threshold in this instance, unlike para 3) and there is no requirement to disclose the name of the recipient.

Paragraph 6   This requirement to consider post-balance sheet events provides the directors with the opportunity to bring the members up to date on the company's position; a 'subsidiary undertaking' is defined in s 258, Sch 10A: s 742; 'unlimited company' is defined in s 1(2)(c).

Paragraph 7   As to the purchase and redemption of a company's own shares, see ss 159–181.

Paragraph 8   As to the definition of 'called-up share capital', see s 737.

Paragraphs 9, 11, 12   In each case, the disclosure obligation is that of the reporting company and, if the accounts are group accounts, the disclosure must relate to the parent company and not to the group. As to the definition of 'employees' share scheme', see s 743.

SCHEDULE 8

FORM AND CONTENT OF ACCOUNTS PREPARED BY SMALL COMPANIES

Sections 246, 248A

Section A
General rules

1.—(1) Subject to the following provisions of this Schedule—

    (a) every balance sheet of a small company shall show the items listed in either of the balance sheet formats set out below in section B of this Part; and

    (b) every profit and loss account of a small company shall show the items listed in any one of the profit and loss account formats so set out;

in either case in the order and under the headings and sub-headings given in the format adopted.

(2) Sub-paragraph (1) above is not to be read as requiring the heading or sub-heading for any item to be distinguished by any letter or number assigned to that item in the format adopted.

2.—(1) Where in accordance with paragraph 1 a small company's balance sheet or profit and loss account for any financial year has been prepared by reference to one of the formats set out in section B below, the directors of the company shall adopt the same format in preparing the accounts for subsequent financial years of the company unless in their opinion there are special reasons for a change.

(2) Particulars of any change in the format adopted in preparing a small company's balance sheet or profit and loss account in accordance with paragraph 1 shall be disclosed, and the reasons for the change shall be explained, in a note to the accounts in which the new format is first adopted.

3.—(1) Any item required in accordance with paragraph 1 to be shown in a small company's balance sheet or profit and loss account may be shown in greater detail than required by the format adopted.

(2) A small company's balance sheet or profit and loss account may include an item representing or covering the amount of any asset or liability, income or expenditure not otherwise covered by any of the items listed in the format adopted, but the following shall not be treated as assets in any small company's balance sheet—

    (a) preliminary expenses;

    (b) expenses of and commission on any issue of shares or debentures; and

    (c) costs of research.

(3) In preparing a small company's balance sheet or profit and loss account the directors of the company shall adapt the arrangement and headings and sub-headings otherwise required by paragraph 1 in respect of items to which an Arabic number is assigned in the format adopted, in any case where the special nature of the company's business requires such adaptation.

(4) Items to which Arabic numbers are assigned in any of the formats set out in section B below may be combined in a small company's accounts for any financial year if either—

    (a) their individual amounts are not material to assessing the state of affairs or profit or loss of the company for that year; or

    (b) the combination facilitates that assessment;

but in a case within paragraph (b) the individual amounts of any items so combined shall be disclosed in a note to the accounts.

(5) Subject to paragraph 4(3) below, a heading or sub-heading corresponding to an item listed in the format adopted in preparing a small company's balance sheet or profit and loss account shall not be included if there is no amount to be shown for that item in respect of the financial year to which the balance sheet or profit and loss account relates.

(6) Every profit and loss account of a small company shall show the amount of the company's profit or loss on ordinary activities before taxation.

(7) Every profit and loss account of a small company shall show separately as additional items—

    (a) any amount set aside or proposed to be set aside to, or withdrawn or proposed to be withdrawn from, reserves;

    (b) the aggregate amount of any dividends paid and proposed.

4.—(1) In respect of every item shown in a small company's balance sheet or profit and loss account the corresponding amount for the financial year immediately preceding that to which the balance sheet or profit and loss account relates shall also be shown.

(2) Where that corresponding amount is not comparable with the amount to be shown for the item in question in respect of the financial year to which the balance sheet or profit and loss account relates, the former amount shall be adjusted and particulars of the adjustment and the reasons for it shall be disclosed in a note to the accounts.

(3) Paragraph 3(5) does not apply in any case where an amount can be shown for the item in question in respect of the financial year immediately preceding that to which the balance sheet or profit and loss account relates, and that amount shall be shown under the heading or sub-heading required by paragraph 1 for that item.

5. Amounts in respect of items representing assets or income may not be set off against amounts in respect of items representing liabilities or expenditure (as the case may be), or vice versa.

Section B
The required formats for accounts

Preliminary

6. References in this Part of this Schedule to the items listed in any of the formats set out below are to those items read together with any of the notes following the formats which apply to any of those items, and the requirement imposed by paragraph 1 to show the items listed in any such format in the order adopted in the format is subject to any provision in those notes for alternative positions for any particular items.

7. A number in brackets following any item in any of the formats set out below is a reference to the note of that number in the notes following the formats.

8. In the notes following the formats—

    (a)   the heading of each note gives the required heading or sub-heading for the item to which it applies and a reference to any letters and numbers assigned to that item in the formats set out below (taking a reference in the case of Format 2 of the balance sheet formats to the item listed under 'Assets' or under 'Liabilities' as the case may require); and

    (b)   references to a numbered format are to the balance sheet format or (as the case may require) to the profit and loss account format of that number set out below.

Balance Sheet Formats

Format 1

A.   Called up share capital not paid (*1*)

B.   Fixed assets

    I   Intangible assets

        1.   Goodwill (*2*)

          2.   Other intangible assets *(3)*

    II Tangible assets

          1.   Land and buildings

          2.   Plant and machinery etc

    III Investments

          1.   Shares in group undertakings and participating interests

          2.   Loans to group undertakings and undertakings in which the company has a participating interest

          3.   Other investments other than loans

          4.   Other investments *(4)*

C. Current assets

    I   Stocks

          1.   Stocks

          2.   Payments on account

    II Debtors *(5)*

          1.   Trade debtors

          2.   Amounts owed by group undertakings and undertakings in which the company has a participating interest

          3.   Other debtors

    III Investments

          1.   Shares in group undertakings

          2.   Other investments

    IV Cash at bank and in hand

D. Prepayments and accrued income *(6)*

E. Creditors: amounts falling due within one year

          1.   Bank loans and overdrafts

          2.   Trade creditors

          3.   Amounts owed to group undertakings and undertakings in which the company has a participating interest

          4.   Other creditors *(7)*

F. Net current assets (liabilities) *(8)*

G. Total assets less current liabilities

H. Creditors: amounts falling due after more than one year

          1.   Bank loans and overdrafts

          2.   Trade creditors

          3.   Amounts owed to group undertakings and undertakings in which the company has a participating interest

          4.   Other creditors *(7)*

I. Provisions for liabilities and charges

J. Accruals and deferred income *(7)*

K. Capital and reserves

    I   Called up share capital *(9)*

II　Share premium account

III　Revaluation reserve

IV　Other reserves

V　Profit and loss account

Balance Sheet Formats

Format 2

ASSETS

A.　Called up share capital not paid (*1*)

B.　Fixed assets

　　I　Intangible assets

　　　　1.　Goodwill (*2*)

　　　　2.　Other intangible assets (*3*)

　　II　Tangible assets

　　　　1.　Land and buildings

　　　　2.　Plant and machinery etc

　　III　Investments

　　　　1.　Shares in group undertakings and participating interests

　　　　2.　Loans to group undertakings and undertakings in which the company has a participating interest

　　　　3.　Other investments other than loans

　　　　4.　Other investments (*4*)

C.　Current assets

　　I　Stocks

　　　　1.　Stocks

　　　　2.　Payments on account

　　II　Debtors (*5*)

　　　　1.　Trade debtors

　　　　2.　Amounts owed by group undertakings and undertakings in which the company has a participating interest

　　　　3.　Other debtors

　　III　Investments

　　　　1.　Shares in group undertakings

　　　　2.　Other investments

　　IV　Cash at bank and in hand

D.　Prepayments and accrued income (*6*)

LIABILITIES

  A. Capital and reserves
    I   Called up share capital *(9)*
    II   Share premium account
    III Revaluation reserve
    IV   Other reserves
    V   Profit and loss account
  B. Provisions for liabilities and charges
  C. Creditors *(10)*
    1. Bank loans and overdrafts
    2. Trade creditors
    3. Amounts owed to group undertakings and undertakings in which the company has a participating interest
    4. Other creditors *(7)*
  D. Accruals and deferred income *(7)*

Notes on the balance sheet formats

(1) *Called up share capital not paid*

(Formats 1 and 2, items A and C.II.3.)

This item may either be shown at item A or included under item C.II.3 in Format 1 or 2.

(2) *Goodwill*

(Formats 1 and 2, item B.I.1.)

Amounts representing goodwill shall only be included to the extent that the goodwill was acquired for valuable consideration.

(3) *Other intangible assets*

(Formats 1 and 2, item B.I.2.)

Amounts in respect of concessions, patents, licences, trade marks and similar rights and assets shall only be included in a company's balance sheet under this item if either—

  (a) the assets were acquired for valuable consideration and are not required to be shown under goodwill; or
  (b) the assets in question were created by the company itself.

(4) *Others: Other investments*

(Formats 1 and 2, items B.III.4 and C.III.2.)

Where amounts in respect of own shares held are included under either of these items, the nominal value of such shares shall be shown separately.

(5) *Debtors*

(Formats 1 and 2, items C.II.1 to 3.)

The amount falling due after more than one year shall be shown separately for each item included under debtors unless the aggregate amount of debtors falling due after more than one year is disclosed in the notes to the accounts.

(6) *Prepayments and accrued income*

(Formats 1 and 2, item D.)

This item may alternatively be included under item C.II.3 in Format 1 or 2.

(7) *Other creditors*

(Format 1, items E.4, H.4 and J and Format 2, items C.4 and D.)

There shall be shown separately—

    (a) the amount of any convertible loans, and

    (b) the amount for creditors in respect of taxation and social security.

Payments received on account of orders shall be included in so far as they are not shown as deductions from stocks.

    In Format 1, accruals and deferred income may be shown under item J or included under item E.4 or H.4, or both (as the case may require). In Format 2, accruals and deferred income may be shown under item D or within item C.4 under Liabilities.

(8) *Net current assets (liabilities)*

(Format 1, item F.)

In determining the amount to be shown under this item any prepayments and accrued income shall be taken into account wherever shown.

(9) *Called up share capital*

(Format 1, item K.I and Format 2, item A.I.)

The amount of allotted share capital and the amount of called up share capital which has been paid up shall be shown separately.

(10) *Creditors*

(Format 2, items C.I to 4.)

Amounts falling due within one year and after one year shall be shown separately for each of these items and for the aggregate of all of these items unless the aggregate amount of creditors falling due within one year and the aggregate amount of creditors falling due after more than one year is disclosed in the notes to the accounts.

Profit and loss account formats

Format 1

(see note (14) below)

1. Turnover
2. Cost of sales *(11)*
3. Gross profit or loss
4. Distribution costs *(11)*
5. Administrative expenses *(11)*
6. Other operating income
7. Income from shares in group undertakings
8. Income from participating interests
9. Income from other fixed asset investments *(12)*
10. Other interest receivable and similar income *(12)*
11. Amounts written off investments
12. Interest payable and similar charges *(13)*
13. Tax on profit or loss on ordinary activities
14. Profit or loss on ordinary activities after taxation
15. Extraordinary income
16. Extraordinary charges
17. Extraordinary profit or loss
18. Tax on extraordinary profit or loss
19. Other taxes not shown under the above items
20. Profit or loss for the financial year

Profit and loss account formats

Format 2

1. Turnover
2. Change in stocks of finished goods and in work in progress
3. Own work capitalised
4. Other operating income
5. (a) Raw materials and consumables
    (b) Other external charges
6. Staff costs:
    (a) wages and salaries
    (b) social security costs
    (c) other pension costs

7. (a) Depreciation and other amounts written off tangible and intangible fixed assets

   (b) Exceptional amounts written off current assets

8. Other operating charges
9. Income from shares in group undertakings
10. Income from participating interests
11. Income from other fixed asset investments *(12)*
12. Other interest receivable and similar income *(12)*
13. Amounts written off investments
14. Interest payable and similar charges *(13)*
15. Tax on profit or loss on ordinary activities
16. Profit or loss on ordinary activities after taxation
17. Extraordinary income
18. Extraordinary charges
19. Extraordinary profit or loss
20. Tax on extraordinary profit or loss
21. Other taxes not shown under the above items
22. Profit or loss for the financial year

Profit and loss account formats

Format 3

(see note (14) below)

A. Charges
    1. Cost of sales *(11)*
    2. Distribution costs *(11)*
    3. Administrative expenses *(11)*
    4. Amounts written off investments
    5. Interest payable and similar charges *(13)*
    6. Tax on profit or loss on ordinary activities
    7. Profit or loss on ordinary activities after taxation
    8. Extraordinary charges
    9. Tax on extraordinary profit or loss
    10. Other taxes not shown under the above items
    11. Profit or loss for the financial year

B. Income
    1. Turnover
    2. Other operating income
    3. Income from shares in group undertakings

   4.   Income from participating interests

   5.   Income from other fixed asset investments (*12*)

   6.   Other interest receivable and similar income (*12*)

   7.   Profit or loss on ordinary activities after taxation

   8.   Extraordinary income

   9.   Profit or loss for the financial year

Profit and loss account formats

Format 4

A. Charges

   1.   Reduction in stocks of finished goods and in work in progress

   2.   (a)   Raw materials and consumables

          (b)   Other external charges

   3.   Staff costs:

          (a)   wages and salaries

          (b)   social security costs

          (c)   other pension costs

   4.   (a)   Depreciation and other amounts written off tangible and intangible fixed assets

          (b)   Exceptional amounts written off current assets

   5.   Other operating charges

   6.   Amounts written off investments

   7.   Interest payable and similar charges (*13*)

   8.   Tax on profit or loss on ordinary activities

   9.   Profit or loss on ordinary activities after taxation

  10. Extraordinary charges

  11. Tax on extraordinary profit or loss

  12. Other taxes not shown under the above items

  13. Profit or loss for the financial year

B. Income

   1.   Turnover

   2.   Increase in stocks of finished goods and in work in progress

   3.   Own work capitalised

   4.   Other operating income

   5.   Income from shares in group undertakings

   6.   Income from participating interests

   7.   Income from other fixed asset investments (*12*)

   8.   Other interest receivable and similar income (*12*)

9.   Profit or loss on ordinary activities after taxation

10. Extraordinary income

11. Profit or loss for the financial year

Notes on the profit and loss account formats

(11) *Cost of sales: distribution costs: administrative expenses*

(Format 1, items 2, 4 and 5 and Format 3, items A.1, 2 and 3.)

These items shall be stated after taking into account any necessary provisions for depreciation or diminution in value of assets.

(12) *Income from other fixed asset investments: other interest receivable and similar income*

(Format 1, items 9 and 10: Format 2, items 11 and 12: Format 3, items B.5 and 6: Format 4, items B.7 and 8.)

Income and interest derived from group undertakings shall be shown separately from income and interest derived from other sources.

(13) *Interest payable and similar charges*

(Format 1, item 12: Format 2, item 14: Format 3, item A.5: Format 4, item A.7.)

The amount payable to group undertakings shall be shown separately.

(14) *Formats 1 and 3*

The amount of any provisions for depreciation and diminution in value of tangible and intangible fixed assets falling to be shown under items 7(a) and A.4(a) respectively in Formats 2 and 4 shall be disclosed in a note to the accounts in any case where the profit and loss account is prepared by reference to Format 1 or Format 3.

PART II
ACCOUNTING PRINCIPLES AND RULES

Section A
Accounting principles

Preliminary

9. Subject to paragraph 15 below, the amounts to be included in respect of all items shown in a small company's accounts shall be determined in accordance with the principles set out in paragraphs 10 to 14.

Accounting principles

10. The company shall be presumed to be carrying on business as a going concern.

11. Accounting policies shall be applied consistently within the same accounts and from one financial year to the next.

12. The amount of any item shall be determined on a prudent basis, and in particular—

    (a) only profits realised at the balance sheet date shall be included in the profit and loss account; and

    (b) all liabilities and losses which have arisen or are likely to arise in respect of the financial year to which the accounts relate or a previous financial year shall be taken into account, including those which only become apparent between the balance sheet date and the date on which it is signed on behalf of the board of directors in pursuance of section 233 of this Act.

13. All income and charges relating to the financial year to which the accounts relate shall be taken into account, without regard to the date of receipt or payment.

14. In determining the aggregate amount of any item the amount of each individual asset or liability that falls to be taken into account shall be determined separately.

Departure from the accounting principles

15. If it appears to the directors of a small company that there are special reasons for departing from any of the principles stated above in preparing the company's accounts in respect of any financial year they may do so, but particulars of the departure, the reasons for it and its effect shall be given in a note to the accounts.

Section B
Historical cost accounting rules

Preliminary

16. Subject to section C of this Part of this Schedule, the amounts to be included in respect of all items shown in a small company's accounts shall be determined in accordance with the rules set out in paragraphs 17 to 28.

Fixed assets

General rules

17. Subject to any provision for depreciation or diminution in value made in accordance with paragraph 18 or 19 the amount to be included in respect of any fixed asset shall be its purchase price or production cost.

18. In the case of any fixed asset which has a limited useful economic life, the amount of—

    (a) its purchase price or production cost; or

    (b) where it is estimated that any such asset will have a residual value at the end of the period of its useful economic life, its purchase price or production cost less that estimated residual value;

shall be reduced by provisions for depreciation calculated to write off that amount systematically over the period of the asset's useful economic life.

19.—(1) Where a fixed asset investment of a description falling to be included under item B.III of either of the balance sheet formats set out in Part I of this Schedule has diminished in value provisions for diminution in value may be made in respect of it and the amount to be included in respect of it may be reduced accordingly; and any such provisions which are not shown in the profit and loss account shall be disclosed (either separately or in aggregate) in a note to the accounts.

(2) Provisions for diminution in value shall be made in respect of any fixed asset which has diminished in value if the reduction in its value is expected to be permanent (whether its useful economic life is limited or not), and the amount to be included in respect of it shall be reduced accordingly; and any such provisions which are not shown in the profit and loss account shall be disclosed (either separately or in aggregate) in a note to the accounts.

(3) Where the reasons for which any provision was made in accordance with sub-paragraph (1) or (2) have ceased to apply to any extent, that provision shall be written back to the extent that it is no longer necessary; and any amounts written back in accordance with this sub-paragraph which are not shown in the profit and loss account shall be disclosed (either separately or in aggregate) in a note to the accounts.

Rules for determining particular fixed asset items

20.—(1) Notwithstanding that an item in respect of 'development costs' is included under 'fixed assets' in the balance sheet formats set out in Part I of this Schedule, an amount may only be included in a small company's balance sheet in respect of development costs in special circumstances.

(2) If any amount is included in a small company's balance sheet in respect of development costs the following information shall be given in a note to the accounts—

    (a) the period over which the amount of those costs originally capitalised is being or is to be written off; and

    (b) the reasons for capitalising the development costs in question.

21.—(1) The application of paragraphs 17 to 19 in relation to goodwill (in any case where goodwill is treated as an asset) is subject to the following provisions of this paragraph.

(2) Subject to sub-paragraph (3) below, the amount of the consideration for any goodwill acquired by a small company shall be reduced by provisions for depreciation calculated to write off that amount systematically over a period chosen by the directors of the company.

(3) The period chosen shall not exceed the useful economic life of the goodwill in question.

(4) In any case where any goodwill acquired by a small company is shown or included as an asset in the company's balance sheet the period chosen for writing off the consideration for that goodwill and the reasons for choosing that period shall be disclosed in a note to the accounts.

Current assets

22. Subject to paragraph 23, the amount to be included in respect of any current asset shall be its purchase price or production cost.

23.—(1) If the net realisable value of any current asset is lower than its purchase price or production cost the amount to be included in respect of that asset shall be the net realisable value.

(2) Where the reasons for which any provision for diminution in value was made in accordance with sub-paragraph (1) have ceased to apply to any extent, that provision shall be written back to the extent that it is no longer necessary.

Miscellaneous and supplementary provisions

Excess of money owed over value received as an asset item

24.—(1) Where the amount repayable on any debt owed by a small company is greater than the value of the consideration received in the transaction giving rise to the debt, the amount of the difference may be treated as an asset.

(2) Where any such amount is so treated—

    (a)   it shall be written off by reasonable amounts each year and must be completely written off before repayment of the debt; and

    (b)   if the current amount is not shown as a separate item in the company's balance sheet it must be disclosed in a note to the accounts.

Assets included at a fixed amount

25.—(1) Subject to the following sub-paragraph, assets which fall to be included—

    (a)   amongst the fixed assets of a small company under the item 'tangible assets'; or

(b) amongst the current assets of a small company under the item 'raw materials and consumables';

may be included at a fixed quantity and value.

(2) Sub-paragraph (1) applies to assets of a kind which are constantly being replaced, where—

(a) their overall value is not material to assessing the company's state of affairs; and

(b) their quantity, value and composition are not subject to material variation.

Determination of purchase price or production cost

26.—(1) The purchase price of an asset shall be determined by adding to the actual price paid any expenses incidental to its acquisition.

(2) The production cost of an asset shall be determined by adding to the purchase price of the raw materials and consumables used the amount of the costs incurred by the company which are directly attributable to the production of that asset.

(3) In addition, there may be included in the production cost of an asset—

(a) a reasonable proportion of the costs incurred by the company which are only indirectly attributable to the production of that asset, but only to the extent that they relate to the period of production; and

(b) interest on capital borrowed to finance the production of that asset, to the extent that it accrues in respect of the period of production;

provided, however, in a case within paragraph (b) above, that the inclusion of the interest in determining the cost of that asset and the amount of the interest so included is disclosed in a note to the accounts.

(4) In the case of current assets distribution costs may not be included in production costs.

27.—(1) Subject to the qualification mentioned below, the purchase price or production cost of—

(a) any assets which fall to be included under any item shown in a small company's balance sheet under the general item 'stocks'; and

(b) any assets which are fungible assets (including investments);

may be determined by the application of any of the methods mentioned in sub-paragraph (2) below in relation to any such assets of the same class.
   The method chosen must be one which appears to the directors to be appropriate in the circumstances of the company.

(2) Those methods are—

(a) the method known as 'first in, first out' (FIFO);

(b) the method known as 'last in, first out' (LIFO);

(c) a weighted average price; and

(d) any other method similar to any of the methods mentioned above.

(3) For the purposes of this paragraph, assets of any description shall be regarded as fungible if assets of that description are substantially indistinguishable one from another.

28. Where there is no record of the purchase price or production cost of any asset of a small company or of any price, expenses or costs relevant for determining its purchase price or production cost in accordance with paragraph 26, or any such record cannot be obtained without unreasonable expense or delay, its purchase price or production cost shall be taken for the purposes of paragraphs 17 to 23 to be the value ascribed to it in the earliest available record of its value made on or after its acquisition or production by the company.

Section C
Alternative accounting rules

Preliminary

29.—(1) The rules set out in section B are referred to below in this Schedule as the historical cost accounting rules.

(2) Those rules, with the omission of paragraphs 16, 21 and 25 to 28, are referred to below in this Part of this Schedule as the depreciation rules; and references below in this Schedule to the historical cost accounting rules do not include the depreciation rules as they apply by virtue of paragraph 32.

30. Subject to paragraphs 32 to 34, the amounts to be included in respect of assets of any description mentioned in paragraph 31 may be determined on any basis so mentioned.

Alternative accounting rules

31.—(1) Intangible fixed assets, other than goodwill, may be included at their current cost.

(2) Tangible fixed assets may be included at a market value determined as at the date of their last valuation or at their current cost.

(3) Investments of any description falling to be included under item B III of either of the balance sheet formats set out in Part I of this Schedule may be included either—

    (a) at a market value determined as at the date of their last valuation; or

    (b) at a value determined on any basis which appears to the directors to be appropriate in the circumstances of the company;

but in the latter case particulars of the method of valuation adopted and of the reasons for adopting it shall be disclosed in a note to the accounts.

(4) Investments of any description falling to be included under item C III of either of the balance sheet formats set out in Part I of this Schedule may be included at their current cost.

(5) Stocks may be included at their current cost.

Application of the depreciation rules

32.—(1) Where the value of any asset of a small company is determined on any basis mentioned in paragraph 31, that value shall be, or (as the case may require) be the starting point for determining, the amount to be included in respect of that asset in the company's accounts, instead of its purchase price or production cost or any value previously so determined for that asset; and the depreciation rules shall apply accordingly in relation to any such asset with the substitution for any reference to its purchase price or production cost of a reference to the value most recently determined for that asset on any basis mentioned in paragraph 31.

(2) The amount of any provision for depreciation required in the case of any fixed asset by paragraph 18 or 19 as it applies by virtue of sub-paragraph (1) is referred to below in this paragraph as the adjusted amount, and the amount of any provision which would be required by that paragraph in the case of that asset according to the historical cost accounting rules is referred to as the historical cost amount.

(3) Where sub-paragraph (1) applies in the case of any fixed asset the amount of any provision for depreciation in respect of that asset—

    (a) included in any item shown in the profit and loss account in respect of amounts written off assets of the description in question; or

    (b) taken into account in stating any item so shown which is required by note (*11*) of the notes on the profit and loss account formats set out in Part I of this Schedule to be stated after taking into account any necessary provision for depreciation or diminution in value of assets included under it;

may be the historical cost amount instead of the adjusted amount, provided that the amount of any difference between the two is shown separately in the profit and loss account or in a note to the accounts.

Additional information to be provided in case of departure from historical cost accounting rules

33.—(1) This paragraph applies where the amounts to be included in respect of assets covered by any items shown in a small company's accounts have been determined on any basis mentioned in paragraph 31.

(2) The items affected and the basis of valuation adopted in determining the amounts of the assets in question in the case of each such item shall be disclosed in a note to the accounts.

(3) In the case of each balance sheet item affected (except stocks) either—

    (a) the comparable amounts determined according to the historical cost accounting rules; or

    (b) the differences between those amounts and the corresponding amounts actually shown in the balance sheet in respect of that item;

shall be shown separately in the balance sheet or in a note to the accounts.

(4) In sub-paragraph (3) above, references in relation to any item to the comparable amounts determined as there mentioned are references to—

    (a) the aggregate amount which would be required to be shown in respect of that item if the amounts to be included in respect of all the assets covered by that item were determined according to the historical cost accounting rules; and

    (b) the aggregate amount of the cumulative provisions for depreciation or diminution in value which would be permitted or required in determining those amounts according to those rules.

Revaluation reserve

34.—(1) With respect to any determination of the value of an asset of a small company on any basis mentioned in paragraph 31, the amount of any profit or loss arising from that determination (after allowing, where appropriate, for any provisions for depreciation or diminution in value made otherwise than by reference to the value so determined and any adjustments of any such provisions made in the light of that determination) shall be credited or (as the case may be) debited to a separate reserve ('the revaluation reserve').

(2) The amount of the revaluation reserve shall be shown in the company's balance sheet under a separate sub-heading in the position given for the item 'revaluation reserve' in Format 1 or 2 of the balance sheet formats set out in Part I of this Schedule, but need not be shown under that name.

(3) An amount may be transferred—

    (a) from the revaluation reserve—

        (i) to the profit and loss account, if the amount was previously charged to that account or represents realised profit, or

        (ii) on capitalisation,

    (b) to or from the revaluation reserve in respect of the taxation relating to any profit or loss credited or debited to the reserve;

and the revaluation reserve shall be reduced to the extent that the amounts transferred to it are no longer necessary for the purposes of the valuation method used.

(4) In sub-paragraph (3)(a)(ii) 'capitalisation', in relation to an amount standing to the credit of the revaluation reserve, means applying it in wholly or partly paying up unissued shares in the company to be allotted to members of the company as fully or partly paid shares.

(5) The revaluation reserve shall not be reduced except as mentioned in this paragraph.

(6) The treatment for taxation purposes of amounts credited or debited to the revaluation reserve shall be disclosed in a note to the accounts.

PART III
NOTES TO THE ACCOUNTS

Preliminary

35. Any information required in the case of any small company by the following provisions of this Part of this Schedule shall (if not given in the company's accounts) be given by way of a note to those accounts.

Disclosure of accounting policies

36. The accounting policies adopted by the company in determining the amounts to be included in respect of items shown in the balance sheet and in determining the profit or loss of the company shall be stated (including such policies with respect to the depreciation and diminution in value of assets).

Information supplementing the balance sheet

37. Paragraphs 38 to 47 require information which either supplements the information given with respect to any particular items shown in the balance sheet or is otherwise relevant to assessing the company's state of affairs in the light of the information so given.

Share capital and debentures

38.—(1) The following information shall be given with respect to the company's share capital—

    (a) the authorised share capital; and

    (b) where shares of more than one class have been allotted, the number and aggregate nominal value of shares of each class allotted.

(2) In the case of any part of the allotted share capital that consists of redeemable shares, the following information shall be given—

    (a) the earliest and latest dates on which the company has power to redeem those shares;

   (b) whether those shares must be redeemed in any event or are liable to be redeemed at the option of the company or of the shareholder; and

   (c) whether any (and, if so, what) premium is payable on redemption.

39. If the company has allotted any shares during the financial year, the following information shall be given—

   (a) the classes of shares allotted; and

   (b) as respects each class of shares, the number allotted, their aggregate nominal value, and the consideration received by the company for the allotment.

Fixed assets

40.—(1) In respect of each item which is or would but for paragraph 3(4)(b) be shown under the general item 'fixed assets' in the company's balance sheet the following information shall be given—

   (a) the appropriate amounts in respect of that item as at the date of the beginning of the financial year and as at the balance sheet date respectively;

   (b) the effect on any amount shown in the balance sheet in respect of that item of—

      (i) any revision of the amount in respect of any assets included under that item made during that year on any basis mentioned in paragraph 31;

      (ii) acquisitions during that year of any assets;

      (iii) disposals during that year of any assets; and

      (iv) any transfers of assets of the company to and from that item during that year.

(2) The reference in sub-paragraph (1)(a) to the appropriate amounts in respect of any item as at any date there mentioned is a reference to amounts representing the aggregate amounts determined, as at that date, in respect of assets falling to be included under that item on either of the following bases, that is to say—

   (a) on the basis of purchase price or production cost (determined in accordance with paragraphs 26 and 27); or

   (b) on any basis mentioned in paragraph 31,

(leaving out of account in either case any provisions for depreciation or diminution in value).

(3) In respect of each item within sub-paragraph (1)—

   (a) the cumulative amount of provisions for depreciation or diminution in value of assets included under that item as at each date mentioned in sub-paragraph (1)(a);

   (b) the amount of any such provisions made in respect of the financial year;

   (c) the amount of any adjustments made in respect of any such provisions during that year in consequence of the disposal of any assets; and

   (d) the amount of any other adjustments made in respect of any such provisions during that year;

shall also be stated.

41. Where any fixed assets of the company (other than listed investments) are included under any item shown in the company's balance sheet at an amount determined on any basis mentioned in paragraph 31, the following information shall be given—

    (a) the years (so far as they are known to the directors) in which the assets were severally valued and the several values; and

    (b) in the case of assets that have been valued during the financial year, the names of the persons who valued them or particulars of their qualifications for doing so and (whichever is stated) the bases of valuation used by them.

Investments

42.—(1) In respect of the amount of each item which is or would but for paragraph 3(4)(b) be shown in the company's balance sheet under the general item 'investments'(whether as fixed assets or as current assets) there shall be stated how much of that amount is ascribable to listed investments.

(2) Where the amount of any listed investments is stated for any item in accordance with sub-paragraph (1), the following amounts shall also be stated—

    (a) the aggregate market value of those investments where it differs from the amount so stated; and

    (b) both the market value and the stock exchange value of any investments of which the former value is, for the purposes of the accounts, taken as being higher than the latter.

Reserves and provisions

43.—(1) Where any amount is transferred—

    (a) to or from any reserves; or

    (b) to any provisions for liabilities and charges; or

    (c) from any provision for liabilities and charges otherwise than for the purpose for which the provision was established;

and the reserves or provisions are or would but for paragraph 3(4)(b) be shown as separate items in the company's balance sheet, the information mentioned in the following sub-paragraph shall be given in respect of the aggregate of reserves or provisions included in the same item.

(2) That information is—

    (a) the amount of the reserves or provisions as at the date of the beginning of the financial year and as at the balance sheet date respectively;

    (b) any amounts transferred to or from the reserves or provisions during that year; and

    (c) the source and application respectively of any amounts so transferred.

(3) Particulars shall be given of each provision included in the item 'other provisions' in the company's balance sheet in any case where the amount of that provision is material.

Details of indebtedness

44.—(1) For the aggregate of all items shown under 'creditors' in the company's balance sheet there shall be stated the aggregate of the following amounts, that is to say—

    (a) the amount of any debts included under 'creditors' which are payable or repayable otherwise than by instalments and fall due for payment or repayment after the end of the period of five years beginning with the day next following the end of the financial year; and

    (b) in the case of any debts so included which are payable or repayable by instalments, the amount of any instalments which fall due for payment after the end of that period.

(2) In respect of each item shown under 'creditors' in the company's balance sheet there shall be stated the aggregate amount of any debts included under that item in respect of which any security has been given by the company.

(3) References above in this paragraph to an item shown under 'creditors' in the company's balance sheet include references, where amounts falling due to creditors within one year and after more than one year are distinguished in the balance sheet—

    (a) in a case within sub-paragraph (1), to an item shown under the latter of those categories; and

    (b) in a case within sub-paragraph (2), to an item shown under either of those categories;

and references to items shown under 'creditors' include references to items which would but for paragraph 3(4)(b) be shown under that heading.

45. If any fixed cumulative dividends on the company's shares are in arrear, there shall be stated—

    (a) the amount of the arrears; and

    (b) the period for which the dividends or, if there is more than one class, each class of them are in arrear.

Guarantees and other financial commitments

46.—(1) Particulars shall be given of any charge on the assets of the company to secure the liabilities of any other person, including, where practicable, the amount secured.

(2) The following information shall be given with respect to any other contingent liability not provided for—

    (a) the amount or estimated amount of that liability;

    (b) its legal nature; and

    (c) whether any valuable security has been provided by the company in connection with that liability and if so, what.

(3) There shall be stated, where practicable, the aggregate amount or estimated amount of contracts for capital expenditure, so far as not provided for.

(4) Particulars shall be given of—

    (a) any pension commitments included under any provision shown in the company's balance sheet; and

(b) any such commitments for which no provision has been made;

and where any such commitment relates wholly or partly to pensions payable to past directors of the company separate particulars shall be given of that commitment so far as it relates to such pensions.

(5) Particulars shall also be given of any other financial commitments which—

(a) have not been provided for; and

(b) are relevant to assessing the company's state of affairs.

(6) Commitments within any of sub-paragraphs (1) to (5) which are undertaken on behalf of or for the benefit of—

(a) any parent undertaking or fellow subsidiary undertaking, or

(b) any subsidiary undertaking of the company,

shall be stated separately from the other commitments within that sub-paragraph, and commitments within paragraph (a) shall also be stated separately from those within paragraph (b).

Miscellaneous matters

47. Particulars shall be given of any case where the purchase price or production cost of any asset is for the first time determined under paragraph 28.

Information supplementing the profit and loss account

48. Paragraphs 49 and 50 require information which either supplements the information given with respect to any particular items shown in the profit and loss account or otherwise provides particulars of income or expenditure of the company or of circumstances affecting the items shown in the profit and loss account.

Particulars of turnover

49.—(1) If the company has supplied geographical markets outside the United Kingdom during the financial year in question, there shall be stated the percentage of its turnover that, in the opinion of the directors, is attributable to those markets.

(2) In analysing for the purposes of this paragraph the source of turnover, the directors of the company shall have regard to the manner in which the company's activities are organised.

Miscellaneous matters

50.—(1) Where any amount relating to any preceding financial year is included in any item in the profit and loss account, the effect shall be stated.

(2) Particulars shall be given of any extraordinary income or charges arising in the financial year.

(3) The effect shall be stated of any transactions that are exceptional by virtue of size or incidence though they fall within the ordinary activities of the company.

General

51.—(1) Where sums originally denominated in foreign currencies have been brought into account under any items shown in the balance sheet or profit and loss account, the basis on which those sums have been translated into sterling shall be stated.

(2) Subject to the following sub-paragraph, in respect of every item stated in a note to the accounts the corresponding amount for the financial year immediately preceding that to which the accounts relate shall also be stated and where the corresponding amount is not comparable, it shall be adjusted and particulars of the adjustment and the reasons for it shall be given.

(3) Sub-paragraph (2) does not apply in relation to any amounts stated by virtue of any of the following provisions of this Act—

    (a) paragraph 13 of Schedule 4A (details of accounting treatment of acquisitions),

    (b) paragraphs 2, 8(3), 16, 21(1)(d), 22(4) and (5), 24(3) and (4) and 27(3) and (4) of Schedule 5 (shareholdings in other undertakings),

    (c) Parts II and III of Schedule 6 (loans and other dealings in favour of directors and others), and

    (d) paragraphs 40 and 43 above (fixed assets and reserves and provisions).

[Dormant companies acting as agents]

51A. Where the directors of a company take advantage of the exemption conferred by section 249AA, and the company has during the financial year in question acted as an agent for any person, the fact that it has so acted must be stated.

PART IV
INTERPRETATION OF SCHEDULE

52. The following paragraphs apply for the purposes of this Schedule and its interpretation.

Historical cost accounting rules

53. References to the historical cost accounting rules shall be read in accordance with paragraph 29.

Listed investments

54. 'Listed investment' means an investment as respects which there has been granted a listing on a recognised investment exchange other than an overseas investment exchange within the meaning of the Financial Services Act 1986 or on any stock exchange of repute outside Great Britain.

Loans

55. A loan is treated as falling due for repayment, and an instalment of a loan is treated as falling due for payment, on the earliest date on which the lender could require repayment or (as the case may be) payment, if he exercised all options and rights available to him.

Materiality

56. Amounts which in the particular context of any provision of this Schedule are not material may be disregarded for the purposes of that provision.

Provisions

57.—(1) References to provisions for depreciation or diminution in value of assets are to any amount written off by way of providing for depreciation or diminution in value of assets.

(2) Any reference in the profit and loss account formats set out in Part I of this Schedule to the depreciation of, or amounts written off, assets of any description is to any provision for depreciation or diminution in value of assets of that description.

58. References to provisions for liabilities or charges are to any amount retained as reasonably necessary for the purpose of providing for any liability or loss which is either likely to be incurred, or certain to be incurred but uncertain as to amount or as to the date on which it will arise.

Staff costs

59.—(1) 'Social security costs' means any contributions by the company to any state social security or pension scheme, fund or arrangement.

(2) 'Pension costs' includes any costs incurred by the company in respect of any pension scheme established for the purpose of providing pensions for persons currently or formerly employed by the company, any sums set aside for the future payment of pensions directly by the company to current or former employees and any pensions paid directly to such persons without having first been set aside.

(3) Any amount stated in respect of the item 'social security costs' or in respect of the item 'wages and salaries' in the company's profit and loss account shall be determined by reference to payments made or costs incurred in respect of all persons employed by the company during the financial year under contracts of service.

General note

Companies generally prepare their individual accounts in accordance with Sch 4: s 226(3); but small companies are permitted to prepare their accounts instead in accordance with Sch 8, or part of Sch 8 and part of Sch 4, or, of course, they may be prepared in accordance with Sch 4: s 246); likewise, a small company preparing group accounts may do so in accordance with this Schedule: see s 248A.

Schedule 8 was inserted in 1997 (see the Companies Act 1985 (Accounts of Small and Medium-sized Companies and Minor Accounting Amendments) Regulations 1997, SI 1997/220) in order to give small companies a stand-alone Schedule setting out the requirements regarding their accounts. The essential difference from Sch 4 is that many matters are aggregated in the balance sheet and profit and loss account or omitted entirely so there is limited disclosure, hence the description of accounts prepared in accordance with this Schedule as 'short form' accounts.

There is no equivalent in Sch 8 of Sch 4, para 36A, which requires the disclosure of any material departure from compliance with applicable accounting standards, but accounts prepared under Sch 8 must still meet the 'true and fair view' standard in s 226, which will constrain any significant departures: see note to s 226, above.

Where advantage is taken of this entitlement to prepare accounts in accordance with this Schedule, the balance sheet must contain a statement that the accounts are prepared in accordance with the special provisions relating to small companies: see s 246(8).

Paragraph 51A See general note to CA 1985, s 249AA, above.

SCHEDULE 8A

FORM AND CONTENT OF ABBREVIATED ACCOUNTS OF SMALL COMPANIES DELIVERED TO REGISTRAR

Section 246

PART I
BALANCE SHEET FORMATS

1. A small company may deliver to the registrar a copy of the balance sheet showing the items listed in either of the balance sheet formats set out in paragraph 2 below in the order and under the headings and sub-headings given in the format adopted, but in other respects corresponding to the full balance sheet.

2. The formats referred to in paragraph 1 are as follows—

Balance Sheet Formats

Format 1

A. Called up share capital not paid
B. Fixed assets
    I   Intangible assets
    II Tangible assets
    III Investments
C. Current assets
    I   Stocks
    II Debtors (1)
    III Investments
    IV Cash at bank and in hand
D. Prepayments and accrued income
E. Creditors: amounts falling due within one year

    F.   Net current assets (liabilities)

    G.   Total assets less current liabilities

    H.   Creditors: amounts falling due after more than one year

    I.   Provisions for liabilities and charges

    J.   Accruals and deferred income

    K.   Capital and reserves

        I   Called up share capital

        II   Share premium account

        III   Revaluation reserve

        IV   Other reserves

        V   Profit and loss account

Balance Sheet Formats

Format 2

ASSETS

    A.   Called up share capital not paid

    B.   Fixed assets

        I   Intangible assets

        II   Tangible assets

        III   Investments

    C.   Current assets

        I   Stocks

        II   Debtors *(1)*

        III   Investments

        IV   Cash at bank and in hand

    D.   Prepayments and accrued income

LIABILITIES

    A   Capital and reserves

        I   Called up share capital

        II   Share premium account

        III   Revaluation reserve

        IV   Other reserves

        V   Profit and loss account

    B.   Provisions for liabilities and charges

    C.   Creditors *(2)*

    D.   Accruals and deferred income

Notes on the balance sheet formats

(1) *Debtors*

(Formats 1 and 2, item C.II.)

The aggregate amount of debtors falling due after more than one year shall be shown separately, unless it is disclosed in the notes to the accounts.

(2) *Creditors*

(Format 2, Liabilities item C.)

The aggregate amount of creditors falling due within one year and of creditors falling due after more than one year shall be shown separately, unless it is disclosed in the notes to the accounts.

PART II
NOTES TO THE ACCOUNTS

Preliminary

3. Any information required in the case of any small company by the following provisions of this Part of this Schedule shall (if not given in the company's accounts) be given by way of a note to those accounts.

Disclosure of accounting policies

4. The accounting policies adopted by the company in determining the amounts to be included in respect of items shown in the balance sheet and in determining the profit or loss of the company shall be stated (including such policies with respect to the depreciation and diminution in value of assets).

Information supplementing the balance sheet

Share capital and debentures

5.—(1) The following information shall be given with respect to the company's share capital—

  (a) the authorised share capital; and

    (b)   where shares of more than one class have been allotted, the number and aggregate nominal value of shares of each class allotted.

(2) In the case of any part of the allotted share capital that consists of redeemable shares, the following information shall be given—

    (a)   the earliest and latest dates on which the company has power to redeem those shares;

    (b)   whether those shares must be redeemed in any event or are liable to be redeemed at the option of the company or of the shareholder; and

    (c)   whether any (and, if so, what) premium is payable on redemption.

6. If the company has allotted any shares during the financial year, the following information shall be given—

    (a)   the classes of shares allotted; and

    (b)   as respects each class of shares, the number allotted, their aggregate nominal value, and the consideration received by the company for the allotment.

Fixed assets

7.—(1) In respect of each item to which a letter or Roman number is assigned under the general item 'fixed assets' in the company's balance sheet the following information shall be given—

    (a)   the appropriate amounts in respect of that item as at the date of the beginning of the financial year and as at the balance sheet date respectively;

    (b)   the effect on any amount shown in the balance sheet in respect of that item of—

        (i)   any revision of the amount in respect of any assets included under that item made during that year on any basis mentioned in paragraph 31 of Schedule 8;

        (ii)   acquisitions during that year of any assets;

        (iii) disposals during that year of any assets; and

        (iv) any transfers of assets of the company to and from that item during that year.

(2) The reference in sub-paragraph (1)(a) to the appropriate amounts in respect of any item as at any date there mentioned is a reference to amounts representing the aggregate amounts determined, as at that date, in respect of assets falling to be included under that item on either of the following bases, that is to say—

    (a)   on the basis of purchase price or production cost (determined in accordance with paragraphs 26 and 27 of Schedule 8); or

    (b)   on any basis mentioned in paragraph 31 of that Schedule,

(leaving out of account in either case any provisions for depreciation or diminution in value).

(3) In respect of each item within sub-paragraph (1)—

    (a)   the cumulative amount of provisions for depreciation or diminution in value of assets included under that item as at each date mentioned in sub-paragraph (1)(a);

  (b) the amount of any such provisions made in respect of the financial year;

  (c) the amount of any adjustments made in respect of any such provisions during that year in consequence of the disposal of any assets; and

  (d) the amount of any other adjustments made in respect of any such provisions during that year;

shall also be stated.

Details of indebtedness

8.—(1) For the aggregate of all items shown under 'creditors' in the company's balance sheet there shall be stated the aggregate of the following amounts, that is to say—

  (a) the amount of any debts included under 'creditors' which are payable or repayable otherwise than by instalments and fall due for payment or repayment after the end of the period of five years beginning with the day next following the end of the financial year; and

  (b) in the case of any debts so included which are payable or repayable by instalments, the amount of any instalments which fall due for payment after the end of that period.

(2) In respect of each item shown under 'creditors' in the company's balance sheet there shall be stated the aggregate amount of any debts included under that item, in respect of which any security has been given by the company.

[General]

9.—(1) Where sums originally denominated in foreign currencies have been brought into account under any items shown in the balance sheet or profit and loss account, the basis on which those sums have been translated into sterling shall be stated.

(2) Subject to the following sub-paragraph, in respect of every item required to be stated in a note to the accounts by or under any provision of this Act, the corresponding amount for the financial year immediately preceding that to which the accounts relate shall also be stated and where the corresponding amount is not comparable, it shall be adjusted and particulars of the adjustment and the reasons for it shall be given.

(3) Sub-paragraph (2) does not apply in relation to any amounts stated by virtue of any of the following provisions of this Act—

  (a) paragraph 13 of Schedule 4A (details of accounting treatment of acquisitions),

  (b) paragraphs 2, 8(3), 16, 21(1)(d), 22(4) and (5), 24(3) and (4) and 27(3) and (4) of Schedule 5 (shareholdings in other undertakings),

  (c) Parts II and III of Schedule 6 (loans and other dealings in favour of directors and others), and

  (d) paragraph 7 above (fixed assets).

[Dormant companies acting as agents]

9A. Where the directors of a company take advantage of the exemption conferred by section 249AA, and the company has during the financial year in question acted as an agent for any person, the fact that it has so acted must be stated.

General note

This Schedule applies only to accounts delivered to the registrar of companies as permitted by s 246(5)(c); and a company delivering accounts in this format may take advantage of the exemptions in s 246(6); and the balance sheet so delivered must contain the statement required by s 246(8).

Paragraph 9A: This provision was added by the Companies Act 1985 (Audit Exemption) (Amendment) Regulations 2000, SI 2000/1430, reg 7, as from 26 May 2000, in relation to annual accounts and reports in respect of financial years ending two months or more after that date. See the note to s 249AA, above.

SCHEDULE 9

SPECIAL PROVISIONS FOR BANKING COMPANIES AND GROUPS

Sections 255, 255A, 255B

PART I
INDIVIDUAL ACCOUNTS

CHAPTER 1
GENERAL RULES AND FORMATS

Section A
General rules

1.—(1) Subject to the following provisions of this Part of this Schedule:

(a) every balance sheet of a company shall show the items listed in the balance sheet format set out below in section B of this Chapter of this Schedule; and

(b) every profit and loss account of a company shall show the items listed in either of the profit and loss account formats so set out;

in either case in the order and under the headings and sub-headings given in the format adopted.

(2) Sub-paragraph (1) above is not to be read as requiring the heading or sub-heading for any item to be distinguished by any number or letter assigned to that item in the format adopted.

(3) Where the heading of an item in the format adopted contains any wording in square brackets, that wording may be omitted if not applicable to the company.

2.—(1) Where in accordance with paragraph 1 a company's profit and loss account for any financial year has been prepared by reference to one of the formats set out in section B below, the directors of the company shall adopt the same format in preparing the profit and loss account for subsequent financial years of the company unless in their opinion there are special reasons for a change.

(2) Particulars of any change in the format adopted in preparing a company's profit and loss account in accordance with paragraph 1 shall be disclosed, and the reasons for the change shall be explained, in a note to the accounts in which the new format is first adopted.

3.—(1) Any item required in accordance with paragraph 1 to be shown in a company's balance sheet or profit and loss account may be shown in greater detail than so required.

(2) A company's balance sheet or profit and loss account may include an item representing or covering the amount of any asset or liability, income or expenditure not specifically covered by any of the items listed in the balance sheet format provided or the profit and loss account format adopted, but the following shall not be treated as assets in any company's balance sheet:

    (i)   preliminary expenses;

    (ii) expenses of and commission on any issue of shares or debentures; and

    (iii) costs of research.

(3) Items to which lower case letters are assigned in any of the formats set out in section B below may be combined in a company's accounts for any financial year if either:

    (a) their individual amounts are not material for the purpose of giving a true and fair view; or

    (b) the combination facilitates the assessment of the state of affairs or profit or loss of the company for that year;

but in a case within paragraph (b) the individual amounts of any items so combined shall be disclosed in a note to the accounts and any notes required by this Schedule to the items so combined shall, notwithstanding the combination, be given.

(4) Subject to paragraph 4(3) below, a heading or sub-heading corresponding to an item listed in the balance sheet format or the profit and loss account format adopted in preparing a company's balance sheet or profit and loss account shall not be included if there is no amount to be shown for that item in respect of the financial year to which the balance sheet or profit and loss account relates.

4.—(1) In respect of every item shown in the balance sheet or profit and loss account, there shall be shown or stated the corresponding amount for the financial year immediately preceding that to which the accounts relate.

(2) Where the corresponding amount is not comparable with the amount to be shown for the item in question in respect of the financial year to which the balance sheet or profit and loss account relates, the former amount shall be adjusted and particulars of the adjustment and the reasons for it shall be given in a note to the accounts.

(3) Paragraph 3(4) does not apply in any case where an amount can be shown for the item in question in respect of the financial year immediately preceding that to which the balance sheet or profit and loss account relates, and that amount shall be shown under the heading or sub-heading required by paragraph 1 for that item.

5.—(1) Subject to the following provisions of this paragraph and without prejudice to note (6) to the balance sheet format, amounts in respect of items representing assets or income may not be set off against amounts in respect of items representing liabilities or expenditure (as the case may be), or vice versa.

(2) Charges required to be included in profit and loss account format 1, items 11(a) and 11(b) or format 2, items A7(a) and A7(b) may however be set off against income required to be included in format 1, items 12(a) and 12(b) or format 2, items B5(a) and B5(b) and the resulting figure shown as a single item (in format 2 at position A7 if negative and at position B5 if positive).

(3) Charges required to be included in profit and loss account format 1, item 13 or format 2, item A8 may also be set off against income required to be included in format 1, item 14 or format 2, item B6 and the resulting figure shown as a single item (in format 2 at position A8 if negative and at position B6 if positive).

6.—(1) Assets shall be shown under the relevant balance sheet headings even where the company has pledged them as security for its own liabilities or for those of third parties or has otherwise assigned them as security to third parties.

(2) A company shall not include in its balance sheet assets pledged or otherwise assigned to it as security unless such assets are in the form of cash in the hands of the company.

7. Assets acquired in the name of and on behalf of third parties shall not be shown in the balance sheet.

8. Every profit and loss account of a company shall show separately as additional items:

    (a) any amount set aside or proposed to be set aside to, or withdrawn or proposed to be withdrawn from, reserves; ...

    (b) the aggregate amount of any dividends paid and proposed;

    (c) if it is not shown in the notes to the accounts, the aggregate amount of any dividends proposed.

Section B
The required formats for accounts

Preliminary

9.—(1) References in this Part of this Schedule to the balance sheet format or to profit and loss account formats are to the balance sheet format or profit and loss account formats set out below and references to the items listed in any of the formats are to those items read together with any of the notes following the formats which apply to any of those items.

(2) The requirement imposed by paragraph 1 of this Part of this Schedule to show the items listed in any such format in the order adopted in the format is subject to any provision in the notes following the formats for alternative positions for any particular items.

10. A number in brackets following any item in any of the formats set out below is a reference to the note of that number in the notes following the formats.

Balance Sheet Format

ASSETS
1. Cash and balances at central [or post office] banks (*1*)
2. Treasury bills and other eligible bills (*20*)
   (a) Treasury bills and similar securities (*2*)
   (b) Other eligible bills (*3*)
3. Loans and advances to banks (*4*),(*20*)
   (a) Repayable on demand
   (b) Other loans and advances
4. Loans and advances to customers (*5*),(*20*)
5. Debt securities [and other fixed income securities] (*6*),(*20*)
   (a) Issued by public bodies
   (b) Issued by other issuers
6. Equity shares [and other variable-yield securities]
7. Participating interests
8. Shares in group undertakings
9. Intangible fixed assets (*7*)
10. Tangible fixed assets (*8*)
11. Called up capital not paid (*9*)
12. Own shares (*10*)
13. Other assets
14. Called up capital not paid (*9*)
15. Prepayments and accrued income

Total assets

LIABILITIES
1. Deposits by banks (*11*),(*20*)
   (a) Repayable on demand
   (b) With agreed maturity dates or periods of notice
2. Customer accounts (*12*),(*20*)
   (a) Repayable on demand
   (b) With agreed maturity dates or periods of notice
3. Debt securities in issue (*13*),(*20*)
   (a) Bonds and medium term notes
   (b) Others
4. Other liabilities
5. Accruals and deferred income
6. Provisions for liabilities and charges
   (a) Provisions for pensions and similar obligations
   (b) Provisions for tax

    (c) Other provisions

7.   Subordinated liabilities *(14)*,*(20)*

8.   Called up share capital *(15)*

9.   Share premium account

10. Reserves

    (a) Capital redemption reserve

    (b) Reserve for own shares

    (c) Reserves provided for by the articles of association

    (d) Other reserves

11. Revaluation reserve

12. Profit and loss account

Total liabilities

MEMORANDUM ITEMS

1.   Contingent liabilities *(16)*

    (1) Acceptances and endorsements

    (2) Guarantees and assets pledged as collateral security *(17)*

    (3) Other contingent liabilities

2.   Commitments *(18)*

    (1) Commitments arising out of sale and option to resell transactions *(19)*

    (2) Other commitments

Notes on the balance sheet format and memorandum items

(1) *Cash and balances at central [or post office] banks*

(Assets item 1)

Cash shall comprise all currency including foreign notes and coins.

Only those balances which may be withdrawn without notice and which are deposited with central or post office banks of the country or countries in which the company is established shall be included in this item. All other claims on central or post office banks must be shown under Assets items 3 or 4.

(2) *Treasury bills and other eligible bills: Treasury bills and similar securities*

(Assets item 2(a))

Treasury bills and similar securities shall comprise treasury bills and similar debt instruments issued by public bodies which are eligible for refinancing with central banks of the country or countries in which the company is established. Any treasury bills or similar debt instruments not so eligible shall be included under Assets item 5, sub-item (a).

(3) *Treasury bills and other eligible bills: Other eligible bills*

(Assets item 2(b))

Other eligible bills shall comprise all bills purchased to the extent that they are eligible, under national law, for refinancing with the central banks of the country or countries in which the company is established.

(4) *Loans and advances to banks*

(Assets item 3)

Loans and advances to banks shall comprise all loans and advances to domestic or foreign credit institutions made by the company arising out of banking transactions. However loans and advances to credit institutions represented by debt securities or other fixed income securities shall be included under Assets item 5 and not this item.

(5) *Loans and advances to customers*

(Assets item 4)

Loans and advances to customers shall comprise all types of assets in the form of claims on domestic and foreign customers other than credit institutions. However loans and advances represented by debt securities or other fixed income securities shall be included under Assets item 5 and not this item.

(6) *Debt securities [and other fixed income securities]*

(Assets item 5)

This item shall comprise transferable debt securities and any other transferable fixed income securities issued by credit institutions, other undertakings or public bodies. Debt securities and other fixed income securities issued by public bodies shall however only be included in this item if they may not be shown under Assets item 2.

Where a company holds its own debt securities these shall not be included under this item but shall be deducted from Liabilities item 3(a) or (b), as appropriate.

Securities bearing interest rates that vary in accordance with specific factors, for example the interest rate on the inter-bank market or on the Euromarket, shall also be regarded as fixed income securities to be included under this item.

(7) *Intangible fixed assets*

(Assets item 9)

This item shall comprise:

  (a) development costs;
  (b) concessions, patents, licences, trade marks and similar rights and assets;
  (c) goodwill; and
  (d) payments on account.

Amounts shall, however, be included in respect of (b) only if the assets were acquired for valuable consideration or the assets in question were created by the company itself.

Amounts representing goodwill shall only be included to the extent that the goodwill was acquired for valuable consideration.

There shall be disclosed, in a note to the accounts, the amount of any goodwill included in this item.

(8) *Tangible fixed assets*

(Assets item 10)

This item shall comprise:
- — land and buildings;
- — plant and machinery;
- — fixtures and fittings, tools and equipment; and
- — payments on account and assets in the course of construction.

There shall be disclosed in a note to the accounts the amount included in this item with respect to land and buildings occupied by the company for its own activities.

(9) *Called up capital not paid*

(Assets items 11 and 14)

The two positions shown for this item are alternatives.

(10) *Own shares*

(Assets item 12)

The nominal value of the shares held shall be shown separately under this item.

(11) *Deposits by banks*

(Liabilities item 1)

Deposits by banks shall comprise all amounts arising out of banking transactions owed to other domestic or foreign credit institutions by the company. However liabilities in the form of debt securities and any liabilities for which transferable certificates have been issued shall be included under Liabilities item 3 and not this item.

(12) *Customer accounts*

(Liabilities item 2)

This item shall comprise all amounts owed to creditors that are not credit institutions. However liabilities in the form of debt securities and any liabilities for which transferable certificates have been issued shall be shown under Liabilities item 3 and not this item.

(13) *Debt securities in issue*

(Liabilities item 3)

This item shall include both debt securities and debts for which transferable certificates have been issued, including liabilities arising out of own acceptances and promissory notes. (Only acceptances which a company has issued for its own refinancing and in respect of which it is the first party liable shall be treated as own acceptances.)

(14) *Subordinated liabilities*

(Liabilities item 7)

This item shall comprise all liabilities in respect of which there is a contractual obligation that, in the event of winding up or bankruptcy, they are to be repaid only after the claims of other creditors have been met.

   This item shall include all subordinated liabilities, whether or not a ranking has been agreed between the subordinated creditors concerned.

(15) *Called up share capital*

(Liabilities item 8)

The amount of allotted share capital and the amount of called up share capital which has been paid up shall be shown separately.

(16) *Contingent liabilities*

(Memorandum item 1)

This item shall include all transactions whereby the company has underwritten the obligations of a third party.

   Liabilities arising out of the endorsement of rediscounted bills shall be included in this item.

   Acceptances other than own acceptances shall also be included.

(17) *Contingent liabilities: Guarantees and assets pledged as collateral security*

(Memorandum item 1(2))

This item shall include all guarantee obligations incurred and assets pledged as collateral security on behalf of third parties, particularly in respect of sureties and irrevocable letters of credit.

(18) *Commitments*

(Memorandum item 2)

This item shall include every irrevocable commitment which could give rise to a credit risk.

(19) *Commitments: Commitments arising out of sale and option to resell transactions*

(Memorandum item 2(1))

This sub-item shall comprise commitments entered into by the company in the context of sale and option to resell transactions.

(20) *Claims on, and liabilities to, undertakings in which a participating interest is held or group undertakings*

(Assets items 2 to 5, Liabilities items 1 to 3 and 7)

The following information must be given either by way of subdivision of the relevant items or by way of notes to the accounts.

The amount of the following must be shown for each of Assets items 2 to 5:

(a) claims on group undertakings included therein; and

(b) claims on undertakings in which the company has a participating interest included therein.

The amount of the following must be shown for each of Liabilities items 1, 2, 3 and 7:

(i) liabilities to group undertakings included therein; and

(ii) liabilities to undertakings in which the company has a participating interest included therein.

Special rules

Subordinated assets

11.—(1) The amount of any assets that are subordinated must be shown either as a subdivision of any relevant asset item or in the notes to the accounts; in the latter case disclosure shall be by reference to the relevant asset item or items in which the assets are included.

(2) In the case of Assets items 2 to 5 in the balance sheet format, the amounts required to be shown by note (20) to the format as sub-items of those items shall be further subdivided so as to show the amount of any claims included therein that are subordinated.

(3) For this purpose, assets are subordinated if there is a contractual obligation to the effect that, in the event of winding up or bankruptcy, they are to be repaid only after the claims of other creditors have been met, whether or not a ranking has been agreed between the subordinated creditors concerned.

Syndicated loans

12.—(1) Where a company is a party to a syndicated loan transaction the company shall include only that part of the total loan which it itself has funded.

(2) Where a company is a party to a syndicated loan transaction and has agreed to reimburse (in whole or in part) any other party to the syndicate any funds advanced by that party or any interest thereon upon the occurrence of any event, including the default of the borrower, any additional liability by reason of such a guarantee shall be included as a contingent liability in Memorandum item 1, sub-item (2).

Sale and repurchase transactions

13.—(1) The following rules apply where a company is a party to a sale and repurchase transaction.

(2) Where the company is the transferor of the assets under the transaction:

   (a) the assets transferred shall, notwithstanding the transfer, be included in its balance sheet;

   (b) the purchase price received by it shall be included in its balance sheet as an amount owed to the transferee; and

   (c) the value of the assets transferred shall be disclosed in a note to its accounts.

(3) Where the company is the transferee of the assets under the transaction it shall not include the assets transferred in its balance sheet but the purchase price paid by it to the transferor shall be so included as an amount owed by the transferor.

Sale and option to resell transactions

14.—(1) The following rules apply where a company is a party to a sale and option to resell transaction.

(2) Where the company is the transferor of the assets under the transaction it shall not include in its balance sheet the assets transferred but it shall enter under Memorandum item 2 an amount equal to the price agreed in the event of repurchase.

(3) Where the company is the transferee of the assets under the transaction it shall include those assets in its balance sheet.

Managed funds

15.—(1) For the purposes of this paragraph 'managed funds' are funds which the company administers in its own name but on behalf of others and to which it has legal title.

(2) The company shall, in any case where claims and obligations arising in respect of managed funds fall to be treated as claims and obligations of the company, adopt the following accounting treatment: claims and obligations representing managed funds are to be included in the company's balance sheet, with the notes to the accounts disclosing the total amount included with respect to such assets and liabilities in the balance sheet and showing the amount included under each relevant balance sheet item in respect of such assets or (as the case may be) liabilities.

Profit and Loss Account Formats

Format 1

Vertical layout

  1. Interest receivable (*1*)

    (1) Interest receivable and similar income arising from debt securities [and other fixed income securities]

(2) Other interest receivable and similar income

2. Interest payable (2)

3. Dividend income

    (a) Income from equity shares [and other variable-yield securities]

    (b) Income from participating interests

    (c) Income from shares in group undertakings

4. Fees and commissions receivable (3)

5. Fees and commissions payable (4)

6. Dealing [profits] [losses] (5)

7. Other operating income

8. Administrative expenses

    (a) Staff costs

        (i)   Wages and salaries

        (ii) Social security costs

        (iii) Other pension costs

    (b) Other administrative expenses

9. Depreciation and amortisation (6)

10. Other operating charges

11. Provisions

    (a) Provisions for bad and doubtful debts (7)

    (b) Provisions for contingent liabilities and commitments (8)

12. Adjustments to provisions

    (a) Adjustments to provisions for bad and doubtful debts (9)

    (b) Adjustments to provisions for contingent liabilities and commitments (10)

13. Amounts written off fixed asset investments (11)

14. Adjustments to amounts written off fixed asset investments (12)

15. [Profit] [loss] on ordinary activities before tax

16. Tax on [profit] [loss] on ordinary activities

17. [Profit] [loss] on ordinary activities after tax

18. Extraordinary income

19. Extraordinary charges

20. Extraordinary [profit] [loss]

21. Tax on extraordinary [profit] [loss]

22. Extraordinary [profit] [loss] after tax

23. Other taxes not shown under the preceding items

24. [Profit] [loss] for the financial year

Format 2

Horizontal layout

A. Charges
   1. Interest payable (*2*)
   2. Fees and commissions payable (*4*)
   3. Dealing losses (*5*)
   4. Administrative expenses
       (a) Staff costs
            (i)   Wages and salaries
            (ii)   Social security costs
            (iii) Other pension costs
       (b) Other administrative expenses
   5. Depreciation and amortisation (*6*)
   6. Other operating charges
   7. Provisions
       (a) Provisions for bad and doubtful debts (*7*)
       (b) Provisions for contingent liabilities and commitments (*8*)
   8. Amounts written off fixed asset investments (*11*)
   9. Profit on ordinary activities before tax
   10. Tax on [profit] [loss] on ordinary activities
   11. Profit on ordinary activities after tax
   12. Extraordinary charges
   13. Tax on extraordinary [profit] [loss]
   14. Extraordinary loss after tax
   15. Other taxes not shown under the preceding items
   16. Profit for the financial year

B. Income
   1. Interest receivable (*1*)
       (1) Interest receivable and similar income arising from debt securities [and other fixed income securities]
       (2) Other interest receivable and similar income
   2. Dividend income
       (a) Income from equity shares [and other variable-yield securities]
       (b) Income from participating interests
       (c) Income from shares in group undertakings
   3. Fees and commissions receivable (*3*)
   4. Dealing profits (*5*)
   5. Adjustments to provisions

    (a) Adjustments to provisions for bad and doubtful debts (9)

    (b) Adjustments to provisions for contingent liabilities and commitments (10)

6.   Adjustments to amounts written off fixed asset investments (12)

7.   Other operating income

8.   Loss on ordinary activities before tax

9.   Loss on ordinary activities after tax

10. Extraordinary income

11. Extraordinary profit after tax

12. Loss for the financial year

Notes on the profit and loss account formats

(1) *Interest receivable*

(Format 1, item 1; Format 2, item B.1)

This item shall include all income arising out of banking activities, including:

    (a) income from assets included in Assets items 1 to 5 in the balance sheet format, however calculated;

    (b) income resulting from covered forward contracts spread over the actual duration of the contract and similar in nature to interest; and

    (c) fees and commissions receivable similar in nature to interest and calculated on a time basis or by reference to the amount of the claim (but not other fees and commissions receivable).

(2) *Interest payable*

(Format 1, item 2; Format 2, item A.1)

This item shall include all expenditure arising out of banking activities, including:

    (a) charges arising out of liabilities included in Liabilities items 1, 2, 3 and 7 in the balance sheet format, however calculated;

    (b) charges resulting from covered forward contracts, spread over the actual duration of the contract and similar in nature to interest; and

    (c) fees and commissions payable similar in nature to interest and calculated on a time basis or by reference to the amount of the liability (but not other fees and commissions payable).

(3) *Fees and commissions receivable*

(Format 1, item 4; Format 2, item B.3)

Fees and commissions receivable shall comprise income in respect of all services supplied by the company to third parties, but not fees or commissions required to be included under interest receivable (Format 1, item 1; Format 2, item B.1).

In particular the following fees and commissions receivable must be included (unless required to be included under interest receivable):

— fees and commissions for guarantees, loan administration on behalf of other lenders and securities transactions;

— fees, commissions and other income in respect of payment transactions, account administration charges and commissions for the safe custody and administration of securities;

— fees and commissions for foreign currency transactions and for the sale and purchase of coin and precious metals; and

— fees and commissions charged for brokerage services in connection with savings and insurance contracts and loans.

(4) *Fees and commissions payable*

(Format 1, item 5; Format 2, item A.2)

Fees and commissions payable shall comprise charges for all services rendered to the company by third parties but not fees or commissions required to be included under interest payable (Format 1, item 2; Format 2, item A.1).

In particular the following fees and commissions payable must be included (unless required to be included under interest payable):

— fees and commissions for guarantees, loan administration and securities transactions;

— fees, commissions and other charges in respect of payment transactions, account administration charges and commissions for the safe custody and administration of securities;

— fees and commissions for foreign currency transactions and for the sale and purchase of coin and precious metals; and

— fees and commissions for brokerage services in connection with savings and insurance contracts and loans.

(5) *Dealing profits losses*

(Format 1, item 6; Format 2, items B.4 and A.3)

This item shall comprise:

(a) the net profit or net loss on transactions in securities which are not held as financial fixed assets together with amounts written off or written back with respect to such securities, including amounts written off or written back as a result of the application of paragraph 34(1) below;

(b) the net profit or loss on exchange activities, save in so far as the profit or loss is included in interest receivable or interest payable (Format 1, items 1 or 2; Format 2, items B.1 or A.1); and

(c) the net profits and losses on other dealing operations involving financial instruments, including precious metals.

(6) *Depreciation and amortisation*

(Format 1, item 9; Format 2, item A.5)

This item shall comprise depreciation and other amounts written off in respect of balance sheet Assets items 9 and 10.

(7) *Provisions: Provisions for bad and doubtful debts*

(Format 1, item 11(a); Format 2, item A.7(a))

Provisions for bad and doubtful debts shall comprise charges for amounts written off and for provisions made in respect of loans and advances shown under balance sheet Assets items 3 and 4.

(8) *Provisions: Provisions for contingent liabilities and commitments*

(Format 1, item 11(b); Format 2, item A.7(b))

This item shall comprise charges for provisions for contingent liabilities and commitments of a type which would, if not provided for, be shown under Memorandum items 1 and 2.

(9) *Adjustments to provisions: Adjustments to provisions for bad and doubtful debts*

(Format 1, item 12(a); Format 2, item B.5(a))

This item shall include credits from the recovery of loans that have been written off, from other advances written back following earlier write offs and from the reduction of provisions previously made with respect to loans and advances.

(10) *Adjustments to provisions: Adjustments to provisions for contingent liabilities and commitments*

(Format 1, item 12(b); Format 2, item B.5(b))

This item comprises credits from the reduction of provisions previously made with respect to contingent liabilities and commitments.

(11) *Amounts written off fixed asset investments*

(Format 1, item 13; Format 2, item A.8)

Amounts written off fixed asset investments shall comprise amounts written off in respect of assets which are transferable securities held as financial fixed assets, participating interests and shares in group undertakings and which are included in Assets items 5 to 8 in the balance sheet format.

(12) *Adjustments to amounts written off fixed asset investments*

(Format 1, item 14; Format 2, item B.6)

Adjustments to amounts written off fixed asset investments shall include amounts written back following earlier write offs and provisions in respect of assets which are transferable securities held as financial fixed assets, participating interests and group undertakings and which are included in Assets items 5 to 8 in the balance sheet format.

CHAPTER II
ACCOUNTING PRINCIPLES AND RULES

Section A
Accounting principles

16. Subject to paragraph 22 below, the amounts to be included in respect of all items shown in a company's accounts shall be determined in accordance with the principles set out in paragraphs 17 to 21.

Accounting principles

17. The company shall be presumed to be carrying on business as a going concern.

18. Accounting policies shall be applied consistently within the same accounts and from one financial year to the next.

19. The amount of any item shall be determined on a prudent basis, and in particular:

(a) only profits realised at the balance sheet date shall be included in the profit and loss account; and

(b) all liabilities and losses which have arisen or are likely to arise in respect of the financial year to which the accounts relate or a previous financial year shall be taken into account, including those which only become apparent between the balance sheet date and the date on which it is signed on behalf of the board of directors in pursuance of section 233 of this Act.

20. All income and charges relating to the financial year to which the accounts relate shall be taken into account, without regard to the date of receipt or payment.

21. In determining the aggregate amount of any item the amount of each individual asset or liability that falls to be taken into account shall be determined separately.

Departure from the accounting principles

22. If it appears to the directors of a company that there are special reasons for departing from any of the principles stated above in preparing the company's accounts in respect of any financial year they may do so, but particulars of the departure, the reasons for it and its effect shall be given in a note to the accounts.

Section B
Valuation rules

Historical cost accounting rules

Preliminary

23. Subject to paragraphs 39 to 44 of this Part of this Schedule, the amounts to be included in respect of all items shown in a company's accounts shall be determined in accordance with the rules set out in paragraphs 24 to 38 of this Part of this Schedule.

Fixed assets

General rules

24. Subject to any provision for depreciation or diminution in value made in accordance with paragraph 25 or 26 the amount to be included in respect of any fixed asset shall be its cost.

25. In the case of any fixed asset which has a limited useful economic life, the amount of:

(a) its cost; or

(b) where it is estimated that any such asset will have a residual value at the end of the period of its useful economic life, its cost less that estimated residual value;

shall be reduced by provisions for depreciation calculated to write off that amount systematically over the period of the asset's useful economic life.

26.—(1) Where a fixed asset investment of a description falling to be included under Assets items 7 (Participating interests) or 8 (Shares in group undertakings) in the balance sheet format, or any other holding of securities held as a financial fixed asset, has diminished in value, provisions for diminution in value may be made in respect of it and the amount to be included in respect of it may be reduced accordingly; and any such provisions which are not shown in the profit and loss account shall be disclosed (either separately or in aggregate) in a note to the accounts.

(2) Provisions for diminution in value shall be made in respect of any fixed asset which has diminished in value if the reduction in its value is expected to be permanent (whether its useful economic life is limited or not), and the amount to be included in respect of it shall be reduced accordingly; and any such provisions which are not shown in the profit and loss account shall be disclosed (either separately or in aggregate) in a note to the accounts.

(3) Where the reasons for which any provision was made in accordance with sub-paragraph (1) or (2) have ceased to apply to any extent, that provision shall

be written back to the extent that it is no longer necessary; and any amounts written back in accordance with this sub-paragraph which are not shown in the profit and loss account shall be disclosed (either separately or in aggregate) in a note to the accounts.

Development costs

27.—(1) Notwithstanding that amounts representing 'development costs' may be included under Assets item 9 in the balance sheet format, an amount may only be included in a company's balance sheet in respect of development costs in special circumstances.

(2) If any amount is included in a company's balance sheet in respect of development costs the following information shall be given in a note to the accounts:

    (a) the period over which the amount of those costs originally capitalised is being or is to be written off; and

    (b) the reasons for capitalising the development costs in question.

Goodwill

28.—(1) The application of paragraphs 24 to 26 in relation to goodwill (in any case where goodwill is treated as an asset) is subject to the following provisions of this paragraph.

(2) Subject to sub-paragraph (3) below the amount of the consideration for any goodwill acquired by a company shall be reduced by provisions for depreciation calculated to write off that amount systematically over a period chosen by the directors of the company.

(3) The period chosen shall not exceed the useful economic life of the goodwill in question.

(4) In any case where any goodwill acquired by a company is included as an asset in the company's balance sheet the period chosen for writing off the consideration for that goodwill and the reasons for choosing that period shall be disclosed in a note to the accounts.

Intangible and tangible fixed assets

29. Assets included in Assets items 9 (Intangible fixed assets) and 10 (Tangible fixed assets) in the balance sheet format shall be valued as fixed assets.

Other fixed assets

30. Other assets falling to be included in the balance sheet shall be valued as fixed assets where they are intended for use on a continuing basis in the company's activities.

Financial fixed assets

31.—(1) Debt securities, including fixed income securities, held as financial fixed assets shall be included in the balance sheet at an amount equal to their maturity value plus any premium, or less any discount, on their purchase, subject to the following provisions of this paragraph.

(2) The amount included in the balance sheet with respect to such securities purchased at a premium shall be reduced each financial year on a systematic basis so as to write the premium off over the period to the maturity date of the security and the amounts so written off shall be charged to the profit and loss account for the relevant financial years.

(3) The amount included in the balance sheet with respect to such securities purchased at a discount shall be increased each financial year on a systematic basis so as to extinguish the discount over the period to the maturity date of the security and the amounts by which the amount is increased shall be credited to the profit and loss account for the relevant years.

(4) The notes to the accounts shall disclose the amount of any unamortised premium or discount not extinguished which is included in the balance sheet by virtue of sub-paragraph (1).

(5) For the purposes of this paragraph 'premium' means any excess of the amount paid for a security over its maturity value and 'discount' means any deficit of the amount paid for a security over its maturity value.

Current assets

32. The amount to be included in respect of loans and advances, debt or other fixed income securities and equity shares or other variable yield securities not held as financial fixed assets shall be their cost, subject to paragraphs 33 and 34 below.

33.—(1) If the net realisable value of any asset referred to in paragraph 32 is lower than its cost the amount to be included in respect of that asset shall be the net realisable value.

(2) Where the reasons for which any provision for diminution in value was made in accordance with sub-paragraph (1) have ceased to apply to any extent, that provision shall be written back to the extent that it is no longer necessary.

34.—(1) Subject to paragraph 33 above, the amount to be included in the balance sheet in respect of transferable securities not held as financial fixed assets may be the higher of their cost or their market value at the balance sheet date.

(2) The difference between the cost of any securities included in the balance sheet at a valuation under sub-paragraph (1) and their market value shall be shown (in aggregate) in the notes to the accounts.

Miscellaneous and supplementary provisions

Excess of money owed over value received as an asset item

35.—(1) Where the amount repayable on any debt owed by a company is greater than the value of the consideration received in the transaction giving rise to the debt, the amount of the difference may be treated as an asset.

(2) Where any such amount is so treated:

    (a) it shall be written off by reasonable amounts each year and must be completely written off before repayment of the debt; and

    (b) if the current amount is not shown as a separate item in the company's balance sheet it must be disclosed in a note to the accounts.

Determination of cost

36.—(1) The cost of an asset that has been acquired by the company shall be determined by adding to the actual price paid any expenses incidental to its acquisition.

(2) The cost of an asset constructed by the company shall be determined by adding to the purchase price of the raw materials and consumables used the amount of the costs incurred by the company which are directly attributable to the construction of that asset.

(3) In addition, there may be included in the cost of an asset constructed by the company:

    (a) a reasonable proportion of the costs incurred by the company which are only indirectly attributable to the construction of that asset, but only to the extent that they relate to the period of construction; and

    (b) interest on capital borrowed to finance the construction of that asset, to the extent that it accrues in respect of the period of construction;

provided, however, in a case within sub-paragraph (b) above, that the inclusion of the interest in determining the cost of that asset and the amount of the interest so included is disclosed in a note to the accounts.

37.—(1) Subject to the qualification mentioned below, the cost of any assets which are fungible assets (including investments) may be determined by the application of any of the methods mentioned in sub-paragraph (2) below in relation to any such assets of the same class.

    The method chosen must be one which appears to the directors to be appropriate in the circumstances of the company.

(2) Those methods are:

    (a) the method known as 'first in, first out' (FIFO);

    (b) the method known as 'last in, first out' (LIFO);

    (c) a weighted average price; and

    (d) any other method similar to any of the methods mentioned above.

(3) Where in the case of any company:

    (a) the cost of assets falling to be included under any item shown in the company's balance sheet has been determined by the application of any method permitted by this paragraph; and

    (b) the amount shown in respect of that item differs materially from the relevant alternative amount given below in this paragraph;

the amount of that difference shall be disclosed in a note to the accounts.

(4) Subject to sub-paragraph (5) below, for the purposes of sub-paragraph (3)(b) above, the relevant alternative amount, in relation to any item shown in a

company's balance sheet, is the amount which would have been shown in respect of that item if assets of any class included under that item at an amount determined by any method permitted by this paragraph had instead been included at their replacement cost as at the balance sheet date.

(5) The relevant alternative amount may be determined by reference to the most recent actual purchase price before the balance sheet date of assets of any class included under the item in question instead of by reference to their replacement cost as at that date, but only if the former appears to the directors of the company to constitute the more appropriate standard of comparison in the case of assets of that class.

Substitution of original amount where price or cost unknown

38. Where there is no record of the purchase price of any asset acquired by a company or of any price, expenses or costs relevant for determining its cost in accordance with paragraph 36, or any such record cannot be obtained without unreasonable expense or delay, its cost shall be taken for the purposes of paragraphs 24 to 34 to be the value ascribed to it in the earliest available record of its value made on or after its acquisition by the company.

Alternative accounting rules

Preliminary

39.—(1) The rules set out in paragraphs 24 to 38 are referred to below in this Schedule as the historical cost accounting rules.

(2) Paragraphs 24 to 27 and 31 to 35 are referred to below in this section of this Part of this Schedule as the depreciation rules; and references below in this Schedule to the historical cost accounting rules do not include the depreciation rules as they apply by virtue of paragraph 42.

40. Subject to paragraphs 42 to 44, the amounts to be included in respect of assets of any description mentioned in paragraph 41 may be determined on any basis so mentioned.

Alternative accounting rules

41.—(1) Intangible fixed assets, other than goodwill, may be included at their current cost.

(2) Tangible fixed assets may be included at a market value determined as at the date of their last valuation or at their current cost.

(3) Investments of any description falling to be included under Assets items 7 (Participating interests) or 8 (Shares in group undertakings) of the balance sheet format and any other securities held as financial fixed assets may be included either:

(a) at a market value determined as at the date of their last valuation; or

(b) at a value determined on any basis which appears to the directors to be appropriate in the circumstances of the company;

but in the latter case particulars of the method of valuation adopted and of the reasons for adopting it shall be disclosed in a note to the accounts.

(4) Securities of any description not held as financial fixed assets (if not valued in accordance with paragraph 34 above) may be included at their current cost.

Application of the depreciation rules

42.—(1) Where the value of any asset of a company is determined in accordance with paragraph 41, that value shall be, or (as the case may require) be the starting point for determining, the amount to be included in respect of that asset in the company's accounts, instead of its cost or any value previously so determined for that asset; and the depreciation rules shall apply accordingly in relation to any such asset with the substitution for any reference to its cost of a reference to the value most recently determined for that asset in accordance with paragraph 41.

(2) The amount of any provision for depreciation required in the case of any fixed asset by paragraph 25 or 26 as it applies by virtue of sub-paragraph (1) is referred to below in this paragraph as the 'adjusted amount', and the amount of any provision which would be required by that paragraph in the case of that asset according to the historical cost accounting rules is referred to as the 'historical cost amount'.

(3) Where sub-paragraph (1) applies in the case of any fixed asset the amount of any provision for depreciation in respect of that asset included in any item shown in the profit and loss account in respect of amounts written off assets of the description in question may be the historical cost amount instead of the adjusted amount, provided that the amount of any difference between the two is shown separately in the profit and loss account or in a note to the accounts.

Additional information to be provided in case of departure from historical cost accounting rules

43.—(1) This paragraph applies where the amounts to be included in respect of assets covered by any items shown in a company's accounts have been determined in accordance with paragraph 41.

(2) The items affected and the basis of valuation adopted in determining the amounts of the assets in question in the case of each such item shall be disclosed in a note to the accounts.

(3) In the case of each balance sheet item affected either:

(a) the comparable amounts determined according to the historical cost accounting rules; or

(b) the differences between those amounts and the corresponding amounts actually shown in the balance sheet in respect of that item;

shall be shown separately in the balance sheet or in a note to the accounts.

(4) In sub-paragraph (3) above, references in relation to any item to the comparable amounts determined as there mentioned are references to:

(a) the aggregate amount which would be required to be shown in respect of that item if the amounts to be included in respect of all the assets covered by that item were determined according to the historical cost accounting rules; and

(b) the aggregate amount of the cumulative provisions for depreciation or diminution in value which would be permitted or required in determining those amounts according to those rules.

Revaluation reserve

44.—(1) With respect to any determination of the value of an asset of a company in accordance with paragraph 41, the amount of any profit or loss arising from that determination (after allowing, where appropriate, for any provisions for depreciation or diminution in value made otherwise than by reference to the value so determined and any adjustments of any such provisions made in the light of that determination) shall be credited or (as the case may be) debited to a separate reserve ('the revaluation reserve').

(2) The amount of the revaluation reserve shall be shown in the company's balance sheet under Liabilities item 11 in the balance sheet format, but need not be shown under that name.

(3) An amount may be transferred

(a) from the revaluation reserve—

(i) to the profit and loss account, if the amount was previously charged to that account or represents realised profit, or

(ii) on capitalisation,

(b) to or from the revaluation reserve in respect of the taxation relating to any profit or loss credited or debited to the reserve;

and the revaluation reserve shall be reduced to the extent that the amounts transferred to it are no longer necessary for the purposes of the valuation method used.

(4) In sub-paragraph (3)(a)(ii) 'capitalisation', in relation to an amount standing to the credit of the revaluation reserve, means applying it in wholly or partly paying up unissued shares in the company to be allotted to members of the company as fully or partly paid shares.

(5) The revaluation reserve shall not be reduced except as mentioned in this paragraph.

(6) The treatment for taxation purposes of amounts credited or debited to the revaluation reserve shall be disclosed in a note to the accounts.

Assets and liabilities denominated in foreign currencies

45.—(1) Subject to the following sub-paragraphs, amounts to be included in respect of assets and liabilities denominated in foreign currencies shall be in sterling (or the currency in which the accounts are drawn up) after translation at an appropriate spot rate of exchange prevailing at the balance sheet date.

(2) An appropriate rate of exchange prevailing on the date of purchase may however be used for assets held as financial fixed assets and assets to be included under Assets items 9 (Intangible fixed assets) and 10 (Tangible fixed assets) in the balance sheet format, if they are not covered or not specifically covered in either the spot or forward currency markets.

(3) An appropriate spot rate of exchange prevailing at the balance sheet date shall be used for translating uncompleted spot exchange transactions.

(4) An appropriate forward rate of exchange prevailing at the balance sheet date shall be used for translating uncompleted forward exchange transactions.

(5) This paragraph does not apply to any assets or liabilities held, or any transactions entered into, for hedging purposes or to any assets or liabilities which are themselves hedged.

46.—(1) Subject to sub-paragraph (2), any difference between the amount to be included in respect of an asset or liability under paragraph 45 and the book value, after translation into sterling (or the currency in which the accounts are drawn up) at an appropriate rate, of that asset or liability shall be credited or, as the case may be, debited to the profit and loss account.

(2) In the case, however, of assets held as financial fixed assets, of assets to be included under Assets items 9 (Intangible fixed assets) and 10 (Tangible fixed assets) in the balance sheet format and of transactions undertaken to cover such assets, any such difference may be deducted from or credited to any non-distributable reserve available for the purpose.

CHAPTER III
NOTES TO THE ACCOUNTS

Preliminary

47.—(1) Any information required in the case of a company by the following provisions of this Part of this Schedule shall (if not given in the company's accounts) be given by way of a note to the accounts ...

(2) Subject to the next sub-paragraph, in respect of every item stated in a note to the accounts the corresponding amount for the financial year immediately preceding that to which the accounts relate shall also be stated and where the

corresponding amount is not comparable, it shall be adjusted and particulars of the adjustment and the reasons for it shall be given.

(3) The last sub-paragraph does not apply to:

(a) paragraphs 55 and 59 of this Part of this Schedule;

(b) paragraph 13 of Schedule 4A;

(c) paragraphs 2, 8(3), 16, 21(1)(d), 22(4) and (5), 24(3) and (4) and 27(3) and (4) of Schedule 5; and

(d) Parts II and III of Schedule 6 as modified by Part IV of this Schedule (loans and other dealings in favour of directors).

General

Disclosure of accounting policies

48. The accounting policies adopted by the company in determining the amounts to be included in respect of items shown in the balance sheet and in determining the profit or loss of the company shall be stated (including such policies with respect to the depreciation and diminution in value of assets).

49. It shall be stated whether the accounts have been prepared in accordance with applicable accounting standards and particulars of any material departure from those standards and the reasons for it shall be given.

Sums denominated in foreign currencies

50. Where any sums originally denominated in foreign currencies have been brought into account under any items shown in the balance sheet format or the profit and loss account formats, the basis on which those sums have been translated into sterling (or the currency in which the accounts are drawn up) shall be stated.

Information supplementing the balance sheet

Share capital and debentures

51.—(1) The following information shall be given with respect to the company's share capital:

(a) the authorised share capital; and

(b) where shares of more than one class have been allotted, the number and aggregate nominal value of shares of each class allotted.

(2) In the case of any part of the allotted share capital that consists of redeemable shares, the following information shall be given:

(a) the earliest and latest dates on which the company has power to redeem those shares;

(b) whether those shares must be redeemed in any event or are liable to be redeemed at the option of the company or of the shareholder; and

(c) whether any (and, if so, what) premium is payable on redemption.

52. If the company has allotted any shares during the financial year, the following information shall be given:

(a) ...

(b) the classes of shares allotted; and

(c) as respects each class of shares, the number allotted, their aggregate nominal value and the consideration received by the company for the allotment.

53.—(1) With respect to any contingent right to the allotment of shares in the company the following particulars shall be given:

(a) the number, description and amount of the shares in relation to which the right is exercisable;

(b) the period during which it is exercisable; and

(c) the price to be paid for the shares allotted.

(2) In sub-paragraph (1) above 'contingent right to the allotment of shares' means any option to subscribe for shares and any other right to require the allotment of shares to any person whether arising on the conversion into shares of securities of any other description or otherwise.

54.—(1) If the company has issued any debentures during the financial year to which the accounts relate, the following information shall be given:

(a) ...

(b) the classes of debentures issued; and

(c) as respects each class of debentures, the amount issued and the consideration received by the company for the issue.

(2) ...

(3) Where any of the company's debentures are held by a nominee of or trustee for the company, the nominal amount of the debentures and the amount at which they are stated in the accounting records kept by the company in accordance with section 221 of this Act shall be stated.

Fixed assets

55.—(1) In respect of any fixed assets of the company included in any assets item in the company's balance sheet the following information shall be given by reference to each such item:

(a) the appropriate amounts in respect of those assets included in the item as at the date of the beginning of the financial year and as at the balance sheet date respectively;

(b) the effect on any amount included in the item in respect of those assets of:

(i) any determination during that year of the value to be ascribed to any of those assets in accordance with paragraph 41 above;

(ii) acquisitions during that year of any fixed assets;

(iii) disposals during that year of any fixed assets; and

(iv) any transfers of fixed assets of the company to and from the item during that year.

(2) The reference in sub-paragraph (1)(a) to the appropriate amounts in respect of any fixed assets (included in an assets item) as at any date there mentioned is a reference to amounts representing the aggregate amounts determined, as at that date, in respect of fixed assets falling to be included under the item on either of the following bases, that is to say:

(a)   on the basis of cost (determined in accordance with paragraphs 36 and 37); or

(b)   on any basis permitted by paragraph 41;

(leaving out of account in either case any provisions for depreciation or diminution in value).

(3) In addition, in respect of any fixed assets of the company included in any assets item in the company's balance sheet, there shall be stated (by reference to each such item):

(a)   the cumulative amount of provisions for depreciation or diminution in value of those assets included under the item as at each date mentioned in sub-paragraph (1)(a);

(b)   the amount of any such provisions made in respect of the financial year;

(c)   the amount of any adjustments made in respect of any such provisions during that year in consequence of the disposal of any of those assets; and

(d)   the amount of any other adjustments made in respect of any such provisions during that year.

(4) The requirements of this paragraph need not be complied with to the extent that a company takes advantage of the option of setting off charges and income afforded by paragraph 5(3) of this Part of this Schedule.

56. Where any fixed assets of the company (other than listed investments) are included under any item shown in the company's balance sheet at an amount determined in accordance with paragraph 41, the following information shall be given:

(a)   the years (so far as they are known to the directors) in which the assets were severally valued and the several values; and

(b)   in the case of assets that have been valued during the financial year, the names of the persons who valued them or particulars of their qualifications for doing so and (whichever is stated) the bases of valuation used by them.

57. In relation to any amount which is included under Assets item 10 in the balance sheet format (Tangible fixed assets) with respect to land and buildings there shall be stated:

(a)   how much of that amount is ascribable to land of freehold tenure and how much to land of leasehold tenure; and

(b)   how much of the amount ascribable to land of leasehold tenure is ascribable to land held on long lease and how much to land held on short lease.

58. There shall be disclosed separately the amount of:

(a) any participating interests; and

(b) any shares in group undertakings that are held in credit institutions.

Reserves and provisions

59.—(1) Where any amount is transferred:

(a) to or from any reserves;

(b) to any provisions for liabilities and charges; or

(c) from any provision for liabilities and charges otherwise than for the purpose for which the provision was established;

and the reserves or provisions are or would but for paragraph 3(3) of this Part of this Schedule be shown as separate items in the company's balance sheet, the information mentioned in the following sub-paragraph shall be given in respect of the aggregate of reserves or provisions included in the same item.

(2) That information is:

(a) the amount of the reserves or provisions as at the date of the beginning of the financial year and as at the balance sheet date respectively;

(b) any amounts transferred to or from the reserve or provisions during that year; and

(c) the source and application respectively of any amounts so transferred.

(3) Particulars shall be given of each provision included in Liabilities item 6(c) (Other provisions) in the company's balance sheet in any case where the amount of that provision is material.

Provision for taxation

60. The amount of any provision for deferred taxation shall be stated separately from the amount of any provision for other taxation.

Maturity analysis

61.—(1) A company shall disclose separately for each of Assets items 3(b) and 4 and Liabilities items 1(b), 2(b) and 3(b) the aggregate amount of the loans and advances and liabilities included in those items broken down into the following categories:

(a) those repayable in not more than three months

(b) those repayable in more than three months but not more than one year

(c) those repayable in more than one year but not more than five years

(d) those repayable in more than five years

from the balance sheet date.

(2) A company shall also disclose the aggregate amounts of all loans and advances falling within Assets item 4 (Loans and advances to customers) which are:

(a) repayable on demand; or

(b) are for an indeterminate period, being repayable upon short notice.

(3) For the purposes of sub-paragraph (1), where a loan or advance or liability is repayable by instalments, each such instalment is to be treated as a separate loan or advance or liability.

Debt and other fixed income securities

62. A company shall disclose the amount of debt and fixed income securities included in Assets item 5 (Debt securities and other fixed income securities) and the amount of such securities included in Liabilities item 3(a) (Bonds and medium term notes) that (in each case) will become due within one year of the balance sheet date.

Subordinated liabilities

63.—(1) The following information must be disclosed in relation to any borrowing included in Liabilities item 7 (Subordinated liabilities) that exceeds 10 per cent of the total for that item:

(a) its amount;

(b) the currency in which it is denominated;

(c) the rate of interest and the maturity date (or the fact that it is perpetual);

(d) the circumstances in which early repayment may be demanded;

(e) the terms of the subordination; and

(f) the existence of any provisions whereby it may be converted into capital or some other form of liability and the terms of any such provisions.

(2) The general terms of any other borrowings included in Liabilities item 7 shall also be stated.

Fixed cumulative dividends

64. If any fixed cumulative dividends on the company's shares are in arrear, there shall be stated:

(a) the amount of the arrears; and

(b) the period for which the dividends or, if there is more than one class, each class of them are in arrears.

Details of assets charged

65.—(1) There shall be disclosed, in relation to each liabilities and memorandum item of the balance sheet format, the aggregate amount of any assets of the company which have been charged to secure any liability or potential liability included thereunder, the aggregate amount of the liabilities or potential liabilities so secured and an indication of the nature of the security given.

(2) Particulars shall also be given of any other charge on the assets of the company to secure the liabilities of any other person, including, where practicable, the amount secured.

Guarantees and other financial commitments

66.—(1) There shall be stated, where practicable:

    (a) the aggregate amount or estimated amount of contracts for capital expenditure, so far as not provided for; ...

    (b) ...

(2) Particulars shall be given of:

    (a) any pension commitments included under any provision shown in the company's balance sheet; and

    (b) any such commitments for which no provision has been made;

and where any such commitment relates wholly or partly to pensions payable to past directors of the company separate particulars shall be given of that commitment so far as it relates to such pensions.

(3) Particulars shall also be given of any other financial commitments, including any contingent liabilities, which:

    (a) have not been provided for;

    (b) have not been included in the memorandum items in the balance sheet format; and

    (c) are relevant to assessing the company's state of affairs.

(4) Commitments within any of the preceding sub-paragraphs undertaken on behalf of or for the benefit of:

    (a) any parent company or fellow subsidiary undertaking of the company; or

    (b) any subsidiary undertaking of the company;

shall be stated separately from the other commitments within that sub-paragraph (and commitments within paragraph (a) shall be stated separately from those within paragraph (b)).

(5) There shall be disclosed the nature and amount of any contingent liabilities and commitments included in Memorandum items 1 and 2 which are material in relation to the company's activities.

Memorandum items: Group undertakings

67.—(1) With respect to contingent liabilities required to be included under Memorandum item 1 in the balance sheet format, there shall be stated in a note to the accounts the amount of such contingent liabilities incurred on behalf of or for the benefit of:

    (a) any parent undertaking or fellow subsidiary undertaking; or

    (b) any subsidiary undertaking

of the company; in addition the amount incurred in respect of the undertakings referred to in paragraph (a) shall be stated separately from the amount incurred in respect of the undertakings referred to in paragraph (b).

(2) With respect to commitments required to be included under Memorandum item 2 in the balance sheet format, there shall be stated in a note to the accounts the amount of such commitments undertaken on behalf of or for the benefit of:

(a) any parent undertaking or fellow subsidiary undertaking; or

(b) any subsidiary undertaking

of the company; in addition the amount incurred in respect of the undertakings referred to in paragraph (a) shall be stated separately from the amount incurred in respect of the undertakings referred to in paragraph (b).

Transferable securities

68.—(1) There shall be disclosed for each of Assets items 5 to 8 in the balance sheet format the amount of transferable securities included under those items:

(a) that are listed and the amount of those that are unlisted; ...

(b) ...

(2) In the case of each amount shown in respect of listed securities under sub-paragraph (1)(a) above, there shall also be disclosed the aggregate market value of those securities, if different from the amount shown.

(3) There shall also be disclosed for each of Assets items 5 and 6 the amount of transferable securities included under those items that are held as financial fixed assets and the amount of those that are not so held, together with the criterion used by the directors to distinguish those held as financial fixed assets.

Leasing transactions

69. The aggregate amount of all property (other than land) leased by the company to other persons shall be disclosed, broken down so as to show the aggregate amount included in each relevant balance sheet item.

Assets and liabilities denominated in a currency other than sterling (or the currency in which the accounts are drawn up)

70.—(1) The aggregate amount, in sterling (or the currency in which the accounts are drawn up), of all assets denominated in a currency other than sterling (or the currency used), together with the aggregate amount, in sterling (or the currency used), of all liabilities so denominated, is to be disclosed.

(2) For the purposes of this paragraph an appropriate rate of exchange prevailing at the balance sheet date shall be used to determine the amounts concerned.

Sundry assets and liabilities

71. Where any amount shown under either of the following items is material, particulars shall be given of each type of asset or liability included therein, including an explanation of the nature of the asset or liability and the amount included with respect to assets or liabilities of that type:

(a) Assets item 13 (Other assets)

(b) Liabilities item 4 (Other liabilities).

Unmatured forward transactions

72.—(1) The following shall be disclosed with respect to unmatured forward transactions outstanding at the balance sheet date:

(a) the categories of such transactions, by reference to an appropriate system of classification;

(b) whether, in the case of each such category, they have been made, to any material extent, for the purpose of hedging the effects of fluctuations in interest rates, exchange rates and market prices or whether they have been made, to any material extent, for dealing purposes.

(2) Transactions falling within sub-paragraph (1) shall include all those in relation to which income or expenditure is to be included in:

(a) format 1, item 6 or format 2, items B4 or A3 (Dealing profits losses),

(b) format 1, items 1 or 2, or format 2, items B1 or A1, by virtue of notes (1)(b) and (2)(b) to the profit and loss account formats (forward contracts, spread over the actual duration of the contract and similar in nature to interest).

Miscellaneous matters

73.—(1) Particulars shall be given of any case where the cost of any asset is for the first time determined under paragraph 38 of this Part of this Schedule.

(2) Where any outstanding loans made under the authority of section 153(4)(b),(bb) or (c) or section 155 of this Act (various cases of financial assistance by a company for purchase of its own shares) are included under any item shown in the company's balance sheet, the aggregate amount of those loans shall be disclosed for each item in question.

(3) ...

Information supplementing the profit and loss account

74. ...

Particulars of tax

75.—(1) ...

(2) Particulars shall be given of any special circumstances which affect liability in respect of taxation of profits, income or capital gains for the financial year or liability in respect of taxation of profits, income or capital gains for succeeding financial years.

(3) The following amounts shall be stated:

(a) the amount of the charge for United Kingdom corporation tax;

(b) if that amount would have been greater but for relief from double taxation, the amount which it would have been but for such relief;

(c) the amount of the charge for United Kingdom income tax; and

(d) the amount of the charge for taxation imposed outside the United Kingdom of profits, income and (so far as charged to revenue) capital gains.

These amounts shall be stated separately in respect of each of the amounts which is shown under the following items in the profit and loss account, that is to say format 1 item 16, format 2 item A10 (Tax on profit loss on ordinary activities) and format 1 item 21, format 2 item A13 (Tax on extraordinary profit loss).

Particulars of income

76.—(1) A company shall disclose, with respect to income included in the following items in the profit and loss account formats, the amount of that income attributable to each of the geographical markets in which the company has operated during the financial year:

(a) format 1 item 1, format 2 item B1 (Interest receivable);

(b) format 1 item 3, format 2 item B2 (Dividend income);

(c) format 1 item 4, format 2 item B3 (Fees and commissions receivable);

(d) format 1 item 6, format 2 item B4 (Dealing profits); and

(e) format 1 item 7, format 2 item B7 (Other operating income).

(2) In analysing for the purposes of this paragraph the source of any income, the directors shall have regard to the manner in which the company's activities are organised.

(3) For the purposes of this paragraph, markets which do not differ substantially from each other shall be treated as one market.

(4) Where in the opinion of the directors the disclosure of any information required by this paragraph would be seriously prejudicial to the interests of the company, that information need not be disclosed, but the fact that any such information has not been disclosed must be stated.

Particulars of staff

77.—(1) The following information shall be given with respect to the employees of the company:

(a) the average number of persons employed by the company in the financial year; and

(b) the average number of persons so employed within each category of persons employed by the company.

(2) The average number required by sub-paragraph (1)(a) or (b) shall be determined by dividing the relevant annual number by the number of months in the financial year.

(3) The relevant annual number shall be determined by ascertaining for each month in the financial year:

(a) for the purposes of sub-paragraph (1)(a), the number of persons employed under contracts of service by the company in that month (whether throughout the month or not); and

(b) for the purposes of sub-paragraph (1)(b), the number of persons in the category in question of persons so employed;

and, in either case, adding together all the monthly numbers.

(4) In respect of all persons employed by the company during the financial year who are taken into account in determining the relevant annual number for the purposes of sub-paragraph (1)(a) there shall also be stated the aggregate amounts respectively of:

- (a) wages and salaries paid or payable in respect of that year to those persons;
- (b) social security costs incurred by the company on their behalf; and
- (c) other pension costs so incurred,

save in so far as those amounts or any of them are stated in the profit and loss account.

(5) The categories of persons employed by the company by reference to which the number required to be disclosed by sub-paragraph (1)(b) is to be determined shall be such as the directors may select, having regard to the manner in which the company's activities are organised.

Management and agency services

78. A company providing any management and agency services to customers shall disclose that fact, if the scale of such services provided is material in the context of its business as a whole.

Subordinated liabilities

79. Any amounts charged to the profit and loss account representing charges incurred during the year with respect to subordinated liabilities shall be disclosed.

Sundry income and charges

80. Where any amount to be included in any of the following items is material, particulars shall be given of each individual component of the figure, including an explanation of their nature and amount:

- (a) In format 1:
    - (i) Items 7 and 10 (Other operating income and charges)
    - (ii) Items 18 and 19 (Extraordinary income and charges);
- (b) In format 2:
    - (i) Items A6 and B7 (Other operating charges and income)
    - (ii) Items A12 and B10 (Extraordinary charges and income).

Miscellaneous matters

81.—(1) Where any amount relating to any preceding financial year is included in any item in the profit and loss account, the effect shall be stated.

(2) The effect shall be stated of any transactions that are exceptional by virtue of size or incidence though they fall within the ordinary activities of the company.

CHAPTER IV
INTERPRETATION OF PART I

General

82. The following definitions apply for the purposes of this Part of this Schedule and its interpretation:

> ...
>
> 'Financial fixed assets' means loans and advances and securities held as fixed assets; participating interests and shareholdings in group undertakings shall be regarded as financial fixed assets;
>
> 'Fungible assets' means assets of any description which are substantially indistinguishable one from another;
>
> 'Lease' includes an agreement for a lease;
>
> 'Listed security' means a security listed on a recognised stock exchange, or on any stock exchange of repute outside Great Britain and the expression 'unlisted security' shall be construed accordingly;
>
> 'Long lease' means a lease in the case of which the portion of the term for which it was granted remaining unexpired at the end of the financial year is not less than 50 years;
>
> 'Repayable on demand', in connection with deposits, loans or advances, means those amounts which can at any time be withdrawn or demanded without notice or for which a maturity or period of notice of not more than 24 hours or one working day has been agreed;
>
> 'Sale and repurchase transaction' means a transaction which involves the transfer by a credit institution or customer ('the transferor') to another credit institution or customer ('the transferee') of assets subject to an agreement that the same assets, or (in the case of fungible assets) equivalent assets, will subsequently be transferred back to the transferor at a specified price on a date specified or to be specified by the transferor; but the following shall not be regarded as sale and repurchase transactions: forward exchange transactions, options, transactions involving the issue of debt securities with a commitment to repurchase all or part of the issue before maturity or any similar transactions;
>
> 'Sale and option to resell transaction' means a transaction which involves the transfer by a credit institution or customer ('the transferor') to another credit institution or customer ('the transferee') of assets subject to an agreement that the transferee is entitled to require the subsequent transfer of the same assets, or (in the case of fungible assets) equivalent assets, back to the transferor at the purchase price or another price agreed in advance on a date specified or to be specified; and
>
> 'Short lease' means a lease which is not a long lease.

Loans

83. For the purposes of this Part of this Schedule a loan or advance (including a liability comprising a loan or advance) is treated as falling due for repayment, and an instalment of a loan or advance is treated as falling due for payment, on the earliest date on which the lender could require repayment or (as the case may be) payment, if he exercised all options and rights available to him.

Materiality

84. For the purposes of this Part of this Schedule amounts which in the particular context of any provision of this Part are not material may be disregarded for the purposes of that provision.

Provisions

85. For the purposes of this Part of this Schedule and its interpretation:
  (a) references in this Part to provisions for depreciation or diminution in value of assets are to any amount written off by way of providing for depreciation or diminution in value of assets;
  (b) any reference in the profit and loss account formats or the notes thereto set out in Section B of this Part to the depreciation of, or amounts written off, assets of any description is to any provision for depreciation or diminution in value of assets of that description; and
  (c) references in this Part to provisions for liabilities or charges are to any amount retained as reasonably necessary for the purpose of providing for any liability or loss which is either likely to be incurred, or certain to be incurred but uncertain as to amount or as to the date on which it will arise.

Scots land tenure

86. In the application of this Part of this Schedule to Scotland, 'land of freehold tenure' means land in respect of which the company *is the proprietor of the dominium utile or, in the case of land not held on feudal tenure,* is the owner; 'land of leasehold tenure' means land of which the company is the tenant under a lease; *and the reference to ground-rents, rates and other outgoings includes feu-duty and ground annual.*

Note: words in italics repealed by the Abolition of Feudal Tenure etc (Scotland) Act 2000, s 76(1), (2), Sch 12, Pt I, para 46(1), (6), Sch 13, Pt I, as from a day to be appointed.

Staff costs

87. For the purposes of this Part of this Schedule and its interpretation:
  (a) 'Social security costs' means any contributions by the company to any state social security or pension scheme, fund or arrangement;
  (b) 'Pension costs' includes any costs incurred by the company in respect of any pension scheme established for the purpose of providing pensions for persons currently or formerly employed by the company, any sums set aside for the future payment of pensions directly by the company to current or former employees and any pensions paid directly to such persons without having first been set aside; and
  (c) any amount stated in respect of social security costs or in respect of the item 'wages and salaries' in the company's profit and loss account shall be determined by reference to payments made or costs incurred

in respect of all persons employed by the company during the financial year who are taken into account in determining the relevant annual number for the purposes of paragraph 77(1)(a).

PART II
CONSOLIDATED ACCOUNTS

Undertakings to be included in consolidation

1.—(1) An undertaking (other than a credit institution) whose activities are a direct extension of or ancillary to banking business shall not be excluded from consolidation under section 229(4) (exclusion of undertakings whose activities are different from those of the undertakings consolidated).

(2) For the purposes of this paragraph 'banking' means the carrying on of a deposit taking business within the meaning of the Banking Act 1987.

General application of provisions applicable to individual accounts

2.—(1) In paragraph 1 of Schedule 4A (application to group accounts of provisions applicable to individual accounts), the reference in sub-paragraph (1) to the provisions of Schedule 4 shall be construed as a reference to the provisions of Part I of this Schedule; and accordingly:

    (a) ...

    (b) sub-paragraph (3) shall be omitted.

(2) The general application of the provisions of Part I of this Schedule in place of those of Schedule 4 is subject to the following provisions.

Minority interests and associated undertakings

3.—(1) The provisions of this paragraph shall have effect so as to adapt paragraphs 17 and 21 of Schedule 4A (which require items in respect of 'Minority interests' and associated undertakings to be added to the formats set out in Schedule 4) to the formats prescribed by Part I of this Schedule.

(2) The item required to be added to the balance sheet format by paragraph 17(2) shall be added either between Liabilities items 7 and 8 or after Liabilities item 12.

(3) The item required to be added to the profit and loss account format by paragraph 17(3) shall be added:

    (a) in the case of format 1, between items 17 and 18; or

    (b) in the case of format 2, between items A11 and A12 or between items B9 and B10.

(4) The item required to be added to the profit and loss account format by paragraph 17(4) shall be added:

    (a) in the case of format 1, between items 22 and 23; or

    (b) in the case of format 2, between items A14 and A15 or between items B11 and B12.

(5) Paragraph 17(5) shall not apply but for the purposes of paragraph 3(3) of Part I of this Schedule (power to combine items) the additional items required by the foregoing provisions of this paragraph shall be treated as items to which a letter is assigned.

(6) Paragraph 21(2) shall apply with respect to a balance sheet prepared under this Schedule as if it required Assets item 7 (Participating interests) in the balance sheet format to be replaced by the two replacement items referred to in that paragraph.

(7) Paragraph 21(3) shall not apply, but the following items in the profit and loss account formats, namely:

    (a) format 1 item 3(b) (Income from participating interests)

    (b) format 2 item B2(b) (Income from participating interests),

shall be replaced by the following two replacement items:

    (i) 'Income from participating interests other than associated undertakings', which shall be shown at position 3(b) in format 1 and position B2(b) in format 2; and

    (ii) 'Income from associated undertakings', which shall be shown at an appropriate position.

4. Paragraphs 18 and 22(1) of Schedule 4A shall apply as if, in substitution for the references therein to paragraphs 17 to 19 and 21 of Schedule 4, they referred to paragraphs 24 to 26 and 28 of Part I of this Schedule.

Foreign currency translation

5. Any difference between:

    (a) the amount included in the consolidated accounts for the previous financial year with respect to any undertaking included in the consolidation or the group's interest in any associated undertaking, together with the amount of any transactions undertaken to cover any such interest; and

    (b) the opening amount for the financial year in respect of those undertakings and in respect of any such transactions

arising as a result of the application of paragraph 45 of Part I of this Schedule may be credited to (where (a) is less than (b)), or deducted from (where (a) is greater than (b)), (as the case may be) consolidated reserves.

6. Any income and expenditure of undertakings included in the consolidation and associated undertakings in a foreign currency may be translated for the purposes of the consolidated accounts at the average rates of exchange prevailing during the financial year.

Information as to undertaking in which shares held as a result of financial assistance operation

7.—(1) The following provisions apply where the parent company of a banking group has a subsidiary undertaking which:

    (a) is a credit institution of which shares are held as a result of a financial assistance operation with a view to its reorganisation or rescue; and

    (b) is excluded from consolidation under section 229(3)(c) (interest held with a view to resale).

(2) Information as to the nature and terms of the operations shall be given in a note to the group accounts and there shall be appended to the copy of the group accounts delivered to the registrar in accordance with section 242 a copy of the undertaking's latest individual accounts and, if it is a parent undertaking, its latest group accounts.

    If the accounts appended are required by law to be audited, a copy of the auditors' report shall also be appended.

(3) ... if any document required to be appended is in a language other than English then, subject to section 710B(6) (delivery of certain Welsh documents without a translation), the directors shall annex a translation of it into English certified in the prescribed manner to be a correct translation.

(4) The above requirements are subject to the following qualifications:

    (a) an undertaking is not required to prepare for the purposes of this paragraph accounts which would not otherwise be prepared, and if no accounts satisfying the above requirements are prepared none need be appended;

    (b) the accounts of an undertaking need not be appended if they would not otherwise be required to be published, or made available for public inspection, anywhere in the world, but in that case the reason for not appending the accounts shall be stated in a note to the consolidated accounts.

(5) Where a copy of an undertaking's accounts is required to be appended to the copy of the group accounts delivered to the registrar, that fact shall be stated in a note to the group accounts.

(6) Sub-sections (2) to (4) of section 242 (penalties, &c in case of default) apply in relation to the requirements of this paragraph as regards the delivery of documents to the registrar as they apply in relation to the requirements of sub-section (1) of that section.

PART III
ADDITIONAL DISCLOSURE: RELATED UNDERTAKINGS

1.—(1) Where accounts are prepared in accordance with the special provisions of this Schedule relating to banking companies or groups:

    (a) the information required by paragraphs 8 and 24 of Schedule 5 (information about significant holdings of the company in undertakings other than subsidiary undertakings) need only be given in respect of undertakings (otherwise falling within the class of undertakings in respect of which disclosure is required) in which the company has a significant holding amounting to 20 per cent or more of the nominal value of the shares in the undertaking; and

    (b) the information required by paragraph 27 of Schedule 5 (information about significant holdings of the group in undertakings other than subsidiary undertakings) need only be given in respect of undertakings (otherwise falling within the class of undertakings in respect of which disclosure is required) in which the group has a significant holding amounting to 20 per cent or more of the nominal value of the shares in the undertaking.

In addition any information required by those paragraphs may be omitted if it is not material.

(2) Paragraph 13(3) and (4) of Schedule 5 shall apply *mutatis mutandis* for the purposes of sub-paragraph (1)(a) above and paragraph 32(3) and (4) of that Schedule shall apply *mutatis mutandis* for the purposes of sub-paragraph (1)(b) above.

PART IV
ADDITIONAL DISCLOSURE: EMOLUMENTS AND OTHER BENEFITS OF DIRECTORS AND OTHERS

1. The provisions of this Part of this Schedule have effect with respect to the application of Schedule 6 (additional disclosure: emoluments and other benefits of directors and others) to a banking company or the holding company of a credit institution.

Loans, quasi-loans and other dealings

2. Where a banking company, or a company which is the holding company of a credit institution, prepares annual accounts for a financial year, it need not comply with the provisions of Part II of Schedule 6 (loans, quasi-loans and other dealings) in relation to a transaction or arrangement of a kind mentioned in section 330, or an agreement to enter into such a transaction or arrangement, to which that banking company or (as the case may be) credit institution is a party.

Other transactions, arrangements and agreements

3.—(1) Where a banking company, or a company which is the holding company of a credit institution, takes advantage of the provisions of paragraph 2 of this Part of this Schedule for the purposes of its annual accounts for a financial year, then, in preparing those accounts, it shall comply with the provisions of Part III of Schedule 6 (other transactions, arrangements and agreements) only in relation to a transaction, arrangement or agreement made by that banking company or (as the case may be) credit institution for—

    (a) a person who was a director of the company preparing the accounts or who was connected with such a director, or

    (b) a person who was a chief executive or manager (within the meaning of the Banking Act 1987) of that company or its holding company.

(2) References in that Part to officers of the company shall be construed accordingly as including references to such persons.

(3) In this paragraph 'director' includes a shadow director.

(4) For the purposes of that Part as it applies by virtue of this paragraph, a body corporate which a person does not control shall not be treated as connected with him.

(5) Section 346 of this Act applies for the purposes of this paragraph as regards the interpretation of references to a person being connected with a director or controlling a body corporate.

General note

Parts I and II of this Schedule reflect the requirements of Sch 4 (form and content of individual accounts) and Sch 4A (form and content of group accounts) as appropriately modified for banking companies and groups; Pt III modifies the operation of Sch 5 (information to be contained in notes to the accounts); and Pt IV modifies the application of Sch 6 in relation to banking companies (defined in s 744) and holding companies of credit institutions (defined in s 262(1)): see notes to ss 255–255B, above.

Part IV   Additional disclosure: emoluments and other benefits of directors and others

Paragraph 2   Banking companies and holding companies of credit institutions are exempt from the disclosure requirements imposed by Sch 6, Pt II, paras 15(a) and (b), 16(a) and (b) with respect to transactions etc within s 330 which require information regarding these matters to be included in the notes to the company's accounts. However, these companies must still comply with Sch 6, Pt II, paras 15(c), 16(c), which require disclosure of material interests of directors of the company or its holding company in any other transaction or arrangement (ie one not within s 330) with the company or a subsidiary of the company. See notes to Sch 6, Pt II, above.

Paragraph 3   Instead of making the detailed disclosures required by Sch 6, Pt II, a company relying on the exemption granted by para 2 above need only comply with the lesser disclosure required by Sch 6, Pt III with respect to transactions etc entered into with the specified officers.

Sch 6, Pt III requires only abbreviated details of the transaction etc to be disclosed in the accounts. However, by ss 343–344, banking companies and holding companies of credit institutions are required (i) to maintain a register of these transactions; and (ii) to make a statement (containing the particulars regarding these transactions) available for inspection by their shareholders before and at the company's annual general meeting. This statement must also be reviewed by the company's auditors. See notes to ss 343–344, above.

SCHEDULE 9A

FORM AND CONTENT OF ACCOUNTS OF INSURANCE COMPANIES AND GROUPS

Sections 255, 255A, 255B

PART I
INDIVIDUAL ACCOUNTS

CHAPTER I
GENERAL RULES AND FORMATS

Section A
General rules

1.—(1) Subject to the following provisions of this Part of this Schedule—
  - (a) every balance sheet of a company shall show the items listed in the balance sheet format set out below in section B of this Chapter; and
  - (b) every profit and loss account of a company shall show the items listed in the profit and loss account format so set out,

in either case in the order and under the headings and sub-headings given in the format.

(2) Sub-paragraph (1) above is not to be read as requiring the heading or sub-heading for any item to be distinguished by any letter or number assigned to that item in the format.

2.—(1) Any item required in accordance with paragraph 1 above to be shown in a company's balance sheet or profit and loss account may be shown in greater detail than so required.

(2) A company's balance sheet or profit and loss account may include an item representing or covering the amount of any asset or liability, income or expenditure not specifically covered by any of the items listed in the balance

sheet or profit and loss account format set out in section B below, but the following shall not be treated as assets in any company's balance sheet—

   (a) preliminary expenses;

   (b) expenses of and commission on any issue of shares or debentures; and

   (c) costs of research.

(3) Items to which Arabic numbers are assigned in the balance sheet format set out in section B below (except for items concerning technical provisions and the reinsurers' share of technical provisions), and items to which lower case letters in parentheses are assigned in the profit and loss account format so set out (except for items within items I.1 and 4 and II.1, 5 and 6) may be combined in a company's accounts for any financial year if either—

   (a) their individual amounts are not material for the purpose of giving a true and fair view; or

   (b) the combination facilitates the assessment of the state of affairs or profit or loss of the company for that year;

but in a case within paragraph (b) above the individual amounts of any items so combined shall be disclosed in a note to the accounts and any notes required by this Schedule to the items so combined under that paragraph shall, notwithstanding the combination, be given.

(4) Subject to paragraph 3(3) below, a heading or sub-heading corresponding to an item listed in the format adopted in preparing a company's balance sheet or profit and loss account shall not be included if there is no amount to be shown for that item in respect of the financial year to which the balance sheet or profit and loss account relates.

3.—(1) In respect of every item shown in the balance sheet or profit and loss account, there shall be shown or stated the corresponding amount for the financial year immediately preceding that to which the accounts relate.

(2) Where the corresponding amount is not comparable with the amount to be shown for the item in question in respect of the financial year to which the balance sheet or profit and loss account relates, the former amount shall be adjusted and particulars of the adjustment and the reasons for it shall be given in a note to the accounts.

(3) Paragraph 2(4) above does not apply in any case where an amount can be shown for the item in question in respect of the financial year immediately preceding that to which the balance sheet or profit and loss account relates, and that amount shall be shown under the heading or sub-heading required by paragraph 1 above for that item.

4. Subject to the provisions of this Schedule, amounts in respect of items representing assets or income may not be set off against amounts in respect of items representing liabilities or expenditure (as the case may be), or vice versa.

5. Every profit and loss account of a company shall show separately as additional items—

   (a) any amount set aside or proposed to be set aside to, or withdrawn or proposed to be withdrawn from, reserves; ...

   (b) the aggregate amount of any dividends paid and proposed,

    (c) if it is not shown in the notes to the accounts, the aggregate amount of any dividends proposed.

6. The provisions of this Schedule which relate to long term business shall apply, with necessary modifications, to business within Classes 1 and 2 of Schedule 2 to the 1982 Act which—

    (a) is transacted exclusively or principally according to the technical principles of long term business, and

    (b) is a significant amount of the business of the company.

Section B
The required formats for accounts

Preliminary

7.—(1) References in this Part of this Schedule to the balance sheet format or profit and loss account format are to the balance sheet format or profit and loss account format set out below, and references to the items listed in either of the formats are to those items read together with any of the notes following the formats which apply to any of those items.

(2) The requirement imposed by paragraph 1 to show the items listed in either format in the order adopted in the format is subject to any provision in the notes following the format for alternative positions for any particular items.

(3) Where in respect of any item to which an Arabic number is assigned in either format, the gross amount and reinsurance amount or reinsurers' share are required to be shown, a sub-total of those amounts shall also be given.

(4) Where in respect of any item to which an Arabic number is assigned in the profit and loss account format, separate items are required to be shown, then a separate sub-total of those items shall also be given in addition to any sub-total required by sub-paragraph (3) above.

8. A number in brackets following any item in either of the formats set out below is a reference to the note of that number in the notes following the format.

9. In the profit and loss account format set out below—

    (a) the heading 'Technical account—General business' is for business within the classes of insurance specified in Schedule 2 to the 1982 Act; and

    (b) the heading 'Technical account—Long term business' is for business within the classes of insurance specified in Schedule 1 to that Act.

Balance Sheet Format

ASSETS

A. *Called up share capital not paid (1)*
B. *Intangible assets*
    1. Development costs
    2. Concessions, patents, licences, trade marks and similar rights and assets *(2)*
    3. Goodwill *(3)*
    4. Payments on account
C. *Investments*
    I   Land and buildings *(4)*
    II   Investments in group undertakings and participating interests
         1. Shares in group undertakings
         2. Debt securities issued by, and loans to, group undertakings
         3. Participating interests
         4. Debt securities issued by, and loans to, undertakings in which the company has a participating interest
    III Other financial investments
         1. Shares and other variable-yield securities and units in unit trusts
         2. Debt securities and other fixed income securities *(5)*
         3. Participation in investment pools *(6)*
         4. Loans secured by mortgages *(7)*
         5. Other loans *(7)*
         6. Deposits with credit institutions *(8)*
         7. Other *(9)*
    IV   Deposits with ceding undertakings *(10)*
D. *Assets held to cover linked liabilities (11)*
Da. *Reinsurers' share of technical provisions (12)*
         1. Provision for unearned premiums
         2. Long term business provision
         3. Claims outstanding
         4. Provisions for bonuses and rebates
         5. Other technical provisions
         6. Technical provisions for unit-linked liabilities
E. *Debtors (13)*
    I   Debtors arising out of direct insurance operations
         1. Policy holders
         2. Intermediaries
    II   Debtors arising out of reinsurance operations

       III Other debtors

       IV Called up share capital not paid (*1*)

  F. *Other assets*

       I   Tangible assets

          1.   Plant and machinery

          2.   Fixtures, fittings, tools and equipment

          3.   Payments on account (other than deposits paid on land and buildings) and assets (other than buildings) in course of construction

       II   Stocks

          1.   Raw materials and consumables

          2.   Work in progress

          3.   Finished goods and goods for resale

          4.   Payments on account

       III Cash at bank and in hand

       IV Own shares (*14*)

       V   Other (*15*)

  G. Prepayments and accrued income

       I   Accrued interest and rent (*16*)

       II   Deferred acquisition costs (*17*)

       III Other prepayments and accrued income

LIABILITIES

  A. *Capital and reserves*

       I   Called up share capital or equivalent funds

       II   Share premium account

       III Revaluation reserve

       IV Reserves

          1.   Capital redemption reserve

          2.   Reserve for own shares

          3.   Reserves provided for by the articles of association

          4.   Other reserves

       V   Profit and loss account

  B. *Subordinated liabilities* (*18*)

  Ba. *Fund for future appropriations* (*19*)

  C. *Technical provisions*

       1.   Provision for unearned premiums (*20*)

          (a)   gross amount

          (b)   reinsurance amount (*12*)

       2.   Long term business provision (*20*) (*21*) (*26*)

          (a)   gross amount

          (b)   reinsurance amount (*12*)

　　3.　Claims outstanding (*22*)
　　　　(a)　gross amount
　　　　(b)　reinsurance amount (*12*)
　　4.　Provision for bonuses and rebates (*23*)
　　　　(a)　gross amount
　　　　(b)　reinsurance amount (*12*)
　　5.　Equalisation provision (*24*)
　　6.　Other technical provisions (*25*)
　　　　(a)　gross amount
　　　　(b)　reinsurance amount (*12*)
D.　*Technical provisions for linked liabilities (26)*
　　(a) gross amount
　　(b) reinsurance amount (*12*)
E.　*Provisions for other risks and charges*
　　1.　Provisions for pensions and similar obligations
　　2.　Provisions for taxation
　　3.　Other provisions
F.　*Deposits received from reinsurers (27)*
G.　*Creditors (28)*
　　I　Creditors arising out of direct insurance operations
　　II　Creditors arising out of reinsurance operations
　　III　Debenture loans (*29*)
　　IV　Amounts owed to credit institutions
　　V　Other creditors including taxation and social security
H.　*Accruals and deferred income*

Notes on the balance sheet format

(1) *Called up share capital not paid*

(Assets items A and E.IV)

This item may be shown in either of the positions given in the format.

(2) *Concessions, patents, licences, trade marks and similar rights and assets*

(Assets item B.2)

Amounts in respect of assets shall only be included in a company's balance sheet under this item if either—

　　(a)　the assets were acquired for valuable consideration and are not required to be shown under goodwill; or
　　(b)　the assets in question were created by the company itself.

(3) *Goodwill*

(Assets item B.3)

Amounts representing goodwill shall only be included to the extent that the goodwill was acquired for valuable consideration.

(4) *Land and buildings*

(Assets item C.I.)

The amount of any land and buildings occupied by the company for its own activities shall be shown separately in the notes to the accounts.

(5) *Debt securities and other fixed income securities*

(Assets item C.III.2)

This item shall comprise transferable debt securities and any other transferable fixed income securities issued by credit institutions, other undertakings or public bodies, in so far as they are not covered by Assets item C.II.2 or C.II.4.

    Securities bearing interest rates that vary in accordance with specific factors, for example the interest rate on the inter-bank market or on the Euromarket, shall also be regarded as debt securities and other fixed income securities and so be included under this item.

(6) *Participation in investment pools*

(Assets item C.III.3)

This item shall comprise shares held by the company in joint investments constituted by several undertakings or pension funds, the management of which has been entrusted to one of those undertakings or to one of those pension funds.

(7) *Loans secured by mortgages and other loans*

(Assets items C.III.4 and C.III.5)

Loans to policy holders for which the policy is the main security shall be included under 'Other loans' and their amount shall be disclosed in the notes to the accounts. Loans secured by mortgage shall be shown as such even where they are also secured by insurance policies. Where the amount of 'Other loans' not secured by policies is material, an appropriate breakdown shall be given in the notes to the accounts.

(8) *Deposits with credit institutions*

(Assets item C.III.6)

This item shall comprise sums the withdrawal of which is subject to a time restriction. Sums deposited with no such restriction shall be shown under Assets item F.III even if they bear interest.

(9) *Other*

(Assets item C.III.7)

This item shall comprise those investments which are not covered by Assets items C.III.1 to 6. Where the amount of such investments is significant, they must be disclosed in the notes to the accounts.

(10) *Deposits with ceding undertakings*

(Assets item C.IV)

Where the company accepts reinsurance this item shall comprise amounts, owed by the ceding undertakings and corresponding to guarantees, which are deposited with those ceding undertakings or with third parties or which are retained by those undertakings.

These amounts may not be combined with other amounts owed by the ceding insurer to the reinsurer or set off against amounts owed by the reinsurer to the ceding insurer.

Securities deposited with ceding undertakings or third parties which remain the property of the company shall be entered in the company's accounts as an investment, under the appropriate item.

(11) *Assets held to cover linked liabilities*

(Assets item D)

In respect of long term business, this item shall comprise investments made pursuant to long term policies under which the benefits payable to the policy holder are wholly or partly to be determined by reference to the value of, or the income from, property of any description (whether or not specified in the contract) or by reference to fluctuations in, or in an index of, the value of property of any description (whether or not so specified).

This item shall also comprise investments which are held on behalf of the members of a tontine and are intended for distribution among them.

(12) *Reinsurance amounts*

(Assets item Da: Liabilities items C.1(b), 2(b), 3(b), 4(b) and 6(b) and D(b))

The reinsurance amounts may be shown either under Assets item Da or under Liabilities items C.1(b), 2(b), 3(b), 4(b) and 6(b) and D(b).

The reinsurance amounts shall comprise the actual or estimated amounts which, under contractual reinsurance arrangements, are deducted from the gross amounts of technical provisions.

As regards the provision for unearned premiums, the reinsurance amounts shall be calculated according to the methods referred to in paragraph 44 above or in accordance with the terms of the reinsurance policy.

(13) *Debtors*

(Assets item E)

Amounts owed by group undertakings and undertakings in which the company has a participating interest shall be shown separately as sub-items of Assets items E.I, II and III.

(14) *Own shares*

(Assets item F.IV)

The nominal value of the shares shall be shown separately under this item.

(15) *Other*

(Assets item F.V)

This item shall comprise those assets which are not covered by Assets items F.I to IV. Where such assets are material they must be disclosed in the notes to the accounts.

(16) *Accrued interest and rent*

(Assets item G.I)

This item shall comprise those items that represent interest and rent that have been earned up to the balance-sheet date but have not yet become receivable.

(17) *Deferred acquisition costs*

(Assets item G.II)

This item shall comprise the costs of acquiring insurance policies which are incurred during a financial year but relate to a subsequent financial year ('deferred acquisition costs'), except in so far as—

(a) allowance has been made in the computation of the long term business provision made under paragraph 46 below and shown under Liabilities item C2 or D in the balance sheet, for—

  (i) the explicit recognition of such costs, or

  (ii) the implicit recognition of such costs by virtue of the anticipation of future income from which such costs may prudently be expected to be recovered, or

(b) allowance has been made for such costs in respect of general business policies by a deduction from the provision for unearned premiums made under paragraph 44 below and shown under Liabilities item C.I in the balance sheet.

Deferred acquisition costs arising in general business shall be distinguished from those arising in long term business.

In the case of general business, the amount of any deferred acquisition costs shall be established on a basis compatible with that used for unearned premiums.

There shall be disclosed in the notes to the accounts—

(a) how the deferral of acquisition costs has been treated (unless otherwise expressly stated in the accounts), and

(b) where such costs are included as a deduction from the provisions at Liabilities item C.I, the amount of such deduction, or

(c) where the actuarial method used in the calculation of the provisions at Liabilities item C.2 or D has made allowance for the explicit recognition of such costs, the amount of the costs so recognised.

(18) *Subordinated liabilities*

(Liabilities item B)

This item shall comprise all liabilities in respect of which there is a contractual obligation that, in the event of winding up or of bankruptcy, they are to be repaid only after the claims of all other creditors have been met (whether or not they are represented by certificates).

(19) *Fund for future appropriations*

(Liabilities item Ba)

This item shall comprise all funds the allocation of which either to policy holders or to shareholders has not been determined by the end of the financial year.

Transfers to and from this item shall be shown in item II.12a in the profit and loss account.

(20) *Provision for unearned premiums*

(Liabilities item C.1)

In the case of long term business the provision for unearned premiums may be included in Liabilities item C.2 rather than in this item.

The provision for unearned premiums shall comprise the amount representing that part of gross premiums written which is estimated to be earned in the following financial year or to subsequent financial years.

(21) *Long term business provision*

(Liabilities item C.2)

This item shall comprise the actuarially estimated value of the company's liabilities (excluding technical provisions included in Liabilities item D), including bonuses already declared and after deducting the actuarial value of future premiums.

This item shall also comprise claims incurred but not reported, plus the estimated costs of settling such claims.

(22) *Claims outstanding*

(Liabilities item C.3)

This item shall comprise the total estimated ultimate cost to the company of settling all claims arising from events which have occurred up to the end of the financial year (including, in the case of general business, claims incurred but not reported) less amounts already paid in respect of such claims.

(23) *Provision for bonuses and rebates*

(Liabilities item C.4)

This item shall comprise amounts intended for policy holders or contract beneficiaries by way of bonuses and rebates as defined in Note *(5)* on the profit and loss account format to the extent that such amounts have not been credited to policy holders or contract beneficiaries or included in Liabilities item Ba or in Liabilities item C.2.

(24) *Equalisation provision*

(Liabilities item C.5)

This item shall comprise the amount of any reserve maintained by the company under section 34A of the Insurance Companies Act 1982.

   This item shall also comprise any amounts which, in accordance with Council Directive 87/343/EEC, are required to be set aside by a company to equalise fluctuations in loss ratios in future years or to provide for special risks.

   A company which otherwise constitutes reserves to equalise fluctuations in loss ratios in future years or to provide for special risks shall disclose that fact in the notes to the accounts.

(25) *Other technical provisions*

(Liabilities item C.6)

This item shall comprise, inter alia, the provision for unexpired risks as defined in paragraph 81 below. Where the amount of the provision for unexpired risks is significant, it shall be disclosed separately either in the balance sheet or in the notes to the accounts.

(26) *Technical provisions for linked liabilities*

(Liabilities item D)

This item shall comprise technical provisions constituted to cover liabilities relating to investment in the context of long term policies under which the benefits payable to policy holders are wholly or partly to be determined by reference to the value of, or the income from, property of any description (whether or not specified in the contract) or by reference to fluctuations in, or in an index of, the value of property of any description (whether or not so specified).

   Any additional technical provisions constituted to cover death risks, operating expenses or other risks (such as benefits payable at the maturity date or guaranteed surrender values) shall be included under Liabilities item C.2.

   This item shall also comprise technical provisions representing the obligations of a tontine's organiser in relation to its members.

(27) *Deposits received from reinsurers*

(Liabilities item F)

Where the company cedes reinsurance, this item shall comprise amounts deposited by or withheld from other insurance undertakings under reinsurance contracts. These amounts may not be merged with other amounts owed to or by those other undertakings.

   Where the company cedes reinsurance and has received as a deposit securities which have been transferred to its ownership, this item shall comprise the amount owed by the company by virtue of the deposit.

(28) *Creditors*

(Liabilities item G)

Amounts owed to group undertakings and undertakings in which the company has a participating interest shall be shown separately as sub-items.

(29) *Debenture loans*

(Liabilities item G.III)

The amount of any convertible loans shall be shown separately.

Special rules for balance sheet format

Additional items

10.—(1) Every balance sheet of a company which carries on long term business shall show separately as an additional item the aggregate of any amounts included in Liabilities item A (capital and reserves) which are required not to be treated as realised profits under section 268 of this Act.

(2) A company which carries on long term business shall show separately, in the balance sheet or in the notes to the accounts, the total amount of assets representing the long term fund valued in accordance with the provisions of this Schedule.

Managed funds

11.—(1) For the purposes of this paragraph 'managed funds' are funds of a group pension fund—

(a) which fall within Class VII of Schedule 1 to the 1982 Act, and

(b) which the company administers in its own name but on behalf of others, and

(c) to which it has legal title.

(2) The company shall, in any case where assets and liabilities arising in respect of managed funds fall to be treated as assets and liabilities of the company, adopt the following accounting treatment: assets and liabilities representing managed funds are to be included in the company's balance sheet, with the notes to the accounts disclosing the total amount included with respect to such assets and liabilities in the balance sheet and showing the amount included under each relevant balance sheet item in respect of such assets or (as the case may be) liabilities.

Deferred acquisition costs

12. The costs of acquiring insurance policies which are incurred during a financial year but which relate to a subsequent financial year shall be deferred in a manner specified in Note (*17*) on the balance sheet format.

Profit and loss account format

I   *Technical account—General business*
1.   Earned premiums, net of reinsurance
   (a) gross premiums written (*1*)
   (b) outward reinsurance premiums (*2*)
   (c) change in the gross provision for unearned premiums
   (d) change in the provision for unearned premiums, reinsurers' share
2.   Allocated investment return transferred from the non-technical account (item III.6) (*10*)
2a. Investment income (*8*), (*10*)
   (a) income from participating interests, with a separate indication of that derived from group undertakings
   (b) income from other investments, with a separate indication of that derived from group undertakings
      (aa) income from land and buildings
      (bb) income from other investments
   (c) value re-adjustments on investments
   (d) gains on the realisation of investments
3.   Other technical income, net of reinsurance
4.   Claims incurred, net of reinsurance (*4*)
   (a) claims paid
      (aa) gross amount
      (bb) reinsurers' share
   (b) change in the provision for claims
      (aa) gross amount
      (bb) reinsurers' share
5.   Changes in other technical provisions, net of reinsurance, not shown under other headings
6.   Bonuses and rebates, net of reinsurance (*5*)
7.   Net operating expenses
   (a) acquisition costs (*6*)
   (b) change in deferred acquisition costs
   (c) administrative expenses (*7*)
   (d) reinsurance commissions and profit participation
8.   Other technical charges, net of reinsurance
8a. Investment expenses and charges (*8*)
   (a) investment management expenses, including interest
   (b) value adjustments on investments
   (c) losses on the realisation of investments
9.   Change in the equalisation provision

10. Sub-total (balance on the technical account for general business) (item III.1)

II   *Technical account—Long term business*
   1.   Earned premiums, net of reinsurance
      (a) gross premiums written (*1*)
      (b) outward reinsurance premiums (*2*)
      (c) change in the provision for unearned premiums, net of reinsurance (*3*)
   2.   Investment income (*8*)(*10*)
      (a) income from participating interests, with a separate indication of that derived from group undertakings
      (b) income from other investments, with a separate indication of that derived from group undertakings
         (aa) income from land and buildings
         (bb) income from other investments
      (c) value re-adjustments on investments
      (d) gains on the realisation of investments
   3.   Unrealised gains on investments (*9*)
   4.   Other technical income, net of reinsurance
   5.   Claims incurred, net of reinsurance (*4*)
      (a) claims paid
         (aa) gross amount
         (bb) reinsurers' share
      (b) change in the provision for claims
         (aa) gross amount
         (bb) reinsurers' share
   6.   Change in other technical provisions, net of reinsurance, not shown under other headings
      (a) long term business provision, net of reinsurance (*3*)
         (aa) gross amount
         (bb) reinsurers' share
      (b) other technical provisions, net of reinsurance
   7.   Bonuses and rebates, net of reinsurance (*5*)
   8.   Net operating expenses
      (a) acquisition costs (*6*)
      (b) change in deferred acquisition costs
      (c) administrative expenses (*7*)
      (d) reinsurance commissions and profit participation
   9.   Investment expenses and charges (*8*)
      (a) investment management expenses, including interest
      (b) value adjustments on investments

    (c) losses on the realisation of investments

10. Unrealised losses on investments (9)

11. Other technical charges, net of reinsurance

11a. Tax attributable to the long term business

12. Allocated investment return transferred to the non-technical account (item III.4)

12a. Transfers to or from the fund for future appropriations

13. Sub-total (balance on the technical account—long term business) (item III.2)

III   *Non-technical account*

1.   Balance on the general business technical account—(item I.10)

2.   Balance on the long term business technical account—(item II.13)

2a. Tax credit attributable to balance on the long term business technical account

3.   Investment income (8)

    (a) income from participating interests, with a separate indication of that derived from group undertakings

    (b) income from other investments, with a separate indication of that derived from group undertakings

       (aa) income from land and buildings

       (bb) income from other investments

    (c) value re-adjustments on investments

    (d) gains on the realisation of investments

3a. Unrealised gains on investments (9)

4.   Allocated investment return transferred from the long term business technical account (item II.12) (10)

5.   Investment expenses and charges (8)

    (a) investment management expenses, including interest

    (b) value adjustments on investments

    (c) losses on the realisation of investments

5a. Unrealised losses on investments (9)

6.   Allocated investment return transferred to the general business technical account (item I.2) (10)

7.   Other income

8.   Other charges, including value adjustments

8a. Profit or loss on ordinary activities before tax

9.   Tax on profit or loss on ordinary activities

10. Profit or loss on ordinary activities after tax

11. Extraordinary income

12. Extraordinary charges

13. Extraordinary profit or loss

14. Tax on extraordinary profit or loss

15. Other taxes not shown under the preceding items

16. Profit or loss for the financial year

Notes on the profit and loss account format

(1) *Gross premiums written*

(General business technical account: item I.1.(a)

Long term business technical account: item II.1.(a))

This item shall comprise all amounts due during the financial year in respect of insurance contracts entered into regardless of the fact that such amounts may relate in whole or in part to a later financial year, and shall include inter alia—

- (i) premiums yet to be determined, where the premium calculation can be done only at the end of the year;
- (ii) single premiums, including annuity premiums, and, in long term business, single premiums resulting from bonus and rebate provisions in so far as they must be considered as premiums under the terms of the contract;
- (iii) additional premiums in the case of half-yearly, quarterly or monthly payments and additional payments from policy holders for expenses borne by the company;
- (iv) in the case of co-insurance, the company's portion of total premiums;
- (v) reinsurance premiums due from ceding and retroceding insurance undertakings, including portfolio entries,

after deduction of cancellations and portfolio withdrawals credited to ceding and retroceding insurance undertakings.

The above amounts shall not include the amounts of taxes or duties levied with premiums.

(2) *Outward reinsurance premiums*

(General business technical account: item I.1.(b)

Long term business technical account: item II.I.(b))

This item shall comprise all premiums paid or payable in respect of outward reinsurance contracts entered into by the company. Portfolio entries payable on the conclusion or amendment of outward reinsurance contracts shall be added; portfolio withdrawals receivable must be deducted.

(3) *Change in the provision for unearned premiums, net of reinsurance*

(Long term business technical account: items II.1.(c) and II.6.(a))

In the case of long term business, the change in unearned premiums may be included either in item II.1.(c) or in item II.6.(a) of the long term business technical account.

(4) *Claims incurred, net of reinsurance*

(General business technical account: item I.4

Long term business technical account: item II.5)

This item shall comprise all payments made in respect of the financial year with the addition of the provision for claims (but after deducting the provision for claims for the preceding financial year).

These amounts shall include annuities, surrenders, entries and withdrawals of loss provisions to and from ceding insurance undertakings and reinsurers and external and internal claims management costs and charges for claims incurred but not reported such as are referred to in paragraphs 47(2) and 49 below.

Sums recoverable on the basis of subrogation and salvage (within the meaning of paragraph 47 below) shall be deducted.

Where the difference between—

    (a) the loss provision made at the beginning of the year for outstanding claims incurred in previous years, and

    (b) the payments made during the year on account of claims incurred in previous years and the loss provision shown at the end of the year for such outstanding claims,

is material, it shall be shown in the notes to the accounts, broken down by category and amount.

(5) *Bonuses and rebates, net of reinsurance*

(General business technical account: item I.6

Long term business technical account: item II.7)

Bonuses shall comprise all amounts chargeable for the financial year which are paid or payable to policy holders and other insured parties or provided for their benefit, including amounts used to increase technical provisions or applied to the reduction of future premiums, to the extent that such amounts represent an allocation of surplus or profit arising on business as a whole or a section of business, after deduction of amounts provided in previous years which are no longer required.

Rebates shall comprise such amounts to the extent that they represent a partial refund of premiums resulting from the experience of individual contracts.

Where material, the amount charged for bonuses and that charged for rebates shall be disclosed separately in the notes to the accounts.

(6) *Acquisition costs*

(General business technical account: item I.7.(a)

Long term business technical account: item II.8.(a))

This item shall comprise the costs arising from the conclusion of insurance contracts. They shall cover both direct costs, such as acquisition commissions or the cost of drawing up the insurance document or including the insurance contract in the portfolio, and indirect costs, such as advertising costs or the administrative expenses connected with the processing of proposals and the issuing of policies.

In the case of long term business, policy renewal commissions shall be included under item II.8.(c) in the long term business technical account.

(7) *Administrative expenses*

(General business technical account: item I.7.(c)

Long term business technical account: item II.8.(c))

This item shall include the costs arising from premium collection, portfolio administration, handling of bonuses and rebates, and inward and outward reinsurance. They shall in particular include staff costs and depreciation provisions in respect of office furniture and equipment in so far as these need not be shown under acquisition costs, claims incurred or investment charges.

Item II.8.(c) shall also include policy renewal commissions.

(8) *Investment income, expenses and charges*

(General business technical account: items I.2a and 8a

Long term business technical account: items II.2 and 9

Non-technical account: items III.3 and 5)

Investment income, expenses and charges shall, to the extent that they arise in the long term fund, be disclosed in the long term business technical account. Other investment income, expenses and charges shall either be disclosed in the non-technical account or attributed between the appropriate technical and non-technical accounts. Where the company makes such an attribution it shall disclose the basis for it in the notes to the accounts.

(9) *Unrealised gains and losses on investments*

(Long term business technical account: items II.3 and 10

Non-technical account: items III.3a and 5a)

In the case of investments attributed to the long term fund, the difference between the valuation of the investments and their purchase price or, if they have previously been valued, their valuation as at the last balance sheet date, may be disclosed (in whole or in part) in item II.3 or II.10 (as the case may be) of the long term business technical account, and in the case of investments shown as assets under Assets item D (assets held to cover linked liabilities) shall be so disclosed.

In the case of other investments, the difference between the valuation of the investments and their purchase price or, if they have previously been valued, their valuation as at the last balance sheet date, may be disclosed (in whole or in part) in item III.3a or III.5a (as the case may require) of the non-technical account.

(10) *Allocated investment return*

(General business technical account:item I.2

Long term business technical account:item II.12

Non-technical account: items III.4 and 6)

The allocated return may be transferred from one part of the profit and loss account to another.

Where part of the investment return is transferred to the general business technical account, the transfer from the non-technical account shall be deducted from item III.6 and added to item I.2.

Where part of the investment return disclosed in the long term business technical account is transferred to the non-technical account, the transfer to the non-technical account shall be deducted from item II.12 and added to item III.4.

The reasons for such transfers (which may consist of a reference to any relevant statutory requirement) and the bases on which they are made shall be disclosed in the notes to the accounts.

CHAPTER II
ACCOUNTING PRINCIPLES AND RULES

Section A
Accounting principles

Preliminary

13. Subject to paragraph 19 below, the amounts to be included in respect of all items shown in a company's accounts shall be determined in accordance with the principles set out in paragraphs 14 to 18 below.

Accounting principles

14. The company shall be presumed to be carrying on business as a going concern.

15. Accounting policies shall be applied consistently within the same accounts and from one financial year to the next.

16. The amount of any item shall be determined on a prudent basis, and in particular—

(a) subject to note (9) on the profit and loss account format, only profits realised at the balance sheet date shall be included in the profit and loss account; and

(b) all liabilities and losses which have arisen or are likely to arise in respect of the financial year to which the accounts relate or a previous financial year shall be taken into account, including those which only become apparent between the balance sheet date and the date on which it is signed on behalf of the board of directors in pursuance of section 233 of this Act.

17. All income and charges relating to the financial year to which the accounts relate shall be taken into account, without regard to the date of receipt or payment.

18. In determining the aggregate amount of any item the amount of each individual asset or liability that falls to be taken into account shall be determined separately.

Departure from accounting principles

19. If it appears to the directors of a company that there are special reasons for departing from any of the principles stated above in preparing the company's accounts in respect of any financial year they may do so, but particulars of the departure, the reasons for it and its effect shall be given in a note to the accounts.

Section B
Current value accounting rules

Preliminary

20. Subject to paragraphs 27 to 29 below—

(a) the amounts to be included in respect of assets of any description mentioned in paragraph 22 below shall be determined in accordance with that paragraph; and

(b) subject to paragraph 21 below, the amounts to be included in respect of assets of any description mentioned in paragraph 23 below may be determined in accordance with that paragraph or the rules set out in paragraphs 30 to 41 below ('the historical cost accounting rules').

21. ...

Valuation of assets: general

22.—(1) Subject to paragraph 24 below, investments falling to be included under Assets item C (investments) shall be included at their current value calculated in accordance with paragraphs 25 and 26 below.

(2) Investments falling to be included under Assets item D (assets held to cover linked liabilities) shall be shown at their current value calculated in accordance with paragraphs 25 and 26 below.

23.—(1) Intangible assets other than goodwill may be shown at their current cost.

(2) Assets falling to be included under Assets items F.I (tangible assets) and F.IV (own shares) in the balance sheet format may be shown at their current value calculated in accordance with paragraphs 25 and 26 below or at their current cost.

(3) Assets falling to be included under Assets item F.II (stocks) may be shown at current cost.

Alternative valuation of fixed-income securities

24.—(1) This paragraph applies to debt securities and other fixed-income securities shown as assets under Assets items C.II (investments in group undertakings and participating interests) and C.III (other financial investments).

(2) Securities to which this paragraph applies may either be valued in accordance with paragraph 22 above or their amortised value may be shown in the balance sheet, in which case the provisions of this paragraph apply.

(3) Subject to sub-paragraph (4) below, where the purchase price of securities to which this paragraph applies exceeds the amount repayable at maturity, the amount of the difference—

  (a) shall be charged to the profit and loss account, and

  (b) shall be shown separately in the balance sheet or in the notes to the accounts.

(4) The amount of the difference referred to in sub-paragraph (3) above may be written off in instalments so that it is completely written off when the securities are repaid, in which case there shall be shown separately in the balance sheet or in the notes to the accounts the difference between the purchase price (less the aggregate amount written off) and the amount repayable at maturity.

(5) Where the purchase price of securities to which this paragraph applies is less than the amount repayable at maturity, the amount of the difference shall be released to income in instalments over the period remaining until repayment, in which case there shall be shown separately in the balance sheet or in the notes to the accounts the difference between the purchase price (plus the aggregate amount released to income) and the amount repayable at maturity.

(6) Both the purchase price and the current value of securities valued in accordance with this paragraph shall be disclosed in the notes to the accounts.

(7) Where securities to which this paragraph applies which are not valued in accordance with paragraph 22 above are sold before maturity, and the proceeds are used to purchase other securities to which this paragraph applies, the difference between the proceeds of sale and their book value may be spread uniformly over the period remaining until the maturity of the original investment.

Meaning of 'current value'

25.—(1) Subject to sub-paragraph (5) below, in the case of investments other than land and buildings, current value shall mean market value determined in accordance with this paragraph.

(2) In the case of listed investments, market value shall mean the value on the balance sheet date or, when the balance sheet date is not a stock exchange trading day, on the last stock exchange trading day before that date.

(3) Where a market exists for unlisted investments, market value shall mean the average price at which such investments were traded on the balance sheet

date or, when the balance sheet date is not a trading day, on the last trading day before that date.

(4) Where, on the date on which the accounts are drawn up, listed or unlisted investments have been sold or are to be sold within the short term, the market value shall be reduced by the actual or estimated realisation costs.

(5) Except where the equity method of accounting is applied, all investments other than those referred to in sub-paragraphs (2) and (3) above shall be valued on a basis which has prudent regard to the likely realisable value.

26.—(1) In the case of land and buildings, current value shall mean the market value on the date of valuation, where relevant reduced as provided in sub-paragraphs (4) and (5) below.

(2) Market value shall mean the price at which land and buildings could be sold under private contract between a willing seller and an arm's length buyer on the date of valuation, it being assumed that the property is publicly exposed to the market, that market conditions permit orderly disposal and that a normal period, having regard to the nature of the property, is available for the negotiation of the sale.

(3) The market value shall be determined through the separate valuation of each land and buildings item, carried out at least every five years in accordance with generally recognised methods of valuation.

(4) Where the value of any land and buildings item has diminished since the preceding valuation under sub-paragraph (3), an appropriate value adjustment shall be made.

(5) The lower value arrived at under sub-paragraph (4) shall not be increased in subsequent balance sheets unless such increase results from a new determination of market value arrived at in accordance with sub-paragraphs (2) and (3).

(6) Where, on the date on which the accounts are drawn up, land and buildings have been sold or are to be sold within the short term, the value arrived at in accordance with sub-paragraphs (2) and (4) shall be reduced by the actual or estimated realisation costs.

(7) Where it is impossible to determine the market value of a land and buildings item, the value arrived at on the basis of the principle of purchase price or production cost shall be deemed to be its current value.

Application of the depreciation rules

27.—(1) Where—

   (a) the value of any asset of a company is determined in accordance with paragraph 22 or 23 above, and

   (b) in the case of a determination under paragraph 22 above, the asset falls to be included under Assets item C.I,

that value shall be, or (as the case may require) be the starting point for determining, the amount to be included in respect of that asset in the company's accounts, instead of its cost or any value previously so determined for that asset;

and paragraphs 31 to 35 and 37 below shall apply accordingly in relation to any such asset with the substitution for any reference to its cost of a reference to the value most recently determined for that asset in accordance with paragraph 22 or 23 above (as the case may be).

(2) The amount of any provision for depreciation required in the case of any asset by paragraph 32 or 33 below as it applies by virtue of sub-paragraph (1) is referred to below in this paragraph as the 'adjusted amount', and the amount of any provision which would be required by that paragraph in the case of that asset according to the historical cost accounting rules is referred to as the 'historical cost amount'.

(3) Where sub-paragraph (1) applies in the case of any asset the amount of any provision for depreciation in respect of that asset included in any item shown in the profit and loss account in respect of amounts written off assets of the description in question may be the historical cost amount instead of the adjusted amount, provided that the amount of any difference between the two is shown separately in the profit and loss account or in a note to the accounts.

Additional information to be provided

28.—(1) This paragraph applies where the amounts to be included in respect of assets covered by any items shown in a company's accounts have been determined in accordance with paragraph 22 or 23 above.

(2) The items affected and the basis of valuation adopted in determining the amounts of the assets in question in the case of each such item shall be disclosed in a note to the accounts.

(3) The purchase price of investments valued in accordance with paragraph 22 above shall be disclosed in the notes to the accounts.

(4) In the case of each balance sheet item valued in accordance with paragraph 23 above either—

   (a) the comparable amounts determined according to the historical cost accounting rules (without any provision for depreciation or diminution in value); or

   (b) the differences between those amounts and the corresponding amounts actually shown in the balance sheet in respect of that item,

shall be shown separately in the balance sheet or in a note to the accounts.

(5) In sub-paragraph (4) above, references in relation to any item to the comparable amounts determined as there mentioned are references to—

   (a) the aggregate amount which would be required to be shown in respect of that item if the amounts to be included in respect of all the assets covered by that item were determined according to the historical cost accounting rules; and

   (b) the aggregate amount of the cumulative provisions for depreciation or diminution in value which would be permitted or required in determining those amounts according to those rules.

Revaluation reserve

29.—(1) Subject to sub-paragraph (7) below, with respect to any determination of the value of an asset of a company in accordance with paragraph 22 or 23 above, the amount of any profit or loss arising from that determination (after allowing, where appropriate, for any provisions for depreciation or diminution in value made otherwise than by reference to the value so determined and any adjustments of any such provisions made in the light of that determination) shall be credited or (as the case may be) debited to a separate reserve ('the revaluation reserve').

(2) The amount of the revaluation reserve shall be shown in the company's balance sheet under Liabilities item A.III, but need not be shown under the name 'revaluation reserve'.

(3) An amount may be transferred

    (a) from the revaluation reserve—

        (i) to the profit and loss account, if the amount was previously charged to that account or represents realised profit, or

        (ii) on capitalisation,

    (b) to or from the revaluation reserve in respect of the taxation relating to any profit or loss credited or debited to the reserve;

and the revaluation reserve shall be reduced to the extent that the amounts transferred to it are no longer necessary for the purposes of the valuation method used.

(4) In sub-paragraph (3)(a)(ii) 'capitalisation', in relation to an amount standing to the credit of the revaluation reserve, means applying it in wholly or partly paying up unissued shares in the company to be allotted to members of the company as fully or partly paid shares.

(5) The revaluation reserve shall not be reduced except as mentioned in this paragraph.

(6) The treatment for taxation purposes of amounts credited or debited to the revaluation reserve shall be disclosed in a note to the accounts.

(7) This paragraph does not apply to the difference between the valuation of investments and their purchase price or previous valuation shown in the long term business technical account or the non-technical account in accordance with note *(9)* on the profit and loss account format.

Section C
Historical cost accounting rules

Preliminary

30. Subject to paragraphs 20 to 29 above, the amounts to be included in respect of all items shown in a company's accounts shall be determined in accordance with the rules set out in paragraphs 31 to 41 below.

Valuation of assets

General rules

31. Subject to any provision for depreciation or diminution in value made in accordance with paragraph 32 or 33 below, the amount to be included in respect of any asset in the balance sheet format shall be its cost.

32. In the case of any asset included under Assets item B (intangible assets), C.I (land and buildings), F.I.(tangible assets) or F.II (stocks) which has a limited useful economic life, the amount of—

    (a)   its cost; or

    (b)   where it is estimated that any such asset will have a residual value at the end of the period of its useful economic life, its cost less that estimated residual value,

shall be reduced by provisions for depreciation calculated to write off that amount systematically over the period of the asset's useful economic life.

33.—(1) This paragraph applies to any asset included under Assets item B (tangible assets), C (investments), F.I (tangible assets) or F.IV (own shares).

(2) Where an asset to which this paragraph applies has diminished in value, provisions for diminution in value may be made in respect of it and the amount to be included in respect of it may be reduced accordingly; and any such provisions which are not shown in the profit and loss account shall be disclosed (either separately or in aggregate) in a note to the accounts.

(3) Provisions for diminution in value shall be made in respect of any asset to which this paragraph applies if the reduction in its value is expected to be permanent (whether its useful economic life is limited or not), and the amount to be included in respect of it shall be reduced accordingly; and any such provisions which are not shown in the profit and loss account shall be disclosed (either separately or in aggregate) in a note to the accounts.

(4) Where the reasons for which any provision was made in accordance with sub-paragraph (1) or (2) have ceased to apply to any extent, that provision shall be written back to the extent that it is no longer necessary; and any amounts written back in accordance with this sub-paragraph which are not shown in the profit and loss account shall be disclosed (either separately or in aggregate) in a note to the accounts.

34.—(1) This paragraph applies to assets included under Assets items E.I, II and III (debtors) and F.III (cash at bank and in hand) in the balance sheet.

(2) If the net realisable value of an asset to which this paragraph applies is lower than its cost the amount to be included in respect of that asset shall be the net realisable value.

(3) Where the reasons for which any provision for diminution in value was made in accordance with sub-paragraph (2) have ceased to apply to any extent, that provision shall be written back to the extent that it is no longer necessary.

Development costs

35.—(1) Notwithstanding that amounts representing 'development costs' may be included under Assets item B (intangible assets) in the balance sheet format, an amount may only be included in a company's balance sheet in respect of development costs in special circumstances.

(2) If any amount is included in a company's balance sheet in respect of development costs the following information shall be given in a note to the accounts—

    (a) the period over which the amount of those costs originally capitalised is being or is to be written off; and

    (b) the reasons for capitalising the development costs in question.

Goodwill

36.—(1) The application of paragraphs 31 to 33 above in relation to goodwill (in any case where goodwill is treated as an asset) is subject to the following provisions of this paragraph.

(2) Subject to sub-paragraph (3) below, the amount of the consideration for any goodwill acquired by a company shall be reduced by provisions for depreciation calculated to write off that amount systematically over a period chosen by the directors of the company.

(3) The period chosen shall not exceed the useful economic life of the goodwill in question.

(4) In any case where any goodwill acquired by a company is included as an asset in the company's balance sheet the period chosen for writing off the consideration for that goodwill and the reasons for choosing that period shall be disclosed in a note to the accounts.

Miscellaneous and supplemental

Excess of money owed over value received as an asset item

37.—(1) Where the amount repayable on any debt owed by a company is greater than the value of the consideration received in the transaction giving rise to the debt, the amount of the difference may be treated as an asset.

(2) Where any such amount is so treated—

    (a) it shall be written off by reasonable amounts each year and must be completely written off before repayment of the debt; and

    (b) if the current amount is not shown as a separate item in the company's balance sheet it must be disclosed in a note to the accounts.

Assets included at a fixed amount

38.—(1) Subject to the following sub-paragraph, assets which fall to be included under Assets item F.I (tangible assets) in the balance sheet format may be included at a fixed quantity and value.

(2) Sub-paragraph (1) applies to assets of a kind which are constantly being replaced, where—

    (a) their overall value is not material to assessing the company's state of affairs; and

    (b) their quantity, value and composition are not subject to material variation.

Determination of cost

39.—(1) The cost of an asset that has been acquired by the company shall be determined by adding to the actual price paid any expenses incidental to its acquisition.

(2) The cost of an asset constructed by the company shall be determined by adding to the purchase price of the raw materials and consumables used the amount of the costs incurred by the company which are directly attributable to the construction of that asset.

(3) In addition, there may be included in the cost of an asset constructed by the company—

    (a) a reasonable proportion of the costs incurred by the company which are only indirectly attributable to the construction of that asset, but only to the extent that they relate to the period of construction; and

    (b) interest on capital borrowed to finance the construction of that asset, to the extent that it accrues in respect of the period of construction;

provided, however, in a case within sub-paragraph (b) above, that the inclusion of the interest in determining the cost of that asset and the amount of the interest so included is disclosed in a note to the accounts.

40.—(1) Subject to the qualification mentioned below, the cost of any assets which are fungible assets may be determined by the application of any of the methods mentioned in sub-paragraph (2) below in relation to any such assets of the same class.

The method chosen must be one which appears to the directors to be appropriate in the circumstances of the company.

(2) Those methods are—

    (a) the method known as 'first in, first out' (FIFO);

    (b) the method known as 'last in, first out' (LIFO);

    (c) a weighted average price; and

    (d) any other method similar to any of the methods mentioned above.

(3) Where in the case of any company—

    (a) the cost of assets falling to be included under any item shown in the company's balance sheet has been determined by the application of any method permitted by this paragraph; and

    (b) the amount shown in respect of that item differs materially from the relevant alternative amount given below in this paragraph;

the amount of that difference shall be disclosed in a note to the accounts.

(4) Subject to sub-paragraph (5) below, for the purposes of sub-paragraph (3)(b) above, the relevant alternative amount, in relation to any item shown in a company's balance sheet, is the amount which would have been shown in respect of that item if assets of any class included under that item at an amount determined by any method permitted by this paragraph had instead been included at their replacement cost as at the balance sheet date.

(5) The relevant alternative amount may be determined by reference to the most recent actual purchase price before the balance sheet date of assets of any class included under the item in question instead of by reference to their replacement cost as at that date, but only if the former appears to the directors of the company to constitute the more appropriate standard of comparison in the case of assets of that class.

Substitution of original amount where price or cost unknown

41. Where there is no record of the purchase price of any asset acquired by a company or of any price, expenses or costs relevant for determining its cost in accordance with paragraph 39 above, or any such record cannot be obtained without unreasonable expense or delay, its cost shall be taken for the purposes of paragraphs 31 to 36 above to be the value ascribed to it in the earliest available record of its value made on or after its acquisition by the company.

Section D
Rules for determining provisions

Preliminary

42. Provisions which are to be shown in a company's accounts shall be determined in accordance with paragraphs 43 to 53 below.

Technical provisions

43. The amount of technical provisions must at all times be sufficient to cover any liabilities arising out of insurance contracts as far as can reasonably be foreseen.

Provision for unearned premiums

44.—(1) The provision for unearned premiums shall in principle be computed separately for each insurance contract, save that statistical methods (and in particular proportional and flat rate methods) may be used where they may be expected to give approximately the same results as individual calculations.

(2) Where the pattern of risk varies over the life of a contract, this shall be taken into account in the calculation methods.

Provision for unexpired risks

45. The provision for unexpired risks (as defined in paragraph 81 below) shall be computed on the basis of claims and administrative expenses likely to arise after the end of the financial year from contracts concluded before that date, in so far as their estimated value exceeds the provision for unearned premiums and any premiums receivable under those contracts.

Long term business provision

46.—(1) The long term business provision shall in principle be computed separately for each long term contract, save that statistical or mathematical methods may be used where they may be expected to give approximately the same results as individual calculations.

(2) A summary of the principal assumptions in making the provision under sub-paragraph (1) shall be given in the notes to the accounts.

(3) The computation shall be made annually by a Fellow of the Institute or Faculty of Actuaries on the basis of recognised actuarial methods, with due regard to the actuarial principles laid down in Council Directive 92/96/EEC.

Provisions for claims outstanding

General business

47.—(1) A provision shall in principle be computed separately for each claim on the basis of the costs still expected to arise, save that statistical methods may be used if they result in an adequate provision having regard to the nature of the risks.

(2) This provision shall also allow for claims incurred but not reported by the balance sheet date, the amount of the allowance being determined having regard to past experience as to the number and magnitude of claims reported after previous balance sheet dates.

(3) All claims settlement costs (whether direct or indirect) shall be included in the calculation of the provision.

(4) Recoverable amounts arising out of subrogation or salvage shall be estimated on a prudent basis and either deducted from the provision for claims outstanding (in which case if the amounts are material they shall be shown in the notes to the accounts) or shown as assets.

(5) In sub-paragraph (4) above, 'subrogation' means the acquisition of the rights of policy holders with respect to third parties, and 'salvage' means the acquisition of the legal ownership of insured property.

(6) Where benefits resulting from a claim must be paid in the form of annuity, the amounts to be set aside for that purpose shall be calculated by recognised actuarial methods, and paragraph 48 below shall not apply to such calculations.

(7) Implicit discounting or deductions, whether resulting from the placing of a current value on a provision for an outstanding claim which is expected to be settled later at a higher figure or otherwise effected, is prohibited.

48.—(1) Explicit discounting or deductions to take account of investment income is permitted, subject to the following conditions:

   (a) the expected average interval between the date for the settlement of claims being discounted and the accounting date shall be at least four years;

   (b) the discounting or deductions shall be effected on a recognised prudential basis;

   (c) when calculating the total cost of settling claims, the company shall take account of all factors that could cause increases in that cost;

   (d) the company shall have adequate data at its disposal to construct a reliable model of the rate of claims settlements;

   (e) the rate of interest used for the calculation of present values shall not exceed a rate prudently estimated to be earned by assets of the company which are appropriate in magnitude and nature to cover the provisions for claims being discounted during the period necessary for the payment of such claims, and shall not exceed either—

      (i)   a rate justified by the performance of such assets over the preceding five years, or

      (ii) a rate justified by the performance of such assets during the year preceding the balance sheet date.

(2) When discounting or effecting deductions, the company shall, in the notes to the accounts, disclose—

   (a) the total amount of provisions before discounting or deductions,

   (b) the categories of claims which are discounted or from which deductions have been made,

   (c) for each category of claims, the methods used, in particular the rates used for the estimates referred to in sub-paragraph (1)(d) and (e), and the criteria adopted for estimating the period that will elapse before the claims are settled.

Long term business

49. The amount of the provision for claims shall be equal to the sums due to beneficiaries, plus the costs of settling claims.

Equalisation reserves

50. The amount of any reserve maintained under section 34A of the Insurance Companies Act 1982 shall be determined in accordance with regulations made under that section.

Accounting on a non-annual basis

51.—(1) Either of the methods described in paragraphs 52 and 53 below may be applied where, because of the nature of the class or type of insurance in question, information about premiums receivable or claims payable (or both) for the underwriting years is insufficient when the accounts are drawn up for reliable estimates to be made.

(2) The use of either of the methods referred to in sub-paragraph (1) shall be disclosed in the notes to the accounts together with the reasons for adopting it.

(3) Where one of the methods referred to in sub-paragraph (1) above is adopted, it shall be applied systematically in successive years unless circumstances justify a change.

(4) In the event of a change in the method applied, the effect on the assets, liabilities, financial position and profit or loss shall be stated in the notes to the accounts.

(5) For the purposes of this paragraph and paragraph 52 below, 'underwriting year' means the financial year in which the insurance contracts in the class or type of insurance in question commenced.

52.—(1) The excess of the premiums written over the claims and expenses paid in respect of contracts commencing in the underwriting year shall form a technical provision included in the technical provision for claims outstanding shown in the balance sheet under Liabilities item C.3.

(2) The provision may also be computed on the basis of a given percentage of the premiums written where such a method is appropriate for the type of risk insured.

(3) If necessary, the amount of this technical provision shall be increased to make it sufficient to meet present and future obligations.

(4) The technical provision constituted under this paragraph shall be replaced by a provision for claims outstanding estimated in accordance with paragraph 47 above as soon as sufficient information has been gathered and not later than the end of the third year following the underwriting year.

(5) The length of time that elapses before a provision for claims outstanding is constituted in accordance with sub-paragraph (4) above shall be disclosed in the notes to the accounts.

53.—(1) The figures shown in the technical account or in certain items within it shall relate to a year which wholly or partly precedes the financial year (but by no more than 12 months).

(2) The amounts of the technical provisions shown in the accounts shall if necessary be increased to make them sufficient to meet present and future obligations.

(3) The length of time by which the earlier year to which the figures relate precedes the financial year and the magnitude of the transactions concerned shall be disclosed in the notes to the accounts.

CHAPTER III
NOTES TO THE ACCOUNTS

Preliminary

54.—(1) Any information required in the case of any company by the following provisions of this Part of this Schedule shall (if not given in the company's accounts) be given by way of a note to those accounts.

(2) Subject to sub-paragraph (3) below, in respect of every item stated in a note to the accounts—

    (a) the corresponding amount for the financial year immediately preceding that to which the accounts relate shall also be stated, and

    (b) where the corresponding amount is not comparable, that amount shall be adjusted and particulars of the adjustment and the reasons for it shall be given.

(3) Sub-paragraph (2) above does not apply to—

    (a) paragraphs 62 and 66 of this Part of this Schedule (assets and reserves and provisions),

    (b) paragraph 13 of Schedule 4A (details of accounting treatment of acquisitions),

    (c) paragraphs 2, 8(3), 16, 21(1)(d), 22(4) and (5), 24(3) and (4) and 27(3) and (4) of Schedule 5 (shareholdings in other undertakings), and

    (d) Parts II and III of Schedule 6 (loans and other dealings in favour of directors and others).

General

Disclosure of accounting policies

55. The accounting policies adopted by the company in determining the amounts to be included in respect of items shown in the balance sheet and in determining the profit or loss of the company shall be stated (including such accounting policies with respect to the depreciation and diminution in value of assets).

56. It shall be stated whether the accounts have been prepared in accordance with applicable accounting standards and particulars of any material departure from those standards and the reasons for it shall be given.

Sums denominated in foreign currencies

57. Where any sums originally denominated in foreign currencies have been brought into account under any items shown in the balance sheet or profit and loss account format, the basis on which those sums have been translated into sterling (or the currency in which the accounts are drawn up) shall be stated.

Information supplementing the balance sheet

Share capital and debentures

58.—(1) The following information shall be given with respect to the company's share capital—

    (a) the authorised share capital; and

    (b) where shares of more than one class have been allotted, the number and aggregate nominal value of shares of each class allotted.

(2) In the case of any part of the allotted share capital that consists of redeemable shares, the following information shall be given—

    (a) the earliest and latest dates on which the company has power to redeem those shares;

    (b) whether those shares must be redeemed in any event or are liable to be redeemed at the option of the company or of the shareholder; and

    (c) whether any (and, if so, what) premium is payable on redemption.

59. If the company has allotted any shares during the financial year, the following information shall be given—

    (a) ...

    (b) the classes of shares allotted; and

    (c) as respects each class of shares, the number allotted, their aggregate nominal value and the consideration received by the company for the allotment.

60.—(1) With respect to any contingent right to the allotment of shares in the company the following particulars shall be given—

    (a) the number, description and amount of the shares in relation to which the right is exercisable;

    (b) the period during which it is exercisable; and

    (c) the price to be paid for the shares allotted.

(2) In sub-paragraph (1) above 'contingent right to the allotment of shares' means any option to subscribe for shares and any other right to require the allotment of shares to any person whether arising on the conversion into shares of securities of any other description or otherwise.

61.—(1) If the company has issued any debentures during the financial year to which the accounts relate, the following information shall be given—

    (a) ...

    (b) the classes of debentures issued; and

    (c) as respects each class of debentures, the amount issued and the consideration received by the company for the issue.

(2) ...

(3) Where any of the company's debentures are held by a nominee of or trustee for the company, the nominal amount of the debentures and the amount at which they are stated in the accounting records kept by the company in accordance with section 221 of this Act shall be stated.

Assets

62.—(1) In respect of any assets of the company included in Assets items B (intangible assets), C.I (land and buildings) and C.II (investments in group undertakings and participating interests) in the company's balance sheet the following information shall be given by reference to each such item—

(a) the appropriate amounts in respect of those assets included in the item as at the date of the beginning of the financial year and as at the balance sheet date respectively;

(b) the effect on any amount included in Assets item B in respect of those assets of—

(i) any determination during that year of the value to be ascribed to any of those assets in accordance with paragraph 23 above;

(ii) acquisitions during that year of any assets;

(iii) disposals during that year of any assets; and

(iv) any transfers of assets of the company to and from the item during that year.

(2) The reference in sub-paragraph (1)(a) to the appropriate amounts in respect of any assets (included in an assets item) as at any date there mentioned is a reference to amounts representing the aggregate amounts determined, as at that date, in respect of assets falling to be included under the item on either of the following bases, that is to say—

(a) on the basis of cost (determined in accordance with paragraphs 39 and 40 above); or

(b) on any basis permitted by paragraph 22 or 23 above,

(leaving out of account in either case any provisions for depreciation or diminution in value).

(3) In addition, in respect of any assets of the company included in any assets item in the company's balance sheet, there shall be stated (by reference to each such item)—

(a) the cumulative amount of provisions for depreciation or diminution in value of those assets included under the item as at each date mentioned in sub-paragraph (1)(a);

(b) the amount of any such provisions made in respect of the financial year;

(c) the amount of any adjustments made in respect of any such provisions during that year in consequence of the disposal of any of those assets; and

(d) the amount of any other adjustments made in respect of any such provisions during that year.

63. Where any assets of the company (other than listed investments) are included under any item shown in the company's balance sheet at an amount determined on any basis mentioned in paragraph 22 or 23 above, the following information shall be given—

(a) the years (so far as they are known to the directors) in which the assets were severally valued and the several values; and

(b) in the case of assets that have been valued during the financial year, the names of the persons who valued them or particulars of their qualifications for doing so and (whichever is stated) the bases of valuation used by them.

64. In relation to any amount which is included under Assets item C.I (land and buildings) there shall be stated—

    (a) how much of that amount is ascribable to land of freehold tenure and how much to land of leasehold tenure; and

    (b) how much of the amount ascribable to land of leasehold tenure is ascribable to land held on long lease and how much to land held on short lease.

Investments

65. In respect of the amount of each item which is shown in the company's balance sheet under Assets item C (investments) there shall be stated—

    (a) how much of that amount is ascribable to listed investments; ...

    (b) ...

Reserves and provisions

66.—(1) Where any amount is transferred—

    (a) to or from any reserves;

    (b) to any provisions for other risks and charges; or

    (c) from any provisions for other risks and charges otherwise than for the purpose for which the provision was established;

and the reserves or provisions are or would but for paragraph 2(3) above be shown as separate items in the company's balance sheet, the information mentioned in the following sub-paragraph shall be given in respect of the aggregate of reserves or provisions included in the same item.

(2) That information is—

    (a) the amount of the reserves or provisions as at the date of the beginning of the financial year and as at the balance sheet date respectively;

    (b) any amounts transferred to or from the reserves or provisions during that year; and

    (c) the source and application respectively of any amounts so transferred.

(3) Particulars shall be given of each provision included in Liabilities item E.3 (other provisions) in the company's balance sheet in any case where the amount of that provision is material.

Provision for taxation

67. The amount of any provision for deferred taxation shall be stated separately from the amount of any provision for other taxation.

Details of indebtedness

68.—(1) In respect of each item shown under 'creditors' in the company's balance sheet there shall be stated the aggregate of the following amounts, that is to say—

    (a) the amount of any debts included under that item which are payable or repayable otherwise than by instalments and fall due for payment or repayment after the end of the period of five years beginning with the day next following the end of the financial year; and

(b) in the case of any debts so included which are payable or repayable by instalments, the amount of any instalments which fall due for payment after the end of that period.

(2) Subject to sub-paragraph (3), in relation to each debt falling to be taken into account under sub-paragraph (1), the terms of payment or repayment and the rate of any interest payable on the debt shall be stated.

(3) If the number of debts is such that, in the opinion of the directors, compliance with sub-paragraph (2) would result in a statement of excessive length, it shall be sufficient to give a general indication of the terms of payment or repayment and the rates of any interest payable on the debts.

(4) In respect of each item shown under 'creditors' in the company's balance sheet there shall be stated—

(a) the aggregate amount of any debts included under that item in respect of which any security has been given by the company; and

(b) an indication of the nature of the securities so given.

(5) References above in this paragraph to an item shown under 'creditors' in the company's balance sheet include references, where amounts falling due to creditors within one year and after more than one year are distinguished in the balance sheet—

(a) in a case within sub-paragraph (1), to an item shown under the latter of those categories; and

(b) in a case within sub-paragraph (4), to an item shown under either of those categories;

and references to items shown under 'creditors' include references to items which would but for paragraph 2(3)(b) above be shown under that heading.

69. If any fixed cumulative dividends on the company's shares are in arrear, there shall be stated—

(a) the amount of the arrears; and

(b) the period for which the dividends or, if there is more than one class, each class of them are in arrear.

Guarantees and other financial commitments

70.—(1) Particulars shall be given of any charge on the assets of the company to secure the liabilities of any other person, including, where practicable, the amount secured.

(2) The following information shall be given with respect to any other contingent liability not provided for (other than a contingent liability arising out of an insurance contract)—

(a) the amount or estimated amount of that liability;

(b) its legal nature;

(c) whether any valuable security has been provided by the company in connection with that liability and if so, what.

(3) There shall be stated, where practicable—

(a) the aggregate amount or estimated amount of contracts for capital expenditure, so far as not provided for; ...

(b) ...

(4) Particulars shall be given of—

(a) any pension commitments included under any provision shown in the company's balance sheet; and

(b) any such commitments for which no provision has been made;

and where any such commitment relates wholly or partly to pensions payable to past directors of the company separate particulars shall be given of that commitment so far as it relates to such pensions.

(5) Particulars shall also be given of any other financial commitments, other than commitments arising out of insurance contracts, which—

(a) have not been provided for; and

(b) are relevant to assessing the company's state of affairs.

(6) Commitments within any of the preceding sub-paragraphs undertaken on behalf of or for the benefit of—

(a) any parent undertaking or fellow subsidiary undertaking, or

(b) any subsidiary undertaking of the company,

shall be stated separately from the other commitments within that sub-paragraph, and commitments within paragraph (a) shall also be stated separately from those within paragraph (b).

71. ...

Miscellaneous matters

72.—(1) Particulars shall be given of any case where the cost of any asset is for the first time determined under paragraph 41 above.

(2) Where any outstanding loans made under the authority of section 153(4)(b),(bb) or (c) or section 155 of this Act (various cases of financial assistance by a company for purchase of its own shares) are included under any item shown in the company's balance sheet, the aggregate amount of those loans shall be disclosed for each item in question.

(3) ...

Information supplementing the profit and loss account

Separate statement of certain items of income and expenditure

73.—(1) Subject to the following provisions of this paragraph, each of the amounts mentioned below shall be stated.

(2) The amount of the interest on or any similar charges in respect of—

(a) bank loans and overdrafts, ... and

(b) loans of any other kind made to the company.

This sub-paragraph does not apply to interest or charges on loans to the company from group undertakings, but, with that exception, it applies to interest or charges on all loans, whether made on the security of debentures or not.

(3)–(5) ...

Particulars of tax

74.—(1) ...

(2) Particulars shall be given of any special circumstances which affect liability in respect of taxation of profits, income or capital gains for the financial year or liability in respect of taxation of profits, income or capital gains for succeeding financial years.

(3) The following amounts shall be stated—

    (a) the amount of the charge for United Kingdom corporation tax;

    (b) if that amount would have been greater but for relief from double taxation, the amount which it would have been but for such relief;

    (c) the amount of the charge for United Kingdom income tax; and

    (d) the amount of the charge for taxation imposed outside the United Kingdom of profits, income and (so far as charged to revenue) capital gains.

Those amounts shall be stated separately in respect of each of the amounts which is shown under the following items in the profit and loss account, that is to say item III.9 (tax on profit or loss on ordinary activities) and item III.14 (tax on extraordinary profit or loss).

Particulars of business

75.—(1) As regards general business a company shall disclose—

    (a) gross premiums written,

    (b) gross premiums earned,

    (c) gross claims incurred,

    (d) gross operating expenses, and

    (e) the reinsurance balance.

(2) The amounts required to be disclosed by sub-paragraph (1) shall be broken down between direct insurance and reinsurance acceptances, if reinsurance acceptances amount to 10 per cent or more of gross premiums written.

(3) Subject to sub-paragraph (4) below, the amounts required to be disclosed by sub-paragraphs (1) and (2) above with respect to direct insurance shall be further broken down into the following groups of classes—

    (a) accident and health,

    (b) motor (third party liability),

    (c) motor (other classes),

    (d) marine, aviation and transport,

    (e) fire and other damage to property,

    (f) third-party liability,

(g) credit and suretyship,

(h) legal expenses,

(i) assistance, and

(j) miscellaneous,

where the amount of the gross premiums written in direct insurance for each such group exceeds 10 million ECUs.

(4) The company shall in any event disclose the amounts relating to the three largest groups of classes in its business.

76.—(1) As regards long term business, the company shall disclose—

(a) gross premiums written, and

(b) the reinsurance balance.

(2) Subject to sub-paragraph (3) below—

(a) gross premiums written shall be broken down between those written by way of direct insurance and those written by way of reinsurance; and

(b) gross premiums written by way of direct insurance shall be broken down—

   (i) between individual premiums and premiums under group contracts;

   (ii) between periodic premiums and single premiums; and

   (iii) between premiums from non-participating contracts, premiums from participating contracts and premiums from contracts where the investment risk is borne by policy holders.

(3) Disclosure of any amount referred to in sub-paragraph (2)(a) or (2)(b)(i),(ii) or (iii) above shall not be required if it does not exceed 10 per cent of the gross premiums written or (as the case may be) of the gross premiums written by way of direct insurance.

77.—(1) Subject to sub-paragraph (2) below, there shall be disclosed as regards both general and long term business the total gross direct insurance premiums resulting from contracts concluded by the company—

(a) in the member State of its head office,

(b) in the other member States, and

(c) in other countries.

(2) Disclosure of any amount referred to in sub-paragraph (1) above shall not be required if it does not exceed 5 per cent of total gross premiums.

Commissions

78. There shall be disclosed the total amount of commissions for direct insurance business accounted for in the financial year, including acquisition, renewal, collection and portfolio management commissions.

Particulars of staff

79.—(1) The following information shall be given with respect to the employees of the company—

(a) the average number of persons employed by the company in the financial year; and

(b) the average number of persons so employed within each category of persons employed by the company.

(2) The average number required by sub-paragraph (1)(a) or (b) shall be determined by dividing the relevant annual number by the number of months in the financial year.

(3) The relevant annual number shall be determined by ascertaining for each month in the financial year—

(a) for the purposes of sub-paragraph (1)(a), the number of persons employed under contracts of service by the company in that month (whether throughout the month or not); and

(b) for the purposes of sub-paragraph (1)(b), the number of persons in the category in question of persons so employed;

and, in either case, adding together all the monthly numbers.

(4) In respect of all persons employed by the company during the financial year who are taken into account in determining the relevant annual number for the purposes of sub-paragraph (1)(a) there shall also be stated the aggregate amounts respectively of—

(a) wages and salaries paid or payable in respect of that year to those persons;

(b) social security costs incurred by the company on their behalf; and

(c) other pension costs so incurred,

save in so far as those amounts or any of them are stated in the profit and loss account.

(5) The categories of person employed by the company by reference to which the number required to be disclosed by sub-paragraph (1)(b) is to be determined shall be such as the directors may select, having regard to the manner in which the company's activities are organised.

Miscellaneous matters

80.—(1) Where any amount relating to any preceding financial year is included in any item in the profit and loss account, the effect shall be stated.

(2) Particulars shall be given of any extraordinary income or charges arising in the financial year.

(3) The effect shall be stated of any transactions that are exceptional by virtue of size or incidence though they fall within the ordinary activities of the company.

CHAPTER IV
INTERPRETATIONS OF PART I

General

81.—(1) The following definitions apply for the purposes of this Part of this Schedule and its interpretation—

'the 1982 Act' means the Insurance Companies Act 1982;

'fungible assets' means assets of any description which are substantially indistinguishable one from another;

'general business' has the same meaning as in the 1982 Act;

'lease' includes an agreement for a lease;

'listed investment' means an investment listed on a recognised stock exchange, or on any stock exchange of repute outside Great Britain and the expression 'unlisted investment' shall be construed accordingly;

'long lease' means a lease in the case of which the portion of the term for which it was granted remaining unexpired at the end of the financial year is not less than 50 years;

'long term business' has the same meaning as in the 1982 Act;

'long term fund' means the fund or funds maintained by a company in respect of its long term business in accordance with the provisions of the 1982 Act;

'policy holder' has the same meaning as in the 1982 Act;

'provision for unexpired risks' means the amount set aside in addition to unearned premiums in respect of risks to be borne by the company after the end of the financial year, in order to provide for all claims and expenses in connection with insurance contracts in force in excess of the related unearned premiums and any premiums receivable on those contracts;

'short lease' means a lease which is not a long lease.

(2) In this Part of this Schedule the 'ECU' means the unit of account of that name defined in Council Regulation (EEC) No 3180/78 as amended.

The exchange rates as between the ECU and the currencies of the member States to be applied for each financial year shall be the rates applicable on the last day of the preceding October for which rates for the currencies of all the member States were published in the Official Journal of the Communities.

Loans

82. For the purposes of this Part of this Schedule a loan or advance (including a liability comprising a loan or advance) is treated as falling due for repayment, and an instalment of a loan or advance is treated as falling due for payment, on the earliest date on which the lender could require repayment or (as the case may be) payment, if he exercised all options and rights available to him.

Materiality

83. For the purposes of this Part of this Schedule amounts which in the particular context of any provision of this Part are not material may be disregarded for the purposes of that provision.

Provisions

84. For the purposes of this Part of this Schedule and its interpretation—

(a) references in this Part to provisions for depreciation or diminution in value of assets are to any amount written off by way of providing for depreciation or diminution in value of assets;

(b) any reference in the profit and loss account format or the notes thereto set out in Section B of this Part to the depreciation of, or amounts written off, assets of any description is to any provision for depreciation or diminution in value of assets of that description; and

(c) references in this Part to provisions for other risks and charges ... are to any amount retained as reasonably necessary for the purpose of providing for any liability or loss which is either likely to be incurred, or certain to be incurred but uncertain as to amount or as to the date on which it will arise.

Scots land tenure

85. In the application of this Part of this Schedule to Scotland—

'land of freehold tenure' means land in respect of which the company is the proprietor of the *dominium utile* or, in the case of land not held on feudal tenure, is the owner;

'land of leasehold tenure' means land of which the company is the tenant under a lease;

and the reference to ground-rents, rates and other outgoings includes feu-duty and ground annual.

Note: It would appear that this provision should have been amended by the Abolition of Feudal Tenure etc (Scotland) Act 2000, see note to Sch 9, para 86.

Staff costs

86. For the purposes of this Part of this Schedule and its interpretation—

(a) 'Social security costs' means any contributions by the company to any state social security or pension scheme, fund or arrangement;

(b) 'Pension costs' includes any costs incurred by the company in respect of any pension scheme established for the purpose of providing pensions for persons currently or formerly employed by the company, any sums set aside for the future payment of pensions directly by the company to current or former employees and any pensions paid directly to such persons without having first been set aside; and

(c) any amount stated in respect of the item 'social security costs' or in respect of the item 'wages and salaries' in the company's profit and loss account shall be determined by reference to payments made or costs incurred in respect of all persons employed by the company during the financial year who are taken into account in determining the relevant annual number for the purposes of paragraph 79(1)(a) above.

PART II
CONSOLIDATED ACCOUNTS

Schedule 4A to apply Part I of this Schedule with modifications

1.—(1) In its application to insurance groups, Schedule 4A shall have effect with the following modifications.

(2) In paragraph 1—

    (a) for the reference in sub-paragraph (1) to the provisions of Schedule 4 there shall be substituted a reference to the provisions of Part I of this Schedule modified as mentioned in paragraph 2 below;

    (b) ...

    (c) sub-paragraph (3) shall be omitted.

(3) In paragraph 2(2)(a), for the words 'three months' there shall be substituted the words 'six months'.

(4) In paragraph 3, after sub-paragraph (1) there shall be inserted the following sub-paragraphs—

    '(1A)   Sub-paragraph (1) shall not apply to those liabilities items the valuation of which by the undertakings included in a consolidation is based on the application of provisions applying only to insurance undertakings, nor to those assets items changes in the values of which also affect or establish policy holders' rights.

    (1B) Where sub-paragraph (1A) applies, that fact shall be disclosed in the notes on the consolidated accounts.'

(5) For sub-paragraph (4) of paragraph 6 there shall be substituted the following sub-paragraphs—

    '(4) Sub-paragraphs (1) and (2) need not be complied with—

      (a) where a transaction has been concluded according to normal market conditions and a policy holder has rights in respect of that transaction, or

      (b) if the amounts concerned are not material for the purpose of giving a true and fair view.

    (5) Where advantage is taken of sub-paragraph (4)(a) above that fact shall be disclosed in the notes to the accounts, and where the transaction in question has a material effect on the assets, liabilities, financial position and profit or loss of all the undertakings included in the consolidation that fact shall also be so disclosed.'

(6) In paragraph 17—

    (a) in sub-paragraph (1), for the reference to Schedule 4 there shall be substituted a reference to Part I of this Schedule;

    (b) in sub-paragraph (2), paragraph (a) and, in paragraph (b), the words 'in Format 2' shall be omitted;

    (c) in sub-paragraph (3), for paragraphs (a) to (d) there shall be substituted the words 'between items 10 and 11 in section III';

    (d) in sub-paragraph (4), for paragraphs (a) to (d) there shall be substituted the words 'between items 14 and 15 in section III'; and

    (e) for sub-paragraph (5) there shall be substituted the following sub-paragraph—

      '(5) Paragraph 2(3) of Part I of Schedule 9A (power to combine items) shall not apply in relation to the additional items required by the foregoing provisions of this paragraph.'

(7) In paragraph 18, for the reference to paragraphs 17 to 19 and 21 of Schedule 4 there shall be substituted a reference to paragraphs 31 to 33 and 36 of Part I of this Schedule.

(8) In paragraph 21—

    (a) in sub-paragraph (1), for the reference to Schedule 4 there shall be substituted a reference to Part I of this Schedule; and

    (b) for sub-paragraphs (2) and (3) there shall be substituted the following sub-paragraphs—

        '(2) In the Balance Sheet Format, Asset item C.II.3 (participating interests) shall be replaced by two items,'Interests in associated undertakings' and 'Other participating interests'.

        (3) In the Profit and Loss Account Format, items II.2(a) and III.3(a)(income from participating interests, with a separate indication of that derived from group undertakings) shall each be replaced by the following items—

           (a) 'Income from participating interests other than associated undertakings, with a separate indication of that derived from group undertakings', which shall be shown as items II.2(a) and III.3(a), and

           (b) 'Income from associated undertakings', which shall be shown as items II.2(aa) and III.3(aa).'

(9) In paragraph 22(1), for the reference to paragraphs 17 to 19 and 21 of Schedule 4 there shall be substituted a reference to paragraphs 31 to 33 and 36 of Part I of this Schedule.

Modifications of Part I of this Schedule for purposes of paragraph 1

2.—(1) For the purposes of paragraph 1 above, Part I of this Schedule shall be modified as follows.

(2) The information required by paragraph 10 need not be given.

(3) In the case of general business, investment income, expenses and charges may be disclosed in the non-technical account rather than in the technical account.

(4) In the case of subsidiary undertakings which are not authorised to carry on long term business in Great Britain, notes (8) and (9) to the profit and loss account format shall have effect as if references to investment income, expenses and charges arising in the long term fund or to investments attributed to the long term fund were references to investment income, expenses and charges or (as the case may be) investments relating to long term business.

(5) In the case of subsidiary undertakings which do not have a head office in Great Britain, the computation required by paragraph 46 shall be made annually by an actuary or other specialist in the field on the basis of recognised actuarial methods.

(6) The information required by paragraphs 75 to 78 need not be shown.

General note

Parts I and II of this Schedule reflect the requirements of Sch 4 (form and content of individual accounts) and Sch 4A (form and content of group accounts) as appropriately modified for insurance companies and groups: see notes to ss 255–255A, above.

Schedule 10 *Repealed by the Companies Act 1985 (Insurance Companies Accounts) Regulations 1993, SI 1993/3246, reg 5(1), Sch 2, para 7.*

SCHEDULE 10A

PARENT AND SUBSIDIARY UNDERTAKINGS: SUPPLEMENTARY PROVISIONS

Section 258

Introduction

1. The provisions of this Schedule explain expressions used in section 258 (parent and subsidiary undertakings) and otherwise supplement that section.

Voting rights in an undertaking

2.—(1) In section 258(2)(a) and (d) the references to the voting rights in an undertaking are to the rights conferred on shareholders in respect of their shares or, in the case of an undertaking not having a share capital, on members, to vote at general meetings of the undertaking on all, or substantially all, matters.

(2) In relation to an undertaking which does not have general meetings at which matters are decided by the exercise of voting rights, the references to holding a majority of the voting rights in the undertaking shall be construed as references to having the right under the constitution of the undertaking to direct the overall policy of the undertaking or to alter the terms of its constitution.

Right to appoint or remove a majority of the directors

3.—(1) In section 258(2)(b) the reference to the right to appoint or remove a majority of the board of directors is to the right to appoint or remove directors holding a majority of the voting rights at meetings of the board on all, or substantially all, matters.

(2) An undertaking shall be treated as having the right to appoint to a directorship if—

    (a) a person's appointment to it follows necessarily from his appointment as director of the undertaking, or

    (b) the directorship is held by the undertaking itself.

(3) A right to appoint or remove which is exercisable only with the consent or concurrence of another person shall be left out of account unless no other person has a right to appoint or, as the case may be, remove in relation to that directorship.

Right to exercise dominant influence

4.—(1) For the purposes of section 258(2)(c) an undertaking shall not be regarded as having the right to exercise a dominant influence over another undertaking unless it has a right to give directions with respect to the operating and financial policies of that other undertaking which its directors are obliged to comply with whether or not they are for the benefit of that other undertaking.

(2) A 'control contract' means a contract in writing conferring such a right which—

(a) is of a kind authorised by the memorandum or articles of the undertaking in relation to which the right is exercisable, and

(b) is permitted by the law under which that undertaking is established.

(3) This paragraph shall not be read as affecting the construction of the expression 'actually exercises a dominant influence' in section 258(4)(a).

Rights exercisable only in certain circumstances or temporarily incapable of exercise

5.—(1) Rights which are exercisable only in certain circumstances shall be taken into account only—

(a) when the circumstances have arisen, and for so long as they continue to obtain, or

(b) when the circumstances are within the control of the person having the rights.

(2) Rights which are normally exercisable but are temporarily incapable of exercise shall continue to be taken into account.

Rights held by one person on behalf of another

6. Rights held by a person in a fiduciary capacity shall be treated as not held by him.

7.—(1) Rights held by a person as nominee for another shall be treated as held by the other.

(2) Rights shall be regarded as held as nominee for another if they are exercisable only on his instructions or with his consent or concurrence.

Rights attached to shares held by way of security

8. Rights attached to shares held by way of security shall be treated as held by the person providing the security—

    (a) where apart from the right to exercise them for the purpose of preserving the value of the security, or of realising it, the rights are exercisable only in accordance with his instructions, and

    (b) where the shares are held in connection with the granting of loans as part of normal business activities and apart from the right to exercise them for the purpose of preserving the value of the security, or of realising it, the rights are exercisable only in his interests.

Rights attributed to parent undertaking

9.—(1) Rights shall be treated as held by a parent undertaking if they are held by any of its subsidiary undertakings.

(2) Nothing in paragraph 7 or 8 shall be construed as requiring rights held by a parent undertaking to be treated as held by any of its subsidiary undertakings.

(3) For the purposes of paragraph 8 rights shall be treated as being exercisable in accordance with the instructions or in the interests of an undertaking if they are exercisable in accordance with the instructions of or, as the case may be, in the interests of any group undertaking.

Disregard of certain rights

10. The voting rights in an undertaking shall be reduced by any rights held by the undertaking itself.

Supplementary

11. References in any provision of paragraphs 6 to 10 to rights held by a person include rights falling to be treated as held by him by virtue of any other provision of those paragraphs but not rights which by virtue of any such provision are to be treated as not held by him.

General note

See note to s 258; and to ss 736, 736A..

SCHEDULE 11

MODIFICATIONS OF PART VIII WHERE COMPANY'S ACCOUNTS PREPARED IN ACCORDANCE WITH SPECIAL PROVISIONS FOR BANKING OR INSURANCE COMPANIES

Section 279

1. Paragraphs 2 to 6 below apply where a company has prepared accounts in accordance with the special provisions of Part VII relating to banking companies and paragraphs 7 to 13 below apply where a company has prepared accounts in accordance with the special provisions of Part VII relating to insurance companies.

Modifications where accounts prepared in accordance with special provisions for banking companies

2. Section 264(2) shall apply as if the reference to paragraph 89 of Schedule 4 therein was a reference to paragraph 85(c) of Part I of Schedule 9.

3. Section 269 shall apply as if:
   (a) there were substituted for the words 'are shown as an asset' in sub-section (1) the words 'are included as an asset'; and
   (b) the reference to paragraph 20 of Schedule 4 in sub-section (2)(b) was to paragraph 27 of Part I of Schedule 9.

4. Sections 270(2) and 275 shall apply as if the references therein to paragraphs 88 and 89 of Schedule 4 were to paragraph 85 of Part I of Schedule 9.

5. Sections 272 and 273 shall apply as if in section 272(3) there were substituted for the references to section 226 and Schedule 4, references to section 255 and Part I of Schedule 9.

6. Section 276 shall apply as if the references to paragraphs 12(a) and 34(3)(a) of Schedule 4 were to paragraphs 19(a) and 44(3)(a) of Schedule 9.

Modifications where accounts prepared in accordance with special provisions for insurance companies

7. Section 264(2) shall apply as if for the words in parentheses there were substituted '('liabilities' to include any provision for other risks and charges within paragraph 84(c) of Part I of Schedule 9A and any amount included under Liabilities items Ba (fund for future appropriations), C (technical provisions) and D (technical provisions for linked liabilities) in a balance sheet drawn up in accordance with the balance sheet format set out in section B of Part I of Schedule 9A)'.

8. Section 269 shall apply as if the reference to paragraph 20 of Schedule 4 in subsection (2)(b) were a reference to paragraph 35 of Part I of Schedule 9A.

9. Sections 270(2) and 275 shall apply as if the reference to provisions of any of the kinds mentioned in paragraphs 88 and 89 of Schedule 4 were a reference to provisions of any of the kinds mentioned in paragraph 84 of Part I of Schedule 9A and to any amount included under Liabilities items Ba (fund for future appropriations), C (technical provisions) and D (technical provisions for linked liabilities) in a balance sheet drawn up in accordance with the balance sheet format set out in section B of Part I of Schedule 9A.

10. Sections 272 and 273 shall apply as if the references in section 272(3) to section 226 and Schedule 4 were references to section 255 and Part I of Schedule 9A.

11. Section 276 shall apply as if the references to paragraphs 12(a) and 34(3)(a) of Schedule 4(d) were references to paragraphs 16(a) and 29(3)(a) of Part I of Schedule 9A.

General note

See note to s 279, above.

Schedule 12 *repealed by the Company Directors Disqualification Act 1986, section 23(2), Schedule 4.*

SCHEDULE 13

PROVISIONS SUPPLEMENTING AND INTERPRETING SECTIONS 324 TO 328

Sections 324, 325, 326, 328 and 346

PART I
RULES FOR INTERPRETATION OF THE SECTIONS AND ALSO SECTION 346(4) AND (5)

1.—(1) A reference to an interest in shares or debentures is to be read as including any interest of any kind whatsoever in shares or debentures.

(2) Accordingly, there are to be disregarded any restraints or restrictions to which the exercise of any right attached to the interest is or may be subject.

2. Where property is held on trust and any interest in shares or debentures is comprised in the property, any beneficiary of the trust who (apart from this paragraph) does not have an interest in the shares or debentures is to be taken as having such an interest; but this paragraph is without prejudice to the following provisions of this Part of this Schedule.

3.—(1) A person is taken to have an interest in shares or debentures if—

- (a) he enters into a contract for their purchase by him (whether for cash or other consideration), or
- (b) not being the registered holder, he is entitled to exercise any right conferred by the holding of the shares or debentures, or is entitled to control the exercise of any such right.

(2) For purposes of sub-paragraph (1)(b), a person is taken to be entitled to exercise or control the exercise of a right conferred by the holding of shares or debentures if he—

- (a) has a right (whether subject to conditions or not) the exercise of which would make him so entitled, or
- (b) is under an obligation (whether or not so subject) the fulfilment of which would make him so entitled.

(3) A person is not by virtue of sub-paragraph (1)(b) taken to be interested in shares or debentures by reason only that he—

- (a) has been appointed a proxy to vote at a specified meeting of a company or of any class of its members and at any adjournment of that meeting, or

(b) has been appointed by a corporation to act as its representative at any meeting of a company or of any class of its members.

4. A person is taken to be interested in shares or debentures if a body corporate is interested in them and—

(a) that body corporate or its directors are accustomed to act in accordance with his directions or instructions, or

(b) he is entitled to exercise or control the exercise of one-third or more of the voting power at general meetings of that body corporate.

As this paragraph applies for the purposes of section 346(4) and (5), 'more than one-half' is substituted for 'one-third or more'.

5. Where a person is entitled to exercise or control the exercise of one-third or more of the voting power at general meetings of a body corporate, and that body corporate is entitled to exercise or control the exercise of any of the voting power at general meetings of another body corporate ('the effective voting power'), then, for purposes of paragraph 4(b), the effective voting power is taken to be exercisable by that person.

As this paragraph applies for the purposes of section 346(4) and (5), 'more than one-half' is substituted for 'one-third or more'.

6.—(1) A person is taken to have an interest in shares or debentures if, otherwise than by virtue of having an interest under a trust—

(a) he has a right to call for delivery of the shares or debentures to himself or to his order, or

(b) he has a right to acquire an interest in shares or debentures or is under an obligation to take an interest in shares or debentures;

whether in any case the right or obligation is conditional or absolute.

(2) Rights or obligations to subscribe for shares or debentures are not to be taken, for purposes of sub-paragraph (1), to be rights to acquire, or obligations to take, an interest in shares or debentures.

This is without prejudice to paragraph 1.

7. Persons having a joint interest are deemed each of them to have that interest.

8. It is immaterial that shares or debentures in which a person has an interest are unidentifiable.

9. So long as a person is entitled to receive, during the lifetime of himself or another, income from trust property comprising shares or debentures, an interest in the shares or debentures in reversion or remainder or (as regards Scotland) in fee, are to be disregarded.

10. A person is to be treated as uninterested in shares or debentures if, and so long as, he holds them under the law in force in England and Wales as a bare trustee or as a custodian trustee, or under the law in force in Scotland, as a simple trustee.

11. There is to be disregarded an interest of a person subsisting by virtue of—

(a) any unit trust scheme which is an authorised unit trust scheme within the meaning of the Financial Services Act 1986;

(b) a scheme made under section 22 or 22A of the Charities Act 1960 or section 24 or 25 of the Charities Act 1993, section 11 of the Trustee

Investments Act 1961 or section 1 of the Administration of Justice Act 1965; or

(c) the scheme set out in the Schedule to the Church Funds Investment Measure 1958.

12. There is to be disregarded any interest—

(a) of the Church of Scotland General Trustees or of the Church of Scotland Trust in shares or debentures held by them;

(b) of any other person in shares or debentures held by those Trustees or that Trust otherwise than as simple trustees.

'The Church of Scotland General Trustees' are the body incorporated by the order confirmed by the Church of Scotland (General Trustees) Order Confirmation Act 1921; and 'the Church of Scotland Trust' is the body incorporated by the order confirmed by the Church of Scotland Trust Order Confirmation Act 1932.

13. Delivery to a person's order of shares or debentures in fulfilment of a contract for the purchase of them by him or in satisfaction of a right of his to call for their delivery, or failure to deliver shares or debentures in accordance with the terms of such a contract or on which such a right falls to be satisfied, is deemed to constitute an event in consequence of the occurrence of which he ceases to be interested in them, and so is the lapse of a person's right to call for delivery of shares or debentures.

PART II
PERIODS WITHIN WHICH OBLIGATIONS IMPOSED BY SECTION 324 MUST BE FULFILLED

14.—(1) An obligation imposed on a person by section 324(1) to notify an interest must, if he knows of the existence of the interest on the day on which he becomes a director, be fulfilled before the expiration of the period of 5 days beginning with the day following that day.

(2) Otherwise, the obligation must be fulfilled before the expiration of the period of 5 days beginning with the day following that on which the existence of the interest comes to his knowledge.

15.—(1) An obligation imposed on a person by section 324(2) to notify the occurrence of an event must, if at the time at which the event occurs he knows of its occurrence and of the fact that its occurrence gives rise to the obligation, be fulfilled before the expiration of the period of 5 days beginning with the day following that on which the event occurs.

(2) Otherwise, the obligation must be fulfilled before the expiration of a period of 5 days beginning with the day following that on which the fact that the occurrence of the event gives rise to the obligation comes to his knowledge.

16. In reckoning, for purposes of paragraphs 14 and 15, any period of days, a day that is a Saturday or Sunday, or a bank holiday in any part of Great Britain, is to be disregarded.

PART III
CIRCUMSTANCES IN WHICH OBLIGATION IMPOSED BY SECTION 324 IS NOT DISCHARGED

17.—(1) Where an event of whose occurrence a director is, by virtue of section 324(2)(a), under obligation to notify a company consists of his entering into a contract for the purchase by him of shares or debentures, the obligation is not discharged in the absence of inclusion in the notice of a statement of the price to be paid by him under the contract.

(2) An obligation imposed on a director by section 324(2)(b) is not discharged in the absence of inclusion in the notice of the price to be received by him under the contract.

18.—(1) An obligation imposed on a director by virtue of section 324(2)(c) to notify a company is not discharged in the absence of inclusion in the notice of a statement of the consideration for the assignment (or, if it be the case that there is no consideration, that fact).

(2) Where an event of whose occurrence a director is, by virtue of section 324(2)(d), under obligation to notify a company consists in his assigning a right, the obligation is not discharged in the absence of inclusion in the notice of a similar statement.

19.—(1) Where an event of whose occurrence a director is, by virtue of section 324(2)(d), under obligation to notify a company consists in the grant to him of a right to subscribe for shares or debentures, the obligation is not discharged in the absence of inclusion in the notice of a statement of—

    (a) the date on which the right was granted,

    (b) the period during which or the time at which the right is exercisable,

    (c) the consideration for the grant (or, if it be the case that there is no consideration, that fact), and

    (d) the price to be paid for the shares or debentures.

(2) Where an event of whose occurrence a director is, by section 324(2)(d), under obligation to notify a company consists in the exercise of a right granted to him to subscribe for shares or debentures, the obligation is not discharged in the absence of inclusion in the notice of a statement of—

    (a) the number of shares or amount of debentures in respect of which the right was exercised, and

    (b) if it be the case that they were registered in his name, that fact, and, if not, the name or names of the person or persons in whose name or names they were registered, together (if they were registered in the names of 2 persons or more) with the number or amount registered in the name of each of them.

    20. In this Part, a reference to price paid or received includes any consideration other than money.

PART IV
PROVISIONS WITH RESPECT TO REGISTER OF DIRECTORS' INTERESTS TO BE KEPT UNDER SECTION 325

21. The register must be so made up that the entries in it against the several names appear in chronological order.

22. An obligation imposed by section 325(2) to (4) must be fulfilled before the expiration of the period of 3 days beginning with the day after that on which the obligation arises; but in reckoning that period, a day which is a Saturday or Sunday or a bank holiday in any part of Great Britain is to be disregarded.

23. The nature and extent of an interest recorded in the register of a director in any shares or debentures shall, if he so requires, be recorded in the register.

24. The company is not, by virtue of anything done for the purposes of section 325 or this Part of this Schedule, affected with notice of, or put upon enquiry as to, the rights of any person in relation to any shares or debentures.

25. The register shall—

    (a) if the company's register of members is kept at its registered office, be kept there;

    (b) if the company's register of members is not so kept, be kept at the company's registered office or at the place where its register of members is kept;

and shall ... be open to the inspection of any member of the company without charge and of any other person on payment of such fee as may be prescribed

26.—(1) Any member of the company or other person may require a copy of the register, or of any part of it, on payment of such fee as may be prescribed.

(2) The company shall cause any copy so required by a person to be sent to him within the period of 10 days beginning with the day after that on which the requirement is received by the company.

27. The company shall send notice in the prescribed form to the registrar of companies of the place where the register is kept and of any change in that place, save in a case in which it has at all times been kept at its registered office.

28. Unless the register is in such a form as to constitute in itself an index, the company shall keep an index of the names inscribed in it, which shall—

    (a) in respect of each name, contain a sufficient indication to enable the information entered against it to be readily found; and

    (b) be kept at the same place as the register;

and the company shall, within 14 days after the date on which a name is entered in the register, make any necessary alteration in the index.

29. The register shall be produced at the commencement of the company's annual general meeting and remain open and accessible during the continuance of the meeting to any person attending the meeting.

General note

Part I Rules for interpretation of the sections and also s 346(4) and (5) Section 324 requires disclosure by a director of any interests he might have in shares or debentures of the company and the group and s 328 attributes to the director any interests of his spouse and children. These provisions are similar to those in ss 208 and 209 requiring the disclosure of interests in shares in a public company, see the notes to those provisions, above.

An interest of any kind whatsoever must be disclosed, even if subject to restraint or restriction (para 1). Other interests which must be disclosed are: an interest under a trust where the trust property comprises an interests in shares and debentures, even if the interest is as a beneficiary under a discretionary trust (para 2); an interest acquired on a contract of purchase (even if the shares to be purchased have not been identified as where the shares form part of a larger holding) (paras 3, 8 and see para 13); interests arising from the right to exercise or control the exercise of rights attaching to any shares or debentures, though not the registered holder (para 3); interests in call or put options (paras 6, 13); joint interests (para 7).

A person must also be treated as interested in any interests in shares or debentures of a body corporate if that person is a shadow director of the company or he has one third of the voting power (para 4) (save where the interests of the body corporate are in its capacity as trustee of any trust relating exclusively to certain retirement benefits schemes or superannuation funds: Companies (Disclosure of Directors' Interests) (Exceptions) Regulations 1985, SI 1985/802, reg 2(e), and (f)).Where that body corporate in turn can exercise the same voting control in another company, then that person is taken to be able to exercise that voting power also (para 5).

Interests which are excluded are those arising by reason only of acting as proxies and as corporate representatives (para 3(3)); interests in reversion or remainder only (where the income of the trust property comprising shares or debentures is payable to another person) (para 9); interests held as bare trustees or nominees (para 10); interests subsisting by virtue of authorised unit trusts and various statutory schemes (para 11); interests held by the Church of Scotland General Trustees (para 12).

For other exclusions, see Companies (Disclosure of Directors' Interests) (Exceptions) Regulations 1985, SI 1985/802, set out in text to s 324(3); also s 324(4), (6).

Part II Periods within which obligations imposed by s 324 must be fulfilled This Part determines the time limits within which a director or shadow director must disclose to the company their interests (and any interests attributed to them under s 328) in shares or debentures of the company or the group for the purposes of s 324(1) and s 324(2).

Essentially, the time period is five days but, in recognition of the breadth of the interests which must be disclosed, the commencement of that period is dependent on the director knowing of the interest in question. See para 14 as to the obligation to disclose an existing interest on appointment under s 324(1); and para 15 as to the obligation to disclose subsequent interests arising on the occurrence of certain events under s 324(2).

Part III Circumstances in which obligation imposed by s 324 is not discharged
This Part identifies specific information which must be contained in the director's
(or shadow director's) disclosure if such disclosure is to discharge his obligations
under s 324(2). In particular, it requires disclosure of the consideration given or
received by the director. Cf Sch 7, para 2A.

**Part IV Provisions with respect to register of directors' interests to be kept under
s 325** A director, if he wishes, may require the company to include clarifying
information about the nature and extent of any interest which he has disclosed (para
23) but the Schedule reflects the statutory position (s 360) that the company takes
no notice of beneficial interests in its shares (para 24). Inspection of the register is
governed by para 25. For provisions relating to the inspection of documents, registers
and fees, see the Companies (Inspection and Copying of Registers, Indices and
Documents) Regulations 1991, SI 1991/1998.

Where the register, and the index to the register, is kept otherwise than in a legible
form (see s 722, 723), the provisions as to the place at which it must be kept and the
place of inspection are subject to the Companies (Registers and Other Records)
Regulations 1985, SI 1985/724.

SCHEDULE 14

OVERSEAS BRANCH REGISTERS

Section 362

PART I
COUNTRIES AND TERRITORIES IN WHICH OVERSEAS
BRANCH REGISTER MAY BE KEPT

Northern Ireland

Any part of Her Majesty's dominions outside the United Kingdom, the Channel Islands or the Isle of Man

Bangladesh	Malta
Cyprus	Nigeria
Dominica	Pakistan
The Gambia	Republic of Ireland
Ghana	Seychelles
Guyana	Sierra Leone
The Hong Kong Special Administrative Region of the People's Republic of China	Singapore
India	South Africa
Kenya	Sri Lanka
Kiribati	Swaziland
Lesotho	Trinidad and Tobago
Malawi	Uganda
Malaysia	Zimbabwe

PART II
GENERAL PROVISIONS WITH RESPECT TO OVERSEAS
BRANCH REGISTERS

1.—(1) A company keeping an overseas branch register shall give to the registrar of companies notice in the prescribed form of the situation of the office where any overseas branch register is kept and of any change in its situation, and, if it is discontinued, of its discontinuance.

(2) Any such notice shall be given within 14 days of the opening of the office or of the change or discontinuance, as the case may be.

(3) If default is made in complying with this paragraph, the company and every officer of it who is in default is liable to a fine and, for continued contravention, to a daily default fine.

2.—(1) An overseas branch register is deemed to be part of the company's register of members ('the principal register').

(2) It shall be kept in the same manner in which the principal register is by this Act required to be kept, except that the advertisement before closing the register shall be inserted in a newspaper circulating in the district where the overseas branch register is kept.

3.—(1) A competent court in a country or territory where an overseas branch register is kept may exercise the same jurisdiction of rectifying the register as is under this Act exercisable by the court in Great Britain; and the offences of refusing inspection or copies of the register, and of authorising or permitting the refusal, may be prosecuted summarily before any tribunal having summary criminal jurisdiction.

(2) This paragraph extends only to those countries and territories where, immediately before the coming into force of this Act, provision to the same effect made by section 120(2) of the Companies Act 1948 had effect as part of the local law.

4.—(1) The company shall—

    (a) transmit to its registered office a copy of every entry in its overseas branch register as soon as may be after the entry is made, and

    (b) cause to be kept at the place where the company's principal register is kept a duplicate of its overseas branch register duly entered up from time to time.

Every such duplicate is deemed for all purposes of this Act to be part of the principal register.

(2) If default is made in complying with sub-paragraph (1), the company and every officer of it who is in default is liable to a fine and, for continued contravention, to a daily default fine.

(3) Where, by virtue of section 353(1)(b), the principal register is kept at the office of some person other than the company, and by reason of any default of his the company fails to comply with sub-paragraph (1)(b) above he is liable to the same penalty as if he were an officer of the company who was in default.

5. Subject to the above provisions with respect to the duplicate register, the shares registered in an overseas branch register shall be distinguished from those registered in the principal register; and no transaction with respect to any shares registered in an overseas branch register shall, during the continuance of that registration, be registered in any other register.

6. A company may discontinue to keep an overseas branch register, and thereupon all entries in that register shall be transferred to some other overseas branch register kept by the company in the same country or territory, or to the principal register.

7. Subject to the provisions of this Act, any company may, by its articles, make such provisions as it thinks fit respecting the keeping of overseas branch registers.

8. An instrument of transfer of a share registered in an overseas branch register (other than such a register kept in Northern Ireland) is deemed a transfer of property situated outside the United Kingdom *and, unless executed in a part of the United Kingdom, is exempt from stamp duty chargeable in Great Britain.*

Note: Words in italics repealed by FA 1990, s 132, Sch 19, Pt VI, to the extent there specified.

PART III
PROVISIONS FOR BRANCH REGISTERS OF OVERSEA COMPANIES TO BE KEPT IN GREAT BRITAIN

9.—(1) If by virtue of the law in force in any country or territory to which this paragraph applies companies incorporated under that law have power to keep in Great Britain branch registers of their members resident in Great Britain, Her Majesty may by Order in Council direct that—

    (a) so much of section 353 as requires a company's register of members to be kept at its registered office,

    (b) section 356 (register to be open to inspection by members), and

    (c) section 359 (power of court to rectify),

shall, subject to any modifications and adaptations specified in the Order, apply to and in relation to any such branch registers kept in Great Britain as they apply to and in relation to the registers of companies subject to those sections.

(2)   The countries and territories to which this paragraph applies are—

    (a) all those specified in Part I of this Schedule, plus the Channel Islands and the Isle of Man,

    (b) Botswana, Zambia and Tonga, and

    (c) any territory for the time being under Her Majesty's protection or administered by the Government of the United Kingdom under the Trusteeship System of the United Nations.

General note

Paragraph 1   Where the register is kept otherwise than in a legible form, see Companies (Registers and Other Records) Regulations 1985, SI 1985/724, regs 2(1), (3)(a), 3; 'officer in default' is defined in s 730(5).

Paragraph 2   As to the maintenance of the register, see s 352; as to the closure of the register, see s 358.

Paragraph 3   As to the jurisdiction to rectify the register, see s 359; the provisions of CA 1948, s 120(2) are replicated in para 4 below.

Paragraph 4   'Officer in default' is defined in s 730(5).

Paragraph 5   The fact that dealings with the shares can only be entered in the register kept in the overseas country or territory has implications for the situs of the shares and the jurisdiction entitled to tax such property; see note to s 352, above. See also para 8.

Paragraph 9   No Orders have been made under this provision.

Schedule 15   *Repealed by CA 1989, s 212, Sch 24 as from 7 January 1991.*

SCHEDULE 15A

WRITTEN RESOLUTIONS OF PRIVATE COMPANIES

Section 381A(7)

PART I
EXCEPTIONS

1. Section 381A does not apply to—
- (a) a resolution under section 303 removing a director before the expiration of his period of office, or
- (b) a resolution under section 391 removing an auditor before the expiration of his term of office.

PART II
ADAPTATION OF PROCEDURAL REQUIREMENTS

Introductory

2.—(1) In this Part of this Schedule (which adapts certain requirements of this Act in relation to proceedings under section 381A)—
- (a) a 'written resolution' means a resolution agreed to, or proposed to be agreed to, in accordance with that section, and
- (b) a 'relevant member' means a member by whom, or on whose behalf, the resolution is required to be signed in accordance with that section.

(2) A written resolution is not effective if any of the requirements of this Part of this Schedule is not complied with.

Section 95 (disapplication of pre-emption rights)

3.—(1) The following adaptations have effect in relation to a written resolution under section 95(2)(disapplication of pre-emption rights), or renewing a resolution under that provision.

(2) So much of section 95(5) as requires the circulation of a written statement by the directors with a notice of meeting does not apply, but such a statement must be supplied to each relevant member at or before the time at which the resolution is supplied to him for signature.

(3) Section 95(6) (offences) applies in relation to the inclusion in any such statement of matter which is misleading, false or deceptive in a material particular.

Section 155 (financial assistance for purchase of company's own shares or those of holding company)

4. In relation to a written resolution giving approval under section 155(4) or (5) (financial assistance for purchase of company's own shares or those of holding company), section 157(4)(a) (documents to be available at meeting) does not apply, but the documents referred to in that provision must be supplied to each relevant member at or before the time at which the resolution is supplied to him for signature.

Sections 164, 165 and 167 (authority for off-market purchase or contingent purchase contract of company's own shares)

5.—(1) The following adaptations have effect in relation to a written resolution—

    (a) conferring authority to make an off-market purchase of the company's own shares under section 164(2),

    (b) conferring authority to vary a contract for an off-market purchase of the company's own shares under section 164(7), or

    (c) varying, revoking or renewing any such authority under section 164(3).

(2) Section 164(5) (resolution ineffective if passed by exercise of voting rights by member holding shares to which the resolution relates) does not apply; but for the purposes of section 381A(1) a member holding shares to which the resolution relates shall not be regarded as a member who would be entitled to attend and vote.

(3) Section 164(6) (documents to be available at company's registered office and at meeting) does not apply, but the documents referred to in that provision and, where that provision applies by virtue of section 164(7), the further documents referred to in that provision must be supplied to each relevant member at or before the time at which the resolution is supplied to him for signature.

(4) The above adaptations also have effect in relation to a written resolution in relation to which the provisions of section 164(3) to (7) apply by virtue of—

    (a) section 165(2) (authority for contingent purchase contract), or

    (b) section 167(2) (approval of release of rights under contract approved under section 164 or 165).

Section 173 (approval for payment out of capital)

6.—(1) The following adaptations have effect in relation to a written resolution giving approval under section 173(2) (redemption or purchase of company's own shares out of capital).

(2) Section 174(2) (resolution ineffective if passed by exercise of voting rights by member holding shares to which the resolution relates) does not apply; but for the purposes of section 381A(1) a member holding shares to which the resolution relates shall not be regarded as a member who would be entitled to attend and vote.

(3) Section 174(4) (documents to be available at meeting) does not apply, but the documents referred to in that provision must be supplied to each relevant member at or before the time at which the resolution is supplied to him for signature.

Section 319 (approval of director's service contract)

7. In relation to a written resolution approving any such term as is mentioned in section 319(1) (director's contract of employment for more than five years), section 319(5) (documents to be available at company's registered office and at meeting) does not apply, but the documents referred to in that provision must be supplied to each relevant member at or before the time at which the resolution is supplied to him for signature.

Section 337 (funding of director's expenditure in performing his duties)

8. In relation to a written resolution giving approval under section 337(3)(a) (funding a director's expenditure in performing his duties), the requirement of that provision that certain matters be disclosed at the meeting at which the resolution is passed does not apply, but those matters must be disclosed to each relevant member at or before the time at which the resolution is supplied to him for signature.

General note

Section 381A makes provision for the use of written resolutions by private companies so enabling them to dispense with the need for formal meetings. Many of the provisions of the statute, presupposing that a particular matter will be dealt with at a meeting, require that various documents be laid before a meeting or disenfranchise certain shareholders from voting at a meeting; requirements which are incompatible with the procedure for written resolutions.

This Schedule amends such provisions to facilitate the use of written resolutions, for example, by requiring documents to be sent to the members along with the written resolution, or by deeming members not to be entitled to vote on certain matters so that their disenfranchisement will not prevent the remaining shareholders from passing a written resolution (unanimity from those entitled to attend and vote being required: s 381A(1)).

Part I Exceptions   Written resolutions may not be used in the specified cases because the director or auditor, as the case may be, is entitled in those circumstances to be heard by the general meeting, see the notes to ss 303 and 391, above.

Part II Adaptation of procedural requirements   The consequences of non-compliance with the requirements of this Part are set out in para 2(2).

SCHEDULE 15B

PROVISIONS SUBJECT TO WHICH SS 425–427 HAVE EFFECT IN THEIR APPLICATION TO MERGERS AND DIVISIONS OF PUBLIC COMPANIES

Section 427A

Meetings of transferee company

1. Subject to paragraphs 10(1), 12(4) and 14(2), the court shall not sanction a compromise or arrangement under section 452(2) unless a majority in number representing three-fourths in value of each class of members of every pre-existing transferee company concerned in the scheme, present and voting either in person or by proxy at a meeting, agree to the scheme.

Draft terms of merger

2.—(1) The court shall not sanction the compromise or arrangement under section 425(2) unless—

    (a) a draft of the proposed terms of the scheme (from here on referred to as the 'draft terms') has been drawn up and adopted by the directors of all the transferor and pre-existing transferee companies concerned in the scheme,

    (b) subject to paragraph 11(3), in the case of each of those companies the directors have delivered a copy of the draft terms to the registrar of companies and the registrar has published in the Gazette notice of receipt by him of a copy of the draft terms from that company, and

    (c) subject to paragraphs 10 to 14, that notice was so published at least one month before the date of any meeting of that company summoned under section 425(1) or for purposes of paragraph 1.

(2) Subject to paragraph 12(2), the draft terms shall give particulars of at least the following matters—

    (a) in respect of each transferor company and transferee company concerned in the scheme, its name, the address of its registered office and whether it is a company limited by shares or a company limited by guarantee and having a share capital;

(b) the number of shares in any transferee company to be allotted to members of any transferor company for a given number of their shares (from here on referred to as the 'share exchange ratio') and the amount of any cash payment;

(c) the terms relating to the allotment of shares in any transferee company;

(d) the date from which the holding of shares in a transferee company will entitle the holders to participate in profits, and any special conditions affecting that entitlement;

(e) the date from which the transactions of any transferor company are to be treated for accounting purposes as being those of any transferee company;

(f) any rights or restrictions attaching to shares or other securities in any transferee company to be allotted under the scheme to the holders of shares to which any special rights or restrictions attach, or of other securities, in any transferor company, or the measures proposed concerning them;

(g) any amount of benefit paid or given or intended to be paid or given to any of the experts referred to in paragraph 5 or to any director of a transferor company or pre-existing transferee company, and the consideration for the payment of benefit.

(3) Where the scheme is a Case 3 Scheme the draft terms shall also—

(a) give particulars of the property and liabilities to be transferred (to the extent these are known to the transferor company) and their allocation among the transferee companies;

(b) make provision for the allocation among and transfer to the transferee companies of any other property and liabilities which the transferor company has or may subsequently acquire; and

(c) specify the allocation to members of the transferor company of shares in the transferee companies and the criteria upon which that allocation is based.

Documents and information to be made available

3. Subject to paragraphs 10 to 14, the court shall not sanction the compromise or arrangement under section 425(2) unless—

(a) in the case of each transferor company and each pre-existing transferee company the directors have drawn up and adopted a report complying with paragraph 4 (from here on referred to as a 'directors' report');

(b) where the scheme is a Case 3 Scheme, the directors of the transferor company have reported to every meeting of the members or any class of members of that company summoned under section 425(1), and to the directors of each transferee company, any material changes in the property and liabilities of the transferor company between the date when the draft terms were adopted and the date of the meeting in question;

(c) where the directors of a transferor company have reported to the directors of a transferee company such a change as is mentioned in sub-paragraph (b) above, the latter have reported that change to every meeting of the members or any class of members of that transferee company summoned for the purposes of paragraph 1, or have sent a report of that change to every member who would have been entitled to receive a notice of such a meeting;

(d) a report complying with paragraph 5 has been drawn up on behalf of each transferor company and pre-existing transferee company (from here on referred to as an 'expert's report');

(e) the members of any transferor company or transferee company were able to inspect at the registered office of that company copies of the documents listed in paragraph 6(1) in relation to every transferor company and pre-existing transferee company concerned in the scheme during a period beginning one month before, and ending on, the date of the first meeting of the members or any class of members of the first-mentioned transferor or transferee company summoned either under section 425(1) or for the purposes of paragraph 1 and those members were able to obtain copies of those documents or any part of them on request during that period free of charge; and

(f) the memorandum and articles of association of any transferee company which is not a pre-existing transferee company, or a draft thereof, has been approved by ordinary resolution of every transferor company concerned in the scheme.

Directors' report

4.—(1) The directors' report shall consist of—

(a) the statement required by section 426, and

(b) insofar as that statement does not contain the following matters, a further statement—

(i) setting out the legal and economic grounds for the draft terms, and in particular for the share exchange ratio, and, where the scheme is a Case 3 Scheme, for the criteria upon which the allocation to the members of the transferor company of shares in the transferee companies was based, and

(ii) specifying any special valuation difficulties.

(2) Where the scheme is a Case 3 Scheme the directors' report shall also state whether a report has been made to the transferee company under section 103 (non-cash consideration to be valued before allotment) and, if so, whether that report has been delivered to the registrar of companies.

Expert's report

5.—(1) Except where a joint expert is appointed under sub-paragraph (2) below, an expert's report shall consist of a separate written report on the draft terms to the members of one transferor company or pre-existing transferee company concerned in the scheme drawn up by a separate expert appointed on behalf of that company.

(2) The court may, on the joint application of all the transferor companies and pre-existing transferee companies concerned in the scheme, approve the appointment of a joint expert to draw up a single report on behalf of all those companies.

(3) An expert shall be independent of any of the companies concerned in the scheme, that is to say a person qualified at the time of the report to be appointed, or to continue to be, an auditor of those companies.

(4) However, where it appears to an expert that a valuation is reasonably necessary to enable him to draw up the report, and it appears to him to be reasonable for that valuation, or part of it, to be made (or for him to accept such a valuation) by another person who—

    (a) appears to him to have the requisite knowledge and experience to make the valuation or that part of it; and

    (b) is not an officer or servant of any of the companies concerned in the scheme or any other body corporate which is one of those companies' subsidiary or holding company or a subsidiary of one of those companies' holding company or a partner or employee of such an officer or servant,

he may arrange for or accept such a valuation, together with a report which will enable him to make his own report under this paragraph.

(5) The reference in sub-paragraph (4) above to an officer or servant does not include an auditor.

(6) Where any valuation is made by a person other than the expert himself, the latter's report shall state that fact and shall also—

    (a) state the former's name and what knowledge and experience he has to carry out the valuation, and

    (b) describe so much of the undertaking, property and liabilities as were valued by the other person, and the method used to value them, and specify the date of the valuation.

(7) An expert's report shall—

    (a) indicate the method or methods used to arrive at the share exchange ratio proposed;

    (b) give an opinion as to whether the method or methods used are reasonable in all the circumstances of the case, indicate the values arrived at using each such method and (if there is more than one method) give an opinion on the relative importance attributed to such methods in arriving at the value decided on;

    (c) describe any special valuation difficulties which have arisen;

    (d) state whether in the expert's opinion the share exchange ratio is reasonable; and

    (e) in the case of a valuation made by a person other than himself, state that it appeared to himself reasonable to arrange for it to be so made or to accept a valuation so made.

(8)   Each expert has the right of access to all such documents of all the transferor companies and pre-existing transferee companies concerned in the scheme,

and the right to require from the companies' officers all such information, as he thinks necessary for the purpose of making his report.

Inspection of documents

6.—(1) The documents referred to in paragraph 3(e) are, in relation to any company—

    (a) the draft terms;

    (b) the directors' report referred to in paragraph 4 above;

    (c) the expert's report;

    (d) the company's annual accounts, together with the relevant directors' report and auditors' report, for the last three financial years ending on or before the relevant date; and

    (e) if the last of those financial years ended more than six months before the relevant date, an accounting statement in the form described in the following provisions.

In paragraphs (d) and (e) 'the relevant date' means one month before the first meeting of the company summoned under section 425(1) or for the purposes of paragraph 1.

(2) The accounting statement shall consist of—

    (a) a balance sheet dealing with the state of the affairs of the company as at a date not more than three months before the draft terms were adopted by the directors, and

    (b) where the company would be required to prepare group accounts if that date were the last day of a financial year, a consolidated balance sheet dealing with the state of affairs of the company and its subsidiary undertakings as at that date.

(3) The requirements of this Act as to balance sheets forming part of a company's annual accounts, and the matters to be included in notes thereto, apply to any balance sheet required for the accounting statement, with such modifications as are necessary by reason of its being prepared otherwise than as at the last day of a financial year.

(4) Any balance sheet required for the accounting statement shall be approved by the board of directors and signed on behalf of the board by a director of the company.

(5) In relation to a company within the meaning of Article 3 of the Companies (Northern Ireland) Order 1986, the references in this paragraph to the requirements of this Act shall be construed as reference to the corresponding requirements of that Order.

Transferor company holding its own shares

7. The court shall not sanction under section 425(2) a compromise or arrangement under which any shares in a transferee company are to be allotted to a transferor company or its nominee in respect of shares in that transferor company held by it or its nominee.

Securities other than shares to which special rights are attached

8.—(1) Where any security of a transferor company to which special rights are attached is held by a person other than as a member or creditor of the company, the court shall not sanction a compromise or arrangement under section 425(2) unless under the scheme that person is to receive rights in a transferee company of equivalent value.

(2) Sub-paragraph (1) above shall not apply in the case of any such security where—

(a) the holder has agreed otherwise; or

(b) the holder is, or under the scheme is to be, entitled to have the security purchased by a transferee company involved in the scheme on terms which the court considers reasonable.

Date and consequences of the compromise or arrangement

9.—(1) The following provisions of this paragraph shall apply where the court sanctions a compromise or arrangement.

(2) The court shall in the order sanctioning the compromise or arrangement or in a subsequent order under section 427 fix a date on which the transfer or transfers to the transferee company or transferee companies of the undertaking, property and liabilities of the transferor company shall take place; and any such order which provides for the dissolution of the transferor company shall fix the same date for the dissolution.

(3) If it is necessary for the transferor company to take any steps to ensure that the undertaking, property and liabilities are fully transferred, the court shall fix a date, not later than six months after the date fixed under sub-paragraph (2) above, by which such steps must be taken and for that purpose may postpone the dissolution of the transferor company until that date.

(4) The court may postpone or further postpone the date fixed under sub-paragraph (3) above if it is satisfied that the steps there mentioned cannot be completed by the date (or latest date) fixed under that sub-paragraph.

Exceptions

10.—(1) The court may sanction a compromise or arrangement under section 425(2) notwithstanding that—

(a) any meeting otherwise required by paragraph 1 has not been summoned by a pre-existing transferee company ('the relevant company'), and

   (b) paragraphs 2(1)(c) and 3(e) have not been complied with in respect of that company,

if the court is satisfied that the conditions specified in sub-paragraph (2) below have been complied with.

(2) Subject to paragraph 11(3) and 12(3), the conditions mentioned in sub-paragraph (1) above are—

   (a) that the publication of notice of receipt of the draft terms by the registrar of companies referred to in paragraph 2(1)(b) took place in respect of the relevant company at least one month before the date of any meeting of members of any transferor company concerned in the scheme summoned under section 425(1);

   (b) that the members of the relevant company were able to inspect at the registered office of that company the documents listed in paragraph 6(1) in relation to every transferor company and transferee company concerned in the scheme during a period ('the relevant period') beginning one month before, and ending on, the date of any such meeting, and that they were able to obtain copies of those documents or any part of them on request during that period free of charge; and

   (c) that one or more members of the relevant company, who together held not less than five per cent of the paid-up capital of that company which carried the right to vote at general meetings of the company, would have been able during the relevant period to require that a meeting of each class of members be called for the purpose of deciding whether or not to agree to the scheme but that no such requisition had been made.

11.—(1) The following sub-paragraphs apply where the scheme is a Case 3 Scheme.

(2) Sub-paragraphs (a) to (d) of paragraph 3 shall not apply and sub-paragraph (e) of that paragraph shall not apply as regards the documents listed in paragraph 6(1)(b), (c) and (e), if all members holding shares in, and all persons holding other securities of, any of the transferor companies and pre-existing transferee companies concerned in the scheme on the date of the application to the court under section 425(1), being shares or securities which as at that date carry the right to vote in general meetings of the company, so agree.

(3) The court may by order direct in respect of any transferor company or pre-existing transferee company that the requirements relating to—

   (a) delivering copies of the draft terms and publication of notice of receipt of the draft terms under paragraph 2(1)(b) and (c), or

   (b) inspection under paragraph 3(e),

shall not apply, and may by order direct that paragraph 10 shall apply to any pre-existing transferee company with the omission of sub-paragraph (2)(a) and (b) of that paragraph.

(4) The court shall not make any order under paragraph (3) above unless it is satisfied that the following conditions will be fulfilled—

   (a) that the members of the company will have received or will have been able to obtain free of charge copies of the documents listed in paragraph 6(1) in time to examine them before the date of the first meeting of the members or any class of members of the company summoned under section 425(1) or for the purposes of paragraph 1;

(b) in the case of a pre-existing transferee company, where in the circumstances described in paragraph 10 no meeting is held, that the members of that company will have received or will have been able to obtain free of charge copies of those documents in time to require a meeting under paragraph 10(2)(c);

(c) that the creditors of the company will have received or will have been able to obtain free of charge copies of the draft terms in time to examine them before the date of the meeting of the members or any class of members of the company, or, in the circumstances referred to in paragraph (b) above, at the same time as the members of the company; and

(d) that no prejudice would be caused to the members or creditors of any transferor company or transferee company concerned in the scheme by making the order in question.

Transferee company or companies holding shares in the transferor company

12.—(1) Where the scheme is a Case 1 Scheme and in the case of every transferor company concerned—

(a) the shares in that company, and

(b) such securities of that company (other than shares) as carry the right to vote at general meetings of that company,

are all held by or on behalf of the transferee company, section 427A and this Schedule shall apply subject to the following sub-paragraphs.

(2) The draft terms need not give particulars of the matters mentioned in paragraph 2(2)(b), (c) or (d).

(3) Section 426 and sub-paragraphs (a) and (d) of paragraph 3 shall not apply, and sub-paragraph (e) of that paragraph shall not apply as regards the documents listed in paragraph 6(1)(b) and (c).

(4) The court may sanction the compromise or arrangement under section 425(2) notwithstanding that—

(a) any meeting otherwise required by section 425 or paragraph 1 has not been summoned by any company concerned in the scheme, and

(b) paragraphs 2(1)(c) and 3(e) have not been complied with in respect of that company,

if it is satisfied that the conditions specified in the following sub-paragraphs have been complied with.

(5) The conditions mentioned in the previous sub-paragraph are—

(a) that the publication of notice of receipt of the draft items by the registrar of companies referred to in paragraph 2(1)(b) took place in respect of every transferor company and transferee company concerned in the scheme at least one month before the date of the order under section 425(2) ('the relevant date');

(b) that the members of the transferee company were able to inspect at the registered office of that company copies of the documents listed in paragraphs 6(1)(a), (d) and (e) in relation to every transferor company or transferee company concerned in the scheme during a period ('the relevant period') beginning one month before, and ending on, the relevant date and that they were able to obtain copies of those documents or any part of them on request during that period free of charge; and

(c) that one or more members of the transferee company who together held not less than five per cent of the paid-up capital of the company which carried the right to vote at general meetings of the company would have been able during the relevant period to require that a meeting of each class of members be called for the purpose of deciding whether or not to agree to the scheme but that no such requisition has been made.

13.—(1) Where the scheme is a Case 3 Scheme and—

(a) the shares in the transferor company, and

(b) such securities of that company (other than shares) as carry the right to vote at general meetings of that company,

are all held by or on behalf of one or more transferee companies, section 427A and this Schedule shall apply subject to the following sub-paragraphs.

(2) The court may sanction a compromise or arrangement under section 425(2) notwithstanding that—

(a) any meeting otherwise required by section 425 has not been summoned by the transferor company, and

(b) paragraphs 2(1)(c) and 3(b) and (e) have not been complied with in respect of that company,

if it is satisfied that the conditions specified in the following sub-paragraph have been complied with.

(3) The conditions referred to in the previous sub-paragraph are—

(a) the conditions set out in paragraph 12(5)(a) and (c);

(b) that the members of the transferor company and every transferee company concerned in the scheme were able to inspect at the registered office of the company of which they were members copies of the documents listed in paragraph 6(1) in relation to every such company during a period beginning one month before, and ending on, the date of the order under section 425(2) ('the relevant date'), and that they were able to obtain copies of those documents or any part of them on request during that period free of charge; and

(c) that the directors of the transferor company have sent to every member who would have been entitled to receive a notice of the meeting (had it been called), and to the directors of each transferee company, a report of any material changes in the property and liabilities of the transferor company between the date when the draft terms were adopted and a date one month before the relevant date.

14.—(1) When the scheme is a Case 1 Scheme and in the case of every transferor company concerned ninety per cent or more (but not all) of—

    (a) the shares in that company, and

    (b) such securities of that company (other than shares) as carry the right to vote at general meetings of that company,

are held by or on behalf of the transferee company, section 427A and this Schedule shall apply subject to the following sub-paragraphs.

(2) The court may sanction a compromise or arrangement under section 425(2) notwithstanding that—

    (a) any meeting otherwise required by paragraph 1 has not been summoned by the transferee company, and

    (b) paragraph 2(1)(c) and 3(e) have not been complied with in respect of that company,

if the court is satisfied that the conditions specified in the following sub-paragraph have been complied with.

(3) The conditions referred to in the previous sub-paragraph are the same conditions as those specified in paragraph 10(2), save that for this purpose the condition contained in paragraph 10(2)(b) shall be treated as referring only to the documents listed in paragraph 6(1)(a), (d) and (e).

Liability of transferee companies for the default of another

15.—(1) Where the scheme is a Case 3 Scheme, each transferee company shall be jointly and severally liable, subject to sub-paragraph (2) below, for any liability transferred to any other transferee company under the scheme to the extent that that other company has made default in satisfying that liability, but so that no transferee company shall be so liable for an amount greater than the amount arrived at by calculating the value at the time of the transfer of the property transferred to it under the scheme less the amount at that date of the liabilities so transferred.

(2) If a majority in number representing three-fourths in value of the creditors or any class of creditors of the transferor company present and voting either in person or by proxy at a meeting summoned under section 425(1) so agree, sub-paragraph (1) above shall not apply in respect of the liabilities of the creditors or that class of creditors.

General note

This Schedule was inserted by the Companies (Mergers and Divisions) Regulations 1987, SI 1987/1991, reg 2(c), Sch, Pt II, and renumbered by CA 1989, s 114(2) as from 1 April 1990.

Certain compromises or arrangements involving the merger or division of public companies as laid down by s 427A are subject to the detailed requirements set out in this Schedule: see the note to that section and to ss 425–427, above.

Schedule 16 *repealed by the Insolvency Act 1986, section 438, Schedule 12*

Schedules 17–19 *repealed by the Insolvency Act 1985, section 235(3), Schedule 10, Part II.*

SCHEDULE 20

VESTING OF DISCLAIMED PROPERTY; PROTECTION OF THIRD PARTIES

Section 619

Part I *repealed by the Insolvency Act 1985, section 235(3), Schedule 10, Part II.*

PART II
CROWN DISCLAIMER UNDER SECTION 656 (SCOTLAND ONLY)

5. The court shall not under section 657 make a vesting order, where the property disclaimed is held under a lease, in favour of a person claiming under the company (whether as sub-lessee or as creditor in a duly registered or, as appropriate, recorded heritable security over a lease), except on the following terms.

6. The person must by the order be made subject—
- (a) to the same liabilities and obligations as those to which the company was subject under the lease in respect of the property at the commencement of the winding up, or
- (b) (if the court thinks fit) only to the same liabilities and obligations as if the lease had been assigned to him at that date;

and in either event (if the case so requires) the liabilities and obligations must be as if the lease had comprised only the property comprised in the vesting order.

7. A creditor or sub-lessee declining to accept a vesting order on such terms is excluded from all interest in and security over the property.

8. If there is no person claiming under the company who is willing to accept an order on such terms, the court has power to vest the company's estate and interest in the property in any person liable (either personally or in a representative character, and either alone or jointly with the company) to perform the lessee's obligations under the lease, freed and discharged from all interests, rights and obligations created by the company in the lease or in relation to the lease.

9. For the purposes of paragraph 5 above, a heritable security is duly recorded if it is recorded in the Register of Sasines and is duly registered if registered in accordance with the Land Registration (Scotland) Act 1979.

SCHEDULE 21

EFFECT OF REGISTRATION UNDER SECTION 680

Section 689

Interpretation

1. In this Schedule—

'registration' means registration in pursuance of section 680 in Chapter II of Part XXII of this Act, and 'registered' has the corresponding meaning, and

'instrument' includes deed of settlement, contract of copartnery and letters patent.

Vesting of property

2. All property belonging to or vested in the company at the date of its registration passes to and vests in the company on registration for all the estate and interest of the company in the property.

Existing liabilities

3. Registration does not affect the company's rights or liabilities in respect of any debt or obligation incurred, or contract entered into, by, to, with or on behalf of the company before registration.

Pending actions at law

4.—(1) All actions and other legal proceedings which at the time of the company's registration are pending by or against the company, or the public officer or any member of it, may be continued in the same manner as if the registration had not taken place.

(2) However, execution shall not issue against the effects of any individual member of the company on any judgment, decree or order obtained in such an action or proceeding; but in the event of the company's property and effects being insufficient to satisfy the judgment, decree or order, an order may be obtained for winding up the company.

The company's constitution

5.—(1) All provisions contained in any Act of Parliament or other instrument constituting or regulating the company are deemed to be conditions and regulations of the company, in the same manner and with the same incidents as if so much of them as would, if the company had been formed under this Act, have been required to be inserted in the memorandum, were contained in a registered memorandum, and the residue were contained in registered articles.

(2) The provisions brought in under this paragraph include, in the case of a company registered as a company limited by guarantee, those of the resolution declaring the amount of the guarantee; and they include also the statement under section 681(5)(a), and any statement under section 684(2).

6.—(1) All the provisions of this Act apply to the company, and to its members, contributories and creditors, in the same manner in all respects as if it had been formed under this Act, subject as follows.

(2) Table A does not apply unless adopted by special resolution.

(3) Provisions relating to the numbering of shares do not apply to any joint stock company whose shares are not numbered.

(4) Subject to the provisions of this Schedule, the company does not have power—

    (a) to alter any provision contained in an Act of Parliament relating to the company,

    (b) without the sanction of the Secretary of State, to alter any provision contained in letters patent relating to the company.

(5) The company does not have power to alter any provision contained in a royal charter or letters patent with respect to the company's objects.

(6) When by virtue of sub-paragraph (4) or (5) a company does not have power to alter a provision, it does not have power to ratify acts of the directors in contravention of the provision.

Capital structure

7. Provisions of this Act with respect to—

    (a) the registration of an unlimited company as limited,

    (b) the powers of an unlimited company on registration as a limited company to increase the nominal amount of its share capital and to provide that a portion of its share capital shall not be capable of being called up except in the event of winding up, and

(c) the power of a limited company to determine that a portion of its share capital shall not be capable of being called up except in that event,

apply, notwithstanding any provisions contained in an Act of Parliament, royal charter or other instrument constituting or regulating the company.

Supplementary

8. Nothing in paragraphs 5 to 7 authorises a company to alter any such provisions contained in an instrument constituting or regulating the company as would, if the company had originally been formed under this Act, have been required to be contained in the memorandum and are not authorised to be altered by this Act.

9. None of the provisions of this Act (except section 461(3)) derogate from any power of altering the company's constitution or regulations which may, by virtue of any Act of Parliament or other instrument constituting or regulating it, be vested in the company.

General note

Paragraph 5   This provision 'converts' the constitution of the company into the format of the memorandum and articles of association (where the company does not adopt a memorandum and articles on registration, which it may do under s 690) but subject to the constraints in para 6.

Paragraph 6   Having converted the company's constitution to the modern format of memorandum and articles of association, that 'conversion' offers the possibility of alteration of various provisions. Sub-paras (4), (5) limit the ability of the company to alter those provisions to the extent specified while sub-para (6) in effect excludes the operation of ss 35 and 35A (which permit members to ratify acts of the directors in excess of the company's constitution and their authority) in cases where paras 4 and 5 apply. If the company cannot alter the provisions which are specified, the members equally cannot ratify acts which are in breach of those provisions. 'Contributory' is defined by IA 1986, s 79 for the purposes of that Act and the CA 1985 as every person liable to contribute to the assets of a company in the event of its being wound up.

As to the meaning of 'this Act', see s 735A(1).

SCHEDULE 21A

BRANCH REGISTRATION UNDER THE ELEVENTH COMPANY LAW DIRECTIVE (89/666/EEC)

Section 690A

Duty to register

1.—(1) A company shall, within one month of having opened a branch in a part of Great Britain, deliver to the registrar for registration a return in the prescribed form containing—

    (a) such particulars about the company as are specified in paragraph 2,

    (b) such particulars about the branch as are specified in paragraph 3, and

    (c) if the company is one to which section 699AA applies, such particulars in relation to the registration of documents under Schedule 21D as are specified in paragraph 4.

(2) The return shall, except where sub-paragraph (3) below applies, be accompanied by the documents specified in paragraph 5 and, if the company is one to which Part I of Schedule 21D applies, the documents specified in paragraph 6.

(3) This sub-paragraph applies where—

    (a) at the time the return is delivered, the company has another branch in the United Kingdom,

    (b) the return contains a statement to the effect that the documents specified in paragraph 5, and, if the company is one to which Part I of Schedule 21D applies, paragraph 6, are included in the material registered in respect of the other branch, and

    (c) the return states where the other branch is registered and what is its registered number.

(4) In sub-paragraph (1) above, the reference to having opened a branch in a part of Great Britain includes a reference to a branch having become situated there on ceasing to be situated elsewhere.

(5) If at the date on which the company opens the branch in Great Britain the company is subject to any proceedings referred to in section 703P(1) (winding up) or 703Q(1) (insolvency proceedings etc), the company shall deliver a return

under section 703P(1) or (as the case may be) 703Q(1) within one month of that date.

If on or before that date a person has been appointed to be liquidator of the company and continues in that office at that date, section 703P(3) and (4) (liquidator to make return within 14 days of appointment) shall have effect as if it required a return to be made under that section within one month of the date of the branch being opened.

Particulars required

2.—(1) The particulars referred to in paragraph 1(1)(a) are —

(a) the corporate name of the company,

(b) its legal form,

(c) if it is registered in the country of its incorporation, the identity of the register in which it is registered and the number with which it is so registered,

(d) a list of its directors and secretary, containing—

(i) with respect to each director, the particulars specified in sub-paragraph (3) below, and

(ii) with respect to the secretary (or where there are joint secretaries, with respect to each of them) the particulars specified in sub-paragraph (4) below,

(e) the extent of the powers of the directors to represent the company in dealings with third parties and in legal proceedings, together with a statement as to whether they may act alone or must act jointly and, if jointly, the name of any other person concerned, and

(f) whether the company is an institution to which section 699A (or the equivalent provision in Northern Ireland) applies.

(2) In the case of a company which is not incorporated in a Member State, those particulars also include—

(a) the law under which the company is incorporated,

(b) (in the case of a company to which either paragraphs 2 and 3 of Part I of Schedule 21C or Schedule 21D applies) the period for which the company is required by the law under which it is incorporated to prepare accounts, together with the period allowed for the preparation and public disclosure of accounts for such a period, and

(c) unless disclosed by the documents specified in paragraph 5—

(i) the address of its principal place of business in its country of incorporation,

(ii) its objects, and

(iii) the amount of its issued share capital.

(3) The particulars referred to in sub-paragraph (1)(d)(i) above are—

(a) in the case of an individual—

(i) his name,

  (ii) any former name,

  (iii) his usual residential address,

  (iv) his nationality,

  (v) his business occupation (if any),

  (vi) particulars of any other directorships held by him, and

  (vii) his date of birth;

 (b) in the case of a corporation or Scottish firm, its corporate or firm name and registered or principal office.

(4) The particulars referred to in sub-paragraph (1)(d)(ii) above are—

 (a) in the case of an individual, his name, any former name and his usual residential address;

 (b) in the case of a corporation or Scottish firm, its corporate or firm name and registered or principal office.

Where all the partners in a firm are joint secretaries of the company, the name and principal office of the firm may be stated instead of the particulars required by paragraph (a) above.

(5) In sub-paragraphs (3)(a) and (4)(a) above—

 (a) 'name' means a person's forename and surname, except that in the case of a peer, or an individual usually known by a title, the title may be stated instead of his forename and surname, or in addition to either or both of them; and

 (b) the reference to a former name does not include—

  (i) in the case of a peer, or an individual normally known by a title, the name by which he was known previous to the adoption of or succession to the title;

  (ii) in the case of any person, a former name which was changed or disused before he attained the age of 18 years or which has been changed or disused for 20 years or more;

  (iii) in the case of a married woman, the name by which she was known previous to the marriage.

(6) Where—

 (a) at the time a return is delivered under paragraph 1(1) the company has another branch in the same part of Great Britain as the branch covered by the return; and

 (b) the company has delivered the particulars required by sub-paragraphs (1)(b) to (f) and (2) to (5) to the registrar with respect to that branch (or to the extent it is required to do so by virtue of Schedule 21B to this Act) and has no outstanding obligation to make a return to the registrar in respect of that branch under paragraph 7 in relation to any alteration to those particulars,

the company may adopt the particulars so delivered as particulars which the registrar is to treat as having been filed by the return by referring in the return to the fact that the particulars have been filed in respect of that other branch and giving the number with which the other branch is registered.

3. The particulars referred to in paragraph 1(1)(b) are—

    (a) the address of the branch,

    (b) the date on which it was opened,

    (c) the business carried on at it,

    (d) if different from the name of the company, the name in which that business is carried on,

    (e) a list of the names and addresses of all persons resident in Great Britain authorised to accept on the company's behalf service of process in respect of the business of the branch and of any notices required to be served on the company in respect of the business of the branch,

    (f) a list of the names and usual residential addresses of all persons authorised to represent the company as permanent representatives of the company for the business of the branch,

    (g) the extent of the authority of any person falling within paragraph (f) above, including whether that person is authorised to act alone or jointly, and

    (h) if a person falling within paragraph (f) above is not authorised to act alone, the name of any person with whom he is authorised to act.

4. The particulars referred to in paragraph 1(1)(c) are—

    (a) whether it is intended to register documents under paragraph 2(2) or, as the case may be, 10(1) of Schedule 21D in respect of the branch or in respect of some other branch in the United Kingdom, and

    (b) if it is, where that other branch is registered and what is its registered number.

Documents required

5. The first documents referred to in paragraph 1(2) are—

    (a) a certified copy of the charter, statutes or memorandum and articles of the company (or other instrument constituting or defining the company's constitution), and

    (b) if any of the documents mentioned in paragraph (a) above is not written in the English language, a translation of it into English certified in the prescribed manner to be a correct translation.

6.—(1) The second documents referred to in paragraph 1(2) are—

    (a) copies of the latest accounting documents prepared in relation to a financial period of the company to have been publicly disclosed in accordance with the law of the country in which it is incorporated before the end of the period allowed for compliance with paragraph 1 in respect of the branch or, if earlier, the date on which the company complies with paragraph 1 in respect of the branch, and

    (b) if any of the documents mentioned in paragraph (a) above is not written in the English language, a translation of it into English certified in the prescribed manner to be a correct translation.

(2) In sub-paragraph (1)(a) above, 'financial period' and 'accounting documents' shall be construed in accordance with paragraph 6 of Schedule 21D.

Alterations

7.—(1) If, after a company has delivered a return under paragraph 1(1) above, any alteration is made in—

(a) its charter, statutes or memorandum and articles (or other instrument constituting or defining its constitution), or

(b) any of the particulars referred to in paragraph 1(1),

the company shall, within the time specified below, deliver to the registrar for registration a return in the prescribed form containing the prescribed particulars of the alteration.

In the case of an alteration in any of the documents referred to in paragraph (a), the return shall be accompanied by a certified copy of the document as altered, together with, if the document is not written in the English language, a translation of it into English certified in the prescribed manner to be a correct translation.

(2) The time for the delivery of the return required by sub-paragraph (1) above is—

(a) in the case of an alteration in any of the particulars specified in paragraph 3, 21 days after the alteration is made; or

(b) in the case of any other alteration, 21 days after the date on which notice of the alteration in question could have been received in Great Britain in due course of post (if despatched with due diligence).

(3) Where—

(a) a company has more than one branch in Great Britain, and

(b) an alteration relates to more than one of those branches,

sub-paragraph (1) above shall have effect to require the company to deliver a return in respect of each of the branches to which the alteration relates.

(4) For the purposes of sub-paragraph (3) above—

(a) an alteration in any of the particulars specified in paragraph 2 shall be treated as relating to every branch of the company (though where the company has more than one branch in a part of Great Britain a return in respect of an alteration in any of those particulars which gives the branch numbers of two or more such branches shall be treated as a return in respect of each branch whose number is given), but

(b) an alteration in the company's charter, statutes or memorandum and articles (or other instrument constituting or defining its constitution) shall only be treated as relating to a branch if the document altered is included in the material registered in respect of it.

8.—(1) Sub-paragraph (2) below applies where—

(a) a company's return under paragraph 1(1) includes a statement to the effect mentioned in paragraph 1(3)(b), and

(b) the statement ceases to be true so far as concerns the documents specified in paragraph 5.

(2) The company shall, within the time specified below, deliver to the registrar of companies for registration in respect of the branch to which the return relates—

(a) the documents specified in paragraph 5, or

(b) a return in the prescribed form—

    (i) containing a statement to the effect that those documents are included in the material which is registered in respect of another branch of the company in the United Kingdom, and

    (ii) stating where the other branch is registered and what is its registered number.

(3) The time for complying with sub-paragraph (2) above is 21 days after the date on which notice of the fact that the statement in the earlier return has ceased to be true could have been received in Great Britain in due course of post (if despatched with due diligence).

(4) Sub-paragraph (2) above shall also apply where, after a company has made a return under sub-paragraph (2)(b) above, the statement to the effect mentioned in sub-paragraph (2)(b)(i) ceases to be true.

(5) For the purposes of sub-paragraph (2)(b), where the company has more than one branch in a part of Great Britain a return which gives the branch numbers of two or more such branches shall be treated as a return in respect of each branch whose number is given.

General note

This Schedule was inserted by the Oversea Companies and Credit and Financial Institutions (Branch Disclosure) Regulations 1992, SI 1992/3179, as from 1 January 1993, to give effect to the Eleventh Company Law Directive (89/666/EEC): see the note to s 690A, above.

Paragraph 1(1)   See s 690A as to the companies within these provisions; as to the meaning of 'branch', see note to that section; the registrar of companies to whom delivery must be made is determined in accordance with s 695A.

Paragraph 1(3)   To avoid the unnecessary duplication of information, if the company's constitutional documents and accounts have been delivered to another branch in the United Kingdom, ie including to the registrar of companies in Northern Ireland, there is no need to submit the documents again to the registrar of companies of that Part where the further branch is being registered; but the information required by sub-paragraph (3)(c) as to that other branch must be given.

Paragraph 2(2)   The provision now applies to any company not incorporated in the European Economic Area: see the European Economic Area Act 1993, s 2. As to the meaning of 'principal place of business', see note to s 698(2), above.

Paragraph 2(3)–(5)   The particulars required as to the directors and secretary are almost identical to the information which must be provided to the registrar of companies by domestic companies (see s 10(2), Sch 1) and included by such companies on the register of directors and secretaries: see the notes to s 289, above.

Para 2(6) To avoid the unnecessary duplication of information, if particulars as to the company and the directors and secretary etc, as specified, have been delivered to the same registrar, and are up to date, there is no need to submit the information again when registering another branch in the same part of Great Britain, provided the number of that other branch is given; and see s 705A(6) as to the obligation of the registrar of companies to ensure that the particulars concerned become part of the registered particulars of each branch concerned.

Paragraph 5 As to the meaning of 'certified copy', see s 698(1); details of the methods of certification are given on Form BR1.

Paragraph 7 Alterations affecting the particulars concerning the branch must be notified within 21 days while alterations affecting the company must be notified within the longer period envisaged by sub-para (2)(b); efforts are made to avoid the unnecessary duplication of information, see sub-para (4).

Paragraph 8 If the company has taken advantage of the possibility under para 1(3) of not submitting constitutional documents and accounts because they have already been delivered with respect to another branch of the company and that branch then closes, the company must deliver the documents afresh or indicate that they have been delivered with respect to another branch.

Any return or document received under paras 1, 7 or 8 must be gazetted by the registrar of companies: s 711(1)(u), (v).

SCHEDULE 21B

CHANGE IN THE REGISTRATION REGIME: TRANSITIONAL PROVISIONS

Section 692A

1.—(1) This paragraph applies where a company which becomes a company to which section 690A applies was, immediately before becoming such a company (referred to in this paragraph as the relevant time), a company to which section 691 applies.

(2) The company need not include the particulars specified in paragraph 2(1)(d) of Schedule 21A in the first return to be delivered under paragraph 1(1) of that Schedule to the registrar for a part of Great Britain if at the relevant time—

    (a) it had an established place of business in that part,

    (b) it had complied with its obligations under section 691(1)(b)(i), and

    (c) it had no outstanding obligation to make a return to the registrar for that part under subsection (1) of section 692, so far as concerns any alteration of the kind mentioned in subsection (1)(b) of that section,

and if it states in the return that the particulars have been previously filed in respect of a place of business of the company in that part, giving the company's registered number.

(3) The company shall not be required to deliver the documents mentioned in paragraph 5 of Schedule 21A with the first return to be delivered under paragraph 1(1) of that Schedule to the registrar for a part of Great Britain if at the relevant time—

    (a) it had an established place of business in that part,

    (b) it had delivered the documents mentioned in section 691(1)(a) to the registrar for that part, and

    (c) it had no outstanding obligation to make a return to that registrar under subsection (1) of section 692, so far as concerns any alteration in any of the documents mentioned in paragraph (a) of that subsection,

and if it states in the return that the documents have been previously filed in respect of a place of business of the company in that part, giving the company's registered number.

2.—(1) This paragraph applies where a company which becomes a company to which section 691 applies was, immediately before becoming such a company (referred to in this paragraph as the relevant time), a company to which section 690A applies.

(2) The company shall not be required to deliver the documents mentioned in section 691(1)(a) to the registrar for a part of Great Britain if at the relevant time—

(a) it had a branch in that part,

(b) the documents mentioned in paragraph 5 of Schedule 21A were included in the material registered in respect of the branch, and

(c) it had no outstanding obligation to make a return to the registrar for that part under paragraph 7 of that Schedule, so far as concerns any alteration in any of the documents mentioned in sub-paragraph (1)(a) of that paragraph,

and if it states in the return that the documents have been previously filed in respect of a branch of the company, giving the branch's registered number.

(3) The company need not include the particulars mentioned in section 691(1)(b)(i) in the return to be delivered under section 691(1)(b) to the registrar for a part of Great Britain if at the relevant time—

(a) it had a branch in that part,

(b) it had complied with its obligations under paragraph 1(1)(a) of Schedule 21A in respect of the branch so far as the particulars required by paragraph 2(1)(d) of that Schedule are concerned, and

(c) it had no outstanding obligation to make a return to the registrar for that part under paragraph 7 of that Schedule, so far as concerns any alteration in any of the particulars required by paragraph 2(1)(d) of that Schedule,

and if it states in the return that the particulars have been previously filed in respect of a branch of the company, giving the branch's registered number.

(4) Where sub-paragraph (3) above applies, the reference in section 692(1)(b) to the list of the directors and secretary shall be construed as a reference to the list contained in the return under paragraph 1(1) of Schedule 21A with any alterations in respect of which a return under paragraph 7(1) of that Schedule has been made.

General note

This Schedule was inserted by the Oversea Companies and Credit and Financial Institutions (Branch Disclosure) Regulations 1992, SI 1992/3179, as from 1 January 1993; see note to s 690A, above. The intention is to facilitate companies moving from the branch registration regime under s 690A and Sch 21A to the place of business regime under ss 691 and 692 and vice versa by allowing, so far as possible, information already registered with the registrar of companies under the old regime to be used for the purposes of the new registration. See notes to those provisions.

Paragraph 1   This provision applies where a company is moving to a branch registration having previously been registered under the place of business regime with that registrar of companies. To avoid the unnecessary duplication of information, if particulars as to the directors and secretary and the company's constitution have been delivered to the same registrar, and are up to date, there is no need to submit the information again when registering as a branch in the same part of Great Britain, provided the registered number of that place of business is given.

Paragraph 2 This provision applies where a company is moving to a place of business registration having previously been registered as a branch with that registrar of companies. To avoid the unnecessary duplication of information, if particulars as to the directors and secretary and the company's constitution have been delivered to the same registrar, and are up to date, there is no need to submit the information again when registering as a place of business in the same part of Great Britain, provided the registered number of the branch is given.

SCHEDULE 21C

DELIVERY OF REPORTS AND ACCOUNTS: CREDIT AND FINANCIAL INSTITUTIONS TO WHICH THE BANK BRANCHES DIRECTIVE (89/117/EEC) APPLIES

Section 699A

PART I
INSTITUTIONS REQUIRED TO PREPARE ACCOUNTS UNDER PARENT LAW

Scope of Part and Interpretation

1.—(1) This Part of this Schedule applies to any institution to which section 699A applies which is required by its parent law to prepare and have audited accounts for its financial periods and whose only or principal branch within the United Kingdom is in Great Britain.

(2) In this Part of this Schedule, 'branch' has the meaning given by section 699A.

Duty to deliver copies in Great Britain

2.—(1) An institution to which this Part of this Schedule applies shall, within one month of becoming such an institution, deliver to the registrar for registration—

    (a) copies of the latest accounting documents of the institution prepared in accordance with its parent law to have been disclosed before the end of the period allowed for compliance with this sub-paragraph or, if earlier, the date of compliance with it, and

    (b) if any of the documents mentioned in paragraph (a) above is not written

1371

in the English language, a translation of it into English certified in the prescribed manner to be a correct translation.

Where an institution to which this Part of this Schedule applies had, immediately prior to becoming such an institution, a branch in Northern Ireland which was its only or principal branch within the United Kingdom it may, instead of delivering the documents mentioned in sub-paragraph (1)(a) under that paragraph, deliver thereunder a notice that it has become an institution to which this Part of this Schedule applies, provided that those documents have been delivered to the registrar for Northern Ireland pursuant to the Companies (Northern Ireland) Order 1986.

3.—(1) An institution to which this Part of this Schedule applies shall deliver to the registrar for registration—

(a) copies of all the accounting documents of the institution prepared in accordance with its parent law which are disclosed on or after the end of the period allowed for compliance with paragraph 2(1) or, if earlier, the date on which it complies with that paragraph, and

(b) if any of the documents mentioned in paragraph (a) above is not written in the English language, a translation of it into English, certified in the prescribed manner to be a correct translation.

(2) The period allowed for delivery, in relation to a document required to be delivered under this paragraph, is 3 months from the date on which the document is first disclosed.

4. Where an institution's parent law permits it to discharge an obligation with respect to the disclosure of accounting documents by disclosing documents in a modified form, it may discharge its obligation under paragraph 2 or 3 by delivering copies of documents modified as permitted by that law.

5.—(1) Neither paragraph 2 nor paragraph 3 shall require an institution to deliver documents to the registrar if at the end of the period allowed for compliance with that paragraph—

(a) it is not required by its parent law to register them,

(b) they are made available for inspection at each branch of the institution in Great Britain, and

(c) copies of them are available on request at a cost not exceeding the cost of supplying them.

(2) Where by virtue of sub-paragraph (1) above an institution is not required to deliver documents under paragraph 2 or 3 and any of the conditions specified in that sub-paragraph ceases to be met, the institution shall deliver the documents to the registrar for registration within 7 days of the condition ceasing to be met.

Registrar to whom documents to be delivered

6. The documents which an institution is required to deliver to the registrar under this Part of this Schedule shall be delivered—

(a) to the registrar for England and Wales if the institution's only branch, or (if it has more than one) its principal branch within the United

Kingdom, is in England and Wales; or

(b) to the registrar for Scotland if the institution's only branch, or (if it has more than one) its principal branch within the United Kingdom, is in Scotland.

Penalty for non-compliance

7.—(1) If an institution fails to comply with paragraph 2, 3 or 5(2) before the end of the period allowed for compliance, the institution and every person who immediately before the end of that period was a director of the institution, or, in the case of an institution which does not have directors, a person occupying an equivalent office, is guilty of an offence and liable to a fine and, for continued contravention, to a daily default fine.

(2) It is a defence for a person charged with an offence under this paragraph to prove that he took all reasonable steps for securing compliance with paragraph 2, 3 or 5(2), as the case may be.

Interpretation

8.—(1) In this Part of this Schedule—

'financial period' in relation to an institution, means a period for which the institution is required or permitted by its parent law to prepare accounts;

'parent law', in relation to an institution, means the law of the country in which the institution has its head office;

and references to disclosure are to public disclosure, except where an institution is not required under its parent law, any enactment (including any subordinate legislation within the meaning of section 21 of the Interpretation Act 1978) having effect for Great Britain or its constitution to publicly disclose its accounts, in which case such references are to the disclosure of the accounts to the persons for whose information they have been prepared.

(2) For the purposes of this Part of this Schedule, the following are accounting documents in relation to a financial period of an institution—

(a) the accounts of the institution for the period, including, if it has one or more subsidiaries, any consolidated accounts of the group,

(b) any annual report of the directors (or, in the case of an institution which does not have directors, the persons occupying equivalent offices) for the period,

(c) the report of the auditors on the accounts mentioned in paragraph (a) above, and

(d) any report of the auditors on the report mentioned in paragraph (b) above.

PART II
INSTITUTIONS NOT REQUIRED TO PREPARE
ACCOUNTS UNDER PARENT LAW

Scope of Part and Interpretation

9.—(1) This Part of this Schedule applies to any institution to which section 699A applies which—

(a) is incorporated, and

(b) is not required by the law of the country in which it has its head office to prepare and have audited accounts.

(2) In this Part of this Schedule, 'branch' has the meaning given by section 699A.

Preparation of accounts and reports

10. An institution to which this Part of this Schedule applies shall in respect of each financial year of the institution prepare the like accounts and directors' report, and cause to be prepared such an auditor's report, as would be required if the institution were a company to which section 700 applied.

11. Sections 223 to 225 apply to an institution to which this Part of this Schedule applies subject to the following modifications—

(a) for the references to the incorporation of the company there shall be substituted references to the institution becoming an institution to which this Part of this Schedule applies; and

(b) section 225(4) shall be omitted.

Duty to deliver accounts and reports

12.—(1) An institution to which this Part of this Schedule applies shall in respect of each financial year of the institution deliver to the registrar copies of the accounts and reports prepared in accordance with paragraph 10.

(2) If any document comprised in those accounts or reports is in a language other than English, the institution shall annex to the copy delivered a translation of it into English, certified in the prescribed manner to be a correct translation.

Time for delivery

13.—(1) The period allowed for delivering accounts and reports under paragraph 12 above is 13 months after the end of the relevant accounting reference period, subject to the following provisions of this paragraph.

(2) If the relevant accounting reference period is the institution's first and is a period of more than 12 months, the period allowed is 13 months from the first anniversary of the institution's becoming an institution to which this Part of this Schedule applies.

(3) If the relevant accounting reference period is treated as shortened by virtue of a notice given by the institution under section 225, the period allowed is that applicable in accordance with the above provisions or 3 months from the date of the notice under that section, whichever last expires.

(4) If for any special reason the Secretary of State thinks fit he may, on an application made before the expiry of the period otherwise allowed, by notice in writing to an institution to which this Part of this Schedule applies, extend that period by such further period as may be specified in the notice.

(5) In this paragraph 'the relevant accounting reference period' means the accounting reference period by reference to which the financial year for the accounts in question was determined.

Registrar to whom documents to be delivered

14. The documents which an institution is required to deliver to the registrar under this Part of the Schedule shall be delivered—

- (a) to the registrar for England and Wales if the institution's only branch, or (if it has more than one) its principal branch within Great Britain, is in England and Wales; or
- (b) to the registrar for Scotland if the institution's only branch, or (if it has more than one) its principal branch within Great Britain, is in Scotland.

Penalty for non-compliance

15.—(1) If the requirements of paragraph 12 are not complied with before the end of the period allowed for delivering accounts and reports, or if the accounts and reports delivered do not comply with the requirements of this Act, the institution and every person who immediately before the end of that period was a director of the institution, or, in the case of an institution which does not have directors, a person occupying an equivalent office, is guilty of an offence and liable to a fine and, for continued contravention, to a daily default fine.

(2) It is a defence for a person charged with such an offence to prove that he took all reasonable steps for securing that the requirements in question would be complied with.

(3) It is not a defence in relation to a failure to deliver copies to the registrar to prove that the documents in question were not in fact prepared as required by this Schedule.

General note

This Schedule was inserted by the Oversea Companies and Credit and Financial Institutions (Branch Disclosure) Regulations 1992, SI 1992/3179, as from 1 January 1993 (see note to s 699A, above); and it sets out the accounting regime applicable to credit and financial institutions within that section.

Part I of the Schedule sets out the accounting disclosure requirements, essentially requiring the disclosure of accounts to the registrar of that part of Great Britain where the principal branch is situated, in cases where the institution is required to prepare and have audited accounts under its parent law.

Part II of the Schedule requires an incorporated institution within s 699A and which is not required by its parent law to prepare and have audited accounts, to deliver s 700 accounts to the registrar. As to s 700 accounts, see the notes to that section. The Schedule then contains provisions equivalent to ss 701–703: see notes to those provisions.

Any document delivered under this Schedule must be gazetted by the registrar of companies: s 711(1)(x).

SCHEDULE 21D

DELIVERY OF REPORTS AND ACCOUNTS: COMPANIES TO WHICH THE ELEVENTH COMPANY LAW DIRECTIVE APPLIES

Section 699AA

PART I
COMPANIES REQUIRED TO MAKE DISCLOSURE UNDER PARENT LAW

Scope of Part

1. This Part of this Schedule applies to any company to which section 699AA applies which is required by its parent law to prepare, have audited and disclose accounts.

Duty to deliver copies in Great Britain

2.—(1) This paragraph applies in respect of each branch which a company to which this Part of this Schedule applies has in Great Britain.

(2) The company shall deliver to the registrar for registration in respect of the branch copies of all the accounting documents prepared in relation to a financial period of the company which are disclosed in accordance with its parent law on or after the end of the period allowed for compliance in respect of the branch with paragraph 1 of Schedule 21A or, if earlier, the date on which the company complies with that paragraph in respect of the branch.

(3) Where the company's parent law permits it to discharge its obligation with respect to the disclosure of accounting documents by disclosing documents in a modified form, it may discharge its obligation under sub-paragraph (2) above by delivering copies of documents modified as permitted by that law.

(4) If any document, a copy of which is delivered under sub-paragraph (2) above, is in a language other than English, the company shall annex to the copy delivered a translation of it into English, certified in the prescribed manner to be a correct translation.

3. Paragraph 2 above shall not require documents to be delivered in respect of a branch if—

    (a) before the end of the period allowed for compliance with that paragraph, they are delivered in respect of another branch in the United Kingdom, and

    (b) the particulars registered under Schedule 21A in respect of the branch indicate an intention that they are to be registered in respect of that other branch and include the details of that other branch mentioned in paragraph 4(b) of that Schedule.

Time for delivery

4. The period allowed for delivery, in relation to a document required to be delivered under paragraph 2, is 3 months from the date on which the document is first disclosed in accordance with the company's parent law.

Penalty for non-compliance

5.—(1) If a company fails to comply with paragraph 2 before the end of the period allowed for compliance, it, and every person who immediately before the end of that period was a director of it, is guilty of an offence and liable to a fine and, for continued contravention, to a daily default fine.

(2) It is a defence for a person charged with an offence under this paragraph to prove that he took all reasonable steps for securing compliance with paragraph 2.

Interpretation

6.—(1) In this Part of this Schedule—

    'financial period', in relation to a company, means a period for which the company is required or permitted by its parent law to prepare accounts;

    'parent law', in relation to a company, means the law of the country in which the company is incorporated;

and references to disclosure are to public disclosure.

(2) For the purposes of this Part of this Schedule, the following are accounting documents in relation to a financial period of a company—

    (a) the accounts of the company for the period, including, if it has one or more subsidiaries, any consolidated accounts of the group,

    (b) any annual report of the directors for the period,

    (c) the report of the auditors on the accounts mentioned in paragraph (a) above, and

    (d) any report of the auditors on the report mentioned in paragraph (b) above.

PART II
COMPANIES NOT REQUIRED TO MAKE DISCLOSURE
UNDER PARENT LAW

Scope of Part

7. This Part of this Schedule applies to any company to which section 699AA applies which is not required by the law of the country in which it is incorporated to prepare, have audited and publicly disclose accounts.

Preparation of accounts and reports

8. A company to which this Part of this Schedule applies shall in respect of each financial year of the company prepare the like accounts and directors' report, and cause to be prepared such an auditors' report, as would be required if the company were a company to which section 700 applied.

9. Sections 223 to 225 apply to a company to which this Part of this Schedule applies subject to the following modifications—

    (a)   for the references to the incorporation of the company there shall be substituted references to the company becoming a company to which this Part of this Schedule applies, and

    (b)   section 225(4) shall be omitted.

Duty to deliver accounts and reports

10.—(1) A company to which this Part of this Schedule applies shall in respect of each financial year of the company deliver to the registrar copies of the accounts and reports prepared in accordance with paragraph 8.

(2) If any document comprised in those accounts or reports is in a language other than English, the company shall annex to the copy delivered a translation of it into English, certified in the prescribed manner to be a correct translation.

(3) A company required to deliver documents under this paragraph is respect of a financial year shall deliver them in respect of each branch which it has in Great Britain at the end of that year.

(4) Sub-paragraph (3) above is without prejudice to section 695A(3).

11. Paragraph 10 shall not require documents to be delivered in respect of a branch if—

    (a)   before the end of the period allowed for compliance with that paragraph, they are delivered in respect of another branch in the United Kingdom, and

(b) the particulars registered under paragraph 1 of Schedule 21A in respect of the branch indicate an intention that they are to be registered in respect of that other branch and include the details of that other branch mentioned in paragraph 4(b) of that Schedule.

Time for delivery

12.—(1) The period allowed for delivering accounts and reports under paragraph 10 is 13 months after the end of the relevant accounting reference period, subject to the following provisions of this paragraph.

(2) If the relevant accounting reference period is the company's first and is a period of more than 12 months, the period allowed is 13 months from the first anniversary of the company's becoming a company to which this Part of this Schedule applies.

(3) If the relevant accounting reference period is treated as shortened by virtue of a notice given by the company under section 225, the period allowed is that applicable in accordance with the above provisions or 3 months from the date of the notice under that section, whichever last expires.

(4) If for any special reason the Secretary of State thinks fit he may, on application made before the expiry of the period otherwise allowed, by notice in writing to a company to which this Part of this Schedule applies extend that period by such further period as may be specified in the notice.

(5) In this paragraph 'the relevant accounting reference period' means the accounting reference period by reference to which the financial year for the accounts in question was determined.

Penalty for non-compliance

13.—(1) If the requirements of paragraph 10 are not complied with before the end of the period allowed for delivering accounts and reports, or if the accounts and reports delivered do not comply with the requirements of this Act, the company and every person who immediately before the end of that period was a director of the company is guilty of an offence and liable to a fine and, for continued contravention, to a daily default fine.

(2) It is a defence for a person charged with such an offence to prove that he took all reasonable steps for securing that the requirements in question would be complied with.

(3) It is not a defence in relation to a failure to deliver copies to the registrar to prove that the documents in question were not in fact prepared as required by this Act.

General note

This Schedule was inserted by the Oversea Companies and Credit and Financial Institutions (Branch Disclosure) Regulations 1992, SI 1992/3179, as from 1 January 1993 (see note to s 699AA, above); and it sets out the accounting regime applicable to companies registered under the branch regime (other than with respect to credit and financial institutions which are within s 699A).

Part I　Companies required to make disclosure under parent law　　If a company is required by the law of the place of incorporation to prepare, have audited and publicly disclose its accounts then, in respect of each branch, it must deliver all the documents (individual accounts, groups accounts, directors and auditors' reports) disclosed in accordance with that parent law, modified as permitted by that law, within three months of the date of disclosure in accordance with that law (paras 2, 4). A translation of any document not in English must also be provided (para 2(4)).

　　For companies incorporated within the European Union and subject to the requirements of the 4th and 7th Directives, the effect will be to require the delivery of full accounts, subject to whatever modifications (as permitted by the Directives) have been adopted by their parent law. For companies not incorporated within the European Union, the position will vary from country to country and, in some cases, the parent law may require the disclosure of only minimal information. If the parent law requires, say, only a summary to be publicly disclosed then only that summary need be delivered to the registrar under these provisions.

Paragraph 5　　As to penalties, see s 730, Sch 24; the penalties extend to a failure to provide a translation as required by para 2(4).

Paragraph 6　　If the disclosure required by the parent law is only to the company's shareholders, this is not public disclosure for these purposes.

Part II　Companies not required to make disclosure under parent law　　If a company is not required by the law of the place of incorporation to prepare, have audited and publicly disclose its accounts, it must deliver accounts prepared in accordance with s 700 (paras 7, 8). As to s 700 accounts, see the notes to that section. The remainder of this Part of the Schedule contains provisions equivalent to ss 701–703, see notes to those provisions.

Paragraph 10　　It is thought that the word 'is' in sub-para (3) should read 'in'.

Any document delivered under this Schedule must be gazetted by the registrar of companies: s 711(1)(y).

SCHEDULE 22

PROVISIONS OF THIS ACT APPLYING TO UNREGISTERED COMPANIES

Section 718

Provisions of this Act applied	Subject matter	Limitations and exceptions (if any)
In Part I—		
section 18	Statutory and other amendments of memorandum and articles to be registered	Subject to section 718(3)
sections 35 to 35B	Company's capacity; power of directors to bind it	Subject to section 718(3)
section 36	Company contracts	Subject to section 718(3)
sections 36A and 36B	Execution of documents	Subject to section 718(3)
section 36C	Pre-incorporation contracts, deeds and obligations	Subject to section 718(3)
. . .		
section 40	Official seal for share certificates, etc	Subject to section 718(3)
section 42	Events affecting a company's status to be officially notified	Subject to section 718(3)
. . .		
In Part IV, sections 82, 86 and 87	*Allotments*	*Subject to section 718(3)*
In Part V—		
section 185(4)	Exemption from duty to prepare certificates where shares etc issued to clearing house or nominee	Subject to section 718(3)
section 186	Certificate as evidence of title	Subject to section 718(3)
Part VII, with—	⎫	Subject to section 718(3)
Schedules 4 to 9	⎪	
Schedule 9A . . ., and	⎬ Accounts and audit	
Schedules 10 and 10A	⎪	
In Part IX—	⎭	
section 287	Registered office	Subject to section 718(3)
sections 288 to 290	Register of directors and secretaries	—
In Part X—		
section 322A	Invalidity of certain transactions involving directors, etc	Subject to section 718(3)

Provisions of this Act applied	Subject matter	Limitations and exceptions (if any)
sections 343 to 347	Register to be kept of certain transactions not disclosed in accounts; other related matters	Subject to section 718(3).
Part XA	Control of political donations by companies	Subject to section 718(3).
In Part XI		
section 351(1), (2) and (5)(a)	Particulars of company to be given in correspondence	Subject to section 718(3).
sections 363 ... to 365	Annual return	Subject to section 718(3).
sections 384 to 394A	Appointment, ..., etc, of auditors	Subject to section 718(3).
Part XII	Registration of company charges; copies of instruments and register to be kept by company	Subject to section 718(3).
Part XIV (except section 446)	Investigation of companies and their affairs; requisition of documents	—
Part XV	Effect of order imposing restrictions on shares	To apply so far only as relates to orders under section 445.
Part XVI	Fraudulent trading by a company	—
In Part XXIV—		
sections 706 to 710A, 713 and 715A	Miscellaneous provisions about registration	—
section 711	Public notice by registrar of companies with respect to certain documents	Subject to section 718(3).
In Part XXV—		
section 720	Companies to publish periodical statement	Subject to section 718(3).
section 721	Production and inspection of company's books	To apply so far only as these provisions have effect in relation to provisions applying by virtue of the foregoing provisions of this Schedule.
section 722	Form of company registers, etc	
section 723	Use of computers for company records	
section 723A	Rights of inspection and related matters	
section 725	Service of documents	
section 730, with Schedule 24	Punishment of offences; meaning of 'officer in default'	
section 731	Summary proceedings	
section 732	Prosecution by public authorities	
Part XXVI	Interpretation	To apply so far as requisite for the interpretation of other provisions applied by section 718 and this Schedule.

General note

See note to s 718 as to unregistered companies.

Entry relating to Pt IV repealed for certain purposes by FSA 1986, s 212(3), Sch 17, Pt 1, see SI 1986/2246, 1988/740, 1988/1960.

SCHEDULE 23

FORM OF STATEMENT TO BE PUBLISHED BY CERTAIN COMPANIES UNDER SECTION 720

Section 720

* The share capital of the company is   , divided into   shares of each.

The number of shares issued is

Calls to the amount of   pounds per share have been made, under which the sum of   pounds has been received,

The liabilities of the company on the first day of January (*or* July) were—

> Debts owing to sundry persons by the company.
>
>> On judgment (in Scotland, in respect of which decree has been granted), £
>>
>> On specialty, £
>>
>> On notes or bills, £
>>
>> On simple contracts, £
>>
>> On estimated liabilities, £
>
> The assets of the company on that day were—
>
> Government securities [*stating them*]
>
> Bills of exchange and promissory notes, £
>
> Cash at the bankers, £
>
> Other securities, £

* If the company has no share capital the portion of the statement relating to capital and shares must be omitted.

SCHEDULE 24

PUNISHMENT OF OFFENCES UNDER THIS ACT

Section 730

Section of Act creating offence	General nature of offence	Mode of prosecution	Punishment	Daily default fine (where applicable)
6(3)	Company failing to deliver to registrar notice or other document, following alteration of its objects	Summary	One-fifth of the statutory maximum	One-fiftieth of the statutory maximum.
12(3B)	Person making false statement under section 12(3A) which he knows to be false or does not believe to be true	1. On indictment 2. Summary	2 years or a fine; or both 6 months or the statutory maximum; or both	
18(3)	Company failing to register change in memorandum or articles	Summary	One-fifth of the statutory maximum	One-fiftieth of the statutory maximum.
19(2)	Company failing to send to one of its members a copy of the memorandum or articles, when so required by the member	Summary	One-fifth of the statutory maximum	
20(2)	Where company's memorandum altered, company issuing copy of the memorandum without the alteration	Summary	One-fifth of the statutory maximum for each occasion on which copies are so issued after the date of the alteration	
28(5)	Company failing to change name on direction of Secretary of State	Summary	One-fifth of the statutory maximum	One-fiftieth of the statutory maximum.
30(5C)	Person making false statement under section 30(5A) which he knows to be false or does not believe to be true	1. On indictment 2. Summary	2 years or a fine; or both 6 months or the statutory maximum; or both	
31(5)	Company altering its memorandum or articles, so ceasing to be exempt from having "limited" as part of its name	Summary	The statutory maximum	One-tenth of the statutory maximum.
31(6)	Company failing to change name, on Secretary of State's direction, so as to have "limited" (or Welsh equivalent) at the end	Summary	One-fifth of the statutory maximum	One-fiftieth of the statutory maximum.

Section of Act creating offence	General nature of offence	Mode of prosecution	Punishment	Daily default fine (where applicable)
32(4)	Company failing to comply with Secretary of State's direction to change its name, on grounds that the name is misleading.	Summary	One-fifth of the statutory maximum	One-fiftieth of the statutory maximum.
33	Trading under misleading name (use of "public limited company" or Welsh equivalent when not so entitled); purporting to be a private company	Summary	One-fifth of the statutory maximum	One-fiftieth of the statutory maximum.
34	Trading or carrying on business with improper use of "limited" or "cyfyngedig"	Summary	One-fifth of the statutory maximum	One-fiftieth of the statutory maximum.
43(3B)	Person making false statement under section 43(3A) which he knows to be false or does not believe to be true	1. On indictment 2. Summary	2 years or a fine; or both 6 months or the statutory maximum; or both	
49(8B)	Person making false statement under section 49(8A) which he knows to be false or does not believe to be true	1. On indictment 2. Summary	2 years or a fine; or both 6 months or the statutory maximum; or both	
54(10)	Public company failing to give notice, or copy of court order, to registrar, concerning application to re-register as private company	Summary	One-fifth of the statutory maximum	One-fiftieth of the statutory maximum.
80(9)	Directors exercising company's power of allotment without the authority required by section 80(1)	1. On indictment 2. Summary	A fine The statutory maximum	
81(2)	Private limited company offering shares to the public, or allotting shares with a view to their being so offered	1. On indictment 2. Summary	A fine The statutory maximum	
82(5)	Allotting shares or debentures before third day after issue of prospectus	1. On indictment 2. Summary	A fine The statutory maximum	

Section of Act creating offence	General nature of offence	Mode of prosecution	Punishment	Daily default fine (where applicable)
86(6)	Company failing to keep money in separate bank account, where received in pursuance of prospectus stating that stock exchange listing is to be applied for	1. On indictment 2. Summary	A fine The statutory maximum	
87(4)	Offeror of shares for sale failing to keep proceeds in separate bank account	1. On indictment 2. Summary	A fine The statutory maximum	
88(5)	Officer of company failing to deliver return of allotments, etc, to registrar	1. On indictment 2. Summary	A fine The statutory maximum	One-tenth of the statutory maximum.
95(6)	Knowingly or recklessly authorising or permitting misleading, false or deceptive material in statement by directors under section 95(5)	1. On indictment 2. Summary	2 years or a fine; or both 6 months or the statutory maximum; or both	
97(4)	Company failing to deliver to registrar the prescribed form disclosing amount or rate of share commission	Summary	One-fifth of the statutory maximum	
110(2)	Making misleading, false or deceptive statement in connection with valuation under section 103 or 104	1. On indictment 2. Summary	2 years or a fine; or both 6 months or the statutory maximum; or both	
111(3)	Officer of company failing to deliver copy of asset valuation report to registrar	1. On indictment 2. Summary	A fine The statutory maximum	One-tenth of the statutory maximum.
111(4)	Company failing to deliver to registrar copy of resolution under section 104(4), with respect to transfer of an asset as consideration for allotment	Summary	One-fifth of the statutory maximum	One-fiftieth of the statutory maximum.
114	Contravention of any of the provisions of sections 99 to 104, 106	1. On indictment 2. Summary	A fine The statutory maximum	

Section of Act creating offence	General nature of offence	Mode of prosecution	Punishment	Daily default fine (where applicable)
117(7)	Company doing business or exercising borrowing powers contrary to section 117	1. On indictment 2. Summary	A fine The statutory maximum	
117(7A)	Person making false statement under section 117(3A) which he knows to be false or does not believe to be true	1. On indictment 2. Summary	2 years or a fine; or both 6 months or the statutory maximum; or both	
122(2)	Company failing to give notice to registrar of reorganisation of share capital	Summary	One-fifth of the statutory maximum	One-fiftieth of the statutory maximum.
123(4)	Company failing to give notice to registrar of increase of share capital	Summary	One-fifth of the statutory maximum	One-fiftieth of the statutory maximum.
127(5)	Company failing to forward to registrar copy of court order, when application made to cancel resolution varying shareholders' rights	Summary	One-fifth of the statutory maximum	One-fiftieth of the statutory maximum.
128(5)	Company failing to send to registrar statement or notice required by section 128 (particulars of shares carrying special rights)	Summary	One-fifth of the statutory maximum	One-fiftieth of the statutory maximum.
129(4)	Company failing to deliver to registrar statement or notice required by section 129 (registration of newly created class rights)	Summary	One-fifth of the statutory maximum	One-fiftieth of the statutory maximum.
141	Officer of company concealing name of creditor entitled to object to reduction of capital, or wilfully misrepresenting nature or amount of debt or claim, etc	1. On indictment 2. Summary	A fine The statutory maximum	
142(2)	Director authorising or permitting non-compliance with section 142 (requirement to convene company meeting to consider serious loss of capital)	1. On indictment 2. Summary	A fine The statutory maximum	

Section of Act creating offence	General nature of offence	Mode of prosecution	Punishment	Daily default fine (where applicable)
143(2)	Company acquiring its own shares in breach of section 143	1. On indictment	In the case of the company, a fine In the case of an officer of the company who is in default, 2 years or a fine; or both	
		2. Summary	In the case of the company, the statutory maximum In the case of an officer of the company who is in default, 6 months or the statutory maximum; or both	
149(2)	Company failing to cancel its own shares, acquired by itself, as required by section 146(2); or failing to apply for re-registration as private company as so required in the case there mentioned	Summary	One-fifth of the statutory maximum	One-fiftieth of the statutory maximum.
151(3)	Company giving financial assistance towards acquisition of its own shares	1. On indictment	Where the company is convicted, a fine Where an officer of the company is convicted, 2 years or a fine; or both	

Section of Act creating offence	General nature of offence	Mode of prosecution	Punishment	Daily default fine (where applicable)
		2. Summary	Where the company is convicted, the statutory maximum Where an officer of the company is convicted, 6 months or the statutory maximum; or both	
156(6)	Company failing to register statutory declaration or statement under section 155	Summary	The statutory maximum	One-fiftieth of the statutory maximum.
156(7)	Director making statutory declaration or statement under section 155, without having reasonable grounds for opinion expressed in it	1. On indictment 2. Summary	2 years or a fine; or both 6 months or the statutory maximum; or both	
169(6)	Default by company's officer in delivering to registrar the return required by section 169 (disclosure by company of purchase of own shares)	1. On indictment 2. Summary	A fine The statutory maximum	One-tenth of the statutory maximum.
169(7)	Company failing to keep copy of contract, etc, at registered office; refusal of inspection to person demanding it	Summary	One-fifth of the statutory maximum	One-fiftieth of the statutory maximum.
173(6)	Director making statutory declaration under section 173 without having reasonable grounds for the opinion expressed in the declaration	1. On indictment 2. Summary	2 years or a fine; or both 6 months or the statutory maximum; or both	
175(7)	Refusal of inspection of statutory declaration and auditors' report under section 173, etc	Summary	One-fifth of the statutory maximum	One-fiftieth of the statutory maximum.

Section of Act creating offence	General nature of offence	Mode of prosecution	Punishment	Daily default fine (where applicable)
176(4)	Company failing to give notice to registrar of application to court under section 176, or to register court order	Summary	One-fifth of the statutory maximum	One-fiftieth of the statutory maximum.
183(6)	Company failing to send notice of refusal to register a transfer of shares or debentures	Summary	One-fifth of the statutory maximum	One-fiftieth of the statutory maximum.
185(5)	Company default in compliance with section 185(1) (certificates to be made ready following allotment or transfer of shares, etc)	Summary	One-fifth of the statutory maximum	One-fiftieth of the statutory maximum.
189(1)	Offences of fraud and forgery in connection with share warrants in Scotland	1. On indictment 2. Summary	7 years or a fine; or both 6 months or the statutory maximum; or both	
189(2)	Unauthorised making of, or using or possessing apparatus for making, share warrants in Scotland	1. On indictment 2. Summary	7 years or a fine; or both 6 months or the statutory maximum; or both	
191(4)	Refusal of inspection or copy of register of debenture-holders, etc	Summary	One-fifth of the statutory maximum	One-fiftieth of the statutory maximum.
210(3)	Failure to discharge obligation of disclosure under Part VI; other forms of non-compliance with that Part	1. On indictment 2. Summary	2 years or a fine; or both 6 months or the statutory maximum; or both	
211(10)	Company failing to keep register of interests disclosed under Part VI; other contraventions of section 211	Summary	One-fifth of the statutory maximum	One-fiftieth of the statutory maximum.
214(5)	Company failing to exercise powers under section 212, when so required by the members	1. On indictment 2. Summary	A fine The statutory maximum	

Section of Act creating offence	General nature of offence	Mode of prosecution	Punishment	Daily default fine (where applicable)
215(8)	Company default in compliance with section 215 (company report of investigation of shareholdings on members' requisition)	1. On indictment 2. Summary	A fine The statutory maximum	
216(3)	Failure to comply with company notice under section 212; making false statement in response, etc	1. On indictment 2. Summary	2 years or a fine; or both 6 months or the statutory maximum; or both	
217(7)	Company failing to notify a person that he has been named as a shareholder; on removal of name from register, failing to alter associated index	Summary	One-fifth of the statutory maximum	One-fiftieth of the statutory maximum.
218(3)	Improper removal of entry from register of interests disclosed; company failing to restore entry improperly removed	Summary	One-fifth of the statutory maximum	For continued contravention of section 218(2) one-fiftieth of the statutory maximum
219(3)	Refusal of inspection of register or report under Part VI; failure to send copy when required	Summary	One-fifth of the statutory maximum	One-fiftieth of the statutory maximum.
221(5) or 222(4)	Company failing to keep accounting records (liability of officers)	1. On indictment 2. Summary	2 years or a fine; or both 6 months or the statutory maximum; or both	
222(6)	Officer of company failing to secure compliance with, or intentionally causing default under, section 222(5) (preservation of accounting records for requisite number of years)	1. On indictment 2. Summary	2 years or a fine; or both. 6 months or the statutory maximum; or both	

Section of Act creating offence	General nature of offence	Mode of prosecution	Punishment	Daily default fine (where applicable)
231(6)	Company failing to annex to its annual return certain particulars required by Schedule 5 and not included in annual accounts	Summary	One-fifth of the statutory maximum	One-fiftieth of the statutory maximum.
232(4)	Default by director or officer of a company in giving notice of matters relating to himself for purposes of Schedule 6, Part I	Summary	One-fifth of the statutory maximum	
233(5)	Approving defective accounts	1. On indictment	A fine	
		2. Summary	The statutory maximum.	
233(6)	Laying or delivery of unsigned balance sheet; circulating copies of balance sheet without signatures	Summary	One-fifth of the statutory maximum	
234(5)	Non-compliance with Part VII, as to directors' report and its content; directors individually liable	1. On indictment	A fine	
		2. Summary	The statutory maximum	
234A(4)	Laying, circulating or delivering directors' report without required signature	Summary	One-fifth of the statutory maximum	
236(4)	Laying, circulating or delivering auditors' report without required signature	Summary	One-fifth of the statutory maximum.	
238(5)	Failing to send company's annual accounts, directors' report and auditors' report to those entitled to receive them	1. On indictment	A fine	
		2. Summary	The statutory maximum	
239(3)	Company failing to supply copy of accounts and reports to shareholder on his demand	Summary	One-fifth of the statutory maximum	One-fiftieth of the statutory maximum.
240(6)	Failure to comply with requirements in connection with publication of accounts	Summary	One-fifth of the statutory maximum	

Section of Act creating offence	General nature of offence	Mode of prosecution	Punishment	Daily default fine (where applicable)
241(2) or 242(2)	Director in default as regards duty to lay and deliver company's annual accounts, directors' report and auditors' report	Summary	The statutory maximum	One-tenth of the statutory maximum.
251(6)	Failure to comply with requirements in relation to summary financial statements	Summary	One-fifth of the statutory maximum.	
288(4)	Default in complying with section 288 (keeping register of directors and secretaries, refusal of inspection)	Summary	The statutory maximum	One-tenth of the statutory maximum.
291(5)	Acting as director of a company without having the requisite share qualification	Summary	One-fifth of the statutory maximum	One-fiftieth of the statutory maximum.
294(3)	Director failing to give notice of his attaining retirement age; acting as director under appointment invalid due to his attaining it	Summary	One-fifth of the statutory maximum	One-fiftieth of the statutory maximum.
305(3)	Company default in complying with section 305 (directors' names to appear on company correspondence, etc)	Summary	One-fifth of the statutory maximum	
306(4)	Failure to state that liability of proposed director or manager is unlimited; failure to give notice of that fact to person accepting office	1. On indictment 2. Summary	A fine The statutory maximum	
314(3)	Director failing to comply with section 314 (duty to disclose compensation payable on takeover, etc); a person's failure to include required particulars in a notice he has to give of such matters	Summary	One-fifth of the statutory maximum	
317(7)	Director failing to disclose interest in contract	1. On indictment 2. Summary	A fine The statutory maximum	

Section of Act creating offence	General nature of offence	Mode of prosecution	Punishment	Daily default fine (where applicable)
318(8)	Company default in complying with section 318(1) or (5) (directors' service contracts to be open to inspection); 14 days' default in complying with section 318(4) (notice to registrar as to where copies of contracts and memoranda are kept); refusal of inspection required under section 318(7)	Summary	One-fifth of the statutory maximum	One-fiftieth of the statutory maximum.
322B(4)	Terms of unwritten contract between sole member of a private company limited by shares or by guarantee and the company not set out in a written memorandum or recorded in minutes of a directors' meeting	Summary	Level 5 on the standard scale	
323(2)	Director dealing in options to buy or sell company's listed shares or debentures	1. On indictment 2. Summary	2 years or a fine; or both 6 months or the statutory maximum; or both	
324(7)	Director failing to notify interest in company's shares; making false statement in purported notification	1. On indictment 2. Summary	2 years or a fine; or both 6 months or the statutory maximum; or both	
326(2), (3), (4), (5)	Various defaults in connection with company register of directors' interests	Summary	One-fifth of the statutory maximum	Except in the case of section 326(5), one fiftieth of the statutory maximum.
328(6)	Director failing to notify company that members of his family have, or have exercised, options to buy shares or debentures; making false statement in purported notification	1. On indictment 2. Summary	2 years or a fine; or both 6 months or the statutory maximum; or both	
329(3)	Company failing to notify investment exchange of acquisition of its securities by a director	Summary	One-fifth of the statutory maximum	One-fiftieth of the statutory maximum.

Section of Act creating offence	General nature of offence	Mode of prosecution	Punishment	Daily default fine (where applicable)
342(1)	Director of relevant company authorising or permitting company to enter into transaction or arrangement, knowing or suspecting it to contravene section 330	1. On indictment 2. Summary	2 years or a fine; or both 6 months or the statutory maximum; or both	
342(2)	Relevant company entering into transaction or arrangement for a director in contravention of section 330	1. On indictment 2. Summary	2 years or a fine; or both 6 months or the statutory maximum; or both	
342(3)	Procuring a relevant company to enter into transaction or arrangement known to be contrary to section 330	1. On indictment 2. Summary	2 years or a fine; or both 6 months or the statutory maximum; or both	
343(8)	Company failing to maintain register of transactions, etc, made with and for directors and not disclosed in company accounts; failing to make register available at registered office or at company meeting	1. On indictment 2. Summary	A fine The statutory maximum	
348(2)	Company failing to paint or affix name; failing to keep it painted or affixed	Summary	One-fifth of the statutory maximum	In the case of failure to keep the name painted or affixed, one-fiftieth of the statutory maximum.
349(2)	Company failing to have name on business correspondence, invoices, etc	Summary	One-fifth of the statutory maximum	
349(3)	Officer of company issuing business letter or document not bearing company's name	Summary	One-fifth of the statutory maximum	
349(4)	Officer of company signing cheque, bill of exchange, etc on which company's name not mentioned	Summary	One-fifth of the statutory maximum	
350(1)	Company failing to have its name engraved on company seal	Summary	One-fifth of the statutory maximum	

Section of Act creating offence	General nature of offence	Mode of prosecution	Punishment	Daily default fine (where applicable)
350(2)	Officer of company, etc, using company seal without name engraved on it	Summary	One-fifth of the statutory maximum	
351(5)(a)	Company failing to comply with section 351(1) or (2) (matters to be stated on business correspondence, etc)	Summary	One-fifth of the statutory maximum	
351(5)(b)	Officer or agent of company issuing, or authorising issue of, business document not complying with those subsections	Summary	One-fifth of the statutory maximum	
351(5)(c)	Contravention of section 351(3) or (4) (information in English to be stated on Welsh company's business correspondence, etc)	Summary	One-fifth of the statutory maximum	For contravention of section 351(3), one-fiftieth of the statutory maximum.
352(5)	Company default in complying with section 352 (requirement to keep register of members and their particulars)	Summary	One-fifth of the statutory maximum	One-fiftieth of the statutory maximum.
352A(3)	Company default in complying with section 352A (statement that company has only one member)	Summary	Level 2 on the standard scale	One-tenth of level 2 on the standard scale.
353(4)	Company failing to send notice to registrar as to place where register of members is kept	Summary	One-fifth of the statutory maximum	One-fiftieth of the statutory maximum.
354(4)	Company failing to keep index of members	Summary	One-fifth of the statutory maximum	One-fiftieth of the statutory maximum.
356(5)	Refusal of inspection of members' register; failure to send copy on requisition	Summary	One-fifth of the statutory maximum	
363(3)	Company with share capital failing to make annual return	Summary	The statutory maximum	One-tenth of the statutory maximum.

Section of Act creating offence	General nature of offence	Mode of prosecution	Punishment	Daily default fine (where applicable)
364(4)	Company without share capital failing to complete and register annual return in due time	Summary	The statutory maximum	One-tenth of the statutory maximum.
366(4)	Company default in holding annual general meeting	1. On indictment 2. Summary	A fine The statutory maximum	
367(3)	Company default in complying with Secretary of State's direction to hold company meeting	1. On indictment 2. Summary	A fine The statutory maximum	
367(5)	Company failing to register resolution that meeting held under section 367 is to be its annual general meeting	Summary	One-fifth of the statutory maximum	One-fiftieth of the statutory maximum.
372(4)	Failure to give notice, to member entitled to vote at company meeting, that he may do so by proxy	Summary	One-fifth of the statutory maximum	
372(6)	Officer of company authorising or permitting issue of irregular invitations to appoint proxies	Summary	One-fifth of the statutory maximum	
376(7)	Officer of company in default as to circulation of members' resolutions for company meeting	1. On indictment 2. Summary	A fine The statutory maximum	
380(5)	Company failing to comply with section 380 (copies of certain resolutions etc to be sent to registrar of companies)	Summary	One-fifth of the statutory maximum	One-fiftieth of the statutory maximum.
380(6)	Company failing to include copy of resolution to which section 380 applies in articles; failing to forward copy to member on request	Summary	One-fifth of the statutory maximum for each occasion on which copies are issued or, as the case may be, requested	

Section of Act creating offence	General nature of offence	Mode of prosecution	Punishment	Daily default fine (where applicable)
381B(2)	Director or secretary of company failing to notify auditors of proposed written resolution	Summary	Level 3 on the standard scale.	
382(5)	Company failing to keep minutes of proceedings at company and board meetings, etc	Summary	One-fifth of the statutory maximum	One-fiftieth of the statutory maximum.
382B(2)	Failure of sole member to provide the company with a written record of a decision	Summary	Level 2 on the standard scale.	
383(4)	Refusal of inspection of minutes of general meeting; failure to send copy of minutes on member's request	Summary	One-fifth of the statutory maximum	
387(2)	Company failing to give Secretary of State notice of non-appointment of auditors	Summary	One-fifth of the statutory maximum	One-fiftieth of the statutory maximum.
389(10)	Person acting as company auditor knowing himself to be disqualified; failing to give notice vacating office when he becomes disqualified	1. On indictment 2. Summary	A fine The statutory maximum	One-tenth of the statutory maximum.
389A(2)	Officer of company making false, misleading or deceptive statement to auditors	1. On indictment 2. Summary	2 years or a fine; or both 6 months or the statutory maximum; or both	
389A(3)	Subsidiary undertaking or its auditor failing to give information to auditors of parent company	Summary	One-fifth of the statutory maximum	
389A(4)	Parent company failing to obtain from subsidiary undertaking information for purposes of audit	Summary	One-fifth of the statutory maximum	
391(2)	Failing to give notice to registrar of removal of auditor	Summary	One-fifth of the statutory maximum	One-fiftieth of the statutory maximum.

Section of Act creating offence	General nature of offence	Mode of prosecution	Punishment	Daily default fine (where applicable)
392(3)	Company failing to forward notice of auditor's resignation to registrar	1. On indictment 2. Summary	A fine The statutory maximum	One-tenth of the statutory maximum.
392A(5)	Directors failing to convene meeting requisitioned by resigning auditor	1. On indictment 2. Summary	A fine The statutory maximum	
394A(1)	Person ceasing to hold office as auditor failing to deposit statement as to circumstances	1. On indictment 2. Summary	A fine The statutory maximum	
394A(4)	Company failing to comply with requirements as to statement of person ceasing to hold office as auditor	1. On indictment 2. Summary	A fine The statutory maximum	One-tenth of the statutory maximum.
399(3)	Company failing to send to registrar particulars of charge created by it, or of issue of debentures which requires registration	1. On indictment 2. Summary	A fine The statutory maximum	One-tenth of the statutory maximum.
400(4)	Company failing to send to registrar particulars of charge on property acquired	1. On indictment 2. Summary	A fine The statutory maximum	One-tenth of the statutory maximum.
402(3)	Authorising or permitting delivery of debenture or certificate of debenture stock, without endorsement on it of certificate of registration of charge	Summary	One-fifth of the statutory maximum	
403(2A)	Person making false statement under section 403(1A) which he knows to be false or does not believe to be true	1. On indictment 2. Summary	2 years or a fine; or both 6 months or the statutory maximum; or both	
405(4)	Failure to give notice to registrar of appointment of receiver or manager, or of his ceasing to act	Summary	One-fifth of the statutory maximum	One-fiftieth of the statutory maximum.

Section of Act creating offence	General nature of offence	Mode of prosecution	Punishment	Daily default fine (where applicable)
407(3)	Authorising or permitting omission from company register of charges	1. On indictment 2. Summary	A fine The statutory maximum	
408(3)	Officer of company refusing inspection of charging instrument, or of register of charges	Summary	One-fifth of the statutory maximum	One-fiftieth of the statutory maximum.
415(3)	Scottish company failing to send to registrar particulars of charge created by it, or of issue of debentures which requires registration	1. On indictment 2. Summary	A fine The statutory maximum	One-tenth of the statutory maximum.
416(3)	Scottish company failing to send to registrar particulars of charge on property acquired by it	1. On indictment 2. Summary	A fine The statutory maximum	One-tenth of the statutory maximum.
419(5A)	Person making false statement under section 419(1A) or (1B) which he knows to be false or does not believe to be true	1. On indictment 2. Summary	2 years or a fine; or both 6 months or the statutory maximum; or both	
422(3)	Scottish company authorising or permitting omission from its register of charges	1. On indictment 2. Summary	A fine The statutory maximum	
423(3)	Officer of Scottish company refusing inspection of charging instrument, or of register of charges	Summary	One-fifth of the statutory maximum	One-fiftieth of the statutory maximum.
425(4)	Company failing to annex to memorandum court order sanctioning compromise or arrangement with creditors	Summary	One-fifth of the statutory maximum	
426(6)	Company failing to comply with requirements of section 426 (information to members and creditors about compromise or arrangement)	1. On indictment 2. Summary	A fine The statutory maximum	

Section of Act creating offence	General nature of offence	Mode of prosecution	Punishment	Daily default fine (where applicable)
426(7)	Director or trustee for debenture holders failing to give notice to company of matters necessary for purposes of section 426	Summary	One-fifth of the statutory maximum	
427(5)	Failure to deliver to registrar office copy of court order under section 427 (company reconstruction or amalgamation)	Summary	One-fifth of the statutory maximum	One-fiftieth of the statutory maximum.
429(6)	Offeror failing to send copy of notice or making statutory declaration knowing it to be false, etc	1. On indictment 2. Summary	2 years or a fine; or both 6 months or the statutory maximum; or both	One-fiftieth of the statutory maximum.
430A(6)	Offeror failing to give notice of rights to minority shareholder	1. On indictment 2. Summary	A fine The statutory maximum	One-fiftieth of the statutory maximum
444(3)	Failing to give Secretary of State, when required to do so, information about interests in shares, etc; giving false information	1. On indictment 2. Summary	2 years or a fine; or both 6 months or the statutory maximum; or both	
447(6)	Failure to comply with requirement to produce documents imposed by Secretary of State under section 447	1. On indictment 2. Summary	A fine The statutory maximum	
448(7)	Obstructing the exercise of any rights conferred by a warrant or failing to comply with a requirement imposed under subsection (3)(d)	1. On indictment 2. Summary	A fine The statutory maximum	
449(2)	Wrongful disclosure of information or document obtained under section 447 or 448	1. On indictment 2. Summary	2 years or a fine; or both 6 months or the statutory maximum; or both	

Section of Act creating offence	General nature of offence	Mode of prosecution	Punishment	Daily default fine (where applicable)
450	Destroying or mutilating company documents; falsifying such documents or making false entries; parting with such documents or altering them or making omissions	1. On indictment 2. Summary	7 years or a fine; or both 6 months or the statutory maximum; or both	
451	Making false statement or explanation in purported compliance with section 447	1. On indictment 2. Summary	2 years or a fine; or both 6 months or the statutory maximum; or both	
455(1)	Exercising a right to dispose of, or vote in respect of, shares which are subject to restrictions under Part XV; failing to give notice in respect of shares so subject; entering into agreement void under section 454(2), (3)	1. On indictment 2. Summary	A fine The statutory maximum	
455(2)	Issuing shares in contravention of restrictions of Part XV	1. On indictment 2. Summary	A fine The statutory maximum	
458	Being a party to carrying on company's business with intent to defraud creditors, or for any fraudulent purpose	1. On indictment 2. Summary	7 years or a fine; or both 6 months or the statutory maximum; or both	
461(5)	Failure to register office copy of court order under Part XVII altering, or giving leave to alter, company's memorandum	Summary	One-fifth of the statutory maximum	One-fiftieth of the statutory maximum.
651(3)	Person obtaining court order to declare company's dissolution void, then failing to register the order	Summary	One-fifth of the statutory maximum	One-fiftieth of the statutory maximum.
652E(1)	Person breaching or failing to perform duty imposed by section 652B or 652C	1. On indictment 2. Summary	A fine The statutory maximum	

Section of Act creating offence	General nature of offence	Mode of prosecution	Punishment	Daily default fine (where applicable)
652E(2)	Person failing to perform duty imposed by section 652B(6) or 652C(2) with intent to conceal the making of application under section 652A	1. On indictment 2. Summary	7 years or a fine; or both 6 months or the statutory maximum; or both	
652F(1)	Person furnishing false or misleading information in connection with application under section 652A	1. On indictment 2. Summary	A fine The statutory maximum	
652F(2)	Person making false application under section 652A	1. On indictment 2. Summary	A fine The statutory maximum.	
685(6A)	Person making false statement under section 685(4A) which he knows to be false or does not believe to be true	1. On indictment 2. Summary	2 years or a fine; or both 6 months or the statutory maximum; or both	
686(3A)	Person making false statement under section 686(2A) which he knows to be false or does not believe to be true	1. On indictment 2. Summary	2 years or a fine; or both 6 months or the statutory maximum; or both	
691(4A)	Person making false statement under section 691(3A) which he knows to be false or does not believe to be true	1. On indictment 2. Summary	2 years or a fine; or both 6 months or the statutory maximum; or both;	
697(1)	Oversea company failing to comply with any of sections 691 to 693 or 696	Summary	For an offence which is not a continuing offence, one-fifth of the statutory maximum For an offence which is a continuing offence, one-fifth of the statutory maximum	One-fiftieth of the statutory maximum.

Section of Act creating offence	General nature of offence	Mode of prosecution	Punishment	Daily default fine (where applicable)
697(2)	Oversea company contravening section 694(6) (carrying on business under its corporate name after Secretary of State's direction)	1. On indictment 2. Summary	A fine The statutory maximum	One-tenth of the statutory maximum.
697(3)	Oversea Company failing to comply with Section 695A or Schedule 21A	Summary	For an offence which is not a continuing offence, one fifth of level 5 of the standard scale For an offence which is a continuing offence one fifth of level 5 of the standard scale	£100
703(1)	Oversea company failing to comply with requirements as to accounts and reports	1. On indictment 2. Summary	A fine The statutory maximum	One-tenth of the statutory maximum.
703R(1)	Company failing to register winding up or commencement of insolvency proceedings etc	1. On indictment 2. Summary	A fine The statutory maximum	£100
703R(2)	Liquidator failing to register appointment, termination of winding up or striking-off of company	1. On indictment 2. Summary	A fine The statutory maximum	£100
720(4)	Insurance company etc failing to send twice-yearly statement in form of Schedule 23	Summary	One-fifth of the statutory maximum	One-fiftieth of the statutory maximum.
722(3)	Company failing to comply with section 722(2), as regards the manner of keeping registers, minute books and accounting records	Summary	One-fifth of the statutory maximum	One-fiftieth of the statutory maximum.

Section of Act creating offence	General nature of offence	Mode of prosecution	Punishment	Daily default fine (where applicable)
Sch 14, Pt II, para 1(3)	Company failing to give notice of location of overseas branch register, etc	Summary	One-fifth of the statutory maximum.	One-fiftieth of the statutory maximum
Sch 14, Pt II, para 4(2)	Company failing to transmit to its registered office in Great Britain copies of entries in overseas branch register, or to keep a duplicate of overseas branch register	Summary	One-fifth of the statutory maximum	One-fiftieth of the statutory maximum.
Sch 21C, Pt I, para 7	Credit or financial institution failing to deliver accounting documents	1. On indictment 2. Summary	A fine The statutory maximum	£100
Sch 21C, Pt II, para 15	Credit or financial institution failing to deliver accounts and reports	1. On indictment 2. Summary	A fine The statutory maximum	£100
Sch 21D, Pt I, para 5	Company failing to deliver accounting documents	1. On indictment 2. Summary	A fine The statutory maximum	£100
Sch 21D, Pt I, para 13	Company failing to deliver accounts and reports	1. On indictment 2. Summary	A fine The statutory maximum	£100

Notes

The statutory maximum is £5,000, the sum prescribed (for England and Wales) by the Magistrates' Courts Act 1980, s 32 and (for Scotland) by the Criminal Procedure (Scotland) Act 1995, s 225.

The standard scale (of fines for summary offences) is laid down (for England and Wales) by the Criminal Justice Act 1982, 37 and (for Scotland) by the Criminal Procedure (Scotland) Act 1995, s 225.

Entries relating to ss 81(2), 82(5), 86(6), 87(4), 97(4) repealed by the Financial Services Act 1986, s 212(3), Sch 17, to a limited extent, see SI 1986/2246, 1988/740.

SCHEDULE 25

COMPANIES ACT 1981, SECTION 38, AS ORIGINALLY ENACTED

Section 132(7)

38. Relief from section 56 in respect of group reconstructions

(1) This section applies where the issuing company—

    (a) is a wholly-owned subsidiary of another company ('the holding company'); and

    (b) allots shares to the holding company or to another wholly-owned subsidiary of the holding company in consideration for the transfer to it of shares in another subsidiary (whether wholly-owned or not) of the holding company.

(2) Where the shares in the issuing company allotted in consideration for the transfer are issued at a premium, the issuing company shall not be required by section 56 of the 1948 Act to transfer any amount in excess of the minimum premium value to the share premium account.

(3) In subsection (2) above 'the minimum premium value' means the amount (if any) by which the base value of the shares transferred exceeds the aggregate nominal value of the shares allotted in consideration for the transfer.

(4) For the purposes of subsection (3) above, the base value of the shares transferred shall be taken as—

    (a) the cost of those shares to the company transferring them; or

    (b) the amount at which those shares are stated in that company's accounting records immediately before the transfer;

whichever is the less.

(5) Section 37 of this Act shall not apply in a case to which this section applies.

General note

See note to s 132(7).

APPENDIX I—COMPANIES ACT 1948

TABLE A

COMPANIES ACT 1948 TABLE A

FIRST SCHEDULE

TABLE A
PART I

REGULATIONS FOR MANAGEMENT OF A COMPANY LIMITED BY SHARES, NOT BEING A PRIVATE COMPANY

Notes

The Table A which applies to any company is the Table A in force at the date of the company's registration, and if Table A is altered, the alteration does not affect a company registered before the alteration takes effect; see CA 1985, s 8(2), (3). Accordingly, Table A to the 1948 Act, which is specifically preserved by the Companies Consolidation (Consequential Provisions) Act 1985, s 31(8), is set out below both in its original form and in its form as amended at different dates.

Part I of Table A applies (subject to the savings set out in CA 1980, s 88(4)) in relation to private companies limited by shares as it applies in relation to public companies so limited (per CA 1980, Sch 3, para 36(1)).

Interpretation

1. In these regulations:—

'the Act' means the Companies Act, 1948.

'the seal' means the common seal of the company.

'secretary' means any person appointed to perform the duties of the secretary of the company.

'the United Kingdom' means Great Britain and Northern Ireland.

Expressions referring to writing shall, unless the contrary intention appears, be construed as including references to printing, lithography, photography, and other modes of representing or reproducing words in a visible form.

Unless the context otherwise requires, words or expressions contained in these regulations shall bear the same meaning as in the Act or any statutory modification thereof in force at the date at which these regulations become binding on the company.

Share Capital and Variation of Rights

2. Without prejudice to any special rights previously conferred on the holders of any existing shares or class of shares, any share in the company may be issued with such preferred, deferred or other special rights or such restrictions, whether in regard to dividend, voting, return of capital or otherwise as the company may from time to time by ordinary resolution determine.

3. Subject to the provisions of *section 58 of the Act, any preference shares* may, with the sanction of an ordinary resolution, be issued on the terms that they are, or at the option of the company are liable, to be redeemed on such terms and in such manner as the company before the issue of the shares may by special resolution determine.

Notes

Paragraph 3   For the words in italics there are substituted the words 'Part III of CA 1981, any shares' by CA 1981, Sch 3, in relation to any company registered on or after 3 December 1981.

4. If at any time the share capital is divided into different classes of shares, the rights attached to any class (*unless otherwise provided by the terms of issue of the shares of that class*) may, whether or not the company is being wound up, be varied with the consent in writing of the holders of three-fourths of the issued shares of that class, or with the sanction of an extraordinary resolution passed at a separate general meeting of the holders of the shares of the class. *To every such separate general meeting the provisions of these regulations relating to general meetings shall apply, but so that the necessary quorum shall be two persons at least holding or representing by proxy one-third of the issued shares of the class and that any holder of shares of the class present in person or by proxy may demand a poll.*

Notes

Words in italics repealed by CA 1980, Sch 4, in relation to any company registered on or after 22 December 1980.

5. The rights conferred upon the holders of the shares of any class issued with preferred or other rights shall not, unless otherwise expressly provided by the terms of issue of the shares of that class, be deemed to be varied by the creation or issue of further shares ranking pari passu therewith.

6. The company may exercise the powers of paying commissions conferred by section 53 of the Act, provided that the rate per cent or amount of the commission paid or agreed to be paid shall be disclosed in the manner required by the said section and the rate of the commission shall not exceed the rate of 10 per cent of the price at which the shares in respect whereof the same is paid are issued or an amount equal to 10 per cent of such price (as the case may be). Such commission may be satisfied by the payment of cash or the allotment of fully or partly paid shares or partly in one way and partly in the other. The company may also on any issue of shares pay such brokerage as may be lawful.

7. Except as required by law, no person shall be recognised by the company as holding any share upon any trust, and the company shall not be bound by or be compelled in any way to recognise (even when having notice thereof) any equitable, contingent, future or partial interest in any share or any interest in any fractional part of a share or (except only as by these regulations or by law otherwise provided) any other rights in respect of any share except an absolute right to the entirety thereof in the registered holder.

8. Every person whose name is entered as a member in the register of members shall be entitled without payment to receive within two months after allotment or lodgment of transfer (or within such other period as the conditions of issue shall provide) one certificate for all his shares or several certificates each for one or more of his shares upon payment of 2s 6d for every certificate after the first or such less sum as the directors shall from time to time determine. Every certificate shall be under the seal [or under the official seal kept by the company by virtue of section 2 of the Stock Exchange (Completion of Bargains) Act 1976] and shall specify the shares to which it relates and the amount paid up thereon. Provided that in respect of a share or shares held jointly by several persons the company shall not be bound to issue more than one certificate, and delivery of a certificate for a share to one of several joint holders shall be sufficient delivery to all such holders.

Notes

Paragraph 8 Words in square brackets inserted by the Stock Exchange (Completion of Bargains) Act 1976, s 2(3), in relation to any company registered on or after 2 February 1979.

9. If a share certificate be defaced, lost or destroyed, it may be renewed on payment of a fee of 2s 6d or such less sum and on such terms (if any) as to evidence and indemnity and the payment of out-of-pocket expenses of the company of investigating evidence as the directors think fit.

10. *The company shall not give, whether directly or indirectly, and whether by means of a loan, guarantee, the provision of security or otherwise, any financial assistance for the purpose of or in connection with a purchase or subscription made or to be made by any person of or for any shares in the company or in its holding company nor shall the company make a loan for any purpose whatsoever on the security of its shares or those of its holding company, but nothing in this regulation shall prohibit transactions mentioned in the proviso to section 54(1) of the Act.*

Notes

(Paragraph 10 repealed by CA 1981, Schedule 4, in relation to any company registered on or after 3 December 1981.)

Lien

11. The company shall have a first and paramount lien on every share (not being a fully paid share) for all moneys (whether presently payable or not) called or payable at a fixed time in respect of that share, *and the company shall also have a first and paramount lien on all shares (other than fully paid shares) standing registered in the name of a single person for all moneys presently payable by him or his estate to the company*; but the directors may at any time declare any share to be wholly or in part exempt from the provisions of this regulation. The company's lien, if any, on a share shall extend to all dividends payable thereon.

Notes

Words in italics repealed by CA 1980, Sch 4, in relation to any company registered on or after 22 December 1980.

---

12. The company may sell, in such manner as the directors think fit, any shares on which the company has a lien, but no sale shall be made unless a sum in respect of which the lien exists is presently payable, nor until the expiration of fourteen days after a notice in writing, stating and demanding payment of such part of the amount in respect of which the lien exists as is presently payable, has been given to the registered holder for the time being of the share, or the person entitled thereto by reason of his death or bankruptcy.

13. To give effect to any such sale the directors may authorise some person to transfer the shares sold to the purchaser thereof. The purchaser shall be registered as the holder of the shares comprised in any such transfer, and he shall not be bound to see to the application of the purchase money, nor shall his title to the shares be affected by any irregularity or invalidity in the proceedings in reference to the sale.

14. The proceeds of the sale shall be received by the company and applied in payment of such part of the amount in respect of which the lien exists as is presently payable, and the residue, if any, shall (subject to a like lien for sums not presently payable as existed upon the shares before the sale) be paid to the person entitled to the shares at the date of the sale.

Calls on Shares

15. The directors may from time to time make calls upon the members in respect of any moneys unpaid on their shares (whether on account of the nominal value of the shares or by way of premium) and not by the conditions of allotment thereof made payable at fixed times, provided that no call shall exceed one-fourth of the nominal value of the share or be payable at less than one month from the date fixed for the payment of the last preceding call, and each member shall (subject to receiving at least fourteen days' notice specifying the time or times and place of payment) pay to the company at the time or times and place so specified the amount called on his shares. A call may be revoked or postponed as the directors may determine.

16. A call shall be deemed to have been made at the time when the resolution of the directors authorising the call was passed and may be required to be paid by instalments.

17. The joint holders of a share shall be jointly and severally liable to pay all calls in respect thereof.

18. If a sum called in respect of a share is not paid before or on the day appointed for payment thereof, the person from whom the sum is due shall pay interest on the sum from the day appointed for payment thereof to the time of actual payment at such rate not exceeding 5 per cent per annum as the directors may determine, but the directors shall be at liberty to waive payment of such interest wholly or in part.

19. Any sum which by the terms of issue of a share becomes payable on allotment or at any fixed date, whether on account of the nominal value of the share or by way of premium, shall for the purposes of these regulations be deemed to be a call duly made and payable on the date on which by the terms of issue the same becomes payable, and in case of non-payment all the relevant provisions of these regulations as to payment of interest and expenses, forfeiture or otherwise shall apply as if such sum had become payable by virtue of a call duly made and notified.

20. The directors may, on the issue of shares, differentiate between the holders as to the amount of calls to be paid and the times of payment.

21. The directors may, if they think fit, receive from any member willing to advance the same, all or any part of the moneys uncalled and unpaid upon any shares held by him, and upon all or any of the moneys so advanced may (until the same would, but for such advance, become payable) pay interest at such rate not exceeding (unless the company in general meeting shall otherwise direct) 5 per cent per annum, as may be agreed upon between the directors and the member paying such sum in advance.

Transfer of Shares

22. The instrument of transfer of any share shall be executed by or on behalf of the transferor and transferee, and, *except as provided by sub-paragraph (a) of paragraph 2 of the Seventh Schedule to the Act*, the transferor shall be deemed to remain a holder of the share until the name of the transferee is entered in the register of members in respect thereof.

Notes

Words in italics repealed by CA 1967, Sch 8, Pt III in relation to any company registered on or after 27 January 1968.

23. Subject to such of the restrictions of these regulations as may be applicable, any member may transfer all or any of his shares by instrument in writing in any usual or common form or any other form which the directors may approve.

24. The directors may decline to register the transfer of a share (not being a fully paid share) to a person of whom they shall not approve, and they may also decline to register the transfer of a share on which the company has a lien.

25. The directors may also decline to recognise any instrument of transfer unless:—

> (a) a fee of 2s 6d or such lesser sum as the directors may from time to time require is paid to the company in respect thereof;
>
> (b) the instrument of transfer is accompanied by the certificate of the shares to which it relates, and such other evidence as the directors may reasonably require to show the right of the transferor to make the transfer; and
>
> (c) the instrument of transfer is in respect of only one class of share.

26. If the directors refuse to register a transfer they shall within two months after the date on which the transfer was lodged with the company send to the transferee notice of the refusal.

27. The registration of transfers may be suspended at such times and for such periods as the directors may from time to time determine, provided always that such registration shall not be suspended for more than thirty days in any year.

28. The company shall be entitled to charge a fee not exceeding 2s 6d on the registration of every probate, letters of administration, certificate of death or marriage, power of attorney, notice in lieu of distringas, or other instrument.

Transmission of Shares

29. In case of the death of a member the survivor or survivors where the deceased was a joint holder, and the legal personal representatives of the deceased where he was a sole holder, shall be the only persons recognised by the company as having any title to his interest in the shares; but nothing herein contained shall release the estate of a deceased joint holder from any liability in respect of any share which had been jointly held by him with other persons.

30. Any person becoming entitled to a share in consequence of the death or bankruptcy of a member may, upon such evidence being produced as may from time to time properly be required by the directors and subject as hereinafter provided, elect either to be registered himself as holder of the share or to have some person nominated by him registered as the transferee thereof, but the directors shall, in either case, have the same right to decline or suspend registration as they would have had in the case of a transfer of the share by that member before his death or bankruptcy, as the case may be.

31. If the person so becoming entitled shall elect to be registered himself, he shall deliver or send to the company a notice in writing signed by him stating that he so elects. If he shall elect to have another person registered he shall testify his election by executing to that person a transfer of the share. All the limitations, restrictions and provisions of these regulations relating to the right to transfer and the registration of transfers of shares shall be applicable to any such notice or transfer as aforesaid as if the death or bankruptcy of the member had not occurred and the notice or transfer were a transfer signed by that member.

32. A person becoming entitled to a share by reason of the death or bankruptcy of the holder shall be entitled to the same dividends and other advantages to which he would be entitled if he were the registered holder of the share, except that he shall not, before being registered as a member in respect of the share, be entitled in respect of it to exercise any right conferred by membership in relation to meetings of the company:

Provided always that the directors may at any time give notice requiring any such person to elect either to be registered himself or to transfer the share, and if the notice is not complied with within ninety days the directors may thereafter withhold payment of all dividends, bonuses or other moneys payable in respect of the share until the requirements of the notice have been complied with.

Forfeiture of Shares

33. If a member fails to pay any call or instalment of a call on the day appointed for payment thereof, the directors may, at any time thereafter during such time as any part of the call or instalment remains unpaid, serve a notice on him requiring payment of so much of the call or instalment as is unpaid, together with any interest which may have accrued.

34. The notice shall name a further day (not earlier than the expiration of fourteen days from the date of service of the notice) on or before which the payment required by the notice is to be made, and shall state that in the event of non-payment at or before the time appointed the shares in respect of which the call was made will be liable to be forfeited.

35. If the requirements of any such notice as aforesaid are not complied with, any share in respect of which the notice has been given may at any time thereafter, before the payment required by the notice has been made, be forfeited by a resolution of the directors to that effect.

36. A forfeited share may be sold or otherwise disposed of on such terms and in such manner as the directors think fit, and at any time before a sale or disposition the forfeiture may be cancelled on such terms as the directors think fit.

37. A person whose shares have been forfeited shall cease to be a member in respect of the forfeited shares, but shall, notwithstanding, remain liable to pay to the company all moneys which, at the date of forfeiture, were payable by him to the company in respect of the shares, but his liability shall cease if and when the company shall have received payment in full of all such moneys in respect of the shares.

38. A statutory declaration in writing that the declarant is a director or the secretary of the company, and that a share in the company has been duly forfeited on a date stated in the declaration, shall be conclusive evidence of the facts therein stated as against all persons claiming to be entitled to the share. The company may receive the consideration, if any, given for the share on any sale or disposition thereof and may execute a transfer of the share in favour of the person to whom the share is sold or disposed of and he shall thereupon be registered as the holder of the share, and shall not be bound to see to the application of the purchase money, if any, nor shall his title to the share be affected by any irregularity or invalidity in the proceedings in reference to the forfeiture, sale or disposal of the share.

39. The provisions of these regulations as to forfeiture shall apply in the case of non-payment of any sum which, by the terms of issue of a share, becomes payable at a fixed time, whether on account of the nominal value of the share or by way of premium, as if the same had been payable by virtue of a call duly made and notified.

Conversion of Shares into Stock

40. The company may by ordinary resolution convert any paid-up shares into stock, and reconvert any stock into paid-up shares of any denomination.

41. The holders of stock may transfer the same, or any part thereof, in the same manner, and subject to the same regulations, as and subject to which the shares from which the stock arose might previously to conversion have been transferred, or as near thereto as circumstances admit; and the directors may from time to time fix the minimum amount of stock transferable but so that such minimum shall not exceed the nominal amount of the shares from which the stock arose.

42. The holders of stock shall, according to the amount of stock held by them, have the same rights, privileges and advantages as regards dividends, voting at meetings of the company and other matters as if they held the shares from which the stock arose, but no such privilege or advantage (except participation in the dividends and profits of the company and in the assets on winding up) shall be conferred by an amount of stock which would not, if existing in shares, have conferred that privilege or advantage.

43. Such of the regulations of the company as are applicable to paid-up shares shall apply to stock, and words 'share' and 'shareholder' therein shall include 'stock' and 'stockholder'.

Alteration of Capital

44. The company may from time to time by ordinary resolution increase the share capital by such sum, to be divided into shares of such amount, as the resolution shall prescribe.

45. The company may by ordinary resolution—
- (a) consolidate and divide all or any of its share capital to shares of larger amount than its existing shares;
- (b) sub-divide its existing shares, or any of them, into shares of smaller amount than is fixed by the memorandum of association subject, nevertheless, to the provisions of section 61(1)(d) of the Act;
- (c) cancel any shares which, at the date of the passing of the resolution, have not been taken or agreed to be taken by any person.

46. The company may by special resolution reduce its share capital, any capital redemption reserve fund or any share premium account in any manner and with, and subject to, any incident authorised, and consent required, by law.

General Meetings

47. The company shall in each year hold a general meeting as its annual general meeting in addition to any other meetings in that year, and shall specify the meeting as such in the notices calling it; and not more than fifteen months shall elapse between the date of one annual general meeting of the company and that of the next. Provided that so long as the company holds its first annual general meeting within eighteen months of its incorporation, it need not hold it in the year of its incorporation or in the following year. The annual general meeting shall be held at such time and place as the directors shall appoint.

48. All general meetings other than annual general meetings shall be called extraordinary general meetings.

49. The directors may, whenever they think fit, convene an extraordinary general meeting, and extraordinary general meetings shall also be convened on such requisition, or, in default, may be convened by such requisitionists, as provided by section 132 of the Act. If at any time there are not within the United Kingdom sufficient directors capable of acting to form a quorum, any director or any two members of the company may convene an extraordinary general meeting in the same manner as nearly as possible as that in which meetings may be convened by the directors.

Notice of General Meetings

50. An annual general meeting and a meeting called for the passing of a special resolution shall be called by twenty-one days' notice in writing at the least, and a meeting of the company other than an annual general meeting or a meeting for the passing of a special resolution shall be called by fourteen days' notice in writing at the least. The notice shall be exclusive of the day on which it is served or deemed to be served and of the day for which it is given, and shall specify the place, the day and the hour of meeting and, in case of special business, the general nature of that business, and shall be given, in manner hereinafter mentioned or in such other manner, if any, as may be prescribed by the company in general meeting, to such persons as are, under the regulations of the company, entitled to receive such notices from the company:

Provided that a meeting of the company shall, notwithstanding that it is called by shorter notice than that specified in this regulation, be deemed to have been duly called if it is so agreed—

(a) in the case of a meeting called as the annual general meeting, by all the members entitled to attend and vote thereat; and

(b) in the case of any other meeting, by a majority in number of the members having a right to attend and vote at the meeting, being a majority together holding not less than 95 per cent in nominal value of the shares giving that right.

51. The accidental omission to give notice of a meeting to, or the non-receipt of notice of a meeting by, any person entitled to receive notice shall not invalidate the proceedings at that meeting.

Proceedings at General Meetings

52. All business shall be deemed special that is transacted at an extraordinary general meeting, and also all that is transacted at an annual general meeting, with the exception of declaring a dividend, the consideration of the accounts, balance sheets, and the reports of the directors and auditors, the election of directors in the place of those retiring and the appointment of, and the fixing of the remuneration of, the auditors.

53. No business shall be transacted at any general meeting unless a quorum of members is present at the time when the meeting proceeds to business; save as herein otherwise provided *three members present in person shall be a quorum.*

Notes

For the words in italics there are substituted the words 'two members present in person or by proxy shall be a quorum' by CA 1980, Sch 3, in relation to any company registered on or after 22 December 1980.

54. If within half an hour from the time appointed for the meeting a quorum is not present, the meeting, if convened upon the requisition of members, shall be dissolved; in any other case it shall stand adjourned to the same day in the next week, at the same time and place or to such other day and at such other time and place as the directors may determine, *and if at the adjourned meeting a quorum is not present within half an hour from the time appointed for the meeting, the members present shall be a quorum.*

Notes

Words in italics repealed by CA 1980, Sch 4, in relation to any company registered on or after 22 December 1980.

55. The chairman, if any, of the board of directors shall preside as chairman at every general meeting of the company, or if there is no such chairman, or if he shall not be present within fifteen minutes after the time appointed for the holding of the meeting or is unwilling to act the directors present shall elect one of their number to be chairman of the meeting.

56. If at any meeting no director is willing to act as chairman or if no director is present within fifteen minutes after the time appointed for holding the meeting, the members present shall choose one of their number to be chairman of the meeting.

57. The chairman may, with the consent of any meeting at which a quorum is present (and shall if so directed by the meeting), adjourn the meeting from time to time and from place to place, but no business shall be transacted at any adjourned meeting other than the business left unfinished at the meeting from which the adjournment took place. When a meeting is adjourned for thirty days or more, notice of the adjourned meeting shall be given as in the case of an original meeting. Save as aforesaid it shall not be necessary to give any notice of an adjournment or of the business to be transacted at an adjourned meeting.

58. At any general meeting a resolution put to the vote of the meeting shall be decided on a show of hands unless a poll is (before or on the declaration of the result of the show of hands) demanded—

    (a) by the chairman; or

    (b) by at least *three* members present in person or by proxy; or

    (c) by any member or members present in person or by proxy and representing not less than one-tenth of the total voting rights of all the members having the right to vote at the meeting; or

    (d) by a member or members holding shares in the company conferring a right to vote at the meeting being shares on which an aggregate sum has been paid up equal to not less than one-tenth of the total sum paid up on all the shares conferring that right.

Unless a poll be so demanded a declaration by the chairman that a resolution has on a show of hands been carried or carried unanimously, or by a particular majority, or lost and an entry to that effect in the book containing the minutes of the proceedings of the company shall be conclusive evidence of the fact without proof of the number or proportion of the votes recorded in favour of or against such resolution.

    The demand for a poll may be withdrawn.

Notes

For the word in italics there is substituted the word 'two' by CA 1980, Sch 3, in relation to any company registered on or after 22 December 1980.

59. Except as provided in regulation 61, if a poll is duly demanded it shall be taken in such manner as the chairman directs, and the result of the poll shall be deemed to be the resolution of the meeting at which the poll was demanded.

60. In the case of an equality of votes, whether on a show of hands or on a poll, the chairman of the meeting at which the show of hands takes place or at which the poll is demanded, shall be entitled to a second or casting vote.

61. A poll demanded on the election of a chairman or on a question of adjournment shall be taken forthwith. A poll demanded on any other question shall be taken at such time as the chairman of the meeting directs, and any business other than that upon which a poll has been demanded may be proceeded with pending the taking of the poll.

Votes of Members

62. Subject to any rights or restrictions for the time being attached to any class or classes of shares, on a show of hands every member present in person shall have one vote, and on a poll every member shall have one vote for each share of which he is the holder.

63. In the case of joint holders the vote of the senior who tenders a vote, whether in person or by proxy, shall be accepted to the exclusion of the votes of the other joint holders; and for this purpose seniority shall be determined by the order in which the names stand in the register of members.

64. A member of unsound mind, or in respect of whom an order has been made by any court having jurisdiction in lunacy, may vote, whether on a show of hands or on a poll, by his committee, receiver, curator bonis, or other person in the nature of a committee, receiver or curator bonis appointed by that court, and any such committee, receiver, curator bonis or other person may, on a poll, vote by proxy.

65. No member shall be entitled to vote at any general meeting unless all calls or other sums presently payable by him in respect of shares in the company have been paid.

66. No objection shall be raised to the qualification of any voter except at the meeting or adjourned meeting at which the vote objected to is given or tendered, and every vote not disallowed at such meeting shall be valid for all purposes. Any such objection made in due time shall be referred to the chairman of the meeting whose decision shall be final and conclusive.

67. On a poll votes may be given either personally or by proxy.

68. The instrument appointing a proxy shall be in writing under the hand of the appointer or of his attorney duly authorised in writing, or, if the appointer is a corporation, either under seal, or under the hand of an officer or attorney duly authorised. A proxy need not be a member of the company.

69. The instrument appointing a proxy and the power of attorney or other authority if any, under which it is signed or a notarially certified copy of that power or authority shall be deposited at the registered office of the company or at such other place within the United Kingdom as is specified for that purpose in the notice convening the meeting, not less than 48 hours before the time for holding the meeting or adjourned meeting, at which the person named in the instrument proposes to vote, or, in the case of a poll, not less than 24 hours before the time appointed for the taking of the poll, and in default the instrument of proxy shall not be treated as valid.

70. An instrument appointing a proxy shall be in the following form or a form as near thereto as circumstances admit—

    '   Limited

I/We,   , of   , in the county of   , being a member/members of the above-named company, hereby appoint   of , or failing him, of as my/our proxy to vote for me/us on my/our behalf at the [annual or extraordinary, as the case may be] general meeting of the company, to be held on the   day of 19 , and at any adjournment thereof.

Signed this   day of   19 .'

71. Where it is desired to afford members an opportunity of voting for or against a resolution the instrument appointing a proxy shall be in the following form or a form as near thereto as circumstances admit—

' Limited

I/We, , of , in the county of , being a member/
members of the above-named company, hereby appoint of , or
failing him, of as my/our proxy to vote for me/us on my/our behalf
at the [annual or extraordinary, as the case may be] general meeting of the
company, to be held on the day of
19 , and at any adjournment thereof.

Signed this day of 19 .

This form is to be used $\frac{\text{*in favour of}}{\text{against}}$ the resolution. Unless otherwise
instructed, the proxy will vote as he thinks fit.

*Strike out whichever is not desired.'

72. The instrument appointing a proxy shall be deemed to confer authority to
demand or join in demanding a poll.

73. A vote given in accordance with the terms of an instrument of proxy shall
be valid notwithstanding the previous death or insanity of the principal or
revocation of the proxy or of the authority under which the proxy was executed,
on the transfer of the share in respect of which the proxy is given, provided that
no intimation in writing of such death, insanity, revocation or transfer as
aforesaid shall have been received by the company at the office before the
commencement of the meeting or adjourned meeting at which the proxy is used.

[**73A.** Subject to the provisions of the Companies Acts 1948 to *1980* a
resolution in writing signed by all the members for the time being entitled to
receive notice of and to attend and vote at general meetings (or being
corporations by their duly authorised representatives) shall be as valid and
effective as if the same had been passed at a general meeting of the company
duly convened and held.]

Notes

Paragraph 73A   Added by CA 1980, Sch 3 in relation to any company registered
on or after 22 December 1980; for the year in italics there is substituted the year
'1981' by CA 1981, Sch 3 in relation to any company registered on or after 3
December 1981.

Corporations acting by Representatives at Meetings

74. Any corporation which is a member of the company may by resolution of
its directors or other governing body authorise such person as it thinks fit to
act as its representative at any meeting of the company or of any class of
members of the company, and the person so authorised shall be entitled to
exercise the same powers on behalf of the corporation which he represents
as that corporation could exercise if it were an individual member of the
company.

Directors

75. The number of the directors and the names of the first directors shall be determined in writing by the subscribers of the memorandum of association or a majority of them.

76. The remuneration of the directors shall from time to time be determined by the company in general meeting. Such remuneration shall be deemed to accrue from day to day. The directors may also be paid all travelling, hotel and other expenses properly incurred by them in attending and returning from meetings of the directors or any committee of the directors or general meetings of the company or in connection with the business of the company.

77. The shareholding qualification for directors may be fixed by the company in general meeting, and unless and until so fixed no qualification shall be required.

78. A director of the company may be or become a director or other officer of, or otherwise interested in, any company promoted by the company or in which the company may be interested as shareholder or otherwise, and no such director shall be accountable to the company for any remuneration or other benefits received by him as a director or officer of, or from his interest in, such other company unless the company otherwise direct.

Borrowing Powers

79. The directors may exercise all the powers of the company to borrow money, and to mortgage or charge its undertaking, property and uncalled capital or any part thereof, and [, subject to section 14 of CA 1980] to issue debentures, debenture stock, and other securities whether outright or as security for any debt, liability or obligation of the company or of any third party:

    Provided that the amount for the time being remaining undischarged of moneys borrowed or secured by the directors as aforesaid (apart from temporary loans obtained from the company's bankers in the ordinary course of business) shall not at any time, without the previous sanction of the company in general meeting, exceed the nominal amount of the share capital of the company for the time being issued, but nevertheless no lender or other person dealing with the company shall be concerned to see or inquire whether this limit is observed. No debt incurred or security given in excess of such limit shall be invalid or ineffectual except in the case of express notice to the lender or the recipient of the security at the time when the debt was incurred or security given that the limit hereby imposed had been or was thereby exceeded.

Notes

Words in square brackets inserted by CA 1980, Sch 3 in relation to any company registered on or after 22 December 1980.

Powers and Duties of Directors

80. The business of the company shall be managed by the directors, who may pay all expenses incurred in promoting and registering the company, and may exercise all such powers of the company as are not, by the *Act* or by these regulations, required to be exercised by the company in general meeting, subject, nevertheless, to any of these regulations, to the provisions of the *Act* and to such regulations being not inconsistent with the aforesaid regulations or provisions, as may be prescribed by the company in general meeting; but no regulation made by the company in general meeting shall invalidate any prior act of the directors which would have been valid if that regulation had not been made.

Notes

For the words in italics there are substituted the words 'Companies Acts 1948 to 1980' in both places by CA 1980, Sch 3 in relation to companies registered on or after 22 December 1980; in the text as substituted the year '1980' is substituted by the year '1981' by CA 1981, Sch 3 in relation to companies registered on or after 3 December 1981.

81. The directors may from time to time and at any time by power of attorney appoint any company, firm or person or body of persons, whether nominated directly or indirectly by the directors, to be the attorney or attorneys of the company for such purposes and with such powers, authorities and discretions (not exceeding those vested in or exercisable by the directors under these regulations) and for such period and subject to such conditions as they may think fit, and any such powers of attorney may contain such provisions for the protection and convenience of persons dealing with any such attorney as the directors may think fit and may also authorise any such attorney to delegate all or any of the powers, authorities and discretions vested in him.

82. The company may exercise the powers conferred by section 35 of the Act with regard to having an official seal for use abroad, and such powers shall be vested in the directors.

83. The company may exercise the powers conferred upon the company by sections 119 to 123 (both inclusive) of the Act with regard to the keeping of a dominion register, and the directors may (subject to the provisions of those sections) make and vary such regulations as they may think fit respecting the keeping of any such register.

84.—(1) A director who is in any way, whether directly or indirectly, interested in a contract or proposed contract with the company shall declare the nature of his interest at a meeting of the directors in accordance with section 199 of the Act.

(2) A director shall not vote in respect of any contract or arrangement in which he is interested, and if he shall do so his vote shall not be counted, nor shall he be counted in the quorum present at the meeting, but neither of these prohibitions shall apply to—

    (a) any arrangement for giving any director any security or indemnity in respect of money lent by him to or obligations undertaken by him for the benefit of the company; or

    (b) to any arrangement for the giving by the company of any security to a third party in respect of a debt or obligation of the company for which the director himself has assumed responsibility in whole or in part under a guarantee or indemnity or by the deposit of a security; or

(c) any contract by a director to subscribe for or underwrite shares or debentures of the company; or

(d) any contract or arrangement with any other company in which he is interested only as an officer of the company or as holder of shares or other securities;

and these prohibitions may at any time be suspended or relaxed to any extent, and either generally or in respect of any particular contract, arrangement or transaction, by the company in general meeting.

(3) A director may hold any other office or place of profit under the company (other than the office of auditor) in conjunction with his office of director for such period and on such terms (as to remuneration and otherwise) as the directors may determine and no director or intending director shall be disqualified by his office from contracting with the company either with regard to his tenure of any such other office or place of profit or as vendor, purchaser or otherwise, nor shall any such contract, or any contract or arrangement entered into by or on behalf of the company in which any director is in any way interested, be liable to be avoided, nor shall any director so contracting or being so interested be liable to account to the company for any profit realised by any such contract or arrangement by reason of such director holding that office or of the fiduciary relation thereby established.

(4) A director, notwithstanding his interest, may be counted in the quorum present at any meeting whereat he or any other director is appointed to hold any such office or place of profit under the company or whereat the terms of any such appointment are arranged, and he may vote on any such appointment or arrangement other than his own appointment or the arrangement of the terms thereof.

(5) Any director may act by himself or his firm in a professional capacity for the company, and he or his firm shall be entitled to remuneration for professional services as if he were not a director; provided that nothing herein contained shall authorise a director or his firm to act as auditor to the company.

85. All cheques, promissory notes, drafts, bills of exchange and other negotiable instruments, and all receipts for moneys paid to the company, shall be signed, drawn, accepted, endorsed, or otherwise executed, as the case may be, in such manner as the directors shall from time to time by resolution determine.

86. The directors shall cause minutes to be made in books provided for the purpose—

(a) of all appointments of officers made by the directors;

(b) of the names of the directors present at each meeting of the directors and of any committee of the directors;

(c) of all resolutions and proceedings at all meetings of the company, and of the directors, and of committees of directors;

and every director present at any meeting of directors or committee of directors shall sign his name in a book to be kept for that purpose.

87. The directors on behalf of the company may pay a gratuity or pension or allowance on retirement to any director who has held any other salaried office or place of profit with the company or to his widow or dependants and may make contributions to any fund and pay premiums for the purchase or provision of any such gratuity, pension or allowance.

Disqualification of Directors

88. The office of director shall be vacated if the director—

- (a) ceases to be a director by virtue of section 182 or 185 of the Act; or
- (b) becomes bankrupt or makes any arrangement or composition with his creditors generally; or
- (c) becomes prohibited from being a director by reason of any order made under section 188 of the Act [*or under section 28 of CA 1976*]; or
- (d) becomes of unsound mind; or
- (e) resigns his office by notice in writing to the company; or
- (f) shall for more than six months have been absent without permission of the directors from meetings of the directors held during that period.

Notes

Words in square brackets inserted by CA 1976 in relation to any company registered on or after 1 June 1977, and repealed by CA 1981, Sch 4 in relation to any company registered on or after 3 December 1981.

Rotation of Directors

89. At the first annual general meeting of the company all the directors shall retire from office, and at the annual general meeting in every subsequent year one-third of the directors for the time being, or, if their number is not three or a multiple of three, then the number nearest one-third, shall retire from office.

90. The directors to retire in every year shall be those who have been longest in office since their last election, but as between persons who became directors on the same day those to retire shall (unless they otherwise agree among themselves) be determined by lot.

91. A retiring director shall be eligible for re-election.

92. The company at the meeting at which a director retires in manner aforesaid may fill the vacated office by electing a person thereto, and in default the retiring director shall if offering himself for re-election be deemed to have been re-elected, unless at such meeting it is expressly resolved not to fill such vacated office or unless a resolution for the re-election of such director shall have been put to the meeting and lost.

93. No person other than a director retiring at the meeting shall unless recommended by the directors be eligible for election to the office of director at any general meeting unless not less than three nor more than twenty-one days before the date appointed for the meeting there shall have been left at the registered office of the company notice in writing, signed by a member duly qualified to attend and vote at the meeting for which such notice is given, of his intention to propose such person for election, and also notice in writing signed by that person of his willingness to be elected.

94. The company may from time to time by ordinary resolution increase or reduce the number of directors, and may also determine in what rotation the increased or reduced number is to go out of office.

95. The directors shall have power at any time, and from time to time, to appoint any person to be a director, either to fill a casual vacancy or as an addition to the existing directors, but so that the total number of directors shall not at any time exceed the number fixed in accordance with these regulations. Any director so appointed shall hold office only until the next following annual general meeting, and shall then be eligible for re-election but shall not be taken into account in determining the directors who are to retire by rotation at such meeting.

96. The company may by ordinary resolution, of which special notice has been given in accordance with section 142 of the Act, remove any director before the expiration of his period of office notwithstanding anything in these regulations or in any agreement between the company and such director. Such removal shall be without prejudice to any claim such director may have for damages for breach of any contract of service between him and the company.

97. The company may by ordinary resolution appoint another person in place of a director removed from office under the immediately preceding regulation, and without prejudice to the powers of the directors under regulation 95 the company in general meeting may appoint any person to be a director either to fill a casual vacancy or as an additional director. A person appointed in place of a director so removed or to fill such a vacancy shall be subject to retirement at the same time as if he had become a director on the day on which the director in whose place he is appointed was last elected a director.

Proceedings of Directors

98. The directors may meet together for the despatch of business, adjourn, and otherwise regulate their meetings, as they think fit. Questions arising at any meeting shall be decided by a majority of votes. In case of an equality of votes, the chairman shall have a second or casting vote. A director may, and the secretary on the requisition of a director shall, at any time summon a meeting of the directors. It shall not be necessary to give notice of a meeting of directors to any director for the time being absent from the United Kingdom.

99. The quorum necessary for the transaction of the business of the directors may be fixed by the directors, and unless so fixed shall be two.

100. The continuing directors may act notwithstanding any vacancy in their body, but, if and so long as their number is reduced below the number fixed by or pursuant to the regulations of the company as the necessary quorum of directors, the continuing directors or director may act for the purpose of increasing the number of directors to that number, or of summoning a general meeting of the company, but for no other purpose.

101. The directors may elect a chairman of their meetings and determine the period for which he is to hold office; but if no such chairman is elected, or if at any meeting the chairman is not present within five minutes after the time appointed for holding the same, the directors present may choose one of their number to be chairman of the meeting.

102. The directors may delegate any of their powers to committees consisting of such member or members of their body as they think fit; any committee so formed shall in the exercise of the powers so delegated conform to any regulations that may be imposed on it by the directors.

103. A committee may elect a chairman of its meetings; if no such chairman is elected, or if at any meeting the chairman is not present within five minutes after the time appointed for holding the same, the members present may choose one of their number to be chairman of the meeting.

104. A committee may meet and adjourn as it thinks proper. Questions arising at any meeting shall be determined by a majority of votes of the members present, and in the case of an equality of votes the chairman shall have a second or casting vote.

105. All acts done by any meeting of the directors or of a committee of directors or by any person acting as a director shall, notwithstanding that it be afterwards discovered that there was some defect in the appointment of any such director or person acting as aforesaid, or that they or any of them were disqualified, be as valid as if every such person had been duly appointed and was qualified to be a director.

106. A resolution in writing, signed by all the directors for the time being entitled to receive notice of a meeting of the directors, shall be as valid and effectual as if it had been passed at a meeting of the directors duly convened and held.

Managing Director

107. The directors may from time to time appoint one of more of their body to the office of managing director for such period and on such terms as they think fit, and, subject to the terms of any agreement entered into in any particular case, may revoke such appointment. A director so appointed shall not, whilst holding that office, be subject to retirement by rotation or be taken into account in determining the rotation of retirement of directors, but his appointment shall be automatically determined if he cease from any cause to be a director.

108. A managing director shall receive such remuneration (whether by way of salary, commission or participation in profits, or partly in one way and partly in another) as the directors may determine.

109. The directors may entrust to and confer upon a managing director any of the powers exercisable by them upon such terms and conditions and with such restrictions as they may think fit, and either collaterally with or to the exclusion of their own powers and may from time to time revoke, withdraw, alter or vary all or any of such powers.

Secretary

110. [Subject to Section 21(5) of CA 1976] the secretary shall be appointed by the directors for such term, at such remuneration and upon such conditions as they may think fit; and any secretary so appointed may be removed by them.

Notes

Words in square brackets inserted by CA 1976, Sch 2 in relation to any company registered on or after 18 April 1977.

111. No person shall be appointed or hold office as secretary who is—

    (a) the sole director of the company; or

    (b) a corporation the sole director of which is the sole director of the company; or

    (c) the sole director of a corporation which is the sole director of the company.

112. A provision of the Act or these regulations requiring or authorising a thing to be done by or to a director and the secretary shall not be satisfied by its being done by or to the same person acting both as director and as, or in place of, the secretary.

The Seal

113. The directors shall provide for the safe custody of the seal, which shall only be used by the authority of the directors or of a committee of the directors authorised by the directors in that behalf, and every instrument to which the seal shall be affixed shall be signed by a director and shall be countersigned by the secretary or by a second director or by some other person appointed by the directors for the purpose.

Dividends and Reserve

114. The company in general meeting may declare dividends, but no dividend shall exceed the amount recommended by the directors.

115. The directors may from time to time pay to the members such interim dividends as appear to the directors to be justified by the profits of the company.

116. *No dividend shall be paid otherwise than out of profits.*

Notes

Words in italics substituted by CA 1980, Sch 3, in relation to any company registered on or after 22 December 1980, as follows—

'No dividend or interim dividend shall be paid otherwise than in accordance with the provisions of Part III of CA 1980 which apply to the company.'

---

117. The directors may, before recommending any dividend, set aside out of the profits of the company such sums as they think proper as a reserve or reserves which shall, at the discretion of the directors, be applicable for any purpose to which the profits of the company may be properly applied, and pending such application may, at the like discretion, either be employed in the business of the company or be invested in such investments (other than shares of the company) as the directors may from time to time think fit. The directors may also without placing the same to reserve carry forward any profits which they may think prudent not to divide.

118. Subject to the rights of persons, if any, entitled to shares with special rights as to dividend, all dividends shall be declared and paid according to the amounts paid or credited as paid on the shares in respect whereof the dividend is paid, but no amount paid or credited as paid on a share in advance of calls shall be treated for the purposes of this regulation as paid on the share. All dividends shall be apportioned and paid proportionately to the amounts paid or credited as paid on the shares during any portion or portions of the period in respect of which the dividend is paid; but if any share is issued on terms providing that it shall rank for dividend as from a particular date such share shall rank for dividend accordingly.

119. The directors may deduct from any dividend payable to any member all sums of money (if any) presently payable by him to the company on account of calls or otherwise in relation to the shares of the company.

120. Any general meeting declaring a dividend or bonus may direct payment of such dividend or bonus wholly or partly by the distribution of specific assets and in particular of paid up shares, debentures or debenture stock of any other company or in any one or more of such ways, and the directors shall give effect to such resolution, and where any difficulty arises in regard to such distribution, the directors may settle the same as they think expedient, and in particular may issue fractional certificates and fix the value for distribution of such specific assets or any part thereof and may determine that cash payments shall be made to any members upon the footing of the value so fixed in order to adjust the rights of all parties, and may vest any such specific assets in trustees as may seem expedient to the directors.

121. Any dividend, interest or other moneys payable in cash in respect of shares may be paid by cheque or warrant sent through the post directed to the registered address of the holder or, in the case of joint holders, to the registered address of that one of the joint holders who is first named on the register of members or to such person and to such address as the holder or joint holders may in writing direct. Every such cheque or warrant shall be made payable to the order of the person to whom it is sent. Any one of two or more joint holders may give effectual receipts for any dividends, bonuses or other moneys payable in respect of the shares held by them as joint holders.

122. No dividend shall bear interest against the company.

Accounts

123. The directors *shall cause proper books of account to be kept with respect to—*

- *(a) all sums of money received and expended by the company and the matters in respect of which the receipt and expenditure takes place;*
- *(b) all sales and purchases of goods by the company; and*
- *(c) the assets and liabilities of the company.*

Proper books shall not be deemed to be kept if there are not kept such books of account as are necessary to give a true and fair view of the state of the company's affairs and to explain its transactions.

Notes

For the words in italics there are substituted the words 'shall cause accounting records to be kept in accordance with section 12 of CA 1976' by CA 1976, Sch 2, in relation to any company registered on or after 1 October 1977.

124. *The books of account shall be kept at the registered office of the Company, or, subject to section 147(3) of the Act, at such other place or places as the directors think fit, and shall always be open to the inspection of the directors.*

Notes

Substituted by CA 1976, Sch 2 in relation to any company registered on or after 1 October 1977, as follows—

'The accounting records shall be kept at the registered office of the company or, subject to section 12(6) and (7) of CA 1976, at such other place or places as the directors think fit, and shall always be open to the inspection of the officers of the company.'

125. The directors shall from time to time determine whether and to what extent and at what times and places and under what conditions or regulations the accounts and books of the company or any of them shall be open to the inspection of members not being directors, and no member (not being a director) shall have any right of inspecting any account or book or document of the company except as conferred by statute or authorised by the directors or by the company in general meeting.

126. The directors shall from time to time, in accordance with *sections 148, 150 and 157 of the Act*, cause to be prepared and to be laid before the company in general meeting such profit and loss accounts, balance sheets, group accounts (if any) and reports as are referred to in those sections.

Notes

For the words in italics there are substituted the words 'sections 150 and 157 of the Act and sections 1, 6 and 7 of CA 1976' by CA 1976, Sch 2 in relation to any company registered on or after 1 October 1977.

127. A copy of every balance sheet (including every document required by law to be annexed thereto) which is to be laid before the company in general meeting, together with a copy of the auditors' report [and directors' report], shall not less than twenty-one days before the date of the meeting be sent to every member of, and every holder of debentures of, the company and to every person registered under regulation 31. Provided that this regulation shall not require a copy of those documents to be sent to any person of whose address the company is not aware or to more than one of the joint holders of any shares or debentures.

Notes

Words in square brackets inserted by CA 1976, Sch 2, in relation to any company registered on or after 1 October 1977.

Capitalisation of Profits

128. The company in general meeting may upon the recommendation of the directors resolve that it is desirable to capitalise any part of the amount for the time being standing to the credit of any of the company's reserve accounts or to the credit of the profit and loss account or otherwise available for distribution, and accordingly that such sum be set free for distribution amongst the members who would have been entitled thereto if distributed by way of dividend and in the same proportions on condition that the same be not paid in cash but be applied either in or towards paying up any amounts for the time being unpaid on any shares held by such members respectively or paying up in full unissued shares or debentures of the company to be allotted and distributed credited as fully paid up to and amongst such members in the proportion aforesaid, or partly in the one way and partly in the other, and the directors shall give effect to such resolution:

Provided that a share premium account and a capital redemption reserve fund may, for the purposes of this regulation, only be applied in the paying up of unissued shares to be *issued* to members of the company as fully paid bonus shares.

Notes

For the word in italics there is substituted the word 'allotted' by CA 1980, Sch 3 in relation to any company registered on or after 22 December 1980.

[**128A.** The company in general meeting may on the recommendation of the directors resolve that it is desirable to capitalise any part of the amount for the time being standing to the credit of any of the company's reserve accounts or to the credit of the profit and loss account which is not available for distribution by applying such sum in paying up in full unissued shares to be allotted as fully paid bonus shares to those members of the company who would have been entitled to that sum if it were distributed by way of dividend (and in the same proportions), and the directors shall give effect to such resolution.]

Notes

Added by CA 1980, Sch 3 in relation to any company registered on or after 22 December 1980.

129. *Whenever such a resolution as aforesaid shall have been passed* the directors shall make all appropriations and applications of the undivided profits resolved to be capitalised thereby, and all allotments and issues of fully-paid shares or debentures, if any, and generally shall do all acts and things required to give effect thereto, with full power to the directors to make such provision by the issue of fractional certificates or by payment in cash or otherwise as they think fit for the case of shares or debentures becoming distributable in fractions, and also to authorise any person to enter on behalf of all members entitled thereto into an agreement with the company providing for the allotment to them respectively, credited as fully paid up, of any further shares or debentures to which they may be entitled upon such capitalisation, or (as the case may require) for the payment up by the company on their behalf, by the application thereto of their respective proportions of the profits resolved to be capitalised, of the amounts or any part of the amounts remaining unpaid on their existing shares, and any agreement made under such authority shall be effective and binding on all such members.

Notes

For the words in italics there are substituted the words 'Whenever a resolution is passed in pursuance of regulation 128 or 128A above' by CA 1980, Sch 3 in relation to any company registered on or after 22 December 1980.

Audit

130. Auditors shall be appointed and their duties regulated in accordance with *sections 159 to 162 of the Act.*

Notes

The regulation set out above applies to any company registered before 27 January 1968.

For the words in italics there are substituted the words 'sections 159 to 161 of the Act and section 14 of the Companies Act 1967' by CA 1967, in relation to any company registered between 27 January 1968 and 17 April 1977; for the words in italics there are substituted the words 'section 161 of the Act, section 14 of CA 1967 and sections 13 to 18 of CA 1976' by CA 1976, in relation to any company registered between 18 April 1977 and 2 December 1981; and for the words in italics there are substituted the words 'section 161 of the Act, sections 14 and 23A of CA 1967, sections 13 to 18 of CA 1976 and sections 7 and 12 of CA 1981' by CA 1981, in relation to any company registered between 3 December 1981 and 30 June 1985.

Notices

131. A notice may be given by the company to any member either personally or by sending it by post to him or to his registered address, or (if he has no registered address within the United Kingdom) to the address, if any, within the United Kingdom supplied by him to the company for the giving of notice to him. Where a notice is sent by post, service of the notice shall be deemed to be effected by properly addressing, prepaying, and posting a letter containing the notice, and to have been effected in the case of a notice of a meeting at the expiration of 24 hours after the letter containing the same is posted, and in any other case at the time at which the letter would be delivered in the ordinary course of post.

132. A notice may be given by the company to the joint holders of a share by giving the notice to the joint holder first named in the register of members in respect of the share.

133. A notice may be given by the company to the persons entitled to a share in consequence of the death or bankruptcy of a member by sending it through the post in a prepaid letter addressed to them by name, or by the title of representatives of the deceased, or trustee of the bankrupt, or any like description, at the address, if any, within the United Kingdom supplied for the purpose by the persons claiming to be so entitled, or (until such an address has been so supplied) by giving the notice in any manner in which the same might have been given if the death or bankruptcy had not occurred.

134. Notice of every general meeting shall be given in any manner hereinbefore authorised to—

    (a) every member except those members who (having no registered address within the United Kingdom) have not supplied to the company an address within the United Kingdom for the giving of notices to them;

    (b) every person upon whom the ownership of a share devolves by reason of his being a legal personal representative or a trustee in bankruptcy of a member where the member but for his death or bankruptcy would be entitled to receive notice of the meeting; and

    (c) the auditor for the time being of the company.

No other person shall be entitled to receive notices of general meetings.

Winding up

135. If the company shall be wound up the liquidator may, with the sanction of an extraordinary resolution of the company and any other sanction required by the Act, divide amongst the members in specie or kind the whole or any part of the assets of the company (whether they shall consist of property of the same kind or not) and may, for such purpose set such value as he deems fair upon any property to be divided as aforesaid and may determine how such division shall be carried out as between the members or different classes of members. The liquidator may, with the like sanction, vest the whole or any part of such assets in trustees upon such trusts for the benefit of the contributories as the liquidator, with the like sanction, shall think fit, but so that no member shall be compelled to accept any shares or other securities whereon there is any liability.

Indemnity

136. Every director, managing director, agent, auditor, secretary and other officer for the time being of the company shall be indemnified out of the assets of the company against any liability incurred by him in defending any proceedings, whether civil or criminal, in which judgment is given in his favour or in which he is acquitted or in connection with any application under section 448 of the Act in which relief is granted to him by the court.

PART II
REGULATIONS FOR THE MANAGEMENT OF A PRIVATE COMPANY LIMITED BY SHARES

1. *The regulations contained in Part I of Table A (with the exception of regulations 24 and 53) shall apply.*

2. *The company is a private company and accordingly—*

(a) *the right to transfer shares is restricted in manner hereinafter prescribed;*

(b) *the number of members of the company (exclusive of persons who are in the employment of the company and of persons who having been formerly in the employment of the company were while in such employment and have continued after the determination of such employment to be members of the company) is limited to fifty. Provided that where two or more persons hold one or more shares in the company jointly they shall for the purpose of this regulation be treated as a single member;*

(c) *any invitation to the public to subscribe for any shares or debentures of the company is prohibited;*

(d) *the company shall not have power to issue share warrants to bearer.*

3. *The directors may, in their absolute discretion and without assigning any reason therefor, decline to register any transfer of any share, whether or not it is a fully paid share.*

4. *No business shall be transacted at any general meeting unless a quorum of members is present at the time when the meeting proceeds to business; save as herein otherwise provided two members present in person or by proxy shall be a quorum.*

5. *Subject to the provisions of the Act, a resolution in writing signed by all the members for the time being entitled to receive notice of and to attend and vote at general meetings (or being corporations by their duly authorised representatives) shall be as valid and effective as if the same had been passed at a general meeting of the company duly convened and held.*

6. *The directors may at any time require any person whose name is entered in the register of members of the company to furnish them with any information, supported (if the directors so require) by a statutory declaration, which they may consider necessary for the purpose of determining whether or not the company is an exempt private company within the meaning of subsection (4) of section 129 of the Act.*

Note. Regulations 3 and 4 of this Part are alternative to regulations 24 and 53 respectively of Part I.

Notes

(Part II repealed by CA 1980, Schedule 4, in relation to any company registered on or after 22 December 1980.)

(Paragraph 6 repealed by CA 1967, Schedule 8, Part III, in relation to any company registered on or after 27 January 1968.)

APPENDIX II—COMPANIES ACT 1985

TABLE A

COMPANIES ACT 1985 TABLE A

(SI 1985/805, SCHEDULE)

TABLE A
REGULATIONS FOR MANAGEMENT OF A COMPANY
LIMITED BY SHARES

INTERPRETATION

1. In these regulations—

'the Act' means the Companies Act 1985 including any statutory modification or re-enactment thereof for the time being in force.

'the articles' means the articles of the company.

'clear days' in relation to the period of a notice means that period excluding the day when the notice is given or deemed to be given and the day for which it is given or on which it is to take effect.

['communication' means the same as in the Electronic Communications Act 2000.]

['electronic communication' means the same as in the Electronic Communications Act 2000.]

'executed' includes any mode of execution.

'office' means the registered office of the company.

'the holder' in relation to shares means the member whose name is entered in the register of members as the holder of the shares.

'the seal' means the common seal of the company.

'secretary' means the secretary of the company or any other person appointed to perform the duties of the secretary of the company, including a joint, assistant or deputy secretary.

'the United Kingdom' means Great Britain and Northern Ireland.

Unless the context otherwise requires, words or expressions contained in these regulations bear the same meaning as in the Act but excluding any statutory modification thereof not in force when these regulations become binding on the company.

Notes

Definitions in square brackets inserted by the Companies Act 1985 (Electronic Communications) Order 2000, SI 2000/3373, art 32(1), Sch 1, para 1, as from 22 December 2000.

SHARE CAPITAL

2. Subject to the provisions of the Act and without prejudice to any rights attached to any existing shares, any share may be issued with such rights or restrictions as the company may by ordinary resolution determine.

3. Subject to the provisions of the Act, shares may be issued which are to be redeemed or are to be liable to be redeemed at the option of the company or the holder on such terms and in such manner as may be provided by the articles.

4. The company may exercise the powers of paying commissions conferred by the Act. Subject to the [provisions] of the Act, any such commission may be satisfied by the payment of cash or by the allotment of fully or partly paid shares or partly in one way and partly in the other.

5. Except as required by law, no person shall be recognised by the company as holding any share upon any trust and (except as otherwise provided by the articles or by law) the company shall not be bound by or recognise any interest in any share except an absolute right to the entirety thereof in the holder.

Notes

Paragraph 4   Word in square brackets substituted for original word 'provision' by the Companies (Tables A to F) (Amendment) Regulations 1985, SI 1985/1052 with effect from 1 August 1985.

SHARE CERTIFICATES

6. Every member, upon becoming the holder of any shares, shall be entitled without payment to one certificate for all the shares of each class held by him (and, upon transferring a part of his holding of shares of any class, to a certificate for the balance of such holding) or several certificates each for one or more of his shares upon payment for every certificate after the first of such reasonable sum as the directors may determine. Every certificate shall be sealed with the seal and shall specify the number, class and distinguishing numbers (if any) of the shares to which it relates and the amount or respective amounts paid up thereon. The company shall not be bound to issue more than one certificate for shares held jointly by several persons and delivery of a certificate to one joint holder shall be a sufficient delivery to all of them.

7. If a share certificate is defaced, worn-out, lost or destroyed, it may be renewed on such terms (if any) as to evidence and indemnity and payment of the expenses reasonably incurred by the company in investigating evidence as the directors may determine but otherwise free of charge, and (in the case of defacement or wearing-out) on delivery up of the old certificate.

LIEN

8. The company shall have a first and paramount lien on every share (not being a fully paid share) for all moneys (whether presently payable or not) payable at a fixed time or called in respect of that share. The directors may at any time declare any share to be wholly or in part exempt from the provisions of this regulation. The company's lien on a share shall extend to any amount payable in respect of it.

9. The company may sell in such manner as the directors determine any shares on which the company has a lien if a sum in respect of which the lien exists is presently payable and is not paid within fourteen clear days after notice has been given to the holder of the share or to the person entitled to it in consequence of the death or bankruptcy of the holder, demanding payment and stating that if the notice is not complied with the shares may be sold.

10. To give effect to a sale the directors may authorise some person to execute an instrument of transfer of the shares sold to, or in accordance with the directions of, the purchaser. The title of the transferee to the shares shall not be affected by any irregularity in or invalidity of the proceedings in reference to the sale.

11. The net proceeds of the sale, after payment of the costs, shall be applied in payment of so much of the sum for which the lien exists as is presently payable, and any residue shall (upon surrender to the company for cancellation of the certificate for the shares sold and subject to a like lien for any moneys not presently payable as existed upon the shares before the sale) be paid to the person entitled to the shares at the date of the sale.

CALLS ON SHARES AND FORFEITURE

12. Subject to the terms of allotment, the directors may make calls upon the members in respect of any moneys unpaid on their shares (whether in respect of nominal value or premium) and each member shall (subject to receiving at least fourteen clear days' notice specifying when and where payment is to be made) pay to the company as required by the notice the amount called on his shares. A call may be required to be paid by instalments. A call may, before receipt by the company of any sum due thereunder, be revoked in whole or part and payment of a call may be postponed in whole or part. A person upon whom a call is made shall remain liable for calls made upon him notwithstanding the subsequent transfer of the shares in respect whereof the call was made.

13. A call shall be deemed to have been made at the time when the resolution of the directors authorising the call was passed.

14. The joint holders of a share shall be jointly and severally liable to pay all calls in respect thereof.

15. If a call remains unpaid after it has become due and payable the person from whom it is due and payable shall pay interest on the amount unpaid from the day it became due and payable until it is paid at the rate fixed by the terms of allotment of the share or in the notice of the call or, if no rate is fixed, at the appropriate rate (as defined by the Act) but the directors may waive payment of the interest wholly or in part.

16. An amount payable in respect of a share on allotment or at any fixed date, whether in respect of nominal value or premium or as an instalment of a call, shall be deemed to be a call and if it is not paid the provisions of the articles shall apply as if that amount had become due and payable by virtue of a call.

17. Subject to the terms of allotment, the directors may make arrangements on the issue of shares for a difference between the holders in the amounts and times of payment of calls on their shares.

18. If a call remains unpaid after it has become due and payable the directors may give to the person from whom it is due not less than fourteen clear days' notice requiring payment of the amount unpaid together with any interest which may have accrued. The notice shall name the place where payment is to be made and shall state that if the notice is not complied with the shares in respect of which the call was made will be liable to be forfeited.

19. If the notice is not complied with any share in respect of which it was given may, before the payment required by the notice has been made, be forfeited by a resolution of the directors and the forfeiture shall include all dividends or other moneys payable in respect of the forfeited shares and not paid before the forfeiture.

20. Subject to the provisions of the Act, a forfeited share may be sold, re-allotted or otherwise disposed of on such terms and in such manner as the directors determine either to the person who was before the forfeiture the holder or to any other person and at any time before sale, re-allotment or other disposition, the forfeiture may be cancelled on such terms as the directors think fit. Where for the purposes of its disposal a forfeited share is to be transferred to any person the directors may authorise some person to execute an instrument of transfer of the share to that person.

21. A person any of whose shares have been forfeited shall cease to be a member in respect of them and shall surrender to the company for cancellation the certificate for the shares forfeited but shall remain liable to the company for all moneys which at the date of forfeiture were presently payable by him to the company in respect of those shares with interest at the rate at which interest was payable on those moneys before the forfeiture or, if no interest was so payable, at the appropriate rate (as defined in the Act) from the date of forfeiture until payment but the directors may waive payment wholly or in part or enforce payment without any allowance for the value of the shares at the time of forfeiture or for any consideration received on their disposal.

22. A statutory declaration by a director or the secretary that a share has been forfeited on a specified date shall be conclusive evidence of the facts stated in it as against all persons claiming to be entitled to the share and the declaration shall (subject to the execution of an instrument of transfer if necessary) constitute a good title to the share and the person to whom the share is disposed of shall not be bound to see to the application of the consideration, if any, nor shall his title to the share be affected by any irregularity in or invalidity of the proceedings in reference to the forfeiture or disposal of the share.

TRANSFER OF SHARES

23. The instrument of transfer of a share may be in any usual form or in any other form which the directors may approve and shall be executed by or on behalf of the transferor and, unless the share is fully paid, by or on behalf of the transferee.

24. The directors may refuse to register the transfer of a share which is not fully paid to a person of whom they do not approve and they may refuse to register the transfer of a share on which the company has a lien. They may also refuse to register a transfer unless—

   (a) it is lodged at the office or at such other place as the directors may appoint and is accompanied by the certificate for the shares to which it relates and such other evidence as the directors may reasonably require to show the right of the transferor to make the transfer;

   (b) it is in respect of only one class of shares; and

   (c) it is in favour of not more than four transferees.

25. If the directors refuse to register a transfer of a share, they shall within two months after the date on which the transfer was lodged with the company send to the transferee notice of the refusal.

26. The registration of transfers of shares or of transfers of any class of shares may be suspended at such times and for such periods (not exceeding thirty days in any year) as the directors may determine.

27. No fee shall be charged for the registration of any instrument of transfer or other document relating to or affecting the title to any share.

28. The company shall be entitled to retain any instrument of transfer which is registered, but any instrument of transfer which the directors refuse to register shall be returned to the person lodging it when notice of the refusal is given.

TRANSMISSION OF SHARES

29. If a member dies the survivor or survivors where he was a joint holder, and his personal representatives where he was a sole holder or the only survivor of joint holders, shall be the only persons recognised by the company as having any title to his interest; but nothing herein contained shall release the estate of a deceased member from any liability in respect of any share which had been jointly held by him.

30. A person becoming entitled to a share in consequence of the death or bankruptcy of a member may, upon such evidence being produced as the directors may properly require, elect either to become the holder of the share or to have some person nominated by him registered as the transferee. If he elects to become the holder he shall give notice to the company to that effect. If he elects to have another person registered he shall execute an instrument of transfer of the share to that person. All the articles relating to the transfer of shares shall apply to the notice or instrument of transfer as if it were an instrument of transfer executed by the member and the death or bankruptcy of the member had not occurred.

31. A person becoming entitled to a share in consequence of the death or bankruptcy of a member shall have the rights to which he would be entitled if he were the holder of the share, except that he shall not, before being registered as the holder of the share, be entitled in respect of it to attend or vote at any meeting of the company or at any separate meeting of the holders of any class of shares in the company.

ALTERATION OF SHARE CAPITAL

32. The company may by ordinary resolution—

   (a) increase its share capital by new shares of such amount as the resolution prescribes;

(b)   consolidate and divide all or any of its share capital into shares of larger amount than its existing shares;

(c)   subject to the provisions of the Act, sub-divide its shares, or any of them, into shares of smaller amount and the resolution may determine that, as between the shares resulting from the sub-division, any of them may have any preference or advantage as compared with the others; and

(d)   cancel shares which, at the date of the passing of the resolution, have not been taken or agreed to be taken by any person and diminish the amount of its share capital by the amount of the shares so cancelled.

33. Whenever as a result of a consolidation of shares any members would become entitled to fractions of a share, the directors may, on behalf of those members, sell the shares representing the fractions for the best price reasonably obtainable to any person (including, subject to the provisions of the Act, the company) and distribute the net proceeds of sale in due proportion among those members, and the directors may authorise some person to execute an instrument of transfer of the shares to, or in accordance with the directions of, the purchaser. The transferee shall not be bound to see to the application of the purchase money nor shall his title to the shares be affected by any irregularity in or invalidity of the proceedings in reference to the sale.

34. Subject to the provisions of the Act, the company may by special resolution reduce its share capital, any capital redemption reserve and any share premium account in any way.

PURCHASE OF OWN SHARES

35. Subject to the provisions of the Act, the company may purchase its own shares (including any redeemable shares) and, if it is a private company, make a payment in respect of the redemption or purchase of its own shares otherwise than out of distributable profits of the company or the proceeds of a fresh issue of shares.

GENERAL MEETINGS

36. All general meetings other than annual general meetings shall be called extraordinary general meetings.

37. The directors may call general meetings and, on the requisition of members pursuant to the provisions of the Act, shall forthwith proceed to convene an extraordinary general meeting for a date not later than eight weeks after receipt of the requisition. If there are not within the United Kingdom sufficient directors to call a general meeting, any director or any member of the company may call a general meeting.

NOTICE OF GENERAL MEETINGS

38. An annual general meeting and an extraordinary general meeting called for the passing of a special resolution or a resolution appointing a person as a director shall be called by at least twenty-one clear days' notice. All other extraordinary general meetings shall be called by at least fourteen clear days' notice but a general meeting may be called by shorter notice if it is so agreed—

(a) in the case of an annual general meeting, by all the members entitled to attend and vote thereat; and

(b) in the case of any other meeting by a majority in number of the members having a right to attend and vote being a majority together holding not less than ninety-five per cent in nominal value of the shares giving that right.

The notice shall specify the time and place of the meeting and the general nature of the business to be transacted and, in the case of an annual general meeting, shall specify the meeting as such.

Subject to the provisions of the articles and to any restrictions imposed on any shares, the notice shall be given to all the members, to all persons entitled to a share in consequence of the death or bankruptcy of a member and to the directors and auditors.

39. The accidental omission to give notice of a meeting to, or the non-receipt of notice of a meeting by, any person entitled to receive notice shall not invalidate the proceedings at that meeting.

PROCEEDINGS AT GENERAL MEETINGS

40. No business shall be transacted at any meeting unless a quorum is present. Two persons entitled to vote upon the business to be transacted, each being a member or a proxy for a member or a duly authorised representative of a corporation, shall be a quorum.

41. If such a quorum is not present within half an hour from the time appointed for the meeting, or if during a meeting such a quorum ceases to be present, the meeting shall stand adjourned to the same day in the next week at the same time and place or [to] such time and place as the directors may determine.

42. The chairman, if any, of the board of directors or in his absence some other director nominated by the directors shall preside as chairman of the meeting, but if neither the chairman nor such other director (if any) be present within fifteen minutes after the time appointed for holding the meeting and willing to act, the directors present shall elect one of their number to be chairman and, if there is only one director present and willing to act, he shall be chairman.

43. If no director is willing to act as chairman, or if no director is present within fifteen minutes after the time appointed for holding the meeting, the members present and entitled to vote shall choose one of their number to be chairman.

44. A director shall, notwithstanding that he is not a member, be entitled to attend and speak at any general meeting and at any separate meeting of the holders of any class of shares in the company.

45. The chairman may, with the consent of a meeting at which a quorum is present (and shall if so directed by the meeting), adjourn the meeting from time to time and from place to place, but no business shall be transacted at an adjourned meeting other than business which might properly have been transacted at the meeting had the adjournment not taken place. When a meeting is adjourned for fourteen days or more, at least seven clear days' notice shall be given specifying the time and place of the adjourned meeting and the general nature of the business to be transacted. Otherwise it shall not be necessary to give any such notice.

46. A resolution put to the vote of a meeting shall be decided on a show of hands unless before, or on the declaration of the result of, the show of hands a poll is duly demanded. Subject to the provisions of the Act, a poll may be demanded—

    (a) by the chairman; or

    (b) by at least two members having the right to vote at the meeting; or

    (c) by a member or members representing not less than one-tenth of the total voting rights of all the members having the right to vote at the meeting; or

    (d) by a member or members holding shares conferring a right to vote at the meeting being shares on which an aggregate sum has been paid up equal to not less than one-tenth of the total sum paid up on all the shares conferring that right;

and a demand by a person as proxy for a member shall be the same as a demand by the member.

47. Unless a poll is duly demanded a declaration by the chairman that a resolution has been carried or carried unanimously, or by a particular majority, or lost, or not carried by a particular majority and an entry to that effect in the minutes of the meeting shall be conclusive evidence of the fact without proof of the number or proportion of the votes recorded in favour of or against the resolution.

48. The demand for a poll may, before the poll is taken, be withdrawn but only with the consent of the chairman and a demand so withdrawn shall not be taken to have invalidated the result of a show of hands declared before the demand was made.

49. A poll shall be taken as the chairman directs and he may appoint scrutineers (who need not be members) and fix a time and place for declaring the result of the poll. The result of the poll shall be deemed to be the resolution of the meeting at which the poll was demanded.

50. In the case of an equality of votes, whether on a show of hands or on a poll, the chairman shall be entitled to a casting vote in addition to any other vote he may have.

51. A poll demanded on the election of a chairman or on a question of adjournment shall be taken forthwith. A poll demanded on any other question shall be taken either forthwith or at such time and place as the chairman directs not being more than thirty days after the poll is demanded. The demand for a poll shall not prevent the continuance of a meeting for the transaction of any business other than the question on which the poll was demanded. If a poll is demanded before the declaration of the result of a show of hands and the demand is duly withdrawn, the meeting shall continue as if the demand had not been made.

52. No notice need be given of a poll not taken forthwith if the time and place at which it is to be taken are announced at the meeting at which it is demanded. In any other case at least seven clear days' notice shall be given specifying the time and place at which the poll is to be taken.

53. A resolution in writing executed by or on behalf of each member who would have been entitled to vote upon it if it had been proposed at a general meeting at which he was present shall be as effectual as if it had been passed at a general meeting duly convened and held and may consist of several instruments in the like form each executed by or on behalf of one or more members.

Notes

Paragraph 41 Word in square brackets inserted by the Companies (Tables A to F) (Amendment) Regulations 1985, SI 1985/1052.

VOTES OF MEMBERS

54. Subject to any rights or restrictions attached to any shares, on a show of hands every member who (being an individual) is present in person or (being a corporation) is present by a duly authorised representative, not being himself a member entitled to vote, shall have one vote and on a poll every member shall have one vote for every share of which he is the holder.

55. In the case of joint holders the vote of the senior who tenders a vote, whether in person or by proxy, shall be accepted to the exclusion of the votes of the other joint holders; and seniority shall be determined by the order in which the names of the holders stand in the register of members.

56. A member in respect of whom an order has been made by any court having jurisdiction (whether in the United Kingdom or elsewhere) in matters concerning mental disorder may vote, whether on a show of hands or on a poll, by his receiver, curator bonis or other person authorised in that behalf appointed by that court, and any such receiver, curator bonis or other person may, on a poll, vote by proxy. Evidence to the satisfaction of the directors of the authority of the person claiming to exercise the right to vote shall be deposited at the office, or at such other place as is specified in accordance with the articles for the deposit of instruments of proxy, not less than 48 hours before the time appointed for holding the meeting or adjourned meeting at which the right to vote is to be exercised and in default the right to vote shall not be exercisable.

57. No member shall vote at any general meeting or at any separate meeting of the holders of any class of shares in the company, either in person or by proxy, in respect of any share held by him unless all moneys presently payable by him in respect of that share have been paid.

58. No objection shall be raised to the qualification of any voter except at the meeting or adjourned meeting at which the vote objected to is tendered, and every vote not disallowed at the meeting shall be valid. Any objection made in due time shall be referred to the chairman whose decision shall be final and conclusive.

59. On a poll votes may be given either personally or by proxy. A member may appoint more than one proxy to attend on the same occasion.

60. (*An instrument appointing a proxy shall be in writing*) [The appointment of] a proxy shall be ... executed by or on behalf of the appointor and shall be in the following form (or in a form as near thereto as circumstances allow or in any other form which is usual or which the directors may approve)—

'   PLC/Limited

I/We,   , of   , being a

member/members of the above-named company, hereby appoint

of   , or failing him,

of   , as my/our proxy to vote in my/our name[s]
and on my/our behalf at the annual/extraordinary general meeting of the
company to be held on   19   , and at any
adjournment thereof.

Signed on   19   .'

61. Where it is desired to afford members an opportunity of instructing the proxy
how he shall act the (*instrument appointing*) [appointment of] a proxy shall be
in the following form (or in a form as near thereto as circumstances allow or in
any other form which is usual or which the directors may approve)—

'   PLC/Limited

I/We,   , of   , being a

member/members of the above-named company, hereby appoint

of   , or failing him,

of   , as my/our proxy to vote in my/our name[s]
and on my/our behalf at the annual/extraordinary general meeting of the
company to be held on   19   , and at any
adjournment thereof.

This form is to be used in respect of the resolutions mentioned below as
follows:

Resolution No 1 *for *against

Resolution No 2 *for *against.

*Strike out whichever is not desired.

Unless otherwise instructed, the proxy may vote as he thinks fit or abstain
from voting.

Signed this   day of   19   .'

62. (*The instrument appointing*) [The appointment of] a proxy and any authority
under which it is executed or a copy of such authority certified notarially or in
some other way approved by the directors may—

(a)   [in the case of an instrument in writing] be deposited at the office
or at such other place within the United Kingdom as is specified in
the notice convening the meeting or in any instrument of proxy sent
out by the company in relation to the meeting not less than 48 hours
before the time for holding the meeting or adjourned meeting at
which the person named in the instrument proposes to vote; or

[(aa) in the case of an appointment contained in an electronic
communication, where an address has been specified for the purpose
of receiving electronic communications—

(i)   in the notice convening the meeting, or

(ii) in any instrument of proxy sent out by the company in relation to the meeting, or

(iii) in any invitation contained in an electronic communication to appoint a proxy issued by the company in relation to the meeting,

be received at such address not less than 48 hours before the time for holding the meeting or adjourned meeting at which the person named in the appointment proposes to vote;]

(b) in the case of a poll taken more than 48 hours after it is demanded, be deposited [or received] as aforesaid after the poll has been demanded and not less than 24 hours before the time appointed for the taking of the poll; or

(c) where the poll is not taken forthwith but is taken not more than 48 hours after it was demanded, be delivered at the meeting at which the poll was demanded to the chairman or to the secretary or to any director;

(*and an instrument of proxy which is not deposited or delivered*) [and an appointment of proxy which is not deposited, delivered or received] in a manner so permitted shall be invalid.

[In this regulation and the next, 'address', in relation to electronic communications, includes any number or address used for the purposes of such communications.]

63. A vote given or poll demanded by proxy or by the duly authorised representative of a corporation shall be valid notwithstanding the previous determination of the authority of the person voting or demanding a poll unless notice of the determination was received by the company at the office or at such other place at which the instrument of proxy was duly deposited [or, where the appointment of the proxy was contained in an electronic communication, at the address at which such appointment was duly received] before the commencement of the meeting or adjourned meeting at which the vote is given or the poll demanded or (in the case of a poll taken otherwise than on the same day as the meeting or adjourned meeting) the time appointed for taking the poll.

Notes

Regulation 60   Words in square brackets substituted and words omitted revoked by the Companies Act 1985 (Electronic Communications) Order 2000, SI 2000/3373, art 32(1), Sch 1, para 2 as from 22 December 2000. The previous wording is indicated by italics and brackets.

Regulation 61   Words in square brackets substituted by SI 2000/3373, art 32(1), Sch 1, para 3 as from 22 December 2000. The previous wording is indicated by italics and brackets.

Regulation 62   Words in first and fourth pairs of square brackets substituted, para (aa) and words in second, third and fifth pairs of square brackets inserted by SI 2000/3373, art 32(1), Sch 1, para 4 as from 22 December 2000. The previous wording is indicated by italics and brackets.

Regulation 63   Words in square brackets inserted by SI 2000/3373, art 32(1), Sch 1, para 5 as from 22 December 2000.

NUMBER OF DIRECTORS

64. Unless otherwise determined by ordinary resolution, the number of directors (other than alternate directors) shall not be subject to any maximum but shall be not less than two.

ALTERNATE DIRECTORS

65. Any director (other than an alternate director) may appoint any other director, or any other person approved by resolution of the directors and willing to act, to be an alternate director and may remove from office an alternate director so appointed by him.

66. An alternate director shall be entitled to receive notice of all meetings of directors and of all meetings of committees of directors of which his appointor is a member, to attend and vote at any such meeting at which the director appointing him is not personally present, and generally to perform all the functions of his appointor as a director in his absence but shall not be entitled to receive any remuneration from the company for his services as an alternate director. But it shall not be necessary to give notice of such a meeting to an alternate director who is absent from the United Kingdom.

67. An alternate director shall cease to be an alternate director if his appointor ceases to be a director; but, if a director retires by rotation or otherwise but is reappointed or deemed to have been reappointed at the meeting at which he retires, any appointment of an alternate director made by him which was in force immediately prior to his retirement shall continue after his reappointment.

68. Any appointment or removal of an alternate director shall be by notice to the company signed by the director making or revoking the appointment or in any other manner approved by the directors.

69. Save as otherwise provided in the articles, an alternate director shall be deemed for all purposes to be a director and shall alone be responsible for his own acts and defaults and he shall not be deemed to be the agent of the director appointing him.

POWERS OF DIRECTORS

70. Subject to the provisions of the Act, the memorandum and the articles and to any directions given by special resolution, the business of the company shall be managed by the directors who may exercise all the powers of the company. No alteration of the memorandum or articles and no such direction shall invalidate any prior act of the directors which would have been valid if that alteration had not been made or that direction had not been given. The powers given by this regulation shall not be limited by any special power given to the directors by the articles and a meeting of directors at which a quorum is present may exercise all powers exercisable by the directors.

71. The directors may, by power of attorney or otherwise, appoint any person to be the agent of the company for such purposes and on such conditions as they determine, including authority for the agent to delegate all or any of his powers.

DELEGATION OF DIRECTORS' POWERS

72. The directors may delegate any of their powers to any committee consisting of one or more directors. They may also delegate to any managing director or any director holding any other executive office such of their powers as they consider desirable to be exercised by him. Any such delegation may be made subject to any conditions the directors may impose, and either collaterally with or to the exclusion of their own powers and may be revoked or altered. Subject to any such conditions, the proceedings of a committee with two or more members shall be governed by the articles regulating the proceedings of directors so far as they are capable of applying.

APPOINTMENT AND RETIREMENT OF DIRECTORS

73. At the first annual general meeting all the directors shall retire from office, and at every subsequent annual general meeting one-third of the directors who are subject to retirement by rotation or, if their number is not three or a multiple of three, the number nearest to one-third shall retire from office; but, if there is only one director who is subject to retirement by rotation, he shall retire.

74. Subject to the provisions of the Act, the directors to retire by rotation shall be those who have been longest in office since their last appointment or reappointment, but as between persons who became or were last reappointed directors on the same day those to retire shall (unless they otherwise agree among themselves) be determined by lot.

75. If the company, at the meeting at which a director retires by rotation, does not fill the vacancy the retiring director shall, if willing to act, be deemed to have been reappointed unless at the meeting it is resolved not to fill the vacancy or unless a resolution for the reappointment of the director is put to the meeting and lost.

76. No person other than a director retiring by rotation shall be appointed or reappointed a director at any general meeting unless—

    (a) he is recommended by the directors; or

    (b) not less than fourteen nor more than thirty-five clear days before the date appointed for the meeting, notice executed by a member qualified to vote at the meeting has been given to the company of the intention to propose that person for appointment or reappointment stating the particulars which would, if he were so appointed or reappointed, be required to be included in the company's register of directors together with notice executed by that person of his willingness to be appointed or reappointed.

77. Not less than seven nor more than twenty-eight clear days before the date appointed for holding a general meeting notice shall be given to all who are entitled to receive notice of the meeting of any person (other than a director retiring by rotation at the meeting) who is recommended by the directors for appointment or reappointment as a director at the meeting or in respect of whom notice has been duly given to the company of the intention to propose him at the meeting for appointment or reappointment as a director. The notice shall give the particulars of that person which would, if he were so appointed or reappointed, be required to be included in the company's register of directors.

78. Subject as aforesaid, the company may by ordinary resolution appoint a person who is willing to act to be a director either to fill a vacancy or as an additional director and may also determine the rotation in which any additional directors are to retire.

79. The directors may appoint a person who is willing to act to be a director, either to fill a vacancy or as an additional director, provided that the appointment does not cause the number of directors to exceed any number fixed by or in accordance with the articles as the maximum number of directors. A director so appointed shall hold office only until the next following annual general meeting and shall not be taken into account in determining the directors who are to retire by rotation at the meeting. If not reappointed at such annual general meeting, he shall vacate office at the conclusion thereof.

80. Subject as aforesaid, a director who retires at an annual general meeting may, if willing to act, be reappointed. If he is not reappointed, he shall retain office until the meeting appoints someone in his place, or if it does not do so, until the end of the meeting.

DISQUALIFICATION AND REMOVAL OF DIRECTORS

81. The office of a director shall be vacated if—

    (a) he ceases to be a director by virtue of any provision of the Act or he becomes prohibited by law from being a director; or

    (b) he becomes bankrupt or makes any arrangement or composition with his creditors generally; or

    (c) he is, or may be, suffering from mental disorder and either—

        (i) he is admitted to hospital in pursuance of an application for admission for treatment under the Mental Health Act 1983 or, in Scotland, an application for admission under the Mental Health (Scotland) Act 1960, or

        (ii) an order is made by a court having jurisdiction (whether in the United Kingdom or elsewhere) in matters concerning mental disorder for his detention or for the appointment of a receiver, curator bonis or other person to exercise powers with respect to his property or affairs; or

    (d) he resigns his office by notice to the company; or

    (e) he shall for more than six consecutive months have been absent without permission of the directors from meetings of directors held during that period and the directors resolve that his office be vacated.

REMUNERATION OF DIRECTORS

82. The directors shall be entitled to such remuneration as the company may by ordinary resolution determine and, unless the resolution provides otherwise, the remuneration shall be deemed to accrue from day to day.

DIRECTORS' EXPENSES

83. The directors may be paid all travelling, hotel, and other expenses properly incurred by them in connection with their attendance at meetings of directors or committees of directors or general meetings or separate meetings of the holders of any class of shares or of debentures of the company or otherwise in connection with the discharge of their duties.

DIRECTORS' APPOINTMENTS AND INTERESTS

84. Subject to the provisions of the Act, the directors may appoint one or more of their number to the office of managing director or to any other executive office under the company and may enter into an agreement or arrangement with any director for his employment by the company or for the provision by him of any services outside the scope of the ordinary duties of a director. Any such appointment, agreement or arrangement may be made upon such terms as the directors determine and they may remunerate any such director for his services as they think fit. Any appointment of a director to an executive office shall terminate if he ceases to be a director but without prejudice to any claim to damages for breach of the contract of service between the director and the company. A managing director and a director holding any other executive office shall not be subject to retirement by rotation.

85. Subject to the provisions of the Act, and provided that he has disclosed to the directors the nature and extent of any material interest of his, a director notwithstanding his office—

    (a) may be a party to, or otherwise interested in, any transaction or arrangement with the company or in which the company is otherwise interested;

    (b) may be a director or other officer of, or employed by, or a party to any transaction or arrangement with, or otherwise interested in, any body corporate promoted by the company or in which the company is otherwise interested; and

    (c) shall not, by reason of his office, be accountable to the company for any benefit which he derives from any such office or employment or from any such transaction or arrangement or from any interest in any such body corporate and no such transaction or arrangement shall be liable to be avoided on the ground of any such interest or benefit.

86. For the purposes of regulation 85—

    (a) a general notice given to the directors that a director is to be regarded as having an interest of the nature and extent specified in the notice in any transaction or arrangement in which a specified person or class of persons is interested shall be deemed to be a disclosure that the director has an interest in any such transaction of the nature and extent so specified; and

    (b) an interest of which a director has no knowledge and of which it is unreasonable to expect him to have knowledge shall not be treated as an interest of his.

DIRECTORS' GRATUITIES AND PENSIONS

87. The directors may provide benefits, whether by the payment of gratuities or pensions or by insurance or otherwise, for any director who has held but no longer holds any executive office or employment with the company or with any body corporate which is or has been a subsidiary of the company or a predecessor in business of the company or of any such subsidiary, and for any member of his family (including a spouse and a former spouse) or any person who is or was dependent on him, and may (as well before as after he ceases to hold such office or employment) contribute to any fund and pay premiums for the purchase or provision of any such benefit.

PROCEEDINGS OF DIRECTORS

88. Subject to the provisions of the articles, the directors may regulate their proceedings as they think fit. A director may, and the secretary at the request of a director shall, call a meeting of the directors. It shall not be necessary to give notice of a meeting to a director who is absent from the United Kingdom. Questions arising at a meeting shall be decided by a majority of votes. In the case of an equality of votes, the chairman shall have a second or casting vote. A director who is also an alternate director shall be entitled in the absence of his appointor to a separate vote on behalf of his appointor in addition to his own vote.

89. The quorum for the transaction of the business of the directors may be fixed by the directors and unless so fixed at any other number shall be two. A person who holds office only as an alternate director shall, if his appointor is not present, be counted in the quorum.

90. The continuing directors or a sole continuing director may act notwithstanding any vacancies in their number, but, if the number of directors is less than the number fixed as the quorum, the continuing directors or director may act only for the purpose of filling vacancies or of calling a general meeting.

91. The directors may appoint one of their number to be the chairman of the board of directors and may at any time remove him from that office. Unless he is unwilling to do so, the director so appointed shall preside at every meeting of directors at which he is present. But if there is no director holding that office, or if the director holding it is unwilling to preside or is not present within five minutes after the time appointed for the meeting, the directors present may appoint one of their number to be chairman of the meeting.

92. All acts done by a meeting of directors, or of a committee of directors, or by a person acting as a director shall, notwithstanding that it be afterwards discovered that there was a defect in the appointment of any director or that any of them were disqualified from holding office, or had vacated office, or were not entitled to vote, be as valid as if every such person had been duly appointed and was qualified and had continued to be a director and had been entitled to vote.

93. A resolution in writing signed by all the directors entitled to receive notice of a meeting of directors or of a committee of directors shall be as valid and effectual as if it had been passed at a meeting of directors or (as the case may be) a committee of directors duly convened and held and may consist of several documents in the like form each signed by one or more directors; but a resolution signed by an alternate director need not also be signed by his appointor and, if it is signed by a director who has appointed an alternate director, it need not be signed by the alternate director in that capacity.

94. Save as otherwise provided by the articles, a director shall not vote at a meeting of directors or of a committee of directors on any resolution concerning a matter in which he has, directly or indirectly, an interest or duty which is material and which conflicts or may conflict with the interests of the company unless his interest or duty arises only because the case falls within one or more of the following paragraphs—

(a) the resolution relates to the giving to him of a guarantee, security, or indemnity in respect of money lent to, or an obligation incurred by him for the benefit of, the company or any of its subsidiaries;

(b) the resolution relates to the giving to a third party of a guarantee, security, or indemnity in respect of an obligation of the company or any of its subsidiaries for which the director has assumed responsibility in whole or part and whether alone or jointly with others under a guarantee or indemnity or by the giving of security;

(c) his interest arises by virtue of his subscribing or agreeing to subscribe for any shares, debentures or other securities of the company or any of its subsidiaries, or by virtue of his being, or intending to become, a participant in the underwriting or sub-underwriting of an offer of any such shares, debentures, or other securities by the company or any of its subsidiaries for subscription, purchase or exchange;

(d) the resolution relates in any way to a retirement benefits scheme which has been approved, or is conditional upon approval, by the Board of Inland Revenue for taxation purposes.

For the purposes of this regulation, an interest of a person who is, for any purpose of the Act (excluding any statutory modification thereof not in force when this regulation becomes binding on the company), connected with a director shall be treated as an interest of the director and, in relation to an alternate director, an interest of his appointor shall be treated as an interest of the alternate director without prejudice to any interest which the alternate director has otherwise.

95. A director shall not be counted in the quorum present at a meeting in relation to a resolution on which he is not entitled to vote.

96. The company may by ordinary resolution suspend or relax to any extent, either generally or in respect of any particular matter, any provision of the articles prohibiting a director from voting at a meeting of directors or of a committee of directors.

97. Where proposals are under consideration concerning the appointment of two or more directors to offices or employments with the company or any body corporate in which the company is interested the proposals may be divided and considered in relation to each director separately and (provided he is not for another reason precluded from voting) each of the directors concerned shall be entitled to vote and be counted in the quorum in respect of each resolution except that concerning his own appointment.

98. If a question arises at a meeting of directors or of a committee of directors as to the right of a director to vote, the question may, before the conclusion of the meeting, be referred to the chairman of the meeting and his ruling in relation to any director other than himself shall be final and conclusive.

SECRETARY

99. Subject to the provisions of the Act, the secretary shall be appointed by the directors for such term, at such remuneration and upon such conditions as they may think fit; and any secretary so appointed may be removed by them.

MINUTES

100. The directors shall cause minutes to be made in books kept for the purpose—
    (a) of all appointments of officers made by the directors; and
    (b) of all proceedings at meetings of the company, of the holders of any class of shares in the company, and of the directors, and of committees of directors, including the names of the directors present at each such meeting.

THE SEAL

101. The seal shall only be used by the authority of the directors or of a committee of directors authorised by the directors. The directors may determine who shall sign any instrument to which the seal is affixed and unless otherwise so determined it shall be signed by a director and by the secretary or by a second director.

DIVIDENDS

102. Subject to the provisions of the Act, the company may by ordinary resolution declare dividends in accordance with the respective rights of the members, but no dividend shall exceed the amount recommended by the directors.

103. Subject to the provisions of the Act, the directors may pay interim dividends if it appears to them that they are justified by the profits of the company available for distribution. If the share capital is divided into different classes, the directors may pay interim dividends on shares which confer deferred or non-preferred rights with regard to dividend as well as on shares which confer preferential rights with regard to dividend, but no interim dividend shall be paid on shares carrying deferred or non-preferred rights if, at the time of payment, any preferential dividend is in arrear. The directors may also pay at intervals settled by them any dividend payable at a fixed rate if it appears to them that the profits available for distribution justify the payment. Provided the directors act in good faith they shall not incur any liability to the holders of shares conferring preferred rights for any loss they may suffer by the lawful payment of an interim dividend on any shares having deferred or non-preferred rights.

104. Except as otherwise provided by the rights attached to shares, all dividends shall be declared and paid according to the amounts paid up on the shares on which the dividend is paid. All dividends shall be apportioned and paid proportionately to the amounts paid up on the shares during any portion or portions of the period in respect of which the dividend is paid; but, if any share is issued on terms providing that it shall rank for dividend as from a particular date, that share shall rank for dividend accordingly.

105. A general meeting declaring a dividend may, upon the recommendation of the directors, direct that it shall be satisfied wholly or partly by the distribution of assets and, where any difficulty arises in regard to the distribution, the directors may settle the same and in particular may issue fractional certificates and fix the value for distribution of any assets and may determine that cash shall be paid to any member upon the footing of the value so fixed in order to adjust the rights of members and may vest any assets in trustees.

106. Any dividend or other moneys payable in respect of a share may be paid by cheque sent by post to the registered address of the person entitled or, if two or more persons are the holders of the share or are jointly entitled to it by reason of the death or bankruptcy of the holder, to the registered address of that one of those persons who is first named in the register of members or to such person and to such address as the person or persons entitled may in writing direct. Every cheque shall be made payable to the order of the person or persons entitled or to such other person as the person or persons entitled may in writing direct and payment of the cheque shall be a good discharge to the company. Any joint holder or other person jointly entitled to a share as aforesaid may give receipts for any dividend or other moneys payable in respect of the share.

107. No dividend or other moneys payable in respect of a share shall bear interest against the company unless otherwise provided by the rights attached to the share.

108. Any dividend which has remained unclaimed for twelve years from the date when it became due for payment shall, if the directors so resolve, be forfeited and cease to remain owing by the company.

ACCOUNTS

109. No member shall (as such) have any right of inspecting any accounting records or other book or document of the company except as conferred by statute or authorised by the directors or by ordinary resolution of the company.

CAPITALISATION OF PROFITS

110. The directors may with the authority of an ordinary resolution of the company—

- (a) subject as hereinafter provided, resolve to capitalise any undivided profits of the company not required for paying any preferential dividend (whether or not they are available for distribution) or any sum standing to the credit of the company's share premium account or capital redemption reserve;
- (b) appropriate the sum resolved to be capitalised to the members who would have been entitled to it if it were distributed by way of dividend and in the same proportions and apply such sum on their behalf either in or towards paying up the amounts, if any, for the time being unpaid on any shares held by them respectively, or in paying up in full unissued shares or debentures of the company of a nominal amount equal to that sum, and allot the shares or debentures credited as fully paid to those members, or as they may direct, in those proportions, or partly in one way and partly in the other: but the share premium account,

the capital redemption reserve, and any profits which are not available for distribution may, for the purposes of this regulation, only be applied in paying up unissued shares to be allotted to members credited as fully paid;

(c) make such provision by the issue of fractional certificates or by payment in cash or otherwise as they determine in the case of shares or debentures becoming distributable under this regulation in fractions; and

(d) authorise any person to enter on behalf of all the members concerned into an agreement with the company providing for the allotment to them respectively, credited as fully paid, of any shares or debentures to which they are entitled upon such capitalisation, any agreement made under such authority being binding on all such members.

NOTICES

[**111.** (*Any notice to be given to or by any person pursuant to the articles shall be in writing except that a notice calling a meeting of the directors need not be in writing.*) Any notice to be given to or by any person pursuant to the articles (other than a notice calling a meeting of the directors) shall be in writing or shall be given using electronic communications to an address for the time being notified for that purpose to the person giving the notice.

In this regulation,'address', in relation to electronic communications, includes any number or address used for the purposes of such communications.]

112. The company may give any notice to a member either personally or by sending it by post in a prepaid envelope addressed to the member at his registered address or by leaving it at that address [or by giving it using electronic communications to an address for the time being notified to the company by the member]. In the case of joint holders of a share, all notices shall be given to the joint holder whose name stands first in the register of members in respect of the joint holding and notice so given shall be sufficient notice to all the joint holders. A member whose registered address is not within the United Kingdom and who gives to the company an address within the United Kingdom at which notices may be given to him [, or an address to which notices may be sent using electronic communications,] shall be entitled to have notices given to him at that address, but otherwise no such member shall be entitled to receive any notice from the company.

[In this regulation and the next, 'address', in relation to electronic communications, includes any number or address used for the purposes of such communications.]

113. A member present, either in person or by proxy, at any meeting of the company or of the holders of any class of shares in the company shall be deemed to have received notice of the meeting and, where requisite, of the purposes for which it was called.

114. Every person who becomes entitled to a share shall be bound by any notice in respect of that share which, before his name is entered in the register of members, has been duly given to a person from whom he derives his title.

115. Proof that an envelope containing a notice was properly addressed, prepaid and posted shall be conclusive evidence that the notice was given.[Proof that a notice contained in an electronic communication was sent in accordance with guidance issued by the Institute of Chartered Secretaries and Administrators shall be conclusive evidence that the notice was given.] A notice shall, ... be deemed to be given at the expiration of 48 hours after the envelope containing it was posted [or, in the case of a notice contained in an electronic communication, at the expiration of 48 hours after the time it was sent].

Notes

Regulation 111 Substituted by the Companies Act 1985 (Electronic Communications) Order 2000, SI 2000/3373, art 32(1), Sch 1, para 6 as from 22 December 2000. The previous wording is indicated by italics and brackets.

Regulation 112 Words in square brackets inserted by SI 2000/3373, art 32(1), Sch 1, para 7 as from 22 December 2000.

Regulation 115 Words in square brackets inserted by SI 2000/3373, art 32(1), Sch 1, para 8 as from 22 December 2000; words omitted (*'unless the contrary is proved'*) revoked by the Companies (Tables A to F) (Amendment) Regulations 1985, SI 1985/1052.

116. A notice may be given by the company to the persons entitled to a share in consequence of the death or bankruptcy of a member by sending or delivering it, in any manner authorised by the articles for the giving of notice to a member, addressed to them by name, or by the title of representatives of the deceased, or trustee of the bankrupt or by any like description at the address, if any, within the United Kingdom supplied for that purpose by the persons claiming to be so entitled. Until such an address has been supplied, a notice may be given in any manner in which it might have been given if the death or bankruptcy had not occurred.

WINDING UP

117. If the company is wound up, the liquidator may, with the sanction of an extraordinary resolution of the company and any other sanction required by the Act, divide among the members in specie the whole or any part of the assets of the company and may, for that purpose, value any assets and determine how the division shall be carried out as between the members or different classes of members. The liquidator may, with the like sanction, vest the whole or any part of the assets in trustees upon such trusts for the benefit of the members as he with the like sanction determines, but no member shall be compelled to accept any assets upon which there is a liability.

INDEMNITY

118. Subject to the provisions of the Act but without prejudice to any indemnity to which a director may otherwise be entitled, every director or other officer or auditor of the company shall be indemnified out of the assets of the company against any liability incurred by him in defending any proceedings, whether civil or criminal, in which judgment is given in his favour or in which he is acquitted or in connection with any application in which relief is granted to him by the court from liability for negligence, default, breach of duty or breach of trust in relation to the affairs of the company.

General note

The Table A which applies to any company is the Table A in force at the date of the company's registration and, if Table A is altered, the alteration does not affect a company registered before the alteration takes effect: see s 8(2),(3).

As to the articles of association and the role of Table A, see notes to ss 7–9.

See note to CA 1985, s 258, above and to ss 736, 736A, above.

Index